722.99

Psychology for A Level

Mike Cardwell
Liz Clark
Claire Meldrum

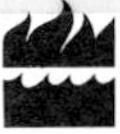

Collins Educational
An Imprint of HarperCollins*Publishers*

Published by Collins Educational
An imprint of HarperCollins*Publishers* Ltd
77–85 Fulham Palace Road
Hammersmith
London W6 8JB

© HarperCollins*Publishers* Ltd 1996

First published 1996
Reprinted 1996 (three times)

ISBN 0 00 322442 2

All rights reserved. No part of this publication may be reproduced, stored in a retrieval system, or transmitted in any form or by any other means, electronic, mechanical, photocopying, recording or otherwise, without the prior permission of the Publisher.

A catalogue record for this book is available from the British Library.

Commissioned by Emma Dunlop
Production managed by Hugh Hillyard-Parker (National Extension College)
Edited by Ros Connelly, Ivan Deith
Index compiled by Ann Marangos
Cover by Moondisks
Page design by Hilary Norman
Typesetting by Liz Gordon, Cambridge
Illustrations by Anna Hancock, Gary Stoker and Maureen Carter

Permissions

The Publisher, authors and editors would like to thank the organisations listed below for permission to reproduce material from their publications. Full bibliographic information for all sources is given in the 'References' section at the end of the book.

Chapter 2
24 Table 2.1: Cambridge University Press
26 Table 2.2: Penguin Books Ltd
27 Table 2.3: from *Close Relationships* by Kelley *et al.* Copyright © 1983 by W.H. Freeman and Company. Used with permission.
28 Table 2.4: Allyn and Bacon Inc.
31 Fig. 2.1: Random House Inc.
41 Table 2.7: Reprinted by permission of John Wiley & Sons Ltd

Chapter 3
45 Fig. 3.1: Carnegie Press
57 Table 3.3: The Academy of Management, USA
63 Table 3.4: Sage Publications Ltd

Chapter 4
70 Fig. 4.1: Appleton Century Crofts
72 Table 4.1: Duke University Press
73 Table 4.2: © 1968 by the American Psychological Association. Reprinted with permission
77 Fig. 4.2: Prentice Hall
79 Fig. 4.3: © 1987 by the American Psychological Association. Reprinted with permission

Chapter 7
151 Table 7.1: Methuen & Co Ltd

Chapter 10
219 Table 10.3: Routledge

Chapter 11
235 Fig. 11.2: © 1985 by the American Psychological Association. Reprinted with permission.
252 Table 11.6: Chapman & Hall

Chapter 12
267 Fig. 12.3: Philip Allan Publishers Ltd
275 In Focus: *The Times*

Chapter 13
293 Fig. 13.7: Prentice-Hall Inc.

Chapter 14
304 Fig. 14.1: © 1951 by the Trustees of the University of Illinois. Used with permission of the University of Illinois Press
320 Fig. 14.11: from 'The origin of form perception' by Robert L. Fantz. Copyright © 1961 by Scientific American Inc. All rights reserved.
321 Fig. 14.12: Scientific American Inc.

Chapter 15
336 Table 15.1: Chapman & Hall Ltd

Chapter 16
359 Fig. 16.1: American Psychological Association

Chapter 19
421 Table 19.2: Reproduced with permission of The McGraw-Hill Companies

Chapter 20
441 Fig. 20.1: from *The Seasons of a Man's Life* by Daniel J. Levinson *et al.* Copyright © 1978 by Daniel J. Levinson. Reprinted by permission of Alfred A. Knopf Inc.
443 Table 20.4: Simon & Schuster
454 Table 20.9: Kübler-Ross extract reprinted with the permission of Simon & Schuster from *On Death and Dying* by Dr. Elisabeth Kübler-Ross. Copyright © 1969 by Elisabeth Kübler-Ross; Baywood Publishing Co Inc. (for Fulton extract); International Universities Press (for Murray-Parkes extract)

Chapter 22
481 Table 22.1: Blackwell
490 Fig. 22.4: Benjamin Cummings
493 Table. 22.2: Cambridge University Press

Chapter 26
568 In Focus: *The Independent* (article text); Mars Corporation (for the photographic image)
581 Table 26.3: Croner
595 Table 26.5: Sage
596 In Focus: Harvester Wheatsheaf

Chapter 27
602 Table 27.1: British Psychological Society
607 Table 27.2: *The Psychologist*
611 Fig. 27.1: *New Scientist*
613 Fig. 27.2: *Animal Behaviour*
615 In Focus: *The Independent*

Chapter 28
627 Fig 28.1: University of Nebraska Press
630 In Focus: Copyright © 1972 by Scientific American Inc. All rights reserved.

Chapter 29
646 Fig 29.2: British Psychological Society
647 Fig 29.4: Blackwell Publishers
648 Fig 29.5: Blackwell Publishers

Chapter 30
662 In Focus: British Psychological Society
663 In Focus: Academic Press Inc.
692 Appendix 3: McGrawHill
695 Appendix 4: Addison Wesley Longman Ltd
696 Appendix 5: American Statistical Association
698 Appendix 7: American Statistical Association

Chapter 32
719 Table 32.1: Associated Examination Board
720 Table 32.2: Associated Examination Board
724 Table 32.1: Associated Examination Board

Chapter 33
738 Table 33.1: Routledge
742 Fig. 33.4: Plenum Publishing Corporation
744 Fig. 33.5: Crown copyright – reproduced with the permission of the Controller of HMSO

Every effort has been made to contact copyright holders, but if any has been inadvertently overlooked, the Publisher will be pleased to make the necessary arrangements at the first opportunity.

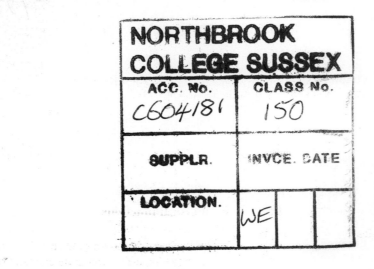

NORTHBROOK COLLEGE SUSSEX
ACC. No. C604181
CLASS No. 150
SUPPLR.
INVCE. DATE
LOCATION. WE

Contents

Acknowledgements

Producing a textbook with 33 chapters is a substantial undertaking, involving a large number of people. The editors owe a great debt of gratitude to all those who have been involved, not least the authors, the expert readers and all those friends and family members who have provided much-needed support and encouragement when flagging spirits brought on by tight deadlines and long days and nights threatened to overwhelm.

With this in mind, Mike Cardwell would like to thank Chris and Alex, who put up with his self-absorption with characteristic good humour and understanding. Liz Clark particularly wishes to thank her husband, who had to be incredibly patient and put up with being well down the list of priorities, only hearing the never-ending promise of 'It's nearly finished – only a few more days now!' Claire Meldrum would like to single out Stuart, who provided support and encouragement throughout this project. His willingness to take on the lion's share of domestic duties and responsibilities while the book was being written, was much appreciated. Claire's thanks also go to friends and colleagues at City College Norwich who never grumbled about her preoccupation with the book and who provided a sympathetic ear when anxiety about deadlines surfaced.

We would also like to extend our thanks to all those teachers whose encouragement and anticipation has made the production of this text a truly worthwhile enterprise. In addition, we would like to acknowledge the cooperation of the Associated Examination Board for their permission to use adapted versions of Board documents throughout this text.

Finally, our thanks to Emma Dunlop at Collins Educational, who brought a personal involvement to the project that is recognised and appreciated by all authors; to Patrick McNeill, whose infectious enthusiasm and belief in this project started the whole ball rolling; to Hugh Hillyard-Parker and colleagues at the National Extension College, who remained helpful and calm about design issues even when we put them under extraordinary pressure; and to Victoria Ingham, also at Collins Educational. They never ceased to believe in us and the entire project and, without their never-ending enthusiasm, this book might have taken a lot longer in its gestation!

Editor and author biographies

Mike Cardwell, BSc, PGCE, MEd, is Senior Lecturer in Psychology at Filton College, Bristol and the Chief Examiner for AEB A- and AS-level psychology. As well as being Editor of the *Psychology Review*, he is also a regular contributer to student conferences. Mike is the author of both the *A Level Psychology Revise Guide* and *The Complete A-Z Psychology Handbook* and the co-author of a range of titles, including *The Landsdowne Lectures, A Concise Introduction to Psychology* and *A Level Psychology Masterclass*. In the time he has away from the psychological field, Mike tends to head for the stands at Anfield!

Liz Clark, BA, PhD, is Head of Distance Learning at the Royal College of Nursing. She has published a range of open learning texts, including *Introduction to Psychology, Communication and Group Behaviour, The Social Development of Children* and *The Developing Person*, and is a member of the Editorial Board of *Social Sciences in Health: The International Journal of Research and Practice*. Liz has also contributed to edited texts on the application of psychology to nursing and health care, and acted as consultant for the National Extension College. She admits, when she has a moment, to being an avid follower of *The Archers*!

Claire Meldrum MA, MSc, PGCE is a lecturer at City College, Norwich and has fifteen years' teaching experience in both HE and FE behind her. At present she is teaching psychology at degree level, A level and on 'Access to HE' courses, as well as being an A-level examiner for AEB psychology. She has published three papers in the field of educational psychology and is the co-editor of *Psychology for Nurses and Health Care Professionals*. She is a member of the British Psychological Society (BPS) and of the Special Group in Health Psychology.

George Balfour, MA, BSc, is a lecturer in psychology at the University of Newcastle-upon-Tyne and cites his main interest as developmental psychology. He is a team leader for the AEB psychology A level, and also serves on the advisory board of the *Psychology Review*.

Phil Banyard is a lecturer at Nottingham Trent University, as well as the Chief Examiner in A-level psychology for the Oxford & Cambridge Examinations and Assessment Council. He has already published three major psychology titles, *Psychology: Theory and Application, Introducing Psychological Research* and *Applying Psychology to Health*, and is the organiser of training events for psychology teachers around the Nottingham area. He is an avid Nottingham Forest supporter.

John Cartwright, BSc, MSc, lectures at University College, Chester and is the Principal Examiner in Environmental Science for the NEAB. A regular contributer to the *Psychology Review*, he has also published *Risk* (Satis 16–19, ASE) and *Resources and Environment – Notes for Teachers* for the NEAB.

David Clarke, BA, MA, PGCE, AFBPsS, CPsychol, lectures at Priestly College in Warrington and has long been a team leader for AEB A-level psychology, Paper 1. He is also Principal Examiner for OCSEB for A-level psychology Paper 5 and an Associate Editor of *Psychology Teaching Review*. Having been Secretary of Association for the Teaching of Psychology (ATP) for three years, and a committee member for ten, he is also a Chartered Psychologist and an Associate Fellow of the BPS.

Graham Davies, BA, MSc, PGCE, is a lecturer at Eastbourne College of Arts and Technology and the Principal Coursework Moderator for AEB AS- and A-level psychology. He leads AEB's team of Regional Coursework Advisers and is an Examiner for both the Perspectives and Research Methods elements of the new syllabus. He has published various journal articles and is a speaker and workshop leader for a number of psychology conferences. A committee member and former Chair of the ATP, Graham currently edits the ATP journal, *Psychology Teaching* and, in the spare time he can find, is a keen mountain-climber.

Roger Davies, BSc, MSc, MPhil, PGCE, AFBPsS, CPsychol, is Senior Lecturer at the Behaviour and Evolution Group at University College, Chester. He is also team leader for the AEB Paper 1 and the co-author of three psychology textbooks. He is currently working on a text on evolutionary psychology, as well as carrying out further research into facial asymmetry and attractiveness. Roger also reviews articles on educational technology, a subject in which he takes an active interest, and is a member both of the Association for the Study of Animal Behaviour and the BPS.

Simon Green, BSc, PhD, is Senior Lecturer in Psychology at Birkbeck College, University of London. He was the Chief Examiner for AEB psychology between 1983 and 1986 and remains a Senior Examiner today. He is the author of two psychology titles, *Principles of Biopsychology* and *A Textbook of Psychology*, and has contributed articles both to other psychology textbooks and the *Psychology Review*. Simon is also the editor of the *Principles* series and a member of the BPS.

Pat Hasan, SRN, BSc, is Senior Lecturer and Scheme Tutor in Psychology at the University of Hertfordshire and is also committed to teaching psychology to nurses on P2000 courses. She has already contributed to and edited a number of books and articles within the field of psychology, and is currently completing her PhD thesis investigating the relation between cognition and communication in pre-school children with Down's Syndrome.

Peter Hayes, BSc, PhD, is Senior Psychology Lecturer at University College, Chester, as well as a part-time lecturer in Cognitive Psychology for the Open University. His research publications are in the area of everyday memory, cognition and emotion and he is currently also interested in researching frontal functioning and amnesia.

Paul Humphreys, MSc, BA, is Senior Lecturer in Psychology at Worcester College of Higher Education and the Editor of the *Psychology Review*. He is not only the author of *Understanding Psychology* and *Starting Statistics* and co-author of *BPS Manual of Psychology Practicals*, but also author of the *Fast Forward* and *Masterclass* psychology cassettes. Previously the Chief Examiner for AS- and OA-level psychology for the AEB, he is now the Chief Examiner for A Level. Paul is a member of both the ATP and... Liverpool FC!

David Messer, BSc, PhD, is a Professor of Psychology and author of both *The Development of Communication* and *Mastery Motivation in Early Childhood*. He is also Co-Editor of the *Journal of Reproductive and Infant Psychology*, Associate Editor for *First Language* and Conference Reports Editor for the *Psychologist*. David is currently interested in research into language and cognitive development, and children's sleeping difficulties.

Lesley Messer, BSc, PhD, is affiliated to the Open University and is pursuing her longstanding interest in developmental psychology.

Pamela Prentice, BA, MEd, NRHP, is a lecturer in A-level psychology at Filton College, Bristol and a tutor for the AEB Counselling certificate and diploma courses. She is both an AEB A-level examiner and a moderator for the OCN Counselling courses, and her name will be well known to readers of the *Psychology Review* as a regular columnist. Among the many societies she is involved with are the BPS and the British Association for Counselling, and she is an active national committee member of the ATP. Pamela is a practising Counselling Psychologist with the NHS and, in her spare time, a dedicated follower of Italian fashion!

Alison Wadeley, BSc, PGCE, MPhil, is Head of Psychology at Filton College, Bristol. She has had long experience as both an Examiner and Principal Moderator for the AEB and is currently a reviser for A-level psychology. Alison has published three textbooks, *Perspectives in Psychology*, *A GCSE Psychology Revise Guide* and *A Level Psychology Exam Kit*, and co-authored *The BPS Manual of Psychology Practicals*. As well as being Editor of the *Psychology Review*, she is an active member of the ATP.

Jane Willson, BA, BSc, is a lecturer at City College, Norwich and is currently co-authoring *Private Eyes*, an investigation of children's interaction with screen-based technology. She is a Senior Examiner for the AEB and a member of the ATP.

Introduction

Over a year ago, when we started discussing this book, we all agreed that what we wanted to produce was a user-friendly text which would cover all aspects of the new 1998 Associated Examination Board (AEB) psychology syllabus. The wide range of this new syllabus and its inclusion of many up-to-date aspects of psychology led us to the conclusion that it was important that the chapters were written by people who were experts in their field as well as being experienced teachers of psychology. In this way we hope to have done justice to the psychological content of the syllabus while at the same time recognising the need to pitch the material at a level which is accessible to the A-level reader.

How to use this book

In addition to the usual features that you would expect to find in a textbook such as an *Index* and list of *References*, we have also included a *Glossary* of syllabus and examination terms – as well as a number of other features within each chapter which we hope will facilitate the use of the book and make it easier to relate its content to the requirements of the AEB syllabus.

Each chapter starts with a *Preview* of contents and ends with a *Summary* to enable you to peruse quickly the topics covered therein. Within the body of the chapters, you will find *Activities* which are designed to help you test your knowledge, apply psychological findings to real-life situations, try out practical exercises and consider the ethical implications of research.

The *Essay/Exam questions* at the end of each chapter have been carefully constructed to resemble closely the format and type of mark apportioning which you will find in the A-level exam itself. These questions will provide a useful guide to aid your essay writing skills and will give you an idea of the type of questions you will encounter in the examination itself.

Although every effort has been made to cover all aspects of the AEB syllabus, we recognise that many readers will want to explore in more depth certain topics which they find particularly interesting. For this reason, advice about *Further reading* is given at the end of each chapter.

This book is designed specifically for the AEB A-level syllabus and this fact has defined its content. Because this syllabus covers the major topics and controversies in modern psychology so does the book. Before you use this text as part of your study programme, it is worth spending some time carefully assessing what is involved in the syllabus and the examination. Detailed accounts of the syllabus and information about the examination are available from the AEB (address given at the end of this introduction) and so we shall only sketch out the main points here.

The syllabus and the examination

What is the difference between the modular and the terminal routes?

You may be following a course where you take all your examinations at the end of the course (the terminal assessment route) or where you have examinations at various points throughout the course (the modular assessment route). Whether one route is better than the other is open to debate. The point for you to remember is that the content of the course is the same regardless of the route taken and the examination content is also the same.

There are four modules in the course, each comprising two sections of the syllabus and each worth 20 per cent of the total marks:

- Social psychology and Comparative psychology
- Bio-psychology and Atypical development and abnormal behaviour
- Cognitive psychology and Developmental psychology
- Perspectives and Research methods.

If you are following the *terminal assessment route*, the first two modules constitute one written paper and the second two modules constitute the second written paper. Each written paper, therefore, is worth 40 per cent of your final examination mark. If you are taking an AS-level course, you will take the Perspectives and Research methods module plus one other. Each module on the AS course is therefore worth 40 per cent of your final examination mark.

If you are taking the *modular assessment route* on an A-level course, a maximum of *two* module papers may be taken *during* the course and the remaining *two* module papers taken *at the end* of the course. If you are taking an AS-level course, *one* module paper is taken during the course and the remaining *one* at the end.

As an A-level student, you will also be required to carry out and write up two pieces of research as the coursework element of your course (one piece if you are taking the AS-level course). This is worth 20 per cent of the marks of the final examination. To aid you in this requirement, we have included a chapter especially concerned with coursework and the writing up of reports (see Chapter 31).

What is involved in the syllabus?

As you can see from the Contents page, each section of the syllabus has a number of different subsections. For example, Social psychology has the following four subsections:

- Social cognition
- Social relationships
- Social influence
- Pro-and anti-social behaviour.

These subsections reflect different areas of interest in social psychology. Because of the way the syllabus has been designed you may find that you do not study *all* the subsections in a given section. This is perfectly alright, as teachers are free to design their own flexible course within the boundaries laid down by the syllabus. You may find, for example, that your teacher does not cover Social cognition as an area, but chooses to spend more time on some other part of the syllabus.

If you are designing your own course of study, however, it is worth bearing two things in mind:

1. Random selection of subsections rarely gives a true feel of what psychology is about. Your teachers will know what subsections go best together. If you are involved in designing your own course of study, seek your teacher's advice.
2. Examination questions are asked on a 'one per subsection' basis, and so it pays to be fully conversant with all the topics within a particular subsection. Remember that each chapter in this book represents one complete subsection of the syllabus and, therefore, the material on which one examination question will be set.

Although there is a certain flexibility in the syllabus as regards which subsections you choose to study, it is important that you study *at least one* subsection from each of the sections (Social, Developmental, etc.) and *all* the subsections concerned with Research Methods. Remember that this is the bare minimum and not a recommended route through the syllabus.

The syllabus is designed to provide assessment of four different skills. These are:

A *Knowledge and understanding* (assessed in all areas of the syllabus but mainly in the written papers. This constitutes 46 per cent of the final examination mark).

B *Interpretation and commentary* (assessed in all areas but mainly in the written papers. This constitutes 38 per cent of the final examination mark).

C *Research skills* (assessed in the research projects that comprise your coursework. This constitutes 11 per cent of the final examination mark).

D *Quality of language* (assessed throughout the syllabus and constituting 5 per cent of the final examination mark).

You will find advice on how to maximize these marks at various points in this book, but Chapter 32 (Examination techniques) will show you how you can do well where it really matters, that is, in the examination itself. You will also find the *Further reading* section at the end of each chapter useful to extend your understanding of the syllabus topics discussed within the chapter.

The future

While all of us engaged in this project are pleased, even relieved, to see the publication of this first edition, we are aware also that this is just the beginning. The book arose out of a need to respond to a major change in the psychology syllabus which is studied by more than 20,000 people per year. In turn, that change in the syllabus had arisen out of a recognition that modern psychology is changing rapidly.

Psychologists today, for example, are much more aware of social and cultural issues which might affect their work than they were even a few years ago. Similarly, research techniques once considered too sociological or anthropological for psychologists are now being embraced by many involved in social and developmental psychology. The subject matter of psychology is not static. The discipline is dynamic, and as new topics emerge and new means for investigating them are developed so this book will need to reflect these developments. Therefore, before the ink is even dry on this edition, we are already anticipating the second edition. To this end, we invite you to write to us, care of the Publisher, to let us know what you think about this text. How well does it meet your needs? What would you like to see added or changed in the next edition? Are there supplementary materials which would be helpful? Please feel free to let us know what you think. Your feedback will help us to keep improving *Psychology for A level.*

Mike Cardwell
Liz Clark
Claire Meldrum

For details about syllabuses or any other documents concerning A-level psychology, contact:

The Associated Examination Board
Publications Department
Stag Hill House
Guildford
Surrey
GU2 5XJ

Part 1

Social Psychology

Chapter 1

Social cognition

David Clarke

Preview

In this chapter we shall be looking at:

- social cognition and related theories and research, including social identity and social representation theories
- attribution theory and biases in the attribution process
- the origins and maintenance of prejudice and discrimination
- the reduction of prejudice and discrimination.

Introduction

Psychologists interested in social cognition are concerned with understanding the ways in which people attempt to make sense of their social world. In this chapter we will look at social cognition and related areas of research. In particular, we will examine:

- social identity theory – which looks at how social contexts affect our social behaviours
- the theory of social representations – which examines the way we understand and share beliefs about our social experiences.

In addition to these two theories, we will also look at attribution theory. This focuses on the way in which we try to explain our own and other people's behaviours. We will consider a number of theories of attribution and the evidence that has been claimed for them from psychological research studies. Our consideration of attribution theory will include an examination of some of the biases that have been identified in the attributional process.

Finally, we will consider prejudice and discrimination, and examine attempts to explain the origins and maintenance of these phenomena. We will also describe and evaluate some of the attempts made to reduce them.

Social cognition

The importance of social cognition was first recognized by Fritz Heider and George Kelly. According to Heider (1958), people generally have a strong desire to form a coherent understanding of the world and to control their social environment. Heider argued that in order for us to do this we behave like 'naive psychologists', applying common sense to our world so that we can explain our own and others' behaviour. Kelly (1955) saw people as acting like 'scientists' in trying to understand and predict their world, and he suggested the existence of 'constructs which we use to classify people, objects and events in the world'.

According to Leyens and Dardenne (1996), *social cognition* can be defined as the way in which we perceive, interpret and judge the behaviour of others in everyday interactions. To understand social cognition, we need to look first at the structure and mechanisms we use to perceive our social world. We also need to look at the processes by which we acquire information about other people and the ways in which we apply this information. *Schema theory* will help us achieve the first objective, and the use of *heuristics* and *social categorization* the second.

Schema theory

Fiske and Taylor (1992) have defined a *schema* as a cognitive structure that represents a person's general knowledge about a given concept or 'stimulus domain'. A schema can be seen as a prior expectation about an event which determines what aspects of that event we attend to, what we categorize for further use, and what we discard as unimportant. *Schemata* (the plural of schema) serve a number of useful functions. For example, they simplify detail, speed up processing, help us to interpret and remember, and allow us to evaluate new information. Many social schemata exist. These include *self schemata, role schemata, person schemata* and *script schemata.*

Script schemata, for example, are schemata about events. According to Schank and Abelson (1977), they are a sort of 'mental program' of how we ourselves and others are likely to behave in a particular situation. For example, there is a likely sequence of events that occurs when we go to a restaurant for a meal. First, we are seated by a waiter who then brings us a menu. After looking at the menu, we order some food from it and, possibly, a drink. When the food has been cooked and served, we eat it. Finally, we pay for what we have eaten and drunk. We know how we are likely to behave in this situation and we know how those who are with us and those who are serving us are likely to behave. The 'going to the restaurant' script schema thus provides us with the means for successfully interacting with others in society because we understand what they are likely to do – and this understanding allows us to predict their likely behaviour.

❖ Activity 1 ❖

Social schemata

This activity involves making a number of lists:

1. First, list ten characteristics that summarize *you* as a person. What do you think is individual and special about you? In order to do this, you will need to consult your *self schemata.*
2. List five characteristics which you feel are characteristic of (a) your mother or father and (b) your best friend. How are they similar and how are they different? To construct these lists, you will need to consult your *person schemata.*
3. List five characteristics which you feel are typical of (a) a teacher and (b) a policeman. How are they similar and how are they different? These lists require you to access your *role schemata.*

As Hamilton (1981) has observed, we also have schemata for members of an identifiable group, and we call these 'stereotypes'. According to Aronson (1988), to stereotype someone is 'to assign identical characteristics to any person in a group, regardless of the actual variation among members of that group'. As we will see when we look at prejudice and discrimination, stereotypes are often negative. However, we should also remember that they can be positive or, indeed, neutral. In order to see what gender-role stereotypes you possess, try the following activity.

❖ Activity 2 ❖

Which of the following do you think is more typical of a man or a woman?

Personality traits:

1 Independence

2 Warmth

3 Competitiveness

4 Emotionality

Role behaviours:

5 Meal provider

6 Financial provider

7 Taker of initiative with the opposite sex

8 Provider of care for children

Physical characteristics:

9 Muscular

10 Small-boned

11 Graceful

12 Deep voiced

Deaux and Lewis (1983) found that numbers 2, 4, 5, 8, 10 and 11 were seen as being typical of women and 1, 3, 6, 7, 9 and 12 of men. How do your stereotypes compare with those found by Deaux and Lewis?

We mentioned earlier that schemata are concerned with how knowledge is represented in memory. Unfortunately, the information that is stored in memory is so vast and complex that it is impossible for us to have all of it available and ready for use all of the time. According to Fiske and Taylor (1992), when we apply the knowledge in our memory to the perception of our social world, we act as 'cognitive misers' – that is, we take short cuts in order to process social information more efficiently. The two main types of short cut are called *heuristics* and *categorization.*

Heuristics

According to Stratton and Hayes (1993), heuristics are 'problem solving strategies which involve taking the most probable or likely option ... [heuristics] provide a way of reducing a complex task to a manageable set of tasks'. For Tversky and Kahneman (1974), heuristics are short cuts and strategies that we use to modify and reduce complex information about the social world. Whereas schemata contain our knowledge, heuristics help us to *apply* that knowledge.

One type of heuristic is that of *representativeness.* This is what we use to compare whether or not a new 'stimulus' matches an existing schema. Representativeness helps us to decide quickly whether a person is a member of a particular group because he or she matches a typical example (or 'prototype') of that group. If an individual possesses one or more matching features, then we conclude that he or she belongs to that group. Suppose, for example, that we hold a particular stereotype about nurses, and we are told that a given individual is a female who is caring. If we were asked to guess that person's occupation, we might be inclined to select nursing because of the two important elements in our stereotype of nurses which that person possesses. Using such short cuts often results in accurate conclusions about people. However, we should note that in some cases such short cuts lead to inaccurate conclusions.

A second heuristic is *availability* which is the characteristic that comes to mind first from all other possibilities. If, for example, you were asked to describe a politician, one of the features that might be most readily available (at least to some of us) might be their inability to be truthful!

Both representativeness and availability serve a useful function in that they enable us to rate the likelihood or frequency of something being the case in a shorthand way. A more detailed discussion of heuristics can be found in Fiedler (1996).

Social categorization

Another way in which we take short cuts in processing social information is by categorizing incoming information into meaningful units that can be stored for future use. A *category* is a set of objects that (are perceived to) have in common one or more characteristics (Hewstone *et al.* 1996). In interpersonal perception, we use categories such as male–female, young–old, and black–white. No matter how little information we have or how contradictory it may be, and no matter how many times our initial impressions have been wrong, we still categorize.

Such categories include *prototypes* which, as we noted above, are typical examples of what we expect someone in a category to be like. For example, if you are asked to imagine a librarian, rugby player, or grandmother, you could probably conjure up prototypical images of these people – that is, images that best represent the category in question. Although categorization into meaningful units is efficient in that it allows us to process a great deal of information in a relatively short period of time and with a minimum amount of effort, the generalizations involved inevitably contain an element of distortion. This is because it is not possible to process *every* item of social data. This distortion manifests itself in the form of biases and errors in judgement.

Two of these errors are the *confirmatory bias* and the *false consensus bias*. The former is the tendency to seek information that is consistent with existing categories. For example, if we are told that a nurse is female and this matches our stereotype for nurses, we may seek other information that confirms our stereotyped notions about nurses, perhaps ignoring other non-confirming information. The false consensus bias is where we assume that if we know something about our own attitudes and behaviours, then we also know about the attitudes and behaviour of others. Thus, we tend to assume that other people behave and think as we do. Both of these biases are evident in many cognitive processes and we will return to them later when we look at attribution theory and prejudice and discrimination.

Social identity theory

In this chapter so far, we have been concerned with social information processing by individuals. However, another major influence on our perception and understanding of the social world is the people around us. It is important to look at the ways in which other people and the groups to which they belong affect our perceptions. This is the concern of *social identity theory* (SIT) which Hayes (1993, p. 159) defines as: 'how membership of social groups forms a significant part of the self-concept and can determine reactions to other people and events, such that people respond primarily as group members and not as individuals'.

Tajfel (1982) sees personal and social identity as being different, the latter dealing with the processes by which we learn from our group membership who we are and what we are worth.

Categorization

Fundamental to our social identity is the process of categorization. Earlier on, we noted that people act as 'cognitive misers' when categorizing in order to cut down on the amount of information that must be processed. We tend to group people into social categories on a range of dimensions. These include universal and national (such as female–male and English–Welsh, for example) and membership of specific groups (such as our friends and family).

The group to which we belong is called the 'ingroup' or 'we-group' – a select group in which all members feel a strong sense of identity within the group, a sense of élitism about the group and a tendency to act so as to exclude others. These others are referred to as the 'outgroup' or 'they-group'. In essence, the outgroup is a group comprising any or all people not in one's ingroup.

We also noted earlier on in this chapter that while putting people into groups can speed up social information processing, it may lead to biases and inaccuracies. The same effects extend to the group level. The *'ingroup favouritism effect'* refers to treating ingroup members more favourably than outgroup members. The term *'negative outgroup bias'* refers to the unfavourable treatment that members of the outgroup receive. It occurs because we perceive greater differences between the ingroup and the outgroup than actually exist.

We process more thoroughly information about those who belong to our ingroup than information about those who belong to an outgroup. One consequence of this is the *'outgroup homogeneity effect'* where we assume that members of an outgroup are no more than 'undifferentiated items in a unified social category'. By contrast, members of our ingroup are seen as possessing individual variations to which we apply sub-categories.

Tajfel (1970) has argued that categorization not only applies to major distinctions (such as males and females) but to *any* divisions of individuals into groups (see *In Focus* below for one example of this).

Social comparison

Another aspect central to SIT is that of social comparison. Festinger's (1954) social comparison theory was an attempt to explain the process of comparison of abilities and attitudes between individuals. However, SIT is much more than this, claiming that not only do we compare ourselves with other individuals, but we also compare our group with other groups and this provides us with feedback about their relative strengths and weaknesses. When we compare groups in this way we expect the comparison to favour the group to which we belong. If it does, we feel good; if it does not, we feel disappointed. Such feelings contribute to our self-esteem, which is the third central aspect in social identity theory.

In Focus

The minimal group paradigm

Tajfel (1970) has demonstrated how easily people will discriminate against others whom they perceive to be in a different group. Some schoolboys from Bristol were placed into groups in a purely random fashion. There was no face-to-face contact between any of the boys. Under the pretext that they were participating in an experiment on decision-making, the boys were required to allocate points, which could later be converted to money, to both their own group (the ingroup) and another group (the outgroup). Ingroup favouritism was shown with the boys allocating more points to their own group. Most interestingly, the boys maximized the *differentials* between the groups, even when this meant disadvantaging their own group in terms of the absolute number of points allocated.

Although it is tempting to conclude that the very act of categorizing people as members of even the most nominal (minimal) group is sufficient to cause ingroup favouritism and outgroup discrimination, the minimal group paradigm has been criticized. For example, the members of the groups in Tajfel's studies may have been subjected to 'demand characteristics' (see Chapter 29) and felt that they had little choice but to discriminate against the outgroup members. Nevertheless, the findings from minimal group studies are remarkably robust, having been replicated many times in several countries and using adult as well as child participants.

Self-esteem

Self-esteem is a term used to describe the degree to which we value ourselves. In part, self-esteem is arrived at by comparing ourselves with other people and other groups. Two groups are particularly influential. The first is the *peer-group*, i.e. those people we perceive as being like ourselves. The second, the *reference group*, are those who set the social norms we try to emulate. As Eiser (1986) has observed, people will 'tend to engage in intergroup comparisons which are seen as likely to make a positive contribution to their social identity and will tend to avoid comparisons which are seen as likely to make a negative contribution'.

People need a positive social identity to enhance their self-esteem. This is achieved by comparing some feature of their ingroup with the same feature possessed by the outgroup. However, and as we have already seen, when we belong to a group, we are biased in favour of it and so tend to disparage the qualities/ideas of alternative groups when making our comparisons. As a result, we see the ingroup in a positive way.

Our positive social identity is also reinforced when members of the ingroup are successful in some way and we feel proud because we are a member of that group. By contrast, when the ingroup is unsuccessful we feel deflated. When the England Cricket Team wins a test match series, at least some of us feel proud.

However, repeated exposure to failure within our ingroup could lead us to change groups, although this depends on the type of group we are a member of and other factors. For example, whilst we might be able to switch our allegiance to a successful rather than unsuccessful cricket team, we cannot easily change our nationality! Instead, we are much more likely to try and explain the failure so that the group has an apparently legitimate excuse. So, when the England Cricket Team loses yet another test match, the adverse environmental conditions (such as the hot weather in India (!) or the consumption of prawn curry) have been invoked as explanations for failure. These explanations – some of which are more plausible than others – for the causes of failure take us into the domain of attribution theory, which we will consider later on in this chapter.

Social representations

As we have seen, examining how people understand the world involves looking at individual constructs (such as schemata, social categorizations, and identities) or considering our membership of, and interaction with, groups. Another approach is provided by social representation theory. According to this theory, we do not necessarily strive for a full and accurate explanation of 'the world' on every occasion. Rather, as 'cognitive misers', we settle for a representation of it. Moscovici (1981) defines *social representations* as shared beliefs held by groups of people to explain their social experience.

For example, suppose a number of people hear (but do not see) a car accident. They rush to the scene and find that whilst no one is injured, two cars are badly damaged. They then discuss why the accident occurred. Because no one actually witnessed the accident, explanations will vary as to the probable cause, and everyone will have their own suggestions derived from their existing knowledge and experiences of such situations. However, as a result of talking to others and through the information this provides, people may change their views. The outcome will be a conclusion which a group of people consider an acceptable explanation for the event. It is, therefore, a *social representation*.

As well as taking into account individual explanations, social representation theory also considers the way in which people interact with others in society, particularly those with whom they identify such as their peers and/or reference group. Indeed, such explanations may well be shared amongst members of an ingroup. Such groups and processes operate at a number of levels. These may be small as in the case of the people who discussed the accident we described above, or quite large as in the case of political parties. Of course, different groups of any composition can provide radically different explanations for the same events.

We can use social representation theory to account for the common sense explanations, or what Kruglanski (1980) calls 'lay epistemology', that people use to explain their knowledge of the world. In one study, Moscovici and Hewstone (1983) noted that scientific knowledge is often hard to grasp when it is presented in scientific form. However, through 'personification', in which theories become associated with particular people, and 'figuration', in which images and metaphors represent the concept in question, scientific knowledge seems to become more accessible. For example, people think that they 'know about' the theory of relativity because they can associate with the name of Einstein (personification). Likewise, people converse about psychoanalysis by visualizing a three-storey building with the id in the basement, the ego on the ground floor and the superego on the top floor (figuration).

Section summary

Social cognition is concerned with how we process information. One way in which we do this is by comparing a stimulus, such as a person, with our existing schemata. We have many schemata, such as those about ourselves, other people, scripts, and the roles we and others play. When we process information about a person, some psychologists believe that we are lazy and do not process all information. Instead, we behave as 'cognitive misers' and take short cuts by putting people into categories and using heuristics or 'rules of thumb'. In taking such short cuts, we generalize. This leads to biases in our social perception. Two such biases are the confirmatory and false consensus biases.

Social identity theory examines the ways in which we compare ourselves with others. Comparison of our ingroup with outgroups provides us with a sense of belonging and this affects our self-esteem. Social representation theory holds that we perceive events in the world around us and, based on our experiences and the responses of others, we form a common-sense and shared interpretation of events which we perceive around us. Therefore, any event will be perceived in the light of any personal, local and national circumstances which apply to that event.

Attribution theory

At the beginning of this chapter we noted that according to Heider (1958), people have an overwhelming desire to form a coherent understanding of their world and control their social environment. One aspect which is fundamental to this is that of *causality* – that is, the factors or conditions which cause particular events or behaviours to occur. An 'attribution' is the process by which people use available information to make inferences about the causes of a particular behaviour. The conditions which affect how each of us attributes causes for our own and others' behaviour is called 'attribution theory' (Jones 1977).

In this section we will look at what research tells us about the attributions we make about our own behaviour and that of others. In order to do this, we will also need to consider aspects of social cognition. As noted earlier, when we process social information we take short cuts and consequently do not process information as accurately as we could. As a result, biases occur in the attributional process. Consider, for example, the real-life example mentioned in Activity 3.

❖ Activity 3 ❖

You may have read about the 1996 'Brit-pop' awards in which Jarvis Cocker, the lead singer with the group Pulp, interrupted the stage act of Michael Jackson. Amongst other things, Cocker exposed his buttocks to the audience. Why did Jarvis Cocker behave in the way he did? Was he drunk? Was he making some sort of a protest? Was he upset that Pulp had failed to win the major awards? Was it an attempt to discredit the awards system? Or was it perhaps a bet with a fellow artist? Try to think of as many reasons as you can for Cocker's behaviour.

According to attribution theorists, our explanations for a person's behaviour will generally refer either to factors stemming from *within* that person or to factors that are *external* to that person, such as the environment. When we explain people's behaviour in terms of it being a result of 'something about them' we are making a 'dispositional attribution'. When behaviour is explained in terms of something about the environment or social world, we are making a 'situational attribution'.

Look at the explanations you came up with for Jarvis Cocker's behaviour. You can probably identify some as being dispositional attributions and others as situational.

Attributional theories

A number of attribution theories have been developed. These include Kelley's (1972) *co-variation model*, and his subsequent (1973) refinement to it, the *causal schemata model*. Rather than being seen as competitors, each seeking to explain the same thing in the best way, it is more fruitful to see attributional theories as being complementary and differing according to the kind of explanation that is required and the information that is available to the person doing the explaining. In this section, we will look at the two theories developed by Kelley.

The co-variation model

Kelley's co-variation model applies to the explanations we give for the behaviour of people we know. Kelley argues that when we make such attributions we take two factors into account. The first of these is what we know about the person and his or her previous behaviour. The second is the way in which the person's behaviour compares with that of other people. According to the principle of co-variation, we take three types of causal information into account when arriving at an explanation. The extent to which these three types of information co-vary results in us making a dispositional (or internal) attribution, a situational (or external) attribution, or a combination of the two.

- The first type of causal information is *consensus*. This refers to the extent to which other people behave in the same way towards the same stimulus as the person whose behaviour we are trying to explain. For example, suppose that we are asked to explain why a person is afraid of a dog. If most people are afraid of this particular dog, then consensus is *high*. However, if few people are afraid of the dog, consensus is *low*.
- The second type of information is *consistency*. This refers to the extent to which the person in question has behaved in the same way in the past towards the stimulus in question. If the person has been afraid of the dog on other occasions, consistency is *high*. However, if he or she has not shown fear before then consistency is *low*.
- The third type of information is *distinctiveness*. This refers to the extent to which the person behaves in the same or a similar way to other stimuli. If, for example, the person is not afraid of other dogs, then the behaviour of being afraid of this dog is a highly distinctive one. Thus, distinctiveness is *high*. If the person is afraid of all other dogs and, perhaps,

all other animals, then the behaviour of being afraid of this dog is not particularly distinctive. Hence we can say that distinctiveness is *low*.

Kelley argued that if consensus was low, consistency was high, and distinctiveness was low, then we would tend to make a dispositional (or internal) attribution for behaviour. So, if John was afraid of the dog and we knew that very few other people were afraid of the dog, that John had been afraid of the dog before, and that John was afraid of other dogs as well as this one, we would tend to explain his behaviour in terms of something about him. Perhaps, for example, we would describe him as being 'timid'.

If consensus, consistency and distinctiveness were all high, Kelley argued that an attribution to the 'entity' would be made. For example, suppose that Peter failed to win a prize on a particular radio quiz show, everyone else he knew had failed to win a prize on the same quiz, Peter had also failed to win a prize on the quiz when he had taken part in it before and Peter had won prizes on other quiz shows. We would explain his behaviour in terms of the quiz show. Perhaps, for example, his failure could be explained in terms of the quiz being very difficult.

In circumstances, however, when consensus is low, consistency is low, but distinctiveness is high, Kelley argued that the cause of behaviour would be most likely to be attributed to a particular set of circumstances. For example, suppose that Julie makes a donation to a particular charity. No one else makes a donation, Julie has not donated to this charity before, and Julie does not usually give her money away. In this case, Julie might be making her contribution because of some special circumstances. Perhaps she has seen a TV programme describing the plight of the people being helped by this particular charity.

Kelley's theory has been tested in a number of experiments in which people are given a behaviour to explain (such as 'Frank laughed at the comedian') along with information about consensus, consistency and distinctiveness. Generally, the results of such experiments have supported Kelley's proposals and shown that when the three types of information are manipulated, people tend to make the attributions predicted by Kelley.

There are, however, several problems with the co-variation model. For example, Garland *et al.* (1975) have shown that when given a choice about the information necessary to arrive at an attribution, some people choose information about things like 'personality' and/or the context in which the behaviour is occurring rather than consensus, consistency or distinctiveness information. Indeed, in one study, it was discovered that people *only* use information about distinctiveness and consistency when no information about context or situation is available.

We should also note that Kelley's theory is cognitively expensive, as it takes a great deal of mental effort to assess information on consensus, consistency, and distinctiveness (even when these sources of information are readily available: see below). As noted before in this chapter, we tend to act as 'cognitive misers' and rather than spend time searching for information we often jump to 'quick and easy' conclusions regarding the causes of behaviour.

Causal schemata

Largely because of the criticisms that were made of the co-variation model, Kelley advanced a second attribution theory which applies to behaviour observed on a single occasion and about which there is no consensus, consistency or distinctiveness information. Kelley argued that if we do not know a person and have no information about their previous behaviour then we can only rely on our *causal schemata*. Causal schemata are, according to Kelley (1972), 'general conceptions a person has about how certain kinds of causes interact to produce a specific kind of effect'.

One type of causal schema is that of *multiple sufficient causes*. This applies when a behaviour may have a number of causes for it and when we are satisfied that any one of them is a *sufficient* explanation of it.

For example, suppose that your neighbours have just moved house. They might have moved because they want to live in a larger or smaller house, because they want a bigger garden, because the house is about to be repossessed or because they do not like you playing music loudly and having parties every weekend. Each cause is sufficient in itself to explain the behaviour of moving house.

On some occasions, however, we may have reason to favour one in particular of the sufficient explanations, which leads us to add weight to it and dismiss or discount the others. Kelley calls this the *'discounting principle'*. For example, suppose that a well-known celebrity appears on television advertising a particular brand of aftershave. The celebrity may really like the aftershave and be advertising it for that reason. He may, however, be doing the manufacturer a favour because of a personal friendship with the head of the company. It might even be the case that the celebrity had been paid £100,000 to endorse the aftershave. It is likely that most of us would discount two of the three sufficient causes presented above, and opt for the last one.

A second type of causal schemata is that of *multiple necessary causes*. These apply when two or more factors are *necessary* for an attribution to be made to explain a behaviour. For example, in order to be successful in the London Marathon it is not sufficient to wear running shoes; the runner must also be fit. Both of these aspects are necessary for successful performance, and if the marathon was completed we would conclude that the runner not only wore running shoes, but was also a physically fit athlete.

Kelley's attribution theories, along with others we have not discussed, assume that we are motivated to explain the behaviour of others in a logical and rational manner. Because these two theories describe the ways in which we *should* make attributions they are referred to as *normative models* of the attribution process. However, as we have stressed on a number of occasions, people do not process every piece of social information in a logical and rational manner. The short cuts we take when arriving at explanations for behaviour lead to biases in our processing of information. It is to *biases* in the attributional process that we turn next.

Biases in the attributional process

Psychologists have discovered that people can be biased in a number of ways when they make attributions. An *attributional bias* can be defined as a distortion in perception or judgement about the causes of our own or other people's behaviour. This section looks at several of these biases.

The fundamental attribution error

Ross (1977) defines the *fundamental attribution error* (FAE) as 'the tendency to underestimate the importance of situational determinants and overestimate the degree to which actions and outcomes reflect the actor's dispositions'. What this means is that we have a tendency to make internal (or dispositional) attributions for people's behaviour even when external (or situational) attributions are equally likely to explain the behaviour. For example, if someone was to spill coffee over us, our explanation of his or her behaviour would probably be in terms of 'being clumsy' even when a situational explanation (the person had been pushed by somebody else) was equally likely. It has been suggested that our 'miserly' approach to cognitive processing leads us to ignore situational influences unless we are directly alerted to them. This results in us emphasizing factors concerned with the person. If we are satisfied that our dispositional attribution is adequate, then we feel we have no need to make matters more complex by considering additional information.

Support for this view was obtained by Ross *et al.* (1977). In their experiment, participants were randomly assigned to be either questioners or contestants in a general knowledge quiz. The questioners were allowed to make up questions based on their own specialized knowledge which, of course, would mean that contestants would often struggle to provide correct answers. The 'quiz' was observed by other participants and at the end of it the observers, questioners, and contestants were asked to rate the general knowledge of the questioners and contestants.

Both the observers and contestants considered the questioners to have superior knowledge. The questioners, however, did not consider themselves to have superior knowledge. Ross and his colleagues argued that the observers and contestants had ignored the fact that the questioners had an unfair situational advantage (they had compiled the questions) and had over-estimated dispositional factors in making their judgements. In another experiment, Bierbrauer (1979) had participants watch a film of Milgram's obedience experiments in which one participant (the 'teacher') apparently gives a series of increasingly severe electric shocks to another (the 'learner') – see Chapter 3 for more details. When asked to explain the behaviour of the teacher, participants underestimated situational factors (such as the presence of the experimenter) in favour of dispositional ones (such as 'the teacher was cruel') in their explanations.

Although the FAE has been demonstrated in a number of studies, it has been argued that it is neither fundamental nor an error. According to Fiske and Taylor (1992), there are circumstances in which the FAE does not occur. One of these is when the discounting principle (see p. 12) is used. Rather than use the term 'error', Fiske and Taylor have argued that the word 'bias' is more appropriate since the FAE refers to a systematic distortion of our cognitions rather than to something that is actually wrong.

Actor/observer biases

Before we look at the actor/observer bias, try Activity 4.

❖ Activity 4 ❖

Imagine you are in a psychology lesson and as your teacher walks around the classroom, he or she trips up. How would you explain this behaviour? Now think about it from your teacher's viewpoint. How do you think your teacher would explain the behaviour?

The FAE occurs when we are explaining the behaviour of other people. Thus, when we are *observers* of behaviour we tend to make dispositional attributions about causes rather than situational ones. For example, when we see someone trip up whilst walking down the street, we tend to explain that behaviour in dispositional terms ('what a clumsy person!'). Suppose, however, that *we* were to trip up whilst walking down a street. Would we explain our own behaviour in dispositional terms? According to the evidence, the answer is 'no'; when we

In Focus

The fundamental attribution error

The FAE has a number of implications. One of these is that once a dispositional attribution has been made it is difficult to reverse. For example, Ross *et al.* (1974) led female students to believe that they had done either quite well or quite poorly on a novel problem-solving task. The students were then debriefed and were told that their scores had been falsified and that what they had been told previously was not necessarily correct. Later, the students were asked to rate their ability at the task, estimate how many correct responses they had made, and predict how well they thought they would do on the task in the future. The results showed that those initially told they had done quite well gave themselves higher ratings and estimates than those initially told they had done poorly. This occurred even though all participants had been told that the initial information they had been given was not necessarily correct.

are the *actors*, we tend to explain our behaviour in situation terms. In the case of tripping up whilst walking down the street, we might explain our behaviour in terms of 'uneven paving stones'.

Jones and Nisbett (1971) have argued that one reason for the differences between actors' and observers' attributions is that different aspects of information are available to those concerned. The actor, who has performed the behaviour, has more direct information available about the event than does the observer. The observer may be at some distance from the actor and may not be able to see the actual situational cause (in the example we used above, the uneven paving stone). The actor also knows more about his or her own previous behaviour than does the observer. We may know, for example, that we have very rarely tripped up while walking down the street. The observer, by contrast, does not have this knowledge and may assume that the behaviour is typical of the person observed. Finally, the focus of attention is different for the actor and observer. Actors focus outwards away from themselves towards the situation and so are likely to locate the cause of their behaviour there (actor bias). Observers, on the other hand, focus their attention on the actor, bypassing situational factors, and are, therefore, more likely to attribute the cause of behaviour to the actor (observer bias).

Attributions of success and failure

Although the actor/observer bias suggests that we emphasize situational factors in explaining our own behaviour, there are occasions on which this bias can be overturned. One of these is when we are asked to explain why we were successful at something, such as passing an examination. The actor/observer bias suggests that such behaviour would be explained in situational terms, such as 'an easy examination paper'. As we know, though, most people do not explain their successes in this way. People who pass exams usually explain their success by reference to all the hard work they did, how intelligent they are, and so on. These, of course, are dispositional attributions.

It seems, then, that we are quite happy to make dispositional attributions for behaviour when we are successful, and this has been termed the 'self-enhancing bias'. However, we tend to avoid taking responsibility when we are unsuccessful (the 'self-protecting bias'). Miller and Ross (1975) use the general term 'self-serving bias' to describe these and they have been demonstrated in a number of experiments. For example, Johnson *et al.* (1964) asked teachers to attribute responsibility for the performance of their pupils. The researchers found that teachers saw poor performance by their pupils as the responsibility of the pupils. However, this view changed when the children improved over time, such that the teachers saw themselves as being responsible for their pupils' improved performance!

There are a number of reasons why the self-enhancing and self-protecting biases should operate. For example, denying responsibility for unsuccessful outcomes allows us to protect our *self-esteem* whereas taking responsibility for success enhances it. Taking responsibility for success also allows us to present ourselves in the best possible light to others. The self-serving bias also operates at a *group* level. Thus, if we are a member of a team we tend to explain the successes of the team in dispositional terms. Successes of other teams (or outgroups) tend to be explained in situational terms, whereas failures of other teams tend to be explained in dispositional terms (Hewstone *et al.* 1982).

Self-handicapping

One extension of the self-serving bias is what is called 'self-handicapping' (Berglas and Jones 1978). Before we look at this, answer the questions in Activity 5.

❖ Activity 5 ❖

Think about the time immediately before an examination when you are waiting to go into the examination room. Your fellow students are all there and you begin talking about your prospects in the exam. What sorts of things do you and your fellow students talk about? Do you talk about how little revision you've done and how, as a result of this, your chances in the exam are very slim? Are there any other reasons people come up with for possible failure in the exam.

In some cases we might accept responsibility for failure if it can be attributed to a factor that is evident to others and we know that we can control that factor and thus improve our performance at a later date. However, when this is not possible we may invent reasons for the failure *before* the event has taken place. This is called self-handicapping. Self-handicapping is a strategy we use to maintain an image of competence when things go wrong. In exams, for example, we may know that we don't have the ability to pass. By self-handicapping, we are able to provide a creditable explanation for likely failure in situational rather than dispositional terms.

Section summary

Attribution is the process by which people use available information to explain the causes of behaviour. There are a number of theories of attribution which seek to explain the attributional process. There are a number of biases in the attribution process which influence the way in which behaviours are likely to be explained.

Prejudice and discrimination

Zimbardo *et al.* (1995) have defined *prejudice* as 'a learned attitude toward a target object, involving negative affect (dislike or fear) and negative beliefs (stereotypes) that justify the attitude' (p. 518).

Discrimination is defined by Zimbardo and his colleagues as 'the behavioural intention to avoid, control, dominate or eliminate those in the target group'. (p. 518).

There is no doubting the existence of prejudice in modern society, and many people have been victims of prejudiced attitudes because of their sex, age, disability, physical appearance and/or membership of an ethnic group. Some people have also been victims of discrimination. Much of the early research in this area of social psychology was conducted by Allport (1954), who outlined five behavioural stages of ethnic prejudice. These are:

1. anti-locution or verbal denigration such as the telling of racist jokes
2. avoidance of the ethnic group by, for example, segregation
3. discrimination, or the inequitable treatment or exclusion of those belonging to an ethnic group
4. physical attack, that is, actual violence against people and their property
5. extermination of the ethnic group, as for example, in the case of the attempts by Nazis to exterminate the Jewish race.

Prejudice is an example of an attitude and, as such, has three components:

- The *affective* component refers to our feelings or emotions towards the target group.
- The *cognitive* component refers to the beliefs, thoughts, and ideas we have about the members of the target group.
- The *behavioural* component is our predisposition to behave in certain ways towards the target group.

Usually, these three components are in balance: for example, if our beliefs about the target group are negative, our feelings and behaviours are also negative. This is because we prefer consistency in our social world and this allows us to interact successfully in it.

In some cases, however, the components may not be in balance. In their theory of 'reasoned action', Fishbein and Ajzen (1975) argued that although attitudes are frequently correlated with both behavioural intentions *and* actual behaviour, this is not always the case. Thus, a person may hold prejudiced beliefs but may not necessarily apply those beliefs by engaging in discrimination. Equally, discrimination may occur without this reflecting prejudice. In many schools, for example, physical education is taught separately to boys and girls, an example of discrimination without prejudice.

In this section we will focus on *racism*, which is one of the most pervasive forms of prejudice and discrimination. Racism can be defined as any attitude, action or institutional structure that exerts power unjustly over others because of their race. It is important to note that our definition includes reference to both individual *and* institutional racism where, as Cray (1995) has observed, the political and economic structure of an organization is such that it discriminates. Jobanputra (1995) has argued that psychology itself has always been affected by the racism of society in general. For Bhavnani and Phoenix (1994) three forms of racism are most evident:

- *Biological racism:* This assumes that some groups are naturally inferior to others, and has been most clearly demonstrated through the use of IQ testing in which attempts have been made to demonstrate white superiority.
- *Common sense racism:* This refers to work on Social Identity Theory in which it is often assumed that members of the ingroup will automatically discriminate against the outgroup (a point we will return to later on in this chapter).
- *New or modern racism:* This does not view other groups as being explicitly deficient in physical or intellectual terms (as is the case in biological racism) but attempts to justify inequalities in more subtle ways, such as viewing people as being 'different' in terms of their culture and in espousing non-traditional values. For Jobanputra (1995), this type of racism is the most harmful because it can be cleverly disguised and therefore be more difficult to detect and 'prove'.

Origins and maintenance of prejudice and discrimination

Psychologists, sociologists and historians have all advanced theories concerning the origins and maintenance of prejudice and discrimination. Sociological theories are concerned with broad patterns of sociocultural factors. Historical theories stress the importance of economic conflicts in the past. Psychologists have advanced explanations at the individual, group and societal levels.

Personality theories of prejudice

One group of psychological theories attributes the primary cause of racism to personality factors. The most famous example of this type of theory was advanced by Adorno *et al.* (1950). According to them, the origins of prejudice lie in what they termed the 'authoritarian personality'. Using a variety of tests, they found that people concerned with power, authority and obedience also tended to be highly *ethnocentric*, that is, considered only members of their own national, ethnic or religious groups as being acceptable. Adorno *et al.* argued that prejudice arises from the possession of specific personality characteristics which lead those who possess them to react with hostility towards certain groups who do not possess those characteristics.

One of the questionnaires developed by Adorno *et al.* measured 'potentiality for fascism' (the F-scale). Some of the items appearing on the questionnaire are shown below, and respondents are asked to decide if they agree or disagree with them:

- 'Most of our social problems would be solved if we could somehow get rid of the immoral, crooked and feeble-minded people.'

- 'Obedience and respect for authority are the most important virtues a child should learn.'
- 'An insult to our honour should always be punished.'
- 'It is only natural and right that women be restricted in ways in which men have more freedom.'

Although personality theories were once fashionable as ways of explaining the origins and maintenance of prejudice and discrimination, they fell into disrepute for a number of reasons. For example, although Adorno *et al.*'s theory explains why some people are more likely to be prejudiced than others, it fails to explain why large numbers of people (and even whole societies) can become prejudiced. The F-scale itself has also been criticized on the grounds that the 'authoritarian' response is always indicated by agreement with the items on the questionnaire. This, it has been argued, may lead to 'response acquiescence', that is, the tendency to agree with the remainder of the items on a questionnaire, irrespective of their content, once the first few have been agreed with.

According to Rokeach (1960), the authoritarian personality is not only associated with extreme right wing political conservatism, but also with extreme political conservatism on the left. Rokeach prefers to explain prejudice in terms of 'dogmatism' rather than the authoritarian personality. Dogmatic individuals are those who have a highly organized set of attitudes which are resistant to change in the light of new information. They are, therefore, rigid and intolerant thinkers.

Frustration/aggression and scapegoating theories of prejudice

According to Dollard *et al.* (1939), being frustrated (which is defined as being blocked from achieving a desirable goal) leads to aggression. As far as prejudice is concerned, scapegoating theories argue that when we are frustrated we need to find a target on which we can vent our feelings of anger. However, because the real cause of our anger might not be a suitable target, we displace it onto something towards which we already feel negatively.

A number of laboratory studies have shown that when people are 'frustrated' in some way they show an increase in prejudice (e.g. Miller and Bugelski 1948, Weatherley 1961). Outside the laboratory, Hovland and Sears (1940) found that as the economic conditions in the southern states of America worsened, white people took out their frustration on black people as shown by the increased number of lynchings that occurred. We should note, however, that this interpretation has been questioned by a number of researchers who point out that while frustration may exacerbate discrimination, it does not cause prejudice.

Social cognition and prejudice

Earlier on in this chapter we noted that because it is impossible to process every aspect of incoming information individually, we take short cuts and categorize information. When asked to recall a person's characteristics, we may do so according to the general category in which we placed them, that is, we tend to recall through stereotypes. We also tend to accept information which confirms the stereotype and refute information which challenges it. For example, when a prejudiced person meets a pleasant or likeable member of a rejected group, that member is perceived to be 'an exception to the rule' rather than as evidence of a misconception. As a result, our stereotypes remain unchanged, the bias in our processing becomes self-confirming, and prejudice is maintained.

According to Billig (1985), social cognition theories see stereotyping as an almost inevitable consequence of social information processing. Although Billig accepts that it is functional for us to *categorize*, he points out that we have the ability to *particularize*. In Billig's view, the focus of research attention should be 'category selection', that is, identifying the categories used by prejudiced and non-prejudiced thinkers.

❖ Activity 6 ❖

In an early study, Katz and Braly (1933) demonstrated the existence of stereotypes about members of different ethnic groups. Subsequent research showed that whilst certain stereotypes had changed over time, they were still prevalent (Karlins *et al.* 1969).

From the list of words below, select five that you think are typical of:

(a) Americans (b) Germans (c) West Indians (d) Chinese.

Place them in order, putting the word you think is most typical first. You may use the same words to describe the members of different nationalities.

Superstitious	Industrious	Sly	Intelligent	Musical
Scientifically minded	Materialistic	Ignorant	Stolid	Methodical
Ambitious	Loyal to family	Impulsive	Passionate	Lazy
Religious	Sportsmanlike	Sensual	Happy-go-lucky	Tradition-loving

Now compare your responses with those of other people. Do you see any similarities? Karlins *et al.* found that in 1969 Americans were mostly seen as 'materialistic' whereas 'industrious' was the stereotype most typical of Germans. West Indians were seen as 'musical' and the Chinese as 'loyal to family'.

Social identity theory and prejudice

Tajfel (1982) believes there are three aspects to prejudice. The first of these is *categorization.* According to Tajfel, the mere categorization of people into groups is sufficient for discrimination to occur, irrespective of any individual differences within the group. The second is *assimilation.* This is when children learn about and absorb the attitudes and values of the society in which they live. The third is *search for coherence.* This involves a need to understand and make sense of our social world. One way of achieving this is through social representations which we outlined earlier on in this chapter.

Social identity theory suggests that we use categorization in order to enhance our self-esteem. When we compare ourselves with others, we highlight any qualities which support our own ingroup values (termed 'ingroup favouritism') and we point out any weaknesses that may appear to exist in the outgroup (termed 'negative outgroup bias'). *Ethnocentrism* occurs when the ingroup considers itself to be at the centre of everything, and any outgroup is judged according to the ingroup's standards. In relation to mental illness, for example, the white ingroup has adopted a *Eurocentric* approach in defining mental illness in terms of the norms of white European cultures. For Pettigrew (1979), ethnocentrism is the ultimate attributional bias because group members see their own desirable behaviour as being dispositional and stable, whilst for any outgroup, desirable behaviour is attributed to situational factors. The reverse of this is true in the case of undesirable behaviour.

Social representations and cultural factors

The theory of social representations suggests that prejudiced explanations derive from the norms of the community or other social institutions of which a person is a part. People are inclined to modify their attitudes so that they come into line with those held by the people with whom they identify (e.g. peer and reference groups). If our reference groups hold prejudiced attitudes, we may adopt these in order to be accepted.

If people conform to the norms of the society they are in, prejudice may maintain itself by becoming part of a cultural ideology. As well as varying from country to country, such ideologies also vary within regions of the same country. For example, Middleton (1976) has shown that there is a difference between the northern and southern states of America; those from the latter show more extreme prejudice against black people than those from the former.

Intergroup conflict

In any society, the resources that people value are always in short supply. Competition between people for those resources inevitably creates winners and losers. Those who are successful may see themselves as superior and wish to protect their gains. However, the losers who would also like to be successful may see the winners as enemies because of their success. This sort of competition can be seen at all levels in society and, if the situation continues over a period of time, full-blown prejudice is likely to develop between the competing groups.

According to Deutsch (1973), there are three consequences of intergroup conflict:

- Communication becomes unreliable and impoverished. Neither group trusts the other, and both may resort to the use of propaganda.
- Perceptions of the members of each group become distorted, such that ingroup favouritism and negative outgroup bias occur.
- The belief develops that the only way to resolve conflict is through the use of superior force (see *In Focus* below).

Reducing prejudice

The reduction of prejudice is clearly an important goal for society. Traditionally, the way to reduce prejudice was to take one of two approaches, using either education (or socialization) or intergroup contact.

Reducing prejudice through education

Changing attitudes through education has, unfortunately, not met with much success. Targeting the home can only work when parents realise that their views are prejudiced – and often they think such views are justified. So what can be done? One possibility is to enrich the school curriculum to enable children to be exposed to other viewpoints (see *In Focus* on p. 20).

In Focus

Intergroup conflict (Sherif *et al.* 1961)

In a classic study, Sherif *et al.* (1961) demonstrated just how easy it is for intergroup conflict to develop. In the first stage of their study, boys who had arrived at a summer camp were randomly divided into two groups. For the first week, each group worked separately and on their own. One of the groups called themselves 'the Rattlers' and the other called themselves 'the Eagles'. In the second stage of the study, the groups were set against each other. Although the researchers had planned to introduce intergroup rivalry through various tasks, the tasks were not needed. For example, when the Rattlers won a tug of war competition, the Eagles responded by burning the Rattlers' flag! The Rattlers retaliated by raiding the Eagles' camp, damaging their property.

By the end of the second week the two teams were arch enemies. Support for their own group (the ingroup) was high. In written tests, the ingroup were considered to be 'friendly', 'tough' and 'brave'. The outgroup, however, were perceived in strongly negative ways and were described as 'sneaky', 'bums' and 'cowards' (strong terms for the 1950s). In a very short time, then, the competitive structure created by the Sherifs had led to hostility between the groups. In the third stage of the study, the researchers attempted to reduce the prejudice that had developed (see 'Reducing prejudice' above).

In Focus

Brown eyes, blue eyes

A classroom-based study conducted by Elliott (1977) attempted to show children what it was like to be discriminated against. One day Elliott, a school teacher, told her pupils that blue-eyed children were 'inferior'. Within a day, the blue-eyed children in the class were doing poorly at their work and described themselves as 'sad', 'bad', 'stupid' and 'mean'. In the meantime, the brown-eyed pupils in the class had become what Elliott described as 'nasty, vicious, discriminating little third graders'. Fights broke out because one child called another 'blue eyes'. The following day, Elliott told the children that she had made a mistake and it was actually brown-eyed children who were inferior and not those with blue eyes. Within a very short time, attitudes and behaviours reversed completely! On the third day, the children were told the truth of the matter.

Studies such as Elliott's give children direct experience of what it is like to be discriminated against. It was believed that the effects of the experience would be temporary because school-based studies are done in isolation from the home environment. However, in a ten-year follow-up of the original pupils in her class, Elliott (1990) found that they were more tolerant of group differences and were actively opposed to prejudice.

Another classroom-based study was carried out by Aronson *et al.* (1978). These researchers believed that the competitive nature of school ensures children will not learn to like and understand each other. Aronson *et al.* argued that rather than compete, children must cooperate in the pursuit of common goals. In the 'jigsaw' technique, each member of a group is given a different section of material to learn. Group members have to interact with each other, learning their part and communicating it to the others. The parts then combine to produce a whole. Aronson and his colleagues found that whilst it took some children longer than others to realise the value of cooperation, children from all races cooperated and learned from each other. The strategy appeared to be effective because it made the children *mutually interdependent* as well as teaching them about cooperation.

Reducing prejudice through intergroup contact

The second major approach to the reduction of prejudice is that of enhancing intergroup contact. The aim of this approach is to increase contact between different groups. As in the case with the jigsaw approach (which also involves contact), research indicates that mere contact between groups is not sufficient, and that it must be interdependent and cooperative rather than competitive.

Early studies showed that when contact is increased, prejudice is reduced. For example, Stouffer *et al.* (1949) showed that mixed race units in the American army produced less prejudice than segregated race units. This occurred because actual contact allowed negative stereotypes to be removed, increased cooperation rather than competition, and led to the formation of a single ingroup fighting a common enemy. In another study, Deutsch and Collins (1951) showed that a group of white residents moved to an integrated housing programme showed less prejudice towards blacks than white residents who moved to a segregated housing programme.

The results of studies such as these led other researchers to set up situations in which people could be manipulated into being prejudiced and were then exposed to strategies designed to reduce prejudice. Consider, for example, the study conducted by Sherif *et al.* The researchers found that bringing the leaders of the two groups of boys together did not produce any effect, nor did bringing the groups together. For example, when the groups were invited to eat together they simply threw food at one another. Mere contact, then, was not enough to reduce prejudice.

What did seem to be effective was the creation of *superordinate goals*, that is, goals which can only be achieved through cooperation. Thus, when the water supply was damaged and the Rattlers and the Eagles had to work together to repair it, and when a truck 'broke down' and both groups had to pull it with ropes to get it restarted, the prejudiced feelings that had developed were significantly reduced. Indeed, at the end of the summer camp a party took place which was enjoyed by both groups together.

So how do these approaches relate to social cognition and categorization? We have already pointed out that through equal status contact people have the opportunity to gain direct experience of other groups. However, unless this is prolonged (as in the case of an integrated housing project), it has been found that negative stereotypes will actually be reinforced rather than reduced.

Increased contact can help to reduce prejudice, however, in three ways:

- It can lead to the recognition of similarities between groups.
- Negative stereotypes can be changed if sufficient information about a group is provided.
- The outgroup homogeneity effect may be challenged.

According to Fiske (1989), when people are instructed to pay close attention to others, they do perceive those others in terms of *personal* rather than *stereotypical* attributes. In fact, Fiske and Neuberg (1990) suggest that we can engage in a number of strategies, ranging from total dependence on stereotypes (least cognitive effort involved) to dependence on the unique features of a person (most cognitive effort involved). Dependence on the unique features of a person matches Billig's idea of particularization. What is important is to address how we prevent people from taking short cuts in their cognitions and focus instead on individual differences.

If intergroup contact is possible, then new ingroups may form, but contact alone is not enough. According to Cook (1978), five factors are necessary for prejudice reduction:

- *Equal-status participants:* prejudice will continue if one group regards itself as being superior. If members of different groups can be brought together on equal terms, a basis for cooperative action is provided and prejudiced attitudes may be revised.
- *Exposure to non-stereotypical individuals:* the more people we meet who do not fit into our stereotypes about their group, the more likely that our prejudices about the group will change.
- *Personal acquaintance*: getting to know someone on a personal basis may reduce the 'outgroup homogeneity effect' (see p. 7); this, in turn, may help us to appreciate members of the so-called 'outgroup' as individuals.
- *Environmental support for intergroup contact:* contact can only be effective if there is support from the authorities and the community.
- *Cooperation between groups:* if the groups are placed in a position where there is a common (or 'superordinate') goal, then prejudice will be reduced.

A major problem in this area of research is that reducing intergroup conflict can only be achieved if it is possible for both groups to have their needs satisfied. According to Deaux *et al.* (1993), it is necessary to look at the reward structure when considering the interaction between two individuals or two groups. A *competitive reward structure*, for example, is totally inappropriate for prejudice reduction since success for one person must therefore mean failure for the other. Much more appropriate for the reduction of prejudice is a *cooperative reward structure*. In this, an individual or a group can only achieve success if the other individual or group also achieves success. A cooperative reward structure was employed by Aronson and his colleagues in their jigsaw technique study, and by Sherif *et al.* when they devised superordinate goals for the Rattlers and the Eagles.

Section summary

Prejudice is comprised of an affective, cognitive, and behavioural component, the last of these being the potential to behave in a discriminatory way. Many theories have attempted to explain the origins and maintenance of racial prejudice. Some of these theories emphasize individual factors such as personality and frustration/aggression whereas others identify factors associated with social information processing. Yet others emphasize group explanations such as social identity theory and intergroup contact. There have been several attempts to devise strategies to reduce prejudice. Although some of these have produced desirable effects, the reduction of prejudice is very difficult to achieve.

Chapter summary

- Social cognition is concerned with how we process information about our social environment. The use of schemata and heuristics are outlined.
- Social identity theory explains how group membership can affect our self-esteem and how categorization and social comparison contribute to our social identity.
- Social representations are the shared beliefs held by groups of people. Such beliefs contribute to the perceptions of individuals.
- The process of attribution is concerned with how people infer the causes of behaviour. Kelley's two models are described and evaluated. Biases in the attribution process are considered.
- Prejudice and discrimination are serious problems in society. Theories concerning the origins of prejudice are discussed and attempts to reduce it are considered.

Essay questions

1 Discuss psychological explanations of the attribution process. *(24 marks)*

2 (a) Consider psychological insights into the reduction of prejudice and discrimination. *(12 marks)*

(b) Assess the effectiveness of strategies for reducing prejudice and/or discrimination that arise from these insights. *(12 marks)*

3 Discuss the role of social representations in social cognition. *(24 marks)*

Further reading

Hatcher, D. (1995) 'The psychology of racism', *Psychology Teaching* (New Series No. 4), Association for the Teaching of Psychology.

Includes six up-to-date and easy to read articles on racism and psychology.

Gross, R. (1995) *Themes, Issues and Debates in Psychology*. London: Hodder and Stoughton.

Contains an excellent chapter on attribution.

Hayes, N. (1995) *Psychology in Perspective*, Basingstoke: Macmillan.

If you want to know more about social identity and social representation theories, Chapter 6 of this book provides a simple explanation of them and their importance in what is called European social psychology.

Chapter 2

Social relationships

Paul Humphreys

Preview

In this chapter we shall be looking at:

- theories of social/interpersonal relationships
- the formation, maintenance and dissolution of relationships
- components of relationships
- effects of relationships
- individual, social and cultural variations in the nature of relationships.

Introduction

If we think about the times in our lives which we associate with great happiness and great sadness, it is highly likely that the majority of them have involved us with other people. They might include falling in love for the first time, a moment of support or help from a close friend when we most needed it, the loss of a loved one, the birth of our children, the pain of a divorce or being told that our parents were splitting up. Even the significant moments in our personal histories which we might think of as personal triumphs or disasters (e.g. getting good A-level results; missing a critical volley in the final of a tennis competition) involve at least some social dimension (e.g. the class you studied with, or your opponent in the tennis final and your friends standing by the side of the court willing you to win). It follows from this that one of the most important aspects of psychology – and social psychology in particular – is the study of the relationships we have with others.

We may define a social relationship as an encounter with another person or with other people which endures through time. It is likely to be characterized by rules, roles and giving and taking. It may be institutionalized (as in the case of marriage). It may be permanent or impermanent, formal or informal. One thing we can say with confidence is that at least some of our relationships with others will constitute the most important aspects of our social lives.

In Focus

◆

The study of social relationships within psychology

Despite what has just been said about the importance of social relationships in our lives, it is only relatively recently in the history of psychology that this topic has been regarded as worthy of study. Perhaps psychologists previously believed that the dynamics of relationships such as friendship, love, and family ties and feuds could not easily be studied by the scientific method or that they were somehow too trivial to be of importance to academics and intellectuals. Relationships were regarded as being too much 'of the real world' or too 'populist' (just as media analysts for many years regarded soap operas as unworthy of study).

The picture has now changed greatly. Social relationships have emerged as a (relatively) unified field with its own journals, conferences and handbooks. Michael Argyle and Steve Duck (who now works in the USA) are particularly influential British social psychologists who have helped to establish social relationships within the mainstream of psychology.

Theories of relationships

Why do we engage in relationships? What do we get out of it for ourselves and what do we give to others? Why do we seek to begin some relationships and end others? What determines which are the relationships from which we derive the most, or least, satisfaction?

These are just some of the questions which psychologists have considered in their attempts to build general explanatory models of relationships. Some critics (e.g. Moghaddam *et al.* 1993) have argued that the questions which have most typically been asked may themselves reflect cultural and gender biases. This point of view, along with that put forward by the so-called postmodernists, is considered throughout the chapter.

As a starting point we may consider the different theories in terms of their level of analysis. Doise (1986) has argued that psychological analysis may be carried out on four levels (see Table 2.1).

In 'real-world' relationships, it may well be that relationships are 'located' at several levels (even at the same time). For example, I may have a loving relationship with someone who satisfies my sexual needs (1), with whom I share mutual pleasures of domestic companionship (2), who provides me with the support of a new family (3) and to whom I am married (4)! Therefore, to understand or explain this relationship, one needs to analyse its function at each level.

Table 2.1 Levels of psychological analysis

	Level	Example
1	Intrapersonal (i.e. within a person)	e.g. personality factors, cognitive styles
2	Interpersonal (i.e. between people)	e.g. helping others such as family and loved ones
3	Positional (i.e. between groups)	e.g. displaying hostility towards an out-group
4	Ideological (i.e. at a societal or cultural level)	e.g. belief in a dominant cultural value such as romantic love

Source: adapted from Doise 1986

Socio-biological theories

In non-human relationships, such as those found among insects or birds, much is genetically programmed. However, the further we move up the phylogenetic (evolutionary) scale, the less this appears to be the case. Some efforts have been made to explain aspects of relationships between people (such as love-making – usually called mating in this context! – and dominance) in purely genetic terms. Wilson (1986) argues that human sexual attraction and behaviour may be explained through an understanding of 'survival efficiency'. He argues that there is a 'bargaining' between men and women which characterizes and defines our sexual relationships. It is, he says, in the 'interests' of the male to impregnate as many women as possible, as this increases the chances of his genes being handed down as copiously as possible into the next generation. The reasons for this lie in the vast number of sperm that a man is capable of producing in his life time. Conversely, a woman may produce only one egg per month. Whereas the male is capable of fathering an almost infinite number of children in a relatively short period of time, the woman usually carries just one pregnancy at a time. The best chance of her genes surviving into the next generation is for her to ensure the healthy survival of the (relatively) few offspring that she is capable of producing during her reproductive lifetime. This, it is claimed, explains why men are what Woody Allen called 'ever-ready cocksmen', whereas women focus their energies on 'getting a good man and tying him down'! (Chapter 22 explores the reproductive strategies of animals in more detail.)

Evaluation of the sociobiological model

- There is always a danger in generalizing from non-humans to humans.
- The above example presumes that sexual attraction and behaviour is 'about' reproduction. For many people most sexual unions are *not* directed towards bearing children. Many people now elect to be childless.
- The example presumes heterosexuality.
- The theory is highly deterministic and accords little importance to our self-awareness, free will and the way in which we regulate most of our behaviours.
- There is an ethical concern that the model may be seen to support gender stereotypes which are divisive, and to endorse or 'authenticate' behaviours which perpetuate the so-called 'double standard', allowing men sexual 'privileges' and freedoms which women are denied.

Reinforcement and need satisfaction

It is possible that the reason why we spend so much of our time in social relationships is because we find them rewarding (i.e. positively reinforcing) or because we find life alone unpleasant and unrewarding. This explanation is based on the idea of operant conditioning (see Chapter 8).

Argyle (1992) points out that individuals who are rewarding are liked most, that is, those who are friendly, helpful and cheerful. Positive non-verbal signals, such as smiling, are signs of liking and are particularly important.

Of course, the reinforcements that a person can employ in social relationships may be more than affirmation and approval. People can distribute many other 'rewards' including love, sex, respect, status, information, help, money or goods (Foa and Foa 1975).

A different way of looking at how relationships may be reinforcing is to consider how they may satisfy our social needs. Argyle (1994) has identified motivational systems which he claims are at the roots of social behaviour (see Table 2.2). Read through the table and think about how far you agree with Argyle.

Table 2.2 Human motivations affecting social behaviour

Needs/motives	*Means by which they are achieved*
Biological needs	e.g. collective eating and drinking behaviours
Dependency	e.g. being comforted or nurtured
Affiliation	e.g. seeking the company and approval of others
Dominance	e.g. making decisions for other people, being 'bossy'
Sex	e.g. flirting; making love
Aggression	e.g. football violence
Self-esteem and ego-identity	e.g. being 'valued' by others

Source: adapted from Argyle 1994

Evaluation of reinforcement and social needs explanations

- Most of the general criticisms which can be levelled against behaviourist models (e.g. environmental determinism and failure to credit consciousness and free will) apply here.
- Hays (1985) found that in examining student friendships, as much value was given to rewarding the other person as being rewarded oneself. The key factor was the totality of both giving and receiving, not merely the latter in isolation.
- Participants in relationships are often more concerned with equity and fairness in rewards and demands rather than with the desire to maximize their own benefits (see later section on equity theory).
- Many social relationships which are more commonly found in non-Western collectivist cultures show little concern for the receipt of reinforcements. For example, Hill (1970) showed that kinship bonds are very influential, resilient and are not dependent upon reinforcement.
- There is evidence of gender as well as cultural differences. It has been shown that in many cultures women are socialized into being more attentive to the needs of others (such as husbands and children), rather than being oriented towards the gratification of their own needs (Lott 1994). It could be argued, of course, that this 'meeting the needs of others' may in itself be reinforcing. Many feminist scholars, however, would take issue with this on many levels including a moral/ethical one.

❖ Activity 1 ❖

Note down three important social relationships in which you are involved. Under each of the three, list the social needs you feel are met by these different relationships. In being explicit in this way and producing lists, you may be surprised at the similarities and differences in these relationships.

Reinforcement and need satisfaction are also important in the next group of theories.

The 'economic' theories

Since their introduction in the late 1950s, economic theories have been highly influential and have generated a great deal of empirical research. They are so called because they assume a view of social relationships analogous to economic activity, such as cost/benefit analysis: What do I gain? What do I lose? What do I give? What do I receive?

Economic theorists argue that we 'run' our relationships according to a balance sheet principle – we aim to maximize our gains or profits and minimize our losses. The majority of these theories are exchange theories because they employ a metaphor of typical market-place activity where we haggle/negotiate and try to drive the best bargain we can. We exchange the rewards we give to others for the ones that we wish them to give to us whilst at the same time trying to 'stay ahead' (receiving more than we give). Blau (1964) argued that our social interactions are 'expensive' (they take energy, time, commitment and other 'valuable', finite personal resources) and so what we get out of the relationships must at least pay us back in equal amount (but preferably give us a profit).

Social exchange theory

This was the first of the economic theories and was developed by Thibaut and Kelley (1959). The theory was concerned with the construction of so-called 'payoff matrices'. These are the calculations of the possible activities a couple could engage in and the profits and losses for each person for all the possible permutations of activities. The couple then become 'locked' into a relationship because of their dependence upon the other person to play their parts in the activities.

On the basis of this, Thibaut and Kelley proposed a four-stage model of long-term relationships (see Table 2.3).

Thibaut and Kelley also saw the importance of influences beyond an analysis of the relationship itself (called the 'reference relationship'). They introduced two 'reference' levels: comparison level (CL) and comparison level for alternatives (CL alt.). CL is concerned with the past and the present, that is, the comparison made is between the rewards and costs of the reference relationship and what we have been used to. If the reference relationship compares favourably, we are motivated to stay in the relationship. CL alt., on the other hand, is concerned with possible alternative relationships. Here we compare the

Table 2.3 Thibaut and Kelley's four-stage model of long-term relationship

Stage	Description
1 *Sampling*	We explore the rewards and costs 'located' in a variety of relationships. This may be done directly (by involvement) or indirectly by observing others.
2 *Bargaining*	We set out our stall at the beginning of a relationship. There is negotiation as the couple 'cost-out' the relationship and establish sources of profit and loss.
3 *Commitment*	We begin the process of 'settling into' a relationship. The exchange of rewards starts to become 'regularized' and relatively predictable.
4 *Institutionalization*	The interactions are established, and norms and mutual expectations are in place. The couple have 'settled-down'.

Source: adapted from Thibaut and Kelley 1959, Kelley *et al.* 1983

reference relationship with others which we *could* be in. If we feel that we could do better in another relationship, we may be motivated to finish the current one.

The social exchange model was modified in several respects by Homans (e.g. 1974). Out of his distributive justice hypothesis (we expect what we get out of a relationship to be proportional to what we have invested in it – otherwise we feel 'cheated'), a major redrawing of social exchange theory began to take shape which eventually resulted in equity theory.

Equity theory

Equity does not necessarily mean equality; rather it refers to *balance* and *stability*. Furthermore, equity may be defined by each member of the social relationship or by outsiders, and these definitions may, of course, differ. Walster *et al.* (1978) offered four principles of equity theory (see Table 2.4).

Evaluation of 'economic' exchange theories

- Many of the studies associated with exchange theories have been characterized by rather contrived methodologies which have little ecological (or real-world) validity. Argyle (1988) points out that social exchange theory 'has led mainly to very artificial experiments... Research on real-life relationships has been hampered by the difficulty of scaling rewards' (p. 224). The majority of methods and techniques used to test exchange theories were short-term and did not examine the dynamics of relationships through time (i.e. only fairly immediate effects and consequences were identified). Later work (e.g. Kelley *et al.* 1983) did, however, address this concern.
- There is a lack of consistent empirical support. For example, Clark and Mills (1979) have identified two different styles of couples: the communal couple and the exchange couple. In the former, giving is motivated by concern and positive regard for the other; only in the latter is there the kind of 'score-keeping' predicted by exchange theory. Murstein has developed a measuring tool – the exchange orientation scale – for identifying people who are score-keepers. These exchange types are suspicious, fearful, paranoid and insecure compared with the giving and trusting types (Murstein *et al.* 1977, quoted in Gross 1992).

Table 2.4 Walster *et al.*'s principles of equity theory

- In relationships, people try to maximize their rewards and minimize negative experiences within any relationship.
- The distribution of rewards is negotiated to ensure fairness. This may be achieved through trade-offs or compensations (i.e. a 'favour' or 'privilege' for one person is paid back by an equivalent favour or privilege).
- Unfair (or inequitable) relationships produce dissatisfaction. Not surprisingly the dissatisfaction is felt most acutely by the 'loser' and the greater the degree of perceived unfairness, the greater is the sense of dissatisfaction.
- As long as the 'loser' feels there is a chance of restoring equity and is motivated to save the relationship, he or she will endeavour to re-establish the equity. Furthermore, the greater the degree of inequity the loser perceives, the greater will be the effort at realignment.

Source: adapted from Walster *et al.* 1978

- There is no clear agreement amongst the research studies on equity theory. For example, Hatfield *et al.* (1979) showed that equity may be more important for females than for males and Murstein *et al.* (1977) also showed that equity is an issue of concern only in 'problematic' marriages. Both of these factors (i.e. gender and 'health' of relationship) were confirmed as important more recently in a longitudinal study of 736 married couples, carried out by Van Yperen and Buunck (1990).
- Work carried out in societies other than North America tend to give little support for equity theory. For example, Lujansky and Mikula (1983) found no equity effects upon romantic relationships in Austria, while Gergen *et al.* (1980) found that whereas American students preferred equity (a constant ratio of rewards to inputs), European students preferred equality. Moghaddam *et al.* (1993) argue that the emphasis upon exchange and equity is a reflection of the dominant values of North America, where these theories of social relationships were developed. They claim that these theories reflect the highly individualistic, capitalist and marketplace economic orientation, and Protestant work ethic of North America.

In Focus

Study of romantic love among girls (Simon *et al.* 1992)

Simon *et al.*'s study was concerned with the ways in which girls talked about the centrality of romantic love in their lives, how these norms were communicated and negotiated between the girls, and how they were 'policed'.

The study is a particularly intriguing one as it shows the process of 'enculturation', or 'how the work of culture is done'. Critics of macro-social psychology often argue that culture and ideology should be studied by sociologists rather than psychologists, but this study demonstrates clearly how culture is enacted and negotiated at Doise's personal and interpersonal levels (see Table 2.1).

The study was carried out in a school in mid-western USA. Data were collected over a period of three years by a variety of methods including participant observation, audio- and video-recording and in-depth group interviews. Most of the time, the focus of the study was upon the naturally occurring conversations of the girls.

On analysing their huge amount of data, the researchers identified five norms:

- Romantic relationships should be important, but not everything, in life.
- One should have romantic feelings only for someone of the opposite sex.
- One should not have romantic feelings for a boy who is already attached.
- One should have romantic feelings for only one boy at a time.
- One should always be in love.

The 'assimilation' of culture is not automatic and may be resisted. Whereas some of the norms were highly developed and generally accepted (e.g. the norms of heterosexuality and monogamy), others were not held by all group members and still were being negotiated.

Finally, the study shows the 'techniques' used for norm-establishment and dealing with non-believers:

- Humour was frequently used to introduce and 'test-out' new ideas – through joking and teasing the girls pointed out their friends' norm violations in an indirect, non-threatening manner.
- The norms were always 'on the agenda' because of their inclusion in day-to-day conversation.
- Confrontation (with consequential tension and conflict) was used if the other strategies did not 'work'.

None the less, there were girls who did not wholly 'buy into the package'. Thus we see the negotiation of ideology through human activity in social relationships.

- Again considering the cross-cultural validity of the 'economic' models, Moghaddam *et al.* (1993) believe that Western and non-Western relationships are dominated by different concerns and features. They argue that North American relationships are predominantly individualistic (concerned with the needs of the self rather than those of a broad group of people), voluntary (rather than determined by kin or family) and temporary (with the majority of relationships able to be terminated). Conversely, most non-Western relationships are collective, obligatory and permanent. They argue that the economic/exchange theories are only relevant in Western cultures.

You will recall that we earlier introduced Doise's levels of analysis model. So far we have concentrated upon the intra- and inter-personal levels. To end this section let us briefly explore explanations at the ideological level of analysis by examining a study by Simon *et al.* (1992) (see *In Focus* on p. 29)

Section summary

Many different theories of interpersonal and social relationships have been produced. They focus upon several aspects of relationships, such as why people engage in them, what they derive from being in them and what they contribute to them. They also address the question of why we remain in some relationships and leave others. The theories can be located at various 'levels of analysis' and Doise's model of four levels of social psychological analysis was used as one way of 'placing' the relationship models we considered. Sociobiological, reinforcement and economic theories were outlined and evaluations were offered for each model. One common concern was the extent to which the theories could be applied to cultures other than the North American/Western European ones in which they were developed.

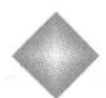

Stages of relationships

Duck and Sants (1983) (quoted in Hayes 1994) criticize much of the research that we have considered so far, claiming that it approaches the study of relationships with inappropriate assumptions. They tackle these by asserting the following:

- Relationships should be seen as changing and dynamic rather than static.
- The interpretations given to events and occurrences by the people involved are crucial. The events themselves are important only because of what they are taken to mean.
- A relationship should not be studied as if it were an object in itself. It arises out of the interaction of the people involved.
- People in relationships are rarely, if ever, dispassionate information processors.

With these points in mind, let us now turn to a developmental consideration of social relationships. Two stage models of social relationships are outlined in Fig. 2.1.

Both of these models offer a stage/developmental way of looking at personal or intimate relationships. Stage models have also been developed for other types of relationships (e.g. friendship).

Perlman and Duck (1987) offer two criticisms of stage models:

- There seems to be little agreement between the different stage theories (e.g. on the nature of the stages or their order). It could, of course, be the case that no one particular theory is 'right' for all personal relationships and thus agreement between the different theories may not be an issue at all. At the moment we are simply not in a position to make this judgement.
- The concept of stage 'shift' may be inappropriate. It may be that development in relationships is substantially a continuous, rather than discontinuous, process (after Hinde 1979).

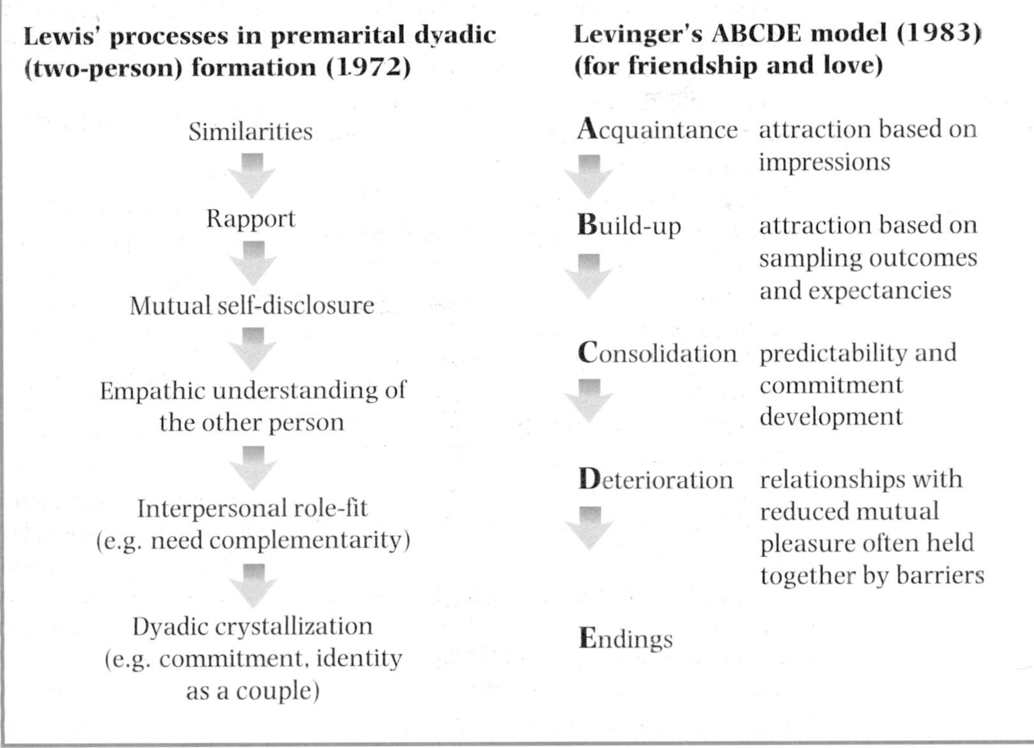

Figure 2.1 Two stage models of relationship development *Source: adapted from* Brehm 1985

Early stages: formation of relationships

Argyle (1988) uses Levinger's five-stage model (see Fig. 2.1) which addresses acquaintance, build-up, consolidation, deterioration and ending. Acquaintance would seem to be synonymous with social relationship formation and Argyle divides it into four aspects, examined below.

Physical attractiveness

Few readers will need to be told that in Western culture, at least, physical attractiveness is very highly valued. A vast array of American studies have shown that it is one of the major determinants of whether we express a wish to develop a relationship (romantic or platonic) with another person. However, there have been criticisms of many of these studies as they tend to concentrate exclusively upon dyadic (two-person) and very short-term (e.g. one meeting or 'date') relationships. In the latter it could be argued that the partners have very little else to 'go on', other than what they 'can see'.

Frequency of interaction

Much of the early work into friendship and attraction (e.g. Festinger *et al.* 1950) emphasized the importance of proximity (or physical/geographical closeness) and the frequency of interaction which is very often associated with this. A later study illustrated the power of familiarity which arises out of continued contact: Saegert *et al.* (1973) found that women who were simply in the company of certain other women as part of a series of drink-tasting studies, came to prefer them to those whom they met only once.

Despite the wealth of supportive evidence showing the importance of this factor, which Zajonc (1968) calls 'exposure', there does appear to be ambivalence about the direction of the effect. Do we like people more because we spend time with them, or do we spend more time with them because we like them?

Furthermore, frequency of interaction does not always lead to greater liking. Warr (1965) demonstrated that it can also produce more disliking. Thus it may be that frequency of interaction results in greater intensity of feelings between people but that these feelings may be either positive or negative.

Similarity

There is considerable evidence to support the view that 'alikes' rather than 'opposites' attract. It would appear that similarity of values, attitudes, beliefs and cognitive constructs are common indicators of strong friendships and attraction (e.g. Lea and Duck 1982).

Rubin (1973) gives the following reasons why we are attracted to those who are similar to us:

- We are 'drawn' to the possibility of engaging in the same activities.
- We seek social validation of our beliefs.
- If we like ourselves, it should logically follow that we will like others who are similar to us.
- It may facilitate communication if certain fundamentals are shared.
- We may presume that people who are similar to us will like us.

In arguing for the view that opposites attract, Kerckhoff and Davis's Filter Theory of Mate Selection (1962) takes a longitudinal view of relationships and contends that in the early stages of a relationship similarity in values may be important but in the later stages of an established relationship complementarity of needs is more important.

Reinforcement

We met this earlier when examining theories of social relationships (see p. 25).

Maintaining relationships

Many of the factors associated with maintaining relationships (such as the effects of rules in relationships and dealing with conflict) will be dealt with in the section on components of relationships.

Dindia and Baxter (1987) interviewed fifty married couples and asked about their maintenance strategies. Partly because of the nature of the questions asked and partly because of the behaviours of the couples, two types of strategies emerged: *maintenance* and *repair*. Repair strategies are those used to make good damage, as discussed in Activity 2. Maintenance strategies may be likened to preventative medicine.

Dindia and Baxter identified a total of forty-nine different strategies. The maintenance ones (such as 'spending time together in the evenings', 'talking about the day', 'telephoning when I'm away') tended to focus on doing things together, whereas the repair strategies – e.g. 'talking over the problem' or 'issuing an ultimatum' – tended to focus on the nature or mechanics of the relationships itself, and thus were more inward-looking and analytical.

There were interesting differences in the responses given by the couples who had been married for long periods compared to those who had only recently married. The former reported using fewer maintenance strategies than the relatively newly-weds. There are a number of possible explanations for this. It may be related to the beneficial effects of familiarity (we know the other so well), a lot of the groundwork will already have been done and the relationship will 'run itself', or there may be a negative 'taking-for-grantedness' in the relationship. It may, however, be an issue of awareness: perhaps the long-term partners are so used to the relationship and the things that they do within it, that maintenance becomes 'second nature' and somewhat invisible to them, and, therefore, it was not reported to the researchers.

❖ Activity 2 ❖

Think for a moment about a close relationship you have (perhaps a friendship, perhaps a strong relationship with a member of your family). Think about a 'crisis' (or time of difficulty, if 'crisis' is too strong) in the relationship and how you and the other person(s) in the relationship went about making good the damage and restoring the 'health' of your relationship.

Many studies of relationship maintenance assume that the people involved are committed to the survival of the relationship. The problem of this assumption is highlighted by a study carried out by Ayres (1983) who was also concerned with the strategies people use to maintain their relationships. The study showed that the strategies vary according to the 'direction' the people want the relationship to move in: escalation, reduction or no-change.

- Avoidance strategies tended to be used by those people resisting an attempt by the other to change the relationship.
- Balance strategies (such as putting in more or less effort) were used by those who wanted a relationship to change. The level of effort depended on the desired direction of change).
- Directness usually involved talking about issues and was generally associated with a desire for the status quo.

The end of a relationship

The ending of a relationship can be one of the most emotionally demanding times of our lives. We must, however, be mindful of the different needs of the people in the relationship. For every broken heart in a romance, there may be a liberated, free agent! It can also be the case, of course, that a relationship ends even though both partners wish it to continue or even develop (e.g. lovers thwarted by parental prohibition, geographical separation or the death of one of the partners).

There are many reasons for relationships ending. Some of those studied by psychologists are listed in Table 2.5.

Duck (1981) offered two categories of causes for relationships breaking down:

- predisposing personal factors (e.g. distasteful personal habits, emotional instability)
- precipitating factors, such as:
  - exterior influences on breakdown (e.g. a rival)
  - process/behavioural/management features (e.g. incompatible working hours)
  - emergent properties of relationships that cause decline (e.g. 'the relationship was going nowhere' or 'it just got too intense')
  - attributions of blame (e.g. 'what went wrong?', 'who was to blame'?).

Table 2.5 Reasons for relationships ending

- conflict (see section on components of relationships)
- breaking agreed rules (e.g. about confidentiality, support, fidelity)
- dissatisfaction or boredom with the relationship
- lack of stimulation or novelty
- an attractive alternative relationship (see exchange models)
- costs outweighing rewards (see exchange models)
- perceived changes in the relationship
- interference from other relationships
- problems of abuse (e.g. alcohol, sexual, monetary)
- changes in *self* or other person
- falling out of love
- saving face (e.g. finishing a relationship before the other person does).

❖ Activity 3 ❖

Think of the relationships in which you have been involved and which *you* ended. Were there common reasons or was each one different?

Now think of relationships which *the other person* ended. Were there common reasons or was each one different?
If there was a common reason, what does this tell you about yourself?

Duck (1988) has developed a four-phase model of the termination of close or intimate relationships.

1. The *intra-psychic* phase – This is where one of the partners or friends becomes increasingly dissatisfied with the relationship. If the dissatisfaction is sufficiently great there is 'progression' to the next phase.
2. The *dyadic* phase – Here the other person becomes involved. If the dissatisfaction is not acceptably resolved there is progression to the next phase.
3. The *social* phase – This is where the break-up is 'aired' and made public, for example to friends and family. It is also where the social implications (such as care of children) are negotiated. If the relationship is not saved here (perhaps by the intervention of family) it goes to the final stage.
4. The *grave-dressing* phase – Here the ex-partners begin the organization of their post-relationship lives and begin publicizing their own accounts of the breakdown and what (if any) is the nature of the new relationship with the ex-partner. The self-serving attributional bias (see Chapter 1) is frequently employed by partners who develop their own versions of where the blame for breakdown actually lies.

Evaluation of 'stages of relationships' material

The cross-cultural critique

We may consider critiques of the 'relationship life span' material from two perspectives. The first is one we have addressed before, that concerning cross-cultural issues.

Moghaddam *et al.* (1993) contend that whereas social relationships in Western cultures tend to be individualistic, voluntary and temporary, those in non-Western cultures tend to be collective, obligatory and permanent. It follows from this distinction that a great deal of what we have just been considering is simply not applicable or relevant to non-Western cultures. Moghaddam *et al.* go on to say, 'The cultural differences in interpersonal relationships reminds us that scientists, like everyone else, are socialized within a given culture. As a result, their theories and research are inevitably affected by this cultural experience. The cultural values and environmental conditions in North America have led North American social psychologists to be primarily concerned with first-time acquaintances, friendships, and intimate relationships, primarily because these appear to be the relationships most relevant to the North American urban cultural experience' (p. 103). They suggest that in non-Western cultures where people cannot enter and leave relationships 'at will', key questions for research might be:

- What mechanisms are there within interpersonal relationships that serve to ensure positive interactions?
- How do people resolve or remove the conditions that adversely influence their relationships?
- How are people able to tolerate differences and incompatibilities within their relationships?

The postmodern critique

In recent years the postmodern critique, originally developed in the arts such as literature in the immediate post-Second World

War period, has been something of a growth industry in psychology (see Kvale 1992, for example). What does the term mean? Petkova (1995) identifies three types of meanings:

- As referring to a postmodern age – The modern world had faith in science as our new God. The postmodern 'world' (literally, after-the-modern world) has developed a more critical stance to science, having witnessed the construction of the atomic bomb and global environmental pollution. Science has failed to produce a cure for HIV/AIDS, let alone one for the common cold, and is now increasingly seen as a human exercise rather than an 'uncovering' of natural truths.
- As a cultural expression – This contends that all human understanding is time- and place-specific. In other words, ideas/theories and explanations are influenced by the time and place in which they emerge.
- Postmodern thought – There is no longer a belief that there is objective reality (or truth), merely that people negotiate meanings through their interactions (for example their conversations and their disagreements).

The postmodern critique has many contributions to make to our study of social relationships. Let us consider one of these at the moment and return to others later.

Wood and Duck (1995) argue that much of the research into what we have called 'relationship life span', has merely reflected the taken-for-granted assumptions of the researcher. In other words, if we construct our enquires in such as way that a presumption of relationship formation, maintenance and breakdown is built in (for example, through the questions we ask) then it should not surprise us when this is 'mirrored back' to us in the outcomes. To put it crudely, we see what we expect to see.

Section summary

Duck and Sants (1983) argued against a mechanistic view of relationships which portrays them as products rather than processes. Relationships were then looked at from a developmental perspective and three phases were identified: formation, maintenance and dissolution. Factors involved in each of these phases were examined. Finally, a cross-cultural and a postmodern critique on the developmental perspective were offered.

Components of relationships

❖ Activity 4 ❖

Consider three of your social relationships (either current or past) and write down what things you typically do (or did) in those relationships. Is there a correlation between how much time you spend on the various activities and how important they are within the relationship? Are there significant differences between the activities, according to what kind of relationships they take place in (e.g. friendships versus family) or are the majority of activities common?

The current *Concise Oxford Dictionary* defines component as 'a part of a larger whole'. Therefore we may consider this to be concerned with what happens *within* relationships. In other words, what are the constituent parts of a relationship?

Argyle (1988), after acknowledging that much will depend upon the type of relationship being studied, addresses the following 'features' of relationships.

Activities

What do people in relationships do? Argyle and Furnham (1983) found that the most common activities in marriages were: being in bed together, watching television, domestic jobs, games, informal meals, shopping, intimate conversation and arguing.

There appear to be gender differences in the nature of relationships. Nardi (1992), for example, describes women's friendships as 'expressive', men's as 'instrumental' (i.e. talking versus doing things); women's as 'face-to-face', men's as 'side-by-side'; women's as more concerned with disclosure and intimacy.

Nardi notes two interesting differences between the same-sex friendships of lesbians and the same-sex friendships of gay men. Gay men are more likely than lesbians to have sex with casual friends (for gay men it is often the case that sexual intimacy precedes psychological intimacy whereas for lesbians the reverse is typically true) and gay men are significantly less likely to continue to maintain friendship with an ex-lover than are lesbians.

Nardi argues, however, that there is a danger of regarding gender differences as 'set in stone' and we should be mindful that there are just as many (if not more) differences within, as opposed to between the genders and that the differences which are frequently found may have as much to do with social forces (e.g. work roles, family, marital status) as factors 'within the individual'. For example, it may be argued that men's friendships are constrained by an overwhelming desire to avoid being seen as homosexual. Segal (1990) states that the possible imputation of homosexual interest causes heterosexual men to be aware of and assert their difference from both women and homosexual men.

This is well illustrated by Williams (1992) who compared friendships between North American Indians and Asians. One of his findings was that as the homophobia of North America increasingly permeated the lives of the North American Indians, male-male friendships became less intense than those in past generations. He says, 'American Indian men's alienation from each other is a 'miner's canary' to warn us of the even more extreme alienation going on among mainstream Americans. Friendships among heterosexual men are one of the main casualties of homophobia' (p. 197).

Goals and conflicts

Argyle and Furnham (1983) asked participants to rate their degree of satisfaction with a number of relationships. The major factors which emerged as important within relationships were:

- material and instrumental help
- social and emotional support
- common interests.

They found that 'the spouse is the greatest source of both satisfaction and conflict; the work superior, on the other hand, is typically a major source of conflict but a low source of reward. Neighbours are low on both' (p. 232).

What about goals? Argyle (1992) regards these as what people are trying to achieve in a relationship. Research (e.g. Argyle *et al.* 1981) in which participants were asked to rate the importance of goals for different relationships has shown that three major goals usually emerge:

- own physical well-being
- social acceptance
- task goals specific to the situation.

They also asked the participants to rate whether each goal helped, hindered or was independent of the other goals. Links between goals, both within and between persons, were found. For example, in studying nurses, it was found the nurses' goal of looking after and caring for the patient (task goal) led to the well-being of the patient (other person) but conflicted with their own physical well-being (see list above).

Rules

Argyle and Henderson (1985) define rules as 'shared opinions or beliefs about what should and should not be done'. These rules may be formal or informal, general (to all relationships and/or situations) or specific, restrictive or facilitatory, universal or culturally specific, etc. They argue that the most important kinds of rules are:

- rewardingness (the basic assumption of exchange theories) – e.g. giving attention and ego-support to the other person
- intimacy rules (about the permitted levels and forms of intimacy within a relationship) – e.g. restrictions on certain forms of physical contact
- coordination and avoiding difficulties (leading to the satisfaction of goals) – e.g. meeting the other person 'halfway' when trying to make decisions affecting both parties.
- rules of behaviour with third parties – e.g. 'standing up' for the other person in public.

Argyle and Henderson (1985) argue that rules have two major functions in relationships. First, they regulate behaviour to minimize potential sources of conflict which may disrupt the relationship (Regulatory rules). Second, they act as a check on exchange of rewards, which motivate people to stay in the relationship (Reward rules). We have already questioned the latter in our evaluation of exchange theories. But surely there can be no question about the other function of rules which Argyle and Henderson give (to avoid conflict because it is disruptive to relationships)? Not so. Wood and Duck (1995) state that 'Conflict is too often regarded as an aberration that must be 'managed'. Yet it is not necessarily symptomatic of relational difficulty and may in fact be highly constructive in many instances' (p. 17). In a study of intimacy by Wood *et al.* (1994) respondents described conflict as energizing relationships, heightening individuality, inspiring trust and enriching intimacy.

Power and roles

We may define power as the potential or capacity to get others to behave as desired (see Chapter 3). Stratton and Hayes (1993) define a role as the part that each individual is expected to play in a social situation. Thus, we can see that the two may be regarded as substantially interdependent.

One area of interest in the power/roles interplay is that of the power relationships between men and women. Argyle (1988) says, 'For a long time, and in most cultures,

Activity 5

Argyle *et al.* (1985) investigated relationship rules in four countries (Britain, Italy, Hong Kong and Japan). They presented their respondents with a list of 33 rules considered general to all relationships, and a further 12 rules specific to particular relationships (e.g. 'intimate'). Twenty-two types of relationships were also presented to respondents who then rated the importance of each rule for each relationship. The rules listed below are those chosen by respondents as applying to most relationships. The order shown, however, is not the order found by Argyle *et al.* Try to place the rules into rank order, showing which rules were chosen as important for most relationships. The order found by Argyle *et al.* is given on the next page. The first rule was found in all 22 relationships, the last in only 11.

(a) should address the other person by their first name
(b) should not criticize the other person publicly
(c) should stand up for the other person in their absence
(d) should not discuss with another person things said in confidence
(e) should not indulge in sexual activity with the other person
(f) should seek to repay debts, favours or compliments no matter how small
(g) should share news of success with the other person
(h) should respect the other's privacy
(i) should look the other person in the eye during conversation.

wives had an 'expressive' and nurturant role inside the home, while husbands had an 'instrumental' role in finding food, earning money, building houses and dealing with the world outside. Pressure from women is causing these roles to change in three ways: more women have jobs, and sometimes have better jobs than their husbands; they have more equal pay; and they do less of the housework than before, though they still do most of it' (p. 236).

Many critical psychologists (not to mention feminists) would take issue with the notion that 'the lot' of women has significantly improved. For example, although it is true that more women do have paid employment outside the home, many of these jobs are part-time, temporary and poorly paid. Furthermore, it may be the case that far from being 'liberated' from the home they are forced to go out to work because of the increase in male unemployment.

One of the preferred methods of the postmodern writers and researchers is discourse analysis. Although it is impossible to offer an easy definition of this approach, there are some common features which we can identify. Discourse analysis:

- is qualitative rather than quantitative
- is concerned with readings of 'texts' (such as conversations or interviews, or writings such as letters or autobiographies)
- is generally concerned with 'naturally occurring events' (such as people talking) rather than contrived events (such as experimental manipulation)
- is concerned with the relationships between researcher and participants, and aims to establish greater parity and equality between them than is found in most 'traditional' research
- states there can be no one, true reading or interpretation of events; for example, think about the two different accounts ex-husbands and wives may give following the breakdown of their relationship
- focuses upon language and the use that is made of it
- claims that psychological factors (such as the self or gender) are not products that 'live' within a person and are displayed in our behaviour, but rather they are created within the interpersonal activity between people.

Answer to Activity 5
The order of importance that Argyll *et al.* found was: h, d, i, b, e, f, c, g, a.

Evaluation of components of relationships research

Wood and Duck (1995) claim that the calls to rethink research reflect a larger cultural and intellectual shift into postmodernity. They offer the following five 'implications of postmodern thinking' for the study of social and personal relationships:

- *Profound contextuality:* Relationships should always be seen in their 'embedded' environments, not as stand-alone things. You will recall that this is similar to the point made earlier by Duck and Sants (1983) – relationships are processes not products.
- *Decentered selves:* Rather than seeing the self as a stable inner core, postmodernists see it as inconsistent and dependent upon circumstances. Back in 1892 William James said that a person has as many selves as there are people viewing it. If this is true then we should not expect to see relationships between people as either predictable or constant.
- *Understudied relationships*: Not only has there been an emphasis upon certain types of relationships (such as heterosexual, romantic partnerships) as noted before, but many others have been neglected, such as homosexual relationships and 'virtual' relationships (e.g. those on the Internet).
- *Language as presentational*: Language does not merely 'reflect' things, but actually creates them. This issue has a long history in psychology, such as in the linguistic determinism/relativity debate (e.g. the Whorfian Hypothesis).
- *Situated accounts, not laws; perspectives, not truths:* Science is a social enterprise with the scientist just one player among many. There are no universal truths to be uncovered, merely a variety of ways of 'making sense' of the world.

In Focus

Discourse analysis

The following study is a synopsis of a discourse analysis study carried out by Gavey (1992) which gives us a view of power within relationships. Her study of 'coerced heterosexual behaviour' used interview data from only a small sample of six women, but postmodernists contend that psychologists have for too long been slaves to the need for large numbers of participants and have been blind to the depth which can be achieved in small-scale analyses. Gavey observes that the women were not chosen because they identified themselves as having any particular problems or experiences, 'in fact, several expressed the reservation that their experiences of sex with men had been very ordinary, and that they might not have anything to say that would be of interest to me' (p. 330). It is also worth noting that all the women were consulted by Gavey after she had written her first draft, to ensure that what she had written was acceptable to them.

She identified the following 'discourses' (statements which create and justify that which they speak about).

1 **What is normal (or 'what's wrong with me?')**

Elaborate steps may be taken by lovers to meet, or time together may be so limited that 'the inevitability of sex (usually sexual intercourse) taking place is predictable'; for example:

Lee: 'You'd hardly get in, book into a motel room... go to a huge amount of trouble to get rid of my child, for him to put his work on hold and... living in a small town to sort of creep around the back streets and make sure no one had seen you. Then to have done all that and then say, "I'm sorry, actually, I just wanted a cuddle and a cup of tea".'

Many of the women believed that the coercion was normal, and their reluctance or resistance abnormal, for example:

Pat: 'I know perfectly well that if I really said "absolutely no, no, no, not under any circumstances", then he wouldn't have persisted, but then the other thing to that is that maybe I wouldn't actually say "absolutely no" in case he never came back again.'

Chloe: 'The argument stands out as the most important thing. Things like being called a f****** bitch and having the door slammed. And always trying to explain that it didn't mean that I didn't care because I didn't want to have sex, but never ever succeeding.'

2 **Nurturance and pragmatism**

Lee: 'He pleaded. And wanted to have sex with me. And so, I'd land up feeling sorry for him... It was pathetic.'

Lee: 'He kept saying, just, just let me do this or just let me do that and that will be all. And this could go on for an hour... I just wanted to go to sleep... I can just feel that sexual energy, he's no sooner going to go to sleep than fly to the moon. So after maybe an hour of me saying "no", and him saying "oh, come on, come on", I'd finally think, "Oh my God... for a few hours rest peace and quiet, I may as well".'

Power indeed.

Section summary

In this section there is a deliberate contrasting of 'traditional' relationships research (e.g. experimental or questionnaire design, large sample sizes and quantitative analysis) versus the discursive, discourse analysis work which Burman and Parker (1993) contend is 'sweeping across social psychology'.

What people do in relationships was considered by examining the following: activities; goals and conflicts; rules; power and roles. The section concluded with a critique from Wood and Duck (1995).

Effects of relationships

Finally, let us turn our attention to the consequences and outcomes of relationships. We have indirectly dealt with much that is relevant to this section already. Remember that one of the norms that Simon *et al.* (1992) found among their adolescent girls was 'one should always be in love'. The effects of sexual coercion we have just seen described by Gavey (1992). When Klinger (1977) asked the question 'What is it that makes your life meaningful?', the two most frequently given answers were close friends and romantic partners. Social relationships may also, of course, be sources of great anguish and personal misery.

Happiness

What is happiness? Argyle (1992) says 'If people are asked what they mean by this word they give two kinds of answer. Some describe it in terms of positive emotions – joy, fun, euphoria. Others describe it in terms of satisfaction and contentment with life as a whole – job, spouse, home and so on – a reflective state of mind. "Happiness" includes both components' (p. 282). Let us consider what has been found about the effects of social relationships on these two aspects of happiness.

Positive emotions

Argyle (1992) asks why it is that friends, in particular, produce joy. He offers three possible explanations:

- shared enjoyable experiences (such as going to parties; eating and drinking)
- positive feedback that is exchanged (e.g. from non-verbal signals such as smiling and touching)
- synchrony and coordination (it may be that we mirror the moods of others we are with to positive effect). Locke and Horowitz (1990), showed that participants who were either 'normal or mildly depressed' enjoyed time spent with another person if that person were in a similar mood to themselves).

It could be argued that the first two of these explanations are firmly rooted in an adherence to the economic/exchange models which we looked at earlier, and as such may be subjected to the same general criticisms and concerns which were directed at them. Furthermore, we should be mindful that the majority of the research in this field has been carried out on what we have earlier called 'voluntary' relationships (e.g. friendship and love); consequently the findings may not have applicability to cultures which are characterized by 'obligatory' relationships.

Positive states of mind

Despite these troubled times for the institution of marriage, it has been shown that marriage is strongly associated with happiness, although much of the quoted evidence is not particularly contemporary. For example, see the findings of Veroff *et al.* (1981) in Table 2.6.

Set against this, women with children reported negative feelings concerning marriage, such as boredom, loneliness and aggression (Harding 1985).

One of the great difficulties in interpreting findings of research into the relationships between marriage and positive states of mind concerns the direction of the effect (are people

Table 2.6 Happiness of married, single and divorced people

Percentage describing themselves as 'very happy'

	Men	*Women*
Married	35.0	41.5
Single	18.5	25.5
Divorced	18.5	15.5

Source: Veroff *et al.* 1981

happy because they are married or do they get married because they are already happy with a relationship?). Furthermore, we may not be comparing like with like. It may be the case that there are important psychological (and other) differences between those people who marry and those who cohabit or live alone. One of the difficulties in addressing this question is that very little work has been carried out on cohabitation. Cunningham and Antrill (1995) state that since Newcomb's review of the field in 1987 almost nothing has been published in journals concerning cohabitation with the word psychology in the title. Their own study shows commitment to be the central distinction between those who marry and those who cohabit: 'uneasiness about a lifetime commitment to the present partner or to the institution of marriage continually arises in surveys of cohabitors. Women's uneasiness about the institution of marriage now often stems from their awareness that it is still one of the major sites of gender inequality.'

Mental health

We have already noted in several places that social relationships are not only the sources of many of our greatest pleasures in life, but they are also associated with some of our moments of greatest despair. We may address an issue of even greater significance: do social relationships contribute to mental ill health?

Table 2.7 Mental hospital admissions and marital status

Marital status	*Mental hospital admission per 100,000*
Single	770
Married	260
Widowed	980
Divorced	1,437

Source: Cochrane 1988

Argyle and Henderson (1985) state that divorced and separated people are more likely to be mentally ill or commit suicide than married people. They quickly add, however, 'part of the explanation of the high rate for the divorced and separated is that many of them get divorced because of these mental disturbances'. This again highlights the difficulties of establishing the direction of effect (as we said above with regard to happiness). However, there is considerable evidence to show that there *is* a correlation between mental health and personal relationships (see Table 2.7).

Relationships as social support

Argyle (1988, 1992) focuses upon the influence of the 'social support' provided by relationships on mental health. He talks of the 'buffering hypothesis' whereby good, effective social support can 'absorb' some of the effect of harmful and threatening life events (such as unemployment). He offers three reasons why social support might relieve distress:

- It may enhance self-esteem and self-confidence.
- It may have a positive emotional effect (for example, being shown affection may make us feel more valued).
- 'A problem shared is a problem halved' – perhaps not literally, but knowing that others are there at times of need may make us feel more comfortable.

Much of what we have noted earlier about gender and cultural differences will almost certainly have considerable influence in this final, important aspect of social relationships. For example, women tend to have more expressive (and by implication, more supportive) relationships than men. Non-Western cultures have greater institutionalized social support through more permanent and collective relationships.

Section summary

This section focused on two effects of relationships: happiness and mental health. Critical reference was made at the end to gender and cultural differences.

Chapter summary

- Several social/interpersonal models of relationships have been produced. The main ones are biological/evolutionary; exchange (the so-called economic theories) and cultural (or ideological). Many of the assumptions and features of the models have been accused of gender and culture bias.
- Partly as a response to what is perceived as the mechanistic and reductionist nature of several of the models, considerable work has been carried out on the 'life span' of relationships, i.e. using a developmental perspective. This is generally viewed in terms of stages or phases (e.g. formation, maintenance, dissolution). The majority of work has been carried out on dyads (two persons) and has concentrated upon the early stages of relationships. The applicability of this research to non-Western cultures (where relationships tend to be collective, obligatory and permanent rather than individualistic, voluntary and temporary) is questioned.
- Recently, much of the work in social psychology on the components of relationships (what people do within them) has been informed by a postmodern, discursive (e.g. discourse analysis) perspective.
- Relationships have consequences for the people within them.Throughout the chapter many of these effects are considered but the final section focuses specifically upon two: happiness and mental health. Although it is often difficult to be sure about the direction of effect, some effects of belonging to social relationships do emerge from the research.

Essay questions

1 Critically consider two theories of interpersonal relationships. *(24 marks)*

2 (a) Describe research evidence relating to either the formation or maintenance of relationships. *(12 marks)*

(b) Critically evaluate the research you have described in part (a). *(12 marks)*

3 Discuss individual, social and cultural variations in the nature of relationships. *(24 marks)*

4 Critically consider what psychological research has told us about the effects of interpersonal relationships. *(24 marks)*

Further reading

Argyle, M. (1992) *The Social Psychology of Everyday Life*, London: Routledge.
Duck, S. (1988) *Relating to Others*, Milton Keynes: Open University Press.

These two books, written by the two British authors who have done so much to establish social relationships as a 'legitimate' topic within social psychology, offer lucid and concise accounts of research in the field.

Wilkinson, S. and Kitzinger, C. (eds) (1994) *Heterosexuality*, London: Sage.

An intriguing set of contemporary papers, the vast majority of which are within the new 'Postmodern Zeitgeist'.

Moghaddam, F.M., Taylor, D.M. and Wright, S.C. (1993) *Social Psychology in Cross-Cultural Perspective*, New York: W.H. Freeman.

Puts North America and Western Europe in their place! It shows us just how much psychology is dominated from these locations and how narrow this focus can often be.

Wood, J.T. and Duck, S. (eds) (1995) *Understudied Relationships: Off the Beaten Track*, Thousand Oaks, USA: Sage.

The title says it all.

Chapter 3

Social influence

David Clarke
Claire Meldrum

Preview

In this chapter we shall be looking at:

- research relating to conformity, obedience and independent behaviour
- theories of and research into the basis of social power, including the roles of both leaders and followers
- theories and research concerning collective behaviour, including that of crowds and mobs.

Introduction

Social influence is the process by which an individual's attitudes, beliefs or behaviours are modified by the presence or actions of others (Saks and Krupat 1988). Conformity and obedience are two forms of social influence. We will also look at how some people resist both conformity and obedience to authority and continue to act independently. In this chapter we will explore how group pressure may cause the former and how authority figures may command the latter. Leaders are those with the power to exert especial social influence over others. We will examine how different styles of leadership interact with the behaviour of those who are led. Finally, we will discuss the way in which being a member of a crowd might affect an individual's behaviour.

Conformity

Conformity is defined by Aronson (1988) as 'a change in a person's behaviour or opinions as a result of real or imagined pressure from a person or group of people'. Zimbardo *et al.* (1995) define it as a 'tendency for people to adopt the behaviour, attitudes and values of other members of a reference group'. You may find it easier to identify with Aronson's definition which focuses upon the kind of experience most of us have had at one time or another: the feeling that others are putting pressure on us to change our minds or behaviour. However, Zimbardo *et al.*'s definition proposes that we tend to go along with those people with whom we compare ourselves when we are evaluating our status (i.e. our reference groups). If you accept that the process of conformity can occur without your being aware of it, then you may prefer the wording of Zimbardo *et al.*'s definition.

❖ Activity 1 ❖

Think back to an occasion when you have conformed to the views or behaviours of others.

- What was it about the situation that caused you to conform?
- Were you aware at the time that you were under pressure to conform?

Although most people think of themselves as autonomous individuals, they nevertheless tend to go along with (conform to) the social norms (rules and expectations) that their groups and societies have evolved. The social norms that indicate how we ought to behave may be explicit (e.g. a 'No Smoking' sign in a restaurant), or they may be implicit (e.g. the unspoken but well understood norm in this country of not standing too close to strangers).

According to Insko *et al.* (1985), there are two powerful psychological needs that lead people to conform to such norms rather than rebel against them:

- the desire to be liked which underlies *normative social influence* – we conform because we think that others will approve and accept us
- the desire to be right which forms the basis for *informational social influence* – we look to others, whom we believe to be correct, to give us information about how to behave, particularly in novel or ambiguous situations.

Abrams and Hogg (1990) claim that each of these two types of social influence is underpinned by the process of *self-categorization*; conformity enables us to maintain our membership of a group with which we identify (see Chapter 1 for more information on the process of categorization).

As long ago as 1958, Kelman identified three types of conformity (that is, three responses to social influence):

- *Compliance*: publicly conforming to the behaviour or views of others but privately maintaining one's own views. Compliance may result from normative social influence.
- *Identification*: where one adopts the views or behaviour of a group both publicly and privately because one values one's group membership. However, the new attitudes and behaviours are dependent on the presence of the group and are often temporary, no longer maintained if one leaves the group.
- *Internalization*: a true change of private views to match those of the group. Internalization may be the result of informational social influence. What distinguishes this type of conformity from identification is that the new attitudes and behaviours have become part of one's value system and are not dependent on the presence of the group.

❖ Activity 2 ❖

Revisit the occasion you thought of for Activity 1. Using Kelman's three types of conformity, decide which type best applies in your case: compliance, identification or internalization.

There are occasions when people appear not to conform. There are at least two ways of explaining their behaviour:

- The person might be displaying true *independence*, that is, being unresponsive to the norms of the group. An example of this type of behaviour might be the case of a student who ignores the dress norms of her fellow students and who dresses only to please herself. Note that sometimes this student might dress like her friends if their dress sense happened to coincide with hers. She is not reacting against their code; she is just unaffected by it.
- *Anticonformity*, on the other hand, occurs when someone consistently opposes the norms of the group. Anticonforming

behaviour is not uncommon, such as deliberately choosing to dress or wear one's hair in a way that is different from others. It may seem paradoxical, but anticonformity is, in fact, a type of conformity as it is determined by the norms of the group; if the group favours long hair, anticonformists will wear theirs cut short; if the group decides that short hair is cool, anticonformists will wear theirs long.

The Sherif study

Sherif (1935) investigated the emergence of group norms using the autokinetic effect. This is an optical illusion experienced when a person is placed in a totally dark room in which a stationary point of light appears to move because the person's perceptual system has no frame of reference for it. Sherif asked individual participants to judge how far the light appeared to move on a number of trials. Each individual's estimates were relatively stable but between participants there was considerable variation. When the same participants then worked in groups of three, announcing their estimates aloud, their judgements converged until a group norm emerged. When Sherif altered his procedure so that participants made their first judgements in the group situation, he found that group norms emerged even more quickly than in the previous procedure. The study showed that when faced with an ambiguous situation, the participants looked to others in the group for guidance, that is, they experienced informational influence. Furthermore, this occurred even though they were asked to give their *own* estimates and despite the fact that, at the end of the study, they stated that they had not seen themselves as members of a group.

Strictly speaking, Sherif was studying the process of norm formation in new groups, not the process of conformity. Nevertheless, his results suggest that people will adjust their judgements to bring them into line with those of other people even when they do not perceive themselves and the others as constituting a group.

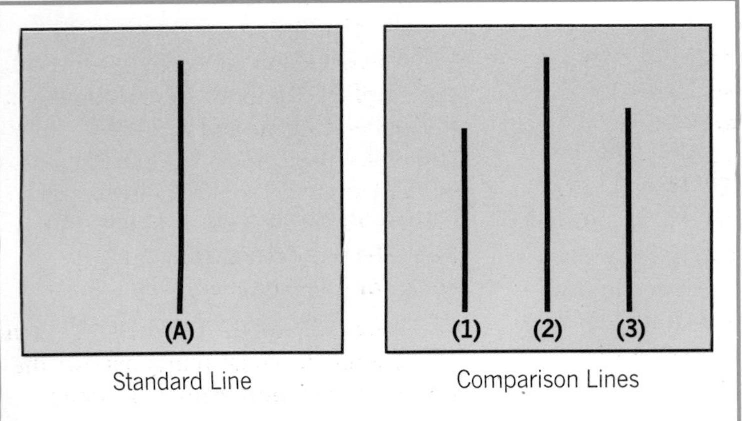

Figure 3.1
A sample of the stimulus material used in Asch's experiments on conformity

The Asch studies

Asch (1952) argued that the convergence of judgements found in the Sherif study was attributable to the ambiguity of the situation. What would happen, Asch wondered, if participants were exposed to normative social influence in a situation where there could be no doubt about the correct answer to a question? In Asch's original study he showed a pair of cards to people seated around a table. On one card was a 'test' line and on the other, three lines of differing lengths. The participants' task was to say aloud which of the three lines (1, 2 or 3) matched exactly with the test line (see Fig. 3.1). The correct judgements were always obvious. Fifty male college students were studied in the first round of experiments.

Apart from one naive participant, all other members of the group were confederates (accomplices) of the experimenter. Asch used groups of seven to nine confederates. He instructed them to give the same wrong answer unanimously on twelve of the eighteen trials. All participants sat at a table with the naive participant answering last but one. How many participants would conform to the group, deny the evidence of their own eyes and give the wrong answer when it was their turn?

Main results of Asch studies

- On 32 per cent of the critical trials (those when the confederates had given the wrong answers), naive participants conformed. This might not strike you as a particularly high figure, but remember that the correct answer was always obvious.
- 74 per cent of naive participants conformed at least once.
- Thirteen out of fifty participants never conformed. Some of these 'independent' participants were confident in their judgements. More often, however, they experienced tension and doubt but managed to resist the pressure being exerted by the unanimous majority (see the section on independent behaviour, p. 53, for more about this issue).
- During debriefing interviews with his participants, Asch found that conformity occurred at three levels:
  - A few participants experienced *distortion of perception* and were unaware that their estimates had been distorted by the majority.
  - Most participants experienced a *distortion of judgement:* they thought that their perception must be inaccurate and for that reason they yielded to the majority view.
  - Some participants did not undergo a distortion of perception or think that their judgement must be wrong. Rather they yielded to the majority (*distortion of action*) because they could not bear to be in a minority of one and risk being ridiculed or excluded by the group.
- Asch sums up these findings from the debriefing interviews thus: 'Independence and yielding [conformity] are not psychologically homogeneous … [they] can be the result of different psychological conditions.' (Asch 1952, p. 179)

In addition to his interest in individual differences, Asch was also interested in how variations to situational factors might affect levels of conformity.

Effects of varying Asch's procedures

- *A non-unanimous majority*: Asch found that levels of conformity dropped dramatically when just one other participant dissented from the majority and supported the naive participant. In a number of studies investigating the effects of dissenters, Allen and Levine (1968) showed that a dissenter only had to give a different answer from the majority, even a different wrong answer, for conformity levels to be reduced. Morris and Miller (1975) found that when the dissenter's judgement was heard near the beginning of the procedure there were lower levels of conformity than when it was given nearer the end. A unanimous majority of three was more effective in producing conformity than a majority of eight with one dissenter.
- *The size of the majority*: When the majority consisted of only two people, conformity responses in naive participants dropped to 12.8 per cent of their total judgements. Optimum conformity effects (32 per cent of responses) were found with a majority of three. Increasing the size of the majority beyond three did not increase the levels of conformity found. Baron and Byrne (1994) suggest that people may suspect collusion if the majority rises beyond three or four. When only one confederate was used, no conformity effects were elicited.
- *Losing or gaining a partner*: The effect of losing a partner was tested by having the naive participant start with a 'partner' who responded correctly to begin with but who 'deserted' to the majority in the middle of the procedure. This resulted in conformity levels of 28.5 per cent on critical judgements. When a participant who had started the procedure as a minority of one received a 'partner' part way through, this reduced conformity responses to 8.7 per cent.
- *The nature of the task*: As Asch reduced the clarity of the task or increased its difficulty, the levels of conformity increased.

- *Mode of response*: When Asch asked his participants to write their answers rather than call them out loud, conformity levels dropped sharply. This illustrates the difference between *public compliance* (overtly adhering to social norms) and *private acceptance* (actually thinking as others do).

Evaluation of conformity studies

Numerous studies have confirmed Asch's basic findings. Some of these used different tasks and different procedures. One of the best known was that carried out by Crutchfield (1955). He thought that the face-to-face arrangement of participants in the Asch procedure might be responsible for the levels of conformity found. Therefore, he arranged his participants in booths out of sight of each other, but all able to see the stimulus cards. This enabled him to collect data in a more economical fashion by running several naive participants at the same time. Participants sat individually in booths with a row of switches and lights in front of them. They had to press the switch which corresponded to their judgement when their turn came to answer. They were told that the lights on the display panel showed the responses of the other participants. In fact, the experimenter controlled these lights and each participant saw an identical display. Despite the absence of an actual face-to-face group, Crutchfield found 30 per cent conformity levels when using Asch's line comparison tasks. When the task was made more difficult, conformity increased.

Asch's experimental situation is accused of being unlike real life (lacking ecological validity). Why choose a task where the correct answer was obvious? Remember that Asch wanted to investigate pure public conformity. He did not want a situation where participants might genuinely have doubts about the correct response. In his later studies, he actually showed that conformity levels were higher when the answers were less obvious. Several studies examining conformity in real-life situations have demonstrated how others act as a source of influence, especially when people are uncertain how to act.

Asch is sometimes accused of not specifying what caused the conformity that he observed, i.e. was it normative or informational influence? Nevertheless during his post-experimental interviews, he did establish that different psychological processes were at work for different individual participants: distortions of *perception, judgement* or *action*. Crutchfield also was interested in individual differences and how these might affect conformity. His participants were drawn from business and military men on a three-day assessment course where they had been tested for a number of qualities including intelligence, leadership ability and ego strength. The participants who scored highly on these characteristics displayed lower levels of conformity during Crutchfield's study. It may, therefore, appear tempting to claim that there is a conforming type of personality. However, there has been a lack of evidence subsequently to support Crutchfield's findings and many social psychologists (e.g. McGuire 1968) think that to engage in such a search would be unproductive and misguided.

Some observers have suggested that Asch's findings tell us more about the historical and cultural climate of the United States in 1951 than they do about fundamental psychological tendencies and some more recent studies of conformity have failed to confirm Asch's findings. For example, Larsen (1974) found significantly lower rates of conformity among American students than Asch had two decades earlier. Perrin and Spencer (1981) who replicated Asch's procedure, using British students, found only one conforming response in 396 trials. They proposed that this dramatic reversal of Asch's findings could be explained in terms of the cultural changes that had occurred in the interim. In the 1950s the USA was very conservative, involved in the Korean war and its educational institutions were more hierarchical than they are today. By the time of the Larsen study in 1974, the USA had undergone considerable social change, including a period of student militancy. Another factor that might have influenced the Perrin and Spencer results is the type of students used. They were drawn from engineering, chemistry and mathematics courses and it is possible that the knowledge and skills acquired in their courses had equipped them to resist conformity pressures during a task of this sort. Another study by Perrin and Spencer (1981), using youths on probation as participants and using probation officers as the confederates and experimenters, demonstrated levels of conformity similar to those found by Asch in 1951. The researchers suggested that where the perceived costs for people of not yielding are high, conformity effects would still be demonstrated.

Asch is sometimes criticized for implying that conforming behaviour is intrinsically 'bad'. Clearly there are dangers involved if people are too conformist. Nevertheless, without widespread conformity, society could not function effectively. Conformity to pro-social norms, such as helping others in distress, is obviously highly desirable.

❖ Activity 3 ❖

Consider the ethical issues raised by Asch's research, e.g. issues to do with deception and participant distress. Refer to Chapter 27 for a discussion of ethical issues in psychology.

Minority social influence

The research of Asch (1952) was concerned with the influence of majorities. There are, however, numerous examples in life where small minorities or even lone dissenters have influenced majority opinion. These people may be dismissed initially by the majority as eccentrics or extremists. However, under certain circumstances, these small groups or individuals can become very influential eventually.

Experiments on minority influence

Moscovici *et al.* (1969) asked six participants to estimate the colour of 36 slides. All the slides were blue but their brightness was varied by adding filters. Each participant had good eyesight. Two of the six participants were accomplices of the experimenter. They called the slides green on all trials, that is, they constituted a consistent minority. Results showed that naive participants called the slides green (i.e. they conformed to the minority) in 8.42 per cent of the trials and 32 per cent of all naive participants reported a green slide at least once. Although these levels of conformity are nothing like as high as those found by Asch in his studies of majority influence, they do indicate that minorities can exert social influence.

Moscovici (1985) has identified the behavioural styles which minorities must possess if they are to exert social influence on majorities:

- They must be consistent in their opposition to the majority.
- They must not appear dogmatic by rigidly reiterating the same arguments. They need to demonstrate a degree of flexibility.
- They will be more influential if they are propounding views that are consistent with current social trends.

Section summary

Because we look to other people for guidance and approval, we are likely to conform to their attitudes and behaviours in many situations. Conformity may occur at one of three levels: compliance, identification or internalization. Sherif has demonstrated how norms may emerge in small groups, while Asch has shown how a unanimous majority of three can produce optimum conformity effects. Not only are majorities influential; Moscovici has shown how even small minorities who act consistently may exert social influence. The influence on behaviour of social roles has been demonstrated in the prison simulation study of Philip Zimbardo.

In Focus

Conformity to social roles

To investigate how readily people would adopt a new role and exercise the power that went with it, Zimbardo *et al.* (1973) recruited 25 male volunteers to participate in a two-week study of prison life. Volunteers, who would be paid $15 a day during the study, were clinically examined, judged to be both physically and mentally healthy and allocated randomly to the roles of prisoners or guards. Local police were recruited to help and 'prisoners' were arrested at their homes, without any warning, taken blindfolded to the 'prison' (basement of Stanford University, California), stripped, showered (deloused) and given prison smocks to wear and their numbers to memorize. From then on they were referred to by number only. The 'guards' wore khaki shirts and trousers, dark glasses and carried long wooden batons. The guards conformed to their perceived roles with such zeal that the study had to be discontinued after 6 days. Many prisoners exhibited passive behaviour, depression, crying and anxiety.

How can we account for such findings? According to Zimbardo, these results demonstrate how easily people can come to behave in uncharacteristic ways when placed in new situations and given new roles. The adoption of new role-related behaviours might have been facilitated by the stereotypic expectations that the participants brought with them of how guards and prisoners should behave. Another possible explanation is that the volunteers might have tried to be 'good subjects' and behaved in the ways they thought the researcher wanted.

Many criticisms have been levelled against this study, including the following made by Savin (1973):

- Participants did not give fully informed consent; they did not know, for example, they would be arrested at home, although they did sign an agreement drawn up by Stanford University to act as volunteers.
- Participants were humiliated and dehumanized by the initiation procedure when they arrived at the 'prison'.
- The ends do not justify the means and this study became 'too real' for those participating; it should not have been carried out.

In answer to these criticisms, Zimbardo claimed that the reality of this study and its findings made people uneasy because they preferred not to consider that they might have behaved in the same way.

Obedience

'It has been reliably established that from 1939 to 1945, millions of innocent persons were slaughtered on command; gas chambers were built, death camps were guarded, daily quotas of corpses were produced with the same efficiency as the manufacture of appliances. These inhumane policies may have originated in the mind of a single person, but they could only have been carried out on a massive scale if a very large number of persons obeyed orders.' (Milgram 1963, p. 371).

Similarly appalling events have occurred since then (e.g. the My Lai massacre during the Vietnam war; the slaughter of Kurds by supporters of Saddam Hussein; the attempted genocide of Rwandan Tutsis by their compatriots, Hutus). The list seems endless. What induces people to obey their leaders' orders to torture and kill other human beings, even those who have been their neighbours and who have done them no harm?

Milgram's studies of obedience

Stanley Milgram (1963, 1973) carried out a series of studies to try to shed some light on this distressing aspect of human behaviour. In all, he studied over 1000 participants who were representative of the general population in his controversial series of experiments. He discovered that the blind obedience of the Nazis in the Second World War was unlikely to have been a product of their 'Germanic personality'. Rather he found that under certain situational influences any one of us might obey orders that went against our conscience.

Milgram's original procedure

Forty male participants were recruited by means of newspaper advertisements. Each was paid $4.50 for volunteering. Participants believed that they were taking part in a study on the role of punishment in learning and memory. The study took place in a laboratory at Yale University in the USA. Each participant was introduced by the experimenter (who wore a grey lab coat to reinforce his authority) to another participant and they each drew lots to determine who would be the 'teacher' and who would be the 'learner'. In fact, the draw was fixed so that the real participant was always the teacher and the other person, an accomplice of the researcher, was always the learner. The teacher's role was to administer a shock each time the learner made a mistake on a simple learning task. The learner was strapped into an 'electric chair' in a room next door to where the teacher sat. The teacher was told that the shocks were painful but not dangerous and he was given a sample shock of 75 volts to feel the amount of pain it caused. The accomplice (learner) was a mild-mannered 50-year-old man who mentioned that he had had a heart complaint in the past but that he was willing to participate in the study none the less. His task was to memorize pairs of words. When tested, the 'learner' would indicate his choice using a light system. The teacher sat in front of the shock generator which had thirty levers, each of which indicated the level of shock to be given. The first shock was 15 volts. Each subsequent shock was increased by another 15 volts. Shocks ranged from 15 volts to 450 volts (labelled 'Danger: Severe Shock XXX').

To begin with, the accomplice answered correctly but then began to make mistakes. As the level of shock administered increased, the accomplice was heard to protest until, at 180 volts he shouted that he could bear the pain no longer. At 300 volts he screamed and complained that his heart was troubling him. At 315 volts he refused to continue and from then on he made no responses to the teacher's requests that he answer. In reality, of course, the accomplice never received any shocks. His responses and pleadings were prerecorded.

You will not be surprised to learn that this procedure was very stressful for the 'teacher' participants. Most protested and wanted to stop. Many showed signs of extreme anxiety, biting their lips and trembling. However, whenever the teacher hesitated, the experimenter gave standardized prods to encourage him to continue:

- Prod 1: 'Please continue' or 'Please go on'
- Prod 2: 'The experiment requires that you continue'
- Prod 3: 'It is absolutely essential that you continue'
- Prod 4: 'You have no other choice, you must go on'.

The experiment continued either until the teacher refused to continue or until 450 volts were reached and given four times. All participants were then debriefed and taken to meet the learner.

Milgram's results

- Most participants dissented verbally but obeyed behaviourally.
- All participants went to at least 300 volts.
- When the learner was in the next room to the 'teacher' and answering via the light system, 65 per cent of the participants went to the end of the shock generator, i.e. they believed that they had administered 450 volts!

Milgram was as surprised by these results as anyone. Prior to conducting his study, he had asked a number of people, including psychiatrists, how far they thought the participants would go in a study of this sort. They predicted that only a tiny handful would proceed to 450 volts. They were wrong. What was it about the situation that caused the participants to obey? In order to answer this question, Milgram systematically varied a number of the features of his procedure. These variations and their consequences for the participants' behaviour are listed below in Table 3.1.

It is clear from the results given in Table 3.1 that obedience levels can be manipulated by controlling situational variables. Where participants were unsure how to disobey or what the consequences of disobedience might be, they tended to obey. When others modelled disobedience for them, they were quick to follow suit. When participants were forced to see as well as hear the consequences of their actions (i.e. the learner's distress) they were less likely to obey the experimenter. When they were less closely supervised by the experimenter, obedience levels declined. When someone else 'did the dirty work' of throwing the switches, obedience levels soared. A study by Rosenhan (1969), using school children as participants, showed that when the relative status of the experimenter to the participant is increased, obedience levels rise (to 80 per cent in this case). Milgram also pointed out that the participants felt that they had 'contracted' to help with the study and so felt obligated to continue even when the going got tough. Similarly, they found it difficult to decide to disengage at any particular point in the procedure because each voltage increment was fairly small.

❖ Activity 4 ❖

List the particular features of Milgram's procedure that you think most contributed to the high levels of obedience he found. What variations to this procedure do you think would (a) reduce, and (b) increase obedience?

Look at Table 3.1 to compare your ideas with what Milgram found.

Evaluating Milgram's work

Milgram's work has been criticized both on ethical and methodological grounds. Baumrind (1964) believed that Milgram showed insufficient respect for his participants, that there were inadequate steps taken to protect them and that his

Table 3.1 Variations on Milgram's basic procedure

Variation	*Obedience rate (those going to 450 volts)*
Venue moved to seedy offices in nearby town	47.5%
Teacher and learner in same room	40%
Teacher had to force learner's hand on to plate to receive shock	30%
Teacher given support from two other 'teachers' (confederates) who refuse to continue	10%
Teacher paired with an assistant (confederate) who threw the switches	92.5%
Experimenter instructs and prods teacher by telephone from another room	20.5%

procedures had the potential for causing long-term harm. The studies, it has been claimed, involved lack of informed consent, deception and possible psychological harm to his participants. Milgram (1964) responded to Baumrind's comments by distributing a questionnaire to participants. Eighty-four per cent replied that they were glad they had been involved and claimed it had been an enriching and instructive experience. Only 1.3 per cent reported negative feelings. A year after the study, a university psychiatrist interviewed 40 participants and reported no evidence of emotional harm that could be attributed to participation in the study. (See Chapter 27 for further discussion of ethical issues relating to Milgram's work.)

Orne and Holland (1968) suggested that Milgram's studies were lacking in both *experimental realism* (the extent to which the situation forces participants to take the study seriously) and *mundane realism* (or ecological validity, the extent to which the situation relates to real life). They argued that participants did not believe they were really giving electric shocks and that they were not really distressed, just pretending in order to please the experimenter and to continue to play their role in the study. Milgram disputed both these claims.

Given the criticism that Milgram's studies were artificial, it is interesting to look at the results of a study by Hofling *et al.* (1966) which showed that blind obedience to an authority figure can occur just as readily in a real-life situation. The situation used was a hospital. They arranged for a nurse (the participant) to receive a phone call from an unknown doctor who asked her to administer 20 milligrams of a drug called Astroten to a patient so that it would have taken effect before he arrived. If the nurse obeyed she would be breaking several hospital rules:

- giving twice the maximum dose allowable for this drug
- administering a drug not on the ward stock list for that day
- taking a telephone instruction from an unfamiliar person
- acting without a signed order from a doctor.

Despite all this, 95 per cent of the nurse participants started to give the medication (a harmless placebo, in fact) until they were stopped by another nurse who had been stationed nearby but out of sight. When interviewed afterwards, all the nurses said that they had been asked to do this type of thing before and that doctors became annoyed if they refused.

Why do people obey authority?

Legitimate authority

One suggestion is that we feel obligated to those in power because we respect their credentials and assume they know what they are doing. Legitimate social power is held by authority figures whose role is defined by society, which usually gives the person the right to exert control over the behaviour of others, and others usually accept it (see the study by Hofling). Although respect for authority permits orderly social interaction, there is the danger that it may be so deeply ingrained in us that we obey, even when we believe we are being asked to do something that is unethical or immoral.

Milgram's agency theory

Milgram accepted that perceived legitimacy enhanced the power of an authority figure. In addition, however, he proposed his *agency theory*. This states that people operate on two levels:

- as *autonomous* individuals, behaving voluntarily and aware of the consequences of their decisions
- on the *agentic level*, seeing themselves as the agents of others.

At this agentic level, Milgram argued, people mindlessly accept the orders of the person seen as responsible in the situation. In effect, their responsibility is to the person in charge and not to the target of their actions. Milgram believed that this explained the behaviour of the participants in his study; they denied personal responsibility, merely 'doing what they were told'. You probably know that when those responsible for atrocious crimes during the Second World War were asked why they did what they did, their answer was simply: 'I was only obeying orders' (Arendt 1963).

What causes people to operate in the agentic state? Milgram suggested that it is part of the socialization process: we train children from a very early age to be obedient to authority at home, in school and in society. Many rules and regulations exist to reinforce obedience, so that eventually we tend to accept unquestioningly what we are told to do because most requests are perceived to be both reasonable and appropriate.

Buffers

Milgram suggested another mechanism by which people may be able to cope with the likely stress of obeying an immoral or unethical command. Remember that the participants in his studies did not enjoy what they were doing! He suggested that the moral strain is reduced through the use of '*buffers*'. In the original Milgram study, the 'teacher' and 'learner' were in different rooms, the teacher buffered (protected) from seeing his victim. In some real-life situations where obedience is required, the person merely has to press a button – the resulting destruction may not even be observed. In other cases, those carrying out orders are not told full details of their mission. This was the case with the air crew who dropped the atomic bomb on Hiroshima.

Passivity

Moriarty (1975) suggested that the desire many people have to avoid confrontation may result in *passivity*. Laboratory and field studies have confirmed that people will, for example, tolerate loud and intrusive music rather than confront the offender. Is it any wonder, then, that people tend passively to obey those they perceive as being in authority?

Section summary

In his original study, Milgram showed that 65 per cent of participants were willing to give electric shocks as punishment to a 'learner' seated in an adjacent room whenever he gave a wrong answer on a memory test. Factors that have been shown to increase levels of obedience include: the perceived legitimacy of the authority figure; the adoption of an agentic state; being buffered (protected) from the results of one's actions; unwillingness to cause a fuss by disobeying.

Independent behaviour

At this point it might seem that the pressures to conform or obey are irresistible. This is not so. Remember that some of Asch's participants held out against the normative social influence exerted by the majority; 13 out of 50 never conformed. Asch, using post-experimental interviews, distinguished three main categories of independent behaviour:

- Independence based on *confidence* that their perceptions were correct: These people were aware of being isolated but were resilient in coping with the conflict that brought. This probably contributed in part to the results found by Perrin and Spencer (see p. 48) when they used mathematics, engineering and science students as participants.
- Independence accompanied by *withdrawal*: These participants reported the need to act as individuals no matter what the others did. They tried to isolate themselves from the others by avoiding eye contact.
- Independence accompanied by *tension and doubt*: These participants felt they had to deal with the requirements of the task no matter what discomfort they were experiencing.

Therefore, we see that the reasons for independent behaviour are no more homogeneous than those for conforming behaviour. Asch's findings still beg the question 'Do some people possess certain characteristics that enable them to resist group pressure or to disobey a malevolent authority?' There is very limited evidence concerning such individual factors. Crutchfield's early results concerning differences in intelligence, for example, have not received support. Two reasons for individuals resisting majority pressure, however, have been investigated more recently:

- The desire for *individuation*, i.e. to be distinguished in some way from others: Maslach *et al.* (1987) claim that while we want to be like others generally, we still wish to be individuals in certain respects. Therefore, sometimes we will risk the disapproval of the group in order to proclaim our unique individuality.
- The desire to maintain *control* over events in our lives: Burger (1992) has demonstrated that people who score highly in desire for personal control are more likely to resist conformity pressures than those who have a lower need to feel in control.

Resisting pressures to obey

Remember, also, that some of Milgram's participants refused to continue giving shocks when they thought the learner was in distress. One such participant, when asked why she refused to continue, said that she had experienced too much pain in her own life, having grown up in Nazi Germany, and did not wish to inflict pain on someone else. According to Milgram, the triggering of painful memories had 'awakened' her from her agentic state. She felt responsible for any harm produced.

Among the other factors proposed to enable people to resist pressure from authority figures are:

- exposing people to the actions of *disobedient models*, that is seeing others refuse to obey instructions from an authority figure (Milgram 1973)
- *questioning* the motives and expertise of authority figures (Baron and Byrne 1994)
- *educating* people about the dangers of blind obedience. One particularly nice example of the effectiveness of education arose during a study by Gamson *et al.* (1982). Participants, working in groups, refused to obey the requests of the experimenter and one person actually quoted Milgram's findings as a reason for disobedience.

❖ Activity 5 ❖

Think of an occasion when you have demonstrated independent behaviour. How did you feel at the time? What were the consequences of your behaviour?

Section summary

Pressure to conform or obey is not irresistible. Those who desire control in their lives or those who need to think of themselves as different from others may be less susceptible to social influence. Resistance to social influence may be increased also if we are encouraged to question the motives of those in authority or if we see others disobey.

Social power

Social influence can take the form of *social power*: the potential or capacity to get others to behave as desired. Parents exert power over their children, doctors over their patients and teachers over students. At a more subtle level, of course, children, patients and students can exercise power by manipulating their parents, doctors and teachers respectively. French and Raven (1959) referred to six different types of power that people may use. Table 3.2 lists

Table 3.2 Forms of social power and Kelman's processes of influence

Type of power	*Process of influence*
1 **Reward:** power to reward	Compliance
2 **Coercive:** power to punish	Compliance
3 **Referent:** power achieved because others wish to identify with person	Identification
4 **Legitimate:** power from recognized position in the social structure	Related to compliance, but rewards and punishment need only be implied
5 **Expert:** power from possessing superior knowledge	Related to internalization: induced behaviour accepted at level of true belief, but mainly on grounds of faith, rather than real understanding
6 **Informational:** power from having information in accord with others' beliefs or values	Internalization

Source: French and Raven (1959)

❖ Activity 6 ❖

Refer to the six types of power outlined in Table 3.2. Try to identify six people whom you know either personally or through the media, each of whom possesses at least one kind of power. You should be able to match a person to each of the six types of power. What roles do these people occupy in relation to you?

these six and shows how they relate to Kelman's processes of social influence.

This approach to classifying social power has been applied and tested in a number of both real-world and simulated situations. For example, Raven and Haley (1980) found support for the categories in a study using hospital personnel. They found that doctors and nurses favoured the use of informational power as a means of persuading fellow colleagues to follow hospital policy regarding infection control. Reward and coercive power were used most when someone of high status was trying to influence someone of lower status. Rodin and Janis (1982) have demonstrated also how useful referent power can be for health practitioners who are trying to persuade people to undertake weight reduction programmes.

Schriesheim *et al.* (1991), however, suggest that a better way of conceptualizing social power is found by using only two categories:

- position power, including coercive, reward, legitimate and informational power
- personal power, including persuasive power (power to convince) and charismatic power (power to enthuse).

Power and leadership are closely related. Many of the types of power so far described are possessed by leaders. The following section examines the nature of leadership, how leaders emerge, what constitutes effective leadership and the significance of the behaviour of those who follow.

Leadership and followership

Leadership is an important ingredient in group activities. When we hear of businesses or schools or sports teams failing to perform well, the accusation of poor leadership is often to the fore. Some people would even go so far as to claim that good leadership is the single most important factor in the performance of a group. People find it more difficult, however, to define 'good leadership'. Psychologists tend to focus their definitions on the process of social influence. For example, Hollander (1985) defines leadership as the 'process of influence between a leader and followers to attain group, organisational, or societal goals'. Yukl (1989) defines it as 'the process through which one member of a group (its leader) influences other group members toward the attainment of specific group goals'. Note that Hollander's definition implies the ability of followers to influence leaders as well as vice versa.

Two main issues have dominated thinking on leadership over the last fifty years:

- How do leaders emerge? Do some people possess the personal qualities which destine them for leadership? Or is it the case that some people who possess certain skills happen to find themselves in the right place at the right time to emerge as leaders?
- What constitutes effective leadership? Can we identify an ideal leadership style? Or is it a case of horses for courses?

Emergence of leaders

Are leaders born or are they made? Those who believe that leaders are born suggest that some individuals possess a number of unique characteristics enabling them to realize their destiny as leaders. These so-called 'great person theories' led to years of research that tried to identify the traits that leaders shared and which distinguished them from followers. The findings from these early studies were such that most social psychologists gave up the search and concluded that there were no consistent differences in personal qualities between followers and leaders.

Recent research in business settings, however, has found that leaders do differ from others in some important respects. Kirkpatrick and Locke (1991) have identified *flexibility* as a key trait in those who emerge as successful leaders. See Table 3.3 for a list of the traits they found among many business leaders.

Therefore, according to Kirkpatrick and Locke (1991, p. 58): 'Leaders are not like other people. They do not have to be great men or women ... but they do need to have the "right stuff" and this stuff is not equally present in all people.'

A very different approach to the emergence of leaders was that conducted by Bales and Slater (1955). By observing small discussion groups they identified two types of leaders who tended to emerge in most groups: the *task specialist* who was concerned with the group achieving its goal, and the *social-emotional specialist* who was primarily concerned with the relationships among group members. These two types of emergent leaders may complement each other in the group's activities. The relative importance of either type of leader would depend upon the nature of the group and its task. This idea is discussed further in the next section. Other researchers turned their attention to leadership effectiveness.

Leadership style and effectiveness

Early research on leadership style

One of the earliest studies looking into the effectiveness of different leadership styles was conducted by Lewin *et al.* (1939). In their study, they investigated the effect of authoritarian, democratic and *laissez-faire* adult leaders on the behaviour of 10-year-old boys during an after-school model making club.

Table 3.3 Characteristics of successful leaders

Traits	*Description*
Drive	Desire for achievement; energy
Honesty and integrity	Trustworthiness; reliability
Leadership motivation	Desire to influence others to reach goals
Self-confidence	Trust in own abilities
Cognitive ability	Intelligence
Expertise	Knowledge of relevant matters
Creativity	Originality
Flexibility	Adaptability to needs of followers and to changing situation

Source: adapted from Kirkpatrick and Locke (1991)

- One group of boys had a *democratic* leader who expressed an interest in what the boys were doing and discussed the activities with them.
- A second group had an *autocratic* leader who was task-oriented, told the boys what they would make and with whom they could work.
- The third group had a *laissez-faire* leader who left the boys to their own devices and only gave them help when they asked for it.

The results showed that boys in the democratic group were more satisfied, organized, independent and efficient than those in the other two groups. In the autocratic group they were more submissive and were aggressive toward each other when things went wrong, although the quality of work was equivalent to that in the democratic group. When the autocratic leader left the room, arguments broke out and work stopped. In the *laissez-faire* group very little work was completed whether the leader was present or not. By switching the styles of leadership that the boys were experiencing, Lewin *et al.* were able to establish that it was indeed the style of leadership that was causing the different outcomes and not the personality of the boys or the leaders.

Does this mean that a democratic style of leadership is best in all situations? This seems unlikely, given the diverse functions of groups, e.g. compare the type of leadership required from someone running a charity shop staffed by volunteers with that required from an army officer in charge of a group of soldiers fighting in a war. The following sections will look at the two most influential approaches to the study of effective leadership (contingency theory and normative theory), the first of which emphasizes the need to study both the behaviour of leaders and the situations in which their behaviour is exercised.

Contingency theory

A number of contingency theories of leadership have been proposed. The best known of these is that of Fiedler (1967). His contingency model proposes that effective leadership is dependent on a match between the leader's behavioural style and the extent to which the situation gives control to that leader. Fundamental to the model is the view that leaders are either task-oriented or relationship-oriented. Fiedler identified liking for a least-preferred co-worker (LPC) as an important characteristic of leaders. Those who perceive a LPC in favourable terms are described as high-LPC leaders (people-oriented). Those who perceive a LPC in unfavourable terms are described as low-LPC leaders (task-oriented). Which kind of leader is more effective is, according to Fiedler, dependent on how much control leaders have over their subordinates. Three factors are seen as determining this level of (what he termed) situational control:

- how much support a leader already has from followers
- how clearly structured are the group's goals and roles
- how effectively the leader can make subordinates comply.

According to Fiedler, low-LPC leaders are most effective when situational control is either very low or very high. That is, for example, when group goals are ambiguous and when firm leadership is required if the

❖ Activity 7 ❖

Use the scales below, adapted from Fiedler's own measure of LPC, to determine your own leadership style. In pencil, circle your score for each characteristic.

Think of a group of people you have worked with in the past, perhaps at school or at work. Recall the one person you found it most difficult to work with. Again, use the scale below and circle the characteristics of that person.

Pleasant	8	7	6	5	4	3	2	1	Unpleasant
Friendly	8	7	6	5	4	3	2	1	Unfriendly
Rejecting	1	2	3	4	5	6	7	8	Accepting
Tense	1	2	3	4	5	6	7	8	Relaxed
Distant	1	2	3	4	5	6	7	8	Close
Cold	1	2	3	4	5	6	7	8	Warm
Supportive	8	7	6	5	4	3	2	1	Hostile
Boring	1	2	3	4	5	6	7	8	Interesting
Quarrelsome	1	2	3	4	5	6	7	8	Harmonious
Gloomy	1	2	3	4	5	6	7	8	Cheerful
Open	8	7	6	5	4	3	2	1	Guarded
Backbiting	1	2	3	4	5	6	7	8	Loyal
Untrustworthy	1	2	3	4	5	6	7	8	Trustworthy
Considerate	8	7	6	5	4	3	2	1	Inconsiderate
Nasty	1	2	3	4	5	6	7	8	Nice
Agreeable	8	7	6	5	4	3	2	1	Disagreeable
Insincere	1	2	3	4	5	6	7	8	Sincere
Kind	8	7	6	5	4	3	2	1	Unkind

Add the numbers you have circled to arrive at a score.

Score 18–57: A task-oriented leader.
Score 58–63: A combination of the two approaches.
Score 64–144: A relationship-oriented leader.

Source: adapted from Fiedler and Chemers (1984)

task is to be performed, or when situational control is very high and a more *laissez-faire* approach may be appreciated by subordinates. High-LPC leaders, on the other hand, are most effective when situational control is moderate.

Many laboratory studies (e.g. Strube and Garcia 1981) have provided support for Fiedler's theory, but real-life studies have been less supportive (e.g. Peters *et al.* 1985). The validity of the LPC score has been challenged. How does it relate to actual leadership behaviour? A person's LPC score may change over time. There are problems in measuring accurately the true levels of situational control in real-life groups and organizations. Furthermore, Fiedler's model focuses heavily on actual performance and overlooks employee satisfaction.

Normative theory

According to Vroom and Yetton (1973) an important aspect of leaders' effectiveness will be the extent to which they permit their followers to participate in decision-making. What is an appropriate amount of participation will depend on two factors: how crucial it is that the decision be of high quality, and how important it is that the decision be accepted by the followers as well as the leader.

Vroom and Yetton's theory proposes that an *autocratic* style of leadership may be most appropriate in two situations:

- when the quality of the decision is vitally important
- when the decision will work, even without the agreement of the followers.

However, when the cooperation of subordinates is essential for a decision to be effective, then a *participative* style of leadership will be more successful. Therefore, the key to effective leadership is allowing the *appropriate* amount of participation.

When managers have been surveyed about decision styles, the normative model has received support. When subordinates have been surveyed, however, a preference for participative leadership has been found, even when the model would predict that an autocratic style would be preferred (Field and House 1990). In general, people have strong preferences for participative procedures.

Furthermore, not all managers will be successful using a participative style in every situation where the model might recommend this. In cases where managers have to resolve conflicts, only those who are skilful in such tasks should use a participative approach. Therefore, the evidence to date suggests that the normative model of leadership effectiveness requires modifications to take account of individual differences in the skills of leaders and the widespread preferences that people have for participating in decision-making.

Leaders, followers and expectations

You may well be familiar with the concept of the self-fulfilling prophecy: the idea that the expectations which we hold of others may contribute to producing behaviour in line with these expectations. For example, teachers who have high expectations of their students may interact with them in such a way that the students achieve high standards of performance. In 1960, McGregor proposed that managers held two distinctly different views of their subordinates, referred to by him as Theory X or Theory Y. Those who subscribed to Theory X believed that workers were lazy and only worked if they had to. Therefore, the manager's role was to coerce workers to keep them up to scratch. Those who subscribed to Theory Y believed that workers could enjoy their jobs and would work hard if they were appreciated. The manager's job in this case was to encourage and guide. House (1971) found that if people were treated with respect as responsible adults they would respond positively, especially if the manager/leader was able to facilitate the fulfilling of their followers' own personal goals as well as those of the group.

Smith and Peterson (1988) claim that the most effective leaders are those who exemplify the values of the group and who provide good role models for their followers. In other words, through their behaviour

In Focus

Charismatic (transformational) leaders

Charismatic leaders have the determination, energy, confidence and ability to inspire followers to extraordinary lengths. They are sometimes called transformational leaders because they have the ability to transform social, political or economic reality. The following behavioural characteristics have been identified in transformational leaders (see Greenberg and Baron 1995):

- They articulate a *vision* (e.g. an image of what a group or organization could become).
- They map out a *plan* for attaining their vision (i.e. they tell their followers how to get from their present position to the envisioned one).
- They define the *purpose* of their movement to give meaning to their actions.
- They take above average *risks* to achieve their goals.
- They demonstrate high levels of *confidence* in self and followers and excellent *communication skills.*
- They are expert at *impression management* (i.e. able to enhance their appeal to others).

The followers of transformational leaders tend to behave in particular ways. They:

- engage in performance beyond the levels normally to be expected
- demonstrate high levels of devotion and loyalty to the leader
- show enthusiasm for the leader and the leader's ideas
- are willing to sacrifice personal interest for sake of the wider collective goal.

these leaders demonstrate their expectations of others.

Of course, leaders may well not have the same expectations of all their followers. Let us consider again the case of managers and those who are answerable to them. Where workers have performed well in the past, managers are likely to have high expectations of them. Thus, we see the way in which follower-behaviour can affect the attitudes (and consequently the behaviours) of leaders. Followers also may expect their leaders to adopt a participative style of management even when they are clearly lacking the interpersonal skills to do so

❖ Activity 8 ❖

- Can you identify any charismatic (transformational) leaders?
- Do (did) they possess the behaviours listed above?
- Do (did) their followers behave as described above?

successfully. By trying to fulfil these expectations, unskilled managers may exacerbate an already bad situation. The relationship, therefore, that exists between leaders and followers is reciprocally determined (Hollander 1985).

When leaders lack confidence in the ability or motivation of some of their followers, but retain confidence in others, they are effectively establishing an out- and an in-group (see Chapter 1 for more details). The dangers inherent in such a process include ignoring the individuality of out-group members and being more likely to make dispositional attributions for any failures made by an out-group member. Deluga and Perry (1991), not surprisingly, have found that in-group members are more satisfied with their jobs than out-group members.

Training programmes have been developed to help improve relationships between managers and workers where matters have deteriorated. Scandura and Graen (1984) report improvement in both group productivity and job satisfaction when employees have attended such courses.

Section summary

Leaders possess the social power to influence others. This power may derive from their position or from personal qualities. Some leaders are task specialists, while others are more social-emotional specialists. Flexibility has been identified as a key trait among those who become successful leaders. According to contingency theory, the most effective style of leadership will depend upon both the behaviour of the leader and the situation in which this behaviour happens. Normative theory outlines the conditions where a participative style of leadership is the most effective. The expectations which leaders have of their followers and vice versa play an important role in determining the productivity and job satisfaction of work groups.

Collective behaviour

People collect together for a variety of reasons, e.g. to wait for a bus, to watch a film, to support a football team, to shop in a supermarket. There is nothing particularly remarkable in such common everyday experiences and Sears *et al.* (1991) have defined a crowd simply as 'people in physical proximity to a common situation or stimulus'. Although collective behaviour may not be governed by formally established norms, the behaviour expected of people in such situations is known and usually conformed to.

Peaceful crowds

On the majority of occasions when people collect together in crowds, it is for peaceful purposes and social cohesion will often be enhanced, e.g. when people gather to express collective congratulations on the occasion of a royal wedding or the return of a victorious football team. Benewick and Holton (1987) interviewed people who had attended an open-air mass when the Pope visited Britain in 1982. There were upward of 80,000 people in this crowd. Nearly everyone interviewed commented on the feeling of unity they experienced from being in such a crowd. There was no violence.

Perhaps it is understandable that psychologists should be more interested in occasions when crowds become violent. It is important, however, to remember that peaceful gatherings of people are far more common than violent assemblies.

The psychology of 'the mob'

LeBon (1895) was the first to propose that crowds *per se* could be dangerous. He believed that, when in a crowd, people feel invincible and anonymous, losing any sense of responsibility. He believed that crowds displayed impulsiveness, irritability and an inability to reason. This irrational crowd behaviour was viewed as homogeneous, reflecting a 'mental unity' that bound the crowd together. The spread of this unified, mindless behaviour he called '*social contagion*'. The result was a 'mob'. Turner and Killian (1957) criticized LeBon's theory on two counts:

- Crowd behaviour is not homogeneous; not all members of a crowd behave in the same way.
- They disagreed with the use of the terms 'irrational' and 'emotional'; they suggested that the terms 'unpredictable' and 'spontaneous' would be more appropriate to describe the behaviour of crowds.

The 'baiting' or taunting crowd has been reported in some American studies and lends support to the notion of the crowd as a mob. Mann (1981) has recorded 10 incidents of crowds urging a potential suicide to jump. These incidents tended to occur during evenings and when the crowd was some distance from the person being taunted. It has been suggested that the concept of deindividuation (first expounded by Zimbardo in 1969) might help explain this type of behaviour. Zimbardo

In Focus

Brown's types of crowds

Brown (1965) identified a number of different types of crowds:

- The *acquisitive crowd* is concerned with acquiring some economic gain. Shoppers are a good example, particularly during the January sales when crowds 'fight' to buy goods at bargain prices.
- An *escaping crowd* is one intent on escape from a dangerous situation. This type of crowd can be further divided into panicky and non-panicky. To prevent panic occurring in an escaping crowd during an emergency, exits need to be sufficient in number and clearly marked.
- An *expressive crowd* is peaceful, intent on having a good time and enjoying a shared experience. For example, people assembled for an open-air concert would form an expressive crowd.
- An *aggressive crowd* is frequently referred to as a mob, having antisocial intent. There are numerous examples of the behaviour of 'lynch mobs' in the southern states of America. It is estimated that more than three thousand black people have been lynched since 1882, the most recently recorded being in 1955.

❖ Activity 9 ❖

Does this classification of crowds by Brown adequately cover the different types of crowd that can exist? Think about crowds you have been part of or have witnessed, whether in person or on the television.

distinguished between *individuated* behaviour which is rational and conforms to acceptable social standards, and *deindividuated* behaviour which is based on primitive urges and does not conform to society's norms. According to Zimbardo, being part of a crowd can diminish awareness of individuality. In a large crowd each person is faceless and anonymous. There is diminished fear of retribution and a diluted sense of guilt. Conditions that increase anonymity serve to minimize concerns about evaluation by others and thus weaken normal controls based on guilt, shame and fear. The larger the group the greater the anonymity and the greater the difficulty in identifying a single individual.

An explanation of crowd unrest which makes use of concepts such as deindividuation and which explains crowd behaviour in terms of mob psychology, carries with it serious risks. This was vividly and tragically illustrated in 1989 at Hillsborough stadium where nearly 100 football supporters were crushed to death. Banyard (1989) reported how the beliefs of the police that a crowd equals a mob meant that they failed to take measures which might have saved lives.

Crowds of football supporters are often labelled as 'mobs' because of their hostile intentions toward supporters of the other team. However, in studies such as those by Marsh *et al.* (1978) it has become clear that football fans, far from comprising mindless mobs, operate within a strong social structure and their behaviour is often highly patterned. Of course, there is violence from time to time, but this is seldom the 'free-for-all' violence that the media portrays. Rather, most hostile fan behaviour is ritualized. For example, it is common after a match to chase other supporters, who are threatened with shouts of what aggressive actions will take place when they are caught, but on most occasions the aggression remains verbal.

Why some crowds become violent

As already mentioned, most crowds are peaceful. This is true even when the crowd is involved in a demonstration of some kind.

❖ Activity 10 ❖

What advice would you offer to those in charge of crowd control at a demonstration in order to prevent violence happening? Compare your suggestions with those of Waddington *et al.* below.

Waddington *et al.* (1987) have investigated what acts as a flash point to turn a peaceful demonstration into a violent one when perceived long-term grievances are converted into violent expression. They recommend that the following guidelines be adhered to in order to police demonstrations successfully:

- let crowds police themselves where possible
- establish good liaison between police and organizers
- use minimum force to avoid provocation
- train crowd managers in effective interpersonal communication
- police must be seen to be accountable for their actions.

If these guidelines are followed then some major sources of grievance will be removed and outbreaks of violence are less likely. Waddington *et al.* (1987) argue that public disorder is not caused by some form of mob psychology that overtakes a crowd. Rather they think it is both predictable and avoidable. See Table 3.4 for the different levels of analyses which they believe are necessary in order to understand why crowds may become violent.

Social identity theory and crowd behaviour

Reicher (1984) has suggested that some violent incidents involving crowds can best be understood in terms of social identity theory rather than in terms of mob psychology (see Chapter 1 for a fuller account of social identity theory). For example, in 1980 in the St Paul's district of Bristol the police raided a cafe one afternoon following allegations of illegal drinking. Two men were arrested. As the police tried to leave, bricks were thrown at them by a crowd and when police reinforcements arrived they were also attacked by the crowd of some three thousand who overturned cars and set them alight.

Table 3.4 Levels of analyses of crowd behaviour

Level of analysis	*Example*
Structural	the role of unemployment in producing frustration
Political	any sources of political grievance such as a lack of political representation
Cultural	shared social representations (see Chapter 1) such as those concerning the role of the police in relation to one's own group
Contextual	events leading up to the demonstration such as perceived long-term discrimination
Spatial	way in which the geography of certain locations may make confrontation more likely (e.g. allowing no escape routes)
Interactional	nature of the interactions of people involved

Source: adapted from Waddington *et al.* (1987)

LeBon might have interpreted this in mob terms.

Reicher, on the other hand, suggested that a closer look at the event made it clear that mob rule and deindividuation did not provide an explanation. Apparently the behaviour of the crowd was selective and restrained:

- The violence was restricted to the St Paul's district.
- There was minimal damage to property.
- Only police cars were damaged (and a few suspected of being unmarked police cars).
- Any other outbreaks of violence were quickly stopped.

Reicher argued that the actions of the crowd were influenced by their social identity as members of the community who saw the police as an illegitimate foreign presence which had to be removed. The crowd, the St Paul's residents, were the in-group and their behaviour against the out-group was perceived by them to be rational. Similar observations have been made concerning the riots in Liverpool and in Moss Side, Manchester during the 1980s (Banyard and Hayes 1994).

Section summary

Most gatherings of people are peaceful. However, from time to time, crowds do become violent. According to LeBon, crowds are potentially dangerous and liable to behave irrationally as people lose their individuality and become a mindless mob. This view of collective behaviour has been criticized and the dangers of subscribing to such a view are discussed. Waddington *et al.* have recommended guidelines that police could use to minimize the chance of violence erupting during demonstrations. They also point out the need to take account of the social context of demonstrations in order to predict whether or not violence is likely to occur.

Chapter summary

- Behaviour and attitudes may be influenced by majority and minority groups, and by the social roles we occupy. The findings of Sherif, Asch, Moscovici and Zimbardo are discussed.
- The circumstances under which people are most and least likely to obey an authority figure are described and Milgram's research is discussed.
- Different forms of social power are outlined and related to the role of leadership.
- The reciprocal nature of leader-follower relations has been established and Contingency and Normative theories of leadership are discussed.
- The nature of collective behaviour is outlined and the dangers of likening a crowd to a mindless mob are emphasized.

Essay questions

1 (a) Outline some of the reasons why people conform. *(6 marks)*

(b) Outline and critically evaluate studies of conformity. *(18 marks)*

2 (a) Describe some of the findings from research investigations of obedience in humans. *(12 marks)*

(b) Assess the implications of this type of research. *(12 marks)*

3 (a) Outline research evidence on the emergence of leaders. *(6 marks)*

(b) Discuss psychological insights into leadership effectiveness. *(18 marks)*

4 Critically consider research relating to the behaviour of crowds. *(24 marks)*

Further reading

Greenberg, J. and Baron, R.A. (1995) *Behaviour in Organisations*, London: Prentice-Hall.

An up-to-date American text providing very good coverage of leadership and followership.

Hayes, N.J. (1993) *Principles of Social Psychology*, Hove: Erlbaum.

This is easily read, with a section on collective behaviour.

Baron, R.A. and Byrne, D. (1994) *Social Psychology: Understanding Human Interaction* (7th edn), Boston: Allyn and Bacon.

An excellent, well established text which provides many applied examples of social psychology research.

Chapter 4

Pro- and antisocial behaviour

David Clarke

Preview

In this chapter we shall be looking at:

- explanations and research relating to altruism and bystander behaviour
- social psychological theories of aggression
- implications of research for the reduction of aggressive behaviour
- media influences on pro- and antisocial behaviour.

Introduction

Often people do favours for one another: they help, sacrifice, share and even save other people's lives. Often such help may involve great risk, with little or no gain to the helper. Sometimes, on the other hand, people behave in distinctly unpleasant ways: they injure, rob, rape and even murder other people. Why do people behave in either prosocial or antisocial ways? Some social psychologists propose that the society in which we live and features of modern life determine our behaviours. Another explanation is that behaviour results from an interaction of physiological arousal (e.g. how alert/emotional we are) and cognitive processing (e.g. how we assess a situation). Some psychologists think that our propensity to behave in a pro- or antisocial way is inherited (part of our genetic make-up), while others believe we learn all our behaviour (whether pro- or antisocial), from parents and significant others. An important consideration in this area of study is the extent to which the media influence our behaviour. A number of studies have shown that exposure to television violence is positively correlated with violent behaviour. Other studies suggest that any relationship is weak and that viewers can discriminate between real life and fictional violence. It is also argued by some that television can be used to reduce aggression and encourage prosocial behaviour.

Prosocial behaviour

Consider the following real-life examples of behaviour.

- Shortly after Christmas in 1981, while postwoman Karen Green was at work she was assaulted by three men and two women, all of whom were drunk. While she spent 15 minutes struggling, people telephoned the police several times but no one directly intervened. Finally, she was forced into a car and driven away. Her body was found two days later. Why did no one help directly?
- In the case above, people at least telephoned for help. In 1964, New Yorker Kitty Genovese was returning home from work. As she neared home, a man jumped out of the shadows and attacked her. She screamed and tried to defend herself. Although 38 people heard her screams and many looked out of their windows and saw the attack, which lasted for over half an hour, no one went to her rescue and no one called the police. Why not?
- On 13 January 1982, moments after take-off in Washington DC, a commercial jet hit a crowded bridge and plunged into the icy waters of the Potomac river. A 28-year-old man named Lenny Skutnik stopped and watched from the shore as rescuers tried to pull survivors out of the river. When Priscilla Tirado lost her grip on a helicopter lifeline and started to sink, Skutnik risked his own life by jumping into the water and pulling her to safety. Why did he behave in this prosocial way?

Activity 1

Make a list of some situations, however trivial, in which you could have helped someone.

Why did you help in some cases, but not in others?

What is prosocial behaviour? A definition of terms is important:

- *Helping* is a general term which describes giving assistance to another person.
- *Altruism* is more specific and considers the motives for helping. Walster and Piliavin (1972) define altruism as 'helping behaviour that is voluntary, costly to the altruist and motivated by something other than the expectation of material or social reward'. Altruism is therefore different from helping in that there is a regard for the interest of others, without apparent concern for one's self-interest.
- Both altruism and helping are forms of *prosocial behaviour* which can be defined as 'any actions that benefit another regardless of the benefits or self sacrifices of the actor' (Wispe 1972).

Traditional explanations of prosocial behaviour

Natural selection

According to the principles of natural selection, only behaviour that gives animals some survival or reproductive advantage will be performed. Altruistic behaviour appears to give no such advantage (according to Walster and Piliavin's definition) and so animals should not behave altruistically. However, acts of altruism have been observed in many species of animal (e.g. rabbits, bees, wasps, termites, birds and dolphins). This is described as the 'paradox of altruism'. However, it is believed by some that the survival of one's *genes* is more important than the survival of the *individual animal.* Thus an animal may sacrifice itself to save the genes of its relatives, i.e. its kin. Socio-biologists such as Wilson (1975) argue that altruism is built into the genetic code of humans as well as other animals. Rushton (1989) goes even further and proposes that we are more likely to help those who are genetically similar to ourselves, judged by their physical similarity, because we have inherited our ancestors' assumption that this would be the most effective guarantee that family genes would survive.

Learning theory

Learning theorists have argued that prosocial behaviour is learned in the same way as any other behaviour, with prosocial acts more likely to occur when they are rewarded. Moss and Page (1972) have shown that helping behaviour decreases when it is punished. Midlarsky *et al.* (1973) suggest that the best way to teach children prosocial behaviour is to have them observe it and then reward them when they copy it.

Norm theories of prosocial behaviour

Socialized norms

Norm theorists argue that prosocial behaviour is that which benefits society as a whole; we help others because we are motivated to act in accordance with an internalized set of norms (standards) for behaviour. Social norms represent consensus about which behaviours are acceptable and encouraged in society, and which are unacceptable and discouraged. Gouldner (1960) suggested a 'reciprocity norm' whereby we help those who have helped us. Berkowitz and Daniels (1963), on the other hand, suggested a *social responsibility norm* whereby we help those in need because they are dependent on us. Norms such as these are essential for successful interaction amongst people in any society. This being the case, in an emergency all witnesses should offer help, because of either the norm of reciprocity or the norm of social responsibility. They don't, however. This may be because individuals are faced with other conflicting norms: the norm of 'mind your own business', for example. On the other hand, it may be because these norms are too general and do not obviously apply to specific situations. In response to these criticisms, Schwartz (1977) suggested we consider *personalized norms.*

Personalized norms

Personalized norms relate to an individual's feelings of moral obligation. Schwartz explained how such norms become activated for an individual who becomes aware of another's need and perceives that there are actions he or she could take to help. The person may then feel a moral obligation to help because of existing personal norms about the desirability of helping others. The person then begins to assess the costs involved and may enter a defence stage, attempting to deny responsibility. Finally, the person makes a *response,* i.e. helping or not helping.

One advantage of the Schwartz model is that it specifies how motivation to help is activated in a situation and how defences come into play to determine whether or not help will be given. However, this theory suffers from the same problem as other norm theories: the number of norms is large and they may be in conflict (e.g. the 'social responsibility' norm conflicting with the 'minding-your-own-business' norm). Do other factors influence our decision about whether or not to help?

Empathy and arousal in prosocial behaviour

Consider the situation of Lenny Skutnik mentioned earlier. He witnessed a horrific accident which doubtless evoked powerful emotions in him. As he watched Priscilla Tirado struggle for her life, he presumably felt that he had to do something. Fortunately for the drowning woman, he did not walk away and try to forget what he had seen. This would have been one way of trying to reduce his heightened state of arousal. In this case, however, Lenny Skutnik released himself from his emotional state by jumping into the river and saving the woman. According to the *negative-state relief model* (Cialdini *et al.* 1981), we help others, not for altruistic reasons, but rather for egoistic reasons, in order to make ourselves feel better, e.g. by reducing our feelings of sadness or anxiety. Although some limited evidence has been offered in support of this theory (e.g. Cialdini *et al.* 1987), there have been many criticisms levelled against it. Prime among these comes from Batson *et al.* (1981) who proposed the *empathy–altruism theory*.

According to Batson, much of our helping behaviour in emergency situations is motivated by an unselfish desire to help the person in need. This desire arises from our ability to empathize with others. When we observe that someone needs help we can imagine what it must be like to be in that situation. By adopting the perspective of the person in need, we are motivated to offer help in order to reduce the person's distress. Therefore, according to the empathy–altruism theory, we may offer help for purely altruistic reasons and not merely as a means of making us feel better. Several experiments (e.g. Batson *et al.* 1983), where empathic concern for a victim has been manipulated, have provided support for this theory.

More recently, it has been suggested by Smith *et al.* (1989) that while empathy does lead to helping behaviour, it is not for purely altruistic reasons. They have proposed an *empathic joy model* of helping which states that 'prosocial behaviour is motivated by the joy one experiences when observing that someone else's needs have been met' (in Baron and Byrne 1994, p. 421). Another term for this is 'helpers' high' (Luks 1988), which is experienced not only by those who offer help but also by those who have been required to give it (Williamson and Clark 1992).

In order for helpers to experience empathic joy, they must obtain some feedback about the effects of their helping. If the empathic joy model is the best predictor of helping behaviour, then people should be less willing to offer help when they expect no such feedback. The results of an experiment conducted by Smith *et al.* (1989) indicated that empathic joy is an essential part of prosocial behaviour (see *In Focus* below). Nevertheless, it would be wrong to conclude that the role of egoistic motives in apparently altruistic behaviour had been resolved. Current research in social psychology continues to investigate this issue.

❖ Activity 2 ❖

1 Think of a situation where you gave help. What were your feelings at the time? Why did you help? How did you feel afterwards?

2 Think of a situation where you did *not* give help. What were your feelings that time? Why did you not help and how did you feel afterwards?

3 Which of the three models outlined above best describes your feelings on each of these two occasions?

In Focus

Testing competing models

Smith *et al.* (1989) tested the competing models by comparing empathy-altruism, negative state relief and empathic joy explanations of prosocial behaviour. They created an experimental situation in which an observer had the opportunity to help an unhappy stranger by offering her advice. The experimenters created feelings of high or low empathy by providing information that the stranger was very similar to or very dissimilar from the observer. In addition, some participants were told that feedback about effects of the advice would be given; others were told they would receive no feedback. According to the empathic joy theory, feedback would be necessary for helping to occur, but according to the empathy–altruism or negative-state relief models, feedback would *not* be essential. As the experimenters hypothesized, the highest level of helping occurred in the high empathy plus feedback condition, thus providing support for the empathic joy model.

Source: Baron and Byrne 1994, p. 423

Cognitive explanations of prosocial behaviour

Whereas norm theories consider personal and social values, and empathic, arousal theories emphasize emotions, cognitive models consider helping or not helping to be the result of a logical decision-making process: how the observer perceives and evaluates a situation and, on the basis of balancing the pertinent factors, makes a decision whether or not to help.

Latané and Darley's cognitive model

Latané and Darley (1970) formulated a five-stage model to explain why bystanders at emergencies sometimes do and sometimes do not offer help. At each stage in the model the answer 'No' results in no help being given, while the answer 'Yes' leads the individual closer to offering help (see Fig. 4.1).

Several studies support the existence of these decision-making stages.

- Shotland and Huston (1979) have identified five characteristics which lead us to perceive that an event is an emergency that requires our assistance:

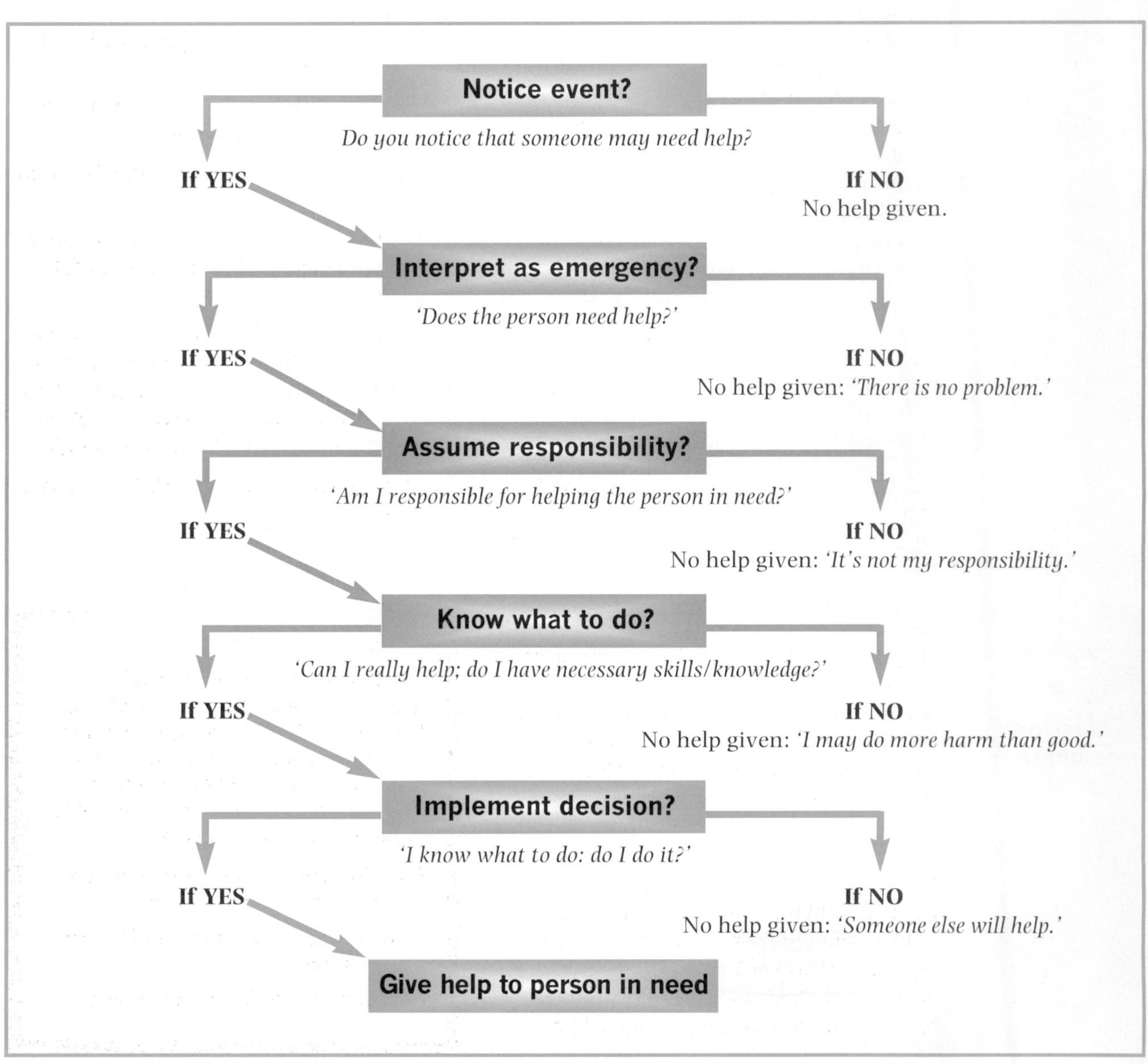
Notice event?
Do you notice that someone may need help?
If YES
If NO
No help given.
Interpret as emergency?
'Does the person need help?'
If YES
If NO
No help given: 'There is no problem.'
Assume responsibility?
'Am I responsible for helping the person in need?'
If YES
If NO
No help given: 'It's not my responsibility.'
Know what to do?
'Can I really help; do I have necessary skills/knowledge?'
If YES
If NO
No help given: 'I may do more harm than good.'
Implement decision?
'I know what to do: do I do it?'
If YES
If NO
No help given: 'Someone else will help.'
Give help to person in need

Figure 4.1 Cognitive model of prosocial behaviour *Source: adapted from* Latané and Darley 1970

- Something happens which is sudden and unexpected.
- There is clear threat of harm to the victim.
- The harm will persist or worsen if no one intervenes.
- The victim is helpless and needs outside assistance.
- Some form of effective assistance is possible.

❖ Bickman (1972) has shown that the more ambiguous the situation, the less likely it is that help will be offered.

❖ Maruyama *et al.* (1982) found that increasing personal responsibility leads to an increase in helping, whereas when people are in a group with a leader, group members tend to believe that the *leader* should be the one to act.

❖ Clark and Word (1974) have demonstrated the importance of necessary skills, and found that those with 'electrical' experience helped those who had apparently suffered an electric shock.

It has been shown, however, that where there are no other people present, individuals will still help despite their lack of competence. Where other people are present, a new set of factors apply in determining whether or not help will be given. These are known as 'bystander effects' and are considered in greater depth later in this chapter.

Latané and Darley's model, therefore, has received considerable support from a wide range of research. It is, however, criticized for not taking account of individual differences in the personality factors among potential helpers. These factors are outlined later in the section 'Characteristics of the potential helper'.

Cost/benefit analysis

An alternative cognitive theory is the cost/benefit analysis, originally outlined by Homans (1961) but developed by Piliavin *et al.* (1981) to explain the results of their 'subway samaritan study' (detailed later in this section). This theory suggests that whether we help or not depends on the outcome of weighing up both the costs and benefits of helping. The *costs of helping* may include:

❖ effort: e.g. helping may be physically demanding

❖ time: e.g. we may be late for work or an appointment

❖ loss of resources: e.g. we may damage clothes or lose earnings

❖ risk of harm: e.g. we may risk life and limb

❖ negative emotional response: e.g. we may feel physically sick.

All these factors are weighed against the *benefits of helping* such as:

❖ social approval: e.g. thanks from victim (and crowd, if there is one)

❖ self-esteem: e.g. feeling that one is a kind person

❖ positive emotional response: e.g. feelings (such as elation) elicited by successful rescue.

It is argued by Piliavin *et al.* that such a cost/benefit analysis is performed to reduce negative emotional arousal, and in addition to the above factors, the *costs of not helping* must also be assessed. These may include:

❖ disapproval: e.g. no rewards from victim or crowd

❖ Activity 3 ❖

Calculate your own cost/benefit analysis. Imagine you are driving a car to work with two friends as passengers and you see one car crash into another on the road ahead. Would you stop or not? List all the possible costs/benefits involved in stopping to help.

Now also consider whether your decision to stop would be influenced by:

- your recognizing the driver of the car which crashed
- your being late for an appointment.

- damaged self-esteem: e.g. feelings that one is not a kind person
- negative emotional response: e.g. not helping may cause feelings of guilt.

The Piliavin *et al.* model has been supported by a number of studies which demonstrated that increasing various costs will lead to a decrease in helping, whilst increasing the benefits will lead to an increase in helping.

Who helps whom?

Do we decide whether to give help because of the type of person we are or because of the type of person the victim appears to be?

Characteristics of the person in need

Undoubtedly we perceive certain types of people to be more deserving of help than others. We help those to whom we are related and those for whom we feel responsible. For example, you may recall that in 1995 Philip Lawrence went to the aid of one of his pupils who was being bullied by youths from another school. One attacker stabbed Philip Lawrence who died from the wounds inflicted. More generally, research (e.g. Piliavin *et al.* 1981) has shown that:

- We are more likely to help those who are perceived to be similar to ourselves.
- We are more likely to help those we perceive as needing help, e.g. children and elderly people.
- We are more likely to help those to whom we are physically attracted.
- We are less likely to help those who are not attractive, particularly those who are disfigured (unless we are also disfigured).
- We are less likely to help those whom we perceive as responsible for their own plight.

Characteristics of the potential helper

Is there a helping personality? In an attempt to answer this question, Bierhoff *et al.* (1991) compared the personal characteristics of those who witnessed a road traffic accident and provided first aid with those who witnessed such an accident and did not provide help. The results of this study are shown in Table 4.1 below.

Milgram (1970) proposed a *stimulus overload* theory, suggesting that people from cities are so familiar with emergency situations that they treat them as everyday occurrences – these situations are less likely to attract interest and so people do not help. People from small towns, however, do not witness emergencies very often, so that when these situations occur, their novelty is more likely to attract attention and help.

Table 4.1 Components of the helping personality

Characteristics of those who help	*Characteristics of those who do not help*
had high internal locus of control	had low internal locus of control
held belief in a 'just world'	held less belief in a 'just world'
felt socially responsible	felt less socially responsible
possessed ability to empathize	possessed less ability to empathize
were less egocentric	were more egocentric

Source: adapted from Bierhoff *et al.* 1991

The mood of a bystander may affect whether or not help is given. Being in a good mood may lead to helping if the consequences of helping are likely to be pleasant and where there is little ambiguity about help being needed. If, however, the need is ambiguous and the consequences of helping are likely to be unpleasant, then people in a good mood tend not to help. According to Isen (1984), this is because they do not want to spoil the good mood they are currently enjoying. Likewise, being in a bad mood may help or hinder prosocial behaviour. There is the possibility that the bad mood, if it is due to guilt, might be alleviated by helping someone. However, if people are focused on their own worries, they may be less responsive to the needs of others (e.g. Cialdini *et al.* 1982).

Steele and Southwick (1985) have shown that the consumption of alcohol leads to helping behaviour, because the alcohol reduces inhibitions and awareness of potential dangers. McGovern (1976) suggested that individuals who fear embarrassment are less likely to help and Satow (1975) found that, when others are watching, people who scored high on 'need for approval' were more likely to help than those with low scores. A number of these suggestions relate to the inhibitory effect the presence of others has on an individual, details of which we will look at next.

The influence of others (bystander effects)

In the Kitty Genovese incident there were thirty-eight witnesses, yet no one helped or called the police. Darley and Latané (1968) suspected that the fact that the number of possible helpers was so large might actually have contributed to their lack of intervention. A number of studies have investigated this phenomenon.

Bystander effects in the laboratory

In their 'epileptic seizure' study, Darley and Latané (1968) used male students seated in cubicles connected by an intercom system. They had volunteered to take part in a discussion on college life. The students were led to believe that they were either alone with one other participant, who later would be heard to have an epileptic seizure, or that they were joined by either one or four other participants besides the apparant seizure victim. Therefore, there were three conditions in the experiment. Once the discussion was underway, the victim clearly announced that he was experiencing a seizure. Help was less likely and slower to happen when participants believed that other potential helpers were present (see Table 4.2 for results).

Table 4.2 Bystander effects

Group size (number of people)	*% responding during fit*	*% responding at any point*	*Average response time (in seconds)*
1	85	100	52
2	62	85	93
5	31	62	166

Source: Darley and Latané 1968

In Focus

If people won't help others in emergencies, will they help themselves?

Latané and Darley (1970) performed another study, the 'smoke-filled room experiment', which demonstrates the power of the bystander effect. In this study whilst participants are in the waiting room completing questionnaires, smoke begins to fill the room. This continues until the room is full of thick, white smoke. In the condition where experimental accomplices are present with the participants, of all those tested, only one took any action! One possible explanation is that this result is a product of the experimental situation – some participants reported that they thought the smoke was introduced to see how it affected their ability to fill in the questionnaires! Most, however, looked to the others present in the room for some guidance as to how to act. Since the accomplices did nothing, the participants did nothing – a powerful demonstration of the bystander effect.

Explaining bystander effects

Latané and Nida (1981) proposed three main reasons to explain the influence on helping of other people being present.

- *Audience inhibition:* We may be inhibited about offering help if we think that bystanders might disapprove, especially if we value their good opinion.
- *Diffusion of responsibility*: When only one person is present then that person is 100 per cent responsible for giving help. When there are two people present then responsibility is divided. If there are ten bystanders the onus of responsibility is diffused amongst all ten. In the Kitty Genovese case witnesses assumed someone else had phoned for the police. Support for the notion of diffusion of responsibility comes not only from the Latané and Darley study mentioned earlier, but also from 'social loafing' research (Latané *et al.* 1979) where it has been demonstrated that the more people who are present, the less effort each individual makes.
- *Pluralistic ignorance*: When making a decision whether or not to help, we look to see what other bystanders are doing. If one person defines the situation as an emergency and helps, we are likely to follow and give assistance. If no one offers to give help then we may conclude that the situation is not an emergency and do nothing. In effect, each bystander looks to the behaviour of others as a guide to his or her own behaviour. In the Kitty Genovese case, since no one was seen to be intervening, this tended to define the situation as one not requiring intervention from anyone (see also *In Focus* above).

Bystander effects in the natural environment

Latané and Darley (1970) found that when a person dropped some books in a lift, the probability of receiving help decreased with the number of people present: 40 per cent were offered help when there was one other passenger, but only 15 per cent when there were six others. Not all studies carried out in a natural environment, however, have found that large numbers mean little helping.

Piliavin *et al.* (1969) conducted a study to investigate the effects on helping of the type of person who is in need. They looked at the effect on help offered of (a) the victim appearing ill or drunk, and (b) the race of the victim (black or white).

During a seven-and-a-half minute journey on a busy New York subway train, the 'victim' accomplice collapsed on the floor of the train and remained there until someone helped. The major findings of the study are as follows: (a) those appearing to be ill were more likely to be helped than those appearing to be drunk; (b) the race of the 'victim' had little effect on the helper. In addition, the expected diffusion of responsibility effect (mentioned earlier) did not occur. Why is this? It is suggested by Piliavin *et al.* that in the laboratory studies participants could *hear* but not *see* the 'victim', whereas in this study participants could both see and hear the 'victim'. Participants could also see what bystanders were *actually* doing.

Section summary

There are a number of explanations of prosocial behaviour including those based on genetic determinism, learning theory, norm theories, and the roles of arousal and empathy. Cognitive theories propose that helping (or not helping) behaviour is the result of a logical decision-making process. Other explanations focus on the characteristics of the person in need or the characteristics of the helper. Laboratory studies have generally found that helping was decreased when passive bystanders were present and that this was due to audience inhibition, diffusion of responsibility and pluralistic ignorance.

Antisocial behaviour

'Antisocial acts are those that show a lack of feeling and concern for the welfare of others' (Baron and Richardson 1994). Successful social interaction and the smooth running of society can only exist if most people do not behave antisocially. Most societies, therefore, have laws, enforced via a police force and a legal system, to discourage, condemn and punish antisocial acts. Aggressive acts are usually viewed as one of the most disturbing types of antisocial behaviour.

Defining aggression

Different types of aggressive behaviour have been identified:

- *Antisocial aggression:* defined by Penrod (1983) as 'all behaviour that is intended to inflict physical or psychological harm on another individual who does not want to be so treated'.
- *Prosocial aggression:* e.g. when the police shoot a terrorist who has murdered hostages and is threatening others.
- *Sanctioned aggression:* such as self-defence, e.g. when a woman injures a rapist while defending herself.

A further distinction is that between aggressive behaviours which are overt and aggressive feelings, such as anger, which are covert. Frustration frequently makes people angry, but angry people do not always behave aggressively.

Social learning and aggression

According to Berkowitz (1989) and Bandura (1965), although the aggressive behaviour of lower animals can be explained in terms of instinctual drives, aggression in humans is the product of learning. They claim that aggressive behaviour is learned either through direct experience or by observing others. *Imitation or observational learning* occurs when a child who sees a role model behaving in a particular way reproduces that behaviour. Bandura *et al.* (1961) had one group of children observe an adult behaving aggressively to a bobo doll (a large, inflated doll), whilst a second group observed the adult in the same room displaying no aggressive behaviour towards the doll. When allowed to play in the same room, each group imitated the behaviour of its model. In other words the former group displayed high levels of aggression compared with the latter group (see *In Focus* on p. 76).

❖ Activity 4 ❖

- Have you ever been reinforced for being aggressive? If so, what form did the reinforcement take?
- Have you ever been punished for being aggressive? If so, what form did the punishment take?
- Do you think aggressive behaviour is learned?

In Focus

Do children learn aggression?

Bandura (1965) divided sixty-six nursery school children into three groups. All three groups watched a film where an adult model kicked and punched a bobo doll.

- Condition 1: Children saw the adult model being rewarded by a second adult.
- Condition 2: Children saw a second adult telling off the adult model for the aggressive behaviour.
- Condition 3: The adult model was neither rewarded nor punished.

The children were then allowed to play in the room with the bobo doll whilst experimenters watched through a one-way mirror. Results showed that children in Condition 1 behaved most aggressively, and those in Condition 2 behaved least aggressively. However, an important distinction must be made between learning and performance. All the children *learnt* how to behave aggressively but those in Condition 2 did not *perform* as many aggressive acts until later, when they were offered rewards to do so. When this happened, they quickly showed that they had learned (acquired) as many aggressive techniques as the children in Condition 1.

Studies such as this have been criticized because of their artificiality.

However, children do not imitate everything other people do. The type of role they see model is crucial and studies have shown that the more important, successful, powerful and liked the role model is, the more likely the person is to be imitated. Parents fulfil all these criteria in a child's early years. Later on, one's peers are more likely to be one's influential models.

If a child learns by imitation, then such learning is likely to be repeated if the behaviour is *positively reinforced*, whilst behaviours either not rewarded, or actually punished, are less likely to be repeated. Positive reinforcement helps to develop aggressive behaviour since children are often rewarded for such behaviour.

According to the social learning view of aggression, whether or not a person behaves aggressively in a group situation depends upon a number of factors, including past experiences and perceptions about what is appropriate (see Fig. 4.2).

Social determinants of aggressive behaviour

Frustration and aggression

Dollard *et al.* (1939) formulated the frustration–aggression hypothesis which asserted that when frustration occurs, (i.e. when something interferes with the achievement of a goal), the outcome is always aggression.

In order to test this hypothesis, Buss (1961) devised an 'aggression machine' to measure the intensity of an aggressive response. Participants believed they would be delivering an electric shock to a victim as a punishment in a learning task. (Of course, no shocks were actually received.) Buss caused some participants to be frustrated (e.g. by interfering with their attempts to win money) before the task began. Buss found that 'frustrated' participants gave more 'shocks' than 'unfrustrated' participants. However, it is not merely frustration that leads to aggression. The manner in which one's goals are interrupted may also be important. For example, Kulik and Brown (1979) asked students to telephone people (who were accomplices of the experimenter) to ask for donations to a charity. When called and asked to donate, all accomplices refused. Some were polite and gave reasonable explanations for not giving; others were insulting and gave no reason at all. Kulik and Brown found that the students making the calls were apparently more frustrated by the latter response and used more aggressive language, even venting their anger on the

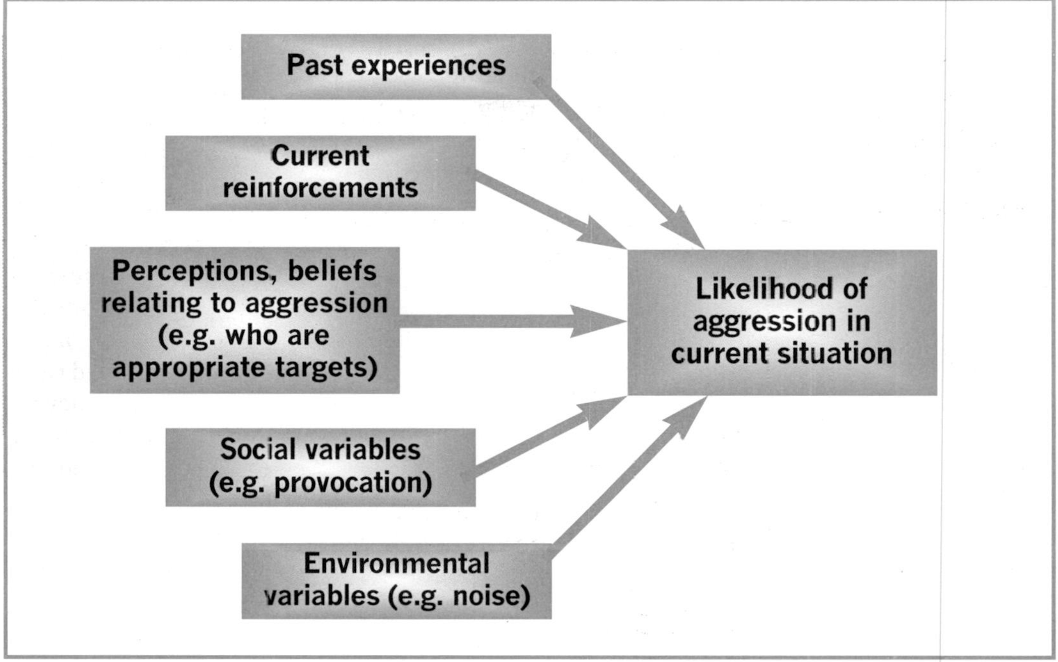

Figure 4.2 The social learning view of aggression *Source: adapted from* Bandura 1986

telephone itself by slamming down the receiver.

Berkowitz (1989) has shown that even when frustration is strong, unexpected and illegitimate, it does not inevitably lead to aggression because people's higher level cognitive processes enable them to reflect upon the cause of their frustration and choose what is an appropriate response.

❖ Activity 5 ❖

List a number of things that cause you frustration. Try to put them into categories (such as those to do with work, environment, family, etc.). Do your frustrations always lead you to behave aggressively? If not, why not?

Environmental cues and frustration–aggression

Modifying the original frustration–aggression hypothesis, Berkowitz (1962) stated that two factors were important prerequisites for aggressive behaviour:

- a readiness to act aggressively, usually created by frustration
- external cues that trigger the expression of aggression.

Initially, Berkowitz, along with LePage (1967), suggested that the mere availability of weapons could increase aggression, and this 'weapons effect' hypothesis has received some support from subsequent research.

Berkowitz later suggested that frustration may lead to aggression when there are either *aggressive cues* (such as a weapon) or *aversive environmental stimuli* (see below) in the environment.

Other environmental factors

- *Temperature:* Bell and Baron (1974) have shown that there is a critical range of uncomfortably warm ambient temperatures (between 81° and 85° Fahrenheit) which facilitates aggressive responses in humans, but that at extremely high or extremely low temperatures aggression is reduced.
- *Noise:* In laboratory studies, Donnerstein and Wilson (1976) have found that unpredictable and uncontrollable bursts of noise increased the aggression of angry participants. In real life, excessive noise caused by neighbours has led to a number of aggressive incidents. In one

extreme example, Peter Thurston was jailed for 22 years for firebombing his noisy neighbours. Apparently 'he was so driven by the relentless noise of parties within that block which spanned over a decade, that he planned and executed this terrible attack'. (*Daily Mirror* 1995).

- *Provocation and attack*: studies have shown that physical provocation and attack lead to strong counter attacks. Studies by Geen (1968) have shown that verbal insult, particularly when it is intentional, elicits even higher levels of aggression than does frustration.
- *Deindividuation:* according to Zimbardo (1970) when people are in a deindividuated state (have lost their sense of personal identity and responsibility), they are more likely to behave aggressively because they are less likely to be identified and have diminished self-awareness (see Chapter 3).

To this list Berkowitz (1983) added foul odours, frightening information, irritating cigarette smoke and disgusting images!

Personal causes of aggressive behaviour

Type A behaviour

Type A behaviour (according to Friedman and Rosenman 1974) is exhibited by someone who is highly motivated, competitive, assertive, time conscious and aggressive. *Type B behaviour* does not exhibit these characteristics. Studies by Strube *et al.* (1984) have shown that Type As are more likely to engage in hostile aggression. Type As and those suffering from an accumulation of everyday hassles (Kanner *et al.* 1981) are also more likely to suffer extreme frustration when, for example, they are held up in traffic. They are also more likely to demonstrate their 'road rage' by behaving aggressively not only in the form of rude gestures, but in terms of actual bodily harm inflicted upon those perceived to have caused the problem. Type As are also more likely to have road accidents than Type Bs (Evans *et al.* 1987) (see Fig. 4.3).

In Focus

Does alcohol consumption lead to aggression?

The commonly held view is that violence is increased by the consumption of alcohol. In a review of studies by Hull and Bond (1986) the overwhelming conclusion supported this view. Why is this? One suggestion is that the alcohol reduces the constraints preventing aggressive behaviour, but interestingly, as shown by Steele and Southwick (1985) the removal of inhibitions can also lead to an increase in helping behaviour. To account for these apparent contradictions, Taylor and Sears (1988) have proposed that alcohol interferes with normal cognitive functioning. In their study, all-male participants consumed what they thought was a large amount of alcohol. One group consumed alcohol and the other consumed liquid that smelled and looked alcoholic but was not. Participants then competed in a reaction time test against each other where an electric shock was given to the loser. An accomplice of the experimenter initially encouraged participants to give ever-increasing shocks and left the room after a period of time. Results showed that the level of shocks remained consistent throughout for the non-alcoholic group, whilst the 'alcoholic group' initially gave larger shocks when encouraged by the accomplice but later reduced the level of shock when the accomplice left the room. Taylor and Sears concluded that alcohol influences normal cognitive functioning to the extent that we are more likely to take into account social or situational cues which suggest what form of behaviour is appropriate in the circumstances. This could be either pro- or antisocial behaviour.

Figure 4.3 Type A behaviour pattern and aggression *Source:* Evans et al. 1987

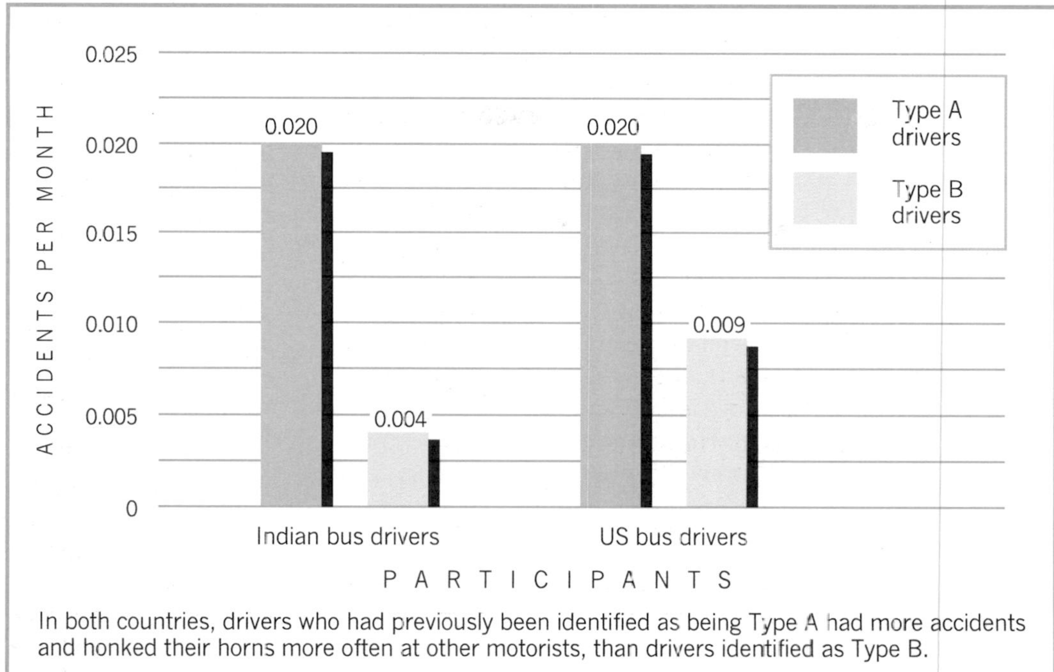

In both countries, drivers who had previously been identified as being Type A had more accidents and honked their horns more often at other motorists, than drivers identified as Type B.

The excitation transfer theory

Another explanation for aggressive behaviour is that provided by Zillmann (1983) in his *excitation transfer theory*. This states that whatever its cause, heightened physiological arousal takes time to dissipate. During this time if a situation arises which might normally have caused mild annoy-ance, any residual arousal is transferred to the new situation, and anger and aggression become more likely. Zillmann and Bryant (1974) had participants pedal cycles to create either a high or low physiological arousal condition and following this had them play in a game where an accomplice verbally abused them. Later the participants had the opportunity to deliver a harsh noise in the abuser's headphones. Zillmann's theory was supported: those in the high arousal condition gave the higher levels of noise to the abuser. In a later study, Bryant and Zillmann (1979) found that even one week later, those who had been in the high arousal condition demonstrated more aggressiveness.

Attribution and aggression

When directly provoked, people often respond in kind. For example, if someone is rude to us, we may well reciprocate. However, this is not inevitable. How we *interpret* other people's behaviour will influence how we respond to it. If we know that there are mitigating factors for the rudeness (e.g. the person has been under exceptional stress) or that the behaviour is unintended (e.g. caused by a mental disorder and beyond the person's control) then we are much less likely to lose our temper and respond aggressively. In other words, how we *attribute* the cause of a provocative act will influence how we respond to it (Kremer and Stephens 1983) – see *In Focus* on p. 80.

Gender differences in aggression

Are males more aggressive than females? Well, yes and no. Men tend to be more *physically* aggressive than women but women are at least as likely as men to indulge in *indirect* or non-physical forms of aggression, such as malicious gossiping.

What causes men to be more physically aggressive? The answer appears to be twofold.

- Girls are taught from an early age that physical aggression is unfeminine and should be avoided. Boys, on the other

In Focus

The social construction of aggression

'Almost every behaviour, even a failure to act (as in the case of giving help), can become aggression if someone judges that the actor intended harm to the victim. Conversely, cases of extreme violence need not be identified as aggression [e.g. cases of self-defence].' (Hewstone 1988, p. 280)

Furthermore, when we describe a behaviour as aggressive, we imply that the perpetrator should be punished in some way because he or she has violated a social norm. The same act, on the other hand, may sometimes be deemed appropriate and may even attract praise or reward.

Camino and Trocolli (1980, cited by Leyens and Fraczek 1984) reported that the judgement of an action as aggressive or violent was dependent upon the sociopolitical beliefs of the person making the judgement. Some viewed police treatment of demonstrators as violent while others did not. People with positive attitudes towards the police were more likely to condone the actions taken by them. Blumenthal *et al.* (1972) have shown, however, that students who hold negative attitudes towards police were highly critical of the way student demonstrations were policed, and judged many police actions to be aggressive. Ferguson and Rule (1983) have listed three criteria which people tend to use when they are deciding whether or not an action is aggressive: intention to harm, actual harm and norm violation.

hand, are taught that aggression is appropriate. Many social psychologists, therefore, claim that the different socializing experiences of males and females explain the difference in expressed aggression.

- Levels of testosterone (male sex hormone) correlate positively with levels of aggressive behaviour in males (though not in females). Furthermore, levels of physical aggression are the same in heterosexual and homosexual men, thus weakening the argument that gender roles may influence levels of aggression (Gladue 1991).

Although men may be somewhat hormonally predisposed to show more physical aggression than women, this does not mean that males are *compelled* or doomed to be aggressive. Biology is not destiny and techniques for controlling aggression do exist, as we shall see later on.

Cultural diversity and antisocial behaviour

Examination of murder rates from around the world reveals some interesting statistics. Scott (1992) shows that whereas Norway has 0.9 murders per 100,000 people, Japan has 1.2, Britain 1.4, the United States 9.9, and New Guinea 683! Such figures must be the result of varying social and cultural factors, including differences in socially acceptable reactions to frustration. Osterwell and Nagano-Hakamura (1992) have shown that whereas Israeli mothers believe aggression is provoked and, therefore, should be expressed, outside the family, Japanese mothers believe it is a natural part of growing up and should, therefore, be expressed within the family. Similarly Kaufman *et al.* (1990) have shown that when they were an ethnic minority in American schools, Hispanic school children were more moody but not more aggressive, whereas Anglo children were not more moody but were more aggressive.

Cultural differences in aggression are due not only to the *microculture* (groups within a wider culture), but also to the wider society as a whole. Consider the following information: in nations that had recently been at war, Archer and Gartner (1976) discovered that there was a dramatic increase in post-war homicide rates. Following World War II, France had an increase of 51 per cent, Italy 133 per cent and the Netherlands 13 per cent. Archer and Gartner (1976) also noted that during the Vietnam War, the murder rate in the United States more than doubled after a thirty-year decline. Since war is sanctioned aggression, it is interesting to see the effect this has on society as a whole.

Reducing and controlling aggressive behaviour

Fundamental to maintaining peace and order in any society is the control of aggression. This can be done on two levels:

- at a *societal* level, through sanctions imposed by legitimate authority
- at an *individual* level, through learning appropriate behaviours and ways of thinking.

Controlling aggression with punishment

To address whether punishment imposed by legitimate authority is effective, we need to consider whether the threat of arrest and possible imprisonment acts as a deterrent for the majority of the population. For a large portion of the population, punishment is more of an *additional* reason for not behaving aggressively towards another, rather than the single most important reason. For other people, the threat of such punishment is not a deterrent at all – as is reflected in the slowly upward trend in crime statistics.

Bower and Hilgard (1981) suggest that punishment can be a successful deterrent if:

- the punishment is *prompt*, i.e. it follows the aggressive act as soon as possible
- it is *intense* and highly aversive
- it is *probable*, i.e. is almost always applied.

In considering the effect of punishment on models, Bandura (1965) has shown that even if children observe models being punished for behaving aggressively, they still behave more aggressively than children who have not seen any aggression in the first place. Social learning theorists believe that environmental conditions which control the acquisition and maintenance of aggressive behaviours should be the target of attempts at control, such as reducing violence on television or presenting more prosocial models. Deaux *et al.* (1993, p. 279) have claimed that 'we cannot eliminate all aggressive models from our society, [but] we may be able to reduce aggression by adding more unaggressive models to the environment'.

Alternative 'learning' strategies

Aggression can be reduced by teaching adults various strategies to counter it. One such strategy, known as the use of 'incompatible responses', is based on the belief that it is impossible to do two incompatible things at once or have two incompatible emotions at the same time. A person, for example, who is happy is much less likely to behave aggressively. Therefore, if we can induce angry people to feel empathy or to see the funny side of the situation, they will behave less aggressively (e.g. Zillman 1983).

Toch (1985) observes that much of the violence in society appears to be caused by a lack of social skills. Toch claims that failure to deal skilfully with provocation from others may exacerbate the situation, making aggression more likely. Similarly, an inability to express our wishes clearly so that others repond as we would wish, may result in our becoming increasingly frustrated. He suggests that social-skills training can teach us both to avoid potentially explosive situations and to express ourselves more effectively. Schnieder (1991) has demonstrated the effectiveness of such training in reducing aggressive behaviour in school children.

Another strategy is to raise awareness of the attribution process. On the one hand, there are those who perceive hostile intent where none is present and on the other, there are those with the skill to diffuse potentially hostile responses by providing mitigating information. Studies have shown that providing a simple apology can be effective in reducing aggression. Ohbuchi *et al.* (1989) found participants were much less aggressive when they received either a public or private apology than when they received no apology for a person's bad behaviour.

Catharsis and aggression reduction

According to Freud, aggressive urges arise from bodily processes and must periodically be released. If not released, the aggression can cause tension, pain and irrational behaviour. He believed that aggression should be directed into socially acceptable activities through sublimation, e.g. sports, competitions, etc. Dollard *et al.* (1939) also believed that 'the expression of any act of aggression is a catharsis that reduces the instigation of all other acts of aggression'. 'Letting off steam' and 'getting it out of your system' are typical expressions describing catharsis. It is claimed that catharsis works by reducing tension levels and thereby reducing the likelihood that aggression will escalate.

Several activities which are often claimed as useful in safely redirecting aggression have been researched. Most evidence suggests that taking part in so-called 'cathartic' activities is ineffective in reducing aggressive behaviour. Overall it is concluded that aggression is not reduced by:

- attacking inanimate objects (Mallick and McCandless 1966)
- watching filmed or televised violence (Geen 1978)
- attending competitive sporting events – studies suggest that, if anything, *more* rather than less aggression results from such activities (Arms *et al.* 1980)
- using verbal rather than physical violence. Verbal aggression is not the route to peace and harmony, but rather to outbreaks of more serious violence (Carlson *et al.* 1989).

Contrary to popular belief, catharsis is *not* an effective means of reducing aggression.

Section summary

Aggressive behaviour may be caused by frustration aggravated by aggressive cues (such as weapons) and aversive stimuli (such as temperature and noise). Other factors, such as the consumption of alcohol, levels of physiological arousal and Type A behaviour, also contribute.

According to social learning theorists, aggression is learned through imitation and reinforcement. There are cultural differences in the rates of aggressive behaviour, and it was suggested that this is due to differing socialization practices.

The role of punishment, alternative learning strategies and catharsis as a means of reducing aggression have been examined.

Media influences on prosocial and antisocial behaviour

We have seen that observational learning and reinforcement are important in learning aggressive or helping behaviour. What then, is the role of the media in this process? In particular, what is the role of television? The widely held view of the media as a source of aggression is reinforced by many experts:

- 'Watching movie or television aggression increases the likelihood of the observers engaging in similar aggressive actions.' (McGee and Wilson 1984, p. 504)
- 'There is now overwhelming evidence that excessive violence on television causes aggressive behaviour in children.' (Report of National Institute of Mental Health 1982).

First, let us consider what is meant by the term 'television violence' and how much of it there is.

Defining television violence

How is television violence defined? How much violence is there on television? What do viewers, rather than researchers, consider to be violent television?

How much violence is there on television?

According to Cumberbatch (1987), television violence is the portrayal of 'any action of physical force with or without a weapon against oneself or another person, animal or inanimate object, whether carried through or merely attempted and whether the action caused injury or not'.

In Britain the BBC's Audience Research Department began research in 1972, which culminated in a large-scale study supervised by Cumberbatch (1987). Taking into account all forms of violence, the study found there were 1.68 violent acts per hour, rising to 1.96 acts when verbal threats were included.

In recent years, however, there has been a significant increase in the types of television available, such as that provided by cable and satellite networks. Whereas terrestrial channels are governed by the 9 pm 'watershed', encrypted channels have more freedom, e.g. on Sky Movies on Sunday 3 December 1995 between 8 a.m. and 8 p.m., of the six films shown, five had a PG (parental guidance) certificate. American cartoons, often with a high violence content and once comprising a very small percentage of viewing time on terrestrial channels, now (via The Disney Channel and The Cartoon Network) provide children with virtually non-stop opportunities to observe violent acts!

What viewers consider as violence

According to Cumberbatch there is a difference between what researchers and viewers perceive as violence. He suggests that viewers, particularly children, can be highly discriminating. Children view cartoons as containing hardly any violence at all, because cartoons are not a true reflection of reality. What do parents consider to be violent programmes? Messenger-Davies (1989) discovered that although most parents (60 per cent) thought that watching violent television made children more aggressive, 75 per cent thought that *Magnum*, *Minder* and *The A-Team* were harmless, even for those under 5 years old.

❖ Activity 6 ❖

1 List, on your own, as many examples of violent television programmes as you can. When you have finished, compare your list with someone else's. How similar are they? Can you explain any differences? For example, are the dissimilarities caused by differences in what you watch or differences in interpreting programme content?

2 In your opinion do adults and/or children differentiate between real-life violence and fictional violence? Do you think the ability to differentiate in this way matters?

Television and aggression

Studying the effects of television violence

The effects of television violence have been investigated in a number of ways. In controlled *laboratory* conditions, a number of studies have shown that when children were exposed to violent programmes they showed violent behaviours. Following the studies of Bandura (1965) where participants watched filmed violence in a laboratory, Berkowitz (1969) used a procedure where participants were given either a single electric shock or seven electric shocks (creating an 'angry' group) following their performance on a problem-solving task. The participants were then shown a seven-minute film which was either non-aggressive or aggressive. When given the opportunity to give electric shocks to an accomplice of the experimenter, those from the 'angry' group who had watched the aggressive film, delivered the most shocks. These results support the view that aggression can be triggered by a stimulus in the environment, especially if a person is already aroused. In this case, the aggressive film was the catalyst. Although laboratory studies provide a controlled environment, they have little ecological validity and usually involve relatively small, unrepresentative samples. In real life, children watch a variety of programmes, over a period of time and in very different environments.

The use of *field experiments* would appear to overcome some of the problems encountered in laboratory studies. However, the studies performed to date tend to have design flaws. In a study by Parke *et al.* (1977) male juvenile delinquents living in institutions were used. The boys lived in small groups (cottages). Base-line measures of aggressive behaviour were taken first. Subsequently boys in one cotttage watched violent films, while boys in another cottage watched non-violent films. Increases in some forms of aggressive behaviour were recorded for those who had watched the violent films. However, there are methodological problems associated with such field experiements. The boys allocated to each condition belonged to a pre-existing group and therefore we cannot be sure that the two groups were equivalent in all important respects. And, of course, young offenders are hardly representative of young people in general.

Hennigan *et al.* (1982) looked at the changes in crime rates following the introduction of television to areas where it was previously unavailable. Although it was found that there was no change in violent crime, this analysis only focused on reported crimes and did not consider any changes in domestic violence or violence at school, or changes in unreported crimes.

Other field studies have used the *correlation method*, that is, investigating whether there is a relationship between the amount of violent television viewed and levels of aggressive behaviour. However, the studies had problems with sampling, measuring aggression and estimating how much violence had been watched previously. By no means all studies have positively correlated watching television violence with violent behaviour. Where correlations have been found, they need to be interpreted with caution (see *In Focus* on p. 85).

To try to establish some evidence of causality, Milavsky *et al.* (1982) performed a three-year *longitudinal* study of some 3,200 children. Some small positive correlations *were* found between viewing habits and aggressive behaviour but there was no firm evidence relating the watching of television violence to violent behaviour. Family background and social environment were better predictors of aggression than television viewing habits.

Despite lack of firm evidence from correlational and other studies, several psychologists (e.g. Wood *et al.* 1991) support the view that exposure to media violence contributes to the occurrence of aggressive behaviour. How this might occur is outlined next.

Proposed effects of watching violence on television

- *Disinhibition:* people's inhibitions are reduced as violence becomes a part of everyday life, not only through television but also through the availability of aggressive cues in the environment (e.g. the 'weapons effect' as outlined by Berkowitz and Le Page 1967).
- *Arousal:* watching a violent programme increases the level of physiological arousal. Although this may not lead to the performance of aggressive behaviour immediately afterwards, the arousal may be transferred to some other situation after a period of time (Zillmann 1983).
- *Desensitization:* refers to our decreased sensitivity to stimuli that are presented constantly over a period of time. The concern is that a viewer who watches too much television violence becomes adapted to it. Further violence becomes less objectionable because the viewer has become desensitized to it (e.g. Drabman and Thomas 1974).
- *New cognitions:* Repeated exposure to violence could prime us to perceive future information or events in terms of aggressive intent where aggression was not, in fact, intended.
- *Imitation:* social learning theorists argue that television is a powerful source of modelling. In real life there are examples of serious crime which are said to be the

In Focus

Violence on TV and aggressive behaviour

'Among studies which have focused on violence, arguably the most ambitious of correlational studies was carried out by Belson (1978)... on 1,565 boys aged 13 to 16 in London. It attempted to measure children's exposure to television violence in their earlier years and to link this to self-reported violent behaviour, through a sophisticated system of matching those who were more exposed to television violence with those who were less exposed to television violence. This matching was done according to over 200 different measures... Belson concluded that boys with high levels of exposure to television violence commit 49 per cent more acts of serious violence than those who see little. He then went on to list policy recommendations and suggested that violence should be reduced on television especially in 'plays or films in which violence occurs in the context of close personal relationships', 'programmes presenting fictional violence of a realistic kind' and so on.

'This sounds like the kind of impressive data providing the specific recommendations needed to clean up television. Unfortunately, closer examination of the vast array of data Belson presents advises more caution. For example, the graphs for the full sample show that the results are far from as simple as his conclusions imply. In these graphs, where exposure to television violence is plotted against violent behaviour, it is clear that the relationship is curvilinear. Thus very low viewers of television violence are slightly *more* aggressive than moderate viewers. More importantly, very high viewers of television violence are *less* aggressive than the moderate-to-high exposure group. Moreover, in Belson's data, exposure to non-violent television is also linked to aggressive behaviour, as indeed are comics/comic books and even newspaper readership.'

Source: Cumberbatch 1991, p. 179

result of imitating TV programmes. In the United States a famous case was that of John Hinckley who, in 1981, after watching the film *Taxi Driver* some twelve times, shot President Reagan. In Britain there is the case of Michael Ryan who shot and killed many people in the village of Hungerford. Numerous videotapes depicting violence were later discovered at his home. It is argued that exposure to media violence provides viewers with new ideas and techniques about which they previously knew nothing.

Conclusions: effects of violent television

The conclusion from a large number of studies is that observing violence on television is no more than a contributory factor in aggressive behaviour. Other factors may be equally, if not more, influential. Durkin (1985) suggested that children's own personalities and aspirations affect their responses to what they viewed. To conclude, Messenger-Davies (1989) states: 'What children get from television depends on what children bring to it. Depending on how old they are, how bright they are, how tired they are, what sort of family they belong to, what sort of skills they already have, television will affect them differently.'

Video violence

Recently there has been growing concern over the effects of viewing violent videotapes. Tragic real-life events have reinforced the concern expressed, especially about the effects on the behaviour of children – for example, the case of the two 10-year-old killers of James Bulger, Thompson and Venables, who regularly watched adult horror movies, particularly the notorious *Child's Play 3*. A second case is that of a 15-year-old boy who carried out two armed robberies and whose father blamed violent videos for his son's descent into crime. The gist of the concern about so-called 'video nasties' is summarized in the following quotation of Newson: 'Over the past few years, considerable anxiety has been expressed by those professionally concerned with children about the effects of "horror", "sex and violence", "soft porn" and similar scenes experienced by children via videos seen in their own or their friends' homes.' (Newson 1994, p. 273)

It has also been pointed out that, unlike traditional 'horror' stories, in video nasties the viewer is encouraged to identify with the perpetrator rather than the victim of the violence.

Television and prosocial behaviour

We have seen studies demonstrate that when an adult encourages or condones aggressive behaviour, children are more likely to be aggressive. Studies have also shown that if an adult condemns the violence viewed, children are less likely to behave aggressively. Eron et al (1983) compared two groups of 8- and 9-year-old children who watched significant amounts of television violence. In the experimental group they taught the children that violence on television is unrealistic; that most people don't behave in such ways; that watching television violence is undesirable; that children should not imitate the violence they see and that most people find alternative ways to resolve conflicts. The control group did not receive such teaching. Results showed that over a two-year period not only were the children in the experimental group less aggressive than the children in the control group but they behaved in much more socially desirable ways.

Midlarsky *et al.* (1973) demonstrated that, if a child observes altruistic behaviour and the model is rewarded, then the child is likely to repeat the helping behaviour. Further studies along this line have produced encouraging results. Stein and Friedrich (1972) exposed children for four weeks to television involving one of three types of programme: aggressive, neutral or prosocial. Those in the prosocial condition subsequently showed more helpfulness, cooperation and affection than those in the other conditions.

Baran (1979) found that 8- to 10-year-olds who had watched an episode of *The Waltons* where helping behaviour was prominent in the storyline later exhibited more helping behaviours than those who had not watched this episode. Sprafkin and Rubinstein (1979) discovered that children who prefer and often watch prosocial programmes tend to behave more prosocially at school than classmates who rarely watch such programmes. Forge and Phemister (1987) have found that when children of nursery-school age are exposed to prosocial programmes such as *Sesame Street*, they are more likely to behave in altruistic ways than children who have not had experience of such programmes. (In fact the American government created the Children's Television Workshop in 1968 to produce television programmes that would stimulate interest and intellectual development. Its first production, *Sesame Street* is now broadcast to nearly seventy countries worldwide. Not only did *Sesame Street* promote prosocial values, it was also associated with improved intellectual ability.)

Studies by Messenger-Davies (1989) reveal that watching television serves many useful purposes: it informs children, helping to structure their lives:

- It provides common interests with friends and family, promoting family togetherness, discussion and argument.
- It gives children ideas for play and work.
- It is a form of entertainment.

Gunter and McAleer (1990) draw the same conclusions, claiming that television can have socially desirable effects through educational programmes, entertainment and drama productions. It is claimed that good informative programmes can introduce children to a wide range of people, places and ideas, and that such viewing helps children to keep in touch with their peers who watch the same programmes.

❖ Activity 7 ❖

Messenger-Davies suggests that television informs and educates, and brings families together, stimulating discussion and argument.

How many programmes can you name which:

1 inform and educate children
2 provide whole-family entertainment
3 provide a focus for discussion among your friends?

Section summary

Investigating the relationship between viewing television violence and aggressive behaviour is fraught with problems. Laboratory and field studies have been conducted, and although there is public concern over the effect of TV violence, it has proven difficult to establish causal links between viewing habits and levels of aggression. The ways in which any effects might be mediated have been outlined. Television, it is claimed, may also have beneficial effects in encouraging prosocial behaviour among viewers.

Chapter summary

- ❖ Whether or not a person behaves in a prosocial way depends on a number of factors:
  - personal and social norms
  - empathizing with the person in need
  - receiving feedback about the effect of one's helping
  - how the emergency situation is appraised
  - a cost/benefit analysis of helping
  - characteristics of both the helper and the victim
  - the behaviour of bystanders.
- ❖ The role of social factors in aggressive behaviour is considered. These include social learning, the role of frustration and environmental factors.
- ❖ There are individual (personal) causes affecting aggression. These include factors as diverse as Type A behaviour (personality), levels of arousal, gender and alcohol consumption.
- ❖ Cultural differences in levels of aggression have a role in the social construction of what constitutes aggressive behaviour.
- ❖ Research on reducing aggression includes a consideration of punishment, learning alternative behaviours and cathartic activities.
- ❖ Finally, the chapter looked at the role of the media as a source of pro- and antisocial behaviour and considered methodological problems.

Essay questions

1 Describe and evaluate research into bystander behaviour. *(24 marks)*

2 Discuss social psychological factors thought to elicit aggressive behaviour in people. *(24 marks)*

3 Describe and evaluate the evidence of the influence of the media on either aggressive behaviour or prosocial behaviour. *(24 marks)*

Further reading

Baron, R.A. and Byrne, D. (1994), Social *Psychology: Understanding Human Interaction* (7th edn), London: Allyn and Bacon.

Chapters 10 and 11 provide good coverage of both pro- and antisocial behaviour.

Eisenberg, N. (1985) *Altruistic Emotion, Cognition and Behaviour*, Hillsdale, New Jersey: Erlbaum.

Good American review of contrasting theories of prosocial behaviour.

Messenger-Davies, M. (1989) *Television Is Good for Your Kids*, London: Hilary Shipman Ltd.

Considers the positive side of the debate and is easy to read.

Newson, E. (1994) 'Video violence and the protection of children', *The Psychologist*, 7(6), pp. 272–4.

Up-to-date summary of the main concerns about television violence.

Part 2

Bio-psychology

Chapter 5

Neural and hormonal processes

Simon Green

Preview

In this chapter we shall be looking at:

- the neuron and electrical and chemical neurotransmission
- the organization of the nervous system: peripheral, somatic and autonomic nervous systems
- the central nervous system and an outline of brain structures and their functions
- interactions between central and autonomic nervous systems and the endocrine system
- drug effects on behaviour, including clinical drugs and drugs of abuse.

Introduction

All complex animals, including worms, squid, fish, frogs, lizards, birds and mammals such as rats, monkeys, apes and humans, possess a nervous system and an endocrine system. Even across these very different animals, some features show similarities, such as the presence of neurons and synapses or the secretion of particular hormones. They tend, however, to be organized in very different ways; for instance, some animals have brains and some do not. The description that follows applies to mammalian systems (so-called 'warm-blooded' animals, including shrews, rats , dogs, cats, horses and primates such as monkeys, apes and humans). Where the brain is concerned we shall concentrate on humans.

The basic unit of the nervous system is the neuron and we begin by describing how the neuron works in relation to the transmission of information in the nervous system. We shall then cover the organization and functions of different parts of the nervous system and we shall also be looking at the relationships between the nervous system and the endocrine, or glandular, system. The final section deals with some of the effects of drugs on behaviour and how we can explain these effects in terms of brain chemistry; we will cover both clinically used drugs and drugs of abuse.

Nervous system: the basic structure

The nervous system of the body can be divided into various subsystems, such as the central nervous system (CNS) and the autonomic nervous system (ANS). Before considering the organization and functions of these subsystems, we first need to look at their basic structure.

The nervous system is made up of billions of specialized cells called neurons. As with all cells in the body, neurons have their own particular characteristics and it is these characteristics that allow neurons to carry out their specialized functions. These functions concern information transmission in the nervous system.

Neurons and electrical transmission

Neurons are usually elongated (see Fig. 5.1), with a set of short processes on one side of the cell body (the dendrites) and a single longer branching process on the other (the axon). The cell body contains the nucleus, in which we find the chromosomes, the genetic material of the body. Every cell in the body contains an identical set of chromosomes and, besides allowing us to pass characteristics on to our offspring, the genetic material also controls the activity of the cell containing it. We still do not know how the same set of chromosomes allows a blood cell to function as a blood cell and a neuron to function as a neuron.

Figure 5.1
The neuron

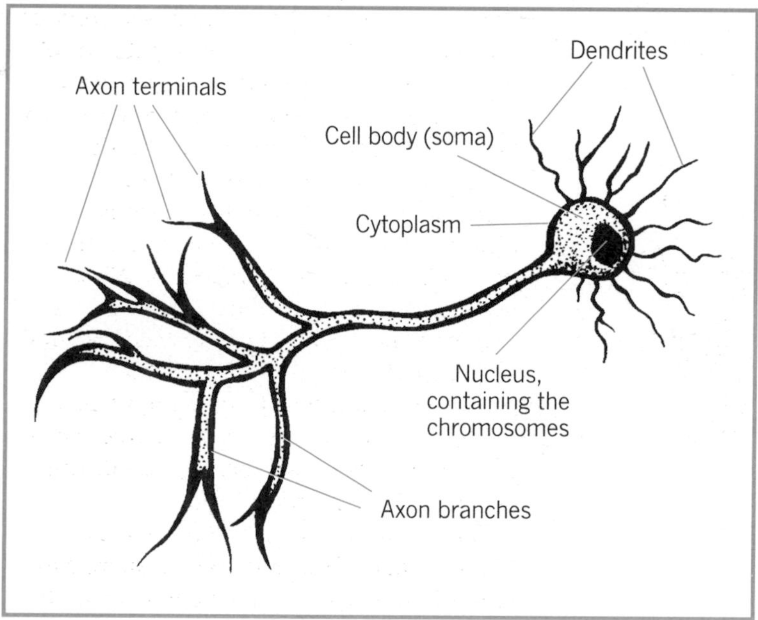

The outer covering of the neuron is the cell membrane. This is a complicated layered structure made up of protein and fat molecules and is crucial to information transmission. The fluid inside the neuron (cytoplasm) and the fluid surrounding it (extra-cellular fluid) contain concentrations of electrically-charged particles known generally as ions. These include both positively-charged ions such as potassium and sodium and negatively-charged ions such as chloride. When the membrane is in its resting state, the high concentration of potassium ions inside and the high concentration of sodium and chloride ions outside produces an imbalance in the electrical charge across the membrane. This is called the resting electrical potential and is measured at −70 millivolts (a millivolt is a thousandth of a volt).

When the membrane is disturbed, channels within it open and sodium ions rush into the neuron from outside. This causes a sudden and radical shift in the resting potential from −70 to +40 millivolts (Fig. 5.2); after peaking at +40 mV, the membrane returns to its resting state, the whole process taking about 4 milliseconds. This rapid and violent swing in the membrane potential is called an action potential. It is another feature of the structure of the neuronal cell membrane that when an action potential is produced by some sort of stimulation at one point, it automatically travels along the membrane, a process called propagation. If we use a thin wire or glass electrode to record electrical activity from a point on the neuronal membrane, then the action potential is picked up as a momentary blip of electrical potential. Before and after the action potential (also referred to as a nerve impulse), that point on the membrane is at its resting potential. If nerve impulses are repeatedly

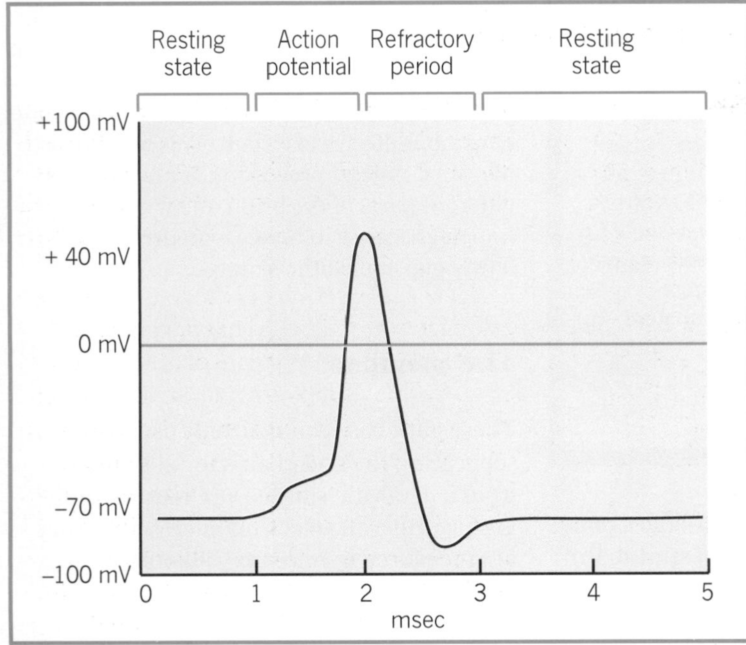

Figure 5.2
The action potential

stimulated, they travel in sequence along the membrane and will be recorded by our electrode as a sequence of blips. As each nerve impulse disturbs the membrane for about 4 msecs, then the maximum rate or frequency at which impulses can travel along the membrane is 250 per second.

Many neurons in the nervous system operate in this way. However, others have become modified to allow even higher rates of transmission. These neurons, including most of those in the brain, have axons covered in a fatty layer called a myelin sheath (Fig. 5.3). At intervals in the sheath the axon membrane is exposed; these points are called Nodes of Ranvier and by complicated electrical processes the nerve impulse can 'jump' from node to node. This is known as saltatory conduction and is much faster than conventional propagation of impulses along the neuronal membrane. Faster transmission clearly increases the rate of information processing and myelination was an important step in the evolution of advanced brains.

Figure 5.3
Myelinated neuron

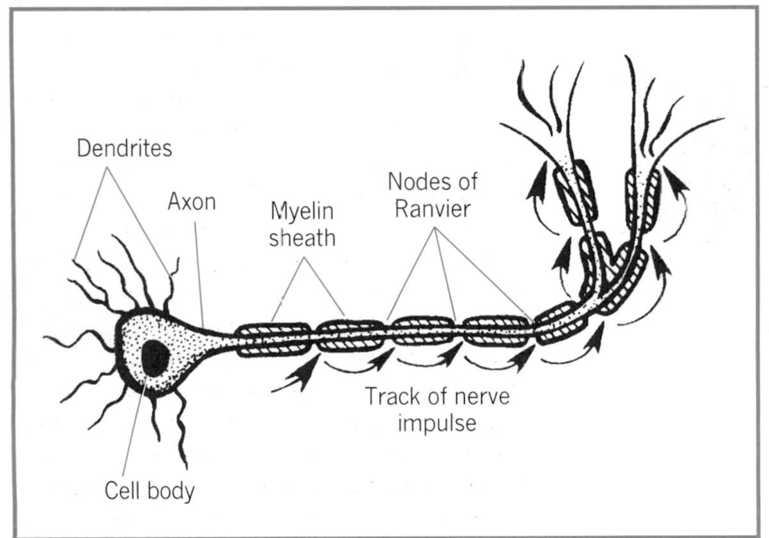

Each impulse, wherever recorded, has exactly the same electrical properties as any other. This is important as we know that information handled by the nervous system, which is in effect everything it does, including sensation and perception, memory, language, thought, emotions, personality, movement and control of the body's physiological systems, is coded by these nerve impulses. As they are electrically identical, then different types of information must be coded by the frequency and patterning of impulses (whether they come in steady streams, or in bursts of activity) and where in the nervous system they occur.

A simple example of our dependence on this electrical code comes from sensory processes. We can only be aware of stimuli in the world around if they can trigger electrical impulses in the nervous system. To do this we have specialized cells, called sensory receptors, whose job it is to convert the energy of the stimulus into patterns of nerve impulses travelling along neurons. For instance, in the visual system we find a layer of visual sensory receptors in the retina at the back of the eye. These receptors then connect with neurons making up the optic nerve, which in turn travels from the eye to the brain. When light (which is a form of electro-magnetic energy) from an object in the world around us reaches the visual receptors, they respond by stimulating nerve impulses in the optic nerve. The pattern and frequency of these impulses therefore represents the object in the nervous system.

So we can see, hear, taste, smell, etc., because each of these sensory systems has specialized receptors which can respond to

❖ Activity 1 ❖

With a small pin, gently prick the skin under your heel. Now repeat with the skin on your hand. Is the sensation different? The skin under the heel contains relatively few receptors and the sensation is quite dull. The skin of the hand contains many more sensory receptors per square millimetre and the sensation is sharper and more intense. Our sensory experience depends upon the type and number of sensory receptors we possess.

particular types of stimulus. It follows, of course, that we can be aware of stimuli in the world around only if we have receptors for them. We cannot hear ultrasonic sounds because we do not possess hearing or auditory receptors for that frequency of high-pitched sounds; bats can, because they do have such receptors.

Information in the nervous system is carried along neurons in the form of trains or sequences of nerve impulses. In the nervous system there are something of the order of fifteen to twenty billion neurons, most of them in the brain. If these neurons were physically connected, nerve impulses would automatically travel to all parts of the system, as neurons are specialized to transmit impulses, and the whole system would be one enormous electrical circuit. This would not allow specialized processing, for instance, in different parts of the brain and it doesn't happen because in between neurons there is a tiny gap, called the synapse.

The synapse

These gaps between neurons, usually separating the end of an axonal branch from a dendritic surface, are minute. Only visible under the electron microscope, they are measured in microns (billionths of a metre), but even so they represent a physical gap which the electrical nerve impulses cannot automatically jump. Conduction or transmission across the synapse has to involve other processes and these are chemical in nature.

Within the end of each axon branch (the presynaptic terminal) are sets of vesicles, spherical structures containing molecules of chemicals called neurotransmitters (Fig. 5.4). When nerve impulses travelling along the axon reach the presynaptic terminal, vesicles

Figure 5.4
The synapse

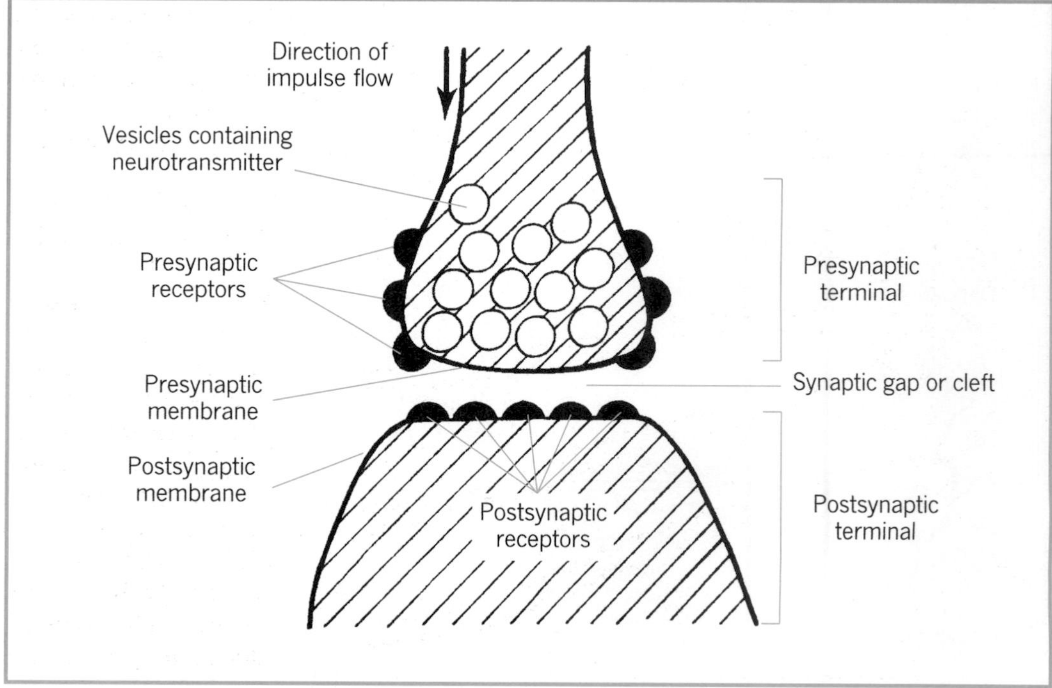

are stimulated to move to the end membrane of the terminal. Their chemical structure allows them to merge with the membrane and, as they do, their contents – the neurotransmitters – are released into the synaptic gap. Because the gap is so small, the molecules of neurotransmitter can drift or diffuse over to the membrane of the dendrite. On this postsynaptic membrane we find receptors. These are molecules attached to the membrane, with a structure which matches that of the neurotransmitter molecule, in the same way that the shape of a key fits the appropriate lock. Neurotransmitter molecules attach themselves to receptors and although the combination is very brief, it is sufficient to disturb the postsynaptic membrane, allowing ions to pass through it. This passage of ions is the basis of the nerve impulse, as described earlier, but the combination of a single neurotransmitter molecule with a single receptor is not enough to shift the membrane potential far from its resting state and a nerve impulse is not stimulated.

For a nerve impulse to be stimulated, a minimum number of combinations must take place in the same region of the postsynaptic membrane, which then disturbs the resting potential sufficiently for an action potential to be triggered. Action potentials, or nerve impulses, are all-or-nothing events in the sense that they either happen or do not happen. For the resting potential to be sufficiently shifted for a nerve impulse to occur, either a train of impulses must arrive at the presynaptic terminal in a short space of time, so that the combined release of neurotransmitter molecules destabilizes the postsynaptic membrane (this is called temporal summation); or several presynaptic terminals which contact the same region of the postsynaptic membrane (see Fig. 5.5) must all be active at the same time (this is called spatial summation). Either way, activity in the postsynaptic neuron cannot easily be predicted by activity in a presynaptic neuron and we can see this change in the frequency and patterning of impulses as they cross (or do not cross) the synapse as a vital aspect of information processing in the brain. It is an opportunity for information, in the form of nerve impulses, to be integrated with other pathways, lost (if it does not cross a synapse, a nerve impulse simply ceases to exist), or processed in other complex ways.

It is important to remember that although a single synapse can be fairly straightforward in operation, their overall organization is not. The 15 to 20 billion neurons in the nervous system make on average about a thousand synaptic connections each, so the complications of the neuronal network are almost unimaginable.

Figure 5.5
Spatial summation

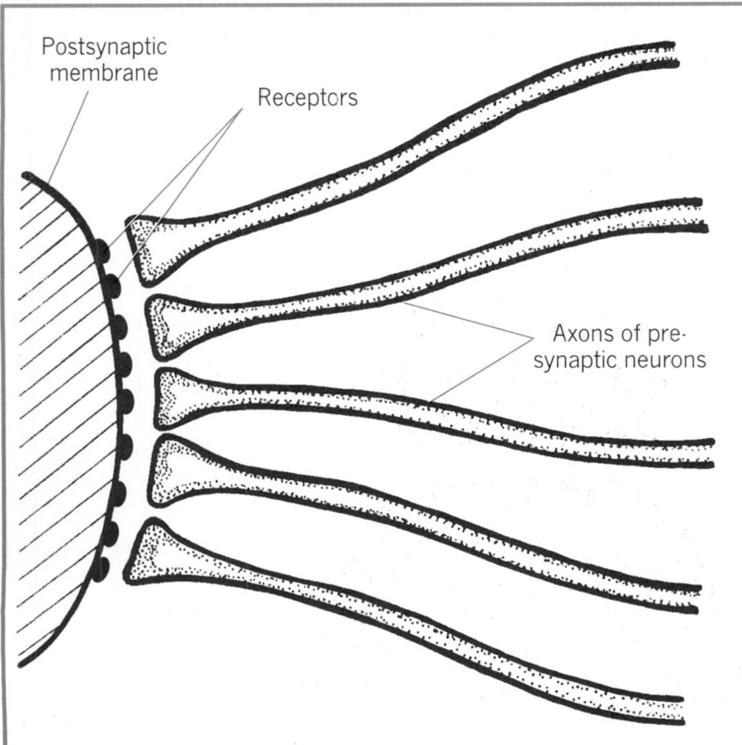

Neurotransmitters and drugs

The chemicals transmitting the nerve impulse across the synapse are called neurotransmitters. It is a general principle that the axon terminals of any given neuron will release the same neurotransmitter at their synapses, although different neurons may release different neurotransmitters. We have identified many of these chemicals (Table 5.1), so we can now characterize neurons by the neurotransmitters they release, such as dopamine-releasing (dopaminergic), acetylcholine-releasing

Table 5.1 Synaptic neurotransmitters

Classical neurotransmitters	
Acetylcholine	
Noradrenaline	Monoamines
Dopamine	Monoamines
Serotonin (5-hydroxytryptamine)	Monoamines
Amino acid neurotransmitters	
Glycine	
Glutamate	
GABA (Gamma-amino-butyric-acid)	
Possible neurotransmitters/neuromodulators	
Enkephalin	
Substance P	
Vasopressin	
Cholecystokinin	

Neuromodulators are found within neurons, but may function to regulate the release of classical neurotransmitters such as acetylcholine and dopamine, rather than act as transmitters in their own right.

(cholinergic) and noradrenaline-releasing (noradrenergic) neurons. In a similar way, we can also identify the receptors for these neurotransmitters (because a receptor has to have a matching molecular structure), such as dopamine, noradrenaline and acetylcholine receptors.

Our knowledge of the molecular make-up of neurotransmitters and receptors is vital to our understanding of drug effects on behaviour. Although most drugs were introduced before we knew anything about chemical transmission at the synapse, it now turns out that many of the most dramatic examples of drugs influencing behaviour involve actions at the synapse. Some drugs have similar molecular structures to neurotransmitters and stimulate the same receptors, while others increase the release of the neurotransmitter from the presynaptic terminal. These agents, which increase transmission at the synapse, are called agonists. Some drugs have similar structures and combine with the receptor, but without stimulating it; they simply prevent the natural neurotransmitter from having its own stimulating effect. These agents, which block the synapse and reduce transmission, are called antagonists. The effects of these drugs are described in more detail later in the chapter.

Section summary

The nervous system is made up of billions of cells called neurons. Neurons are elongated, with processes called dendrites and axons. They are specialized to conduct electrical impulses along their length and these impulses represent information in the nervous system. Between neurons is the synapse, a tiny physical gap. Impulses are transmitted across the synapse by chemical neurotransmitters secreted from the presynaptic neuron; synaptic neurotransmission allows a considerable amount of filtering and processing of information to occur. Specific neurotransmitters and receptors have been identified and can be used to explain the effects of drugs on brain function.

Organization of the nervous system

As we have seen, the unit of the nervous system is the neuron. Nerve impulses are transmitted electrically along the neuron itself and chemically across the synaptic gaps between neurons. Basic though these processes are to nervous system function, the types of behaviour psychologists are interested in are more concerned with the overall organization and structures of the nervous system, rather than with individual neurons. Apart from anything else, we simply cannot deal with fifteen billion neurons separately.

For ease of description we divide the whole nervous system into various sub-systems (see Fig. 5.6). It is important to remember, however, that the nervous system works in a highly organized and integrated way and no one of the subsystems functions independently of any of the others.

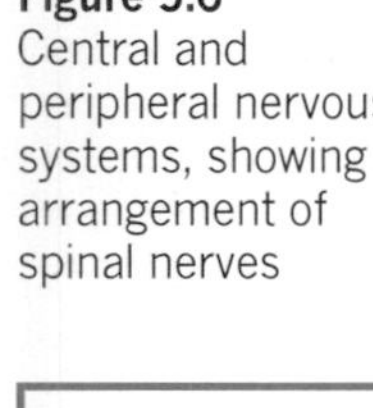

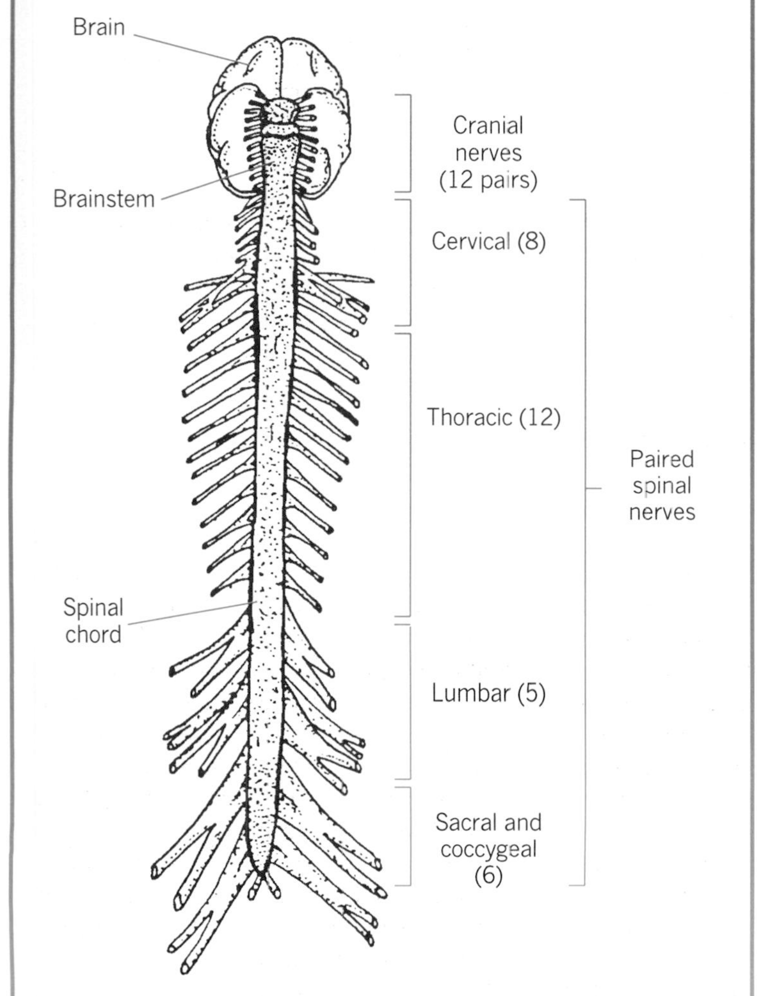

Figure 5.6 Central and peripheral nervous systems, showing arrangement of spinal nerves

Peripheral nervous system

Neuronal fibres (axons or dendrites, usually the long axons) travelling around the body are organized into bundles and covered in a protective sheath; these are nerves and in humans nerves may be made up of hundreds of thousands or even millions of fibres. The spinal cord is protected by the vertebrae and the spinal nerves emerge from the spinal cord between the vertebrae. They then travel to all parts of the body, as shown in Fig. 5.6.

A single spinal nerve may contain many different types of fibre. Some will be carrying sensory information to the brain from receptors on the skin or on internal organs and these are called sensory or afferent fibres or pathways. Others will be carrying commands from the brain out to the muscles of the skeleton, to the muscles of the heart and digestive tract, or to the glands of the body. These are motor or efferent fibres or pathways. To make some sense of this complex arrangement, the fibres are allocated to one of two systems, the somatic nervous system or the autonomic nervous system.

Somatic nervous system

One part of the somatic nervous system consists of afferent fibres carrying sensory information from receptors in the skin, body muscles and joints. Examples of this input would be touch, pain, pressure, heat and cold. The other part of the somatic system is made up of efferent fibres carrying motor commands to the striped muscle of the skeleton. So, if you touch a hot radiator and rapidly withdraw your hand, the sensation of heat and pain and the avoidance movement are examples of somatic nervous system activity.

Autonomic nervous system (ANS)

If we regard the somatic nervous system as dealing with stimuli in the external world and reactions to them, then we can regard the ANS as dealing with our internal world or environment. It is a purely motor system, controlling the activity of a range of internal organs and systems. These include heart muscle, the smooth muscle of the circulatory system and the gut and various glands such as the salivary glands and the adrenal medulla. To allow for precise control, the ANS has two subdivisions, the sympathetic and the parasympathetic. Fibres of both systems run to the same structures, but on the whole have opposite effects. When you go for your early morning jog, activity in the sympathetic branch increases your heart rate and blood pressure and slows down digestive activity; when you relax watching television in the evening, activity in the parasympathetic branch decreases your heart rate and blood pressure and stimulates digestive activity.

Usually the two subdivisions are in balance. When the sympathetic branch becomes dominant, we see a pattern referred to as peripheral physiological arousal, associated with situations demanding activation and energy expenditure. When the parasympathetic branch is dominant, the pattern is one of physiological relaxation and energy conservation.

A key feature of the ANS is that this regulation of our internal physiological systems, or metabolism, is largely automatic and proceeds outside conscious awareness; you do not consciously instruct your heart to speed up when you play tennis, or to slow down when you relax in the bath. The ANS also has a central role in homeostasis, that is the maintenance of a constant internal environment. Perhaps the simplest example is the control of body temperature. When the outside temperature falls, the ANS conserves heat by narrowing peripheral blood vessels and reducing sweat gland activity and generates heat by increasing the metabolism of stored fats and carbohydrates; when the outside temperature is high, the ANS expands peripheral blood vessels and promotes sweating and slows down internal metabolism. Obviously we also have conscious adaptation techniques, such as sitting in the shade or next to a fire, but the main reason humans and other mammals can exist in such a wide range of environments is the possession of a sophisticated ANS.

❖ Activity 2 ❖

Run up the stairs. Take your pulse and then check it every minute for three minutes. The increase is produced by the sympathetic branch of the ANS in response to the physical exercise and the decrease as you relax is produced by the parasympathetic branch.

Now think of something exciting (taking A level examinations!), or something you are currently worried about; take your pulse and you will note how it increases. This is again produced by the sympathetic branch of the ANS, but this time it is in response to your internal thoughts and anxieties. The brain assumes that the reaction to excitement or stress will involve physical activity, so it instructs the ANS to prepare the body for energy expenditure.

The cranial nerves

Closely related to the spinal nerves of the peripheral nervous system are the cranial nerves. In the same way that the spinal nerves serve the sensory and motor functions of the body, so the cranial nerves serve the sensory and motor functions of the head region. The key difference in their organization is that whereas the spinal nerves connect with the spinal cord outside the brain, the cranial nerves connect directly with the brain, so their points of origin are contained within the skull.

The twelve pairs of cranial nerves carry a variety of somatic and autonomic nervous system functions. Some are specialized, such as the olfactory nerve and the optic nerve, carrying sensory information from the smell receptors in the nose and the visual receptors of the eye respectively. Others are mixed, carrying sensory information into the brain, motor commands to the muscles of the face, mouth and throat and they may also contain fibres of the autonomic nervous system regulating organs in the chest cavity, including the heart.

Section summary

The nervous system is divided into the central and the peripheral nervous systems. The peripheral nervous system is made up of the spinal nerves, which emerge from the spinal cord in pairs. Each nerve contains a mixture of neuronal fibres. Some belong to the somatic nervous system, which carries sensory information from the skin into the central nervous system and motor commands from the central nervous system to the muscles of the skeleton. Other fibres in the spinal nerves belong to the autonomic nervous system (ANS), which regulates the activity of internal organs and glands. The cranial nerves are the equivalent of the spinal nerves but connect directly with the brain; they handle sensory and motor processes for the receptors and musculature of the head region.

The central nervous system (CNS)

The CNS is made up of the brain and the spinal cord. Although the spinal cord (Fig. 5.6) clearly has a major role in carrying sensory information from the spinal nerves up towards the brain and motor commands from the brain out to the muscles of the body, it contains millions of fibres in a complex organization. It is not a simple collection of ascending and descending pathways, but within it we find some sophisticated processing of, for instance, pain information.

Damage to the spinal cord affects sensation and our ability to control the muscles of the skeleton, as sensory messages from the body are prevented from reaching the brain (and so we are unaware of them) and commands to the muscles organized by the brain cannot reach their targets. Severe damage may lead to motor paralysis and sensory loss (anaesthesia), with the degree of loss depending on how high up the spinal cord the damage occurs. If the cord is affected low down, only the lower spinal nerves are cut off and effects are restricted perhaps to the abdomen and legs (Fig. 5.6). High spinal damage can produce complete paralysis of the limbs (tetraplegia) and complete body anaesthesia. This is because the brain is cut off from all sensory input from the body and from the skeletal muscles of the limbs. You might wonder how the patient survives at all; it is because the control of the heart and respiration depends on fibres of the somatic and autonomic nervous system travelling in the cranial nerves. You may recall that these nerves emerge from the brain itself and are therefore unaffected by spinal cord damage.

It is an unfortunate general property of neurons that once damaged they die and are not replaced. This means that brain or spinal cord injuries leading to significant behavioural problems, whether motor paralysis or difficulties with speech or memory, often have permanent effects. However, surviving neurons in the same neighbourhood as the damaged ones can sometimes 'sprout' new branches to their axons and make new synaptic connections and a great deal of current research is aimed at ways of encouraging this process. New connections may aid recovery of behavioural functions.

The brain

This section gives an overall outline description of the brain; many of structures mentioned will be discussed in more detail in later chapters.

Depending on what classification system you use, the brain can be divided into tens or hundreds of areas and structures. Luckily, as psychologists, we are interested more in the larger components and a manageable breakdown is presented in Fig. 5.7. The classic picture of the human brain (Fig. 5.8) is not obviously divided into fore-, mid- and hindbrain. In fact the arrangement is best seen in the developing nervous system in the embryo, where the brain grows as three linked chambers. These eventually become the major subdivisions of the adult brain, but during the course of development, the forebrain grows much larger than the other parts and finally grows backwards and covers them. They can, however, all be identified in the adult brain.

The hindbrain

The medulla oblongata and the pons of the hindbrain (see Fig. 5.9) can be seen in simple terms as extensions of the spinal cord within the skull. They contain millions of fibre pathways carrying sensory information up to the cortex and motor commands out to the muscles and glands of the body. However, they also contain some specialized structures. Running through their core is the reticular formation, a network of some millions of neurons; this is part of the ascending reticular activating system (ARAS), which is vital to the arousal and alertness of the brain. We will meet it again in connection with the control of sleep and waking.

Also embedded within the pons and medulla are autonomic nuclei. A 'nucleus' refers to a cluster of neuronal cell bodies, whose axons then tend to run together towards their destinations. The autonomic nuclei are the origin for autonomic nervous system fibres which emerge through cranial and spinal nerves to control the internal functions of the body. Together with the reticular formation, this means that the medulla and pons contain structures vital to the biological survival of the organism; without them, life itself would not be possible.

Jumping ahead a little, the midbrain also contains parts of the ARAS and some autonomic nuclei and is often classified with the pons and medulla as the brainstem. There are various tests which doctors can do to see if these brainstem mechanisms are functioning properly; if they are not working, the situation is referred to as brainstem death and the patient is defined

Figure 5.7 The subdivisions of the brain

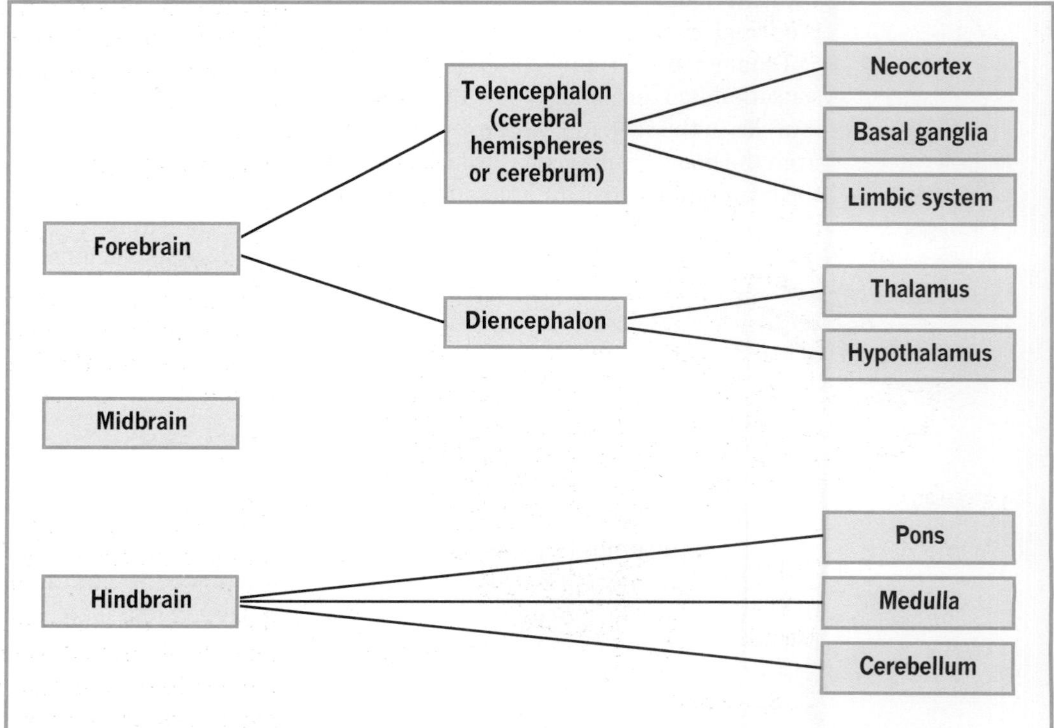

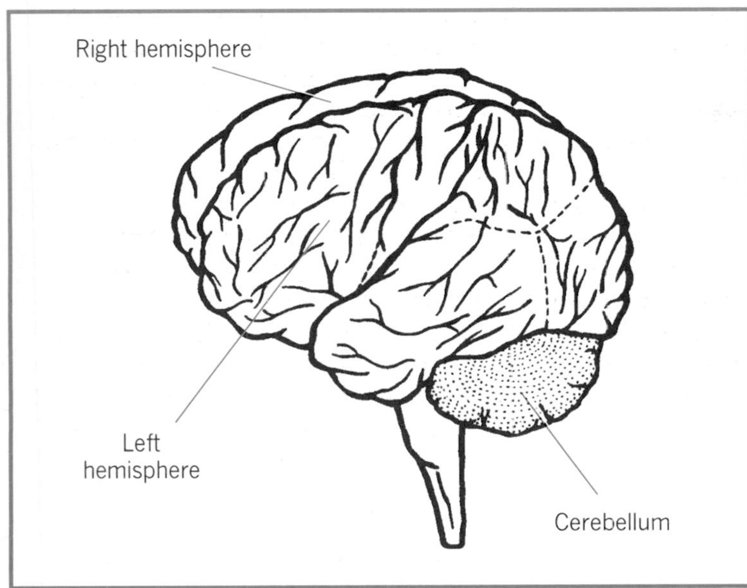

Figure 5.8
The human brain

as dead. Although rather clinical, brainstem death has become an important concept in an era when patients can be kept 'alive' for many years on life support systems.

The third major component of the hindbrain is the cerebellum (see Fig. 5.9). This is a large structure containing billions of neurons and seems to be mainly involved in the fine control and coordination of muscular activity. Damage to the cerebellum leads to difficulties with posture and control of movements, involving limbs, the head and the eyes. There is also some evidence that the cerebellum may have a role in some of the simpler forms of learning and memory (Thompson 1986).

Figure 5.9
Cross section of the brain

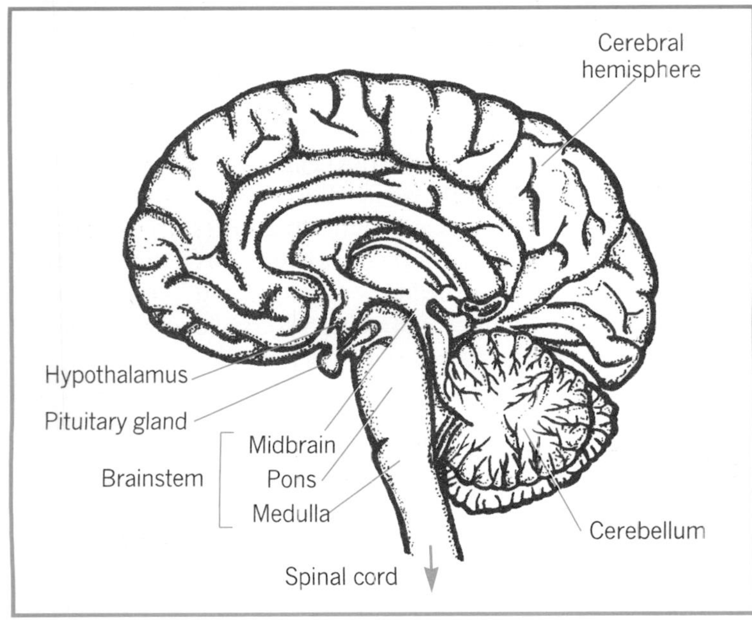

The midbrain

This has already been mentioned as part of the brainstem. It is the smallest of the subdivisions of the brain, but does contain some structures of interest. The superior colliculi form part of the visual system pathways and are probably involved in the control of eye movements. The inferior colliculi play a role in the auditory, or hearing, system, possibly in relation to locating sounds in space. The substantia nigra is a nucleus that projects a pathway to the basal ganglia of the forebrain and we shall discuss it in more detail shortly.

It is important to note that most of the structures of the brain are paired, with one in each half, or hemisphere. If you split the brain lengthways (a sagittal section), then each half contains one superior colliculus, one inferior colliculus and one substantia nigra. Like the rest of the body, the brain is bilaterally symmetrical, in that dividing it lengthways produces two mirror-image halves. Some of the implications of this arrangement are dealt with in the next chapter.

The forebrain

The forebrain is the subdivision that, as psychologists, we are most interested in. It contains many structures of interest and to cope with them we must first subdivide it once more, into the diencephalon and the cerebral hemispheres.

Diencephalon

The diencephalon contains the hypothalamus and the thalamus. The hypothalamus is a small structure in the base of the brain (Fig. 5.9). It is connected by a stalk (the infundibulum) to the pituitary gland which lies just below it in the cranial cavity. The hypothalamus controls the hormonal secretions of the pituitary, which in turn regulate the activities of many other glands in the body. In this way, the hypothalamus is directly involved in sexual and reproductive behaviour, stress, growth and the body's general physiological systems. The hypothalamus is also directly connected by neuronal pathways to the autonomic centres in the brainstem. This involves it in the activities of the ANS, such as homeostatic regulation of the body's metabolic processes. We can demonstrate the role of the hypothalamus through the effects of electrical stimulation of various sites within it. Depending on the precise site, we can observe:

- release of adrenocorticotrophic hormone from the pituitary, which in turn stimulates the release of hormones from the adrenal gland.
- increases in heart-rate and blood pressure, via the autonomic centres in the brainstem.
- stimulation of feeding in non-hungry rats
- inhibition of feeding in hungry rats
- sexual behaviour in male and female rats.

The thalamus lies above the hypothalamus. It is a larger structure and can be divided into several functional units or nuclei, several of which are involved in sensory processes. All sensory pathways except smell or olfaction travel to the thalamus, which then projects the information on to the cerebral cortex. As we shall see with vision, some processing also takes place in the thalamus, so it is not simply a passive relay station.

Other parts of the thalamus have functions related to general arousal and cognitive functions such as memory. There is evidence that damage to thalamic nuclei can produce a severe amnesic state.

Cerebral hemispheres

Technically called the telencephalon, the cerebral hemispheres are the most recently evolved and complex regions of the brain. They have grown proportionately larger through evolution and in primates, including humans, they dominate the rest of the brain. Although the cerebral cortex in turn dominates the cerebral hemispheres, they also contain two other important systems, the limbic system and the basal ganglia.

- *Limbic system*

  This is a network of structures linked by neuronal pathways and it includes the hippocampus, septum, amygdala and mammillary bodies. It was originally thought that the system operated as an integrated unit, especially in relation to emotion and arousal, since lesions or stimulation in animals can lead to rage, aggression or placidity. Nowadays it is clear that each of the component structures has additional important functions of its own. For instance, the hippocampus plays a central role in aspects of learning and memory, while the amygdala is involved in fear and anxiety.

- *Basal ganglia*

  The basal ganglia are made up of the globus pallidus, the caudate nucleus and the putamen; the caudate and the putamen together are referred to as the striatum. They are connected with the cortex and with midbrain and hindbrain structures such as the cerebellum and have important functions in relation to the control of movement. Damage does not paralyse the individual, but can cause problems with control and coordination.

Cerebral cortex

Functions of the cortex are dealt with in detail in the next chapter. For the moment, though, we need to cover its outline organization and structure.

The cortex has evolved as a thin covering over the forebrain. It is about 3 mm thick and consists of six layers of neurons. This concentration of neurons means that the cortex contains about 99 per cent of all the neurons in the forebrain and is the site of most of our higher cognitive abilities. The different layers of cells are distinguished by their size, shape, organization and input/output pathways and this layered arrangement seems basic to the way the

In Focus

Parkinson's Disease

There is a neuronal pathway running from the substantia nigra of the midbrain (mentioned earlier) up to the striatum, labelled the nigro-striatal pathway from its points of origin and termination. In 1817, James Parkinson described the motor disorder which now bears his name. Parkinson's disease consists of a tremor, especially of the limbs, a rigidity of skeletal muscles and a slowness in starting and continuing movements. It was soon established that the disease was associated with a destruction of the nigro-striatal pathway (incidentally, we still do not know the cause of the disorder). In the 1960s, researchers were able to show that the neurons making up the nigro-striatal pathway, with their cell bodies clustering in the substantia nigra and their axons travelling up to the striatum, all released the neurotransmitter dopamine at their synaptic junctions. So the pathway degenerating in Parkinson's disease was a dopamine pathway. This explained the effectiveness of some drugs, at least in the early stages of the disease. Drugs which work, such as L-DOPA and apomorphine, increase activity in dopamine pathways. As long as some of the dopamine neurons remain intact, the drugs can increase their activity and overcome the symptoms of the disorder. Unfortunately, once the pathway has deteriorated too far, the drugs become less effective.

There are other basal ganglia movement disorders, such as Huntington's chorea and tardive dyskinesia, but Parkinson's has been the most studied. Interestingly, in the treatment of schizophrenia we use drugs which block dopamine activity (dopamine antagonists); an unfortunate side effect of these drugs, especially in the early days when less was known of brain chemistry, was the appearance of severe movement abnormalities very similar to Parkinson's. What was happening, of course, was that the drugs, besides helping to relieve the symptoms of schizophrenia, were also blocking the nigro-striatal dopamine pathway and so producing a drug-induced Parkinsonism. Schizophrenic patients are now given combinations of drugs to help prevent these movement side effects, but clinical observations of schizophrenia and Parkinson's disease have contributed to our knowledge of dopamine's role in the brain and emphasized the functions of the basal ganglia in regulating movement.

cortex works. Cortex is found in all mammals and wherever it is found it has this six-layered structure.

Because the cortex has to have this thin sheet-like arrangement, it cannot increase in amount by becoming thicker. So, as evolutionary pressure is towards the development of more and more cortex, it has increased by increasing the surface area of the brain. In animals with complex brains the surface of the brain has infolded or invaginated and this process provides more surface area for the cortex to grow over. In humans it means that only about a third of the cortex is visible on the surface of the brain, with the rest buried within the infoldings. An infolding is called a sulcus and the surface area of cortex between sulci is called a gyrus.

To handle the complex functions of the cortex we need to be able to subdivide it into manageable chunks. This is done by dividing the whole of the cerebral hemispheres into lobes. Remember that the hemispheres include cortex, basal ganglia and limbic system and so the lobes are made up of surface cortex and structures of the basal ganglia and limbic systems; as these lie underneath the cortical covering, they are collectively referred to as subcortical structures. The lobes of the hemispheres are shown in Fig. 5.10 and consist of the frontal, parietal, temporal and occipital lobes; these provide our basic classification of cortical areas.

The cortex contains centres for many of our higher cognitive functions, such as language and thought, consciousness,

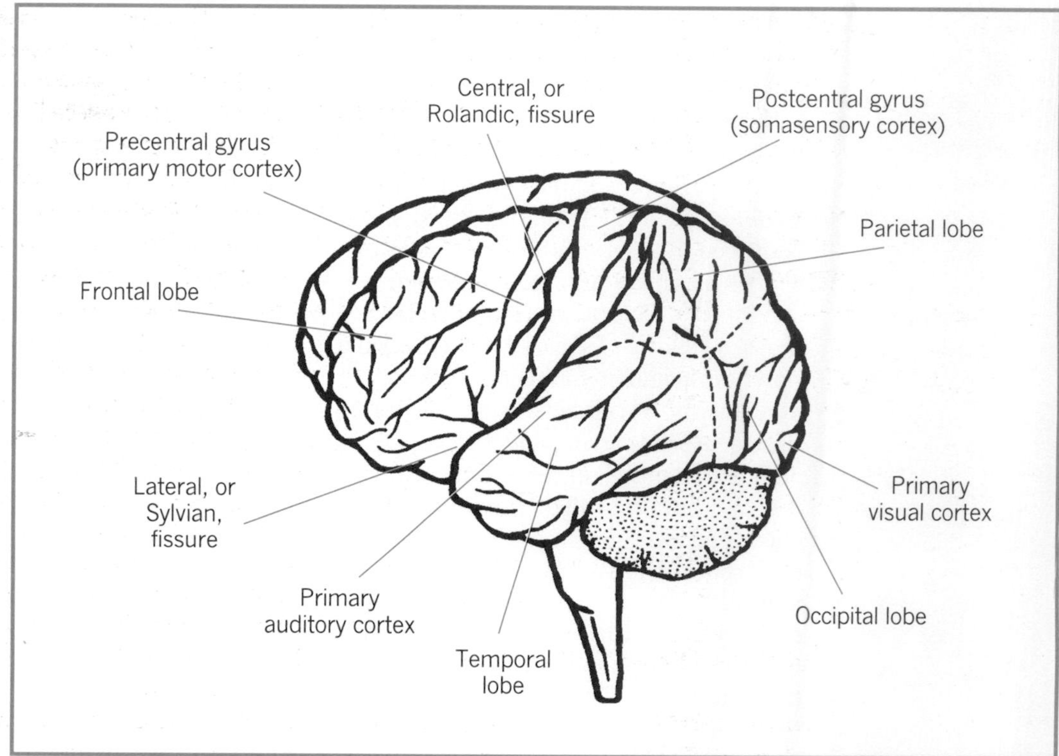

Figure 5.10 Side view of the brain

planning and problem solving, as well as the highest levels of sensation and perception and the production of complex movements. We will look at some of these in the next chapter, but at this stage we can ask how the different levels of organization in the nervous system relate to each other and also how the nervous system interacts with the endocrine system and the autonomic nervous system.

Section summary

The central nervous system is made up of the brain and spinal cord. The brain can be divided into hind-, mid- and forebrain. Hindbrain structures are involved in arousal and other basic biological functions and the coordination of movement. The midbrain is small, although it does contain some visual and hearing relay centres. The forebrain is the most highly developed and is divided into the diencephalon and the cerebral hemispheres. The diencephalon is made up of the hypothalamus and the thalamus, which are involved in homeostatic, sensory, arousal and memory functions. The cerebral hemispheres include the limbic system, basal ganglia and cerebral cortex. They contain centres for high level cognitive, motor and sensory functions.

Interactions between systems

Although the central nervous system, autonomic nervous system and endocrine systems are usually described as though they function independently, the exact opposite is the case. Each is continuously active and their activities are carefully coordinated. There are occasions when one seems more or less dominant, but these are rare and most examples of behaviour will involve activation of all three systems.

The main reason for the coordinated interactions of these systems takes us back to the hypothalamus, briefly discussed earlier. The hypothalamus is part of the central nervous system. Below it lies the pituitary gland, the master gland of the endocrine system, which is controlled by the hypothalamus. In addition, neuronal pathways run from the hypothalamus to the autonomic nervous system (ANS) centres in the brainstem, allowing the hypothalamus to regulate ANS activation if necessary. We can demonstrate the involvement of the hypothalamus in endocrine and ANS functions by stimulating it using thin wire electrodes. Depending on exactly which part of the hypothalamus we stimulate, we can increase or decrease hormone release from the pituitary gland, or increase or decrease ANS arousal.

We discussed the ANS earlier. Before considering some examples of interactions between the three systems, we will look at the endocrine system in more detail.

The endocrine system

Endocrine glands release hormones directly into the circulatory system. This is contrasted with the exocrine glands, such as tear ducts, sweat glands and the salivary glands, whose secretions do not pass directly into the blood supply. Table 5.2 outlines the major endocrine glands of the body and their hormonal secretions. I mentioned earlier that the pituitary gland releases a number of hormones whose function is to regulate the secretions of other glands; Table 5.3 lists the hormones secreted by the two lobes of the pituitary, the anterior and posterior and their targets.

You can see from Table 5.3 that the endocrine system is centrally involved in general processes such as metabolism (the body's overall physiological activity) and energy regulation, which are basic to all of our active behaviours, as well as the more specific mechanisms of reproduction and growth. As it is controlled from the pituitary, which in turn is regulated by the hypothalamus, links between the endocrine system and the central nervous system are direct and integrated, with, as we shall see, the ANS also forming part of the overall nervous system/endocrine system network.

Table 5.2 The endocrine glands

Pituitary	see Table 5.3
Testes and ovaries	release testosterone and oestrogen, which have many effects on the body, including the growth of secondary sexual characteristics such as breast development and muscle growth
Thyroid	releases thyroxin, affecting many physiological functions and increasing metabolic rate and bodily growth
Parathyroid	releases calcitonin which increases calcium retention in bones
Adrenal cortex	releases corticosteroids which have many effects on the body, mobilising glucose for energy expenditure and reducing the body's immune responses
Adrenal medulla	releases adrenaline and noradrenaline, increasing physiological arousal via activation of the sympathetic branch of the ANS
Pancreas	releases insulin and glucagon, with effects on liver, muscle and fat cells to increase glucose uptake
Lining of the intestine	secretes a number of hormones which regulate activity of the intestine and also help in the control of food intake and meal size

Table 5.3 Hormones released by the pituitary gland

Hormone	Action
Anterior lobe (adenohypophysis)	
Growth hormone	promotes growth by stimulating protein synthesis in all cells of the body
Thyroid-stimulating hormone (thyrotropin)	stimulates thyroid gland to release thyroxin, which helps regulate the body's metabolic rate
Adrenocorticotrophic hormone (ACTH)	stimulates adrenal cortex to release corticosteroids in states of arousal and stress
Follicle-stimulating hormone and Luteinising hormone	act together to promote testosterone release and sperm cell growth in males and oestrogen release and egg cell production in females
Prolactin	promotes milk production by action on female mammary glands
Posterior lobe (neurohypophysis)	
Vasopressin (anti-diuretic hormone)	promotes water retention by direct action on kidney tubules
Oxytocin	stimulates uterine contractions during labour.

It is important to remember that these systems are continually active, with changes caused by behaviour superimposed on this baseline level of hormone secretion and ANS activation.

The three systems and behaviour

Homeostasis was briefly described earlier and refers to the maintenance of a constant internal physiological environment. This allows an animal to be far more independent of the external environment and to live and behave in circumstances which a non-homeostatic animal would find disabling. Hunger and the regulation of food intake is an important part of homeostasis and represents a good example of the interplay between the CNS, ANS and endocrine systems. This is dealt with in detail in Chapter 8.

Temperature regulation is a simpler example of homeostatic regulation. Body temperature is controlled around a set-point of 98.6° Fahrenheit, rather like the thermostatic control of a central heating system. The CNS component focuses on the hypothalamus. In the preoptic area of the hypothalamus we find neurons whose activity is sensitive to the temperature of the local blood supply. If this temperature varies from the body's set-point, the hypothalamus activates a network of coping responses. Some of these are behavioural, such as moving to a hotter or cooler place, or removing or adding clothing. Some of them involve activation of ANS centres in the brainstem. In hot weather, increased sweating, panting and dilation of skin blood vessels helps reduce temperature, while in the cold sweating is inhibited, blood vessels contract and shivering occurs to generate heat through muscle activity. These are all controlled by the ANS, in turn regulated by the hypothalamus.

There is also an endocrine component. The body's metabolism generates heat as a by-product; in cold weather, metabolism is increased by the release of thyroxine and appetite and food intake are stimulated, while in hot weather metabolism slows and appetite is suppressed.

Temperature regulation involves conscious behaviour and automatic ANS and endocrine responses, controlled from the hypothalamus in the CNS. Other forms of behaviour involve a greater CNS component.

We react to environmental circumstances in many ways, but we hope the response is appropriate and effective. Many situations require the cognitive processes found in the forebrain, especially the cortex and limbic system. We perceive the world around and evaluate it using our memories of similar circumstances. If the results of this perception and evaluation require action of some sort, the hypothalamus is activated by these higher brain systems and in turn produces the appropriate pattern of endocrine and ANS arousal.

For instance, a fearful stimulus is perceived and recognized by cortical and limbic mechanisms. The initial emotional and physical reactions – perhaps fear and avoidance – are organized in the forebrain, but the hypothalamus will simultaneously organize the necessary endocrine and ANS responses. The pituitary stimulates the thyroid gland and the adrenal cortex to release more thyroxin and corticosteroids to increase metabolism to provide for possible energy expenditure. At the same time ANS sympathetic arousal increases heart-rate and blood pressure, diverts blood to brain, and heart and skeletal muscles, increases sweating and the release of adrenaline from the adrenal medulla and generally prepares the animal for effective and rapid action.

The overall picture is of higher brain centres determining the necessary reactions to a given situation, with the hypothalamus then organizing the endocrine system and the ANS to provide the required physiological activation. We return to this integration of CNS, endocrines and ANS in Chapter 8 in relation to stress, where we see that sometimes the reactions are not always appropriate. Usually, though, the three systems are efficiently synchronized and it is hard to imagine any behaviours which do not involve all three. Perhaps calm and reflective thought is one circumstance where endocrine and ANS arousal are unnecessary; even then, the systems are still actively regulating the body's metabolic processes, continually maintaining homeostasis.

Section summary

The central nervous system, the ANS and the endocrine system function together in many aspects of behaviour. The main centre integrating their activities is the hypothalamus, which directly controls secretions from the pituitary gland and ANS nuclei in the brainstem. Examples of behaviour involving all three systems include homeostatic regulation of body temperature and responses to fearful stimuli. Connections between the hypothalamus and higher brain centres ensure that the pattern of endocrine and ANS activation is matched to the needs of the animal as it reacts to its environment.

Drugs and behaviour

Drugs are chemicals which have a biological effect on the body's tissues. The drugs that psychologists are interested in are those producing changes in behaviour through their effect on the brain, known generally as psychoactive drugs.

Ever since humans appeared on the face of the earth they have used drugs in various ways. The earliest drugs, such as alcohol and extracts from fungi and plants, probably had important roles in religious rituals, but today we have a far wider range of agents available with a variety of uses. For our purposes, these can be divided into drugs used to treat clinically-abnormal behaviour and drugs used for recreational purposes.

❖ Activity 3 ❖

Do you consider yourself a drug taker? Most people don't. Now tick any of the following you have taken in the last fortnight:

☐ paracetamol	☐ coffee
☐ aspirin	☐ tea
☐ alcohol	☐ nicotine

All of these contain active ingredients which can act on brain mechanisms to alter perception or behaviour. Indeed, many would classify alcohol and nicotine as drugs of abuse, with the capability to induce dependence and a withdrawal syndrome.

The study of the effects of drugs on brain and behaviour is known as psychopharmacology. Before considering some examples, you should briefly review the earlier material in this chapter on synapses and synaptic neurotransmitters. Most drug-induced changes in behaviour can now be related to alterations in the activity of the brain's naturally-occurring neurotransmitter systems and particularly important is the role of the synaptic receptors. You may recall that each neurotransmitter has a specific receptor associated with it and it is the combination of the neurotransmitter with the receptor that allows the action potential to cross the synaptic gap.

Psychopharmacology of clinical drugs

Depression

There are three main groups of antidepressant drugs. Two of them, the tricyclics and the monoamine oxidase inhibitors (MAOIs) have been in use for at least thirty years, while the third group, specific serotonin re-uptake inhibitors (SSRIs), are a fairly recent development.

Both tricyclics and MAOIs seem to act by increasing activity in serotonin and noradrenaline systems in the brain. After combining with a postsynaptic receptor, molecules of neurotransmitter are either broken down by another chemical called an enzyme, or reabsorbed into the presynaptic terminal for reuse, via a reuptake mechanism. Tricyclics work by blocking this reuptake mechanism in serotonin and noradrenaline neurons; this fools the neuron into assuming that there is little neurotransmitter in the synapse and in response it manufactures and releases more, leading to an overall increase in synaptic activity.

MAOIs inhibit or block the enzyme, monoamine oxidase, which normally breaks down serotonin and noradrenaline. This means that more of the neurotransmitter remains available in the synapse to combine with receptors, so increasing synaptic transmission.

SSRIs also work by blocking reuptake mechanisms, but in this case they seem to be specific to serotonin neurons. One of them, Prozac, whose chemical name is fluoxetine, has become famous (or notorious, depending on your point of view) as a 'happiness' drug. SSRIs seem to be as effective as the older drugs and also have fewer toxic side effects. However, it is also the case that no antidepressant works for all people with clinical depression and all clinical drugs have some unwelcome physical side effects. The most common problems encountered include digestive problems, headaches and giddiness.

Anxiety

There are many anxiety conditions, including obsessive-compulsive disorder, phobias and generalized anxiety. Only the last has proved reliably treatable with drugs, but due to its wide occurrence drugs for generalized anxiety are the most prescribed in the world (it has been estimated that around 500 million people have taken a course of anti-anxiety drugs in the last 25 years). Up to the 1960s treatment was with one of the barbiturate drugs, which have severe problems of physical addiction and dependence.

In the mid-1960s, drugs from the benzodiazepine (BZ) family were introduced. They proved to have fewer side effects and were less liable to produce dependence and rapidly took over from the barbiturates. These drugs, such as librium (chlordiazepoxide), valium (diazepam) and mogadon (nitrazepam), can be effective against anxiety and are also sleep-inducers or hypnotics.

BZs are unusual in that there seems to be in the brain a specific BZ synaptic receptor, i.e. along with dopamine, serotonin, acetylcholine receptors, etc. we also have other synaptic mechanisms. As there is a BZ receptor we may assume that there is a naturally-occurring BZ-like neurotransmitter, although this remains to be discovered. The BZ drugs presumably act by mimicking the action of the natural neurotransmitter.

BZ receptors do not occur in isolation from other receptors and neurotransmitters and it seems that one of the main effects of stimulating them with BZ drugs is to reduce serotonin neurotransmission in the brain; it has been suggested that this is the basis for their anti-anxiety action. You should remember, though, that the complexity of the brain means that any simple hypothesis, for instance linking anxiety and depression with serotonin increases and decreases, is almost certain to be an over-simplification.

Schizophrenia

Earlier in the chapter we saw how the anti-schizophrenic drugs could produce movement side effects identical to naturally occurring Parkinson's disease, confirming the involvement of the neurotransmitter dopamine in both conditions. Drugs used in schizophrenia (also called antipsychotics or neuroleptics) come from several groups; chlorpromazine (trade name largactyl) is a phenothiazine, haloperidol (haldol) a butyrophenone and flupenthixol (depixol) a thioxanthine.

All these drugs have in common an ability to block dopamine receptors and so reduce dopamine neurotransmission in the brain. This has led directly to the hypothesis that schizophrenia is caused by an overactivity in brain dopamine pathways, although it should be remembered that only around 50 to 60 per cent of patients respond significantly to drug therapy. This implies that the non-responsive patients may have a different type of brain abnormality.

Clinical psychopharmacology: general considerations

When reading about drug effects on abnormal behaviour, it is easy to assume that the treatments are very effective and very safe. The medical model of abnormal behaviour tends to emphasize the benefits and minimize the risks of physical treatments in general and drugs in particular. However, it is important to remember that no drug treatment is 100 per cent effective for any of the clinical problems we have discussed. Many patients do not respond to drug treatment and many who do also have to endure a range of physical side effects, as all drugs affect a number of biological systems in the body. In addition, any drug taken regularly for long periods can produce psychological or physical dependence.

This is a particular problem with antidepressants and antianxiety agents. Librium and valium, for instance, do not have high dependency-inducing potential when compared to, say, barbiturates and heroin, which can produce dependence after a few days or weeks. However, because librium and valium used to be taken by millions of people for months and years at a time, they did lead to dependency developing. This could be psychological – 'I cannot function without my pills' – or, more seriously, physical. This would show itself through the occurrence of a withdrawal syndrome when the patient tried to stop taking them; they might experience trembling, sweating, diarrhoea, increased anxiety, etc.

These symptoms occur because the brain has become used to the chemical environment produced by constantly taking the drug. Remove the drug and the brain has to readjust to a new chemical situation and it is this that leads to withdrawal symptoms. In fact, many people may continue taking the drug simply to prevent the unpleasant symptoms of withdrawal.

Nowadays it is generally accepted that these drugs should only be prescribed for short periods of time, with regular drug-free periods to prevent dependence developing.

On a positive note, we should also emphasize that drugs can be very effective. Schizophrenics who respond well can lead normal lives in the community because of their drug therapy, while many anxious and depressed people find drugs vital in coping with particularly severe episodes. Drug therapy is usually less time-consuming and expensive than psychoanalytic and humanistic approaches, although the argument that they are only suppressing symptoms and not dealing with the underlying psychological problems is a powerful one.

Psychopharmacology of drugs of abuse

The term 'drug of abuse' refers to drug usage which goes beyond socially defined limits. It is culturally specific; for instance, chewing coca leaves (the source of cocaine) is perfectly acceptable in parts of South America while illegal in Western societies, while alcohol is an acceptable recreational drug in the West but banned in Muslim countries.

The assessment of drugs is based on social norms and on their behavioural and physiological effects. Besides specific actions on mood and experience, we also have to consider the concepts of dependence and tolerance. Dependence was mentioned above. In the context of drugs of abuse, it refers generally to a situation where someone continues to take a drug because of the pleasurable effects it has and persists despite any negative social or physical consequences. If a physical withdrawal syndrome occurs when drug-taking stops abruptly, the person has become physically dependent. Heroin, morphine and alcohol produce severe physical dependence and a withdrawal syndrome which can include symptoms such as restlessness, craving for the drug, sweating, fever, chills, vomiting and pains in the joints. Cannabis, cocaine, amphetamine and hallucinogenics usually produce only a mild withdrawal syndrome.

Psychological dependence can be more of a problem with drugs of abuse. Despite perhaps little or nothing in the way of physical withdrawal symptoms, the loss of the perceived pleasurable effects of the drug leads to unhappiness and psychological craving if the drug is withdrawn. Of course, many drugs produce both physical and psychological dependence.

Tolerance refers to the need to take increasing amounts of the drug to maintain the desired pharmacological effect. It is found most commonly with heroin, morphine and alcohol, but far less so with, for instance, cocaine and amphetamine.

Opioids

Extracts of the Oriental poppy have been used for many centuries for their ability to induce euphoria (happiness) and reduce pain. Opium is one of these extracts obtained from the dried juice of the seed capsule and contains a mixture of active ingredients, the most important one of which is morphine. The term opioid therefore refers to a group of morphine-like drugs, such as its close relative heroin and codeine.

Opioids are powerful pain-relievers, or analgesics, and morphine and heroin also produce a euphoric state, which is the main reason they are abused. They lead to rapid physical and psychological dependence and tolerance develops quickly. Side effects can be mild, such as constipation, or severe, leading to death in the case of respiratory depression.

Cannabis

This is another drug with a long history of human usage. It is derived from the hemp plant, cannabis sativa, but is not a pure compound as the various parts of the plant contain around sixty psychoactive chemicals or cannabinoids and, however it is prepared, the final drug will contain many of these. The most important of them is tetrahydrocannabinol (THC).

Cannabis is the most popular illegal recreational drug and every few years there is a campaign for it to be made legal, on the basis that its effects are largely harmless and

In Focus

How opioids work

One of the most interesting aspects of opioid drugs is their mode of action. In the 1970s, a brain synaptic receptor was discovered that appeared to be specific for the opioid group of drugs. Soon after, a naturally-occurring or endogenous opioid was identified in the brain that functions as a neurotransmitter combining with the opioid receptor. These opioid systems are found, as you would expect, in areas of the brain dealing with pain perception and emotion; drugs such as morphine and heroin produce their behavioural effects by stimulating the brain's natural opioid system. The endogenous opioids, incidentally, are in two groups called enkephalins and endorphins.

Experimental work has also shown that our natural opioid system can be activated in a variety of ways. The analgesic effects of acupuncture seem to involve release of endogenous opioids in the brain, while a similar mechanism may explain the pleasurable effects of physical exercise.

that it does not lead on to the 'harder' drugs of abuse. Besides producing feelings of relaxation and euphoria, though, cannabis can cause memory problems, confusion with time, apathy and inertia and high doses may lead to paranoia and delusions. The most severe physical side effects are the increased risk of lung cancer and heart disease in cannabis smokers.

Moderate usage is not associated with significant dependence or tolerance, although these can occur with higher doses. Overall, in fact, cannabis seems no more dangerous than alcohol in terms of personal and social consequences, but it is part of the 'drug culture' and it is impossible to conclude that using it will not lead to experimenting with other drugs.

Partly because all preparations of cannabis contain many active ingredients, it has proved impossible to determine its specific effects on the brain. THC does not appear to combine with neurotransmitter receptors, but there are suggestions that it can have a general influence on the neuronal cell membrane. You may recall that the structure of the cell membrane is the basis for the transmission of action potentials along the neuron, so THC may affect neuronal activity in a non-specific way by interfering with the normal functions of the membrane.

Hallucinogens

These are drugs which produce hallucinations with increased sensory awareness. Some, such as mescaline, occur naturally, while others, such as lysergic acid diethylamide (LSD), are synthesized. Hallucinations are almost always visual and there can be associated sensory confusions where colours are 'heard' and sounds 'seen'. Sometimes the experiences are accompanied by anxiety and panic.

Hallucinogenics do not cause significant physical or psychological dependence, although tolerance can occur to their effects. Their actions in the brain involve the serotonin system, as it was shown many years ago that LSD blocks serotonin receptors and leads to a reduction in serotonin neurotransmission. There is evidence that all hallucinogenics act in a similar way.

Psychostimulants

These are drugs such as amphetamine and its relatives and cocaine. They produce a sense of euphoria, increased energy and motivation and decreased fatigue. Negative features can include anxiety, panic and psychotic episodes including visual hallucinations and paranoia. Physically psychostimulants, especially cocaine, affect the blood supply to the heart, leading in a significant proportion of cases to severe heart damage.

Although tolerance develops to most of the effects of psychostimulants, they do not appear to produce substantial physical dependence. However, psychological dependence can be a major problem.

Both amphetamine and cocaine increase activity in dopamine pathways in the brain. Cocaine blocks the reuptake mechanism for dopamine (as with the serotonin reuptake inhibitors discussed earlier), while amphetamine increases the release of dopamine from neuronal terminals into the synapse.

Designer drugs

These are drugs synthesized in illicit laboratories and designed to mimic the classic drugs of abuse. Several of the most recent developments are variations on the amphetamine model; ecstasy, for instance, is methylenedioxymethamphetamine (MDMA) and has most of the positive and negative properties of amphetamine itself. In addition, these drugs are not systematically tested, so any severe toxic effects only become apparent when the drug hits the market. There have been several highly-publicized cases of sudden death and non-fatal severe physical reactions to ecstasy and while some are due to associated behaviour such as drinking too much water (this reduces blood sodium levels, which can lead to coma), others are related to direct actions of the drug on the body and brain. Work with animals suggests that MDMA can act as a direct toxin, destroying brain neurons.

The danger in these compounds was best shown by a designer drug produced in California in the early 1980s. It was a morphine derivative, sold as heroin, but somewhere along the way the production process had gone wrong. The drug was contaminated with methyl-phenyl-tetrahydropyridine (MPTP), a toxin which destroys dopamine neurons in the brain. In particular, neurons of the nigro-striatal dopamine pathway were lost; you may remember that this is the cause of Parkinson's disease and people who took this designer drug ended up with drug-induced Parkinsonism.

Section summary

The study of drugs and behaviour is known as psychopharmacology. Clinical psychopharmacology covers drugs used to treat conditions such as depression and anxiety. Advances in our knowledge of brain chemistry allow us to explain many of the effects of these drugs, including problems of dependence and withdrawal. Drugs of abuse such as heroin, cannabis and cocaine also act on brain neurotransmitters, but in some cases they can produce severe physical dependence. A more recent problem is the designer drug, produced in illicit laboratories. Dangerous in themselves, they may also be contaminated with toxic chemicals.

Chapter summary

- The nervous system is made up of billions of neurons. These elongated cells are specialized to transmit information in the form of electrical impulses. Between neurons is the synapse, a small gap. Transmission of the impulse across the synapse is by means of chemicals called neurotransmitters.
- The nervous system is divided into the central nervous system and the peripheral nervous system. The peripheral nervous system is made up of the spinal nerves. These contain neuronal fibres carrying sensory information from the skin into the central nervous system and motor commands out to muscles and glands. The peripheral nervous system is in turn divided into the somatic and the autonomic nervous systems.
- The brain is made up of the hind-, mid- and forebrain. The forebrain is the most advanced, containing systems involved in homeostasis, movement, sensation, perception, memory and learning. The cerebral cortex controls our highest cognitive functions, such as language, personality and consciousness.

- The central nervous system, the autonomic nervous system and the endocrine system work together in regulating many aspects of behaviour, such as temperature control and emotional reactions. The hypothalamus in the forebrain is vital to this integration as it has direct control over the autonomic nervous system and the pituitary gland.
- Psychopharmacology is the study of drugs and behaviour. Advances in brain chemistry means that we can explain many of the effects of clinically-used drugs and drugs of abuse in terms of their actions on brain neurotransmitters. In both categories there can be problems of dependence and withdrawal.

Essay questions

1 (a) Outline the organization of the autonomic nervous system and the endocrine system. *(12 marks)*

(b) Assess the effects that either of these has on behavioural functions. *(12 marks)*

2 Distinguish between the processes involved in neuronal and synaptic transmission. *(24 marks)*

3 Describe and evaluate research into the effects of any two drugs on behaviour. *(24 marks)*

Further reading

Green, S. (1994) *Principles of Biopsychology*, Hove: Erlbaum.

A concise and readable introduction to the nervous system and behaviour.

Bloom, F.E. and Lazerson, A. (1988) *Brain, Mind and Behaviour* (2nd edn), New York: Freeman.

A comprehensive and beautifully illustrated text, especially good on neuronal function and the organization of the nervous system.

Chapter 6

Cortical functions

Simon Green

Preview

In this chapter we shall be looking at:

- the various methods used to investigate how the brain works
- the organization of sensory and motor functions in the cortex
- the localization of cognitive abilities, such as language, across the cerebral hemispheres
- the contribution of studies of patients with 'split brains' to our understanding of cortical functions
- different specializations of the two hemispheres
- the mechanisms and processes underlying visual perception, including the structure of the visual system and the development of cortical visual areas.

Introduction

The functions of the cortex represent the final frontier for neuroscientists. It is the most complex of brain structures, containing over 90 per cent of all the neurons of the forebrain and is involved in all our higher cognitive abilities, as well as attributes such as consciousness and personality. Although we know a reasonable amount about some functions, such as sensation, perception and language, others remain mysterious. It is also unusual in that some aspects of cortical organization are specifically human, related to the evolution of language, while others, such as visual perception, can be modelled using findings from work with animals. In this chapter we cover some of the methods used to investigate brain function and then review the overall organization of the cortex. This is followed by a detailed description of split-brain studies and how the model of hemisphere organization emerging from that work is modified by research using normal subjects. Finally, we look at the pathways and processes underlying visual perception.

Methods used to investigate brain function

How do you know where you are?

Many of the procedures used today by brain researchers involve implanting electrodes (usually made of very thin wire) accurately into the brain. In other areas, too, such as neurosurgery (performing operations on the brain), there is a need to know exactly where structures are located within the brain. For humans and all experimental animals we now have stereotaxic atlases; when the skull is fixed (painlessly) in a rigid steel frame, or stereotax, the atlas can be used to provide three-dimensional coordinates for any brain structure. The surgeon or researcher can then carry out their procedure confident that they are in the correct area.

The two basic processes underlying information transmission in the nervous system are electrical conduction along the neuron and chemical transmission across the synapse. Although there are many other methods for investigating functions of the brain, two major categories are based on these fundamental processes.

Electrical stimulation and recording

There are by now many examples of how thin wire electrodes can be used to stimulate brain neurons artificially in order to produce effects on behaviour. As the brain does not possess pain receptors, this technique can be used in conscious human patients as well as in non-human animals. For instance, Penfield (1958) stimulated the temporal lobe in humans and some patients reported experiencing very vivid memories from their childhoods. Stimulation in the visual cortex can produce a sensation of flashes of light and similarly auditory cortex stimulation may lead to a 'buzzing' sensation.

Besides trying to mimic the brain's natural electrical activity, we can also record it. Thin electrodes can record the activity of single neurons (single unit recording), a procedure which has proved invaluable in the study of, for instance, the visual cortex, as we shall see later. Larger electrodes record from clusters of thousands or millions of neurons and often involve measuring evoked potentials. These are neuronal responses correlated with the regular presentation of stimuli such as light flashes or auditory tones. As there is so much background electrical 'noise' in the brain the response to a single stimulus does not stand out, so a computer is used to analyse the responses evoked by a series of stimuli and the characteristic evoked potential emerges from this analysis. This can be used to identify areas of the brain involved in sensory processes.

The electroencephalograph (EEG), introduced by Berger in 1929, records the electrical activity of billions of cortical neurons using a number of small metal electrodes on the surface of the skull. This has the advantage of being a 'non-invasive' procedure, with no need to penetrate brain tissue itself. The disadvantage is that we are still not sure how the activity of all those neurons combines to produce the final EEG pattern.

We do know that an EEG can be synchronized, with a recognizable and repeated wave form, or desynchronized with an apparently random pattern of waves and spikes. It also has a frequency, or number of waves or spikes per second (measured as hertz). Certain patterns correlate highly with behavioural states; alertness and activity produce a fast desynchronized EEG, while drowsiness leads to a synchronized pattern which gradually slows as sleep becomes deeper. Chapter 7 covers this in more detail.

Chemical stimulation and recording

In the earlier discussion of the synapse we saw how neurotransmitters combine with specific receptors in the brain. We also saw how many of the most dramatic effects of drugs on behaviour can be explained by our knowledge of how they interact with brain synaptic receptors. However, we can also design drugs which are highly specific for particular categories of these synaptic receptors; either they can stimulate the receptor (stimulants or agonists), or by combining with the receptor they inactivate it (blockers or antagonists). So if we wish to investigate the role of dopamine pathways in behaviour, we can give animals drugs which specifically stimulate or block dopamine receptors. By observing the behavioural effects we can then draw some conclusions on what the dopamine system may be doing. Similarly, if we suspect that the acetylcholine system is involved in memory, drugs which stimulate cholinergic receptors should improve memory and learning in animals, while cholinergic antagonists, which block the receptors, should impair memory and learning.

Another chemically-based technique is to measure levels of neurotransmitters in the brain. This is technically very difficult to do and the procedure is not common. One example would be the attempt to measure levels of dopamine in the brains of schizophrenics. The brain is removed at autopsy and the dopamine extracted and measured, to test the theory that schizophrenia is associated with high levels of dopamine. Few positive results have been reported, partly because most of the patients have been on drug therapy for years which could itself upset dopamine activity. More recently, attempts have been made to use computer-based techniques such as PET scans (see later) to measure, for instance, numbers of dopamine receptors in the living brain. This would seem a more promising approach, as schizophrenic patients can be studied before they are put on drug therapy.

Physical destruction of brain tissue

This was the original approach to the experimental study of brain function in non-human animals and is still very popular. At first, techniques were primitive, using needle points or knife cuts. Nowadays, localized areas of damage, or lesions, are usually performed using thin wire electrodes. A current is passed through which heats the tip of the electrode and the heat creates a small sphere of destruction around the tip.

Several decades ago large lesions, or ablations, were popular and the frontal lobotomy (destruction of the frontal lobe) was even used in humans as a 'treatment' for schizophrenia. As more was discovered about the links between brain structure and behaviour, interest shifted to smaller units of the brain. Whereas in the past we might have ablated the whole amygdala, now we would confine damage to small areas within the amygdala such as the central nucleus. One of the latest lesion techniques used in research with non-human animals involves chemicals called neurotoxins. These are specific to particular neurotransmitters, so when injected into a part of the brain, they destroy only those neurons releasing that neurotransmitter at their synapses.

❖ Activity 1 ❖

Lesions to the hippocampus in rats can prevent maze learning. List some of the psychological processes involved in memory and learning, such as perception, short-term and long-term memory and retrieval. Do you think it is justified to conclude from lesion experiments that the hippocampus is the site of memory in rats?

Modern non-invasive procedures

Like the EEG these are procedures which do not require direct interference with brain tissue. The era began with computed axial tomography, or the CAT scanner, in the early 1970s. This procedure uses multiple X-rays and a computer to produce pictures of horizontal sections through the brain. A later technique was magnetic resonance imaging or MRI scanning (Fig. 6.1). The procedure involves placing the head in a powerful magnetic field and bombarding the brain with radio waves.

Molecules in the brain vibrate in response to the radio waves and emit radio waves of their own. These are recorded, computerized and assembled into a three-dimensional picture of brain structures. The level of detail is on the whole better than with the CAT scanner and it also avoids subjecting the patient to X-rays. A more complicated but more valuable procedure is positron emission tomography (PET scanning). The usual procedure involves injecting radioactive glucose into the bloodstream. This reaches the brain and, as glucose is used as an energy source by cells, it is taken up by neurons. The brain is then scanned by a battery of detectors which pick up the radioactivity emitted by the glucose (doses of radioactivity are tiny and harmless); parts of the brain which are more active take up more glucose and emit more radioactivity and a computer can then draw up an activity map of the brain. The procedure can be used to identify, for instance, those parts of the brain which are most active during speech, or problem solving, or recognizing faces, etc. This ability to correlate activity in different brain areas with psychological functions makes PET scanning the most useful of current computer-based techniques. However, it should be remembered that all these procedures are hospital-based, time-consuming and very expensive.

Figure 6.1
A sagittal section of a human brain using MRI scanning

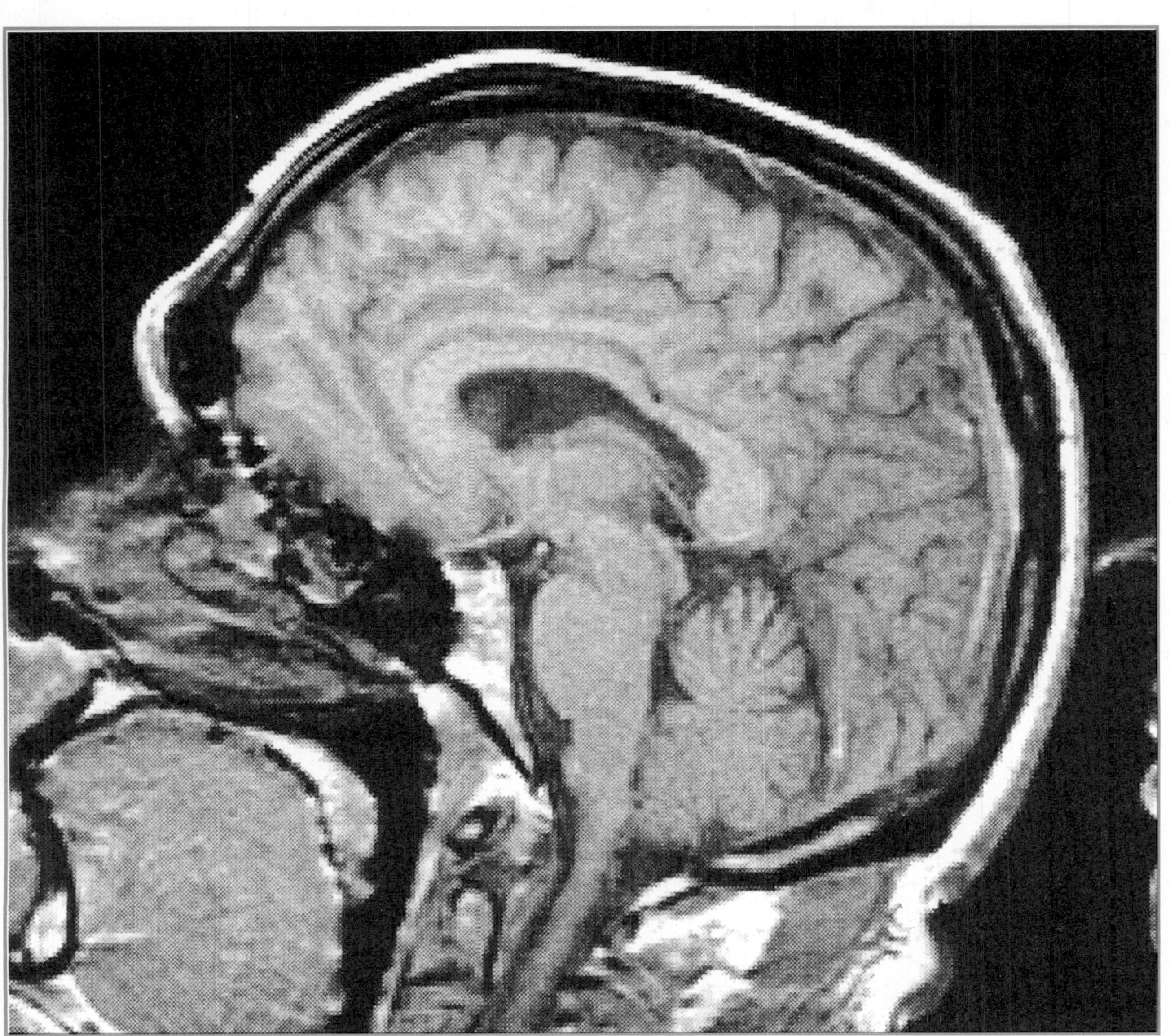

However, as data from the human brain accumulates, it means that we will gradually rely less on animal-based research.

Section summary

Researchers and neurosurgeons use a stereotaxic atlas to locate structures within the brain to be stimulated or lesioned. As neuronal transmission uses electrical and chemical processes, both electrical and chemical recording and stimulating techniques have been developed. Electrical stimulation has been used to mimic normal brain function, while recordings can be made from single neurons or from clusters of thousands of neurons. The electro-encephalograph (EEG) records activity from the cortex. Chemical stimulation uses drugs or specially designed chemicals, while recording concentrates on measuring levels of neurotransmitters. Physical destruction of brain tissue using electrical lesions is less common now and involves only small areas. Recent non-invasive procedures such as CAT and PET scanners produce pictures of the living brain and reduce our reliance on animal-based research.

Localization of function in the human brain

Although it may seem obvious that behavioural functions should be localized to particular structures and regions of the brain, there is in fact no particular reason why they should be. If we approached the brain knowing only the arrangement of neurons and how they worked, we would have no immediate way of knowing, for instance, how language might be organized. Would it be spread over large regions of cortex, or would it be restricted to small, highly specialized areas?

The principle of localization of function states that psychological functions are located in specialized areas, so that damage to the relevant area causes a drastic loss of that function. It can be contrasted with the view that functions are widespread, or distributed, across large regions of the brain, so that damage to any one small area causes only minimal loss of function.

Of course we have by now collected a huge amount of experimental data which goes a long way towards answering this question. The organization of the hypothalamus (which was discussed in the last chapter) suggests that here we have a structure which has important specialized functions localized within it and there is no suggestion that temperature control, for instance, is distributed across large amounts of brain. In fact, many of the more physiological functions of the brain are strictly localized and it is only when we consider the higher cognitive functions of the cerebral cortex that the picture becomes more confused.

Lashley (1929; see *In Focus* on next page) demonstrated that there was a vague localization of maze memory to the visual cortex, although he was working only with memory and other cognitive functions may be organized differently. He did show that the extreme localization found, for instance, in the hypothalamus did not necessarily hold for functional localization in association cortex.

Functional organization of the cortex

The cortex contains most of the neurons in the forebrain and controls many complex functions. The simplest way to approach the organization of these functions is to divide them into different categories:

- Sensory functions, such as vision and hearing, are related to the processing of sensory input.
- Motor functions are concerned with the planning and execution of movement.

In Focus

Lashley's laws of cortical organization

In the 1920s and 30s Karl Lashley was investigating the brain mechanisms of memory in the rat. He called the physical basis of memory the engram and spent many years searching for the site within the brain where the engram was located. For instance, he would train rats to learn a complicated maze and then show that a lesion taking out most of the visual cortex would remove the memory, or engram, so that the rat would no longer remember the maze. So the engram was presumably somewhere in the visual cortex. He then repeated the study several times, each time removing only a small part of the visual cortex, reasoning that the engram must be in one of these smaller zones. In fact, none of these smaller lesions affected memory for the maze and Lashley had to conclude that the engram does not exist in a highly localized form but is spread across cortical regions. He summarized his findings in two laws of cortical organization:

- The Law of Mass Action states that lesions affect memory in proportion to their size, as the cortex works together as a whole.
- The Law of Equipotentiality states that all areas of the cortex have equal roles in memory storage, so that damage to different areas has similar effects.

- There is a large category of cognitive functions such as language, thought, planning and problem solving, personality, etc., which together make up our higher cognitive abilities.

A practical reason for dividing functions into these categories is that we have known for many years that sensory and motor functions are localized in specialized areas of the cortex, so much so that we can categorize these areas as sensory and motor cortex respectively. As we shall see, labelling areas of cortex as sensory or motor leaves a lot of cortex to be described. These areas of cortex are called association cortex, an old-fashioned term based on the idea that the functions of these areas in some way 'associate' sensory input with motor output.

It has been known since the early years of the century that electrical stimulation or lesions of various parts of the cortex in animals can affect sensory and motor abilities and this has been confirmed by the effects of accidental damage to the cortex in humans, or by some rare cases where electrical stimulation has been carried out on human patients (this is usually to check that a subsequent surgical procedure will not damage, or impair, important functions).

The result of all this work is that we can map these sensory and motor functions on to the cortical surface of the hemispheres. Fig 6.2 shows such a map. In each of the areas, electrical stimulation will mimic the function to a greater or lesser extent, while damage will impair the function. You will immediately notice that our most complex and important sensory abilities, vision and hearing, have specialized cortical areas dedicated to them; this is because visual and auditory (hearing) processing is far more sophisticated than, say, the perception of touch or taste and requires more neuronal material. Stimulation in these areas produces either visual sensation (perhaps a flash of brightness) or auditory sensation (perhaps a buzzing noise), while damage may impair vision or hearing.

The somatosensory cortex in the postcentral gyrus (so-called because it lies behind the central fissure, one of the brain's main anatomical landmarks) contains our general body senses, mainly dealing with stimuli on the skin such as touch, pressure, heat, cold and some aspects of pain. Stimulation here gives rise to the experience of touch or pressure on part of the skin. It seems that there is a point-for-point representation of the body

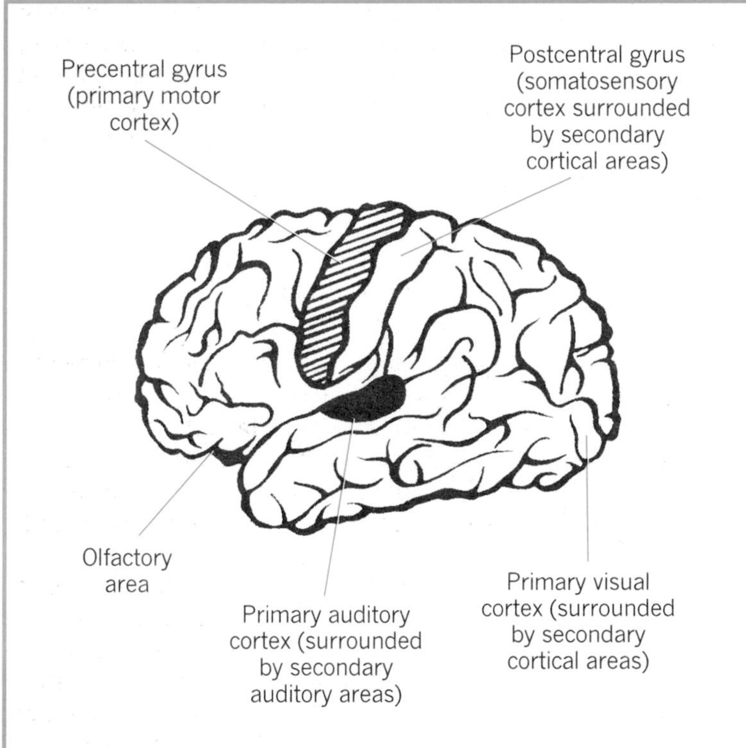

Figure 6.2 Side view of left hemisphere showing sensory and motor areas

surface on the cortical surface, an arrangement called a topographical map; as you stimulate parts of the somatosensory cortex, so the reported sensation of touch moves up and down the body. The map is upside down, with the skin of feet and legs dealt with by the cortex at the top of the brain. Damage to somatosensory cortex leads to a loss of sensation (anaesthesia) from the body.

Visual, auditory and somatosensory cortex represent the target zones for neuronal pathways carrying sensory information from receptors into the central nervous system. As the receiving areas for these pathways they are called primary sensory cortex. Of course there are a number of stages between basic sensation and complex perception and after arrival at primary cortex sensory information is passed on to secondary and even tertiary cortical areas where increasingly complex processing occurs. Auditory, visual and somatosensory cortex are surrounded by these secondary and tertiary areas, where sensation becomes perception. You can see this transition in the effects of brain damage. If the primary visual cortex is involved, loss can be profound, as without primary areas the visual input cannot be transmitted on for further processing. If secondary or tertiary areas are involved, basic visual abilities may be intact, but some high level ability, such as face recognition, may be lost. The study of such syndromes (patterns of symptoms) seen after damage to cortical areas outside primary cortex is called cognitive neuropsychology, with the aim of using the pattern of cognitive loss after brain damage to build models of how normal cognitive functions are organized. We see later how such work has led to current models of how visual sensation and perception are organized in the brain.

The precentral gyrus in the frontal lobe (Fig. 6.2) contains motor cortex. This is the origin of pathways running eventually to the muscles of the skeleton to produce movement. Damage here can lead to paralysis, while stimulation can produce movement of individual muscle fibres. As with somatosensory cortex, motor cortex contains a topographical map of the body, also upside-down, with muscles of the feet and legs controlled from areas at the top of motor cortex. As our most complex muscular control involves the muscles of the throat, larynx, pharynx and tongue used in speech, this area takes up proportionately more cortical surface. It is also important to remember the other parts of the motor system. In Chapter 5 we met the cerebellum and the basal ganglia, which have important roles in integrating and fine-tuning movement; damage to those areas impairs smooth control but does not eliminate movement completely.

A note on pathways

Figure 6.2 shows only the left hemisphere. However, a map of the sensory and motor functions of the right hemisphere would look exactly the same, only the other way round. Humans, like all mammals, are what is called bilaterally (bilateral means two-sided) symmetrical; if divided vertically, you end up with two mirror-image halves. The presence of two legs, two arms and two cerebral hemispheres reflects this bilateral symmetry, which also explains why we usually find brain structures in pairs, one on each side.

The arrangement of sensory and motor pathways connecting the hemispheres with the body is determined by this fundamental organizational principle. Motor and somatosensory pathways connect each hemisphere with only one side of the body. For reasons which are unknown these pathways are crossed, with the left hemisphere connecting to the right side of the body and the right hemisphere to the left. Cortical damage to the left hemisphere therefore produces a right-sided paralysis and loss of sensation. This arrangement is called a crossed or contralateral pathway.

The visual and auditory systems have a more complicated arrangement. Each eye and ear have pathways connecting them with both hemispheres, i.e. a combination of crossed (contralateral) and uncrossed (ipsilateral – meaning 'same side') pathways. This means that damage to only one hemisphere will not destroy vision or hearing completely, as the other hemisphere is still functionally connected to both eyes or ears. We discuss the visual pathways in more detail later.

Despite vision and hearing having crossed and uncrossed pathways, in relation to the hemispheres themselves the arrangements are perfectly symmetrical. For sensory and motor functions the two hemispheres have similar organizations, i.e. they show functional symmetry and describing one effectively describes the other.

They also show significant localization of function, with small areas of cortex carrying out specialized and specific functions. But of course the problems met by Lashley were in the area of memory and it is to the higher cognitive functions we now turn.

Cortical organization of cognitive functions

Taking out the sensory and motor cortical areas leaves large parts of the cortex unaccounted for (see Fig. 6.2). As mentioned above, these are referred to as association cortex and it is here that we assume that higher cognitive functions will be located.

The search for these began in the earliest days of brain research in the nineteenth century, when the systematic study of brain-damaged patients started. Two of the most remarkable observations were made by Paul Broca and by Karl Wernicke, who were interested in how language was organized in the brain. In 1861 Broca reported on a patient admitted to hospital after suffering a stroke. Tests showed that although he could understand speech, following instructions and answering simple questions with head movements, the only recognizable word he could actually say was 'tan'. There was no fluent speech at all. Broca found eight similar cases with similar symptoms of a lack of speech production coupled with normal speech understanding or comprehension. This syndrome is called Broca's aphasia; aphasia is the technical term for any speech problem encountered

❖ Activity 2 ❖

Lift your left arm. Which hemisphere is controlling the movement? Now raise your right leg and answer the same question. Now read the last sentence. Is it easy to work out which hemisphere is controlling your lips, tongue, larynx and pharynx when you talk? Probably not. These are muscles controlled from the motor cortex, but their role in speech means that control must be highly detailed and fine-tuned. Because of this, they are the only examples where control of muscles on both sides of the body is located in one hemisphere. Can you guess which? Because of the left hemisphere role in language, the left hemisphere motor cortex has taken over control of our speech musculature on both sides of the body.

after brain damage. Alternative terms for Broca's aphasia are expressive or motor aphasia.

At roughly the same time Wernicke, using similar methods, identified a syndrome with the opposite pattern of symptoms; patients did not seem to comprehend speech, but could produce reasonably well-organized sequences of speech. As they could not understand speech, what they said was unrelated to any question or comment spoken to them. This syndrome is called Wernicke's aphasia, or alternatively sensory or receptive aphasia.

Broca and Wernicke were interested in the brain mechanisms of language and so the brains of the patients were examined after they had died. Broca consistently found that his patients had suffered damage to an area low down in the cortex of the frontal lobe, now known as Broca's area (see Fig. 6.3).

Wernicke's patients had damage to an area in the temporal lobe close to the primary auditory cortex (Fig. 6.3), now called Wernicke's area. Work since then, right up to recent studies using PET scans, generally confirms the original findings of Broca and Wernicke: damage to Broca's area severely impairs speech but leaves the comprehension of speech intact, while damage to Wernicke's area affects comprehension but leaves speech production quite fluent.

It seems that Wernicke's area in the temporal lobe contains a store of the sound representations of words which we use to recognize incoming speech. Broca's area is thought to contain the motor plans for words, i.e. the pattern of muscle movements of the throat and tongue, etc., which are specific to each word. When we wish to speak, instructions are passed from Wernicke's area to Broca's area to activate the relevant motor plans, which are then transmitted the short distance to the motor cortex in the prefrontal cortex, which sends instructions down the motor pathways to the muscles themselves. When Wernicke's area is damaged we lose the store of word

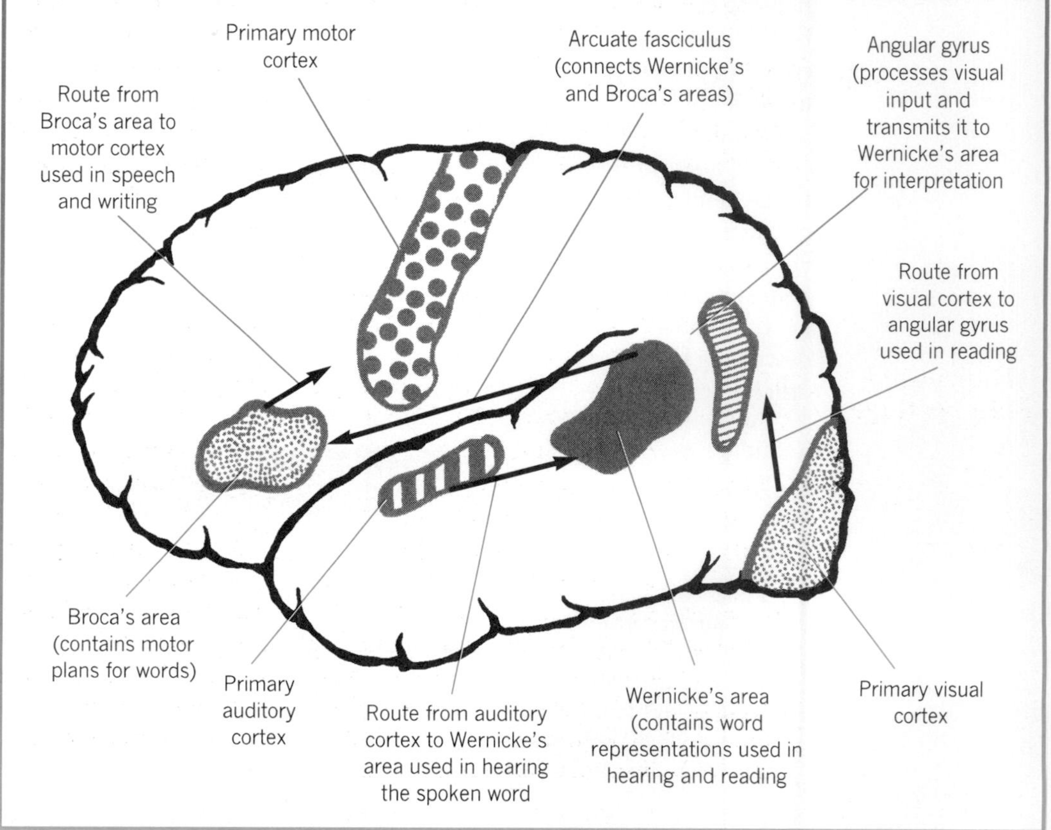

Figure 6.3 Language mechanisms in the left hemisphere

representations and so cannot recognize incoming speech, but as Broca's area is intact motor plans can still be activated and speech produced. I am sure you can work the opposite pattern out for yourselves.

Besides the significant finding that speech production and comprehension seemed to be localized to particular areas of the cortex, Broca and Wernicke also confirmed a suggestion that had been made earlier in the century, that brain damage affecting language usually involved the left hemisphere. Damage to the right hemisphere rarely had any effect on language. The conclusion was that our language mechanisms are found only in the left hemisphere.

Thousands of research studies since those pioneering observations have confirmed this general pattern, with some exceptions which we meet later in the chapter. The significance of the finding was that, in contrast to sensory and motor functions, language was not organized symmetrically across the two hemispheres of the brain, but represented a hemisphere asymmetry of function. From these beginnings, the study of hemisphere asymmetries of function has become one of the main research themes in psychology. Before looking at some of the findings, however, we should have a more general look at other functions of association cortex.

Studies of damage to the frontal lobes (see *In Focus*) has led to the idea of a frontal lobe syndrome, with symptoms of impulsivity, a failure to plan ahead or to follow plans through to a conclusion, perseveration (repeating the same actions) and sometimes apathy and indecision. There can be a loss of creative or abstract thought. However, the frontal cortex is such a large area that it may well contain a wide range of complex functions and it might be better to map the whole area in detail rather than to study the effects of major damage. Generally it seems to control our capacity for forward planning and goal-directed behaviour. In relation to hemisphere asymmetries, apart from Broca's area, usually found only in the left frontal cortex, there is little evidence for asymmetries of other frontal functions.

The association cortex of the parietal lobe contains many functions related to perception. Damage can lead to problems with object recognition and apraxias, which are particular problems with skilled sequences of actions, for instance in assembling a set of parts into a complete object.

In the right hemisphere parietal lobe there appears to be an area specialized for face recognition, while damage to other areas in the right parietal cortex can lead to unilateral neglect. This is a bizarre

In Focus

The case of Phineas Gage

The frontal lobes contain the largest proportion of association cortex of any of the lobes making up the hemispheres. One of the earliest and most dramatic cases of frontal lobe damage studied was that of Phineas Gage. In 1848, he was working on the construction of the American railroad, where his job was to tamp down the explosive charges used to blow rocks out of the way. One of the charges exploded prematurely and blew the tamping iron (a metal rod, several feet long) through his cheekbone and out through the top of the skull. Gage suffered severe injuries, losing much of his frontal association cortex.

Amazingly Gage not only survived (he only lost consciousness for a few minutes and actually signed off from work before going to the doctor), but lived for 13 years afterwards. Even the behavioural effects were less than you might expect after losing so much brain tissue. His general cognitive functions such as memory, attention and perception, were intact. He was, however, more impulsive, less conscientious and had fewer social inhibitions than before. Planning ahead was impossible and he found it difficult to hold down a job, even for a time becoming an exhibit in a circus.

syndrome in which patients ignore the space on their left, i.e. on the opposite side to the lesion. They will draw only one half of a clock, with all the numbers crowded together, or only dress one side of their body. It seems that the parietal lobe is concerned with our perception of and orientation within the surrounding space.

Another important language structure found in the parietal lobe is the angular gyrus (Fig. 6.3). This area of cortex is vital to the visual aspects of language involved in reading and writing, as it works with Wernicke's area to convert the visual input into the brain's language code. Damage can lead to a loss of both reading and writing, while damage which disconnects the angular gyrus from the visual cortex (which, of course, is where visual input, including the read word, first reaches the cortex) produces a strange syndrome known as alexia (absence of reading) without agraphia (absence of writing), or pure word blindness. Because the written word cannot reach the angular gyrus, it cannot be read. However, as the gyrus itself is intact, together with the pathways running to Wernicke's area and on to Broca's area, the planning and production of writing can still happen. So patients can write, but not read back what they have written! Although the angular gyrus can be identified in the right hemisphere, the loss of language function occurs only after damage to the left hemisphere.

It is important to remember that these syndromes observed after brain damage happen even though basic sensory and motor pathways are working properly. For instance, testing shows that patients with aphasia or dyslexia have normal vision and motor control, so the symptoms must be due to difficulties with higher level cognitive processes. It is these that the psychologist is interested in.

The temporal lobe association cortex contains the secondary and tertiary auditory cortex and Wernicke's area, described earlier. It also contains regions of secondary and tertiary visual cortex, radiating out from the visual cortex of the occipital lobe. Damage to the temporal lobe can therefore affect auditory perception (e.g. identifying sounds or voices), language, referred to previously and high level visual perception such as identifying and categorizing stimuli, e.g. being able to recognize that the object seen is an apple and that an apple is a fruit.

These are functions of the cortical surface of the temporal lobe. Under the surface are subcortical structures and buried within the temporal lobe are parts of the limbic system such as the hippocampus and the amygdala. Besides other functions, the limbic system plays an important role in relation to emotion. Because of the links between the limbic system and temporal lobe cortex, damage to the cortex alone can affect not just how we identify stimuli but also weaken our emotional response to it. Responses become distant and strictly neutral. The association cortex of the occipital lobe is almost completely dedicated to visual processing, so much so that occipital cortex is often simply referred to as visual cortex. Damage to these areas affects visual perception and we shall see some examples later in this chapter.

Section summary

Early work by Lashley suggested that processes such as memory were not highly localized in the brain. However, sensory and motor processes are located to specific areas of the cortex, which can be mapped out. Each hemisphere has areas dedicated to the motor control and general body senses of the opposite side of the body. The auditory and visual cortex of each hemisphere are connected to both ears or eyes. Studies of association cortex began with Broca and Wernicke's work on language, which they located to the left hemisphere in the first demonstration of an asymmetry of hemisphere function. Damage to association cortex produces high level loss of cognitive abilities such as aphasias, apraxias, the frontal lobe syndrome and perceptual problems. These syndromes occur even though basic sensory and motor processes are intact.

Hemisphere asymmetries and the split brain

The historical work of Wernicke, Broca and others demonstrated that some of the functions of association cortex, such as language, seemed to be located in only one hemisphere; this is called an asymmetry of function, in comparison to sensory and motor functions which are organized symmetrically across the hemispheres. Since then a vast number of experimental studies on normal and brain-damaged patients has reinforced and extended these original findings. One of the most dramatic series of studies was that of Roger Sperry, which began in the 1950s and continued until his death in 1980.

Sperry's subjects were patients suffering from epilepsy. Epilepsy comes in many forms, but always involves an uncontrolled discharge of electrical activity in the brain. The discharge may originate in an area of scar tissue following accidental brain damage, often at birth, or during brain surgery, or perhaps from a developing cyst or tumour; when such a point of origin can be identified, it is called a focus and sometimes it can be removed surgically. In other cases of epilepsy there is no clear focus, but probably some imbalance in excitatory and inhibitory influences in the brain.

Whatever the cause, once the discharge begins it is automatically transmitted along neuronal pathways, as this is what they are specialized to do. Severe epilepsy can involve many brain circuits and lead to convulsions and loss of consciousness and a patient may have several attacks a week or even a day. It is therefore a disabling condition. Nowadays we have many drugs for the control of epilepsy, although there are still patients who do not respond and are very handicapped. In the 1940s there were far fewer drugs and many more patients suffering severely from the effects of epilepsy.

It is a feature of most types of epilepsy that the attack usually begins in one hemisphere or the other. Connecting the hemispheres is the largest pathway in the brain, the corpus callosum, consisting of some 300 million neuronal fibres. This pathway interconnects areas of the cortex in each hemisphere, ensuring that the hemispheres communicate with each other and synchronize their activities. The corpus callosum also allows epileptic discharges to spread to the other hemisphere and in the 1940s an operation was devised to prevent this spread; the corpus callosum was cut. In this way the epilepsy was confined to only one hemisphere and its effects reduced.

Strangely the operation (technically called a commissurotomy as the corpus callosum is the largest of the commissures, those pathways travelling between the hemispheres rather than contained within one of them) seemed to have little effect on the patient. Sensory, motor and cognitive functions continued as before, but there was an improvement in their epilepsy.

Sperry was intrigued by this: surely the largest pathway in the brain must have important functions and its removal should affect behaviour. He decided to study these patients using careful experimental procedures based on the anatomy of the visual pathways. These are outlined in Fig. 6.4. Light strikes the retina at the back of the eye, which contains millions of visual receptor cells (these processes are dealt with in detail later in this chapter). The receptors trigger activity in axons making up the optic nerve (see Fig. 6.4), which runs via the thalamus on to primary visual cortex in the occipital lobe.

As Fig. 6.4 shows, it is a feature of the retina of each eye that the receptors in the outer half connect with fibres running to the visual cortex in the hemisphere on the same side of the brain – an ipsilateral (same-side) pathway. Receptors contained within the inner half of each retina project to the visual cortex in the opposite hemisphere – a contralateral (crossed) pathway. So each retina projects in a systematic way to both hemispheres, with the crossed pathways passing from one side to the other at the optic chiasma. Figure 6.4 also shows how a stimulus presented out to the right of the subject (known as the right visual field, or

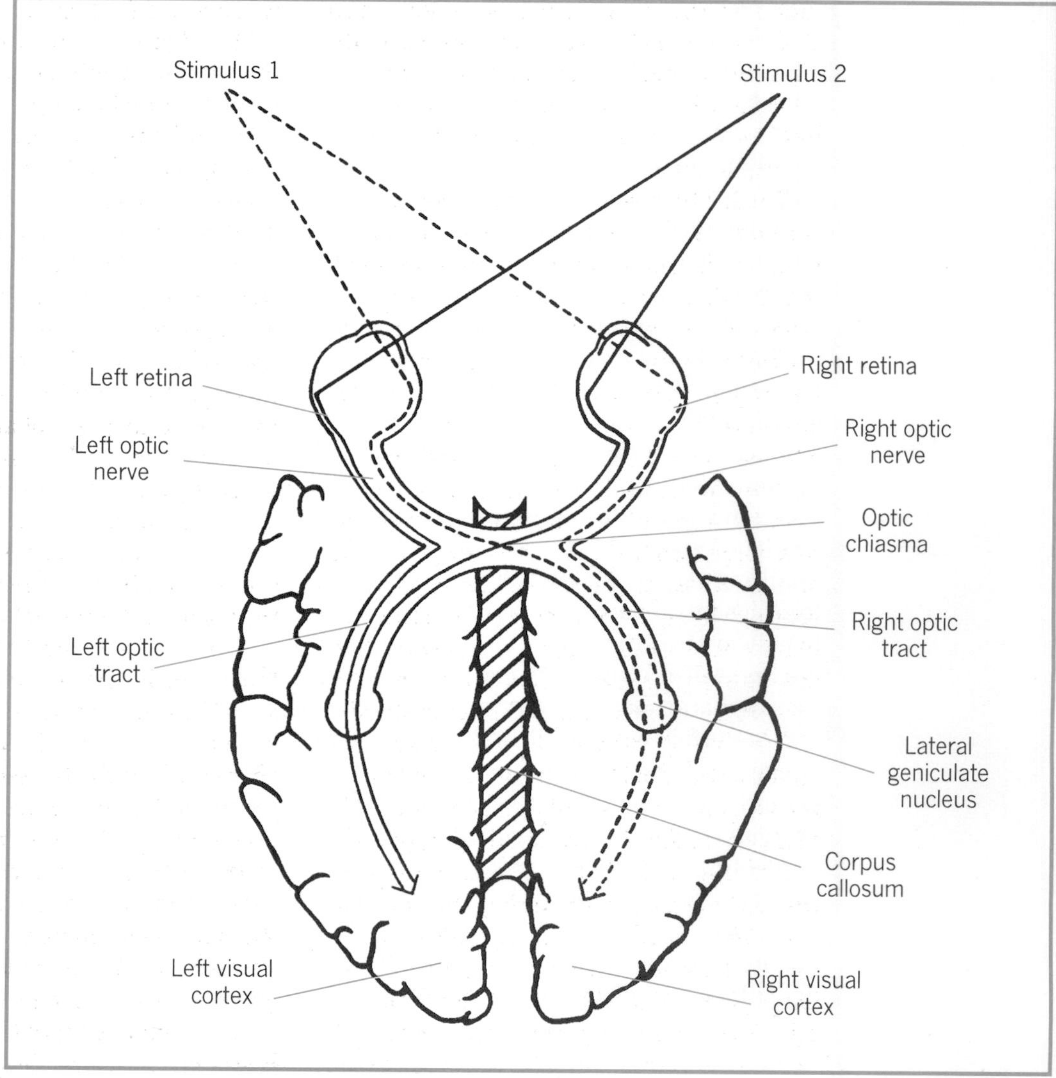

Figure 6.4 Outline of the visual pathways

RVF) is picked up. With the eyes pointing (or fixated) straight ahead, it hits the left side of the left eye and the left side of the right eye; look carefully and you will see that these parts of each retina both project to the visual cortex of the left hemisphere. So a stimulus in the RVF, with both eyes fixated straight ahead, is seen first by the left hemisphere and by the same geometrical argument a stimulus out to the left of the subject (in the left visual field, LVF) is seen first by the right hemisphere.

In normal subjects any information reaching one hemisphere first is rapidly and automatically transferred to the other hemisphere via the corpus callosum. In patients who have had a commissurotomy, known informally as split-brain patients, the information cannot pass to the other hemisphere as the corpus callosum has been cut. So this experimental procedure, referred to as the divided field, enabled Sperry to present visual stimuli and know that they would be confined to the hemisphere to which they were transmitted. What sort of things could he demonstrate?

The split-brain subject sits in front of a screen. A word is flashed up briefly in the subject's RVF (if the exposure of the stimulus is too long, the eyes automatically move towards the stimulus, which may then be seen by both hemispheres). The word is transmitted to the left hemisphere and if you ask the subject to report what they saw, they will say the word. Repeat the study with the LVF. The word travels to the right hemisphere. When asked to report what they have seen, the subject denies having seen anything. Can you work out the explanation?

The left hemisphere in most people contains the language system, i.e. it can read words and speak. The word presented in the RVF goes to the left hemisphere, is read and reported by the subject. The word presented in the LVF goes to the right hemisphere, which does not have a highly developed language system and certainly cannot speak. Therefore the subject has nothing to report. In fact the experiment involves a spoken response which itself has to emerge from the left hemisphere; with the corpus callosum cut, the left hemisphere does not know what is going on in the right hemisphere, so the subject's left hemisphere language system cannot comment on stimuli presented to the right hemisphere.

This type of early study allowed Sperry to confirm that the left hemisphere controls reading and speech and that the right hemisphere apparently could not process verbal stimuli at all. But he was worried that as long as he used verbal questions and responses – 'what was the stimulus you saw?' – he was not giving the right hemisphere a fair chance; if it could not talk, it could not respond at all, so in fact he had no idea what was going on in it. So he introduced a variation.

You may remember that the motor pathways are completely crossed, with each hemisphere controlling the muscles of the opposite side of the body. So the right hemisphere controls the left arm and hand and it was this system that Sperry used to test the right hemisphere. The experiment described above is repeated, except that in this case the left hand is placed behind a screen (so the subject cannot see what it is doing) among a collection of different objects. A word such as 'orange' is presented in the RVF. It goes to the left hemisphere and when the subject is asked whether they saw anything, they say 'orange'. Then 'banana' is presented in the LVF. This goes to the right hemisphere and when asked for a spoken response the subject denies seeing anything. However, the left hand behind the screen emerges triumphantly holding a banana it has selected from the range of objects!

It appears that the right hemisphere can understand simple concrete nouns and understand their meaning. This has activated the left hand, controlled by the right hemisphere, to select out the appropriate object. Meanwhile the left hemisphere, which can talk but has no access to the right hemisphere, has not seen the word and does not know why the left hand is holding a banana. When asked what is going on, the subject, using their left hemisphere to produce a spoken reply, will seem confused, or sometimes even deny that the left hand is theirs! The split brain represents a disconnection syndrome, in which brain damage disconnects normally integrated functions. Ask a normal subject, with their eyes shut, to say whether two objects, one in each hand, are the same and they can do it easily. Ask a split-brain patient and they cannot even say whether they have an object in the left hand.

Using the left hand response system meant that Sperry and other researchers could test the right hemisphere with various types of stimulus, while the left hemisphere could continue using its language mechanisms. Sperry concluded that the right hemisphere had some simple reading ability, in that it could read concrete nouns (i.e. object names) but not abstract words and could not produce language (writing or speaking). However, it was better at recognizing pictures and shapes, especially faces.

Work on the split brain demonstrated that although the right hemisphere may not be very linguistic, it had important functions related to processing pictures and shapes, or visuo-spatial stimuli. This division of the hemispheres into a verbal and linguistic left and a visuo-spatial right has become a basic model of brain function, supported in general by many thousands of subsequent studies with normal subjects. Before looking at some of this later work, there are some problems with the split brain that should be mentioned.

Evaluation of split-brain studies

- Because it is such a drastic treatment, very few commissurotomies have ever been done; only about eighty overall and they are extremely rare nowadays. Only about twenty have been given much psychological testing and most of the data has come from fewer than ten of them. Can we base models of brain function on such a small sample?
- Epilepsy is caused by some sort of brain abnormality and patients have to live with it for many years before surgery takes place. They are also likely to be on drug therapy and it is hard to argue that these were 'normal' subjects before surgery. In fact, some of the later patients showed good evidence of right hemisphere expressive language, by writing with the left hand. So do we conclude that bilateral (two-sided) language organization is the norm, or that these particular brains have been reorganized because of the presence of some sort of abnormality and should not be used to model the normal brain?
- There are too many uncontrolled variables for the split-brain patients to be considered a uniform group. Patients vary in sex, age of onset of epilepsy, cause of the epilepsy, age at which surgery was performed and age at testing.

For the reasons listed above, it is unjustified to use experimental findings only from split-brain patients to build models of normal brain function. However, they have been very important, for various reasons:

- From Sperry's earliest work it seemed probable that the right hemisphere, previously thought to be unimportant compared to the verbal left hemisphere, did contain important cognitive functions related to visuo-spatial stimuli.
- The split-brain patient shows the central role of language in our conscious self-awareness. When asked to comment on their situation, the patient always refers to the experiences of the left hemisphere. Only under special experimental conditions can the right hemisphere clearly express itself.
- Sperry was intrigued by the role of the corpus callosum in brain function. The disconnection syndromes seen in the split-brain patient suggest that the role of this major pathway is to enable each hemisphere to be aware of activities in the other. Each hemisphere seems to have its own specialized functions and in the intact brain the corpus callosum allows these to be coordinated and integrated, producing an integrated personality. Thus we can reflect (using left hemisphere language) on our visuo-spatial abilities (in the right hemisphere).
- One underestimated contribution of Sperry's was his development of the divided visual field technique to test the hemispheres separately. As we shall see, this has become one of the most used procedures.

Before discussing work with non-split-brain people, you may wonder how the split-brain patient manages in everyday life and the answer is, much better than you might imagine. The key is the organization of the visual system. Each eye projects to both hemispheres and if the eyes are moved to scan the whole visual field, all the stimuli will be transmitted to both hemispheres. When reading, for instance, head movements are exaggerated as all the text must be seen by the left side of each retina (Fig. 6.4) so it goes to the left hemisphere language mechanisms. A problem can arise with coordinating the hands, for instance in striking a match. With eyes shut, the person would not know that the left hand held the matchbox, as explained above, so coordination is dependent on the eyes. The most bizarre problem reported is a tendency for the right-hemisphere/left-hand system to have its own views; one patient selected some trousers to wear and then found her left hand independently choosing a second pair!

Hemisphere asymmetries: non-split-brain studies

In parallel with the split-brain work, thousands of studies were carried out on normal subjects. Many of these relied on two basic techniques, Sperry's divided field and dichotic listening. As normal subjects have an intact corpus callosum, the divided field cannot be used unmodified, as a single stimulus presented to one hemisphere is rapidly communicated to the other. The simple modification is to present two stimuli at once, one in each visual field. With brief exposure (less than 100 milliseconds), usually only one is reported by the subject. If words are used, the word presented in the RVF and going directly to the left hemisphere and its language mechanisms would be the one registered by the subject; this is called an RVF superiority. If pictures or faces are used, then the one in the LVF going first to the right hemisphere is reported; this hemisphere is better at analysing such stimuli and although the results have to be passed to the left hemisphere to be verbally reported, this is faster than the processing of the stimulus in the RVF going to the left hemisphere, which cannot deal with it and has to pass it across to the right hemisphere to be analysed. Visuo-spatial stimuli therefore give an LVF advantage.

The results of the many studies done with the divided visual field are reasonably consistent:

- Words, letters and digits give an RVF advantage, indicating superior processing by the left hemisphere.
- Recognizing faces and patterns, discriminating brightness and colours and depth perception, all give an LVF advantage, indicating right hemisphere processing.

Dichotic listening is a similar procedure for the auditory system. A pair of sounds is presented simultaneously through headphones. Although each ear projects to both hemispheres, the crossed, contralateral, pathway is dominant, so stimuli in the left ear are processed by the right hemisphere and vice-versa. If words are used, the one in the right ear going to the left hemisphere is usually reported, giving a right ear advantage (REA). If non-verbal sounds such as animal noises are used (a sort of auditory equivalent of visuo-spatial stimuli), then the one in the left ear tends to be the one identified and reported; this is a left ear advantage, or LEA.

Summarizing findings from dichotic listening studies:

- Spoken words, digits, normal and backwards speech and nonsense syllables all give an REA (left hemisphere advantage).
- Recognizing environmental sounds and most aspects of music perception give an LEA (right hemisphere advantage).

So the pattern of visual field superiorities and ear advantages can give us a picture of how the hemispheres process a range of stimuli. Table 6.1 summarizes some of the findings.

Attempts have been made to characterize the hemispheres on the basis of such findings. As words and digits come in as a sequence of stimuli spread over time, the left hemisphere is seen as better at sequential or time-based processing and at segmenting and analysing input into its component parts (think of understanding speech, where we take in the sequence of sounds, but to understand them we need to identify each unit, be it phoneme or whole word, and then put the sentence together after analysing the parts). Pictures and faces are usually identified as one whole stimulus with all the features processed immediately in parallel; so the right hemisphere is seen as better at Gestalt or parallel processing. 'Gestalt' means an integrated whole stimulus, not just a collection of parts.

Some theorists have gone further, seeing the left hemisphere as analytic, scientific and rational and the right hemisphere as creative, artistic and emotional. There is little solid experimental evidence for these speculations. As the role of the corpus callosum is to coordinate the activities of the two hemispheres, it is unlikely that any complicated human activity involves only one of them independently. Science, for

Table 6.1 Suggested characteristics of the two hemispheres

Left hemisphere	*Right hemisphere*
Verbal	Visuo-spatial
Sequential processing	Simultaneous, parallel positioning
Analytic	Gestalt, holistic
Rational	Emotional
Deductive	Intuitive, creative
Convergent thought	Divergent thought
Scientific	Artistic

instance, involves producing hypotheses and theories, which is clearly a creative enterprise.

Although the original work of Wernicke and Broca, and Sperry's experiments on the split brain, can be criticized for studying too few subjects and involving uncontrolled variables, the basic picture of hemisphere specialization that emerged has been confirmed by later, better controlled studies. Language is localized to the left hemisphere, while the right hemisphere is specialized for the processing of visuo-spatial stimuli, of which the best example is faces. Other approaches, such as assessing the effects of lateralized (one-sided) brain damage, give further support; left hemisphere damage through a stroke or accidental brain injury can affect language, leaving face recognition intact, while right hemisphere damage can produce the opposite pattern.

What emerges is the picture of a 'standard' brain, with left hemisphere language and right hemisphere visuo-spatial ability. But how standard is this brain? The left hemisphere controls language and the right hand, the dominant hand in most people; do left-handers show the same pattern of asymmetries? Does gender make any difference?

❖ Activity 3 ❖

If you are right-handed, close your eyes and stand on your right leg. Now repeat the exercise while talking (recite a poem, or describe the functions of the cerebral hemispheres!). Some people find standing on the right leg more difficult if they are simultaneously talking; in theory both right leg balancing and talking are left hemisphere functions and interfere with each other. What type of task might interfere with left leg balancing? If you are left-handed, what result would you predict?

Handedness, gender and hemisphere asymmetries

Depending on precisely how it is assessed, around 10 to 15 per cent of the population are left-handed. As right-handers seem to have a left hemisphere which controls language and the right hand, it would seem logical that left-handers should have right hemisphere language, i.e. the reverse pattern. In fact the picture is more complicated. Around 70 per cent of left-handers have left hemisphere language, around 15 per cent have language in the right hemisphere and in 15 per cent language seems to involve both hemispheres, i.e. bilateral representation. In general, left-handers are less lateralized in regard to language than right-handers.

Does this have any implications for cognitive abilities? There were early suggestions that left-handers might be worse at visuo-spatial tasks than right-handers, because the spread of language into the right hemisphere somehow interferes with visuo-spatial abilities. However, there is no convincing evidence for overall differences in cognitive abilities between left- and right-handers. Interestingly, left-handers are over represented amongst mathematicians and architects, but also amongst people with dyslexia and those suffering from mental retardation. There are speculations that these observations are related to the unusual pattern of hemisphere development in left-handers.

There is some evidence that females show a different pattern of hemisphere asymmetries to males, specifically a higher frequency of bilateral representation. This has been used to explain the superiority of females in language-based intelligence tests and their poorer performance on visuo-spatial tasks. The increased development of verbal skills, involving both hemispheres, it is argued, interferes with the development of visuo-spatial skills in the right hemisphere. Although this biological argument has become popular, there is little experimental evidence for it and it ignores the wide range of social and cultural pressures during development which can influence cognitive abilities. For instance, there is a powerful correlation, regardless of sex, between academic performance in a particular subject and previous experience of that subject. This does not seem surprising, but learning experience is often ignored by biological theorists.

As left-handers and females can show patterns of reduced asymmetry for language, you might argue that female left-handers should be the least asymmetrical of all. This is not consistently the case. Performance on tests of hemisphere asymmetries, such as the divided field and dichotic listening, seems to involve a complicated interaction between gender and handedness. It also reflects the fact that differences in hemisphere organization between any two individuals, regardless of handedness or gender, are probably greater than any systematic differences between groups of left- and right-handers, or between males and females.

Section summary

In some patients with severe epilepsy the corpus callosum is cut to prevent electrical discharges passing between the hemispheres. Roger Sperry studied split-brain subjects using a special experimental procedure called the divided field. He was able to confirm that language is lateralized to the left hemisphere, but was also able to show that the right hemisphere has superior visuo-spatial skills. The split-brain studies can be criticized, but they have made a major contribution to the study of hemisphere asymmetries of function. Work on non-split-brain subjects has extended Sperry's findings. The left hemisphere is seen as a sequential or analytic processor, while the right hemisphere processes stimuli in parallel as Gestalts. Left-handers and females have a lesser degree of hemisphere asymmetry, but the practical significance of this is unclear.

Visual perception

Vision has evolved into our most complicated and valuable sensory system. There are many aspects to the study of vision. We can see colour, shape, movement and depth. Despite being seen from changing distances and angles, object size and shape are usually perceived as constant. Again at the perceptual level there are the phenomena of perceptual illusions and the Gestalt laws of perceptual organization. Brain damage can produce intriguing effects such as blind sight and prosopagnosia (loss of the ability to recognize faces). All of these depend on or can be explained by the way our visual system is organized, from the eye and the visual receptors up to the visual areas of association cortex. It is a complicated system, but it demonstrates some basic features of how perception emerges from sensation and if you can understand this then it will also help you to understand psychological models of perception (see Chapter 14).

The eye, visual receptors and visual pathways

Visual receptor cells are found in the retina, a layer covering the inside of the eye (see Fig. 6.5).

Light passes through the transparent cornea and is focused by the lens onto the retina. The receptors come in two forms: rods are specialized for vision in poor light conditions and cones for colour and high detail vision in bright light. There are about 125 million rods and about 6 million cones in the retina, but the cones are concentrated at the fovea, the centre of the visual field, i.e. if you look straight ahead, what you focus on is received on the fovea and seen very clearly. Towards the edge of your visual field vision becomes less clear as the number of cones decreases.

Rods and cones contain slightly different forms of a molecule called rhodopsin. This molecule reacts to light (electro-magnetic energy) by changing its structure and in a complex sequence of chemical events this triggers an action potential, or nerve impulse, in neurons synapsing on to the receptor. In this way the stimulus – light energy – is converted or transduced into nerve impulses. Rod rhodopsin is reactive to low light levels, so in bright light it is overstimulated and therefore inactive. When we suddenly move from bright light to dim light, the time it takes to adjust is the time it takes for the rod rhodopsin to be reformed and be able to react again to light.

The nerve impulse triggered by a receptor travels through several layers of nerve cells which make up the retina. The axons of the final layer – the ganglion cells – make up the optic nerve, which leaves the rear of the eye (Fig. 6.5). As there are 131 million visual receptors and only about one million optic nerve fibres, you can see that there is much processing and integration of information even in the retina. To put it another way, if we record nerve impulses in an individual axon of the optic nerve, they represent a combination of activity in some tens or hundreds of visual receptors.

We looked at the visual pathways earlier in the chapter (Fig. 6.4). You will recall that the optic nerves from the two eyes meet at the optic chiasma, where fibres from the inner half of each retina cross to the other side of the brain, while fibres from the outer halves remain on the same side. This means that after the chiasma each optic tract (inside the brain we have tracts or pathways rather than nerves) is made up of fibres from the outer half of one eye and the inner half of the other, or using the terms introduced earlier, each tract represents either the right or left visual field (Fig. 6.4).

After the optic chiasma the optic tracts project to a part of the thalamus called the lateral geniculate nucleus. From here they run to the primary visual cortex of the occipital lobe (Fig. 6.2). All cortex is made up of six layers of neurons. Axons making

Figure 6.5 Cross section through the eye

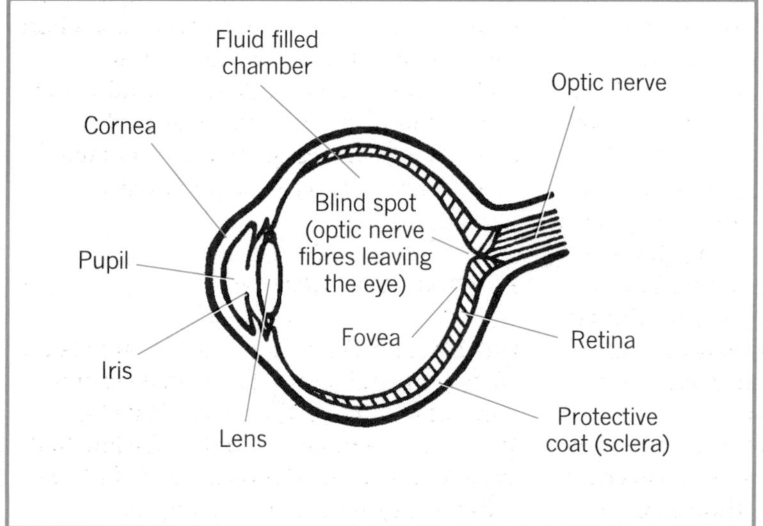

❖ Activity 4 ❖

Look at the visual pathways (Fig. 6.4). At what point would damage to the pathway cause a loss of vision in one eye? What would be the effects of damage to the visual cortex in the left hemisphere (this pattern of visual impairment is called homonymous hemianopia)?

up the optic tract reach the visual cortex and synapse onto the cells making up layer IV and from here visual information is distributed vertically to other cortical layers and then horizontally from primary visual cortex to surrounding areas of secondary and tertiary visual cortex. It is in these areas that complex perception takes place, but the groundwork takes place earlier in the system.

Retinal receptive fields

One of the main techniques used to study the functions of the visual system concentrates on recording electrical activity from single neurons. Researchers use special apparatus to stimulate the retina with visual stimuli of various shapes and sizes. Simultaneously, electrodes record activity from neurons at different stages along the visual pathway, such as fibres of the optic nerve, neurons in the lateral geniculate nucleus and neurons in the visual cortex. The aim is to identify the type of stimulus which maximally activates the neuron from which recordings are being made. Although the technique was introduced by other groups, it was its use by Hubel and Wiesel, over some thirty years, which unravelled many secrets of the visual system (they received the Nobel Prize in 1981, jointly with Roger Sperry).

Some examples may make it clearer. If you see a penguin, the image of the penguin has been focused by the lens on to the retina. Does a neuron carry the image of the penguin into the brain and up to the visual cortex? This would be demonstrated if, say, an optic nerve axon was activated maximally by a stimulus the shape of a penguin on the retina. In fact, right up to the cells of layer IV in the cortex, neurons respond best to tiny spots of light on the retina. The type of stimulus activating a given cell defines its retinal receptive field, i.e. that area of the retina which, when stimulated, results in maximum activation of that cell.

Of course, a large stimulus like a penguin covers a large retinal area and so will cover the receptive fields of many thousands of neurons. Put another way, the representation of the penguin in the early stages of visual processing is a pattern of activation across thousands of neurons, each responding to the stimulation of its particular tiny circular retinal receptive field.

Working through the visual pathways, from layer IV neurons to other layers of the visual cortex and then on into surrounding secondary and tertiary cortex, we find cells with more complex retinal receptive fields. So-called complex cells in the cortex respond best to line stimuli on the retina – lines, edges, or boundaries between light and darker zones – while hypercomplex cells respond to angles between lines and simple shapes. What seems to be happening is that many neurons earlier in the system synapse on to a single cell later in the system and this cell responds to a combination of the receptive fields of the preceding neurons; the way the combination occurs allows the circular receptive fields found early in the system to become the linear fields of complex and hypercomplex neurons.

Although the details are very complicated, the principle that stands out is that a stimulus received on the retina is not processed intact. In fact it is the very opposite, as it is broken down at the first stage into very basic and primitive features. Then, as they pass through the system, these basic features are actively re-assembled into the experience of the whole object. As neurons in the cortex respond to more and more detailed features of the stimulus, it is logical to ask if there is a single neuron somewhere that responds to a complete penguin. Although we do not know for certain it is thought unlikely. The final stages of perception probably involve coordinated activity across several cortical areas.

Innate or acquired?

Outside layer IV, neurons in primary visual cortex respond best to lines or edges at a particular point on the retina. Hubel and Wiesel also demonstrated that the line had to be at a specific orientation and that the cells were systematically arranged.

Recording from neurons as they slowly penetrated the cortical layers, they were able to show that all the cells in this vertical column of cortex responded to lines at different positions on the retina, but all with the same orientation. If they repeated the recording with a column a millimetre away, the neurons again responded to lines of the same orientation, but this time the orientation was shifted round slightly from the first column.

Hubel and Wiesel concluded that these orientation columns were a basic organizational feature of the visual cortex, which was made up of millions of such columns covering all orientations and retinal positions. Orientation columns are fundamental to our ability to recognize shapes. Are we born with them, or does their selective response to line orientation develop through experience? The answer is clearly that they depend on experience. Blakemore and Mitchell in 1973, using cats, showed that exposure to either vertical or horizontal lines for a short period in the first weeks of life would produce visual cortical neurons which in the adult responded only to vertical or horizontal lines. It has also been shown that other aspects of perception, such as depth perception, similarly depend upon early visual experience to develop properly. The general implication is that our perceptual abilities depend upon a wired-in inherited set of visual pathways whose function is modified by early experience.

Colour vision and parallel processing

Visual perception is a huge area, deserving a text book to itself and as you have seen it is complex even when simplified. The outline of visual processing given above refers to the perception of shape, based upon the neurons detecting specific features of the stimulus such as lines, angles and orientations. Colour vision is equally complex and will not be covered in detail here. However, a couple of observations will clarify some of the principles behind visual processing. As mentioned earlier, cone receptors in the retina are responsible for our colour vision. They contain the photochemical rhodopsin and the precise version of the chemical a neuron possesses determines the wavelength of light it responds to. Cones can contain one of three versions: one responds best to light in the red region of the colour spectrum, one responds to green and the third to blue. It was established centuries ago that all the colours we can see can be produced by mixing the three primary colours of red, green and blue, in the right amounts.

The three types of cone receptor – red, green and blue – provide a physiological confirmation of this idea. Each will be separately stimulated by light of the appropriate wavelength from a stimulus. Later in the visual system the relative level of stimulation across the populations of different cone receptors will be integrated

In Focus

◆

Blindsight

Weiskrantz (1986) has worked for some years on the phenomenon of blindsight. People suffering extensive damage to the primary visual cortex are blind, with no conscious visual experience. Weiskrantz found that if asked to discriminate colours, or the direction a stimulus was moving in, some 'blind' patients could perform significantly above chance. The whole exercise must have seemed very bizarre to them, as there was no conscious awareness of the stimuli. It seems that under these special circumstances, with the main visual pathway to the visual cortex destroyed, we can use an alternative pathway connecting the retina to visual cortical areas beyond the damaged primary area. This pathway has not yet been identified and although it can support some visual processing there is no suggestion that it could compensate for the drastic loss of vision in the blind person.

into the perceptual experience of a single colour – the colour of the stimulus. This model, based on the three types of cone receptor, is called the trichromatic theory of colour vision.

The processing of colour is therefore similar to that of shape. The colour of a stimulus is not passed intact from the retina into the brain, but broken down early in the process into its basic features of 'redness', 'greenness' and 'blueness'. The colour experienced is then synthesized in the cortex from the results of this basic analysis. Incidentally, some people suffer from colour blindness, particularly problems with seeing red and green; this may reflect problems with those particular cone receptors.

Shape and colour seem to be dealt with separately by the visual system and other studies show that movement is another stimulus property with its own pathways up to the cortex. This suggests that parallel processing is a fundamental characteristic of the visual system and it has been shown to operate right up to visual association cortex. Patients with damage to secondary and tertiary cortex may lose colour vision, with shape and movement perception left intact (a condition known as achromatopsia); some may lose movement perception, where stimuli are seen when still, but disappear when they move (akinetopsia). At some point of course, all these properties have to be integrated into our usual perception of stimuli with simultaneous shape, colour and movement. The details of this final stage are still vague.

The visual system breaks stimuli down into basic features at an early stage of processing and actively re-synthesizes them at later stages. Separate parallel pathways simultaneously process different properties, which are then integrated at cortical level. It is likely that these fundamental characteristics of perception as an active process involving parallel processing apply to other sensory systems as well.

Section summary

Visual receptors are found in the retina at the back of the eye. The two types of receptor are stimulated by either dim or bright light. Pathways run from the retina to the lateral geniculate nucleus of the thalamus and on to the visual cortex. Each neuron along the pathway responds to a particular light stimulus on the retina, called its retinal receptive field. Hubel and Wiesel showed that simple cortical cells respond to lines on the retina, while complex cells respond to angles and shapes. The ability of cortical cells to detect features of the stimulus is not innate, but acquired shortly after birth. Different populations of cone receptors in the retina are responsible for colour vision. As lesions to the cortex can selectively eliminate colour vision or movement perception, it seems that the visual system analyses and processes stimulus features in parallel, resynthesizing the whole stimulus at cortical level.

Chapter summary

- There are many methods for studying brain function, including electrical and chemical stimulation and recording, and physical destruction of brain tissue. Recent non-invasive techniques provide insights into the living human brain.
- Sensory and motor functions are localized to particular areas of the cortex. Although each hemisphere is associated with the opposite side of the body, the arrangement of sensory and motor functions within each hemisphere is identical.
- Cognitive functions such as language can be asymmetrically organized across the hemispheres. Damage to association cortex can produce aphasias, apraxias and problems with perception even though basic sensory and motor processes are intact.

- Sperry's work on the split brain showed that the right hemisphere had superior visuo-spatial abilities, while the left hemisphere contained language mechanisms.
- Subsequent studies on non-split-brain subjects demonstrated that the left hemisphere is an analytical sequential processor, while the right hemisphere processes stimuli as Gestalts, in parallel.
- The visual system analyses stimuli into basic features such as shape and colour, and resynthesizes the whole stimulus at cortical level. Feature detection in the visual system is acquired rather than innate.

Essay questions

1. Discuss the contribution of split-brain studies to our knowledge of hemisphere functional asymmetries. *(24 marks)*
2. There have been historical disputes on whether perception is an 'active' or a 'passive' process. Discuss the extent to which neurophysiological research supports either of these views. *(24 marks)*
3. Discuss the contribution of studies of aphasic patients to models of language mechanisms in the brain. *(24 marks)*

Further reading

Green, S. (1994) *Principles of Biopsychology*, Hove: Erlbaum.

Gives clear and comprehensive coverage of all the areas covered in this chapter.

Springer, S.P. and Deutsch, G. (1993) *Left Brain, Right Brain*, New York: Freeman.

Besides covering hemisphere functional asymmetries in great detail, this text also contains topics such as methodology in brain research, language disorders and some speculations on the nature of consciousness.

Chapter 7

Awareness

Simon Green

Preview

In this chapter we shall be looking at:

- types of bodily rhythms and internal body clocks
- brain mechanisms of sleep and dreaming
- functions of sleep and dreaming
- altered states of awareness
- phenomena and theories of hypnosis.

Introduction

We all experience altered states of awareness, even if we don't drink to excess or take drugs. About one third of our lives is spent in the altered state of sleep, which besides involving changes in awareness also represents one of our basic biological rhythms. The first part of the chapter therefore introduces bodily rhythms in general and then describes brain mechanisms involved in the control of sleep and dreaming. There are many theories about why we sleep and dream, and these are considered in later sections. Altered states of awareness can be produced by drugs and are also found in some clinical conditions such as schizophrenia and autism. These are discussed after a review of models of consciousness and self-awareness. Finally, the phenomena and controversies surrounding hypnosis are debated.

Bodily rhythms

The natural world is full of rhythms, such as the regular cycle of the seasons, the rise and fall of the tides, and the rising and the setting of the sun. The body also has its rhythms, some obvious such as the menstrual cycle and the alternation of sleeping and waking, others less obvious such as the regular variations in body temperature over a single day.

Many of these rhythms are clearly related to the physical properties of the world we live in. The cycle of the seasons depends on the earth's orbit around the sun. The alternation of day and night is due to the earth's rotation about its axis, and tidal flow reflects the gravitational influence of the moon on the earth. It would therefore be logical to assume that the rhythms we observe in living organisms are directly controlled by these external stimuli. But in fact the situation is more complicated than that. For instance, beach-living algae (single-celled plants) stay under the sand at high tide, burrow to the surface as the water recedes to allow for photosynthesis in the sunshine and then tunnel back under just before the tide returns. Is this regular rhythm controlled by tidal flows? A simple way to test this is to keep the algae in a laboratory with constant light and no tides. Despite the absence of environmental stimuli, they still burrow to the surface just after the time of high tide at their home beach and tunnel back under just before the tide returns.

The heliotrope ('sunseeking') plant opens its leaves during the day and closes them at night. It shows this pattern even if kept indoors in the dark, in time with the actual day/night cycle outside. In countries with fierce winters, the squirrel population hibernates. If these squirrels are kept in a laboratory in a constant warm environment, with alternating 12-hour periods of light and dark, they go through the hibernation routine at the appropriate time of year, increasing food intake and body weight and decreasing body temperature. In addition, they awake as spring approaches in the world outside.

These examples suggest that rhythmic activities can be inbuilt, or endogenous, so that they persist even when the environmental stimuli are absent. Algae are single cells and the controlling pacemaker is probably in the genetic material of the cell nucleus. Squirrels are mammals with complex brains, and hibernation is a complex activity probably controlled from pacemakers in the brain. However, even with these endogenous pacemakers, behaviour in the real world has to be adapted to external events such as winter or night-time, so that leaf opening or hibernation occurs at exactly the right time. Where external events have a role in rhythmic activities, they are called *zeitgebers* ('time-givers') and much of the research into biological rhythms has been aimed at unravelling the relationship between endogenous pacemakers and these *zeitgebers*.

Types of rhythm

As already mentioned, there are many biological rhythms in the natural world. A general classification divides them into three groups:

- *Ultradian* rhythms have a frequency of more than one complete cycle every 24 hours; an example we meet later is the oscillation between sleep stages during a single night's sleep.
- *Infradian* rhythms occur less than once every 24 hours, for instance hibernation in squirrels and the human menstrual cycle.
- *Circadian* rhythms occur once every 24 hours. The human sleep/waking cycle is a good example and many other physiological systems, such as body temperature, operate to the same rhythm. The opening and closing of the heliotrope's leaves is also a circadian rhythm.

❖ Activity 1 ❖

Think about your own sleep patterns.

- Do you sleep early and rise early, sleep late and rise late, or some combination?
- Do you need 6, 8 or 10 hours' rest at night? Or more, or fewer?
- Are you a 'morning' person, functioning more effectively soon after waking, or an 'evening' person, ready for action when twilight comes?
- Do you sometimes nap during the day?

Compare your pattern with someone else you know and you will find differences. Although inbuilt and generally similar across people, biological rhythms show individual differences in their precise patterning.

Pacemakers

Endogenous pacemakers, sometimes referred to as biological clocks, probably represent an inherited genetic mechanism. For example, regular rhythms of activity and rest can be measured in the unborn human embryo which has never been exposed to the outside world. But, as pointed out earlier, these rhythms have to respond to *zeitgebers* if the behaviour they control is to be fully coordinated with the external world. One of the most influential *zeitgebers* is light, and its role in fine-tuning bodily rhythms has been reasonably well mapped out.

Probably the most important pacemaker in the brain of birds and reptiles is the pineal gland. This structure contains light receptors which respond to external light penetrating the thin layer of skull that lies above the pineal. In turn, they influence the activity of neurons in the pineal. These neurons have a natural rhythmic activity and also convert the neurotransmitter serotonin into the hormone melatonin. Melatonin is then released into the general circulation, acts on many of the body's organs and glands, and seems to be responsible for the rhythmic nature of many activities. For instance, it acts on brainstem sleep mechanisms to help synchronize the phases of sleep and waking, and it has been shown that injections of melatonin can produce sleep in sparrows. The manufacture and release of melatonin is regulated by the amount of light falling on the pineal, decreasing as light increases. Research has shown, for instance, that chickens wake and become active as dawn breaks and melatonin secretion falls (Binkley 1979). This also means that their waking, although controlled by the biological clock in the pineal, is adjusted to the actual time that morning begins, which of course varies throughout the year.

In mammals, including humans, the pathways are more complicated. The main biological clock seems to be a small area in the hypothalamus, the supra-chiasmatic nucleus (SCN), whose neurons have an inbuilt circadian rhythmic firing pattern. This nucleus regulates the manufacture and secretion of melatonin in the pineal gland via an inter-connecting pathway. Another pathway connects the retina of the eye to the SCN. This allows the amount of light falling on the retina to influence the activity of SCN neurons and, indirectly, the release of melatonin from the pineal. So the link between light and melatonin production is maintained.

The pineal and the SCN function jointly as endogenous pacemakers or biological clocks in the brain. There are many bodily rhythms, and it is likely that there are other structures involved in maintaining their regularity, as we shall see later in relation to sleep.

The sensitivity of the pineal and SCN to light, and the role of melatonin in controlling sleep and activity amongst other things, mean that despite the endogenous nature of the clocks, their activity is synchronized with the light/dark rhythm of the world outside. Occasionally, slightly bizarre studies have allowed us to look at the effects of removing light as a *zeitgeber* and allowing these biological clocks to run free (see *In Focus* below).

In Focus

Michel Siffre's free-running biological clock

The most famous study of free-running biological clocks involved a French cave explorer, Michel Siffre, who in 1972 spent six months in an underground cave in Texas separated from natural light/dark cycles. He was wired up so that various body functions could be recorded. When he was awake, the experimenters put his lights on; when he went to bed, they turned the lights off. He ate and slept whenever he wanted. At first his sleep-waking cycle was very erratic, but it settled down to a fairly regular pattern with a periodicity of between 25 and 30 hours. When he emerged, it was the 179th day, but by his 'days' it was only the 151st.

Such studies show that subjects with free-running biological clocks settle to a rhythmic sleeping/waking pattern of about 25 hours, i.e. slightly longer than under normal conditions. So we can draw two conclusions:

- Our endogenous mechanisms can control sleep/waking cycles in the absence of light.
- The presence of light as a *zeitgeber* is necessary to re-set the clock every day so that the biological rhythm is perfectly coordinated with the external world.

As mentioned earlier, light affects melatonin secretion in chickens, triggering the chicken's waking routine. Something similar may well be happening in humans.

Such studies indicate how we use stimuli around us to coordinate our biological clocks. The gradual lengthening and shortening of the days is reflected in gradual shifts in rhythms of activity and sleep/waking cycles. These biological processes are also influenced by other stimuli, such as outside temperature and social patterns. Eskimos have regular sleep/waking cycles, even though they have continuous daylight in summer and continuous darkness in winter, showing that for them the social rhythms of life are the dominant *zeitgebers*.

Jet lag and shift work

Usually *zeitgebers*, such as light or social behaviour patterns, change only slowly, if at all. However, there are times when they change radically and quickly, and the usual coordination between our biological rhythms and the outside world breaks down. Modern civilization has led to two common examples, jet travel and shift work.

If you travel by plane from England to the USA, leaving at noon, you arrive at about 7 p.m. UK-time, but it would be 2 p.m. USA-time. All your physiological rhythms are working to UK-time, so that at 6 p.m. USA-time you are ready to sleep, with a falling body temperature and decreasing bodily arousal. This dislocation of our physiological rhythms from the outside world produces the sensation of jet lag that many people experience and which lasts as long as it takes for them to re-synchronize. Studies have shown that the quickest way to achieve this is to follow the local *zeitgebers* rather than your body, i.e. in the example above you should force yourself to stay awake until 11 p.m. USA-time and also adjust your meal times and socializing patterns. If you follow your biological clocks, adjustment takes much longer.

Strangely, jet lag is more severe travelling West to East (USA to the UK), than from East to West. This may be because it is easier to adjust the body clocks when they are ahead of local time (called 'phase delay') than when they are behind (a situation when they have to 'phase advance'). Because of its role in controlling body rhythms, melatonin has been studied as a possible treatment for jet lag and other desynchronization problems and although nothing very systematic has yet emerged it may eventually lead to an effective therapy.

Organizations and industries that work around the clock require their employees to do shift work. A classic pattern is to divide the day into three eight-hour shifts: midnight to 8 a.m., 8 a.m. to 4 p.m., 4 p.m. to midnight. Switching shifts obviously disrupts links between *zeitgebers* (light/dark, meals, social life, etc.) and biological rhythms and, as with jet lag, some time is necessary for readjustment. Many shift patterns require a turn around every week, with workers moving back one shift every time. The work with jet lag suggests that a week is barely enough time to allow for such a major resynchronization, so that workers are in a permanent state of 'jet lag', impairing performance and increasing stress. The backwards movement is the same as West to East jet travel, leading to the more difficult phase-advance situation.

Czeisler *et al.* (1982) found exactly this pattern in a Utah Chemical plant and recorded a high rate of health problems, sleep difficulties and work-related stress. He persuaded them to change to a phase delay system (moving a shift forwards every time) and to increase the shift rotation from 7 days to 21 days, allowing more time for adjustment. After nine months of the new system, worker satisfaction was significantly increased and factory output was higher.

The problems of jet lag and shift work are due to the way we have artificially dislocated the normal coordination between our biological clocks and the external world. We are the results of a long evolutionary history, in which the alternation of day and night has shaped the lives of all organisms. It is therefore no surprise that we should still be under the same influence. Sometimes, though, problems arise even when the relationship is not artificially disrupted.

Seasonal affective disorder (SAD) has become recognized as a clinical depression in humans that occurs during the autumn and winter months. You may recall how the hibernation of squirrels is an example of an infradian biological rhythm, adjusted to the changes in the seasons to allow the animal to survive times when food is hard to find. Although this seems largely a genetically preprogrammed behaviour, it has evolved under the influence of climatic conditions. Seasonal changes also affect people, with some developing SAD over the winter months. The key changes which trigger SAD in susceptible individuals could be external *zeitgebers* such as day length or temperature, or could be a relic of some evolutionary, ancient, inherited tendency towards a hibernation-like state. This might interact with the *zeitgebers* to produce the depressive state. Unlike the case of the squirrel, day length and light do seem important in SAD. One therapy that is effective in a proportion of SAD cases is light treatment, involving exposure to bright white light for at least an hour or so every day. This must be influencing the activity of the supra-chiasmatic nucleus, the pineal and the release of melatonin, but the precise way in which this direct interference with our biological clocks has an anti-depressant action is not understood.

Section summary

Bodily rhythms are found throughout the natural world, in both plants and animals. Evidence suggests that these rhythms are natural, controlled by endogenous pacemakers or biological clocks. These clocks can be set by external stimuli, referred to as '*zeitgebers*', such as light and dark. In mammals the main biological clock is the supra-chiasmatic nucleus, which responds to light falling on the eye by altering the release of melatonin from the pineal gland. Bodily rhythms can be disrupted by jet travel and shift work, leading to behavioural disorganization and stress. Day length changes are involved in seasonal affective disorder, which can be treated by exposure to bright artificial light during the day.

Sleep: circadian and ultradian rhythms

The 24-hour cycle of sleeping and waking is our most obvious biological rhythm. We spend around 30 per cent of our lives sleeping and for centuries have wondered about its function. Other bodily processes, such as body temperature, urine flow and release of hormones from the pituitary and adrenal glands, also show a circadian rhythm, with one peak and one trough every 24 hours. However, it is the sleep/waking cycle that has been most studied. One of the features of sleep is that there are several different identifiable types of sleep which we move between throughout the night in a regular pattern (see Fig. 7.1). This is an example of an ultradian rhythm.

One of the earliest debates in this area was whether sleep was simply the state the body fell into when it was not active, i.e. sleep as a passive process. You have probably read enough now to see that this is unlikely. The brain contains biological clocks which actively regulate physiological and behavioural processes. In the cave studies, sleep/waking patterns settled down to a consistent pattern despite the absence of

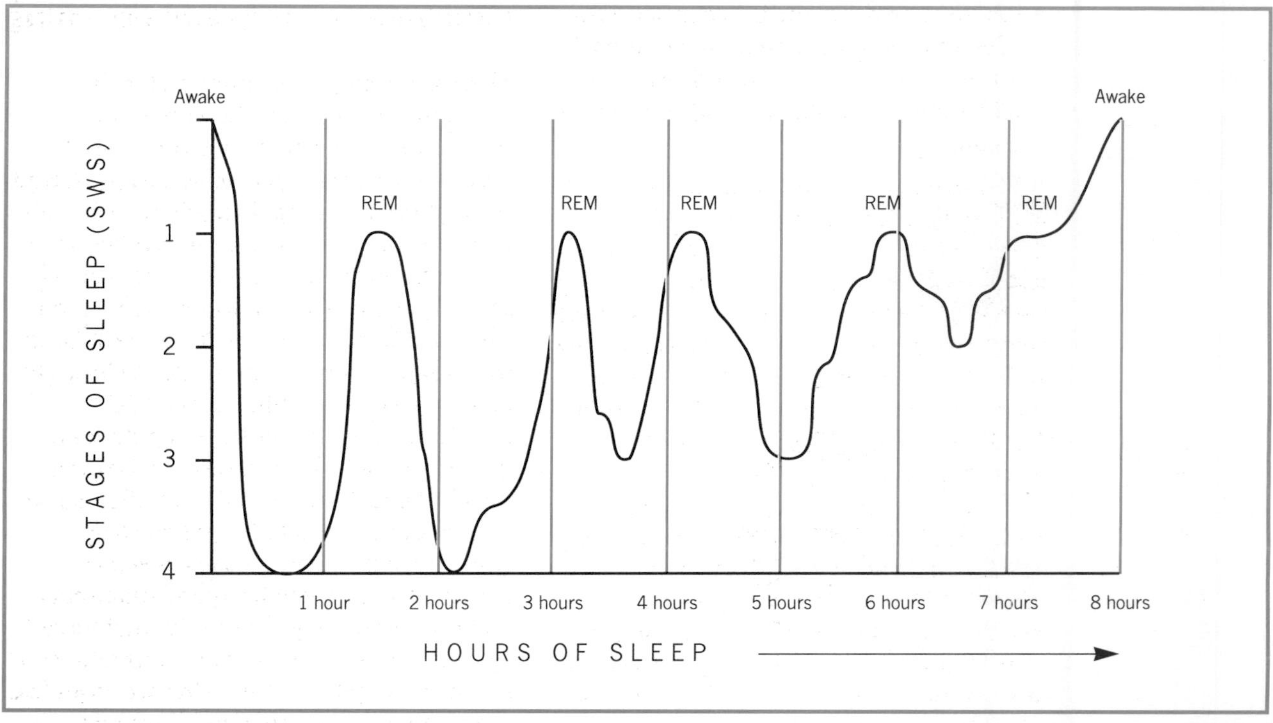

Figure 7.1
Pattern of sleep over one night

zeitgebers, while states such as hibernation are induced by the brain at the appropriate time of year. Biological rhythms in general reflect active control by brain mechanisms and sleep is unlikely to be different. The problem is to identify the specific brain mechanisms involved in sleep and to explain how they interact with the world outside. This may give us some idea of the functions of sleep.

Sleep – stages and types

The introduction of the electroencephalograph (EEG) in the 1930s was a crucial step in the investigation of sleep. Using it, Dement and Kleitman in the 1950s were able to demonstrate that sleep, far from being a quiet and peaceful phenomenon, consisted of clearly differentiated stages of brain activity. There are various approaches to defining the stages, but whichever is used, the EEG observations themselves are similar.

- Chapter 6 described how the EEG pattern can be either synchronized or desynchronized. When it is synchronized, there is a repeated wave form with a particular frequency (measured as cycles per second, or Herz, Hz), while when desynchronized, there is no consistent wave form.
- The waking, alert EEG consists of fast desynchronized activity.
- As we relax prior to sleep, the EEG becomes synchronized and alpha waves appear with a characteristic frequency of 8 to 12 Hz. Heart rate slows, muscle tension reduces and body temperature begins to fall.
- In stage 1 of sleep proper, the alpha waves disappear to be replaced by slower and smaller desynchronized activity.
- In stage 2, the EEG becomes synchronized with larger and slower waves interrupted by bursts of fast spiking activity, the sleep spindles. These last for a second or two and consist of high frequency (12 to 16 Hz) waves.
- Stage 3 is dominated by large slow delta waves (1 to 3 Hz), with spindles becoming less common. Heart rate, respiration and metabolic rate continue to fall.

- Finally, in stage 4 the EEG consists only of delta waves, metabolic rate is at its lowest and the arousal threshold (how difficult is it to wake the subject up) is at its highest.

These are known as the stages of 'slow-wave sleep' or SWS, as the EEG is characterized by synchronized slow-wave activity. However, sleep is a dynamic process and, after 30 minutes or so in stage 4 SWS, we ascend through the sleep stages to the light SWS of stage 2. At this point, about an hour and a half after sleep onset, the EEG suddenly shifts into the fast, desynchronized pattern of the aroused subject. Here arousal thresholds are at their highest and the skeletal muscles completely relax leaving the person effectively paralysed. Heart rate and respiration increase and rapid movements of the eyes occur. For this reason, this stage of sleep is called 'rapid eye movement' sleep, or REM. It is sometimes also referred to as 'paradoxical' sleep, as it combines features of bodily relaxation with an aroused EEG and the rapid eye movements.

After 15 minutes or so in REM we move back into light SWS and then descend into the deeper stages 3 and 4. This cyclical pattern (Fig. 7.1) repeats itself every ninety minutes or so (the ultradian rhythm mentioned earlier), giving five or six cycles per night. Towards morning we spend more time in light SWS, which seems to trigger more phases of REM. As we shall see, REM is associated with dreams and so we tend to dream more as morning approaches.

As mentioned earlier in the chapter, cycles of rest and activity can be recorded in the developing embryo and it has been shown that the sleep cycle of the new-born baby does not vary much over the first year. The rhythms of sleep are controlled by our endogenous biological clocks, although, as the baby grows, the activity of the clocks will become synchronized with the outside world, especially the light-dark cycle.

The sleep/waking cycle and the patterning of the stages of sleep are fundamental biological rhythms. So, what are their functions?

Functions of sleep and dreaming

There is no simple explanation for the functions of sleep and there are many hypotheses based on a wide range of observations and experiment. Sleep is found throughout the animal kingdom, although it can be hard to recognize in reptiles and other cold-blooded animals, since arousal states in these groups depend so much on external temperature and it can be difficult to distinguish sleep from inactivity brought on by the cold. In addition, the EEG recordings used to identify sleep stages in mammals come from the cerebral cortex, which is poorly developed in reptiles, so we are not even sure what reptilian sleep would look like in EEG terms. Sleep is clearly identifiable in birds and mammals and this alone suggests that it must have some function. There are humans who can get by on very little sleep – in rare cases less than an hour – but in general we all need between 6 and 8 hours. If it is universal, what happens if animals are deprived of it?

Rats deprived of sleep for around 21 days die, but this is complicated by the very stressful procedures they are put through

Activity 2

Think back to a time when you experienced significant sleep deprivation, perhaps an all-night party or foolishly revising during the night before an examination.

- Did you notice any effects the following day? These could have been feelings of tiredness, problems with concentration and perhaps difficulties with memory.
- The following night, did you sleep for much longer than usual, or only a little?

Excitement and stress can override our biological pacemakers and keep us awake when the body wants to sleep and arousal can minimize the psychological effects of sleep deprivation. Eventually we do have to recover some of the lost sleep, but usually only a fraction of what was lost.

in order to keep them awake. There have been many studies of voluntary sleep deprivation in humans and these provide more reliable data.

Sleep deprivation and restoration explanations

In a thorough review of the area, Horne (1988) concludes that studies of sleep deprivation in normal subjects show only the range of effects seen in the schoolboy, Gardner (see *In Focus*), together with some sleep recovery concentrated in stage 4 SWS and REM. Although the effects of sleep deprivation are not dramatic, they do involve cognitive abilities such as perception, attention and memory, while the recovery of stage 4 SWS and REM suggests that these are the critical phases. Horne therefore proposes that, in humans, *core sleep*, consisting of stage 4 SWS and REM, is essential for normal brain functioning, while the lighter stages of SWS are not essential and he refers to them as *optional sleep*. During core sleep the brain recovers and restores itself after the activities of the day (some details of what is being restored are covered later).

This hypothesis is similar to the restoration model put forward by Oswald (1980). He suggests that the high level of brain activity seen in REM reflects brain recovery, while an increase in the body's hormone activities during SWS reflects restoration and recovery in the body. They both agree that REM is essential for brain repair and this is supported by the high proportion of REM seen in the newborn baby, where it makes up 50 to 60 per cent of sleep time, gradually falling to the normal proportion of about 25 per cent as the child grows. The months before and after birth are a time of rapid brain growth and development so that, if REM is a time when such processes occur, it is logical that the baby should show increased REM sleep (see Fig. 7.2).

The difference between the two approaches lies in the proposed functions of slow-wave sleep. As total sleep deprivation produces few obvious effects on the body, Horne (1988) thinks that body restoration is not the purpose of sleep. He suggests that this occurs during periods of relaxed wakefulness, leaving core sleep to provide for the brain. However, Horne is specifically discussing human studies and it is quite possible that the sort of division put forward by Oswald could apply to non-human animals. As there are significant differences between species in the precise details of the sleep/waking cycle, it is possible that no single hypothesis could cover them all.

REM sleep deprivation and neurochemical explanations

Besides total sleep deprivation, many studies have investigated specific deprivation of REM sleep. In rats and cats this involved the now discredited 'flowerpot technique'. The animal was placed on an upturned flowerpot surrounded by water, with no possibility of escape. It would fall asleep and then pass into a phase of REM. You will

In Focus

Sleep deprivation record

The record for total sleep deprivation is held by a 17-year-old schoolboy, Randy Gardner, who in 1964 stayed awake for 264 hours (11 days). If sleep is a critical function, you might expect such deprivation to have severe effects. In fact Gardner did have blurred vision and incoherent speech, some perceptual disturbances such as imagining objects were people and a mild degree of paranoia, imagining that others thought him stupid because of his cognitive problems. He did not suffer from psychosis (a complete breakdown of mental functioning) and recovered quickly when he eventually slept. The first night he slept for 15 hours and in fact over that and following nights recovered only about a quarter of his lost sleeping time. Recovery was specific to particular stages, as two-thirds of stage 4 SWS and a half of REM sleep were recovered, but little of the other SWS stages.

Figure 7.2 Changes in proportions of SWS and REM sleep with age

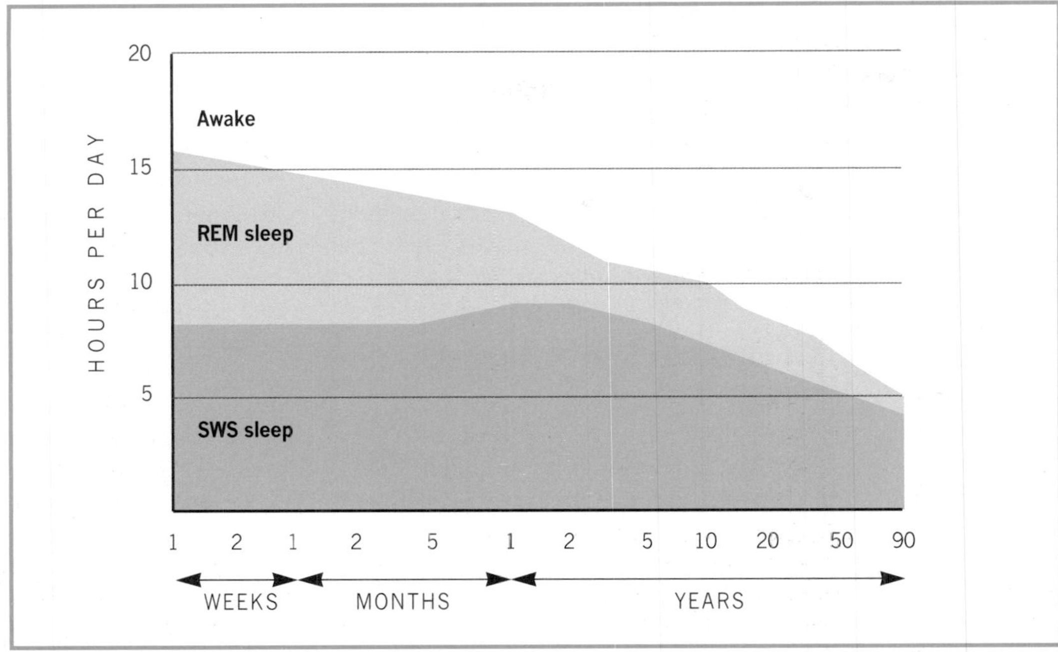

recall that in REM the skeletal muscles relax. In the flowerpot animal, as the neck muscles relax, the head falls into the water and the animal wakes up. Over a long period the animal becomes deprived of sleep in general and REM in particular. It is also permanently wet and highly stressed, which is why any results were very unreliable (and why the procedure is no longer used).

In humans, REM deprivation is achieved by monitoring the EEG recordings and waking the participants up when they enter a phase of REM. One of the earliest observations was that, after some nights of REM deprivation, there would be some REM rebound, i.e. an increase in REM sleep which partially compensated for the lost REM. This is entirely consistent with the findings from Randy Gardner and other studies of total sleep-deprivation.

This observation can be combined with those concerning the effects of drugs in the treatment of depression. Drugs (described in Chapter 5) such as the monoamine oxidase inhibitors (MAOIs) and tricyclics, besides their antidepressant action, also cause a drastic reduction in REM sleep. More interestingly, when drug treatment is discontinued, there is no REM rebound as you normally find after REM deprivation.

A possible explanation for this is that REM rebound occurs because the subject has been deprived of whatever it is that occurs during REM sleep and needs to make up the loss. If there is no rebound, perhaps it is because the treatment causing the loss of REM is itself providing whatever is necessary. What do the drugs do in the brain? Although they may have different mechanisms of action, antidepressants always increase levels of the neurotransmitters noradrenaline and serotonin. Therefore, it has been proposed by Stern and Morgane (1974) that the normal function of REM sleep is to enable levels of neurotransmitters to be restored after the day's exertions. An ordinary person deprived of REM suffers a loss of neurotransmitters that they make up when allowed to sleep normally by increasing the amount of REM sleep – REM rebound. A depressed person given antidepressants shows a decrease in REM because the drugs are themselves increasing neurotransmitter levels, removing the need for REM sleep and for any REM rebound when drug treatment stops.

This account is closely related to the restoration hypotheses of Oswald and Horne. REM sleep restores neurotransmitter levels, while REM deprivation causes a loss of noradrenaline and serotonin, and this also causes problems with any behavioural functions in which they are involved, such as perception, memory and attention. Total sleep deprivation would have similar effects because REM is also lost under these conditions. We return to neurotransmitters and sleep later, but for now we need to look at a very different approach.

Evolutionary and ecological approaches

Although sleep can be identified, with difficulty, in reptiles, it is found in its characteristic complexity only in birds and mammals. Even in mammals there are profound differences in total sleep time, amounts of SWS and REM, and cyclical organization. Many variables contribute to these differences, such as primitiveness (assessed in terms of brain development), body size and ecological niche (i.e. lifestyle). This variety has led to a number of hypotheses on the general functions of sleep across the animal kingdom.

Meddis (1979) proposes that sleep evolved to keep animals inconspicuous and safe from predators when normal activities were impossible. The importance of the predator or prey status is emphasized by the observation that predators (lions, tigers, etc.) sleep for much longer than prey animals (cattle, gazelle, etc.). It is as though the more dangerous your world, the less time you can afford to spend sleeping and vulnerable. One slight complication is that prey animals tend to be herbivores, needing to spend huge amounts of time grazing in order to take in sufficient food and simply have less time to sleep, although, of course, it still makes sense to be as inconspicuous as possible when not feeding.

The precise ecological niche an animal occupies can also affect the organization of sleep. Aquatic mammals such as dolphins and porpoises have particular problems, because prolonged sleep under water is dangerous, given that they are air breathers. The Indus dolphin gets around this by apparently sleeping for seconds at a time repeatedly throughout the 24-hour day. The bottlenose dolphin sleeps with one hemisphere of the brain at a time, alternating throughout the night; vigilance is never completely lost.

In land mammals, total sleep time is also related to body weight. Squirrels and shrews, for instance, sleep for about fourteen hours a day, cows and sheep for about four. The smaller an animal is, the greater its metabolic rate. Metabolic rate is an index of the activity in the body's physiological systems and the higher it is, the faster the body uses up energy resources. So, sleep in smaller mammals may be important for conserving these resources as well as keeping them safe from predators.

Because of the way sleep duration and patterning seems to depend on brain development, body size, lifestyle, etc., it is unlikely that any single explanation could account for the function of sleep in all animals. As sleep itself has many stages, it is even likely that different stages have different functions. For instance, REM sleep is most clearly identifiable in birds and mammals, which are warm-blooded (homiotherms), and not in reptiles, which are cold-blooded (poikilotherms). It has therefore been suggested that REM, during which brain metabolism is increased, evolved as a means of maintaining the brain's temperature during a period when it might otherwise fall to dangerous levels. The peculiar characteristics of REM sleep have generated much interest and a number of detailed hypotheses.

Section summary

Using the EEG we can identify four stages of slow-wave sleep (SWS) and a stage of REM or paradoxical sleep associated with dreaming. Sleep deprivation studies show that stage 4 of SWS and REM sleep are important for normal growth and function of the brain. Neurochemical approaches show that REM sleep is important for the functioning of brain neurotransmitter pathways. Sleep patterns also depend on lifestyle and ecological niche, as they vary greatly between different species. Overall, there is unlikely to be a single explanation for the functions of sleep.

Functions of REM sleep and dreaming

The most distinctive feature of REM sleep is dreaming. Although people woken up during SWS may report dreaming, they are much more likely to do so if they are woken during a phase of REM. Dreams can be bizarre and dramatic phenomena and it is easy to assume that they must have some deep meaning. Before looking at some of the possibilities, we must first draw a distinction between REM sleep and dreaming. REM sleep is a physiological state of the brain and body, defined using measures of the EEG, eye movements, muscle tone, etc. There can be *physiological theories* of REM sleep, such as the restoration of neurotransmitter levels described earlier, which are entirely independent of dreams and dream content. Theories which concentrate on the content and imagery of dreams themselves are *psychological theories* and it is important to keep this distinction clear.

Freud and dreams

Freud (1955) viewed the imagery of dreams as symbolic of hidden needs, wishes and fears stored in the unconscious. He referred to the remembered imagery of dreams as the 'manifest content', while the hidden meanings were the 'latent content'. Dream analysis was an important component of Freud's psychotherapeutic technique, in which he would interpret the symbolism of the dream imagery, usually in terms of repressed sexual desires. By bringing these to the surface they could be resolved and the patient's conflicts and neuroses removed.

Unfortunately, the whole technique depended on subjective report by the client and the personal interpretation of Freud. There is no independent confirmation of the link between dream imagery and repressed sexual content and indeed it is hard to imagine any scientific way of assessing the meaning of dream imagery. However, this has not prevented others putting alternative views.

Crick and Mitchison

Computer metaphors, popular for describing the brain, have also been applied to dreams. Crick and Mitchison (1983) propose that during dreaming the brain is 'off line'; during this phase it sifts through the information gathered during the day's waking activities and throws out unwanted material. According to this model, we dream to forget by a process of 'reverse learning'. The actual content of dreams is an accidental by-product and has no deep meaning or significance. Although this approach seems quite plausible, there is no direct experimental evidence for it and it stands only as an imaginative metaphor.

Evans

Evans (1984) also proposes that during dreams the brain is dealing with the day's input, but he argues that it is reorganizing the material and integrating it with stored memories. This allows the possibility that some problem-solving may occur during REM, as a particular dilemma encountered during the day can be worked on by the brain during dreaming sleep, making connections between current problems and past experience. An example often quoted (Borbely 1986) is of the chemist Kekule, who was trying to work out the structure of benzene. He dreamt of a snake swallowing its own tail and this gave him the solution of a continuous ring. Although anecdotes like this are interesting, there is little convincing experimental support for Evans' explanation.

Hobson

Dreaming is associated mostly with REM sleep and it is one of the striking characteristics of REM that during this phase the brain is as physiologically active as when we are awake. This activity has stimulated the idea that during REM and dreaming something important must be happening, as in the models of Crick and Mitchison, and Evans outlined above. A similar approach is taken by Hobson (1988), whose activation-synthesis hypothesis of dreaming, in contrast to some other researchers, is based on many years of intricate electrophysiological research into the brain mechanisms of REM.

The activation component of the hypothesis concerns the regular switching on of REM sleep as part of the endogenous cycle of sleep stages. The REM mechanism is based in the brainstem and when activated, it inhibits skeletal muscles (producing the characteristic 'paralysis' of REM) and excites activity in the forebrain via pathways ascending from the brainstem. As part of this forebrain activation, sensory and motor information is internally and automatically aroused and forms the bases for our dream experience. The dream itself represents a synthesis, or organization into a coherent structure, of this sensory and motor information, with a considerable input from the individual's past experiences and expectations.

The activation-synthesis hypothesis states that dreaming is an automatic part of the brain's sleep mechanisms and can be seen as an endogenous process with a large genetic component. It may have no significance beyond the brain's natural drive to organize material into coherent streams. However, activation-synthesis also allows for the brain to integrate sensory and motor information with individual memories and expectations, and this can happen in novel and creative ways. So the model can also account for any creative problem-solving aspect of dreams.

The model proposed by Hobson is similar in some ways to the approaches mentioned earlier, but differs in its breadth and in the way it is based on extensive experimental work. In fact, its breadth is a major problem in trying to validate it. Since dreams can be either meaningless or creative, it faces the difficulty of being able to explain any type of dream experience. This is not a problem confined to this model; dream research always runs up against the need for subjective interpretation of dream symbolism and it is virtually impossible to do this in a scientifically rigorous way. However, Hobson does provide a convincing account of the brain mechanisms underlying REM and dreaming and by basing psychological interpretation on the physiology of REM and dream states, makes it that much more convincing.

❖ Activity 3 ❖

Think back to dreams you have had. Are they usually coherent and understandable, or are they bizarre and intriguing or even frightening? Do you assume they are significant in some way, perhaps dealing with current anxieties or telling you the winner of the 3.30 at Kempton Park?

Compare them with a friend's; do you share similar imagery and do you have the same attitude towards them? Try to slot your experiences into one of the theories discussed above. Which offers the most convincing explanation?

Brain mechanisms of sleep

The role of endogenous clocks in the patterning of sleep/waking cycles was described earlier. However, the range of brain structures and pathways involved in them extends far beyond the pineal gland and supra-chiasmatic nucleus. Early work in the 1940s and 1950s concentrated on the functions of the reticular formation (RF) in the brainstem. This is a network of millions of neurons making up the core of the brainstem whose general function is to control, or modulate, the activity level of the brain, especially the cortex. Activity in the RF is influenced by levels of external stimulation and by internally generated thoughts, anxieties, etc. Studies soon showed that lesions of the RF could produce permanent sleep, while electrical stimulation would activate the cortex, arouse the animal and increase alertness.

In the 1960s the French neurophysiologist Jouvet analysed the system in more detail. He showed that damage to regions of the RF could have selective effects on sleep. Lesions of the locus coeruleus eliminated REM sleep, while lesions to the raphé nuclei eliminated slow-wave sleep; large lesions of the raphé nuclei prevented any sleep at all. He was also able to show that lowering brain levels of the neurotransmitter serotonin had similar effects to raphé lesions, and concluded that slow-wave sleep depends upon serotonin pathways running from the raphé nuclei up to the forebrain. The raphé nuclei may also be the site of action of melatonin released from the pineal gland and known to be involved in sleep regulation.

Neurotransmitter control of REM is more complicated. We covered some of the material earlier and it seems that noradrenaline is involved in some aspects of REM. There is also evidence that acetylcholine plays a role and, given that REM has many manifestations (eye movements, skeletal paralysis, cortical activation, etc.), it is not surprising that two or more transmitters should be involved. REM is inherently more complicated than slow-wave sleep.

Besides forebrain-endogenous clocks and brainstem sleep and arousal centres, there are other structures linked into our sleep circuits. It has been known for many years that electrical stimulation of some brain areas can induce sleep in a waking animal. This means that sleep is not a 'passive' state the brain falls into when nothing is happening but an 'active' state imposed on the brain under certain conditions. Sites from which sleep can be triggered are called 'hypnogenic centres' and they can be found in the brainstem and in the forebrain near the hypothalamus and the frontal cortex. Bremer's (1977) suggestion is that hypnogenic centres receive inputs from the brain's endogenous clocks and from the reticular formation. Normally they impose sleep in line with circadian rhythms, but this can be overridden by arousing inputs from the reticular formation. This would happen, for instance, at times of stress or anxiety, or if we are at a very good party (see Fig. 7.3).

A final contribution to the control of sleep may come from chemicals circulating in the bloodstream. These chemicals, two of which are Factor S and delta-sleep-inducing-peptide (DSIP), have been extracted from sleeping

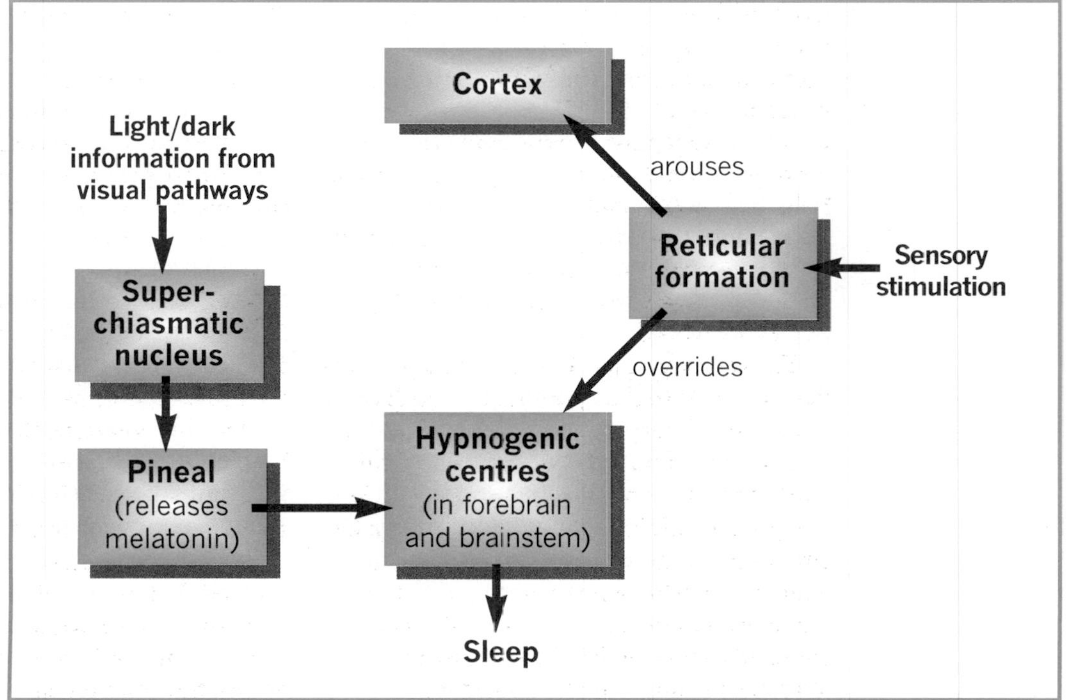

Figure 7.3 Brain mechanisms of sleep: activity of hypnogenic centres is a balance betwen inputs from brain pacemakers and the reticular formation

animals and shown to produce sleep when injected into awake animals. They are complex molecules with a number of effects on the body. Horne (1988) suggests that they may not have a major role in producing sleep, but may be able to regulate or modulate sleep rhythms. We have no idea how they interact with the brain mechanisms and circuits outlined above.

Section summary

Psychological theories of dreaming began with Freud's view that dreams represent repressed material, usually sexual. Modern approaches often use computer metaphors, seeing dreams as processing the day's information input. The most detailed explanation is offered by the activation-synthesis model which sees dreams as an automatic part of our sleep mechanisms, but with no symbolic significance. Theories of dreaming are difficult to test experimentally, as they rely on subjective reports and interpretation. Brain mechanisms of sleep involve the neurotransmitters serotonin and noradrenaline in the reticular formation, hypnogenic centres which actively impose sleep on the brain, and biological clocks.

Consciousness

We would all agree that sleep involves changes in the state of consciousness. What we may not agree on is a definition of consciousness itself. Is consciousness a solely human characteristic? In that case, is your cat or dog unconscious? Is consciousness the same as self-awareness, the ability to think about and reflect on our own actions? There are many approaches to explaining consciousness.

Freud and the unconscious

It was one of Freud's enduring contributions to bring consciousness and the unconscious into the mainstream of psychology. 'Conscious' refers to what we are aware of at any given time; the 'preconscious' refers to material just beyond consciousness which can be made conscious with little effort; and the 'unconscious' to deeply repressed material which can influence our thoughts, emotions and behaviour, but of which we are normally unaware. Analytical techniques are designed to bring this repressed material to conscious awareness so conflicts and neuroses can be resolved. Although many would disagree with the detail of this structuring of consciousness, the general observation that we can distinguish consciousness or self-awareness from the unconscious is unarguable. The distinction has even crept into cognitive psychology, where automatic processing is seen as preconscious or unconscious, and controlled processing as involving working memory and conscious awareness.

Consciousness and self-awareness

Most people would agree that the highest level of awareness is self-awareness – the sense of 'self' and the ability to introspect about ourselves and the world around us. This is found most highly developed in humans, where it is tied into our formidable language skills. You may recall Sperry's (1982) split-brain studies (see Chapter 6), in which the left hemisphere possessed language. When asked to comment on their performance in Sperry's experimental tasks, participants were only aware of what their verbal left hemisphere had been doing. If the non-verbal right hemisphere had controlled responding, for instance reaching with the left hand, the participant could not explain what was going on, to the extent of sometimes denying that the hand was their own! It seems from this that language is the vehicle for our conscious self-awareness, but other studies suggest a more complicated situation (see *In Focus*).

In Focus

◆

Non-verbal self-awareness

Imagine a chimpanzee with a splodge of paint on its forehead. It sits in front of a mirror. After some disturbance, as its first reaction is usually to treat the mirror image as an intruder, the chimpanzee settles down and eventually feels its forehead to investigate the splodge, using the mirror to guide its movements. Some chimpanzees will use a mirror to inspect their teeth, showing that they realize in some sense that the image in the mirror is themselves. Orang utans have been shown to react like this, but other higher primates, such as gorillas, gibbons and monkeys, do not. They behave as if the image is another animal, while mammals such as cats and dogs do not seem to 'see' the two-dimensional image as an animal at all. The ones that do 'realize' are showing some self-awareness in the absence of developed language skills.

A parallel can be drawn with the human right hemisphere, which in the split-brain work could read simple words and select appropriate objects, perform complex visuo-spatial tasks, cope with the world holistically rather than analytically, and generally demonstrate a different and 'non-linguistic' form of consciousness.

In an attempt to bring some order to this difficult field, Oakley (1985) has suggested a three-way division of awareness, shown in Table 7.1.

- At the lowest level we have reflex systems and simple associative learning such as classical conditioning. This he calls 'simple awareness'.
- The next level he refers to as 'consciousness', which consists of representational systems. By these he means mechanisms by which the brain can represent external events, using information-processing systems such as complex learning, reasoning and memory. All these help the animal to know about the world and Oakley considers this stage to reflect the emergence of 'mind'.
- The final level of awareness in Oakley's system is self-awareness, the awareness of one's inner life and of being aware. This representation of ourselves leads to the formation of the self-image and our concept of our 'self'. It also means that we can accept that others have similar systems, which leads to complex communication and to the ability to understand the internal worlds of other people.

Table 7.1 Oakley's levels of awareness

Type of awareness	*Where found*
Simple awareness (e.g. reflexes, classical conditioning)	Simple nervous systems Subcortical structures in advanced nervous systems
Consciousness (e.g. complex learning, reasoning, memory)	Advanced nervous systems – limbic system and cortex
Self-awareness (e.g. self-image, self-concept)	Highly evolved cortex – in humans and other primates

Levels of awareness are linked to brain development. Simple awareness is found in all animals with even the most basic of nervous systems and in higher animals the necessary mechanisms are located in subcortical regions. Consciousness requires a complex brain, with forebrain structures such as the limbic system and the cortex as found in rats, cats and dogs. Self-awareness is a property of a highly evolved cortex and as such is found in humans and possibly, as discussed above, in some non-human primates.

This model is not universally accepted but it does provide a framework for talking about awareness systematically. Information processing is seen as a way of representing the world internally, and consciousness emerges when this representation becomes sufficiently complex, using learning, memory and reasoning to organize behaviour. On this basis, cats, dogs, monkeys and the human right hemisphere are all conscious. Self-awareness is the highest level of awareness and matches what many people think of as our distinctive human subjective consciousness. Oakley thinks that in humans the left and right hemispheres contain two different representational systems, one analytic and the other holistic, with perhaps separate self-representations and separate self-awarenesses. The evidence for the right hemisphere's self-awareness comes from split-brain work and as such is not totally convincing (see Chapter 6 for an evaluation of the split-brain studies). A general advantage of Oakley's system is that levels of awareness are separated from considerations of language, although language clearly makes self-representation (thinking about oneself) much easier.

A final point to make is that this view of awareness and consciousness sees them as properties of the brain, with higher levels emerging as the brain evolves. There is no distinction between mind and brain, with consciousness and self-awareness simply aspects of brain function which have evolved as means of representing the world internally, and so organizing and guiding behaviour more effectively.

Altered states of awareness

The systems described above emerge from the brain and can be affected by natural or imposed changes in brain function. The simplest way to alter someone's state of awareness is to hit them hard over the head, producing unconsciousness. A less damaging way is to let them fall asleep. After the drowsy stage dominated by alpha waves they enter slow-wave sleep and then REM, during both of which they are far less reactive and far less aware of the external world. This emphasizes how dependent we are on patterns of brain activity for our consciousness and self-awareness, and there are many dramatic conditions which lead to subtle changes in awareness.

Drugs

Drugs have been used since humans colonized the world to induce altered states of awareness. The hallucinogens such as LSD and mescaline (see Chapter 5) can produce a profound loss of self-awareness along with hallucinations and delusions, and were taken, especially in the 1960s, in the hope that they would reveal new and creative levels of awareness. There is no strong evidence that they did, although our knowledge of the pharmacology of hallucinogens has allowed us to link their effects to the brain neurotransmitter serotonin.

Psychosis

Some abnormal conditions such as schizophrenia and manic-depressive psychosis are characterized by a fragmentation of the mind that often includes a loss of self-awareness and insight, together with symptoms of hallucinations and delusions. Again, these are almost certainly caused by variations in neurotransmitter function or by structural damage affecting the high-level circuits controlling our conscious self-awareness. At the psychological level, Frith (1992) has proposed that the symptoms of schizophrenia are caused by a loss of representational processes. He points out that one result of the way we can represent ourselves and the world we inhabit is that we know where things come from. If our arm moves, we know it is us moving it and if we hear thoughts in our head, we know they are our thoughts. This is part of our high-level representational system (self-awareness in Oakley's model). If it breaks down, then we may attribute the movement or the 'thoughts' to outside agencies, perhaps leading to the delusion that outside forces are moving our arm, or that we are hearing voices talking to us. There is as yet no direct evidence for this hypothesis but it does emphasize that schizophrenia, besides any brain malfunction, is also characterized by profound changes in awareness.

Autism

A more subtle change is seen in childhood autism, a disorder dominated by a failure to make effective social and emotional contact with other people. Frith (1989) has proposed a 'theory of mind' explanation. Part of the self-awareness system discussed above allows us to put ourselves in the position of other people; we assume their minds work like ours, meaning that we can understand and interpret their actions, and thus effectively communicate. If this level of awareness does not develop, we are left stranded. A example often quoted is the Smartie box test. In this test, you show a child a full box of Smarties. As he or she watches, you tip the smarties into a drawer and refill the box with marbles. You then ask the child to predict what another child would say if brought into the room, shown the box and asked what was in it. The standard child would say 'Smarties'. They know they have been switched, but they also know that the second child hasn't seen the switch. The autistic child says 'marbles', because that is what is in the box and they cannot put themselves in the position of the second child who hasn't seen the switch; they have a defect in the highest levels of representation and awareness.

Dissociative identity disorder

A final example of the way consciousness and awareness can be fragmented is in many ways the most dramatic. Multiple personality was once treated with suspicion and scepticism, but has now been accepted as a genuine category of abnormal behaviour and is referred to as 'dissociative identity disorder' (DID). Dissociative identity disorder is defined as the existence of two or more fully integrated egos, or 'alters', within an individual, that have different styles of being, behaving and feeling, independent of each other. So much so, that the different alters may be completely unaware that others exist. It should be distinguished from schizophrenia, which involves a fragmentation of thoughts and feelings within an individual and not the manifestation of separate identities. Perhaps the best way to describe it is in terms of one of the most famous cases (Thigpen and Cleckley 1954; see *In Focus* on next page).

Nowadays we are sure that DID exists as a recognizable condition, although in one or two celebrated cases it seems to have been manufactured as a defence for accused criminals, in which cases it can be hard to disprove. Validated cases seem to emerge in childhood although diagnosis is not usually until adolescence. It is often associated with other abnormal behaviour and experiences such as depression, phobias and suicidal ideas.

Explanations of DID, whether psychodynamic or via learning theory, concentrate on the need to cope with early stressful events such as child physical or sexual abuse or infantile sexual conflicts. Psychodynamic approaches would emphasize the splitting off of that 'personality' experiencing the trauma by repression into the unconscious. Learning theorists would explain DID as a complex learnt avoidance response. Psychoanalytic treatment is often successful and DID provides some of the best evidence for the existence of Freudian concepts such as repression and the unconscious. There seems little doubt that patients with DID have 'forgotten' large parts of earlier experiences.

In Focus

The case of Eve White

Eve White had been in therapy for some months. She was a shy and retiring figure, suffering from headaches and blackouts. Then, instantaneously, another personality emerged during one of the sessions. This personality was carefree and extrovert, and referred to herself as Eve Black. Although each personality talked about and wanted to learn more about the other, they were independent and intact personalities in their own right, with their own memories, attitudes and emotions. At a later stage a third personality, Jane, appeared. She was more mature and capable than Eve White, for whom she developed a deep affection. The three personalities could be present in the same therapy session at different times and it was during one of these that a final integrated personality emerged. This was more identified with Jane, but with aspects of the others. The patient decided she could live with this personality, but did change her name to Evelyn White to emphasize that it was not the same as any of the others.

It should be noted that this account is based on the therapist's notes. A later book written by the patient herself (Sizemore and Pittillo 1977) claimed that the patient's personality continued to fragment after therapy stopped. Eventually twenty-one independent personalities made their appearance, usually emerging in threes as the previous set faded. She apparently came to a final resolution by realizing that the personalities were aspects of herself and not complete strangers.

The existence of DID contradicts our belief that the human body is inhabited by a single personality, or mind, or psyche. More positively, it supports the view that the brain is capable of an extraordinary amount of complex processing and integration of life experiences. Remember with the split-brain studies (see Chapter 6), how in one patient the right-hemisphere/left arm system seemed to have a 'mind' of its own, choosing clothes that the woman did not want to wear. This observation may in some small way be linked to the phenomenon of DID.

We usually know ourselves as integrated and unitary personalities through our conscious self-awareness. The existence of the altered states described above need not alter this self-perception, which may be the brain's way of ensuring consistency in behaviour. Could we cope and behave effectively with a shifting view of our self and self-image? However, the fact that we see ourselves as 'one' does not mean that there are no other levels and types of consciousness buried within us.

Section summary

Consciousness and self-awareness are not easy to define. Oakley has proposed three levels of awareness, ranging from simple awareness to consciousness and on to self-awareness. Higher levels of awareness emerge as the nervous system becomes more complex, so that self-awareness is found only in humans and possibly in chimpanzees and orang utans. Altered states of awareness can be caused by drugs and are also associated with clinical conditions such as schizophrenia, autism and dissociative identity disorder. Evidence shows that although we perceive ourselves as integrated personalities there are other levels of consciousness within us.

Hypnosis

Hypnosis can be defined as an altered state of consciousness or awareness in which the hypnotized person can be influenced to behave and to experience things differently than in the ordinary waking state (Rubin and McNeil 1983). An alternative definition would be that it represents a social interaction in which one person responds to suggestions made by another person for experiences involving alterations in perception, memory and voluntary action (Kihlstrom 1985).

These two definitions are quite similar, but do differ in one critical assumption. The first assumes that hypnosis represents an altered state of consciousness compared with normal, while the second makes no such assumption. This difference reflects the main controversy in the area. Before we can discuss the issues in detail, we need to consider some of the features of hypnosis.

Inducing hypnosis

A hypnotist will ask an individual to focus on a particular spot or object and then run through a brief relaxation procedure, suggesting that arms and legs are gradually becoming heavier and lethargic and that the person is feeling drowsy. Then they are given a series of suggestions to test hypnotic susceptibility, graded from simple to difficult. Examples from the Stanford Hypnotic Susceptibility Scale would be:

- arm lowering: it is suggested that an outstretched arm is becoming heavier; the arm should gradually fall
- mosquito hallucination: it is suggested that a mosquito is buzzing around the person's head; they try to brush it away
- age regression: the person is asked to imagine being back at school and may be asked to recall the experience or write a passage which should appear in an age-related style
- arm immobilization: the participant is unable to move an arm after the suggestion that it is immovable
- posthypnotic amnesia: events occurring during hypnosis will not afterwards be recalled by the person unless a prearranged signal is given.

There are twelve items in the scale and susceptibility to hypnosis is measured by how far up the scale the participant goes. Using this type of procedure, it has been shown that about 15 per cent of people are highly susceptible, about 10 per cent highly resistant while the rest show varying degrees of susceptibility. Stage hypnotists use a variety of other entertaining techniques such as post-hypnotic suggestion, in which the participant is instructed during hypnosis that when they hear a trigger word after the session they will act in a certain way, such as barking when they hear the word 'Denmark'.

Hypnosis and personality

Highly susceptible individuals often show similar traits. They tend to become easily absorbed in imagination and fantasy. They also have a positive attitude towards hypnosis and expect to be influenced by hypnotic suggestions. Resistant individuals are less imaginative and fantasy-prone and do not expect to be influenced (McIlveen 1995). This distinction becomes important when we discuss theories of hypnosis later.

Practical applications of hypnosis

Hypnotic recall

Witnesses to crimes are sometimes hypnotized on the assumption that material unavailable to normal recall may be recovered under hypnosis. They may be encouraged to visualize the incident as if it were a television programme with freeze-frame control. McIlveen (1995) has summarized some of the potential drawbacks with this procedure:

- Suggestions from the hypnotist may be incorporated into memory and 'recalled' as factual by the witness.
- Hypnotized witnesses sometimes recall details which are incorrect.
- The witness is often more confident of details recalled under hypnosis than standard witnesses, which can mislead police and juries.
- Social pressure to recall material encourages guesswork.

Nowadays, evidence uncovered using hypnosis would not be used without independent corroboration.

Hypnotic regression

Breuer and Freud (1895) pioneered the use of hypnosis in uncovering repressed childhood memories as an aid to resolving adult conflicts and neuroses. Many hypnotized people can recall impressive detail of their childhoods which they assumed were forgotten. Unfortunately, it is often impossible to confirm the accuracy of these memories; memory as such is a reconstructive process (see Loftus and witness memory, Chapter 15) and is therefore vulnerable to error. It may also be influenced by suggestions from the therapist.

This issue has become a major problem for psychology, as cases of childhood sexual abuse are sometimes based on hypnotic regression. This introduces the possibility of the so-called 'false memory syndrome' in which, however convincing and convinced the individual may be, the recovered memories could, in fact, be inaccurate. Without independent corroboration it is virtually impossible to assess the reliability of memories regained through hypnotic regression. A recent report from the British Psychological Society (Andrews *et al.* 1995) concluded that recovered memories can be accurate, but could not suggest a straight-forward way of validating them.

Hypnotic reincarnation

This is a more dramatic version of hypnotic regression, in which individuals claim to recall previous lives, often with impressive detail of time and place. Although they usually claim never to have been in that place or to know anything of that way of life, close examination often reveals discrepancies in their accounts. Wagstaff (1981) reports a case of a man who believed he had been a seaman in Nelson's time, speaking under hypnosis in naval jargon. It turned out that he liked reading seafaring novels set in that period. It may be that hypnotic reincarnation is related to the high levels of fantasy and imagination associated with susceptibility to hypnosis.

Hypnosis and pain

There is no doubt that hypnotic procedures are effective in controlling pain in a range of clinical settings (Wadden and Anderton 1982), such as dentistry, childbirth and with burn victims. The controversy is not whether it works, but how. The techniques of hypnosis include relaxation and an expectation that pain will not be felt, which in turn reduces anxiety. It may be that these effects themselves reduce the experience of pain. A further complication is that 'pain' involves the physical sensation, the emotional response or feeling and the reporting of the pain to the hypnotist or doctor. It is still unclear which of these is affected by hypnosis, although studies with the cold pressor test (which is discussed later) suggest that the effect is not on the physical impact, but on the subjective emotional response.

Theories of hypnosis

These can be divided into two main types:

- *State theorists* believe that hypnosis involves special processes and is qualitatively distinct from the non-hypnotized condition.
- *Non-state theorists*, while not disputing the phenomena of hypnotism, explain it in terms of processes operating in other situations.

Hypnosis as an altered state of consciousness

The most popular of these approaches is that of Hilgard (1977), whose dissociation model proposes that in hypnosis, experiences are dissociated or separated from conscious awareness. Hilgard sees our cognitive processes as having a central control which directs a variety of sub-systems. These subsystems, such as conscious awareness, memory and the sensation of pain, can be separated from each other by 'amnesic barriers' through hypnotic suggestion, which can thus determine which experiences are accessible to conscious awareness. The hypnotized person moves his or her arm, brushes away a mosquito or endures painful stimuli because these actions and experiences have become separated from conscious awareness.

An important feature of Hilgard's model is the 'hidden observer'. This is a component or segment of consciousness which remains aware during the hypnotic experience, providing a route to awareness and able to comment on the actions and feelings of the hypnotized participant. It can be demonstrated using the cold pressor test (see *In Focus* below) and in other ways. For instance, Hilgard (1973) induced hypnotic deafness in a participant but also suggested that he should raise a finger when asked if there was any part of him that could still hear. Deafness was convincingly established, but the finger did rise when the question was asked. In Hilgard's view, this is the hidden observer monitoring the situation and replying to the question without the participant's awareness.

Non-state explanations of hypnosis

This approach accepts hypnotic phenomena but proposes that they can be explained using well-established psychological principles. The most important are presented below:

- *Compliance and demand characteristics:* The participant enters a social contract with the hypnotist, leading to the expectation that they will be hypnotized and should comply with suggestions. If it is a public show, there are additional social pressures not to 'spoil' the performance. The situation has powerful demand characteristics, as studied by Orne (Spanos 1982).
- *Role expectation*: Participants often believe in hypnosis and accept that they will fulfil the role of a hypnotized subject.

In support of their position, non-state theorists point to other observations:

- All hypnotic phenomena can be imitated by non-hypnotized people, indistinguishably from the hypnotized (Barber 1979). However, this does not seem a powerful argument: people can imitate clinical depression successfully, but that is not to say that clinical depression does not exist. The crucial point is that the hypnotized person believes they are in a different state, while the imitator does not (McIlveen 1995).

In Focus

The cold pressor test

The cold pressor test is widely used as a measure of pain sensitivity. People have to keep their arm in ice-cold water for as long as possible, which under normal circumstances is about 25 seconds. Hypnotized people can extend this to about 40 seconds. However, when Hilgard (1977) asked the hidden observer to write down ratings of the level of pain they were much higher than the participant's verbal report. The hypnotic suggestion apparently induces an amnesic barrier between the segment of consciousness responding to the suggestion and the intensity of the pain itself. The hidden observer, however, remains aware of the true level of pain. Whether the hidden observer exists or not, these observations do suggest that conscious self-awareness can be dissociated from other aspects of experience and behaviour.

- No measure of brain activity successfully distinguishes between the hypnotized and non-hypnotized states consistently (Sarbin and Slagle 1972). Some researchers feel that hypnosis is associated with specific changes in brain electrical activity (Crawford and Gruzelier 1992), but findings are hard to replicate and are often found in states of relaxation and meditation. Again, this may not be critical. It is possible that we are looking at the wrong measures or in the wrong part of the brain for hypnotic phenomena.
- Hypnotic induction and relaxation training can lead to similar levels of hypnotic susceptibility. Expert ratings also failed to distinguish self-reports of subjects experiencing hypnotic induction from those experiencing relaxation training, and the authors (Council and Kenny 1992) conclude that the state of consciousness produced by the two procedures is indistinguishable.
- People most susceptible to hypnotic induction score highly on measures of fantasy and imagination, suggesting that these are important elements in the hypnotic experience.

Conclusions

There is no clear answer to the state versus non-state controversy. The state theory is almost impossible to disprove, as you can always argue that the precise markers for the altered state have not yet been discovered. Some phenomena, such as hypnotic-induced pain relief and the 'hidden observer' are not easy to explain in conventional psychological terms. As Gregg and Wagstaff (1990) conclude, regardless of the view you take, at least the hypnotized subject is no longer seen as a passive automaton blindly following instructions, but as an active agent in the procedure. There is also the final argument, that if hypnosis works to alleviate pain, for instance, the academic argument is in practical terms irrelevant.

Section summary

Hypnotized people can be influenced to behave differently than in the ordinary waking state. There is controversy, though, over whether it is actually a different state of awareness. Scales measuring susceptibility show that about 15 per cent of people are highly susceptible and that these score highly on measures of fantasy and imagination. Hypnotic regression and recall are vulnerable to problems of independent verification, but hypnosis is valuable in clinical pain relief. Theories of hypnosis divide into state and non-state explanations. State theories propose that different areas of experience and behaviour can be separated from conscious awareness. Non-state approaches explain hypnosis using established psychological principles such as compliance. Evidence cannot yet distinguish between the two.

Chapter summary

- Bodily rhythms are controlled by endogenous biological clocks which can be set by external triggers or *zeitgebers* such as light and dark. Rhythms can be disrupted by jet travel and shift work leading to behavioural disorganization and stress, while day-length changes can lead to winter depression.
- EEG studies identify four stages of slow-wave sleep and a stage of REM sleep associated with dreaming. Stage 4 SWS and REM are important for normal growth and development of the brain. Sleep patterns also depend on lifestyle and ecological niche and vary greatly between species.
- Freud's theory saw dreams as representing repressed material. Modern approaches often use computer metaphors, but all theories of dreaming

are difficult to test experimentally. Brain mechanisms of sleep involve brain neurotransmitters, hypnogenic centres and biological clocks.

- Oakley proposes three levels of awareness, with higher levels emerging in more complex nervous systems. Self-awareness is found in humans and perhaps in chimpanzees and orang utans. Altered states of awareness can be caused by drugs and are also found in some clinical conditions. We all contain different levels of consciousness within us.
- Explanations of hypnotic phenomena divide into state and non-state. The first approach sees hypnosis as an altered state of awareness. Non-state theorists use psychological principles such as compliance, obedience and personality to explain behaviour under hypnosis. Evidence at present cannot decide between the two views.

Essay questions

1 Discuss psychological insights into the functions of sleep. *(24 marks)*

2 Using studies of altered states of awareness, discuss approaches to the psychology of consciousness. *(24 marks)*

3 Describe and evaluate theories of hypnosis. *(24 marks)*

Further reading

Borbely, A. (1986) *Secrets of Sleep*, London: Penguin.

A readable survey of sleep, dreaming and biological rhythms.

Oakley, D.A. (1985) *Brain and Mind* (Edited collection), London: Methuen.

A fairly high-level set of papers for those interested in theoretical approaches to consciousness and self-awareness.

McIlveen, R. (1995) 'Hypnosis', *Psychology Review*, 2 (November), pp. 8–12.

McIlveen, R. (1996) 'Applications of hypnosis', *Psychology Review*, 2 (February), pp. 24–7.

These two articles present a clear and concise account of the phenomena, theories and applications of hypnosis.

Chapter 8

Motivation, emotion and stress

Simon Green

Preview

In this chapter we shall be looking at:

- physiological approaches to motivation, emphasizing the role of homeostatic physiological drives
- psychological models of motivation
- the role of physiological and psychological factors in emotion
- the effects of stress on health
- methods of coping with stress.

Introduction

Motivation and emotion are often discussed together in psychology textbooks. They are both terms which are used to explain large areas of human experience, particularly the arousing and directing of behaviour. Everybody has a general idea what the terms mean. Unfortunately, psychology has to define terms in ways that are clear and unambiguous, and this sometimes produces research and theories which can seem a long way from everyday life. Much of the work on the physiology of motivation and emotion has been done with non-human animals, and so we also have to consider whether applying the results to humans is justified. Therefore, the first sections of this chapter deal with physiological and psychological approaches to motivation and emotion. Stress is also linked to arousal and emotion, but research has focused on the negative effects of stress and how individuals can cope with it. This work is covered in the final section.

Motivation

Motivation is that area of psychology concerned with the arousing and directing of behaviour. An extreme view would be that all behaviour has some purpose, i.e. it is directed towards some particular goal. Sometimes the purpose seems obvious, such as making and eating a meal when hungry, or revising hard to prepare for an exam. Sometimes the motivation for a particular behaviour is less clear; walking the Derbyshire dales or listening to old Beatles records would be examples of simple behaviours with no easily defined motivation (such as hunger or academic success). The clearest examples of motivated behaviour come from the study of primary or physiological drives, and are associated with the concept of *homeostasis.*

Claude Bernard (1856) in the nineteenth century was the first to emphasize the importance to survival of the maintenance of a constant internal environment. The internal environment of the body consists of such systems as the oxygen content of the blood, the concentration of various nutrients such as glucose, the water balance of the body, and body temperature. All of these systems can only fluctuate within narrow limits if health and survival are to be maintained. This stable equilibrium of body systems is called 'homeostasis', a term introduced by Cannon (1932).

As a system departs from the stable state, for instance as we expend energy or go out into the cold, the body tries to restore homeostatic equilibrium through physiological and behavioural mechanisms. For instance, if we have not eaten for some time we develop a bodily or tissue need for food. This need leads to a drive to eat, and eating reduces the drive and restores homeostasis. This sequence is a simple example of behaviour motivated by a primary physiological drive aroused by a tissue need, and a whole class of motivated behaviours is represented by these homeostatic primary drives (see Fig. 8.1).

Figure 8.1
A simple model of motivation – homeostatic drive-reduction

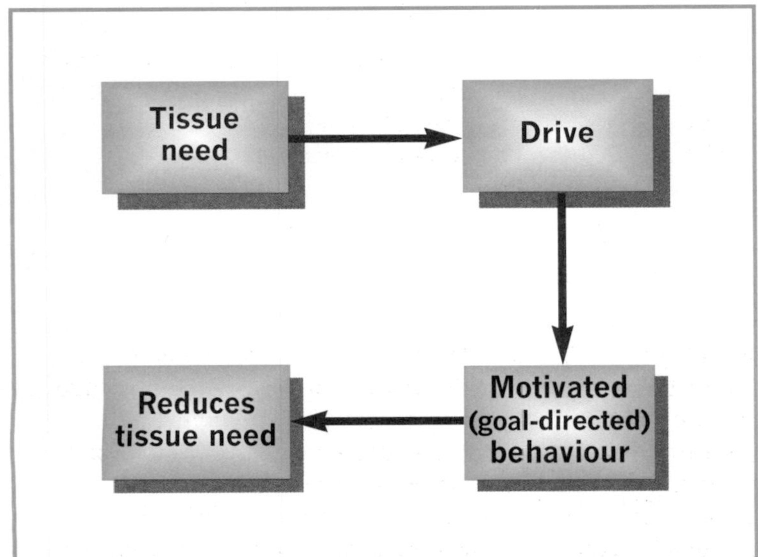

In fact many approaches to motivation try to explain more complicated behaviours using similar models, in which the behaviour is driven by an internal state of 'need'. More recent approaches place emphasis on the *environment* we live in, and the role it plays in arousing and guiding our behaviour. It has even been shown that the behaviour associated with basic homeostatic drives, such as food-seeking, can be influenced by the environment, and that they are not always entirely biological. Homeostatic drives represent the physiological approach to the study of motivation. The simple picture of a tissue deficiency leading to a specific need which in turn arouses the appropriate behaviour is very appealing, and many thousands of experiments have been done to see if this is indeed the case. Most of these have been done on non-human animals, especially rats, and hunger has been the drive most studied.

Hunger

We go without food for some hours, we feel hungry, we eat, the hunger drive disappears. The overall picture looks simple, but even at this level there are complications. Our diet is made up of carbohydrates such as sugar, proteins, fats and small amounts of trace elements and amino acids vital to cellular function throughout the body. So, when we feel hungry, what do we feel hungry for? The most important need is for the foods we use for energy, in particular carbohydrates and fats. The energy content of these foods is measured in calories, and the best index of caloric intake is body weight, as calories taken in but not immediately used in cellular and muscular activity are stored as fat.

One of the most impressive aspects of food intake regulation is that body weight is usually maintained within fairly narrow limits, apart from the dynamic phases of growth and during pregnancy (although it is fair to say that at least in the West, obesity is now becoming a widespread problem). So, although we need a balanced diet, research has focused on the regulation of caloric intake and body weight.

In Focus

Davis' cafeteria study

The extreme position on control of food intake by homeostatic drives would be that, if given free choice, we would select a balanced diet. In 1928 Davis gave human infants a selection of food dishes and allowed them to choose what they wanted at meal times. He reported that they chose a balanced diet and thrived during this 'cafeteria' study. However, he included only simple plain foods, without sweet extras like ice cream and chocolate. We all have favourite foods and will eat them even when there is no specific need. Rats will press bars to receive saccharine, a sweet-tasting but non-nutritive substance, and will overeat sugary foods if they are available (Morgan 1965). Children eat more Smarties if they are multi-coloured than if they are all one colour. In general, taste and appearance can outweigh the physiological needs of the body.

This regulation seems to anticipate needs, as we take meals according to routines set by social and cultural patterns (breakfast, lunch, dinner) and, again talking about relatively prosperous societies, we do not wait until we feel desperately hungry before eating. This anticipatory function is a departure from the simple homeostatic model. Meals themselves are usually short-lasting, and certainly end before the food can have been fully absorbed with an effect on body weight. This last observation means that although body weight may be important in the long-term regulation of food intake, it does not decide the size of individual meals. There must be other factors which determine food intake in the short-term, and these include the presence of food in the mouth, stomach, and small intestine. They are jointly referred to as peripheral factors.

❖ Activity 1 ❖

Think about your own eating habits.

- When were you last very hungry?
- Have you eaten anything in the last few hours that you didn't really need?
- What was the attraction of it?
- If you eat chocolate do you eat it for dietary reasons or because of the sweet taste?

Our diet is not only determined by basic homeostatic drives.

Short-term regulation of food intake

❖ *Presence of food in the mouth*

In one study, participants swallowed a rubber tube and could then press a button to inject a liquid diet directly into the stomach. After a few days they established a regular intake which maintained body weight, but they found the meals unsatisfying and wanted to taste and chew the food (Spiegel 1973), implying that taste is an important feature but not strictly necessary for regulation of meal size. This is supported by a study of sham-feeding using rats. Everything the rats swallowed passed out of the oesophagus (via a tube) before it could reach the stomach. In these circumstances rats ate far more than they normally would, showing that the presence of food in the mouth is not itself sufficient to regulate intake.

❖ *Presence of food in the stomach*

The Spiegel study shows efficient regulation of food injected directly into the stomach. The earliest suggestion that the stomach is central to food intake regulation was by Cannon (Cannon and Washburn 1912). Stomach contractions were recorded in humans using a balloon swallowed by participants and then inflated so that contractions altered the air pressure of the balloon. The hunger pangs reported by the participants correlated with stomach contractions.

A more direct study by Deutsch *et al.* (1978) in rats used a reversible block of the passage between the stomach and the small intestine. Rats with the block in place ate a normal sized meal, even though food did not pass beyond the stomach. This demonstrates that signals of fullness (or satiety as it is technically known) travel from the stomach to the brain, probably via the vagus nerve. The system is sensitive to the quality of food as well as quantity, as the rats would eat less bulk of a high calory food but more of a low calory food. Although the presence of food in the stomach is an important part of our regulatory apparatus, there is no evidence that patients with substantial parts of the stomach removed, because of ulceration or cancer, suffer problems with food intake. There must be alternative regulatory mechanisms.

- *Cholecystokinin (CCK)*

  CCK is a hormone released into the bloodstream from the duodenum (that part of the small intestine immediately following the stomach) in response to the presence of food in the duodenum. Injections of CCK shorten meal size in rats and humans (Antin *et al.* 1978, Pi-Sunyer *et al.* 1982), and it has been put forward as a satiety hormone. Intriguingly CCK also functions as a synaptic neurotransmitter in the brain, and it is tempting to see its effect on satiety and meal size as involving brain pathways. However, there is no direct evidence for this and it is more likely that CCK operates in combination with other factors such as the presence of food in the stomach (McHugh and Moran 1985).

The taste of food in the mouth and the presence of food in the stomach and small intestine all contribute in varying degrees to the regulation of food intake. After passing through the gastro-intestinal system, the products of digestion diffuse into the blood supply. One of the main products of carbohydrate digestion is the sugar glucose, and blood glucose levels have been a popular choice for the regulation of food intake. It is unlikely that changes in blood glucose occur fast enough to affect the size of a single meal, but they may certainly affect the feelings of hunger that develop between meals.

Blood glucose and hunger

Levels of glucose in the blood are controlled by food intake and by the hormone insulin, released from the pancreas gland. Insulin promotes the conversion of glucose to fats and the storage of fats in fat storage cells called adipocytes. Therefore the levels of blood glucose are closely related to levels of insulin; if insulin levels are low, as in diabetes, less glucose is stored in cells and blood levels are high (very high levels lead to hyperglycaemic coma, one of the dangers of diabetes), but when blood insulin rises more glucose is stored and less circulates in the bloodstream. Artificial increases in blood glucose via injections decrease food intake (Tordoff *et al.* 1982), while insulin levels are lowest at night, when appetite decreases, and higher during the day, causing lower blood glucose levels and increasing appetite (LeMagnen 1981).

Effects of glucose on appetite depend upon specialized receptors called glucoreceptors, found in the lining of blood vessels, in the liver and in the brain, especially the hypothalamus. In this way the brain is constantly aware of blood glucose levels. However, this neat relationship between appetite and glucose is probably not the whole answer. In normal people, levels of glucose in the blood do not vary dramatically even after long periods without food. Part of homeostasis involves maintaining steady levels, so that if less is eaten, stored fats are converted to glucose in the bloodstream; if more sugar is taken in the diet, insulin activity increases to convert blood glucose into stored fats in cells. It is unlikely that glucose levels change often enough and regularly enough to explain our eating patterns. Probably of more importance are the central mechanisms of hunger and feeding.

The hypothalamus and feeding centres

In 1942 Hetherington and Ranson demonstrated that lesions of part of the hypothalamus called the ventro-medial (VMH) nucleus caused dramatic over-eating in rats, so that they became massively obese. A few years later Anand and Brobeck (1951) showed that lesions of the lateral nucleus of the hypothalamus (LH) inhibited eating so that rats lost weight. These two studies and many others since suggest that the hypothalamus contains two centres, one in the ventromedial nucleus which normally stopped feeding at the appropriate time – a satiety centre – and one in the lateral hypothalamus which normally stimulated feeding – a feeding centre.

Although these centres are obviously critical in the control of feeding, they can only act if they know the state of the body's energy reserves, so that feeding is related to need. Glucoreceptors alert them to levels of blood glucose, and this probably plays a part. More popular in recent years has been the concept of body-weight set-point. This is the idea that our feeding systems try to maintain our body-weight around a set-point or target weight. The best index of body-weight is the amount of fat stored in the adipocytes (fatty tissue), and Nisbett (1972) suggested that the hypothalamus monitors (through sensory nerves) fat levels and maintains them around a set level. Lesions to the hypothalamus shift this body-weight set-point: VMH lesions raise the level so that rats overeat and become obese, while LH lesions lower it so that rats stop eating to reduce their body-weight.

The body-weight set-point seems to be determined by inherited factors and early nutritional experience. Nisbett's model therefore implies that the obese human is not showing weakness of will or self-indulgence, but simply working to maintain a high target weight. While this is undoubtedly true of some, there are many other factors involved (see *In Focus* below), and even in animals there is little direct experimental evidence for the model. However, the impressive regulation of body-weight in most people and animals does point to some kind of set-point, and Nisbett's ideas are the most convincing in this area.

We have dealt with hunger in some detail. It is a classic homeostatic drive, but there is no simple relationship between need and intake. Diet depends on inherited factors, habit, taste, gastro-intestinal and brain mechanisms, and energy expenditure. Although basically physiological, psychological variables influence food selection in

In Focus

Obesity and anorexia

A peculiarity of the VMH obese rat is that it is not more motivated to eat, and in fact will eat less of a peculiar-tasting food than hungry controls. Schachter (1971) performed an experiment with obese humans to see how motivated they were. Normal-weight and obese participants were allowed equal access to shelled and unshelled almond nuts. The controls ate roughly similar amounts of both types, but obese participants ignored the unshelled nuts and ate only the shelled. Schachter concluded that when food is accessible, the obese rat or human eats more than normal, but when it is hard to get at, they eat less.

Although human obesity may reflect specific brain mechanisms, it is much more likely to represent general physiological variables, as discussed earlier in the chapter, or psychological variables. The opposite syndrome, anorexia nervosa, is found most commonly in females between 12 and 18. It appears to be a pathological desire to be thin and has no simple explanation. The most convincing explanations are psychological, involving self-concept and family dynamics, plus the influence of idealized female forms seen in the media. The most effective treatments are behavioural or psychodynamic therapies, but they have to overcome the problem that many anorexics refuse to see themselves as being abnormally thin.

normal individuals and may be heavily involved in abnormal states such as obesity and anorexia. Other approaches emphasize the psychological aspects even more.

Hull and drive-reduction

Hull (1943) produced one of the grandest theories in the whole of psychology. It represents a combination of physiological homeostatic drives and psychological principles of learning based on drive-reduction, and so could be classified as a half-way house between purely physiological and purely psychological approaches to motivation. His central thesis is that all behaviour is motivated, and that all motivation originates in the satisfaction of homeostatic drives such as hunger, thirst and temperature control. Homeostatic drives are reduced by the appropriate stimulus, e.g. food, water, warmth. These stimuli serve to reinforce the behaviour that led to them, and the animal learns the behaviour because it is reinforced. Thus Hull's is a theory of motivation and learning through drive-reduction.

An obvious question is how such a theory could cope with complex human behaviour. This requires the introduction of secondary reinforcers. Imagine a baby being fed by its mother. The food she provides satisfies the homeostatic drive of hunger and is called a primary reinforcer. However, because of her constant association with food, the mother acquires reinforcing properties of her own, and becomes a secondary reinforcer to the baby. The child then learns to behave in ways which bring contact with the secondary reinforcer, i.e. mum. It is then a short step to seeing the mother's approval as an important reinforcer for behaviour, and, although it may seem silly now, to see Alexander the Great's motivation for conquering the known world as a way of seeking his mother's approval. This view of motivation was taken seriously by psychologists for many years (in fact in this respect Hull has a lot in common with Freud!).

Actually Hull's theory failed through more basic weaknesses. His fundamental prediction was that animals do not learn unless there are drives which are reduced through reinforcement. Rats will not learn their way through a maze unless they are, for instance, hungry and find food at the end. As early as 1948 Tolman had shown that rats learn mazes by developing cognitive maps without drive-reduction or reinforcement, and now we know that spatial learning is a highly developed ability in most animals and does not depend on drives and reinforcements (Olton 1976).

Hull failed to address the complexity of human motivations (virtually all his work was on rats) and placed too much emphasis on homeostatic drives and too little on higher cognitive processes. This was not entirely his fault. At the time he was working, cognitive psychology did not exist as a discipline. To deal with motivation properly we have to look at psychological approaches.

Section summary

Homeostatic drives provide a relatively simple model of motivated behaviour. However, even hunger depends upon a range of interacting factors. Food intake and meal size are affected by the sight, smell and taste of food, and the presence of food in the mouth and stomach. The hormone insulin controls levels of blood glucose which may contribute to longer-term regulation of food intake. There are feeding and satiety centres in the hypothalamus which seem to regulate body-weight around a pre-determined set-point. Hull's drive reduction model proposed that all learning is based upon the satisfaction of homeostatic drives, but was too limited to account for some types of animal learning and for complex human motivations.

Motivation: psychological approaches

An old-fashioned view of motivation divided it into extrinsic and intrinsic motives. With extrinsic motives you could identify a clear reward or reinforcement for the behaviour. Behaviourists have shown, especially in rats, that almost any behaviour can be learnt on the basis of reward. Other behaviours, even in rats, seem to have no obvious external reward and these are referred to as intrinsically motivated. Monkeys will learn to open a closed window simply to see out for thirty seconds (Butler 1953), or will do wire puzzles for hours on end with no extrinsic reward (Harlow 1950). These behaviours can be seen as motivated by curiosity and manipulative drives respectively, and are clearly distinct from homeostatic drives. There is no tissue deficiency leading to a drive state, and no obvious physiological explanation.

Similarly in humans there are many behaviours without a close link to physiology, and various psychological theories have been put forward to explain them.

Murray's Needs

One major problem with drives such as curiosity and manipulation is that they are simply descriptions of the behaviour, and in theory anyone could make up their own list of drives or motives. Murray (1938) used his Thematic Apperception Test (TAT) to provide a more reliable set of human social motives. The TAT, still used in personality testing today, consists of twenty pictures of people in various situations. The participant is asked to use his or her imagination to write a story about each picture, and then the stories are analysed in terms of the types of motivation represented. From these analyses Murray produced a list of twenty social motives, or psychogenic needs, as he called them. These include:

- *achievement:* to accomplish difficult tasks, to overcome obstacles, to rival and overcome others
- *affiliation:* to cooperate and win affection from others
- *aggression:* to overcome others forcefully, by attacking, injuring or killing
- *deference:* to admire and support a superior
- *nurturance:* to protect, console, comfort and nurse the weak, ill or disabled
- *play:* to behave for fun, with no other purpose, especially in games and sports
- *understanding:* to seek or give answers to problems and to analyse and theorize.

Murray's list sounds convincing and it is based on the TAT. But this itself is a projective test and relies on Murray's own analysis. No one would question that these motives are ones which humans would recognize as important, but it would be more convincing if other evidence was available to give them objective validity. In fact Achievement motivation has been extensively studied by McClelland (1961) who developed original ways of assessing levels of Need for Achievement (nAch) in the stories children write. Using a rating scale, he measured achievement imagery in these stories (e.g. references to ambition, successful careers at school, college and in work), and related levels to, for instance, child-rearing practices, showing that mothers of high nAch boys placed earlier demands on the boy's self-reliance and independence.

On a grander scale, McClelland measured levels of nAch in children's reading books from 1925 across forty countries and found a significant correlation with economic growth between 1929 and 1950. He proposed that a society's future economic progress could be predicted by the achievement imagery used in its children's literature; adult levels of nAch are decided partly by the achievement imagery they are exposed to as a child.

McClelland's work has given nAch more validity as one of the central human motives. Others in Murray's list have not been studied so intensively and so lack a degree of validity, and this lack of experimental verification is a consistent feature of models of human motivation. However, Maslow has at least tried to describe the relationships between different types of motive or need.

Maslow's hierarchy of needs

Maslow (1954) proposed that there are two sets of human needs. One set concerns basic survival needs, such as those related to homeostasis, physiological needs and physical safety. The second set concerns self-actualization, the realization of an individual's full potential especially, as shown in creativity and use of the intellect.

Maslow arranges the various needs in a hierarchy (Fig. 8.2), as he states that the basic survival needs have to be satisfied before you can ascend the hierarchy and begin to satisfy creative and intellectual drives. Also, the higher up the hierarchy you go, the more difficult it is to satisfy the needs, as they become psychological rather than physiological, and long-term rather than short-term. In fact Maslow would argue that many of us do not reach our full human potential, or self-actualize, and as his examples of successful self-actualizers include Einstein and Abraham Lincoln, it is not too surprising!

He does associate 'peak experiences' with self-actualization. These are the moments when individuals are totally lost in themselves and are oblivious to other needs or to other people. Such moments are usually confined to the activity of the moment (work, sport, childbirth, etc.) and are difficult to reach consistently.

Maslow's approach has positive and negative features:

- It has a uniquely human emphasis; only humans can self-actualize or engage in high-level cognitive and aesthetic activities. In this way it is an advance on the largely animal-based physiological and reward-based models of motivation.

Figure 8.2
Maslow's hierarchy of needs

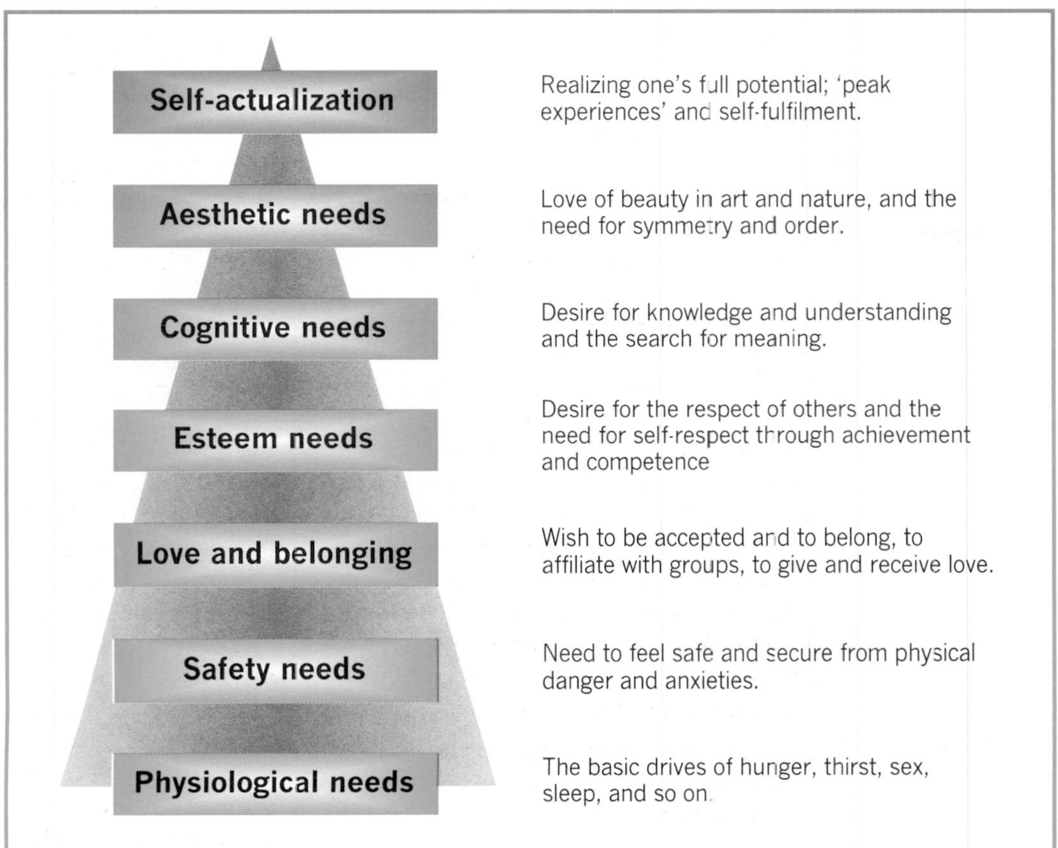
Self-actualization
Realizing one's full potential; 'peak experiences' and self-fulfilment.
Aesthetic needs
Love of beauty in art and nature, and the need for symmetry and order.
Cognitive needs
Desire for knowledge and understanding and the search for meaning.
Esteem needs
Desire for the respect of others and the need for self-respect through achievement and competence
Love and belonging
Wish to be accepted and to belong, to affiliate with groups, to give and receive love.
Safety needs
Need to feel safe and secure from physical danger and anxieties.
Physiological needs
The basic drives of hunger, thirst, sex, sleep, and so on.

- There is no evidence that the needs operate as a strict hierarchy. In fact, it is a cliché that great artists like Van Gogh would paint rather than eat or earn the money to eat, and some activities such as pot-holing or mountain climbing deliberately flirt with risk and danger.
- There is little direct empirical evidence for the model, and indeed it is hard to imagine how one would collect such evidence.
- It provides a framework for discussing the richness and complexity of human motivation that goes beyond homeostatic models and the simple lists of Murray.

Activity 2

Think about your own life.

- Why are you studying at college?
- Do you have a long-term plan that motivates you?

Look at Maslow's hierarchy.

- Can you identify with the types of drives he describes, and can you imagine or have you experienced self-actualizing?
- Do you believe the hierarchy is a realistic model of your own motivational structure?

Motivation: physiological and psychological approaches

We have discussed various approaches to the study of motivation and now we can draw some general conclusions:

- Much behaviour is aimed at satisfying primary physiological drives such as hunger and thirst. However, the link between the drive and behaviour is not always direct. Eating, for instance, is influenced by psychological factors and by the sight, taste and smell of food as well as by tissue need. We also eat according to habit and custom, and usually anticipate need rather than respond to it.
- Physiological theories are limited to behaviours related to survival and have great problems with even simple non-physiological behaviours such as curiosity and manipulation. Explanations involving secondary reinforcers are clumsy and unconvincing.
- Psychological approaches, such as Murray's and Maslow's, try to understand complex human motivations in a realistic way. Their major weakness is the lack of objective experimental data, but they provide more convincing descriptions of human motivation than does the biological approach.

Section summary

Psychological approaches to human motivation are based on identifying specific drives. Murray's thematic apperception test has been used to list twenty such drives or needs, but most have little objective validity. McClelland has demonstrated the usefulness of the Need for Achievement, showing that nAch imagery in children's stories correlates with later economic success. Maslow's hierarchy of needs emphasizes the richness of human motivation but has little empirical support. Physiological and psychological approaches to motivation each have their advantages and disadvantages.

Emotion

We all experience emotions, and we all know what they are – fear, anger, love, sorrow, etc. We can work out that they have different aspects. We feel angry, we act angrily, and our arousal level goes up; emotions involve subjective experience (the 'feeling'), behaviour and physiological changes. But can you define 'emotion'? Kleinginna and Kleinginna (1981) reviewed a variety of definitions and came up with a synthesis:

'Emotion is a complex set of interactions among subjective and objective factors, mediated by neural (nervous) and hormonal systems which can (a) give rise to feelings of arousal, pleasure/displeasure; (b) generate cognitive processes; (c) activate widespread physiological adjustments to the arousal conditions; and (d) lead to behaviour that is often, but not always, expressive, goal-directed, and adaptive.'

Besides being so general as to be not of much practical use, there are problems in using this definition to compare, for example, anger and sorrow. Anger fits the definition quite well, but does sorrow involve 'widespread physiological adjustments', and does it lead to behaviour that may be goal-directed and adaptive? Arnold (1960) suggested a sequence of events in emotional situations:

- perception of the situation
- appraisal – an assessment of the situation as beneficial or potentially harmful
- emotion – a 'felt' tendency towards a beneficial stimulus or away from a harmful stimulus
- expression – physiological changes in the body associated with the emotion
- action – behavioural approach or withdrawal.

To make sense of research into emotion, psychologists have sensibly left the problem of a concise definition on the sidelines, and concentrated on other, clearer questions. These involve the relationships between the subjective experience or feeling, the behaviour associated with the emotion along with physiological changes in the body, and cognitive processes such as perception and appraisal. The earliest systematic theory of emotion illustrates these questions and has provided the basis for most subsequent work.

James-Lange theory of emotion

Working independently, William James (1884) and a Danish psychologist named Lange (1885) put forward similar models of emotion, now known jointly as the James-Lange theory. The theory is counter-intuitive. Their idea was that the perception of an emotion-arousing stimulus (for instance, a hungry bear) leads to a behavioural response, probably running away. This response involves changes in the body's physiological systems (increased arousal in the autonomic nervous system and in skeletal muscles). The brain detects these physiological changes and interprets them as the emotion of fear. In the classic phrase, we do not run because we are scared; we are scared because we run (see Fig. 8.3).

Figure 8.3 Models of emotion: James-Lange (A) and Cannon-Bard (B)

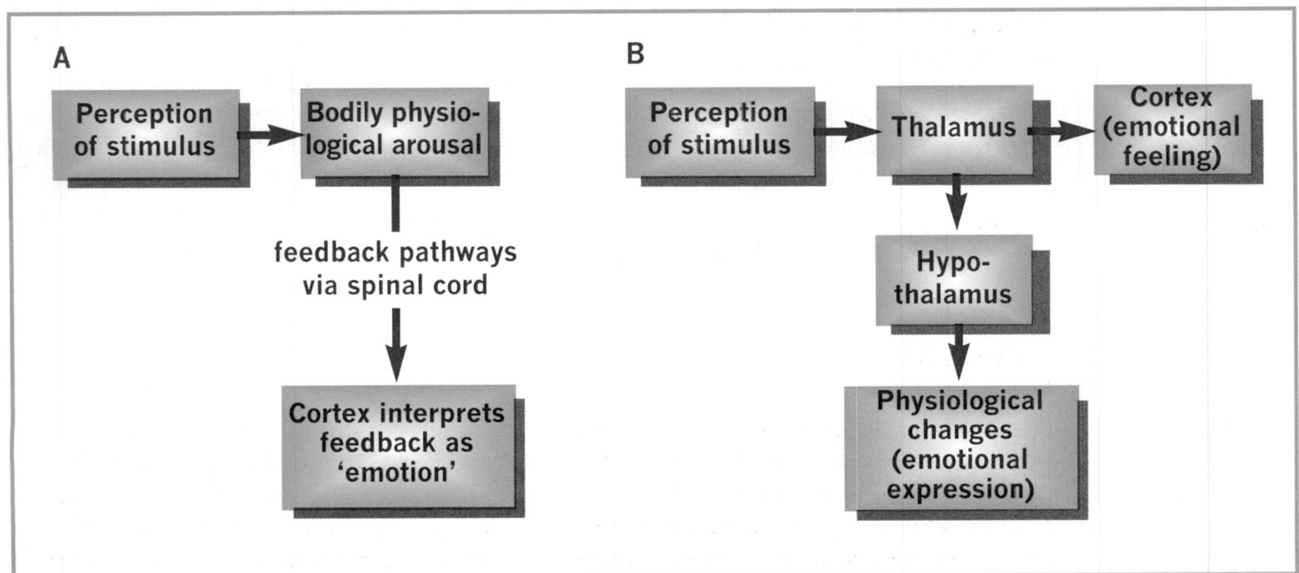

This sequence of events goes against commonsense, which would say that the perception and appraisal of the bear leads *simultaneously* to the feeling of fear and the response of running away. What the James-Lange theory is emphasizing is the central role of feedback to the brain of peripheral physiological arousal in generating emotional states, and it is on this particular aspect that it has been most heavily criticized.

Cannon (1929) presented several major criticisms:

- If the emotion felt depends upon bodily arousal, then each separate emotion would have to be associated with a different pattern of arousal. Although extreme emotions such as anger and fear can be distinguished on the basis of physiological changes, usually such differences between emotions are subtle, if they exist at all.
- Physiological changes occur too slowly following perception of the stimulus to account for the emotional feeling, which occurs almost instantaneously.
- Feedback from the body passes to the brain through the spinal cord. If the spinal cord is damaged, bodily changes and feedback are prevented, so there should be no emotional experience. Cannon quotes a study (Dana 1921) of a patient with spinal damage who reported a normal range of emotions. However, Hohmann (1966) reported on 25 such patients who did experience reductions in feelings of anger and fear, in line with predictions from the James-Lange theory.
- If bodily arousal was necessary and sufficient to produce emotion, then physical exercise or taking stimulant drugs should produce emotional feelings. Running up the stairs is not usually an emotional experience, but work on drugs is less clear cut. Cannon quotes a study by Maranon (1924), who injected participants with the drug adrenaline (known as epinephrine in the USA) which produces bodily physiological arousal. None of the 210 participants felt real emotions, although 29 per cent reported that they felt 'as if' they were afraid or angry. Cannon concluded that the James-Lange theory was contradicted, as the induced arousal did not produce real emotions as the theory predicted.

As an alternative to the James-Lange model, Cannon proposed a central theory of emotions (see Fig. 8.3). Known as the Cannon-Bard theory, it proposes that peripheral arousal is unnecessary for emotional feelings. Incoming stimuli are processed through the thalamus in the brain. Messages then pass from the thalamus upwards to the cortex, which is where conscious emotional experience occurs, and messages are also sent downwards to the hypothalamus and then on to the body, producing physiological arousal and muscular activity. If the spinal cord is damaged, messages cannot reach the body from the brain and arousal does not occur, but messages still ascend from the thalamus to the cortex and so emotional feelings are preserved.

Although not taken seriously today, the Cannon-Bard theory did anticipate limbic models of emotion, which we consider later. In the meantime we return to efforts to untangle the role of bodily arousal in emotional states. Remember that Maranon's participants experienced 'as if' emotional states, so the arousal induced by the injection of adrenaline did not just produce a pattern of generalized arousal, but led to specific reactions, even if they were not 'real' emotions. To try and clarify the situation Schachter and Singer (1962) performed one of the most famous studies in psychology.

Cognitive labelling theory

Schachter and Singer proposed that the debate about the role of arousal in emotional states had largely ignored the important role of cognitive factors. When we feel emotional, it is always about something, whether it is an external stimulus or internal thoughts and memories. A crucial stage in any emotional experience is therefore cognitive appraisal when a stimulus is perceived and evaluated.

Perception of the stimulus may also lead to bodily physiological arousal and, according to Schachter and Singer, it is the combination of arousal and cognitive appraisal that leads to the experience of emotion. For instance, if the arousal is produced by the sight of a grizzly bear, the cognitive appraisal of the situation leads us to interpret the arousal as the emotion of fear. If the arousal is produced by your brother dyeing your favourite T-shirt brown, cognitive appraisal leads to the interpretation of the arousal as the emotion of anger.

In Schachter and Singer's view, physiological arousal is necessary for emotional experience but needs to be labelled or interpreted by cognitive appraisal of the situation. So they follow James-Lange in emphasizing the role of arousal, although they do not propose that patterns of arousal vary between emotions. We feel different emotions because of cognitive labelling, and the same pattern of arousal can occur in different emotional states. If we see cognitive appraisal as based in the brain, Schachter and Singer are also emphasizing central mechanisms in emotion, so their position is a combination of the James-Lange bodily arousal theory and the Cannon-Bard central theory.

One clear prediction from the cognitive labelling theory is that if a state of unexplained bodily arousal is induced in participants, they will look around and try to explain it in terms of their environment. If this cognitive appraisal involves an emotional element, then they will label their state of arousal as an emotional experience. This may sound similar to Maranon's experiment mentioned earlier, but don't forget that those people knew they had been injected with adrenaline, and so had a cognitive interpretation for their arousal state that did not involve emotions. Schachter and Singer intended to induce a completely unexpected and unexplained state of arousal, and then manipulate the environment to try and produce different emotional states.

As in Maranon's study, adrenaline was used to produce a physiological arousal state, but Schachter and Singer deceived their male participants by telling them they were receiving a vitamin supplement called 'suproxin' as part of an experiment on vision. There was also a control group receiving a non-active placebo but which was otherwise treated in the same way as the experimental groups. Participants given injections of adrenaline were either told to expect the real physiological consequences such as increased heart-rate, dry mouth and palpitations, were misinformed as to the physical effects of the injection, or were left ignorant. The experimental situation was manipulated in two ways. In the euphoria condition, accomplices of the experimenters acted in a manically happy way, flying paper aeroplanes and playing with balls of paper. In the anger condition, an accomplice became progressively more angry as he and the participant filled in a highly personal questionnaire ('Do members of your family require psychiatric care?').

The emotional state of the participants was assessed using observers watching through one-way mirrors and by self-reports after the episodes with the accomplices, i.e. measures of emotional behaviour and emotional experience. The main predictions were:

- The group told to expect physiological arousal after the injection would have a cognitive explanation of their state, and would not need to explain it using the behaviour of the accomplices. This is similar to Maranon's study, and changes in emotion would not be predicted.
- The group given the inactive placebo would not experience bodily arousal and therefore would have no arousal state to explain or label. They should not report changes in emotion.
- The group given adrenaline but left ignorant as to the effects *would* experience an unexplained state of bodily arousal. To interpret it they would use cognitive appraisal of the environment; if they are with an accomplice behaving euphorically they should label their state as euphoria, and if they are with an angry accomplice, they should label the

state as anger. The critical predictions Schachter and Singer make are that more emotional change should be seen in the adrenaline-ignorant group than in the placebo group, and that the emotion experienced would depend on which accomplice the participant was with. (The misinformed group were included for complex control reasons and will not be considered further here.)

Schachter and Singer reported results in line with their predictions. Participants given no explanation for the arousing effects of the injection showed more emotional change than the placebo group, reacting more euphorically or angrily in line with their accomplice's behaviour.

This seems a neat combination of the James-Lange and Cannon-Bard positions. Bodily arousal is necessary but not sufficient for emotion, which depends upon an interaction between bodily arousal and the central processes of cognitive appraisal. Therefore emotion is produced by a combination of peripheral and central factors.

There are, however, some problems with this classic study:

- The first statistical analyses produced significant differences between adrenaline-ignorant and placebo groups only for the observer ratings in the Anger condition. (Remember that there are four predicted differences, for observer ratings and self-reports in the two conditions of anger and euphoria.)
- When Schachter and Singer eliminated participants in the adrenaline-ignorant group who they thought had worked out that the injection was responsible for their state of arousal, they found just one more significant difference, for observer ratings for the Euphoria condition.
- No significant differences were found for the self-report data on participants' emotional feelings (observer ratings are of emotional behaviour).
- Therefore adrenaline may simply make participants more likely to imitate an accomplice's behaviour, without changing the actual emotional state.
- There was no assessment of participants' emotional state before the study, which may have interacted with the experimental manipulations.
- Unexplained bodily arousal is an unusual state in real life, and so is drug-induced arousal. The study is far removed from natural emotions, and this reduces its validity.
- Attempts to replicate the experiment (which for largely ethical reasons have been rare) have been unsuccessful (Marshall and Zimbardo 1979, Maslach 1979).

Schachter and Singer's study therefore does not settle the dispute on the role of arousal and cognition in emotion. On the positive side, it did emphasize the major role of cognitive processes such as perception and appraisal.

The debate continues (see *In Focus* on p. 173), with some researchers taking extreme positions. Lazarus (1984), for instance, defines emotions as depending upon cognitive appraisal of the environment, while Zajonc (1984) proposes that cognitive processes and emotions can be independent. He gives the example of babies who can show emotions such as fear and disgust in the absence of high-level cognitive abilities. However, babies are scared or disgusted by something which they have sensed or perceived, and it seems to be splitting hairs to say that their emotions do not depend on some cognitive assessment of their environment. Strongman (1987) gives some general conclusions:

- Bodily physiological arousal can be important, intensifying emotional experience in states such as fear and anger, but it is not necessary for all emotional experience. Emotions such as sadness occur in the absence of arousal.
- Cognitive processes such as perception and appraisal are basic and necessary for emotion.
- The huge range of human emotions means that simple models of the links between emotion, arousal and cognition are unrealistic.

In Focus

Bodily arousal and attraction

In 1974 Dutton and Aron reported their suspension bridge study. Male participants visiting a Canadian canyon were questioned by an attractive female on their reactions to the scenery. As part of the interview they were asked to make up a story about an ambiguous picture of a woman. The level of sexual imagery in the story was scored, and it was found that participants interviewed on a high suspension bridge included more sexual imagery in their stories than those interviewed on a stable wooden bridge. The interpretation was that the bodily arousal produced by the fear and anxiety of the high suspension bridge had intensified the sexual attractiveness of the interviewer, and this was reflected in the stories. Accepting that the sexual imagery of the story is an indirect way of measuring sexual attraction, the study does suggest that arousal can intensify emotions.

Physiological theories

We have so far considered mixed approaches to the study of human emotion. The James-Lange model gives more emphasis to bodily physiological processes but does involve evaluation of feedback, while Schachter and Singer represent an interaction between physiological arousal and psychological processes of cognitive appraisal. One research tradition which lies almost completely in the physiological arena is based largely on work with non-human animals, and has led to the limbic theory of emotion.

The Limbic Theory of Emotion

The limbic system is a set of structures in the forebrain interconnected by neural pathways (see Chapter 5). It includes the hippocampus, the septum, the amygdala and the cingulate gyrus, and also has close links with the hypothalamus. Lesions and electrical stimulation of limbic system structures have effects on emotions in animals such as rats, cats and monkeys. In 1939, Kluver and Bucy reported on a syndrome seen after removing the temporal lobe of the forebrain in monkeys. They became quieter and tamer, tended to put objects in their mouths ('orality') and showed increased sexual activity. This is known as the Kluver-Bucy syndrome, and the critical damage is to the amygdala buried deep within the temporal lobe. Lesions to the amygdala in rats and monkeys reduce aggressive behaviour, while damage to the septum increases it (King and Meyer 1958).

In 1937 Papez proposed a relationship between the anger and rage seen in people with rabies and damage to the hippocampus caused by rabies, and suggested that the hippocampus and the other limbic system structures acted together to control the expression of emotional behaviour. MacLean (1949) supported and extended these ideas, and the joint Papez-MacLean limbic model of emotion has been extremely influential.

There is no doubt that lesions and stimulation of limbic structures in non-human animals can affect emotion, and findings have been used to justify using surgical procedures to change emotional behaviour in humans. Altering behaviour through brain surgery is called psychosurgery and, although it has largely died out now, in the 1950s and 1960s it was quite popular. The amygdala was removed in aggressive human psychiatric patients (including children) in the hope that, as in monkeys, aggression would be reduced (Kiloh *et al.* 1974). The frontal lobotomy, used up to the 1950s to 'treat' schizophrenia, was based on similar operations shown to tranquillize monkeys, i.e. make them more manageable. There is no evidence that any of the psychosurgical procedures had consistent and specific effects on extreme emotional behaviour although the frontal lobotomy could sedate patients, making them easier to control.

Despite the wealth of evidence linking limbic structures to emotion in non-human animals, there are problems with applying it to human emotional behaviour:

- A vital part of human emotions is emotional experience, i.e. the feeling. Experiments using animals can only study behaviour, i.e. expressed emotion.
- Because of this, the limbic model deals mainly with a few high-intensity emotions which are easy to recognize, such as rage and fear. It is a very limited model.
- The human brain is more highly evolved and complex than the brains of rats, cats and monkeys. Although it is a reasonable hypothesis that our limbic system will be involved in emotion, the precise details may well differ between species. There is as yet little direct experimental evidence on limbic function in humans, for obvious ethical reasons.

Activity 3

Consider some of your own emotions. Try to rank them in order of the bodily arousal associated with them. Are there any independent of arousal? Think of a clear emotional experience; do you think it is possible for the bodily reaction to occur before you feel the emotion?

Section summary

The James-Lange theory of emotion said that emotions depend upon bodily physiological arousal. Cannon criticized their ideas and instead proposed a central model which located emotions in brain structure. In an attempt to reconcile the two approaches, Schachter and Singer tried to demonstrate that emotions depend upon the cognitive labelling of generalized arousal states, a combination of central and peripheral mechanisms. Their main study can be criticized as being flawed and artificial, but they did correctly emphasize the role of cognitive appraisal and evaluation in emotion. These processes are essential to emotional experience, but bodily arousal probably is not. The limbic theory of emotion is based mainly on work with non-human animals and deals with extreme emotions such as rage and aggression, and its application to human emotions is therefore limited.

Stress

What is it? Although the term 'stress' has been in common use throughout the last century, it rarely occurred in the psychological literature before the end of the Second World War (Pollock 1988). Now, however, many thousands of research papers are published every year on the subject, and it is also a daily topic of conversation in the public at large. There are several widely held beliefs about stress, which we shall be discussing during this section:

- Life today is more stressful than it used to be.
- Stress is linked to ill health in a directly causal way.
- Stress is therefore bad for you.
- Some individuals are more susceptible to stress than others.

The central role that stress now plays in research and in our daily lives should mean that it is easy to define. But it is not. There have been several approaches to conceptualizing stress which illustrate some of the problems:

- *Stress as external stimuli*: Stress represents the effects of environmental events or stimuli ('stressors') on the body. This model, derived from engineering and the Law of Elasticity, emphasizes the role of external stressors on a passive body. Up to a point the body's 'elasticity' allows it to cope with the stressor, but if strained beyond a given limit the negative effects of stress are seen.
- *Stress as the body's response:* The physiological model emphasizes the

changes within the body produced by external stressors, and sees stress as a pattern of physiological changes within the body. It has been popularized by the work of Selye, which we deal with later.

- *The transactional model of Cox* (1975) combines the two views above. Stress involves external stimuli (the engineering model), the body's physiological responses (stress as response), but also includes key psychological processes mediating between the two to determine the level of stress experienced. These processes include the perception of the environmental demands being made on the individual and the perception of his or her own coping resources. It leads to a definition of stress:

A state of stress exists when there is a mismatch between how a person perceives the demands being made upon them and how they perceive their ability to cope with those demands (see Fig. 8.4).

This general definition of stress refers to the subjective feeling that you are under pressure. It does not state that stress always has negative consequences, such as anxiety and physical illness. In fact, most people agree that stress can be arousing and positive, as when months of pressurized studying produces a successful exam result! Selye (1956) coined the term 'eustress' for these beneficial effects.

However, most of the research into stress has focused on the supposed link with anxiety, depression and physical illnesses such as heart disease, raised blood pressure, gastric ulcers and psychosomatic illnesses – the latter include asthma, migraine headaches, eczema, and digestive problems ('psyche' meaning mind, and 'soma' meaning body; hence, bodily conditions produced or intensified by processes in the mind). It should be emphasized that these conditions can also have purely physical causes. As we progress through the chapter, this question of stress and illness is repeatedly addressed. It is a common belief that the two are directly linked, but there are those who feel that it has not been demonstrated convincingly and that the whole concept of stress needs revamping (Pollock 1988). However, the general definition given above would still hold, as it does not specifically predict a clear relationship between stress and illness.

The current popularity of stress research has its origins in the work of Hans Selye in the 1930s and 1940s, and his ideas are still relevant today.

Figure 8.4
Simplified view of Cox's transactional model of stress

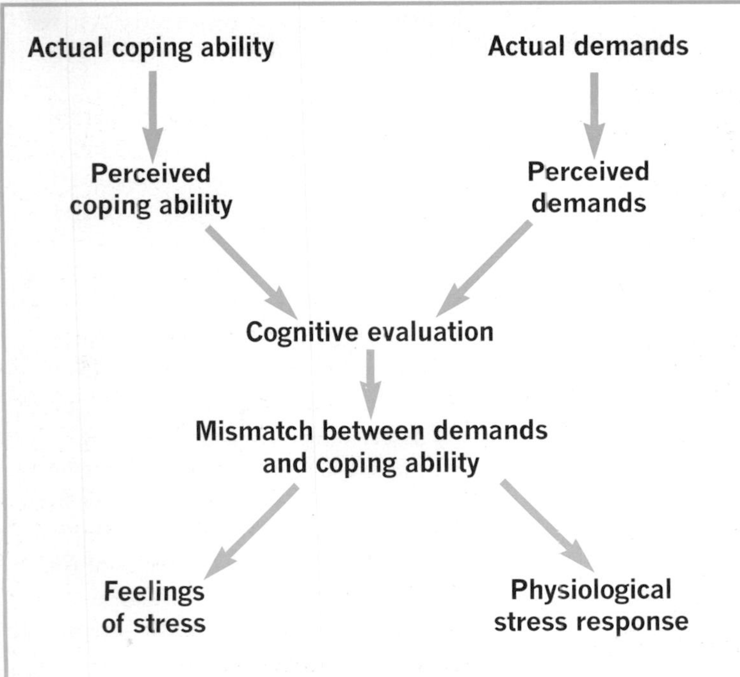

The General Adaptation Syndrome

During his time as a medical student and then as a doctor, Selye observed that patients seemed to experience the same bodily or physiological reactions regardless of the illness or injury they were suffering from. He formed these observations into his general adaptation syndrome, which he regarded as the non-specific way the body responds to any physical stressor. It mainly involves the largely automatic responses of the autonomic nervous system (ANS) and the endocrine system (see Chapter 6), and has three stages:

- *Alarm:* The sympathetic branch of the ANS is activated, increasing heart-rate and blood pressure, directing blood flow to the muscles, and releasing adrenaline and noradrenaline from the adrenal medulla. These hormones maintain and intensify sympathetic activity. The pituitary gland also releases the hormone ACTH, which acts on the adrenal cortex to release corticosteroids. These chemicals, such as cortisone and corticosterone, have many effects on the body, especially glucose metabolism and the immune system.

- *Resistance:* If the stressor persists, the body tries to cope with the demands by maintaining the high levels of physiological arousal.
- *Exhaustion:* Eventually the body's defence systems become exhausted. Although heart-rate and blood pressure may return to normal, blood levels of adrenal hormones are still high and responses to even mild additional stressors become exaggerated. It is at this stage that psychosomatic disorders such as heart disease, gastric ulcers, permanently raised blood pressure and digestive problems can occur.

Selye's physiological model of the stress process has been enormously influential.

Its main feature is that a range of very different stressors would trigger common physiological systems and produce the general adaptation syndrome. Chronic (long-lasting) stress would lead to psychosomatic disorders. But even at this stage we can identify some problems:

- Patients with the same illnesses or injuries do not all react by developing stress-related disorders. There are individual differences.
- Even in patients who do develop psychosomatic complaints, some go down with heart disease, some with ulcers, some with asthma, etc. This must mean that although the same bodily arousal systems are involved in the general adaptation syndrome in all people, the precise way prolonged activation leads to illness must involve other physiological or psychological processes.

It is undeniable that external physical stressors of the type studied by Selye can activate the body's arousal systems, and it seemed likely that this arousal could lead to serious consequences for the individual. A significant development of Selye's ideas was the realization that psychological stressors could have similar physiological effects.

The systems outlined under the general adaptation syndrome are activated when the body is preparing for physical action. Increases in heart-rate and blood pressure increase the oxygen supply to the muscles of the skeleton, while hormone changes increase the availability of glucose to be burnt up by muscle activity. This is an adaptive process when the reaction to a stressful situation is a physical response such as running away or fighting. Evolution in the way humans live together means that nowadays we are more often stressed by less clear-cut situations, such as the frustration of being in a traffic jam, worrying about examinations or paying the mortgage, or coping with raising a family on a small income. These situations still activate our arousal systems in preparation for muscular activity, but of course for most of them there is no obvious muscular response. So we sit in the car getting more and more frustrated, or lie awake in the middle of the night worrying about money problems or examinations. This means that the increases in blood levels of glucose and fatty acids intended to be burnt up in muscle activity now have nowhere to go, and may contribute to the furring up of the arteries and the development of high blood pressure and heart disease. In general terms, we have arousal systems which evolved to cope with one set of stressors but which are not perfectly adapted to the modern stressors of late twentieth-century Western civilization. There is no evidence that life today is any more stressful than it has ever been; the nature of stressors has changed and we are simply more conscious of the problem.

Although it is worth emphasizing the earlier point that many people survive lives of consistent stress without developing psychosomatic disorders, the assumption that the degree of life stress is related to later illness has led to systematic attempts to quantify the impact of life events.

The Holmes-Rahe Social Readjustment Rating Scale (SRRS)

Holmes and Rahe (1967) developed their scale after studying the records of five thousand hospital patients. They noticed that significant life events often seemed to cluster in the months preceding the illness or injury, and produced a list of 43 such events (see Table 20.5). A panel of judges was used to produce ratings of how much change in someone's life each event would lead to, and a rank order emerged with 'death of spouse' at the top (value 100) and 'Christmas' and 'minor violations of the law' at the bottom (12 and 11 respectively). Holmes and Rahe equated life change with stress, and predicted that high levels of life change (calculated by simply adding up the values of all events experienced) over a 12-month period would lead to an increased chance of health breakdown over the following two years; a score of 300 or more was seen as critical.

Studies have shown some small but significant correlations between score on the SRRS and later health problems, although some findings are negative. The approach itself has some obvious problems:

- The ratings for individual life events are arbitrary and may vary from person to person. Some people violently dislike holidays and Christmas, and find them very stressful. Others might find marital separation a relief from a highly dysfunctional and stressful marriage. Each person could have a separate rating scale, as this mechanical approach ignores the individual perception of a situation which determines how stressful it is.
- The relationship between SRRS score and health is only correlational and may tell us nothing about causality. Depression, for instance, may lead to life problems rather than being caused by them.
- Holmes and Rahe include a wide range of health problems, from psychological disorders, through heart disease and diabetes, to accidents and injuries. It is difficult to imagine a convincing causal chain between the stress of life events and this varied collection of outcomes.

On the other hand it does emphasize some commonly accepted truths about life stress:

- The degree of life stress experienced can affect health, even if the relationship is not straightforward.
- Life events vary in the impact they can have on the individual.

There have been other attempts to approach systematically the links between life events and stress. Lazarus' group produced the Hassles and Uplifts scale (Kanner *et al.* 1981), in which hassles are the less dramatic but more common problems of everyday life such as worries about health or money; uplifts are positive events such as good health or rewarding relationships. Scores on the scale correlate with psychological symptoms such as depression and anxiety (obviously the greater the hassles score relative to uplifts the more the chance of a negative outcome). Little work has been done on psychosomatic disorders in relation to this scale.

The creation of these scales reflects the powerful belief that stressful life events influence our general wellbeing. Although low correlations are sometimes found, it is equally the case that many people undergoing apparently severe life stress show no psychological or health problems. If stress can be damaging, why do these individuals seem protected? Or, to take the reverse position, why are some people more vulnerable?

❖ Activity 4 ❖

Look at your own life and rank the life events you have experienced in order of their stressful impact on you. Does it match the SRRS? How would you go about devising a life events scale that would be less arbitrary than the SRRS?

Section summary

Early models of stress concentrated either on stress as external stimuli or stress as the body's physiological response. The transactional model emphasizes the individual's perception of themselves and the world around them. Selye's general adaptation syndrome describes the body's response to stress but does not account for individual differences in reactions. Life events can be stressful, and the Social Readjustment Rating Scale tries to relate the degree of life event stress to health breakdown. The scale can be arbitrary, and again fails to take individual differences into account.

Individual differences and stress

Personality

In the 1960s Friedman and Rosenman (1974) studied the personalities of patients suffering from coronary heart disease, and proposed that a particular type of personality was vulnerable to this stress-related illness. This personality was characterized by constant time-pressure, doing several tasks at once, being intensely competitive in work and social situations, and being easily frustrated with the efforts of others (Table 8.1). This has become known as the Type A personality.

Since their original work, many surveys have been done on the Type A personality. While significant positive correlations have been found between Type A score and heart disease they are never very high, and some psychologists question the value of the concept (Evans 1990). Friedman later introduced a measure of anger and hostility into the concept of Type A behaviour (Booth-Kewley and Friedman 1987) which increased the correlation with heart disease. However, it is still striking that many Type A personalities seem to survive happily with their supposedly risky life style. So we can conclude that other physical and psychological factors must be involved, and there is clear evidence that control is one of the most important (examples of Type A behaviour can be seen in Table 8.1).

Control

The degree of experimental control possible in animal studies has produced convincing evidence that perceived control over a situation is critical in the level of stress experienced (see *In Focus* on next page).

The Brady and Weiss studies show clearly the importance of feedback on

Table 8.1 Type A behaviour pattern

Time pressure	• working against the clock • doing several things at once • irritation and impatience with others • unhappy doing nothing
Competitive	• always plays to win at games and at work • achievements measured as material productivity
Anger	• Self-critical • hostile to the outside world • anger often directed inwards

In Focus

Stress in monkeys and rats

In 1958 Brady *et al.* conducted their 'executive monkey' study. Monkeys received electric footshocks at 20-second intervals for periods of six hours at a time, with six hours rest in between. Shocks were not signalled. Monkeys were run in pairs with one in each pair – the executive – able to press a lever to postpone shock for 20 seconds. The other monkey could not press the lever, but received any footshocks (a yoked control). On this type of schedule not all shocks can be avoided, and after many sessions Brady and his colleagues found that many of the executives died of gastric ulceration. They concluded that the shocks themselves were not that stressful, as the yoked controls were healthy, but it was the added stress of trying to avoid the shocks that fatally stressed the executives.

Weiss (1972) repeated Brady *et al.*'s studies with rats. He found that feedback on successful avoidance (sounding a tone) drastically reduced ulceration in executives, below that of the yoked controls. Without feedback (as in Brady's set-up) levels of ulceration were comparable for the two groups. This was different to Brady's findings, but Weiss noticed that Brady and his colleagues had used their most active monkeys as executives. When Weiss used his most active rats as executives in the no-feedback condition his results were the same as Brady's; the executives ulcerated more than controls.

The conclusions to these studies are that feedback on successful coping responses significantly reduces stress, and that individual differences, such as basic activity level, affect vulnerability to stress-induced illness. It is easy to see how these conclusions can be applied to humans.

It should be noted that because of the stressful conditions used, this type of unethical experiment could not be carried out today.

successful responding in reducing levels of stress, as it gives a sense of control over the situation. Seligman (1975) demonstrated the consequences of a total lack of control in his work on learnt helplessness. Rats given inescapable footshocks failed to learn to escape from avoidable footshocks on a later test. Seligman showed that learnt helplessness also occurs in humans (Hiroto and Seligman 1975). Using loud noise as a stressor, they found that participants exposed to uncontrollable bursts of noise performed poorly on a later task in which the noise was controllable; they had learnt from the earlier experience that they could not control the noise. Seligman suggests that the experience of life as being uncontrollable is an important factor in the development of psychological depression, and some of the coping strategies discussed later are aimed at increasing a sense of being in control of life events.

Control is also an important element in Kobasa's concept of the Hardy personality. Hardiness has three components:

- a sense of personal control over events in one's life
- a sense of commitment and purpose
- a perception of life events as challenges and opportunities rather than threats.

People scoring highly on hardiness have been shown (Kobasa 1979) to suffer less stress-related illness than those with low scores.

The evidence that aspects of personality such as a sense of control and commitment can reduce susceptibility to stress helps explain why some apparently vulnerable individuals cope with stressful situations successfully. A Type A personality, besides being rushed and competitive, may also have a strong sense of personal control and commitment, and may see life as a series of positive challenges to be overcome rather than endured. This combination may protect them from the negative effects of their Type A lifestyle. One of the criticisms of the Type A concept is that it does not include measures of self-perception, i.e. how do you see yourself? You may remember from the definition of stress at the start of the chapter that perception of yourself and the world around you is central, and if you do not see yourself as stressed then you may not suffer the negative effects of an apparently stressful world.

Today many people feel stressed and although some stress-related disorders such as raised blood pressure and heart disease can have a genetic component, and are also related to a lack of exercise, diet, and smoking, it is certainly the case that stress-reduction techniques are becoming increasingly popular and are often effective.

Coping with stress

Some of the simplest ways of coping with the negative effects of stress have just been mentioned. Stop smoking, maintain a healthy diet and take regular exercise. This will help prevent overweight and keep the immune system (the body's main defence against infection) in good trim. Beyond these commonsense approaches there are a wide range of physiological and psychological techniques available.

Drugs

Stress increases the heart-rate and blood pressure, which can lead directly to cerebro-vascular accidents such as strokes and brain haemorrhages. In people who have survived such emergencies or who are at high risk through chronic (long-lasting) high blood pressure, drugs called beta-blockers are often prescribed. These act directly on the autonomic nervous system to reduce physiological arousal.

If stress is associated with anxiety or depression then anxiolytic drugs such as Librium or Valium, or antidepressants such as Tofranil or Prozac, may be used. Although these may be effective in the short term, psychological strategies usually offer a better long-term solution. All drugs have side effects and can also lead to problems of psychological and physical dependence (see Chapter 5), so psychological therapies are preferable if they are effective.

Biofeedback

Physical effects of stress on heart-rate or blood pressure or the increase in muscle tension that can lead to migraine headaches, can be recorded using hand-held monitors. These provide feedback to the patient, who is then taught techniques to reduce the levels. Muscle relaxation or altered posture can be surprisingly effective in reducing blood pressure, although more common techniques involve whole body relaxation and meditation. In this way the patient learns, through biofeedback, physical and psychological methods to reduce bodily arousal.

Biofeedback can be technically difficult and expensive to set up, but, once trained, the patient becomes independent of the monitor as obviously the procedures are effective even if arousal isn't being recorded! However, in some people the feedback that they are coping successfully is essential if the learnt techniques are not to extinguish.

Psychological approaches

Psychological approaches to coping with stress are many and varied. In general, relaxation and meditation are effective in reducing physiological arousal. However, the effects can be short lasting unless meditation is a regular feature of the lifestyle, in which case it can lead to a change in self-perception – *'I am now a calm and relaxed person'*.

Stress involves the perception and assessment of external events and internal thoughts and anxieties. The most effective strategies for permanently altering reactions to stressors involve changing perceptions as well as training in practical coping techniques. In this way they are categorized as cognitive-behavioural approaches, and a good example is Kobasa's system (Kobasa 1986). We have already met her concept of the Hardy personality, and she suggests three stages in developing and increasing Hardiness:

- *Focusing*: the individual is trained to identify signs of stress such as muscle tension and increased heart-rate, and so recognize sources of stress.

- *Reconstructing stressful situations:* the individual is helped to analyse a recent stressful situation, concentrating on ways it could have turned out better and ways it could have turned out worse. The aim is to give them a realistic perception of their life stresses.
- *Compensation through self-improvement:* the individual is encouraged to take on challenges that they can cope with. The experience of successful coping is a form of assertiveness training, and besides helping them to deal with other unavoidable stressors it prevents the development of learnt helplessness-like tendencies.

A similar programme has been put forward by Meichenbaum in his stress-inoculation training (Meichenbaum and Cameron 1983), which also has three components:

- *Conceptualization:* the individual analyses and identifies sources of stress in their life and the ways they have tried to cope with them.
- *Skills training and rehearsal:* the therapist helps the individual to acquire general coping strategies such as relaxation and a realistic appraisal of demands, and specific problem-centred techniques, such as study skills for examinations or better interpersonal communication.
- *Application and follow-up:* newly-acquired skills are practised in the therapeutic environment under the supervision of the therapist. After returning to the real world there are regular follow-up sessions and more training if necessary.

If we go back to our original definition of stress we can see what these approaches have in common. Stress arises when there is a discrepancy between perceived demands on us and our perceived coping responses. The best strategy for reducing stress therefore is to remove the discrepancy by making sure the demands are being realistically assessed and simultaneously improving our coping skills. Identifying sources of stress checks the first stage; perhaps an examination is not so difficult, or money worries are not so severe as you thought at 3 o'clock in the morning. Of course they may be, but often we do exaggerate the demands upon us and it is crucial to be realistic.

Learning and developing coping skills then handles the second part of the stress equation. Kobasa and Meichenbaum use cognitive techniques to alter our perceptions of demands upon us and behavioural techniques to learn and use effective coping strategies. Note that experience of successful coping is an essential feature – the reinforcement this provides also helps alter our perception of ourselves, so eventually we develop a sense of control over events rather than being at their mercy.

This type of analysis makes it sound as though stress reduction is easy but many other factors have a part to play. As adults we have had years to learn our responses to stress, and we may have inherited particular patterns of physiological response. Inappropriate learnt responses to stress such as anger, avoidance or acceptance of failure can be difficult to break down, and in some cases only a deeper analysis through psychotherapy could remove self-destructive strategies. If your nervous system is particularly reactive or you have inherited a tendency towards high blood pressure then stress reduction can be an uphill struggle anyway. The advantage of the cognitive-behavioural approach is that it acknowledges the central role of cognitive processes, such as perception and self-evaluation, in the overall picture of stress. This distinguishes it from the older-fashioned ideas of Selye and Holmes-Rahe, which see the link between life events and the psychological and physiological reactions to stress as direct, without room for individual differences in personality and cognition.

Section summary

Friedman and Rosenman described the Type A personality as one particularly vulnerable to stress-related heart disease. Although there is a relationship, it does not seem to be highly significant. A sense of control and commitment are important in protecting against the effects of stress even in Type As. Physical methods for coping with stress include drugs such as beta-blockers and biofeedback. The most effective psychological techniques use cognitive-behavioural procedures to produce realistic assessments of an individual's life stresses and to teach effective behavioural coping strategies. The emphasis is on changing perceptions, in line with the transactional model of stress.

Chapter summary

- Homeostatic drives provide useful models of motivation, but even hunger is controlled by a range of peripheral and central mechanisms. Important are the presence of food in the stomach, hormones such as CCK and insulin, and feeding and satiety centres in the hypothalamus.
- Psychological approaches have produced lists of human drives but suffer from a lack of experimental verification. A notable exception is the work of McClelland on the Need for Achievement. Maslow's hierarchy of needs does emphasize the uniquely human attributes of creativity and self-actualization.
- Work on human emotion has concentrated on the roles of bodily arousal and central cognitive approaches in emotional states. Arousal plays a part in some emotions but may not be involved in others. Cognitive appraisal and evaluation of the situation are essential to emotion. Studies with non-human animals show that the limbic system is important for intense emotions such as fear and anger.
- Stress research has focused on the possible effects of stress on health. Much of it has ignored individual differences in reactions to stress. The Type A personality is vulnerable to heart disease, but a sense of personal control and commitment seems to protect against stress-related health breakdown. Coping strategies include drugs and biofeedback, while cognitive-behavioural techniques aim to alter perceptions as well as behaviour.

Essay questions

1 Compare and contrast physiological and psychological approaches to the study of motivation. *(24 marks)*

2 Discuss the role of cognition in emotion. *(24 marks)*

3 Discuss factors which may influence the effects of stress on people. *(24 marks)*

Further reading

Green, S. (1994) *Principles of Biopsychology*, Hove: Erlbaum.

Covers motivation, emotion and stress clearly and in reasonable detail.

McIlveen, R. and Gross, R.D. (1996) *Biopsychology*, London: Hodder & Stoughton.

A recently written text that addresses all the topics in this chapter.

Strongman, K.T. (1987) *The Psychology of Emotion* (3rd edn), Chichester: Wiley.

Very detailed but a comprehensive survey of the history and current state of affairs in emotion research.

Part 3

Atypical Development and Abnormal Behaviour

Chapter 9

Atypical development

David Messer
Lesley Messer

Preview

In this chapter we shall be looking at:

- theories and research about learning difficulties, including:
  - the definition of learning difficulties
  - the causes of learning difficulties
  - problems associated with learning difficulties
  - children with Down's syndrome
- the effects of physical and sensory disability, including cerebral palsy, visual impairment and hearing impairment
- emotional, behavioural and educational problems, including attention-deficit hyperactivity disorder, autism and developmental dyslexia.

Introduction

There are many forms of atypical development in children. Indeed, one could even argue that because every child develops in a set of unique circumstances there is no such thing as typical development and no distinction should be made between typical and atypical children. But the danger with this argument is that important differences between children are ignored and we may fail to assist the optimal development of certain groups of children. This chapter will begin with a consideration of the topic of learning difficulties. This is followed by a discussion of physical disabilities and lastly there is an examination of three forms of atypical development which illustrate a range of behaviours and thinking in children.

Any form of atypical development needs to be considered not just in relation to the child, but also in relation to the family and wider culture. The diagnosis or discovery of some form of disability is usually a stressful and emotional time for parents. They may experience a range of different reactions including shock, disbelief, anger, bereavement, inadequacy, embarrassment, guilt or fear. It may take months or years for families to come to terms with the disability. On the other hand, it is also true that some families find caring for their atypical child a satisfying and very rewarding experience.

Theories and research about learning difficulties

The definition of learning difficulties

Learning difficulties are usually classified on the basis of a child's intelligence quotient (IQ) score. The discussion of intelligence in Chapter 26 shows that measurement of this capacity is controversial. It is not surprising therefore that a definition of learning difficulties which is based on IQ has met with criticism. One common definition of learning difficulties involves a person having an IQ of less than 70. Ninety-five per cent of children have an IQ score between 70 and 130. A score of 70 has been chosen to identify learning difficulties because this value is two standard deviations below the mean score of 100. Thus, the choice of 70 is not based on functioning, but on statistical considerations and this has lead to further criticisms of this definition. However, in practice, a person with an IQ below 70 is often going to face some problems functioning in an everyday context because of their limited abilities. This probably explains why this method of identification has persisted despite the apparent psychological arbitrariness of the definition.

There have been attempts to base definitions of learning difficulties on the ability of a person to live independently relative to their age. This involves an assessment of the ability to feed, dress oneself and so on. Although this can be seen as a more satisfactory approach, the problem is that the assessment relies on the reports of carers and this may be subject to various biases.

A last point to be made about the definition and use of terms in relation to learning difficulties is that these have changed over time because of the wish of both professionals and parents to avoid words which have negative associations. Originally words such as 'idiot' and 'imbecile' were used. The term 'mental retardation' replaced these with the following classification being used:

❖ Activity 1 ❖

Write down a list of skills and abilities which you feel are important for individuals to possess in order to lead independent lives. Then rank these in terms of their importance. If possible, discuss your list and rankings with someone else on your course and try to agree a joint list of skills/abilities and their rankings.

- Mildly mentally retarded individuals had an IQ of between 50 and 70.
- Severely mentally retarded individuals had an IQ between 25 and 50
- Profoundly retarded individuals had an IQ below 25.

The term 'mentally retarded' is now also falling into disuse and is being replaced by the following: learning difficulties, special needs or developmental delay. The term 'learning difficulties' is usually used as a general description, and when a particular disability is being discussed the preferred expression is 'children with learning difficulties' or 'children with Down's syndrome' (rather than 'Down's syndrome children'). In the past, the word 'abnormal' was often used, but this is now generally considered to be inappropriate because it has negative associations and raises the whole question of what is 'normal' and 'abnormal'.

The causes of learning difficulties

Learning difficulties are often classified according to whether the cause is genetic or environmental. Inherited disabilities are usually caused by both parents having recessive genes for the disability. This means that the parents themselves carry a gene for the disability, but they also possess a dominant gene which ensures that the recessive characteristic does not result in their having the disability. If both parents are carriers and the condition obeys the classic laws of inheritance, then there is a 1 in 4 chance of any child possessing the learning disability. It is also possible for one parent to have a dominant gene for the condition (see Chapter 22).

Phenylketonuria (PKU) is caused by the inheritance of a recessive gene from both parents. This condition involves a child being unable to process certain proteins chemically, with the result that harmful waste products accumulate and damage the developing nervous system after birth. Learning difficulties occur without intervention. However, if detected early, the child's diet can be altered and any major intellectual impairment can be avoided. This is one reason why, shortly after birth, a small, test sample of blood is taken from the heel of all babies in Britain. PKU illustrates the process of inheriting a genetic disorder, and it also illustrates the fact that genetic dispositions interact with environmental influences. A suitable environment, in the form of a restricted diet, can minimize the effects of PKU. Thus, the inheritance of a genetic disability does not mean that the environmental conditions cannot influence development.

There are few dominant genes that cause learning difficulties in children. A dominant gene which causes an early disability is likely to be eliminated from a population because the individuals will be less likely to reproduce. One dominant gene which causes problems in later life is Huntington's chorea, a condition which involves the degeneration of the nervous system with an onset usually after the age of 40. One should also note, that not all genetic disorders operate according to the classic laws of inheritance. In many cases, characteristics are the result of the influence of several genes (e.g. eye colour). In such cases it is much more difficult to work out the inheritance of a disorder.

Chromosomal abnormalities can be another cause of learning difficulties, and many are not directly inherited from either parent. Genetic abnormalities are most often caused by additional or absent genetic material. One of the most common is Down's syndrome where there is usually an extra chromosome on the 21st pair. It seems likely that the extra chromosome occurs because of an error in the process of

In Focus

Research with children who have learning difficulties

An important general issue about such research is the choice of comparison groups. Early studies tended to match children who had learning difficulties with those of a similar *chronological age*. Usually these comparisons revealed that children with learning difficulties did not achieve the same level of performance as children of a similar age – an unsurprising finding!

A more usual comparison, in recent research, is between children with learning difficulties and a group of a similar mental age (MA) as assessed by an IQ test. This means that the two groups should have similar cognitive abilities, but are likely to differ in age, the children with learning difficulties being older than those in the other group. Such comparisons can be used to answer questions such as, whether language is less developed than one would expect on the basis of the children's general mental age. Unfortunately, there are still problems with the interpretation of these comparisons. Children with learning difficulties may lack the motivation to attempt IQ tests. They may also be less attentive and less able to sustain attention during a relatively long testing session (Harter and Zigler 1974). Thus, mental age scores may underestimate the cognitive abilities of children with learning difficulties. This means that caution should always be exercised when interpreting comparisons based on mental age.

cell division. Thus, the condition is not inherited from the genes of the parents, but is caused by an extra chromosome being present in the fertilised cell. As with PKU, the degree of learning difficulties in children with Down's syndrome is influenced by environmental conditions – children who experience stimulating and caring environments are more likely to make better cognitive progress.

Since the growth of a foetus in the womb is a time of rapid cell division, this is a time when environmental influences can cause learning difficulties. These influences are termed 'teratogens', of which there are many. Some occur because of an illness in the mother during pregnancy, such as German measles (rubella). The severity of the effects depends on when the mother was ill with this virus; the greatest risk is in the fourth to the sixth week of pregnancy. During this time the developing nervous system is especially susceptible to damage.

The use of drugs by the mother (e.g. heroin, alcohol) may also cause learning difficulties. Other chemical causes include radiation, lack of oxygen and problems from pollutants such as mercury. It is important to recognize that the influence of these teratogens depends on when the foetus experienced them and the amount of exposure. Each teratogen has a reasonably specific influence on various parts of the body (e.g. rubella affects the central nervous system, hearing and heart). However, teratogens do not seem to affect all foetuses to the same extent and in the same way. Furthermore, the severity of the effects is influenced by the general health status of the mother, with the foetuses of younger and older mothers being more susceptible.

Physical damage to the brain at any stage of development can be a cause of learning difficulties. It is also the case that the pervasive effects of a poor environment, when coupled with unstimulating care, can result in learning difficulties (see also Chapter 17) and this is known as psychosocial deprivation. For example, the presence of low intellectual functioning of individuals in certain deprived areas, such as rural regions of the Appalachian mountains in the USA, has been attributed to poor environmental conditions (e.g. poor care, poor housing conditions, poor nutrition and lack of educational materials).

Issues associated with learning difficulties

We have already discussed issues surrounding the use of terms to describe people with learning difficulties. This is important because of the possibility of labelling. It has been found that giving a label to a teacher about a child's abilities may result in changes in the child's performance which reflect the label; this has been shown to occur in mainstream classrooms (Rosenthal 1985). The use of labels creates expectations which can affect behaviour towards the labelled children. For example, a range of studies suggests that when teachers (and other adults) speak to children with learning difficulties, they tend to be more directive and less responsive than to non-delayed children.

A related issue is whether children with learning difficulties should attend specialist or mainstream schools. The argument for specialist schools is that they provide greater expertise in educational matters. The arguments against are that:

- they may inadvertently promote low expectations
- the children are deprived of contact with others
- there is often stigma attached to special schools.

It is argued that such problems are less likely in mainstream schools, and that they prepare children better for an independent life. In Britain there has been a move away from specialist schools to integration in mainstream schools, but this does not mean that all the problems have been solved. One problem of integration is that of social rejection and isolation. Furthermore, it should be borne in mind that some children may benefit from one form of education and others from a different form.

A further issue is that of statementing. The 1981 Education Act requires Education Authorities to identify children with special needs, to ensure where possible that they can attend mainstream schools, and to make additional provision when a child's needs cannot be met in a mainstream school. This reflected a wish to move away from the labelling of children and towards identifying their individual needs. The formal assessment or statement of special needs is usually produced by a range of professionals including educational psychologists. Approximately two per cent of pupils in England and Wales have been identified as having special needs by the process of statementing. Controversy occurs when Education Authorities do not consider statementing, or where there is disagreement over the best provision for a child.

In Focus

Children with Down's syndrome

The extra chromosome in children with Down's syndrome has consequence for both health and abilities. These children have a higher incidence of respiratory and heart problems, together with a susceptibility to infections. It has been suggested that cognitive abilities often do not surpass those of a five-year-old and the maximum potential is usually reached by 12 to 15 years (Rondal 1988). However, more and more children with Down's syndrome are making very good progress and statistics about ability levels are probably outdated. For example, many children with Down's syndrome can be taught to read and this seems to have a positive effect on their other abilities. It is extremely important to recognize that the degree of disability is highly variable, so that there will always be exceptions to any generalization.

How is it best to characterize the development of children with Down's syndrome? There has been debate about whether it is different or delayed. Such discussions have implications for intervention, because if development is delayed then progress will be similar to that in other children, but will be slower and not reach such a high level. Intervention should, therefore, be based on processes that aid the development of all children. Alternatively, if development is different then interventions should be designed to build on the strengths of the children and take account of their weaknesses.

Cicchetti and Mans-Wagener (1987) have presented evidence for delay in social and cognitive processes, and Fowler (1988) has claimed that language development is slower, but otherwise is the same as in other children. The delay position does seem to describe the broad outline of development. However, when more detailed observations are made, this description becomes less convincing. For example, Miller (1988) argues that there is an increasing gap between speech and cognitive abilities, so that speech becomes delayed and different in form. This means that taken as a whole, the development of children with Down's syndrome is different from that of other children. Rondal (1988) reports that older children with Down's syndrome tend to use a greater range of words than non-delayed children at a similar mental age. This was interpreted as being due to the children with Down's syndrome having greater experience of speech (because they were chronologically older) and as a result they have more opportunities to learn more words.

Thus, there is support for both the delay and difference descriptions of children with Down's syndrome. In relation to this, Rondal (1988) has argued that even though one dimension of communication may follow the same *sequence* of development, it may be 'out of step' with related abilities. When this is the case, he argues that the pattern of development as a whole should be considered different.

Section summary

The definition and the use of terms to describe children with special needs are sensitive and controversial topics. Learning difficulties can be caused by genetic and by environmental processes, and there is a growing realization that both of these processes play a part in determining a child's level of abilities. The choice of comparison groups is an important research issue, as this will influence the type of conclusions that can be drawn from a study.

Effects of physical and sensory disability

In general, the term 'disability' has replaced that of 'handicap' in the discussion of physical and sensory abilities. One general message from the study of these children is that some individuals can make remarkable progress. For example, Richard Boydell, who was not able to speak because of cerebral palsy, was given, at the age of 30, a foot-operated typewriter. Within nine days he was able to compose elegant grammatical sentences (Fourcin 1975). Another famous individual was Helen Keller, who was both deaf and blind but learned to communicate through the use of touch spelling. Three forms of physical disability are examined in this section: cerebral palsy, visual impairment and hearing impairment.

Cerebral palsy

Cerebral palsy involves movement disabilities caused by damage to the brain early in life; this affects about 0.2 per cent of the population. The damage can be from: anoxia (lack of oxygen to the brain), internal bleeding in the brain, excessive jaundice in the first few weeks, injury or infections. There is no clear relation between the damage and the type of disability, making prediction about later development difficult. The severity varies considerably, both in the parts of the body that are affected and in the type of problems that occur. For example, it is estimated that only about half of children with cerebral palsy can walk by the time they are five years old. Cerebral palsy may also be associated with other disabilities involving cognitive processes, vision, hearing and the production of sounds.

Cerebral palsy involves damage to the immature nervous system. Because of this, disabilities may be caused not only by specific damage to parts of the nervous system, but also by the way the damage influences and interacts with subsequent development (e.g. difficulty in speaking can affect other processes). In general, a child with cerebral palsy is likely to show:

- delay in the acquisition of new skills
- continuation of infant behavioural patterns (including some reflexes)
- the presence of motor patterns not usually seen in other children.

All this makes accurate diagnosis complicated, especially as there may be difficulties in assessing cognitive capacities because of the motor disabilities. Various terms are used in the classification of cerebral palsy and some of these are shown in Table 9.1.

Children with cerebral palsy often have problems with producing sounds and this interferes with the development of communication. The difficulties in communication can result in an underestimation of the ability of that person. However, as has already been mentioned in the case of Richard Boydell, some individuals have overcome their profound disabilities and are able to make use of alternative methods of communication. The presence of such abilities is remarkable given the absence of understandable speech throughout the person's development. These abilities suggest that Piaget was incorrect in supposing that children need to be able to act

Table 9.1 Terms used to describe cerebral palsy

A large range of terms are used, and sometimes there may be differences of opinion about which is the most appropriate to describe a particular condition. This is because of the range in severity and type of disabilities.

quadriplegia	disabilities involving all four limbs
disaplegia	disabilities involving two limbs
paraplegia	disabilities involving both legs
hemiplegia	movement difficulties on one side of the body
spastic cerebral palsy	rigidity in one or more limbs and often there are difficulties with voluntary movements
athetoid cerebral palsy	there are unusual, and uncontrollable movements
ataxic cerebral palsy	difficulties with balance, voluntary movements are often clumsy.

on their environment to develop more advanced cognitive capacities.

Several treatment methods are used, but there is an absence of studies evaluating their effectiveness. One method that has attracted considerable attention is conductive education, which originates from the work of Andras Peto in Hungary. The residential programme involves intensive sessions involving groups of 15 to 20 children with similar needs. The children practise movements which are designed to assist their motor development. The emphasis is on children acquiring better motor co-ordination through control of their own movements. The success of this programme is still the subject of debate. A different type of approach has been utilized by Margaret Rood who advocates the stimulation of muscle groups in various ways (e.g. stroking, brushing, slow and quick muscle stretch). This is related to helping children to progress through a sequence of motor accomplishments. It is also suggested that eclectic approaches are necessary which draw on the strengths of different programmes and are adapted to the needs of individual children.

Visual impairment

There is a variety of forms and degrees of visual impairment. In this section we will concentrate on children who have very little or no visual perception. Children who are visually impaired often have other disabilities; the early studies failed to take account of this and typically reported delays in development which may have been due to other factors. For this reason we discuss the more recent work.

Severely visually-impaired infants have no access to the information provided by faces or facial expression that signal the very existence of adults. Their contact with people must be through vocalizations and touch, and for many visually-impaired infants these modalities appear sufficient to provide a basis for communication. One of the pioneers of this research was Selma Fraiberg. She recognized that the absence of eye contact and cues from infant gaze about the direction of attention makes interaction especially difficult, and that this is compounded by reduced facial expressiveness. The latter may be caused by the absence of visual models and by the

In Focus

Fraiberg's discussion of reactions to children who are blind

Fraiberg was in the forefront of research about children who are blind. She wrote in 1979:

> 'I gradually became aware of many differences in my behavior toward blind infants . . . many of these feelings are still with me and catch me with surprise. Yet I think I am reasonably without prejudice toward the blind.' *(pp. 149–50)*

Fraiberg then discussed her reactions to Toni, a child with blindness, and to Lennie, a severely neglected child who had been incorrectly diagnosed as blind.

> 'I did very little talking when I was with Toni. This troubled me. Toni was an endearing and responsive child. Lennie depressed me. I enjoyed holding Toni. I had to overcome feelings of revulsion when I held Lennie. But I talked to Lennie. What was the reward? When I searched my memory again, I came up with two pictures. When I talked to Lennie long enough, I elicited brief moments of visual fixation of my face and a meeting of eyes. When I sustained his fixation long enough, I elicited a ghost of a smile.
>
> 'Later... when I was with Toni, I talked to her more frequently, but I always had the sense of something missing, something that should be coming back from Toni. There was of course no fixation of my face. And something else was missing. Although Toni smiled frequently in response to her mother's voice, she rarely smiled in response to us.'

This eloquent passage illustrates the difficulties of communicating with a child who is visually impaired, and the benefits of recognizing such limitations and devising appropriate strategies.

need to pay more attention to the process of communicating (see *In Focus*).

Fraiberg suggested that parents should pay particular attention to the hands of visually-impaired children, because the manipulation of objects (rather than direction of gaze) gives vital information about a child's interest and preferences. Fraiberg reports that visually-impaired children can make normal progress in the use of speech if such interventions are used. Given that severely visually-impaired children cannot see the things that adults talk about, it is surprising that the onset of their first words has been reported to be delayed only by several months, and that this is within the normal range of variation.

A study by Mulford (1987), which carefully screened the children to exclude those with other disabilities, found no major delays in vocabulary growth. Although the significant milestones in speech may be reached at appropriate ages, there appear to be some subtle differences concerning the quality of speech and type of conversations. The words used by visually-impaired children are broadly similar to those of sighted children, but there are differences. Visually-impaired children tend to have more names of household objects and fewer names for animals, presumably because of differences in the ease of locating these things (Dunlea 1989). For a visually-impaired child it may be easier to share and refer to past events than to aspects of the 'here and now'. Andersen *et al.* (1993) suggest that this results in the ability to use the past tense of verbs (e.g. play-*ed*) before sighted children, and the delay in learning words about locations (e.g. in, on, under).

A problem that has often been noted in severely visually-impaired children is the reversal of the meaning of personal pronouns (e.g. you, I). A visually-impaired child might say 'you wanna go outside?' as a request for him/herself to go outside (Fraiberg 1977). Andersen *et al.* suggest that this may be because visually-impaired children are using speech before they fully understand its meaning. Similar problems occur in the use of some words about location (e.g. this, that, here, there) which children may use interchangeably (Andersen *et al.* 1993).

An area where the lack of visual input has unexpected consequences is in the production of speech sounds. (Before reading further, please carry out Activity 2.)

❖ Activity 2 ❖

Say the sounds b, m and f to yourself. Now say the sounds j, k, h and x to yourself. What do you notice about your mouth movements?

It has been reported that babbling in visually-impaired and sighted children occurs at a similar age, around six to seven months. However, Mills (1987) found that visually-impaired infants aged between one and two years made more errors with sounds that have highly visible mouth movements (e.g. b, m, f). No difference was found between the children in the use of sounds where there is no obvious mouth movement (e.g. j, k, x, h), suggesting that this finding is not the result of a general delay. This implies that seeing mouth movements helps infants to produce the sounds and learn words. This conclusion is reinforced by Mulford's (1987) findings that visually-impaired children have fewer words in their vocabulary which include a sound with visible mouth movements.

Hearing impairment

Hearing impairment is a far from uniform condition. There are different degrees of auditory impairment and variation in the age of onset. There are also differences in the language environment. The parents of about ten per cent of hearing-impaired children are also hearing impaired and use sign language, but the majority of hearing-impaired children have hearing parents who, initially at least, do not know a sign language. In relation to this subject, the term *language* is used to refer to both oral (i.e. spoken) and sign languages, while *speech* is used to refer to oral communication only.

The teaching of language to hearing-impaired children has sometimes been the cause of heated arguments between advocates of different methods of teaching children language. The major methods are outlined in Table 9.2.

The oralist tradition

The oralist tradition has as its goal making the hearing-impaired child an effective communicator with hearing individuals. As a result, emphasis is placed on using hearing aids, developing skills in lip reading and on the complex training to achieve the ability to produce recognizable words. In the past, the use of sign languages has been actively discouraged by advocates of the oral approach, as it was thought to interfere with the development of lip reading and producing words. Such discouragement has received criticism because it threatens the language of the hearing-impaired community, and is often seen as an outside attack on a system which works very well for many hearing-impaired individuals. There are a number of reports of the successful use of the oralist method (e.g. Quigley and Paul 1987). However, it also seems that a large proportion of children using this method fail to develop the ability to produce recognizable words. Thus, although oralist methods are successful in some cases, there are also many hearing-impaired children who are not able to communicate effectively after having received this method of training.

Sign language

The traditional alternative to the oralist tradition comes from advocates of the acquisition of sign language. Sign languages are equivalent to and as complex as oral languages (Klima and Bullugi 1979). The grammar of sign languages does not correspond to spoken English, but is independent and different from it. In sign

Table 9.2 The main types of communication systems used with hearing-impaired children

Oral English	
Aural-oral	Concentration on visual and auditory capacities, by using any minimal hearing, lip-reading and sound-production capacities.
Cued speech	Handshape and hand location are used to provide information about those sounds which are very difficult to identify from lip reading (e.g. m, p and b).
Sign languages	
Languages which rely on gestures. These languages have their own grammar and do not simply match the grammar of the language of the hearing community. ASL refers to American Sign Language; BSL refers to British Sign Language.	
Manually coded English	
These systems are designed to reflect the structure of English rather than that of a sign language. The systems are designed to be used at the same time as speech.	
Finger spelling	Twenty-six specific handshapes matching the letters of the alphabet. The slowness of the method has limited its use.
Signed English	Signed items correspond to English words; these are employed with sign markers which give the 14 most common grammatical functions. Finger spelling is used for some words where there is no sign equivalent.
Pidgin signed English	This involves the informal use of signs in an English-based structure; more complex grammatical elements are omitted (e.g. plurals and the tenses of verbs). This is much like the way someone who is learning English as a second language might communicate at first.

languages there are commonly four major components: the hand shape; the hand location in relation to the body; the hand movement; and the orientation of the hand (Stokoe 1960). Each of these can influence the meaning of the communication.

In cases where hearing-impaired children have hearing-impaired parents, sign language is readily acquired. A problem for hearing-impaired children of hearing parents, is that the rest of the family are not usually fluent in signing, and as a result the input will be less than ideal.

Quigley and Paul (1987) argue that sign languages enable effective communication to occur in the hearing-impaired community, and provide a good starting point for the subsequent development of reading and writing skills.

Sign systems

A third more recent approach to communication is the use of sign systems which correspond to the words and the structure of an oral language (see items about manually coded English in Table 9.2). Their main advantage is that it is relatively easy for parents and teachers to learn them. However, the sign *systems* are not as rich as sign *languages*, and even when using the simpler system, adults often fail to include a number of relevant grammatical elements. Quigley and Paul (1987) comment that despite their extensive use, there is little evidence for sign systems resulting in competent reading and writing skills. It is often suggested that sign systems should be used with speech, but there are numerous comments about the difficulty of this because signs are slower to produce than words. For these reasons there is concern that sign systems may not provide an adequate basis for the development of communication.

Total communication

Related to the use of sign systems is the method of *total communication* which has been defined in various ways, but is perhaps best seen as a readiness to use any available methods to communicate effectively (Stewart 1992). This has been a popular approach to teaching, and sometimes has been regarded as simply the use of signs together with speech to communicate. In practice, sign languages are rarely employed in total communication programmes. Stewart (1992) suggests that the result is pidgin signed English (i.e. a very simple form of language with many grammatical elements missing) and that adults tend to use whatever method of communication is easiest for them, rather than what is most suitable for the hearing-impaired person. Gregory and Barlow (1989) have also questioned the effectiveness of hearing parents using total communication. They worry that it may be difficult for parents to simplify the signing in the same way they would a spoken language, and that unless the whole family learns to sign, the child may become isolated from conversation.

The acquisition of signs

In a minority of cases hearing-impaired children are born to hearing-impaired parents. Here the acquisition of sign language occurs at a similar rate to oral language, and may even be faster (Schlesinger and Meadows 1972). This has surprised many researchers as one might expect such children to be disadvantaged, because it would seem easier to relate sounds of words to objects, than to relate visual stimuli (a sign) to an object. Examination of communication with hearing-impaired infants has revealed that parents simplify their signing and, in particular, signs are adapted in ways that make them more visible. For instance, the sign may be made where the infant can see it rather than in the correct position in relation to the adult's body. Adults also appear to use more single signs and produce fewer signs (Harris 1991) than one would expect from speech communication to hearing children.

Gregory and her colleagues have argued (e.g. Gregory and Barlow 1989) that there is better attunement when hearing-impaired infants have hearing-impaired mothers rather than hearing mothers. She suggests that this stems from hearing mothers having to adapt to a different mode of communication, not simply from a lack of proficiency with signing. For instance, hearing-impaired mothers, in comparison to hearing mothers, spent more time with the same focus of attention as the child (94 per cent vs 75 per cent) and were more likely to 'reply' to a child's behaviour (50 per cent vs 23 per cent). Gregory and Barlow reason that less effective pre-linguistic communication has consequences for later language development.

The effects of hearing impairment

Many hearing-impaired children have difficulties learning to read. Conrad (1979) reported that only two to three per cent of children with profound hearing loss achieved the appropriate age norms for reading, and half of school leavers had reading ages below eight years. Not surprisingly, the children who were better readers tended to have better hearing and a better understanding of English. More surprising was the finding that children with a severe hearing impairment with parents who are also hearing-impaired, also tended to be good readers (Conrad 1979). One suggestion is that this is due to sign language helping with the acquisition of reading, not because there is any direct similarity between the two languages, but because an understanding of any language will help with reading.

There has been interest in the effect of a lack of language on the cognitive development in children who are hearing-

In Focus

Cognitive superiority

Hearing-impaired and hearing Chinese children who were just starting to write were shown a moving point of light which traced the outline of a character from the Chinese alphabet. Because this was presented on a video screen, the children never saw a complete image of the character. The hearing children found it very difficult to draw the characters on paper, while the hearing-impaired children, who were used to sign language, found the task easier (Fok and Bellugi 1986).

A similar finding is that hearing-impaired children are better than hearing children at recognizing faces. The hearing-impaired children who took part in the study all had a member of their family who was also hearing-impaired and were therefore likely to have been exposed to sign language. The children were given a picture of the front view of a face and had to pick out the same face from:

1 six frontal views
2 six views at an angle
3 six views when the lighting was different from the original.

Hearing-impaired children aged three years could perform as well as six-year-old hearing children on these tasks (Bellugi *et al.* 1990).

Both of these findings would appear to show that the needs of hearing-impaired children to attend to movement and faces result in their being better at recognizing certain forms of information.

impaired. Furth (1966) conducted a number of such investigations in the early 1960s. More recently, these studies have been criticized as largely ignoring the issue of hearing-impaired children having a sign language (Gregory 1995). In contrast, the *In Focus* shows that children with hearing impairment may be better than hearing children at some tasks.

Section summary

Across all three forms of physical disability – cerebral palsy, visual impairment and hearing impairment – the development of children in terms of both their ability to communicate and their intelligence is an indication of the resilience of development in the face of limited opportunities. The findings also suggest that development may be aided by children being able to use different forms of information in their environment to compensate for their disability.

Emotional, behavioural and educational problems

In this section we will examine attention-deficit hyperactivity disorder (ADHD), autism and developmental dyslexia. Emotional and behavioural problems are most apparent in ADHD where the children tend to be excitable and distractable. In contrast, a prominent feature of autism is the difficulty in social activities, and in dyslexia the ways of processing information.

Attention-deficit hyperactivity disorder (ADHD)

The key characteristics of ADHD listed in DSM-IV (see Chapter 10) are:

- poor sustained attention, with the result that long tasks are difficult to accomplish
- inappropriate overactivity
- impulsivity (the child acts before thinking).

Typically children with ADHD have normal IQ, but may not do well at school because of their difficulties in adapting to a classroom environment. Despite its name. ADHD does not simply imply that these children are more active than other children. They may be no more active in free-play situations, but they do tend to be more active in structured situations, such as in the classroom. As a result, a child's behaviour in school may mistakenly be perceived as disruptive, especially if, as sometimes occurs, there has been a failure to diagnose ADHD.

A number of explanations and methods of treatment have been proposed for ADHD. A biological explanation has been put forward by Whalen (1989) that children with ADHD need to obtain extra stimulation because they have minimal brain damage (i.e. damage to the brain which cannot be detected). Confirmation of this hypothesis was thought to come from the finding that the attention of children with ADHD was improved when they were given stimulant medications (e.g. amphetamines such as Ritalin). This paradoxical effect appeared to confirm the hypothesis because extra stimulation in the form of drugs appeared to make the children calmer. However, a study by Rapoport *et al.* (1978) revealed that a similar effect also occurred in children without ADHD. Because of these findings, the hypothesis about minimal brain damage continues to be investigated.

A different and widely publicized theory is that additives in the diet are the cause of ADHD. The use of a suitable diet without additives (e.g. the Feingold diet) appears to reduce the effects of ADHD in some children, although the claim still remains controversial (Conners *et al.* 1980).

It has also been suggested that parental behaviour causes ADHD. However, comparison of patterns of interaction when the children were receiving medication and when they were not, revealed that mothers react to their children in different ways at these two times (the mothers did not know when their children were receiving medication). Thus, the pattern of interaction seems to have been caused by the child, rather than the adult's behaviour being the cause of ADHD.

At present there is no single explanation of ADHD which is generally accepted. This may be because the condition is the result of a number of different causes in different children. However, there are two forms of treatment which are reasonably successful. Medication involving stimulants appears to improve the behaviour of about 75 per cent of children with ADHD. The children are less impulsive, disruptive and oppositional as well as showing better attention. It is estimated that somewhere between one and two per cent of children in the United States receive this type of medication. Even though there are immediate beneficial effects with medication, there are worries about its long-term effects, about the ethics of such treatment and the side effects (such as insomnia, and loss of appetite). Furthermore, the effects of medication on behaviour only last while the medication continues to be administered.

Behaviour therapy is also used as a method of treatment. This uses a system of rewards for accomplishing target behaviours (see Chapter 12). This seems to be effective in the short term (O'Leary 1980). The disadvantage of this approach is that the effects are not long lasting and that learning often does not generalize to other situations.

Autism

Autism is a condition which has attracted considerable attention. It was the subject of the film *The Rain Man*, as well as a number of television documentaries. However, autism in the form identified by Kanner (1943) is a rare condition (0.002 per cent of children, Gilberg 1990). Despite its rarity, the puzzling and intriguing nature of the disorder has resulted in much media and research interest.

As with other disabilities, there is a range in the severity of autism. Some children show withdrawal from social interaction, a dislike of changes in their environment so that they may become angry or distressed if objects are moved in their room, and either a lack of speech or speech that is not particularly communicative.

Drawing by an autistic child, Nadia, aged 5 years.
Source: Selfe 1983

Such characteristics were described by Kanner (1943) in his identification of the condition. A feature of autism which is often commented on by observers and by some of the individuals themselves is a difficulty in understanding the way other people act. Children with autism generally perform poorly on IQ tests and have scores below 70 (DeMyer *et al.* 1974). However, a few children with autism show average or above average functioning in areas such as:

- drawing skills
- remembering names and dates
- performing complex calculations
- the ability to play a musical instrument.

Explanations of childhood autism

Why do children with autism have impaired social abilities? There have been a number of answers to this question. Originally the parents were blamed and thought to have impersonal relationships with their children (Kanner 1943), but evidence has accumulated against this explanation. Although it is unusual for other children in the family to have autism, carefully conducted twin studies have revealed a genetic cause of the condition (Szatmari and Jones 1991).

One explanation that we will discuss is the idea that children with autism lack the ability to think about mental states (e.g. liking, reasoning, believing) in themselves and others, and this provides one account of why these children have social difficulties. According to this explanation, children with autism lack a theory of mind (ToM), i.e. an understanding that other people have mental states which can involve different ideas from their own. There is much current interest in this possibility and about the way that such ideas can explain many features of autism. For a child to possess a theory of mind (ToM), they must be able to understand that someone else may have a different perspective or knowledge to their own. The classic study in this area involved testing children's understanding of stories in what has become known as the false belief task. One such story was as follows. Maxi puts his chocolate in a green cupboard and then goes to play outside. Unknown to Maxi, his mother moves the chocolate to a blue cupboard. The child is asked where they think Maxi will look for the chocolate when he comes back. All children younger than 4 years typically say the blue cupboard and therefore do not seem to take account of the

❖ Activity 3 ❖

Imagine that you are unable to understand what other people are thinking about and that you simply assume that they have the same sorts of thoughts as yourself. Make a list of the ways that this would alter how you relate to other people. For instance, would you lie to them, be pleased to see them, etc.?

fact that Maxi does not know that the chocolate has been moved. Among investigators in this area it is generally agreed that the ability to answer questions like this signals an important cognitive and social development. It shows that children can now view people and what people know in a very much more sophisticated way (see also Chapter 18).

Children with autism typically fail ToM tasks even when their mental age is above four years. A number of investigators have claimed that many of the problems experienced by children with autism (e.g. inability to deceive, lack of personal relationships, difficulty with communicating) can be attributed to a lack of ToM (e.g. Baron-Cohen *et al.* 1985). Consequently, it has been suggested that they have what is termed 'mind blindness', i.e. an inability to understand the mental states of themselves and others.

Why do children with autism fail to develop a theory of mind? One explanation is that children with autism have difficulties in forming alternative ideas about the world. Leslie (1987) has developed a model of pretend play which suggests that at about 18 to 20 months, children are able to decouple their thoughts from reality. This means that they can pretend, for example, that a banana is a telephone. He suggested that pretence is possible because of the operation of a *decoupler*, a cognitive process which allows children to go beyond what they perceive, to think about alternative possibilities in their world. Prior to about 18 months, when the decoupler becomes available, infants are supposed to perceive the world in a literal way. The activation of the decoupler changes this and allows new cognitive operations involving pretending. According to this model, the absence of pretend play, the inability to tell lies and other related characteristics in children with autism (Wulff 1985) are due to their inability to decouple their thoughts from reality.

One problem with this hypothesis, however, is that pretend play is present at 2 years, yet most studies report that a ToM emerges at around 4 years. Leslie (1987) originally suggested that this age difference can partly be accounted for by the additional complexity of the ToM task, especially the need to make inferences about another person's beliefs. Furthermore, the age gap between these two processes may be smaller than was originally thought, and may simply be due to young children's problems in remembering all the compo-nents in the ToM tasks (Lewis *et al.* 1994). Leslie has also suggested that the ToM task may require a deeper understanding of the way that mental states can be the cause of actions, and that this is needed for successful performance in ToM tasks.

There are also suggestions that autism may be caused by a more basic deficit: the lack of an ability to understand the emotions of people. Hobson (1993) suggests that children with autism, unlike other children, fail to understand or identify the facial expressions they see. As a result, they live in a world where they do not notice the emotions of others, and fail to develop an understanding that other people can have different ideas from themselves. If you do not know that other people experience emotions, then it will be very difficult to understand that other people have different feelings and beliefs from you. Hobson argues that such understanding is necessary to enable children at a later age to be able to engage in pretend play and similar activities, and thus this hypothesis can also be used to explain the reason why children with autism fail to develop pretend play and later a ToM.

So far, research investigations have not been able to determine which is the better explanation of autism. Hobson (1993) points out that given many of the similarities between Leslie's and his own ideas, it will be difficult to identify a critical test to distinguish between them. For instance, in children with autism there is a striking absence in the words that refer to attention and to cognitive states (Jordan 1993); both accounts would predict this. Similarly, children with autism seem unable to decouple themselves from reality and as a result have difficulty in deceiving; again such findings can be explained by both accounts (Sodian and Frith 1990).

In relation to all these arguments, it is important to return to the range of abilities of children with autism. Tager-Flusberg (1992) has observed that in many studies between 20 and 50 per cent of the children with autism are able to pass the false belief task. Such a finding has largely been ignored even though it indicates that a ToM explanation may not be appropriate for all children with autism.

The research into children with autism has had an important impact on the way psychologists think about early development. At present there is some uncertainty about the precise cause of the difficulties in children with autism. However, discussion of this issue has been associated with the development of more detailed models about the way that cognition, emotion and communication are inter-related.

Developmental dyslexia

Most people know that dyslexia involves problems with reading and spelling. The more precise definition of dyslexia is a topic which has created considerable controversy. Part of the reason for this is that some authorities maintain that children with dyslexia process information in a different way to other children, while others argue that the reading and spelling difficulties are on a continuum, the children with dyslexia simply being at one end of this continuum. This difference has important implications, as some Education Authorities accept the continuum theory and argue that children with dyslexia do not have special needs and do not therefore need special provision.

In general terms dyslexia is usually seen as a reasonably specific difficulty with reading and spelling, and that this difficulty would not be expected on the basis of a child's other abilities. The reading and spelling difficulties often involve:

- losing track of what is being read
- difficulty in saying unfamiliar words
- the reversal and rotation of written letters
- the omission of syllables.

However, Fawcett (1994) has argued that there may be other associated difficulties, like forgetfulness and clumsiness. The term 'developmental dyslexia' is used to distinguish it from acquired dyslexia, a condition with similar characteristics, but which is the result of some form of neurological damage.

Various hypotheses have been put forward to account for different types of dyslexia. One problem when investigating these ideas has been to separate the causes from the consequences of the condition. For example, an early idea was that children with dyslexia had perceptual problems which meant that they had a poor visual memory. Indeed, a number of studies reported that children with dyslexia were poorer at remembering words and letters. However, such a finding does not tell us whether this problem is the cause of dyslexia or is a consequence of poor reading skills. Vellutino (1979) tested the ability of children with dyslexia to remember and write down both English words and words written in Hebrew. The children with dyslexia were worse than children of the same age at the first task, but performed as well as children of the same age in the second task. Consequently, the findings suggest that children with dyslexia do not have a visual memory problem, but they are less good at processing English words because of delays in reading. Findings such as these led to a move away from the visual hypothesis. Interestingly, more recent work (Fawcett and Nicolson 1994) has suggested that children with dyslexia have difficulties processing transient information, i.e. information which is only presented for a very brief time. This may be related to research evidence which suggests that there is a general impairment to short-term memory (Ellis and Miles 1977).

Another explanation is that children with dyslexia have problems with the processing of speech sounds (these speech sounds are called phonemes, which are the smallest sound that can be identified in speech, e.g. b, p, t). Various studies point to the difficulties that children with dyslexia have with verbal memory tasks involving information about sounds. For example, Olson *et al.* (1989) compared children with

In Focus

Five different views about dyslexia (from Fawcett and Nicolson 1994)

Unsympathetic headteacher (of child with dyslexia, aged 7): 'He's not dyslexic – he's just a silly little boy who won't concentrate for more than 10 seconds. What he needs is a good kick up the backside!'

Exasperated (but supportive) teacher (of a 14-year-old): 'This year Ben has put in the minimum of effort. He arrives at lessons ill prepared, his homework is rarely, if ever, handed in and his work is scrappily presented. He is his own worst enemy!'

Baffled parent: 'Alan just keeps losing things – he put his coat in the locker so it wouldn't get lost, but then he lost the key, and now he can't even remember which locker it was – he'd lose his own head if it wasn't joined on!'

Depressed parent: 'The depressing thing is that although we've gone over the word 20 times this weekend, he still doesn't seem to be any better at spelling it!'

Desperate parent: 'He's been in the remedial reading group for five years now, but I'm sure he's reading worse now than when he was eight years old.'

dyslexia and matched children with a similar reading age on their ability to move the sound from one part of a word to another (e.g. they used a complicated task that involved removing the first sound of a word and adding it to the end of the word and also adding –ay, so pig would become ig-pay). Children with dyslexia were worse than the other children when they performed this task, which suggests that they had problems with processing speech sounds.

Rack *et al.* (1994) have argued that such difficulties affect reading skills and there are findings which support this argument. Olson *et al.* (1989) were able to show that children with dyslexia were less accurate and slower at reading non-words (words made up by the experimenters) than children with a similar reading age. This suggests that the children with dyslexia have problems in being able to translate the letters they see into the appropriate sounds. When the two groups of children were asked to identify which of a pair of words was spelt correctly (e.g. sammon-salmon), children with dyslexia were better than the matched group, indicating that in tasks which involve visual recognition, children with dyslexia can perform as well as other children. However, not all studies have found such effects (Rack *et al.* 1992). Furthermore, it is interesting to note that Rack *et al.* (1994) argue, in relation to explaining the pattern of behaviour in dyslexia, that the reversal errors often present in these children (reading 'saw' instead of 'was') are common in *all* children and may not be a unique feature of dyslexia.

The finding of phonological problems in children with dyslexia is particularly interesting because other research indicates that these skills help children to learn to read. Bryant and Bradley (1985) tested nursery school children before they started to read on their ability in rhyming and alliteration (being able to identify the same sounds in different words), so that the children's skills were not affected by their reading ability and experience. Bryant and Bradley found a correlation between these skills and later reading abilities when the children were eight or nine years old. This suggests that skills in dealing with speech sounds help the development of reading. These conclusions have been reinforced by an intervention study which revealed that training pre-school children in processing speech sounds helped their later reading (Lundberg *et al.* 1988).

Another explanation of dyslexia is that it involves a deficit in automaticity (Fawcett and Nicolson 1994). Automaticity refers to the process by which a skill changes from having to involve conscious thought, to one in which the whole process can be conducted without conscious monitoring and control (much like the change from playing a piano note by note, to the fluent performance of a skilled pianist). To support their argument, Fawcett and Nicolson quote the finding that children with dyslexia not only have problems in moving to an automatic pairing of sight and sound when reading, but also have difficulties in balancing, and in acquiring other new skills. These investigations about speech perception have been important in suggesting the types of problem that children with dyslexia have in processing information. Even so, there continues to be a debate about the precise nature of these problems.

Section summary

The psychological research about ADHD, autism and dyslexia has focused on the causes of these conditions. In all three conditions there remains uncertainty about the precise reason for the disability. However, research has provided a much fuller description of the conditions and has identified important explanations which need to be further evaluated.

Chapter summary

- Atypical development raises many issues for parents, carers and research workers. We still know remarkably little about many of the forms of atypical development.
- Research investigations have identified many features of atypical development which are contrary to widely perceived notions about this process:
  - (a) In cases where there is a genetic cause of a condition, the environment often has an important role in influencing the degree of disability.
  - (b) The examination of cerebral palsy, visual impairment and hearing impairment has revealed that, despite the fact that these conditions have a wide-reaching effect on the way children interact with their social and physical environment, children can achieve levels of performance equivalent to others without the disability.
  - (c) The discussion of ADHD, autism and dyslexia has illustrated that atypical development involves very different dimensions of behaviour: ADHD concerns levels of activity and attention; autism concerns the inability to relate to others; dyslexia involves an inability to process certain forms of information.
- The study of atypical development has implications for our understanding of typical development (e.g. because it can highlight the way certain abilities are necessary for typical development). In the same way, the study of typical development can be important for the understanding of atypical development; it can provide information about the usual way that development occurs.
- Children with atypical development, like all children, have their own strengths and weaknesses.
- Because in many cases there remains uncertainty about the definition of a disability, attention needs to be paid to *all* the characteristics of the child, not just to the *label* given to some of their abilities.
- The challenge for the parent, carer and researcher is to recognize and work in relation to the diversity of different patterns of development.

Essay questions

1 Discuss some of the psychological effects of *one* physical and *one* sensory disability.* *(24 marks)*

2 Describe and evaluate research into the causes of any *one* emotional or behavioural problem in children (e.g. ADHD, autism).** *(24 marks)*

3 (a) What do psychologists mean by the term 'learning difficulties'? *(6 marks)*

(b) Outline and evaluate *two* explanations of learning difficulties in children. *(18 marks)*

* Please note: in the AEB exam, the term 'handicap' may be used in place of 'disability' or 'impairment', to conform to the wording used in the AEB syllabus. In this chapter, we have preferred to use the terms 'disability' and 'impairment', so as not to cause any offence.

** In this chapter we have implied that dyslexia is an educational, rather than an emotional or behavioural, problem in children. However, since the AEB syllabus includes dyslexia in this latter category, it would be permissible to base your answer to this question on dyslexia.

Further reading

Bancroft, D. and Carr, R. (1995) *Influencing Children's Thinking*, Oxford: Blackwell.

An up-to-date and accessible book with chapters about dyslexia, hearing impairment, Down's syndrome and autism.

Lewis, V. (1987) *Development and Handicap*, Oxford: Blackwell.

A good coverage of visual impairment, hearing impairment, Down's syndrome and autism.

Chapter 10

Conceptions and models of abnormality

Pamela Prentice

Preview

In this chapter we shall be looking at:

- definitions of abnormality
- classification systems (ICD and DSM)
- models of abnormality
- cultural and sub-cultural definitions of abnormality.

Introduction

This chapter will consider a range of definitions and models of abnormality in relation to what are often called 'mental disorders'.

Definitions of abnormality refer to ways in which abnormality has been defined and classified. Whilst most of these definitions have practical value, this chapter will consider how they are often hampered by operational or ethical difficulties. The models of abnormality outlined in this chapter offer coherent, yet differing, perspectives on the origins of abnormal behaviour and psychological functioning. Each orientation, in turn, leads to quite different ideas about treatment methods for mental disorders. This chapter will also consider cultural and subcultural definitions of abnormality.

Cultural definitions refer to differences *between* cultures in the way that abnormal behaviour is defined and classified. Subcultural definitions refer to the ways in which ethnicity, gender and social class, for example, affect how abnormal behaviour is defined and classified *within* a culture.

Definitions of abnormality

There are many definitions of abnormality and in this section four definitions will be discussed. These are:

- statistical infrequency (deviation from the norm)
- violation of moral standards
- deviation from the expected
- personal suffering, distress and dysfunction.

Statistical infrequency (deviation from the norm)

According to this definition, any behaviour which is statistically infrequent is regarded as abnormal. It is assumed that personality traits and behaviour can be placed into a normal distribution pattern and that most people do not stray very far from the 'norm' or average. This method is used to assess mental retardation and mental genius, on the assumption that intelligence can be measured by IQ tests, in which scores are plotted against a normal distribution pattern. The main problem here is that positively valued deviations (e.g. higher IQ) tend not to be viewed as 'abnormal'. As Davison and Neale (1994) point out, many behaviours that are statistically infrequent, such as great athletic ability, are not generally regarded as abnormal.

Violation of moral standards

Szasz (1972) suggested that 'madness' is manufactured solely in order to label those people in society who do not conform to the rules of society or to conventional standards of morality. Society sets up rules for behaviour and if anyone breaks those rules then they are regarded as deviant. Historically, unmarried women who became pregnant were interned in mental institutions, as were homosexual people. A diagnosis of insanity has been used in Russia as a way of detaining political dissidents, and in Japan as a threat to ensure a strong work ethic. In present day Western culture, the term 'mental disorder' is not generally used to define 'deviant' behaviour, either political or sexual. There have been criminal cases (e.g. murder or sexual crimes) where the perpetrator has pleaded the insanity defence, but this is not a matter of course. A recent example of invoking the insanity defence is given below. There are types of behaviour that are generally regarded as unacceptable, such as rape and mass murder, where it is difficult to accept that such violation of others could possibly be normal. In such cases there is a tendency to regard those people as abnormal, believing that their extreme anti-social behaviour must be inherent in their personality.

Deviation from the expected

On a day-to-day basis we distinguish between normal and abnormal behaviour according to what is expected in a given situation. Much of our behaviour is context specific and out of context it may seem bizarre. For example, what would you think if you were walking through the park and someone sitting on a bench suddenly jumped up and started singing and dancing?

In Focus

The insanity defence

Lorena Bobbitt pleaded temporary insanity and was acquitted in January 1994 of the charge of maliciously wounding her husband. In June 1993 she had taken a kitchen knife and cut off his penis whilst he slept. She claimed that she had suffered many years of abuse by John Bobbitt and that after one episode of abuse she suffered a brief psychotic episode in which she was compelled to commit the act.

In Focus

The genetic defence for psychopathic murderers

There is a current suggestion that sociopaths and psychopaths may have a genetic defect and that this is the cause of their anti-social and often violent behaviour. This could be viewed as a mitigating circumstance for the apparently cold-blooded murderer or rapist. A number of defence lawyers in the USA have recently put forward the genetic argument in defence of their client. They have provided phenotype data (family trees) showing an ancestry of violent criminals, suggesting that the accused was not exercising free-will, but acted as a result of a genetic defect. So far this defence has not resulted in acquittal.

You would probably think that this person was rather odd. But if you then saw a film crew you would contextualize the scene, assume the person was an actor and perhaps stay around to watch.

❖ Activity 1 ❖

Refer to the example of 'singing and dancing' behaviour in the text. Drawing on your own experience, provide examples of unexpected behaviours and how you interpreted or explained them.

At a practical, everyday level, deviation from the expected can be a useful way to identify mental problems. We learn what to expect from individuals on a day-to-day basis and if their behaviour deviates drastically from this, then we become alarmed on their behalf. This may be vital to the receipt of suitable help because, for example, people with clinical depression are often unable to motivate themselves to seek assistance, and people suffering from schizophrenia are characterized by a lack of insight regarding their problem. An important point to note here is the shift in emphasis from the *person* to the *behaviour* that is being regarded as abnormal.

Personal suffering, distress and dysfunction

People with clinical depression or anxiety often experience considerable suffering and distress and a general dysfunction in their everyday activities, such as being unable to go to work. But these are not true definitions of 'abnormality'. They are more a way of determining the extent of a person's problems and the likelihood that they might need professional help. A student experiencing anxiety and distress about a forthcoming exam may behave uncharacteristically, but this would not necessarily be regarded as abnormal behaviour. Conversely, a sociopath might exhibit abnormal behaviour, such as violence and aggression, but be unlikely to experience personal suffering, distress, or any general dysfunction. Comer (1995) points out that psychological abnormality is not necessarily indicated by dysfunction alone; for example, some people protest against social injustice by depriving themselves of necessities, such as food. It is when abnormal behaviour interferes with daily functioning, such that people lose the ability to work or the motivation to care for themselves properly, that the behaviour becomes pathological.

Classification systems

The statistical definition of 'abnormality', mentioned earlier in this chapter, is a way of viewing abnormal behaviour in terms of the degree to which behaviour strays, or deviates, from the population 'norm'. Classification systems also adopt statistical criteria, but these are based upon the presence [or absence] of certain symptoms, rather than population norms. A cluster of symptoms which are found to occur regularly together is called a syndrome. Agreement is reached among clinicians as to whether a particular syndrome constitutes a category of mental disorder. A list of categories with their symptom descriptions forms a classification system.

ICD and DSM

The major classification system is the International Classification of Diseases published by the World Health Organization (WHO), currently in its tenth revision (ICD-10), published in 1993. ICD is an official system for coding known diseases into categories that can be identified at an international level. The primary function of ICD is to facilitate the collection of basic health statistics. Mental disorders were not included until the sixth revision in 1952 (ICD-6). Various countries have developed their own classification systems, such as the American Psychiatric Association –

In Focus

DSM-IV definition of mental disorder

'In DSM-IV, each of the mental disorders is conceptualized as a clinically significant behavioural or psychological syndrome or pattern that occurs in an individual and that is associated with present distress (e.g. a painful symptom) or disability (i.e. impairment in one or more important areas of functioning) or with a significantly increased risk of suffering death, pain, disability or an important loss of freedom. In addition, this syndrome or pattern must not be merely an expectable and culturally sanctioned response to a particular event, for example the death of a loved one. Whatever its original cause, it must currently be considered a manifestation of a behavioural, psychological or biological dysfunction in the individual. Neither deviant behaviour (e.g. political, religious or sexual) nor conflicts that are primarily between the individual and society are mental disorders unless the deviance or conflict is a symptom of a dysfunction in the individual, as described above.'

Source: DSM-IV 1994, pp. xxi-xxii

Diagnostic and Statistical Manual of Mental Disorders (DSM) and the Chinese Classification of Mental Disorders (CCMD).

The American Psychiatric Association (APA) first published DSM as a variant of the mental disorders section of ICD-6, because there was some disagreement about the mental disorders taxonomy. The APA take an operational approach by including diagnostic criteria, so that the manual will also serve clinical practice. DSM is the most widely used diagnostic system in British psychiatry, bearing in mind that ICD does not include diagnostic criteria.

DSM avoids the use of the term 'abnormal' since it does not serve any purpose in either diagnosis or treatment. Instead the term 'mental disorder' is used,

Table 10.1 Major categories of mental disorder listed in DSM-IV

Clinical Disorders	**Personality Disorders**
Schizophrenia and other Psychotic Disorders	Antisocial Personality Disorder
Mood Disorders	Paranoid Personality Disorder
Anxiety Disorders	Schizoid Personality Disorder
Somatoform Disorders	Schizotypal Personality Disorder
Factitious Disorders	Borderline Personality Disorder
Dissociative Disorders	Narcissistic Personality Disorder
Sexual and Gender Identity Disorder	Avoidant Personality Disorder
Sleep Disorders	Dependent Personality Disorder
Eating Disorders	Obsessive-Compulsive Personality Disorder
Impulse-Control Disorders	
Adjustment Disorders	**Mental Retardation**
Disorders First Diagnosed in Infancy, Childhood or Adolescence	
Delirium, Dementia and Amnesic and other Cognitive Disorders	

although tentatively because it lacks a consistent operational definition that covers all situations. The overriding factors in determining whether individuals might require professional help are their degree of functioning in their daily life and the extent of their personal suffering and distress. Therefore, along with the statistical symptom criteria, DSM also incorporates the personal distress or dysfunction definition of abnormality. DSM is currently (1994) in its fourth edition (DSM-IV). The DSM-IV definition of mental disorder is shown on the previous page and Table 10.1 lists the major categories of mental disorder in DSM-IV.

Assessment procedures

In order to diagnose a problem, assessment procedures are required and usually include some or all of the following:

- clinical interview (to ascertain information from the client/patient regarding their problem)
- careful observation of the client's behaviour, mood states, etc. (usually during the interview)
- medical records
- psychometric tests.

Psychometric tests include IQ tests, which are often used to differentiate between mental retardation and mental disorder. Cognitive tests, which engage verbal, spatial and problem-solving abilities, are used to test for cognitive impairments.

Using DSM-IV, classification and diagnosis are made according to a multi-axial assessment, consisting of five axes (see Table 10.2). The first two involve classification according to symptoms and the remainder relate to other factors that are taken into consideration when making a diagnosis.

Table 10.2 Multi-axial assessment in DSM-IV

Axis I: 'Clinical Disorders' and Axis II: 'Personality Disorders' and 'Mental Retardation'

Classification is defined according to a set of symptoms which have been identified as present in a particular disorder. Diagnosis is made according to a symptom count from the defined list, the greater the number of symptoms, the more likely the diagnosis.

Axis III: 'General Medical Conditions'

These might be relevant to the understanding or management of the disorder. It may be that the mental disorder is a consequence of a physiological condition, for example pregnancy complications or infectious diseases.

Axis IV: 'Psychosocial and Environmental Problems'

These are taken into consideration when making a diagnosis. Such problems might include bereavement, marital discord, unemployment, poverty, illiteracy, sexual or physical abuse.

Axis V: 'Global Assessment of Functioning Scale'

Psychological, social and occupational functioning is considered on a hypothetical continuum of mental illness, from (100) superior functioning in a wide range of activities, to (70) some mild symptoms, to (50) some serious symptoms, to (1) persistent danger of seriously hurting self or others.

Practical and ethical implications

Classification raises a number of practical and ethical implications. These include:

- the purpose of classification
- reliability and validity
- labelling.

The main purpose of classification systems, in particular ICD, is to initiate consensus or agreement on a universal definition for specific disorders or syndromes. This helps to ensure that whenever research is undertaken on a disorder with a particular set of symptoms, the disorder can be universally recognized. Without agreed definitions (labels) it would be difficult for researchers and clinicians to communicate. An additional purpose of the DSM classification system is to assist clinicians to diagnose a person's problem (or set of symptoms) as a particular disorder. This may also enable a clinician to use available information on a given disorder to decide upon an appropriate course of treatment.

For a classification system to be of any real value then, it must be accurate. In technical terms it must be judged to have reliability and validity. Davison and Neale (1994) explain three kinds of validity in relation to classification systems – aetiological, concurrent and predictive:

1. *Aetiological validity* is met when the same causal factors for a particular disorder are found in all people with that disorder. For example, if a disorder is thought to be genetically determined, then there should be a family history of that disorder in all who suffer from it.
2. *Concurrent validity* is met when other symptoms, that are not part of the disorder itself, are nevertheless characteristic of those with the disorder, for example, finding that most people with schizophrenia have difficulties in personal relationships.
3. *Predictive validity* means that classification categories should predict the prognosis, or outcome, of a disorder.

Validity also relies heavily on the *reliability* of a category. The consistency with which clinicians agree upon a diagnosis for a particular set of symptoms is known as inter-rater reliability. For a classification system to be useful, therefore, those using it must be able to agree when a person should or should not be given a particular diagnosis (Davison and Neale 1994). Psychiatric diagnosis is notoriously unreliable and studies show that even very experienced psychiatrists only agree about 50 per cent of the time (see Spitzer and Williams (1985) for a review of the process of diagnosis). In the 1960s and 1970s there was a great deal of concern that psychiatrists too readily gave a diagnosis of schizophrenia. There was even greater concern that many people were being admitted to mental hospitals when they were not mentally ill, and once admitted they were detained and given treatment without their informed consent. This was supported in a famous study by Rosenhan (1970) and is explained briefly below. In response to criticism, the APA have

In Focus

On being sane in insane places (Rosenhan 1970)

Rosenhan asked nine pseudopatients (colleagues) to present themselves at mental hospitals throughout the United States, displaying one symptom of psychosis, that of hearing voices, but otherwise to appear sane. In all cases the pseudopatients were diagnosed with schizophrenia, admitted for treatment and retained for up to 30 days. After publication of his findings, Rosenhan conducted a subsequent study in which he publicly announced that he would send more pseudopatients. In fact he sent none, but nevertheless hospital admission statistics for schizophrenia were considerably lower during this period. Rosenhan concluded that psychiatrists cannot tell the sane from the insane.

tightened up reliability and validity within the current DSM-IV, although imperfect inter-rater reliability is inevitable when there is a large element of social judgement. The APA is careful to add a rejoinder that there is no assumption in DSM-IV that each category of mental disorder is a completely discrete entity. It is recognized that the boundaries are blurred between mental disorders because symptoms overlap.

There are also difficulties in identifying the boundary between mental disorder and no mental disorder. The APA, therefore, points out that DSM-IV is a guideline for clinicians and not meant to be used in a 'cookbook' fashion by rigidly adhering to a 'recipe'. DSM-IV diagnosis is merely the first step in a comprehensive evaluation and considerable additional information about the person being assessed is invariably required. Retaining someone in a mental hospital without their consent is still possible in the UK, under Sectioning laws, but this is restricted to a short period, after which the person's consent is required. People cannot any longer be retained indefinitely against their will, other than in a psychiatric prison. Indeed, with the current move within the NHS towards care in the community and the closing of mental hospitals, the situation has reversed. In-hospital care is now largely restricted to psychiatric wards within general hospitals and demand far exceeds current provision, which means that mentally ill people may not always get the treatment they need.

Goffman (1968) maintained that labelling someone as mentally ill carried a stigma that might stick long after the person had recovered from the problem. Scheff (1966) suggested that once labelled, a person was likely to accept the diagnosis and behave accordingly because he or she would be rewarded for adopting the role and punished for trying to escape from it. The APA is aware of these problems and is careful to point out in DSM-IV that clinicians should use DSM to classify and diagnose a disorder, rather than a person. So, for example, a person could be diagnosed as suffering from schizophrenia, but not labelled as schizophrenic. There is, to some extent, an inevitability about labelling. First, when people are absent from work, employers expect an explanation and this usually entails labelling the problem. Second, people suffering from mental problems, as with physical problems, are usually confused and concerned about their condition, as are their families, and they naturally seek to label the problem. Without a professional label people invent their own, often letting their imagination run wild and creating unwarranted fears. Despite this, psychologists, in the main, disagree with the principle of classification, because they think it forces people into categories, whilst ignoring individual differences and therefore overlooking important information. Many psychologists also regard the labelling of a set of symptoms as unnecessary for psychological treatment.

Section summary

Although the concept of 'abnormal' as distinct from 'normal' behaviour may be useful as a general guide for identifying whether someone may require professional assistance, its use is limited because it is difficult to determine what is 'normal', other than at a statistical level. Classification systems, such as ICD and DSM, enable consensus to be reached among clinicians about what symptoms constitute a particular disorder. DSM also includes diagnostic criteria, although it has been criticized on the grounds of low validity and poor reliability. This is, however, continually being improved. The concept of labelling someone with a mental disorder has been criticized on ethical grounds, but there are, nevertheless, a number of practical advantages.

Models of abnormality

There are five major conceptual models, each of which offers different explanations for the origins of mental disorders. Psychiatrists usually adopt the medical model, mental disorder as an 'illness', whilst psychologists tend to reject the concept of 'mental illness' in favour of models such as the psychodynamic, behavioural, cognitive or humanistic. The adoption of a particular conceptual model is very important because it will influence the type of research that is conducted and also the methods of treatment adopted.

Medical model

Assumptions of the medical model

The medical model has dominated the field of mental health for the past 200 years. It is a biological approach, which regards abnormality of mental functioning as an 'illness' or 'disease'. This is because mental disorders are thought to be related to physical malfunctioning in the brain. Some mental disorders are thought to have an organic basis, such as a brain tumour, or poisoning due to alcohol or drug abuse. Mental disorders which do not have a clear organic cause are often referred to as functional disorders, although they are still thought to be physical in origin, because symptoms occur as a consequence of chemical changes in the brain. Why these changes take place is not yet clear, but they may be due to a genetic defect or to life stress. It should be noted that the distinction between organic and functional is no longer made in DSM-IV (1994), but it is still in common usage among practitioners.

Evaluation and implications

- *Biochemical theory:* It is now known that some chemical drugs affect particular neurotransmitters, producing the symptoms of certain mental disorders. Since these drugs can also relieve the symptoms of certain disorders, it seems likely that a chemical imbalance is at the root of the problem. However, some psychologists disagree, believing the chemical imbalance to be the effect, rather than the cause, of mental problems. Many psychologists criticize psychiatry for focusing its attention primarily on symptoms.
- *Genetic research:* This research has highlighted a possibility that some people may be genetically at risk of developing a mental disorder, but so far the only strong evidence relates to conditions such as schizophrenia and manic-depression. Since no preventive measures to arrest the onset of these psychoses have yet been developed, the publicity surrounding such research may unfortunately serve to create further anxiety in relatives of a diagnosed person. Furthermore, by focusing attention and research funding on genetics, attention is distracted from environmental influences, which are thought to play a significant role in mental disorders.
- *The concept of 'no blame':* A diagnosis of mental 'illness' implies that the person is in no way responsible for the abnormality of functioning and as such is not to blame. This is generally thought to be more humane and likely to elicit a much more sympathetic response from others. However, anti-psychiatrists, such as Szasz (1972), point out that, even more than physical illness, mental illness is something that people fear, largely because it is something they do not understand. In general, people do not know how to respond to someone diagnosed as mentally ill. There may also be fears that the person's behaviour might be unpredictable and potentially dangerous. Therefore sympathy is more likely to give way to avoidance of the person, which in turn leads to the person feeling shunned.

- *Personal responsibility:* While the concept of 'illness' may remove blame, people become patients, handing over responsibility for their 'wellness' to professionals, who may or may not accurately diagnose the problem. Prescribed treatment may not be appropriate and yet there is an expectation that patients will comply with medication, despite the fact that, as the British National Formulary (index of pharmaceutical drugs and preparations) indicates, most medication carries side effects and often long-term dependency upon the drugs.
- *Implications for diagnosis and treatment:* Those adopting the medical model generally make use of ICD and DSM classification systems for defining and diagnosing mental disorders. Physical treatments are regarded as the most appropriate, since mental problems are viewed as physical illnesses (see Chapter 16 for types of physical treatment).

Psychodynamic model

Assumptions of the model

Psychodynamic theory, as a major orientation in psychology, is outlined in Chapter 25. It may be useful to refer to this to help you understand how psychodynamic theory has been applied to explain mental disorders. The psychodynamic model emphasizes the internal dynamics and conflicts which occur at an unconscious level. In his 'Introductory lectures on psychoanalysis' (1915 to 1918), Freud stated that humans are born with insatiable, demanding instincts (the id) and are subsequently socialized into the moral standards of their culture (the superego). The well-adjusted person develops a strong ego, that is able to 'manage' the personality, by allowing both the id and the superego expression at appropriate times. If the ego is weakened then the personality may be dominated by either the id or the superego, whichever is the stronger. If id impulses emerge unchecked, then they are expressed in destructiveness and immorality and this may result in conduct disorders in childhood and psychopathic behaviour in adulthood. A powerful superego rigidly enforces defence mechanisms, such that the person will be deprived of even socially acceptable pleasures. This will create neurosis, which could be expressed in the symptoms of anxiety disorders, such as phobias and obsessions. Psychological disturbance, therefore, results from the inability of the ego to manage conflict within the psyche.

Although psychical conflict can occur at any time in our life, it is most marked in early childhood because the ego is not developed fully enough to mediate between the id and the superego. Nor is it developed fully enough to deal with external events such as maternal absences, parental shortcomings and competition with siblings. Events in childhood of a traumatic or confusing nature are pushed into the unconscious through the defence mechanism of repression, because they are too painful for the ego to bear, or because the child hasn't developed sufficient knowledge of the world to make sense of the event (A. Freud 1936). Defence mechanisms, such as repression and displacement, have a powerful, yet unconscious, influence upon our behaviour. Whilst useful for protecting the ego, they do not offer a long-term solution, because distressing feelings do not disappear when they are repressed. They find expression in dreams and irrational behaviour and may eventually erupt and express themselves in psychological and psychosomatic problems. According to Freud, the behaviour of all people is to some extent 'abnormal' in that none of us is free from the dynamic conflicts relating to our unconscious drives, nor from the influence of repressed memories. Therefore it is perfectly 'normal' to experience anxiety. Abnormality is therefore both inevitable and beyond our conscious control.

Evaluation and implications

- *Scientific status:* Psychodynamic theory has proved to be difficult to subject to scientific, empirical analysis and as such some theorists claim that the theory is lacking in validity. However, Kline (1988) claims that a theory is not invalidated because it cannot be tested scientifically; it merely means that no-one has yet found a way to do it. Many of the observations made by psychodynamic theorists, such as those concerning the use of defence mechanisms, appear to be borne out in everyday life. Although early traumatic experiences may not necessarily emerge in adulthood as psychological problems, research indicates that many people with psychological problems do recollect experiences of emotional trauma in childhood.
- *Psychic determinism:* The model holds that abnormal behaviour results from unconscious psychic conflict related to innate, biological drives. The model also holds that early relationships with parents are important to psychological development. For these reasons it has been claimed the theory is 'deterministic' in the sense that individuals appear to have very little conscious involvement in their own personality development. The implicit assumption, therefore, is that people are not to blame for their *own* abnormal behaviour, but may be partially responsible for the development of abnormal behaviour in their offspring. This may prove to be a heavy burden for parents who feel they have 'done their best' and, according to the model, may also be grappling with their own inner emotional conflicts.
- *Implications for treatment:* Freud was instrumental in changing ways of thinking about the mentally ill, by pointing out that physical symptoms could have psychological causes. He developed a method of treatment for psychological distress (which is explained in Chapter 16) and from this many other psychodynamic therapies have evolved. These involve investigating unconscious psychodynamic processes, in order to facilitate insight into the conflicts and anxieties that are the underlying causes of abnormal behaviour.

Behavioural model

Assumptions of the model

Behaviourism, as a major orientation in psychology, is outlined in Chapter 25. It may be useful to refer to this to help your understanding of how this approach has been used to explain mental disorders. Advocates of the behavioural model would not use the term 'mental disorder' since they have no interest in mental structures, only in overt behaviour. Accordingly, they argue, abnormal behaviour is learnt in the same way as most other behaviour, through stimulus-response mechanisms and operant conditioning. The behavioural model provides explanations for the emergence of specific, maladaptive, or dysfunctional behaviours such as phobias, anxiety, depression and obsessive-compulsive disorders. (See Chapter 15 for more detail about these disorders).

- *Classical conditioning* (Pavlov 1927, 1941) explains how behaviour is learned through the association of an event in the environment (stimulus) with a physiological reaction (response) in the individual. Phobias, pathological fears of objects or situations, are thought to develop in this way. For example, a person may climb to the top of a high building and, when looking down, experience nausea and dizziness. This may develop into a fear of heights which is so strong that it becomes a phobia. In classical conditioning, it is not the object, or the situation, which is the cause of the fear (e.g. spiders or heights) but the conditioned response to the object or situation. For example, it is the response of feeling sick and dizzy when looking down from a high building that causes the fear of heights, not the height itself.

- *Operant conditioning* (Skinner 1974) explains how our behaviour is influenced by the consequences of our own actions. We learn the likely consequences of our own actions at a very early age through rewards and punishments from those who are caring for us. Conduct disorders and anti-social personality disorders have been explained in operant conditioning terms. If childhood aggression is rewarded, then that behaviour is likely to be repeated and reinforced again and again. Behaviours that may appear maladaptive to others may be functional or adaptive to the individual. For example, anxiety or depression might procure secondary gain in the form of attention and concern from others. If a child grows up in a violent environment, then, as explained by Social Learning Theory (Bandura 1973), the child learns anti-social behaviour by observing violent behaviour in others.

The behavioural model emphasizes individual differences; we are all subject to our own unique learning experiences, which means that the gap between 'normal' and 'abnormal' is reduced. According to Skinner (1953), cross-cultural studies reveal that what is regarded as abnormal in one culture may be regarded as normal in another. For example, hallucinations are viewed as a symptom of psychosis in the western world, whereas in some African tribes these are regarded as 'visions'.

Evaluation and implications

- *Scientific status:* Many studies have been conducted to test out the behavioural model, such as the famous study by Watson and Raynor (1920) who conditioned a young boy named 'Little Albert' to fear white rats. However, because of the ethical considerations surrounding conditioning research with humans, many of the more recent studies have been carried out on animals and it is an open question whether such research can be extrapolated to humans. (See Chapter 8 for more details about animal studies and behaviourism.)
- *Rejection of the 'illness' model:* The behavioural model provides explanations for psychological problems which overcome the ethical considerations of labelling someone as 'ill' or 'abnormal'. Instead it looks at whether behaviour is 'adaptive' or 'maladaptive'. This model also allows individual and cultural differences to be taken into account. Providing the behaviour is presenting no problems to the individual, or to other people, then there is no reason to regard the behaviour as a mental disorder. However, whilst this philosophy is embodied in the theoretical model, it is not always adhered to in practice. Behavioural methods of re-shaping behaviour have been forced on people who are not in a position to give informed consent, for instance, because they are institutionalized. (For a fuller account of the ethical considerations of the behavioural model, see Chapter 16.)
- *Symptoms versus cause:* Advocates of the psychodynamic model claim that the behavioural model focuses only on symptoms and ignores the causes of abnormal behaviour. They claim that symptoms are merely the tip of the iceberg – the outward expression of deeper underlying emotional problems. Whenever symptoms are treated without any attempt to ascertain the deeper underlying problems, then the problem will only manifest itself in another way, through different symptoms. This is known as 'symptom substitution'. Behaviourists counter this criticism by claiming that they need not look beyond the symptoms because the symptoms *are* the disorder. Thus, there is nothing to be gained by searching for internal causes, either psychological or physical.
- *Implications for treatment:* Behavioural therapy takes a practical problem-solving approach. The role of the therapist is to identify maladaptive learning, to facilitate the unlearning of maladaptive responses, and then to educate the person into more adaptive learning strategies. (Chapter 16 provides a more detailed account of behavioural therapies.)

Cognitive model

Assumptions of the model

The cognitive approach to understanding abnormality was founded by Albert Ellis (1962) and Aaron Beck (1963), who thought that the weakness of the behavioural model was that it did not take mental structures into account. The rationale behind the cognitive model is that the *thinking* processes between stimulus and response are seen as responsible for the *feeling* component of the response. The cognitive model holds that emotional problems can be attributed directly to distortions in our cognitions or thinking processes. These take the form of negative thoughts, irrational beliefs and illogical errors, such as polarized thinking and overgeneralization. These maladaptive thoughts, it is claimed, usually take place automatically and without full awareness. Ellis (1962) maintained that everyone's thoughts are rational at times and irrational at other times. Psychological problems occur only if people engage in faulty thinking to the extent that it has become maladaptive for themselves and others around them (see Fig. 10.1).

Evaluation and implications

- *Scientific status:* Research has shown that many people suffering from mental disorders do exhibit thought patterns associated with maladaptive functioning. For example, Gustafson (1992) found that maladaptive thinking processes were displayed in many people with psychological disorders, such as anxiety, depression and sexual disorders.

  However, Beck (1991) himself has pointed out that, although cognitive processes are involved in many psychological disorders, they may well be a consequence rather than a cause of their problems.
- *Model for living:* The cognitive approach offers a 'model for living' which promotes psychological well-being and avoids the stigma of 'mental illness'. However, the cognitive model has been criticized because it suggests that everyone should be self-sufficient; this tends to devalue social support systems. It lays the blame for psychological problems firmly within the individual, rather than with the social environment. Consequently, attention may be drawn away from the need to improve social conditions which have a significant effect on quality of life.
- *Implications for treatment:* Cognitive therapy takes a practical, problem-solving approach, by scientifically challenging and changing faulty cognitions. The methods are to teach people to recognize their maladaptive thinking patterns, and to counter these by replacing them with more adaptive ones. (See Chapter 16 for a fuller account of cognitive therapy.)

Humanistic model

Assumptions of the model

The humanistic model is based on the work of Carl Rogers (1951) and of Abraham Maslow (1968). The model proposes that people are able to make choices in life freely and that in the main those choices are channelled towards fulfilment and

Figure 10.1 Rationale behind cognitive theory

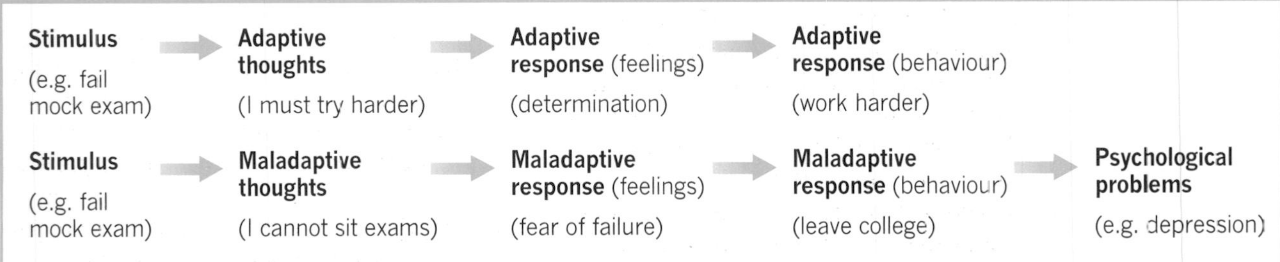

Figure 10.2
Congruence and incongruence

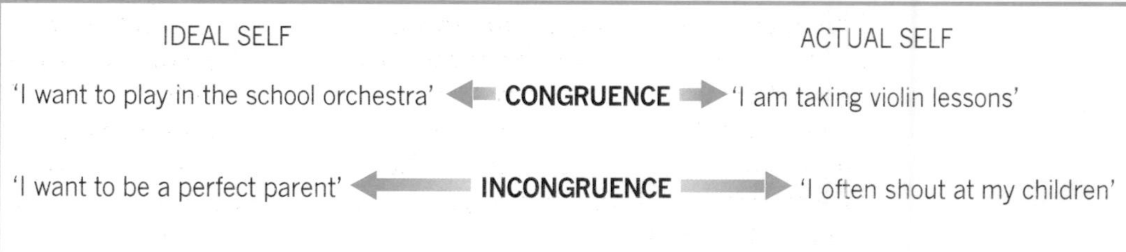

happiness and a healthy sense of self-worth. Rogers maintained that the development of self-worth begins in infancy. Humans have a basic need to feel nurtured and valued by significant people in their lives, such as parents. This nurturing comes in the form of love, praise and acceptance – what Rogers called positive regard. Rogers claims that if this is given freely, without conditions (unconditional positive regard), then people will develop a healthy sense of self-worth, recognizing their abilities and their difficulties. However, when there are conditions placed upon positive regard, such as 'We will love you only if . . . you are a good girl', then those people learn that they cannot be accepted and loved unless they fulfil standards set by others. As the child grows up conditions for acceptance become self-imposed and are often too rigid and impossible to meet. Children who receive only negative regard, such as criticism and blame, develop low self-esteem. Such people are usually quick to recognize faults in themselves and to take blame readily upon themselves, but they are very reluctant to accept their good qualities and to praise themselves. Rogers maintains that, in order to avoid this, parents should criticize the behaviour not the child, e.g. 'That was a naughty thing to do' rather than 'You are a bad boy.'

Humans establish a healthy sense of well-being by maintaining reasonable consistency between ideal-self and actual behaviour – what Rogers called congruence. However, the person's self-imposed conditions of worth, developed in childhood, may create a discrepancy between these. In striving for self-fulfilment, people often set themselves goals, or ideal standards, that are difficult or even impossible to meet and thus set themselves up for failure. Rogers called this incongruence; the greater the gap between ideal-self and actual-self, the greater the incongruence. He maintained that this can generate feelings of low self-worth, which in turn can affect psychological well-being and can even lead to maladjustment. Figure 10.2 shows examples of congruence and incongruence.

Strictly speaking, humanistic theory does not offer a 'model of abnormality' because it is diametrically opposed to any form of classification. Humanistic psychologists believe that it is fruitless to differentiate between 'normal' or 'abnormal', because people are unique individuals with their own idiosyncratic modes of behaviour. Therefore, everyone's experience of problems is individual and it is this unique experience that is important and not the labels attached to it.

Evaluation and implications

- *Scientific status:* It is often thought that humanistic theory is even more difficult than psychodynamic theory to subject to scientific analysis, although Rogers maintained that his theory grew out of research. He employed a large research team and claimed that his theories were testable empirically. Most of the research has examined the validity of therapeutic skills and these are addressed in Chapter 16. The main difficulty is that Rogers' research relied heavily on self-report measures of psychological functioning, yet many mental disorders are characterized by a lack of insight.
- *Person-centred:* The humanistic model offers an optimistic view by focusing on mental health and well-being, rather than illness, and on personal growth, rather than mental disorder.

Although some would argue that this is overly optimistic, it is regarded as the most ethical of all the models because of its particular emphasis on the *person* rather than on the *label*. This avoids any of the problems associated with labelling, such as stigma and misdiagnosis.

- *Personal and parental responsibility:* The belief in personal responsibility carries an implicit assumption that people *ought* to be able to help themselves (self-cure), which may not always be the case, especially for someone with a severe psychological problem. The emphasis on personal freedom and the reluctance to diagnose, if adhered to too rigidly, may mean that some disorders requiring medical assistance go untreated. The humanistic model also places much of the responsibility on significant others in the child's life, but it is very difficult for parents to provide consistent unconditional positive regard and always to limit their criticizing to the behaviour, rather than the person.
- *Implications for treatment:* Humanistic therapy, often called 'person-centred therapy', concentrates on the *person* rather than the *problem* and in particular on levels of incongruence (i.e. distorted self-perceptions and low self-worth). Given the human tendency towards growth and self-fulfilment, the aim of therapy is to facilitate the human capacity for self-cure. A fuller account of humanistic therapy is provided in Chapter 16.

Section summary

Each of the models explains the origins of abnormality in different ways. However, these models are not necessarily mutually exclusive, since each is effectively examining a different aspect of the individual. The medical model focuses on the physical dimension, whilst the psychodynamic model emphasizes the psychological dimension.The behavioural model observes that learned behaviour can be maladaptive while the cognitive model claims that thoughts can be irrational and therefore also maladaptive. The humanistic model focuses on the person's ability to fulfil their potential and, like the psychodynamic model, claims that early environmental experience is important to later development. Each of the models is subject to certain practical and ethical considerations.

Cultural and subcultural definitions

Conceptions of abnormality differ *between* cultures and this can have an enormous influence on the diagnosis and treatment of mental disorders. Subcultural differences relating to ethnicity, social class or gender *within* our own culture, are also thought to influence diagnosis and treatment.

Culture bound syndromes

Some abnormalities, or disorders, are thought to be culture specific. For example, the disorder *shenjing shuairuo* (neurasthenia) accounts for more than half of psychiatric outpatients in China. It is listed in the second edition of the Chinese Classification of Mental Disorders (CCMD-2) but it is not included in the American diagnostic classification system for mental disorders (DSM) used in the western world. Tseng (1986) questions whether this reflects a high prevalence of the disorder in China, or whether it is merely related to diagnostic procedures. Many of the symptoms of neurasthenia listed in CCMD-2 are similar to the symptoms that would meet the criteria for a combination of a mood disorder and an anxiety disorder under DSM-IV. The APA have now formally recognized 'culture bound syndromes' by including a separate listing in the appendix of DSM-IV (1994). However, as Fernando (1988) points out, many of these 'exotic' conditions actually occur quite frequently, but as long as they are limited to 'other' cultures then they will not be admitted into mainstream western classification. Western psychiatry maintains that most of these are merely variants of known syndromes and do not warrant new diagnostic entries.

Depression, which is common in our own culture, appears to be absent in Asian cultures. In trying to understand the reason for this, it has been observed that Asian people tend to live within an extended family, which means that they have ready access to social support. However, as Rack (1982) points out, Asian doctors report that depression is equally common among Asians, but that Asians consult their doctor for physical problems only and rarely with 'emotional' distress. They do not see this as the responsibility of the doctor and instead they tend to sort it out within the family. They might seek help for the physical symptoms of depression, such as tiredness, sleep disturbance and appetite disturbance, but would probably not mention their mood state. Socio-cultural differences in the prevalence of depression may, therefore, reflect the statistical likelihood of seeking professional help for emotional states.

One of the major difficulties with studies using diagnostic data is that figures are based on hospital admissions, which may not reflect the true morbidity rates for particular ethnic groups or particular disorders. Low admission rates found in many minority ethnic groups may reflect cultural beliefs about mental health. Cohen (1988) explains that in India, mentally ill people are cursed and looked down on. Rack (1982) points out that in China, mental illness also carries a great stigma and therefore the Chinese are careful to label only those whose behaviour is indisputably psychotic (i.e. where thinking and emotion are so impaired that the individual is out of contact with reality).

Culture bias in mental health

Research statistics have shown that there are significant differences in the prevalence rates for mental disorders between different ethnic or cultural groups in Britain. For instance, there is an over-representation of black (African-Caribbean) immigrants among those diagnosed with schizophrenia, of between two to seven times the rate for whites (e.g. Cochrane 1977). Cochrane and Sashidharan (1995) claim that this does not appear to be confined to first generation immigrants, because studies (e.g. Thomas *et al.* 1993) indicate that, if anything, the relative risk may be greater in the second generation. In contrast, Cochrane (1983) reports that he has found rates of admission for schizophrenia among South Asians (from India, Pakistan, Bangladesh, Hong Kong) to be comparable to whites. However, for less severe disorders, admission rates for South Asians and African-Caribbeans were significantly less than for whites.

An immediate explanation for these differences is that diagnostic figures merely reflect high or low morbidity rates for a particular disorder in the population of the country of origin. However, this cannot explain the high figures for schizophrenia diagnosis among African-Caribbeans in Britain because, as Cochrane (1983) points out, this has not been found to the same extent anywhere else in the world. How, then, can these differential diagnoses be explained?

Cultural stereotyping in British psychiatry

Fernando (1988) claims that stereotyped ideas about race are inherent in British psychiatry. For example, there are stereotypes of black violence and the belief that blacks cannot 'use' help and are therefore not suitable for open hospitals. Research has shown that the compulsory detaining of African-Caribbean patients in secure hospitals is higher than for any other group. Ineichen *et al.* (1984) examined hospital admissions in Bristol and found that non-white groups (West Indian plus other non-white) accounted for 32 out of 89 compulsory admissions, but only 30 out of 175 voluntary admissions. In a survey conducted by McGovern and Cope (1987) on hospital-detained psychotic patients in Birmingham, it was found that two-thirds were African-Caribbean (both migrants and British born), with the remaining one-third white and Asian. Table 10.3 lists some British research of practical importance, cited in Fernando (1988).

Culture 'blindness' in diagnosis

Cochrane and Sashidharan (1995) point out that it is a common assumption that the behaviours of the white population are normative and that any deviation from this by another ethnic group reveals some racial or cultural pathology. Conversely, as Rack (1982) points out, if a member of a minority ethnic group exhibits a set of symptoms that is similar to that of a white British-born patient, then they are assumed to be suffering from the same disorder, which may not actually be the case. For example, within the culture of one ethnic group it might be regarded as normal to see or hear a deceased relative during the bereavement period. Under DSM-IV criteria this behaviour might be misdiagnosed as a symptom of a psychotic disorder. Cochrane and Sashidharan (1995) suggest that practitioners are almost forced into assuming that mental illnesses such as schizophrenia, depression and neurosis, which are commonly found in European patients, are also found in non-European patients. They claim, furthermore, that the system does not easily allow for other disorders to be identified, which do not conform to those recognized in white patients, because British psychiatry is 'shot through with Eurocentric bias'. They claim that so-called 'culture bound syndromes' receive academic discussion, but they are

Table 10.3 Research studies on ethnicity and mental health

British research of practical importance
1 Over-diagnosis of schizophenia in: West Indian and Asian immigrant in-patients (Cochrane 1977; Carpenter and Brockington 1980; Dean *et al.* 1981) Patients of West Indian ethnicity admitted compulsorily in Bristol (Harrison *et al.* 1984) and in Birmingham (McGovern and Cope 1987)
2 Excess of compulsory admission of: Patients of West Indian ethnicity in Bristol (Harrison *et al.* 1984) and in Birmingham (McGovern and Cope 1987)
3 Excessive transfer to locked wards of: West Indian, Indian and African patients (Bolton 1984)
4 Excessive admisson of 'offender patients' of: People of West Indian ethnicity in Birmingham (McGovern and Cope 1987)
5 Overuse of ECT for: Asian in-patients in Leicester (Shaikh 1985) Black immigrant patients in East London (Littlewood and Cross 1980)

Source: Fernando 1988, p. 74

doubtful that this influences clinical practices in GP surgeries or busy hospitals.

Stressful life-experiences

Fernando (1988) points out that being a member of a minority ethnic group could be stressful owing to the exploitation, deprivation and harassment often experienced and, therefore, it might be expected that there would be a higher incidence of psychological problems among people from minority ethnic groups. However, ethnic differences are not reflected in the statistics which attempt to correlate stress and psychological problems in minority ethnic groups. Nevertheless, as Cochrane and Sashidharan (1995) point out, racism and prejudice have a significant impact upon psychological well-being. They also explain that migration from third world to first world countries means that the first generation of migrants is likely to be exposed to economic uncertainty, substandard housing and harsh working conditions, which in themselves may have mental health implications. These may then mistakenly be attributed to ethnicity.

Social class and mental health

It has long been established that there is an association between social class and mental illness. For example, major psychiatric disorders, such as schizophrenia, are diagnosed more often in people from socially disadvantaged backgrounds. Conversely 'neurotic' disorders are diagnosed more often in people from higher socio-economic groups. Several reasons have been suggested for these differences.

Stressful life-experiences

The literature has indicated that the higher prevalence of severe mental disorders in socially disadvantaged groups is largely due to their exposure to more stressful life experiences, compared with those in more advantaged social groups. The first large-scale survey to support this hypothesis was the Midtown Manhattan Study (Srole *et al.* 1961, and Langner and Michael 1962). The study found the lowest levels of psychiatric impairment in the upper classes, slightly more in the middle classes and the highest levels in the lower classes. When symptoms of disorders were mild to moderate, the levels were very similar in all three social classes, with the highest level of mental well-being in the upper classes. These findings were supported in a British study (Cochrane and Stopes-Roe 1980), which also found that lower social status was associated with higher risk of psychological problems.

A major study by Brown and Harris (1978) found a high incidence of depression among working-class housewives in Camberwell, London. The main vulnerability factors they identified were long-term periods of adverse circumstances, together with the cumulative effect of short-term life events, combined with factors such as lack of paid employment. However, the major finding in such studies was that high levels of stress correlate with greater susceptibility to mental disorder, regardless of social class. It has been proposed, therefore, that there are additional factors associated with social class and mental problems. For instance, those in the middle and upper classes have more 'positive' life-experiences to offset the 'negative' and those in the lower classes have less control over their environment.

Coping resources

The Brown and Harris (1978) study also revealed that, when faced with stressful events, the lack of a close confiding relationship was a strong indicator of vulnerability to mental illness, suggesting that social support may be an effective 'coping resource'. It has been noted that those in the middle and upper classes more readily access 'coping resources' than those in the lower classes. Therefore the greater prevalence rates for less severe 'neurotic' disorders in the higher socio-economic groups may simply reflect their greater tendency to take advantage of professional services for psychological problems. Cochrane (1995) explains that people living in high-rise flats are more prone to psychological problems than those in 'traditional' accommodation. People who have been rehoused in tower blocks report a drop in the quality of relationships with neighbours. This may be an important factor in mental health, because neighbours are a potential source of social support. However, Cochrane points out that neighbours can also be a source of irritation and even fear. Halpern (1995) claims that if a neighbourhood becomes labelled as a dumping ground for 'problem families' then people who were not originally a 'problem' themselves may develop adverse reactions which may affect their mental health.

The 'drift' hypothesis

An explanation for the higher incidence of serious mental disorder in lower socio-economic groups, is that the early onset of a major mental disorder, such as schizophrenia, might reduce the chances of establishing a career. The person may then subsequently 'drift' down the socio-economic scale. This indicates that social class is largely a consequence of, rather than a contributory factor in, mental disorder. Support for this is found in cases where the initial onset of schizophrenia has occurred later in life. It has been noted that many such individuals had previously established a good career.

Cochrane (1983) points out that the higher incidence of schizophrenia in poor areas could reflect the number of people who move to those areas after the onset of their illness, because it is all they can afford, rather than that they had lived there all their lives.

Bias in classification and diagnosis

A study by Umbenhauer and DeWitte (1978) investigated the effects of social class upon the attitudes of mental health professionals. They found that upper-class people received more favourable clinical judgements and were more likely to be offered psychotherapy than lower-class people. On the other hand, Johnstone (1989) pointed to studies showing that, regardless of symptoms, more serious diagnoses were given to lower-class patients. They were more likely to spend longer periods in hospital and more likely to be considered as having a poorer prognosis. Working-class patients were more likely to be prescribed physical treatments, such as ECT and drugs and less likely to be offered psychotherapy. Johnstone asserted that health professionals justify this by claiming that working-class patients were less able to benefit from verbal therapies because they were less articulate. She concluded that working-class patients, who were the least powerful and who experienced the most social and economic hardship, ended up receiving the 'disabling' rather than the 'empowering' psychiatric treatments. This served to deprive them even further of any remaining autonomy and independence and also served to 'diffuse legitimate protest' about the likely social origins of their problems, such as unemployment and poverty.

Whilst there was a great deal of research conducted in the 1960s and 1970s on social class and mental illness, over the past ten to fifteen years this has declined. It is unlikely that social class bias has disappeared completely. The recent political climate, however, has raised the profile of gender and culture above that of social class.

Gender bias in mental health

Mental health statistics indicate that certain mental disorders are diagnosed more frequently in men while others are diagnosed more frequently in women. It has been suggested that this can be explained through biological differences. However, this view has been challenged by those who claim that the differences merely reflect stereotyped judgements among mental health professionals.

❖ Activity 2 ❖

True or false?

Read the following statements and consider whether you think they are true or false.

1 Regardless of how we define psychological disorders, men are more likely than women to have problems.
2 Women are more likely than men to suffer from social phobias, or excessive fear of social situations.
3 Females constitute around 95% of people who have specific fears (e.g. fear of snakes or fear of the dark).
4 Men are more likely than women to suffer from an alcohol-related disorder.
5 Women are more likely to be diagnosed with obsessive-compulsive personality disorder.
6 Men are more likely to be diagnosed with anti-social personality disorder.

(The answers are at the end of the chapter.)

Biological differences

Schizophrenia is more prevalent in males, but equally prevalent in both sexes beyond the female menopause. It has been noted that this is when female oestrogen levels subside, which has led to the suggestion that oestrogen may be a protective hormone against psychosis. However, there is, as yet, insufficient evidence to support this claim. It has long been thought that women suffer more from depression because of fluctuations in hormonal states related to the menstrual cycle, childbirth, the use of oral contraceptives and the menopause. An extensive review by Weissman and Klerman (1981) found mixed support for this belief, but in the main they concluded that there is insufficient evidence to relate mood changes to hormonal changes.

Stereotyped judgements

Broverman *et al.* (1981) thought that since certain behavioural characteristics have traditionally been ascribed to either male or female genders, it is likely that clinical diagnosis of mental disorders will reflect these distinctions. They conducted an important study on 'sex-role stereotypes and clinical judgements' and found that clinicians have different concepts of health for men and women and that these differences do tend to parallel the sex-role stereotypes prevalent in our society. They asked 46 male and 33 female mental health professionals (clinically trained psychologists, psychiatrists and social workers) to rate the characteristics of the healthy man, the healthy woman and the healthy adult. They found that the healthy adult and the healthy man were rated in a similar way, as assertive, decisive and relatively independent. The healthy woman was regarded as more submissive, dependent and emotional than the healthy man.

In the light of their study, Broverman *et al.* suggest that a double standard of mental health exists within clinical diagnosis, with certain behavioural characteristics thought to be pathological in members of one sex, but not in the opposite sex. It is generally believed that health consists of good adjustment to one's environment. Men and women are trained from birth to fulfil different social roles, and therefore healthy adjustment for a woman is to accept the behavioural norms for her sex, even though these behaviours may be considered less healthy for the generalized healthy adult. If the 'adjustment' notion of health is accepted then it would be maladaptive for a woman to exhibit characteristics that are considered to be 'healthy' for men but not for women. One of the dangers of mental health professionals adopting the adjustment notion of health is that they actively reinforce and perpetuate sex-role stereotypes.

Gender and the environment

Howell (1981) points out that women's experience in this culture predisposes them to depression and therefore clinicians are diagnosing a *situation* rather than a *person*. Cochrane (1995) explains that depression can be related to the long-term effects of child abuse and also to gender role socialization, which produces increased female vulnerability. He points out the adverse effects on women of power relationships and sex discrimination. Despite the vast amount of evidence relating women's depression to socio-cultural factors, clinicians continue to ignore environmental circumstances and convey the message that the problem lies in the person's illness (Johnstone 1989). Johnstone believes this also applies to men. She points out that unemployed men have a high rate of psychiatric breakdown and by labelling the problem as a mental disorder, not only does the person have the stigma of a psychiatric label, but the problem is seen only in individual terms, rather than in the wider political and social context. Bennett (1995) believes that the socialization of men in industrialized societies has created masculine stereotypes that alienate men from seeking help for psychological problems.

Gender bias in DSM

Gender differences are particularly marked in the prevalence rates for specific personality disorders (see Table 10.4). It has been suggested that this differential diagnosis may reflect gender bias in the diagnostic system, rather than actual differences. In a study by Hamilton *et al.* (1986) clinicians were given client descriptions consistent with the symptoms of Histrionic Personality Disorder (see Table 10.4), which has traditionally been diagnosed more in females than males. In the descriptions the sex of the client was varied but the symptoms were identical.

Table 10.4 DSM-IV diagnostic description for personality disorders more prevalent in males or females

Histrionic Personality Disorder *(diagnosed more frequently in females)* A pervasive pattern of excessive emotionality and attention seeking.
Dependent Personality Disorder *(diagnosed more frequently in females)* A pervasive and excessive need to be taken care of that leads to submissive and clinging behaviour and fears of separation.
Narcissistic Personality Disorder *(diagnosed more frequently in males)* A pervasive pattern of grandiosity (in fantasy or behaviour), need for admiration and lack of empathy.
Obsessive-Compulsive Personality Disorder *(diagnosed more frequently in males)* A pervasive pattern of preoccupation with orderliness, perfectionism and mental and interpersonal control, at the expense of flexibility, openness and efficiency.

In Focus

Sexism in assessment and diagnosis

Worell and Remer (1992) claim that sexism occurs in assessment and diagnosis in four ways:

Disregarding environmental context

Assessment and diagnosis focus primarily on traits and behaviours of the individual without regard to the environmental context, such as poverty, patriarchy and powerlessness. Judgements are often made without taking into account the person's response to the environment, and so, if the clinician holds strong gender stereotypes, behaviour can either be dismissed as an over-reaction, or regarded as abnormal or pathological.

Differential diagnosis based on gender

If female and male clients present the same symptoms but different diagnoses are made, then gender bias is occurring. This is most likely to happen if symptoms mirror traditional sex-role stereotypes and if diagnostic classifications use descriptions such as 'dependent' or 'submissive', which are more likely to be associated with a female stereotype.

Therapist misjudgement

Because of sex-role stereotyping, therapists may have pre-conceived ideas about particular symptoms and may therefore perceive those symptoms more readily in either males or females. Because people are often unaware that they hold stereotypical beliefs, therapists may be unaware that they are making these assumptions.

Theoretical orientation sex bias

Diagnosis is often made on the basis of the therapist's own theoretical orientation. If that orientation is sex-biased, then it is more likely that the assessment made by the therapist will also be biased.

Clinicians consistently rated female clients as more histrionic than males. Narcissistic Personality Disorder (see Table 10.4) is diagnosed more frequently in males, but does this statistic truly reflect the prevalence of the disorder in males? The diagnostic symptom criteria in DSM-IV list behaviours which reflect stereotypical male gender roles much more than female – for example, 'shows arrogance', 'has a sense of entitlement', 'has a grandiose sense of self-importance'.

Section summary

What constitutes abnormal behaviour, and in turn what would be regarded as a pathological problem, has been found to differ between cultures. As a consequence, there are no universal definitions for 'abnormality'. This indicates that the concept of 'abnormality' should perhaps be regarded as a social construction.

There are many ways in which bias can occur in mental health. Culture bias can occur if cultural differences are not taken into account by the clinician. Stereotyped views relating to culture, social class or gender may influence the over-diagnosis or under-diagnosis of certain disorders and the type of treatment received. It is believed by many psychologists that the extent of racial, class and gender bias that exists within society finds expression through the agency of mental health professionals who have enormous powers of social control.

Chapter summary

- There are various ways in which abnormality can be defined and these offer a useful general guide for distinguishing forms of functioning which might be regarded as pathological. However, their use is limited because there are no universal definitions of 'normality' and 'abnormality'.
- Classification systems, such as DSM-IV and ICD-10, have been devised to provide consensus on what constitutes a pathological syndrome, and to provide symptom information for diagnostic purposes. DSM has been subjected to criticism in the past on the grounds of poor reliability and validity and the ethics of labelling someone as 'abnormal' or 'mentally ill'.
- Models of abnormality are based on very different assumptions about the nature of human functioning and the origins of psychological disorders. Each model offers quite different therapeutic strategies, based upon their relative orientations. Since each model is addressing a different aspect of functioning it is possible that they all have a valid place in explaining abnormality of psychological functioning.
- Cultural and subcultural differences are clearly very important factors to be taken into consideration when defining and classifying psychological problems. Epidemiological research has indicated different trends in the diagnosis and treatment of certain mental disorders according to gender, ethnic, and socio-economic groups. It has been suggested that these differences are largely due to stereotyped views held by clinicians about culture, social class or gender.

Essay questions

1 Describe and evaluate some of the ways in which psychologists have defined abnormality. *(24 marks)*

2 Critically consider both practical and ethical considerations for adopting classification systems for mental disorder. *(24 marks)*

3 (a) Choosing any one model of abnormality, describe the assumptions of this approach to normality and abnormality. *(12 marks)*

(b) Evaluate this model in terms of its ethical and practical implications. *(12 marks)*

4 Discuss cultural and subcultural differences in definitions, classification and diagnosis of abnormality. *(24 marks)*

Answers to Activity 2

1 False

2 False

3 True

4 True

5 False

6 True

Further reading

Comer, R.J. (1995) *Abnormal Psychology* (2nd edn), USA: W.H. Freeman & Company.

Davison, G.C. and Neale, J.M. (1994) *Abnormal Psychology* (6th edn), New York: John Wiley.

Rosenhan and Seligman (1995) *Abnormal Psychology* (3rd edn), New York: W.W. Norton & Company.

Comer (1995), Davison and Neale (1994) and Rosenhan and Seligman (1995) all provide broader accounts of conceptions and models of abnormality. The coverage of classification systems is especially readable in Comer.

Rack, P. (1982) *Race, Culture and Mental Disorder*, London: Tavistock/Routledge.

Written in a clear style, this provides an interesting in-depth account of the topic, mixing empirical research with polemical narrative.

Worell, J. and Remer, P. (1992) *Feminist Perspectives in Therapy*, Chichester: John Wiley.

An interesting account of the female experience of the mental health profession, written from a feminist perspective, with supporting empirical research.

Chapter 11

Psycho-pathology

Pamela Prentice

Preview

In this chapter we shall be looking at:

- anxiety disorders, including phobias and post-traumatic stress disorder
- eating disorders, including anorexia nervosa and bulimia nervosa
- affective (mood) disorders, including depression (unipolar) and manic-depressive psychosis (bipolar)
- schizophrenia.

Introduction

This chapter will look at the psychopathology of mental disorders. The specific disorders mentioned in the preview above will be outlined briefly to provide the reader with some understanding of each disorder. The medical profession and the psychology profession have long been trying to understand the causes of mental disorders, not least in order to provide suitable treatment for alleviation.

The main purpose of this chapter is to examine different views, or theories, of the aetiology (explanation of cause) for each of the disorders. The aetiologies will be split into two major groups, namely genetic/neurological and social/psychological. The first represents the medical model, which views mental disorders as an 'illness' or a 'disease', while the second represents the view that mental disorders are a psychological dysfunction, relating to the interaction between individuals and their environment. You will find that some explanations seem more plausible than others for some types of disorder, but not for others. As yet, no one aetiology has been accepted as *the* complete explanation for any single mental disorder and an open mind on a combination of aetiologies seems more appropriate.

Anxiety disorders

Anxiety is something that everyone feels from time to time. It can relate to immediate concerns, such as attending an interview or sitting examinations, or to longer-term concerns about the future. When anxiety becomes so intense that it interferes with a person's ability to function in her or his daily life, then it can be regarded as an anxiety disorder. Anxiety disorders are the most prevalent of all adult mental disorders. The *Diagnostic and Statistical Manual of Mental Disorders*, fourth edition (DSM-IV 1994) has classified anxiety disorders into a number of specific categories according to symptomatology. This text will focus on two specific types of anxiety disorder – phobias and post-traumatic stress disorder.

Phobias

Specific (simple) phobias are, as the term implies, fears relating to something specific and, although they are often referred to as *simple* phobias, they are far from simple. Almost everyone has aversions to certain things, the most common being spiders, snakes, rodents or a fear of heights. This is quite normal and it is only when the aversion becomes an excessive and unreasonable fear that it is classified as a phobia. Table 11.1 lists some specific phobias.

Social phobia is an excessive fear of social situations. Most people are nervous about public speaking, but someone with a social

Table 11.1 Specific (simple) phobias

	fear of		*fear of*
Arachnophobia	spiders	Phasmophobia	ghosts
Ophidiophobia	snakes	Xenophobia	strangers
Helminthophobia	worms	Pediophobia	children
Ailurophobia	cats	Androphobia	men
Cynophobia	dogs	Gynophobia	women
Hippophobia	horses	Oneirophobia	dreams
Musophobia	mice	Sciophobia	shadows
Apiphobia	bees	Achluophobia	darkness
Acrophobia	heights	Phengophobia	daylight
Aerophobia	flying	Tachophobia	speed
Claustrophobia	enclosed spaces	Keraunophobia	thunder
Ochlophobia	crowds	Astraphobia	lightning
Autophobia	being alone	Hydrophobia	water
Kenophobia	empty rooms	Pyrophobia	fire
Ergasiophobia	work	Homichlophobia	fog
Scholionophobia	school	Algophobia	pain
Bibliophobia	books	Spermophobia	germs
Graphophobia	writing	Necrophobia	death

Source: extracted from Melville 1978

phobia is afraid of any activity performed in public, such as eating in public or going into a public lavatory. Agoraphobia, a fear of public places, is especially debilitating because it can result in people being afraid to go out of their home, which means they are unable to go to work, or even to shop for provisions. Many people with agoraphobia are also prone to panic attacks when they venture into public places. With the increase in air travel, fear of flying is becoming one of the most common phobias and many airlines now offer therapy programmes based on systematic desensitisation (see Chapter 12, 'Therapeutic approaches').

Genetic/neurological explanations

To determine a genetic link for anxiety disorders, or indeed for any other disorder in humans, research has focused on three areas of study:

- *Family history studies* examine the recurrence of a particular disorder between and within generations. One of the major problems with family history studies is that they usually rely on interviews with the family members of someone already diagnosed with a particular disorder. This means that accounts are retrospective and subjective, and without the benefit of diagnostic criteria. Some studies have examined medical records, but these would exclude anyone suffering from a disorder who did not present for treatment.
- *Adoption studies* look at the occurrence of a disorder when a child with affected biological parents is adopted at an early age by 'healthy' parents.
- *Twin studies* examine the rate of concordance of a disorder (i.e. whether both twins are affected). A comparison is made between monozygotic (MZ) twins, who have identical genetic make-up, and dizygotic (DZ) twins, who are no more genetically alike than any other siblings.

The rationale behind both adoption and twin studies is an attempt to separate genetic factors from environmental factors. Since anxiety has evolutionary advantages for survival, it is likely that a fear response is at least partly genetic. Research has focused mainly on family studies with first-degree relatives (parents, children, siblings) and in a few studies, with second-degree relatives (aunts, uncles, nieces, nephews). There have been a small number of twin studies and virtually no adoption studies.

Family studies have focused mainly on agoraphobia. A study by Solyom *et al.* (1974) of 47 phobic patients, found a family history of psychiatric disorder in 45% of the cases (with 30% of their mothers having phobias), in contrast to only 19% in families of a non-phobic control group of patients. Noyes *et al.* (1986) found a higher than normal rate of agoraphobia (11.6%) and panic disorder (17.3%) in first-degree relatives, using the family interview method. Another family interview study by Fyer *et al.* (1990) of 49 first-degree relatives of people with a specific phobia found that 31% of relatives were also diagnosed with phobias, but only two people had the same type. Reich and Yates (1988) found a 6.6% rate for relatives of people with social phobia compared with 2.2% in controls. When categorising people into those with animal-types of phobias and those with non-animal types of phobias, they found a much higher frequency of the same type of phobia in relatives compared with controls.

A twin study by Slater and Shields (1969) found 41% concordance in 17 MZ twin pairs versus 4% in 28 DZ twin pairs, for any type of anxiety disorder. A more recent study conducted by Torgersen (1983) found 31% concordance in 13 MZ twin pairs for panic disorder and agoraphobia versus zero concordance in 16 DZ twin pairs, although none of the concordant twins shared the same phobia.

Although most of the family studies show that the relatives of those with phobias are more likely to suffer phobias themselves compared with relatives of non-phobic controls, these differences are not statistically significant. There are methodological difficulties with family studies, the main problem being that in most instances family members share the same environment. Twin studies offer more reliable data, which support the genetic hypothesis, but unfortunately very few have been conducted. The lack of empirical research, particularly in recent years, is a good indication that there is very little support for the genetic transmittance of anxiety disorders.

Neurological theories are based on the functioning of the autonomic nervous system. Research indicates that people who develop phobias are those who generally maintain a high level of physiological arousal, which makes them particularly sensitive to their external environment. This suggests an interaction between arousal level and conditioning, but the question is whether high arousal levels are the cause of, or the consequence of the phobia. Asso and Beech (1975) favour the former argument, suggesting that a high level of physiological arousal makes it easier to acquire a conditioned response. However, Lader and Mathews (1968) found that high levels of arousal are more significant only in the cases of agoraphobia and social phobia, whereas conditioning is more significant in the case of specific phobias. (See next section for a fuller account of the conditioning of phobias).

Social/psychological explanations

The *classical conditioning* explanation for phobias proposes that first a panic attack occurs, in response, for instance, to being trapped in a lift. This results in an association being established between anxiety and that lift. Subsequently this anxiety becomes generalised to all lifts. Consequently, the person will actively avoid using lifts in the future. In terms of operant conditioning, avoidance of lifts is further reinforced by the reduction in anxiety experienced when the person adopts alternative strategies, such as using the stairs.

The conditioning explanation for phobias has been extensively researched and is supported by early studies on humans and animals which would now be regarded as unethical. You are probably familiar with the classic study by Watson and Raynor (1920) where they apparently conditioned a 10-month-old boy, named Little Albert, into developing a phobia towards a white rat, using classical conditioning techniques. Although there has been considerable support for the behaviourist explanation of phobias, more recent studies have failed to replicate their findings, including an attempt by Watson and Raynor themselves.

Some phobic reactions are more common than others and this has been accounted for by the suggestion that there are species-specific biological predispositions to fear certain stimuli, dating back to our ancestors. This has been researched by Seligman (1971), who proposed the concept of biological 'preparedness', suggesting that all species are innately 'prepared' to avoid certain stimuli because they are potentially dangerous. A famous study by Garcia and Koelling (1966) showed that rats could be conditioned easily to avoid life-threatening stimuli, such as shocks or toxic liquids, but not to avoid stimuli which carried no adverse consequences, such as flashing lights. Human phobias, such as fear of the dark or fear of heights, are consistent with this theory. However, this does not necessarily lend support for biological preparedness. The ease with which certain phobias can develop could equally be accounted for in *social learning* terms, that is through modelling our behaviour on others and in particular on our parents. If certain stimuli are potentially dangerous, then from an early age we observe others avoiding these. In the same way we also learn that certain stimuli are commonly avoided within a given culture, which can explain apparent phobias for stimuli that are not necessarily life-threatening, for example, snakes and large spiders, most of which are not dangerous. Further criticism of the theory of 'biological preparedness' comes from a study by McNally and Steketee (1985) where they found that in 91 per cent of cases of snake and spider phobias, the cause for concern was not a fear of being harmed, but rather a fear of having a panic attack. The exception was in the case of dog phobias, where most people were afraid of being bitten.

The *cognitive explanation* for phobias extends the behavioural view of the conditioning of physiological reflexes to the cognitive domain of 'thinking'. Leading theorists in this field, such as Albert Ellis (1962) and Aaron Beck (1963), suggest that catastrophic thoughts and irrational beliefs contribute to the development of a phobia. For example, an experience of feeling 'hemmed in' in a crowded lift might be maintained later on by thoughts and beliefs such as 'I might suffocate if I were trapped in a lift'. This then turns into a fear of lifts, which is then generalized to other similar situations, resulting in the onset of claustrophobia. Therefore it is not only an initial exposure to a fearful situation which initiates the phobia, as proposed by conditioning theory. Rather it is also the person's irrational thoughts about the future possibility of a fearful situation.

The *psychoanalytic view* is that phobias are associated with unconscious sexual fears (or 'id' impulses) and that they operate through the defence mechanisms of *repression* and *displacement*. The original source of the fear is repressed into the unconscious and the fear is then displaced onto some other person, object or situation. Thus the fear appears to be irrational because there is no conscious explanation for it. Freud's theory of phobias rests on his 1909 case study of a boy named Little Hans who developed a fear of horses (Freud 1909). Freud believed that the boy's phobia was directly related to his unconscious fear of his father, associated with the Oedipal phase. Although there is no empirical evidence to support Freud's theory directly, cross-cultural studies (e.g. Whiting 1966) do indicate that anxieties and phobias are more common in cultures characterised by strict upbringing and punishment.

Bowlby (1973) suggested that all anxiety disorders can be explained by his theory of 'Attachment'. For instance, agoraphobia relates to a fear of losing someone to whom the person has become attached (most often the mother). He maintained that the origins lie with 'separation anxiety' in early childhood, particularly where parents are overprotective. However, with respect to phobias, studies tend to show a lack of consistency. For example, Parker (1979) found that being overprotected during early childhood correlated with the development of social phobias later on. On the other hand, the development of agoraphobia was found to correlate with having parents who had tended to display a lack of affection. Many studies indicate no relationship at all between parental rearing styles and types of anxiety disorders.

❖ Activity 1 ❖

Find out what you can about the two studies of Little Hans (Freud 1909) and Little Albert (Watson and Raynor 1920). Which do you think offers the most plausible explanation for phobias?

❖ Activity 2 ❖

First identify any of your own fears and phobias. Now think about the most likely explanation, taking account of all the above aetiological theories.

Major life events have long been regarded as a major contributing factor in anxiety disorders. Holmes and Rahe (1967) explained the cumulative effects of major life events, and the work of Kobasa (1979) highlighted the effects of everyday minor hassles. Kleiner and Marshall (1987) found that in a group of agoraphobics, 84 per cent had experienced family problems prior to the onset of their first panic attack and this finding has been confirmed by a number of other studies. However, some people who experience the most adverse life events do not develop an anxiety disorder.

)iathesis-stress model explanation

The diathesis-stress model proposes an interaction between various factors and may explain individual differences in susceptibility to stress and anxiety. It is suggested that we all have our own individual tolerance thresholds which form a predisposition to stress; this is known as our *diathesis* or *vulnerability* factor. The origin of this predisposition to vulnerability is not certain. It may be genetically inherited, or alternatively it may be acquired through early experience; explanations include psychodynamic, behavioural and cognitive. The interaction between this vulnerability factor and the degree of life stress a person encounters (major life events and/or minor hassles) is thought to determine the likelihood that anxiety will reach a degree where it becomes dysfunctional (see Fig. 11.1).

Figure 11.1
Diathesis-stress model

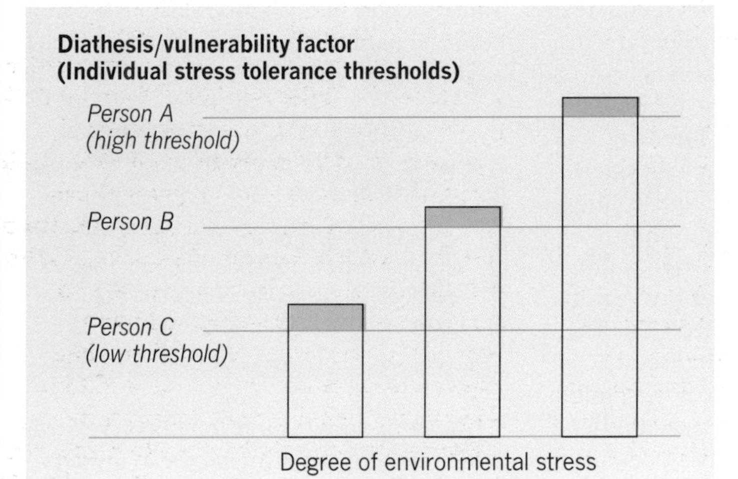

Explanation
When environmental stressors penetrate the tolerance threshold for an individual, this results in physical or mental symptoms (illustrated by the darker shaded areas).

- A small number of stressors, such as minor ailments or failing a driving test, may penetrate the stress tolerance of person C (who has a low threshold).
- Additional stressors may penetrate the stress tolerance threshold of person C and also person B (who has a medium threshold.
- The cumulative effect of many stressors, or one significant or life-threatening event, may penetrate the stress tolerance threshold of persons C and B and even of person A (who has a high threshold).

Post-traumatic stress disorder (PTSD)

Anxiety disorders are usually associated with objects and events which most people do not find threatening. There are, however, some events which would be threatening for almost everyone, such as an aeroplane crash or an earthquake. People who encounter a very traumatic experience usually suffer from *acute stress disorder*, which is a temporary reaction and most people recover within a short while and continue with their lives. However, some people do not recover and go on to develop the pathological disorder known as *post-traumatic stress disorder* (PTSD).

Although PTSD was not listed in DSM until 1980, it is not a new disorder. It was noted in the First World War that armed combat could produce symptoms known as 'shell shock', but it was not until after the Vietnam War that PTSD was classified as a specific disorder. Since then, PTSD has been associated with exposure to any extremely traumatic event, such as a natural disaster, fire, serious accident, violent personal assault, kidnapping, terrorist attack, being diagnosed with a terminal illness, or being a witness to a serious accident or crime. PTSD can appear immediately after the trauma, or its onset can be delayed for several months or even years. According to DSM-IV, children are as susceptible to PTSD as adults and there appear to be no gender, age or cultural differences in susceptibility to PTSD. Certain traumatic events are, however, more likely to occur in one group than another. For example, sexual assault and armed combat are more likely to be gender specific.

Symptoms of PTSD include the persistent re-experiencing of the event through frightening dreams and flashback episodes, which are usually triggered by cues that are associated with or resemble the traumatic event. The person persistently avoids anything, anywhere, or anyone associated with the trauma, and there may even be an inability to recollect the traumatic event. There may also be changes in the person's general behaviour in that they may lack concentration and become easily startled,

In Focus

Case study of post-traumatic stress disorder

Susan, a 23-year-old clerical worker, had always been happy and carefree. She enjoyed her work, had lots of friends and was engaged to be married. Recently, however, she had become morose and distant. She no longer wanted to go out with friends and she was unable to concentrate at work. Her friends noticed that she had begun to cry a lot and was easily startled. She was also frequently angry with her boyfriend for no apparent reason. She began to withdraw from relationships with people and called off her engagement. Susan eventually went to see a counsellor, to whom she revealed that, six months before, she had been raped by her boss one evening when she was working late. He was married and had warned her not to tell anyone or she would be fired. Afterwards, at home in her flat, Susan had tried to scrub away the effects of the rape in the shower. For several days she felt dirty and cheap, but couldn't tell anyone, especially her boyfriend, because she was worried that he wouldn't believe her. She even began to doubt herself, believing that maybe she had in some way 'asked for it'. She resolved to put it behind her and get on with her life. This she managed to do quite well for over two months, but then she began having nightmares about being stalked by someone who wanted to harm her. Even when awake she was often overcome by violent images that would intrude on her thoughts.

irritable and angry. There is also a loss of interest in activities, a detachment from others and an inability to experience feelings of love. The case study mentioned above should give you some idea of the experience of post-traumatic stress disorder.

The very definition of PTSD implies that the disorder is caused by the stressful exposure to a traumatic event, which would appear to rule out alternative explanations. Certainly the reason for the onset of the disorder is clear: it follows a traumatic event, even when there has been a delayed onset of six months or more. Risk factors for PTSD have been identified, such as the level of severity of the traumatic event and/or how great the exposure was to the traumatic event. However, this does not explain why some people recover quickly from a traumatic event, regardless of its level of severity or the length of exposure, and why other people develop PTSD.

Neurological explanations

The view of endrocrinology is that trauma causes long-term alterations and abnormalities in specific brain systems. The suggestion is that exposure to an extremely traumatic event has an adverse effect on the normal physiological stress reaction of autonomic arousal, which triggers the release of adrenaline and serotonin in order to prepare for 'fight' or 'flight'. Van der Kolk (1988) says that there is an absence of resiliency in those suffering from PTSD, as if autonomic arousal is no longer a preparation for an emergency, but a precipitant of responses which bear no relationship to the present stimulus. Laboratory studies on survivors of extreme stress, including Vietnam war veterans, show that when exposed to trauma cues (visual, auditory and imaginary), there is a consistently higher physiological reactivity (e.g. in heart rate, temperature, pulse, respiration) than in controls. One suggestion is that the experience of the trauma damages the noradrenergic system, which then raises levels of noradrenaline making the person more prone to being startled and to express emotion. Evidence for this position comes from Kosten *et al.* (1987) who found higher than normal levels of noradrenaline in PTSD hospital patients.

In the case of prolonged stressful events over a long period of time, the suggestion is that the persistent secretion of neurotransmitters leads to a diminished supply of noradrenaline, which makes the person less resilient even to minor stressful events. 'Noradrenergic burnout' is accompanied by a decrease in learning ability, memory functions and motivation. In addition to human studies, support also comes from animal conditioning studies on 'learned helplessness', which showed that when animals were exposed to inescapable shock there were deficits in motivation, learning ability and memory, characteristic of depression in humans. Van der Kolk (1988) found significant excretions of dopamine and noradrenaline in parts of the brain and changes in costisol and adrenaline levels. When there was prolonged exposure to the shock, there was an eventual depletion of noradrenaline.

Whilst new discoveries in neuro-endocrinology are providing answers for specific symptoms of PTSD, they still cannot explain individual differences in susceptibility to the disorder. For this reason, research has also focused on the psychological aspects of stress.

Social/psychological explanations

The more traditional *behavioural* account for PTSD is based on Pavlov's theory of classical conditioning (Pavlov 1927, 1941). Pavlov found that, over a period of time, repeated dosages of overwhelming excitation mobilized innate reflexive responses in the form of a defensive reaction (fear response). These primary responses were then linked by association to cues in the environment. The cues then became the conditioned stimuli, which would by themselves elicit a conditioned response. Pavlov called this 'traumatic mental imprinting'.

In *cognitive* psychology, PTSD can be explained in terms of 'state or situation dependent memory'. Anything which elicits a fearful, emotional response, or any situation which resembles the original traumatic event, can trigger the memory of the actual event. With PTSD it is as if everything exposed to every one of our senses (sight, smell, etc.) at the time of the original trauma, is somehow imprinted alongside the original trauma, much like a whirlpool or a hurricane sucking in everything within its reach. In cognitive-behavioural terms, people who experience a traumatic event often feel that life is no longer predictable. This, in turn, produces a belief that they are no longer in control of any aspect of their life. Irrational thoughts develop, for example that the disaster was somehow their own fault. This results in faulty coping methods such as avoidance, blaming, catastrophizing, isolation from others and the abuse of drugs and alcohol. Lazarus (1991) maintains that these inadequate coping strategies fail to reduce the effects of the traumatic event and can actually increase the experience of the stress, which in turn leads to PTSD.

The growing recognition of PTSD has generated a resurgence of interest in the *psychodynamic* view. This view explains the often delayed onset of PTSD; for example, the studies of Archibald *et al.* (1963) on survivors of the Normandy campaign, showed that the onset of PTSD had been delayed by fifteen years in some people. Horowitz (1975) suggested that the traumatic event was suppressed or dissociated because it was too painful for the conscious mind to contemplate, but there remained an internal struggle to integrate the trauma into the person's existing beliefs about him/herself and the world.

A more recent application of the psychodynamic approach to PTSD proposes that someone who has experienced emotional trauma in childhood is more vulnerable to trauma in later life. This would explain individual differences in the effects of exposure to the same traumatic events. There is support for this in that, for example, rape victims are more likely to develop PTSD if they had psychological problems prior to the traumatic event (Sales *et al.* 1984). Bremner *et al.* (1993) have shown that PTSD is also more prevalent in those who in childhood experienced poverty, parental separation or divorce, physical or sexual abuse, mental illness in a family member, or any other catastrophic event. They suggest that abused children tend to dissociate themselves from the memory of the abuse and that this becomes a habitual way of dealing with any difficult or traumatic event in life, which then sets the stage for the development of PTSD. However, it could equally be argued from a psychodynamic perspective that such people should be less susceptible because they have built up strong defence mechanisms.

Diathesis-stress model explanation

A more pragmatic view is that psychological factors interact with environmental factors in a cumulative fashion. A person who is more vulnerable because of past experiences is more likely to be affected by stressful events. This vulnerability increases with the intensity and duration of the traumatic event, increasing the likelihood of PTSD. One's level of vulnerability could also be explained in terms of the strength of available social support systems, since it has been found that those who have a strong support system, who are loved and cared for, are more likely to recover from a traumatic experience, such as rape. Conversely, it was found that Vietnam war veterans with a weak social support system were more likely to develop PTSD.

Early DSM criteria for PTSD stated that the person must have experienced an event which was 'beyond the range of usual human experience', but this has been deleted from DSM-IV because many of the events are becoming more usual. Parson (1993) regards PTSD as a public health problem deriving from the increase in aircraft and railroad incidents, drug-instigated violence, terrorist activity, child abuse (physical and sexual), and brutal rape which he says is the fastest growing crime in the United States. Fig. 11.2 shows the extent of the psychological effects of rape. DSM-IV now states that the person must have experienced, witnessed, or been confronted with an event or events that involved actual or threatened death or serious injury, or a threat to the physical integrity of self or others.

Section summary

To search for a *cause* is probably the wrong way to try to understand PTSD. Certainly a traumatic event precipitates the disorder, which may trigger neuro-chemical malfunction, but if this were the sole cause then everyone experiencing the same traumatic event would develop PTSD. Psychological and socio-cultural factors do not in themselves cause the disorder, but they may play an important role in the person's vulnerability to develop the disorder. A recent article by Scott and Stradling (1994) has even suggested that PTSD can occur without the trauma. They cite clinical case examples of people who have all the symptoms of PTSD in the absence of a single, acute dramatic trauma of any kind. An explanation could be that PTSD can occur, not only from trauma, but also through prolonged exposure to stressors. They suggest that the DSM classification should be amended to distinguish between post-traumatic stress disorder (PTSD) and prolonged-duress stress disorder (PDSD).

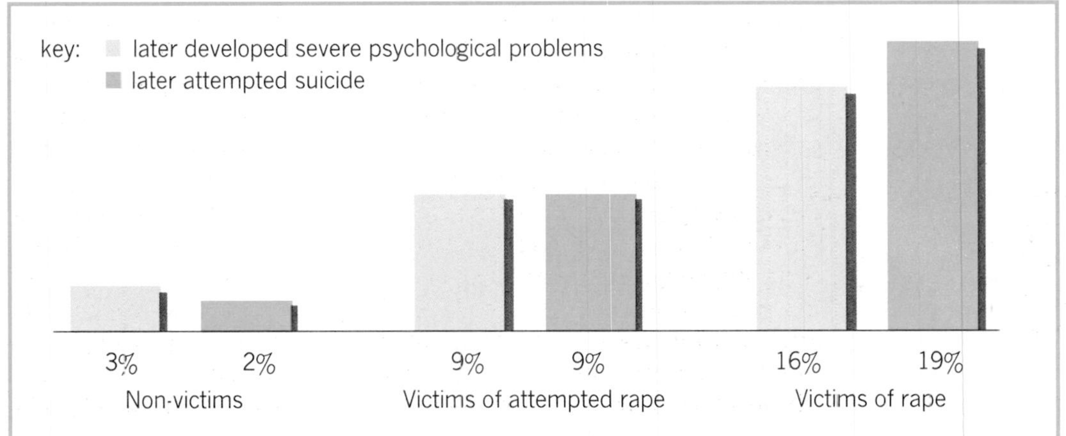

Figure 11.2 Percentages of victims of rape and attempted rape who later developed symptoms of PTSD and percentages of those who later attempted suicide *Source: adapted from study by* Kilpatrick *et al.* 1985, cited in Comer 1995, p. 224.

Eating disorders

Anorexia nervosa

Anorexia nervosa comes from the term anorectic, describing nervous loss of appetite. However, *loss of appetite* does not mean that the person is never hungry. Indeed, people with anorexia usually have normal appetites and may often be very hungry, but will nevertheless behave as if they have lost their appetite. The main characteristic of anorexia is a refusal to maintain a minimum average expected body weight. Even though the person is under-weight, there is an intense fear of gaining weight or becoming fat. There is also a disturbance in the way anorexic people perceive their body weight and shape; they believe themselves to be overweight or deny that they are seriously underweight. Ninety per cent of cases of anorexia occur in females, usually between the ages of 13 and 18. Anorexia rarely begins before puberty and in its diagnosis it is expected that, in females, there would have been an absence of at least three consecutive menstrual cycles. DSM-IV states that anorexia occurs in 0.5% to 1.0% of females in late adolescence and early adulthood.

The course and outcome of anorexia are variable. Around 20% of anorexics have one single episode with full recovery, while around 60% follow an episodic pattern of weight gain and relapse over a number of years. The remaining 20% continue to be severely affected and in many cases hospitalization is required to restore weight, as well as fluid and electrolyte balance. For some, it is a chronic unremitting course until death. The mortality rate of those admitted to hospital is over 10%, with deaths occurring from starvation, suicide or electrolyte imbalance.

Bulimia nervosa

Bulimia nervosa is characterized by episodes of binge eating, followed by inappropriate behaviours designed to compensate for weight gain, such as self-induced vomiting, misuse of laxatives, diuretics, enemas, medications, excessive exercise or fasting. With bulimia, unlike anorexia, the person is usually within the normal weight range but, like anorexia, this is accompanied by a disturbance in self-perception of body weight, size, or shape. Ninety per cent of cases are female. This condition is more common in a slightly older age group than anorexia. Between 1.0% and 3.0% of bulimic women are in their twenties and thirties and it frequently follows on from months or years of anorexia.

Genetic/neurological explanations for eating disorders

There is an increased risk of eating disorders among first-degree biological relatives (parents, children and siblings) of sufferers (DSM-IV 1994), with a number of studies showing a much higher prevalence rate than in the general population. However, since relatives usually share the same environment, this does not necessarily indicate a genetic base. Twin studies provide more reliable evidence. Holland *et al.* (1984)

In Focus

◆

Princess Diana's confession of bulimia

In a television interview on the BBC programme *Panorama* in 1995, Princess Diana confessed that she had suffered from bulimia for many years, although she had managed to hide it because bulimia does not involve weight loss. The Princess said that she and other sufferers inflict it upon themselves because their self-esteem is at such a low ebb and they have no sense of value or worth. The Princess explained that bulimia is a 'cry for help, although it is often giving the wrong signals'.

In Focus

Consequences of anorexia and bulimia

Anorexia and bulimia are very serious, life-threatening disorders. Not only is there a high mortality rate through starvation or suicide, there are other long-term consequences, some of which may lead to death. The consequences of starvation, vomiting and the use of laxatives are listed below:

Starvation

Amenorrhoea (absence of menstruation)

Brittle bones which break easily

Muscles become weak

Difficulty in concentrating and thinking straight

Broken sleep

Constipation

Depression

Loss of interest in sex

Vomiting

Stomach acid dissolves the enamel on teeth

Puffy face (due to swollen salivary glands)

Irregular heartbeats

Muscle weakness

Kidney damage

Epileptic fits

Laxatives

Persistent stomach-pain

Swollen fingers

Damage to bowel muscles which may lead to long-term constipation

Taken mainly from the free publication by the Royal College of Psychiatrists on anorexia and bulimia.

found a 55% concordance rate for MZ twins, compared with only a 7% concordance rate in DZ twins for anorexia nervosa. Kendler *et al.* (1991) found a similar result for bulimia nervosa, with a 23% concordance rate in MZ twins compared with 8.7% in DZ twins. It has been suggested that the genetic element may be a pre-morbid personality. In many cases of anorexia and bulimia, there is a family history of mood or personality disorders.

Eating disorders are not accounted for by any known physical disease, although they may be associated with a biochemical imbalance. Research in the biological field has focused on the *hypothalamus.* According to Keesey and Corbett (1983) the *lateral hypothalamus* (LH) and the *ventromedial hypothalamus* (VMH) work alongside each other to provide a 'weight thermostat'. When activated, the LH produces hunger and the VMH depresses hunger. If weight falls below the set point on the 'thermostat', the LH is activated and if weight rises above the set point, the VMH is activated. Once either the LH or the VMH is activated, the hypothalamus will send messages to areas of the brain responsible for thinking and behaviours that will satisfy whichever is activated (LH or VMH). A malfunction in this part of the hypothalamus offers a possible explanation for eating disorders, although there is as yet no conclusive evidence.

Amenorrhoea (loss of menstrual cycle) can occur *before* weight loss, according to DSM-IV, which suggests a primary disorder of low endocrine levels, again associated with a hypothalamus dysfunction. Also, the endocrine levels of anorexics of around 19 years of age are similar to those of a healthy 9-year-old. However, post-mortems have not revealed lesions of the hypothalamus. The problem with this type of research is that it is difficult to differentiate between the cause and the effect, since the behavioural symptoms of anorexia and bulimia have a direct, and significant, adverse effect on the person's physiology, which, in turn, may affect their bio-chemistry.

Social/psychological explanations

Socio-cultural factors have been associated with anorexia and bulimia. It has been noted that these disorders are more prevalent in industrialized societies, mainly Europe, USA, Canada, Australia, Japan, New Zealand and South Africa. In these societies there is an abundance of food and yet, at the same time, being attractive is associated with being slim. DSM-IV states that immigrants from cultures where these disorders are rare have been found to develop anorexia just as frequently as those born in industrialized societies, once these ideals of attractiveness are assimilated. However, since few studies have been conducted in non-industrialized cultures, it is difficult to provide an adequate comparison. Advertising in teenage magazines and on television provides a message that 'slim is beautiful'; it is not surprising that so many people turn to diets with such frequency. The layperson's view of anorexia is therefore 'slimming that got out of hand'.

Classical conditioning incorporates the layperson's view, suggesting that slimming becomes a 'habit', just like any other habit, through stimulus-response mechanisms. The person first goes on a diet and after a while receives admiration from others, either for their endeavour or their new slimmer appearance. Operant conditioning comes into play as this admiration further reinforces the dieting behaviour. Rewards may also come in the form of the attention gained from parents by not eating. Not eating can even be an effective way of punishing parents.

Freud maintained that eating is a substitute for sexual expression and therefore, in *psychoanalytic* terms, anorexia could be viewed as the person's way of repressing sexual impulses. Hilde Bruch has been particularly influential in applying psychodynamic theory to anorexia. She suggests (1979) that anorexia is associated with psychosexual immaturity in a number of ways. One suggestion is that women have fantasies of oral impregnation and confuse fatness with pregnancy. They then unconsciously believe that eating will lead to pregnancy and therefore starve themselves. Another suggestion is that eating becomes equated with taking on an adult sexual role and that those women who cannot face this, starve themselves in order either to remain children or to regress to childhood. Bruch (1987) suggests that there is a mutual reward to be gained by both mothers and daughters. The mother may become over-anxious about her daughter and therefore curtail her independence and thus retain her 'child'. For the daughter, her behaviour has secured a way of continuing to be dependent upon her mother.

Eating disorders have been strongly related to early traumatic experiences, and psychotherapy studies indicate that a large proportion of patients report early experience of sexual abuse. The suggestion is that such experiences are repressed into the unconscious and express themselves in adolescence and adulthood through the symptoms of anorexia or bulimia. Sexual abuse in childhood can lead to a rejection by victims of their own bodies; in adolescence this rejection can turn to disgust and an unconscious desire to destroy their bodies. It is, however, difficult to obtain evidence to support or refute these ideas.

In *humanistic* terms, eating disorders relate to family relationships, and in particular to the adolescent's struggle to gain a sense of individual identity. In some family relationships, the parents exert such a strong level of control that children grow up without a sense of their own identity and consequently with a low self-esteem. In adolescence, this control is maintained through roles within the family, such as the mother cooking the meals and the daughter dutifully eating them. This may form the arena in which the daughter struggles for her identity by refusing to eat.

Anorexia is much more prevalent in middle-class families, particularly among those whose parents have a professional background. It is also more prevalent in those who go on to higher education. Consequently, it is suggested that family pressure to 'succeed' may be too great for some young people and may lead to psychological problems, such as depression and anorexia.

In *Family Systems Theory*, Minuchin (1978) suggests that the development of anorexia serves the function of preventing dissension within the family. For example, it may be the adolescent's way of preventing a marriage break-up by diverting attention onto her/himself. In so doing, the hope is that joint concern for the child will bring the parents back together. The ways in which families may be involved in eating disorders have been explained in psychodynamic, humanistic and family systems terms. Family relationships are thought to be a central feature in eating disorders, so much so that family therapy (based largely on family systems theory) is currently the most significant form of intervention for eating disorders.

Section summary

There is little evidence to suggest that eating disorders are caused by any known disease. Although there is some evidence for a genetic link, it is difficult to isolate this from environmental influences. Biochemical imbalances are equally as likely to be the effect as the cause, of eating disorders. Currently, the bulk of the evidence trying to explain eating disorders comes from social/psychological theories, particularly those concerned with early sexual abuse, socialization of gender and family relationships.

In Focus

Case study of anorexia nervosa

Jenny was in her first year at university but abandoned the course and returned home having been diagnosed with anorexia nervosa. This was not the first diagnosis. As a child she was chubby and remembers several hurtful remarks from teachers. Jenny is the middle child of three siblings and recalls a sense of always being left out as a child and of not getting her needs met, especially by her mother. She also recalls that she was sent to ballet lessons, piano lessons and singing lessons, and although she enjoyed these, there was always an expectation that she would do better than she felt able to do. Although Jenny is currently back to a normal weight, she is totally preoccupied with food. For several years her dreams have been symbolic of her disorder, for example drowning in a pool of spaghetti. She also makes a ritual of the way that she eats food, daydreams about food and is constantly reading recipes for meals. She feels that she desperately needs to understand her psychological condition.

Affective (mood) disorders

Depression (unipolar)

We all feel depressed from time to time and this is quite normal. Usually it is short lived and does not interfere too much with our everyday functioning, in that we carry on going to work or college, even though we might not feel too much like socializing. This is not depression in the clinical sense. Clinical depression is when everyday functioning is seriously impaired.

Depression is an *affective* (mood) disorder, characterized by feelings of sadness and a general withdrawal from those around us. The degree of impairment varies and can range from mild to so severe that the person may not be able to feed or clothe him/herself or maintain personal hygiene. Depression can be so serious that it leads to suicide. Table 11.2 lists some of the main symptoms of depression.

It has long been thought that there are two quite discrete categories of depression, *reactive* and *endogenous*, with quite different aetiologies. Reactive, as the term implies, is a reaction to stressful events outside ourselves, such as the death of a family member, or redundancy, or even failing exams, whereas endogenous depression is thought to arise from within the person, independent of external events. Whilst reactive depression can range from mild to quite serious, endogenous depression is usually very severe.

Although the categories of reactive and endogenous are in common use by clinicians, they are not contained in either ICD10 or DSM-IV (see Chapter 10), which only serves to emphasize the difficulties associated with classification and diagnosis.

Table 11.2 Symptoms of depression

Cognitive	*Behavioural*	*Emotional*	*Physical*
Low self-esteem	Decrease in sexual activity	Sadness	Loss of weight
Guilt	Loss of appetite	Irritability	Loss of energy
Self dislike	Disordered sleep patterns	Apathy (no interest or pleasure in activities)	Aches and pains
Loss of libido (no interest in sex)	Poor care over self and others		Sleep disturbance
Negative thoughts	Suicide attempts		Menstrual changes
Suicidal thoughts			
Poor memory			
Lack of ability to think and concentrate			

DSM-IV lists two sub-types of depressive disorder, *major depressive disorder* (MDD), which is severe but can be short-lived, and *dysthymic disorder* (DD), which may be less severe but is more chronic. If the depressive episode has lasted for two consecutive years with less than two months without symptoms, then dysthemic disorder is diagnosed. Major depression can become a psychotic illness when very severe, i.e. the person experiences delusions or hallucinations (see Table 11.5).

In Focus

Case study of major depression

Jonathan is a 37-year-old building worker who was brought to the psychiatric clinic by his wife. Although Jonathan has been functioning normally for the past several years, he suddenly became severely disturbed and depressed. At the time of admission, Jonathan was agitated and suicidal, even going so far as buying a gun to kill himself. He had lost his appetite and had developed insomnia during the preceding two weeks. He had become hypersensitive in his dealings with neighbours, co-workers and family, insisting that others were being over-critical of him. This was the second such episode in Jonathan's history, the first having occurred five years earlier following the loss of his job because of a massive layoff in his business.

- What symptoms of major depression are shown in Jonathan's behaviour?
- What information would you need in order to determine whether Jonathan's depression is endogenous or reactive in nature?

(Taken from Halgin and Whitbourne 1993)

Table 11.3 Symptoms of mania

Cognitive	*Behavioural*	*Emotional*	*Physical*
No insight	Increase in work and social activity	Elevated mood	Increased energy
Increased sexual desire		Irritable	Little sleep needed
Reckless decisions	Increase in sexual activity		
Expansive ideas	Reckless actions		
Grandiose delusions	Rapid speech, more talkative		
Persecutory delusions	Easily distracted		
Hallucinations (visions, voices)			

Manic-depressive psychosis (bipolar)

Manic-depression is classified as a psychotic disorder, characterized by major mood swings between severe depression and a state of mania, hence the classification as a bipolar disorder. Table 11.3 lists some of the symptoms of mania. Note that two of the symptoms are delusions and hallucinations, which are also found in schizophrenia. They must be absent when the manic state is absent, otherwise schizophrenia, rather than mania, may be suspected.

Genetic/neurological explanations

There is very little substantial evidence for genetic factors in unipolar depression, but quite strong evidence in bipolar (manic-depression). Family history studies indicate that first degree biological relatives (parents, siblings and children) of those with severe psychotic depression have a morbidity risk of between 4 and 24%, whereas the risk is only 1 to 2% in the general population (DSM-IV 1994). However, once again the difficulty with family studies is that those concerned generally share the same environment.

In Focus

◆

Genius and manic-depression

Many well-known, gifted and talented people throughout history have experienced extreme mood swings, some of whom are listed here. It is believed that during a state of mania, creative energy is heightened far beyond normal human capabilities. It has even been suggested that manic-depression is responsible for the progression of human civilization!

Romantic poets:	Coleridge, Keats
Composers:	Mahler, Handel, Schumann
Politicians:	Winston Churchill, Abraham Lincoln, Theodore Roosevelt
Authors:	Virginia Woolf, James Joyce

In Focus

DNA markers for manic-depression among the Amish community

Perhaps the strongest evidence for genetic factors in manic-depression comes from linkage studies in molecular genetics, which try to identify DNA markers (mutations on a chromosome) occurring through many generations. The most well-known of these studies is one with the Amish community in Pennsylvania, conducted by Egeland *et al.* (1987). This is a small inbred community, with a high incidence of manic-depression. The study indicates that manic-depressive psychosis is related to two markers, the insulin gene and the cellular oncogene Ha-ras-1, on the short arm of chromosome eleven. Unfortunately, to date this has not been supported in replication studies conducted by Berrettini *et al.* (1990), nor in an Icelandic kinship study conducted by Hodkinson (1987). This is a new and interesting area of study, but much more work is required before any significance can be assessed.

Twin studies provide more convincing evidence. Price (1968) looked at seven twin studies and found much higher concordance rates for manic-depressive psychosis in identical (MZ) twins than in non-identical (DZ) twins. The most revealing factor was that the concordance rate for MZ twins was almost the same for those reared together and those reared apart (see Table 11.4).

Adoption studies also provide genetic evidence. A study by Cadoret (1978) looked at 126 adopted children, eight of which were born to a parent with manic-depression, but adopted by a healthy couple neither of whom suffered from depression. Three of those eight later developed a major affective disorder, compared to only eight of the remaining 118 children. In a study of 71 adoptees treated for major depressive disorders, Wender *et al.* (1986) found a high concordance for manic depression with biological parents, but not with adoptive parents.

Whilst genetic evidence for manic-depression (bipolar) is strong, no study has yet shown a 100% concordance rate, indicating that the genetic component might be a predisposing factor, but that there may also be additional precipitating causes. In contrast, genetic evidence is weak for major depressive disorder and dysthemic disorder (unipolar). However, DSM-IV states that there is a high incidence of unipolar depression in the offspring of those with bipolar depression.

The biochemical theory of depression emerged in the 1950s, when it was discovered that a certain class of drugs,

Table 11.4 Concordance rates for manic-depressive psychosis

	concordance rate
Dizygotic twins (119 pairs)	23%
Monozygotic twins – reared together (97 pairs)	68%
Monozygotic twins – reared apart (12 pairs)	67%

(based on Price 1968 – 7 studies)

known as Tricyclic drugs, was effective in treating depression. Since then it has been proposed that depression is linked to a disturbance of amine metabolism (brain chemistry). Three specific neurotransmitters are thought to be involved: noradrenaline (closely linked to adrenaline), serotonin (a brain substance which can be interfered with by hallucinogenic compounds such as LSD and magic mushrooms) and dopamine.

It is thought that tricyclic drugs increase reduced noradrenergic function, but so far there is no conclusive evidence to support such a view. Post-mortems of depressed patients have not revealed an abnormality of noradrenaline concentration (Cooper 1988). Serotonin serves to modulate neural activity and it is thought that if the level of serotonin is too low, then it allows wild fluctuations in other neural activity, producing mania or depression. However, it cannot be ruled out that the serotonin levels fluctuate as a result of the increase or decrease of motor activity in a state of mania or depression. Dopamine is thought to be especially involved in the depression of old age, because the dopamine content of the brain diminishes considerably over the age of forty-five. However, the synthetic drug L-dopa (which replicates the action of dopamine) has no specific antidepressant effect.

Another biological explanation has emerged from endocrinology. Levels of the hormone cortisol are found to be high in those suffering from depression and techniques known to suppress cortisol secretion have been found to be successful in depressive patients (Carroll 1982). This suggests that there is overactivity in the hypothalamic-pituitary-adrenal cortex. However, this may be due to the stress of being ill, because increased cortisol secretion is a function of the stress response.

Endocrine (hormonal) changes could account for pre-menstrual, post-natal and menopausal depression. These types of depression can be very serious indeed, leading to suicide attempts. In the case of post-natal depression, psychotic elements often appear, such as fantasies and loss of contact with reality. Some mothers with severe post-natal depression may harm or even kill their newborn child. Cooper (1988), however, found little difference between the number of women suffering from depression just after childbirth and a control group of non-pregnant women of a similar age. Pre-menstrual depression occurs in the week prior to menstruation and 25% of women are seriously affected, although most are not of diagnosable severity. An oestrogen-progesterone imbalance has been suggested (Dalton 1964), oestrogen levels being too high and progesterone levels too low. At menopause, oestrogen levels drop. Hormone replacement therapy appears to be reasonably effective for treating many (but not all) women who suffer from menopausal depression. Both oestrogen and progesterone increase greatly during pregnancy and then fall rapidly after childbirth, which may account for post-natal depression. However, research evidence for these hormone-imbalance theories is inconclusive (Clare 1985).

Nevertheless, if hormonal changes are not implicated, then it is difficult to explain why these depressive states occur more frequently during periods of hormonal change. One of the problems in trying to ascertain hormonal links with depression,

In Focus

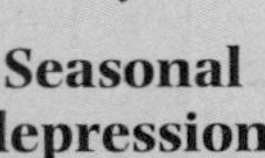

Seasonal depression

Depression can be seasonal: that is, the person suffers a regular period of depression at a specific time of year. Winter depression is the most common and is thought to relate to changes in the number of daylight hours. Explanations are that either the person is not exposed to enough natural light, or that they are adversely affected by too much artificial light. Special daylight light bulbs can now be purchased and appear to be effective for those suffering from this type of depression.

is that there are invariably social changes occurring at the same time. A possible explanation is that hormonal changes interact with a genetic predisposition to depression, together with excessive tiredness and a stressful domestic situation.

Social/psychological explanations

The *psychodynamic* view relates depression in adulthood to the early relationship with parents and in particular to the repression of early trauma. Hostile feelings towards parent(s), it is claimed, are redirected towards the self in the form of self-accusation, or self-hatred. These feelings may arise from a lack of love and care, support and safety, or from child abuse.

John Bowlby, in his theory of maternal deprivation (see Chapter 17), suggested that separation from or loss of the mother in early childhood could result in severe depression in adulthood. Support for this view comes from carefully conducted studies by Hinde (1977), who examined the effects of separating infant rhesus monkeys from their mother. These monkeys (both mother and child) very quickly displayed behaviours similar to the symptoms of depression in humans. However, Paykel (1981) subsequently reviewed fourteen studies and found the evidence inconclusive because seven studies supported the hypothesis and seven did not support the hypothesis. It should also be borne in mind that it may be unwise to use studies of primates to support aetiological theories of disorders in humans.

Major life events, such as bereavement, unemployment, divorce and serious illness are thought to be significant precipitating factors in reactive depression, though not in endogenous depression. In 1978, Brown and Harris published a very influential book, entitled *The Social Origins of Depression*, which was the result of a study of depression among housewives in Camberwell, London. They identified two types of precipitating factors for depression – severe life events and long-term difficulties. These factors came into play when the person also experienced vulnerability factors – lack of paid employment outside the home, two or more children under the age of five, early loss of mother and, especially, lack of a close confiding relationship.

The life events theory has received a great deal of support and is now incorporated into the DSM diagnostic criteria under Axis IV where social and environmental circumstances are assessed. However, it does not explain why many patients do not report critical life events at the onset of their depression or why many people have ongoing psychosocial stressors but do not become clinically depressed. The diathesis-stress model provides a solution: life events may be precipitating factors which interact with other vulnerability factors.

Lewinsohn's (1974) *behavioural theory* of social reinforcement suggested that depression is a consequence of a reduction in positive reinforcement. For example, if someone experiences a bereavement, or loses his or her job, then there is less opportunity for enjoying pleasant experiences and receiving positive reinforcement. Depression may then occur. There is also a secondary gain, in that depressive behaviour may be positively reinforced by others in the form of their sympathy and concern. However, this cannot explain why the depression does not cease long after sympathy from others has waned.

One of the most notable behavioural explanations for reactive depression is Seligman's (1974) theory of Learned Helplessness. In the course of investigating the effects of Pavlovian fear conditioning in dogs, Seligman found that, when placed in an inescapable and unavoidable stressful situation, the dog failed to initiate escape behaviour in another stressful situation where escape was possible. Seligman suggested that people are generally able to influence many aspects of their environment, but sometimes things just happen, irrespective of their own behaviour. If this occurs too often then people lose their motivation and just give up, because they have learned that they are helpless in life situations.

Maier and Seligman (1976) tested this theory with humans, subjecting people to inescapable noise, shock and unsolvable problems and found that they later failed to escape from similar situations where escape was possible. These results were not always replicated, however, and some studies showed that helplessness actually facilitated subsequent performance (Wortman and Brehm 1975). Like many of the behavioural theories, learned helplessness was seen to be inadequate as a complete explanation because it does not take cognitions into account. Allied to this, gender differences were found in studies involving insoluble problems, the predominant female response being depression and the predominant male response being anger.

In view of the inadequacy of the learned helplessness account, Seligman later reformulated his theory in *cognitive, attributional* terms (Abramson, Seligman and Teasdale 1978). This revised theory suggested that when people experience failure, they usually try and attribute a cause to that failure. Causal explanations operate on three dimensions of judgement:

- internal–external (personal or environmental)
- stable–unstable (always so, or just on this occasion)
- global–specific (all encompassing, or specific to this situation).

A maladaptive style is to attribute all negative events to internal, stable, global causes. These causal explanations can then lead to expectations, which in turn can lead to symptoms of depression (see Fig. 11.3).

Research in support of the attributional theory of helplessness comes from studies using the Attributional Style Questionnaire, devised by Seligman, which gives scores for internality, stability and globality of an individual's expectations. A study, conducted on grade aspirations in college students, showed that most of those with poor results were depressed after the exams. Two days later, however, those who made unstable, specific attributions about their failure had recovered, whereas those who had made stable, global attributions remained depressed. However, most of Seligman's studies were conducted on college students, rather than on clinically depressed patients. Furthermore, one of the key elements of the helplessness theory is that depressed people believe they have little control over their lives, yet Ford and Neale (1985) found that depressed students did not underestimate their degree of control.

Beck (1991) maintains that there are three components to depression:

1 negative views of the self
2 negative views of one's ongoing experience of the world
3 negative views about the future.

He called these the cognitive triad. Thus the person sees him/herself as:

1 worthless and helpless
2 living in a world full of obstacles
3 contemplating a future continuing in much the same way.

As these components interact they interfere with normal cognitive processing, leading to impairments in perception, memory and problem-solving abilities, with the person becoming completely obsessed with automatic negative thoughts, or schemas, such as 'I am worthless' and 'I can't ever do anything right'. These faulty cognitions can, in turn, lead to depression.

Figure 11.3 An example of attributional judgements leading to depression

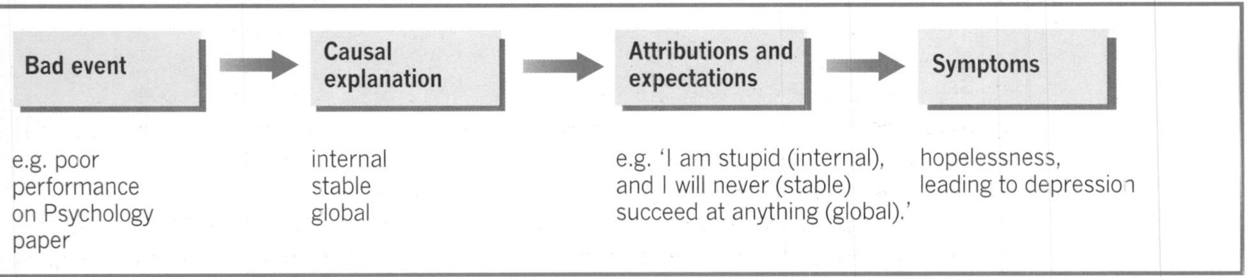

Beck maintains that there is strong evidence that stable temperament and behavioural tendencies are present at birth, based on the evolutionary strategies of fight, flight, freeze, or faint as alternative reactions to threat. Beck claims that inherited strategies can be strengthened or weakened by the environment and that negative schemas may be acquired in childhood as a result of traumatic events and negative treatment.

Section summary

A genetic tendency for unipolar depression is not supported in twin and family studies, but there is strong evidence for a genetic component in manic-depressive psychosis. There is no conclusive evidence for a biochemical or hormonal link with depression, although antidepressant drugs can offer an effective treatment for many depressed people. Psychological and social factors appear to provide the most plausible accounts for unipolar depression. The diathesis-stress model explains how factors within the individual can interact with external environmental factors, accounting for individual differences in susceptibility to depression. The vulnerability element may be inherited temperament, or it may develop through adverse life experience, conditioning, or negative ways of thinking.

Schizophrenia

Schizophrenia is the condition most often associated with the term 'madness'. It is not a split personality, it is a group of psychotic disorders that are characterized by a loss of contact with reality. Symptoms are mainly disturbances of thought processes, but also extend to disturbances of emotion and behaviour. There are two major symptom categories, one of which relates to *acute* schizophrenia, characterized by what are known as *positive* symptoms, such as hallucinations and delusions. The other relates to *chronic* schizophrenia, characterized by what are known as negative symptoms, such as apathy and withdrawal. A further distinction has been made between Type I (positive/acute) as a *functional* disorder and Type II (negative/chronic) as an *organic* disorder. DSM-IV has now moved away from these definitions and classified schizophrenia into three main sub-types, which are *paranoid, disorganized* and *catatonic.* Table 11.5 incorporates symptoms from both the traditional distinctions and DSM-IV classifications.

Schizophrenia is a serious psychotic disorder. DSM-IV (1994) states that estimates of prevalence vary in different studies and have ranged from 0.2% to 2.0% and that these rates are similar throughout the world. Although it can emerge later in life, the onset of schizophrenia for men is usually in the late teens or early twenties and for women onset is usually in the late twenties. It can suddenly strike, for example, a young person at university or just starting a career with a bright future. Around one third have a single, or just a few brief acute episodes and recover fully, whilst around another third have an episodic pattern of acute symptoms throughout life, maintaining a reasonable level of functioning whilst in remission. For the remaining third there is an unremitting course which deteriorates from acute to chronic symptoms. Treatment can reduce the effects of acute symptoms and some people recover spontaneously, but, as yet, there is no known cure for schizophrenia, despite the vast amount of money spent on research worldwide. See *In Focus* on p. 248 for three case studies of schizophrenia.

Genetic/neurological explanations

Family studies have been conducted since the 1900s in an attempt to identify a genetic link with schizophrenia. Of the more recent studies, Kendler *et al.* (1985) have shown that first-degree relatives of those with schizophrenia are 18 times more at risk than the general population.

Table 11.5 Symptoms of acute and chronic schizophrenia incorporating DSM-IV types

<table>
<tr><th>DSM-IV</th><th>Type I – functional
Acute (positive) symptoms</th><th>Type II – organic
Chronic (negative) symptoms</th></tr>
<tr><td>Paranoid type</td><td>Delusions of grandeur
Delusions of persecution
Auditory hallucinations</td><td></td></tr>
<tr><td>Disorganized type</td><td colspan="2">Disorganized speech
Disorganized behaviour
Inappropriate affect
Flat emotions</td></tr>
<tr><td>Catatonic type</td><td></td><td>Apathy
Loss of drive
Cataleptic stupor and bizarre postures
Excessive motor activity
Echolalia</td></tr>
</table>

Explanation of symptoms	
Delusions of grandeur:	Beliefs that they are someone grand or famous, such as The Messiah, Albert Einstein or Elvis Presley, or beliefs that they have special magical powers.
Delusions of persecution:	Beliefs that people are plotting against them, that they are being spied upon, talked about by strangers or deliberately victimized.
Auditory hallucinations:	Voices heard in the absence of external stimuli, which are often critical, warning of danger or giving commands.
Disorganized speech:	Inappropriate speech, for example: 'It's raining... fruit trees in summer... acts of Jupiter in a sea of haze... I should go and get my coats and hats... cosmic laws interjecting with... apples, oranges, pears...'
Disorganized behaviour:	Severe disruption in the ability to perform daily living activities, such as showering, dressing, preparing meals.
Inappropriate affect:	Silliness and laughter which are out of context, e.g. laughing when being told terrible news.
Flat emotions:	No emotional response can be elicited to any stimulus; face is immobile, eyes are lifeless, speech is toneless, often staring vacantly.
Apathy:	Loss of interest in normal goals.
Loss of drive:	Feeling drained of energy and unable to initiate or complete a course of action.
Cataleptic stupor:	Standing motionless like a statue in bizarre postures.
Excessive motor activity:	Moving in odd and disturbing ways (e.g. sudden movement, odd gestures, strange grimaces) that are apparently purposeless and not influenced by external stimuli.
Echolalia:	Repetitive echoing of words spoken by others, or the accentuated imitation of the mannerisms of other people.

In Focus

Case studies of schizo-phrenia

Catatonic schizophrenia

Maria is a 19-year-old college student who has been psychiatrically hospitalized for more than a month. For days prior to her admission, and for the weeks since her arrival in the hospital, Maria has been mute. Rigidly posturing her body and staring at the ceiling, she spends most of the day in a trance-like state that seems impenetrable. Her family and college acquaintances have been mystified. In trying to sort out why and when she began showing such odd behaviour, the only incident that could be recalled was Maria's ranting and raving, just prior to going into the catatonic state, that one of her lecturers was a 'demon'.

What type of catatonic behaviour is shown by Maria's staring and mutism?

Disorganized schizophrenia

Joshua is a 43-year-old man who can be found daily standing near the steps of a local bank on a busy street corner. Every day he wears a yellow T-shirt, worn-out hiking shorts and orange trainers. Rain or shine, day in and day out, Joshua maintains his 'post' at the bank. Sometimes he can be seen 'conversing' with imaginary people. Without provocation he sobs miserably, and at other times he explodes in shrieks of laughter. Police and social workers keep taking him to shelters for the homeless, but Joshua manages to get out and be back on the street before he can be treated.

What behaviours shown by Joshua suggest that he has disorganized schizophrenia?

Paranoid schizophrenia

Esther is 31-year-old unmarried woman who lives with her elderly mother. A belief that the outside world is filled with radio waves that will insert evil thoughts into her head keeps Esther from leaving the house. The windows in her bedroom are 'protected' with aluminium foil that 'deflects the radio waves'. She often hears voices that comment on these radio signals. For example, one comment was the slow, deep voice of an elderly man who angrily stated, 'We're going to get these thoughts into your head. Give up the fight!'

What behaviours of Esther's would lead you to consider her as having paranoid schizophrenia?

Source: adapted from Halgin and Whitbourne 1993, pp. 280–281

Unfortunately, family studies cannot differentiate between genetic and environmental influences.

Twin studies compare the concordance rates for MZ and DZ twins. Many studies have been conducted and they all show a much higher concordance rate in MZ than in DZ twins. Twins, however, also share the same environment, which has led researchers to seek out MZ twins reared apart where at least one twin has been diagnosed with schizophrenia. Obviously these are few in number and there is an added problem in that one of the reasons for separation might be a problem in the family. Gottesman and Shields (1982) used the Maudsley twin register and found 58% (seven out of twelve MZ twin pairs reared apart) were concordant for schizophrenia. If the genetic hypothesis is correct, then the offspring of a non-affected discordant MZ twin should still be high-risk. A study by Fischer (1971) found that 9.4% of such offspring developed schizophrenia, which is a much higher incidence than in the general population. Figure 11.4 illustrates the level of risk for developing schizo-phrenia, for different relatives of schizophrenics. Dworkin (1987) separated twin data into positive (acute) symptoms and negative (chronic) symptoms and found a stronger genetic component for negative symptoms.

Twin and family studies continue to provide reliable evidence that the degree of

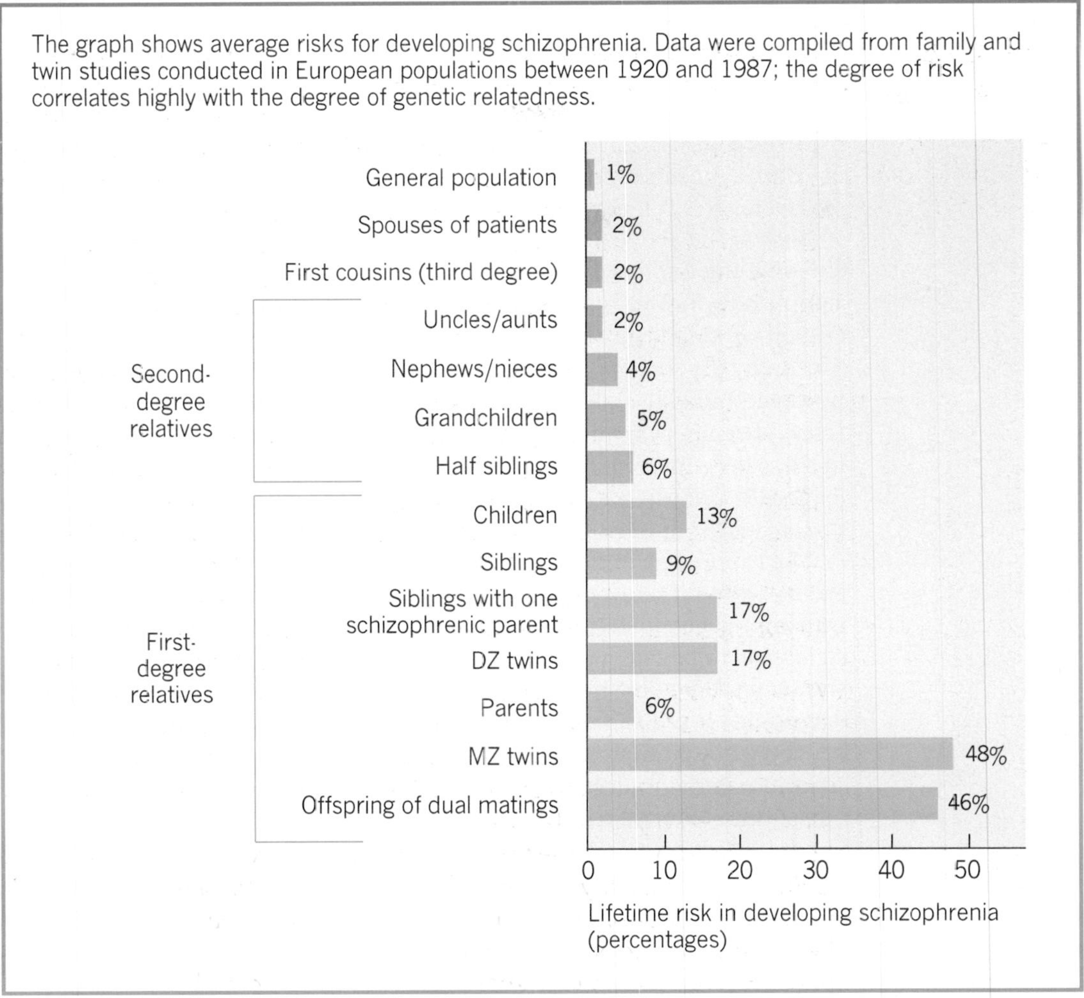

Figure 11.4 Genetic risk of developing schizophrenia *Source: Zimbardo et al. 1995*

risk increases with the degree of genetic relatedness (see Fig. 11.4); however, no study has yet shown 100% concordance. So far, all the genetic research mentioned has been conducted retrospectively, i.e. with people who have already been diagnosed with schizophrenia. Currently, however, there are a number of large-scale prospective (longitudinal) studies being conducted with high-risk families.

In the Israeli High Risk study, which Marcus began in 1967, fifty high-risk children were identified (where one or both parents had been diagnosed with schizophrenia) and fifty matched control children were identified (children of a similar age and background, but neither parent had been diagnosed with schizophrenia, or any other mental disorder). Within each group half were raised on a kibbutz (where all the children are reared together and separate from their parents) and half in a traditional family setting. The age range of children at the start of the study was 8.1 to 14.8 years. At a thirteen year follow-up, twenty-two of the high-risk group had been diagnosed with schizophrenia and only four of the control group. Sixteen of those diagnosed were from the kibbutz and ten from traditional families (Marcus *et al.* 1987).

The Finnish Adoption study, which Tienari began in 1969, identified adopted-away offspring of biological mothers who had been diagnosed with schizophrenia (112 index cases), plus a matched control group of 135 adopted-away offspring of mothers who had not been diagnosed with any mental disorder. Adoptees ranged from 5 to 57 years at the start of the study and all had been separated from their mother before the age of 4. So far, the study has reported that 7% of the index adoptees have developed schizophrenia, compared to 1.5% of the controls (Tienari *et al.* 1987).

Both of the above longitudinal studies are still ongoing and many of the people in the sample have not yet passed through the critical period for the onset of schizophrenia. The data they have provided so far, however, indicate a genetic link for schizophrenia. Diagnosis is a major problem in these longitudinal studies because diagnostic criteria are continually being updated and changed.

The rationale behind a biochemical theory is that if schizophrenia can be transmitted genetically, then either structural or biochemical abnormalities should be detectable in the brains of those diagnosed for schizophrenia. Research into neurochemical functioning has focused on serotonin and noradrenaline, but results have been inconclusive.

More convincing evidence has come from research on dopamine receptors. Interest in dopamine arose when it was found that phenothiazines (neuroleptic, anti-psychotic drugs which reduce the symptoms of schizophrenia) serve to inhibit dopamine activity and that L-dopa (a synthetic dopamine-releasing drug) can induce symptoms resembling paranoid (acute) schizophrenia in non-psychotic people. An interesting corollary concerning Parkinson's disease and schizophrenia has been noted. Symptoms of Parkinson's disease, such as shaking of the limbs, are common side-effects of anti-psychotic medication and Parkinson's disease is known to be associated with low levels of dopamine (see Fig. 11.5).

Studies on amphetamines have provided further support for the dopamine hypothesis. The symptoms of amphetamine psychosis are similar to paranoid schizophrenia and one of the actions of amphetamines is the release of dopamine at central synapses. Amphetamines have also been shown to worsen the symptoms of schizophrenia. In a study by Randrup and Munkvan (1966) behaviour similar to that found in those suffering from schizophrenia was induced in rats by administering amphetamines and the effects were then reversed by neuroleptic drugs. Further support comes from post-mortems of patients with schizophrenia, which have revealed a specific increase of dopamine in the left amygdala (Falkai *et al.* 1988) and increased dopamine receptor density in the caudate nucleus putamen (Owen *et al.* 1978).

Given the findings from post-mortems, and assuming that dopamine is the important factor in the action of anti-psychotic drugs, then it would be expected that dopamine metabolism is abnormal in schizophrenia patients. With the development of positron emission tomography (PET scans), metabolic activity can now be monitored in live brains. PET scan research conducted by Wong *et al.* (1986) revealed that dopamine receptor density in the caudate nuclei is indeed greater in those with schizophrenia than in controls. However, this has not been supported in subsequent studies and despite extensive research on dopamine receptors in the brains of schizophrenia patients,

Figure 11.5 Dopamine links with schizophrenia and Parkinson's disease

Disorder	Symptoms	Drug	Action	Effect
Schizophrenia	disordered thought and behaviour	Phenothiazine →	decreases dopamine →	reduces disordered thought and behaviour causes stiffness and tremors
Parkinson's disease	stiffness and tremors	L-dopa →	increases dopamine →	reduces stiffness and tremors

no consensus has yet been reached. Unfortunately, neither post-mortems nor PET scans can reveal whether increased dopaminergic activity causes schizophrenia, or whether schizophrenia interferes with dopamine metabolism.

❖ Activity 3 ❖

Based on information given in the previous paragraphs, which of the following statements seem more likely to be correct?

a) High levels of dopamine cause schizophrenia.

b) High levels of dopamine induce symptoms of schizophrenia.

c) Schizophrenia causes high levels of dopamine to be produced.

d) There is no connection at all between schizophrenia and dopamine activity.

Structural abnormalities in the brain of schizophrenic patients have long been suspected, but whereas previously work was confined to post-mortems, advancement in technology has meant that live brains of schizophrenic patients can be examined. Magnetic resonance imaging (MRI) has been a tremendous breakthrough because it provides a picture of the brain. MRI studies show quite definite structural abnormalities in the brains of many patients with schizophrenia, such as decreased brain weight and enlarged ventricles (the cavities in the brain that hold cerebrospinal fluid) (Brown *et al.* 1986). Abnormalities are also found in the frontal and prefrontal cortex, the basal ganglia, the hippocampus and the amygdala (Buchsbaum 1990).Young *et al.* (1991), using MRI, found a number of structural differences between schizophrenics and controls, particularly in the asymmetry of the brain. For example, in controls the amygdala was smaller on the left than the right, but in the schizophrenia group asymmetry was absent. Young *et al.* found that the degree of abnormality correlated with the severity of the symptoms. These findings lend support to the view of Kraepelin (who was the first to identify and label 'schizophrenia' at the end of the last century) that schizophrenia resulted from a process of brain degeneration.

There are conflicting views as to whether these structural abnormalities result from a genetic defect, or from birth complications. Pollin and Stabenau (1968) claim that with MZ twins discordant for schizophrenia, there is a higher frequency of birth complications in the affected twin. In contrast to this, a recent study by Lewis *et al.* (1990) found lesions in an unaffected twin, but not in the affected twin. These findings raise the possibility that some forms of brain damage may actually protect against schizophrenia.

The critical period for the onset of schizophrenia is not usually before adolescence. Therefore, if the lesion owing to a genetic defect and/or brain damage precedes the onset of clinical symptoms this suggests that schizophrenia is a developmental disorder. However, there is still very little evidence of progressive structural brain changes which means that the causal direction of the hypothesis is still in question – whether structural abnormalities predispose to schizophrenia, or whether the onset of clinical symptoms cause structural changes (Weinberger 1988). According to Iacono *et al.* (1988) dopamine deficiency may be the cause of ventricular enlargement.

❖ Activity 4 ❖

Taking the preceding evidence into account, do you think that the three biological aetiologies (genetic, biochemical and neurological) are mutually exclusive? Or can you suggest how they might fit together to explain schizophrenia?

Social/psychological explanations

In the 1950s and 1960s it was thought that people suffering from schizophrenia were from *dysfunctional* families. There was even a strong belief that schizophrenia was caused by a dysfunction of communication within the family. The term schizophrenogenic families (coined by Fromm-Reichmann 1948) was used to describe families with high emotional tension, with many secrets, close alliances and conspiracies. An associated suggestion was the double-bind situation where children are given conflicting messages from parents who express care, yet at the same time appear critical (Bateson *et al.* 1956). It was thought that this led to confusion, self-doubt and eventual withdrawal. This theory went into decline because of a failure to replicate findings across studies. Another reason for the loss of interest in it in the 1970s was the convincing evidence that was appearing for a genetic predisposition in schizophrenia.

The main problem, however, was that families were studied retrospectively, long after the person's mental disorder may have affected the family system. Living with someone who is suffering from schizophrenia is difficult and distressing for the whole family. Routines are disrupted, often with one parent having to give up paid employment to care for the person. As families struggle to cope with schizophrenia, to suggest that they have caused the disorder is at least unhelpful and at most highly destructive.

By the mid-1970s, psychologists had become more interested in the part the family might play in the *course* rather than the *cause* of schizophrenia. Vaughn and Leff, working at the Medical Research Council in London, published a paper in 1976 suggesting that the extent of expressed emotion within a family was a strong predictor of relapse rates among discharged patients. Their research was stimulated by an earlier study by Brown (1972) showing that schizophrenic patients who returned to homes where a high level of emotion was expressed (High EE), such as hostility, criticism, over-involvement and over-

Table 11.6 Results of prospective studies of expressed emotion (EE)

Author	*Location*	*No. of subjects*	*Follow-up*	*Relapse rate High EE*	*Relapse rate Low EE*
Vaughn and Leff (1976)	S. London	37	9 months	50%	12%
Leff and Vaughn (1981)*	S. London	36	2 years	62%	20%
Vaughn *et al.* (1984)	Los Angeles	54	9 months	56%	28%
Macmillan *et al.* (1986)	N. London	67	2 years	63%	39%
Leff *et al.* (1987)	Chandigargh (India)	76	1 year	33%	14%
Budzyna-Dawidowski *et al.* (1989)	Cracow (Poland)	36	1 year 2 years	32% 72%	9% 18%
Cazzullo *et al.* (1989)	Milan (Italy)	45	9 months	58%	21%
Barrelet *et al.* (1990)	Geneva	41	9 months	32%	0%

* Follow-up of same patients as Vaughn and Leff (1976)

Source: extracted from Bebbington and Kuipers 1992, *cited in* Kavanagh 1992 concern, showed a greater tendency to relapse than those returning to Low EE homes. Vaughn and Leff (1976) found similar results, with 51% relapse in those in High EE homes and only 13% relapse in those in Low EE homes. Vaughn and Leff included in their study the amount of time spent in face-to-face contact with relatives after discharge and found that relapse rates increased as face-to-face contact increased, but only with High EE relatives. The study also included data on whether or not the patient was on medication and it was found that the relapse rate increased to 92% in High EE homes with increased contact coupled with no medication. It should be noted, however, that no study has since replicated these particular results relating to medication.

Twenty years on, EE has now become a well established 'maintenance' model of schizophrenia and many prospective studies have been conducted which support the expressed-emotion hypothesis across many cultures (see Table 11.6). So well accepted has this model become that treatment programmes for schizophrenia usually include education and training for family members in controlling levels of EE. However, despite the widely-held acceptance of the EE model, it is not without its critics. Firstly, many schizophrenic patients are either estranged from their families, or have minimal contact and yet there is no evidence that such people are less prone to relapse (Goldstein 1988). There is no reason why this should negate the model, however, because presumably any social involvement could be regarded as high or low EE. Adopting this view is less accusing to families, suggesting that they are more in focus simply because they are usually the first and most frequent point of contact. Added to this, it has been suggested that high EE may well develop as a response to the burdens of living with schizophrenia.

Diathesis-stress model explanation

Since the 1980s the diathesis-stress model has been applied to schizophrenia. The reasoning behind this theory is that those individuals who develop schizophrenia may be genetically predisposed. In addition, however, the research on 'expressed emotion' has revealed that they are also extremely sensitive to psychosocial elements in their environment. Therefore, stressful events in the environment, such as major life events, traumatic experiences, or dysfunctional families, may act as a 'trigger' in a high-risk individual (see Fig. 11.6).

Support for the 'diathesis-stress' model also comes from prospective longitudinal studies. As research gathered further evidence for genetic factors, it was also becoming clear that schizophrenia did not always develop in those thought to be genetically vulnerable. This led researchers back to the environment in the search for precipitating factors.

The Finnish Adoption Study undertaken by Tienari (1987) also investigated environmental factors by assessing the quality of parenting through a battery of tests and interviews. All of the schizophrenic cases reported occurred in families rated as 'disturbed'. Furthermore, where the rearing environments were rated as 'healthy' in the high-risk sample, the occurrence of schizophrenia was well below general population rates. However, this cannot be

Figure 11.6 Diathesis-stress model for schizophrenia

Predisposing factors +	**trigger** →	**outcome**
Genetic predisposition plus (or expressed as)* increased sensitivity to psychosocial factors	adverse family circumstances *and/or* major life events *and/or* traumatic experiences	schizophrenia

* This may be a separate factor or it may be the phenotypic expression of the genetic predisposition.

seen as evidence for a purely environmental aetiology because low-risk children from 'disturbed' families did not develop schizophrenia.

The Israeli High Risk Study (Marcus 1987) investigated environmental factors by assessing the parents on hostility, inconsistency and over-involvement. All the reported cases of schizophrenia had poor parenting ratings. However, all of these cases also showed signs of neuropsychological abnormalities at the time of initial assessment (thirteen years previously), which raises the question of whether these abnormalities had influenced the parent-child interaction.

These studies are ongoing and many of the children have not yet passed through the critical period for the onset of schizophrenia. However, the evidence so far strongly supports the diathesis-stress model.

❖ Activity 5 ❖

1 Assuming there is a genetic predisposition to schizophrenia, what environmental factors might prevent the manifestation of the actual disorder?

2 What environmental factors might influence the severity and course of schizophrenia?

3 What ethical issues might arise from a prospective study investigating the causes of schizophrenia?

Section summary

Although the severity of any disorder is specific to the individual, most people would agree that schizophrenia is probably the most serious of all mental disorders. Because of this, a vast amount of financial resources has been invested in research throughout the world and yet the origins of the disorder still remain elusive. However, research has come a long way in providing an understanding of schizophrenia and the pieces of the aetiological puzzle may be beginning to take shape. The current view holds that genetic inheritance predisposes, or renders a person vulnerable (high risk) to the disorder, with biochemical and neurological factors being expressions of the predisposition. Added to this, there are probably additional precipitating factors involved, especially social/family factors. In the near future it may even be possible to integrate all of the aetiological theories.

❖ Activity 6 ❖

Could you recognize someone suffering from schizophrenia?

The next time you see a vagrant lying in a doorway, or someone walking along the street talking strangely to themselves, look again with a little more sympathy. They may be suffering from schizophrenia, with no one to care for them.

Chapter summary

- This chapter has looked at different types of mental disorders. There are many explanations of the causes of specific disorders and some have been supported by empirical evidence more strongly than others. However, this does not inevitably make these explanations more correct.
- Twin and family studies have provided strong, although not yet conclusive, evidence for a genetic link with manic-depression and schizophrenia. A genetic link has not been firmly established for anxiety disorders, eating disorders and unipolar depression.
- Neurological research has highlighted possible physical abnormalities linked with schizophrenia, mood disorders and eating disorders, but only very tentatively with anxiety disorders.

- Social/psychological explanations, including the psychodynamic, behavioural and cognitive, are prominent for anxiety disorders, eating disorders and unipolar depression. Research on expressed emotion has offered valuable insights into environmental effects on the *course* rather than the *cause* of schizophrenia.
- The diathesis-stress model offers an explanation which accounts for individual differences, by suggesting a predisposition to vulnerability which interacts with environmental factors, such as stressful life events.
- You may have found that you could identify with some of the social/psychological explanations, from your own experiences in life. It is hoped, after reading this chapter, that the reader will think and act even more sympathetically with regard to the suffering of people with mental disorders.

Essay questions

1 Describe and evaluate the evidence that schizophrenia is a genetic disorder. *(24 marks)*

2 Critically consider the view that anorexia nervosa is the result of 'slimming that got out of hand'. *(24 marks)*

3 Discuss the influence of genetic and/or neurological factors on mental illness. *(24 marks)*

4 (a) Describe any one mental disorder. *(10 marks)*

(b) Discuss social/psychological explanations given for this disorder. *(14 marks)*

Further reading

Comer, R.J. (1995) *Abnormal Psychology*, New York: Freeman. Chapters 6, 8, 12 and 15.

Davison, G.C. and Neale, J.M. (1994) *Abnormal Psychology*, New York: John Wiley. Chapters 6, 9, 14 and 15.

Comer (1995) and Davison and Neale (1994) both provide readable, comprehensive accounts of the disorders discussed in this chapter.

Oltmanns, T.F., Neale, J.M. and Davison, G.C. (1995) *Case studies in Abnormal Psychology* (4th edn), New York: John Wiley.

This book provides extended, detailed case studies to illustrate mental disorders.

For more concise illustrations, look at Comer (1995), Davison and Neale (1994) or **Rosenhan, D.L and Seligman, M.E.P.** (1989) *Abnormal Psychology* (2nd edn), London: Norton.

Chapter 12

Therapeutic approaches

Pamela Prentice

Preview

In this chapter we shall be looking at:

- somatic (biological) treatments
- psychodynamic therapies
- behavioural therapies
- cognitive-behavioural therapy
- humanistic (person-centred) therapy
- ethical issues in therapy and intervention.

Introduction

There are considerable ethical issues involved with therapy and intervention, which are of particular concern to those involved in mental health, either as recipients or practitioners. A number of these issues will be considered later in this chapter. Prior to that, a number of different therapies and treatments for abnormal behaviour will be outlined, each one based on a particular theoretical orientation regarding the basis of human nature and the causes of psychological problems. Explanations for the causes of abnormal behaviour are outlined in Chapter 10 and are essential prior reading for an understanding of the therapies outlined in this chapter.

Somatic (biological) treatments

Somatic treatments follow from biological explanations for abnormal behaviour; that is mental disorder viewed as illness and mainly due to a biochemical imbalance. Somatic treatments are, therefore, designed to redress biochemical imbalance. This is achieved through the administration of chemical drugs and, in some cases, electro-convulsive therapy (ECT).

Drug treatments (chemotherapy)

Drugs believed to be beneficial for mental disorders are classified into three main types: anti-anxiety (benzodiazepines); antidepressant (tricyclics, serotonin reuptake inhibitors and monoamine-oxidase inhibitors); anti-manic (lithium salts) and anti-psychotic (phenothiazines), all of which operate on the central nervous system.

- *Anti-anxiety drugs*: Benzodiazepines are minor tranquillizers and include Librium and Valium. They were introduced in the 1950s and 1960s and soon became the most prescribed drugs in the world.
- *Antidepressant drugs*: These are stimulants and fall into three categories: tricyclics, serotonin reuptake inhibitors and monoamine-oxidase inhibitors (MAOIs), which were the first antidepressants on the market. The first MAOI was Iproniazid, and its antidepressant effect was discovered by accident when it was tried as a new drug for tuberculosis and found to induce euphoria. It was widely used as a treatment for depression in the late 1950s, but it was found to have a toxic effect if combined with other drugs and certain foods and drinks. It was quickly superseded by the tricyclics, such as Tofranil, which are milder antidepressants, with fewer severe side effects. Prozac is the newest of the antidepressant drugs, which selectively inhibits the re-uptake of serotonin. The neurotransmitter, serotonin, is thought to play a part in mood regulation, inducing relaxation and controlling aggression.
- *Anti-manic drugs*: These are used to control the mania in those suffering from manic-depression. They were discovered through the work of John Cade, an Australian physician. He conducted lithium carbonate tests on guinea pigs, after inducing mania by injecting urine from manic patients. Cade then tested his lithium preparation on manic patients and found that their manic euphoria had calmed within a few days. By the 1970s lithium carbonate had become the routine treatment for manic-depression.
- *Anti-psychotic drugs*: Phenothiazines are used in treatment for schizophrenia. They are major tranquillizers which sedate the person and ameliorate delusions and hallucinations. An excess of the neurotransmitter dopamine has been linked with schizophrenia (see Chapter 10) and one of the actions of phenothiazine drugs is that they bind to dopamine receptors and block the build up of dopamine.

Appropriateness and effectiveness

Drug treatments have been especially beneficial in restoring faith in the medical profession as the front line for treating mental disorders, after Freud had cast a shadow of doubt on the physical origins of mental problems. Outcome studies indicate that drugs are reasonably effective for treating certain mental disorders and they are readily available, easily administered and cost-effective (see Table 12.1).

Benzodiazepines (anti-anxiety drugs) were eagerly taken up by GPs because they offered a safe way to alleviate anxieties in patients. They did not lead to fatality when taken in overdose, unlike opioids, such as morphine and laudanum. These were the only drugs previously available and doctors were loath to prescribe them because of the dangers of addiction, severe side effects, overdose and potential fatality. Drugs also offered a quick and easy solution for GPs who could write a prescription rather than engaging in counselling (for which few GPs are trained), thereby reducing patient consultation time. Unfortunately, benzodiazepines did not prove to be such a magic solution after all because they create dependency on the drug, sometimes for many years after the initial problem has been resolved. The frequency and willingness with which GPs prescribed benzodiazepines in the 1960s and 1970s has resulted in the recent development of self-help groups for people trying to overcome their long-term dependency. Most GPs are now careful to restrict such drugs to short courses.

The effectiveness of antidepressants was tested by Spiegel (1989) who found that around 65 per cent of depressed patients improved with tricyclics, although there are potential side effects, the most serious being cardiac problems. MAO inhibitors are equally effective and have the same side effects. They are used with extreme caution because, in addition, they can be fatal if taken with other forms of medication. However, Thase *et al.* (1991) claim that they may be the only recourse for treating depressive episodes in manic-depression.

Table 12.1 Effectiveness and side effects of drug treatments

Drug treatment	*Disorder*	*Effectiveness*	*Side effects*
Anti-anxiety			
Benzodiazepines	anxiety specific phobias panic	short-term improvement little improvement some improvement	become less potent over time as the body builds up tolerance and requires larger dosages, which can lead to physical dependency on the drug.
Antidepressants			
Tricyclics	depression agoraphobia	moderate improvement moderate improvement	cardiac problems, tremor, rash, mania, confusion, weight gain, memory loss, fatigue.
Serotonin reuptake inhibitors (e.g. Prozac)	depression	moderate improvement moderate improvement	nausea, nervousness, anxiety, insomnia, fever, convulsions, diarrhoea, sexual dysfunction, mania, suicidal morbidity.
MAO inhibitors	depression social phobia agoraphobia	moderate improvement moderate improvement moderate improvement	hypertension, dizziness, fatigue, tremors, nervousness, convulsions, rashes, weight gain, mania, hallucinations, toxicity, may be fatal if taken with other antidepressants.
Anti-psychotic			
Lithium salts	manic-depression	substantial improvement	cardiac problems, vomiting, convulsions, tremors, gastrointestinal problems, toxicity.
Phenothiazines	schizophrenia	partial improvement	irregular heartbeat, low blood pressure, immobility of face, uncontrolled fidgeting, tremors, spasms, impotence, epileptic seizures, tardive dyskinesia.

Prozac was hailed as the 'wonder drug' for depression when it was first introduced in the late 1980s and is presently the most prescribed of all antidepressants. However, it has recently become a media target because there have been so many anecdotal reports of serious side effects, including a preoccupation with violence and suicide (Steiner 1991).

Psychological therapies have traditionally been thought to be less effective for psychotic disorders and drugs continue to be the main form of treatment. Anti-psychotic drugs have provided a breakthrough in treating the symptoms of schizophrenia, such as delusions and hallucinations. Prior to the introduction of phenothiazines in the 1950s schizophrenia was considered untreatable and patients were interned in mental institutions. As Rosenhan and Seligman (1995) vividly explain, the back wards of mental hospitals were called 'snake pits', filled with inmates who were unreachable or mutely catatonic, or were wild with delusions and straitjacketed, or were 'giggling out' unrelated words. All previous attempts to treat schizophrenia, such as insulin shock, ECT and various drugs, had failed, until the introduction of phenothiazines. These drugs have enabled many patients to live a reasonably normal life in the community. Community care has, however, proved inadequate for many people with schizophrenia, one of the problems being poor compliance with medication. Research indicates that if anti-psychotic drugs are stopped abruptly and too soon then symptoms recur (Davis *et al.* 1993). This has led to the 'revolving door syndrome' of continual discharge into the community and readmission into hospital.

Phenothiazines have considerable side effects, which may explain non-compliance with medication. They operate on dopamine receptors and, when administered to psychotic patients, can induce symptoms similar to those in Parkinson's disease, such as stiffness, immobility and tremors. The most serious side effect is tardive dyskinesia, which includes uncontrollable, frog-like sucking and smacking of the lips. It is thought that phenothiazines destroy a part of the brain and, once begun, this process is irreversible. It occurs in around 30 per cent of those taking the drug and the risk increases with prolonged usage (Gualtieri 1991).

Lithium salts (e.g. lithium carbonate), the drugs used for manic-depression, are effective for around 80 per cent of patients (Rosenhan and Seligman 1995). Prior to their introduction, 15 per cent of manic-depressives committed suicide and a large proportion were unable to function properly in daily life because of their extreme mood swings. Many patients, however, are loath to take medication because they like being in a euphoric state (Johnson *et al.* 1989)

❖ Activity 1 ❖

Do you think the potential benefits (effectiveness) of drug treatment outweigh the potential costs (side effects), described in Table 12.1? Remember, if you, or a member of your family, were suffering from a mental disorder, you might think differently.

and because lithium carbonate has side effects. It is toxic and can lead to gastrointestinal and cardiac problems, and even death. Another problem is that if a person starts on lithium and then discontinues it, its future use can increase the risk of manic-depressive episodes (Suppes *et al.* 1991).

It has now become clear that drugs do not necessarily offer a long-term cure, because in many cases symptoms recur when the drugs are no longer taken. It is believed by many psychologists that biochemical imbalance is the result of, rather than the cause of, abnormal functioning. This leads to the claim that drugs merely treat the symptoms (e.g. the anxiety or depression), but they do not address the cause of the problem (e.g. why the person is anxious or depressed). Consequently, they can only provide short-term alleviation. Given that there are also numerous side effects from drugs, as shown in Table 12.1, one wonders whether the benefits could ever outweigh the costs, particularly if the initial problems still remain. Many people, however, prefer drugs. This may be because taking tablets is a familiar activity, whereas psychological treatment is unfamiliar territory and many people feel cautious, or even threatened, by the thought of it.

For psychological therapies to be effective, the client or patient must have some insight, in so much as they must recognize that they have a problem. Some people suffering from chronic psychotic disorders have no insight and therefore psychological treatment is difficult, although for many psychotic patients insight is regained during periods of remission from acute psychotic episodes. With the assistance of phenothiazines, which reduce psychotic symptoms such as delusions and hallucinations, psychotic patients can be 'more available' to psychological therapies, such as insight therapies and family therapy. Short courses of antidepressant drugs can be worthwhile in cases of severe clinical depression, because without these, patients often have no motivation to engage in psychological treatment. Antidepressants may even be essential, as a first line of treatment for severe clinical depression, because of the high risk of suicide. These examples illustrate ways that somatic treatment and psychological treatment can work together, rather than as alternative forms of treatment.

Electro-convulsive therapy (ECT)

ECT was originally developed by Cerletti and tested as a treatment for schizophrenia in 1938. It was found to be ineffective in reducing psychotic symptoms, but very effective in alleviating severe depression. ECT involves the passage of electrical current through the brain by the application of between 70 and 130 volts which induces a convulsion or epileptic seizure. It is thought that the convulsion acts upon neurochemical transmission in a way that improves the person's mood state. The original procedure was bilateral, i.e. the current passed through both cerebral hemispheres of the brain. The patient was awake prior to the seizure. The contortions of the body produced by the original procedure have now been minimized by a newer procedure, where a strong muscle relaxant and an anaesthetic are given prior to treatment. The procedure used now is also unilateral, passing the current through the non-dominant hemisphere only (Abrams *et al.* 1991).

Appropriateness and effectiveness

ECT is a controversial treatment, not least because the medical profession is still unsure of how it works – an analogy has been drawn with kicking the side of the television set to make it work. ECT has, however, been successful in treating severe depression in patients where all other methods have failed and many argue that this is sufficient justification for its use, especially if it prevents suicide. It is a very quick form of treatment, in contrast to drugs or psychological therapies and Klerman (1988) maintains that ECT may be the optimal treatment for severe depression. Studies indicate that 60 to 70 per cent of patients improve with ECT (e.g. Sackeim 1988), although a large proportion of these become depressed again the following year (Sackeim *et al.* 1993).

In Focus

Psychosurgery

Psychosurgery is an extreme form of somatic treatment. It involves the cutting of neural tissue in the brain and was designed to change a psychological condition. The first technique was the lobotomy, developed in the 1940s as a cure for schizophrenia. This involved severing the connection between the frontal cortex and the lower centres of the brain. In the 1960s this procedure was replaced by the prefrontal leukotomy, thought to be less extreme, which involved drilling two holes in either side of the skull and inserting a pointed instrument to sever nerve fibres. A more recent procedure is the cingulotomy, where a tiny cut is made in the cingulum nerve fibres, using an electrode needle which is guided by magnetic resonance imaging, making the procedure much more precise.

Psychosurgery continues to be regarded as the most controversial of all treatments for mental disorders. The procedure is irreversible because neural tissue has been destroyed and there is no guarantee that the procedure will have a beneficial effect. Significant detrimental effects were found with the earlier lobotomy operation, such as withdrawal, stupors, seizures and even death. The more recent leukotomy procedure is less severe, but there are still dangers involved. According to Beck and Cowley (1990), the procedure is beneficial in some cases of severe anxiety, depression and obsessive-compulsive disorders. Nowadays, psychosurgery is performed only in extreme cases when all other forms of treatment have failed and where, because of the disorder, the person is likely to cause harm to themselves or others.

When ECT was first introduced there were dangerous side effects, such as bone fractures, memory loss and confusion. There are no detectable changes in brain structure with the newer unilateral procedure and, as the technique is continually improved, side effects are being reduced. Nevertheless, ECT remains controversial; it requires consent from the patient or close relative and is only used when other methods have failed. Although techniques are improving, there continues to be a decline in the use of ECT. Comer (1995) suggests three reasons for this:

- Applying an electrical current to the brain is a frightening and forceful form of intervention and even with the newer techniques there are still side effects, especially with repeated use.
- ECT has a history of abuse, being used as a means of punishing or controlling people in mental hospitals with some people having received hundreds of ECT treatments.
- There are now very effective antidepressant drugs which provide a more attractive alternative.

Psychodynamic therapies

The aim of psychodynamic therapy is not to 'cure' the patient's psychological problems, in the way that the medical profession might hope to find a cure for cancer. Rather, the aim is to enable the person to cope better with inner emotional conflicts that are causing disturbance. The purpose of therapy is to uncover unconscious conflicts and anxieties which have their origins in the past, in order to gain insight into the causes of psychological disturbance (see *In Focus* for an example). After bringing these conflicts into consciousness, the client is encouraged to work through them by examining and dealing with them in the safety of the consulting room, and, in so doing, release the power they exert over behaviour – a process known as *catharsis*. An important aspect of this is that confusing or traumatic childhood experiences can be better understood with the benefit of adult knowledge.

In psychodynamic therapy, a variety of techniques are employed to facilitate the process of catharsis, which include the following:

- *Free association*: The client is asked to recline on a chair or couch (with the therapist out of sight) and allow the free flow of feelings, thoughts or images. As these come to mind, clients express them in words, without censorship.

In Focus

Case study of a phobia

Mary was referred for treatment because of a fear (phobia) of vomiting. She was so afraid of vomiting that she was unable to eat in public. This became even more serious when she found it difficult to eat at all. She was, by then, displaying all the symptoms of anorexia nervosa. She was treated with 'systematic desensitization' (a behavioural treatment believed to be very effective for phobias and which is explained in the next section of this chapter). In Mary's case this had no effect and she was then given psychodynamic therapy. During therapy Mary recollected that she had been sexually abused as a child by her father. The usual scenario was that her father would return after an evening's drinking. He would first visit the bathroom where he could be heard to vomit and then he would enter Mary's bedroom. The psychodynamic explanation was that this traumatic experience in early childhood had been repressed into the unconscious, only to reveal itself in the form of a phobia in later life.

The analyst must listen, suspending their own values and judgements and interrupting from time to time to ask the client to reflect upon the significance of associations. The reasoning is that associations should arise from, and therefore reflect, internal dynamic conflict.

- *Word association*: The client is read a list of words one at a time and asked to reply with whatever comes instantly to mind. The analyst pays particular attention to unusual responses, hesitations and mental blanks, which may indicate repression.

❖ Activity 2 ❖

Try the word association test in pairs, with one responding and the other speaking the words and noting the responses. Devise your own list of around eight words such as the following:

Dark	Mother	Earth	Death
Child	Home	Water	Moon

- *Dream analysis*: Freud believed that our unconscious drives are expressed uncensored in dreams, although they are disguised in symbolic form in order to protect the conscious mind. The role of the analyst is to help the client interpret their dreams' significance. In Freudian psychoanalysis, dreams are interpreted as wish-fulfilment, usually of a sexual or aggressive nature. In Adlerian therapy, dreams are viewed as an attempt to avoid feelings of inferiority, the most common dreams being of flying or falling. In Jungian analysis, dreams are an attempt to solve particular problems or to anticipate the future.
- *Transference:* This occurs when the client redirects feelings (e.g. of hostility) towards the therapist, which are unconsciously directed towards a significant person in their life (usually a parent) but which have been censored from the conscious mind. Transference is important because it indicates that repressed conflict is coming very close to conscious awareness. Transference must occur naturally, however, and the therapist must neither encourage nor prevent it. The aim is to identify the source (person) of the transference and the circumstances surrounding the repression.
- *Projective tests*: There are many types of projective test, the most well-known being the Rorschach Ink Blot (see Fig. 12.1) and the Thematic Apperception Test (or TAT) (see Fig 12.2). The client is asked to describe what they see in the ink blot or to tell a story around the picture. These are used as tools to uncover recurrent themes that may reveal the unconscious needs and motives of the person.

❖ Activity 3 ❖

Try out the projective tests for yourself.

- Look at the ink blot and write down anything that comes into your mind.
- Weave a short story around the picture.

Now analyse what you wrote and try to identify any significance. Alternatively, ask someone else also studying psychology to analyse what you wrote.

Appropriateness and effectiveness

Psychodynamic therapy is generally conducted over a number of years, which makes it expensive and this has restricted its availability. More modern brief psychodynamic therapies have emerged, however, and their focus has been much more on current, rather than past concerns. Psychodynamic therapy has been regarded as appropriate for psychological problems traditionally labelled as 'neuroses', such as anxiety disorders, depression and eating disorders, although its use may be limited

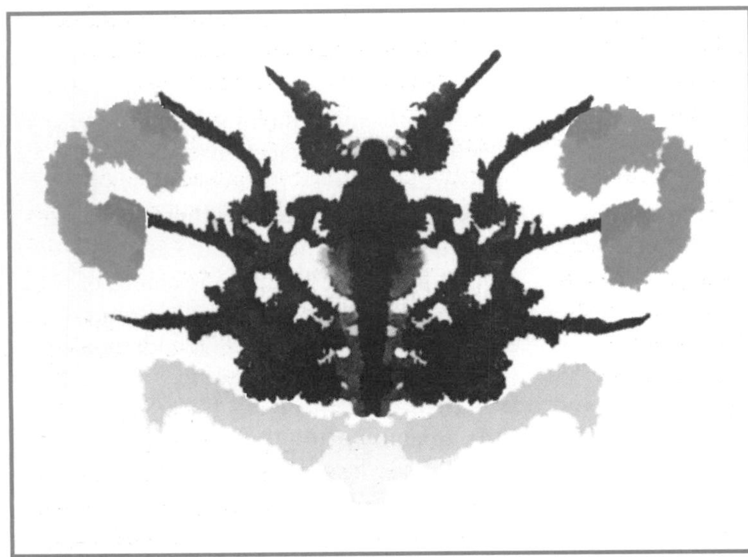

Fig. 12.1
Projective test:
Rorschach Ink Blot

Fig. 12.2
Projective test: Picture from the Thematic Apperception Test, introduced in 1935 by Henry Murray and his associates at the Harvard Psychological Clinic.
Like the Rorschach, this projective test is designed to reveal unconscious conflicts and concerns.

with depression because patients are generally apathetic and fatigued. Comer (1995) cites the American Psychiatric Association's concern about 'transference' with patients suffering from depression, because of their tendency towards extreme dependency on important people in their lives. Comer also points out that psychodynamic techniques may be detrimental to the treatment of obsessive-compulsive disorder, because 'free association' may inadvertently increase the person's tendency to ruminate and over-interpret. Psychodynamic therapy was traditionally believed to be of little benefit for patients with schizophrenia, because their loss of contact with reality would prevent them from using insight therapy. With the introduction of phenothiazines, however, patients with schizophrenia can now be much more 'available' to psychotherapy and it has been shown to be beneficial (Boker 1992).

Probably the most quoted indictment against psychodynamic therapy came from Eysenck (1952) who claimed that it simply does not work. He reviewed two outcome studies, incorporating waiting list controls, which showed that 66 per cent of the control group improved spontaneously, whereas only 44 per cent of psychoanalysis patients improved. Eysenck's papers were subsequently reviewed by Bergin (1971) who found that patients in one of the control groups were in fact hospitalized and those in the other group were being treated by their GP. He also found that by selecting different outcome criteria, improvement in the psychoanalysis group increased to 83 per cent and the control groups dropped to 30 per cent.

Corsini and Wedding (1995) claim that, depending on the criteria involved, 'cures' range from 30 to 60 per cent. The concept of 'cure' is, however, inappropriate, and Bolger (1989) makes the point that much of the evaluative research is based on the medical model of problem behaviour which assumes that a psychological disorder follows a course similar to that of a disease. It is now generally accepted that there are methodological difficulties in evaluating the effectiveness of psychodynamic therapy. It generally spans several years and the point at which it is assessed may be crucial to a measurement of efficacy. Corsini and Wedding (1995) also explain that there are too many variables involved to enable a controlled and statistically valid outcome study. Comparisons may be made between symptoms at the beginning and termination of treatment, but during the course of therapy other complications may arise as a direct result of insight during therapy. Because treatment is over such a long period, there may also be other factors occurring in the client's life during the course of therapy which impact upon the outcome. Life may have been favourable for some clients and unfavourable for others. Effectiveness is a subjective concept, measurable only by the extent to which clients themselves feel that their condition has improved. Freud himself was quite modest about the therapeutic claims of psychoanalysis (Freud 1937). Despite difficulties in evaluation, psychodynamic therapies continue to thrive and the newer brief therapies have made this type of therapy more accessible and affordable.

Behavioural therapies

Behavioural therapies, which emerged in the 1950s, are a logical extension to behaviourism as applied to the field of psychopathology. The main assumption of the behavioural view is that abnormal behaviour is acquired in the same way as normal behaviour, through the principles of classical and operant conditioning, and social learning theory. Therefore, just as it is learned, it can equally be unlearned. Over the past thirty or forty years a number of therapeutic techniques have been developed out of the learning paradigm, with the overall aim of encouraging adaptive strategies to enable the person to function more effectively in the environment. The first stage in behavioural therapy is a 'functional analysis' to assess the person's level of functioning, identify the stimulus antecedents to maladaptive responses, and to decide upon the most appropriate treatment techniques. Techniques derived from classical conditioning and operant conditioning are described below.

Techniques derived from classical conditioning

- *Systematic desensitization*: This technique, devised by Wolpe (1958), was developed specifically to countercondition fears, phobias and anxieties. The therapist works with the client to compile a hierarchical list of feared situations, starting with those that arouse minimal anxiety, progressing to those that are the most frightening. The person is first encouraged to relax and then to progress through graded exposure from the least fearful situation to the more difficult situations over a number of sessions. The principle behind this technique is to replace the conditioned fear response with one of relaxation. It is the pairing of relaxation with the feared stimulus which induces the desensitization. This technique can be conducted *in vitro* (through imagined imagery) or *in vivo* (real-life).
- *Flooding* (also known as 'implosion'): Quicker and often thought to be more effective than systematic desensitization, the philosophy is that if someone refuses to face up to their fear, that fear will never be overcome and may even grow in strength. Flooding is a technique whereby the person is asked to remain with the fear, experiencing the full impact of their anxiety state. Physiologically it is not possible to maintain a state of high anxiety for a very long period, and so eventually it will

subside. This transition through the anxiety shows the person that they are still safe and that nothing dreadful has happened to them. Thus the fear should be extinguished. For ethical reasons, this technique is conducted mainly *in vitro* and the therapist should first ensure that the person is in good physical health.

- *Aversion therapy*: Aversion therapy was developed from studies with animals which showed that the pairing of an unpleasant stimulus, such as an electric shock, with a neutral stimulus can produce negative reactions, or 'aversion' to the neutral stimulus. This has formed the basis of 'aversion therapy', which was developed to deal with habits and addictions. Here the therapist attempts to attach negative feelings to stimuli that are considered inappropriate. An example of this is smoking. This is achieved through pairing the taste of tobacco with a feeling of nausea, for example by inserting a nausea-inducing substance into cigarettes. The major problem with this technique is that it is doubtful that aversion will continue once the negative pairing has been discontinued.

Techniques derived from operant conditioning

- *Token economy*: Token economy is a behaviour modification programme based on Skinner's principle of behaviour shaping through positive reinforcement. In exchange for desirable behaviour, the person will receive rewards in the form of tokens, which can be exchanged for goods, outings or privileges. Token economy has been applied extensively in institutions, mainly with psychotic patients, and with people who have severe learning difficulties. Although it has been claimed that it is difficult to sustain the modified behaviour beyond the institution, the intention is that positive reinforcement will be elicited naturally from others in the environment as a consequence of correct behaviour.
- *Social skills training*: Bandura's (1969) 'social learning theory' is an extension of operant conditioning, to include learning through observing and modelling the behaviour of others. Originally, Bandura applied the concept of 'modelling' as a treatment for phobias, but more recently, modelling has been applied widely in the development of social skills training, particularly in assertiveness and interpersonal skills training. The technique involves behaviour rehearsal in the form of role-play and feedback. People are encouraged to practise appropriate responses to replace maladaptive responses in the safety of a role-play situation. Skills training is thought to be particularly helpful for people with a low self-esteem, for those who are anxious in social situations and for those who are often exploited by others.

Appropriateness and effectiveness

Behavioural therapies based on classical conditioning are considered to be very appropriate methods of treatment for anxiety disorders, such as phobias and post-traumatic stress disorder and for addictions, although they are not regarded as suitable for psychotic disorders, such as schizophrenia. These methods are widely adopted by clinical psychologists within the NHS and are relatively quick, usually taking just a few months, by contrast to psychodynamic therapies which usually last several years. They are also very effective in group therapy. The treatment is structured, the goals are clear, and clinical progress is measurable.

The efficacy of behavioural techniques has been shown to be quite high. McGrath *et al.* (1990) claim that systematic desensitization is effective for around 75 per cent of people with specific phobias. Comer (1995) cites an interesting study on 'flooding', conducted by Hogen and Kirchner (1967). Twenty-one people with a phobia for rats were asked to imagine themselves having their fingers nibbled and being clawed by rats. After treatment, twenty were able to open a rat's cage and fourteen could actually pick up the rat. *In vivo* techniques are found to be more effective for specific phobias than *in vitro* (Menzies and Clarke 1993). Agoraphobia is one of the most difficult phobias to treat, yet 'systematic desensitization' has facilitated improvement for between 60 and 80 per cent of cases (Craske and Barlow 1993). However, improvements are shown to be only partial and in 50 per cent of cases relapses occur.

Critics of behaviourist methods point out that quite often people with phobias have no recollection of any traumatic experience involving the object of their fear. Psychoanalytic theorists claim that this is because the phobia is merely a symptom, a conscious manifestation of the underlying cause, a signal from the unconscious that something is wrong. Bandura (1969) argues that if 'underlying' is defined as 'not immediately obvious' then behaviour therapists indeed do look for underlying causes. The task is for the therapist to work with the client to find the most significant causes. According to social learning theory, phobias can develop through observing those fears in significant others and modelling behaviour upon those observations. Bandura has supported the effectiveness of using 'modelling' in the treatment of phobias in a clinical study of 48 nursery children with dog phobias (Bandura and Menlove 1968) and with adults with snake phobias (Bandura *et al.* 1969), claiming a 90 per cent success rate.

Programmes of behaviour modification, such as 'token economy', do not offer a cure for mental disorders; they are merely intended to enable patients to 'fit' better into their social world. For example, chronic psychiatric patients often have no motivation to maintain personal hygiene and therefore tokens can be earned for washing, brushing hair, etc. The intention is to give the person back some dignity. The natural rewards that will eventually replace the tokens to reinforce the behaviour are that others will be more sympathetic towards them. Token economy has been widely adopted in psychiatric institutions with psychotic patients and found to be very effective in reducing inappropriate behaviour (Emmelkamp 1994). It has been suggested, however, that the so-called success of this therapy may have more to do with its requirement for closer interaction between patient and nurse, suggesting that it is the attention that is therapeutic rather than the technique. Behavioural methods have provided an opportunity for nursing staff to become far more involved in treatment, which may have increased their investment in helping the patient. Despite its scientific status, behaviourist methods are still prone to some of the problems of evaluation encountered by all therapeutic approaches.

❖ Activity 4 ❖

You may recall that in the case study previously described (*In Focus* on p. 261), Mary did not find systematic desensitization very helpful because her vomit phobia had a deeper underlying cause. Re-read the case study, however, and consider the following:

- Does the case-study of Mary lend support for the psychodynamic view – that the traumatic experience of sexual abuse had been repressed into the unconscious, only to reveal itself as a phobia in later life, or does it lend support to the behaviourist view – that a conditioned association had been established between vomiting and sexual abuse?
- Alternatively, can you present a case for a combination of the two explanations?

Cognitive-behavioural therapy

Cognitive-behavioural therapy began in the 1960s with the work of Ellis (1962), who founded rational-emotive therapy (RET) which was subsequently developed into rational-emotive-behaviour therapy (REBT). Beck (1976) later developed a cognitive therapy for depression and Meichenbaum (1975) developed a cognitive-behavioural therapy for stress management, which he called stress inoculation training (SIT). The rationale for all cognitive-behavioural therapies is that thoughts (cognitions) interact with and have an enormous influence on emotions and behaviour. When these thoughts are persistently negative and irrational, they can result in maladaptive behaviour. Ellis (1962) maintained that people can become habituated to their disturbed thoughts and this results in problems such as anxiety and depression. Ellis (1991) devised the ABC model (see Fig. 12.3) to illustrate how irrational, self-defeating thoughts can lead to maladaptive behaviour. Although cognitive therapists do not disregard what has happened in the past, the focus of therapy is on the person's current state of functioning.

Cognitive-behavioural therapy is *active* and *directive*, and it involves a collaborative enterprise between therapist and client. The aim of therapy is to help the client to

❖ Activity 5 ❖

Think about a recent activating event (A). Did you follow the rational or the irrational route, as illustrated in Fig. 12.3?

Figure 12.3 An example of the ABC model in action *Source:* Prentice (1995), adapted from Ellis (1991)

A: Activating event

Linda gets a low mark in her mock exam for A level psychology.

B: Beliefs (about A)

Rational thoughts
Linda tells herself that she could have done better but did not put in enough revision.

Irrational thoughts
Linda tells herself that she should have done well and this means she will fail in her final exams.

C: Consequences (of B)

Desirable emotions
Linda feels disappointed with her own efforts.

Undesirable emotions
Linda feels that she must be awful at psychology.

Desirable behaviour
Linda resolves to put in more effort for her final exams.

Undesirable behaviour
Linda decides to give up college.

identify their negative, irrational thoughts and to replace these with more positive, rational ways of thinking. A therapy session includes both cognitive and behavioural elements, with homework between sessions.

- *Cognitive element:* The therapist encourages the client to become aware of beliefs which contribute to anxiety or depression, or are associated with a general dysfunction in daily life. This involves direct Socratic questioning, such as: 'Tell me what you think about...' The therapist does not comment upon the irrational or biased nature of these beliefs, instead they are treated as hypotheses and examined for validity. Diagrams (such as the ABC model) can be used to help the client understand better where their faulty cognitions are leading them. The therapist and client also conduct a cost-benefit analysis, examining the advantages and disadvantages of particular beliefs.
- *Behavioural element:* The therapist and client decide together how these hypotheses can be reality-tested through experimentation. Experiments can be conducted through role-play during the session or better still through homework assignments. The aim is that by actively testing out possibilities, clients will themselves come to recognize the consequences of their faulty cognitions. The therapist and client then work together to set new goals for the client in order that more realistic and rational beliefs are incorporated into ways of thinking. These are usually in graded stages of difficulty so that clients can build upon their own success.

Appropriateness and effectiveness

Like the older behavioural therapies, cognitive-behavioural therapies are structured, with clear goals and measurable outcomes. They are increasingly becoming the most widely employed therapy by clinical psychologists in the National Health Service (NHS), not least because they are short term and therefore economic. Meichenbaum (1975) has concentrated on stress management and his techniques have been widely employed in industry. Cognitive-behavioural therapies appeal to clients who find insight therapies (which delve into inner emotional conflicts) too threatening. Although they are subject to the criticism that they do not address underlying causes, cognitive therapies attempt to empower clients, by educating them into self-help strategies. However, despite this, many clients do become dependent upon their therapist.

Ellis (1980) maintains that REBT is appropriate for any kind of psychological problem, such as anxiety disorders, sexual problems and depression, but not for severe mental disturbance, where the person cannot be treated with talking therapies. He maintains that REBT helps clients to 'cure' themselves in an *elegant* way because it can be incorporated into their way of life. Haaga and Davison (1989) found REBT to be effective for anger, aggression, depression and antisocial behaviour, although not as effective as systematic desensitization in reducing anxiety. Engels, Garnefski and Diekstra (1993) examined quantitative data on 28 controlled studies which showed REBT to be superior to placebo and no treatment, but only equally effective when compared with systematic desensitization, or combination therapies (those combining REBT with some form of behaviour therapy). A more recent appraisal by Haaga and Davison (1993) suggests that there are difficulties in evaluating the effectiveness of REBT because of the difficulty in defining and measuring 'irrational beliefs'.

Beck's work has centred mainly on depression. He devised the Beck Depression Inventory, which is an assessment scale for depression, and from this many more have been devised, such as the Suicide Intent Scale. These scales have been widely adopted by clinical psychologists to monitor depression in clients, and employed by researchers for outcome studies. Beck has subsequently applied his techniques to phobias and anxieties (Beck *et al.* 1985) and to personality disorders (Beck *et al.* 1990). The concept of irrational beliefs has been tested and supported empirically (e.g. Beck 1991). In outcome studies on depression, cognitive therapies have been found to be equally or more effective than drugs (e.g. Hollon *et al.* 1992). Long-term follow-up studies have also shown that the relapse rate is lower in those who received cognitive therapy (Evans *et al.* 1992).

Cognitive-behavioural therapy is thought to be particularly effective for depression and anxiety disorders and sexual problems. It is also widely employed in stress management. In the main, cognitive therapies are appropriate only for those who have developed good problem-solving skills and are capable of gaining reasonable insight into their problems. However, both Beck and Meichenbaum see a role for cognitive-behavioural therapy with psychotic patients. Hole, Rush and (1979) worked with chronic schizophrenia patients encouraging them to reality-test their delusions, and they found that in half of the patients they could reduce the pervasive nature of delusions. One of the major symptoms of acute schizophrenia is 'inner speech' and this is usually of a controlling nature (telling the person what to do). Meichenbaum and Cameron (1973) developed a programme wherein patients are trained to develop more adaptive controlling statements in their 'inner speech'. Cognitive techniques for schizophrenia are continually being developed and refined (e.g. Kingdon and Turkington 1994) and although they do not offer a cure for schizophrenia, they are effective in 'normalizing' symptoms.

Humanistic therapy

Humanistic therapy is better known as 'person-centred therapy' and originated largely from the work of Carl Rogers (1951). Rogers did not hold with the interventionist techniques of the psychodynamic, or behaviourist schools. He believed they created dependence upon the therapist and was convinced that the major element of concern in the therapeutic relationship was the distribution of power. He introduced the term 'person-centred' to underline the fact that this approach was first and foremost a means to access the personal power of the individual client to become more autonomous, spontaneous and confident in themselves.

Humanistic person-centred therapy is, like psychodynamic therapy, an insight therapy in that it involves delving into deeper emotions. Rogers, however, believed that therapy should focus on the present, rather than the past, because it is now that the person is grappling with problems. Although he does not dispute that events in the past have a huge influence on our behaviour, he was more concerned with what is happening in clients' lives now and how therapy can effect future changes by encouraging people to recognize and value their capacity to direct their own life. Rogers believed that for this to occur therapy needs the right climate, which rests not on techniques, but on the relationship between the therapist and the client. Rogers proposed three core conditions which he claimed are both necessary and sufficient for this relationship. These three core conditions – warmth, genuineness and empathy – are qualities which should be exhibited and communicated by the therapist. When they are experienced by clients to a significant degree, they should be able to discover within themselves the resources needed to effect personal change and reintegration. According to Rogers, interventions by a therapist, however well intentioned, run counter to person-centred therapy.

- *Warmth:* The first condition is 'warmth' (or 'unconditional positive regard'), which means that the therapist must have respect for the client and display complete acceptance of the person in their own right, at that moment in time. This must also be accompanied by a non-judgemental attitude towards the client.

- *Genuineness:* The second and most important condition, according to Rogers, is 'genuineness', meaning that the therapist must show themselves to be a 'real' person, with their own thoughts and feelings, which should be expressed where appropriate. This is enhanced by 'self-disclosure', which would be deemed totally inappropriate in psychoanalytic therapy, where the therapist must remain a 'blank' in order to facilitate 'transference'. Rogers adopts quite the opposite view in that he believes that the client must feel that the therapist is emotionally involved and completely transparent.
- *Empathy:* The third condition is 'empathic understanding'. By this Rogers meant that the therapist must enter the client's inner world. He suggested that this could be achieved through genuine, attentive listening and by restating what the client says, in order to clarify its emotional significance. Rogers believed this required intense concentration on the part of the therapist, along with an ability to be sensitive to what is currently going on for the client just below the level of awareness. The therapist must sense the pleasure and the hurt of the client as if they, the therapist, were pleased or hurt.

Appropriateness and effectiveness

Rogers recognized that most people need help at some time or other in their life, although they would not regard their condition as pathological. He therefore took the monopoly on therapy away from the arena of 'specialist expertise', such as clinical psychologists, psychiatrists and psychotherapists, and made therapy much more accessible. Client-centred therapy is now strongly represented within 'counselling' and is probably the most widely adopted therapy in this country and the United States. Counsellors adopting a basically Rogerian approach are increasingly employed in sectors such as Social Services, the Health Service, industry, commerce and education, as well as the voluntary agencies such as those counselling on marriage, bereavement, drugs, AIDS, and so on. The growth of person-centred counselling could be seen to vouch for its own effectiveness, or at the very least, the growing need for a therapy which is less intrusive and non-interventionist.

Like all insight therapies, person-centred counselling is difficult to evaluate for effectiveness because there are too many variables to take into account. Most of the early research was focused on Rogers' insistence that the three core conditions are both necessary and sufficient for an effective therapeutic outcome. For example, Mitchell (1977) found that 'genuineness' was of central importance, but in a later analysis she found that it was not genuineness *per se* which correlated with a positive client outcome, but rather a 'lack of genuineness' which mitigated against a positive client outcome, by interfering with the helpful effects of 'warmth' and 'empathy'.

Studies have also focused on a range of different settings. For example, Dryden *et al.* (1989) cite studies by Rose and Marshall (1974) who evaluated counselling for truancy and delinquency in a number of schools and found that pupils responded favourably. Ashurst and Ward (1983) found counselling in medical general practice to be effective.

There are limitations to the scope of counselling, however. Counselling is best suited to those clients who are able to discuss their emotional concerns in detail and who are motivated to focus on their subjective experience. As Rogers himself pointed out, person-centred therapy may not be very effective for severe psychological disorders, such as schizophrenia. However, counselling may be useful for someone with schizophrenia, for example, along with their family, in providing support and guidance for coping with such a severe mental disorder. *Milieu therapy* is an innovative humanistic approach, designed specifically for institutionalized chronic psychiatric patients and appears to have met with some success (see *In Focus* on the next page).

In Focus

Milieu therapy

Milieu therapy, pioneered by Maxwell Jones (1953), is based on the idea that if psychiatric patients are to make clinical progress, then the social milieu of institutions must change. In milieu therapy, a therapeutic community is created in psychiatric wards, where people are not treated as patients, but 'residents'. Each person is valued as an individual and participates alongside staff on institutional planning in an atmosphere of mutual respect. The purpose is not to offer a 'cure' for disorders such as chronic schizophrenia, but to promote independence and responsibility, and to restore self-respect. Milieu therapy has been introduced in many psychiatric institutions in Britain and the US and is an effective 'half way house' for patients who are to be discharged into the community.

Section summary

Each of the therapies outlined in this chapter offers quite different methods of treatment for mental disorders, based upon their respective model of abnormality. Somatic treatments, based on the medical model, address physical symptoms of mental disorder, such as biochemical imbalance, whilst all of the other therapies address social and psychological factors thought to precipitate mental disorder. Some therapies are easier than others to test for efficacy, but this does not necessarily mean that they are more effective. Many therapists nowadays take an eclectic approach. They are trained in a number of different therapies and draw on any of these where they are thought to be most appropriate.

Ethical issues in therapy and intervention

Ethical issues relating to therapy and intervention are quite considerable. Some of these have already been considered in Chapter 10 concerning:

- reliability and validity of diagnosis
- labelling as mentally ill
- the insanity defence
- cultural and subcultural differences in defining abnormality.

A number of ethical issues concerning the rights of patients/clients are further considered here:

- confidentiality
- informed consent
- compliance with medication/treatment
- choice of therapy
- choice of goals
- abuse of power
- cultural issues in therapy.

Confidentiality

Confidentiality is a means of providing the client with safety and privacy. It enables the client to feel comfortable when revealing personal, and often very intimate, details of themselves on the understanding that these will not be divulged to others. For this reason, any limitation on the degree of confidentiality is likely to diminish the usefulness of therapy. Many people, however, are under the misapprehension that therapy is completely confidential between client and therapist and cannot be revealed to a third party. Whilst most practitioners are bound by a code of ethics which prevents them from discussing their clients with all and sundry, confidentiality is not restricted to therapist-client. Therapists usually work within an agency setting, such as the NHS, or a voluntary agency, where case-notes are kept and where information may be communicated to other professionals who are directly involved in the case of the individual concerned. However, this is usually restricted to information regarding the problem and the treatment, rather than any personal matters that might be discussed. Most therapists receive regular supervision in which individual cases are discussed and clients should be informed of this at the outset.

Confidentiality and the law

Cohen (1992) provides an account of legal issues in relation to counselling and psychotherapy. If a therapist judges that clients may be a danger to themselves or to others, then the therapist may feel morally obliged to inform an appropriate body, but there is no duty under criminal law for the therapist to report a criminal offence that a client has committed or intends to commit. The Police and Criminal Evidence Act (1984) protects client records to a degree, because access to records requires a search warrant signed by a judge. There are, however, certain exceptions, such as the Prevention of Terrorism Act (1989), relating to Northern Ireland, where statutory laws override confidentiality. The Act requires disclosure to assist in the prevention or investigation of an act of terrorism. Therapists are also bound by legislation to disclose child abuse to the authorities, or to assist inquiries into child welfare under the Children Act (1989). Because of these restrictions, both moral and legal, most agencies provide written information, and therapists should ideally explain their boundaries of confidentiality to a client before commencing therapy. Suicide and suicidal attempts are no longer a crime and, for the therapist, there is a complicated balance to maintain between preserving life and respecting a client's autonomy.

Informed consent

Common law states that before any course of treatment is administered, agreement should be obtained from the patient or client. Consent alone, however, is not sufficient. Ideally it should be 'informed' consent, which means that the person is capable of making the decision and has agreed to treatment in full knowledge of what is involved. Some of the factors that should be taken into consideration are listed in Table 12.2.

Costs vs benefits

Any costs or side effects associated with treatment or therapy should be justified in terms of benefits. A therapist may act in good faith when informing a client about the likelihood of *harmful effects*, but this information may be inconclusive or incomplete, because knowledge is continuously being updated through research. Added to this, it is not really known how some therapies work (e.g. ECT

Table 12.2 Informed consent

Clients/patients should be entitled:

1 To be informed about the range of therapies and treatments available for their problem and to have these explained to them, including the likely length and frequency of treatments.

2 To be told the probability of success for treatments and therapies.

3 To be informed about the likelihood of physical or mental harm that could result directly from treatment, or any potential side effects.

4 To have the right to terminate treatment or therapy at any time.

5 To be informed about confidentiality.

6 To be told about the likely cost of therapy or treatment.

and many pharmacological preparations). If the therapist has doubts about whether he or she is the right person to treat a client, or thinks that the client might better benefit from *alternative types of treatment* to the one he or she is offering, then the therapist has an ethical obligation to inform the client. For example, Corsini and Wedding (1995) suggest that although someone suffering from clinical depression can be treated solely with psychotherapy, for some patients antidepressant medication or ECT may be the best treatment.

Probability of success

Unfortunately, in therapies for mental disorders it is very difficult for a clinician to assess the *probability of success*, even for somatic treatments. First of all, it depends very much on the individual client; their commitment to therapy together with the extent and severity of their problems. Clients may present with one problem, but during therapy other issues often arise that are more complex than the presenting problem. The apparent success or failure of a therapy may depend upon the point in time that effectiveness is being assessed. Some therapies are relatively brief, such as systematic desensitization, whereas others are lengthier. Psychodynamic therapies, for example, often span a number of years, during which the client's personal circumstances may change considerably. This may be related or unrelated to the therapy.

Problems with informed consent

There are many reasons why people may not be able to give informed consent. Many people comply without question because they see the GP or clinician as the 'expert'. People with clinical depression are often unable to motivate themselves to ask questions. Even when information is offered, they may find it difficult to absorb the information in their existing state of mind. Informed consent may not be possible for certain people, for example young children or people with severe learning difficulties. In such cases, a parent or guardian may be asked to give informed consent on their behalf. People with disorders such as schizophrenia may not be able to give informed consent owing to a lack of insight into their problem and a loss of contact with reality. For this reason, it has been possible for clinicians to administer biological treatments, in the form of medication, ECT and even psychosurgery, without informed consent from the patient. Recent studies, such as one conducted by Grisso and Applebaum (cited in Davison and Neale 1994) found that there was clearly a wide range of understanding among schizophrenia patients relating to their treatment. In view of this, they claim that each patient should be assessed individually on their ability to give informed consent, before allowing other individuals to take such decisions on their behalf. The whole issue of informed consent is, however, fraught with difficulty because, as Irwin *et al.* (1985) found in their study, only about a quarter of patients who had said they understood the benefits and side effects of their treatment, actually did understand when questioned specifically.

Psychosurgery has come under attack more than any other treatment for mental disorders. Comer (1995) explains that psychosurgery was performed on tens of thousands of people in the 1950s as a response to overcrowding in mental institutions and the absence of effective treatments for many serious mental disorders. Comer (1995) also explains that

❖ Activity 6 ❖

The film *One Flew Over the Cuckoo's Nest* (of the book of the same name by Ken Kesey) provides a vivid portrait of the consequences of enforced biological treatment, culminating in psychosurgery. You should be able to rent the video or buy the book. Please note: the Mental Health Act for England and Wales (1983) states that for psychosurgery the patient's consent is now required, along with a second opinion by an independent doctor.

In Focus

Sectioning laws

Patients can be admitted to a psychiatric hospital without giving their consent under sectioning laws included in the Mental Health Act (1983) for England and Wales.

Section 2 of the Act allows for 28-day compulsory admission and detention for assessment, which may be followed by medical treatment. Section 2 may be implemented when it is thought:

(a) that the patient suffers from a mental disorder that requires assessment and treatment, and

(b) that detention is necessary for the patient's own health or safety or the protection of others.

To invoke Section 2, application must be made by the patient's nearest relative, or an approved social worker, together with the medical recommendations of two doctors.

Section 3 is a compulsory treatment order for up to six months, which may be renewed for a further six months and subsequently for twelve months at a time. The grounds for a treatment order are that:

(a) medical treatment in hospital is appropriate owing to the nature or degree of mental illness, mental impairment, or psychopathic disorder

(b) such treatment is likely to alleviate or prevent deterioration of the condition

(c) treatment is necessary for the health and safety of the patient or the protection of others and it cannot be provided unless the person is detained.

Section 4 can be invoked in an emergency. A detention order for 72 hours would be invoked by one doctor and an approved social worker. This is then usually converted into a Section 2 order.

there was concern in the US about the suspected use of psychosurgery to control perpetrators of violent crimes. The lobotomy also became a civil rights issue with claims that it was being used as a means of silencing political activists and of controlling difficult mental patients in institutions.

Compliance with medication/treatment

Disturbing films like *One Flew over the Cuckoo's Nest*, along with accusations levelled at the medical profession by the anti-psychiatry movement in the 1960s, instilled doubts about the true purpose of somatic treatments. Are they administered to alleviate suffering in the patient or to sedate patients so they are more compliant with institutional regimes? As a result, there has recently been greater emphasis on voluntary agreement and the right to refuse treatment. There are, however, two sides to this debate – the right to refuse versus the consequences of non-compliance.

For example, some schizophrenia patients are genuinely very dangerous unless sedated with major tranquillizers. Ensuring that such patients stay on their regime of drugs was not too difficult in the days of mental institutions, but in the current climate of civil rights and care in the community this is not so straightforward. Issues of compliance with medication have become high profile in recent years as a result of the killing in 1993 of an innocent bystander by a schizophrenia patient (see *In Focus* on the next page

Choice of treatment

Treatment administered to someone who has been detained under sectioning laws is usually decided by the consultant psychiatrist. Voluntary patients, on the other hand, should have the right to choose their treatment. But is this the case? On financial grounds, clients may be restricted

In Focus

Fatal stabbing by schizophrenia patient

In Torquay on September 1993, Andrew Robinson stabbed a nurse in the face and neck. She remained conscious but paralysed and died five days later. Robinson suffered from paranoid schizophrenia and had a 15-year history of violence. This has led to a government inquiry into community care, which has recommended new powers of supervision for mental patients in the community and legal powers to enforce compliance with medication. The National Association for Mental Health (MIND) has expressed concern that the government may use this one isolated case as a basis for an overhaul in the law.

Source: The Times, 17 January 1995

to what is available within their local health authority. In the main, these tend to be somatic treatments (drugs or ECT) or cognitive-behavioural therapies. Psychodynamic therapies are less available within the NHS because they are usually longer term and therefore more expensive than other forms of treatment. Waiting lists for psychological treatments are currently very long in most NHS mental health units. Consequently, drug treatments are the most immediate option.

Theoretically, when finance is not an obstacle, clients are able to 'shop around'. Choosing a therapy, though, is very difficult for someone who is not aware of theoretical orientations, techniques and therapeutic goals, and this includes a large proportion of the population. People are also, to some extent, cautious about psychological therapies because the concept is alien to them and they don't know what to expect. Drug treatment is much more familiar, since most people are used to taking tablets, but there are considerable side effects, some serious. Undertaking some background research can enable people to make a more informed choice about the type of treatment, but then choosing a therapist can be a minefield, because, currently, there are no statutory regulations regarding the level of training required for private practice.

Devine and Fernald (1973) demonstrated that the role of choice and commitment to a particular type of treatment hugely influenced the therapeutic outcome. Clients with snake phobias were shown films of four types of treatment. The clients were then split into three groups:

- The first group were allowed to select their preferred treatment.
- The second group were randomly assigned to a treatment.
- The third group were required to undergo a non-preferred treatment.

The most successful therapeutic experience was found in the first group, who were given the treatment of their choice. Devine and Fernald concluded that this was because a sense of control had been exercised over the therapeutic process. In contrast, clients who were forced into a non-preferred treatment merely complied without any real commitment.

Choice of goals

Ideally the client and therapist should set the goals of therapy, and this is often the case. However, in some cases the goals are set by the therapist and may actually go against the patient's wishes. This has been a particular criticism levelled at some behavioural therapies. Token economy has been widely administered in institutions. Here the choice of goals is set by the institution, which decides what is regarded as desirable behaviour, often designed to serve the institution on the pretext of serving the recipient. Whenever goals are imposed by others, then desirable behaviour is inevitably influenced by personal or institutional bias, even when the goal is truly believed to be for the client's own good. One of the major criticisms of token economy is that, in order to be effective, important reinforcements need to be controlled, which may violate basic human rights, such as restrictions on food, privacy and freedom of movement. Comer (1995) explains that boundaries have now been set on basic rights that clinicians cannot violate, but this may reduce the impact of token economy programmes. One of the saddest consequences of token economy programmes is that people become dependent on the regime and find it very difficult to think for themselves when outside the institutional setting. This has been the case with many people who have recently found themselves back in the community after prolonged institutional care.

When agreeing to a particular therapy, the client, and to some degree the therapist, cannot always anticipate what may occur during the course of therapy. This has been a major criticism of behavioural therapies, in particular the technique of 'flooding'. Even when conducted *in vitro* (using the imagination, or video films) rather than *in vivo* (real life) there may be dangerous consequences of hyperventilation, raised blood pressure or heart attacks. As such, this procedure should not be undertaken without adequate training and medical supervision. Aversion therapy has also come under attack because it breaches ethical guidelines in its use of induced pain or nausea as aversive stimuli.

Psychodynamic therapies have not escaped criticism, but here the major cause for concern is emotional rather than physical. For example, a psychoanalyst may guide a client towards an insight that may prove emotionally distressing, yet is necessary for recovery from their current problem. The distress surrounding the new insight may prove to be greater than the distress of the current problem. Psychodynamic therapists abiding by a professional code of ethics should warn their client of this danger before engaging in therapy, and therapists should never work beyond their competency in dealing with what may arise in therapy. Recovered memories of child abuse have been the subject of much debate and legal wrangling over the past few years, in discussions of what has become known as 'false memory syndrome' (see *In Focus* below).

In Focus

False memory syndrome (FMS)

Many patients have claimed they have uncovered traumatic memories during therapeutic sessions. The debate over whether recovered memories during therapy are accurate representations of events that have happened in childhood is one of modern psychology's most contentious issues. Is it possible to recover previously forgotten memories of childhood trauma and what might be the consequences of such recollections? Critics of the notion of recovered memories have cast doubt on their validity on two counts. Firstly, they point to the somewhat bizarre or unlikely nature of many of the recollections, and secondly, they question the use of techniques such as suggestion and hypnotic regression to extract these memories. The consequences of either side of the FMS argument pose ethical problems for the therapist. First, if these are *false* memories (often about sexual abuse), then there is concern over the consequences of parents being falsely accused of abusing their children. Second, if these are *true* memories, there may be harmful effects on the people who have actually been abused in childhood in not being believed (Andrews *et al.* 1995).

A further ethical issue is now emerging as a direct result of the proliferation of media articles on 'false memory syndrome' over the past few years. These have created a climate of disbelief about the credibility of disclosures of child sexual abuse to the extent that adult survivors are now discouraged from disclosing and seeking help for themselves (Toon *et al.* 1996).

Abuse of power

The 'expert'

A psychiatrist, clinical psychologist or psychotherapist is held to be an 'expert' and consequently patients or clients can see them as being in a position of power. Dryden (1990) explains that therapists can easily be seduced into abusing this power unless they are adequately trained to recognize and take corrective action when it is likely to occur. One form of abuse identified by Dryden is ideological conversion, which is analogous to brainwashing. Supporters of false memory syndrome (FMS) have suggested that a client may succumb to the belief because the suggestions come from an authority figure. Toon *et al.* (1996) report that FMS supporters accuse therapists in private practice of even inducing false memories for financial gain, because the therapy will take longer. Toon *et al.* point out, however, that there is no clear evidence, as yet, to demonstrate the existence of therapist-induced false memories. Masson (1989) attacked all therapies and therapists, claiming that the imbalance of power creates a temptation for therapists to abuse, misuse, profit from and bully the client. Holmes (1994) largely agrees, but maintains that this accusation could also be levelled at other professionals, such as lawyers, teachers and priests. What is important is that, whilst there is potential for exploitation, professionals are bound by codes of practice, with disciplinary procedures that include expulsion.

Sexual contact

Some clients idealize their therapist. They may bestow on the therapist attributes that they admire or fear through a process of 'transference'. It is not uncommon for clients to believe they are in love with their therapist and that this love is reciprocated. This should be dealt with sensitively by the therapist. Abuse occurs when the therapist takes advantage of this and becomes sexually involved with their client or patient. Reviewing a number of studies in the US of psychiatrists, psychologists and social workers, Garrett (1994) found between 2 and 7 per cent were having sexual relations with clients. A large survey has recently been undertaken by the British Psychological Society Division of Clinical Psychology (Garrett and Davis 1994) with questions designed to collect a variety of data. Included were questions on attitudes towards, and incidence of, sexual contact with patients. The experience of sexual attraction was reported in 56.5 per cent of respondents, the majority of whom were male, and of these respondents 87 per cent were not unduly concerned about this attraction. Four per cent of the total sample admitted to having actually engaged in sexual contact; two per cent in sexual intercourse and two per cent in other forms of erotic contact. In many cases the sexual contact was only once and many of the cases were with discharged patients. However, one respondent reported that there were 'too many occasions to count' and another admitted to sexual contact with five current patients. Codes of Practice, for example those of The American Psychiatric Association and The British Association for Counselling, preclude sexual relations between therapist and client. Most codes of practice prescribe a time lapse following the termination of therapy and the start of any intimate relationship.

Cultural issues in therapy and intervention

Most psychological therapists have been trained in theory and practice which have central European or US origins. The question is whether this training prepares therapists to work with clients of different cultural backgrounds. It has been argued that this may be the reason why it has been asserted that, for example, black people do not respond well to traditional methods of psychotherapy (Jones 1985). White therapists are reluctant to believe that they may be racist because they regard themselves as sensitive, caring people. However, as Lago and Thompson (1989) point out, white people have been exposed to a whole range of mechanisms, perceptions and experiences throughout their lives, and black people have experienced centuries of oppression, exploitation and discrimination.

Given this set of circumstances, cross-race therapy can prove to be very difficult even with specialist training. Ideally, clients should be given a choice of therapist, choosing someone of their own cultural background if they so wish. In reality, however, this choice is rarely available. Sue and Sue (1990) claim that black clients find self-disclosure difficult with a white therapist because of their past experience of prejudice and discrimination. Grant (1994) cites three types of racial reaction among white psychotherapists:

- The 'illusion of colour-blindness': treating a black client 'as if' they were white is a form of denial of that person's unique experience. Grant maintains that colour-blind therapists may be unable to accept colour differences for fear of finding racism within themselves.
- There is the assumption that black people's problems revolve around their being black.
- Some psychotherapists believe that they understand the black person's mind and that all the black client need do is place their trust in the white therapist.

Grant (1994) points out that these kinds of racial reaction are offensive to most black clients. For these reasons, Grant suggests that black people tend to respond more favourably to black therapists.

Section summary

A number of ethical issues in therapy and intervention have been outlined in this chapter, but this is by no means a complete list. So important are ethical issues in therapy, that it is essential for practitioners to work within a formal code of ethical guidelines, such as those laid down by the British Psychological Society or the British Association for Counselling. When writing an essay on ethical issues in therapy and intervention, it is quite valid to bring in the difficulties and controversies associated with classification and diagnosis (see Chapter 10), because they have a direct impact on informed consent and choice of goals.

Chapter summary

- Medical (somatic) treatment consists mainly of drugs, which are prescribed to redress biochemical imbalance. They are reasonably effective in the short-term, although there are numerous adverse side effects. Dependency can be created if drugs are taken over a long period of time. With severe depression, ECT has been found to be effective for some patients, but again there are adverse side effects.
- Psychodynamic (insight) therapies attempt to uncover unconscious anxieties and conflicts in order to disable their power over behaviour. Although their success is difficult to test empirically, they are thought to be very effective for certain disorders, such as anxiety and depression.
- Behavioural therapies attempt to identify maladaptive learning and to modify it into more adaptive behavioural strategies. Techniques such as systematic desensitization are thought to be effective for phobias. Behaviour modification programmes have been subjected to ethical scrutiny on the grounds that the goals are set by the institution and may not serve the interests of the recipient.
- Cognitive-behavioural therapy extends the behavioural model to the realms of thinking and attempts to replace distorted irrational thoughts with more rational ways of thinking. It has been found to be effective for coping with anxiety. Beck's cognitive therapy has been found to be more effective than any other therapy for depression.

- Humanistic (person-centred) therapy aims to improve perceptions of self-worth and to enhance the human capacity to realize full potential. The growth of person-centred counselling in education, voluntary agencies and commerce vouches for its usefulness.
- Because therapists are dealing with people who are disturbed and distressed, there are inevitably ethical issues to be taken into consideration. This chapter has outlined some of the major issues, including confidentiality, informed consent, choice of goals and abuse of power.

Essay questions

1 Critically consider somatic treatments for mental disorders. *(24 marks)*

2 Describe and evaluate two psychological therapies. *(24 marks)*

3 Discuss ethical issues in relation to therapy and intervention. *(24 marks)*

Further reading

Corsini, R.J. and Wedding, D. (1995) *Current Psychotherapies* (5th edn), Illinois: F.E. Peacock Publishers.

An American text which covers traditional, along with more recent theories and applications of therapy. Suitable for undergraduates and those with a special interest in therapy.

Dryden, W. (1996) *Individual Therapy: A Handbook*, Milton Keynes: Open University Press.

A British text with a chapter for each therapy written by different authors. The chapters are slim and most, but not all, are written in a clear style that is interesting and informative. The latest edition was published in 1996.

Nelson-Jones, R. (1995) *The Theory and Practice of Counselling* (2nd edn), London: Cassell.

Another British text, which has recently been revised. It provides well-written accounts of a variety of theories and how they are developed in practice. Self-assessment questions are included. This text is especially suited to those wishing to pursue a career in counselling.

Part 4

Cognitive Psychology

Attention and performance limitations
Peter Hayes

Perceptual processes
Peter Hayes

Memory
Peter Hayes

Language and thought
Jane Willson

Cognitive Psychology: Overview

'Cognition' literally means 'knowing' and concerns the way we understand the world around us. Most people would agree that the main aim of psychology is to understand people's thinking and behaviour. However, this is a very general way of thinking about psychology and most psychologists try to restrict themselves to particular types, or levels, of explanation. In our everyday lives we demonstrate a wide range of behaviour which includes things such as recognizing familiar people and particular objects, remembering telephone numbers and birthdays, reading books, doing mental arithmetic, playing chess and so on. Many of these examples of human behaviour are similar in that they involve information from the world being acquired through the senses, stored in memory and used in everyday behaviour. Cognitive psychologists are interested in explaining the mental activity which accompanies particular behaviour. However, rather than trying to understand the cognitive system as a whole, cognitive psychologists often try to break it down into more manageable parts, and investigate those individual parts.

An analysis of behaviours such as those mentioned above shows that some of them place a greater emphasis on the acquisition of knowledge, some on its storage and some on the use of knowledge. This sort of analysis allows us to split cognitive psychology into topic areas such as attention, perception, memory, language and thinking. It is important, however, to remember that although this split is useful in some ways, it is also arbitrary and there will be a considerable overlap between these areas. For example, try to imagine anything you can do without memory. This relates to a more general issue in cognitive psychology which involves a consideration of how these individual areas can be pulled together to give an idea about the overall nature of cognition. Consequently, the cognitive psychology chapters in this book consider some of the influential research in the individual areas of attention, perception, memory, thinking and language. However, they also consider some of the more general issues in cognitive psychology, such as the interrelationship between the different topic areas.

Chapter 13

Attention and performance limitations

Peter Hayes

Preview

In this chapter we shall be looking at:

- the nature of the information-processing approach
- the concept of attention
- auditory attention
- visual attention
- performance deficits.

Introduction

In this chapter we shall look at some of the research which has investigated people's ability to allocate their mental resources to the performance of everyday tasks. The chapter will begin by considering the nature and usefulness of what is known as the information-processing approach to the explanation of mental activity. It will then:

- consider the general concept of 'attention'
- introduce and explain more specific concepts such as focused (selective) and divided attention
- evaluate a number of theoretical ideas and research findings in the areas of both auditory and visual attention.

Finally, the chapter will consider performance deficits and the relationship between attention and other aspects of human information-processing. Some explanations will seem more plausible than others and in many areas the explanations are far from complete. Research in cognitive psychology is an ongoing activity.

The nature of the information-processing approach

Abstract models

Cognitive psychology is based on what is known as the *information-processing approach*. With this type of approach, the brain is likened to an information-processing device, such as a telephone exchange or a computer, through which information is acquired, stored, retrieved and used in some way. As we cannot observe mental activity directly, one important feature of cognitive psychology is the use of *abstract models* to try to explain the different stages through which information might be processed. Psychologists often use metaphors, such as abstract information-processing models, to help develop their theoretical understanding of any psychological activity. An abstract model can be thought of as a 'way of thinking' about mental activity. In other words it does not 'exist' in any sense other than as a theoretical metaphor.

The structures proposed in any abstract model may not necessarily have any physical equivalence to the biological make-up of the brain. If you could open up a person's head you would not find any perceptions or memories as such. However, the activity of the brain gives us the experience of these things and cognitive psychologists try to develop the most appropriate way of thinking about how this is achieved, by describing the internal cognitive structures and processes which may be involved in these sorts of activity.

❖ Activity 1 ❖

Consider the stages of information-processing which might be required in order for you to hear the music of your favourite band on your CD player. It does not matter if you do not know much about the technical processes which are actually involved. Write down, in order, as many different processing stages as you can, starting with the group playing the music and finishing with you hearing the music. For example, you might start with the vocals/instruments, go on to the microphones/amplifiers, and so on.

Processing and representation

Cognitive psychologists are concerned with how the knowledge involved in mental activity is represented and processed. *Processing* simply means the various ways the brain deals with information and how it is passed between various hypothetical cognitive structures. The notion of *representation* is quite a difficult concept to grasp. Marr (1982) sums it up well using the concept of the number three. This can be represented in different ways, such as 'three', '3' or 'III'. However, although the representations are different, they all describe the same concept. Another analogy we can use involves considering what happens to information during a long-distance telephone call. First, we speak into the mouthpiece of the telephone, producing sound waves. The telephone then converts these sound waves into electrical activity which is passed down a cable to a radio station. The radio station converts the electrical activity into radio waves and transmits them to a receiving station. The receiving station reverses the process and the recipient of the call hears our words. At all stages in this process the actual information (what we are saying) remains the same. However, at each stage information is represented in different ways: that is, as sound waves, electrical activity and radio waves. One of the tasks of the cognitive psychologist is to try to understand the different ways in which information can be processed and represented within the cognitive system.

Early researchers in cognitive psychology began with a very simple information-processing model, splitting it into three basic stages:

- input processes – research investigated the registration (recording) of sensory information
- translation processes – research dealt with the elaboration, manipulation and selection of information for storage in memory
- output processes – research concentrated on how appropriate responses to incoming information are produced.

This basic information-processing model is illustrated in Fig. 13.1.

Figure 13.1. Broadbent's generic model of the information-processing system

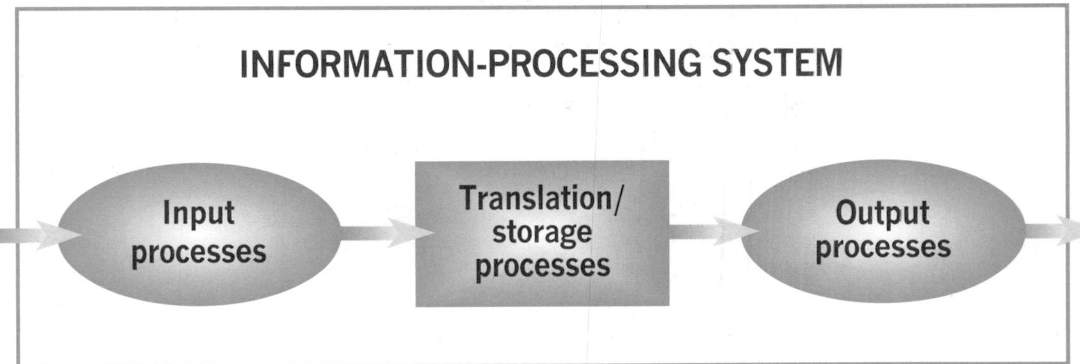

❖ Activity 2 ❖

Reconsider the stages of information processing which you identified in the last activity. Go back to the model (Fig. 13.1) and write down the different ways the music might be represented at each of the stages you noted. How many different types of representation can you identify? Try beginning with sound waves.

Methodology in cognitive psychology

After developing their abstract information-processing models, cognitive psychologists need to devise methods of evaluating them. There are various ways they can do this. One major technique is using traditional experimentation. Cognitive psychologists often devise experiments to test and further develop their models, using measures such as reaction time and slips and errors. Reaction time can be seen as a measure of the amount of information processing which is required to complete a task; if there are two conditions in an experiment, and one takes longer for subjects to complete, we can then assume that it requires more extensive information processing. Other techniques include introspection, studies of brain-damaged people and the important technique of computer simulation of human information processing (see *In Focus* over the page).

The concept of attention

Attentional capacity

Attention is a concept which almost everyone understands at an intuitive level. However, it is difficult to define precisely. Wilding (1982) suggested that processes such as focusing, selection and concentration are central to the mental effort necessary for attention, but he also emphasized that factors such as arousal, alertness and the limited capacity of our mental resources will also affect our attentional abilities. The world presents us with a continuous stream of sensory information. However, we do not register information in the same way as an audio or video cassette player records material. Our capacity for information processing seems to be limited. If we had to 'attend' to all the information bombarding our senses we would have no time to do anything else, so we have to take a selective approach. Mental capacity is also quite a difficult concept to define, but can be thought of as the total amount of *mental resources* a person has available at any one time. In other words, there is only so much information we can take in from the

In Focus

Computer modelling in cognitive psychology

One of the major influences on the development of cognitive psychology came with the invention of the digital computer and the idea of a computer programme. The actual hardware, or architecture, of the computer was seen as relatively unimportant, because the same programme could be run on different machines. This distinction between the computer and the programme is crucial to cognitive psychology. It enables people to be described as general purpose information-processing organisms, born with a certain hardware (brain), and programmed through socialization and experience. A further important distinction can be made between what is often called 'pure *artificial intelligence*' (AI) and 'computer simulation'.

Pure AI is often more concerned with getting a computer to demonstrate human-like behaviour without necessarily 'thinking' like a human being – in other words, doing some of the things people do, but in different ways. A good example would be developing a robotic system to work on a production line. Unlike a human being, the robot would be unaffected by fatigue or boredom. With computer simulation the computer is used as a tool in order to evaluate models of human information-processing. The development of a computer programme to test a model of human information-processing requires theoretical precision and is a good test of the practical, or logical, aspects of any theory. If the theory is not precise theoretically or is not logical, it will be impossible to test it using computer simulation. An early attempt at computer simulation is Newell *et al.*'s (1958) model called General Problem Solver.

senses, draw upon from memory or utilize in behaviour at any given time. Therefore, the best way to define attention might be as a process by which we *focus* and *concentrate* our *limited mental resources* on a *selection* of the *information* which reaches our senses.

❖ Activity 3 ❖

To illustrate the previous point, have a tape recorder with you next time you are studying. Switch the tape to record and then try to forget about it while you are studying. At the end of the session, play back the tape. You might be surprised by some of the sounds you hear, such as the rustling of paper, the tick of a clock, background noise from an adjacent room, and so on. In fact you might hear many sounds which had previously gone unnoticed.

Focused and divided attention

We have all experienced difficulty in attending to tasks. Often the reason for this is that our thoughts are continually being diverted to another unrelated task, e.g. trying to read a book whilst worrying about impending exam results. On the other hand, it is sometimes quite easy to focus on what we are doing or even attend to several things at the same time, e.g. driving a car whilst listening to music and planning the weekend activities. People are continually subjected to vast amounts of information impinging on their senses, but they also have the ability to attend selectively to particular aspects of this information. The ability to focus on specific sensory input is known as *selective*, or *focused attention* – many tasks that are *difficult* or *new* require this type of information processing. The ability to attend to more than one task at a time is known as *divided attention* – many *simple* or *well-practised* tasks require this type of information processing.

❖ Activity 4 ❖

In this exercise you should listen to some music on your CD or cassette player. Try to focus on the overall piece of music and then try to focus more directly on the various instrumentalists or singers. When you do this you should find it possible to switch your attention between the overall piece of music and the individual instruments. Although the music does not alter in any specific way, it can take on a different quality each time you refocus your attention.

The distinction between focused and divided attention is not as clear cut as it might at first seem. On occasions, you may be focusing your attention selectively until an unexpected event suddenly causes a distraction (e.g. if a noisy sibling comes into the room while you are reading). On the other hand, you may be dividing your attention quite easily between several tasks when suddenly something happens which forces you to focus your total attention on only one of the tasks (e.g. if a dog runs in front of your car as you are driving along listening to music). Other factors concerning the situation or the individual may also affect attentional processing. Some individuals seem better able to focus their attention than others and some may be more highly motivated by particular tasks. Factors such as tiredness can also affect people's ability to allocate attention.

Section summary

Most people understand what is meant by the term 'attention', but it is nevertheless quite difficult to obtain a precise definition of the concept. People cannot attend to all the information which reaches their senses and need to be selective in using their mental resources. Attentional capacity appears to be limited and people need to use active strategies to utilize it to the full. On some occasions, people can quite easily divide their attention between different tasks, while at other times, a single task may require their full attentional capacity. Whether we focus our attention on one task or divide it across several depends on the nature of the task(s), the nature of the situation and the nature of the individual who is attending.

Auditory attention

Information-processing models of attention

Early applications of information processing in cognitive psychology treated people as if they were information-transmission *channels* (see Fig. 13.1). People's ability to process information was seen to depend on factors such as the number of messages transmitted, the way they were coded and the amount of interference, or incidental information, affecting the information processor. This type of approach focuses on the transmission of information through the information-processing system and leads to questions such as:

- Which information reaches the later stages of processing and which is discarded early?
- At what point in the system does selection of information occur?
- How is this selection carried out?
- What are the constraints on information processing?

The approach emphasizes the idea that mental activity can be broken down into different *stages of processing* and is concerned overall with *how much* information people can handle and *how fast* they can handle it.

Models of focused (selective) attention

Early selection models

Broadbent (1958) was one of the first theorists to put forward a reasonable explanation of focused auditory attention. He was initially concerned with attentional problems of air traffic controllers and argued that by using careful observation of attentional overload it was possible to test models of focused attention. He was influenced particularly by the work of Cherry (1953) who had studied what is called the '*cocktail party phenomenon*'. This term refers to people's ability to switch their attention selectively between the different conversations which might be taking place in a social setting, such as a cocktail party. The terminology might seem a little old-fashioned to students today, but it does highlight the ability of people to switch between competing conversations and to select one for further attention.

Cherry investigated the cocktail party phenomenon by using '*dichotic listening tasks*' in which participants were required to listen to two different messages at the same time (a different message played to each ear through headphones). Cherry also asked his participants to repeat one of the messages out loud (known as '*shadowing*'), and then asked them questions about the other message. He found that participants could tell him nothing about the meaningful content of the non-shadowed message (they did not even notice a change of language), but they could tell him if it was a man's or a woman's voice, or if it changed from a voice to a pure tone. Participants appeared to have blocked out the meaningful content of the non-shadowed message, and were only aware of its general physical characteristics.

This finding suggests that we might deal with auditory messages in at least two stages. The first stage may be able handle several messages at once, but is only involved in the processing of general physical properties, such as the type of voice (male or female). The second stage can only deal with one

❖ Activity 5 ❖

Think back to a large party or gathering you have recently attended. Many different conversations were probably taking place at any one time, with people able to take part in their own conversations while ignoring others. Why is it that in a situation like this, your attention might suddenly be caught by something said in another group's conversation? What type of information breaks through the background noise to divert your attention from your own conversation?

In Focus

Broadbent's (1954) split-span procedure

Broadbent's split-span procedure involved participants recalling digits presented simultaneously in pairs, with one digit going to one ear and the other digit going to the other ear. Between the presentation of each pair of digits there was an interval of half a second. Following the presentation, participants were asked to recall the digits in one of two ways:

- 'pair by pair' – reporting the first pair of digits presented, then the second and finally the third
- 'ear by ear' – reporting the three digits heard by one ear followed by the three digits heard by the other ear.

Broadbent found that 'ear-by-ear' reports were easier for participants, and produced more accurate responses, than 'pair-by-pair' reports. This procedure is illustrated in Fig. 13.2.

On the basis of these findings, Broadbent argued that the ears act as separate channels which can only be attended to one at a time. He suggested that in the pair-by-pair condition the participants had to switch between channels more often than in the ear-by-ear condition. Subsequently Broadbent presented the first *filter model of selective attention* (see Fig. 13.3).

message at a time, but processes this at a deeper and more meaningful level. It is only at this second stage that the words and content of a message are recognized. Furthermore, between these two stages there must be a selection system which passes on one of the incoming messages. Broadbent (1954) developed a similar dichotic listening technique, which is known as the *'split-span procedure'* (see *In Focus*).

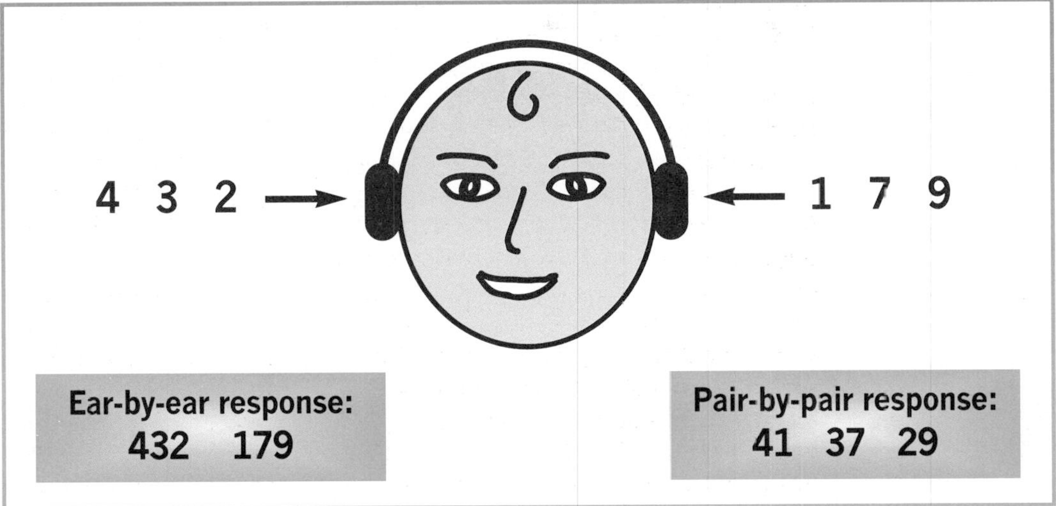

Figure 13.2 Broadbent's (1954) split-span procedure

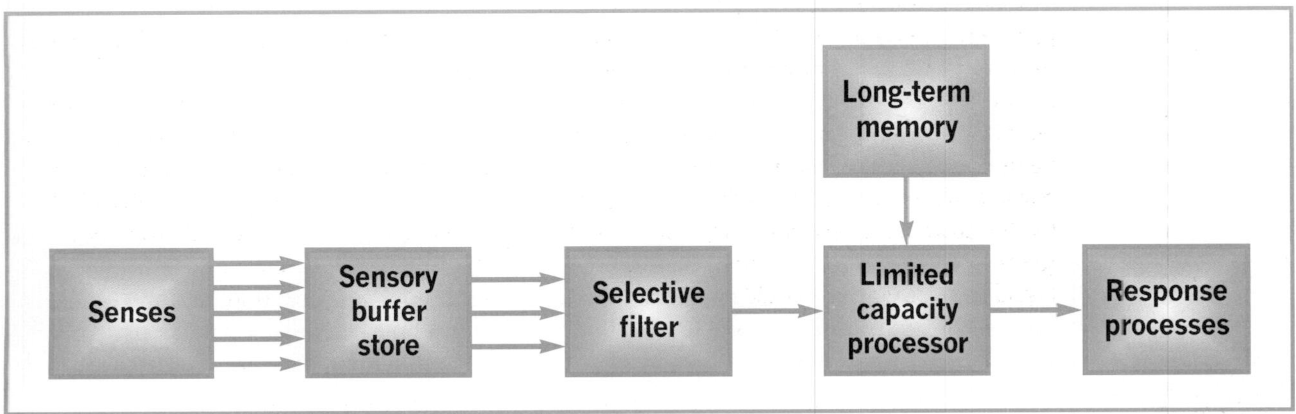

Figure 13.3 Broadbent's (1958) filter model of selective attention

In his model Broadbent had a sensory buffer, a selective filter and a limited capacity attentional processor. He argued that the sensory buffer has the ability to hold the physical characteristics of information, while the person is attending to other information. In the next stage of the model, the selective filter accepts some inputs and rejects others on the basis of physical properties, and in the final stage, the limited capacity processor concentrates on processing the most important information. One important aspect of Broadbent's model is that selection of the single channel is not based on meaning. Each ear is seen to represent a separate channel and the brain can fully process only one channel at a time. Consequently, this type of model was known as a single channel model. The importance of Broadbent's theory lies less in the model itself than in the wider interest and research it generated. In fact, there were immediate problems for the model in that it is very difficult to determine the exact nature of a 'channel'. Subsequent research investigated where precisely in any model the filter, or *bottleneck*, should be placed. Further problems for the model were posed by a study conducted by Gray and Wedderburn (see *In Focus* on the next page).

In Focus

◆

Gray and Wedderburn's (1960) version of the split-span procedure

In their experiment, Gray and Wedderburn modified Broadbent's original split-span technique. They used an almost identical procedure to Broadbent, but made one slight modification. Instead of using just digits, they simultaneously presented material from two categories, digits and words. Participants had to report either 'ear by ear' (as in Broadbent's original experiment) or 'category by category'. Gray and Wedderburn found that if the material in either ear was semantically (meaningfully) related, as in 'dear cousin Albert', participants reported this relationship as easily as they reported the ear by ear presentation (see Fig. 13.4).

Figure 13.4 Gray and Wedderburn's (1960) version of the split-span procedure

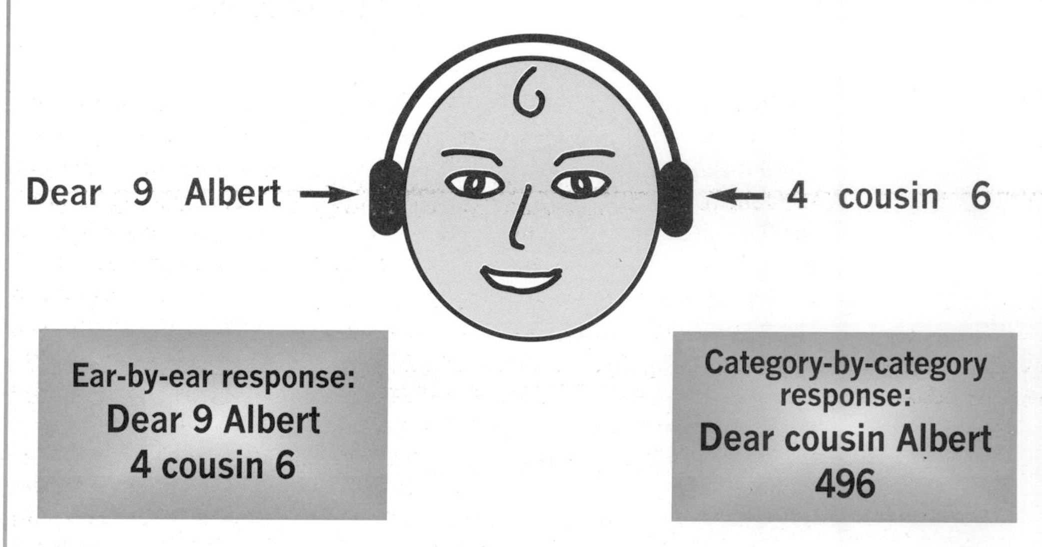

Gray and Wedderburn's finding creates serious problems for Broadbent's model. It contradicts the notion that the ear of arrival determines the channel, or that switching between channels presents much difficulty. Since meaning determines the switching, this also contradicts Broadbent's ideas that filtering was dependent on the physical properties of the message (think back to Activity 5 and consider the things which determine your switch of attention, meaning or physical properties?). This finding resulted in a number of people (e.g. Treisman 1960) initiating investigations into how the content of an unattended message might affect shadowing.

Treisman (1960, 1964) varied the presentation of the material in the unattended ear to see how this affected the shadowing of the material in the attended ear. In one of her experiments she used bilingual participants. These participants had to shadow a message in one ear, which was presented in English, while ignoring a message in the other ear, which was presented in the participants' second language, French. In fact, both messages had the same meaning and, although the French version lagged slightly behind the English version, participants noticed that both messages had the same meaning. Clearly, the participants were processing some of the meaning in the unattended message. As with Gray and Wedderburn's finding, this suggested that the meaning of a message can be recognized prior to any focusing of attention. People seem to have the ability to switch from message to message if the content of one message is related to the content of the other message.

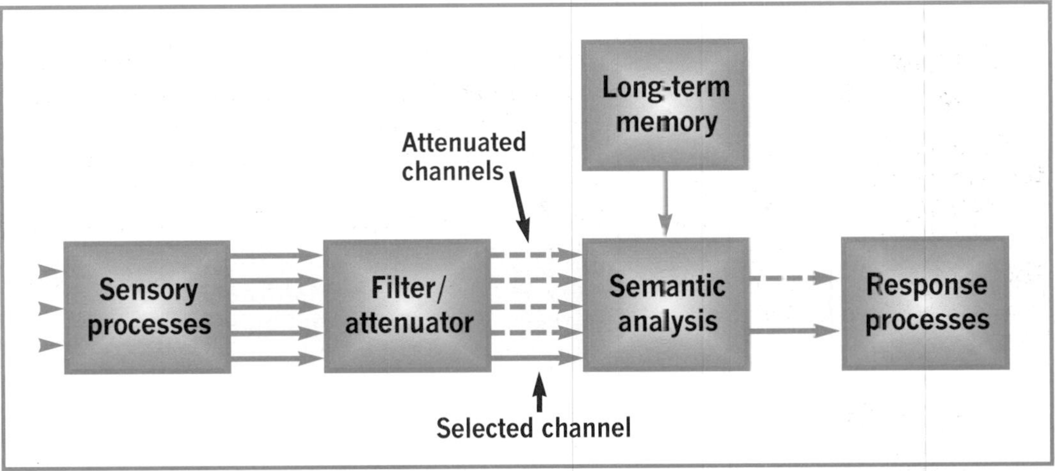

Figure 13.5 Treisman's (1964) attenuator model of selective attention

or if it is more meaningful than the message which was the original focus of attention. These ideas led Treisman (1964) to revise Broadbent's model and suggest that perhaps the filter does not block the unattended message, but attenuates it – that is, passes it on, but in a weaker, or depleted form (see Fig. 13.5).

Treisman's model has a two-stage filter. The first stage selects information based on its physical characteristics, and the second stage selects information in terms of its meaning. This model accounts for the cocktail party phenomenon better than Broadbent's model, allowing for the possibility of switching to one of the attenuated channels if it contains meaningful information. Nevertheless, there are two main problems for the Treisman model:

- Although the functions of attenuation are reasonably clear, the operating principles (how it does it) are not clear. She does not give a precise definition of 'attenuation'.
- Both Treisman's and Gray and Wedderburn's findings suggest that an analysis of the semantic meaning of an attenuated channel may require much more extensive processing than is allowed for in Treisman's model.

Late selection models

Both Treisman's and Broadbent's models agree that the bottleneck occurs during the early stages of information processing. An alternative view is that all incoming information receives at least some simple semantic analysis, and only after this does selection occur. This notion of late selection was first proposed by Deutsch and Deutsch (1963) and was later refined by Norman (1968). The main idea behind these models is that all stimuli gain access to semantic analysis and all are matched to information in long-term memory. The item which is the most salient at any particular time is then selected for further analysis and made subject to conscious attention. Other stimuli will only be attended to if their relevance exceeds that of the stimulus currently being processed. All, or most, information is processed in the early stages of information processing and only at the late stage of response selection does a bottleneck occur. A summary of the late selection model is given in Fig. 13.6.

Various studies have tried to differentiate between early and late selection models. For example, Lewis (1970) supported late selection models by showing that semantically related words presented in the unattended channel could affect processing in the attended channel. This indicates that two channels can be processed in parallel up to a level at which the meaning of the words in each channel was being processed. MacKay (1973) also showed that the meanings of ambiguous words could be determined by information in the unattended channel. For example, an

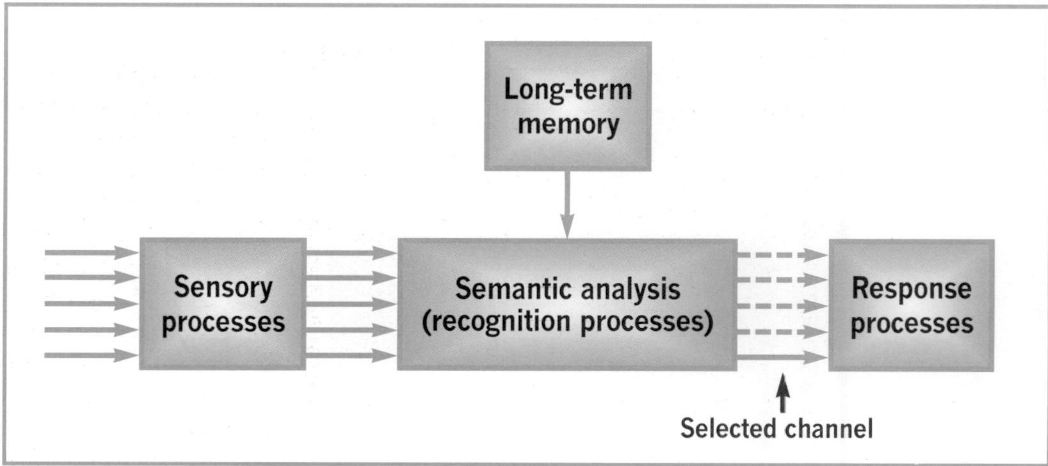

Figure 13.6 The Deutsch/Norman late selection model of selective attention

ambiguous message in the attended ear could be about a 'bank'. The message in the unattended ear could concern either rivers or financial institutions, and this would influence participants' interpretation of the meaning of 'bank'. However, the late selection models have also received their share of criticism. Treisman and Geffen (1967) showed that attended messages were more easily recognized later on than non-attended messages. This casts doubt on the suggestion from late selection models that 'all' information receives some level of processing. Treisman and Geffen point out how uneconomical it would be for all information to be processed for meaning.

Very soon people began to question whether or not single channel filter models were an appropriate way of thinking about focused attention. It soon became obvious that both early and late selection processes may be involved in focused attention. Johnston and Heinz (1978) put forward evidence suggesting that focused attention is more flexible than proposed by either early or late selection models. They suggest that attention may be focused at several stages of processing and selection occurs as early as possible, depending on the task demands.

Early attention research is a good example of how cognitive psychologists make use of abstract theoretical models in developing their theoretical ideas. Research began with observations from the world (air traffic controllers), a theory was derived and a model was constructed (Broadbent). Predictions were made, the model was tested and amendments were made. Finally, the models could not account for all the empirical evidence, so new models (better ways of thinking about attention) were developed.

Divided attention

Dual task performance

All the theories discussed so far assume there is some type of single processor dealing with one channel at a time. An alternative view is that there may be a number of separate processors which can operate in parallel, a multi-processor view of focused (selective) attention. Allport *et al.* (1972) have shown that skilled musicians can accurately shadow prose at the same time as playing sheet music, and Shaffer (1975) has shown that skilled typists can shadow prose accurately while typing a foreign language. These findings suggest that concurrent tasks only interfere with each other, and need to be selectively attended to, if they are competing for the resources of the same processor. In other words, in certain circumstances we have the ability to '*divide*' our overall attentional capacity between different tasks.

These studies also show that different types of input can be processed in parallel with equal accuracy and suggest that processing capacity is determined by the

❖ Activity 6 ❖

Think of some of the things you find easy to do at the same time. Now think of some of the things you find difficult to do at the same time. Are there any patterns of similarities and differences in the tasks you have identified? Is this pattern consistent or does it change as a result of other factors, such as how you are feeling at any particular time?

nature, as well as the amount, of input. This raises questions about *interprocess conflict* (processes which are competing for the same resource allocation) and relates to real-life experiences when at times we can easily do two things at once, and at other times this becomes difficult, or impossible.

Capacity models of attention

Since the 1960s, researchers have tended to concentrate on which tasks require more attention than others, and why. Most theorists still accept the notion of an overall limited capacity of attention, but modern theories talk about resource allocation, rather than single channel processing, and emphasize the flexible nature of the allocation of attention (e.g. Kahneman 1973). Attentional capacity is now viewed as dynamic so that the total capacity can be increased, or decreased, by factors such as levels of arousal. An increased level of arousal is thought to increase our attentional capacity, but once a critical level has been reached, attentional capacity drops off dramatically.

Kahneman also introduced the concept of *mental effort*, which relates to how

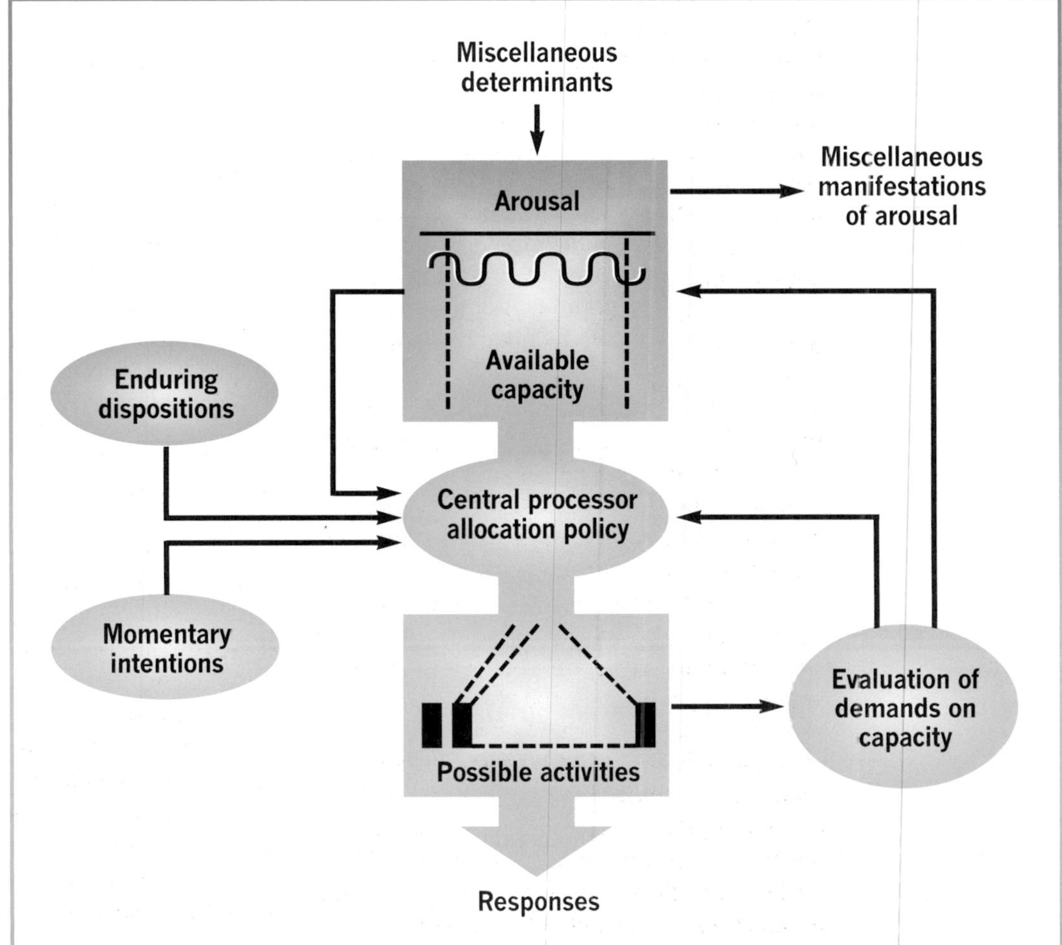

Figure 13.7 Kahneman's capacity model of attention *Source:* Kahneman 1973

demanding of attention a particular task might be. He proposed a general model of attention which includes the notion of some activities requiring more attention than others, the idea of arousal affecting our overall attentional capacity and the possibility of several activities being performed at the same time if our overall capacity is not exceeded (see Fig. 13.7).

According to Kahneman's model, the central processor coordinates and allocates the finite attentional resources available. It monitors how much demand is being placed on the attentional system. If demand becomes excessive, and mental effort exceeds a critical level, it determines where attention will be directed. The allocation of attention by the central processor is influenced by 'enduring dispositions' (e.g. how well you normally handle similar situations), 'momentary intentions' (e.g. how interested you are in the task) and an evaluation of demands on capacity (how much capacity is currently available). According to Kahneman, therefore, attentional ability is determined by a number of internal and external factors. In a similar vein, Neisser (1976) also suggested that attention should be seen as a skill which can be developed rather than a fixed resource. In other words, the more skilful we become at a task, the less attention we have to allocate to that task, and performance may eventually become *'automatic'*.

Automaticity

The idea of automatic processing is crucial to the notion of divided attention and capacity models of attention. Posner and Snyder (1975) suggest that performance on a task is automatic if it can occur without the intention or awareness of the performer and does not interfere with other mental activities. This idea has been elaborated by Shiffrin and Schneider (1977) in their differentiation between controlled and automatic processes (see *In Focus* below).

Shiffrin and Schneider point out that the development of automaticity is important in

In Focus

Shiffrin and Schneider's (1977) distinction between attentional and automatic processing

Shiffrin and Schneider (1977) reported a series of studies which explored the nature of automatic, or non-conscious, information processing. Their investigations led them to differentiate between two general modes of human information processing: 'attentional' and 'automatic'. They suggested that the two modes of processing have the following general features.

Automatic processing	*Attentional processing*
These processes are not hindered by capacity limitations.	These processes are of limited capacity and require focused attention.
These processes are fast, can operate in parallel and many processes can be active at any one time.	These processes are serial in nature and, in line with single channel theories, each has to be dealt with singly.
Tasks only reach automatic status through considerable practice and are difficult to modify once learnt.	Tasks which are attentionally processed can be learnt quickly and can be modified relatively easily.
Automatic processing usually takes place at a non-conscious level.	Attentional processes are usually consciously directed to a task.
Automatic processing is unavoidable; it always occurs when appropriate stimulus is present.	

many everyday tasks (e.g. cycling). Some tasks can be performed with virtually no conscious effort and automaticity usually improves with practice. Finally, although we can make a distinction between automatic and attentional processing, it is often difficult to decide whether processing is entirely automatic or is partly attentional. Often there seems to be a degree of both types of processing involved. Consider the case of the Stroop task (Stroop 1935), where people read aloud the colour in which a word is printed. When the word is itself the name of a colour, this interferes with the task. For example, when the word 'red' is printed in green, people find it more difficult to identify the colour green. This Stroop effect is usually explained in terms of automatic processing: people cannot avoid processing the *word* 'red', even though it is irrelevant to this task. However, Kahneman and Henik (1979) found the effect to be much greater when the distracting word was superimposed on the colour which was to be identified, rather than when placed in an adjacent position on the page. Perhaps the Stroop effect is not as fully automatic as originally thought.

Norman and Shallice (1980) distinguish between what they call *fully-automatic processing*, *partially-automatic processing* and *controlled processing*. Automaticity may, therefore, be better viewed as a continuum, ranging from completely automatic to completely controlled processing.

To date, none of the models discussed has provided a complete model of attention. In fact, some theorists (e.g. Kahneman and Treisman 1984) have suggested that all have some merit, and have used a combination of the ideas in their theorizing. Ideas of dual task performance and allocation of attention have also been taken up in many other areas of research, such as in Baddeley and Hitch's (1974) Working Memory model (see Chapter 15). However, there are still a lot of questions which remain unanswered. For example, Allport (1980) emphasizes the role of novelty and practice in allocating attention, and has questioned the appropriateness of the idea of a limited capacity central processor. He suggests that individual areas of processing might involve the use of specialist subsystems of relatively unlimited capacity. Nevertheless, many of the original ideas have been taken up in other areas of research, and many modern cognitive models incorporate some sort of limited-capacity attentional component.

Section summary

Research in the area of auditory attention began with the development of simple information-processing models. The first models were the early selection models. However, these models could not adequately explain how attentional switching could be based on meaning. Late selection models attempted to address this problem, but again these models could not adequately explain experimental findings. Researchers then began to consider attention as an overall resource which could be increased or decreased as a result of a number of factors. Some of these factors related to the task in hand and some to the person undertaking the task. Furthermore, attentional resources could be allocated at different stages of processing. Modern theories of attention are far more diverse and attention is currently conceptualized as one component within more general information-processing models.

Focused visual attention

Visual and auditory attention

Most attentional research has been conducted in the area of auditory attention, and much of this research has utilized dual task techniques in which the ears are seen to correspond to separate information-processing channels. However, there has also been a substantial amount of research on visual attention. Some of this has shown important similarities between focused auditory and focused visual attention, but there are also important differences between these processes. In the case of auditory attention, we appear to be able to attend selectively to information in either ear. However, with visual attention, the biological make up of the visual system means that we cannot attend selectively to the input to one eye while ignoring the input to the other. Information entering both eyes must be combined prior to any stage of processing involving visual attention. Therefore, in the case of visual attention, the visual system must utilize a single input channel. La Berge (1983) has suggested that visual attention might be best conceptualized using a variable beam spotlight analogy. Using this analogy, everything in the beam of the spotlight can be seen quite clearly, but anything outside the beam is much more difficult to detect. However, the beam can be enlarged or decreased to cover different areas of the visual field. If the beam is decreased, a small area is seen, but in great detail. On the other hand, if the beam is enlarged, more can be seen, but in less detail.

Although we cannot switch visual input channels, this does not mean we cannot shift our visual attention (change the position of the visual 'beam'). By moving our eyes, or head, we can shift our attention to different areas of our *visual field*.

For example, at present your visual attention is focused on this section of the book. However, you should be able to 'see' other things in the periphery of your vision and by simply moving your eyes you can change the focus of your attention.

This points to a further important difference between visual and auditory attention.

In the case of visual attention, the sense organs (the eyes) can be directed to the focus of attention, but in the case of auditory attention the sense organs (the ears) cannot shut out some sounds and focus on others. Both ears convert all the sound energy they receive and the selection of items for attention must occur after the basic auditory information has been processed. In the case of visual attention, selection of items for attention can occur much earlier in the process as the eyes move across the visual field. With visual attention, it does not make sense to think in terms of the 'number of channels' which can be processed at any one time. Therefore, in visual attention, capacity is seen to be limited by the 'number of items' of visual input which can be processed at any one time, and much of the research in this area has concentrated on the *visual search* procedure.

Visual search

One of the first theorists to utilize the visual search task to investigate visual attention was Neisser (see *In Focus*).

From his research, Neisser concluded that participants could process many items at the same time without being completely 'aware' of the exact nature of the distractor items (e.g. the type of background letters). He went on to suggest that there may be different levels of recognition with visual processing and that some aspects of recognition occur below the level of consciousness. Neisser (1967) later suggested that there must be a *'pre-attentive'* stage of visual processing, evoked automatically by 'features' (e.g. angles or curves) in the visual input. Therefore, Neisser argues that feature detection is important in the early stages of visual attention and is an automatic process which works pre-attentively. This idea is supported by Johnston and Dark (1986) who provided evidence that the processing of items outside the 'attentional spotlight beam' is primarily based on the primitive physical features of those items.

In line with Neisser's thinking, Gibson (1969) demonstrated that if feature detection is a major process in visual perception, then in letter recognition letters sharing similar features may be confused, i.e. angular letters will be confused with other angular letters (e.g. 'V's with 'W's) and curved letters with other curved letters (e.g. 'O's with 'Q's). This suggests that visual features may be central in early

In Focus

Neisser's (1963) visual search procedure

In a number of different experiments, Neisser gave participants arrays of individual items and embedded in each array was one target item. An example of this technique is given below.

Y U D K S L K X Z W

K B P I W Q L N S H

J P T E W M F A W L

N L O Y T 7 N C H E

J F A O P W E S G E

D G T P O R T I G D

Participants have to work through this array of letters and detect the target item (in this case the number '7'). Neisser knew how many letters participants had to work through before they came to the number, and could calculate how long it took to compare each letter with the number.

Neisser conducted numerous experiments in which the type of target and background items were varied. For example, participants might have to detect an angular letter (e.g. 'V') among other angular letters (e.g. 'X's, 'W's and 'K's) or among curved letters (e.g. 'G's, 'Q's, and 'D's). When the distractor (background) items were also angular, participants took longer to detect the 'V'.

stages of visual processing. However, later research has shown that this idea may be too simplistic, as demonstrated in Activity 7.

There are a number of reasons why the task in Activity 7 might create problems for readers. People could be automatically converting the *visual representations* of letters into *phonological representations*. Therefore the 'OF's sound like 'OV's and people fail to detect the 'F's. Demonstrations such as this indicate that the sound of letters may also result in confusions in visual search tasks. Another explanation might be that in reading we *automatically* process frequently occurring words as *whole units* and find it difficult to focus on component letters. Reicher (1969) demonstrated what he called the 'word superiority effect'. In his experiment, participants were presented with words (e.g. NEAT) and non-meaningful letter strings made up of the same letters (e.g. ATNE). They had to decide if particular letters were present in those items. Reicher found that participants could detect particular letters more easily if they came from real words rather than from the non-meaningful letter strings. This suggests that stored knowledge of words (meaningful units) was being used to help participants complete the task. Therefore, although feature detection is clearly involved in visual attention, expectations and *stored knowledge* also have a role to play. These ideas are discussed in more detail in Chapter 14.

❖ Activity 7 ❖

Read the following sentence and count the number of 'F's.

FISH FINGERS ARE THE PRODUCT
OF MANY YEARS OF DEVELOPMENT
IN THE AREA OF FOOD PROCESSING.

You should have counted six 'F's in the sentence. However, do not worry if you missed some because people often find tasks such as this quite difficult. People often miss the 'F's in the word 'of', which occurs three times in the sentence. Try this out with friends and family.

Section summary

Focused visual and auditory attention share some similarities, but there are also some important differences between the two processes. The visual system utilizes single channel input and attentional processes appear to be activated much earlier in visual than in auditory processing. In visual processing, attentional capacity is seen to be determined by the number of items, rather than the number of channels, which can be processed at any one time. Research into focused visual attention has tended to utilize the visual search task. Findings have indicated that some aspects of visual recognition occur automatically and that feature detection is a key process in visual recognition. However, other evidence indicates that processing of features is also mediated by expectations and stored knowledge.

Performance deficits

In addition to devising controlled experiments to develop and test their theoretical models of attention, cognitive psychologists can also learn a great deal about attentional processes by studying the nature of everyday attentional errors. This is also a good example of the interrelationship between the different sub-areas of cognitive psychology, because attentional errors often reflect lapses in memory. Memory is not only concerned with recall of past events. We also use our memory to remember plans and keep track of ongoing actions (see Chapter 15). This is often called *prospective memory* and is concerned with remembering to do things. Failure to keep track of plans and intentions is usually called *absent-mindedness* and gives rise to what are called *slips of action.*

Attentional slips and errors

Diary study techniques

Cognitive psychologists have utilized a number of techniques in their study of absent-mindedness. For example, questionnaires can be used to assess the frequency with which certain things are forgotten. Another method which has been used, which also relies on self-assessment, is the diary study technique. In diary studies, participants are asked to keep daily records of the memory errors they make. One important diary study in this area was carried out by Reason (see *In Focus*).

The first point to make about Reason's study is that some of the distinctions between the categories are not very clear. For example, some of the errors classified as

In Focus

Reason's (1979) diary study of slips of action

Reason (1979) conducted a diary study in which 35 participants kept a diary record of their slips of action over a two week period. The study revealed 400 errors and Reason divided them into five categories:

- Storage failures (40% of total errors): forgetting that an action had already been performed and doing it again (e.g. putting the sugar in a cup of tea twice).
- Test failures (20% of total errors): forgetting the goal of a sequence of actions and switching to a different goal (e.g. starting off making a cup of tea and ending up making a cup of coffee).
- Subroutine failures (18% of total errors): component actions of a sequence being omitted, or wrongly ordered (e.g. putting the boiling water in the tea pot without having put in the tea).
- Discrimination failures (11% of the errors): confusing the objects involved in different actions (e.g. taking a fork instead of a spoon to stir your tea).
- Programme assembly failures (5% of total errors): wrongly combining actions from different sequences (e.g. opening a new packet of tea and placing the wrapping in the teapot and tea in the waste bin).

The remaining 6% of errors were unclassifiable.

'discrimination failures' are not that different from errors classified as 'programme assembly failures'. A second problem is that a particular type of slip may be more disruptive and noticeable. Therefore, these errors may be reported as happening more frequently. However, a subsequent larger study by Reason and Mycielska (1982) arrived at very similar categories.

❖ Activity 8 ❖

Over a two week period try to keep a written record of all the slips of action you make. If possible you could also try to get one or two members of your family and/or one or two friends to keep a record of their attentional errors. At the end of the period, try to categorize the errors in the same way as Reason and consider whether your errors fit into his classification system.

Reason explained the error patterns by arguing that attentional processing works at three levels:

- a superficial level concerned with routine automatic tasks which require little conscious thought (the majority of errors seem to occur at this level)
- a deeper level of processing involving a realization that a routine is incorrect and that more attention and knowledge is required to correct the situation (errors can occur at this level if you misread a situation and then realize that your actions do not fit the current context)
- an even deeper level of processing in which you have to bring all your knowledge to bear and use all your conscious control to solve a problem (a further problem at this level is that by now you might have reached a critical point and fear or panic may not allow clear thinking).

Reason has used these ideas to look at disasters such as Chernobyl and has concluded that, unless an understanding of the nature of human errors is allowed for in the design of new technology, these accidents are not only possible, but inevitable.

Dual task limitations

A key finding from the Reason study is that the majority of errors seem to occur in highly practised, over-learned, routines. These action sequences often involve automatic processing and are carried out with little conscious monitoring. Therefore, they are less prone to dual task limitations (see page 292 on dual task monitoring). Automatic actions have the advantage of releasing attentional resources to be used in the performance of parallel activities. However, they can also lead to errors. There is a tendency for a more commonly performed task to take over from one performed less often, particularly if both tasks share a component stage. Slips of action often occur at junctions between stages when there can be a switch over to an incorrect procedure, e.g. walking or driving in the wrong direction because that is the way most often taken. In addition to these 'habit intrusions', people can also lose track of a sequence of actions resulting in actions being repeated or omitted. Some people are more prone to these kinds of errors than others, and everyone finds that slips and lapses can increase with tiredness and stress. Norman (1981) has proposed an explanation of attentional slips and lapses based directly on one of the most important theoretical ideas in cognitive psychology, known as schema theory.

Schema theory

The notion of *schemas* was first put forward by Bartlett (1932). They can be thought of as organized sets of mental representations which incorporate all our knowledge of particular objects, concepts or events. According to schema theory, if the same incoming information is experienced repeatedly it eventually becomes incorporated into a generalized schematic representation. Schema theory attempts to explain how we organize knowledge from past experience to help us interpret, or guide, new information coming in from the senses. Rumelhart and Norman (1983) list five main characteristics of schemas:

- Schemas incorporate all the knowledge we have acquired through past experiences, including generalizations and learnt facts (e.g. our knowledge of what to do in exams).
- Schemas represent knowledge of all kinds ranging from simple feature knowledge (e.g. the features of a triangle) to more complex abstract knowledge (e.g. the meaning of justice).
- Schemas can be linked together into related systems containing other schemas and subschemas (e.g. a schema for chairs can be a subschema of a schema for 'items used for sitting on', which in turn can be part of a general schema for furniture).
- Schemas have slots which can be filled with fixed or variable values (e.g. a fixed value for a car could be that it has an engine and a variable value could be the size of the engine). Furthermore, variable values can be filled by the most probable value (default value) if any information is not given or is missing (e.g. you might assume a car has four wheels if you do not know it is a Reliant Robin).
- Various schemas at different levels may be engaged in recognizing new inputs (e.g. in your first week at university you might incorporate various schemas of educational and social experience to help you with new found independence and the transition into higher education). A good example of the influence of schemas in human information processing can be seen in a study carried out by French and Richards (see *In Focus*).

According to Norman's (1981) model of attentional slips and lapses, action sequences are controlled by schemas. He suggests that several schemas can be activated simultaneously and linked into related sets. The highest level, or parent schema, corresponds to the overall intention, or goal (e.g. going to school). Subordinate, or child, subschemas correspond to the component actions in the sequence (e.g. going to the bus stop, catching the bus, getting off the bus and walking to school). Each schema, or subschema, has its own activation level which is determined by both external (the current situation) and

In Focus

French and Richards' (1993) study of schema-driven attentional errors

In this experiment, French and Richards had three conditions.

- Condition 1: participants were shown a clock with roman numerals and asked to study the clock for one minute. After the time had elapsed, the clock was taken away and participants were then asked to draw the clock from memory.
- Condition 2: the same procedure was followed with the exception that participants were told they would be required to draw the clock from memory.
- Condition 3: the clock was left in full view of the participants and they were instructed merely to produce a drawn copy of the clock.

In the standard form of roman numerals the number four is represented as IV, but on clocks with roman numerals the four is almost invariably represented as IIII. French and Richards found that in both the conditions in which participants had to draw the clock from memory, a significant majority reverted to the conventional IV notation. In Condition 3, however, all the participants used the correct IIII notation. French and Richards explained these results in terms of schema theory and the strong influence of schematic knowledge on the way people process information. In Conditions 1 and 2, the strong influence of schematic knowledge of roman numerals appeared to have affected participants' memory retrieval.

internal events (plans and intentions). Each schema also has a set of triggering conditions, and a given schema is activated if the activation level is sufficiently high and the current situation matches the triggering conditions. According to Norman, slips can occur as a result of faulty specification of the overall intention (another schema has a higher level of activation than the one associated with the original intention) or faulty triggering (the current situation, or context, triggers an alternative schema). An example of faulty specification might be starting off going to visit an aunt you have not seen for some time and ending up around the corner at a friend's house which you visit more frequently. An example of faulty triggering could be deciding to walk to school instead of catching the bus, but, as you are passing the bus stop, the bus arrives and before you have realized what you are doing, you are on the bus. However, although a useful explanation of attentional slips and errors, Norman's model is not without its problems. As with Reason's classification, some errors do not fall neatly into either of the categories and may result from a combination of factors (e.g. a combination of both faulty specification and faulty triggering). Nevertheless, schema theory remains a useful way of thinking about attentional slips and errors and will be discussed in more depth in Chapter 15.

Section summary

A complementary approach to experimental studies of attentional processing involves an investigation of everyday attentional errors. One way of carrying out such an investigation is through diary studies in which participants keep a written record of any errors they might make. These errors can then be categorized and used to aid theoretical understanding of attentional processes. Although there are problems in classifying errors, studies which have been carried out using this technique have proved to be useful in the development of models of attentional errors. Many errors seem to occur during automatic, or partially automatic action sequences, and schema theory has proved useful in explaining the information processing underpinning these errors.

Chapter summary

- Research in the area of attention is a good example of how science progresses and develops, and was among the first to utilize information-processing models. Early researchers made observations of the world and developed simple information-processing models to try to explain how people might allocate mental resources. The models were tested and further developed as a result of empirical findings.
- This scientific progression saw the development of various models of auditory attention. The first models of attention were simple filter models which were then superseded by attenuator models and late selection models. However, none of the models could offer a complete explanation of auditory attention and researchers began to question whether attention could be seen as an 'all-or-nothing' process.
- Research into auditory attention then began to focus on the flexible nature of resource allocation and comparisons have been made between auditory and visual attention.
- Researchers have also investigated performance deficits and the relationship between attention and other aspects of human information processing, such as memory.
- To date, there is no comprehensive theory of attention, and the modern view is to consider attention as one component in a more general model of human information processing.

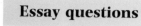

Essay questions

1 Critically consider research relating to divided attention. *(24 marks)*

2 (a) Outline the nature of automatic processsing. *(6 marks)*

(b) Describe and evaluate research evidence relating to automatic processing. *(18 marks)*

3 Discuss research studies into performance deficits *(24 marks)*

Further reading

Eysenck, M.W. and Keane, M.T (1995) *Cognitive Psychology: A Student's Handbook* (2nd edn), Hove: Lawrence Erlbaum Associates.

Gives a more detailed coverage of attention using similar terminology to that used in this chapter.

Best, J. B. (1995) *Cognitive Psychology* (4th edn), St. Paul, Minneapolis: West Publishing Company.

This probably gives attention more coverage than Eysenck and Keane, but organizes the topic in a different way.

Chapter 14

Perceptual processes

Peter Hayes

Preview

In this chapter we shall be looking at:

- basic perceptual processes, including perceptual organization
- theories of visual perception
- social and developmental aspects of visual perception.

Introduction

This chapter considers research which has investigated people's ability to translate physical information from the senses into the psychological experience of perception. It focuses primarily on visual processing and begins by considering the basic processes of visual perception and perceptual organization. We will then consider theories of perception, including constructivist and direct theories. Finally, we will evaluate how these theories have been used in explanations of perceptual development and of social variations in perception.

Basic perceptual processes

Perceptual processing

The world around us is filled with people and objects which we can see, hear, touch, smell or taste. We receive this information through sense organs in the body, such as the eyes, ears and nose. These sense organs contain sensory receptors which detect the physical properties of the world around us, such as light and sound, and pass this information on to the brain and central nervous system (CNS). The brain and CNS then convert this information into our perceptual experiences of the world. Cognitive psychologists are interested in explaining the mental activity required to convert physical information from the environment into the psychological experience of perception. There has been a vast amount of research into perceptual processing, but most has tended to focus on the visual modality.

Visual processing

Visual processing is fast and effortless, but we are rarely aware of the processes which

Figure 14.1
Dallenbach's (1951) fragmentary picture

❖ Activity 1 ❖

Look at Fig. 14.1 and see if you can detect the object depicted in the figure. If you cannot, go to the end of the chapter to find the answer. Having done this, consider the following questions:

- ❖ If you had difficulty in detecting the object, why was this?
- ❖ Now you know the answer, can you see the object as anything else?

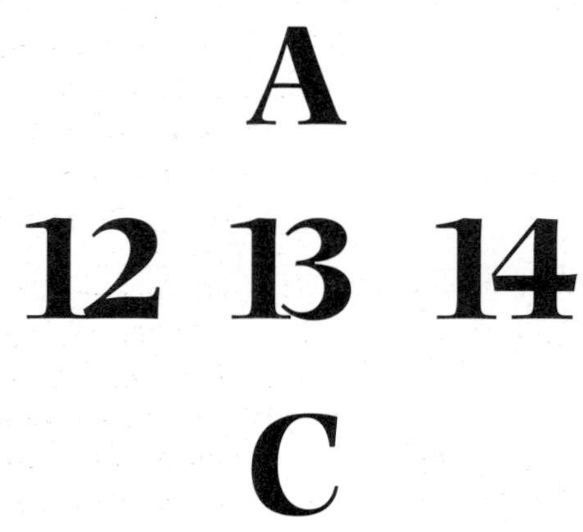

Figure 14.2
Illustration of the role of context in visual perception

underpin visual perception and this makes it difficult to study. However, when our visual processing lets us down, we appreciate how much time and effort it actually takes. One way of showing this is to slow processing down by providing impoverished input to the visual system.

In investigating visual perception it is clear that while sensory input can be fragmentary, disorganized and ambiguous, we can see objects and figures which appear to have structure, stability and meaning. This suggests that there is a gap between the sensory input and what we actually perceive. Perceptual interpretations can be incorrect, suggesting that processing involves some sort of guesswork which is going beyond the available information. Figure 14.2 illustrates the way perception is influenced by context. In Fig. 14.2, the middle character can be seen as a 'B' in the vertical context and a '13' in the horizontal context.

Perception requires a great deal of information about the world, which is stored and represented in memory. Memory and perception are interrelated, and involve the use of internal representations of the world. We can think of perception as drawing on stored information, while, at the same time, continually adding to, and modifying, this information.

Psychophysical and behaviourist studies of visual perception

Early studies of perception were carried out in the psychophysical tradition by pioneers of psychology such as Wundt and Fechner. Psychophysics is concerned with the changes in psychological response which result from variations in physical stimuli. Psychophysicists believe that perceptual processing can be broken down into sensory elements. Rather than asking people to recognize objects and events, they investigate elementary perceptual sensations, such as responses to stimuli consisting of tones and lights. In a typical psychophysical experiment, participants would be presented with light sources of different frequencies and asked to describe (i.e. 'introspect about') which colour they perceived. Psychophysicists are concerned with identifying which changes of light frequency result in changes of colour perception.

Psychophysicists were criticized for their use of such introspective techniques and later approaches focused on learning to discriminate. The behaviourist emphasis was on how various stimuli could control a discriminative response. In other words, how people learn to match stimuli (e.g. input light frequency) with a particular response (e.g. colour name). Both psychophysical and behaviourist approaches claimed that perceptual processing could be broken down into sets of basic elements. Support for this idea comes from neuro-biological studies of the visual system.

Neurological studies of visual perception

The picture to emerge from studying the biology of perception is that the visual system consists of the eyes, various brain structures and the neural pathways connecting these structures. There are two main pathways involved in visual perception. One pathway travels from the eye to an area of the thalamus called the lateral geniculate nucleus (LGN) in the mid-brain area, and then travels to the striate, or visual, cortex. However, before this pathway reaches the LGN, some nerve fibres branch off and travel to the superior colliculus of the tectum to form the other visual pathway. Evidence suggests that the two pathways are associated with two distinct perceptual functions: the collicular pathway is involved in locating objects and bringing them to central vision; the cortical pathway is involved in identifying and analysing objects. Further evidence concerning the role of the cortical pathway comes from Hubel and Wiesel's (1962) work using single-cell recordings of individual nerve cells.

Hubel and Wiesel investigated cells in the retina, LGN and striate cortex. They found that different types of stimuli activate different cells in the visual system and suggested that, as we go deeper into the visual system, cells need increasingly complex visual features in order to respond. These cells are the building blocks of perception and perception may be the product of this rudimentary analysis. If we were to extrapolate from this approach, we could have cells which respond to stimuli such as particular people (e.g. a grandmother cell), or particular objects (e.g. a yellow Volkswagen cell). There is some support for this idea in that cells have been identified which respond to very specific stimuli. Desimone *et al.* (1984) showed that certain cells in the monkey cortex respond to face-shaped stimuli. These ideas suggest that one of the basic processes involved in perception is feature detection. Studies of perceptual organization, however, suggest this may be an oversimplification.

Perceptual organization

Perceptual constancy

Visual perception begins with light being projected on to the light-sensitive receptor cells of the retina. This two-dimensional information provides the input for visual processing, and perception involves interpreting this retinal image to form an accurate perception of the outside world. We know that this process must involve interpretation because much perception remains constant, despite fluctuations in the retinal image. The clearest example of this can be seen in size constancy. Size constancy refers to the fact that although objects may be at different distances and create different-sized retinal images, they are perceived as having a constant size (see Fig. 14.3).

Figure 14.3 shows how the same object, at different distances from the eye, projects different-sized retinal images. As we move closer to or further away from an object, it will project different-sized images on to the retina. However, it will appear to maintain a constant size. The perceptual system compensates for fluctuations in the retinal image to create a stable perception. As well as compensating for fluctuations in the size of the retinal image, the perceptual system maintains constancy in terms of shape,

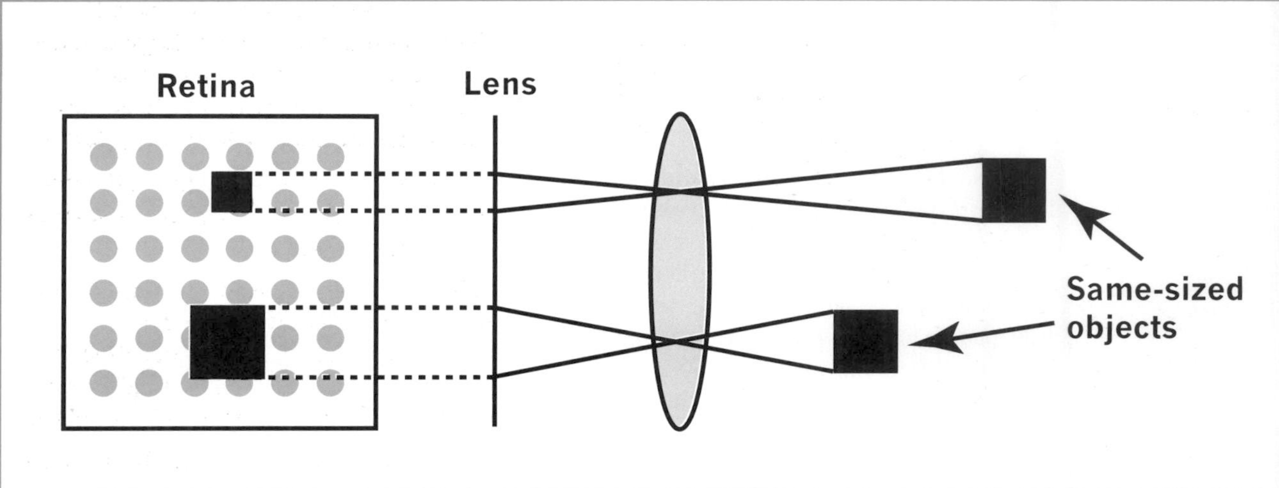

Figure 14.3 Illustration of the different-sized retinal images projected from same-sized objects

location, colour and brightness. Size constancy can be effectively demonstrated in an exercise described by Gregory (1972) – see Activity 2.

❖ Activity 2 ❖

Hold out one of your hands at arms length and the other at half the distance with the back of your hands facing your eyes. Despite the difference in distance, both hands will look the same size. However, if you now move the nearer hand closer to the eye and move it to overlap the other hand, you should find that it covers it completely. This shows that, although both hands looked the same size, they were projecting different sized retinal images.

Perception of space (depth perception)

The perception of space, or depth, is crucial in everyday life. In order to go about our day-to-day activities, we need to comprehend the distance between ourselves and objects in the world, and the spatial relationships between those objects. Sekular and Blake (1994) use the term 'absolute distance' to refer to the distance between ourselves and other objects, and 'relative distance' to refer to the distance between two objects. We need to estimate absolute distance to stop ourselves bumping into objects, and relative distance to do things such as putting a record on a turntable. These seem like simple tasks, but require the complex process of turning a two-dimensional retinal image into a three-dimensional perception.

Although we have described Fig. 14.4 in the caption as an 'impossible figure', it is not really an impossible figure, but simply a two-dimensional line drawing. The problem is that people use three-dimensional knowledge to try to impose depth onto the figure. Furthermore, this seems to be an automatic process. One of the main sources of information about depth and space comes from visual cues derived from objects in the world. Some of these cues will be 'monocular', i.e. they can be utilized by one eye, and some are 'binocular', i.e. they require processing by both eyes.

Eysenck and Keane (1995) highlight some of the main cues which are used in estimating depth. Monocular cues include:

❖ Activity 3 ❖

Look at Fig. 14.4 and see if you can determine what is depicted in the drawing.

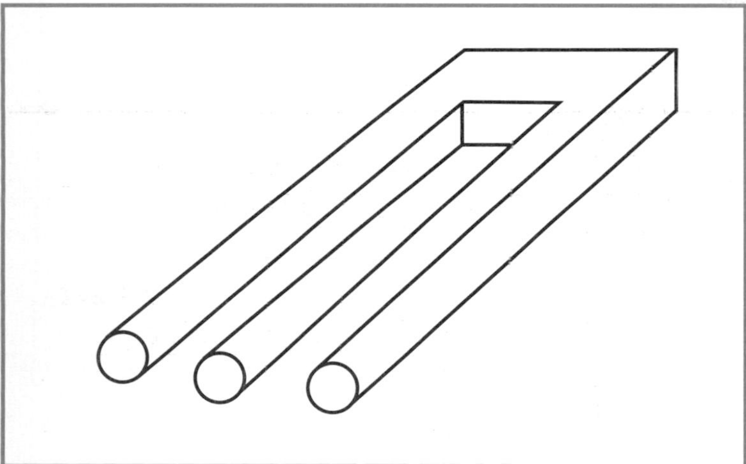

Figure 14.4 Illustration of an 'impossible' figure

- *Linear perspective:* parallel lines appear to come closer together as they recede into the distance.
- *Aerial perspective*: more distant objects are less well-defined than nearer objects.
- *Texture*: different surfaces reflect light in different ways, and changes in texture give indications of depth.
- *Interposition*: Nearer objects hide parts of objects further away, and give cues about relative distance.
- *Shading*: three-dimension objects cast shadows and the presence of shading gives impressions of depth.
- *Familiar size*: people can use stored knowledge about the normal size of objects to estimate the distance between themselves and those objects.
- *Motion parallax*: objects at different distances create differential changes in the retinal image *as they move* relative to the observer – closer objects create larger changes in the retinal image than objects further away. This results in objects which are further away seeming to move more slowly than objects which are closer.

Eysenck and Keane also highlight three important binocular cues to depth used by the visual system. These are:

- *Convergence:* refers to the way the eyes need to turn inwards to a greater extent to focus on closer objects compared with those further away.
- *Accommodation:* refers to the way the lenses of the eyes change shape when we are focusing on objects at different distances. For near objects, the lenses thicken; for distant objects, they flatten.
- *Stereopsis:* the retinal images of the two eyes show some disparity, giving further indications of depth.

The visual system needs to combine and integrate the different depth cues to facilitate three-dimensional perception. Bruno and Cutting (1988) highlight three possible processes which could be involved:

- *Additivity:* information from the different cues is simply added together.
- *Selection:* information from one cue takes priority over other cues.
- *Multiplication:* information from different cues interacts in a multiplicative way.

Bruno and Cutting give evidence to support the additivity theory, but the relative importance of the various cues to depth has been the subject of some debate. Marr (1982) made extensive use of stereopsis in his computer model of vision. Nevertheless, there is evidence that other factors are also important. Gregory (1973), using his 'hollow face illusion', showed that people can ignore stereoptic information. When shown a picture of a hollow mould of a face, people perceive it as a normally contoured face, indicating that expectations about human faces can override depth cues. Furthermore, other cues to depth come from movement.

Perception of movement

As we move around our environment, we need to avoid some moving objects and make contact with others. In order to interact safely with our environment, we need to perceive accurately the movement of the various objects around us. An indication of the importance of perceiving movement comes from the case study of a woman, LM, reported by Zihl *et al.* (1983). As a result of brain damage, LM had severely impaired perception of movement. As she walked along the street, she could

❖ Activity 4 ❖

Return to Fig. 14.1. If you had difficulty in detecting the object, the process in you which was affected was probably your ability to select the figure from the background. You should now consider what information was missing from the scene and how this interfered with your ability to select figure from ground.

see cars getting closer, but they were not moving in the conventional sense. It was as though a car was in one place at one time, and then suddenly in another place at another time. The simple act of pouring water into a teapot became extremely difficult, because she could not see the water level rising in the pot. However, most people are very good at perceiving movement. In fact, the processes involved in the perception of movement seem quite exceptional. The skill required to play ball games is evidence of this exceptional ability, and further insights come from studies of biological movement.

Most people can decide quickly whether other people are running or walking. Furthermore, evidence suggests that this ability is powerful enough to overcome dramatic reductions in visual input. Johansson (1975) conducted a study in which actors were dressed in black and had lights attached to their joints. They were then filmed whilst moving around in a darkened setting so that only the lights were visible. Johansson found that most observers could perceive the moving actors and describe accurately their posture and movements. Further research has shown that people can make extremely precise discriminations based on the limited information from such point-light displays. Using a similar methodology, Kowalowski and Cutting (1978) showed that most people could even identify the sex of the actors.

Johansson concluded that the perception of biological movement is an innate ability. However, the experience of apparent motion suggests this may be an oversimplification. Apparent motion is most clearly evident in television and films when we get the impression of continuous motion from a rapid series of still images. Braddick (1980) suggests that some aspects of apparent motion are dependent on higher level cognitive processes, which utilize expectations based on stored knowledge about the properties of particular objects. Clearly, some aspects of perception are innate and some are learned. Furthermore, some processes are dependent on expectations based on experience, and some are driven by the properties of the visual input.

Figure 14.5 Examples of the Gestalt laws of organisation

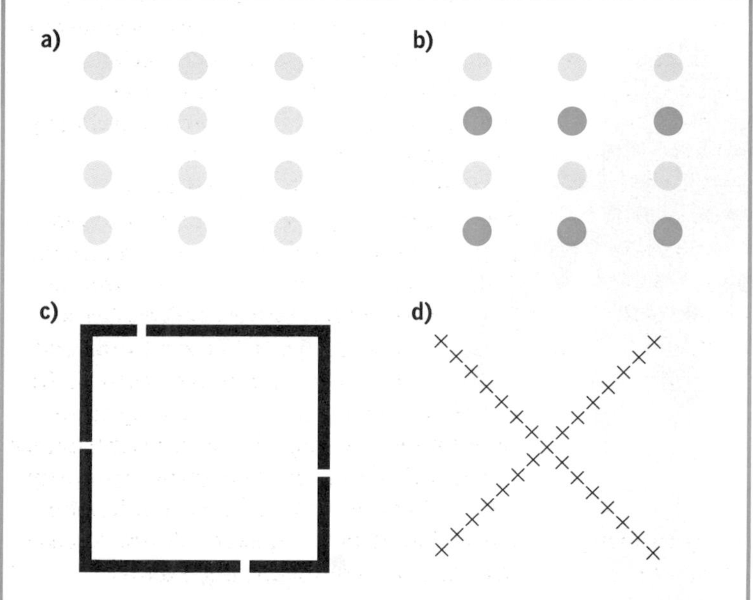

Gestalt studies of visual perception

The Gestalt approach is best known for its claim that the whole is greater than the sum of its component parts. Gestalt psychologists, such as Koffka and Kohler, argued that figures and objects are seen as organized structures, which have properties unique to the whole structure, known as 'emergent properties'. Using a series of demonstrations, they showed that things are not seen in terms of individual features, but in their holistic shape. They noted that every perception is organized into a figure and a background, and that holistic figures standing out from the background had well-

In Focus

The Gestalt laws of perceptual organization

Gestalt psychologists demonstrated a number of laws of organization. Some of these are illustrated in Figure 14.5.

- In (a), the dots are usually seen as three vertical columns, which demonstrates the *law of proximity* (items close together are grouped as part of the same perceptual whole).
- In (b), the dots now look like four horizontal rows, which demonstrates the *law of similarity* (similar items are grouped together). One interesting point to note is that the proximity between the dots is exactly the same in (a) and (b). This suggests that similarity might have a stronger effect than proximity. Gestalt psychologists never fully resolved issues such as this, and their lack of comprehensive explanations was one of the reasons which led to the demise of the approach.
- In (c), the shape is usually perceived as a square, despite the missing sections. This demonstrates the *law of closure* (we ignore missing information to give figures holistic shape).
- In (d), the shape is usually seen as two crossing lines, rather than two V-shapes, demonstrating the *law of continuity* (items which follow smoothly on from one another are grouped together).

The *law of common fate* also describes how things which move, or change, together are grouped together. Another principle is *transposition*, which describes how component elements, or features, of an object can change without the overall pattern, or shape, of an object changing. All the individual laws are component factors of the more general *Law of Pragnanz*, which is a tendency towards perceiving 'good shape'.

defined contours, depth and solidarity. Segregation of figure from ground was seen as one of the basic and innate characteristics of perception.

The main theme of Gestalt research was setting out laws of perceptual organization (see *In Focus* above). There are a number of problems for the Gestalt ideas. The most crucial is their failure to explain why certain things happen (as in the differential effects of proximity and similarity). Although the approach is descriptive rather than explanatory, the Gestalt laws have played a role in many subsequent theories of perception. Within the information-processing approach, psychologists (e.g. Pomerantz 1981) have tried to explain the operating principles which underpin the laws, and others (e.g. Marr 1982) have built them into their models.

Empirical investigations of Gestalt theories

Navon (1977) conducted a study showing that holistic, or global, structures are perceived more readily than their component parts (see *In Focus* on p. 310).

Navon's study showed that global configurations (holistic shapes) are processed more readily than their component parts (features). In other words, people primarily process the overall shape of objects rather than individual features. To use a more general analogy, people first detect the forest and are then able to identify individual trees, rather than identifying individual trees and building up to the recognition of the forest.

Pomerantz (1981) argues that this conclusion is too inflexible, since the relative precedence of global over feature processing depends on the viewing conditions and the nature of the task. Pomerantz describes a study in which subjects had to pick the odd feature out of a configuration of features. In one condition, he found that adding extra information as context improved performance and he called this the 'configural superiority effect'. However, in a second condition, he found that adding context could *also* impede performance. Pomerantz argued that

In Focus

Navon's (1977) study of 'global processing'

Navon devised configurations made up of *local elements* (features) which either matched, or mismatched, *global features* ('Hs' made up of 'Hs' or 'Ss'– see Fig. 14.6).

Navon gave participants a series of these configurations and asked them to detect the presence of particular letters. He showed that mismatches between the global shape and feature letters did not affect the participants' ability to detect the presence of the large letters, but it did affect their ability to detect the small letters.

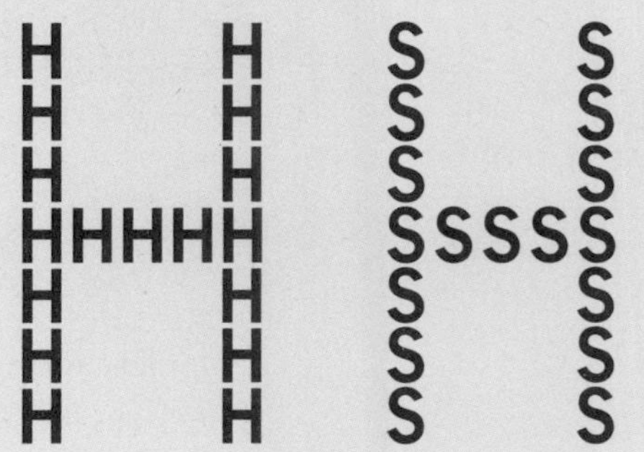

Figure 14.6
Illustration of Navon's (1977) stimuli

whether adding context facilitated or impeded performance depended on the type of configuration resulting from the addition of context. This fits with our intuitive experience of the world. Context can often aid our perception (as in Fig. 14.2), but occasionally it can impede perception (as in the case of camouflage). Therefore, global properties sometimes, but not always, take precedence over local details (features) in perceptual processing. Holistic *and* feature processing must frequently interact in perception.

Section summary

Demonstrations of visual processing show that visual perception is an active process involving the interpretation of sensory input. Early psychophysical and behaviourist research attempted to split the overall process of perception into perceptual units and to investigate those units. Evidence from neurological studies suggests the units of perception may be visual features. However, studies of perceptual constancy, and studies of the perception of shape and movement, indicate that this idea may be an oversimplification. Perceptual organization was investigated by Gestalt theorists, who emphasized holistic aspects of perception. However, this approach could not offer an adequate explanation of perception, and further theoretical development came through the application of the information-processing metaphor.

Theories of visual perception

Top-down and bottom-up processing

With the development of the information-processing approach, psychologists had the language to enable them to put forward more comprehensive explanations of perception. This type of approach focuses on the transmission of information through the information-processing system, and one important concept for perception is *direction* of information flow. Sensory information comes from the outside world and must be processed into the cognitive system. However, other information, derived from memory, originates *within* the cognitive system. Psychologists distinguish between top-down and bottom-up processing. Bottom-up, or data-driven, processing is concerned with physiological processing from the senses, processed upwards in the direction of the cognitive system. Theories emphasizing bottom-up processing focus on how perception is influenced by the properties of incoming sensory information. Top-down, or conceptually driven, processing is concerned with high-level processing, originating in the cognitive system, and being processed downwards in the direction of the senses. Theories emphasizing top-down processing focus on how perception is influenced by the properties of stored information (memory).

Constructivist and direct theories of visual perception

Constructivist theories

The constructivist approach emphasizes the role of constancy in perception. Ames (1952) used perceptual constancies to stress the active and adaptive character of perception in his theory of 'transactional functionalism'. He argued that perception involves a process of going beyond the information in the retina to construct a suitable representation of the world. He demonstrated this with his 'Ames Room' illusion (see Fig. 14.7).

In Fig. 14.7, the two people are actually the same size, but the depth cues give the impression that one of them is larger than the other. Perception involves a process of actively constructing the world, and this

> **❖ Activity 5 ❖**
>
> Go back to Figs 14.1 and 14.2 and reconsider the issues raised. One of the figures emphasizes issues concerning sensory input (bottom-up processing) and the other emphasizes issues concerning stored knowledge (top-down processing). an you work out which is which? (The answer is given at the end of the chapter.)

construction involves the use of inferences based on stored knowledge. This type of illusion supports the argument that people use non-conscious assumptions in perception, and such assumptions form part of their internal representations of the world.

One important model of representation is schema theory (see Chapter 15). Schemas are organized packages of knowledge about particular objects, activities and events in the world. Inferential processing is seen to rely heavily on the top-down, or conceptually driven, influence of schematic knowledge acquired through learning from repeated experiences of objects and events. In other words, we interpret incoming sensory information in terms of what we already

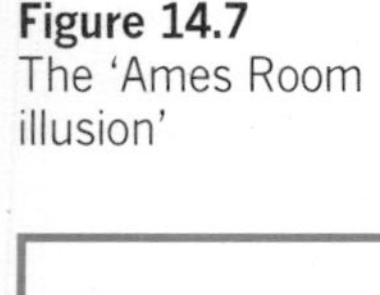

Figure 14.7
The 'Ames Room illusion'

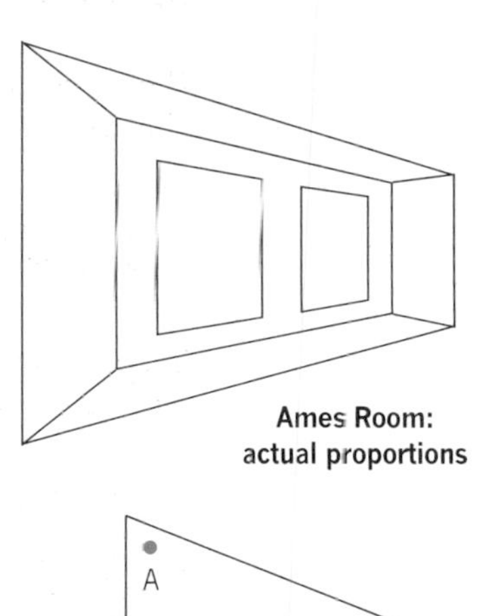

Ames Room: actual proportions

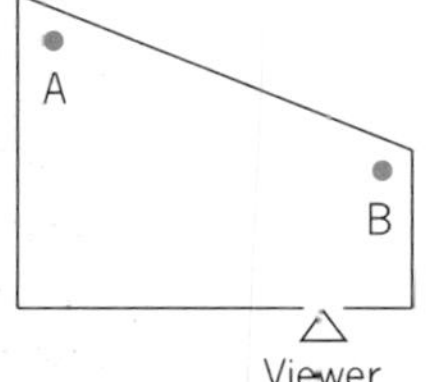

Ames Room: view from above
In position A, the girl appears much smaller than she does in position B. The distorted dimensions of the room conceal its depth.

know. However, these inferences can be incorrect (e.g. when distance cues are misleading, as in the Ames room studies).

Gregory (1972) emphasizes the fragmentary nature of visual information in the retinal image. The information in this image is often ambiguous and the visual system has to 'go beyond' the given information and fill in the gaps to resolve the ambiguity. Gregory makes extensive use of visual illusions in his research, and argues that perception is an active process of using stored schematic knowledge to suggest and test hypotheses. In other words, perceptions are internally constructed hypotheses, based on cues from sensory information, which are tested against sensory input. He argues that visual illusions reflect misplaced hypotheses.

Direct theories

The inferential, or constructivist, approach is not without its critics, most notably Gibson (1966). In his theory of direct perception, Gibson argues that the constructivists do not allow for the fact that the information in the retinal image is extremely elaborate and detailed. He argues that, when all the information in the retina is taken into account, many of the so-called problems of perception disappear, and there is no need to resort to explanations involving representations and stored knowledge.

Most image-processing approaches see the input to visual perception as a two-dimensional (2D) retinal image. Gibson, however, sees the input as being a complex pattern of light, which is constructed by the surfaces from which it has been reflected. Different surfaces reflect light in different ways (smooth surfaces reflect evenly, rough surfaces unevenly, and different objects reflect different colour frequencies). Gibson argues that all this information is captured in the pattern of light which reaches the perceiver's eye. He calls this the 'optic array' and it can be thought of as a number of tiny, cone-shaped beams, each coming to a point at the eye and each containing different mixtures of light wavelengths. According to Gibson, this provides invariant information about the world. It makes the layout of objects in space unambiguous, and this can be picked up 'directly' by the perceiver. Furthermore, there will also be systematic changes in the pattern of reflected light across the line of sight of the eyes, giving what Gibson calls a 'texture gradient' (see Fig. 14.8).

Figure 14.8 Illustration of a typical Gibsonian texture gradient

Figure 14.8 shows an example of a texture gradient which gives the impression of surfaces receding into the distance.

Gibson suggests that another important source of information is movement. As we move around the environment, the pattern of light reflected from surfaces will change and set up dynamic patterns in the optic array. Gibson calls this the 'optic flow'. He argues that this type of information gives people direct and unambiguous cues about their relationship to the environment. Consequently, he sees no need for processes to transform incoming information into intermediate representations, or to supplement it by drawing on stored knowledge. According to Gibson, therefore, there is no need to use information-processing explanations of perception.

Gibson's theory seems well suited to skilled tasks in which the perceiver must have precise information which needs to be translated immediately into some action (e.g. playing some sports). However, it has difficulty in accounting for visual illusions (particularly, naturally occurring illusions, such as the illusion of water on the road during a hot day). Gibson's only defence against this criticism is that illusions are unfair tests of perception. His approach is better thought of as complementary to other approaches, rather than as a replacement, and his most useful contribution has been to highlight the fact that input to the visual system is much richer than was traditionally assumed. His influence can be seen in the work of later researchers, such as Marr (1982), who used Gibson's ideas while retaining many of the assumptions of the information-processing viewpoint.

Interactive theories of visual perception

Constructivist or direct?

In some ways Gibson's ideas contradict the constructivist ideas and he used the term 'direct perception' to emphasize the difference between his theory and the constructivist approach. However, many of the differences between the two approaches are accentuated by philosophical differences and semantic usage. It is interesting to note that Gregory sees many perceptual hypotheses occurring non-consciously, and being applied 'directly' to perceptual input. This is not very different from Gibson's ideas concerning the direct use of perceptual features. The main difference between the two approaches is their differential emphasis on direction of information flow. Direct theorists emphasize bottom-up processing, whereas constructivists emphasize top-down processing.

Few contemporary theorists would support either extreme viewpoint. Visual perception clearly involves a combination of both types of processing. Modern theorists try to assess the relative degree to which both types of processing are involved in particular perceptual activities. One major problem with purely top-down approaches is that they are not very precise about how conceptual information interacts with sensory input. A further related problem is that they say little about the issue of how knowledge is represented in the cognitive system. A major problem with purely bottom-up approaches is that sensory input, on its own, is frequently insufficient to elicit appropriate interpretations. A further problem is that, even when there may be sufficient information, there would need to be an exhaustive search of stored representations before any interpretation could be made. It does not make sense to assume that we have to work through all our knowledge before we can recognize something and so we must somehow use processes which *restrict* the search area.

Neisser's cyclic model of perception

One model which tries to reconcile the direct and constructivist approaches is Neisser's (1967) cyclic model of perception. Neisser proposes mechanisms which restrict conceptual search to areas in which likely interpretations of sensory input might be found. He argues that perception involves what he calls 'analysis by synthesis'. In Neisser's perceptual cycle, perception is initiated by sensory input which gives the perceiver an impression of the world. Attentional mechanisms are activated which determine what sensory information is focused upon, and consequently what is interpreted. In the model, perception is seen as an active and cyclic process and Neisser proposes the following processes:

- *Sampling*: Automatic processes operate to produce a preliminary representation of the sensory input (bottom-up processing). These are guided by the organizational properties of the stimulus (figure/ground, proximity, closure, similarity, and so on), and this is done pre-attentively.
- *Directing*: if the preliminary representation signifies some significant stimulus, attention is directed towards it, and in conjunction with contextual information, is used to guide the construction of a perceptual hypothesis (top-down processing). At this stage, the perceiver constructs, or synthesizes, an intermediate representation and compares this with the preliminary representation constructed from the sensory input (interaction of top-down and bottom-up processing).
- *Modifying*: if there is a match, the constructed intermediate representation is accepted, and used as a basis for

updating stored knowledge. If there is a mismatch, alternative intermediate representations are constructed and tested until a match is finally accepted.

Neisser's model successfully manages to:

- account for the extraction of holistic properties and features
- incorporate Gestalt principles
- account for the processing of sensory, contextual and conceptual information
- incorporate automatic, constructivist and conscious processes.

However, there are problems in that the model is not stated in sufficiently explicit terms. It is not clear in what form representations are stored or how stored knowledge interacts with sensory input. Neisser's model accounts for many of the functions of perception, but lacks a detailed specification of the processes which underpin these functions. Marr (1982) argues that a full explanation of visual perception needs at least three different levels of explanation:

- the 'hardware level', which specifies biological processes that are not open to consciousness and is concerned with the mechanisms of vision (i.e. relates to the neurology of the brain).
- the 'algorithmic level', which specifies the processes and representations involved in perception and is concerned with how a visual task can be implemented (i.e. relates to traditional issues in psychology).
- the 'computational level', which specifies the functions of perception and is concerned with the task analysis (i.e. what the system is doing, what information it needs and why).

Marr suggests that the computational level is the most important. According to Marr, if you cannot specify precisely the functions of perception, you will never explain its processes. A great deal of information about visual perception has been gleaned from experimental investigations, and further insights into the role of the different types of processing involved in perception have been gained from computer simulation of visual processing.

Computer models of visual perception

Computer simulation

Cognitive psychologists are interested in the knowledge representations and processes involved in cognition. One way of investigating processing is through controlled scientific experiments. A complementary approach is to develop artificial intelligence (AI) computer programs which simulate the knowledge and processes of human information-processing (see Chapter 13). All computer models of cognition start from the assumption that computers have no knowledge. The researcher has to provide all the information (knowledge) for the database and precise programming instructions (processes) to make it work. Greene (1986) argues that computer models have three main advantages for psychologists:

- Cognitive processes have to be stated explicitly, forcing psychologists to be clear in their theorizing.
- The act of working out exactly what information and rules are required to make a program function, in itself, can reveal a lot about the knowledge and processes involved in human information-processing.
- Running a program is a good test of whether or not a model of cognition can actually work.

Early computer models

Computer simulation has contributed much to our understanding of visual perception and researchers have tried to simulate visual functions (segregating a figure from the background). The human visual system is capable of a wide range of functions, and one strategy is to try to design a comprehensive model of perception which models the whole system (Marr 1982). An alternative approach is to investigate specific visual functions. Early work often confined itself to the problem of specifying the knowledge and processes required in object recognition. Programs were designed to analyse scenes, e.g. to identify the presence of individual blocks within a heap of block-shaped objects. In line with major theoretical thinking at the time, these programs tending to emphasize either top-down (constructivist) or bottom-up (direct) processing.

Roberts' (1965) program analysed photographs of different blocks. It looked for evidence of the presence of particular blocks by using top-down processing of stored knowledge to influence the bottom-up processing of visual features. The program worked through a sequence of stages. In the first stage, the program identified edges and surface boundaries (visual cues). In the next stage, stored knowledge (known as prototypes) was used to hypothesize about which figures were being indicated by the visual cues. The program then selected a prototype and compared it with the visual cues. If a match was made, the hypothesis was accepted, if not, alternative cues were selected and other prototypes considered until a match was found. In its limited domain, the program worked quite well. It selected figure from ground and perceived a 2D input as a 3D scene. However, it relied heavily on top-down processing, and the images it produced were often poor because the top-down knowledge it utilized was poor.

Guzman's (1969) SEE program also dealt with attempts to discover how many blocks were present in a scene comprising jumbled blocks. However, Guzman's program relied more heavily on bottom-up processing, i.e. it tried to identify objects by analysing the details of the input data. However, this bottom-up knowledge was of poor quality. Attempts to improve it resulted in programs providing too many alternatives from which to make a decision. Later modifications led to an increasing dependence on stored (top-down) information.

Marr's model

Marr (1982) argues that, if perception has different functions in different organisms, the first thing that needs to be asked of a visual system is what its functions or purposes are. He calls this the *task analysis*, and suggests that computer programs which simulate human vision must roughly correspond with its functions. Marr's approach to perception built on the work of early AI researchers, but he also takes account of a number of other important empirical and theoretical ideas. He argues that computer vision is much more difficult than earlier theorists had appreciated and needs to use much richer visual cues. In early models, processing was controlled by hypotheses (top-down knowledge), but Marr's model only needs to resort to top-down processing in ambiguous situations. Central to Marr's model is the notion of *representation*. He suggests that perception involves a variety of sub-systems, all working independently, and whose combined outputs give some sort of final representation.

Marr sees the main function of vision as representing 3D shape, and the visual problem as the extraction of useful information from an input image of a scene. He sees vision as requiring the processing of a sequence of representations, with each representation being derived from previous ones using an appropriate set of processes. He argues that this sequence of operations can be grouped under three headings, according to the descriptions, or representations, dealt with (see Fig. 14.9).

In this model, information is passed through three stages of processing, with the output of one stage being the input of the next stage, and each dealing with a particular form of representation.

- The *first stage* deals with *image representations*. Information from the retina is made more explicit to form a representation which Marr calls the *primal sketch*. The program forms this representation by analysing the geometrical distribution, and organization, of intensity changes in the retinal image. The intensity levels at each point (pixel) in the image are determined, and blobs, lines, edges, terminations, groupings, etc., are identified. This can be seen to be analogous to modelling the Gestalt laws of organization.

- The *second stage* deals with *scene-surface representations*. It is concerned with making the orientation and surfaces of the image more explicit to form a representation which Marr calls the *2.5D sketch*. It makes use of information such as contours, shading, texture, stereoptic and movement information. This is also seen to be the final stage of early bottom-up processing. This stage then acts as a buffer store, in which partial visual solutions (representations) can be stored while other processing proceeds.
- The *final stage* deals with *volume representations*. It is concerned with making shape, and spatial organization in the image more explicit to form a final representation which Marr calls the *3D model*. Here, stored representations are accessed to facilitate recognition. Once an initial match is made, conceptually driven (top-down) information is used to refine the analysis of the image. The 3D shape representations are evaluated using top-down knowledge, and if criteria are met, the representation is accepted and recognition occurs.

In Marr's model, each representation is delivered by a specific vision module, and each module is specified in terms of its input representation (the starting information), its output representation (the derived representation which acts as the input to the next module), and the solution to one or more visual problems (a description of the processes which form the output representation from the input representation). Marr's work emphasizes bottom-up processing, but not at the expense of top-down processing. Stored knowledge is used in the final stage of the model, the formation of the 3D model. However, Marr's model cannot be seen as a complete model of perception. It does not overcome the fundamental problem in this area which is explaining exactly how top-down and bottom-up processes interact to facilitate perception. This issue may never be fully resolved until we have a more comprehensive understanding of the way knowledge is represented in the cognitive system.

Figure 14.9 Summary of Marr's (1982) model of vision

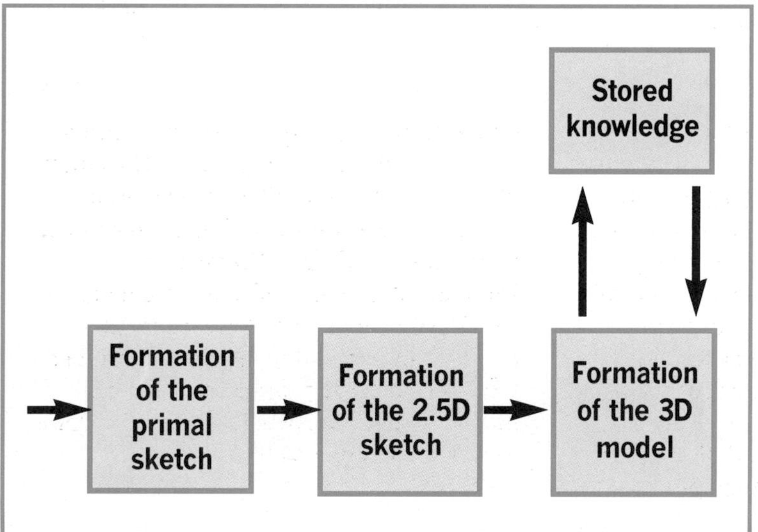

Section summary

The information-processing approach led to the development of two general explanations of visual perception, known as constructivist and direct theories. Constructivist theories emphasize top-down processing and the role of stored knowledge in maintaining perceptual constancy from fragmentary sensory input. Direct theories emphasize the role of bottom-up processing and the richness of sensory information. Neither theory offers a complete explanation of perception, and theorists have developed models which combine both processes.

Experimental work has enhanced our understanding of the processes involved in visual perception, and this has been further supplemented by knowledge gained from computer models of vision. To date, we have not developed a complete model of perception and a more comprehensive explanation may require a better understanding of how knowledge is represented in the cognitive system.

Social and developmental aspects of perception

Social and cultural variations in perception

Lack of visual experience

The evidence discussed in previous sections suggests that incoming sensory information is actively interpreted in terms of stored information. This implies that, if our stored knowledge is relatively sparse, perceptual interpretation might prove difficult. Nowhere should this be more apparent than in situations where perceptual processing undergoes a fundamental change, as in people who have been blind since birth but later have had their sight restored. Gregory and Wallace (1963) describe the experience of a patient known as SB (see *In Focus* below).

There are processes of perception which are present at birth, but the study of SB indicates that innate aspects of perception must be mediated by perceptual experience, and evidence of this should be found in cross-cultural studies of perception. Different cultural experience should lead to different perceptual interpretations.

Cross-cultural studies

Cross-cultural studies of visual perception have focused on testing different cultural groups using similar materials. They have often used visual illusions, and, in particular, variations of illusions demonstrating interpretations of line lengths (see Fig. 14.10).

Figure 14.10 illustrates a number of line illusions in which people appear to use configural features to make erroneous judgements about the length of lines. In (a), known as the Müller-Lyer illusion, the line with the outgoing arrow-fins is seen as longer, but the lines are actually of the same length. In (b), the vertical line is seen as longer, but both lines are the same length. In (c), known as the Ponzo illusion, the central lines are seen as progressively shorter as you move down the figure, but they are all in fact the same length. Typically, these illustrations have been taken to indicate people's non-conscious use of depth cues. However, in (d) there are no depth cues, but the line in the 'dumbbells' is seen as longer than the line in the 'spectacles', whereas they are in fact the same length. It seems that many factors might contribute to the experience of an illusion.

A number of early cross-cultural studies of European and various other cultures indicated there were cultural differences in susceptibility to perceptual line illusions. This suggests that physical environment might be a factor in people's susceptibility to visual illusions. Segall *et al.* (1963) spent a number of years studying people from various cultural settings, including native

In Focus

Gregory and Wallace's (1963) case study of SB

SB had been blind since birth but had his sight restored by an operation in his early fifties. After his operation, he could recognize objects and linguistic stimuli as long as he had previously experienced them by touch (e.g. capital letters learned from Braille, but not lower case letters). However, it soon became clear that SB was behaving like a newborn baby when it came to recognizing objects by sight alone. For example, he could not understand why he could not reach through a top-storey window and touch the ground. The study of SB suggests that not all processes in perception are innate and some need to be learned. According to Gregory and Wallace, SB had passed the critical age for developing some of the basic processes involved in perception and had developed a reliance on tactile processing which interfered with the development of normal visual processing mechanisms.

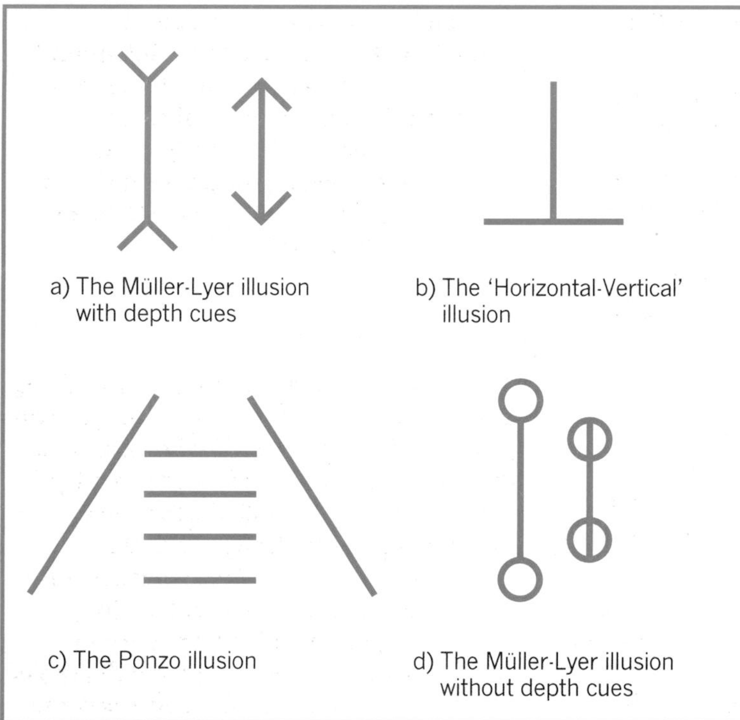

Figure 14.10 Examples of line illusions

Africans, white Africans, Americans and Filipinos and discovered a number of cultural differences in susceptibility to line illusions. For example, African tribes who lived in open country giving long lines of vision were more likely to be fooled by the illusions than tribes who lived in a jungle environment giving short lines of vision. This suggests that the environment is linked to, and may determine, our perceptual abilities.

Segall *et al.* also found support for their argument when they compared various cultures living in either rural or urban environments. Rural African Zulus were less likely to be fooled by angular illusions than urban Europeans and rural Tongan children were less likely to be fooled by the Ames Room illusion than European children. Segall *et al.* attempted to explain these cultural and social differences by proposing their 'carpentered world hypothesis'. They suggested that past experience is central to perceptual ability and this is determined by our physical environment. In Western cultures the physical environment is mainly artificial and uses more straight lines and angles than the natural world. Consequently, as a result of our past cultural experience, we constantly use this information to interpret perceptual input in terms of depth (turn back to Fig. 14.4). There is further support for this idea from cross-cultural studies of size constancy. Turnbull (1961) investigated size constancy in African pygmies who lived in a dense rainforest environment. Turnbull removed some of the pygmies from their natural environment and took them to a plains environment. They were asked about buffalo grazing at a distance and they suggested to Turnbull that the buffalo were 'insects'. Turnbull argued that the pygmies had no experience of viewing objects from a distance and interpreted the buffalo as small animals because of the small retinal image they generated.

This environmentally deterministic view has its critics and a number of studies have provided contrary evidence. In studies using line illusions, Jahoda (1966), with Ghanaians, and Gregor and McPherson (1965) with Australian Aborigines, found no support for the 'carpentered world hypothesis'. Furthermore, as with Gestalt studies, research using visual illusions relies on introspective reports which are susceptible to bias in terms of the relationship between thought and language (see Chapter 16). One of the main cultural differences between people is the language they use. Nevertheless, these studies have indicated that, although there are biological influences, *some* aspects of perception are influenced by the environment.

Perceptual development

Infant visual perception

At birth, human infants are totally dependent on their caregivers. The infant has the basic 'hardware' of vision, but needs to 'fine-tune' it through experience to allow perception to occur. Exactly what proportion of perceptual ability is present at birth and what needs to be learned through experience has been the subject of some debate in psychology. This area is one in which the 'nature–nurture' debate has been most evident. Infant perception is more difficult to study than adult perception for two reasons:

- The infant has not got the language to describe its perceptual experience.
- Visual acuity (clarity of vision) is only about 5 per cent of that of adults.

Given these factors, alternative methods of study to those used with adults are required when looking at infant perception.

Methods of studying infant perception

Infant behavioural responses are quite limited. However, a number of different techniques have been used to study infant perception. These include:

- *Visual evoked potentials (VEP)*: electrodes are attached to the scalp and changes of electrical activity in the brain are measured. If presenting different stimuli results in different patterns of electrical activity, it can be assumed the infant can discriminate between the stimuli.
- *Optokinetic nystagmus (OKN)*: the tracking response that occurs when a moving stimulus is shown to the infant is monitored. If an infant can track a stimulus, it can differentiate that stimulus from its background.
- *Sucking rate*: a dummy with a sensor records the rate at which sucking occurs. If a stimulus causes the sucking rate to increase, it can be assumed that the infant can detect the stimulus.
- *Heart and breathing rate*: changes are measured as stimuli are presented to the infant. A change in either rate when different stimuli are presented indicates the infant can discriminate between the stimuli.
- *Spontaneous visual preference (SVP)*: the amount of time the infant spends 'looking' at different stimuli is measured. If an infant prefers to spend more time looking at one stimuli rather than another, this indicates that the infant can discriminate between the two stimuli. A variation on SVP is the 'habituation' technique in which a stimulus is continually presented to the infant until it ceases to attract its attention. A new, but similar, stimulus can then be presented and, if this results in an increase in looking time, the infant can be assumed to be able to discriminate between the two stimuli.

Early visual preference

The most widely used technique in studying infant perception is SVP. The technique was pioneered by Fantz (1961) who discovered that infants prefer to look at patterned, as opposed to plain, stimuli. Furthermore, increasing the complexity of stimuli increases looking time. This tendency has been used in measuring infant acuity. Infants are presented with a pattern of stripes on a grey background and the size of the stripes is varied. As the stripes become narrower, the infant has more difficulty in detecting them until he or she cannot discriminate the stripes from the background. The point at which the infant ceases to discriminate the stripes indicates the level of acuity. Other research (e.g. Fantz *et al.* 1975) has indicated that infants prefer to look at moving, three-dimensional and curved patterns. Fantz (1961) also showed that infants preferred to look at face-like stimuli (see Fig. 14.11).

Figure 14.11 shows that infants preferred patterned ((a) and (b)) to non-patterned stimuli, and a face-like stimulus to a 'scrambled' face-like stimulus. This led Fantz to suggest that infants have an innate propensity for face recognition and added further fuel to the nature–nurture debate.

Direct (nature) theories of infant perception

Many studies in infant perception (e.g. Fantz 1961) indicate that aspects of perception, such as face recognition, are present at birth. Furthermore, some researchers have made stronger claims by suggesting that basic cognitive processes, such as depth perception, are innate. These ideas link to

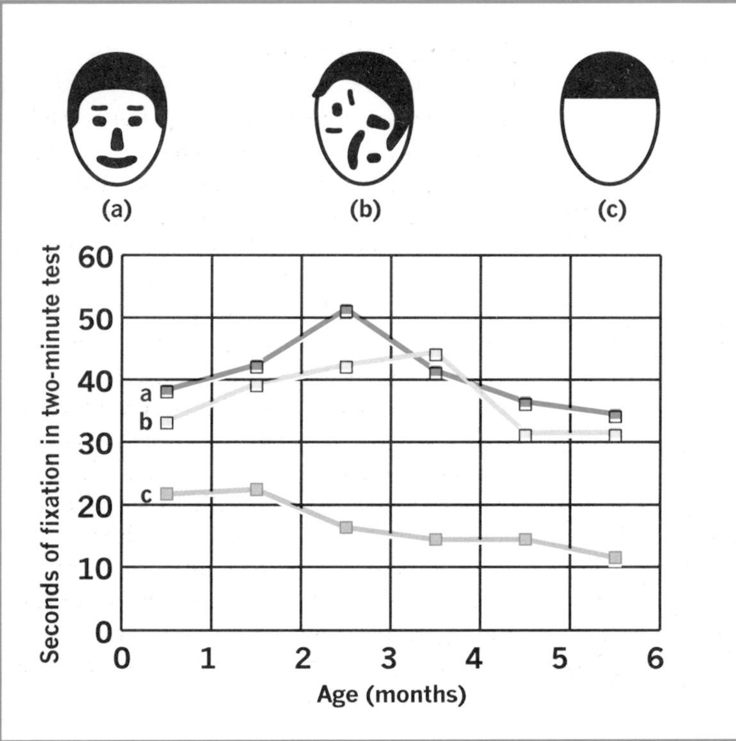

Figure 14.11
Looking time for Fantz's (1961) face stimuli
Source: Scientific American

J.J. Gibson's (1966) theory concerning direct vision. Gibson sees no need for the use of stored knowledge in perception. Experience, therefore, would have no role to play. This idea was supported in a study by E.J. Gibson and Walk (1960) (see *In Focus*).

Gibson and Walk took the findings of their 'visual cliff' study as support for the view that depth perception is an innate ability. However, the children used in the study were at least 6 months of age and so aspects of the ability may have been learned. Nevertheless, innate aspects of infant perception are also supported by the studies of Bower (1966). Bower trained infants (2 months' old) to turn their heads at the sight of a particular shape using operant conditioning techniques. He found that conditioned responses still occurred when the object was presented at different orientations and concluded that shape constancy was present at birth. This finding was supported in a study by Slater and Morison (1985), using SVP with 2-day-old babies. Some aspects of perception, therefore, are clearly present at birth or develop very quickly.

Constructivist (nurture) theories of infant perception

Despite the evidence to support innate aspects of perception, other psychologists emphasized the learned aspects and how knowledge develops within the child. Most notable of these was Piaget (1954). Piagetian theory is covered in more depth in Chapter 18, but some aspects of his theory are important in infant perception. Piaget believed that, throughout development, cognitive structures are being adjusted as a result of environmental experience. According to Piaget, these structures are not innate, but are generated from ongoing activity. In the early 'sensori-motor' stages, infants are seen to develop basic 'action schemas' and this primitive knowledge base is elaborated at later stages. His theory gives central importance to the role of action in perceptual development, and puts infants at the centre of their own development. As with evidence from cross-cultural studies, this supports a 'nurture' view of perceptual development, i.e. our perceptual abilities are influenced by aspects of the environment in which they develop.

In Focus

E.J. Gibson and Walk's (1960) 'visual cliff' experiment

Gibson and Walk constructed a glass-topped table with two halves. One half of the table had glass covering a checkerboard design immediately beneath the glass, and the other half had the same design four feet below the glass. The depth cues from the apparatus give the impression of a 'drop' on one side of the table. Gibson and Walk placed a number of babies on the table and the mothers of the babies encouraged them to crawl across the table top over the 'drop' (see Fig. 14.12).

Gibson and Walk discovered that, although it was perfectly safe to do so, most of the infants refused to cross over the 'visual cliff' despite encouragement from their mothers.

Figure 14.12 Gibson and Walk's (1960) 'visual cliff' study

Section summary

Studies of lack of perceptual experience and cross-cultural studies of perception indicate that many aspects of perceptual processing need to be learned. Furthermore, some theorists in the area of infant perception also emphasize learning. However, others emphasize the role of innate perceptual abilities and evidence suggests that some types of visual organization (e.g. shape constancy) are present at birth. Nevertheless, these basic perceptual abilities need to be refined through experience. As with the debate concerning the relative roles of top-down and bottom-up processing, the best conclusion to date in the nature–nurture debate is that both innate and learnt factors affect perceptual development and the relative degree to which each is involved has yet to be clarified fully.

Chapter summary

- Early approaches to perception emphasized perceptual *units*, but studies of perceptual organization indicate that *holistic factors* are influential in perceptual processing.
- Theories of perception, such as constructivist and direct, have emphasized direction of information flow in perceptual processing. However, none of top-down, bottom-up or interactive models can explain the interaction between sensory input and stored knowledge. Further insights into perceptual processing have been gained from computer modelling.
- Studies of social and cultural differences in perception and studies of perceptual development have been examined within the context of the nature–nurture debate. Both innate and learned factors affect our perceptual development.

Answers to activities

Activity 1

The object in Fig. 14.1 is a cow, its face taking up most of the left half of the diagram.

Activity 5

- Figure 14.1 emphasizes the need for adequate sensory input (bottom-up processing).
- Figure 14.2 demonstrates how stored knowledge about context influences perception (top-down processing).

Essay titles

1. Compare constructivist and direct theories of visual perception. *(24 marks)*
2. Evaluate the role of perceptual organization in visual perception. *(24 marks)*
3. Evaluate the relative importance of innate and learned factors in visual perception. *(24 marks)*

Further reading

Eysenck, M.W. and Keane, M.T. (1995) *Cognitive Psychology: A Student's Handbook* (3nd edn), Hove: Lawrence Erlbaum Associates.

This provides a detailed coverage of perception, but is intended as a book for undergraduate students.

Roth, I.A. and Bruce, V. (1995) *Perception and Representation: Current Approaches* (2nd edn), Buckingham: Open University Press.

Gives a detailed coverage of perception in student-friendly language.

Gregory, R.L. (1972) *Eye and Brain* (2nd edn), London: Wiedenfield and Nicholson.

Theoretically quite dated, but gives wonderful examples of illusions and descriptive aspects of visual perception.

Eysenck, M.W. (1993) *Principles of Cognitive Psychology*, Hove: Lawrence Erlbaum Associates.

Chapter 2 of this book provides an easy-to-read account of perception.

Chapter 15

Memory

Peter Hayes

Preview

In this chapter we shall look at:

- the structural model of memory
- the working memory model
- organization in long-term memory
- practical aspects of memory
- theories of forgetting.

Introduction

In this chapter we shall review the research which has investigated people's ability to retain information. We will begin by evaluating structural models of memory. We will then consider the working memory model of short-term memory and the organization of knowledge in long-term memory, concluding by considering research into memory in everyday life, and forgetting.

Memory processes

Memory is involved in all aspects of our lives and, although it is difficult to get a precise definition of memory, it can be thought of as the ability to retain information and demonstrate retention through behaviour. Memory has three important functions:

- making sense of who you are
- making sense of the current situation
- making plans for the future.

Psychologists are interested in the structures and processes of memory. The structures comprise the various subsystems of memory, and processes are the different activities occurring both within and between those subsystems. A number of factors influence memory. We remember

Activity 1

Make a list of all the activities which require memory in the period between your getting up and leaving for school, college or work. Now try to make a list of any activities you can undertake without using memory. These tasks should emphasize the centrality of memory in our lives.

information if it is distinctive (different from other memories), elaborate (rich in detail), connected (integrated with other knowledge) or salient (personally important). Memory has three basic processes:

- *Encoding*: the acquisition of knowledge and creation of an internal representation to be stored.
- *Storage*: the retention and integration of this internal representation within the organization of existing knowledge.
- *Retrieval*: the re-accessing, or reconstructing, of an internal representation for some behavioural activity through *recognition* or *recall*. Recognition involves a direct match between an item of sensory information and an item of stored knowledge. Recall involves bringing a stored representation to consciousness for use in a behavioural activity.

If any of these processes break down, the result is failure to remember, or forgetting.

❖ Activity 2 ❖

Look at a family photograph album and find a photograph of a family member whom you know. Immediately you see the person you will probably recognize who it is. Now try to remember as much as you can about the person. To do this you need *to generate* information, which involves the more active process of recall.

The structural model of memory

Memory stores

This structural approach treats memories as 'memory traces', with specific locations, or stores, in the cognitive system. Encoding involves placing the trace in a store, and retrieval involves relocating the trace. Memory stores deal with different types of information, for different lengths of time, and researchers differentiate between sensory, short-term and long-term stores. Early approaches to memory investigated the memory stores and their capacity for retention of material.

Sensory memory (SM)

Our perceptual systems are bombarded with enormous amounts of information and our limited-capacity attentional processes are selective in dealing with incoming information. Some items are selected for further processing (sensory registration). Most sensory-memory traces fade away quickly, but some are maintained for a short length of time in a sensory buffer store. Visual information is retained in iconic and auditory information in echoic SM. Sperling (1960) tested iconic memory by presenting participants with arrays of letters for short periods of time (50 milliseconds). He found that people could retain about four items for up to a second in iconic memory. Similarly, Triesman (1964), using shadowing techniques, showed that information fades from echoic memory in about two seconds without additional processing. (See Chapter 13 for an account of the shadowing technique.)

Short-term memory (STM)

Psychologists distinguish between information retained in consciousness after perception and information which has faded from consciousness. The former represents the contents of short-term and the latter long-term memory. Support for this idea comes from studies of brain-damaged people (Baddeley and Warrington 1970). Patients suffering from Korsakoff's syndrome (amnesia caused by alcohol abuse) show immediate retention of information to be intact, but have an impaired ability to remember information from the past. STM has an extremely limited capacity and is prone to distraction or displacement of information. Miller (1956) suggests the capacity of STM

❖ Activity 3 ❖

Quickly read through this list of numbers once. On completion, cover them up and write them down in the same order.

3 7 2 8 6 5 1 4 9

The number you have correctly recalled, in the right order, is a rough measure of your immediate memory span.

Now, quickly read through this next list of numbers once. On completion, cover them up, count backwards from ten, and then write them down.

1 5 6 9 2 4 8 3 7

This task is more difficult and demonstrates the fragility of storage in STM.

is seven, plus or minus two items. He called this the 'magic number seven'.

Brown (1958) and Peterson and Peterson (1959) both investigated the capacity of STM using a similar methodology, now known as the Brown-Peterson technique. The technique involves presenting participants with trigrams, which are nonsense syllables consisting of three letters, such as GHT, BAV, for a short time (3 seconds) and testing recall after a delay of between 0 and 20 seconds. However, during this retention interval participants have to count backwards, which prevents them rehearsing the trigrams. Typical results of Brown-Peterson experiments show rapid forgetting over a short interval and after 18 seconds, only a small amount of information (approximately 10 per cent) is retained. Peterson and Peterson argued that the results could be explained in terms of the *decay* of the STM trace (counting backwards prevented rehearsal and allowed the memory trace to fade). However, Reitman (1974) points out that findings can be explained in terms of displacement (items in STM were displaced by new information). Therefore, we can conclude that STM stores hold approximately seven items of information for a brief length of time (less than 30 seconds) unless maintained by attentional processes. Information will decay, or can be displaced by other information, unless rehearsed and passed on to long-term memory (LTM).

Long-term memory (LTM)

Once information reaches LTM, it is relatively stable. LTM is thought of as having an essentially unlimited capacity and can hold information for very long periods of time. Forgetting occurs with decay through lack of activation of information or through interference from other memories. The culmination of this early work can be seen in the Atkinson and Shiffrin (1968) modal model of memory (see Fig. 15.1).

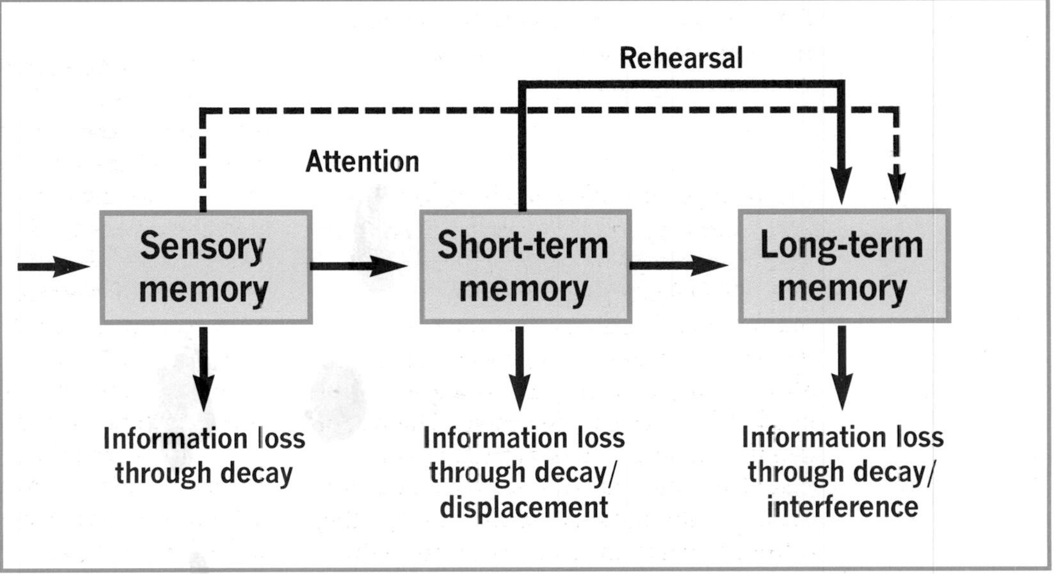

Figure 15.1 Summary of the Atkinson and Shiffrin (1968) modal model of memory

In Focus

◆

Shallice and Warrington's (1970) case study of KF

KF was a man in his twenties who had a motor-cycle accident. As a result of this, he suffered damage to the left parieto-occipital region of his brain. This left him with an impaired STM digit span. On some occasions he could recall two items, but often only one. However, he showed normal long-term learning and a normal LTM for information since his accident. Given that everything which gets to LTM has to go through a unitary short-term store, this evidence creates problems for the modal model. If the STM is damaged, you would expect people to have difficulty in getting information into LTM. However, KF showed that this is not always the case. Either there are different routes through STM or it is too complicated to be represented by a single unitary store.

In this model, the stores are modality specific (iconic and echoic SM stores). Information enters sensory memory where most will decay, but a small amount is passed on to STM, which deals with a limited amount of information for a short length of time using attentional processes. These processes are subject to interference, but, through other processes such as rehearsal, some information eventually reaches LTM. Once in LTM, information is durable and long-lasting, although it can fade or be affected by information from other memories.

An evaluation of the structural model

There are a number of problems for this model. One problem came to light in Shallice and Warrington's (1970) case study of the patient KF (see *In Focus* above).

A further problem for the modal model is its passive view of memory, and theorists have emphasized the active processing involved in recall. Contemporary researchers suggest that STM is better understood by considering capacity as limited by processing (allocation of attention) rather than structural constraints (amount of space available). However, Eysenck and Keane (1995) point out that the model has served an important function by providing a systematic account of the structures and processes of memory. It still makes sense to differentiate between the memory stores, each of which has a different capacity, duration and forgetting mechanism. Furthermore, each is affected differently by different types of brain damage. Many theorists have used the modal model as the basis for their theorizing.

Section summary

Early approaches to memory looked at the capacity and durability of hypothetical memory stores. Researchers investigated the capacity of sensory, short-term and long-term memory stores, and this led to the development of the structural model of memory. Problems for this model have since been identified and many researchers have now moved away from this passive view to investigate the more *active* processes involved in memory. However, the model has served an important function in providing the basis for current models of memory.

The working memory model

Baddeley and Hitch (1974) argued that structural approaches were inadequate in explaining the diversity of processing involved in STM. The working memory model emphasizes *active* processing, and the unitary STM store of the modal model is replaced with a system containing a number of separate processors. In the original working memory model, there were three components:

- a *central executive*
- a *visuo-spatial scratchpad* (dealing with visual material)
- an *articulatory-loop* (dealing with verbal material).

As a result of subsequent research, a further component, the *primary acoustic store*, was added (see Fig. 15.2).

The central executive is at the top of the hierarchical system and has the function of allocating processing resources to the other components. Each component has a specialized function and deals with a different type of information-coding (representation):

- The central executive is involved in all tasks requiring attention. It has a limited capacity and can store information briefly. It processes information from any sensory modality, with any type of coding, and can allocate processing resources to any of the other components.
- The visuo-spatial scratchpad deals with visual and/or spatial material, and information is represented as visual features such as size, shape and colour (a sort of inner eye).
- The articulatory-loop is a verbal rehearsal component used to hold the words we are preparing to speak out loud. It organizes verbal material in a serial and temporal fashion and deals with the articulation of this material. Information is represented as it would be spoken (a sort of inner voice).
- The primary acoustic store deals with auditory information. It links with the articulatory-loop and auditory information can enter directly, or indirectly via the articulatory-loop. Information is represented as auditory features such as pitch and amplitude (a sort of inner ear).

Figure 15.2 Summary of the Baddeley and Hitch (1974) working memory model of short-term memory

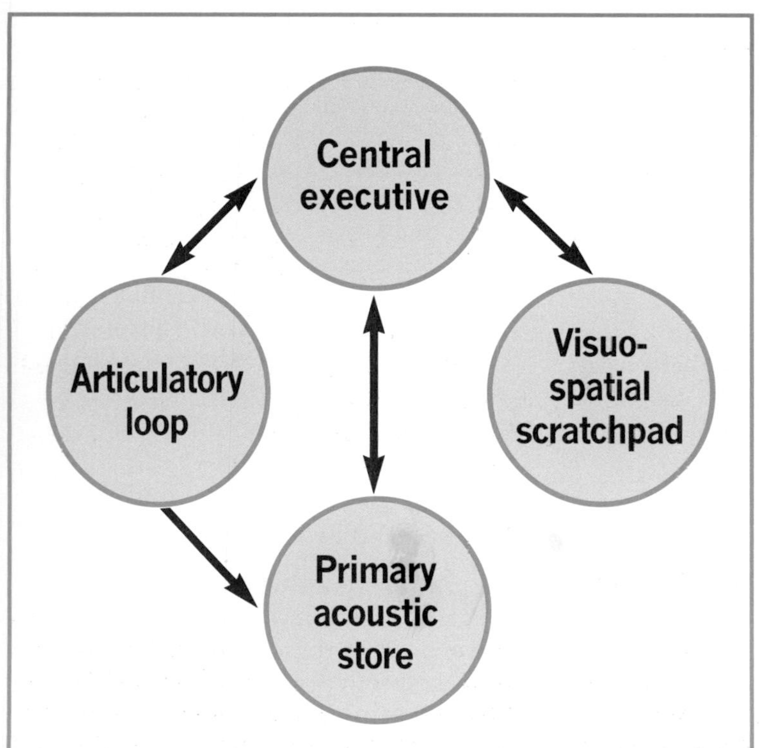

Working memory research

Methodology

Researchers have utilized the dual-task technique in investigating the working memory model. The assumption behind the technique is that processors have a limited capacity to process information. If two tasks make use of the same component, or processor, when done concurrently performance on one or both of the tasks will be worse than when the two tasks are done separately. On the other hand, if the two tasks make use of different components, both should be done concurrently as well as if they were done separately. One widely used version of the dual-task technique is called *articulatory suppression*. Suppression techniques involve loading one of the components (e.g. the articulatory-loop) and investigating how this affects performance on a task. An assumption of the technique is that if you get someone to repeat something out loud (such as 'la, la, la'), this uses up the resource allocation of the articulatory-loop, and it cannot be used for any other task. If suppression results in a detrimental performance on an additional task, it can then be assumed that, under normal conditions, that task involves the use of the suppressed component.

❖ Activity 4 ❖

Turn to a section of this book you have not yet read and pick out a long paragraph. Now read the paragraph, but at the same time say 'the' 'the' 'the' out loud continually as you are reading. You will probably find that you had difficulty in following and comprehending the text, suggesting that articulatory suppression affected your reading ability. However, you can probably read your favourite magazine whilst singing out loud and experience no difficulty. Why might this be? Later sections give clues as to the possible reasons for this.

The articulatory-loop

Researchers have provided insights into the functioning of the articulatory-loop. Baddeley *et al.* (1975) found than memory span for short words was greater than for long words. This implies that the articulatory-loop holds a certain number of syllables (not words). This is known as the 'word-length effect', but it only occurs if the articulatory-loop is involved in the processing. Baddeley *et al.* found that if words are presented visually, and the articulatory-loop is suppressed, the word-length effect disappears (participants recalled equal numbers of long and short words). They also found that people can recall as many words as they can read out loud in approximately two seconds. They argue that the articulatory-loop is a time-based system which has a capacity limited to the amount of information a person can articulate in approximately two seconds. If an item is not articulated within two seconds, it fades from the store.

The primary acoustic store

In the original working memory model there was no primary acoustic store. However, Baddeley and Lewis (1981) presented participants with a series of nonsense words. All of the words were grammatically possible words, but some were letter strings which sounded like real words (e.g. 'brane' and 'trane') and some were ones which did not sound like real words (e.g. 'slint' and 'prane'). Participants had to decide which non-words sounded like real words. They found that articulatory suppression did not affect their participants' ability to do this. The fact that people can make this decision without using the articulatory-loop suggests that there are acoustic as well as articulatory processes involved in reading. In other words, we use an acoustic code as well as an articulatory code, and consequently there needs to be a separate processor to do this. Hence the formulation of the primary acoustic store.

The visuo-spatial scratchpad

The functioning of the visuo-spatial scratchpad is less well understood than that of the articulatory-loop, and it is more difficult to identify its features. However, Baddeley and Lieberman (1980) argued that we need to distinguish between visual and spatial information (blind people may lack visual processing, but still have spatial knowledge). They used a concurrent (dual)-task technique to investigate the relative roles of visual and spatial processing. In their experiment, they had three conditions: no concurrent task, a concurrent visual task and a concurrent spatial task. There were detrimental effects on both concurrent tasks, suggesting that the visuo-spatial scratchpad is involved in processing both visual and spatial information. However, the two types of concurrent task led to different detriments (spatial interference was more disruptive). Therefore, they concluded that the visuo-spatial scratchpad might be more of a spatial than visual store and spatial processing might take priority.

The central executive

The central executive has a limited capacity and is involved in all tasks demanding attention. Often the involvement of the central executive is inferred if the suppression of other components is not detrimental to a task. More direct evidence of its role is gained from studies using the dual-task technique. If two tasks are dissimilar (e.g. a psychomotor task – tracing a path – and an intelligence task), but interfere with each other, then it is feasible to assume that both are competing for the limited attentional resources of the central executive. Hunt (1980) conducted such a study and found that these tasks did interfere with each other. It seems unlikely that they involve the use of the same specific processing systems (articulatory-loop or visuo-spatial scratchpad), and therefore it is assumed that both are competing for the attentional resources of a general processing component (the central executive).

Applications of the working memory model

Working memory research has given insights into the internal workings of short-term memory, but a further value of the model is that it gives a useful conceptual framework for investigating the role of STM in tasks requiring attention. Research has investigated areas such as problem-solving and many language tasks (e.g. reading). Investigations of articulatory suppression in reading tasks have given mixed results. For example, suppression sometimes affects performance a great deal and at other times much less. Levy (1978) conducted a study which investigated the effects of articulatory suppression on participants' comprehension of written material. In one condition, she gave participants a series of visually presented sentences for them to read while engaging in articulatory suppression. She found that articulatory suppression did not affect participants' ability to remember the gist, or general meaning of, a sentence, but it did affect their ability to remember the precise wording. Therefore, it appears that the articulatory-loop is not essential for the extraction of meaning in reading, but is involved in word-by-word recall.

Evidence suggests that we resort to the articulatory-loop when the central executive becomes overloaded. Although the articulatory-loop is useful at preserving the order in which verbal items are processed (word-by-word recall), articulation is not an essential part of the reading process. The articulatory-loop is a back-up system which can be used if reading becomes difficult. If reading is straightforward, visual information may be comprehended directly without utilizing the articulatory-loop. However, if reading becomes difficult, we can resort to phonological processing (that is, sounding out the words in our head).

Limitations of the working memory model

The main problem with the working memory model is that the component we know the least about (the central executive) is the most important. It has a limited capacity, but nobody has shown the exact nature of this capacity. Richardson (1984) argues that there are problems in specifying the precise functioning of the central executive. He points out that the term 'central executive' is vague, can be used to explain any kind of results and can present a circular argument (if we give participants a task with articulatory suppression and this affects performance, we assume the articulatory-loop is utilized in the task, but if performance is not affected, we assume the central executive is normally utilized in the task). Hence it is difficult to falsify the model.

Allport (1980) argues that the idea of a central processing system should be replaced with one containing specific processing mechanisms only. Baddeley (1981) also argues that one research task is to identify as many specific processing mechanisms as possible (as with the primary acoustic store) and break down the central executive even further. If we accept this argument, the central executive is the area of STM which has yet to be explained fully, and we may end up eventually with a system of separate processing mechanisms. However, Eysenck (1986) argues that a central system is necessary, because a system based solely on specific processors would be chaotic.

Section summary

The working memory model has proved useful in explaining the role of STM in many cognitive activities. A problem with the model, however, is that little is known about its major component, the central executive, and many explanations of research findings are circular. However, the working memory model is the best model of STM available currently.

Organization in long-term memory

Activity 1 emphasized the centrality of memory to our everyday activities. We have vast amounts of knowledge stored in our memory system. However, Activity 2 showed that we can access this knowledge quickly and apparently effortlessly. We clearly do not have to trawl through *all* our knowledge to access appropriate information. This implies that stored knowledge must be highly organized to allow us to retrieve the appropriate information for a given situation. This organization will be determined by the way that information is encoded into memory, and the way knowledge is organized will determine the type of process required to access that information on a future occasion.

Encoding and levels-of-processing theory

Craik and Lockhart (1972) argued that LTM traces are determined by encoding processes. They treat encoding as the central feature of memory, and differentiate between two types of processing: Type I (rote repetition) and Type II (meaningful analysis). Only Type II processing leads to good memory performance. Craik and Lockhart argue that processing varies in depth, and the depth, or level, of processing will determine the persistence of the LTM trace. Shallow sensory processing leads to weak memory traces and deeper, meaningful processing leads to more elaborate, longer lasting, stronger, memory traces.

Rowe (1974) showed that *semantic* (meaningful) encoding leads to more effective learning than *phonemic* (sound) encoding, which in turn is more effective than *visual* (physical features) encoding. The assumption is that semantic processing is somehow a deeper sort of encoding. One technique used extensively in this area is giving people different orienting tasks to perform on stimulus material. With this technique, researchers attempt to demonstrate that different orienting tasks require different levels of processing. A good example of a study using different orienting tasks is that carried out by Hyde and Jenkins (1973) (see *In Focus*).

In Focus

Hyde and Jenkins' (1973) levels-of-processing study

Hyde and Jenkins used five different orienting tasks. Participants were presented with lists of words for three seconds and had to complete one of the following tasks:

1 Rate the word for pleasantness.

2 Estimate the frequency of use of the word.

3 Detect the presence of particular letters in the word.

4 Decide the appropriate part of speech of the word (noun, verb, adjective, etc.).

5 Make decisions as to whether or not the words fits into sentence frames (e.g. it is the..., it is...).

Hyde and Jenkins argued that conditions 1 and 2 required semantic processing whereas the others did not. Their results supported this prediction and, in these conditions, participants remembered more words than in the other conditions.

An evaluation of levels-of-processing theory

Many studies have supported the idea that encoding activity has influential effects on recall, but there are problems with Craik and Lockhart's ideas about Type I and Type II processing. There is no disagreement with the notion of Type II processing leading to better performance, but research has shown that Type I processing (rote rehearsal) can also affect memory performance. Glenberg *et al.* (1977) showed that rote rehearsal improved recognition of stimuli, but it did not enhance free recall. This poses problems for Craik and Lockhart in that rote rehearsal *can* improve one type of retrieval (i.e. recognition). Furthermore, semantic processing is unlikely to be the only thing affecting LTM. The theory is really more descriptive than explanatory, and does not explain why deep processing is so effective. Anderson and Reder (1979) have shown that deep, or semantic, processing is more *elaborate* than shallow, or non-semantic, processing, while Eysenck (1979) and Jacoby and Craik (1979) have demonstrated the importance of *distinctive*, or unusual, *processing* in enhancing memory recall. Therefore, there are many aspects of input processing that can affect memory and enhance recall.

In contrast to structural approaches to memory, levels-of-processing emphasizes the active aspects of encoding. However, there are difficulties in specifying the exact nature of a 'level'. A further problem arises in that most of the evidence for the approach comes from orienting tasks, and we can never be sure that participants are not using alternative processing in these tasks. Evidence concerning the differential effects of encoding is quite robust, but Eysenck (1986) argues that the emphasis on encoding in levels-of-processing theory is too narrow. He argues that learning and memory will be affected by at least four general factors:

- the nature of the task given to the subject
- the type of material to be remembered
- the individual knowledge of the subject
- the nature of the test used to measure memory performance (e.g. recall or recognition).

Retrieval processes

The use of retrieval cues is central to efficient memory operation. Retrieval needs to be guided to allow us to retrieve appropriate information in a particular situation. Our memory needs to be interrogated, using selective retrieval cues, to access appropriate areas of memory and prevent unwanted access to irrelevant information. Researchers have investigated the effectiveness of different retrieval cues in accessing memories using 'cued-recall'. In free-recall studies, participants are given items to remember and are free to recall as many items as they can with no help. In cued-recall, participants are given a cue to help in their recall; for example, participants are given a list of words and then given cues associated with the words, e.g. target word 'table', cue word 'chair'.

Encoding specificity

One important idea about retrieval from LTM is Tulving and Thomson's (1973) *encoding specificity principle* (ESP). The ESP states that a cue will be successful in retrieving a memory if, and only if, the information contained in the cue was encoded on the original memory trace. In other words, information specific to a cue must be encoded as part of the original memory trace if that cue is to facilitate retrieval. According to the ESP, memory traces are accessed directly (information provided by the cue is directly matched with the memory trace). However, another way of thinking about retrieval is to consider it as a more active process than the direct access process of the ESP. Recall may involve the active use of a cue to create, or generate, alternative items until one is recognized. Models which advocate this type of processing are known as 'generate-recognize' models.

The main difference between the two approaches is that ESP emphasizes elaboration in encoding, while generate-recognize models emphasize elaboration in retrieval. Ogilvie *et al.* (1980) showed that recall can improve over a delay, which creates problems for the ESP, and theorists have to suggest that memory traces are still being created long after the target items were presented. However, Ogilvie *et al.* also found that some items which participants failed to recognize in the first phase of the experiment were recalled at a later stage. This is called 'recognition failure' and creates problems for the generate-recognize approach, which sees recognition as an essential stage in recall (cues are generated and one is recognized). Therefore, recall without recognition should not occur. This poses no problems for the ESP because it makes no distinction between recognition and recall. However, in his dual-route model, Jones (1978) suggests there may be two separate routes for retrieval – a direct access route (similar to the ESP), and a generate-recognize process. Therefore, recall may involve a sequential process of direct access followed by generate-recognize, if direct access fails.

Episodic and semantic memory

The knowledge stored in LTM comes in various forms and Cohen and Squire (1980) propose that it can be separated into two parts: procedural and declarative memory. Procedural memory is knowledge about how to do things, whereas declarative memory is knowledge about things (specific items or facts). Tulving (1972) also proposes that declarative (propositional) memory can be divided into two other separate, though related, components: *semantic* (facts, ideas and concepts) and *episodic* memory (particular personal events). Support for this idea comes from studies of amnesia. Many amnesiacs show severely impaired memory for episodes in their lives, but have largely unimpaired language abilities, and perform normally on intelligence tests.

Semantic organization in LTM

Bousfield (1953) gave early evidence of semantic (meaningful) clustering in free recall. In his experiment, participants were given lists of words to remember. The lists contained items from different semantic categories (animals, vegetables, professions and names of people). Bousfield found that, although the words were presented

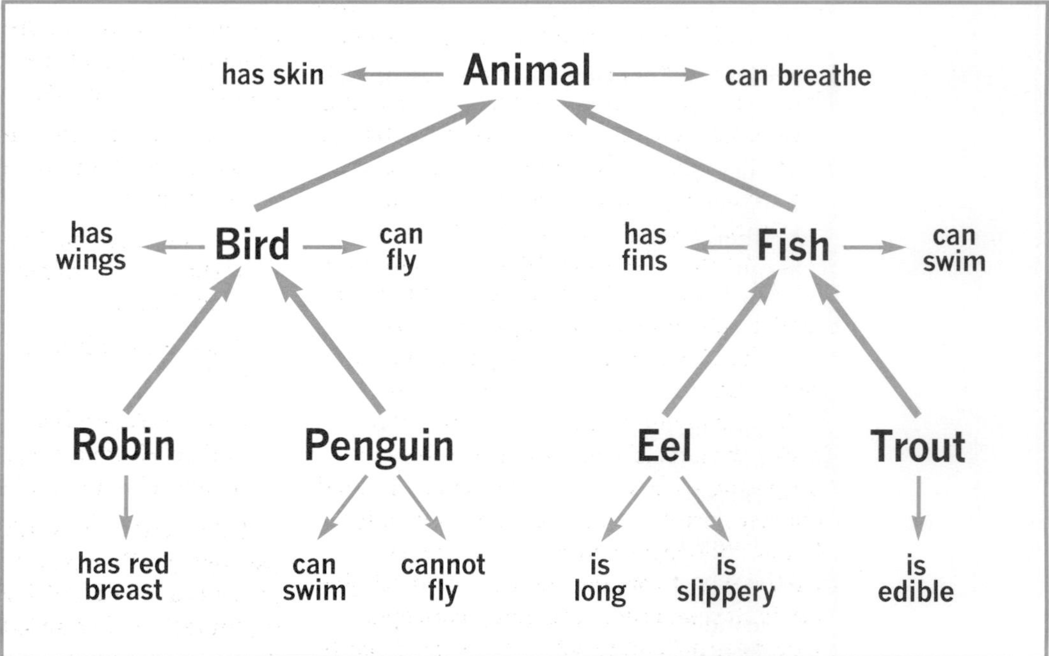

Figure 15.3 Schematic diagram of part of a Collins and Quillian (1969) hierarchical semantic network

randomly, during recall participants tended to remember clusters of items belonging to the same category (for example, cat would be followed by items such as mouse, dog, horse and cow). Bousfield suggested that this was evidence of semantic organization in LTM, and this led to the development of models of the organization of knowledge in memory. One of the earliest of these models was the Collins and Quillian (1969) model of conceptual hierarchies.

Collins and Quillian argued that knowledge in LTM is organized in *hierarchical semantic networks*. A network is a structure of pieces of information (nodes) with interconnecting links, or pathways. The links represent semantic associations between the nodes, which are hierarchically organized with specific concepts (e.g. robins) at the bottom of the hierarchy and general concepts (e.g. animals) at the top. Figure 15.3 shows part of a semantic network for the concept 'animal'.

According to Collins and Quillian, retrieval of factual information involves searching through this semantic hierarchy. Consequently, the more levels of the hierarchy that need to be passed through in retrieval, the longer it should take to access information. Collins and Quillian tested their ideas using sentence verification tasks. In these tasks, participants have to say if a sentence is true or false, e.g. 'robin can fly' (true) or 'robin can swim' (false). Collins and Quillian's results tended to support their ideas: participants took longer to verify sentences such as 'a robin is an animal' than sentences such as 'a robin is a bird'. However, problems for the idea come from typicality effects. People can verify sentences such as 'a robin is a bird' more quickly than sentences such as 'a penguin is a bird'. According to Collins and Quillian's model, this should not happen, because both decisions require a search through the same number of levels in the hierarchy.

This led Collins and Loftus (1975) to revise the idea of semantic hierarchies by proposing a network model in which related concepts are not organized hierarchically, but in interconnected semantic clusters. However, network models depend on defining attributes, and there are many concepts which are difficult to define in terms of clearly identifiable attributes (what are the defining attributes of 'game'?). Consequently, some theorists have suggested another theory – schema theory – which can provide a better account of organization in semantic memory.

Schema theory

Schema theory is discussed more fully in Chapters 13 and 14, but, in brief, Cohen (1986) suggests schemas influence memory in four ways:

- The selection of information to be remembered is guided, and information not relevant to the current schema may be ignored.
- Information in memory is abstracted and transformed from the specific to the general (people remember the 'gist' of things).
- Knowledge is integrated and interpreted in terms of existing schematic knowledge and we can use schemas to fill in missing information and to make inferences.
- Memories are normalized and distorted to make them fit with past experiences.

Evaluation of schema theory and episodic and semantic memory

A good deal of empirical evidence in memory has been interpreted in terms of schema theory, but there are a number of problems with the idea:

- It is vague in explaining whether its processes occur during encoding, storage or retrieval.
- It emphasizes the inaccuracies in memory at the expense of memories recalled in clear detail.
- It is not clear how schemas are acquired in development.
- It is not clear where one schema ends and another begins, and how we know which schema to select at any one time.

Schema theory is still influential within psychology. However, Schank (1982) presents a model which retains the schematic organization of knowledge, but *within* a hierarchical framework. He suggests we have a hierarchical organization in memory, ranging from the specific at the lower levels, to the general at the higher levels. Representations become more general and schema-like as you move up the hierarchy. Lower-level memories are not retained for long, and event memories gradually become absorbed into higher-level generalized memories, which store the common features of repeated events. Details of events are retained if they are unusual or important. Therefore, this model allows for storing memories of both specific events and generalized schemas. Instead of a rigid distinction between episodic and semantic memory, LTM is organized at many levels ranging from the specific to the general.

Tulving (1972) argued for a clear distinction between separate episodic and semantic memory stores. However, the two types of information are clearly related, and Schank's model provides a better account of the organization in LTM than original schema theory. There is a close relationship between episodic and semantic knowledge (everything in semantic memory must at some stage have been in episodic memory), and these days, few accept Tulving's absolute distinction (see Baddeley 1992). Further evidence of the interrelationship between episodic and semantic memory comes from studies of everyday memory. Everyday experiences are the source of knowledge, and general knowledge allows us to interpret everyday events (we use a combination of top-down, conceptually driven, and bottom-up, data-driven, processing).

Section summary

The highly organized nature of knowledge in LTM suggests that processes at encoding will determine the organization of LTM, and this organization will determine retrieval processes. Theorists have begun to specify the nature of these processes in some detail. Distinctions can be made between the different types of knowledge stored in LTM. Early approaches focused on the hierarchical organization of semantic memory, but problems have been identified with this idea. Schema theory has also been very influential in understanding the organization of knowledge in semantic memory, and recent ideas have indicated problems in making a rigid distinction between episodic and semantic memory.

Practical aspects of memory

Everyday memory

Neisser (1978) discussed the 'thundering silence' with which researchers replied to questions about the role of memory in everyday life. He pointed out that a hundred years had been spent in the laboratory, concentrating on theoretical questions about the underlying mechanisms and structures of memory. While these are important issues, ordinary questions about the everyday functioning of memory had received little consideration. Neisser used the term 'ecological validity' to emphasize that theorizing needed to be applied to the world outside the laboratory.

❖ Activity 5 ❖

Before reading further, look at the *In Focus* on 'Memory for medical information' (p. 335), then consider what strategies you might use to improve patients' memories for medical information. After you have done this, compare your ideas with the list provided in Table 15.1.

Methods of studying everyday memory

In experimental studies, factors which may affect the results are controlled rigorously. However, the things we experience in everyday life are not isolated lists of meaningless items. They are complex experiences embedded in a context of ongoing events and surrounding objects.

In Focus

Memory for medical information

There now exists a considerable body of evidence to show that both hospital and general practice patients are poor at remembering what their doctors tell them. One of many studies which illustrates this was carried out by Bain (1977) who analysed how much patients could recall an hour after a consultation with their general practitioner (GP). The results are shown below:

Type of information	*% of patients who failed to recall what their GP told them*
Name of drug	37
Frequency of dose	23
Duration of treatment	25

Ley (1988) has summarized the findings from a number of studies using GP and hospital patients. He found considerable variation in the amount of information remembered. Average amounts of information accurately recalled ranged from 40 to 90 per cent. Ley found that recall was influenced by many factors. You will not be surprised to learn that possessing medical knowledge and being intelligent improved patients' recall. Less predictable perhaps was the finding from most studies (e.g. Anderson *et al.* 1979) that higher levels of anxiety were *positively* associated with better recall. Other factors found to improve recall were:

- the primacy effect – information given first is remembered best
- the perceived importance of the information.

In hospital studies, an inverse relationship was found between patients' recall and the amount of information given by the doctor – that is, the more bits of information to be remembered, the greater the *proportion* forgotten. However, in studies of GP patients, this relationship was not found. The reason for this is not clear, but Ley speculates that the greater predictability of information given by GPs may have something to do with it.

Although research findings are inconsistent, the balance of evidence to date shows that older people up to the age of about 70 are no more likely to forget medical information than are younger people. This is contrary to some predictions about the effects of ageing on memory.

We often find that everyday memory studies lack the control of many experimental studies. However, theorists investigating everyday memory still need to apply rigorous techniques. Researchers need to focus questions on particular aspects of memory and devise methods of testing and measurement.

Cohen (1986) points out that everyday memory research is often more concerned with the contents of memory than its mechanisms. Therefore, many of its methods are concerned with quantifying the contents of memory, and two general methodologies have been used extensively in this area:

- The use of self reports, or introspections, which require participants to make ratings of their memories, or observations about its functioning.
- Naturalistic experimentation in which the researcher devises experiments which are more representative of memory functioning in everyday life. This involves using naturalistic materials such as faces, stories or events, instead of lists of words or nonsense syllables.

Both methodologies, however, have potential problems:

Table 15.1 Recommendations for improving patients' memory for medical information

1 Give the most important information first, i.e. exploit the primacy effect.

2 Simplify information, e.g. by using short words and short sentences.

3 Use explicit categorization, e.g. 'Now I am going to tell you:

(a) what the problem is

(b) what tests we need to do

(c) what the treatment will be', and so on.

4 Stress and/or repeat important points or ask patients to repeat them.

5 Be specific, e.g. 'You must lose four kilos' rather than 'You need to lose weight'.

6 Use reminders, e.g. letters and telephone calls about appointments.

Source: adapted from Ley 1988

- We need to be cautious about the use of self reports, because only part of people's mental activity is open to consciousness.
- Even in naturalistic experiments, the experimental situation is never exactly representative of everyday life.

Everyday memory researchers have to accept these limitations, but these are compensated for by the interest and relevance of their research.

Memory for scenes and events

Memory for scenes

Brewer and Treyens (1981) investigated people's memory for objects in a room. They argued that memory for a scene will be influenced by the schema which is most appropriate to that scene. Brewer and Treyens predicted that people would remember objects they would expect to find in a particular room and not objects they would not expect to find there (i.e. context would be more influential than distinctiveness). In the experiment, participants were asked to wait for 35 seconds in a university office and were then taken to another room. When they arrived in the other room, they were given the unexpected task of writing down everything they had seen in the office. Participants did well at recalling items which would normally be found in the room, and poorly at recalling items which would not normally be there. They also recalled items which were likely to be in a typical office, but which were not actually present in the office used in the experiment. Brewer and Treyens concluded that the memory for the scene was strongly influenced by a pre-existing schema. This and many other studies emphasize the role of stored knowledge in the forming of everyday memories.

Memory for events: eye-witness testimony

Many studies have demonstrated that memories for events are susceptible to the influence of misleading information. Loftus (1975) conducted a series of experiments in which she tested the idea that, in memory for events, new information is integrated with pre-stored memory representations (schemas). She showed that people's memory for an event they had witnessed can be falsified if they are later given misleading information (see *In Focus* on next page).

Loftus claims that new information is incorporated into the original memory

In Focus

Loftus' (1975) study of eye-witness testimony

Loftus (1975) showed participants a film of a car accident. They were then split into two groups and asked a series of questions about the event. One group was asked questions all of which incorporated information consistent with what they had seen (e.g. 'How fast was the white sports car going when it passed the stop sign?'). The other group was asked the same questions except for one which contained misleading information ('How fast was the white sports car going when it passed the barn?'). The film had shown the car passing a stop sign, but there had been no barn, and mentioning a barn implied there had been one. A week later participants were asked new questions about the accident. The final question was 'Did you see a barn?'. The results showed that more people in the second group answered this question incorrectly and said they had seen a barn. For these participants, the fictitious barn had been integrated into the memory for the event. This suggests that false information had been added to the memory representation. In a further study, Loftus *et al.* (1978) also showed that correct information could be deleted and replaced by subsequent false information.

trace, updating it and erasing any original information which is inconsistent with the new information. Once the misleading information is incorporated into the original memory, people cannot distinguish the differing sources of the information. However, in a further study (Loftus 1979) she also showed that participants were less likely to be misled if the false information was blatantly incorrect. Loftus and her colleagues are not without their critics. Bekerian and Bowers (1983) argue that if you ask questions in a structured way, you can get back to the original memory trace.

Early research focused on inaccuracies in eye-witness reports. Recently this emphasis has changed and attention has turned to how eye-witness testimony can be improved, e.g. Geiselman *et al.*'s (1985) work using the cognitive interview to enhance eye-witness reports and Christianson's (1992) work on differentiating between central and peripheral details in eye-witnessing. Christianson argues that participants can be misled about peripheral detail, but not about details central to the event. However, Loftus (1993) has shown recently how a completely false memory can be experimentally induced, which adds further doubt about the accuracy of memories for scenes and events.

❖ Activity 6 ❖

Think back to a party which you have attended. Focus on the memory and make it as clear as possible. Can you 'see' yourself in the memory? Many of you will find that you *can* see yourself. However, unless you were looking in a mirror, you could not have seen yourself at the time. What kind of a memory can this be? It must be a 'reconstructed' memory built from a combination of information from the event plus information from subsequent recall of the event. Try this out with friends and family. (It also works well with memories for weddings.)

Autobiographical memory

Diary studies of autobiographical memory

Autobiographical memory concerns people's memory of personal experiences and events from their past. Insights into the nature of autobiographical memory came from Linton's (1982) six-year diary study of her own memory (see *In Focus* overleaf).

Linton's findings indicate that many events are forgotten with time, but some remain memorable. The first of a sequence of events, for example, may be recalled because it represents an important

In Focus

Linton's (1982) diary study of autobiographical memory

Each day for six years Linton recorded two events which occurred during the day. Every month she recalled the memories and estimated the order in which they occurred and on what date. She also rated each event for personal importance and emotionality, both at the time of writing and recall. Linton identified two main types of forgetting. The first involved repetitions of similar occurrences. Over time there was a decrease in the distinctiveness of these events. However, Linton observed that the first and most recent occurrences of an event remained distinctive. She also noticed a second type of forgetting in which episodes were forgotten altogether. At the end of the sixth year, Linton found that she could not remember 30 per cent of the events at all, even though written in her diary, and that forgetting increased with time. Linton also found little relationship between her initial ratings of emotionality and importance, and subsequent recall.

milestone in a person's life. Robinson (1992) suggests that first-time experiences are a key feature in the organization of autobiographical memory. Conway (1992) argues that autobiographical memory is organized around life themes (e.g. 'when I was in sixth-form', 'when I lived in London') and Robinson suggests that first-time experiences may reflect changes in life themes (key stages in a person's life). Therefore, they are remembered clearly. Repeated events are not remembered because they tend to become less distinctive, and more schematic, with time. Therefore, it becomes difficult to remember one occasion of a repeated event as episodes become integrated into a general memory schema.

One interesting aspect of Linton's study is that she found little relationship between initial ratings of emotionality and importance, and recall. This is counter-intuitive because experience suggests we remember important events. However, Linton noticed that initial ratings of emotionality and importance did not always correspond with later ratings of these things. She found that events which seemed significant at the time sometimes turned out to be trivial later. Linton suggests that events endure in memory if they are perceived as important, or emotional, at the time of the event and *also* retain the same significance later in life. Hayes *et al.* (1992) have also shown that if the recall of the event generates some of the same emotional feeling that was felt at the time of the event, it is more likely to be remembered.

Flashbulb memory

Some events are recalled in great detail and are called 'flashbulb memories'. Brown and Kulik (1977) investigated memories of events such as the assassinations of J.F. Kennedy and Martin Luther King, and discovered that people could remember the events clearly. However, more interestingly, they could also relate a lot of apparently trivial details about the circumstances when they first heard the news. Typically they could remember who they were with, what activities they were engaged in, and so on. People do not usually retain this type of information for very long. It is obviously important that we remember major world events, but it is not clear why we remember apparently trivial details.

Brown and Kulik drew on a concept from Livingston (1967) to explain flashbulb memories. Livingston argued that if an event is surprising or emotional, lower brain systems become activated. This activation spreads to cortical areas and this increased cortical activation causes all recent events to be permanently recorded in memory. Brown and Kulik argue that when we hear about these nationally important events a neural mechanism, such as the one described by Livingston, is activated. This leads to the whole scene being imprinted on memory (similar to taking a flashbulb photograph). They support their claim by pointing out that all flashbulb memories have a similar structure in that people remember where they were (place), what

❖ Activity 7 ❖

Think back to a highly memorable event such as the Dunblane massacre that occurred in March 1996. Can you remember when you first heard about the incident? If you can, you may also be able to remember how you heard about it, what you were doing, who you were with, and so on. This would be a typical flashbulb memory.

they were doing (activity), who told them (informant) and what they felt (effect).

The concept of flashbulb memory has its critics. Neisser (1982) argues that there is no need to postulate a special neural mechanism to account for the similarities in structure of flashbulb memories. He suggests the structural features are products of narrative conventions (traditional schemas which govern the format of story telling). In other words, these are the things we would typically talk about when describing an event to someone else. Neisser argues that these detailed memories result from frequent rehearsal after the event, rather than from some special neural mechanism. He suggests that many so-called flashbulb memories, although recounted in good faith and in great detail, are found to be inaccurate when checked.

Other researchers (e.g. Thompson and Cowan 1986), have pointed out that the vast majority of flashbulb memories are more or less accurate and any errors are minor reconstructive errors. Recent research by Conway *et al.* (1994) into memories about the resignation of Margaret Thatcher has also supported the existence of flashbulb memories after a one-year interval. However, importance and rehearsal are interrelated and difficult to isolate at an empirical level. Banaji and Crowder (1989) argue that everyday memory research has failed to add anything to our understanding of memory. They point out that it is difficult to generalize from the findings of everyday memory research. Still other psychologists (e.g. Conway 1991) refute this claim and emphasize some of the important findings to come from everyday memory research.

Section summary

Research into everyday memory has included investigations of patients' memories, eye-witness testimony, autobiographical memories and flashbulb memories. Researchers disagree about the usefulness of everyday memory research in improving our understanding of memory processes.

Theories of forgetting

Everyday forgetting

Structured forgetting

For much of our lives we are exposed to information from the outside world. However, most has little relevance to our daily activities and retaining it in memory has little value. Therefore, forgetting has a functional role in cognitive processing. We need to forget information of little value and retain potentially useful information. In earlier sections, we saw how forgetting can occur through processes linked to the structure of memory. Forgetting can occur through *decay*, *displacement* and *interference*.

Forgetting through decay, displacement and interference

Decay and displacement are relatively straightforward ideas. Many theories of memory assume we have memory traces. According to *trace theory*, when information enters memory a subset of neurons are activated. Memories are retained for as long as this set of neurons remains activated. The activation of the neurons can be maintained through rehearsal, or frequent recall of the information. If the activation is not maintained, the memory trace is thought to fade, or *decay*. Decay occurs in STM, which can only hold information for brief periods of time. However, decay can also occur in LTM if information is not recalled (reactivated) for a long period of time. Displacement occurs when new information utilizes the same set of neurons as old information. In other words, the old information stored on the memory trace is displaced, or overwritten, by new information. Displacement is thought to occur in both short-term and long-term memory.

Psychologists have identified two main types of *interference* which can result in forgetting. One type occurs when new material interferes with material you have already learned. This is known as *'retroactive interference'*. Displacement could be seen as a type of retroactive interference, in that new information interferes with existing memories. However, displacement is an all-or-nothing process, and interference may result in the distortion of existing memories, rather than replacing them entirely. The other type of interference is known as *'proactive interference'*, and occurs when material you have already learned interferes with new information. Old memories distort the processing of new information and we interpret this information in terms of what we already know. There have been many empirical demonstrations of both retroactive and proactive interference. However, theoretical explanations of the effects have tended to be weak. The most plausible explanation of both types of interference comes through schema theory. As we saw in earlier sections, we ignore information if it does not fit with an activated schema (proactive interference) and schemas are tuned and refined by new experiences (retroactive interference).

Reality monitoring

In Chapter 13 we also saw how forgetting can occur through slips of attention. One of the main findings from this research is that the majority of errors occur in highly practised routines which are carried out with little conscious monitoring. People have two sorts of memory:

- externally derived memories (products of actual experiences)
- internally generated memories (products of thinking, planning and imagining).

One problem for psychologists is how people detect whether a particular memory originated in the outside world or in their heads (i.e. how they determine whether an event was actually experienced or merely imagined). An explanation of this ability, proposed by Johnson and Raye (1981), is called 'reality monitoring'. Reality monitoring is usually effective, but occasionally we cannot remember whether we have actually done something we intended to do. This uncertainty reflects a breakdown in reality monitoring and can occur in various ways:

- A memory of a planned act is mistaken for a memory of an act that actually took place.
- Something which happened in a dream is confused with something that actually occurred.
- Stories from our past are embroidered, and later we cannot distinguish fact from fantasy.

Given that memory representations are the joint product of external information and stored schemas (bottom-up and top-down processing), it is not surprising that confusions occur. Johnson (1985) argues that externally derived and internally generated memories differ in their features. She suggests that memories of real events comprise more sensory information than imagined events. They contain detail such as information about sound, smell, colour, and context. Therefore, it is normally possible to distinguish between real and imagined events, because the memory traces of real events are much richer in detail. Internally-generated memories lack this detail and are more schematic in nature (i.e. they contain more top-down information, such as memories about most dreams).

Confusions in reality monitoring occur with automatic actions because we may fail to attend to, and consequently fail to encode, sensory detail. Therefore, these memory traces lack the sensory information which usually accompanies real events, and are not so easily distinguishable from those of imagined events (Johnson and Raye 1981). Furthermore, if an imagined event is unusually vivid and rich in detail, it is difficult to distinguish it from an actual event (Johnson *et al.* 1979). Mitchell *et al.* (1986) also showed that poor reality monitoring is a feature of amnesia, and is particularly evident in Alzheimer's patients.

Amnesia

Traditional approaches

There are two general forms of amnesia:

- *organic* amnesia (caused by brain damage)
- *psychogenic* amnesia (forgetting with no apparent physical cause).

Organic amnesia often falls within the area of neuropsychology, whereas psychogenic amnesia often falls within the realm of psychoanalysis. Organic disorders can be further divided into *global* amnesia, in which a large component of memory is affected, and *specific* amnesia, in which the loss of memory is localized to quite a small area. Psychologists also refer to *anterograde* amnesia, which describes difficulty in remembering things since an illness or trauma, and *retrograde* amnesia, which refers to difficulty in remembering things prior to an illness or trauma. Traditional neuropsychology has a number of basic features:

- It takes brain-damaged people and classifies them by specific syndromes.
- It compares patients classified by a syndrome with normal people and specifies the deficits associated with that syndrome.
- It tries to localize the syndrome to a particular area of the brain, which is then seen as functional in terms of the abilities missing in patients.

Cognitive neuropsychology

Recently a new approach to amnesia has been developed, known as 'cognitive neuropsychology' (Ellis and Young 1988). Cognitive psychologists have found important differences between patients who had been grouped together under the same syndrome. They provide detailed case studies of single patients, and data from the patients are used to develop theories of normal cognitive processing (e.g. Shallice and Warrington's study of KF discussed in the earlier *In Focus*). Neuropsychologists look at syndromes, but cognitive neuropsychologists look at specific types of amnesia.

Memory is dependent on the processes of encoding, storage and retrieval, and cognitive neuropsychologists look for deficits in these processes in brain-damaged people. An *encoding amnesia* should leave storage and retrieval intact, but not allow new memory registration. Registration problems should result in anterograde amnesia, but not retrograde amnesia. Scoville and Milner (1957) describe the case of HM who had his temporal lobes and part of his hippocampus and amygdala removed to alleviate life-threatening epilepsy. This cured his epilepsy but left him deeply amnesic. He showed severe anterograde amnesia, but his memory for events before the operation was good. Therefore he fits the pattern of someone with registration problems.

If patients have *retrieval amnesia*, they should be able to lay memory traces down, but not retrieve anything. Korsakoff patients (whose amnesia is caused by alcohol abuse) demonstrate severe retrograde amnesia and often have deficits of anterograde memory. However, Korsakoff patients are not ideal patients to study because their brain damage is often widespread. Some psychologists have suggested they have retrieval problems, but others have argued they have registration problems. The evidence to support the retrieval hypothesis is severe retrograde amnesia, but a major problem is in determining when the amnesia began. Patients may have long histories of alcohol abuse going back twenty or thirty years before they became clinically amnesic.

Amnesia leads to severe social problems. Social relations cannot be formed, books read or TV programmes watched. Patients cannot remember simple sequences of events. If memory aids are given, patients forget they have been given them. Little can be done to help these people, but their perceptual motor skills and basic language abilities are often normal (providing those skills were developed prior to the accident). Cognitive neuropsychology has advanced our understanding of amnesia further by trying to explain symptoms in terms of deficits in cognitive processes instead of simply in terms of damage to areas of the brain.

Section summary

People cannot remember all the information that impinges on their sensory systems, and much is forgotten. Some forgetting occurs as a result of the structural constraints of the memory system and some as a result of integrating new information with previously stored knowledge. Slips and errors of memory can occur when everyday activities are carried out with little sensory processing and conscious attention. However, abnormal forgetting occurs in some people, often as a result of brain damage. Studies of amnesiacs add to our understanding of normal memory processing, and emphasize the key role of memory in our everyday lives.

Chapter summary

- Structural approaches to memory offered a number of insights into hypothetical memory structures. Later theorists emphasized the active processes of memory.
- The working memory model has offered new insights into the nature of STM and its role in activities requiring attention.
- Theorists have also looked at the organization of LTM, the representation of different types of knowledge and the active processes involved in encoding and retrieval.
- Recent research has investigated the role of memory in everyday life. However, although important insights have been gained in this area, the approach is not without its critics.
- A great deal of research has been conducted in the area of forgetting, including structured and abnormal forgetting, which emphasizes the crucial role of memory in our everyday lives.

Essay questions

1. Describe the structural approach to memory and evaluate the usefulness of this type of approach. *(24 marks)*
2. Discuss studies of forgetting. *(24 marks)*
3. Evaluate the contribution of everyday memory studies to our overall understanding of memory functioning. *(24 marks)*

Further reading

Eysenck, M.W. and Keane, M.T. (1995) *Cognitive Psychology: A Student's Handbook* (3rd edn), Hove: Lawrence Erlbaum Associates.

Gives detailed general coverage of memory. This is primarily an undergraduate text.

Cohen, G., Kiss, G and Le Voi, M.E. (1993) *Memory: Current Issues* (2nd edn), Buckingham: Open University Press.

Gives detailed coverage of memory in student-friendly language.

Baddeley, A.D. (1990) *Human Memory: Theory and Practice*, Hove: Lawrence Erlbaum Associates.

Gives comprehensive coverage of memory research.

Collins, A.F., Gathercole, S.E., Conway, M.A. and Morris, P.E. (eds) (1993) *Theories of Memory*, Hove: Lawrence Erlbaum Associates.

Good contemporary view of memory, but terminology can be a bit complex.

Chapter 16

Language and thought

Jane Willson

Preview

In this chapter we shall be looking at:

- theories relating to language acquisition
- explanations of language production and comprehension
- models of thought
- theories relating to the relationship between language and thought.

Introduction

In this chapter we will consider the nature of human language and the ways in which psychologists have sought to explain the processes involved in producing, understanding and acquiring language. Language is a highly complex system of communication based on words which have meaning. These words can be strung together according to a set of grammatical rules and used to create an infinite number of sentences. The flexibility, richness and complexity of human language sets it apart from other animal communication systems but that very complexity poses an enormous challenge to psychologists attempting to explain the underlying processes.

Just as humans have developed a highly sophisticated system of language, they have also outstripped other species in their ability to think and reason. All the processes involved in memory, attention and perception could legitimately be considered 'thought' processes. However, when cognitive psychologists refer to *models of thought* they usually mean particular types of goal-directed thinking, such as problem-solving and reasoning, and so discussion will be limited to those areas in this chapter.

We will also be looking at theoretical attempts to establish the links between language and thought, and will consider briefly some of the social and cultural factors that can influence these processes.

Language acquisition

Although language acquisition is one of the most remarkable of human achievements, it is not yet clear precisely how this is accomplished. In this part of the chapter, we shall consider explanations provided by:

- learning theory
- nativist theory
- interactionist theories.

Learning theory

The earliest attempts to explain language development were largely founded on the common-sense notion that it was a relatively uncomplicated process dependent on imitation and reinforcement. A formal theory of language acquisition based on this idea was put forward by Skinner (1957). He referred to language as 'verbal behaviour' because he believed that it was acquired by exactly the same mechanisms of operant conditioning and reinforcement that governed all other aspects of human behaviour. According to this theory, infants, motivated by a survival need to communicate, begin to emit random verbal sounds. If these are reinforced by adults (e.g. by smiling or nodding approval), the sounds will be repeated, but if they are not reinforced, they will extinguish. In addition, children sometimes use echoic responses simply to imitate what they have heard and these imitations are also reinforced. Through a process of selective reinforcement, adults gradually shape their children's language into correct usage. This extreme form of learning theory has a number of serious flaws:

- Most children achieve language competence even though their environments are very different.
- Language seems to be learnt at roughly the same rate and in the same sequence, regardless of environment.
- Adults generally correct only truth and meaning in children's utterances, not syntax (Brown and Hanlon 1970), and on the occasions when they do attempt to correct grammar, it has either little effect (Bellugi 1970) or it is positively detrimental to progress (Nelson 1973).
- Certain words (e.g. 'No!') are clearly understood by children before they try to produce them.
- The pattern of acquisition of irregular verb and noun forms does not occur as learning theory would predict. There is often a U-shaped development where performance begins well, becomes temporarily worse and then improves again. It is as though the child has to learn the general rules and then learn exceptions to those rules (Kolota 1987).
- Children often produce new utterances which they have never heard before and Skinner's theory cannot account for this creativity.

While Skinner's extreme view of language acquisition receives little support, there is some evidence that the type of language the child hears spoken does have an effect on development. Children who listen to more spoken language are known to develop vocabulary faster than those who hear less (Engel *et al.* 1975). It seems also that children whose carers use language responsively show more rapid language development (Olsen *et al.* 1986). One particular type of parental language that has attracted interest is the use of *motherese*

❖ Activity 1 ❖

Try to 'listen in' to a carer (usually, but not always, a mother) talking to a young child. A queue at a supermarket checkout is often a good location to do this if you have no other access to a young family. See if you notice anything about the tone, pitch, choice of words, sentence structure, and so on, that is different from language used between adults.

(see Snow 1994). This is a simplified way of talking to children using shorter, slower, clearly segmented speech which includes more repetition and redundancy than is usual in adult speech.

This child-directed speech gradually fades as children get older and levels of comprehension improve. The evidence concerning the role of motherese in language development is unclear but it seems likely that motherese is helpful, at least at an early stage. However, this does not provide an adequate explanation of the process of language acquisition since children who are not exposed to motherese still manage to learn a complex grammar, even if they do so at a slower rate.

While learning theory undoubtedly offers an explanation for certain aspects of language acquisition such as pronunciation and understanding of word meanings, it is too simplistic to account for the complexity and the rapidity of the achievement.

Nativist theory

Given that language development appears to follow a very similar pattern across cultures, it would seem likely that the ability is somehow 'wired in'. The best-known theorist to take this position is Chomsky (1957), who argued that children learn language by acquiring a set of rules or grammar. He maintained that this could not occur as a result of environmental exposure alone because much of what they hear spoken is 'degenerate output'. In other

In Focus

Deep and surface structures

Chomsky believed that we possess an innate understanding of grammar that allows us to distinguish between acceptable sentence structure and meaningless strings of words. One aspect of our grammar is a set of rewrite rules which enables us to analyse sentences into their lowest level constituents (e.g. noun phrases, verb phrases, nouns, verbs). A constituent is a unit of language that can be replaced with a single word without altering the basic grammatical structure of the sentence although it might alter the meaning. For example, in the sentence *'The friendly, little girl spoke to the grumpy, old woman'*, *'the friendly, little girl'* is a constituent because it could be replaced with *'Emma'* while *'the friendly, little'* is not a constituent because it cannot be replaced by one word; *'spoke to the grumpy, old woman'* can be replaced simply by *'spoke'* so this, too, is a constituent, whereas *'to the'* is not. We can use these constituents to generate novel sentences and to avoid producing non-sentences. However, this phrase-structure grammar alone cannot account for all our linguistic competence and in 1965 Chomsky revised his theory to include the concept of transformational grammar, which converts deep structure (the underlying meaning of a sentence) into surface structure (the actual words that are written or spoken). Chomsky recognized that sentences could have different surface structures but similar deep structures. For example:

The boy ate the apple.

The apple was eaten by the boy.

On the other hand, sentences can have similar surface structures but quite different deep structures. For example:

He is easy to please.

He is eager to please.

Occasionally, a sentence can have one surface structure but two underlying deep structures (as in the case of an ambiguous sentence). For example:

Teachers should stop drinking in classrooms.

Visiting relatives can be a nuisance.

Chomsky proposed that people use transformational rules to convert surface structure to deep structure when trying to understand language, and to convert deep structure into surface structure when producing language.

words, the adults surrounding them produce language which consists of false starts, hesitations, slips of the tongue and blurred word boundaries (i.e.it is not clear where one word ends and another begins). He also believed that language acquisition cannot be dependent on intelligence or experience because it occurs at a time when the child is incapable of complex cognitions. Chomsky thought that children acquire language readily because they are biologically equipped to do so and possess an innate mechanism which is programmed to recognize grammatical structure. This Language Acquisition Device (LAD) is not specific to a particular language, such as English or Chinese, but rather sets limits on what is permissible in any acquired language. Chomsky believes that there are *linguistic universals* which are features common to all languages, for example phonological elements such as vowels and syllables and syntactic structures such as nouns, verbs, plurals, tenses. These similarities between languages exist at what Chomsky calls 'the deep structure' level whereas differences between languages exist at 'surface structure' level (see *In Focus* on the previous page). Children have an innate ability to use transformational rules which allow them to transform deep structure into surface structure and vice versa.

A more recent formulation of the innate approach has been put forward by Slobin (1985) who believes that infants possess a basic system of general processing strategies ('operating principles') which account for their 'language-making capacity'. He thinks that infants are pre-programmed to pay attention to the beginnings and endings of sounds and that they also tune in to particular repetitions or regularities in the language heard.

This kind of view of language acquisition seems able to explain more aspects of the process than the learning theory account but there are still a number of criticisms:

- Learning must play some part in the acquisition process, otherwise, for example, children would not progress from saying 'gived' to 'gave'.
- Exposure to spoken language would seem to be a necessary prerequisite.
- It does not adequately account for single word utterances which have no grammar.
- It ignores social and cognitive factors.
- There is some evidence (e.g. Akiyama 1984) that world languages are not as similar as Chomsky supposed.

❖ Activity 2 ❖

Take five minutes to write down as many different world languages as you can recall (for example, Spanish, Mandarin). How many did you identify? Do you think that you are close to the total? See the end of the chapter for the answer.

Interactionist theories

Most contemporary theorists have rejected the extreme versions of both the nativist and learning approaches outlined above and have opted instead for an interactionist view which stresses the role of maturation *and* experience. This view encompasses two broad types of theory: cognitive and social-interactionist.

Cognitive theory

According to theorists such as Piaget, language is dependent on other cognitive and perceptual processes and follows cognitive stages of development. Early language, in his view, is egocentric and characterized by three distinct types of early speech:

- *echolalia* – where children simply repeat utterances
- *monologues* – where children appear to be thinking out loud
- *collective monologues* – where two or more children give the appearance of engaging in dialogue but are, in fact, simply producing monologues.

A prerequisite for language development is the understanding of certain key concepts. For example, children need to attain the stage of object permanence before they can acquire concepts of objects and nouns. This could account for the rapid increase in vocabulary size at around the age of 18 months. Corrigan (1978), however, showed that once the effect of age had been controlled, there was no correlation between the development of object permanence and language. The increase in words could simply reflect increased memory capacity. There is, however, some evidence to suggest that the emergence of relational words such as 'up', 'more', 'gone', does depend on object permanence.

Another feature of the cognitive approach is its emphasis on the child as an active learner. Flavell (1985) has suggested that children seem to be constantly formulating and testing hypotheses about the rules and properties of language. Such rule-searching behaviour is apparent in other areas of development and this lends weight to the argument that language learning is simply part of a wider cognitive process. The cognitive theory is not too far removed from the ideas of theorists such as Slobin. The difference centres mainly on whether the rules are innate or whether they arise from the child's active analysis and exploration of the environment. There is little current research in this area and interest has focused more on the social-interactionist approach.

Social-interactionist theory

While accepting that certain biological and cognitive processes may be necessary for language development, social interactionists believe that these processes alone are not sufficient. They feel that the linguists' preoccupation with grammar obscures the main function of language, which is interpersonal communication. Bruner (1983) contrasted the idea of the LAD with that of the LASS (Language Acquisition Socialization System). He believed that the mother-child relationship serves to develop important social skills, such as turn-taking and mutual gaze, which then play a part in conversational language. Support for the necessity of exposure to language in a social context comes from studies of deprived children. Sachs *et al.* (1981) reported the case of 'Jim' whose parents were both deaf and dumb. Television provided his only exposure to spoken language up to the age of three. Although he produced speech, it was grammatically idiosyncratic and poorly articulated, which suggests that exposure alone is insufficient – there must be some social interaction as well.

It seems irrefutable that language development needs to occur in a social context to be completely effective. The social-interactionist account cannot, however, explain all the features of language acquisition.

Section summary

A number of theories have been put forward to account for the acquisition of language but none has yet been offered that provides a satisfactory explanation of *all* the features of this complex process. Learning, maturational, cognitive and social factors probably all have a part to play but the precise ways in which these various elements combine and interact is not yet fully understood.

Language production and comprehension

Even though we do not yet fully understand the acquisition process, we do know that people become extremely skilled and accurate at producing and understanding language. In order to do so they have to engage as active information processors using many different strategies. In the next section, we shall look at some of the ways in which people achieve this extraordinary cognitive feat.

Language production: speech and writing

Speech

There has been surprisingly little research on speech production, mainly because it is difficult to investigate experimentally. One approach has been to look at the hesitations and slips of the tongue that occur in everyday speech. Speaking requires considerable planning in terms of choosing appropriate words and then putting them together in the form of sentences. Evidence from hesitation-analysis studies lends support to the idea that planning plays an important part in speech production. Goldman-Eisler (1968) has suggested that pauses allow us to plan the content of what we want to say. She found that pauses occur more often and last for longer before words that are less predictable from the preceding context, and concluded that pauses are used to track down elusive words. Harley (1995) has suggested that we know the meaning of what we want to say but cannot always retrieve the appropriate sound. This interpretation fits with the evidence from studies of the 'tip-of-the-tongue' phenomenon (TOT). This is an extended pause where we have a strong feeling that we know the word but cannot access the sound. It implies that retrieval difficulties involve weak links between the semantic (meaning) and phonological (sound) systems. Early research on pauses suggested that they were used only for semantic planning, but it now seems likely that syntactic planning also occurs.

Just as the study of perceptual illusions can throw light on normal perceptual processing, so the analysis of speech errors can help us to understand some aspects of language production. The speech we use in everyday conversation is often flawed. We pause, repeat ourselves, start new sentences before earlier ones have been completed and interject 'filler' words such as 'well', 'um' and 'er'. This happens at all levels, even amongst skilled language users. The type of error most investigated is the slip-of-the-tongue where sounds (phonemes), parts of words (morphemes) or whole words are transposed. There are several types of error (see Table 16.1).

Table 16.1 Examples of typical speech errors

Error class	*Error type*	*Target*	*Utterance*
Phoneme errors	Exchange	fast cars	cast fars
	Anticipation	reading lamp	leading lamp
	Perseveration	dirty hands	dirty dands
	Deletion	underground	undergound
Morpheme errors	Exchange	he picked bunches of flowers	he bunched picks of flowers
	Deletion	she answered 'No'	she answer 'No'
Word errors	Exchange	she took the dog to the vet	she took the vet to the dog
	Blend	shouting and screaming	shreaming
	Substitution	pass me the toast	pass me the plate

❖ Activity 3 ❖

Try keeping a diary for a week in which you record all your slips-of-the-tongue and then classify each error using the information in Table 16.1. You might find that you need friends to point out your errors to you as you will not always notice them yourself. Why do you think this is so?

Garrett (1988) has argued that speech production arises from a series of five independent levels of processing which operate *in sequence:*

- message level – the conceptual stage where the speaker formulates an abstract representation of what is to be said
- functional level – the syntactical planning stage where the grammatical structure of the utterance is represented
- positional level – where words are explicitly ordered
- sound level – where information about pronunciation is generated
- articulatory level – where instructions for the correct articulation of the words can be found.

We construct a syntactic structure for a sentence and then insert words into the appropriate slots.

Garrett's model is consistent with much of the speech error evidence but there are some problems, particularly with his claims that speech production is a serial process and that the levels are independent. Harley (1995) has suggested that the nature of certain speech errors should lead us to conclude that at least some parallel processing is taking place, and that there is interaction between the levels. According to Harley, Dell (1986) has put forward a more complete model. In his theory, processing occurs concurrently across a series of levels during which word representations activate the sound elements to which the words are linked. This model accounts for speech error data and for the feedback that occurs when speakers make alterations mid-sentence as a result of self-monitoring.

Writing

Speaking and writing share many cognitive components but they also differ in a number of ways. The language used in writing is often more formal and uses more complex syntactic and semantic structures. It is also unlikely to contain the kind of errors and hesitations so commonly found in speech. Various cognitive tasks are involved in writing, such as planning, sentence generation and revision.

❖ Activity 4 ❖

Consider how you set about writing an essay. Do you find you are more successful if you write a plan first? If you sometimes use a wordprocessor to prepare an essay, are you more or less likely to start with an outline? Why do you think this is?

Planning seems to play a particularly important role and Hayes (1989) has demonstrated that the amount of planning is highly correlated with the quality of the writing. With the increased use of wordprocessors for producing written text, researchers have begun considering whether people approach writing tasks in the same way as with traditional tools. It seems that the planning stage is more frequently omitted with computers, although more time is spent on editing.

The next stage in the writing process is usually sentence generation where the writer has to turn ideas from the planning stage into sentences. Kaufer *et al.* (1986) asked people to write out their planning outline for an essay. They found that, no matter how elaborate the outline, the essay was always at least eight times longer. Writing, just like speaking, is punctuated by pauses in which the writer deliberates about forms of expression and choices of words. The pattern of pauses seems to depend on the goal of the writer and the nature of the text (Matsuhashi 1982). Once text has been written, it is usually subjected to a revision process. The writer re-examines the goals of the text and assesses how well those goals have been met. Expert writers, not surprisingly, are better at the revision process than less experienced writers. Hayes *et al.* (1987) compared first-year college students with expert writers and found that the students were far more likely to focus on individual sentences and problems of spelling than on the overall organization and coherence of the text.

Language comprehension: listening and reading

Listening

In the first instance, we have to interpret the sounds of speech – a task which is highly complex but which we take for granted. In spoken, as opposed to written, language phonemes do not neatly follow one another and some overlap occurs. This overlap is referred to as *parallel transmission.* For example, if we see the word 'dog', the letters 'd', 'o', 'g' are clearly separated, but in speech the phoneme 'd' is carried into the sound of the 'o', the 'o' influences the sounds of both the 'd' and the 'g', and the 'g' begins to be sounded before the 'o' has been completely transmitted. In order to make sense of spoken language, listeners make use of a number of strategies. They can use context to help them reconstruct sounds missed against a noisy background and to understand unclear pronunciation. In spoken language, there are often no pauses to mark word boundaries.

❖ Activity 5 ❖

Try to tune in to a foreign radio station where a language is being spoken that you do not understand. How easy is it to know when one word starts and another ends?

We take it for granted in our native tongue that we can easily distinguish between words and sounds but this is an ability that is learned through experience and we do not always manage it successfully – consider, for example, the game of Chinese Whispers. Information from the speaker's face and lips provides visual cues that can be helpful and might account for the finding that speech is heard better in face-to-face conversation than on the telephone, no matter how good the line is (Massaro 1989).

Two types of theory have been proposed to account for speech perception. One approach favours the view that humans have a special phonetic mechanism specifically tuned to speech perception (Liberman and Mattingley 1989). The other, for which there seems to be more evidence, proposes a general mechanism which is responsible for processing both speech and non-speech sounds (e.g. Jusczyk 1986).

While the identification of isolated sounds is a necessary component of speech comprehension, it is also clearly important to understand the syntactic and semantic structure of what is being said. One way in which it is thought that we do this is to break sentences down into constituents. Matlin (1994) suggests that understanding a sentence involves several processes which occur *in parallel.* These are:

- hearing the speech sounds
- storing a representation of the speech sounds in short-term memory
- locating the meanings of the words in semantic memory
- organizing the representations of the speech sounds into constituents
- determining the meaning of the constituents
- combining the constituents to figure out the meaning of the whole sentence
- forgetting the exact wording of the constituents, retaining only the gist.

Another method of decoding spoken language is to apply Chomsky's model of transformational grammar which was described earlier in the chapter.

People are remarkably good at understanding spoken language but there are factors which make the process more difficult. Sentences containing negatives take longer to process and become very difficult to unravel if they contain more than one negative. Consider the sentence used by Sherman (1976):

> *'Few people strongly deny that the world is not flat.'*

It also seems that the active rather than the passive forms of sentences are easier to understand. For example, *'The dog chased the cat'* rather than *'The cat is chased by the dog'*. Ambiguous sentences (e.g. *'The chicken is ready to eat'*) also pose problems for listeners, and it is not clear how such sentences are processed. The parallel-distributed processing approach suggests that all possible meanings for an ambiguous item are activated and the correct one is then chosen on the basis of context and frequency. Other approaches assume that context has an influence from the outset and so access is limited to a single interpretation.

Reading

Reading does not depend on initial speech perception but on letter and word identification. Our eyes make very rapid movements (known as 'saccades') in order to bring the centre of the retina over the word to be read and then fixate for brief periods (approximately 250 milliseconds) in order to extract the information necessary for reading. The amount taken in during a fixation is referred to as the 'perceptual span' and typically includes about four letters to the left of the fixation and fifteen to the right, except in languages like Hebrew which are read from right to left. There is a difference between 'good' and 'bad' readers, in that 'good' readers make larger saccadic movements and are less likely to move back to earlier text. It also seems that readers with large working memory capacity are quicker and more accurate at understanding complex or ambiguous sentences (Just and Carpenter 1992).

Three broad types of explanation have been offered to account for word recognition:

- The *direct-access hypothesis* suggests that the visual pattern provides sufficient information for recognition to occur.
- The *indirect-access* hypothesis states that translation into some kind of speech code is required before the reader can access stored word meanings.
- The *dual-encoding* hypothesis, which has the most empirical support, allows for semantic memory being reached through either the sound or the visual route (Van Orden *et al.* 1990).

Reading is not simply a matter of recognizing individual words but also involves drawing inferences based on information stored in memory. (See the suggestions for further reading at the end of the chapter for more detailed coverage of this topic.)

Section summary

Language production and comprehension are complex achievements which involve humans in behaving as active information-processors. There are similarities between the spoken and written forms of language since, for both activities, we need to understand grammatical structure and be able to extract meaning. There are also important differences in that spoken language is acquired with little training whereas reading and writing skills are achieved, if at all, with some effort and considerable instruction. Reading and writing also allow us more time for recapping and revision so we are less likely to make the errors which occur in spoken language.

Models of thought

Problem-solving

This is an everyday activity which is often taken for granted and yet it is a highly complex skill. It is used whenever we need to reach a goal that is not readily available. There is, for example, no problem to be solved in the equation $x = 5 + 2$, because this can be found in a single step (i.e. the goal is readily available). Real problem-solving involves situations such as finding your way to an unfamiliar destination or planning nutritious meals on a restricted budget. Given the wide diversity of tasks that come under the heading of problem-solving, it is not surprising that there is no single adequate theory to explain how we solve all our problems. However, the information-processing approach provides a common framework within which to study problem-solving. This approach arises from the work of Newell *et al.* (1958) which divides problem-solving into a set of stages progressing from the original to the goal state. The stages involve:

- representing the problem
- selecting and implementing operators to tackle the problem
- evaluating progress to assess whether or not the goal state has been achieved.

These stages are flexible and allow the solver to go back to previous states or to set a series of subgoals by which the final goal can be achieved. This approach has the advantage that it provides a broad framework which can then be elaborated to provide more detailed analysis of the specific processes involved in solving particular problems.

Computer modelling of problem-solving has developed from the information-processing approach and this has proved useful in several ways, for example by providing information about the nature of strategies, the importance of a knowledge base and the crucial nature of the representation stage in problem-solving. In 1972, Newell and Simon developed a computer program called General problem-solver or GPS in which they attempted to mimic the processes used by humans in tackling problems. The GPS was used extensively to study a number of different problems but it was eventually discarded by Newell and Simon because it was not as applicable to human problem-solving as they had first assumed, particularly as far as tackling ill-defined problems was concerned.

Methods of problem-solving

Newell and Simon (1972) suggested that problem-solving consisted of searching through the *problem space* which is made up of a number of linked *states* leading to the *goal state*. The solver crosses the problem space by using a range of *permissible operators* which transform one state to another. One way of searching through the problem space which guarantees a solution is to use the *algorithmic method*. This involves a systematic random search in which all possible solutions are tried until the correct one is found. However, this approach can be time-consuming and

❖ Activity 6 ❖

Try solving the following anagram and think about the way you tackled it:

g w n i l k a

An algorithmic method would guarantee a solution but it is highly unlikely that you applied that method. The anagram has seven letters which means that there are $7 \times 6 \times 5 \times 4 \times 3 \times 2 \times 1$ (= 5040) possible permutations. It is more likely that you used a heuristic method. For example, you might have picked out 'ing' because you recognized this as a familiar combination found at the end of English words. You are then left with a much smaller problem space 'w l k a' and the solution 'walking' now becomes quite easy to find.

inefficient, and it is more usual for human problem-solvers to adopt a *heuristic* approach. This is a rule of thumb involving a selective search which looks only at those parts of the problem space most likely to produce a solution.

Psychological research has focused more on heuristics than on algorithms largely because we use heuristics far more frequently. There are different kinds of heuristic strategies available to us, described in the following subsections.

Means-ends analysis

This involves breaking the problem up into a number of subproblems which are solved in turn and which gradually reduce the difference between the original state and the goal state. There is some evidence that people pause at intervals during the problem and work out their strategy for the next few moves. Greeno (1974) gave subjects the Hobbits-and-Orcs problem (shown in Activity 7) and found that they did not progress at a steady pace but, instead, took a long time at the beginning and then, again, before two other critical moves. It seems that they were tackling a subproblem at these points and needed to organize a group of moves. Try to solve the problem in Activity 7 before you read any further.

In dealing with certain problems it is sometimes appropriate actually to *increase* the difference between the original state and the goal state by temporarily moving backwards. For example, in the Hobbits-and-Orcs problem, solvers tend to concentrate on reducing the difference between the original state (all creatures on the left side) and the goal state (all creatures on the right side) and so think only of moving them from left to right. This means that they ignore the crucial step, which they need to solve the problem, of moving creatures backward across the river. So it is sometimes necessary temporarily to violate the difference-reduction strategy of the means-ends approach in order to reach a solution.

❖ Activity 7 ❖

The Hobbits-and-Orcs Problem

Three Hobbits and three Orcs are standing at the side of a river bank. They all want to cross the river but there is just one small boat available which can only carry up to two creatures at a time. The boat cannot be pushed back empty to the other side and always requires one creature to steer it. If Orcs are ever allowed to outnumber the Hobbits, they will attack them and gobble them up. Your task is to find a way of transporting all the creatures across the river while never leaving more Orcs than Hobbits on any river bank.

The solution can be found at the end of the chapter.

Source: adapted from Thomas (1974)

Analogy approach

Another heuristic that can be applied to problem-solving is the use of analogy. In other words, we use a solution to an earlier problem to help us with a new one. This would seem to be a useful approach but research shows that problem-solvers frequently fail to notice a potential analogy and that, even when they do, they often make errors in their interpretation. Novick and Holyoak (1991) have suggested that four processes are required for successful problem-solving using analogies:

- locating the appropriate analogical problem (source problem)
- making appropriate correspondences between parts of the source problem and parts of the target problem
- adapting the procedures that were helpful in the source problem
- developing an abstract schema for the whole class of problems that the source and target problems represent.

If these processes are prerequisites for the successful use of the analogy technique, it is perhaps not surprising that Novick (1988) found experts using analogies more frequently than novices.

Other factors influencing problem-solving

Expertise

The superiority that Novick found for experts over novices has been demonstrated in several studies. Experts differ from novices in many ways such as in terms of their memory for task-related information, their knowledge base, their method of problem representation, their self-monitoring abilities, and their speed and efficiency.

Mental set

This can also influence the way in which problems are solved in that solvers sometimes get locked into a specific way of tackling problems that has been useful in the past even when a solution could be reached in a simpler way. The *In Focus* outlines a well-known experiment on mental set conducted by Luchins (1942).

Functional fixedness

Functional fixedness refers to the tendency people have to assign fixed functions to objects. Duncker (1945) conducted a classic study in which subjects were left alone in a room equipped only with a table, a candle, a box of matches and a box of tintacks. They were instructed, using nothing but the materials available in the room, to support the candle on the wall. Most subjects failed to accomplish the task because they used unsuccessful tactics (e.g. trying to pin the candle to the wall or to fix it using melted wax). The only successful solution involved overcoming functional fixedness by tacking the empty matchbox to the wall and using it as a candle holder.

Problem definition

Another way in which the nature of the problem can be a factor concerns its definition. *Well-defined* problems (e.g. anagrams) have clearly specified

In Focus

Luchins' Water Jar Problem

Participants were asked to imagine that they had three jars A, B and C and an unlimited supply of water. For each problem, Luchins supplied a list of the capacities of all three jars and also specified a particular amount of water to be measured out. The task for the subjects was to use all or some of the jars to measure out the required (goal) amount of water. Try this exercise yourself before you read any further.

Problem	*A*	*B*	*C*	*Goal*
1	22	150	4	120
2	18	125	16	75
3	17	97	9	62
4	39	129	22	46
5	15	66	11	29
6	41	89	7	34

The best way to solve Problem 1 is to fill Jar B and then remove from it one jarful using jar A and then two jarfuls using jar C. The first five problems are all solved best in this way and most people continue to apply this method for the whole exercise. However, in this instance past experience works to the solver's disadvantage because, for Problem 6, there is a more direct method. It is easily solved by subtracting one jarful of C from A. Did you recognize this easier solution?

original and goal states and an easily verifiable solution. Most everyday problems, however, are *ill-defined*, so that neither the original state, the goal state nor the rules are clear. Since ill-defined problems have no single, verifiable answer, there is also no way of telling if the solution is correct. There are various ways to tackle ill-defined problems, including:

- division into subproblems
- imposing more structure
- simply launching into the problem, even though it is poorly understood, and stopping when a solution of sorts is achieved.

Reasoning

Reasoning is a particular kind of logical problem-solving which involves drawing conclusions from given information. A distinction has been drawn between *deductive* and *inductive* reasoning. Deductive reasoning involves drawing conclusions that follow necessarily from given statements but it does not require specialist knowledge about the content of those statements. Inductive reasoning, on the other hand, involves generating a hypothesis consistent with a known body of data. We will now consider two types of deductive reasoning: propositional and categorical.

Propositional reasoning

This involves 'if... , then...' relationships. For example, imagine that a friend says to you: *'If I can get up in time tomorrow, I'll meet you at the bus stop.'* The friend does not turn up the next day, so you make the logical deduction that she has not been able to get up in time. In studies of this type of reasoning, participants are often given two statements and then asked if a third statement follows logically from the first two. There are certain kinds of statement which inevitably lead to an invalid conclusion and others which always lead to a valid conclusion. The following are examples:

- affirming the antecedent:
  If it is snowing, the post will be late.
  It is snowing.
  Therefore, the post will be late. *(Valid)*
- affirming the consequent:
  If it is snowing, the post will be late.
  The post is late.
  Therefore it is snowing. *(Invalid)*
- denying the antecedent:
  If it is snowing, the post will be late.
  It is not snowing.
  Therefore, the post will not be late. *(Invalid)*
- denying the consequent:
  If it is snowing, the post will be late
  The post is not late.
  Therefore, it is not snowing. *(Valid)*

People find it far easier to deal with the propositions that lead to a valid conclusion than those which produce invalid conclusions (Taplin 1971). There are several reasons why people make errors in these reasoning tasks. Johnson-Laird and Byrne (1991) have suggested that people construct *mental models* to represent the premises in the statement but that they fail to look at all the logical possibilities. Another possibility is that they make an *illicit conversion* by incorrectly changing part of the problem into another form. For example, when people tackle reasoning tasks of denying the antecedent (an invalid method), they convert the first statement from *'If p, then q'* to *'If q, then p'*. They then treat the problem using the method of denying the consequent (a valid method) and so wrongly conclude that q is not true. Sometimes errors occur in deductive reasoning because people try to confirm a hypothesis rather than disprove it. A good example of this is the Wason (1960) task (see *In Focus* on the next page).

Why do so many people fail to solve this problem? Wason believed that people have a *confirmation bias* and neglect to seek falsifying evidence. Other theorists (e.g. Evans and Lynch 1973) suggest that it is an example of *matching bias* whereby attention is biased towards items actually mentioned in the rule. These suggestions do not account for the finding that most people solve the problem when it is presented in a less abstract form.

In Focus

◆

The Wason selection task

Try to do the following task. Look at the set of cards below. Every card has a letter on one side and a digit on the other.

You are then given a rule which may be either true or false:

If there is an E on one side of the card then there is a 6 on the other side of the card.

You have to select those cards and *only* those cards which are needed to decide whether the rule is true or false. Work out your answer before you read on.

Most people respond to this by saying either E alone, or E and 6 but the correct answer is actually E and 9. The rule can only be false if there is an E on one side of a card and a number *other than* 6 on the other. You need to turn over the 9 as well to see if a number card that is *not* a 6 has E on the other side. Turning over the 6 card gives you no relevant information because the rule does not state that an E *must* be on the back of a 6. Do not worry if you got it wrong: less than 10% of participants typically arrive at the correct answer and, according to Jackson and Griggs (1988), even a PhD qualification is no guarantee of success.

Categorical reasoning

This type of reasoning is expressed in syllogisms. These are logical tasks consisting of two statements (premises) and a conclusion. They are concerned with membership in categories and use words such as 'all', 'none', 'some'. In studies of categorical reasoning, people are asked to decide whether a conclusion is 'valid', 'invalid' or 'no valid conclusion' – a task which they generally find very difficult. An example of a valid categorical syllogism is:

All As are Bs.
All Bs are Cs.
Therefore, all As are Cs.

The symbols are usually replaced by words, for example:

All women in this class are members of the tennis club.
All members of the tennis club are under 50 years old.
Therefore, all women in this class are under 50 years old.

The premises themselves do not have to be true in order for the conclusion to be valid. The important thing is that the underlying logic is correct. For example:

All teachers are Martians.
All Martians have green legs.
Therefore, all teachers have green legs.

It seems that these tests are more difficult when they include negative words and when they use the passive voice (Lippman 1972). Galotti *et al.* (1986) also showed that time was an important factor and that performance improved, even for skilled logicians, if they were not under time pressure. As in propositional reasoning, a major source of error arises from illicit conversion. The *belief-bias effect* can also lead to errors because people make judgements on the basis of previous knowledge rather than on the basis of logic (Markovits and Nantel 1989). Evans (1989) explained the belief-bias by suggesting that people suspend their usual critical approach in analysing the syllogism if the conclusion fits in with existing beliefs.

Johnson-Laird and colleagues (e.g. Johnson-Laird and Byrne 1991) have proposed a theory to explain how people solve syllogisms. In their studies, people are given two concrete statements and asked to supply their own logical conclusion. By analysing the strategies used, the researchers concluded that people form an internal, pictorial model of the problem and use this to draw a conclusion. However, if they fail to consider alternative models, they may draw the wrong conclusion. People who continue to search for counter-examples to their first model are more successful. This theory has not been universally accepted but it does account for much of the research data (see *In Focus* below).

Section summary

We have considered two particular types of thinking. Problem-solving requires the use of stored knowledge and it has numerous practical applications. People use heuristics and analogies to help them try to reach solutions but they are not always successful. Formal reasoning is rather different in that it only deals with conclusive arguments. We are rarely able to draw conclusions in everyday life with the same certainty.

In Focus

Mental models

Given the premise *'All lions are carnivores'*, you might first imagine a set of lions. Exactly how you imagine them (e.g as images, words or symbols) is not important in Johnson-Laird's model. The critical factor is how the parts of your model fit together. We will use notation similar to that used by Johnson-Laird.

lion

lion

You can then add in the information that lions are carnivores:

lion = carnivore

lion = carnivore

[carnivore]

The brackets indicate that your model recognizes that there are instances of carnivores which are not lions.

You might then think of a famous lion, like Elsa, and add her into your model:

Elsa = lion = carnivore

lion = carnivore

[carnivore]

You are now ready to draw an inference: *Elsa is a carnivore.*

This is a simplified example. What complicates the issue is that syllogisms may give rise to a number of different mental models. Consider the following two premises:

All fish are swimmers.

Some swimmers are happy.

You might represent these premises as:

fish = swimmer

fish = swimmer = happy

fish = swimmer = not happy

You might then conclude: *Some of the fish are happy.*

However, if you leave it there, you will fail to see that there is another model consistent with the premises:

fish = swimmer

fish = swimmer = not happy

not fish = swimmer = happy

not fish = not swimmer = happy

In this model, fish are related only to those swimmers who are not happy, so *none* of the fish are happy. There is, for these two premises, no single conclusion that can be drawn that is consistent with both mental models. Therefore, we can only infer that *there is no valid conclusion.*

Language and thought

There has been considerable interest in the question of the relationship between thought and language and the similarities and differences that exist in thinking between members of different language communities. In this section we shall consider:

- whether there are significant differences between languages
- whether thinking differs between people who speak different languages
- whether there is a causal relationship between thinking and language.

We shall also consider some of the social factors which affect language and thinking.

The linguistic relativity hypothesis

The *relativist* view, most notably espoused by Whorf (1941), focuses on the differences between languages and, in its strong form, asserts that an individual's particular native language determines the way the individual thinks and perceives the world. In its weaker form, the word 'influences' substitutes for 'determines'. However, in both forms the terms 'language' and 'thought' are not precisely defined, and so the hypotheses are difficult to test. In practice, most cross-cultural studies have only considered the effects of language on perception and memory rather than on mental processes such as problem-solving and reasoning.

It has proved difficult to find unequivocal support for this hypothesis in either the strong or the weak form because, even where cognitive differences are found in different language communities, it is difficult to isolate language as the only influence. Education, intelligence, age, experience and environment may all be contributory factors. Much of the evidence cited in support of the theory comes from observations that certain words exist in some languages but not others. Whorf was particularly interested in the languages of North American Indians and noted that the Hopi have a single term to denote a flying object, whereas English distinguishes between birds, insects, planes, helicopters, and so on. Similarly, Eskimos are reported to have several words for specific kinds of snow as do Arabs for sand. The assumption of the theory is that a huge choice of words allows native speakers to perceive and remember specialized categories of objects in a way that is impossible for native speakers of other languages which lack the appropriate vocabulary. However, the basis on which some of these claims are made is dubious. Harley (1995) suggests that Eskimo actually only has two words for types of snow and that English is similar in that it differentiates between slush and sleet. It is, in any case, an enormous inferential leap to assume that people are unable to conceptualize something in the absence of an appropriate linguistic label. A gardening expert, for example, has labels for subspecies of plants which most other people in the same language community do not need to know. These latter are, however, just as capable of perceiving differences between the plants and could learn the labels if they chose to do so. Nor can we assume that the existence of a verbal label ensures complete understanding of a particular concept.

While there is little evidence for the extreme version of the linguistic relativity hypothesis, there is some modest support for the weaker form. In a classic

❖ Activity 8 ❖

Consider the following words: 'soul', 'consciousness' and 'language'. Now try to write down briefly what you think each word means. Compare your answers with those of other people you know. You will probably find that there is no precise, agreed meaning for abstract concepts such as these.

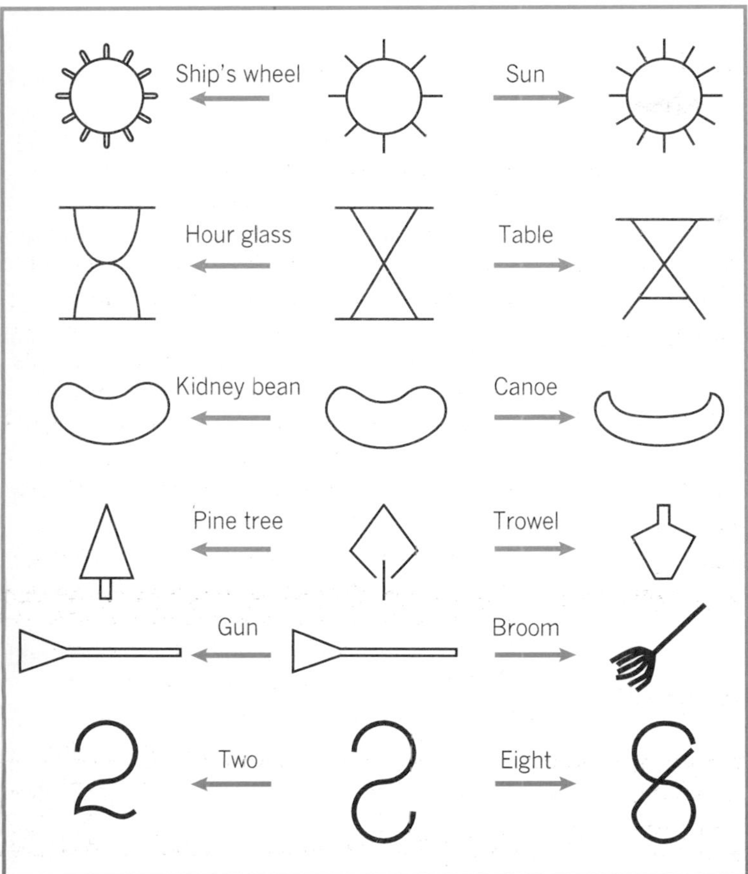

Figure 16.1 Some examples of stimuli and responses showing the effect of verbal labels

Source: adapted from Carmichael *et al.* (1932)

experiment, Carmichael *et al.* (1932) looked at the effects of learning verbal labels on the recall of ambiguous line drawings (see Fig. 16.1). Results showed that recall was affected by the label that had been attached at the first presentation.

Ervin-Tripp (1964) found that Japanese-American bilinguals given word association tests in Japanese produced responses that were typical of Japanese monolinguals. The same individuals, however, responded like American monolinguals when the test was in English. Although this lends support for the Whorfian hypothesis, it was found that responses were also influenced by the nationality of the listener and by the nature of the topic under discussion.

Attempts to investigate the possible effects of grammatical differences between languages have produced inconclusive evidence. Bloom (1981) argued that English speakers, because they have a subjunctive mood, find it easy to reason counter-factually (i.e. *If* she had taken the bus, she *would* have arrived on time). There is no subjunctive mood in Chinese and so Chinese speakers should find counter-factual reasoning more difficult. Liu (1985) refuted this, arguing that such reasoning is possible in Chinese but might take longer to formulate. While this casts doubt on the strong version of the linguistic relativity hypothesis, it does suggest that the facility within a language to express a concept in simple terms reduces processing time.

The evidence from studies investigating the linguistic relativity hypothesis has been difficult to interpret because of the problem of disentangling the language component from other possible influences. There appears to be no support for the strong version but some evidence for the weaker version, since language does seem to influence some habits of thought and also the facility and efficiency with which certain thought can be expressed.

If causal links do exist between thought and language they are likely to be bi-directional. We sometimes invent new words to meet a need and these new words, in turn, might come to affect the way we think. So, for example, 'chairperson' has been coined in order to provide a less gender-specific term than 'chairman', and those who introduced it hoped that use of the term would change views about gender roles.

Piaget and the cognition hypothesis

Unlike Whorf, who was concerned with differences between cultures, Piaget was interested in universal patterns that occur in all children's thought regardless of their native language. He saw language as just one type of symbolic function, much like symbolic play and symbolic imagery. He recognized that language could have a facilitating effect on thinking, but that an understanding of underlying concepts was required before the appropriate verbal tag could be applied. Piaget's views are expressed in more detail earlier in this chapter and in Chapter 18.

Vygotsky and the social context of language

A rather different view has been put forward by Vygotsky (1934). He believed that language and thinking have different roots and develop independently in infancy. At first, any attempts by an infant to use language are for social purposes and not linked to inner thoughts. Thinking, which starts to develop during this same period, is at a fairly basic level and occurs in the absence of language. Vygotsky suggested that, at about the age of two years, social speech and thought without language begin to merge and language starts to play a major role in the child's intellectual and social development. He believed that egocentric speech becomes internalized as inner speech and continues to play an important role in regulating and planning cognitive operations.

So far, we have looked mainly at cognitive factors in the thought-language relationship. It is important not to lose sight of the fact that language is also a tool for social communication. There has been some research on the effects of social context on language. Bernstein (1973) suggested that children's language is influenced by their social environment. He made a distinction between 'restricted code' and 'elaborated code'.

- *Restricted code* is a pattern of speech which uses fairly basic vocabulary and contains mainly concrete description. It can usually only be understood when set in context.
- *Elaborated code*, on the other hand, is not context-bound and uses more complex and abstract words and structures.

Bernstein believed that working-class children use only restricted code, whereas most middle-class children can use both codes, even though they have a greater tendency to adopt the elaborated. It is not entirely clear from the evidence whether this puts working-class children at a disadvantage, although it could cause problems of communication between teachers and pupils if they come from different backgrounds.

One other aspect of the social importance of the relationship between language and thought is the possible effect of language on certain disadvantaged groups in society. Spender (1980) has written about the importance of non-sexist language in reducing gender stereotyping. The assumption of this view is that using neutral terms like 'headteacher' rather than 'headmaster' will influence patterns of thinking about gender roles. This, of course, depends on some form of the linguistic relativity hypothesis being plausible.

There has also been interest in the effects of non-standard forms of language such as the dialects spoken in some black communities (often referred to as 'black English'). Labov (1970) found that speakers can express the same ideas as 'standard-English' speakers and that the two groups can understand each other well. However, black children are at a disadvantage in certain social and educational situations where standard English is the norm. Labov gave an example of a black child being interviewed, first in standard English and then in his local, black English dialect. In the first interview, he had been taciturn and monosyllabic but he became lively and articulate when he was allowed to use his own familiar language.

Section summary

Various attempts have been made to demonstrate a relationship between language and thought. There is some evidence to support all three of the major positions, that is:

- the cognition hypothesis that suggests that some aspects of cognitive development facilitate some aspects of language acquisition
- Vygotsky's theory that thought and language begin to develop independently and then merge to produce a two-way process of social and cognitive development
- the weak version of Whorf's hypothesis that particular languages can influence performance on certain cognitive tasks.

Social factors also seem to play a role in this relationship although there has been less research in this area. The relationship between language and thought is obviously a complex interaction of biological, cognitive, social and cultural factors.

Chapter summary

- The skill with which humans produce and comprehend language is remarkable. Psychologists have been interested both in the process of initial language acquisition and in the mechanisms underlying later, fluent use of the spoken and written word. Various theories have been proposed to account for the acquisition of language, but none has yet provided a complete explanation.
- Theorists looking at language production and comprehension have generally stressed the importance of active information-processing. More research has been conducted into comprehension than production, mainly because the former is easier to study in controlled conditions.
- Both spoken and written forms of language have been investigated and they share certain similarities. However, there are important differences, too, and these help us to understand some of the underlying mechanisms involved in the comprehension and production of language.
- There are a number of types of thinking which have interested psychologists and we have considered two of these: problem-solving and reasoning. We tend to be more successful at the former, perhaps because we use problem-solving more in our everyday life.
- Finally, we drew together the threads of language and thought and considered the relationship between the two cognitive processes. This relationship is a highly complex combination of biological, cognitive, social and cultural factors.

Solutions to activities

Activity 2

There are between 3,000 and 4,000 languages spoken in the world today. If known dialects are included, the number is even higher. Voegelin and Voegelin (1977) have produced an index of the world's languages in which there are over 20,000 entries.

Activity 7

There are several steps involved in the Hobbits and Orcs problem. L represents the left bank and R represents the right bank:

1. Move 2 Orcs, L to R.
2. Move 1 Orc, R to L.
3. Move 2 Orcs, L to R.
4. Move 1 Orc, R to L.
5. Move 2 Hobbits, L to R.
6. Move 1 Orc, 1 Hobbit, R to L.
7. Move 2 Hobbits, L to R.
8. Move 1 Orc, R to L.
9. Move 2 Orcs, L to R.
10. Move 1 Orc, R to L.
11. Move 2 Orcs, L to R.

Essay titles

1 Describe and evaluate **two** theories relating to language acquisition in humans. *(24 marks)*

2 Describe and evaluate research findings relating to both the production and comprehension of language. *(24 marks)*

3 Discuss any **two** models or explanations of human thought. *(24 marks)*

4 (a) Outline **two** theories relating to the relationship between language and thought. *(12marks)*

(b) Assess the extent to which either of these theories is supported by research evidence. *(12 marks)*

Further reading

Eysenck, M.W. (1993) *Principles of Cognitive Psychology*, Hove: Lawrence Erlbaum Associates Publishers.

This covers most of the areas included in this chapter and is written clearly and accessibly.

Harley, T.A. (1995) *The Psychology of Language: From Data to Theory*, Hove: Erlbaum (UK), Taylor and Francis.

This is a comprehensive and up-to-date account of the psychology of language. It is an undergraduate text but it is accessible for A level students who would like more detailed coverage.

Matlin, M.W. (1994) *Cognition* (3rd edn), Orlando: Harcourt Brace Publishers.

This is an excellent, readable book which covers all the topics in this chapter in more detail and includes some very clear examples and illustrations.

Part 5

Developmental Psychology

Chapter 17

Early socialization

David Messer
Lesley Messer

Preview

In this chapter we shall be looking at:

- theories relating to the process of early social development
- research findings relating to social behaviour in humans
- theories and research relating to the development of attachment
- theories and research relating to enrichment and deprivation, including separation, maternal deprivation, isolation and enrichment
- social and cultural variations in child-rearing.

Introduction

Infants are physically helpless and need adults to feed, care for and protect them; without such assistance they cannot survive (psychologists generally use the term 'infant' to refer to children of less than two years, the term 'child' is used to refer to anyone below the age of adolescence). However, adults do much more than simply provide for the physical care of infants. When adults are with infants they invariably are involved in some form of social behaviour – this is one of the delights of having infants. The first section of this chapter outlines theories and findings about early social behaviour, together with a consideration of the process of attachment. The chapter then moves on to discuss enrichment and deprivation, and here again the emphasis is on social rather than physical processes. The last section draws the material together by examining cross-cultural issues, a topic which is also considered at various other points in the chapter.

Early social development: theories and research

General theories

Many of the controversies in developmental psychology stem from two fundamentally different, and often opposing views. These views have been characterized as the 'nature–nurture' debate. On one side is the view that the child begins life with very few or no innate abilities (these are abilities which are present because they are inherited, for example the ability to smile is probably inherited and therefore is innate), and that *experience* produces the child's abilities and characteristics. This is known as the *nurture* or *empiricist* position. On the other side is the argument that many of our characteristics are the result of the general human abilities that we *inherit* (e.g. walking upright), and the more specific characteristics that we inherit from our parents (e.g. what colour eyes we have). This is known as the *nature* or *nativist* position. Today it is rare for any psychologist to adopt these extreme positions, but the impact of such thinking can be seen in theories about social development.

❖ Activity 1 ❖

At birth, an infant appears as a helpless being virtually without social skills. A two-year-old is able to use non-verbal and verbal communication to:

- register approval and disapproval
- enlist help
- greet people
- show interest to others.

Make a list of the different sorts of explanation that can be used to describe the development of social skills (e.g. are social skills innate?).

Specific viewpoints

We all have an idea of what is meant by social behaviour, but there are a number of issues about its definition. If I smile to myself, is this social behaviour? Is an audience needed to make the behaviour 'social'? The answer to these questions will probably have a bearing on the way we think about related behaviours in infants. Similarly, there are differences of opinion amongst psychologists about what is meant by 'socialization'. It can be thought of as a process that allows children to acquire the social skills to function in their society but, as we will see in the next sections, there are different viewpoints about what is 'social behaviour' and the process of socialization.

Learning theory

In the past, the nurture position has been linked to the various forms of learning theory. The strong influence of behaviourism on psychology during the 1930s to 1950s meant that the prevailing belief was that reinforcement could explain many processes in development. However, although reinforcement is undoubtedly an important process in explaining the frequency of particular social behaviours, there is difficulty in using this approach to explain why certain social behaviours occur (e.g. speech), and why they develop in the order that they do (e.g. why smiling develops before pointing). More recently the idea of social learning theory has been introduced. Bandura and Walters (1963) claimed that observational learning could explain many of the processes which were difficult to explain using other versions of learning theory (see Chapter 19). However, this model has not been directly applied to the range of behaviours encountered in early social development.

Piaget and Vygotsky

The ideas of both these theorists are considered fully in Chapter 18. For Piaget, there is little that is special about social development. He believed that social and communicative advances occur as a result of developments in general cognitive abilities. In contrast, Vygotsky argues that social interaction and culture provide the basis for development. A central aspect of Vygotsky's theory is that understanding has to occur in a social context *before* it can be incorporated into a person's cognitive structures, thus giving prominence to the role of social behaviour. In this way it is supposed that social communication develops out of interaction with adults.

Innate capacities

Trevarthen has taken the position that children from an early age have the capacity for 'intersubjectivity'. This can be a difficult idea to understand. He explains it as follows:

> 'For infants to share mental control with other persons they must have two skills. First, they must be able to exhibit to others at least the rudiments of individual consciousness and intentionality. This attribute of acting as agents I call subjectivity. In order to communicate, infants must also be able to fit this subjective control to the *subjectivity* of others: they must also demonstrate *intersubjectivity*.' (Trevarthen 1979, p. 322)

If we regarded infants as little more than automatic biological machines which unthinkingly react to their circumstances, then the idea of intersubjectivity would be meaningless. What Trevarthen is claiming is that even very young infants are conscious that people are fundamentally different from objects, and infants are able to fit their behaviours appropriately with the actions of other people. For example, he claims that mothers and infants tend to take turns in vocalizing just as adults do in a conversation.

Furthermore, Trevarthen sees social and cognitive development as proceeding not through a relationship with a more competent adult, but as the maturation of innate capacities. He believes that infants interact with people in what he terms the *communicative* mode. Actions used in the communicative mode include what Trevarthen calls pre-speech mouth movements: sustained and active movements of the mouth and tongue which often occur when infants are interacting with people. By using these actions infants are believed to convey their mood and intentions to another person.

More recently, Hobson (1993) has suggested that infants are able to perceive the emotions of other people directly. In other words, infants do not have to learn what a smile or an angry shout mean, instead they automatically understand these signals. Hobson supposes that this capacity allows infants to engage in social behaviour and possess intersubjectivity.

Ethological and ecological approaches

Neither the ethological nor the ecological approach provides theories about development, but each provides a separate framework for the study of social development. Ethology is concerned with the study of behaviour in its natural setting together with a consideration of the evolutionary and adaptive influences on the behaviour. Most of the work in ethology has concerned animal behaviour, but this approach, as we will see later, has influenced thinking about the biological basis of infants' attachment to their mother. Critics of ethology have pointed out the problem of discussing evolutionary pressures with no real data about this process, and of the lack of attention paid to cultural processes.

Bronfenbrenner (1979) is usually regarded as the father of the ecological approach. This approach places a child's development in the context of the family, the wider family system and the cultural setting. All these levels are usually seen as having different kinds of impact on development. Thus, the immediate family may develop particular routines and games with a child;

❖ Activity 2 ❖

Make a table in which the headings are the specific viewpoints about early social development (Learning Theory, Piaget, Vygotsky, Trevarthen, Ethological and Ecological). Enter in the rows the answers a supporter of each viewpoint might give to the following questions:

1. Are infants born with social capacities?
2. What is the main process responsible for developing social capacities?
3. What observations support this viewpoint?
4. What do you think are the problems with this viewpoint?

these in turn may be the result of knowledge contained in the wider family system, and these in turn may reflect the values in the culture of the family. The importance of this approach is that it suggests that there are a variety of influences on the development of social behaviour and that social behaviour is the result of processes in both the immediate family and the wider culture (e.g. views about whether girls and boys should be treated differently).

Research findings

Research into the characteristics of newborn babies has revealed that they start life with a preference for social stimuli. Two questions can be asked:

- Do infants have a preference for adults in general?
- Do they have any specific preferences for their mother?

A preference for adults and mothers?

Recent research has revealed that infants prefer the *sound, sight* and *movement* of adults to other comparable stimuli (see Messer 1994). When we speak to pre-school children, we tend to use a higher pitch (similar to a higher musical sound), a more sing-song voice and shorter utterances. Newborn babies prefer to listen to this adult-to-child speech than to normal adult-to-adult conversation.

In addition, young infants find human faces attractive (Fantz 1961) and this seems to be because human faces contain general visual properties which make any stimuli attractive for infants (high contrast between dark and light areas, vertical symmetry, movement and curved rather than straight lines).

Infants are also interested in the movements of adults. Investigators attached light points to a person's limbs and recorded their movements in a darkened room. A computer was used to generate an equivalent set of movements which would not be possible for a human to make. Three-month-old infants preferred to watch the actual human movements rather than the computer-generated ones. These capacities are likely to provide a basis for attention to the things people do and say, and this may be of assistance to the development of both social behaviour and of relationships with people.

In the last twenty years there has also been a series of investigations which have revealed that newborn infants show a preference for the *sound, sight* and *smell* of their mother. One-day-old infants will learn to suck harder and more frequently on a teat to hear the sound of their mother's voice rather than that of a stranger (DeCasper and Fifer 1980). This seems to be a result of *pre-natal* learning. Newborns show preferences for various sounds heard before their birth (Hepper 1991). These include nursery-rhymes, speech transformed so that it sounds similar to what would be heard inside the womb and even the theme tune to the popular TV soap *Neighbours* (presumably a consequence of maternal interest in this programme during pregnancy!).

Even more remarkably, Bushnell *et al.* (1989) have found that infants who were less than 24 hours old, looked longer at their mother than another woman. This occurred when all they could see were the adults' faces and when they were unable to smell their mother. As yet there is no entirely convincing explanation of these findings.

Infants are also attracted to the odour of their mother. MacFarlane (1975) placed, either side of babies' heads, a pad that had been in contact with the breast of their mother and one from another mother. By ten days after birth infants showed a preference by turning towards the pad from their mother. The precise mechanism of this process is not yet clear, but it seems that familiarity with odours may result in such preferences.

These findings indicate that within the first two weeks of life, infants already show a preference for their mother, which may be a result of familiarity. However, it is important to emphasize that these preferences do *not* constitute attachment, as infants below five to seven months do not usually show more distress at the separation from their parents than they would from another adult.

Social capacities and their development

It is apparent that infants are attuned to the characteristics of people. In addition, within the first few months of life infants have an important repertoire of activities and capacities. For example, crying and smiling are two obvious and powerful forms of infant signalling.

Adults find the cries of infants disturbing and they are likely to respond by contact and trying to remove the causes of the distress. Crying is seen by some ethologists as an inherited behaviour which serves an important biological function, summoning the parent when there is a biological need. It is also worth remembering that its power can have unfortunate consequences – unceasing crying is often reported as a precipitating factor in child abuse.

Smiling, like crying, is a powerful signal. Smiles provide information to adults about the things that infants enjoy, and adults will work very hard at social activities to obtain a smile. Smiles can be seen in newborn infants but usually there is no clear external cause. At an early age a simple arrangement of eye dots will make babies smile, but as they become older the more similar a stimulus is to the human face, the more likely it is to cause a smile. By about three months, infants are beginning to smile more at familiar than unfamiliar people (Camras *et al.* 1991). Exposure to the smiling of other people does not seem to be necessary for the development of smiling as children who are blind start to smile at the same age as children with sight (Freeman 1974). However, studies of infants living in institutions where there was less stimulation and social contact than at home found that the infants in institutions started smiling about a month later than those at home (Ambrose 1961).

Infants also exhibit a variety of facial expressions which adults usually interpret as reflecting feelings. Facial expressions which correspond to startle, distress, disgust and simple smiling can be observed in newborns (Izard and Malatesta 1987). By three to four months, facial expressions corresponding to anger, surprise and sadness can be identified. What is unknown is the emotional basis of these very early facial expressions, and the type of relation they have to adult emotions. Interestingly, by the age of two months, different infants will reliably produce similar expressions in the same circumstances, such as distress when being given an injection.

One surprising ability that has been reported in newborns is the ability to imitate actions of others, even when they cannot see their own action, as in the case of tongue protrusion and mouth opening. Meltzoff and Moore (1977) suggested that imitation is possible because newborn infants can translate what they see into actions. Despite some worries about the replicability of these findings (e.g. Hayes and Watson 1981, McKenzie and Over 1983), there has been a growing acceptance of their accuracy. More recently, Meltzoff and Gopnik (1993) have taken the discussion further, putting forward the idea that imitation occurs because infants recognize that adults are 'like them' and that they themselves can perform the same motor actions as adults. As a consequence, the infant's reaction to an adult is 'here is something like me' (p. 336). As imitation has been reported soon after birth, Meltzoff and Gopnik suggest that the infant perception of adults being like themselves must begin at this age. These ideas about imitation have many attractions. Like the ideas about intersubjectivity, they help to explain the feeling of interacting with a communicating partner that most parents report about their young babies. However, there are issues that need to be addressed: Why do infants regard adults as 'like me' when there are many differences between infants and adults? How far can the 'like me' response be extended? To primates? To mammals? Mutual gaze between adult and infant is a form of social behaviour which has a powerful effect on adults.

The occurrence of mutual gaze at about four to eight weeks, gives the adult a feeling of the infant 'knowing and recognizing' them. Later on, from about four months, joint gaze between adult and infant at some third object or event becomes a common feature of social interaction. Often it is the adult who will follow the infant's interest, and match their conversation with this interest.

Another feature of social development is the use of routines. These begin in the first few months when adults will structure an activity so that the infant can make a minimal contribution but still appear to be involved in the process. This might be the giving and taking of a toy, or a game like peek-a-boo. With time, infants take on more and more responsibilities in the routines, and in this way they acquire a framework for developing particular social skills.

Outline the way you would conduct a study to find out whether infants do think adults are like themselves. Remember that finding out whether infants can imitate something is supposed to indicate whether they think it is 'like me'.

Section summary

Infants come into the world with a remarkable repertoire of social abilities. Some of these abilities appear to be the result of pre-natal learning, while others appear to be the result of innate capacities. It is particularly interesting that from the first few weeks of life infants have a preference for the stimuli provided by their mother. Such preferences may help with the development of attachment, a topic to which we will now turn.

The development of attachment: theories and research

The relationship between children and their parents (usually the mother) has been, and continues to be, an issue of great interest to developmental psychologists. The attachment of child to mother was regarded by Freud as a model for later relationships and the issue of separation from parents came to prominence as a result of concerns during and after the Second World War. We will first examine bonding, which is usually considered to be the relationship of mothers to their babies. Then the pattern of attachment of infants to their mothers will be outlined. This is followed by a discussion of theories about the formation of attachment relationships.

Bonding

Until the 1970s, the usual hospital practice in the Western world was to separate newborn infants from their mothers immediately after birth and to reunite them for their first feed. This was supposed to give the mother time to recover. Today, hospital practice is very different. Unless there are medical reasons for the separation, mother and baby are left together (with father) until the mother is taken to the maternity ward. These changes can partly be attributed to the research work of Klaus, Kennell and their colleagues (Klaus and Kennell 1976) – see *In Focus* opposite.

In the years following this work, hospital procedures in the West were changed to allow for extra contact after birth.
In addition, the findings were interpreted as indicating that mothers who did not experience early contact, perhaps for medical or other reasons, would be disadvantaged in developing a relationship with their baby. A failure to 'bond' was thought to have detrimental consequences for a child's social and emotional development. It was even suggested that lack of this early bond in the mother might be a contributory factor to her abusing the child.

Subsequent work has questioned the idea of bonding. One point that has often been made is that the social context of birth varies across human cultures and has varied across historical time. For example, among the Efe people of Zaire, babies are usually given to another mother to breast-feed for the first few days. Their tradition is for someone who is not the biological mother to undertake what we consider to be an intimate activity. In addition, generations of mothers have successfully taken care of their children despite separation at birth. Some mothers, particularly those who experience a painful childbirth, may feel distant from their baby until a few weeks after the birth, but they go on to develop strong bonds with their babies as do parents who adopt a baby.

More importantly, a number of studies failed to replicate the findings of Klaus and Kennell (e.g. Svejda *et al.* 1980), and where replications have been successful, they tend to have been with mothers who are less well educated and of lower social class. It may well be that these mothers feel less confident in hospitals and gain more benefit and confidence from the early contact. Schaffer (1990) in reviewing this work has criticized the idea of bonding as 'super-glue'. He argues that the experimental studies do not provide support for the idea that early contact enhances mother–infant bonds and suggests that the claims about bonding fail to make allowance for the complexity and changing nature of human relationships.

Theories of attachment

Infants are usually considered to be *attached* to someone when they show the following characteristics:

- distress at separation
- an orientation to the person which involves gazing, following and vocalizing
- seeking the person in moments of stress.

At about six to eight months, infants start to show distress at the departure of familiar people and to seek their contact. However, the full range of attachment behaviours is not usually seen until about eight or nine months of age (most studies report quite a range of ages at which these behaviours develop). Infants will also often show fear and wariness of strangers at about the same age that they develop attachments.

One of the first detailed studies of attachment revealed that although the mother was usually the main attachment figure, this was not always the case. Attachments were also formed to fathers,

In Focus

Infant–mother bonding

To examine bonding, Klaus and Kennell (1976) were able to allocate mothers *randomly* either to a treatment group, which had extra contact with their infant after birth, or to a control group, which followed the normal hospital procedure of separation until the first feed. When they were seen at later ages, various positive features were noted about the way the mothers in the treatment group reacted towards their children. These included:

- holding the baby closer
- looking into the infants' eyes more often
- more kissing
- a more relaxed style of cuddling
- being more likely to continue breast-feeding
- at two years, the mother using a greater proportion of questions.

Klaus and Kennell pointed out that in other species, such as goats and sheep, the early contact of the baby animal to the mother is necessary for her to bond to the infant. If this exposure does not take place then the mother is likely to reject the infant animal. By implication it was being suggested that a similar process may occur in humans.

grandparents and others adults (Schaffer and Emerson 1964). Obviously in older children attachment to parents will continue, but the behaviours which reflect this attachment change.

Why are children attached to their parents? Often we accept this process as being such a natural part of development that we do not think about the reasons why attachment develops. In the past, an influential theory about attachment was based on ideas about instrumental learning. A similar idea is contained in Freud's description of the growth of attachment. Here the focus was on the way feeding provides oral gratification which in turn provides a basis for the development of attachment.

However, these theories were shown to be inadequate in the late 1950s and 1960s. Two studies which were very influential in changing views about attachment are summarised below (see *In Focus*).

The failure of learning theory explanations of attachment came about because of the findings from the studies outlined above; this demise was accompanied by a growth of interest in Bowlby's ideas.

Bowlby (1969, 1973) believed that attachment in humans (and other animals) is the result of evolutionary selection pressures. Infants who stay close to their mother are more likely to avoid dangers such as becoming lost, being injured or attacked and, as a result, they are more likely to survive.

Findings from studies of animal behaviour were a powerful influence on Bowlby's thinking. However, although he believed that there was a strong biological basis to human attachment formation, he did not believe that the process was as automatic as in the case of imprinting (see Chapter 23). Rather, he reasoned that the biological need for security has resulted in infants possessing a number of attachment behaviours, such as crying, following, proximity seeking, smiling, clinging and sucking. Bowlby believed that these behaviours are used to achieve the *goal* of a feeling of security and that when infants feel insecure (e.g. when in an unfamiliar house), they will produce these behaviours. He also believed that these behaviours are powerful stimuli to gain an

In Focus

Care and attachment

The first, and perhaps most famous, study to show that attachment is not based on the supply of food was conducted by Harlow and Zimmerman (1959) on infant monkeys. The infant monkeys were placed in a cage with two wire mesh cylinders. On one cylinder the baby monkey could obtain milk from a teat, while the other cylinder was covered with terry cloth towelling. If food was the cause of attachment then one would expect the monkeys to cling to the bare cylinder which supplied the milk. In fact, the monkeys spent most of their time on the cloth covered cylinder and would jump on this cylinder when frightened. The study, which would now be considered unethical, indicated that simply supplying food is not sufficient for the formation of attachment. This work was seen as having important implications for theories about the formation of attachment in both animals and humans.

A second important study, conducted by Schaffer and Emerson (1964), also showed that reinforcement from feeding was not able to account for the formation of attachment of infants to some people. Schaffer and Emerson saw a group of sixty children every month during their first twelve months of life. Observations were conducted in the children's homes. Not only did the study reveal that children formed multiple attachments with mother, father, grandparents and other adults, but the study also revealed that attachments were formed when these other adults took little or no care of the infants' basic needs (e.g. feeding). Instead, attachments seemed to be formed to individuals who were prepared to play, be responsive and interact socially with the child.

adult response. Important to his theory was the idea that the mother provides a secure base for exploration, and that as the infants' feelings of security increase so they are more prepared to move away from the mother (think about the difference in a young child's behaviour when at home and when visiting a strange environment).

A controversial aspect of Bowlby's work was his belief that a mother should be the most important carer and that this care should be provided on a continuous basis. An obvious implication is that mothers should not go out to work. There have been many attacks on this claim. One criticism has been that a wider perspective reveals that mothers are the exclusive carers in only a very small percentage of human societies; often there are a number of people involved in the care of children, such as relations and friends (Weisner and Gallimore 1977). Similarly, van IJzendoorn and Tavecchio (1987) argue that a stable network of adults can provide adequate care and that this care may even have advantages over a system where a mother has to meet all a child's needs. Furthermore, there is evidence that children develop better with a mother who is happy in her work, than a mother who is frustrated by staying at home (Schaffer 1990).

Bowlby's ideas had a great influence on the way researchers thought about attachment. However, one problem with studying attachment was the need to devise a way to measure it. For instance, when children are prepared to wander away from their mother, does this indicate weak attachment, or that the children have a secure relationship with their mother? Does the amount of crying on separation indicate a weak or strong attachment? Preliminary attempts to measure the amount of a single behaviour, and treat it as a *quantity*, like the temperature of a person, were largely unsuccessful.

Ainsworth's strange situation

An important advance in measurement came from an investigation by Ainsworth and her colleagues (Ainsworth and Bell 1970) that indicated that there are different forms of attachment to a parent. Rather than measure the *amount* of attachment, Ainsworth observed the *organization* of attachment behaviour. The observations were made in a laboratory room (see *In Focus* on p. 374) and have been used to classify children into one of three groups: *secure* (also known as type B), and two types of insecure attachment, *avoidant* (type A), and *ambivalent* (type C). In American samples, the proportion of children in these three groups is approximately 70 per cent, 15 per cent and 15 per cent respectively. More recently, a further category labelled *disorganized* has been identified (type D).

In general, studies have found that for a particular child the strange situation classification (SSC) is usually the same at different ages (i.e. it is reliable). When differences occur, these are often associated with changes in the form of care, such as changes in family structure (Melhuish 1993). Two studies have even found similar types of attachment at one year and six years (Main and Cassidy 1988), and a study conducted in Germany found 78 per cent of the children were classified in the same way at these two ages (Wartner *et al.* 1994). Another set of studies provides evidence about validity. These have found that the classification of attachment from the strange situation is related to children's reactions when they are separated in more natural circumstances, such as when a child is left with a baby-sitter (e.g. Smith and Noble 1987).

Other investigations have reported that the security of attachment predicts children's later abilities. Secure infants appear more co-operative with their mother at two years (Matas *et al.* 1978). In addition, infants rated as secure in their second year have been found to be later rated by their nursery school teachers as being more popular, having more initiative, being higher in self-esteem, being less aggressive and being social leaders. Secure children were also rated as more popular by other children (Sroufe 1983). The children in Sroufe's study were also observed again at eleven years. The secure infants were rated as higher in social competence, self-

In Focus

The strange situation

The strange situation takes place in a laboratory with a set arrangement of attractive toys and furniture. The infants have to be mobile and the assessment is typically made with infants between 12 and 18 months of age.

In the strange situation the following sequence of events takes place. All the sessions, except the first one, take three minutes.

1. The mother and child are introduced to the room.
2. The mother and child are left alone and the child can investigate the toys.
3. A stranger enters and stays.
4. The mother leaves the child alone with the stranger, and the stranger interacts with the child.
5. The mother returns to greet and comfort the child.
6. The mother leaves the child with the stranger.
7. The stranger tries to engage the child.
8. The mother returns.

There is a detailed coding scheme to assign children to one of the three categories of attachment. In broad terms, *securely attached* infants (type B) tend to explore the unfamiliar room; they are subdued when the mother leaves and greet her positively when she returns. In contrast, *avoidant* infants (type A) do not orientate to the mother while investigating the toys and room; they do not seem concerned by her absence, and they show little interest in her when she returns. The *ambivalent* infants (type C) often show intense distress particularly when the mother is absent, but they reject the mother by pushing her away, often this occurs when the mother returns. A further group of children was subsequently identified by Main and Cassidy (1988) and this classification group is referred to as *disorganized* (type D). These children show inconsistent behaviour, confusion and indecision. They also tend to freeze or show stereotyped behaviours such as rocking. The methodology used in the strange situation has also been developed to assess attachment in the pre-school and school years.

confidence and self-esteem (Elicker *et al.* 1992). Thus, these and similar studies support the claim that the SSC is measuring a psychologically important characteristic.

In the last decade, many investigations of attachment have been concerned with the claim that the security of attachment is one part of a child's working *model* of themselves and of their parents, involving conscious and unconscious thoughts (Bowlby 1973, Main *et al.* 1985). According to this idea, the SSC provides an assessment of the child's expectations about the way a parent will react during stressful events and their own feelings of security about being separated. It is also supposed that the working model about attachment with the primary caregiver is likely to be extrapolated to other adults.

Bretherton and Waters (1985) suggest that secure children have developed a positive working model of themselves based on their feelings of security derived from a carer who is sensitive, emotionally available and supportive. In contrast, avoidant children are supposed to have a carer who is rejecting, which results in their having a working model of themselves as unacceptable and unworthy. Ambivalent children have carers who are inconsistent and consequently the children tend to have a negative self-image and exaggerate their emotional responses as a way to obtain attention. This hypothesis provides one explanation of the fact that early patterns of attachment are related to later child characteristics. The claim about the working model is not without controversy as any predictability could simply be due to certain positive or negative family characteristics having a continuing impact on attachment and later competencies. In a similar way, arguments have been made that continuing child characteristics such as adaptability and sociability might be responsible for relationships between attachment and later abilities.

An evaluation of the strange situation

What causes the different attachment types? Originally, Ainsworth and Bell supposed that secure attachments were the result of mothers being responsive to children's needs. Their study claimed to show relations between maternal responsiveness and the three types of attachment. However, there were flaws in this study. For example, the raters of maternal responsiveness knew about the eventual type of child attachment. As a result, their scoring of behaviour may have been biased (because the raters should have been unaware of the attachment classification). More recently, a better controlled study by Isabella *et al.* (1989) has claimed to find the relation between responsiveness and attachment as predicted by Ainsworth. Mothers and infants who tended to be responsive to each other at one month and later ages were more likely at twelve months to have a secure relationship. Those that had a more one-sided pattern of interaction tended to have insecure relationships.

More surprisingly, Fonagy and colleagues have found that mothers' pre-natal reports of their relationship with their own mother (concerning parental responsiveness, feelings, etc.) predict the security of attachment their child will have to them (Fonagy *et al.* 1991). It is important to realize that this finding concerns a mother's *perception* of her relationship with her mother and that this may or may not correspond to the reality of the relationship. Even so, this suggests that the way women look at the role of being a mother may influence their own behaviour and this in turn may influence the pattern of attachment.

It would seem that attachment patterns can, at least partly, be predicted from maternal characteristics and behaviour. Such predictability provides evidence for the validity of the strange situation classification (SSC) – behaviour is related to attachment in a way that was predicted from attachment theory. At first sight, these findings about the strange situation suggest we should accept its usefulness without further question. However, it is important to note that there have been criticisms of some of the claims. For instance, it is very difficult to know in most of these studies whether the attachment pattern or some other factor is responsible for the pattern of findings. In the case of the relationship between early social interaction and later attachment patterns, it is possible that the characteristics of the infant influence both the pattern of social interaction and the pattern of attachment. According to this argument, it might be that infants who are better able to engage in social interaction at an early age are also able to form secure relationships at a later age, and at an even later age may have good social skills in a nursery school. Thus, social interaction does not cause the attachment pattern, rather it is the characteristics of infants which influence early social interaction, attachment and later skills.

Another form of this argument is that the behaviour in the strange situation is the result of children's inborn characteristics (temperament). For example, Kagan (1982) has suggested that avoidant infants are difficult to upset, ambivalent infants are easy to stress, and that secure infants are somewhere between these two. Evidence to support the idea of infant temperament as the cause of the differences in behaviour in the strange situation come from several studies. It has been found that newborns who are less able to attend to people and objects are more likely to have insecure attachments at later ages (Waters 1978). Similarly, low Apgar scores (an assessment of physiological status at birth, in terms of breathing, heart rate and so on) are associated with later insecure relationships. Thus, there is a possibility that infant temperament contributes to the form of later attachment.

Other research has revealed that children can have different attachment classifications with different parents. For example, they may be classified as having a secure attachment to their mother and an avoidant relationship with their father (Lamb 1977). This suggests that the attachment classification is not simply a matter of a child's temperament. If it was, then the child should have the same relationship with both mother and father.

Another criticism of the SSC has been that, according to the culture being studied, there is variation in the proportion of children assigned to the three categories. Grossman *et al.* (1985), working in Germany, found a higher proportion of avoidant children (i.e. showing independence), and it was suggested that this may be a result of the greater value placed on this characteristic by parents in this culture. More worrying for the SSC are the findings from Japan where infants very rarely leave their mother; as a result, the strange situation is an unusual and particularly stressful event. Many Japanese infants simply cannot cope with the strange situation and their behaviour is, therefore, very different to that seen in other studies (Miyake *et al.* 1985). Similarly, there is discussion of whether the SSC can be meaningfully applied to children who have extensive non-parental care (Belsky and Isabella 1988). Together, these findings indicate that we should not assume that secure attachments, as diagnosed by the SSC, provide an optimal form of attachment in all cultures (e.g. it is possible that in Germany, avoidant children may be better adapted than secure children). It also seems that the SSC will not always give an appropriate assessment of attachment, as is the case of some Japanese children.

Section summary

Research in early childhood has led to a rejection of the more extreme claims made about bonding. Bowlby's ideas provided a basis for present-day approaches to attachment. Subsequent research into the SSC has produced an impressive array of findings which suggest early attachment is a result of both parental and child characteristics. Findings also indicate that the SSC is a good predictor of later child characteristics. There still remains some uncertainty about the direction of causality (from infant or parents), but we now have a wealth of evidence about the psychological importance of this dimension of behaviour. As we shall see in the next section, the research on attachment has been associated with important advances in our understanding of psychological development.

Enrichment and deprivation: theories and research

Most of us assume that unless it is necessary, young children should not be separated from their mother when, for instance, one of them has to go into hospital. This is such a prevailing assumption that it is easy to forget that thirty years ago attitudes were very different. Parental hospital visits were restricted, children were often placed in unfamiliar day nurseries when their mother went into hospital, and there was little concern about the effects of these separations. The investigations conducted on the effects of separations have provided a scientific basis for the changes in hospital practice, and the wider change in society's attitudes to these matters. Much of the research was conducted some time ago when these separations were common, but the findings are still relevant today. The short-term and the long-term effects of separation have usually been studied separately.

Short-term effects of separation

Research has revealed that the immediate effects of separation on a young child are influenced by the age of the child and the type of care that is provided. As we have already seen, infants below about five months of age appear able to identify their mother, but do not show a marked preference for her

In Focus

Young children's reactions to separation

Robertson and Bowlby (1952) observed that there are three progressive reactions to separation: *protest, despair* and *detachment*. The children in the study, aged between one and four years, were placed by their parents in residential nurseries (often because their mother was entering hospital) or were themselves hospitalized. The initial *protest* involved crying, grizzling and calling the name of the mother, with the children appearing distraught and panic stricken. These behaviours lasted from several hours to about one week. Protest reactions typically gave way to *despair*, where children became apathetic, uninterested in their surroundings, cried occasionally and had a continuing need for their mother. This in turn was followed by *detachment* as the child cried less and became more alert and interested. The detachment at first sight appeared to indicate recovery, but this seems to have been at the cost of suppression of feelings for the mother. When the mother returned, the child responded to her with a lack of interest and often was angry and rejecting.

presence. Therefore it is unsurprising that separations before this age do not seem to have a marked effect. For example, Schaffer and Callender (1959) observed few signs of distress in infants below seven months when they were admitted to hospital, but above this age there was crying, together with disturbances in sleeping and feeding. In cases of complete separation because of adoption, some effects may occur at an even earlier age. Yarrow and Goodwin (1973) collected information about the reactions of infants who were being adopted into a new home. Their conclusion was that few infants show a reaction before three months; that between three and six months there is an increasing proportion of infants who show a reaction (e.g. sleep and feeding disturbances, emotional reactions), and that between seven and sixteen months all infants showed some reaction. On the basis of these and other studies, we can have confidence that at about seven months of age there is an increase in disturbed behaviour following separation. What are young children's reactions to separation? These are outlined below.

In the past, very little used to be done to help the children adjust to their new surroundings. An important study by Robertson and Robertson (1971) showed that given appropriate preparation and care, children could adjust to separation from their mother. The Robertsons were successful in minimizing the distress of four children whom they cared for on separate occasions in their own hom. They prepared the child for the separation – the child visited the Robertsons' home beforehand. When the child was separated, a similar routine was adopted as the child had at home and the Robertsons talked to the child about his or her mother.

Long-term effects of separation

Concerns about the long-term effects of separation were given an impetus by Bowlby's report in 1944 that delinquency was associated with young children's separation from their mother and claims that prolonged separation might lead to an inability to form later relationships. He supposed that the separation was the cause of the delinquency. However, Bowlby's study of delinquent boys was flawed. Later, it was recognized that what he failed to do was find out whether a similar rate of separations occurred in similar adolescents who were not delinquent.

From this and other studies, Bowlby developed the idea that if an infant were unable to develop a 'warm, intimate, and continuous relationship with his mother (or permanent mother-substitute)' (Bowlby 1953, p. 13), then the child would have difficulty forming relationships with other people and be at risk for behavioural disorders.

This became known as the maternal deprivation hypothesis. The hypothesis was criticized because much of the evidence used to support the idea came from studies of children in institutions where they were deprived of social contact, but were also deprived in many other ways. Indeed, a later study by Bowlby (1956) effectively showed that separations do not necessarily lead to later problems. The study concerned children below four years who had been isolated because they had tuberculosis. In the units the children were not seen more than once a week by their parents. The nursing regimes tended to be strict and the care impersonal. Information was obtained about these children when they were between seven and fourteen years old. A control group of children who had not been in the clinics was also studied. There were differences between the two groups, but they were not large and involved characteristics such as the tubercular group showing more daydreaming, being less sociable and less attentive. No differences were found in terms of delinquency or problems in forming social relationships.

An investigation by Rutter (1976) of a different set of data revealed that repeated hospital admissions was a marker for disadvantage and that this, rather than the separations themselves, could account for children who were separated from their parents having a higher risk for later social and emotional problems. Later, Rutter (1981) distinguished between the effects of:

- privation – the lack of any affection bonds, such as in an institution where there is little contact with the infants
- disruption of bonds – where there may be separation caused by death
- distortion of relationships – where there may be stress associated with separation or divorce.

Rutter reports that disruption has the least effect on later development. Thus, it would appear that in itself separation does not necessarily lead to later problems, rather the available evidence points to family stress and associated difficulties as being the cause of later problems.

Disadvantage and deprivation

Many studies have reported that the academic progress of children is related to characteristics of their home environment. For example, the reading and arithmetic ability of British seven-year-olds has been found to be related to the occupation of the father, which in turn is usually taken as a useful indicator of socio-economic status (SES); children from lower-SES families performed less well (Davie *et al.* 1972). There has been considerable debate about what causes these findings. One general explanation of the findings is that the SES differences are due to the cumulative effects of housing conditions, lower income and so on, and that these have a generally negative impact on child development. A more specific explanation is that the effect occurs because the skills being assessed are also the skills that are valued in the home life of the middle- and upper-SES families. As a result, children from lower-SES families are disadvantaged relative to other children.

One example of this explanation concerns the language of the home. Bernstein (1962) suggested that there is a tendency in lower-SES homes to use speech which needs to be understood in relation to the context in which it is said (context-dependent speech). In contrast, he suggested that speech in middle-class homes tends to be less context-dependent so that it can be understood independently of when and where it was said, and this affects both communication and cognitive development. Differences were found in the speech of children from different backgrounds, which supported Bernstein's claims, but these effects could have been due to children from lower-SES families finding the experimental situation more threatening, so that their language became more restricted. Another explanation of SES differences is that they reflect the difficulties children face in adapting to a different sub-culture. Here the emphasis is placed on the equal value of different forms of communication, but that children from lower-SES families are disadvantaged when faced with the unfamiliar culture of a middle-class school system. A further explanation is the presence of prejudice and self-fulfilling prophecies. For example, there is evidence that pupils from ethnic minorities, especially from Afro-Caribbean families, tend to be entered for examinations which are below their level of ability (Eggleston 1985) and this may be because of non-academic considerations such as cooperativeness.

A different form of deprivation is the social isolation caused by living in a rural environment where there is little contact with children outside the immediate family. Hollos (1975) found that such isolated children aged between seven and nine years who were living in Norway did less well than children from towns and villages when given Piagetian social perspective-taking tasks (see Chapter 18). However, they were equally skilled at other cognitive tasks. This suggests there was a particular problem with these social tasks, indicating that home circumstances can affect certain aspects of children's development.

Research by Rutter (1981) identified four specific forms of deprivation and family discord which were associated with behavioural problems:

- family discord
- social deviance of the parents in terms of psychiatric problems or criminal record
- social disadvantage
- poor school environment.

He found that when two or more forms of deprivation were present in the 150 English families he studied, then the incidence of childhood behaviour problems and psychiatric disorders increased dramatically.

When an examination is made of child-rearing conditions which involve a severe lack of stimulation and care, it is not surprising that these forms of deprivation have adverse effects on development. A study by Dennis (1973) of children in a Lebanese orphanage examined the effects of conditions where there was little play or social contact and the children were left alone in their cots for much of the day. At the end of the first year, the children's scores on a development test were half that expected for their age. Children who were adopted before the age of two years showed recovery to normal levels of intelligence, while those who were adopted later did not show as good a recovery (their IQs were about 80). Girls who were kept at the orphanage and later went on to a poorly resourced school, showed extremely low levels of functioning when they were tested at twelve to sixteen years. This study has a number of important messages. One is that the effects of deprivation are reversible, but that continuing adverse circumstances are likely to have a negative effect on the individuals who experience these conditions.

Although various forms of deprivation can be shown to have an adverse effect on development for the majority of children, it is also the case that a few children are *resilient* to such effects. Clarke and Clarke (1996) identify factors which are associated with such resilience, including:

- individual attractiveness
- problem-solving ability
- an internal locus of control (feeling that one can be successful)
- networks of social support
- a supportive peer group
- a capacity for purposeful planning.

Isolation

Over the centuries there have been a number of reports of children who have been raised in isolated and deprived circumstances. What is remarkable about some of the more recent, and better documented, cases is that recoveries have occurred despite extreme deprivation. Recovery, however, does not always occur, and in such cases it is difficult to know whether there were some features of the isolation which prevented recovery (e.g. age at isolation, age of detection, type of isolation) or whether the child had learning disabilities when he or she was isolated. Three of these cases are outlined on the next page (see *In Focus*).

In Focus

Cases of isolation

The first case outlined is that of Isabelle. She had been kept in isolation in a darkened room with her mother who was deaf and without speech (Mason 1942, Davis 1947). Isabelle had not been given an adequate diet and had severe rickets. During her isolation she communicated with her mother using gestures. The mother escaped from the isolation when Isabelle was about six years old. On her admission to hospital Isabelle behaved like a wild animal and only made croaking sounds. After one week in the hospital she started to make speech sounds and seemed to pass rapidly through the normal stages of speech. After 18 months she had a vocabulary of over 2,000 words, could read and write, and could compose imaginative stories.

The second case involves Czechoslovakian, male, identical twins whose mother died after giving birth (Koluchova 1976). The children went to a children's home for eleven months, then spent six months with their aunt, and next went to stay with their father and stepmother. The father was of low intelligence and the stepmother was exceptionally cruel. The boys were never allowed out of the house and were kept either in a small unheated closet or in a cellar. When discovered at seven years, the children could hardly walk, had acute rickets, were very fearful and their spontaneous speech was very poor. After placement in a hospital and then a foster home excellent gains were made. The children are now adults and appear well adjusted and cognitively able (Clarke, personal communication).

Genie, the third case, was found when she was thirteen years old (Curtiss 1977). Her history was one of isolation, severe neglect and physical restraint; she was kept strapped to a child's potty in an attic. Her father punished her if she made any sound. On discovery her appearance was of a six- or seven-year-old child. She was described by Curtiss as 'unsocialized, primitive, and hardly human'; she made virtually no sounds and was hardly able to walk. Genie has not achieved good social adjustment or language despite intervention and being placed with a foster family.

Enrichment

We have already seen that the effects of deprivation can be reversed by a supportive environment. Can enrichment be effective in other circumstances, especially for those children who are disadvantaged? Head Start is the name given to the largest enrichment programme that has been conducted. Head Start was designed to reverse the effects of what was seen as social disadvantage in the United States by providing intensive pre-school education (compensatory education). This was sometimes accompanied by the extra provision of social services, medicine and nutritional advice, as well as involving the children's families in care and education. When children in the pre-school programme entered school, they showed more advanced cognitive and social behaviour than children who were not involved in the programme (Lee *et al.* 1990). However, the initial positive effects disappeared in the years following entry, and this led to doubts about the usefulness of the programme. Such doubts were then challenged by further evaluations which revealed that children in the programme had higher IQs (although this difference declined with increasing age), higher arithmetic and reading skills, as well as being less likely to be assigned to special education classes (Lazar and Darlington 1982). Even older individuals had higher feelings of competence. They were less likely to leave school early and more likely to go to college. The effects have been found to be stronger when the pre-school programme had been followed up with later interventions. The evaluation of the programme, however, continues to be plagued with controversy as the choice of the control groups of children was not strictly random. Furthermore, Haskins (1989) has claimed that in economic terms the programme costs exceeded the gains that were made from savings to social services.

Less controversially, there is a reasonable body of evidence that very young children who receive early help in the development of language do make appreciable progress. Fowler (1990) has carried out a programme which involved concentrating on the use of language, appropriate for the child's level of functioning, in everyday situations. The programme did not involve any unusual teaching activities on the parents' part, rather it simply focused them on language-related games and play. A number of gains were reported, including the finding that children in the programme started using pronouns (e.g. it, him, her) at 18 months, while the usual age for this milestone is about 23 months.

Section summary

The findings about the short-term effects of separations are reasonably clear. If young children are not given adequate support then there follows protest, despair and detachment. The longer-term effects are less clear but suggest that separations in themselves do not necessarily lead to later psychological problems. Deprivation and disadvantage influence children's progress at school, but there is still considerable debate about the precise reasons for this. It would appear that compensatory education can reverse some of these effects and the case studies of isolated children reveal that some can make remarkable recoveries from severe deprivation.

Social and cultural variations in child-rearing

Across the world and across history there have been many different forms of child-rearing. Some of these contrast with our own in terms of the resources that are available. For example, in the deprived families in the north east of Brazil about half of the children die before reaching their fifth birthday. Children who are passive or have clear signs of developmental delay receive minimal care when sick. The infants who are active, demanding and advanced for their age tend to receive more attention. By five years the surviving children are expected to contribute to the family well-being by stealing and scavenging in the case of boys, or by doing chores in the case of girls. Scheper-Hughes (1992) argues that these harsh child-rearing styles reflect an adaptation to unremitting poverty and deprivation.

In other cases the differences are most marked in terms of specific forms of child-rearing. Konner (1977) has reported that in Botswana the Zhun/twsai people hardly ever let their babies cry. This seems to be because the infants live in the same room as the rest of the family. As a result, the infants are breast-fed at the slightest sign of distress.

Other differences between cultures are more general, as in the way that each culture has different expectations for boys and girls in terms of the roles that they are expected to fulfil. What is becoming increasingly accepted in relation to such cultural differences, is that there is no 'right' or 'wrong' way to bring up a child; child-rearing practices should rather be judged in relation to assisting children to adjust to

❖ Activity 4 ❖

It is very easy to adopt a Western perspective and assume that all cultures adapt their care-giving style to the capacities of infants and children. List the ways we adapt to the needs of children. Think about the following points:

- the way we speak to children
- the way a house is adapted and changed for children
- the way products are designed for play.

their culture. This is known as *cultural relativism*. There may, however, be disputes between people from different cultures about what they consider to be acceptable child-rearing practices (for example, the rights of women, the use of physical violence, the exposure of children to advertisements and sexually explicit material).

An important challenge to the assumption that adults modify social interaction in a way adapted to the needs of infants comes from Ochs and Schieffelin (1984). They draw attention to quite different child-rearing practices in Samoa and in Papua New Guinea (see *In Focus* below).

The evidence from these observations has been used to argue that children can acquire language and other cognitive capacities without the types of adaptations made in Western families. In this way, cross-cultural studies can be important in answering questions about the skills that can be acquired without certain child-rearing experiences. In many cases it would be impossible, because of ethical considerations, to conduct experimental studies of these issues.

The observations of Kagan and Klein (1975) in Guatemala also provide evidence about the resilience of child development. The villagers in an isolated mountainous region believed that it was best to confine babies up to one year old in the family home, which was typically dark, small and poorly lit. The infants were rarely talked to and had few play objects. All this was

In Focus

Child-rearing in Samoa and Papua New Guinea

Samoan society is highly stratified according to a person's rank and various features of child-rearing practice appear to reflect this. During the first six months infants are not treated as conversational partners, but are usually 'spoken to' in songs or rhythmical high-pitched vocalizations. Speech tends to be directed at the infant in a loud and sharp voice, and adults do not simplify their speech towards infants. Another feature of Samoan interactions is that low-ranking individuals, including children, are expected to adapt to the needs of higher-ranking individuals. Consequently, childcarers rarely attempt to clarify children's unintelligible utterances. Instead, children are expected to make the clarification for the adult's benefit.

The other pattern of child-rearing described by Ochs and Schieffelin (1984) involves the Kaluli of Papua New Guinea. Their society assigns an important role to conversation. Conversations take place against a complex pattern of relationships based on obligation and reciprocity. However, the Kaluli do not talk about the feelings or thoughts of others, a norm which has consequences for child-rearing practices.

The Kaluli infant's mother is the primary caregiver and she is responsive, attentive and constantly present. Infants are not treated as conversational partners because of the belief that they are not capable of understanding these exchanges. As a result, few utterances are addressed to infants, and those that are involve calling his or her name. Although the mothers do not talk *to* their infants they will talk *for* their infants. For example, if another child addresses an infant, the mother of the infant will reply in a high-pitched voice. Unlike the attempts at conversation in Western families, the speech of the Kaluli mother appears unrelated to the activities of the infant. Ochs and Schieffelin suggest that these exchanges are designed to foster social relationships rather than to teach language. Another feature of these early interactions is that Kaluli mothers do not engage in mutual gaze. Instead, they usually put their infant in a position where they can observe, and be observed by, others.

because the villagers believed that the outside dust, air and sun were harmful. Not surprisingly, the children were quiet, fearful and had very low scores on tests of development. However, children in their second year were allowed outside the home and soon developed into typically active infants, while the older children showed no detectable delay in their later development. Consequently, the cross-cultural study suggests that the lack of early stimulation does not necessarily result in significant developmental delays in later abilities.

Another useful feature of cross-cultural studies is that they can make us think and ask questions about the organization of our own child-rearing practices. It can be argued that the very notion of childhood is related to cultural assumptions about development. In many cultures children will start to contribute to the income of the family early on in life, sometimes as young as five years old, by either tending animals or even being employed. In contrast, Western culture can be considered to provide an extended period of childhood when offspring are both being educated and do not earn an income of their own.

Cross-cultural studies also provide interesting material about the possible effects of different patterns of child-rearing. We have already seen that within Western countries, differences in SES (which we could think of as different sub-cultures) are associated with differences in children's school performance. However, we have also seen that such differences are very difficult to interpret. Not only is it unclear which aspect of child-rearing may be responsible for these differences, but there is also discussion about whether such differences exist and what they tell us about the abilities of children from different SES backgrounds. Similar difficulties are experienced when it comes to interpreting the effect of different patterns of child-rearing.

For example, when interpreting the different behaviours of American, German and Japanese infants in the Strange Situation discussed earlier in this chapter, the differences between national groups are often attributed to different patterns of child-rearing. Japanese child-rearing appears to place greater value on developing close family relationships; young infants are rarely separated from their mothers and the mothers are highly responsive to their needs. In addition, greater prominence is given to allowing children to develop their own group identity and the ability to solve problems within a group. Some of the American styles of child-rearing seem harsh and inappropriate to the Japanese. The fostering of independence, coupled with adults acting as arbiters in disputes, does not correspond with the practice in Japan. Thus, it appears that different patterns of child-rearing are associated with different outcomes in terms of attachment processes. However, it is important to remember that since these are not experimental studies, we cannot be sure that this is a causal relationship. The differences in attachment relationships between cultures could be caused, for the sake of argument, by genetic differences between cultures rather than differences in child-rearing practices.

Differences between cultures in child-rearing have also been related to school achievement. A study of 4,000 children found that children entering school in the United States were doing less well than those from Taiwan and Japan, and that the American children were doing less well in reading and arithmetic in their fifth year of schooling (Stevenson and Stigler 1992). Differences were not found in the intelligence of the children or in their parents' education level. However, observations and interviews with a sample of the families revealed that the American mothers tended to:

- be the most positive about their children's progress
- believe that ability was more important than effort in success at school
- emphasize carrying out chores and play rather than homework and reading for pleasure (17 per cent of the first year school children did chores in Taiwan, 90 per cent did chores in America)
- show less active involvement in homework.

These findings have attracted a great deal of interest, but it should be remembered that there must remain an area of doubt about whether differences in child-rearing styles cause the differences in school achievement.

Section summary

These observations draw attention to the diversity of child-rearing practices that are employed in human societies. They also challenge assumptions that particular features of adult–infant interaction found in the West are essential for later communicative and social development. Other cross-cultural studies suggest that differences in child-rearing practices can have consequences for both social development and success at school.

Chapter summary

- In the first few years of life considerable social and cognitive advances take place; no other period of life sees such advances.
- Theories about early social development give emphasis to different aspects of the way that these advances take place: some highlight the role of innate capacities, some the role of environment, and some a process of interaction.
- The work of Bowlby has provided the essential base for the development of our present-day understanding of attachment.
- Later work with the Strange Situation Classification (SSC) has provided a wealth of information about attachment, but there is still controversy as to the interpretation of some of the findings.
- Related to attachment has been an interest in deprivation and enrichment and we now have a much better understanding of the consequences of these processes.
- Cross-cultural research provides an essential reminder that it is all too easy to make assumptions that child-rearing in other cultures is similar to the forms that we know.

Essay questions

1 'Mother love in infancy and childhood is as important for mental health as are vitamins and proteins for physical health.' (Bowlby 1951) Discuss. *(24 marks)*

2 Describe and critically assess research into the effects of *either* enrichment *or* deprivation on the subsequent development of children. *(24 marks)*

3 (a) Describe any two studies that have demonstrated cultural differences in the rearing of children. *(12 marks)*

(b) To what extent have these differences been shown to affect the socialization of children. *(12 marks)*

Further reading

Schaffer, H.R. (1990) *Making Decisions about Children*, Oxford: Blackwell.

A comprehensive review of the issues of attachment and separation.

Smith, P. and Cowie, H. (1991) *Understanding Children's Development*, Oxford: Blackwell.

A good overview of issues in child development.

Butterworth, G. and Harris, M. (1994) *Principles of Developmental Psychology*, Hove: Lawrence Erlbaum Associates.

A useful introduction to developmental psychology.

Chapter 18

Cognitive development

George Balfour

Preview

In this chapter we shall be looking at:

- three theories of cognitive development (those of Piaget, Vygotsky and information processing) and the evidence on which they are based
- the practical applications of such theories and research to education
- factors which affect the development of performance on intelligence tests.

Introduction

If you were asked to predict how some individual might deal with a particular problem or think about some topic, but were only allowed to ask for one piece of information about them, then quite probably you would ask to know their age. From the moment of birth, what our society expects of us, and indeed what it provides for us, is much influenced by our age. It is likely, too, that our experiences and how we make sense of them are age related. The claim that children's thinking differs at different ages and is different from the thinking of adults will probably seem obvious, and indeed such differences are readily observable. For instance, we would not expect an adult to say 'A sentence is a big word with holes in it', although a 5-year-old did!

Psychologists who study cognitive development are interested in the ways in which children's thinking and understanding change.

Compared to what was known, or more often assumed, in previous centuries our current knowledge of cognitive development is impressive although still incomplete. Our current emphasis on childhood as a special time for learning has not always been shared.

A few hundred years ago, children were thought to be simply miniature adults. In the 17th century the English philosopher John Locke suggested that a child was born '*tabula rasa*', i.e. with a mind like a blank writing slate. It was assumed that the child's environment determined what was written on the slate. This view was quite consistent with behaviourist learning theory, which was particularly influential in the USA until challenged by more cognitive theories in the 1960s. Psychologists have also been interested in intelligence, how it develops, and how it can be measured. Psychologists have devised a variety of intelligence tests, and are interested in the factors that can influence children's performance on intelligence tests. There has been much debate and research about the relative contributions of genetic and environmental factors.

In this chapter we shall consider three influential theories of cognitive development and the evidence on which they are based. We shall then look at how such theory and research has been applied to education. Finally, we shall look at what we know about the factors that affect intelligence test performance.

Three theories of cognitive development

Piaget's theory

Jean Piaget (1896–1980) was born in Switzerland and initially trained as a biologist and zoologist. Yet by the mid-1970s, Piaget's work was more frequently referenced in the psychological literature than that of anyone else, apart from Freud. Piaget's interest in children's development began in the early 1920s in Paris when he was working on the standardization of a children's intelligence test. Piaget became intrigued by the replies he got from children when he asked them questions. To him, younger children did not simply make errors. Rather it seemed to Piaget that older children seemed to organize their thinking in different ways to give better answers to questions.

Piaget began to formulate the theory that intelligence was a particular instance of biological adaptation which permitted an increasingly more efficient interaction between the child and the world. Piaget recognized that mental development was not simply maturational nor was it the passive absorption of environmental experience. Piaget argued strongly that knowledge was discovered and constructed through the child's own activity. This development of the child's knowledge about the world involved a series of transformations of earlier incomplete and erroneous ideas into increasingly more effective understanding.

Piaget spent more than fifty years producing a wealth of good descriptive observations of children, and extensive theory. To appreciate Piaget's contribution, we need to look at the central features of his theory. Piaget noted that all babies are born with similar biological 'equipment' (Piaget used the term 'structures'). These biological structures were the senses, the brain and reflexes (such as sucking and grasping). Piaget argued that the complex cognitive achievements of the older child must in some way be built up from basic reflexes. He introduced the term 'schema' to mean a psychological structure that represented everything that the baby or child knew about an object or an action. Schemas develop from the child's own interactions with the environment. New experiences would lead to new schemas being developed.

How do schemas become more complex? Piaget proposed two ways this might happen. All intelligent organisms organize their experience and adapt to changes in their environment. In Piaget's view, adaptation has two components. These are assimilation and accommodation. Assimilation is the process of fitting new information and experiences into existing schemas, while accommodation is the process of changing the existing schemas when new information cannot be assimilated.

The concepts of assimilation and accommodation help explain the different kinds of thinking that Piaget observed as the child grew older. Piaget believed that cognitive development went through stages. One way to think of a stage is that it is a time of relative stability when a child will show similar ways of thinking across a wide range of situations or problems. But if this thinking is challenged by some new information or experiences that cannot be assimilated, then this may lead to a major reorganization of schemas.

Thus, accommodation would allow understanding at a new level or stage.

Piaget has identified four major stages in the development of the child's thought:

- the sensorimotor stage (0 to 2 years)
- the pre-operational stage (2 to 7 years)
- the concrete operational stage (7 to 11 years)
- the formal operational stage (11+ years).

All the ages given should be regarded as approximate descriptive guidelines. However, the child progresses through the stages in this fixed order and cannot miss out a stage, though there is no guarantee that the final stage especially will always be reached.

The sensorimotor stage (birth to 2 years)

Piaget's descriptive account of the sensorimotor stage is based on his detailed observation of young infants. The knowledge infants have about the world is limited to what they can experience through the senses and what they can do. Piaget identified six substages of sensorimotor development (see Table 18.1).

Within the sensorimotor stage, infants who initially display only reflex behaviours develop into reflective problem-solvers and by the end of the stage they will have learnt much about themselves, other important persons in their world, and the objects and events which occur in their everyday experience.

One crucial development is that of 'object permanence' – the realization that objects continue to exist even when they cannot be seen. Up to about 8 months, 'out of sight' seems to be 'out of mind', as babies do not search for objects that are hidden from view as they watch. A few months later they may look for an object where they have seen it hidden repeatedly, even if they now see it being hidden somewhere new. But by substage 5, object permanence is quite securely developed, and they will search for an object where it was last seen, and express surprise if it is not there.

Table 18.1 The six substages of sensorimotor development

	Substage	Description
1	*Reflexes (0 to 1 month):*	exercise of inborn reflexes such as grasping, sucking and turning towards sounds or lights
2	*Primary circular reactions (1 to 4 months):*	repeating interesting actions on own body (e.g. touching lips)
3	*Secondary circular reactions (4 to 8 months):*	repeating interesting actions on external objects (e.g. grasping and releasing a cot blanket)
4	*Co-ordination of schemas (8 to 12 months):*	combining actions to solve problems (e.g. an object in the way is pushed aside so that another object can be reached)
5	*Tertiary circular reactions (12 to 18 months):*	experimenting with variations on interesting actions (e.g. when sitting in a chair, dropping different objects from different sides of the chair to see what happens)
6	*Mental combinations (18 to 24 months):*	the beginning of symbolic representations – the child can represent the world in his or her mind and is no longer dependent on actual physical exploration and manipulation to solve problems

The pre-operational stage (2 to 7 years)

During the pre-operational stage, Piaget thought that children became increasingly able to use mental symbols to represent objects, events and situations in their world. Despite this substantial advance, Piaget's descriptions of pre-operational intelligence focused mainly on children's limitations. This is because Piaget believed that children could not yet perform what he called operations. Operations are logical mental rules applied to actual objects in the world. For example, addition and subtraction are reversible operations because 'adding 3' can be reversed by 'taking 3 away'.

Piaget argued that such operations are not well established before 7 years so he described younger children as 'pre-operational'. Up to about the age of 4, pre-operational children can develop preconcepts. By this term Piaget meant that children's concepts were too general (e.g. Daddy owns a blue car – therefore all blue cars are called 'Daddy's car'). Children at this age might also show 'animism' – a willingness to give lifelike qualities to inanimate things (e.g. 'The moon wants to hide behind the clouds'). Between 4 and 7 years, Piaget described children's thought as 'intuitive', because their beliefs seem to be based on what they feel or sense is true, but they cannot explain the underlying principles. Piaget has highlighted some fundamental weaknesses in pre-operational children's thought; five are described in Table 18.2.

Piaget considered egocentrism was the most serious deficiency in pre-operational

Table 18.2 Some limitations in pre-operational thought

1 *Egocentrism:*	This means viewing the world and thinking about it from one's own point of view and being unaware that others may have different points of view or thoughts.
2 *Irreversibility:*	Reversible means 'can be returned to the original state'. For example, pouring liquid from one glass beaker to another can be reversed by simply pouring it back. Pre-operational children lack this flexible reversibility of thought.
3 *Centration:*	This refers to the pre-operational child's tendency to focus or centre attention on only one aspect of a task, and ignore other relevant aspects.
4 *Poor classification:*	Pre-operational children have difficulty with 'class inclusion' problems. For example, when shown four roses and two daffodils and asked 'Are there more roses, or more flowers?', Piaget found that pre-operational children said there were more roses.
5 *Transductive reasoning:*	The pre-operational child's inadequately developed preconcepts can lead to inappropriate conclusions in reasoning, e.g. 'Mummy went to hospital and had a baby, so when daddy goes to hospital he will have a baby too.'

Figure 18.1 Piaget's three mountains scene
Source: Davenport (1994)

children's thinking. Piaget's classic 'three mountains task' (see Fig. 18.1) demonstrated such egocentrism. Pre-operational children were asked how the three-dimensional model of a mountain scene would look from an observation position different to their own position. The three mountains were differently coloured and could also be further distinguished by the fact that there was snow on the top of one, a cross on the top of another and a house on the top of the third. The child sat with the three mountains in front of her and a doll was placed behind the first. The child was asked, 'What can the doll see?' Typically, pre-operational children confidently said that the scene would look just the same as from their own viewpoint. This was the case wherever the doll was positioned.

Concrete operational stage (7 to 11 years)

As well as overcoming the restrictions on thought that characterized the pre-operational stage, concrete operational children are also acquiring cognitive operations. A cognitive operation is a complex mental schema which enables the child to reach logical conclusions about the actual world they experience. For the concrete operational child, the pre-operational reliance on intuition and perception is replaced by a confident use of logical rules. Table 18.3 shows three such important abilities.

Table 18.3 Concrete operational abilities

Seriation:	This cognitive operation allows the child to order a set of items in terms of dimensions like height, or width or both together. For example, when given a set of dolls of different heights, the child can arrange them in order so that the tallest doll is at one end of the row, next is the second tallest doll and so on down to the shortest doll at the other end of the row.
Transitivity:	This is the ability to recognize logical relationships within a series. For example, if David is taller than John and John is taller than Mike, then it follows logically that David is taller than Mike.
Classification:	Concrete operational children understand the relationship between subclasses and the whole class. For example, they know that four roses and two daffodils give six flowers. They also understand that three sets of two give a set of six, enabling number skills like multiplication and division to develop.

Figure 18.2 Examples of different types of conservation involving number, volume, substance and area

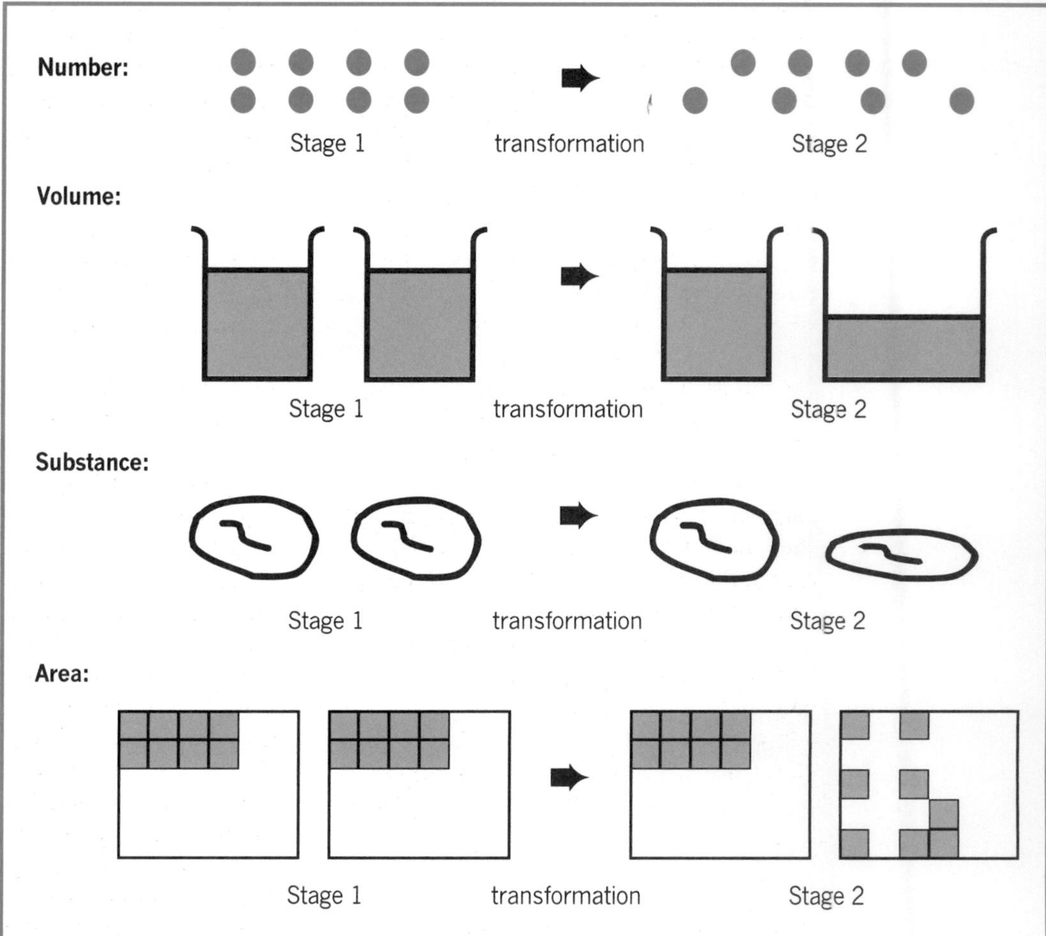

During Stage 1, the child agrees the initial equality of the critical attribute. This is followed by a transformation which destroys the visual similarity, yet does not affect the critical attribute (number, volume, etc.). The child is again asked about the critical attribute. A child is classified as a 'conserver' if he or she affirms the equality of the critical attribute after the transformation has occurred.

One of Piaget's most famous ways of assessing children's thinking was to present them with conservation tasks. Figure 18.2 gives examples of the different types of conservation that have been used. To succeed on a conservation task, the child must realize that although aspects of the display may change, some other important property (or critical attribute) remains constant. For example, a child must realize that the number of counters in a row does not change even when the row is more spaced out, or that the amount of liquid in a glass beaker does not change when it is poured into a glass beaker of a different shape. Failures in conservation tasks demonstrate many of the characteristic features of pre-operational thinking. Thus, pre-operational children may fail on a conservation task because they centre on the row of counters but do not allow for the increased space between the counters. Alternatively, some children may fail by not noticing that the increased length can be reversed by pushing the counters closer together again.

Formal operational stage (11+ years)

With the achievement and use of concrete operational skills, children have an impressive understanding of their world. Yet Piaget argued that their understanding was still limited in the sense that it dealt with the actual world. Piaget thought concrete operational children had difficulty in considering ideas which were hypothetical or abstract.

Formal operational thinkers are also capable of dealing with what Piaget referred to as the 'logic of combinations', which requires carefully planned manipulation of a number of factors, either one at a time or in combinations. In Piaget's pendulum problem, children were shown a simple pendulum consisting of a weight hanging from a string. Their task was to discover which factors affected the frequency of the pendulum swing.

Concrete operational children tend to carry out various experiments; for example, they may alter the length of the string and record the results, but will not usually have a systematic plan. Formal operational thinkers typically develop an overall plan. For example, they keep all the variables constant except one in order to determine its effect, and in this way systematically explore all the possibilities. Formal operational thinking is the final stage in Piaget's theory.

Counter evidence to Piaget's theory

Piaget made the study of children's cognitive development central to psychology. After more than fifty years of studying children, Piaget left us with the most detailed and comprehensive account of cognitive development that currently exists. In general, the results of his observations and experiments are among the most replicable in the whole of psychology.

All good theories should generate research and Piaget's theory has certainly done so. Some of this research has raised important questions about the adequacy of Piaget's account. The central issue has concerned the distinction between *competence* (what a child is capable of doing) and *performance* (how a child performs on a particular task). Piaget was concerned to identify competencies and tended to assume that a child who failed on one task simply lacked the underlying cognitive structures that Piaget believed were needed to succeed on that task. More recent researchers have suggested that Piaget's assumption in this regard was incorrect because a number of other factors can influence a child's performance at a particular time in a particular setting. Subsequent research suggests that a child may have these competencies and may have them earlier than Piaget thought on the basis of his observations and experiments.

Piaget's conclusions about pre-operational deficiencies have been challenged. Influential studies by Donaldson (1978) and her colleagues provide some of the most persuasive evidence. McGarrigle and Donaldson (1974) tested pre-school children in number conservation tasks similar to that used by Piaget, except that one row of beads was 'accidentally' spread out by a 'naughty' teddy glove puppet, who was interfering with the task. The children's ability to conserve was much improved compared to performance on Piaget's

❖ Activity 1 ❖

Carry out Piaget's conservation of volume task with a child aged between 5 and 8 years.

Present two identical glasses with equal amounts of water in them and get the child's agreement that they contain the same amount of water. Then pour the water from one glass into another differently shaped glass. Ask the child 'Does the glass have more water or is there the same amount in each glass?'

Ask the child to explain his or her choice, and try to explore the child's reasoning with follow-up questions. If you can, repeat the task again with a child at a different age. Afterwards, consider whether using different words might have affected the child's replies, and how you might change the task to see if the child's responses change. If you tested two children, how did their responses differ, if at all?

version of the task. Pre-school children understand tasks better when they are presented in natural settings so that they make what Donaldson calls 'human sense'. A task presented in an artificial situation is much more difficult; young children may make errors because they misunderstand the situation, the adults' intentions or the questions asked. In a study by Light *et al.* (1979), only 5 per cent of children conserved when the liquid in a glass beaker was poured into a differently shaped glass beaker. But 70 per cent conserved when the adult drew the children's attention to a crack in the first beaker and suggested that the liquid should be poured into another beaker. Here, the cracked beaker seemed to give a sensible, practical, everyday reason for transferring the liquid into a different beaker.

A study by Borke (1975) (see *In Focus*) shows that several factors are important in assessing the competence of young children.

Evaluation

- Piaget produced the first comprehensive theory of children's cognitive development. The theory has generated a great deal of research.
- Piaget's theory has changed our ideas about children and has had a general influence on educational practice.
- The theory tends to under-emphasize the role of language and social interaction in cognitive development.
- Some important aspects of the theory need to be reconsidered in the light of more recent evidence. Children have been shown to possess important cognitive abilities earlier than Piaget believed.
- Sometimes these abilities have been found so much earlier that Piaget's whole concept of 'stages' is in doubt.

In Focus

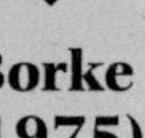

Borke (1975)

A study by Borke (1975) incorporated many factors that are related to young children's ability to succeed in tests of egocentrism. Children aged 3 and 4 were shown three-dimensional displays after a practice session where they became familiar with turning a red fire engine on a turntable so that it fitted the view of Grover, a popular character from *Sesame Street* (an educational TV programme). The three experimental displays were:

1 Piaget's three mountains scene
2 a scene with a lake, boat, horse, cow and house
3 a visually more complex scene involving people and animals in natural settings.

As Grover drove along and stopped to look, the children had to turn their copy of the display on their turntable, so that it matched Grover's view.

Results

Display	*Per cent correct responses*	
	3-year-olds	*4-year-olds*
1	42	67
2	80	80
3	79	95

Only 31 per cent of errors were *egocentric* errors.

It seems that the children's performance, even in the difficult version of the tasks, was improved by several factors including:

- practice, familiarity and interest in the task
- how the child's choice is shown (by turning the display rather than by choosing a picture)
- by the visual discriminability of the scenes – lots of easy-to-recognize, familiar objects provided good cues.

Given these helpful conditions, 3- and 4-year-old children can overcome egocentrism.

Vygotsky's theory

Lev Vygotsky (1896–1934) was an important Russian psychologist and an early critic of Piaget's ideas. Vygotsky's work was not readily available outside the Soviet Union until the 1960s, but since then it has been very influential.

Piaget's account suggests a solitary child making sense of his or her physical environment. Vygotsky argued strongly that the child's intellectual ability and cognitive development took place as the result of social interactions between the child and other people. Children begin with rudimentary abilities and develop more sophisticated cognitive abilities through the teaching of adults. Adults have more knowledge and can provide a supportive context within which the child is guided towards the solution of problems. Children undergo apprenticeships in the skills of their culture; as the children develop, the need for adult help is reduced.

As most social interaction involves language, Vygotsky argued for a close interrelationship between language development and cognitive development from about 2 years of age. Earlier than this, infants can show non-verbal cognitive problem-solving abilities (as in Piaget's sensorimotor stage) and can vocalize to make social contact and express feelings. This 'pre-verbal thought' and 'pre-intellectual speech' gradually come together (e.g. a child may use fingers as a help in counting) until language and thought are closely integrated. However, Vygotsky regarded language as a much more powerful way of dealing with the world.

In one of the relatively few empirical studies that he carried out, Vygotsky argued for the central role of language in concept development. Children were given wooden blocks of varying height and shape, with each block labelled with a nonsense symbol (e.g. 'ZAT' was used to label tall and square blocks). The child's task was to work out what these labels meant. Vygotsky observed that children went through three stages before achieving mature concepts (see Table 18.4).

Vygotsky also distinguished between children's informal concepts and understanding that arose from their own observations and experiences of the world, and the more formal scientific concepts which arose from teaching at school. Vygotsky argued that the role of the adult as teacher was to help the child's extensive but somewhat disorganized informal concepts to become the systematic and organized understanding of the adult (note here the similarities with Piaget's intuitive and operational stages).

Clearly Vygotsky thought that adults and teachers should support children's learning and extend it, and actively challenge children to move on from their present understanding into what Vygotsky referred to as the 'zone of proximal development' (though perhaps 'zone of potential development' would be a better translation). This concept is central in Vygotsky's theory – indeed, he defined intelligence as the

Table 18.4 Vygotsky's stages of concept formation

Stage	Description
1 *Vague syncretic stage:*	Largely trial and error without understanding.
2 *Complexes stage:*	Some appropriate strategies are used but the main attributes are not identified.
3 *Potential concept stage:*	One attribute only (e.g. tall) can be dealt with at a time.
4 *Mature concept stage:*	The child is able to deal with several attributes simultaneously (e.g. tall and square).

capacity to learn from instruction. He saw the teacher's task as one of guiding children from their present level of ability towards their potential level of ability. Vygotsky recognized that different children might have different potential and that the relationship between instruction and learning could be complex. A cooperative interactive relationship between teacher and child was considered to be central to development. Vygotsky also advocated the use of peer teaching. He suggested that a more advanced child might work with a less advanced child to their mutual benefit, because in the course of explaining and helping the other child, the more advanced child might well improve his or her own understanding.

Almost thirty years after the publication of the original edition of Vygotsky's book, *Thought and Language*, the 1962 edition was published with an introduction written by Jerome Bruner, an influential cognitive psychologist and educationalist who saw the importance of Vygotsky's ideas. This helped the book to reach a wide audience of developmental psychologists and educationalists. Bruner also developed Vygotsky's ideas, produced supportive evidence for them and advocated their application within the education system.

Evaluation

- Vygotsky's ideas on cognitive development have had considerable influence.
- Vygotsky emphasized the roles of language and culture, and the crucial role that adults and teachers can have in enabling children to develop their potential.
- Vygotsky argued for a very positive role for education.
- Although Vygotsky produced very little direct empirical evidence, other researchers have provided support for his ideas and their application.

Information processing approach

A recent approach to explaining cognitive development is information processing. This approach owes much to research in memory, selective attention and computer models. It sees all cognitive activities in terms of taking in and processing information.

> **❖ Activity 2 ❖**
>
> Observe a child engaged in any game, e.g. skipping or hide and seek, and think about the various demands being made on the child's perception, memory and attention. Consider how these may change as the child becomes better at the game.

The information processing approach has two main interests. The first is concerned with developments in the basic information processing systems like perception, memory and attention. Much research suggests that some basic components do not develop very much. What does develop, however, are the processes that control and make use of information. The second main interest is to find out how, and why, performance on a task changes. Often, such research suggests improvement is due to the child using more appropriate rules or strategies.

As a developmental approach, information processing assumes that if adults think differently and more successfully than children, this is because the adults can process information more effectively (see Table 18.5).

The first assumption, that the child has limited processing abilities, is supported by the results of many tests of memory recall. For example, people's ability to recall digits after hearing them just once improves with age (adults can usually recall about seven).

Some information processing theorists believe that this is because memory capacity increases as the brain grows and matures. Maturation includes the process of 'myelinization' in which an insulating sheet develops over nerve fibres in the brain, allowing faster transmission of messages.

Table 18.5 Information processing assumptions about the child

1	The child has a limited ability to process information.
2	The child is a novice, without much experience or knowledge.
3	The child is not very skilled at using strategies to improve performance.

The second information processing assumption is that children do less well because they are novices and do not know as much as adults, who have acquired much more knowledge, including better ways to learn. For example, adults have learnt how to 'chunk' several items together to form a meaningful new item. An experiment by Chi (1978), however, challenges the general assumption that adults are more expert because of their greater experience. Chi compared children in local chess clubs who were relative experts at chess with adults who were novices at the game. The children were much better than the adults at recalling chess board positions. Chi's study does, of course, confirm that those with experience and expertise in an area will perform better than those without such advantages.

The third general information processing assumption is that the child is a poor strategist, and does not have good techniques to help memory. Sometimes even 3-year-olds can show some early attempts to aid their memory, e.g. by keeping their hands on the box in which a toy has been hidden. This technique can extend to two hidden objects but if the number increases further, the child runs out of hands, and so its usefulness is limited!

Several specific information processing theories of development can be termed 'neo-Piagetian', because they use information processing ideas to re-interpret aspects of Piaget's theory. We shall consider two such theories now: those of Case and of Fischer.

Case's theory

Case's theory (1992) emphasizes dynamic strategies rather than the schemas of Piaget's theory, and cognitive development is assumed to result from an increase in information processing ability arising from the use of more efficient strategies. Case uses the concept of mental space, or 'M space'. This is rather like the concept of 'working memory' (see Chapter 15) and increases with age, due to three factors:

- Brain maturation, especially myelinization, improves the speed of neural processing.
- Schemas or strategies become more automatic with practice and so need less conscious attention, thus freeing M space for other work.
- Once the schemas are sufficiently automatic, they can become 'central conceptual structures', allowing children to think about their experience in more advanced ways and to develop more efficient ways to solve problems – in effect to move to a new stage of development.

Fischer's skill theory

Like Case, Fischer (1980) begins with ideas that are essentially Piagetian. Fischer argues that a skill is a Piagetian schema that is applied to one task or set of tasks. He suggests that development may be more rapid in some areas, such as number or classification or art, depending on the child's opportunities for experience in these areas. There may well be skill differences between children, depending on their different experiences or learning opportunities.

Fischer identifies three levels of skill performance:

- sensorimotor actions
- representations
- abstractions.

They correspond to Piaget's three main stages (sensorimotor, concrete and formal operational). Children, or adults, do not often perform at their best level. This is because the highest skills of skill performance need extensive support from the environment and require a long period of skill-learning. During this time, the child will become competent in specific tasks and gradually integrate these skills into more general skills. Fischer emphasizes that different skills are heavily dependent on specific experiences and often develop separately. When skills become coordinated using a general principle, then development moves to a higher level, e.g. from representation to abstraction.

Evaluation

- The information processing approach offers a more detailed account of cognitive development by identifying the specific component skills required in a task and studying how these develop.
- Information processing theorists draw on a wide range of research findings.
- Although information processing accounts can be quite explicit, they are often rather narrow and, as yet, task-specific.
- Information processing accounts allow cognitive development across the whole life span. However, the information processing approach has not yet produced a comprehensive theory and some of its explanations (e.g. maturation, experience and organization) are rather general and are shared by other theories.

Section summary

The cognitive theories of Piaget, Vygotsky and information processing have all contributed to our knowledge of how children come to understand their world. There are many points of overlap between the theories, but also differences in emphasis between them.

Research evidence is very important in providing support for each theory. We now have a substantial amount of knowledge about children's cognitive development, although a comprehensive unified theory has not yet been proposed.

Practical applications in education

The theories of cognitive development proposed by Piaget, Vygotsky and information processing allow a major role for environmental influences, although they emphasize different aspects of the environment, both physical and social. As Bruner (1973) has said: 'Some environments push cognitive growth better, earlier and longer than others... it makes a huge difference to the intellectual life of a child simply that he was in school.'

For most children in western societies, the school environment is one in which they spend considerable time, so we shall now look at the applications of these cognitive theories to education. However, much learning can take place at home, with parents and siblings, and many of the applications considered below can be adapted for use either at home or in school.

The theories put forward by Piaget, Vygotsky and information processing have had considerable impact on educational practice, although there are important points of difference between Piaget's rather more 'child-centred' approach, the 'teacher–child' interaction favoured by Vygotsky, and the development of skills, strategies and rules that information processing typically emphasizes. Piaget has said that 'every time we teach a child something we prevent him from discovering it on his own'. Vygotsky, however, did not accept that teachers should wait for the child to be ready to learn and claimed that 'what a child can do with assistance today he/she can do by him/herself tomorrow'.

Piaget's ideas have had most influence in maths and science education. For example, the Nuffield Science approach allows the teacher to provide practical and experimental work before progressing to more abstract and deductive reasoning. The Plowden Report (1967) was much influenced by Piaget's ideas and recommended their incorporation, at least in general terms, into the primary education of 5- to 11-year-olds. Interestingly though, when Davis (1991) asked teachers what had influenced them in their training in classroom practice, she found that although Piaget was invariably named, only rather general ideas were mentioned. As in the Plowden Report, these included active learning, differences in thinking at different ages and the importance of the environment.

❖ Activity 3 ❖

Observe an adult or an older child helping a young child with some activity (e.g. doing a jigsaw). How does the adult or older child help? Does the help seem to fit the child's needs? How does the help offered change as the child becomes more skilled on the task?

Vygotsky believed that children could be helped by adults who know more than the children and can pass on their knowledge in a supportive learning context. The term 'scaffolding' is now used to describe the support the adult provides for the child. This support can be removed when the child has learned. In a study by Freund (1990), 3- to 5-year-olds had to put furniture into the rooms in a doll's house either with their mothers or alone. The children who did the initial tasks with their mothers were much better on a subsequent complex task of furniture sorting than the children who did the initial task alone.

Wood *et al.* (1978) identified two important general strategies mothers can use when helping their children. Wood and colleagues observed 4-year-olds as they tried to make a wooden pyramid from small blocks. The mothers used different levels of support, varying from a general prompt like 'Now you make something' to a very specific instruction such as 'Get four big blocks'. Wood found that the mothers who taught most effectively used two rules to guide their level of help:

- ❖ If the child is failing, then the level of help should be increased.
- ❖ If the child is succeeding, then the level of help should be decreased.

This seems to be just the kind of 'scaffolding' help, and its removal, that is advocated by Vygotsky and aptly summarized by Bruner (1983) when he wrote: 'Where before there was a spectator let there now be a participant.'

Children can obviously learn from parents but children also interact extensively with other children, whether brothers, sisters or their peers at home and at school. What do we know about such interaction? Norman-Jackson (1982) has shown how home play experience with older siblings can transfer to school skills. In this study of low-income black families, it was found that children who learned to read easily at school were likely to have had older brothers and sisters who had played 'school' with them and taught them basic skills such as the alphabet.

Experience of socio-cognitive conflict in a peer group can lead to cognitive development. Howe *et al.* (1991) showed this with children aged between 12 and 14 years who had to make judgements about the trajectory and release point for an object that was to be dropped from an aircraft so as to hit a specific target on the ground. Children were paired either with another child who had similar ideas or with another child who had different initial ideas. It was these latter pairings who made the greatest improvements during the course of the study. A study by Blaye *et al.* (1991) shows the advantages that can come from children working in pairs (see *In Focus*).

At a very general level, all the theories we have considered reflect aspects of information processing within them. But the information processing approach has its own quite distinctive contribution to make to educational practice. Whilst information

In Focus

Blaye *et al.* (1991)

The introduction of computers into classrooms has often resulted in children working in pairs or small groups. Blaye and colleagues studied 11-year-olds, working either alone or in pairs, trying to solve problems presented in the context of a computer adventure game. The task proved difficult and only a few pairs of children and no single children were successful on their first attempts. On their second session, about 50 per cent of the pairs of children working together were successful compared to less than 20 per cent of children working alone. On their third and final session, all children worked individually on a variation of the task. Over 70 per cent of children who had previously worked in pairs were successful compared with only 30 per cent of children who had previously worked individually. Children who worked together on computer tasks, however, did not always outperform those who worked alone. Even when they did so, this advantage did not always transfer to other tasks. None of this research shows individuals outperforming pairs or groups of children. Whether communication through computer networks will lead to the 'real possibility of intellectual coordination with peers in pursuit of joint projects', as suggested by Crooke (1992), remains to be seen.

processing theorists agree with Piaget that children actively explore their world, they are closer to Vygotsky in their recommendations that teachers should take a direct role in instructing children.

Information processing research tries to identify what cognitive abilities and strategies are needed for good performance on a task and how these develop. They also try to find out the difference between 'good' and 'poor' learners. They then try to devise teaching procedures that will improve children's learning. Table 18.6 summarizes some general guidelines for teachers that have been derived from information processing research. Brown and Burton (1978) show how the information processing approach can lead to new teaching applications (see *In Focus* on next page).

Learning to read is probably a child's most important educational achievement. Whether this is best achieved by a 'whole language' or a 'basic skills' approach is much debated. The 'whole language' approach argues that from the start children should be exposed to reading, just as they are to spoken language, in its complete form – for example, in appropriate and meaningful whole stories.

The 'basic skills' approach argues that children should first learn basic rules such as those of translating letters into sounds. There is an information processing position between these extremes.

Learning the basics allows children to deal with new words. As they become more familiar, the process becomes automatic and releases the child's attention for the higher level skills of understanding the meaning of

Table 18.6 Implications of information processing for teachers

1 Know what information is needed and what has to be done with it to be successful.

2 Do not overload short-term memory.

3 Try to find out what rule the child is using if consistent errors are being made.

4 Encourage 'meta cognitive' knowledge about strategies and their usefulness (e.g. 'Why does summarizing in your own words help?').

In Focus

Brown and Burton (1978)

A study by Brown and Burton (1978) shows how some of the guidelines based on the information processing approach can be applied to the study of children's errors in arithmetic tasks. In computer science, a 'bug' refers to an error in a computer programme. Brown and Burton used the term to apply to an error in a child's arithmetic rules. A bug leads to systematic errors, but still implies some understanding, although imperfect. The examples below illustrate the errors that can arise when a subtraction procedure has not quite been applied correctly. In each case, the smaller number has been consistently subtracted from the larger number, regardless of which is on the top line.

625	444
− *478*	− *363*
253	121

Once they had identified such 'bugs', Brown and Burton set up two computerized games to train teachers to recognize and correct these bugs. The games, 'Buggy' and 'Debuggy', give the teacher examples of the bug and the teacher tries to identify the bug. Two benefits have been shown:

- Teachers become more skilful at detecting bugs (i.e. faulty rule use by children).
- Teachers realize that children's errors may be due to the use of systematic but imperfect rules that can be corrected, rather than due to carelessness.

the text. Parents who read to their young children encourage both the basic and higher level skills which lead to successful literacy (Wells 1985). This general point is quite similar to that of Hewison and Tizard (1980) (see *In Focus* below) and shows how different approaches can lead to similar findings.

Psychologists have recently been looking for ways to incorporate the key insights from different theories. These suggest that the ideal situation for children's learning arises from direct experience with appropriate materials in a social context where a child can have the skilled guidance of an expert to develop general skills and strategies. For young children at least, this description can fit the home situation quite well and the home can be an effective learning place. The challenge for education is to be equally successful in the classroom. As the study by Hewison and Tizard (1980) suggests, it is unlikely that we can do without human resources, either inside or outside the classroom.

In Focus

Helping children to read (Hewison and Tizard 1980)

Research by Hewison and Tizard (1980) emphasizes the advantages to the child of relevant experience with a supportive adult. Their study looked at progress over a two-year-period in the reading skills of three initially comparable groups of children, including those from non-literate and non-English-speaking families in twelve inner-London primary schools. One group received no special help in learning to read, other than that normally given in school. A second group was given extra instruction from an additional teacher. The third group had to read to their parents at home for ten minutes each day in addition to their normal school reading experience. This third group made greater progress in reading than the other two groups.

Section summary

Cognitive theories of development and the research they have generated have important applications to educational practice.

Some of the research findings, such as the ways a more knowledgeable other person can assist the child, can be used quite generally either in the home or at school and, for optimal development, in both. One important point is that development and learning can occur throughout the life span. With appropriate materials and teaching help, and the careful consideration of what demands a topic will make on the learner's skills, we can have a positive view of helping children to learn.

The development of measured intelligence

Psychologists have carried out much research on the controversial topic of intelligence.

> **❖ Activity 4 ❖**
>
> Think of as many examples as you can of activities or behaviours that you consider reflect 'intelligence'. Then consider the following questions:
>
> - How do you think that intelligence might be measured?
> - What kinds of test could be used?
> - How might 'intelligence' be measured in very young children?

If you found that doing Activity 4 produced a range of ideas about intelligence, then you may not be surprised to discover that psychologists have not agreed on one definition of intelligence either. They even disagree on whether there is one general kind of intelligence or several different kinds. Although there are a variety of definitions of intelligence, there is, however, considerable agreement that it refers to differences in the ability to acquire information, to think and reason well, and to deal effectively and adaptively with the environment.

Measuring intelligence

The issue of assessing children's intelligence was first tackled by Binet in 1905. Binet had been asked to develop a way of identifying pupils who needed special remedial education. Binet and his colleague Simon developed a test of 'general mental ability' which included a range of both verbal and non-verbal reasoning tasks. The test items varied in difficulty and Binet and Simon were able to determine at what age the average child would succeed with each item. (Working on later versions of these tests, Piaget became interested in the differences in the answers children gave to specific test items.) Binet's developmental approach, which assumed that mental abilities develop over time and older children can generally succeed on more difficult tasks, was so successful in predicting school performance that it became the basis for many other intelligence tests.

A recurrent issue in the assessment of intelligence has been whether there is one general ability which a single score could represent, or whether intelligence is made up of several, or many, different abilities. There have also been tests based on particular theories or approaches, such as Piaget's theory and the information processing approach. There is also a range of tests intended for more specific use, such as to test infants or to test non-verbal abilities, and also some attempt to develop tests that are 'culture-free' or at least 'culture-fair'.

In many intelligence tests, the score is given as an 'intelligence quotient' (IQ). This score enables one individual's performance to be compared with the performance of others. Following Binet, the general principle for calculating IQ has been to establish the child's 'Mental Age'. A child will have a mental age of, say, 8 if that child passes the test items that average 8-year-olds pass (but does not pass the tests that average 9-year-olds pass). If this mental age is divided by the child's actual age, called 'chronological age' (CA), and multiplied by 100 (to remove fractions), then the result is the child's IQ. This means a child of average ability will have an IQ of 100. Scores above or below 100 indicate a child of greater or less than average intelligence.

Factors affecting intelligence test scores

In this section we shall look at what is known about the factors that can affect children's scores on IQ tests. Psychological research has identified quite a number of such factors, but the topic is a difficult one to investigate for various methodological reasons. There is as yet insufficient evidence to come to precise conclusions about the exact contributions any one factor can make, especially in the individual child.

There is no doubt that different children achieve different scores on IQ tests. There is also some evidence that there are differences in test performance between different groups of children. These groups may be ethnic, social class or even gender. One important point to make is that any such differences are based on group averages, and there is typically overlap in the distribution of individual scores between groups.

Research has investigated three general factors that may affect intelligence test performance. These are:

- genetic factors
- environmental factors
- test bias factors.

Genetic factors

The long-standing controversy about the relative contributions of genetic factors ('nature') versus environmental factors ('nurture') has been prominent in the debate about IQ differences. In general terms, it is now widely accepted that each makes a considerable contribution and that the two must interact. But how much variation in IQ scores is due to genetic factors and how much is due to environmental factors? Two general research designs have been used to study genetic factors: kinship studies, especially of twins, and adoption studies.

Kinship studies

Kinship studies look at the correlation in IQ scores between pairs who are genetically related to varying degrees. Much criticism has been directed at earlier studies in this area, on methodological grounds – for example, whether the environments of separated pairs really were different in ways that would affect IQ. Buchard and McGue (1981) have tried to take such criticisms into account in producing a summary of a large number of studies conducted worldwide. Their findings are shown in Table 18.7.

The correlation for identical twins reared apart (0.72) is higher than for fraternal (non-identical) twins reared together (0.60). This indicates that genetic factors are at least partially responsible for differences in IQ scores. However, comparison of three other sets of correlations in Table 18.7 indicates considerable environmental effects. The correlation of identical twins reared

Table 18.7 Summarized IQ correlations

Kinship pair	*Average correlation*
Identical twins reared together	0.86
Identical twins reared apart	0.72
Fraternal twins reared together	0.60
Siblings reared together	0.47
Siblings reared apart	0.24

Source: Buchard and McGue (1981), p. 1056

apart (0.72) is lower than that of identical twins reared together (0.86); the correlation for fraternal twins reared together (0.60) is higher than that for siblings reared together (0.47); and the correlation for siblings reared together (0.47) is higher than that for siblings reared apart (0.24). On the basis of this kind of evidence, it seems that about half of the variation in IQ scores may be due to individual differences in heredity. This is a much more moderate estimate than the controversial claims made earlier (e.g. Jensen 1969).

Adoption studies

Adoption studies allow researchers to compare the IQ correlations of children with both their biological and their adoptive parents. Early adoption studies often suffered from a methodological limitation – selective placement may have taken place. This means that children's adoptive families were 'matched' as closely as possible with their biological parents. When this has occurred, genetic and environmental influences cannot be separated. There are, however, more recent adoption studies where selective placement has been minimal. The *In Focus* describes the Texas Adoption Project (Horne 1983).

In their transracial adoption study, Scarr and Weinberg (1976, 1983) looked at black American children adopted by white families. The adoptive families had higher educational status and income than the children's biological families. The average IQ of the adopted black children was 106, and those adopted within twelve months of birth averaged 110. The average IQ of black American children with similar genetic background but who were not brought up in a middle-class environment was 90. Scarr and Weinberg conclude that heredity does not account for the typically lower IQ scores of black children in low-income black communities.

Environmental factors

Just as there is clear evidence for genetic factors, there is also a considerable amount of evidence for environmental effects on IQ scores. That both genetic and

In Focus

The Texas Adoption Project (Horne 1983)

The Texas Adoption Project was made possible by the data from a large private adoption agency in Texas. The agency had given IQ tests to the unmarried mothers of some 469 children who were adopted after birth by 300 adoptive families. The IQs of the adoptive mothers were also available. The correlation of the adopted children's IQ with their biological mother's IQ was 0.28 and with their adoptive mother's IQ 0.15. While these figures show some genetic contribution, the difference between the correlations is very small. Other research has produced similar results. In statistical terms, the small correlations indicate that the IQ scores of the biological mothers explain 8 per cent of the differences in the adopted children's IQ scores and the IQ scores of the adoptive mothers explain 2 per cent of the differences in the adopted children's scores. Assuming that biological and adoptive fathers contributed similarly, there is still about 80 per cent of the variation in children's IQ scores to be accounted for by individual environmental experiences outside the shared home, such as school. One intriguing possibility here is that genes may influence development by their effect on how a child reacts to particular experiences.

Horne also studied the adopted children of two groups of biological mothers with widely different IQ scores, those with IQs above 120 and those with IQs below 95. When tested in middle childhood, the average IQ of children of biological mothers with lower IQs was 102, but the average IQ of the children of the high-IQ biological mothers was 118. This study clearly shows that both environment and heredity contribute substantially to IQ.

Table 18.8 Environmental factors affecting IQ scores (Sameroff and Seifer 1983)

1 The mother has a history of mental illness.
2 The mother has serious anxiety.
3 The mother has rigid attitudes, beliefs and values about her child's development.
4 There are few positive interactions between mother and infant.
5 The main earner in the household has a semi-skilled job.
6 The mother did not go to High School.
7 The child is from a minority group.
8 The father does not live with the family.
9 The family has suffered more than twenty stressful events before the child was aged 4.
10 There are four or more children in the family.

environmental factors are involved is not in dispute. Recent studies of environmental factors have tried to find which specific aspects of the environment contribute to children's IQ scores, and by how much. We shall look at two such large-scale studies.

Beginning in the 1970s, Sameroff and Seifer (1983) followed several hundred children from birth to adolescence. They have identified ten environmental factors, each of which can lead to a loss of roughly five IQ points, and together can account for almost half the variability in children's IQ scores. The ten factors are listed in Table 18.8.

Caldwell and Bradley (1978) have developed a checklist of items to use when gathering information about the quality of children's home lives, called the Home Observation for Measurement of the Environment (HOME). There are versions of HOME for infancy, pre-school and middle childhood. Each has subscales that relate to aspects of the child's environment. Table 18.9 shows the pre-school version.

Almost all the items have some relation to later achievement. HOME scores can correlate 0.5 with later IQ scores. Low scores in infancy can predict a reduction in IQ scores of up to twenty points. For the pre-school scales, Bradley and Caldwell (1984) found that children who score well on IQ tests are generally from families who:

- are emotionally responsive and involved with the child
- talk to the child
- provide appropriate play materials
- provide opportunities to explore and learn
- expect their child to learn and achieve.

Table 18.9 HOME: Pre-school version

Subscale
1 Pride, affection and warmth
2 Avoidance of physical punishment
3 Language stimulation
4 Stimulation of academic behaviour
5 Stimulation through toys, games and reading material
6 Modelling appropriate social behaviours and encouraging social maturity
7 Variety in daily stimulation
8 Physical environment: safe, clean and conducive to development

Source: Elardo and Bradley (1981)

The correlation between HOME scores and IQ is lower for middle childhood, probably because by then children are spending time in other environments such as school. While these results using HOME scores are consistent with much other research, they are based on correlational data and can say nothing conclusive about causation, especially as these results come from children raised by their biological parents. A longitudinal study by Yeates *et al.* (1979) helps here. They measured the IQ scores of 112 mothers and their children at ages 2, 3 and 4 years and their HOME scores. The best predictor of a child's IQ at age 2 was the mother's IQ, as genetic causes would suggest, but by age 4, HOME scores were the best predictor of a child's IQ. Home environment is therefore important.

Test bias factors

A controversial question raised by differences in IQ test performance, especially between racial or cultural groups, is the extent to which such differences may be due to aspects of the test, including the possibility that:

- the test content samples culturally specific knowledge
- the administration of the test can disadvantage some children
- children's motivation to succeed varies.

On the one hand, IQ tests do predict quite well educational and other aspects of success, so in that sense the tests are not biased. They do not of course give any kind of reasons or explanations for the scores. On the other hand, a wider view of test bias is that the IQ scores of some children will be underestimated because of the kinds of factors mentioned above. This view of bias is that whatever environmental or genetic factors have resulted in the child's actual intelligence, the test used may not measure this accurately and almost always underestimates the child's actual intelligence.

Test content

IQ tests are designed to predict success in a particular culture. Items may have bias because other cultures use different criteria. Luria (1971) gives a clear example. When presented with a classification task involving the four items axe, log, shovel and saw, and asked to identify which one is the odd one out, 'log' is considered to be the odd one out because it is not a tool. 'Log' is, therefore, the 'correct answer' because our culture values the ability to classify. However, Luria found that unskilled Russian peasants chose 'shovel' because it wasn't needed when cutting up the log with the axe and the saw. Cole *et al.* (1971) found that the Kpelle in Nigeria persistently grouped pictures of objects according to their use until they were asked to sort them in the way a stupid person would do so. They then used the categories preferred by Europeans!

Attempts to produce 'culture-free' or 'culture-fair' tests have had mixed success. Some such tests have substantially reduced cultural group differences and some have not, although this could be because the tests were still culturally biased. Williams' (1972) BITCH (Black Intelligence Test of Cultural Homogeneity) indicates an alternative 'strategy'. This test was specifically designed for American Negro children and white children do less well by comparison.

Motivation

IQ scores can improve if the child is familiar with the tester, is given praise for success, and has some test experience, especially of giving correct answers. Zigler *et al.* (1973) found that pre-school children from impoverished backgrounds could gain up to ten IQ points if they had a short play session with the tester beforehand, or were tested a second time. By comparison, middle-class children's scores increased by only three IQ points.

Familiarity with test materials

Performance on some IQ test items may depend on particular opportunities to learn prior to the test. Dirks (1982) found that children's performance on an IQ test item requiring the child to rearrange wooden blocks to copy a design quickly, was related to their experience of a popular but expensive game that made very similar demands. Heath (1989) found that the mothers of black American children typically asked their children 'real' questions, that is questions that did not have one correct, short answer already known by the mother. Such questions helped the children to develop complex verbal skills, but did not prepare them for the kinds of questions they met in the classroom or in IQ tests.

The evidence of test bias suggests that caution is needed in interpreting IQ scores, and particularly the IQ scores of people from minority groups. We need to know much more about the effects of cultural context on IQ test performance.

Section summary

IQ test scores have good predictive power for school success. Evidence has shown that both genetic and environmental factors affect children's IQ scores. The best current estimates suggest that each contributes about 50 per cent of the variability between test scores. Caution is needed when interpreting IQ scores because some cultural groups can be disadvantaged by various kinds of bias within IQ tests.

Chapter summary

- Theories of cognitive development have enriched our understanding of children's thinking and learning. There are both differences of emphasis (e.g. in the role of language, or the use of strategies) and considerable overlap (e.g. in the importance of experience) between the theories. However, one coherent and comprehensive, descriptive and explanatory theory has not yet emerged.
- Theories of cognitive development have generated much empirical research.
- This research has both increased our detailed knowledge about many aspects of the child's developing cognitive skills, and has important applications to education, both at home and in the school.
- Interest in the measurement of children's intelligence has led to the development of the Intelligence Quotient (IQ) – a score that reflects the child's measured intelligence in comparison with other children of the same age.
- Both genetic and environmental factors can contribute substantially to IQ scores, although there are methodological difficulties in assessing the exact contributions of each. Great caution is needed when interpreting IQ scores, particularly those of children from different social and cultural backgrounds.

Essay questions

1 Describe and evaluate any one theory of cognitive development. *(24 marks)*

2 (a) Describe the application of theory and research in cognitive development to education. *(12 marks)*

(b) How successful have such applications been? *(12 marks)*

3 (a) Describe the environmental factors that can influence children's intelligence test scores. *(12 marks)*

(b) Comment on any methodological difficulties that can arise in studies that attempt to assess such environmental factors. *(12 marks)*

Further reading

Donaldson, M. (1978) *Children's Minds*, London: Fontana.

An influential yet readable critique of Piaget.

Wood, D. (1988) *How Children Think and Learn*, Oxford: Blackwell.

A detailed account of the theories of Piaget and Vygotsky, and their potential for learning and classroom practice.

Eysenck, H. J. and Kamin L. J. (1981) *Intelligence: The Battle for the Mind*, London: Macmillan.

Presents arguments and evidence from both sides of the nature–nurture debate.

Sutherland, P. (1992) *Developmental Psychology Today: Piaget and his Critics*, London: Paul Chapman.

Includes readable chapters on Piaget, Vygotsky and information processing, and their educational implications.

Chapter 19

Social behaviour

Pat Hasan

Preview

In this chapter we will be looking at:

- definitions and theories of moral development
- definitions of gender
- theories of gender development
- the development of self-understanding.

Introduction

There is a traditional nursery rhyme which goes like this:

'What are little girls made of?
Sugar and spice and all things nice.
That's what little girls are made of.

'What are little boys made of?
Frogs and snails and puppy dogs'
tails.
That's what little boys are made of.'

The politically incorrect content of this rhyme goes against current thinking which seeks to eliminate such overt gender stereotyping from as many contexts as possible. Few parents would feel comfortable reciting such rhymes at bedtime to their impressionable tiny tots! Nevertheless, the current generation of young children will certainly acquire a sense of gender identity, of being male or female, by the time they are 3 years old. As they develop, they will inevitably conform to gender-based sociocultural roles, often heavily influenced by stereotypes.

Likewise, children are also exposed to rules about what they themselves and those around them, should and should not do in terms of their moral behaviour. Gender differences, stereotyping and sociocultural norms may influence moral development too.

The development of a sense of gender identity and gender role, as well as a moral sense of right and wrong, is an important process for each individual child as they come to discover who they are and what sort of person they will become, i.e. as they come to acquire self-understanding. According to Costanzo (1992) and Shantz and Hobart (1989), both cited in Durkin (1995), there are two primary sub-goals of socialization:

- *individuation* – determining one's own personal uniqueness
- *social connection* – discovering how to relate to, learn from, and function with other people.

It is not surprising then that developmental psychologists consider these developments to be worthy of investigation. As we shall see, they are crucial for the social adjustment and functioning of the developing child, and in turn are reflected in the child's relationships with others in a social situation. This chapter considers each of these processes individually and examines them in more detail. We will clarify what is meant by the terms, moral development, gender and the self, and then discuss the main theories which underpin these developments, including:

- social learning theory (Bandura 1977)
- psychodynamic theory (Freud 1920, Erikson 1980)
- cognitive developmental theories of moral development (Piaget 1932, Kohlberg 1963, 1969, 1985).

Theories of moral development

What is moral development?

Moral development is concerned with the rules about the rightness and wrongness of certain behaviours and how people should behave in relation to others. An inevitable part of socialization across all cultures involves the developing child having to learn sociocultural values and the rules which govern the behaviours associated with them. Traditionally, psychologists have studied three aspects of moral development:

- how children *think* and *reason* about moral issues and how this influences the decisions they make
- how children actually *behave* in a situation where they are required to exercise judgement over the conflict between right and wrong
- how children *feel* about moral issues – would they experience a feeling of guilt if they behaved in a way which they knew to be wrong?

Conveniently, there is a particular theoretical approach which has addressed each of these three aspects of moral development. Cognitive theories, such as those of Piaget, have looked at *thinking* and *reasoning* about moral issues. Some of the learning theories such as classical and operant conditioning, and social learning theories, have been concerned with actual moral *behaviour*, and the psychodynamic theories of Freud and Erikson have shed some light on *feelings* about ethical and moral matters.

Cognitive developmental theories

Piaget's theory of moral development

Jean Piaget (1932) developed a cognitive theory of moral development based on an invariant sequence of stages through which children progress as they think about moral issues. Piaget relied on observation and interview to develop his theory, working with children aged between 3 and 12 years. For example, he observed children playing games of marbles and asked them questions about the rules of the game and what they thought about them. He also told pairs of fictitious stories (see *In Focus*) to children and then asked the question 'Which of the characters was the naughtier and who should be punished the most?' In this way, Piaget was able to question children on a number of moral issues such as theft, lies, punishment and justice.

What did Piaget conclude from the answers which these children gave? He described children before the age of 3 or 4 years as premoral, suggesting that they have no concept of rules as such, and consequently they cannot make judgements about when rules are disregarded or violated. Thereafter, children do begin to reason actively about right or wrong. The first stage of actual moral reasoning, according to Piaget, is the stage of heteronomous morality or moral realism which characterizes children aged between 3 and 6 years. However, during this stage

In Focus

Piaget's stories

Pairs of stories used by Piaget in studies of young children's moral development.

Story 1: A little boy who is called John is in his room. He is called to dinner. He goes into the dining room. But behind the door there was a chair, and on the chair there was a tray with 15 cups on it. John couldn't have known that there was all this behind the door. He goes in, the door knocks against the tray, 'bang' to the 15 cups and they all get broken!

Story 2: Once there was a little boy whose name was Henry. One day when his mother was out he tried to get some jam out of the cupboard. He climbed up on a chair and stretched out his arm. But the jam was too high up and he couldn't reach it and have any. But while he was trying to get it, he knocked over a cup. The cup fell down and broke.

Source: Piaget 1932, p.122

the child's perception of rules is totally inflexible and they believe rules to be fixed and unchanging. Rules are regarded as *absolute,* whether they are the rules of the games they play or those laid down by parents or teachers. Rules must also be obeyed, and failure to obey a rule automatically results in punishment (imminent justice), based on the idea that wrongdoing is instantly punished by God or someone in authority. After hearing the stories which Piaget told during his investigations, children within the age range of 3 to 6 years replied to the question 'Who is the naughtier and who should be punished the most?' by the *consequences* of the action rather than the *intent* (see *In Focus* below).

In Focus

Piaget's stories: children's responses

Below is a characteristic response for a child in the stage of moral realism:

Questioner: 'What did the first boy do?'

Child: 'He broke 15 cups.'

Questioner: 'And the second one?'

Child: 'He broke a cup by moving roughly.'

Questioner: 'Is one of the boys naughtier than the other?'

Child: 'The first one is because he knocked over 15 cups.'

Questioner: 'If you were the daddy, which one would you punish most?'

Child: 'The one who broke 15 cups.'

Questioner: 'Why did he break them?'

Child: 'The door shut too hard and knocked them over. He didn't do it on purpose.'

Questioner: 'And why did the other boy break a cup?'

Child: 'Because he was clumsy. When he was getting the jam the cup fell down.'

Questioner: 'Why did he want to get the jam?'

Child: 'Because he was alone. Because the mother wasn't there.'

Source: Piaget 1932, p.129

We can see that John is regarded by the child in the stage of moral realism as being the naughtier of the two, because the outcome of his behaviour was that 15 cups were broken, although the child recognizes that this was unintentional. Henry only broke one cup, while he was trying to *deceive* his mother, but because the consequences of the action were less in the child's eyes, he is seen as less naughty. According to Piaget, an older child would say that Henry was the naughtiest because he wanted to take the jam, without his mother's permission, and this child is considering intentions. He or she would deny that it mattered that John broke more cups because he did not do it deliberately.

However, Piaget observed a change in the behaviour of the children aged 9 to 11 years. Because of greater cognitive maturity, these children had entered the second stage of moral development which Piaget called the stage of autonomous morality or morality of reciprocity. Children are now more flexible in their thinking and can adopt alternative ways of looking at things. They realize that the rules of games are not necessarily fixed, and that they are free to adapt and change the rules as long as all players agree. Transgressions of an accepted code of behaviour and rule violations are no longer seen as inevitably followed by punishment. Perhaps the greatest cognitive shift is reflected in the older child's ability to take *intention* into consideration when considering the morality of an action, thereby refraining from making judgements which are purely based on the outcome or *consequences* of an action.

From this description of the theory so far, we have left children between the ages of 7 and 9 years unaccounted for. Piaget believed that this was a period of transition between the two stages and that children in this age range will show evidence of features from both.

❖ Activity 1 ❖

Moral realism or autonomous reality?

Devise pairs of stories similar to those used by Piaget. Make sure that you discuss the stories with your teacher and also the ethical guidelines for conducting a project such as this one involving young children. Try to find children known to you who are of the ages necessary to test Piaget's theory – a child aged between 3 and 7, and a child over 10 years old. One child in each age group will be sufficient. If they are willing to cooperate, read them the stories and then ask them the questions such as those described in the *In Focus*. Write down their answers. Do the younger children answer the questions according to Piaget's predictions?

The general developmental progression from a stage of moral realism to a stage of moral reciprocity which Piaget describes has frequently been replicated, at least in Western cultures (Ferguson and Rule 1982). Cross-cultural evidence however, has been less convincing and cultural factors may indeed alter the sequence of rigid stages proposed by Piaget.

In addition, just as Piaget underestimated the cognitive capacities of young children on tasks designed to test for egocentrism and conservation abilities, as reported by Donaldson (1978), (see Chapter 18), the same is true in relation to moral development. All too often a child is credited with a particular developmental stage when really the child's performance is constrained by the methodology used. For example, children may misunderstand the instructions which they are given because they are unnecessarily complex, or the task which they are asked to complete may be beyond that child's current experience of the world. In relation to moral development, if the situation in the moral stories is one which the child is easily able to identify, then even 6-year-olds are able to consider intentions. Taking this further, Chandler *et al.* (1973) have found that if the format of these stories is changed from a verbal to a videotaped presentation, then 6-year-olds recognize the intentions of the actor just as well as older children do. Likewise, Feldman *et al.* (1976) have found that young children are able to make judgements based on intention when the intentions of the characters in the stories are evaluated separately from the outcomes, whereas in Piaget's original stories, the intent of the child is always confused with the consequences of the action.

Overall, more recent research suggests that Piaget may have underestimated the complexity of moral reasoning. A more complex approach to the study of moral reasoning is reflected in the work of Kohlberg (1963, 1969, 1985).

In Focus

Kohlberg's dilemmas

One of the most famous of Kohlberg's dilemmas concerns that of Heinz, described below.

In Europe, a woman was near death from a particular kind of cancer. There was one drug that the doctors thought might save her. It was a form of radium that a druggist in the same town had recently discovered. The drug was expensive to make, but the druggist was charging ten times what the drug cost him to make. He paid $200 for the radium and charged $2000 for a small dose of the drug. The sick woman's husband, Heinz, went to everyone he knew to borrow the money, but he could only get together about $1000 which is half of what it cost. He told the druggist that his wife was dying, and asked him to sell it cheaper or let him pay later. But the druggist said: 'No, I discovered the drug and I'm going to make money from it.' So Heinz got desperate and broke into the man's store to steal the drug for his wife.

After hearing the story, the individual is asked a series of questions, such as:

- Should Heinz have stolen the drug?
- What if Heinz didn't love his wife? Would that change anything?
- What if the person dying was a stranger?
- Should Heinz steal the drug anyway?

Kohlberg and Elfenbein 1975, p. 621

Kohlberg's theory of moral development

Kohlberg's theory builds on Piaget's ideas and extends them to cover adolescence and adulthood. He devised his theory on the basis of analysis of interviews conducted with 10- to 16-year-old boys who were presented with a series of moral dilemmas (see *In Focus* above). Based on their responses, he developed a theory consisting of three broad levels of moral development which are subdivided into six stages (see Table 19.1). Kohlberg believes that the order of these stages is invariant, with each stage building on the moral achievements and concepts of the previous stage.

Kohlberg, however, acknowledges that there is some flexibility in relation to the chronological age at which individuals arrive at each stage and indeed, some adults may never achieve the highest level of moral judgement, that of universal ethical principles. This stage may be reserved for people who are generally regarded as being exceptional, such as Martin Luther King or Mother Teresa. The participants' responses when tested on Kohlberg's dilemmas are assigned to an appropriate stage based on the *reasons* given for the choice that is made when evaluating the problem, rather than on the basis of the choice itself.

- *Stage 1: Punishment and obedience orientation*

  The child judges right and wrong on the basis of whether or not a behaviour is punished, and obeys adults because they are stronger and more powerful.

- *Stage 2: Individualism, instrumental purpose and exchange*

  Here the child begins to indulge in good behaviour because it brings pleasurable rewards to the child which makes him or her feel good; the child avoids bad behaviour because it has the opposite effect. Concern for others emerges here but only in the strictly reciprocal rather self-serving manner of 'If you help me, I'll help you'.

- *Stage 3: Mutual interpersonal expectations, relationships and interpersonal conformity*

  At this stage children begin to consider relationships with others and value qualities such as trust, loyalty and respect. They associate good behaviour with pleasing other people. Children are also able to judge actions based on intentions as well as consequences.

- *Stage 4: Social system and conscience*

  This stage sees the young person broadening their environment from

Table 19.1 Stages of moral development (Kohlberg 1976)

Level 1: Preconventional morality

Stage 1: Punishment and obedience orientation

The child decides what is wrong on the basis of what is punished. Obedience is not valued for its own sake; the child obeys because adults have superior power.

Stage 2: Individualism, instrumental purpose and exchange

The child follows rules when it is in his immediate interest. What is good is what brings pleasant results. Right is also what is fair, what is an equal exchange, a deal or an agreement.

Level 2: Conventional morality

Stage 3: Mutual interpersonal expectations, relationships and interpersonal conformity

The family or small group to which the child belongs becomes important. Moral actions are those that live up to others' expectations. 'Being good' becomes important for its own sake, and the child generally values trust, loyalty, respect, gratitude and keeping mutual relationships.

Stage 4: Social system and conscience (law and order)

A shift in focus from family and close groups to the larger society. Good is fulfilling duties one has agreed to; laws are to be upheld except in extreme cases. Contributing to society is also seen as good.

Level 3: Principled or postconventional morality

Stage 5: Social contract or utility and individual rights

Acting so as to achieve the 'greatest good for the greatest number'. The child is aware that there are different views and values, that values are relative. Laws and rules should be upheld in order to preserve the social order, but they can be changed. Still, there are some basic nonrelative values, such as the importance of each person's life and liberty, that should be upheld no matter what.

Stage 6: Universal ethical principles

The person develops and follows self-chosen ethical principles in determining what is right. Since laws usually conform to those principles, laws should be obeyed, but when there is a difference between law and conscience, conscience dominates. At this stage, the ethical principles followed are part of an articulated, integrated, carefully thought-out and consistently followed system of values and principles.

family, close friends and the peer group to larger social groups which provide him or her with norms of behaviour. The focus is on exercising one's duty, respecting authority, obeying rules and keeping within the law.

Stage 5: Social contract or utility and individual rights

The main shift in reasoning that takes place at this stage is similar to Piaget's description of children realizing that rules can be negotiated and changed if all parties agree. Stage 5 reasoning involves the recognition that if rules are unfair, unjust, inhumane or against an individual's principles and values, then they do not have to be obeyed unquestioningly. For example, there is provision in most Western societies for protest and pressure on government and influential groups to change laws which discriminate against certain sections of the population.

An important focus of the work of Amnesty International is to draw attention to parts of the world that do not afford their citizens the kind of human rights which would be based on this level of moral reasoning.

- *Stage 6: Universal ethical principles*

  This final stage, as previously mentioned, involves individuals who are committed to a system of values and principles to such an extent that when they come up against a situation where their conscience conflicts with the law of the land, their conscience will win over. The moral position of these people is based upon fundamental and universal principles, such as the sacredness of all human life, which seem to drive all of their behaviour. However, few have the 'dream' of people such as Martin Luther King, and Kohlberg himself has suggested that achievement of this stage may be extremely rare amongst the world's population as a whole (Kohlberg 1978). Finally, in an interesting link with the 'obedience to authority' experiments undertaken by Milgram (1974), Kohlberg reported that although small in number, 'people with a Stage 6 moral orientation were less likely to obey the experimenter and administer the strongest shocks to the learner' in this context. Remember Milgram was surprised at the high level of compliance in his experiments, which was contrary to prediction. Likewise, the experiment with nurses carried out by Hofling et al. (1966) also produced surprisingly high levels of compliance, suggesting that compulsion to obey authority is still relatively strong in our society (see Chapter 3). If, as Kohlberg is suggesting, Stage 6 reasoning is a necessary condition for resistance in these situations, we should not be surprised that so many people comply or so few people do not! However one suspects that the relationship is less straightforward than this.

One of the major criticisms of the theories of both Piaget and Kohlberg is that measures of moral reasoning obtained from testing individuals using the appropriate criteria, are often only very weakly correlated with the person's actual behaviour in a real-life situation (Rest 1983). Therefore the predictive value of such measures is questionable. In addition, the method specified by Kohlberg's theory, to code responses or assign an individual to a particular stage, is often criticized for being low in test-retest and inter-rater reliability (Kurtines and Greif 1974). For example, one central concern is whether an individual who is assigned to a particular stage by one researcher would be scored at the same level by someone else or would the second assessment be likely to differ? Rest (1983) highlighted this problem and suggested that frequent revisions in Kohlberg's scoring system and modifications to the theory itself have done little to improve the situation so that a researcher could be confident that this kind of discrepancy would not occur. Rest claims to have developed an objectively designed test of moral reasoning specifically designed to overcome many of the limitations of Kohlberg's theory. In addition, Kohlberg himself has recently questioned the practical value of scoring stories for Stage 6 responses in particular. This final stage has been eliminated from the most recent form of the scoring system (Colby and Kohlberg 1987).

Kohlberg's theory is also often criticized for being culture-bound because it reflects concerns about self-contained individualism typical of middle-class groups in complex urban societies in Western European cultures (Snarey *et al.* 1985). For example, in some cultures, meeting family obligations and submitting to the authority of elders out of respect for their 'elder-statesmen' status, are regarded as reflecting the highest of moral principles, and yet would be scored at lower levels according to Kohlberg's theory.

Shweder (1991, cited in Durkin 1995, p. 498) launched a particularly strong attack on Kohlberg, arguing that 'his research strategies leave him methodologically doomed to impose stage classifications upon informants from other cultures that both distort the meaning of what they have to say, and fail to take account of implicit structures in their views of their own social order'. This then is a major criticism as far as the cross-cultural applications of Kohlberg's theory are concerned.

Finally, one of the most consistent challenges to Kohlberg's theory comes from the work of Gilligan (1982) who suggests that it has a gender bias against women (see also Chapter 26). Because of differences in socialization, Gilligan argues that women tend to base their moral reasoning around issues such as *caring* and *personal relationships* which would merit a Stage 3 response according to Kohlberg's coding system and which would normally place them at a lower level of moral reasoning than men. This is because men are more likely to respond to moral dilemmas along the lines of *justice* and *fairness* which would normally place them at Stage 5 or even beyond.

In a particularly interesting study, Gilligan interviewed women about the moral dilemma of whether or not to terminate a pregnancy. From their responses, she identified three levels of reasoning which were governed by the principles of self-interest, self-sacrifice and care as a universal obligation, respectively. Reasoning at the level of the latter would only equate to Stage 3 according to Kohlberg's criteria. Gilligan argues that it is unfair to judge women to be at a lower level of moral reasoning because they have been socialized differently and have a different moral orientation from males, or a 'different voice' regarding moral issues. Recent versions of Kohlberg's scoring system have been modified in an attempt to counteract this bias (Colby *et al.* 1983).

The basis for these gender differences does seem to reflect somewhat stereotypical ideas about the reasoning of males and females. Although Gilligan produced considerable evidence for her findings, recent researchers have also emphasized that *both* males and females consider issues related to both caring and justice in their moral reasoning (e.g. Galotti 1989, Walker 1989). In fact, a review by Walker (1984) found no consistent gender differences in relation to the scoring on Kohlberg's dilemmas and some recent research has found women scoring higher than men (Funk 1986, Thoma 1986).

Overall, we are presented with a confusing picture, but nevertheless Gilligan's work has been instrumental in raising the important issue of a possible gender bias and thereby highlighting gender issues in the context of research into the development of moral reasoning.

❖ Activity 2 ❖

Gender differences in moral development

Consider a real-life moral dilemma such as termination of pregnancy. Do you think women have a 'different voice' in relation to this issue from men, and if so does 'different' mean 'deficient' in terms of moral reasoning?

Classical conditioning, operant conditioning and social learning theory

Piaget and Kohlberg were concerned with how children and adults *think*. Learning theory and social learning theory is associated with the study of moral *behaviour*. Two approaches that will be discussed here under a general heading of learning theory are classical conditioning (Pavlov 1927, 1955) and operant conditioning (Skinner 1953). Principles of classical and operant conditioning are as relevant to the study of moral behaviour as they are to any other type of behaviour. The classical conditioning approach suggests that learning is based on *association*, whereas the essence of operant conditioning is that learning occurs as a *consequence* of reinforcement or punishment.

Eysenck takes the principles of classical conditioning and suggests that the conscience is no more than a conditioned emotional response (CER). We can see what he means by this in the following example which is cited in Gross (1992).

'If a child is smacked (unconditioned stimulus, UCS) which produces pain and anxiety (unconditioned response, UCR), for stealing, and the child is told, "You must not steal" (conditioned stimulus, CS) just before he or she is smacked, eventually the words "You must not steal" will come to produce anxiety in the child (CR) and finally, when the child even thinks about stealing, this CR will be produced. This anxiety builds up at the thought of the wrongdoing and is a far more effective deterrent than the thought of being caught.' (p. 810)

According to Eysenck, these feelings of anxiety (CERs) represent our ability to resist temptation. However, he also suggests that the conscience also encompasses feelings of the guilt which is felt after committing an action which is morally wrong and it is the timing of the punishment which determines which component of the conscience is activated. Research has shown that 'punishment' that is consistently administered *prior* to a misdeed will result in high resistance to temptation but weak guilt feelings when the wrongdoing does occur. However, when punishment consistently *follows* wrongdoing, the reverse is true.

Nevertheless, it is important to realize that a classical conditioning response to moral behaviour is overly simplistic. Moral behaviour is often more complex than this particular approach allows for, and a classic criticism is that *cognitive* factors are not taken into account. For example, if children are negotiated with and given a reason for not carrying out unacceptable behaviour, in addition to mild punishment, then they are significantly less likely to perform the behaviour than if they were given the punishment alone. Likewise, when a rationale is given, the *timing* of punishment automatically becomes irrelevant.

Skinner's operant conditioning approach, which is based upon the processes of reinforcement and punishment, tries to explain moral behaviour with more emphasis on how it is acquired. At the simplest level, a behaviour that is reinforced increases or becomes stronger, and one that is punished is likely to be weakened or eliminated altogether. Skinner suggested that two kinds of reinforcement, positive and negative, are equally potent in strengthening behaviour. The former involves presenting the child with something he or she likes, and the latter removing something unpleasant which the child does not like. All of these processes have been used to explain children's moral behaviour. If children are reinforced for displaying behaviour which is consistent with sociocultural values and the rules governing socially acceptable behaviour, then they are likely to repeat that behaviour. Moreover, Skinner always maintained that reinforcement, particularly of a positive nature, is a much more effective influence on behaviour than punishment. This is because although the use of punishment serves to make certain behaviours less likely to occur, it cannot be applied independently to promote new behaviours which are desirable for the child to learn.

Although Skinner's approach provides a plausible explanation of moral behaviour, it does not go far enough. Whilst the process of reinforcement can certainly promote morally acceptable behaviour, punishment often only weakens, and may not eliminate unacceptable behaviour altogether. In fact, it can sometimes work in exactly the opposite way. Some children find that they only attract the attention that they crave for when they are being naughty and are consequently smacked or reproached in some way. In this situation, the punishment is acting as a reinforcer and the naughty behaviour is likely to increase.

Using the same argument as we used to highlight the limitations of classical conditioning, there is evidence that a cognitive component should be incorporated within an operant conditioning approach. For example, if verbal explanations are given which elicit the reasoning response in the child as to why a particular reinforcer or punishment is being used, its effectiveness is increased (Gelfand and Hartmann 1980). However, Skinner (1953, 1974) was particularly outspoken about his belief that 'concepts like motive, wish, desire – not to mention cognition – serve more to confuse the picture than to clarify it' (cited in Carver and Scheier 1992, p. 343).

A different perspective on the development of moral behaviour comes from the social learning theory of Bandura (1977) which suggests that children learn much of their behaviour not through reinforcement, punishment or Pavlovian conditioning, but through watching other people in their immediate social environment. Important processes involved here are observing, modelling and imitating role models such as parents or teachers. As far as moral behaviour is concerned, if these role models are displaying appropriate behaviour in terms of morality, children will adopt these behaviours for themselves. Some studies have attempted to link modelling and role playing with Kohlberg's theory to investigate whether moral reasoning can be modified. Bandura and MacDonald (1963) report that shifts to less mature levels of reasoning can be induced by modelling, but the majority of studies of this nature report a shift in an upward direction and an advance in individual moral reasoning through the modelling and role playing of appropriate behaviour (Rest 1983).

However, we must also be mindful of some of the arguments previously discussed in relation to reward and punishment. Physical punishment, such as smacking, if administered in a hostile way, can result in aggressive behaviour from the child through the very same process of modelling.

Social learning theorists have also explored the possibility that moral behaviour might be *situation-specific*. In the early 1930s, Hartshorne and May studied thousands of children in a wide range of different situations to shed some light on this. They found that a child who behaved honestly in all situations was practically non-existent, as was a child who behaved dishonestly in an equally consistent manner. However, there has been some criticism of Hartshorne and May's methodology (Emler 1983). More recent studies have not found such strong evidence for moral behaviour being as situation-specific as they describe.

Unlike Skinner (1953, 1974), social learning theorists have acknowledged and recognized the importance of cognitive factors in helping children to maintain self-control and simultaneously resist temptation. A good example of this is shown in the evidence from a study by Mischel and Patterson (1976). Preschool children were asked to perform a boring task. A mechanical clown had been placed nearby in order to distract them by persuading the children to come and play with him. Some of the children had been specifically trained to resist, by repeating to themselves, 'I'm not going to look at Mr Clown when Mr Clown says to look at him', and these children were able to control their behaviour and continue working on the task for significantly longer than those who had not received such training. Yet in spite of the existence of such studies, social learning theorists traditionally pay less attention to the cognitive component than Piaget and Kohlberg in their cognitive developmental theories.

We have already discussed some of the limitations and criticisms of certain learning theories. As we have seen, the main focus for these theories are the processes of reinforcement, punishment and observational learning. Obviously, the nature of the reinforcers and the punishment used are determined by the circumstances of the individual child and administered by persons in his or her

❖ Activity 3 ❖

Operant conditioning and moral behaviour

Consider your own personal views about the role of reinforcement in promoting socially acceptable behaviour, and punishment in modifying or eliminating unacceptable behaviour, and then talk to three or four parents and/or teachers about their views on these issues. Do they think that reinforcement for good behaviour or punishment for bad behaviour is more effective in producing lasting behaviour change in children?

immediate environment. Likewise, the role models which the child observes are people within that child's social environment. The approach does allow, therefore, for some variation in moral development according to the specific practices adopted by individual families and different cultures. There is no assumption of a universal moral code for all. In other words, there will be differences across individual families and cultures in the kind of behaviours that are modelled as socially acceptable or socially unacceptable. Similarly, there will be differences in the application of reward and punishment within these families.

A consistent limitation of all these theories is that the cognitive component is given less prominence and assumes lesser importance in the development of moral behaviour.

Psychodynamic theories

These theories are principally concerned with the *feelings* associated with morality. According to Sigmund Freud and his psychoanalytic theory, there are three main structures of personality: the id, the ego and the superego. It is the superego which represents the moral component of personality or the *conscience.* The superego is acquired through the process of identification which occurs during the phallic stage – one of Freud's five psychosexual stages of development – when the child is between 3 and 6 years of age approximately.

During this stage, the child resolves the Oedipus complex and identifies with the same-sex parent, with boys repressing their desire for the mother and identifying with the father through fear and castration anxiety. According to Freud, girls have less reason to identify with their rival, the mother, since they feel that they have *already* been punished for 'naughty desires' toward the father, because they do not have a penis, which they think has already been castrated as a punishment. The little girl assumes that the same fate has previously befallen her mother when she was young and that she copes with the rejection she feels from the knowledge that her father prefers her mother, by identifying with the mother. She identifies with her mother through a process of internalization known as anaclitic identification. This involves the child internalizing images of the mother and behaving in a way which would earn the mother's approval, while feeling that her mother would not love her if she did not behave in this way. In the same way that the boy identifies with the aggressor in a defensive way, this process defensively keeps the mother 'alive' inside the girl and may be important for her moral development.

Through identification with the same-sex parent, the child internalizes the parents' standards of right and wrong that reflect sociocultural rules. At the same time, the child internalizes feelings of hostility which were previously directed overtly to the same-sex parent, and these feelings are now experienced unconsciously as guilt. These feelings of guilt, although unconscious, serve to protect the child from wrongdoing and the child conforms to sociocultural rules in order to avoid guilt.

Similar views come from the psychoanalytic theorist Erik Erikson who describes a series of psychosocial stages, rather than Freud's psychosexual stages. At the chronological age of 4 to 5 years, he describes a stage of initiative versus guilt, where a situation analogous to the Oedipal conflict with the same-sex parent causes guilt in the child (see Chapter 20). However, rather than treating the Oedipus complex as the salient feature of this developmental stage as Freud does, Erikson suggests that it is just one feature of what is happening to the child at this age. For example, Erikson suggests that if parents patronize their children or belittle their activities at a time when the child has a naturally enquiring mind and is engaged in much exploratory and fantasy play, then the child will feel guilty about intruding into the parents' lives by engaging in these activities and asking lots of questions. As a consequence, these feelings of guilt constrain the child's natural curiosity, and the whole process, according to Erikson, can be exaggerated when combined with similar feelings generated by the Oedipus complex.

Psychoanalysts also suggest that feelings such as empathy are important contributors to moral development (Damon and Hart 1982). Empathy is experienced as an emotional state with a cognitive component known as perspective taking which is the ability to recognize emotional states in others and anticipate the necessary action required to improve the emotional state of another individual. Selman (1980) has developed a developmental theory of perspective taking which describes a series of stages from 3 years through adolescence. Emotions such as empathy, guilt and anxiety over the contravening of moral standards by others are present early in the developmental process and undergo change throughout childhood and beyond (Damon and Hart 1982).

One major criticism of Freud's concept of the superego or conscience centres around the question of when it comes into existence chronologically. According to Kohlberg (1969), the conscience does not suddenly become operational at the age of 5 or 6 years as Freud suggests. Rather, moral development happens gradually, beginning in childhood and extending into adulthood.

An additional criticism is that Freud's ideas about moral development centre exclusively around relationships within the family, whereas it is currently recognized that developing children are exposed to many other moral influences such as those of the peer group, school and so on. In fact, Freud's theory as we have already seen in relation to Kohlberg, is often criticized for being gender-biased. The whole concept of males having more powerful, dominant personalities because they have a penis, and females being weaker and more submissive because they do not, is indicative of such bias. He also suggests in relation to moral development that females have weaker superegos than males because their motive for identification with the same-sex parent is less strong. However, there is no evidence for this view and studies which have investigated gender differences have often found that females are better able to resist temptation (Hoffman 1979).

Section summary

This section has looked at how children think, feel and behave in relation to moral issues. Three different theoretical approaches to moral development have been examined. The cognitive developmental theories have some methodological flaws associated with their measures affecting their predictive reliability. Subsequent attempts have been made to improve the scoring and coding of responses which was a major cause for concern. Kohlberg's theory in particular has been criticized for being culture-bound and possibly gender-biased. An alternative way of looking at moral development in women has been suggested by Gilligan, who portrays women as having a 'different voice' towards moral issues which is not synonymous with being morally 'deficient'.

In relation to moral behaviour, the classical conditioning approach pays more attention to the role of punishment and suggests that behaviour is learnt through association, whereas operant conditioning stresses the importance of reinforcement, and suggests that learning of appropriate moral behaviour occurs as a consequence of reinforcement. Social learning theories focus on observational learning, where children watch other people in their immediate environment and model appropriate behaviour accordingly. One of the main criticisms of all these theories of learning is that they fail to take account of the mediating influence of cognition and motivation.

The psychoanalytic theory of Freud regards the superego as the moral component of personality, or the conscience. Children internalize parental moral standards through identification with the same-sex parent and conform to sociocultural rules in order to minimize guilt. Erikson suggests that parents may induce guilt in their children by constraining their natural curiosity, and this may combine with the effects of the Oedipus complex to enhance feelings of guilt. A major criticism of these theories is that they focus exclusively on the family, ignoring other sources of influence on the developing child.

Gender development

What is gender?

One interpretation of the term gender is to suggest that it refers to the sociocultural aspect of being male or female rather than the biological dimension, although not every psychologist would make this distinction. Every child has to develop a gender identity, and included in this process is the need to grasp a concept of gender role, which is a set of expectations that prescribe how males and females should think, act and feel. A sense of gender constancy must also be developed and this involves understanding that gender is permanent despite superficial changes. The development of gender identity is an important process in the developing sense of self as the child is constantly hearing him/herself referred to as 'good boy' or 'good girl'. We will now discuss these aspects of gender identity together with the theories which support them.

Gender identity

A basic sense of gender identity seems to be in place by the age of 2 to 3 years, although it is still a long way from being a fully developed concept at this stage. Children of this age have a good idea of their own and other peoples' gender identities.

Dunn and Kendrick (1982) suggest that children are often helped to form these categories through discussions and play within the family. They particularly emphasize the discussions between mother and elder child when a new baby is the focus of attention. In this situation, children typically make remarks which categorize themselves and the newborn in terms of age, size and good or bad behaviour, which helps older children to develop their own sense of identity. If the gender of the baby happens to be different, this often provides a clear topic of conversation, e.g. 'Me boy. Joyce girl. Joyce baby' (cited in Barnes 1995, p. 207).

Gender constancy

The next step in the development of gender identity is the understanding that gender is permanent in spite of changes in age, dress, hairstyle or behaviour (Bem 1989). Although as we have seen, 3-year-olds have a clear idea of whether they are male or female, they may be less sure about whether superficial changes such as those listed above can actually alter a person's gender. There is an inconsistent picture from the literature in relation to the exact age at which gender constancy is acquired. Similar to some of the problems discussed in the context of moral development, the results do seem to depend largely on how the children are assessed. For example, when preschool children were shown *drawings* where gender-inappropriate changes in hairstyle or dress have been made to a boy or girl, very few of them were able to recognize that the gender remains the same despite the changes (Emmerlich *et al.* 1977).

However, if they were shown *photographs* of real children, first in the nude with sexual anatomy visible, and then dressed in gender-inappropriate clothing, almost half the 3- to 5-year-olds, and more than half the girls, knew that the child's gender had not changed in line with the change in clothing (Bem 1989). This was of course largely dependent upon the children recognizing the difference between male and female genitals, and of those who definitely had this ability, 74 per cent passed the test. An additional finding is that when preschoolers are asked whether they *themselves* would change gender if they changed into gender-inappropriate dress, almost all of them realized that they would remain the same (Martin and Halverson 1983). It seems that children grasp this concept earlier when applied to themselves, than when applied to others (Wehren and DeLisi 1983).

There is a consistent theme throughout all of this literature, including that on moral development, which strongly suggests that the way these issues are presented to children is crucial. Presumably when the children were presented with drawings in the Emmerlich *et al.* (1977) study, it is not unreasonable to assume that they may have seen drawings as more easily amenable to change by the person doing the drawing. By contrast, the photographs used in the Bem (1989) study might be regarded as being more permanent by their very nature. This reasoning may, therefore, have been the basis for the children's responses, rather than a lack of understanding about gender constancy.

❖ Activity 4 ❖

The development of gender constancy

Compare the responses of a 2- to 3-year-old child and a 5- to 6-year-old child whom you know well, to the kinds of questions that you think will assess gender constancy. Here are some examples, but add some of your own, after close consultation with your teacher.

- Are you a boy or a girl?
- When you are grown up will you be a man or a woman?
- (To a boy) If you grow your hair really long, would you be a girl?
- (To a girl) If you cut your hair really short, would you be a boy?

Gender-role concept

Children begin to acquire gender-role concepts by the age of 4 or 5 years. Of course these concepts are well stabilized in adults and often heavily influenced by *stereotypes.* In our society, men are traditionally seen as being more ambitious, hard driving, aggressive and competitive, while the female role is seen as more nurturant and emotional (Ruble 1988). According to Serbin *et al.* (1993), it is not until middle childhood that children are able to assimilate into their belief systems stereotypically masculine and feminine characteristics that are typical of their culture. An important cross-cultural study by Whiting and Edwards (1988) found that children in many parts of the world understand and are, therefore, able to manipulate and exploit the differential power of men and women as it is manifest in their particular society and culture, by the age of 7 to 10 years.

Theories which explain gender development

Cognitive developmental theories

It is not surprising that Piaget predicted that children will acquire the concept of gender constancy during the same stage as they acquire conservation (see Chapter 18), at approximately 6 to 7 years of age, simply because the same logic is involved. In its simplest form, the child has to be able to make an inference that something remains the same, although it *looks* different. Kohlberg's (1966) theory of gender-role typing (see Table 19.2) is based on Piaget's theory of cognitive development, predicting that as cognition matures, so does the child's understanding of gender. A simple sense of being male or female and applying the same categorization to others is consistent with pre-operational thought, and the actual understanding of gender constancy is consistent with concrete operational thought.

Recent research has found that the development of gender identity does indeed occur in an order that is consistent with Kohlberg's theory, for both males and females (Martin and Little 1990). In addition, there is evidence that the theory is supported through cross-cultural research as well (Munroe *et al.* 1984). As we have already seen, differences in age-related 'cut-off' points at important stages in children's gender development reported in the literature often depend on the methodology used and the way in which the tasks are presented. This is typical of a great deal of the research based on Piagetian principles.

Table 19.2 Kohlberg's theory of the development of gender typing

Kohlberg suggests that children go through the following stages in developing an understanding of gender:

1 *Basic gender identity*	The child recognizes that he/she is a boy or a girl.
2 *Gender stability*	The child accepts that males remain male and females remain female. Little boys no longer think they might grow up to be a mummy and little girls give up their hopes of becoming Batman.
3 *Gender constancy*	Children recognize that superficial changes in appearance or activities do not alter gender. Even when a girl wears jeans or plays football, or when a boy has long hair or a burning interest in needlepoint, the child's gender remains constant.

Source: Kohlberg 1966, *cited in* Hetherington and Parke 1993, p.547

Gender schema theory

As we have seen, Kohlberg suggests that gender constancy is a necessary prerequisite for gender typing, and his whole approach describes processes which are mediated by the child's own cognitive processing.

A different perspective on gender typing which draws on both the cognitive developmental and social learning approach is gender schema theory (Bem 1981, 1985, 1991, Martin and Halverson 1983). This theory suggests that children develop schemata (the plural of 'schema') or 'theories' which help them to organize and interpret their experience, and it is a general readiness to categorize information based on culturally-defined gender roles which drives this activity.

These gender schemata can affect the way in which children see gender-related situations and a number of studies support this view. Martin and Halverson (1983), for example, showed 5- and 6-year-olds pictures of children performing activities that were either gender-consistent (boys playing with trains) or gender-inconsistent (girls sawing wood). When asked to recall the pictures one week later, children tended to distort the information by changing the sex of the actor in the gender-inconsistent role. Several studies report that girls recall feminine toys and objects more easily than boys, with the same being true in reverse, and children are generally more confident of the accuracy of their recall from gender-consistent pictures, e.g. Martin and Little (1990).

Social learning theory

Social learning theorists such as Bandura (1977), Mischel (1970), and Perry and Bussey (1984), suggest that 'gender-role learning is the outcome of the accumulating learning experiences that the individual has in a particular social environment' (cited in Durkin 1995, p. 174). According to these theorists, children's gender development comes about through observation, modelling and imitation of adults' masculine and feminine behaviour. According to Perry and Bussey (1984), children acquire gender-role stereotypes largely through observational learning. Children also learn through the application of reward and punishment of gender-appropriate and gender-inappropriate behaviours by both adults and their peers. For example, parents may encourage more traditional feminine behaviour in their daughter by saying 'You do look pretty when you wear a dress, instead of jeans'. All of these processes play a significant part in shaping gender roles and encouraging gender-appropriate behaviour.

Important influences in the development of such behaviour are parents, peers, television and the media, and literature. There is evidence that parents are actively shaping their children's preferences from an early age. An interesting line of research compared the decor and content of children's bedrooms. The researchers found that boys' rooms contained more vehicles, machines, soldiers and action-orientated toys compared with girls' rooms which were more likely to house dolls and be decorated with floral and ruffled furnishing (Rheingold and Cook 1975, Pomerlau *et al.* 1990). The interesting part of this research is that little change in these stereotypical findings was reported between the study conducted in 1975 and that conducted in 1990.

Some studies have found differences between mothers and fathers in the types of behaviours which they encourage or reinforce in their sons and daughters. For example, Langlois and Downs (1980) found that mothers were equally tolerant towards both sons and daughters whether or not they were engaging in gender-appropriate play. However, fathers were particularly sensitive to any signs of inappropriate play and were openly hostile towards their child for cross-gender behaviour, particularly when this involved their sons.

As far as observational learning or modelling is concerned, Bandura (1977) suggests that when children pay attention to models, they take into account not only the gender of the model, but also the gender-appropriateness of their behaviour. Usually children will imitate the behaviour of the same-gender model but this is not always so (see *In Focus* below).

As children develop, they encounter other influences apart from parents which provide them with models of either gender-appropriate or sometimes gender-inappropriate behaviour. The influence of television is highlighted by the evidence from a study by Leary *et al.* (1982) which found that children who watched television frequently were more likely to hold stereotypical ideas about gender and race and more likely to conform to gender-role preferences of a culturally appropriate nature. Children's books also provided them with similar gender-role stereotypes as television.

A criticism which is often raised in relation to the process of reinforcement, is that differential reinforcement of gender-typed behaviour cannot explain all the observed differences in this behaviour. For example, boys are not reinforced for aggressive behaviour any more than girls, and yet one of the most frequently observed differences is that boys are found to be physically more aggressive (Parke and Slaby 1983).

In Focus

Why children do not always imitate the same-sex model

In a toy-choice experiment with 4- to 5-year-olds, Masters *et al.* (1979) found that children were less influenced by the model's sex than by the gender label attached to the toy. In this study, children played most with a toy labelled as appropriate to their own gender yet modelled by a member of the opposite gender; it seemed to the authors that children reasoned along the lines that 'if this is so good that even *they* play with it, then this is the toy for me'.

Source: Durkin 1995, p. 176

Also, as we have seen in relation to moral development, one of the main limitations of this approach is one which the social learning theorists themselves acknowledge. They recognize that as well as processes such as reinforcement and modelling, individual motivation, self-regulation and cognitive processes play a crucial role in gender identity development. Taking the example mentioned earlier, if 'looking pretty' is not the prime motivation of the girl in question, and she does not think it important according to her beliefs and values, then rewarding her in such a way will have no effect. However, recently Bandura and colleagues have adapted traditional social learning theory to allow for the mediating effect of cognitive and motivational factors; now called social cognitive theory (Bandura 1986, Bussey and Bandura 1992). They regard one important mediating factor in gender-role development to be the children's ability to regulate their own activities according to the rules relating to gender-appropriate behaviour. This indicates a shift from parental control over this process to a more independent self-evaluation of how children themselves feel when engaged in either gender-appropriate or cross-gender play (see *In Focus* below).

Psychodynamic theories

Freud's theory of psychosexual development which we discussed in relation to moral development, is also relevant here, particularly the process of identification. Between the ages of 3 to 5 years, the child experiences anxiety surrounding his or her attraction to the opposite-sex parent which, according to Freud, is of a sexual nature. Because of the anxiety it generates, the child is driven to resolve this by subsequent identification with the same-sex parent, between the ages of 5 and 6 years. As we have already seen, Freud gives a more detailed explanation of this resolution in the form of the Oedipus complex in boys, than he does for the same experience in girls.

However, as far as gender development is concerned, the process of identification means that the child will use the same-sex parent as a role model, thereby adopting similar behaviours and characteristics which will obviously be influenced by culturally approved norms of masculinity and femininity.

Currently, researchers into gender development are not particularly convinced by Freud's explanation of identification. More recent evidence shows that children become gender-typed earlier than 5-6 years and have no problems identifying with

In Focus

A study to test the relative importance of self-evaluation and gender constancy

Bussey and Bandura (1992) asked pre-schoolers to decide whether they would feel 'real great' or 'real awful' if they played with each of a variety of same-sex or opposite-sex toys. The results showed that between 3 and 4 years both boys and girls developed anticipatory approving self-reactions for same-sex behaviour, and disapproving reactions for cross-sex behaviour. By the age of 4, boys felt great about playing with dump trucks and robots, but were not at all comfortable with kitchen sets and baby dolls; girls showed the opposite preferences. These findings are particularly interesting since the experimenters had arranged things so that the children thought they were registering responses anonymously, so the results cannot be explained easily in terms of demand characteristics or self-presentation. Across a number of tasks, children's self-evaluative reactions were consistent predictors of gender-linked behaviour, whereas gender constancy and gender knowledge scores were not. Bussey and Bandura conclude that children learn early in life the sanctions against cross-sex behaviour, and start to regulate their own behaviour accordingly.

Source: Durkin 1995, p. 184

either masculinity or femininity, even when the same-sex parent is not present in the family. Presumably when Freud was developing his theory, he had no concept of anything other than the nuclear family consisting of mother, father and children.

A more recent alternative perspective within the psychodynamic framework comes from object-relations theorists (Chodorow 1978). These theorists suggest that early relationships, particularly with the mother, because she is *usually* the main caretaker, establish a template for how to relate to other people. As they develop, females do not necessarily have to deviate from this template as it is based on a woman like themselves. As a result, they see femininity and closeness in relationships as inextricably linked. In contrast, males have to distance themselves from the nurturing mother figure in order to develop their masculinity, which in turn becomes defined in terms of a *lack* of closeness in relationships.

Section summary

This section has looked at how children develop a sense of gender identity and come to understand the roles that are considered by society to be appropriate for each gender. The cognitive developmental theories suggest 'stage-like' development where understanding of the concept of gender increases as cognition matures. A well-documented criticism of these theories is that the age-related 'cut-off' points are often determined more by the methodology used and the way the task is presented, rather than by actual chronologically defined stages in the developmental process.

Social learning theory stresses the importance of reinforcement, observational learning, modelling and imitation in relation to gender-role learning. Important influences in the shaping of gender-role behaviour are parents, peers, television and the media, and children's books. One of the main criticisms of social learning theory in relation to gender is the lack of attention directed towards the role of motivational and cognitive processes. However, a recent modification, called social cognitive theory, does allow for self-regulation and self-evaluation on the part of the child in relation to gender-appropriate or cross-gender activities.

The psychoanalytic theory of Freud highlights identification with the same-sex parent as crucial in relation to the development of gender, suggesting that the child will use the same-sex parent as a role model and thereby adopt appropriate masculine or feminine behaviour. One difficulty with this view is that children are able to acquire gender-appropriate behaviour in single-parent families even though the same-sex role model may not be present.

The development of self

'The self, after all, is not a thing; it is not a substance, a material entity that we can somehow grab hold of and place before our very eyes.' (Freeman 1993, cited in Barnes 1995, p. 224)

The above quotation highlights the inherent difficulties of investigating a concept such as 'self' which lacks an objective existence in this way. One of the earliest psychologists to put forward views about the self was William James (who was also a philosopher). He portrayed the self as multifaceted and the product of the many different relationships we have with other people: 'A man has as many social selves as there are individuals who recognize him and carry an image of him in their minds.' (James 1892)

Self: the 'I' and the 'me'

To highlight the fact that the self is unique to the individual and distinct from that of other people whilst at the same time it is the product of social influences and other people's views and opinions, James drew an important distinction between the 'self as subject' of experience – the 'I' which ensures our individuality, and the 'self as object' of knowledge – the 'me' which reflects the social influences. As we shall see, this distinction between the 'I' and the 'me' has influenced the way in which later theorists have studied the self.

The previous section on gender leads us quite conveniently on to this final section of the chapter concerned with self, because gender is a good example of the 'me' or 'self as object' (also referred to by Lewis (1990) as the categorical self). Up to the age of 7 years, children usually define the self in physical terms and will categorize themselves as a girl/boy, with blonde/black hair, who is clever, tall, shy, etc. Many of these categorizations are based on feedback from others which we use to build up a picture of ourselves as others see us.

However, before the process of defining the self in terms of the 'me' or the categorical self begins, a rudimentary stage of self-recognition, often referred to as the existential self or the 'self as subject' – the 'I', needs to have taken place, during which the infant acquires an understanding that he or she is separate and distinct from others. Studies suggest that this early stage of self-recognition is normally complete by around 18 months of age. One way of investigating this has been through mirror studies, such as the one undertaken by Lewis and Brooks-Gunn (1979). In this study, a dot of rouge was applied to the young child's nose and his or her response to their reflection in a mirror was observed. At 18 months, a significant change occurred and the child was observed reaching for the rouge spot on his or her own nose. At a similar age, young children are also able to point to themselves in photographs. All of these factors provide evidence that the child has developed a schema of his or her own face and has begun to distinguish between self and others. Interestingly, this corresponds with the age by which Piaget reported that young children understand object permanence (see Chapter 18), suggesting that this stage of cognitive development is necessary for the development of self-recognition.

The use of feedback to develop categorizations and build up a picture of ourselves as others see us is similar to observing our own reflection in a 'mirror' and has been described by Cooley (1902) as the theory of 'looking-glass self'. Alternatively, we may compare ourselves with others, as occurs when one is told 'you are a good girl', or you realize that you are tall when compared with your friends, or evaluated as 'clever' when compared with other classmates (Bannister and Agnew 1977).

James' distinction between the 'I' and the 'me' can be seen to have exerted considerable influence over the theory of self proposed by Mead in 1934. Mead was also influenced by Cooley's theory of the 'looking-glass self' (Cooley 1902) and stressed in particular the importance of social interaction in the development of knowledge about the self and others, suggesting that, 'It is impossible to conceive of a self arising outside of social experience' (Mead 1934, cited in Barnes 1995, p. 195). Mead conceptualized the 'I' or the existential self as the active ongoing process of doing the experiencing of the world, and suggested that what we experience and interact with is our 'categorical self' or 'me'. In other words, the 'I' is the subject of the interaction or the experience, and not the object, whereas the 'me' is concerned with the content of that experiencing, including the physical descriptions of a person, their behaviour and so on. Moreover, the 'me' was believed to be heavily influenced by the views and perceptions of others whilst the 'I' is capable of dismissing such views, allowing people not to be constrained by others.

The 'me', therefore, becomes the more socialized aspect of self, developing through interaction and comparison with other people and reacting to feedback and evaluation from them. In addition, pretend play is an important feature in the process of this development through which children learn to take on different perspectives (i.e. to role play) such as 'doctor and nurse' or 'mummy and daddy', and thereby learn to react to themselves from the point of view of these other people. The 'me' is able to develop and expand as a result of this kind of role play where the child is pretending to be the other person.

Developments in these two areas of the existential and the categorical self occur rapidly between the ages of 2 and 3 years, particularly within a social context of relationships with others. Once children have a sufficient level of awareness of the existential self, they begin to place themselves, and are simultaneously placed by others, in a whole series of categories that will help to define an individual and unique sense of self for the child. As they develop from the early to the middle and later childhood years, there is a progression from self-descriptions which are based on physical descriptions as we have already discussed, to more psychological descriptions.

In an important literature review, Harter (1983, cited in Barnes 1995) reflects upon the developmental progression of the 'I' evaluating the 'me'. She draws on evidence from a study by Rosenberg (1979) who interviewed 10- to 18-year-olds about themselves with questions designed to investigate how they were seen by themselves and others, what kind of person they would like to be and how they were different from other people.

As would be predicted from Mead's theory, the younger children's descriptions were based upon characteristics which could just as easily be described objectively by others, such as physical attributes, possessions, achievements and membership categories. However, with increasing age, greater emphasis was placed on traits which describe character and emotions, particularly in relation to interactions with others, such as sociable, shy, popular, friendly, attractive, tolerant and so on. Whilst these latter descriptions require more subjective insight, they can still be described fairly accurately in an objective manner by others.

By contrast, the older adolescents in the sample (aged up to 18 years) described themselves far more subjectively in terms of their psychological self, expressing a personal and private individual 'world of emotions, attitudes, wishes and secrets' (Harter 1983, p. 299).

Erikson's theory of psychosocial development

A different theoretical approach to the study of self is Erikson's theory of psychosocial development. This psychoanalytical theory describes the development of self-understanding throughout the lifespan and in this respect can be regarded as a theory of self.

According to Erikson, individuals will come to know and accept themselves through the process of development and recognize their own unified 'self-sameness and continuity in time' (Erikson 1959). At the same time, individuals will identify with the norms and values of society and culture, find their own identity within that framework and also experience a shared identity or 'some kind of essential character with others' (Erikson 1968). Turn now to Chapter 20 for a full description of Erikson's theory. As you read about each of the stages, pause to consider what each tells us about the development of self over the lifespan. For example, during the 'initiative versus guilt' stage, children who are already well aware that they are a person in their own right must subsequently discover what sort of person they will become. Perhaps not surprisingly, Erikson regarded the adolescent stage as being of particular importance in relation to self-identity when the young person struggles with the whole question of who they are and what kind of person they will be. Adolescents are thought to experience an identity crisis and Marcia (1966, 1968), inspired by Erikson, identifies four states of adolescent identity formation. Once the final state of identity achievement is reached, the individual emerges from the crisis with a clear sense of commitment, goals and ideology.

Self-esteem

This can be defined as the view of the self as good and capable and likable (Coopersmith 1967). William James originally suggested that internal psychological factors which we have previously discussed in relation to Harter's study, were the most important in influencing the development of an overall sense of self-worth or self-esteem, particularly individuals' evaluations of achievement and competence in areas where they perceive success to be important. Since then, there have been many attempts to measure self-esteem, many of which have been 'inconsistent and messy' (Bee 1989).

Perhaps one of the better examples is Harter's self-perception profile for children (see Table 19.3) which taps five areas thought to be important to self-esteem:

- scholastic competence and how able the child feels in relation to schoolwork
- athletic competence and how competent the child feels in sports and games
- social acceptance and how popular the child feels with peers
- behavioural conduct and the extent to which the child feels they behave appropriately and acceptably
- physical appearance and how much the child likes their physical characteristics.

A profile of the child's self-esteem in relation to each of these areas can be constructed from their scores. After extensive analysis of children's scores, looking at each of the five areas separately, Harter found that there was a strong correlation between performance in an area which the individual child personally considered to be important, and their overall self-esteem. In other words, success or failure in significant areas affects self-esteem.

Likewise, Harter found that children were also influenced by evaluation from significant others and the nature of this kind of feedback would affect their sense of self-esteem. This is similar to the personality theory of Carl Rogers (1959) which suggests

Table 19.3 Some items from Harter's self-perception profile for children

The green numbers in the boxes represent the scores which would be given for responses in those boxes. These numbers would not be printed on the questionnaires which the children completed.

The children answering the questionnaire have to decide which of the two sets of children described in each item they are more like, and then tick in a box to say whether that is 'really' or 'sort of' true of them.

Really true for me	*Sort of true for me*				*Sort of true for me*	*Really true for me*
1	2	Some kids have *trouble* figuring out the answers in school.	**BUT**	Other kids almost *always* can figure out the answers.	3	4
4	3	Some kids do very *well* at all kinds of sports.	**BUT**	Others *don't* feel that they are very good when it comes to sports.	2	1
4	3	Some kids are popular with others their age	**BUT**	Other kids are *not* very popular.	2	1
1	2	Some kids usually get into *trouble* because of the things they do.	**BUT**	Other kids usually *don't* do things that get them into trouble.	3	4
1	2	Some kids wish their physical appearance was *different*.	**BUT**	Other kids *like* their physical appearance the way it is.	3	4

that feedback from significant others affects how individuals see themselves in terms of their actual and ideal self, and also links to Cooley's work on the 'looking-glass self'.

Comparison with significant others often seems to feature highly in theories which relate to self-esteem. For example, Bannister and Agnew (1977) suggest that self should be regarded as a bipolar construct where having a concept of self automatically implies also having an opposite concept of not-self. In this way we see ourselves as directly compared to other people who are obviously 'not us'. Self-esteem is affected if we constantly compare ourselves or other people compare us against siblings or peers who are 'cleverer', 'prettier', 'more confident' than we are.

However, the significance of others in relation to self-esteem changes as the child develops. Younger children tend to be greatly influenced by evaluations of themselves by adults. This is similar to the way in which they are influenced by adult authority in relation to rules in the moral development literature which we have already discussed. Older children, however, regard evaluation by the peer group and their close friends as much more important (Harter 1986). In a recent study, White (1990) suggests that an important way of raising self-esteem in schools is by stressing the importance of positive feedback from both the teacher and the peer group.

Section summary

Difficulties in investigating a concept which lacks an objective existence have led to a dearth of empirical research into the existential self or 'self as subject', because children are unable to understand this aspect of self as directly related to them. Although young infants can touch the rouge dots on their own noses, realize that they are making the reflection move and causing it to happen on their own, as distinct from other people, this does not mean that they instantly recognize the reflection and understand it as their own self. This understanding gradually develops through routine relationships and through play. By contrast, the development of the categorical self or 'self as object' has been researched more easily in terms of children's self-descriptions and in investigations of gender and moral development, which often take place within the context of the child's increasing knowledge of sociocultural rules and roles.

Self-esteem is also difficult to measure, and factors which either enhance or diminish self-esteem vary in significance from one individual to another.

Finally, a sense of self is not solely dependent upon cognition, but upon social and emotional factors as well, and develops within a social setting of relationships with others and the wider context of sociocultural norms and values.

Chapter summary

- Psychologists have taken a variety of theoretical approaches to investigate how children develop a sense of gender identity and gender role, and a moral sense of right and wrong, and how these processes are important for children when it comes to understanding themselves.
- Cognitive developmental theories of moral reasoning have faced methodological difficulties as well as being criticized for being culture bound and reflecting a possible gender bias against females.
- Some of the learning theory approaches which seek to explain moral behaviour have emphasized different processes, such as association, conditioning, reinforcement, punishment, observation and role models, as being influential in the shaping of this behaviour. The main limitation of these theories is the lack of recognition of the importance of motivational and cognitive factors.

- Psychoanalytic theories have focused on influences and relationships in the family which combine to induce feelings of guilt in the child, and ignore the many other influences within the child's environment. Freud's theory, in particular, is thought to reflect a gender bias in favour of the moral superiority of males.
- Cognitive developmental theories also face methodological difficulties in relation to the investigation of gender development. The methodology used and the way a task is presented can influence children's ability to understand gender constancy.
- Social learning theory points to important influences within the child's social environment, all of which combine to shape gender-role behaviour. These include parental role models, peers, television and literature. A recent modification of this theory allows for the mediating effect of cognitive processes in relation to gender-related behaviour.
- Freud's psychoanalytic theory once again focuses on the process of identification with the parent of the same sex as the child, to explain how he or she adopts appropriate masculine or feminine behaviour, but is unable to account for the fact that problems do not necessarily occur when there is no appropriate role model present in the family.
- Gender is a good example of the categorical self but before this stage of self-understanding is reached, children have to have undergone a process of self-recognition where they see themselves as separate and distinct from others, sometimes termed as the existential self.
- The empirical investigation of the existential self and also research into self-esteem has often proved problematic and difficult to quantify. By contrast, investigation of the categorical self in terms of children's self descriptions has been easier.
- Erikson's theory of psychosocial development offers an important contribution to our understanding of the development of self throughout the life span from a psychoanalytic perspective but, like other psychoanalytic theories, is not easily amenable to empirical testing.

Essay questions

1 (a) Outline any two theories of moral development. *(12 marks)*

(b) Critically assess the evidence on which these theories are based. *(12 marks)*

2 Discuss the view that gender roles are socially constructed. *(24 marks)*

3 Critically consider two theoretical approaches to the study of self-development. *(24 marks)*

Further reading

Durkin, K. (1995) *Developmental Social Psychology*, Oxford: Blackwell.

This is a really excellent general text with detailed chapters on moral development and the development of gender in particular.

Barnes, P. (1995) *Personal, Social and Emotional Development of Children*, Milton Keynes: The Open University.

This book has an excellent chapter by Dorothy Miell on 'Developing a sense of self', containing transcripts of speech from mothers and children in relation to gender development, and useful examples of relevant educational activities.

Chapter 20

Adolescence, adulthood and old age

Alison Wadeley

Preview

In this chapter we shall be looking at:

- adolescence, adulthood and old age: definitions, contexts and methods
- three stage theories of adult personality development
- social theories of successful ageing
- the life events approach to adulthood
- unemployment, parenthood, divorce, loss and bereavement.

Introduction

In a song for his son, John Lennon wrote 'Life is what happens to you while you're busy making other plans' and Woody Allen once remarked 'Life is hard and then you die'. Until the latter half of the twentieth century psychologists had little more to say about development over the entire course of life than this! Adulthood in particular, which for many of us could last for over fifty years, was relatively ignored. In fact, Levinson (1978) remarked that adulthood was 'one of the best kept secrets in our society' (p. ix).

Why has the growth of a developmental psychology of the lifespan been so slow? There are at least two important reasons. One is the undoubted influence of such prominent figures as Freud (1856–1939), Piaget (1896–1980) and Bowlby (1907–90) all of whom emphasized the importance of the early years of life. Another concerns the practical and methodological difficulties of studying the entire lifespan. Psychologists have attempted to deal with these obstacles in various ways and some considerable progress is now being made. Some have succeeded in formulating developmental theories of the entire lifespan while others have focused on specific phases of life, such as old age. Still others have chosen to approach adulthood through studying reactions to the kinds of life events that many adults experience, such as unemployment or becoming a parent.

This chapter takes adolescence and adulthood as its main themes and presents a selection of the existing theories and research in these vast areas. We will begin by clarifying some of the terminology and considering some of the methodological problems faced in studying adolescence and adulthood. We will then look briefly at theories of lifespan or adult development that emphasize personality and social change before going on to consider the impact of specific life events.

Adolescence, adulthood and ageing: definitions, contexts and methods

Adolescence

Adolescence is a transitional period between childhood and adulthood. Biologically, this period begins when the individual enters puberty and ends on reaching sexual maturity. Psychologically, there are a number of levels on which the individual makes the transition to adulthood (e.g. social, emotional and cognitive) and these may not synchronize with each other or with biological maturity, or have clear beginnings and ends. Traditionally, adolescence has been viewed as a time of turmoil or 'storm and stress' but, as we shall see later in this chapter, this is a view which is no longer supported by the evidence. Many of the developmental theories described in this book stop at adolescence but there is still life after puberty!

Adulthood

A general definition of the term 'adulthood' is 'to have matured or to have grown to full size and strength'. In psychology, some theorists have focused their definitions on specific aspects of development. Freud, for example, thought that adults (and adolescents) were in the 'genital stage' of personality development while Piaget suggested that adults (and adolescents) had reached the 'formal operational stage' of intellectual development. Others prefer more general definitions. To them, adulthood is not an unchanging state or even just a steady decline to death. Baltes (1973), for example, prefers to see adulthood as a time of often positive development and change, with gains and losses along the way. This development and change occurs on many different fronts, all working together to affect the whole person.

❖ Activity 1 ❖

The life-line

Take a large piece of paper and draw a straight line across it from left to right. Label the left end of the line 'my birth' and the right end 'my death' and add a rough scale to show age in years. Using the line to indicate 'average', plot and label the past highs and lows of your life so far, so that you have something like a temperature chart. Now project forward and plot the highs and lows you expect to experience in future years.

Are any periods of life:

- 'busier' than others?
- more low than high, or vice versa?

Can cognitive, social, physiological, financial, work or other influences account for the patterns on your life line? Ask a friend to do the same so that you can compare your two life-lines.

Ageing

Ageing measured in terms of time (e.g. in years) is known as *chronological* age and so starts from the moment of conception, but this type of ageing becomes a less useful concept for understanding development once we have matured. There are other types of ageing we should consider:

- ❖ *biological ageing* – changes in bodily functions and in bodily tissues and organs
- ❖ *psychological ageing* – mental reactions to growing older and how one sees oneself, encapsulated in the phrase 'you are as old as you feel'
- ❖ *social ageing* – how individuals relate to society as they grow older.

Neugarten (1968) used the term 'social clock' to describe society's timetable mapping out what we should do at different times of life, e.g. have children, retire. Successful social ageing may depend on whether we are 'in time' with the social clock, as well as on whether society reveres or rejects its older members.

These four types of ageing may synchronize with each other or be out of step; either way they exert an important influence on how we cope with adulthood.

Cohorts and cohort effects

A cohort consists of a group of individuals, or 'generation', who were born during the same time interval and who will, therefore, age together. Each cohort is a specific size and will generally decline in number, usually with a shift to there being more females (who tend to outlive males). A cohort occupies a unique historical niche which usually means that it differs from other cohorts in important ways. This is what we mean by 'cohort effects'. Think of the impact of the motor car, World Wars I and II, television, the contraceptive pill, the AIDS epidemic and advances in computer technology. Cohort size is also important. In very large cohorts, competition for resources, such as jobs or housing, could be fierce and a feeling that times are hard could lead to smaller families. In the UK, the 1960s 'baby boom' cohort will eventually feed into a relatively large older generation. Any conclusions we try to draw about adult development must always be evaluated in the light of the historical context of the cohort, since chronological age alone is only part of the picture.

❖ Activity 2 ❖

Spend a few minutes listing the main social, cultural, historical and other influences on people born in the same year as you. If you can, compare your list with those of people from other cohorts.

Methods used in lifespan developmental research

Our knowledge of adolescence and adulthood is only as sound as the methods used to gather information about them. The usual way of studying age-related changes is to employ either the longitudinal or the cross-sectional research design. The first of these repeatedly studies *the same* group at different points in time, while the second studies a number of *different* age groups all at the same time. They answer essentially the same research questions but in different ways. Each method has its own strengths and drawbacks (see Chapter 29). One important problem in cross-sectional research is in controlling, or accounting for, cohort differences. Longitudinal studies are especially affected by the historical time of testing.

Simple cross-sectional and longitudinal designs are a good starting point for developmental research but are rarely sophisticated enough to give us the depth of understanding we need. More elaborate examples of research design are shown in Table 20.1.

Schaie (1965) combines the three designs in Table 20.1 into his 'most efficient design' which yields a wealth of data and makes possible many different comparisons allowing us to assess the effects of age, cohort and time of testing more thoroughly. The practical difficulties of collecting such data are, of course, quite considerable and use a great deal of time and resources.

We will see in the following sections a number of data collection techniques being used under the umbrella of longitudinal or cross-sectional designs. These techniques have their own strengths and weaknesses which you should bear in mind when assessing the research findings and theories that arise from them.

Table 20.1 Some research designs for studying age-related change

1 *The cohort-sequential design*	Two or more cohorts are taken and studied longitudinally, each over the same age range. Comparison of the cohorts allows us to separate out cohort effects from age effects.
2 *The time-sequential design*	Two or more cross sections covering the same age range are taken at different testing times. Comparisons allow us to separate age effects from historical time of testing effects.
3 *The cross-sequential design*	Two or more cohorts covering different age ranges are taken for comparison and tested at two or more times.

Section summary

Various definitions of adolescence, adulthood and old age have been offered by psychologists, taking into account to varying degrees, biological, social, personality and cognitive factors. Development at any stage of life is often positive although there will inevitably be gains and losses. Research into any stage of the lifespan must take account of cohort effects, which introduce many variables influencing psychologists' conclusions about the effects of age on behaviour. A number of research designs, based generally around the cross-sectional and longitudinal methods, are open to developmental psychologists.

Adolescence

Although we think of adolescence as a 'stage' of development, its boundaries are as blurred as those of any other stage. Individual differences at this, and indeed any, stage of life make it difficult to arrive at general conclusions. The concerns described here are therefore a selection of those thought to be particularly salient to, although not unique to, adolescence, bearing in mind that the young adolescent will still be dealing with concerns relating to childhood and the older adolescent will be dealing with some of the concerns of adulthood. The issues raised are all relevant to the traditional view of adolescence as a period of turmoil.

Identity in adolescence

The idea that establishment of identity is fraught with conflict is at least partly due to the writings of the founder of psychoanalysis, Sigmund Freud, who spoke of an upsurge in sexual instincts at puberty. Blos (1967) took these ideas up and suggested that adolescence was like a second period of individuation, the first occurring in toddlerhood. Just like 'terrible-two'-year-olds, adolescents are said to experience ambivalent feelings towards the main care-givers and show regressive behaviour as they establish themselves as separate individuals.

Unhappy with the emphasis on sexual impulses, Erikson (1968) preferred to focus on psychosocial forces in shaping personality. (Erikson's ideas are discussed more fully as the first of the three stages of adult development later in this chapter.) He suggested that there are eight stages of personality development each presenting a particular psychosocial crisis. These are outlined in Table 20.3. In adolescence the main crisis is that of identity vs. identity diffusion (although it is important to remember that establishing identity is something we do often in our lives). The problem for the individual is to establish 'a subjective sense of an invigorating sameness and continuity' (Erikson 1968, p. 19) – young people need to emerge from this stage with a sense of knowing where they are going and with an inner assuredness, i.e. a firm identity. Erikson also introduced the idea of a psychosocial moratorium during which new identities can be tried out without commitment. This stage can appear to be a crisis because, after it, relative stability usually occurs as the chosen identity is settled on.

For Erikson, then, adolescence is influenced by both physical and social forces. Indeed, in some Western cultures, adolescents would appear to be held in a state of moratorium by laws that block access to the adult world, e.g. the minimum school-leaving age, minimum voting age. Unfortunately, Erikson's ideas are largely theoretical and it has been for others, such as Marcia, to test them empirically.

Marcia (1980) argues that adolescent identity formation involves both crisis and commitment. Crisis occurs through having to re-evaluate old choices and values; commitment happens after this re-evaluation when the individual takes on a set of roles and ideologies. Marcia found four main identity statuses (see Table 20.2). Bee quotes Marcia's view as follows: 'For a fully achieved identity, the young person must both have examined his or her values or goals and have reached a firm commitment.' (Bee 1995, p. 294)

Waterman (1985) combined the findings of several studies of vocational identity status in 11- to 21-year-olds to test these ideas. He found a decrease in diffusion status and an increase in identity achievement with age. Moratorium was quite uncommon but at all ages, 1 in 3 was in foreclosure. Identity achievement was somewhat later than Erikson predicted but this is probably explained by the fact that most of the participants studied were college students who tend to postpone adult status. Munro and Adams (1977) found that 45% of non-college individuals in work had achieved identity status compared to 38% of college students, which is more in line with Erikson's prediction. Other researchers have claimed that identity remains fairly stable in

Table 20.2 Four identity statuses proposed by Marcia (1980), based on Erikson's theory

	High degree of crisis	*Low degree of crisis*
High degree of commitment to a particular role or value	Identity achievement status (crisis is past)	Foreclosure status (crisis not gone through, but a commitment made)
Low degree of commitment to a particular role or value	Moratorium status (in the midst of the crisis and no commitment made)	Identity diffusion status (not in crisis and no commitment made, perhaps because in pre- or post-crisis)

adolescence. Coleman (1974) for example, suggested that adolescents have two identities, one for the present and one for the future. The present one is fairly stable, but the future one becomes increasingly confused and conflicting as the adolescent grows and sees ever increasing choices of identity in the future.

Coleman suggests that the picture of disturbance in adolescence painted by Erikson resulted from it being based on studying atypical and disturbed adolescents. It is also important that we do not ignore cohort effects in such studies since adolescence at different points in history could be a very different experience (e.g. consider post-World War II vs the 1990s). Waterman and Waterman (1975) recommend the use of longitudinal studies of identity formation to help expose cohort effects. In their study they compared identity achievement in fathers and sons, and showed evidence not only for cohort effects but also for the idea that identity achievement could go on into adulthood. One of their studies found foreclosure was the most common identity status in 40- to 65-year-old men but, as they would have experienced childhood and adolescence in the 1930s to 1950s, it is easy to find reasons for this.

In conclusion, Smith and Cowie (1993) query the theoretical validity of Erikson and Marcia's work, especially regarding the idea of 'crisis'. They say:

- Moratorium may not be general but may operate in different areas of life at any one time. We may, for example, experience a vocational moratorium at the same time as achieving a sense of 'political' identity.
- Identity achievement is apparently not confined to adolescence.
- Change tends to be gradual rather than sudden, which tends to defuse the idea of 'crisis'.

Some of these ideas are reflected in Coleman's (1974) focal theory of adolescence which you will find at the end of this section.

Other potential sources of conflict

Adolescence is a period of rapid physical change and adolescents vary in the rate at which they mature. Girls generally enter puberty at any time between 11 and 14 years of age. Most boys enter puberty between 12 and 15 years of age. However, some children mature earlier than this and some later, and it is possible that being at one of these extremes could be a source of turmoil. Smith and Cowie (1993) comment that early maturation in boys can be socially advantageous in groups where physical size and strength are valued. For girls the picture is less clear. Early maturers tend to be less likely than late maturers to go on to tertiary education. They tend to be sexually active, marry and have children earlier. There is also some evidence that they are more likely than late maturers to be involved in taking risks with alcohol or other drugs (although this may be because they tend to mix with older girls). Smith and Cowie quote other research that suggests that early maturers score higher than late maturers in tests of mental ability and school performance, but they warn that these findings could be confounded by other variables. For example, the differences between early and late maturers seem to be linked to social class, as they are more pronounced in lower social class groups. There is also a link with family size, in that puberty tends to arrive later in larger families and in these families, intelligence and school performance also tend to be slightly lower than in smaller families.

In Focus

Rutter *et al.* (1976) on adolescent turmoil

In a study of 2,303 14- to 15-year-olds on the Isle of Wight, Rutter *et al.* (1976) looked for evidence of increased conflict between adolescents and their parents. Parents and teachers answered questionnaires about the teenagers' behaviour and various subsamples of teenagers were selected for interviews and psychiatric assessment. In one part of the research, 200 randomly selected teenagers were compared with 304 others who had scored high on measures of deviancy. These two groups were compared in terms of the amount of conflict between themselves and their parents and in terms of evidence of inner turmoil expressed through their behaviour or the presence of psychiatric disorder, but little support was found for stereotypical adolescent turmoil.

Is adolescence accompanied by conflict and inner turmoil? Rutter *et al.*'s study described above is relevant here. Concerning conflict, in their random sample, 1 in 6 of the parents reported arguments with their sons or daughters about their conduct and 1 in 3 complained about their teenagers' hairstyle or clothing. The teenagers themselves perceived a higher frequency of conflict but rarely reported serious disagreements or criticized their parents. In the 'deviant' group, conflict was generally three times more common and showed itself more often in these teenagers' communications with their parents and in their behaviour (e.g. withdrawal from the family). The general picture was one of good relationships between parents and their teenage children with growing mutual trust and appreciation.

On the subject of inner turmoil, clinical depression was rarely found, although 1 in 5 reported often feeling miserable or depressed, leading Rutter *et al.* to query whether adolescence is any different from other stages of life in this respect. To test this idea, the incidence of psychiatric disorder in a group of 10-year-olds was compared with that in 14- to 15-year-olds and this showed only a modest increase in the teenagers (from about 11% of 10-year-olds to 13% of 14- to 15-year-olds).

One useful source of evidence in this area is cross-cultural research which can show us whether adolescent turmoil is universal. In 1928, Margaret Mead's study of the Samoan people presented a picture of an island paradise in which transition through adolescence was easy and tranquil. She suggested that this resulted from the Samoan extended family life in which disagreements could dissipate more easily. In the confines of the North American smaller, nuclear family, conflict was less easy to escape. She also emphasized the importance of a non-punitive, less repressive child-rearing style amongst the Samoans leading to fewer feelings of guilt and oppression. The young Samoan women that she interviewed described a relaxed attitude to sexual maturation where sexual experimentation was usual and sexual behaviour was promiscuous compared to Western standards at the time. Mead's work seemed to suggest that adolescent turmoil was a cultural phenomenon which was certainly not universal.

❖ Activity 3 ❖

Reflect for a few minutes on your own adolescent years. Do you feel you experienced conflict or inner turmoil relating to your sense of identity, rate of maturation or family relationships? Do you expect other periods in your life to be more, less or equally demanding when compared with the adolescent phase?

Freeman (1983) criticized Mead's conclusions arguing that she was not sufficiently closely involved with the Samoan people and that she saw only what she wanted to see. He argues that she may not have established sufficient trust with the Samoan people to expect total honesty from them. For example, of the fifty 14- to 20-year-old women she interviewed, only eleven claimed to have had heterosexual experience and there was no way of knowing how accurate this figure was. Freeman says more recent studies point to repressive parenting practices and a value being placed on virginity at marriage, especially in higher status families. Unfortunately we may never know whether Mead or Freeman is the more accurate. Mead studied women, while Freeman's research was based on studying males. In addition, between these studies the influence on the Samoans of western ideas from Christian missionaries and American air-base staff would have brought about change.

Finally, in 1974 Bronfenbrenner compared child-rearing patterns in the USSR and the USA, and found that Russian adolescents showed more pro-social behaviour and less of the anti-social behaviour common in the American adolescents. One reason for this finding could be that Russian youths had more opportunities to integrate with adult society early on, whereas the American youths tended to be segregated and discouraged from entering adulthood. The greater degree of conflict shown by the American youths could therefore have resulted from the development of a youth sub-culture distinguishing itself from adults by adopting a different set of values and norms.

Conclusions about 'storm and stress'

The stereotypical picture of the unhappy adolescent tortured by conflict and turmoil is not one borne out by research. In fact, the stereotype is probably more the result of media portrayals of adolescents as rebels. Certainly adolescence can be a stormy period for some but it is not necessarily any more stormy than any other period in life. In addition, adolescent 'storms' could result, not from adolescence itself, but from events which happened earlier in life, e.g. parental neglect. By the time children reach puberty, they may have done most of the groundwork for establishing independence, so that adolescence is a period of consolidation and improving relationships with others rather than one of conflict. There is also little evidence for a great switch of loyalties from the family to the peer group as most adolescents are very selective about their friends!

Coleman's focal theory of adolescence

An attempt to draw together the conflicting findings about adolescence and to offer an explanation for them has been made by Coleman (1974). He suggests that as individuals pass through adolescence, they focus on different aspects of change at different times. Issues to do with biological, cognitive and social change are present all the time, but are not equally important at the same time. For a school leaver entering work, occupational choice would be a point of focus, but for another person contemplating six years of higher education, it may not be so important.

To test these ideas, Coleman and Hendry (1990) examined issues that were important for 800 boys and girls aged 11, 13, 15 or 17 years. Each issue seemed to have a different distribution curve, peaking in importance over a particular age. Concerns about peer relations, for example, peaked earlier than occupational choice. In addition, some adolescents came to these issues earlier than normal and others later. Adolescent life, therefore, can be seen as a mixture of stability and adjustment in different areas of life at different times. The coincidence of a number of important issues all peaking at once could cause problems, but generally, adolescents navigate carefully through this stage of life, choosing whether to engage with particular issues immediately or later. In this way they manage their own life stage and are generally successful in coming through unscathed.

Section summary

Adolescence is a period of transition between childhood and adulthood, accompanied by both physical and psychological changes. Various studies examining the stereotype of storm and stress in adolescence have been carried out focusing on development of a sense of identity, the effect of fast or slow maturation and testing for the presence of conflict and inner turmoil. Cross-cultural research suggests that experiences of adolescence may vary with the cultural setting. Conclusions in all these areas are complicated by the type of adolescent studied and by cohort effects but generally, adolescence seems to be neither more nor less stormy than any other life phase.

Three stage theories of adult personality development

Erik Erikson's 'Eight Ages of Man' (1980)

Erikson's psychodynamic approach to personality development, mentioned in the previous section, was built up over about thirty years. He agreed with several key ideas from Sigmund Freud's psychoanalytic theory but disagreed with others. For example, although he accepted that personality developed in stages and that it consisted of an id, ego and superego, he disagreed that personality was largely laid down in childhood. Instead, he thought that it continued to develop throughout adulthood. He also saw social forces as far more important in shaping personality than sexual ones (hence his approach is known as a psychosocial theory of personality development). In addition, Erikson's theory is more flexible than Freud's, in that he saw greater possibilities for change.

Erikson saw personality development as advancing through eight invariant stages (see Table 20.3), rather like sensitive periods in that certain aspects of personality development are best dealt with at particular stages in life. Nevertheless, problems not resolved earlier on can be revisited later in life and worked through more positively. On the other hand, healthy development can be undone by later experiences. Each stage, which is roughly age-related, presents the individual with a specific psychosocial crisis to be worked through – that is, individuals must resolve a psychological conflict relating to their interactions with others in increasingly wider social settings. Each crisis takes place in a different social setting and if it is dealt with successfully, the individual develops a certain virtue or psychological strength.

For our purposes, the final three stages in Table 20.3 are the most relevant. However, it is important to note that the outcomes of the earlier stages will be carried forward into adulthood (e.g. basic trust is seen as the cornerstone of a healthy personality). Also, some stages (such as identity vs role confusion or intimacy vs isolation) may have to be dealt with repeatedly, especially in times of rapid social change. The final stage (ego integrity vs despair) involves an integration of all that has gone before in the previous stages.

In adulthood, the first major crisis is that of intimacy vs isolation. The main task is to develop a close, meaningful, caring relationship with, usually, one other person and to avoid the isolation that may result from failing to do so. At the same time, individuals need to retain some independence and freedom rather than totally immersing themselves in someone else. In middle adulthood, the main crisis surrounds generativity vs stagnation. Generativity refers to the need to be productive, creative and caring with regard to one's own and future generations. Child-rearing and career may be two avenues for generativity to be satisfied. A feeling of stagnation may lie behind the 'mid-life crisis' when adults may feel that their current life pattern has little purpose or

Table 20.3 Erikson's Psychosocial Stages of Personality Development

Approximate age	*Quality to be developed*	*Social focus*	*Virtue*
0 to 1 year (infancy)	Basic trust vs mistrust	Maternal person	Hope (an optimistic trust that the world will meet one's needs)
2 to 3 years (early childhood)	Autonomy vs shame and doubt	Parental persons	Will (the ability to exercise self-restraint and choice)
4 to 5 years (play age)	Initiative vs guilt	Basic family	Purpose (a sense of goal-directedness)
6 to 12 years (school age)	Industry vs inferiority	Neighbourhood, school	Competence (a sense of confidence in one's own abilities)
13 to 18 years	Identity vs role confusion	Peer groups	Fidelity (the ability freely to pledge loyalty to others)
19 to 25 years	Intimacy vs isolation	Friendships	Love (both romantic and erotic and including the ability to commit oneself to others and maintain the commitment through degrees of compromise and self-denial)
26 to 40 years	Generativity vs stagnation	The household	Care (a sense that certain things in life have meaning and importance, leading one to be productive in life)
41 years +	Ego integrity vs despair	Humankind	Wisdom (a sense that one's life has been worthwhile, arrived at by integrating the outcomes of previous stages)

meaning. In later adulthood the individual faces the ego-integrity vs despair crisis: the end of life is approaching and it is a time to reflect on how one's life has been. A sense of time well spent during a productive and meaningful life will lead to a sense of ego-integrity while a sense of bitterness, opportunities missed and time wasted may lead to despair.

Evaluation

- Erikson's theory has been very influential in establishing the lifespan approach to human development.
- The theory has face validity because it appeals to intuition and common experience.
- Erikson has shown the importance of social influences in personality development. (Some, however, see this as a weakness since successful development is not just restricted to those who conform to the social clock and is still possible in individuals who are 'out of step' with society's expectations.)
- There are some problems with testing such a theory. We would have to depend on extensive self-report, clinical interviews and questionnaires with all their attendant problems. In addition, many of Erikson's ideas are difficult to put into a testable form. These problems mean that there is a lack of sound empirical evidence for the theory.
  The exception, perhaps, is his own cross-cultural research with the Sioux and Yurok Indians, in which he compared different child-rearing practices and the responses of these people to rapid social change. He claimed parents themselves must be fully integrated into their own society and therefore be able to instil in their children a deep sense of purpose and meaning in their actions. If the parents' social order is breaking up around them, this becomes an increasingly difficult task.

Daniel Levinson's 'Seasons of a Man's Life' (1978)

In 1969, Levinson selected a sample of forty men, aged from 35 to 45 years, from a variety of occupational groups. Over a period of two to three months, each participant had between five and ten biographical interviews each lasting one to two hours.

A central idea in this theory is the 'life structure', defined as the 'underlying pattern or design of a person's life at any given time' (Levinson 1978, p. 41). The life structure changes over the lifespan and we build it primarily around our relationships and work. Using transcriptions of detailed interview material, Levinson was able to illustrate that the life structure evolves through a series of alternating stable (*structure-building*) and transitional (*structure-changing*) phases. These he called 'the seasons of a man's life'. An outline of these is given in Fig. 20.1. The lifespan is seen as covering four eras of pre-, early, middle and late adulthood each with specific tasks to be mastered. Where the eras overlap, we experience transitions lasting roughly five years. The ages given in Fig. 20.1 are approximate as there is some variation around them, although it is not thought to be much more than five or six years.

The season's of a man's life

- **Pre-adulthood (0 to 17 years)**
  In this phase, the individual grows from dependent baby to early adulthood.
- **Early adult transition (18 to 22 years)**
  This involves separating oneself from pre-adulthood through increasing moves towards all kinds of independence, e.g. financial, emotional. The individual is able to explore some of life's possibilities, e.g. in terms of occupational choice and personal identity, without yet making firm commitments. It is, as with other transitions, a time of reappraisal.

❖ **Early adulthood (22 to 40 years)**
This can be one of the most dynamic, challenging and stressful periods of adult life. Initially, individuals forge firmer links between themselves and the adult world. Possibilities are still being explored, but now is the time to make some choices and commitments to begin to give the life more structure (although it is important still to leave open possibilities for change). It may now be possible to fulfil some of the 'dreams' of youth, perhaps establishing a home and family, qualifying in one's chosen career and finding a way to balance them all.
A keener sense of time passing by means important decisions about the life structure must be made before it is too late, so there may be some readjustments from time to time. The individual will hopefully settle on a few key choices, find a 'niche' in the adult world, and from its security, continue to grow through contributing constructively to aspects of personal, home and working life. The later part of this phase has been dubbed 'becoming one's own man' or BOOM.

❖ **Mid-life transition (40 to 45 years)**
The sense of passing time and one's own mortality become even more pressing as the physical signs of ageing become more obvious and deaths of one's parents may occur. Initial dreams and plans may or may not be realized and for some (not all), this can be a period of 'mid-life crisis' in which changes must be made in order to avoid extreme disappointment. In this transition, however, BOOM is completed and, with luck, we emerge from it wiser and able to be more loving, caring and reflective, rather than isolated and stagnated.

❖ **Middle adulthood (45 to 60 years)**
In this stage, illusions of immortality and eternal youth will usually disappear. It is a time to build on choices and decisions made during the mid-life transition. For some this may mean a new occupation, perhaps new key relationships. For others the change may be more subtle, so that the existing occupation and relationships remain but the person's attitude to them changes. Typically, adults in this stage are less inward-looking and more concerned with the generations that follow. They have the power, authority and wisdom to make an important and lasting impact on the world and others around them. In a small way, this could mean acting as a mentor to others or becoming more of a family person. On a larger scale the individual could be involved in world politics! For many people, successful progress through this era could make it one of the most satisfying, positive and productive phases of life.

❖ **Late adult transition (60 to 65 years)**
The signs of physical decline are now becoming increasingly obvious and one is becoming 'old' in the eyes of one's culture.

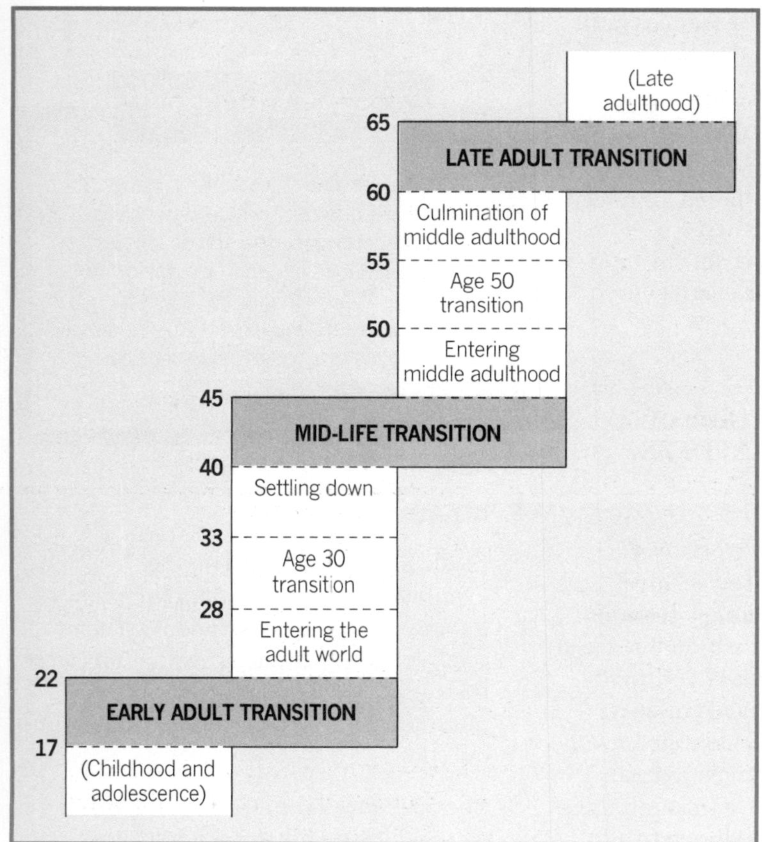

Figure 20.1 Developmental periods in early and middle adulthood *Source:* Levinson 1978

- **Late adulthood (65 years to the end of life)**
A final acceptance that life is finite is now unavoidable and it is important to find a way of accepting and living with how one's life has been, what it is like now and what the future can realistically hold. Again for some, this is a time of crisis, for others a period of calm and reflection and making the most of life.

Evaluation

- There are few quantitative or statistical data to support Levinson's ideas because the information collected was in the form of clinical interview reports. Some would see this as a strength because of the richness of the qualitative data. Others see it as a weakness.
- Levinson's original sample was limited in age and occupational background as well as being all-male. However, in later works published in the 1980s, Levinson claimed his theory held for females (and for different social classes, cultures and historical time periods).
- Most of the interviewees in the study had not reached the age of 45. In fact, information was only gathered for fifteen participants after the age of 45. Consequently the evidence for the later eras is sketchy, being based on a very small group of adults.

Roger Gould's 'Evolution of Adult Consciousness' (1978, 1980)

Gould's ideas stem from his work as a psychiatrist. They are based on medical students' ratings of taped therapy sessions from which a questionnaire was devised and sent to 524 white, middle-class 16- to 50-year-olds who were not clinical patients. From their responses, Gould identified seven age-related stages of adult development. He proposed that, as we move through these stages, we progress from childhood to adult consciousness and we do this by facing and leaving behind four major false emotional assumptions. While we hold these assumptions, they give us an illusion of safety and serve to protect us from anxiety, which is why giving them up can be both difficult and painful. Gould thought that our forties could be particularly difficult, as passing time and a greater sense of our own mortality make facing our false assumptions all the more pressing. The assumptions we have to face and discard are shown in detail in Table 20.4.

By the time we are in our fifties, we should have given up our illusions and developed what Gould calls a sense of 'me' and a feeling that 'I own myself'. There is a contact with one's 'inner core' which gives us a sense of meaning and the personal strength to deal with whatever life still has to bring. We should have dealt with the separation anxiety of childhood, freed ourselves from illusions of absolute safety and learned to stand alone. Individuals who do not reach this stage may feel rootless and that life lacks meaning.

❖ Activity 4 ❖

Take your life line from Activity 1 and, using three different coloured pens for clarity, superimpose the stages suggested by Erikson, Levinson and Gould. How well do they 'fit' your life course? Can you relate the events you expect to experience to the stages or phases suggested by these theories?

Evaluation

- Gould's theory is based on the evaluations of taped patient interviews by only eight medical students. Their relatively inexperienced evaluations were then used as a basis for the questionnaire, which calls its validity into question.
- The 524 questionnaire respondents were white, middle-class adults which tells us little about other types of adults.

Table 20.4 False assumptions to be dealt with in adulthood (Gould 1978, 1980)

Age in years	*False assumption and its components*
Late teens to early twenties	I will always belong to my parents and believe in their world. • If I get any more independent, it will be a disaster. • I can only see the world through my parents' assumptions. • Only they can guarantee my safety. • They must be my only family. • I don't own my body.
Twenties	Doing it my parents' way with willpower and perseverance will probably bring results. But when I am too frustrated, confused or tired, or am simply unable to cope, my parents will step in and show me the way. • Rewards will come automatically if we do what we are supposed to do. • There is only one right way to do things. • My loved ones are able to do for me what I haven't been able to do for myself. • Rationality, commitment and effort will always prevail over other forces.
Late twenties to early thirties	Life is simple and controllable. There are no significant coexisting contradictory forces within me. • What I know intellectually, I know emotionally. • I am not like my parents in ways I don't want to be. I can see the reality of those close to me quite clearly. • Threats to my security aren't real.
Mid thirties to fifty	There is no evil in me or death in the world. The sinister has been expelled. • My work (for men) or my relationship with men (for women) grant me immunity from death and danger. • There is no life beyond this family. • I am innocent.

- There were no attempts to assess the reliability of the questionnaire.
- The detail about life after 60 is sketchy (but this is hardly surprising given the age range of Gould's questionnaire respondents).

Conclusions about stage theories of personality development

Although Erikson, Levinson and Gould have described adult personality development using different terminology, there is general agreement about the overall trends in adulthood, e.g. finding an identity in adolescence, establishing intimacy, making career choices, becoming generative and, finally, looking for a meaning to life and facing death. The forces behind these trends differ in each theory but they share an emphasis on phases or stages that all adults can be expected to move through with varying degrees of success.

The three approaches offer us a much needed framework for understanding certain aspects of adulthood, but there are some important limitations to bear in mind:

- In each case there are some doubts about the soundness of the research on which the ideas are based, particularly with regard to the number and type of participants used and the methods of data collection.
- Some critics think there is a negative over-emphasis on crisis, particularly in mid-life and that this could be because of the nature of the cohorts that were used.
- We cannot be sure how well the three approaches apply to different individuals, societies and cohorts. There could be a great deal of variation within these.
- We must also remember that the changes described in these theories go on against a background of many other age-related changes, e.g. physiological and cognitive/intellectual, that individuals are having to cope with at the same time. (For a discussion of these, see Sugarman 1986.)
- Some researchers think that there is little convincing evidence for stages in adult development and prefer instead to focus on specific life events that affect many adults. We will see something of this later in this chapter.

Section summary

The stage theories of Erikson, Levinson and Gould offer explanations of personality development over the entire lifespan or for specific periods in adulthood. There are broad areas of agreement in these theories although they explain the 'pushes' and 'pulls' of development differently. Methodological criticisms have been raised about all three approaches and all are open to cohort effects. Nevertheless, they have given us some much needed frameworks within which to view personality development in adulthood.

Social theories of successful ageing

The two theories described here emphasize the social context of ageing in later life.

Disengagement theory

Disengagement theory (Cumming and Henry 1961) sees ageing as a gradual and mutual process of separation between individuals and their social roles and interests. This is a natural, and often positive, process whereby in later life peoiple who are ageing become more reflective and self-sufficient, and less absorbed in other people and events. They generally bring this about themselves, but other events, such as loss of spouse and retirement, also encourage disengagement to happen.

There are, however, some problems with this theory:

- People who are apparently disengaging may simply be continuing with a life style that they already had.
- There are plenty of examples of people who actively resist disengagement and who are unhappy when social forces require them to disengage.
- People who are actively socially engaged are often happier than those not so engaged.
- There may be a cohort effect that gives a false impression of disengagement. Later generations of elderly people may be healthier, more financially secure and generally better catered for socially etc. If this proves to be the case, 'disengagement' may disappear.

Activity theory

In direct contrast to disengagement theory, activity theory (Havighurst *et al.* 1968) sees individuals as preferring to remain active and productive in later life, even resisting disengagement from society. Where disengagement is inevitable (e.g. through children leaving home, statutory retirement, reduction in income and changes in physical capabilities), individuals are less likely to be demoralized if they are well prepared and have plenty of substitute activities. However, it is likely that this theory, like disengagement theory, oversimplifies the issues.

In comparing these two theories, it is immediately obvious that there is some value in both but neither is sufficient on its own. People vary considerably in the degree to which they wish to be active or disengaged and in how much choice they have over these things. In fact, successful ageing would appear to result from achieving a mixture of activity and disengagement that suits the individual concerned. We should also consider many other variables (such as health, income, place of residence, sense of control, social support systems, marital status and family) when assessing a person's life satisfaction. Indeed, we would probably find that later life is neither more nor less satisfying than any other stage of life, once we take into account all the ways in which people differ.

Section summary

Activity theory and disengagement theory are two opposing ways of explaining how people adapt to ageing in later life. Taking into account individual differences, it would appear that both approaches are valuable and that the best solution would be to treat them as complementary as opposed to conflicting.

The life events approach to adulthood

Stage theories of adult personality development emphasize similarities between individuals. However, as we have seen, there are wide differences between cohorts, in the lengths of people's lives and in the experiences of each person, and these things make it difficult to arrive at an integrated picture of adult development. One way round this is to adopt a 'life events' approach (advocated by Neugarten (1980) and others) and, therefore, to shift attention to differences between individuals.

Classifying and measuring life events

In general, a life event is a significant milestone or turning point in life to which we need to adjust and which will, consequently, have an effect on our personality. Life events are all 'crises' of a sort but they can be positive as well as negative or even a mixture of both. One way to group them is as follows (for another way, see *In Focus* on the next page).

- Normative, age-graded events: usually biological or social in origin (e.g. birth of first child, menopause, retirement). They affect most people in a particular age range.
- Normative, history-graded events: experienced by most people in a cohort (e.g. war, famine, economic depression).
- Non-normative events: experienced by some but not most people (e.g. accidents, particular illnesses, divorce and localized disasters).

In Focus

The Social Readjustment Rating Scale

One major attempt to classify and measure the effects of life events was made by Holmes and Rahe (1967). They studied 5,000 patient records and listed 43 life events that had occurred in the months preceding illness. With the help of 100 judges, who rated each event in terms of how much change it would entail, they developed the Social Readjustment Rating Scale (SRRS).

On this scale, each event has a value indicating 'life change units' or LCUs. Individuals can be asked to check off all the events that have affected them in, say, the previous year and add the LCUs to arrive at a grand total. See Table 20.5. Links between these scores, which indicate the amount of stress experienced, and stress-related illness can then be researched.

The impact of life events in general

Holmes and Rahe have claimed that scores of 300 LCUs (see *In Focus* above) or over for the preceding year are associated with greater vulnerability to a variety of serious health problems such as myocardial infarction, stroke, TB, diabetes, leukaemia, as well as everyday ailments such as headaches, skin irritations and stomach upsets. Psychologically, links have been drawn with depression, anxiety disorders and increased suicide risk. However, the evidence is mixed and, importantly, we do not always know whether the individual's state of health preceded or followed exposure to a large number of life-changing events. In fact, as correlational evidence is not causal evidence, we should be careful in how we explain these links.

Unfortunately, classifications such as the SRRS are one-dimensional. This means that, although they identify life events, they do not take into account many other factors that could influence how individuals cope. Hultsch and Plemons (1979) provide a model to overcome this problem. They suggest that the following variables should be considered:

- the life event itself – e.g. marriage, divorce, parenting, loss, starting work, losing a job
- the nature of various 'mediating variables' – these include the individual's health, sex, social support network, age, income; all these will affect ability to cope
- how the individual reacts – these are called 'adaptation processes' and include how the individual perceives the event, any preparations made for it, previous experiences of similar events if any and the coping strategies brought to bear on it, e.g. seeking counselling or other support.

❖ Activity 5 ❖

Analyse your own situation, using the SRRS scale shown in Table 20.5.

- How many of the life events listed have you experienced in the last year?
- How appropriate is it for this stage in your life?
- Project ahead 10 years, then 20 years. Does the scale seem more appropriate now?
- Do you think there are stages in life where the listed events are likely to cluster together?

Table 20.5 The Social Readjustment Rating Scale (adapted from Holmes and Rahe 1967)

Rank	*Life event*	*Mean value*
1	Death of spouse	100
2	Divorce	73
3	Marital separation	65
4	Jail term	63
5	Death of a close family member	63
6	Personal illness or injury	53
7	Marriage	50
8	Fired at work	47
9	Marital reconciliation	45
10	Retirement	45
11	Change in health of family member	44
12	Pregnancy	40
13	Sex difficulties	39
14	Gain of new family member	39
15	Business readjustment	39
16	Change in financial status	38
17	Death of close friend	37
18	Change to different line of work	36
19	Change in number of arguments with spouse	35
20	Heavy mortgage repayments	31
21	Foreclosure of mortgage or loan	30
22	Change in responsibilities at work	29
23	Son or daughter leaves home	29
24	Trouble with in-laws	29
25	Outstanding personal achievement	28
26	Spouse begins or stops work	26
27	Begin or end school	26
28	Change in living conditions	25
29	Revision of personal habits	24
30	Trouble with boss	23
31	Change in work hours or conditions	20
32	Change in residence	20
33	Change in schools	20
34	Change in recreation	19
35	Change in church activities	19
36	Change in social activities	18
37	Moderate mortgage or loan	17
38	Change in sleeping habits	16
39	Change in number of family get-togethers	15
40	Change in eating habits	15
41	Vacation	13
42	Christmas	12
43	Minor violations of the law	11

The combination of these variables will result in outcomes that are either functional or dysfunctional. A further consideration is that all this will occur in both individual and socio-historical contexts. This means that an event will happen to the individual at a particular age and at a particular period in time. The occurrence of an event (e.g. childbirth) at an age considered to be out of time with the 'social clock' or at different periods in time will, therefore, also affect the nature of the outcomes, e.g. parenthood happening to an unmarried, younger teenager in the 1950s compared to the 1990s.

Evaluation of the life events approach

As we have seen, stage theories of adult personality development have the disadvantage of playing down individual differences. The life events approach does help to overcome this drawback but it is not without its own problems:

- One shortcoming of the life events approach is its emphasis on crisis and change as the main force behind personality development. Surely the cumulative effects over time of a tedious job or devitalized marriage could also bring about change (although it would be gradual as opposed to rapid). In addition, there appear to be long periods of stability in adulthood that are often far from unpleasant and that could also lead to personal growth.
- The life events approach needs to be flexible enough to cope with historical changes in the 'social clock'. For example, current work patterns are changing, life expectancy is increasing and there are changes in education and health care. These result in life events becoming more and more spread over the life span and consequently, much more 'individual'.

Section summary

Focusing on specific life events in adulthood is one way of bringing order to the vast research field of adult development. One strength of this approach is its focus on individual differences in reactions to life events. Types of life events have been classified and measured in different ways, but our understanding of their impact is complicated by methodological problems such as cohort effects. This approach also tends to emphasize *crisis,* instead of seeing adulthood as holding the potential for positive personal growth.

Specific life events

Bearing in mind the many variables that can affect how individuals react to life events, can we make any general statements about the effects of specific life events? To address this question this section focuses on four events.

- unemployment
- parenthood
- divorce
- loss and bereavement.

Unemployment

The world of work is a rapidly changing place and here, in particular, cohort effects are especially obvious. Older workers are more likely to have dependent children and to feel less able than younger or more independent workers to move geographically to obtain employment. Previous generations may not have faced the prospect of unemployment to the extent that new entrants to the work-force do now.

Those who expected a career for life may find job-loss much harder to cope with than those who now expect to take a series of different jobs. In developed countries there is a marked shift away from goods-producing occupations to service and trade.
More women are moving into the work-force. The explosion in information technology means that some employees need no longer be tied to their place of work. We may now be faced with a completely different approach to work where people are employed on short contracts and expect to face a cycle of employment and unemployment throughout their working lives. They may also need to be much more flexible in what they are prepared to do and come to regard education for work as an ongoing process.

In order to understand the effects of unemployment, it is important to begin by asking what it is that work offers people. Financial rewards are clearly not the whole story since some people prefer low-paid work to no work and others, who are financially secure, choose to work even though they do not need to. Work often gives people an identity and status, and a sense of motivation and purpose. Importantly, it is a source of social contact, satisfying a need to affiliate with others and giving one's life a structure. In Erikson's terms, work is one way in which we may satisfy our generativity needs and it may ultimately contribute to 'ego-integrity'. In Maslow's (1968) view, it may provide opportunities for satisfying a variety of needs including the ultimate need to self-actualize (see Chapter 8).

Some school-leavers may never experience loss of work simply because they cannot find employment at all. Hendry (1989) found that some Scottish youths seeking their first job did not feel optimistic about their prospects of finding work and others were prepared to put up with jobs they disliked, or were over-qualified for, rather than face unemployment. Both unemployment and 'underemployment' were found by O'Brien (1990) to be linked to depression and other psychological problems. However, young adults who felt helpless in the face of unemployment were worse off in this respect than those who felt personally responsible for their employment situation.

Reactions to loss of work are affected by a great many variables. Factors include the sex of the worker, work status, the stage of working life, job satisfaction, how people view the place of work in their lives and the social support systems that are available. Nevertheless, Fryer (1985) suggests that the loss of a job is rarely a pleasant experience. He describes four phases that people may go through as they come to terms with unemployment (see Table 20.6). These are not invariant stages and may differ greatly

Table 20.6 Phases of adjustment to unemployment (Fryer 1985)

Shock	The realization that the job is irretrievably lost is registered.
Optimism	The unemployed person works hard to find another job.
Pessimism	If the job search fails, feelings of helplessness and hopelessness may start to take hold.
Fatalism and depression	The person gives up trying to find work.

between individuals. For example, a person who is not the only 'breadwinner' in a family unit, or someone who is not so personally invested in their work, may cope very well with unemployment compared to people in different circumstances.

On the subject of individual differences in reactions to unemployment, a study by Buss and Redburn (1983) compared the reactions of steelworkers and their managers to the closure of their steel plant in Ohio, USA, over a year between 1978 and 1979. Initially, the steelworkers seemed to feel more dejected than the managers. They felt more helpless and resentful, and that they had few transferable job skills. The managers expected to find new work in management (although not necessarily in a steel plant) and felt that they were more mobile. After a year, the managers were coping less well but still handled unemployment better than the steelworkers. The managers' greater feelings of security, perhaps because they had savings behind them and a greater sense of control, seemed to contribute to this enduring difference in coping. The steelworkers were particularly badly off because they could not see their particular jobs re-opening.

In both the short and long term, links have been drawn between unemployment and mental health problems. It has been argued that mental health problems could play a part in bringing unemployment about, but Fryer (1992) suggested otherwise. After comparing low-paid employed with equally poor unemployed people, evidence was found which showed that unemployment could itself precede a greater incidence of alcoholism and mental health problems. The picture is complicated since any worker under continual stress through threat of unemployment could become ill either before or after losing a job.

Parenthood

Parenthood, like other life events, can be both stressful and rewarding. Unlike some other life events (e.g. marriage), it is irrevocable! In our culture, there may be little preparation for parenthood and little support, other than from a number of often contradictory childcare books. The arrival of a child is also one of the most abrupt transitions experienced by adults.

Parenthood calls for major readjustments in lifestyle and is accompanied by practical issues, such as general fatigue, as well as physical changes (for the mother) and the emotional changes that accompany coming to terms with suddenly being entirely responsible for a helpless and vulnerable baby. Initially, the roles of the new father and mother may become more traditional and polarized and the pre-parenthood balance of the relationship will probably never return. Turner and Helms (1983) suggest a number of reasons why adults choose parenthood. See Table 20.7.

Table 20.7 Reasons for choosing parenthood (Turner and Helms 1983)

Ego expansion	a sense of importance and purpose
Creativity	a sense of achievement (or what Erikson would call successful resolution of the generativity crisis)
Status and conformity satisfaction	fulfilling the expectations of your culture
Control and authority	over your dependants
Love and affection	both given and received
Happiness and security	

Some research has shown that 50 to 80% of adults described the birth of the first child as a moderate to severe crisis (Hultsch and Deutsch 1981). Other research has described the crisis as mild or worse for the mother than for the father (e.g. Leifer 1977). There are many possible reasons for these mixed findings. One is that if the research is questionnaire-based, it tends to result in low return rates and this distorts the sample characteristics. In contrast, interview-based research tends to be more searching and turns up more conflict. In addition, parenthood may have been accidental or entered into as an expression of love or to try to save a failing relationship. Research findings could, therefore, reflect the state of the parental relationship as much as attitudes to parenthood. Finally, the coincidence of parenthood with other life events is, as Hultsch and Plemons remind us, very important.

Satisfaction with parenthood seems to be linked to socio-economic status. Russell (1974) found more dissatisfaction in middle-class parents compared to working-class parents. There are a number of possible reasons for this. Middle-class parents tended to research childcare more by means of books and therefore may have set themselves unrealistic standards. They also tended to resent more the intrusion of the child into their time together. Middle-class women typically found greater personal satisfaction through their careers and, although they welcomed motherhood, it was often at a cost to their career progression. This was often aggravated further by lack of satisfactory childcare and the unwillingness of their employer, partner and partner's employer to recognize both parents' obligations to their children, e.g. when the child was ill.

The arrival of children is typically associated with the early phase of marriage. At that time there may be additional pressures, such as low income and high job pressure, as the parents establish themselves at work. By the time the children are at school, parents may find themselves under the greatest pressure in their career (especially if they are competing with keen, younger, childless colleagues who are cheaper to employ). Parents with adolescent children seemed to be under even greater strain. Bee and Mitchell (1984) reported that the happiest parents were young couples with few financial pressures. In spite of this, 80 to 90% of couples with children said they were very happy and that parenthood had improved their relationship. This was especially true just before the 'empty nest' phase when children were about to be launched into the adult world. For many parents, the 'empty nest' phase was particularly good, being marked by an increase in energy and zest for life and much satisfaction in the adult offspring.

How is the impact of parenthood on women and men different? Sadly, traditional male-female roles appear to hinder both sexes in their capacity as parents. Women still carry the brunt of domestic and parenting tasks even when both partners work outside the home. Women also have to battle with entrenched ideas about 'mother love' and 'maternal instinct' and the 'good mother's role'. Those who have established identities outside motherhood may find a constant conflict of interests between career and parenting and those who immerse themselves in motherhood may have identity problems when the children leave home. Men may be initially more involved in practical aspects of childcare, and just as immersed in their new-borns as women, but they are typically less well prepared for parenthood and may feel left out or inadequate. Both sexes have to adjust to sharing their time and affection differently within the family, but this can be harder for the father initially, if he is less involved than the mother in the daily care of the infant. Levine (1976) suggests that the roles of both fathers and mothers need to be redefined and revitalized so that more of the satisfactions of parenthood are open to both men and women (as well as more of the strains!).

Lugo and Hershey (1979) suggest that many of the negative aspects of the parenthood crisis could be reduced by careful preparation and greater understanding of the different effects on males and females. Much influenced by Maslow (1968), it is suggested that we prepare for parenthood by building a unit that meets our physical and psychological needs, i.e. for survival, security, love, esteem and understanding. If we work on this, parenthood can be a step forward on the road to personal growth and even help us towards self actualization.

Divorce

Next to the death of a spouse, divorce is the most difficult life crisis we are ever likely to experience. Bee and Mitchell (1984) note that divorce is more likely in those who marry younger or older than average, who are childless, whose parents had an unhappy marriage and who married because of unplanned pregnancy.

On the positive side, divorce can be good for you! It may mark the end of a long period of unhappiness and lack of personal growth but, even if the eventual outcome is good, the divorce itself is usually traumatic. Bohannon (1970) suggested six stages in the divorce process. See Table 20.8.

Each of the stages may be accompanied by a conflicting range of emotions including pervasive feelings of failure, ambivalence towards the partner, grief, relief, loneliness and excitement. There may be greater anxiety, loss of self-esteem, less productivity at work and greater vulnerability to mental and physical illness. Carter and Glick (1970) found that divorced people accounted for the highest death rates from TB, cirrhosis of the liver, pneumonia, homicide and accidental falls in males, and from suicide in females. It is important to note, however, that the sample was of people who did not remarry.

Both men and women seem to suffer most during the divorce process itself. The degree of trauma seems to be associated with:

- length of marriage
- the age of the spouses
- the number and ages of any children
- who suggested the divorce
- how it went.

For both sexes, disorganization is a feature of the year following divorce. Both men and women experience a drop in income but women generally seem to suffer more financially from a divorce, especially if they assumed their major role would be as a home-maker or they took a career break in order to rear children and their earnings fell behind. Women also find it less easy to obtain emotional support and there may be negative effects on their career (Hetherington *et al.* 1989). There is some evidence (e.g. Chiriboga 1982) that divorcees over the age of 50 find adjustment

Table 20.8 Stages in the divorce process (Bohannon 1970)

The emotional divorce	The marriage collapses, there is conflict and antagonism.
The legal divorce	The marriage contract is dissolved.
The economic divorce	Decisions are made over money and property.
The co-parental divorce	Custody of and access to children is decided.
The community divorce	Relationships with friends and family are adjusted.
The psychic divorce	There is adjustment to singlehood and autonomy is regained.

harder than do younger ones. People in the older age group seem to feel they have fewer options open to them and find their social life is more difficult. In Chiriboga's study, the older men in particular had trouble envisaging what the future would hold.

Divorcees with children have to deal with their own stress and upset as well as that of their children. In addition, they have to take sole responsibility for discipline and may find it hard to be consistent, so the children's behaviour may deteriorate. Another great source of conflict concerns access rights. Whilst Hetherington *et al.* point out that divorce is never 'good for the children', they say that its effects are less likely to cause serious, long-term damage if there is plenty of frequent and satisfactory contact between the child and both parents, coupled with a minimum disruption to the child's life style and daily routine. Naturally, children of different ages react differently to divorce. Understanding this can help parents to cope better with both the child's unhappiness and their own upset about the child's unhappiness. Some parents cope by arranging for their families to become 'blended', i.e. where step-parents and biological parents both take responsibility for the children's welfare. Difficult though this can be, it does help to maintain contact between divorced parents and their children and to lessen the pressure on both.

For adults, divorce-related disorganization tends to decline after two years, depending on the degree of financial pressure, number and age of children and the emotional support available. Is this reason enough to choose divorce over the possibility of rescuing a strained marriage by counselling or other means? A study by Pearlin (1980) found couples felt more distress during unsatisfactory marriages than they did after they divorced. There is little other evidence, however, and there are clearly many different kinds of marriage and divorce. The existing research does seem to show that at least two years of turmoil are extremely likely, but that prospects are good if the person has a support network. Certainly married people have fewer physical ailments and suffer less from loneliness than divorced or single people, but divorce can be worse in its effect than both marriage and singlehood (Cargan and Melko 1982).

Loss and bereavement

For Erikson (1980), the final life crisis of 'integrity vs despair' is at least partly triggered by anticipation of one's own death. Although death can occur at any age, it is, perhaps, more in our thoughts as we grow older and our peers begin to die. The loss we feel is thus on two fronts: for ourselves and for others.

Elizabeth Kübler-Ross' (1969) pioneering work into how terminally ill and dying people cope with impending death has helped considerably in enabling us to understand and support both the dying person and the bereaved relatives. Her clinical interviews led to a well-known stage theory of dying, although she warns against thinking of these stages as universal or invariant in order. She recommends that the defences of the dying person are not undermined nor should we attempt to push the dying person to stage 5 (see Table 20.9). A sense of control for the patient is central. (Weisman (1972) added that the person should be helped towards an 'appropriate death' that fulfils their expectations and ideals so that they can 'die well'.) In cases where death can be anticipated, Fulton (1970) described four stages of grieving in the person facing bereavement. Collin Murray-Parkes (1972) then described stages of coping with the death of someone close. The stages suggested by Kübler-Ross, Fulton and Murray-Parkes are shown in Table 20.9.

Research by Barrett (1978) has shown that men and women differ in their reactions to the death of a spouse. In a group of 403 community residents aged 62 and over, widowers seemed to experience lower morale and greater dissatisfaction than widows. They needed more domestic help and ate less well. They were less likely to want to talk about their loss and a desire for care and companionship provoked many into thoughts of remarriage. Widows were

Table 20.9 Stages of coping with dying, facing bereavement and dealing with bereavement

Stages of dying (Kübler-Ross 1969)	
Denial	The person resists facing death and may seek other professional opinions or reassurance from religion.
Anger	The person asks 'Why me?' and may feel hostile, resentful and envious of others. There may also be a strong feeling of frustration over unfinished business.
Bargaining	When 'Why me?' is not answered, bargains may be struck with God or fate. Many bargains will be made and broken.
Depression	Denial becomes impossible. Hospitalization may be necessary. There may be physical deterioration and a great sense of loss as well as guilt and worry about letting others down.
Acceptance	In this 'final rest before the long journey', the dying person may feel devoid of feelings, weak and resolute, although not happy.
Stages of grieving in the person facing bereavement (Fulton 1970)	
Depression	Accompanied by extreme upset and anticipatory grief.
Heightened concern	For the ill person, accompanied by the need to deal with unfinished business and discuss things with the dying person. Caring well for them at this point can help to obviate guilt when the person dies.
Rehearsals for the death	Developing coping strategies.
Adjustment to the consequences	New coping strategies along with those developed at stage three can help here.
Stages of grieving after the death has occurred (Murray-Parkes 1972)	
Initial response	Shock, disbelief, extreme sorrow, numbness, coldness and emptiness.
Coping	Anxiety and fear about breaking down completely. The person may turn to tranquillizers, sleeping pills or alcohol, and may show a number of physical and psychological symptoms. These will become more sporadic in the first year or so.
Intermediate phase	Characterized by obsessional reviews ('I could have done more'), trying to explain the loss ('It was God's will') and searching for the presence of the deceased through reminiscing and revisiting certain places.
Recovery phase	In about the second year, a more positive attitude may develop, even pride at having survived the crisis and grown through it.

especially likely to be unhappy if the spouse had been the sole breadwinner. They were more likely to have inadequate incomes and therefore experience greater isolation. (Remember, cohort effects are clearly important in such research. Younger bereaved spouses may have a completely different lifestyle at the outset.)

There is some evidence that older people adjust better and more rapidly to bereavement, but sudden bereavement produces longer and more severe grief at any age, especially if a parent loses a child (Balkwell 1981). Sudden bereavement allows no chance for 'grief work' and detachment to begin. It seems the degree of change demanded by one's new status is crucial. Lopata (1973) found that widows, for example, who had more traditional female roles and were very involved in their community and neighbourhood felt least disruption to their lifestyle. The presence of a supportive social network is also important. Kahn and Antonucci (1980) coined the term 'convoy' to describe the network that accompanies us in life and which provides emotional and practical aid. Those with a complete convoy handle bereavement more effectively, but those who lack a convoy are more prone to illness, emotional disturbance and death after bereavement. It has been suggested that, for men, the spouse fulfils many of the functions of the convoy, so widowhood is potentially more devastating for men than for women whose convoy typically involves more people.

❖ Activity 6 ❖

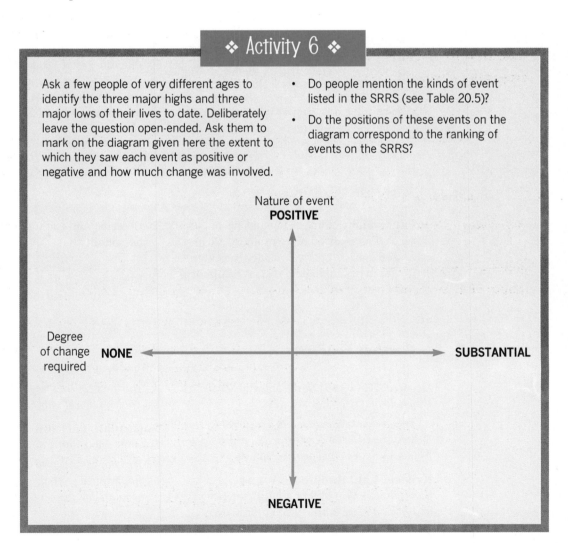

Ask a few people of very different ages to identify the three major highs and three major lows of their lives to date. Deliberately leave the question open-ended. Ask them to mark on the diagram given here the extent to which they saw each event as positive or negative and how much change was involved.

- Do people mention the kinds of event listed in the SRRS (see Table 20.5)?
- Do the positions of these events on the diagram correspond to the ranking of events on the SRRS?

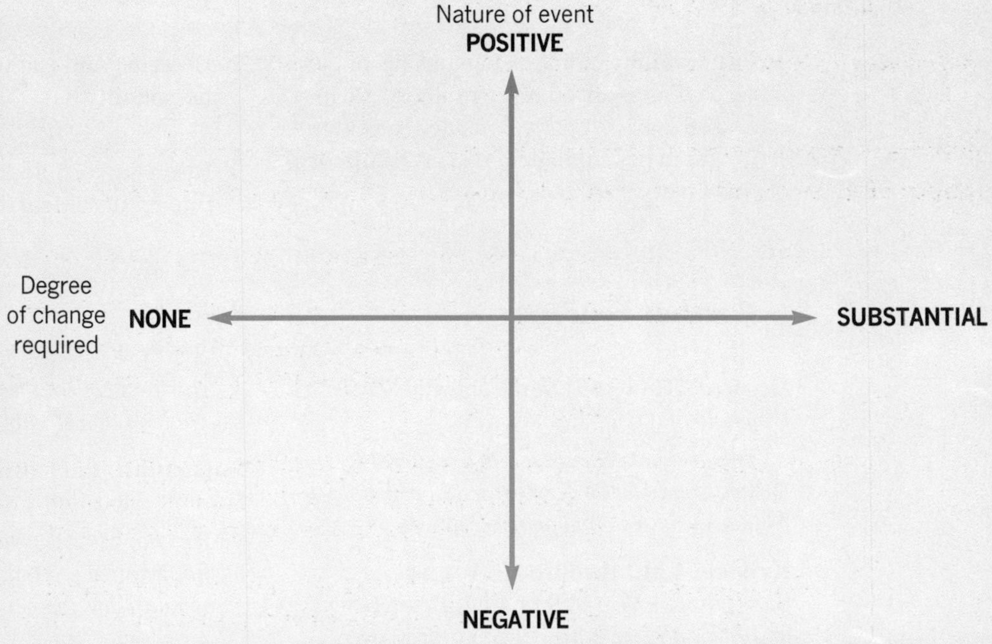

Nature of event
POSITIVE

Degree of change required **NONE** **SUBSTANTIAL**

NEGATIVE

Section summary

Four very different life events have been examined in this section. The effects of *unemployment* or underemployment are seen as being generally negative and linked to an increased incidence of psychological ill-health. *Parenthood* has both positive and negative effects, its impact being mediated by, amongst other things, social class, the phase of marriage and the sex of the parent. *Divorce* is nearly always traumatic and its impact is also mediated by a number of variables. *Loss* of a loved one, particularly a child or spouse, is probably the most traumatic life event of all. Individual differences again are important in how well people cope.

Chapter summary

- Psychologists have taken a variety of approaches to studying the relatively neglected area of lifespan psychology, some producing over-arching theories, others focusing on particular stages of life or specific life events.
- The study of the lifespan is dogged by methodological difficulties, especially those concerning cohort effects and the inherent problems of cross-sectional and longitudinal research.
- Adolescence has traditionally been viewed as a period of 'storm and stress', but research evidence suggests it is no more stressful than any other phase of development.
- Various theories of adult personality development and adaptation to ageing have been offered, all with their own strengths and weaknesses.
- The life events approach to understanding adulthood focuses on individual differences between adults and, although there is an unwelcome emphasis on crisis, much useful research has emerged to help adults understand and cope with life changes.

Essay questions

1 Traditionally, adolescence has been viewed as a period of turmoil or 'storm and stress'. Critically consider the extent to which psychological research supports this view. *(24 marks)*

2 Describe and evaluate theories of personality development in adulthood. *(24 marks)*

3 Discuss psychological research into the impact of critical life events on adults. *(24 marks)*

Further reading

Durkin, K. (1995) *Developmental Social Psychology*, Oxford: Blackwell.

This is an excellent, detailed, general text focusing on lifespan developmental psychology from a social psychology perspective.

Rybash, J.M., Roodin, P.A. and Santrock, J.W. (1991) *Adult Development and Ageing* (2nd edn), New York: Brown.

This text covers lifespan developmental psychology in a simple and accessible way.

Sugarman, L. (1986) *Life Span Development*, London: Methuen.

This book is a classic in its field and contains useful, detailed sections on theories of adult personality development.

Part 6

Comparative Psychology

Chapter 21

Evolutionary determinants of behaviour

Roger Davies

Preview

In this chapter we shall be looking at:

- evolution of behaviour
- competition for resources
- predator–prey relationships
- symbiotic relationships.

Introduction

This chapter is concerned with explaining animal behaviour in terms of how it evolves. To some extent, we could use the word 'evolve' equally well to mean behaviour which an animal *learns* in its lifetime, as well as that which it inherits by way of being a member of a given species. In trial-and-error learning it is those behaviours that lead to successful outcomes for the animal which can be said to 'survive' as part of its day-to-day behavioural repertory. Conversely, behaviours which have led to no such success become 'extinct', that is, the animal is no longer seen to do them. This similar terminology is found in the study of animal learning, as we shall see in Chapter 24, in our discussion of classical and operant conditioning. In the views of the behaviourist B.F. Skinner, the analogy between the evolution of behaviour as a process in heredity and learning was important:

> 'Operant conditioning ... resembles a hundred million years of natural selection or a thousand years of the evolution of a culture compressed into a very short period of time.' (Skinner 1981, p. 502)

However, in this chapter we focus only on the everyday meaning of evolution, that is, the process by which animal behaviour is brought about by means of adaptation through natural selection.

The evolution of behaviour

It is useful to make clear right from the start that the question of whether learning or evolution underlie any given behaviour is meaningless. Any behaviour, however simple or complex, has both an element of inheritance and learning about it. The only point of debate is over the relative importance of the contributions made to a behaviour by *phylogeny* and *ontogeny*.

The term 'phylogeny' refers to the inheritance of species-specific behaviour patterns, e.g. the arching of a cat's back when it is threatened. 'Ontogeny' refers to behaviour which has been acquired during the lifetime of the individual and is not shared with every member of the species. For instance, some cats learn how to open doors by pulling downwards on the handle. Similarly, some blue tits learn how to tear into the caps of milk bottles left on the doorstep (see the photo below).

Whenever a behaviour is seen in all members of a species the strength of inheritance is clear. However, the occurrence of a behaviour in just one or two individuals does not necessarily mean it is '100 per cent learned'. This is because some forms of behaviour are only slight modifications of natural forms. For instance, the opening of the milk-bottle top by blue tits involves similar actions to those they undertake when stripping the bark from trees to reach insects underneath (Fisher and Hinde 1949, Hinde and Fisher 1951, Sherry and Galef 1984). The influence of inheritance in this case is still very strong, and the actions an animal may perform associated with a particular aim, such as to obtain food, are often composed of variations on a theme.

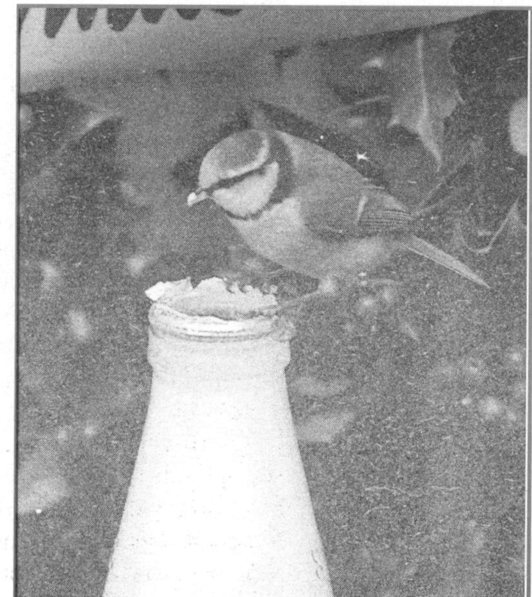
John Paling/Oxford Scientific Films

To illustrate this further, consider the converse situation – that of trying to teach an animal to earn a food reward by having it carry out behaviours it would not normally do. In the case of the blackbird, which feeds by rooting for grubs on the ground, it would not easily learn a task to obtain food while remaining perched. Similarly, birds which seek grubs and insects in tree bark while perched would not readily learn ground-based tasks.

But, however intractable this problem of defining the actions of nature versus nurture seems, in relation to a particular species it is possible to identify where the roots of a given behaviour lie, as this is basically a matter of understanding the species in question well enough, and knowing the range of behaviours seen in related species.

> 'When we see an animal performing an apparently well-adapted action, such as washing a potato before it eats it, we cannot tell whether the behaviour has a long evolutionary history or was learned for the first time a few moments before. That is, we cannot tell without further study'. (Slater and Halliday 1994, p. 3)

The important phrase here is 'we cannot tell without further study'. Although too much of the debate in the past has been rather abstract and theoretical, in the field these problems are not insurmountable.

It is now generally accepted that even in humans no behaviour ever arises for the first time in a void. As an analogy, consider that the evolution of the mammalian eye did not evolve spontaneously from parts which were not present in an earlier form.

Each and every part of the eye existed in a slightly different form, carrying out a slightly different task, in a wide range of other visual systems. Similarly, an animal's behaviour patterns do not spontaneously arise from nowhere. They sometimes comprise elements of behaviours which arise in other circumstances in which that animal is observed. For instance, a lioness may use a biting action to kill prey, to carry her cubs around, to fight off a rival or in friendly play.

Behaviour may take on a more elaborate form than occurred in its ancestors, such as the courtship rituals displayed in many bird species where closely related species may show only rudimentary forms of the ritual. The behaviour may even take on an entirely new function than the one it was previously adapted for, such as the building of bowers by male bower-birds. These are nest-like structures built solely to please the female who seems to chose her mate because of his skill in building the bower. When she has mated with him she then flies off to another nest she has built herself for the purpose of incubating the eggs (Borgia 1985).

The psychologist's interest in the study of evolution is concerned with the function of behaviour, as well as making comparisons between similar forms found in other species. At the very heart of comparative psychology is the aim of learning about human behaviour from these comparisons and contrasts between ourselves and other members of the animal kingdom. In its modern form this approach is known as 'evolutionary psychology'.

Evolution, selection and 'fitness'

Charles Darwin's theory of the process of evolution was as much shaped by his observations of the selective breeding of domesticated animals as it was by his field studies of natural selection. Species of horse, cattle, dogs and other household pets have been bred to accentuate certain of their features which humans either exploit or else find aesthetically pleasing. For instance, horses bred for racing are lighter, leaner

Charles Darwin: the first evolutionary psychologist?

Science Photo Library

and weaker than those bred for farm work. Working horses are tougher, stronger, have more stamina and are less 'temperamental' than those bred to win races. You may own a dog or cat yourself (whether a pedigree or not) which has features that are the result of hundreds of generations of selective breeding. These features may be physical (such as long ears, thick coat, large eyes or drooping jaw) or behavioural (such as running ability, a placid or aggressive temperament, or tracking, hunting or retrieving ability). These diverse breeds possess such qualities as a result of humans systematically mating females with males over many generations in order to produce the most exaggerated forms of the required characteristics. The different breeds become genetically altered from the original, and this is the basis of the 'purity' (i.e. pedigree), of each breed.

Darwin himself became an avid breeder of pigeons so as to study the process by which this type of selection is achieved. His opinion was that the means by which evolution works in bringing about changes in appearance and behaviour of species is similar to the selective breeding of animals

Pedigree dogs, like this boxer, are bred to accentuate certain characteristics

Margot Conte/Oxford Scientific Films

which he witnessed at first hand. The pressures on animals that happen in a natural environment bring about adaptations, i.e. those individuals having the best means of overcoming an extreme circumstance such as of weather, fire, climactic change, floods, predation, competition for scarce resources, and so on, are those more likely to survive.

But the survival of individuals in adverse conditions is only one part of the story. Unfortunately, this is the only part of the mechanism of evolution which seems to stick in people's minds. Indeed, the idea that evolution is a process of selecting out the weakest and least competitive animals, often referred to as 'the survival of the fittest', is usually thought to be all that Darwin had to say. This basic misunderstanding is quite common even today. In fact, the very expression 'survival of the fittest' was not even written by Darwin himself, but by a political economist called Herbert Spencer, when advocating the 'naturalness' of market-place economics. Darwin regarded physical endurance as only one quality that animals must show in their struggle to survive.

In Darwin's theory, 'fitness' is not a quality that individuals possess, such as muscular physique, physical durability or a state of good health. Bodily strength and physical fitness themselves do not guarantee the survival of individuals in an evolutionary sense, however useful these qualities may be in competition with other conspecifics (members of the same species) for scarce resources. In terms of evolution, fitness is linked with reproductive success. It is individuals who leave the most surviving offspring who have the greatest chance of evolutionary success. Darwin took for granted that differential reproductive success was at the centre of the process of evolution. In addition to differences in the relative success of individuals to reproduce is the fitness and survival prospects of their progeny (generally referred to as 'fecundity').

The tendency for organisms to maximize their reproductive output under any circumstances they face is a second aspect of evolution which Darwin emphasized. His views on this topic were formed by reading the work of Thomas Malthus (1766–1834), from a book published in 1798 entitled *An Essay on the Principle of Population*. In this work of political philosophy, Malthus was sounding a note of caution to his contemporaries concerning the provision of food for the poor and unemployed. His argument was that, because there is a natural tendency towards overpopulation (caused by the unwillingness or inability of people to refrain from having large families which they are then unable to support and maintain for themselves), the result of State and Church charities in providing for the poor was counter-productive to the health and welfare of the nation. In Malthus' words: 'Population constantly bears a regular proportion to the food that the earth is made to produce.' (Malthus 1798)

In fact, the 'regular proportion' Malthus had in mind was that while population grows exponentially, food production per unit area of land is only able to expand linearly. In other words, the more that food is harvested to feed the growing population then the faster that population will outpace this food supply until starvation results, because food production must inevitably be exceeded at some point. This argument has been a dilemma for political economists ever since Malthus (Bongaarts 1994), and it had a particular impact on Darwin. To illustrate the exponential rate of increase in a growing population, let us carry out a simple calculation which Darwin himself carried out (see Activity 1).

❖ Activity 1 ❖

At the start, a couple (let's call them Adam and Eve, though by that I do not mean they are the first or only people alive!) have just three children. When these children grow, they in turn will each have three children, as will their own (nine) children, and so on into the future. Remember, a couple having three children are only adding to the population by one surplus individual. For the purpose of this calculation, assume that the only reason for death is old age. Therefore, each child in one generation becomes a parent in the next, followed by becoming a grandparent in the next. Each generation will therefore consist of children, parents and grandparents. We shall fix the point of natural death at the age of grandparents, so in no generation will great-grandparents be alive. The task is to calculate how many direct descendants from Adam and Eve there will be alive after 12 generations. (Assuming there to be three generations per century, this time-scale will be approximately 300 years.) Carry out your own calculations on this problem before referring to Fig. 21.1.

As you can see from the calculations, the direct descendants of Adam and Eve number over a quarter of a million after just twelve generations (300 years). This simple calculation was carried out by Malthus, who also provided particular examples to show how human populations had rapidly increased during good times, i.e. where conditions had been advantageous, such as when there had been no famine, drought, war or disease to act as a natural check upon population growth. Darwin also carried out such calculations, and went so far as to show that after twenty-five generations one couple's descendants would number more than five million (Porter and Graham 1993, p. 318).

Darwin realized that such a vast increase in population would not be in the interest of any animal group whose members are sharing (or, more correctly, competing for) resources in any given habitat. To deplete resources at this rate by the demands of a swelling population would threaten the wellbeing, and quite soon the very survival, of the whole group.

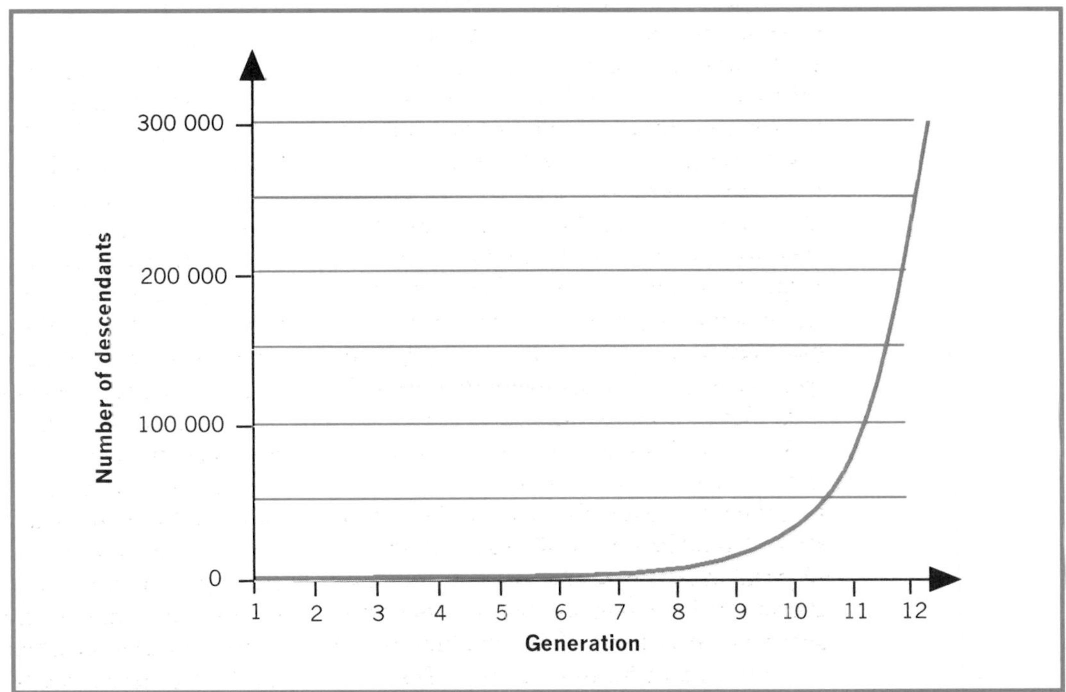

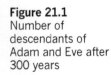

Figure 21.1 Number of descendants of Adam and Eve after 300 years

But Darwin, and Malthus before him, could see that reproductive restraint would never be practised by individuals, though this fact is commonly overlooked even today. The reason for this is that natural selection always acts on the reproductive success of *individuals*, not groups. Although the female of mammalian species, whose young are nurtured within their own body for relatively long periods before birth, may become temporarily infertile during periods of famine (or other extreme stress), it is still true that those individuals who achieve greater reproductive success than others will also have the greater evolutionary success, all things being equal. In purely evolutionary terms, reproductive restraint is not a viable strategy so long as there are others who are unprepared to follow suit. As we shall see next, we cannot really accuse people of selfishness in this regard, since the strongest urge that exists in any species has to be that of procreation.

In addition to the demands made by animal populations on resources such as food, water and shelter, natural selection also operates in predator–prey situations, disease states, and in competition for mates. We shall consider each of these in more detail later.

The evolution of selfishness

Darwin was very aware that his theory of evolution was in many respects contradicted by observable fact. The problems with the 1859 version of this theory were twofold:

- Despite the emphasis on selfishness as the basis of evolutionary success, *altruism* is commonly seen in animal societies. In other words, what *should* figure as an optimal strategy is *not* always predominant.
- There are examples of animal behaviour and morphology (body structure and physiology) which seem to confer no advantage upon the individual. The most often cited instance of this is the tail of the peacock. Peacocks have such long tails (or, more accurately, trains) that their flight and general mobility is impaired. Even more serious is the observation that predators are more able to catch them by grabbing at these long feathers. In this case, what seems to be a *sub-optimal* evolutionary strategy is seen to become *predominant.*

Evolutionary theory has now solved the riddles posed by these two problems. Regarding the first of these, Darwin himself saw no solution and it perplexed him for the rest of his days. The behaviour of social insects, where individuals behave suicidally by attacking aggressive and larger intruders to the nest or hive, seemed inexplicable in terms of *natural selection*. Individuals who pay any cost (calculated in terms of reduction in their reproductive potential) for the benefit of others should receive such a heavy penalty in evolutionary terms that such behaviour would be strongly selected against. This would ultimately lead to extinction, i.e. there would be no descendants left of individuals who acted in this way. This is shown as a simple comparison with others acting selfishly, who would pay no costs, obtain most benefits, and thereby gain more reproductive potential. In short, selfishness should outrun altruism in no time at all in the evolutionary race.

Even more problematic for Darwin's (1859) version of the theory is that there are castes in social insect societies which forego reproductive effort altogether – these individuals, such as the bees illustrated on p. 465, spending their entire lives in caring for the brood of others, usually the single queen of the colony. Such examples of ultimate self-sacrifice were neither understood or seemingly explicable until a century later, as we shall soon see.

The second problem outlined above, that of how structures such as the peacock's train could evolve, was more or less successfully tackled by Darwin in his book entitled *The Descent of Man, and Selection in Relation to Sex*. The basis of so-called *sexual selection* is discussed in detail in Chapter 22. Briefly, a feature will evolve by sexual selection if one sex is attracted to individuals of the opposite sex who possess this feature.

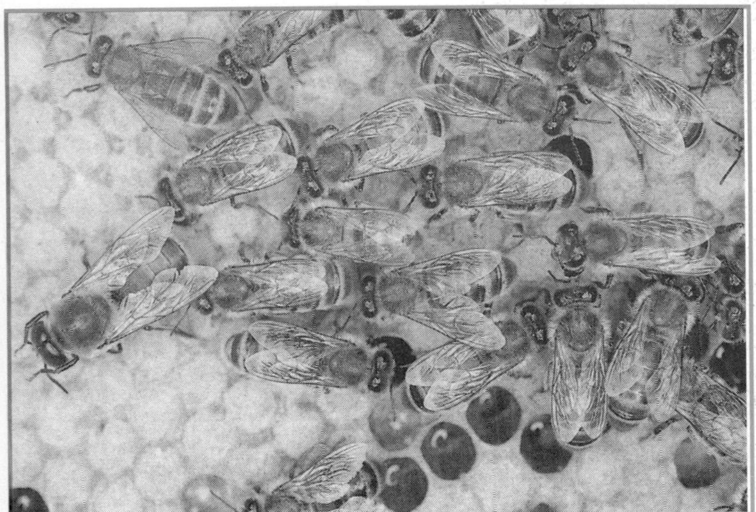

David Parker/Science Photo Library

Worker honey bees (*Apis mellifera*) overseeing the brood chambers

In this case, the feature will serve to facilitate the mating prospects of its bearer. The exact reason why such a preference exists when choosing a mate did not seem to matter very much, since it was evident to naturalists of Darwin's day that mates are selected on a non-random (or 'assortative') basis, i.e. some are more *attractive* than others.

It could simply be that some features are aesthetically more pleasing, in the same way for animals as for humans. We do not usually spend time wondering what it is that makes members of the opposite sex pleasing to us – we just 'like the look' of individuals and this is enough to attract us. Therefore, despite being a physical burden to its owner, a large and spectacular train enables the peacock to be selected by the peahen as her mate. Consequently, those males with the larger and more gorgeous trains will have greater mating success, leaving greater numbers of descendants who are also endowed with large, attractive trains. Males less well-endowed lose in this adornment display and, more importantly, are destined to lose in the evolutionary sense by leaving fewer progeny.

The tendency to choose males with such features will endure in subsequent generations as males are faced with ongoing competition for larger and grander trains. The peahens in their turn continue to accept or reject suitors on the basis of these sexually attractive features. As long as the females continue to find long-tailed males as most attractive, evolution will ensure that tail length (or any other sexually selected feature) will prevail in a *runaway process*. The choosiness of females for these males will also extend to the next generation of females, since there will be either more sons with long trains or more daughters who choose mates owning them (Andersson 1982).

If you are wondering why so much emphasis is placed here on female choice, it is mainly the case that females are the more discriminating in choosing sexual partners. The reason why this is so is discussed in Chapter 22.

Darwin's difficulties resolved

The difficulties arising from these elements of Darwin's theory of evolution were not fully resolved until many decades after his death in 1882. Part of the problem in resolving them was the then lack of knowledge about mechanisms of inheritance, i.e. genetics. Among Darwin's misconceptions was the idea that characteristics were passed between generations by a process of blending, i.e. if a dark-coated female mates with a light-coated male then their offspring will have a coat of intermediate shade. Second, and perhaps crucially, Darwin's reasoning was occurring at the wrong 'level', i.e. he believed that individuals live to reproduce. It is more accurate to consider evolution in terms of the transmission of life's units (i.e. genes) from one generation to the next. Darwin's 'insuperable problem' of the caste system of social insects (see p. 464) can be explained in this way. Among these social insects the high degree of genetic relatedness among sisters means that it is more productive (in terms of increased fitness) for them to help each other than it would be to have their own offspring.

Section summary

This section has focused on the evolution of animal behaviour through natural selection. Not all behaviour has evolved because it confers an adaptive advantage on animals. The essence of Darwin's theory of evolution is that organisms attempt to maximize their reproductive output. Sometimes organisms behave in a way that appears to be less than optimal in that features evolve that appear to compromise the survival of an individual animal. In sexual selection a feature will evolve if one sex is attracted to individuals of the opposite sex who possess that feature. Evolution is now seen not as occurring to benefit an individual animal, but to benefit its genes.

The nature of competition for resources

The exploitation and defence of resources

The acquisition and defence of some resources is common in animal societies. Whether that resource be access to food, water, shelter or a harem of mates, the privileged territory owner usually has to maintain their position through means of threat and, on occasions, actual combat. Why does such territoriality come about?

It follows from what has been said about the tendency of populations to increase to the point of saturation that the demands made on any food resource will be often be great. In many populations these demands may deplete a resource altogether, in which case natural variations in feeding preferences may save some individuals from starvation but not others. This is the classical forum for 'natural' selection, i.e. adaptation in the face of catastrophic change. The giant panda in China faces just such a crisis. Its diet is limited to a once abundant food, a particular type of bamboo shoot. Pandas must eat a large amount of bamboo daily and in order to obtain it, they require a large area over which to range. Not only is the bamboo itself less abundant these days, but there has also been large-scale deforestation of the panda's natural habitat so that the total food available has diminished drastically. There is now very little space for the giant panda to roam in search of food, and less food present when it is located. In reality, the panda has diminishing space left for it on this planet, and the extinction of this unique animal seems both inevitable and imminent.

The giant panda is in a sense engaged in a losing battle with its food supply. Many other animals face this problem for a different reason, which is the constant and severe exploitation of the resource itself. As we have already stated, there is no reason to suppose that any individual animal will refrain from breeding even when food is scarce. The ravages of starvation and drought are the ultimate cost of this incessant urge. But long before food becomes depleted there will be intense competition between individuals for what remains. In the African savannah the dry season brings about this scenario annually.

Giant panda (*Ailurpoda melanoleuca*) – losing the battle for survival?

Daniel J. Cox/Oxford Scientific Films

Chris Catton/Oxford Scientific Films

Black-winged stilts (*Himantopus himantopus*) feeding. Note the even spacing along the shoreline

But even without a large depletion of resources animals constantly engage in daily competition to obtain the best available food, whatever the state of dearth or abundance in supply.

If you have ever fed birds in your garden, or the ducks at the local pond, you will have noticed that however widely you spread the food, and however much you throw down, there is always an intense squabble for individual pieces. Even when there are other pieces nearby, two animals will often fight for their claim to one piece. However, in more natural feeding situations this greedy behaviour does not often arise. Apart from situations such as carnivores gathered around a carcass, animals tend to distribute themselves in a habitat so as to avoid the constant bickering over individual items of food (see photo above).

The distribution of animals in relation to feeding may arise because of claims to space, referred to as territoriality. But in the absence of territorial behaviour animals still tend to avoid congregating in a confined area unless that directly reflects a concentration of food, as in the example of the carcass mentioned above. For instance, wading birds along a shoreline seem evenly distributed, and as newcomers arrive they also distribute themselves evenly among the residents. This tendency of avoiding 'clumping' has the effect of spreading members of a population evenly in relation to food resources.

When there is a choice of habitats available in a given locality, one being a richer resource than the other, the initial immigrants of a species will select the better site. However, as more and more newcomers arrive, competition will escalate at this site. Such competition is avoidable if late arrivals begin to colonize the inferior site, and this is what tends to happen. The dispersion of animals will be in relation to the quality of the food resource, and we would predict a higher density where food is richest. This can be observed to happen in grazing animals such as sheep and cattle, and in bird colonies, and is referred to as an 'ideal free distribution'. Such a pattern of distribution ensures that food can be exploited, i.e. consumed, in the most effective way, and by avoiding costs incurred by bickering and jealous rivalry. In other words, when choice is available, squabbling over food does not usually happen.

But the state of balance between food supply and population numbers, in which there exists a sufficient abundance of the resource to provide for individual needs, is only ever a temporary state of equilibrium. When that equilibrium is lost, intraspecific competition may become intense. One common way that individuals compete for an uncommon or patchy resource is by *interference.* Interference means that individuals who compete for a resource will each be less successful in exploiting that resource owing to the time and energy spent in competitive bouts. Although interference is a measure of loss that each suffers as a result of competition, the stronger individual will tend to lose less of the resource than the weaker one.

In species which are strongly territorial, e.g. blue tits, the red grouse and European robin, this ongoing waste of energy caused by interference may be lessened by maintaining an exclusive territory from which all others are deterred. Though there will still be a regular cost in defending such a space, feeding resources within it can be more effectively (and selfishly) maintained. For instance, Gill and Wolf (1975) estimated that the cost of territorial defence to the golden-winged sunbird amounted to an energy expenditure three times per unit of time of the energy that could be gained by feeding for an equivalent period.

Birds with a higher protein diet, such as insects and grubs, require less overall energy cost in terms of feeding than do nectar feeders. Moreover, when territory defence is shared between male and female, e.g. as in the European robin, then the gains of territory ownership are higher still. Another situation where territorial defence may be enhanced is when the owner allows the presence of a so-called 'satellite' in the territory. The satellite is an intruder who is tolerated as long as they keep 'out of the way', so to speak. This tolerance of the other pays off in that the patrol and defence of the territory is shared, which in effect halves the cost of owning the space (Davies and Houston 1981).

Not only does territorial behaviour limit the immediate access of others, but it also prevents too severe a depletion from occurring to existing resources over the long term. Except in rare instances such as a locust swarm, where a complete ravaging of crops down to bare earth occurs before the swarm moves on to the next wipe-out, animals do not tend to have such a devastating (and sometimes irreversible) effect on their food resources.

Many animals have migratory patterns in which they return to favoured sites annually. It would not be in the interest of these animals to raze a food supply to the ground as locusts and some ant species in the South American rainforest would do. Indeed, many birds are highly beneficial to plant life by assisting in their propagation. Such *symbiotic* relationships, established over evolutionary time, will usually favour a sharing of costs and benefits between plants and the animals that feed on them, since they have a constant and longstanding interest in each other's behaviour and survival, i.e. they have evolved a form of *mutualism*.

Resources, competition and aggression

Psychologists often discuss aggression as though it exists in isolation from the situation in which the behaviour is observed. But aggression is not something which resides inside an organism – it arises out of competition between animals, either for some resource or else in establishing dominance relationships (dominance itself being associated with establishing privileges, priority rights and access to resources). Aggression is the description given to a cluster of behavioural, biological and situational events which are associated with antagonistic encounters.

Not all antagonism between animals needs to be over immediate gains. Aggression directed by two individuals towards one another may originate in previous encounters between them. Therefore, although casual observation of a dispute between individual animals may suggest that aggression arises as an unprovoked, *natural* act on their part, each animal has memories of previous encounters with others which may influence the kind of interactions and relationships they have. In the same way that memory of others underlies the tendency of animals to sustain cooperative, reciprocating relationships, animals remember previous acts of aggression (de Waal 1986). Words such as 'spite' and 'retribution' used to describe a vengeful motive in humans are just as applicable to complex, social-living animals. For instance, hyenas have been witnessed killing a member of a rival group out of spite for not being able to share the kill made by the victim's group. If there is a motive to ensure that cooperation and favours from our allies are to be encouraged, then cheats and enemies must also be discouraged, if not punished, for any disfavours against us, and with the same degree of vigour.

But usually we observe aggression in respect of conflict over immediate gains and advantage to be had. Such conflict can be 'zero-sum', i.e. the type where whatever the winner stands to gain will be equivalent to

Rodger Jackman/Oxford Scientific Films

Frogs in a breeding assembly: male frogs may fight over a female (who is occasionally drowned as a result of their ardour)

whatever the loser stands to lose. For instance, a squabble over who owns a given item of food may mean that the loser must stay hungry. This conflict over the food item could be resolved by both sharing it. The likelihood of such willingness to share rather than fight is partly determined by the relative costs and benefits to each animal, which are in some way assessed and monitored by each of them as the conflict progresses. A hungry animal may not satisfy its need by sharing the food item, and may show a willingness to fight rather than give up any portion of it. If the two combatants are related to one another then there may be more willingness to share food than if they are unrelated. In either case, if both are at risk of starvation we would predict that the squabble will escalate. But, even here, there is everything to lose by embarking upon a protracted, energy-sapping battle with another, possibly stronger, rival. If the item of food offers a smaller energy gain than the cost incurred by fighting, it may yet pay to acquiesce and look elsewhere.

But mortal combat over scarce resources is not unknown, even when that resource does not threaten the individual's survival, such as when fighting over a mate. This has been observed in the bull moose and ibex. In both cases, access to females is worthy of high stakes, the moose because dominant males will herd females into harems and inferior males are then kept away. In wild-living bighorn sheep the females roam in small groups with the rams living a fairly solitary existence. During rutting season the males may encounter one another in their attempts to mate with the females at this time, and show every intention of risking everything to win this high prize. Similarly, Alaskan moose bulls may fight to the point of death or serious injury over ownership of a harem. Evidently, in such cases, a defeated male has every chance of leaving no offspring. Although that is a price which he may be willing to pay for the sake of his own longevity, the calling of his genes produces a stronger imperative which ensures that he will incur *any* cost in order to mate. When there are fewer chances to mate there is likely to be greater tenacity, and willingness to pay higher personal costs (Enquist and Leimar 1990).

London Scientific Films/
Oxford Scientific Films

Ritualized aggression

Rituals are stereotypical behaviour patterns commonly found in conflict and courtship situations in a wide variety of species. In conflict, rituals may be entirely non-contact, such as when Thompson gazelle bucks strut alongside one another in a parallel walk, during which each one assesses the physical attributes of size, strength and willingness to fight the other. Similarly, cats will often face another and arch their backs, erect their fur ('pilo-erection') and spit at one another to signal (and exaggerate) their size and readiness to fight.

Yet other species have trials of strength in which the opponent's strength is directly assessed. For instance, rattle snakes 'wrestle' one another and each attempts to pull the other to the ground. Giraffes club one another's head and neck using their own head, much like two children in a conker tournament! Male (silverback) gorillas thump their chests with their fists so heavily that the sound is drum-like – a fearsome sound and sight for any potential rival to face.

If a mere display of strength is able to scare off an opponent before any fighting commences then it is in both combatants' interest to engage in such displays. The opportunity to 'weigh up' the opposition in some form of ritualized preliminary bouts would circumvent any mortal combat. When one opponent is much the stronger, injury and possible death involved in fighting is an unnecessary risk for both parties. Having established that an opponent is larger, stronger or has more deadly weaponry, the opportunity exists for a face-saving retreat.

Many rituals succeed as mere bluff, and this behaviour is often seen in prey species facing their predator. For instance, the flashing of 'giant eye' spots on the wings of butterflies and moths or on the bodies of a darting fish, may dupe a predator into believing they are faced with a large opponent. When these are flashed at rivals or predators they sometimes produce enough alarm or hesitation to enable escape to be achieved. This leads us on to another aspect of conflict: that between a prey and its predator.

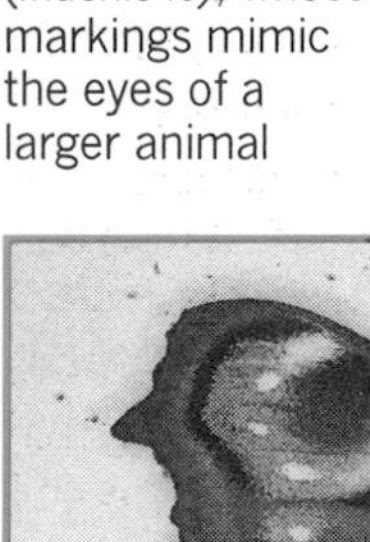

Peacock butterfly (*Inachis io*), whose markings mimic the eyes of a larger animal

David Parker/Science Photo Library

Section summary

Animals frequently compete for resources such as access to food, water, shelter and mates. Animals may be distributed according to territorial space, but at other times may exploit habitats in such a way as to avoid competitive encounters. If the balance between food supply and population numbers becomes unbalanced, intraspecific competition may become intense. The likelihood of animals fighting over a resource is partly determined by the relative costs and benefits to each animal. Some species display ritualized aggression which may function as a trial of strength with another animal, or may serve as an elaborate bluff.

Predator–prey relationships

Few species are fortunate enough to have no stress in their lives caused by predation. Even the mighty African elephant is preyed upon by the hungry human predator – hungry, that is, for the ivory of their tusks. The development of characteristics in prey species may appear odd when viewed purely in an adaptive sense. It can be more easily understood when we consider pressures exerted by the main predators. Any predation is to be avoided at all costs if you are prey, because it is the special vulnerability of the young which predators often exploit. The ability of a prey animal to outrun a predator is unhelpful if the predator can outwit the prey, for instance, by catching it off-guard while grazing, sleeping or being otherwise inattentive.

In perhaps the most filmed of predator–prey chases, that of hyenas, cheetahs or lions hunting down antelope, zebra or wildebeest on an African plain, the cull seems to support the idea of the survival of the fittest. Narrators of such films are often heard to suggest that the predators are doing the prey species a favour by eliminating the slow and the old. But the reality is that individual animals have nothing to gain from the activities of predators, and possibly everything to lose. For instance, among the slow will be the relatively defenceless young, whose flesh is more succulent and tender than that of the old, and whose *fitness*, in this loose sense of the word, is therefore never to be tested.

The pressures upon predator and prey cause them to 'coevolve', i.e. each evolves characteristics which counteract those evolving in the other. For example, prey which are hunted down following a long chase will tend to evolve (owing to the differential survival chances of fast versus slow individuals) greater running speed and more stamina which allows them to outrun the predator. The most successful individuals of the predatory species will also be those able to run the fastest, in this context. Therefore, as natural selection will favour fast-running prey, the pressure upon the predators will be to coevolve in terms of running speed. At some point in this evolutionary process predators may opt for a more subtle strategy involving ambush. But in whatever way it proceeds, the process of coevolution between the characteristics of predators and prey is usually referred to as an 'arms race' (referring to the escalation of nuclear weaponry which occurred in Europe between East and West during the years of the 'Cold War' where countries developed ever more sophisticated weapons in order to counter the military developments in countries they perceived to be potential enemies).

❖ Activity 2 ❖

Next time you watch a natural history film involving a predator–prey chase, try to work out what sort of behaviours the prey have developed to evade capture.

According to Endler (1991), predator–prey pressures may act upon the following different stages in the sequence leading up to capture:

1 encounter
2 detection
3 identification
4 approach
5 consumption.

1 Encounter

Both the predator and prey detection systems need to operate at a great distance. The sensory systems of both the predator and prey will 'coevolve', i.e. become adapted, over evolutionary time, so that each species' ability to detect the other becomes finely attuned to their features (e.g. appearance, sounds or smell). Meddis (1977) suggested that animals sleep because it is an evolved behaviour pattern which keeps animals hidden and out of reach from their predators when they are at their most vulnerable time, e.g. animals that use daylight for vision are relatively helpless by night and would evolve a sleep pattern beginning at dusk. Nocturnal animals use other senses such as smell (olfaction) to navigate their way through the night environment and they sleep when they are at their most vulnerable time – during the daylight hours. The pit viper has organs which are sensitive to infra-red light – typically that emitted as body heat – which enables them to detect small mammals such as mice in complete darkness. Some predators which would normally hunt in daylight (e.g. lions) may use darkness for cover when their prey is in short supply.

2 Detection

Detection of prey is the second stage in prey capture. Vision is most useful in bright daylight, and both predator and prey species may evolve cryptic colourations and markings to avoid being seen. Prey, such as the stick insect (see photo on p. 472), can mimic their surroundings to an extraordinary degree. To avoid detection by

A stick insect from Ecuador: active by night, stick insects remain stationary during the day in imitation of twigs

Dr Morley Read/Science Photo Library

smell, predators may approach downwind. Hearing may be especially acute towards the range of noises made by their predator or prey. Predators often approach both slowly and stealthily to minimize sounds of movement.

3 Identification

Identification is the stage where though the predator (or prey) has been seen, they may be so disguised as to be unrecognized. Some predators have markings which may disguise them as a harmless species (i.e. harmless relative to the prey species). Prey can assume the appearance of an unpalatable species (mimicry).

4 Approach

At the *approach* stage a predator may suddenly rush at the prey over a relatively short distance. Usually prey species have to remain on constant alert against the surprise attack. To help achieve this the prey may flock, herd or school together while feeding. The effect of grouping in this way is to provide for individuals the extra vigilance afforded by numerous pairs of eyes, ears and noses (see photo below).

Michael Fogden/Oxford Scientific Films

Herding together affords these prey animals (springbok) extra eyes, ears and noses – invaluable in vulnerable locations

5 Consumption

Consumption is the final stage of the contest. Predators may evolve the means of reaching edible parts, however protected or armoured the prey's body may be. For instance, gulls may drop shellfish from a height on to the rocks below in order to crack them open. For their part, prey may evade consumption by emitting toxic or irritating substances to repel the predator, even at this late stage. For instance, ants spray formic acid at intruders approaching the nest.

Mimicry: disguise and camouflage

In order to evade capture, some prey may evolve to appear indistinguishable from a poisonous or unpalatable species. This is referred to as 'Batesian mimicry', and it is a fairly common strategy among moths and their caterpillars in evading predation from birds. However, because the poisonous species is mimicked in this way, it becomes at risk from the predator's attention and attack. Such mimicked species are therefore under their own selection pressure to diverge from their original form (a process referred to as 'disruptive selection', meaning that almost *any* change in form will have greater evolutionary success than the original one). It is usually the case that the most noxious prey advertise their noxiousness to predators using bright markings and colouration. Being highly visible in this way is thus a high-risk strategy for any mimicking prey species that are actually palatable!

'Mullerian mimicry' occurs when one species which, though unpalatable, is less so than another. The mimicry here involves a convergence in appearance so as to look more like the *strongly* unpalatable one. In this case the outcome is that both species may gain by their now shared warning signals, since both are intent (in an evolutionary sense) on exploiting signals, e.g. colouration or odour, which give a clear message that they are to be avoided. Such colouration will tend to be bright and ostentatious, the objective being to provide an *honest signal* to advertise, rather than hide, their presence.

Prey may also utilize *behavioural* strategies which help to evade predation, such as crawling under rocks, climbing into trees, digging burrows in the ground or seabed, or literally taking flight, as do birds, bats, flying foxes and insects. The surface of the earth and the seabed has a multitude of hiding places which animals exploit for their own protection and for hiding their vulnerable young.

Section summary

Pressures upon predators and prey cause them to coevolve, so that each evolves characteristics which counteract the evolutionary advantage gained by the other. As evolutionary changes in predators exert pressure on their prey (and vice versa) there is a gradual escalation of the evolutionary 'arms race' between them.

In order to evade capture, some prey have evolved characteristics that render them indistinguishable from poisonous, unpalatable or otherwise dangerous (to the predator) species. In this way, the mimics can produce the same reaction from a predator as would normally be reserved for the more dangerous model.

Symbiosis: a special case of reciprocal altruism

Some species form effective alliances, in evolutionary terms, in which the wellbeing of one benefits the other. Sometimes this relationship is balanced and reciprocated so that each acts as if protectively toward the other. Such mutualism has been discussed earlier in this chapter as that occurring between conspecifics, in which it was concluded that both parties are really showing self-interest by assisting with the other's survival. When the individuals concerned are of differing species the same analysis will apply, i.e. that each has their own self-interest at heart. But interdependency of this kind between species is far from rare in nature, and when the relationship is one of mutual benefit, it is said to be symbiotic.

For example, a number of small 'cleaner' fish species exist by eating ectoparasites from the scales of other, usually much larger, fish. The cleaners may have no other source food and so permanently attend to their host, sometimes even darting in and out of their mouth in order to obtain scraps of food which have become lodged there. The host fish gains from this behaviour by having health-threatening pests removed from their skin. In the absence of cleaners, it has been shown experimentally that the hosts suffer an immediate decline in health, illustrating the value of the relationship to them. In some circumstances, queues of host fish form in the vicinity of cleaners, behaving much like cars passing through a rather busy car-wash! A similar parasite-removal 'service' occurs in the cowbird, an African species which removes insects from the skin and hair of giraffes and other grazing animals. In this case one cowbird may remain on one animal for most of the time.

Symbiotic relationships can also exist between plant and animal species. For instance, ants may become 'protective' of sapling trees by attacking caterpillars which

❖ Activity 3 ❖

Try to find out more about cleaner fish such as the cleaner wrasse. How do you think this behaviour came about in the first place? Why do you think the host fish does not eat the cleaner?

would otherwise damage the tree by gorging on its leaves. In return, the tree exudes a nutritious substance which seems to have no other function than to reward, or at least, induce, the ants into this guardianship role.

We tend to assume in these situations that such reciprocity is not truly altruistic. In other words, the helpful behaviour of one species to another is in effect similar to that between any two individuals. This implies two things:

- The behaviour is based on the self-interest of the individuals concerned – the fact that both gain from such cooperation is not *registered* by the animals – they have merely evolved with a behaviour pattern which has this mutual return effect.
- The balance of interests by the participants in any reciprocal relationship is always open to exploitation by one or other member, or even by a third party.

For example, there are other small fish (e.g. blenny) which have evolved to mimic the appearance and behaviour of cleaners so that they are allowed to approach host fish. But when within close enough range, instead of cleaning the host the mimic takes a bite directly from its flesh. The mimic is, in reality, a parasite taking every advantage of the situation created by the mutual trusting relationship between cleaners and host.

Section summary

Some species form alliances where the well-being of one species also benefits the other. Such reciprocity is not truly altruistic however, as each animal is acting in their own self-interest. These arrangements are also open to exploitation by 'mimics' who take advantage of the mutual trusting relationship between the symbiotic partners.

Chapter summary

- Animals evolve characteristics that confer survival advantages on them and which maximize their reproductive output. Evolution by natural selection and by sexual selection enables animals to adapt successfully to their environment and to increase the numbers of their genes present in the next generation.
- Animals frequently compete for resources. This may take the form of territorial defence or aggressive encounters between conspecifics. When the balance between food supply and population numbers becomes unbalanced, intra-specific competition may become intense. Each animal constantly assesses the costs and benefits of aggression and may choose not to fight or to withdraw from an aggressive encounter if the costs outweigh the benefits.
- Predators and their prey constantly coevolve as each reacts to the evolutionary pressure exerted by changes in the other. Some animals escape being eaten by mimicking the characteristics of a dangerous or unappetizing model so that predators avoid them.
- Some species form symbiotic alliances where animals mutually benefit from the arrangement. The mutual arrangements can be exploited by mimics who take advantage of the established relationship between the symbiotic partners.

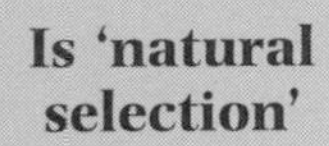

In Focus

◆

Is 'natural selection' still at work?

Perhaps it is no accident that the word 'generation' could also be read as 'gene-ration'. We, the individual animals who make up the natural world, are merely the carriers of genes, even though in different species we package them in relatively unique ways (Dawkins 1976, 1982). In each living organism the genetic material comes to it having survived a tortuous voyage down aeons of time by use of temporary time-travelling vehicles, of which we are merely the latest designs. Many multitudes of genes and gene combinations have fallen by the wayside on this incredible journey through time. On a global scale, perhaps more of these carriers are failing by way of extinction in recent times than ever before (Wilson 1992). There have been disasters on a epic scale in earlier times, such as the decline and fall of the dinosaur empire and the massive extinctions evident in the Burgess Shale, a fossil bed located in the Canadian Rockies (Gould 1989).

But that does not mean that natural selection has stopped functioning. Humans have created new rules for selection involving themselves and most other organisms on the planet today, with the new conditions including overpopulation, environmental pollutants, deforestation, factory-style agricultural production, pesticides, antibiotics, greenhouse gases, nuclear fallout, over-fishing, and a host of other threats to nature's balance. Natural selection will act upon genotypes with as much vigour as it ever did, and take directions which are as unpredictable as ever in the game of evolutionary chance (Gould 1994).

The conditions of life may be much harsher in the future, but it is still likely that genes will survive in carriers in some form or other. They may not continue to build life forms of the kind we are used to seeing today, but that has always been the way of evolution. In terms of evolutionary time humans have been an extremely recent addition to this planet, and we have still not had as much impact on the world as did the dinosaurs. However mightily they once ruled the planet, they are merely fossils today. That fate doubtlessly awaits us too. We might hope to last some of the hundreds of millions of years which they enjoyed on this planet. If recent history is anything to go by, the odds are stacked against our achieving anything like that.

Just to mention one reason for this gloomy prediction, the world now holds a human population of around five and half billion people. If the current growth rate of 1.7 per cent per year continues for another 400 years, the population would swell to five and a half *trillion* people. This figure would permit each person to occupy an area on this planet just a little larger than an average living room of a modern house (Cohen 1995).

E.R. Degginger/Oxford Scientific Films

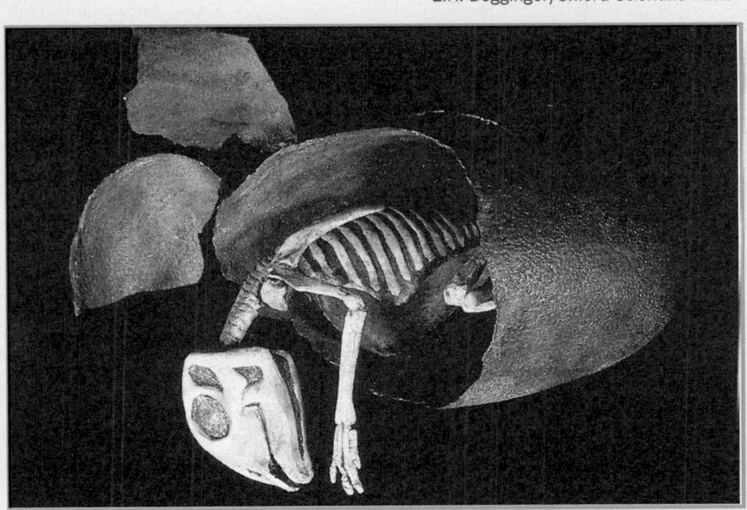

Essay questions

1 Critically consider evolutionary explanations of the behaviour of non-human animals. *(24 marks)*

2 (a) Describe two ways in which animals compete for resources. *(12 marks)*

(b) Assess the implications of each of these. *(12 marks)*

3 Discuss ways in which predator–prey relationships influence the evolution of behaviour patterns. *(24 marks)*

Further reading

Grier, J.W. and Burk, T. (1992) *Biology of Animal Behaviour* (2nd edn), St. Louis: Mosby.

An extremely comprehensive academic text on all aspects of animal behaviour.

Krebs, J.R. and Davies, N.B. (1993) *An Introduction to Behavioural Ecology* (3rd edn), Oxford: Blackwell.

An accessible and well-detailed account of the issues in this chapter.

Chapter 22

Reproductive strategies

John Cartwright

Preview

In this chapter we shall be looking at:

- the nature of sexual reproduction
- consequences of sexual reproduction with regard to the investment of parents in mating and rearing of offspring
- patterns of mating behaviour: systems and strategies
- models and theories of mating
- parent–offspring conflict
- sexual selection, including intra-sexual and inter-sexual
- mate choice in animal (including human) species.

Introduction

Before the mid-1970s, sexual reproduction was usually seen as a way of perpetuating the species through the cooperative endeavour of two individuals. Since then our understanding has been transformed by the rise of socio-biology, behavioural ecology and the 'selfish gene' approach to animal behaviour and comparative psychology (Dawkins 1976). By shifting the focus of attention from the species to the individual, new insights have been gained and we now realize that sex is as much about conflict as cooperation. In this chapter we examine the basic features of sexual reproduction and show how the different strategies employed by individuals of animal species to maximize their reproductive success give rise to a variety of mating systems. The fact that sexual partners make some choice in whom they will mate with is also shown to have profound consequences for the behaviour and physical characteristics of animals. This is the theory of sexual selection first presented by Darwin in 1871 and which has received remarkable experimental confirmation in recent years. It may be possible to comprehend a good deal of human mating behaviour from this evolutionary perspective and there is now a flourishing school of research dedicated to this end.

The nature of sexual reproduction

Why sex?

At first glance, the answer to this question would seem obvious: sexual reproduction is the mechanism by which organisms reproduce. This is true for many species but some animals, such as aphids and Daphnia, are capable of reproducing asexually. The females produce copies of themselves by *parthenogenesis* (reproduction by females without male fertilization) – a very efficient mechanism for making perfect multiple copies in a short time. So the question now becomes: 'why do some reproduce sexually when there is a less troublesome alternative?' The more we think about the 'costs' of sexual reproduction, the less attractive it seems. Sexual reproduction only produces individuals 'half like' yourself, compared to the perfect copies of parthenogenesis. Sex is costly in terms of time, energy and resources used in attracting and defending a mate. Courtship displays and copulation itself are often highly conspicuous and leave the organisms vulnerable to predation.

From a male perspective there is the ever-present danger of cuckoldry (whereby the male assists in raising offspring that are not genetically his own) and in some mating systems, dominant males (usually) monopolize the receptive females and some males never breed at all.

From a female perspective the production of sons is costly since daughters could in principle reproduce parthenogenetically to produce grandchildren whereas males must find a female. Having a population composed of males and females does seem to cut down the rate at which descendants of a mother could multiply.

So if sex is a messy, risky and costly activity, why is it so common? Until relatively recently, the trump card of sex was thought to be the fact that genetic variability was a great asset during times of environmental change. It was thought that sex served the main purpose of stirring up the genes to produce highly variable offspring, so that when the environment changed at least some progeny survived. Investors in stocks and shares know that it is often more prudent to buy shares in a range of companies rather than trust to the fortunes of one. Or to rephrase the old adage, rather than putting all one's eggs in one basket, it is better to put different eggs in different baskets.

This argument still carries some weight, but recent thinking tends to suggest there are reasons other than the risk of physical environmental change for the maintenance of sexual reproduction. A new answer comes from looking at the biological environment and hence the biotic interactions that any organism has to contend with. A typical animal has to be able to run away from predators, move fast enough to catch prey, as well as cope with the constant invasion of parasites.

This line of reasoning is best summed up by the concept of a 'genetic arms race'. To enable the offspring of any animal to outwit their predators and/or prey, it pays to stir, mix and share genes in the hope that a winning combination of advantageous features such as speed, cunning and camouflage emerges. Similarly, an animal's immune system needs to keep one step ahead of parasites who in turn will be evolving just as fast to overcome its defences. Even if the animal feeds on plants, they will be designing ever more unpleasant prickles, stings and chemical weapons to keep it at bay. The animal, in response, may evolve a tougher skin or better enzymes in a better liver to detoxify such substances.

If, on the other hand, the animal feeds on a dead organism, then its food can no longer escape; if the animal chances upon an environment made suddenly available, like a small pond thawing out in spring, there are few competitors. In both cases the best strategy would be to reproduce as quickly as possibly to fill the available niche and sexual reproduction will be an irrelevance.

It is now widely believed that sexual reproduction, and hence the existence of different sexes, has two main functions. One function is the production of genetic diversity; this is partly to cope with spatial and temporal environmental variation but mainly to cope with inter-species competition. Sexually reproducing animals must change quickly to maintain their precarious hold on life. A second function is to enable DNA damage to be repaired. During meiosis, when germ cells divide to produce gametes to carry the genome into the next generation, at the stage when both chromosomes are aligned (see Fig. 22.1a), an enzyme repairs damage to one chromosome using information from its pair. In other words, the spare chromosome in diploid cells acts as a sort of template to enable damage and errors to be corrected. This reduces the number of deleterious mutations that would otherwise appear in the gametes. In a similar way, a 'backup file' on a floppy disc is made of important files on a hard disc.

Males and females

Males and females both provide gametes that will fuse to produce a viable zygote which, with luck and nurture, will grow to adulthood. In a very few cases, such as the protist Paramecium (a microscopic freshwater organism), the gametes are of equal size when they fuse – a condition known as isogamy (literally same gametes). The norm, however, is for one sex to produce a large gamete richly endowed with nutrients and the other to produce a much smaller gamete. In some cases the difference is extreme. The egg of an ostrich (the female gamete) fills the palm of one hand, whereas you would need a microscope to see the male gamete or sperm that fertilized it. This polarization is understandable when we realize that when sexual reproduction began millennia ago, the fusion of gametes was outside the body of the animal, such as is still practised by the bony fish (the teleosts). To increase the probability of a gamete surviving to produce a viable animal that reaches sexual maturity, there are only two basic strategies: invest or compete. The investor endows the gamete with initial biomass to enable it to get a head start over its competitors or survive in a harsh environment. This is a costly process, so the strategy of this sex is to produce a few large gametes. The other strategy is to produce lots of small, highly mobile gametes in the hope that a few reach the larger gametes of the opposite sex before others arrive. The investors produce eggs and are called females, the competitors produce sperm and are called males. This condition is called anisogamy and has profound consequences for animal behaviour.

Figure 22.1a shows the process of spermatogenesis. A diploid cell divides by meiosis to produce four haploid gametes which become incorporated into four spermatozoa.

Figure 22.1b shows the fusion of haploid gametes (sperm and ovum) to produce a zygote which is diploid.

❖ Activity 1 ❖

- Compile a table to show the costs and benefits of sexual reproduction.
- Try to explain why sexual reproduction is most common in the tropics where there is little seasonal change but high biodiversity.
- Aphids such as greenfly can reproduce sexually and asexually. In early summer when the sap is rising on rose bushes they choose to reproduce asexually. Speculate why this is the case.

Section summary

Sexual reproduction carries costs as well as benefits and there are various theories as to why sexual reproduction should exist at all. Current thinking suggests that the prime reason for the maintenance of sexual reproduction in animal species is the enormous genetic diversity produced during the production and fusion of gametes.
The fact that gametes are unequal in size (anisogamy) has profound consequences.

Figure 22.1a
Meiosis and spermatogenesis

This simplified picture shows the fate of one pair of chromosomes from the reproductive cells of a male animal.

A and B represent dominant genes for eye colour and fur colour respectively; a and b represent recessive genes for eye colour and fur colour.

Diploid cell
One pair of chromosomes

Chromosome with two genes
A = black eyes
a = pink eyes
B = brown fur
b = white fur

Duplication

Crossing over

Haploid gametes
One copy of each chromosome

Pink eyes
White fur

Pink eyes
Brown fur

Black eyes
White fur

Black eyes
Brown fur

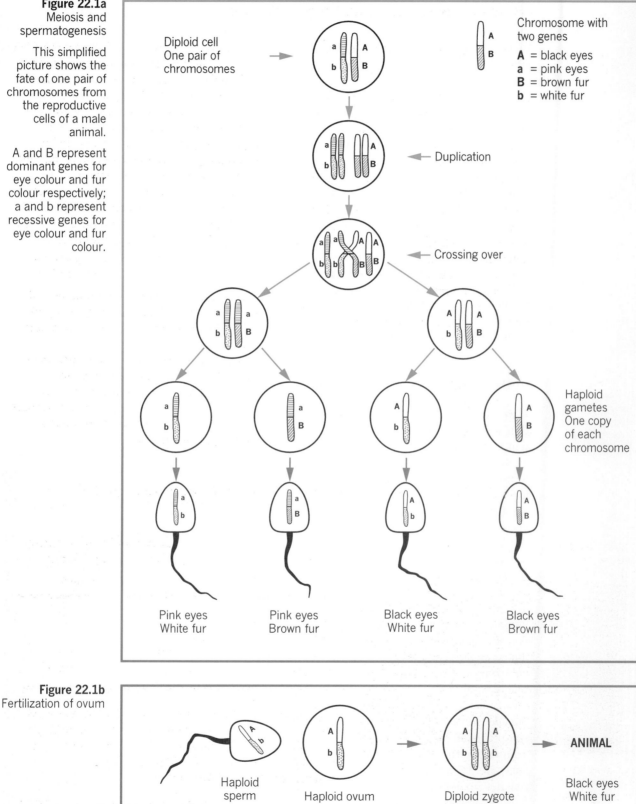

Figure 22.1b
Fertilization of ovum

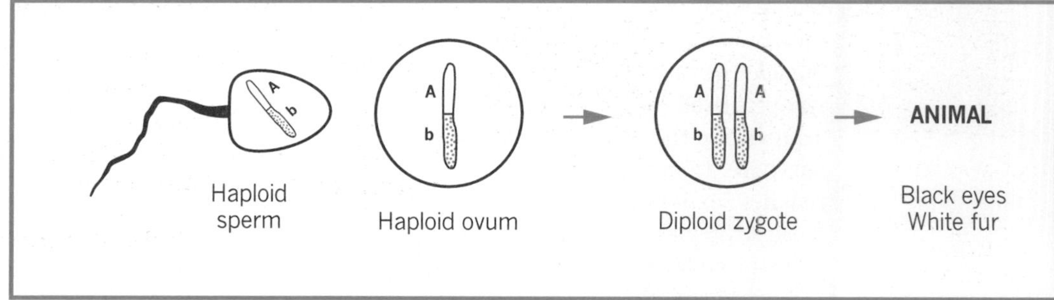

Consequences of sexual reproduction

Anisogamy and reproductive effort

It was Robert Trivers (1985) who gave a cogent expression of the implications of anisogamy as far as the reproductive interests of the two sexes are concerned. Trivers argued that since the parental investment of the female is much greater than that of the male, then the optimum number of offspring for each sex is different. This is particularly the case involving long, energy-demanding pregnancies followed by obligatory maternal care. A female elephant seal, for example, may weigh 650 kg and give birth to a pup weighing 50 kg. In the first five weeks of feeding on its mother's milk, the pup causes its mother to lose as much as 200 kg in weight. The male, in contrast, ostensibly only contributes a few hours' production of sperm cells (gametes) to ensure fertilization. The female, unlike the male, has apparently little to gain from multiple matings. Table 22.1 compares four species in this respect.

The data in Table 22.1 for elephant seals, red deer and humans obviously imply that each male had access to more than one female (polygyny). The figures for Kittiwake gulls, however, show that despite the fact that the gamete of the female is much larger, polygyny does not always follow. Kittiwake gulls are monogamous (one male for one female) and a pair will bond for many seasons. To tackle this theoretically, we need to extend the concept of parental investment to cover total investment in the raising of young. We may say that:

Total reproductive effort = Mating effort + Parental effort

Mating effort covers the production of gametes and the finding and securing of mates. Parental effort covers the care and protection of offspring.

It is due to the fact that both parents of young Kittiwake gulls expend nearly identical levels of reproductive effort on raising chicks that the reproductive success of each sex (as measured by number of offspring) is so similar.

Table 22.1 Maximum number of offspring for four different species

Species	Maximum number of offspring produced during lifetime	
	Male	*Female*
Elephant Seal	100	8
Red Deer	24	14
*Man	888	69
Kittiwake Gull	26	28

*The world record for the number of children produced by any one human male stands at about 888, fathered by Moulay Ismail, an Emperor of Morocco. The record for one female stands at 69 children from 27 pregnancies of a woman in Russia.

Source: Krebs and Davies 1987

Doug Allan/Oxford Scientific Films

Male southern elephant seal courting female (*Mirounga angustirostris*)

In practice it has proved extremely difficult to measure with any precision the total reproductive effort of an individual. From a 'selfish gene' perspective the entire energy expended in the life history of an individual could be interpreted as reproductive effort, since bodies are ways to enable genes to make copies of themselves. In addition, although males of many species apparently leave parental care to the female, their mating effort prior to copulation is often considerable. In the case of the elephant seals considered earlier, males must secure a territory, defend it against rivals and fight them in order to secure a position of dominance in the group. Even when he has acquired a harem, he must be on guard against sneak copulations of subordinate males.

Generally, for most mammals, males put most of their reproductive effort into mating and females most into parental care. Additionally, the total reproductive effort per offspring is usually lower for males, as shown in Fig. 22.2. We must remember though that in these cases a successful male will sire more offspring than the average female and so his total reproductive effort in a breeding season may be similar.

Figure 22.2 Reproductive efforts of successful males and females for typical mammalian species

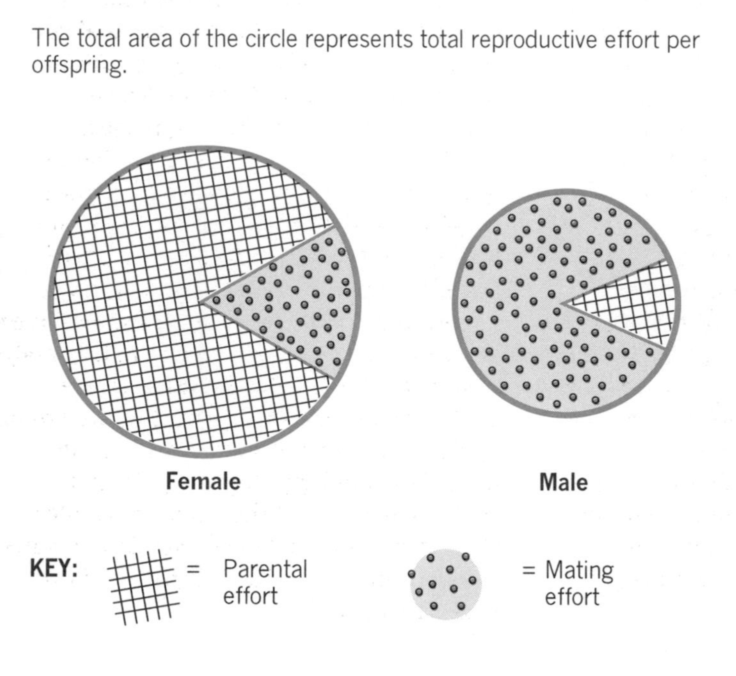

We still need to explain why a female invests more total reproductive effort per offspring and in most cases gives more parental care than a male. Although a female produces a large, expensive egg and in the case of viviparous (live birth) animals carries the foetus, she could still abandon her young and leave the male to expend the extra effort to raise them. Various suggestions have been put forward to explain why this is not usually the case. One is that the cost of desertion is far greater for the female than the male. If a female deserts and the gamete, or egg, or infant fails, it costs her much more in biological terms to produce another than it does a male to produce another spermatozoon. Moreover, it takes females longer to replenish eggs than it does a male to produce sperm. A deserting female runs the risk of not finding another mate before the end of the breeding season. The effect of greater initial investment commits her to ever more investment. This 'cruel bind' serves to drive females to give more parental care. If fertilization is internal, as in birds and mammals, it is obviously easier for the male to desert after copulation, before the egg is laid or the infant born. In fish species (the teleosts), by contrast, where fertilization is frequently external, both parents are free to desert and, as expected, female desertion and male care is more common.

Consequences of differential investment

The implications of unequal investment are that generally it is physically possible for males of most mammalian species to produce more offspring than females. Hence there is a tension between the inclinations of males and females. The male is less strongly committed to parental investment and so will seek ways to father as many offspring as possible, leaving the care to the female. The female, on the other hand, is biologically committed to more investment for each offspring, is limited in the total number that can safely be raised and consequently will be more concerned with the quality of offspring than quantity.

From this reasoning we would predict differences in the mating tendencies of both sexes. We would expect males to be less discriminating in their choice of partner and to have a sexual response that is easily aroused. Males should compete with other males for the limited resource (females). Females, on the other hand, should be more coy and fussy in their choice of mate; they may demand elaborate courtship and should on the whole be less competitive amongst themselves. In this way we can use the idea of the different pattern of investment between males and females to explain the phenomenon of sexual dimorphism (the different shapes and sizes of the two sexes). Where males compete with other males, for example, size carries an advantage and males will tend to be larger than females.

These predictions hold reasonably well for a very wide range of mammalian species including the elephant seals and red deer noted earlier in Table 22.1. They also work for a number of species of lizards.

Reversed sex role species

The concept of reproductive effort can be advanced to cover not only gamete production, gestation and the care and nurturing of young, but also the provision of nuptial gifts and other resources. The theory can then be applied when sex roles are reversed. In these cases the males provide a high level of investment either before or after copulation. In the case of the Mormon cricket and the damselfly (*Coenagrion puella*) the male transfers a protein-rich spermatophore with his sperm during copulation. The female eats this after the transfer of sperm. In areas where food is scarce this nutritious, nuptial gift represents a highly energetic investment. Consequently, as predicted by the analysis earlier, males now become discriminating, and the larger aggressive females fight for access to desirable gift-bearing males.

In a number of bird species such as the emu, lily trotting jacanas and the common British moorhen (*Gallinula choloropu*), although the female, by definition, lays the eggs, after this she invests little or nothing in the way of parental care. Males are left to incubate the eggs and guard the nest – activities which are energetically expensive. Again, consistent with our expectations, females are active in courtship and fight with each other for access to high quality males. In the case of the jacana bird, the female is up to 75 per cent heavier and typically stronger than the average male.

In summary, the sex contributing more in terms of parental investment has the greatest potential for loss if it mates with an inferior partner. Consequently, this sex will adopt a highly discriminating sexual strategy: it may demand an elaborate courtship or some other display of worth from the sex that invests less. The low-investing sex will compete for access to the high investor. The commonest situation is where males invest least and females most.

Exceptions and alternative formulations

The concept of parental investment has made great headway into understanding animal behaviour but is not without its problems. There are puzzling anomalies, such as some pipefish (the *Syngnathidae*), where females compete for males yet females produce the largest gametes. Moreover, some researchers have found 'parental investment' difficult to measure empirically. Recently, Clutton-Brock and Vincent (1991) have suggested that the potential reproductive rate may be a key factor. In the case of the pipefish mentioned above, the males carry the young in a body cavity which is limited in size. Females could produce more offspring but are limited by this 'reproductive bottleneck' in the male. We could say that the potential reproductive rate of the female is greater than that of the male and therefore females compete for males. The full power of this idea remains to be seen.

Section summary

The biological goal of each individual is to maximize his or her reproductive success. The different investments made by males and females in mating and parenting, coupled with the fact that males and females may have different reproductive potentials, means that the interests of the two sexes are rarely the same. This leads to different patterns of behaviour for the two sexes.

Patterns of mating behaviour: systems or strategies?

Given that sexual reproduction throughout the animal kingdom is fundamentally and ultimately the same – the fusion of sperm with an egg – it seems even more puzzling that there should be so many social ways of organizing the same event. Amongst elephant seals, for example, one large dominant male enjoys the sexual favours of a 'harem' of up to 50 smaller females. At the other extreme, albatrosses and swans bond with one partner for life.

There are two basic approaches to making sense of this bizarre variety of mating tendencies. One, the traditional systems approach, is to classify species according to the mating system they illustrate; the other is to concentrate on the sexual strategy employed by individuals in a population. We will examine the systems approach first.

Classification of mating systems

Animal species have traditionally been classified into three basic groups that exhibit monogamy, polygamy or promiscuity. In monogamy (Greek '*gamos*' means marriage), a pair bond is formed between one male and one female. Small passerine (i.e. perching) birds such as sparrows and warblers display annual monogamy whereby the pair bond is renewed each year with a different individual. Swans, albatrosses and eagles exemplify perennial monogamy in that the bond is retained for life.

Within polygamy, a pair bond is formed between one member of one sex and several members of the other. This category may be sub-divided into polygyny in which one male is bonded with several females or polyandry where one female is bonded with several males. Pied flycatchers exhibit serial polygyny in that the males bond with several females during the breeding season but only one at a time. Elephant seals display simultaneous polygyny in that a single male is bonded to a harem of many females simultaneously during the breeding season.

Polyandry is a rarer form of mating but is illustrated by the bird species known as the lily trotting jacana (*Jacana spinosa*) or in some circumstances by the common hedge sparrow or dunnock (*Prunella modularis*).

Finally, promiscuity is characterized by the absence of a pair bond. Males and females meet briefly only to copulate. The male then usually plays no role in caring for offspring which is done exclusively by the female or in many fish species by neither parent. Chimpanzees display highly promiscuous mating behaviour where a female will mate repeatedly with most males in a group.

Problems with the systems approach

There are three main problems with the mating systems approach:

- The classification is usually from the perspective of one sex only. Thus when we say that elephant seals exhibit polygyny we really mean the males have access to many females (poly – gyny) but the females, from their perspective, are largely monogamous i.e. they only mate with one male (unless they succumb to sneak copulations from subordinate males).

- More significantly, the pigeon-holing of whole species into a particular mating system fails to do justice to the fact that some individuals behave in ways outside the normal system of the species. In a study on the common hedgesparrow or dunnock, for example, Davies (1992) observed monogamy, polygyny and polyandry all in the same species.
- The third and final problem is perhaps most important: to suggest that whole species display a particular system is reasoning from the wrong end. In short, it is individuals that behave, not the whole species; the unit of natural selection is the individual, not the group, and individuals behave in a way not to maximize the success of the group but of themselves.

From systems to strategies

Since the 1970s, a more individualistic approach has breathed new life into research concerning mating behaviour. It is now generally agreed that rather than seeing species displaying systems, we should view individuals as employing strategies to maximize their own success, which, if displayed by many members of a species could, as a convenience, be called a system.

Figure 22.3 Mating behaviour as an outcome determined by a context of several factors

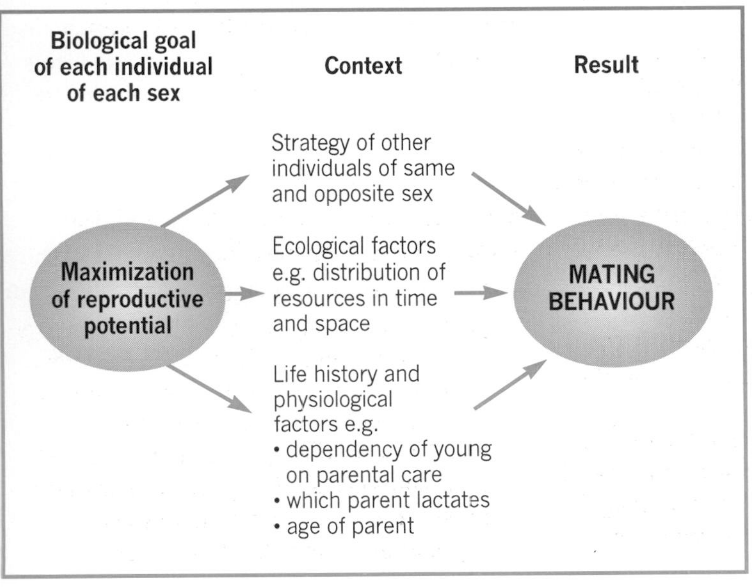

The male:female ratio

It is a tempting idea to think that the ratio of males to females should govern how many mates are acquired by an individual. Perhaps, it is argued, monogamy is found when there are equal numbers of males and females that reach sexual maturity (such as is almost the case with humans), and polygamy when there are more males than females (polyandry) or more females than males (polygyny). Yet even a brief inspection of the data does not support this and for most animals the ratio of males to females remains remarkably close to 1:1, irrespective of the mating system found. It all seems very wasteful and particularly hard on males since polygyny is more common than polyandry. The answer to this apparent paradox was supplied by the geneticist and statistician Fisher in 1930. Fisher argued that if the ratio of sexes should, for some reason, drift from 1:1, those parents who produce offspring of the sex in short supply will fare better in terms of numbers of future grandchildren. The logic is inescapable: if there are more females it pays to produce males, if there are more males then it pays to produce females. Natural selection acts as a strong stabilizing force tending to drive the sex ratio back to 1:1 from any deviations. Whatever the cause of polygamy, it is not a product of an uneven balance in the sexes.

A general model for mating behaviour

If the primary sex ratio is not responsible for any given mating system or pattern of behaviour, then what is? There is no simple answer but probably the best approach to the problem is to view the goal of reproductive success as influenced by a set of key factors. Fig. 22.3 illustrates this approach.

The context of key factors is discussed in the following section.

Strategies of others

Any strategy that best serves the interest of an individual must take account of the behaviour of other individuals in the group. If you are on a picnic with four others, a simple strategy that says 'share your sandwiches whatever others do' would not be in your best interest if no one else shared. On the other hand, if everyone shared, the loss to you of four-fifths of your packed lunch may be more than made up (in variety or even quantity) by the acquisition of four lots of one-fifth of the lunchbox of others.

This simple example serves to illustrate that the individual is not simply pitched in battle against an indifferent environment, but is part of a larger group engaged in a general struggle for resources. This idea has been developed by the eminent mathematical biologist John Maynard-Smith (1976) and is now part of a flourishing school of research in biology and comparative psychology called game theory. Much of the detail of this approach is outside the scope of this chapter but one illustration will be given here.

Females of some species have evolved strategies and mechanisms to elicit more care from a male that would perhaps be tempted otherwise to employ the strategy of 'desert and seek other females'. It is quite common for seabirds such as gulls that breed in dense colonies to show reproductive synchrony whereby females become available for breeding all at the same time. Should a male wander off to find another female, his chances of finding one not already mated are now more remote. In addition, he risks exposing his partner to the advances of other amorously inclined males. His best strategy, given this female counter attack, is probably to stay put and guard his partner.

Life history factors (e.g. condition of young)

If the newly arrived offspring are vulnerable in terms of food requirements or attacks from predators, it may be that successful breeding requires attention and care from both parents. It is no use being a polygamous male, fathering lots of offspring and deserting your females, only to see your offspring perish due to lack of care. This is genetic death as surely as not breeding at all. The fact that monogamy is the predominant mating system in birds is probably due to the vulnerability of the young and the implication that both parents leave more offspring if they cooperate in raising a brood. This reasoning seems to hold good for many sea and shorebirds where males and females share incubation and chickfeeding. The experimental removal of one partner often leads to complete breeding failure.

Most mammals, however, have polygynous mating systems. For grazing animals the male can contribute little in the way of food resources and lactation by the mother provides the crucial calorie input in the first few months of life. Here again the male's reproductive interests are best served by polygynous mating.

Ecological conditions

Among mammalian species where females invest most per offspring, female reproductive success is limited by nutritional constraints. There is now a considerable body of evidence that it is the location of environmental resources (e.g. food, safe areas) that determines the pattern of dispersion and grouping of females and hence the behaviour of males. Some forms of polygyny are termed resource-based in that males control an essential resource which is attractive to the females. In the case of the orange-rumped honeyguide bird (*Indicator xanthonutus*) of Nepal, males establish territories near to the nests of the honeybees that provide the wax which is an essential component of the diet of these birds. Males mate with females that visit their sites.

Lack (1968) used similar ideas to show that monogamy was the rule for every insectivorous sub-family of passerine birds, whereas about 25 per cent of seed-eating and fruit-eating species of passerines were

In Focus

The African elephant

The importance of food localization is illustrated by the African elephant, where female grouping patterns are determined by the patchy distribution of food. Females remain in a localized area of high-quality food supplies and form cooperative, kin-based alliances (it makes good genetic sense to share food with your kin). These kin groups form coalitions and compete with non-related groups of females. Given the 21-month gestation period of the foetus and the long period of calf dependence, adult females only come into oestrus (i.e. sexual receptivity) once every four years. Since a female group may consist of only five related individuals, it would not be a particularly rewarding strategy for a male to live permanently with one group and control a harem. A dominant male would do better by wandering from group to group to find females in oestrus. This is in fact what happens. During 'musth' – the period when male elephants become sexually active – males compete aggressively with other males for access to these female groups. In fights, size carries an advantage and so the male elephant is up to twice the size of the female and by 50 years of age the tusks of the male can be seven times the weight of those of females.

Martyn Colbeck/Oxford Scientific Films

Young 'musth' male African elephant testing female (*Loxodonta africana*)

polygynous. The logic here is that since insects are relatively harder to find and catch and less localized in space than seeds and fruit, insectivorous males are forced to cooperate and remain faithful, whereas desertion by philandering frugivorous (fruit-eating) males leaves females still able to cope in raising a brood alone. Some species seem to be flexible in this respect, and normally monogamous birds may become polygynous in seasons when the environment is prolific in the provision of resources. There is evidence to suggest that even insectivorous male birds will leave the female to raise the brood alone and then mate with another female if the abundance of food in the environment results in a good chance of both broods surviving.

Polyandrous mating can also be partly understood in terms of resource distribution. In the case of some Arctic waders such as the sanderling (*Calidris alba*), the female lays a clutch of eggs which is incubated by the male; she then lays another clutch which she incubates herself. This is a rewarding strategy due to the fact that in the Arctic the breeding season is short but, due to the good supply of insects, very productive. Two clutches are also a good insurance against predation which is heavy. This leads to polyandry if the female chooses to have the second or third clutch of eggs fertilized by another male. This is found in the spotted sandpiper (*Actitis macularia*) where the high productivity on breeding grounds enables the female to lay up to twenty eggs in five clutches. The limiting factor here is not the expense of producing eggs but finding males to incubate them.

Mating as a multifactoral and conditional response

The evidence suggests that ecological conditions play a major role in shaping the mating strategy of each sex. In turn, the strategy of one sex is dependent on the proximity and behaviour of others of the same and opposite sex. The strategy of either sex is also influenced by life history factors such as lactation and gestation.

Their long evolutionary ancestry has probably endowed animals with a basic programme characteristic of the species but with a series of options to fine tune behaviour to prevailing conditions.

We have seen how mating can be interpreted as a mixture of conflict and cooperation between the sexes. These same forces are at work when we examine the relationships between parents and their progeny.

Section summary

Until recently, animal species were assigned to a set of mating systems. Current research suggests that it is more rewarding to look at mating from the point of view of the genetic self-interest of individuals that may possess a flexible repertoire of strategies to suit prevailing conditions. The mating behaviour any individual displays is a strategy that has evolved towards that which leaves the most offspring, under the constraints and conditions found. More studies on animals with variable mating systems will no doubt help deliver an understanding of the conditions that lead to one outcome rather than another.

❖ Activity 2 ❖

Many female mammals announce oestrus by a variety of means. Chimpanzees develop a pink swelling, cows exude odours irresistible to the bulls, and so on. Yet in humans, female ovulation is largely concealed. A slight increase in temperature, undetectable without thermometers, is the only outward sign. Although some other primates, such as the orang utang, likewise conceal ovulation, it is clearly a phenomenon in need of an explanation.

Speculate as to whether concealed ovulation has some adaptive function. Most theories start with the idea that it represents a female strategy to extract male care: if males are unsure as to the period of peak fertility of the female then they are more likely to remain with her for longer periods of time.

Parent–offspring conflict

Infanticide

The easiest conflict to comprehend is perhaps that found in animals where the male practises female defence polygyny. In these systems the male (or a group of males) defends a larger group of females as a permanent harem. Such males, enjoying unrestricted access to a large number of females, have secured a much coveted prize in the attainment of their own reproductive interests and consequently there is much competition for their position. This pattern of mating is observed in lions and langur monkeys and in both cases one of the first acts of males who have taken over the harem is to kill any young they find present. This brings the females back into oestrus and so able to bear the offspring of the victorious males. Such infanticide, repugnant as it may seem to humans, is a biologically successful strategy on the part of the adult male.

In Focus

Lions and infanticide

Studies of lions in the Serengeti region of Tanzania have revealed a remarkable pattern of conflict behaviour but one which is quite consistent with evolutionary explanations (Halliday 1980).

Unlike all other members of the cat family, lions hunt in groups. They lack the speed of cheetahs or the lightning agility of leopards, so instead rely upon cooperative hunting to ambush and outwit large animals such as zebra and wildebeest. A pride of lions usually consists of about ten females and two or three males. The females have been together since birth and are usually sisters or cousins. The adult males are outsiders expelled from their own pride before they reached sexual maturity and are probably half brothers but unrelated to the females. Such males have successfully ousted the previous males controlling the group of females. One of the first acts of the victorious males is to kill all the cubs found in the pride. From a species point of view this brutal act seems wasteful and purposeless, but from the point of view of the male lions it makes sound genetic sense. The cubs in the pride are not only unrelated to the males (and to guard them would be a waste of the males' resources), but additionally the suckling of the cubs prevents the females from coming into oestrus and so impedes the reproductive potential of the males. Once the infanticide is complete, the females come into oestrus and begin to mate with the new males.

Other features of the social behaviour of these animals have adaptive significance. A female who is lactating will allow cubs other than her own to take milk as well. Such parental investment is rewarding to the degree that she is genetically related to them – which of course she is since they are probably the offspring of her sisters.

Lion cubs and mothers *(Panthera leo)*

Selwyn Powers/Oxford Scientific Films

Conflict over weaning

One of the commonest forms of parent – offspring conflict is the struggle between mothers and juveniles over the amount of parental investment. Typically, in the first few months of life the mother is careful to give a great deal of care and often initiates feeding and physical contact. As time passes she becomes more reluctant to invest in the offspring and often resorts to violence to keep the infant at bay. At first glance one would expect their interests to coincide totally: the increase in reproductive fitness is the sole goal of living things, so why should the mother not simply give all the care the infant demands?

The answer is that the mother has other potential offspring to raise. She will view all offspring as roughly equal, so she will best further her reproductive success by producing more and sharing her time and energy between them. The infant however is more self-centred; it will have some interest in the welfare of siblings (they are 'half like' itself), but will be far more concerned with its own welfare.

The infant will try to increase the investment in itself by manipulating the parent. Young herring gulls, for example, although virtually fully grown by about three months, still manage to obtain food from their parents by concealing their size. Begging behaviour involves the young gull stooping and withdrawing its head to give the impression of smaller size. Infant langur baboons have been observed to shriek at their mother and even slap her to elicit food. The spotted flycatcher (*Muscicapa striata*) also reveals the effect of conflict. When the young flycatchers first leave the nest, the parent feeds them without any call. Later they are fed only when calling and after about 16 days the young have to chase parents for morsels of ever decreasing size. Eventually, the young will catch their own food for less energy expenditure.

One further prediction of this theory is that as the parent ages, so the conflict reduces and the amount of care given by the parent increases. This is because near the end of the reproductive life of a parent, future units of reproductive success (i.e. offspring) become less certain. Evidence in support of this comes from studies on red deer, where the condition of the offspring by the first winter relative to the mother improves with the age of the mother, showing that the mother becomes increasingly self-sacrificing as she gets older. Figure 22.4 shows that for the California gull (*Larus californicus*) the number of feedings and defensive acts increases with the age of the parent.

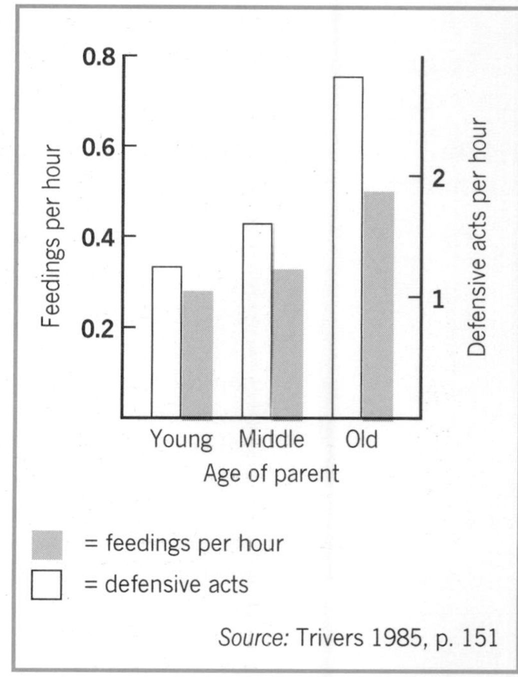

Figure 22.4
Parental investment as a function of age in the Californian gull (*Larus californicus*)

Section summary

Parent–juvenile conflict is easily understood when the parent inherits young not his (or her) own. But even in the case of direct offspring, it is not necessarily in the best reproductive interests of the parent to give all the care that the offspring may crave. A parent may do better by ignoring the last offspring and expending energy on raising some more. Hence a tension exists between the demands of offspring and the future reproductive success of the parents.

Sexual selection

Natural and sexual selection

In a Darwinian world, most features of plants and animals should have some adaptive function in the struggle for existence. Nature should allow no extravagance or waste. So what about the peacock's tail? At first sight it seems a magnificent irrelevance, out of place in Darwin's brutal world. It does not help a peacock fly any faster or better, neither is it used to fight rivals or deter predators. In fact, the main predator of peafowl, the tiger, seems particularly adept at pulling down peacocks by their tails. It would appear to be a positive encumbrance that should have been weeded out by natural selection long before now. Nor is the peacock's tail an exception: many species of animals are characterized by the male (usually) possessing some colourful adornment that serves no apparent function or even seem dysfunctional. Consider the scarlet-tufted malachite sunbird that lives on the slopes of Mount Kenya. The males, unlike the females, have two long tail streamers. Experiments by Evans and Thomas (1992) have shown that artificially shortening the streamers actually increases the success of males in capturing insects for food. Their reproductive success actually declines however since females prefer long-tailed males. We are forced to conclude that long-tailed males are fitter in the Darwinian sense of leaving more offspring.

With characteristic insight, Darwin had provided the answer to this seeming paradox by 1871. In his *Descent of Man and Selection in relation to Sex*, he gave the explanation which is still accepted with refinements today. Individuals possess features which make them attractive to members of the opposite sex. The tail of the peacock has been shaped by sexual selection for the delectation of the peahen.

We must be wary of overstating the distinction between sexual and natural selection. From an evolutionary point of view, it matters not whether you survive to reproduce because you are a fast runner or you reproduce because you are attractive to the other sex. The effect is the same: certain characteristics will enable you to leave more offspring than rival individuals of your species and these characteristics will therefore tend to be maintained.

We need to distinguish two types of sexual selection: 'intra-' and 'inter-'. For reasons already given, the sex ratio usually remains close to 1:1, so where conditions favour polygyny, males must compete with other males. This leads to intra-sexual selection (intra = within one sex). On the other hand, a female investing heavily in offspring or only capable of raising a few offspring in a season or lifetime needs to make sure she has made the right choice. There will be no shortage of males but the implications of a wrong choice for the female are more grave than for the male who will be seeking other partners anyway. Females under these conditions can afford to be choosy. This leads to inter-sexual selection (inter = between sexes).

Intra-sexual selection

Prior to mating

This is probably the easiest form of selection to observe and understand and males fighting males makes good viewing on wildlife documentaries. Bull elephant seals (*Mirounga angustirostris*) rush towards each other, butt their chests and tear each others heads with their teeth. Such fighting has led to a selection pressure in favour of size and consequently male elephant seals are several times larger than females. This difference in size between the sexes is referred to as 'sexual dimorphism' or sometimes as just 'dimorphism'. In the case of the European red deer (*Cervus elaphus*), the males battle with large antlers during the breeding season but during the rest of the year they are tolerant of each other and often move about in groups. Fights are so demanding that few males hold a harem against all comers for more than about four years. The body weight of male deer is about one and a half times that of the females.

The antlers of the red deer are an example of male weaponry. Some of the most spectacular examples of such weapons are found in beetles such as the stag beetle. The males have large horn-like jaws, absent in the females, used only to fight other males.

After mating

It may seem that once mating, i.e. copulation, is over then intra-sexual competition is over: one male must surely have won. The natural world has more surprises in store: some females may mate with many males and retain their sperm in their reproductive tract; such sperm compete inside her to fertilize her egg.

In Focus

Sperm competition, sexual dimorphism and mating systems

The biologist Short suggested that some puzzling differences in the size of male genitalia of the primates can be interpreted consistently in terms of sperm competition theory and that some light is thus thrown on human mating (Short and Balban 1991). Table 22.2 shows data for the weight of testicles and dimorphic ratios for two primates and humans.

When the mating behaviour of chimps and gorillas is considered, the data at first sight appear perplexing. Gorillas are polygynous with successful males guarding a harem of about four females. Chimps live in promiscuous groups where one female may mate with many males. Females advertise their sexual readiness (oestrus) by a pink swelling that males find irresistible.

This information does partly explain the body size differences between chimps and gorillas. For a male gorilla to have exclusive access to four females, he must fight off other suitors. Hence the selective pressure for large body size. Male chimps do not command exclusive access but must share females with other members of the group. Hence there is less male aggression and less advantage in being bigger than your rival. But why the difference in size of testicles? Sperm competition theory provides the answer. Each adult female in the harem of a male gorilla will only come into oestrus once or twice every four years since she will for the rest of the time be pregnant or in lactational anoestrus (female fertility inhibited by breast feeding). Thus, the male will only copulate the few times in the year when an available female is in oestrus.

In the promiscuous system of the chimps however things are very different. Many males may copulate with a single female and the male that deposits the greatest number of good spermatozoa in the reproductive tract of the female will stand the best chance of becoming the father of her offspring. The selective pressure is therefore for males that can produce large volumes of sperm quickly – hence the relatively large testicle size of male chimps.

We can consider the implications of this for human mating behaviour. Short, the discoverer of the testicle effect, draws the following conclusions:

> 'The fact that men are 15 to 20 per cent bigger than women suggests that we are not inherently monogamous. The relatively small size of a man's testes ... the high proportion of morphologically abnormal spermatozoa [i.e. abnormally shaped sperm], and the lack of any cyclical swelling in the female at ovulation suggests that neither are we adapted to a multi-male promiscuous mating system ... The best guess would be that we are basically a polygynous primate in which the polygyny usually takes the form of serial monogamy.' (Short 1991)

In fact, serial monogamy has become extremely common in western societies following the relaxation of divorce laws and changing social mores.

The concept of sperm competition illuminates many features of male and female anatomy in non-human animals. The penis of the damselfly (*Calopteryx maculata*), for example, has appendages designed to remove a competitor's sperm as it injects its own. In the common honey bee (*Apis mellifera*) males produce mating plugs which attempt (often unsuccessfully) to seal off the vagina of the Queen to prevent further injections of sperm from competitors.

Inter-sexual selection

One of the most interesting ideas within Darwin's *Descent of Man* (1871), was the suggestion that choice by one sex could bring about extreme changes in the appearance of the other. Numerous ancillary theories have emerged in recent years to explain why certain features of males and females are found to be attractive. They tend to fall into two schools:

Table 22.2 Comparison of body and testicle size for humans, chimps and gorillas

Species	*Weight of male* (kg)	*Weight of female* (kg)	*Dimorphism* M/F	*Weight of male testicles (g)*
Chimpanzee	50	42	1.2	60
Gorilla	250	62	4.0	10
Humans	70	58	1.2	20

Source: Short and Balban 1991

- the 'good taste' or 'sexy sons' school
- the 'good genes' or 'good sense' school.

The 'good taste' or 'sexy sons' school

This view stems largely from the ideas of Fisher who tackled the problem in the 1930s. Fisher argued that, if at some point in the past an arbitrary drift of fashion led a large number of females in a population to prefer long tails, a runaway effect would result leading to long tails. Once this fashion took hold, it would become despotic and self-reinforcing. Any female that bucked the trend and mated with a male with a shorter tail would leave sons with short tails that were unattractive. Females that succumbed to the fashion would leave 'sexy sons' with long tails and daughters with the same preference for long tails. The overall effect is to saddle males with increasingly longer tails until the sheer expense of producing them outweighs any benefit in attracting females. But since attracting females is fundamental, very long tails indeed could be produced by this process. In Fisher's view, tail length need serve no other purpose – it is truly a fashion accessory.

Indian peacock (*Pavo cristatus*)

Max Gibbs/Oxford Scientific Films

The 'good gene' or 'good sense' school

The 'good gene' theory argues that the taste of males or females for some ornament such as tail length or coloration has some adaptive function. In 1982, Hamilton and Zuk argued that bright colours and extravagant ornaments were 'honest signals' from the male to the female, advertising the fact that the male is largely parasite free since the production of these ornaments is impaired by the presence of parasites.

An idea that has also met with a favourable reception is Moller's view that male ornaments are in reality displays of symmetry (Moller 1992). It takes a great deal of physiological precision to engineer a symmetrical body. Stress or a poor genetic endowment detract from an animal's ability to produce symmetrical appendages.

In Focus

◆

Peacocks and long-tailed birds

Female choice is illustrated by the preference of females of certain species for extravagant ornamentation in the male. Most people know that peahens are rather drab birds in comparison with the magnificent tail ornamentation of the peacock. Studies by Marion Petrie (1994) and others have revealed that the number of copulations achieved by males increases with the size and complexity of his tail. It seems that the more spots a tail has, the more attractive it is to the female. But the more spots also usually implies that the tail is more symmetrical. It is not entirely clear whether females simply prefer spot number or tail symmetry. The work of Petrie also shows that the offspring of fathers with attractive tails are also actually fitter in a physiological sense, so perhaps the tastes of the females are not simply Fisherian whims of fashion.

In a classic study of the long-tailed widow bird (*Euplectes progne*), Malte Andersson showed in 1982 that females have an almost insatiable appetite for tail length. This bird is about the size of a sparrow but males have tails up to a half a metre in length. The female tail is only about 7 cm which is presumably the right length for flight purposes. Andersson divided 36 males into four groups. Some had their tails shortened, some lengthened and some were kept as a control. The control group was divided into those that kept their original tail and those that had their tail cut and glued back together. Figure 22.5 shows the results. Those males with elongated tails were more successful in terms of number of nests than those whose tails were shortened. It is clear that not only have females driven males into producing long tails, but they would, given the choice, prefer them even longer. Notice that the control group also had their tails cut and rejoined. This was to ensure that compensation was made for the effect of the act of cutting on female taste.

Long-tailed widow bird (*Euplectes progne*)

Stan Osolinski/Oxford Scientific Films

Whatever the final outcome of these ancillary theories, Darwin's basic insights concerning sexual selection have been vindicated. The preferences of one sex are impressed on the behaviour and appearance of the other.

❖ Activity 3 ❖

Courtship in the animal world is often a colourful and eventful sight. Amongst bird species, males often perform aerobatic displays or highly athletic song and dance routines. Male peacocks strut and scream, shaking their tail plumage. The male bower bird (*Chlamydera maculata*) builds a bower of twigs decorated with coloured fragments to impress the female.

Compile a list of what you consider to be the functions of courtship.

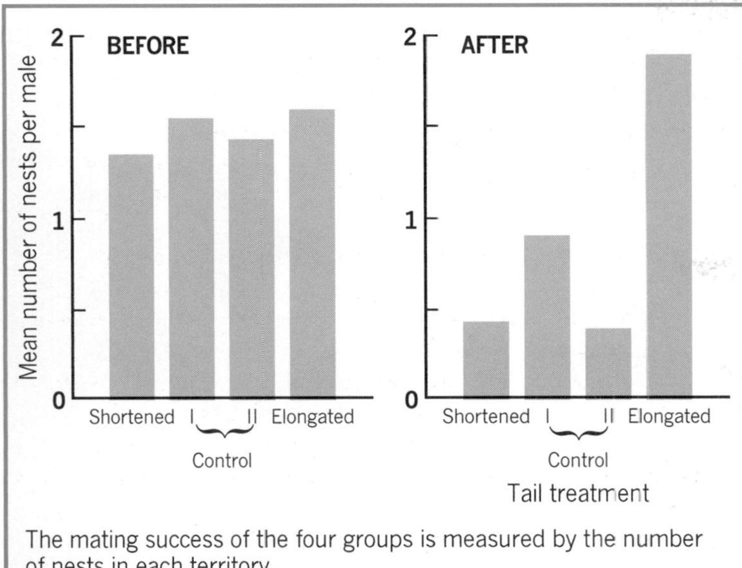

The mating success of the four groups is measured by the number of nests in each territory.

Figure 22.5
Tail length as a sexually-selected feature in long-tailed widow birds
Source: Krebs and Davies 1987

Human mate choice: good genes or good taste?

We finish this chapter by applying the preceding theory to humans and their choice of mate – a subject of never-ending fascination. Because of physical differences, men and women must use different strategies to maximize their reproductive potential. In general, a woman can increase her reproductive success by choosing a high status male who controls sufficient resources to invest materially in her offspring. A man can increase his reproductive success either by taking many wives, if conditions permit, or by choosing a woman who is fertile and demonstrates the potential to be a good mother.

It is reasonable to suppose that this situation would give rise to the following theoretical predictions concerning male and female preferences:

Predictions of male preferences

- The fertility of women is heavily dependent on age and so we would expect men to prefer women in a narrow age band of peak reproductive potential.
- Men use physical characteristics as a guide to age and reproductive ability; these physical traits determine what we mean by attractiveness.

Predictions of female preferences

- Male fertility is less dependent on age and men may remain fertile over a much greater span of years than women. Therefore age should be less important for women than for men as an indicator of attractiveness.
- Women increase their reproductive success by heavily investing in a few offspring. Women should therefore respond positively to men who control resources such as status and income that could be helpful to their offspring.

Evidence on human mate choice

The evidence ranging from common experience to the results of more controlled experiments tends to support the predictions given above.

The 'Lonely hearts' columns of magazines and newspapers provide insight into both what the sexes prefer in a partner and what they think a partner would be looking for in them. Dunbar (1995) and others studied ads placed in American and London newspapers and magazines. The pattern was significant: women seek resources and offer attractiveness, men seek attractiveness and offer resources. The following two examples illustrate this:

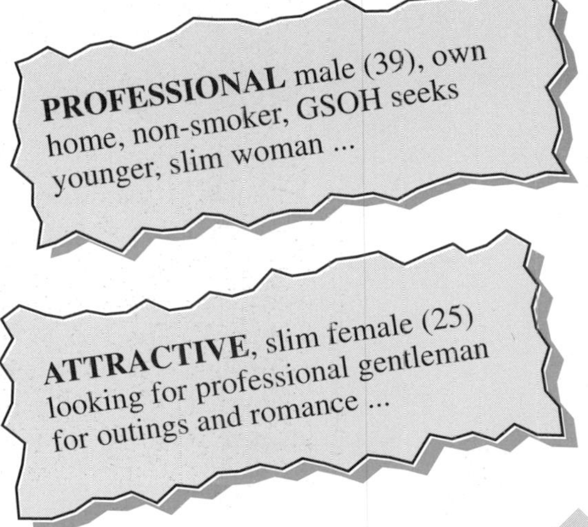

PROFESSIONAL male (39), own home, non-smoker, GSOH seeks younger, slim woman ...
ATTRACTIVE, slim female (25) looking for professional gentleman for outings and romance ...

The same pattern is confirmed by preferences elicited from questionnaires. Buss (1989) demonstrated that the preference amongst men for looks and amongst women for earning capacity held for 37 different cultures. Even women who earned more than average, paid more attention than average to wealth in a prospective partner. Wealthy and powerful women still sought powerful men. Henry Kissinger (US Secretary of State under President Nixon) was perhaps right when he said that the greatest aphrodisiac is power.

©Johansson/Lodge/Outline/Katz Pictures

Hugh Hefner, 'Playboy' empire magnate, at the age of 70, with his wife Kimberly

Good looks equals good genes?

The evidence is now emerging that human beings are a sexually selected species and that many of our traits such as fat distribution, hair colour, eye colour, etc. may not represent adaptations to a hostile environment but features designed to make us appear more attractive to members of the opposite sex. Some features may be 'honest signals' in that they convey real information about the reproductive potential of a prospective mate. Others may be 'dishonest' and part of the attempt of one sex to deceive the other that began long ago and well before the extremely lucrative cosmetics industry of today.

Having reviewed mating behaviour we can begin to understand why, in the words of James and Carol Gould (1989):

> 'Relationships in most of the animal world begin to look as if they have been designed by a hardworking team of bankers, economists, real estate speculators, and advertising executives.'

❖ Activity 4 ❖

1. As a practical exercise, repeat the study of personal ads as carried out by Dunbar and others. Take a local or national newspaper and investigate if Dunbar's findings are repeatable. Do men seek attractiveness and women seek resources? Consider carefully how you will collect and quantify such data and the biases in the sampling procedure.
2. Animal behaviourists use the term 'honest and dishonest signal'. Honest signals convey reliable information about the state of the individual in terms of health, resources, etc. Dishonest signals are designed to mislead or deceive the onlooker. Compile a list of the signals human males and females send each other – clothing and wealth are good starting points. For each one, try to identify whether it is honest or dishonest, and suggest ways in which humans may check the truth-value of these messages.

Section summary

The existence of two sexes with non-identical interests leads to sexual selection – a selective force as powerful in some cases as natural selection. Intra-sexual selection occurs as a result of competition between members of one sex for access to, or control of, members of the other sex. The sex that is competed for is that which limits the reproductive potential of the sex that competes.

In most mammalian species, males will fight with other males to secure females. In some other species, such as some birds and fish, this pattern may be reversed. Inter-sexual selection occurs when individuals of one sex are discriminating in their choice of mate. This leads to an evolutionary pressure for each sex to develop features to attract the other. The discrimination humans exercise in their choice of partners may be a product of sexual selection.

Chapter summary

- This chapter has examined the nature and consequences of sexual reproduction. Sexual reproduction carries costs as well as benefits. The fact that sexual reproduction is more common than asexual reproduction suggests that the benefits of genetic diversity outweigh the costs of locating and securing a mate.
- Individuals behave so as to maximize their reproductive success. The fact that males and females may have different reproductive potentials, coupled with the uneven distribution of mating and parenting effort, means that the interests of the two sexes rarely converge in terms of the number of offspring and number of mates. This leads to different patterns of behaviour for the two sexes.
- The categorizing of animal species according to a mating system has been criticized. Current thinking suggests that it may be more rewarding to look at mating from the point of view of the genetic self-interest of individuals. The mating behaviour any individual displays is a strategy that has evolved towards that which leaves the most offspring under the constraints and conditions found. This may result in a flexible repertoire of strategies to suit prevailing conditions.
- Parent–juvenile conflict has been analysed from the point of view of the interests of parents and offspring. In cases where the parent inherits young that are not his (or her) own, the offspring may be counter to the future reproductive interests of the parent and infanticide may result. Even in the case of direct offspring, it is not necessarily in the best interests of the parent to give all the care that the offspring demands. A parent may do better by ignoring the last offspring and expending energy on producing future progeny.
- Sexual selection is a force as strong in some cases as natural selection. It can be divided into intra- and inter-sexual selection:
  - Intra-sexual selection occurs between members of the same sex for access to members of the other sex.
  - Inter-sexual selection occurs when individuals of one sex are discriminating in their choice of mate. It is likely that the judgements humans make about suitable partners have been conditioned to some extent by inter-sexual selection.

Essay questions

1 Critically consider the nature and consequences of sexual selection in the evolution of animal behaviour. *(24 marks)*

2 (a) Describe some of the different ways in which males and females might invest in the rearing of the young. *(12 marks)*

(b) Assess the significance of male/female differences in investment in the evolution of behaviour in any *two* species. *(12 marks)*

3 Describe and assess the influence of mating strategies on parental care. *(24 marks)*

4 Discuss evolutionary explanations for parent–offspring conflict. *(24 marks)*

Further reading

Ridley, M. (1993) *The Red Queen*, London: Penguin.

A highly readable and exciting book that deals with 'Sex and the evolution of human nature' (the subtitle). Ridley offers a masterly and fascinating synthesis of the most recent research on the topic of sex.

Trivers, R. (1985) *Social Evolution*, New York: Benjamin Cummings.

Much more of a text book than The Red Queen. *It is well illustrated and the central ideas, many of which originated with Trivers, are clearly explained.*

Dawkins, R. (1976) *The Selfish Gene*, Oxford: Oxford University Press.

The book whose title has passed into common language. A bold and forceful statement of the power of biological reductionism and the implications of evolution. The BBC markets two Horizon *programmes on VHS video dealing with Dawkin's work. They are* The Selfish Gene *and* Nice Guys Finish First.

Chapter 23

Kinship and social behaviour

Roger Davies

Preview

In this chapter we shall be looking at:

- genetic and non-genetic explanations for altruism
- sociality in non-human animals
- attachment theory
- signalling systems in non-human animals.

Introduction

Although animals can, and often do, live in isolation, many species show a preference for living in groups. Whether or not animals live in groups depends in large part on the advantages (such as protection from predators or access to resources) that group living brings. Both in smaller kinship groups and in larger social groups, animals have evolved characteristics that enable them to make the most out of social living.

Genetic explanations for apparent altruism

In Chapter 21 we looked at how Darwin was puzzled by the prevalence of altruistic behaviour in the animal world. The point is that in any given circumstance an animal ought (i.e. 'ought' in the terms of increasing its fitness, or reproductive success) to behave selfishly. The reason for this is that altruism, in comparison with a strategy that is selfish, would be less successful and therefore would not evolve in competition with non-altruism.

However, Darwin's paradox was resolved by the work of Hamilton (1963, 1964) who showed in his *Kin selection theory* that evolution does not operate directly on individual organisms but upon their genetic makeup. In other words, any one individual may pass on genes to future generations not just by means of their own reproductive success but also by facilitating the reproductive potential of their relatives (who, by definition, share some genetic material). In theory, the closer this genetic relationship is then the greater the cooperation and altruism each should show towards the other. Hamilton coined the term 'inclusive fitness' to describe the effect of genetic relatedness in determining how individuals would behave altruistically (and, in this case, nepotistically) towards one another.

For instance, Sherman (1981) showed that in Belding's ground squirrel the females who are close relatives (such as mother–daughter or sister–sister) do not fight over burrow sites or over the use of resources within a territory, though their behaviour towards other, unrelated females was highly aggressive. The related females not only show little antagonism to one another but often actively help each other in defending their young from attack by predators or intruders. Related females were seen to give alarm calls at the sight of a predator to warn one another, a behaviour observed only when they were in one another's company; they remained silent at other times.

Altruism can be defined as an act of helping which increases the (reproductive) fitness of the individual who is helped, at some cost to the fitness of the helper. The *cost* of helping is essential to this definition, to understanding both what is being contributed by the helper as well as what is the important gain made by being helped. In both cases, the essential cost and benefit is fitness, which is a measure of reproductive success, i.e. the total contribution made to the gene pool by an individual, including their own offspring and those succoured by all those individuals to whom they are genetically related. Helping a close relative or one of their offspring can therefore be considered to be an example of a selfish commitment to maximizing this inclusive fitness.

But altruism is not confined to acts of helping between related individuals. Consider the following examples.

1. A lamb becomes alarmed by the sight of a dog and rushes to its mother who allows it to suckle.
2. A juvenile male chimpanzee wrestles with a larger male but their play turns more aggressive. A second young male intervenes, and both chase off the larger male.
3. A grouper fish remains motionless with its mouth agape while a tiny fish swims in and out of its mouth collecting morsels of food from inside.
4. An ant returning to its nest having fed encounters a beetle larva near the entrance. The larva prods at the ants mouthparts, and receives a meal of regurgitated food.

What do these instances have in common? By the definition above, each of these qualifies as altruism, though the costs and benefits to helper and helped are not the same throughout. Let us examine them one by one.

Common interest

It might seem 'natural' for a parent to care for its young by providing food and protection. Clearly, there are common interests between two related individuals, and in this case, the mother will usually place herself between the dog and her lamb. The lamb's alarm response of suckling enables her to achieve this. But the lamb is also allowed to suckle from the mother even without the dog being there, and this is also altruistic since it is costly by depleting her own food reserves. Though the lamb may be at a stage when it can graze successfully for itself the mother still does not reject its suckling, and especially when the lamb is in a state of alarm, such as caused by seeing the dog. However, any lamb straying away from its mother will obtain no help from other mothers in the same field. However hard the lamb may try, other mothers will only offer protection and milk to their own lambs, which they recognize by a combination of sound (the lamb's bleating noise) and body smell (which they will have learned by sniffing and licking their lamb in the first minutes after it was born).

Clearly, then, this form of altruism is based upon kinship, i.e. individuals act favourably towards others to whom they are related. But, without a language to express relationship, how could an animal 'know' they are related to another. For instance, a child learns she is a niece to a given adult by firstly being asked to call him 'uncle'. Later on, the brotherly relationship between one parent and the uncle is explained to the child. Without that process, how could the child come to know who are her brothers and sisters, aunts, uncles, cousins or grandparents? The exact way in which animals come to favour relatives over non-relatives has raised some controversy (Grafen 1982,1990), but there are a number of mechanisms by which this could occur (Stuart 1991). To give just two examples:

- spatial proximity (family groups tend to stay together)
- phenotype matching (related individuals have certain characteristics such as smell, appearance or behaviour in common).

In gregarious species which spend time with non-relatives (such as in the case of lambs playing together), kin recognition becomes important. For instance, ground-nesting birds usually recognize their own eggs soon after laying them, whereas tree-nesters are unable to do so (and this makes such species more prone to *brood parasitism*, as we shall see later). In species where the young have a period of dependency (often referred to as 'infancy') the parents and young often form early 'bonds', in which each learns to recognize the other by some salient feature, such as odour or visual cue. The nature of infancy is a period where the infant remains physically close to its parent. In this way, any other young in the brood would naturally be siblings, and so being raised with others is a strong cue to relatedness. This 'natural' mechanism is often exploited by farmers when a sheep in their flock dies giving birth. The farmer brings the surviving lamb to a sheep who has herself just lambed. In the minutes after giving birth herself, the foster mother is allowed to sniff and lick the second lamb as if it were her own. After a few minutes together they will act as mother and offspring for life.

In humans, the *kibbutz* child-rearing arrangement (where infants are raised communally together with their parents acting as caretakers of the crêche on a shift basis) acts much like a full-time nursery class. The 'parents' are usually given special access to their own children during evenings, but the effect on the children is that growing up so closely with other children who are unrelated seems to bring them together in bonds as close as that between true siblings. Having a shared upbringing seems to have the effect of promoting recognition of the others as being close relatives. This is especially noticeable in the kibbutz-reared children during adolescence – the time when people of the opposite sex become interesting playmates for the first time! The *kibbutniks* then seem to reject members of the opposite sex with whom they were raised, preferring to find partners outside their own kibbutz (Shepher 1971, Thornhill 1991).

There are a number of reasons why it is important for an individual to respond differently to kin and non-kin:

- Parents who fails to recognize their own offspring would waste resources on another's young. This does sometimes occur in what is known as 'brood parasitism', discussed shortly.
- If the young are to be protected by the parent they will need to recognize one another quickly so that help can be provided.
- Related individuals who collaborate are more likely to fend off aggression from others who are non-relatives.
- At the time of reaching sexual maturity, it is important that individuals avoid mating with relatives to ensure diversity of genetic material occurs between generations. In addition to this reason, inbreeding itself is believed to have disadvantages which would affect the fitness of offspring.

This raises the question of whether the exact relatedness between individuals matters in this argument: that is, does it matter whether an individual is helping a sister or a cousin? The answer is that it does indeed matter. In addition to the above, helping a distant relative has much less benefit, in terms of inclusive fitness, than does helping a sibling (brother or sister). Remember that any measure of relatedness is also an inverse measure of *unrelatedness.* For instance, stating that you share half your genes with one parent means that half of the genes are not shared, i.e. are unrelated. With a distant relative the majority of your genes are not common to you both. In fact, relationships more distant than siblings means you have much more unshared than shared genetic material.

The extent of relatedness between two individuals is very important in determining how they should interact (Emlen 1995). In the view first expressed by the geneticist J.S. Haldane, a cousin should only receive one-quarter of the help we would normally offer to a brother or sister. For, although we have approximately half our genes different from each of our siblings, a full seven-eighths of our genes are different from our cousin's. In theory, then, it sounds like we have very little in common with our cousin, and should care little for them compared with our brother or sister. But this does not always accord with our psychological experience of these relationships, where a cousin can often feel like our closest friend on earth. Why is this so?

The solution to this is that *gene-environment interactions* make these theoretical statements seem untrue. You may protest that you have a relationship with a cousin that is as close as, or even closer than, your relationship with your brother or sister and this may seem especially so if both you and the cousin are (say) female. However, remember that both you and your cousin are close relatives of your respective parents, and that on one side of each a parent is also closely related (as sister–sister, sister–brother, or brother– brother) to the other's family. In this capacity they will have encouraged you to form a close relationship (in addition to the actual extent of your relatedness), since they each have more to gain from such alliances than do either you or your cousin! A similarity in age between cousins (again, possibly more than usual between siblings) also tends to make cousin relationships closer ones. The point of this discussion is to suggest that the contribution made by genetics to observed altruism can be ascertained from 'relatedness coefficients' (which are measures of approximate gene frequencies shared by various family members with one another). These coefficients are the basal level at which we might predict kin altruism to operate. As we have repeatedly pointed out in this area, evolution *predisposes* the modifying action of experience on an organism, it does not *determine* how things turn out. The very least which this approach provides is a guide to how individuals' life experiences act upon genotypes, modifying the expected patterns of behaviour (in this case altruism) which are found in individual instances.

Reciprocal altruism

This particular explanation for altruistic behaviour was proposed by Trivers (1971). Trivers argued that one animal might show altruistic behaviour towards another if the recipient of this favour reciprocated some time in the future. In a sense then, this involves a 'loan' that will be repaid on some future occasion. Such reciprocating arrangements are not unusual in the animal kingdom. For instance, Wilkinson (1984) found that unrelated vampire bats regurgitate food for one another on their return to the nesting site. While in many instances the recipient of the meal was a relative of the altruist, often they were not. However, the unrelated animals were usually roosting neighbours of the altruist, and Wilkinson went on to show experimentally that the exchanges taking place between unrelated individuals were reciprocated, i.e. they had built up a relationship based upon mutual exchanges of favour. Theoretically, in such a social climate, a cheating strategy (i.e. take the favour but don't return it) would gain more than an honest one. But within the community of vampire bats the cost of being denied a meal having once cheated is very high, since on cold nights an individual going hungry rarely survives.

In Focus

The prisoner's dilemma

Two suspects are arrested by the police and held in separate cells where they cannot communicate with each other. Each is told by the interviewing officer that they only have a weak case against him, and that this would result in only a short prison sentence. However, each is encouraged to inform on the other, with the result that the other prisoner would be given a long prison sentence and the informer would be set free. If, however, both inform on each other, they would both be sent to prison for a moderate sentence. The rewards and costs of each alternative (expressed as a numerical value) for Prisoner A are shown in Fig. 23.1 below:

Figure 23.1 The rewards and costs of informing

Prisoner A \ Prisoner B	Cooperation	Defection
Cooperation	3 (Reward for mutual cooperation)	0 (Sucker's payoff)
Defection	5 (Temptation to defect)	3 (Punishment for mutual defection)

As you might expect, the normal response is for both prisoners to 'squeal' on the other. If prisoner A informs on prisoner B whilst he stays silent the payoff is maximized. Even if prisoner B also informs, it is better to mutually inform (i.e. defect on any cooperative arrangement) than be caught with the 'sucker's payoff', that is to stay silent whilst someone is informing on you.

Axelrod and Hamilton argued that if this situation were repeated time and time again with the same players, it would soon become apparent that the most profitable arrangement for the players would be to cooperate.

Trivers was aware of the possibilities of cheating in such arrangements and suggested that reciprocal altruism would only evolve in species where individuals could recognize each other, and apply sanctions to those who refused to reciprocate. But if cheating is so potentially profitable for an individual, why is it not more common? To solve this problem, Axelrod and Hamilton (1981) turned to game theory analysis (see *In Focus* above).

As a result of the analysis of the strategies used in games such as the prisoner's dilemma, Axelrod and Hamilton put forward a beguilingly simple strategy that would reward cooperation and discourage defection. The strategy, *tit for tat*, called for one animal to cooperate with another (in this discussion, to display altruistic behaviour to another) which would then return the favour. If one party simply returns whatever happened in the previous interaction between the two animals, cooperation would be met with cooperation, defection with return defection. In this way, a cooperative alliance could be formed between two animals that would jointly benefit both. This simple explanation of how cheating is controlled in reciprocal altruism has two major advantages. First, it is retaliatory. Potential defection is discouraged because it would be met with mutual defection and the defecting animal would lose the long-

Rudie H. Kuiter/Oxford Scientific Films

Cleaner fish wrasse (*Labroides dimidiatus)* with cod

term benefits of cooperation. Second, it is conciliatory, in that animals do not miss out on the future benefits of cooperation by holding a grudge against an animal that had once defected.

Mutualism, or return effects

Some cooperative relationships may even involve individuals from differing species, such as cleaner fish who survive by removing either skin parasites from other fish or even, in the case of the grouper, food particles which could harbour bacteria inside the mouth of the host fish. The grouper not only refrains from eating the small fish, but occasionally closes its mouth with it inside when danger looms to threaten the safety of its small companion. Sometimes individuals will cooperate and help one another because, as a team, they can achieve more than by working alone. For instance, lionesses will hunt together in bringing down a wildebeest and other large ungulates which they could not tackle safely alone. Having killed the prey the lionesses will then share it, though not necessarily equally (Caraco and Wolf 1975).

Cuckoo *(Cuculus candrus)* being fed by a dunnock (*Prunella modularis*)

Michael Leach/Oxford Scientific Films

Induced altruism

Some strategies which solicit help from others can be regarded as ploys which are aimed at cheating. This induced altruism is sometimes referred to as 'manipulation' or 'social parasitism'. Such behaviour would include the laying of eggs in another bird's nest ('brood parasitism'), as practised by the cuckoo (Davies and Brooke 1991) and a number of other species, as well as the example of the beetle grub 'begging' for food from the passing ant – Hölldobler (1971) found that the larva of the *Atemelles* beetle mimicks the begging behaviour of ants so as to obtain food from passing workers. Wickler (1968) found a similar instance of deception shown in *Aspidontus*, a fish whose appearance mimmicks the cleaner fish *Labroides*. However, rather than clean the host fish, *Aspidontus* individuals approach it and then bite into its flesh, making off with a morsel of food.

Section summary

Animals sometimes behave in altruistic ways that increase the reproductive fitness of the individual that is helped at some cost to the helper. As a result of this self-sacrificing behaviour, animals may increase their inclusive fitness and are therefore displaying selfishness at a genetic level. Because this form of altruism helps genetic kin, it is generally referred to as 'kin selection'. In reciprocal altruism, animals may help one another but have the favour returned sometime in the future. Essential to the success of this strategy is the idea that animals recognize those who do not return favours and can apply sanctions for such defection. The tit-for-tat strategy works by each animal responding like for like so that a cooperative behaviour is followed by a cooperative behaviour, and a defection is followed likewise by mutual defection. Some animals will cooperate and help one another because as a team they can achieve more than by working alone.

Sociality in non-human animals

Considering the many ways in which animals compete with one another for resources there would seem to be little point or opportunity for social behaviour, in the true sense of sharing or cooperating, to evolve. However, as we have already seen, there are many examples in the animal world where the struggle to obtain resources requires a degree of collaboration. One instance of this has just been mentioned – lionesses hunting cooperatively in bringing down a wildebeest.

Cooperation in defence and attack

Packer (1977) found that in baboon society individuals may band together in order to dominate, or defend against, other stronger individuals. This relationship, or pact, seems to operate in a variety of situations in much the same way as human friendships transcend any given occasion, and serves in bringing about common aims in a variety of situations. In any event if such favours are to be returned then collaboration across spans of time are needed. Such a longitudinal relationship depends upon the individuals concerned having a sophisticated cognitive apparatus, i.e. memory, perception and other information-processing capacities, if they are to deal effectively with the complex sequences of events they encounter (Cosmides 1989).

One such common aim among members of a social group may be in terms of vigilance when there is risk from predation. For instance, Kenward (1978) showed that a goshawk released at varying distances from a flock of wood pigeons is less successful when the wood pigeons are in larger, rather than smaller, flocks. The reason is that individuals in the larger flock have more chance of being alerted to the goshawk's approach than when there are fewer others to be vigilant. The chances of any individual in a group being caught by a single predator are less when the group is large rather than small, an effect which is known as *dilution*. This may explain the tendency of many social living animals to form into huge colonies when feeding or resting, though they may be solitary at other times.

Cooperation in hunting and foraging

Animals that feed on vegetation which is either sparse or difficult to locate will often benefit from group living. Ward and Zahavi (1973) suggest that sharing communal sites enables birds to gather information about good feeding areas in the vicinity. The less successful individuals may acquire knowledge by following others on their daily foraging trips and thereby learn where the sites are which are most likely to provide a good supply of food (Marzluff *et al.* 1996). This process of 'stealing' information from others would be analogous to an act of piracy, and those who lose out by having their food supply shared by incomers should, over evolutionary time, develop tactics which would deceive the potential intruder. However, there may also be another strategy at play here, such as the dilution effect, where the benefits associated with shared foraging outweigh the costs.

For instance, Elgar (1986) found that house sparrows make a loud chirping call from their perch just prior to descending upon a food source. This call has the effect of alerting other sparrows in the locality to the availability of food. Sparrows tend to descend to the ground to feed in numbers and this is believed to enable them to concentrate more on feeding because of being able to share the task of vigilance among them.

It is not being suggested that the cost-benefit calculations which gregarious animals make are similar to those made by humans when assessing the risk associated with some activity such as climbing or driving a car. The mechanisms that bring about specific behaviour patterns which come under the headings of 'sociality' or 'aggression' have evolved to be triggered off automatically when the appropriate environmental cues are present. Despite being more visible, any herd or flock of animals foraging in very great numbers will make a formidable task for a predator who aims to pick off one individual. However, by the same token, only an extremely rich source of food would enable members of so large a group to get enough to eat and sustain their pattern of feeding together. Scanning for predators is a cost which may at times be more expensive than failing to eat when an individual is starving.

This relationship between group size and foraging strategy has been referred to as 'optimality', meaning that predation risks are balanced against feeding time at a point where for each behaviour the gains are maximized against the risks associated with alternative strategies (Pulliam and Caraco 1984). For instance, Fig. 23.2 below shows that a hungry animal in times of shortage is more likely to accept the risks associated with the area to the left of the midpoint (i.e. of group size less than 90 in the chart), whereas when food is plentiful, that same individual may prefer the added benefit of vigilance afforded by being in a large herd or flock and choose the area to the right of midpoint (i.e. of group size larger than 90 in the chart).

This shows that optimal points for foraging behaviour are inherently unstable even in the calculations made by a single individual. But this degree of instability in working with a theoretical model does, in practice, have its drawbacks (Krebs and Davies 1987). For one thing, not all the individuals in a group will obtain an equal payoff for the group's combined vigilance, with the possibility of a cheating strategy known as 'scrounging' becoming successful at the cost of 'producers' (Ranta *et al.* 1996).

However, the benefits from group living go beyond that of optimizing foraging and hunting success, particularly in mammals, so that simple optimality models have been

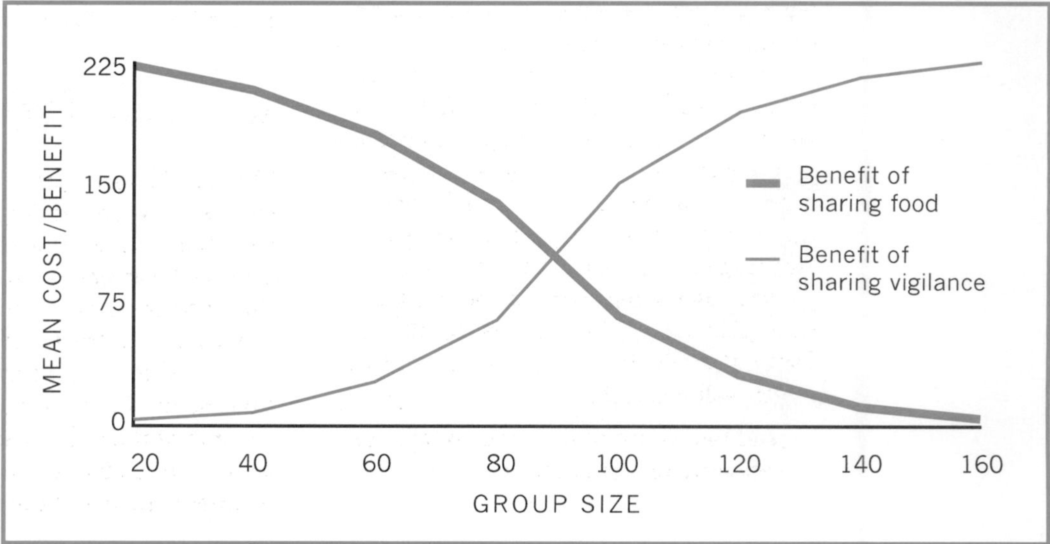

Figure 23.2. The costs and benefits associated with bouts of feeding

difficult to apply in many cases (e.g. Packer *et al.* 1990). Furthermore, it has been difficult to show that for lions there is any benefit to be gained from hunting in groups larger than two (Packer 1986, Mangel and Clark 1988).

Section summary

There are many examples in the animal world where the struggle to obtain resources requires a degree of collaboration. Animals may live in social groups because of the greater vigilance of larger numbers of conspecifics. Cooperation in hunting and foraging may enable animals to benefit from the increased vigilance of larger numbers whilst feeding and also to profit from the information provided by other members of the group. Cooperative feeding also has its costs, with some animals developing cheating strategies at the expense of the more productive members of the group.

Attachment theory

Chapter 22 described how reproductive patterns vary among different species. An important aspect of this variation is whether or not the young of the species in question receive parental care during their early development. Where the young of a species enter the world at a relatively late stage in their development (so-called *precocial* species) they are sometimes entirely independent of any protection by parents from the beginning. If there is either little or no parental care or protection given to the young (as is the case in many frog species, for instance) then the species will often rely upon the production of high numbers of offspring to offset the costs of predation to many of their number.

However, in other species the young enter the world at an early stage in their development and require care and protection during this vulnerable phase in their life. These species are called *altricial*, and the period of dependency of the young on the parents may be very prolonged indeed, as in the case of mammals whose care and protection of each individual offspring can take up a large portion of the parents' own adult lives. In species which show this altricial form of rearing of the young there is the need for a mechanism which will determine:

- that the parent and young are able to recognize one another, and
- that the young, once mobile, will remain relatively close to the parents throughout this period of dependency.

In birds, the first of these problems is not always important, since if the species in question is tree-nesting then the young are unable to stray from the nest until they mature (hence the term 'fly the nest' to describe the final stage of entering adulthood in humans). However, in ground-nesting birds such the tern or goose, the young may become lost among other chicks in the colony of nests which usually surrounds them. In such circumstances a process called *imprinting* is usually found to happen. Imprinting is a phenomenon first described by Douglas Spalding in the nineteenth century, but it was systematically studied by Konrad Lorenz (Lorenz 1937).

Main features of imprinting

Though the exact period varies between species, birds which 'imprint' tend to have a so-called *sensitive period* during which a bond is formed between the offspring and parent. The outcome of the bond, once it has formed, is that the young will tend to follow the parent around. In ducks this will mean that the mother is able to move around the location of the nest, take to the water, move away from danger or engage in any number of other activities without needing to carry or otherwise 'shepherd' her brood along. The fact that they will have imprinted on her in the sensitive period (in the case of ducklings, from between six and twelve hours after hatching) means that they will follow her around wherever she goes.

The imprinting process itself must arise as a consequence of an inherited mechanism, since it is triggered in all young during this particular stage of their development. But imprinting also shows some elements of learning, in that if any large moving object is presented to the duckling during the sensitive period they will imprint upon it instead of the mother, and will begin to follow it around. In Lorenz's early demonstrations of the process of imprinting he showed that the large moving object can be a human. Thereafter, the ducklings will regard this human as the target to be followed. In some species of bird, such as the greylag goose (studied most intensively by Lorenz), imprinting seems to be irreversible, i.e. is a once-only process which is not altered by future experience. Furthermore, the effects of imprinting are both short- and long-term.

The short-term consequences of imprinting are that it forms a bond between mother and offspring which brings about following responses from the young when the mother moves about. But eventually the following behaviour of the young subsides. The long-term consequences of imprinting, however, are not seen until the animal reaches sexual maturity, usually in the first full season after hatching. At this time the social and sexual responses will be seen to be orientated to the object or species which were imprinted upon. In the case of goslings having imprinted upon humans they will now seek out the company of humans rather than their own species. Their sexual preferences also seem to alter away from their own kind, suggesting that the process of imprinting has more deeply ingrained effects than just causing protective bonds between parent and offspring. These longer term consequences seem to do with species recognition, the so-called sexual aspects of imprinting, for which long-term social and sexual preferences were established early on in development.

❖ Activity 1 ❖

What do you think would be the consequences if a young bird of one species (e.g. a bengalese finch) were fostered by a member of a closely related species (e.g. a zebra finch)?

Imprinting is known to occur in a wide range of bird species, with some exceptions, such as the cuckoo. However, the cuckoo female does lay her eggs in the nest of the species in which she herself was fledged, and so even here an element of imprinting seems to be working (Brooke and Davies 1988).

The fact that a process of early learning may take place in a special period of development has long been recognized in a variety of animal species. For instance, in dogs the first 4 to 6 weeks spent in the company of the mother seems to be necessary for the development of normal sexual behaviour when they mature, and also that exposure to humans during this early phase is essential for them to become tame as pets (Scott and Fuller 1965). In ungulates such as sheep and goats, the early learning seems to be a two-way process, with mothers imprinting upon the taste and smell of their offspring soon after birth, in bouts of licking and sniffing which occur in those early minutes (Klopfer *et al.* 1964). This early contact between mother and young has also been proposed to be essential for such bonding in the case of humans (Klaus and Kennell 1975).

Main features of attachment

In monkeys, too, a process of bonding has been recognized as occurring in a sensitive period, which in the case of the rhesus macaques seems to be within the first six months of life (Harlow and Harlow 1962). The Harlows studied the responses of rhesus monkeys to different forms of mothering.

If reared in isolation for the first eight months, the young rhesus develops permanent disorders in development, both in social and sexual orientation. 'Surrogate' mothers lessen the effects, as do periods of daily play with peers. With the surrogate mother present the infant explores its surroundings, whereas in her absence it remains still, passive and fearful. These isolates also show a need for what Harlow termed 'contact comfort' with the surrogate, that is, periods of physical touching. This need seems to be an innate tendency, because it does not depend upon food reinforcement.

These studies of nonhuman primates intrigued psychologists working with troubled children since they raise the possibility that some forms of social maladjustment may be the consequence of failings in the early bonding process between infant and mother. Studies of human bonding suggests that the period of sensitivity to such learning is between six months and four years (Bowlby 1969, Rutter 1981). The common theme running through all cross-species comparisons is that bonding serves a *homeostatic* function, in that it serves to maintain a degree of proximity between parent and offspring which affords protection and succouring of the young.

> 'Attachment behaviour has become a characteristic of many species during the course of their evolution because it contributes to the individual's survival by keeping him in touch with his caregiver(s), thereby reducing the risk of his coming to harm, for example, from cold, hunger or drowning, and, in man's environment of evolutionary adaptedness, especially from predators.' (Bowlby 1981, p. 40)

However, in primates (including humans) the bonding process is in many ways quite unlike the imprinting seen in birds. One principal difference between the bonding processes in attachment and imprinting is the speed at which the event occurs. Imprinting describes a process which may take only minutes to happen whereas in primates the bonding takes many months or years. Furthermore, there are different patterns of behaviour which arise between species as a consequence of failings in the bonding processs. For instance, mallard drakes that are sexually imprinted on geese continue to court them as adults despite lack of success. In finches, however, a preference for their own species usually reappears despite early experience in a process known as 're-imprinting'. Though the effects which have been described in mammals which bond to a parent are quite unlike the imprinted duckling, there are also a number of short-term behavioural effects which they have in common, for instance in the strategies which the young use for signalling distress to the parent, such as by making loud, high-pitched calls, becoming hyperactive and showing other attention-gaining behaviour.

Section summary

Species that imprint tend to do so during a sensitive period during which a bond is formed between offspring and parent. As a result of this bond, offspring will stay close to their parent who will protect them. The imprinting process arises as a result of an inherited mechanism but also involves learning as a result of early exposure to a moving object. Imprinting has both short-term (following) and long-term (in terms of species recognition) consequences for the young animal. Bonding differs from imprinting in that it is a far more gradual process that may take months or years, and failure to bond can produce maladaptive behaviour patterns. In other ways imprinting and bonding are quite similar, particularly in terms of the strategies used for signalling distress to the parent.

Signalling systems in non-human animals

Language is a system of communication in which messages are conveyed between people. But are the elements of human language present in other species? The question of whether language is unique to humans remains controversial. For instance, though some might claim that humans design their own language and communications media (such as Morse Code, the telephone or television), the sounds, sights and smells involved in animal communication are as varied and complex as these human technologies (many of which were, in fact, adapted from what was learned from the biological systems themselves). Moreover, there is much about animal communications that remains unexplored.

The propensity of humans to use spoken language stems from the fact that our brain is designed in many important and unique ways for dealing with auditory communication within a given frequency range corresponding to the human voice (about 1 to 5 kHz). There have been numerous attempts to teach animals to understand human language, but the most productive approach to studying animal communication has been to try to learn the secrets of how *their* communication systems work.

Communication channels

Any communication system involves a *signaller* and a *receiver*. The means by which signals are communicated will depend partially upon the properties of the modality through which the signal is transmitted. For instance, the fabulous display of the peacock is both visual and auditory (the feathers make a fluttering sound during full display), but the effectiveness of colour and movement depends upon the peahen (as receiver) attending to the peacock at the time. To bring about, or to retain, her interest in him, the peacock often has to strut around in front of her, or encircle her so as to intercept her gaze whenever she turns away.

The female in this instance is able to some extent to ignore the visual information provided by the male. But other forms of communication are less easily switched on and off by the receiver. For instance, the bellowing sound made by a band of howler monkeys as they patrol the boundary of their arboreal territory echoes around the South American forests like a foghorn. Only a stone-deaf individual would fail to receive the warning message from such a troup.

Some aquatic species are able to use electricity to communicate. For instance, *Mormyrid* fish (elephant-snouted fish in the lakes of West Africa), whose watery environment is made black by rotting vegetation, communicate their strength and dominance over other males when competing for females (Hopkins 1977, Attenborough 1979). Many moths use chemical signals called *pheromones* to attract mates. In some cases, such as the silkworm moth, the receivers are so sensitive to the airborne chemical message that just one or two molecules are sufficient to trigger a response. Similarly, ants use a chemical signal to communicate sources of food. For instance, the fire ant scout lays a scent trail which excites workers to follow it, eventually leading them towards the food source. In their turn, workers lay their own scent trails so as to maintain the 'pathway' until that food supply has been exhausted.

❖ Activity 2 ❖

Animals tend to evolve signalling systems that work best in their own particular environment. For example, the use of visual communication is clearly advantageous to an animal whose primary habitat is open countryside, but not so good for animals which inhabit dense undergrowth or are nocturnal. What do you think would be the main advantages and disadvantages of the communication channels discussed so far?

In the primates, and in some other mammalian species, touch is an important medium for conveying information. The contact that occurs between chimpanzees during mutual grooming often serves to reassure or pacify individuals who have recently been fighting (Goodall 1990). Harlow and Harlow (1962) also describe the importance of 'contact comfort' in the bonding process between mother and infant rhesus monkey.

The evolution of signals

Many communication systems become ritualized during evolution, that is, the behaviour may become rigidly automatic and will have taken on a new function from that for which it was originally designed. For instance, during courtship, the mandarin drake uses its bill to tap against the brightly coloured markings on its wing tips. This gesture is believed to originate from a preening movement, but now serves to impress the female by emphasizing its wing markings.

Many visual displays are ritualized like this, particularly those occurring during courtship and conflict encounters. A ritualized display is one where two (or more) conspecifics engage in stereotypical sequences of action, each one's responses serving as a stimulus or trigger for the further responses of the other. For instance, the stickleback male engages in a zig-zag dance in front of a pregnant female (carrying a bellyful of unfertilized eggs). His dance may induce her to deposit her eggs in his nest – a shallow pit dug in a stream or river bed, usually under the cover of some light vegetation. After she lays the eggs he swims over and fertilizes them. Each action in this sequence depends upon the previous actions of the other. If the female shows little interest in the male's dance, or she does not approach his nest, the ritual may come to an abrupt end (Tinbergen 1951).

Such ritualization in behaviour sequences serves to 'tune in' each individual to the responsiveness of the other. During courtship rituals this process enables *sexual selection* to occur (described in Chapter 22) where individuals are able to assess the qualities of the other. Furthermore, the existence of the stereotypical behaviour patterns which occur during visual displays serves to prevent cross-breeding between closely related species. The appropriate responses to any one behaviour in such a sequence would only be made by a conspecific – individuals of other species making no such response. This is believed to be important because hybrids arising from cross-breeding are rarely as viable as pure-bred offspring, and are therefore costly errors for parents to make.

Another reason for the evolution of stereotypical, ritualized behaviour patterns is that they create a system which is difficult to infiltrate or exploit by others. A system which is difficult to counterfeit makes it less open to outsiders or cheats to exploit (a process which is referred to as dishonest signalling) (Zahavi 1979). As an analogy, consider how only the very best of forgers are able to reproduce the complex configuration found in a banknote. That is not to say, however, that some forgers and cheats do not get through the system, just that if the task were easier, then more of us would be making paper money!

In conflict situations, too, ritualized bouts enable visual signalling to precede actual combat. This enables an opponent to withdraw when they make the assessment that the other is stronger or bigger than themselves. To learn of this after a fight has started may prove to be immensely costly, adding injury to defeat.

A final example of visual communication is that discussed by Tinbergen and Perdeck (1950) who showed that the orange spot which appears on the mandible of the herring gull bill, serves as a 'target' for the chick's pecking. When the chick pecks at this spot on the parent's bill it triggers the adult to regurgitate food into the nest for the young to eat.

Communication and intentionality

Intentionality of communication does not necessarily imply that either the sender or receiver of a message or signal is making

In Focus

◆

How animals communicate danger

Cheyney and Seyfarth (1990) recorded the sounds made by vervet monkeys in response to the sight of an eagle, leopard and snake. The grunting noises they produce in these situations seem all the same to the untrained human ear. But during playback of these same sounds to the monkeys it was found that their responses were appropriate to the signal being sent (Seyfarth and Cheyney 1992). For instance, vocal signals made when a leopard was seen caused the vervets to run up trees – a sanctuary beyond the reach of any big cat. Playback of the vocalizations made in the presence of a snake caused them to rear up on their hind limbs and stare around them into the undergrowth from where a snake might approach. Vocalizations made in response to an eagle caused the vervets to rush into thicket, a place where a large-winged bird could not enter. There is also evidence that vervet monkeys respond to the alarm calls emitted by starlings, a warning sound which may also be in response to the approach of an eagle (Hauser 1988). In detail, an eagle call sounds like a two-syllable cough, whereas a snake evokes a chuttering sound from the vervets.

The leopard call is also found to be different when made by males and females. The male gives a loud bark whereas the female gives a high-pitched 'chirrup' when a leopard is seen.

conscious decisions. For instance, a pheromone emitted by a male African elephant when in musth (see Chapter 22) serves as a warning to other males that he is likely to be in a highly aggressive state. The biological changes which have occurred in the signalling male are responsible for the message he is emitting. Similarly, people whose cheeks flush red when they are angry or embarrassed are not intentionally producing this signal to warn others. Under these circumstances the receiver *reads the mind* of the sender, using cues from appearance or behaviour which indicate the sender's internal state. Mind-reading is the term given by Krebs and Dawkins (1984) to describe what receivers make of signals that other animals emit – these signals provide some insight into what emotional state the sender is in, and what their likely next action is to be. However, not all signals arise in this way (see *In Focus* above).

Deception in communication

In some encounters between two animals, individuals may engage in a dispute which may have the prospect of escalating into actual combat. One or both individuals may initially signal their determination to fight in order to bluff the other that they mean serious business. Conversely, a weakening in the resolve to fight may be 'leaked' in their body language, signalling to the other that a slight escalation in the dispute will probably bring victory. Under such circumstances the message may either be reliable (an 'honest' signal) or else be deceptive. For instance, an individual hoping to win a dispute by any means short of actual combat may rely heavily upon bluff, perhaps by appearing to be more aggressive, strong or willing to fight than may be true. This strategy will involve dishonest signalling to the opponent.

Another circumstance in which an animal may signal dishonestly is when faced with a predator. For instance, many prey species inflate their body or 'stand tall' when threatened, so as to make themselves look like formidable opposition. On the other hand, appearing carefree while in front of an opponent or predator may also send a specific signal. For example, Thompson's gazelles show a pronounced escape gait known as 'stotting' or 'pronking', in which they leap by 'bouncing' along on all four legs a metre or two into the air (see the photo opposite of a springbok) .

The whole countenance of a gazelle while stotting seems to be one of nonchalance, or

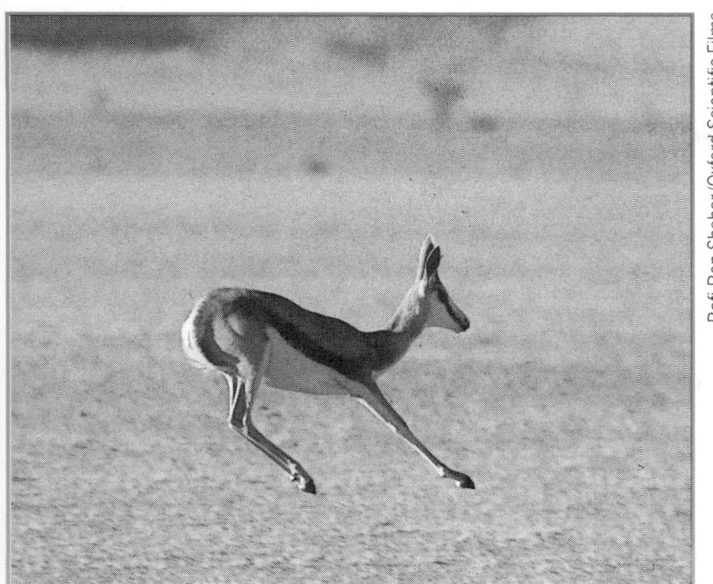
Rafi Ben-Shahar/Oxford Scientific Films

Springbok (*Antidorcas marsupialis*) 'stotting'

even arrogance. This behaviour appears in the presence of some of its many predators, but not all. Of the big cats which prey upon gazelle, most are able to catch them if the chase is over a short distance. However, when predators such as the African hunting dog pack approaches, stotting is seen in many of the herd members. It is believed that this gait signals to the predator that this individual is both strong and fast, and unlikely to be caught if chased. This interpretation is based upon the observation that few of the stotting gazelles are singled out by the dogs, implying that stotting is a clear and honest signal of an individual's ability to escape (Fitzgibbon and Fanshawe 1988), but it is by no means clear whether all the stotting males are signalling honestly.

Sometimes a signal to a predator may take the form of outright bluff, like when a crane or a partridge feigns a broken wing in order to lead a predator such as a fox away from the location of their nest. Recent interest in deceiptfulness in animal communication has been stimulated by the controversy over whether animals have conscious awareness (Griffin 1984, 1991). Some argue that in order to deceive others an individual must have a 'Machiavellian' intent to fool them (Byrne and Whiten 1988). In plain language, animals who are able to 'lie' must presume that those they are deceiving have 'minds' which can be misled.

Dance language of the honeybee

Lindauer (1955) and von Frisch (1967) studied the remarkable communication system in honey bees, known as 'dance language'. Honey bee scouts scour the countryside around the hive looking for sources of nectar. When one scout locates a source it will return to the hive and engage in an excited 'waggle dance', which signals to the workers both the direction (within ±25 degrees) and distance (within ±15 per cent) of the source from the hive. This dance is thought to provide information via sight, sound, vibration and odour, about the quality and location of the food, and is effective even when danced within the darkness of the hive. The waggle dance system is used not just for conveying information about food source, but is also used in other circumstances. For instance, during a swarm, in which a new colony is founded, the dancers seem to convey information about sites they have found which may be suitable for establishing the new hive.

Although it has been suggested by a number of commentators that the bees are merely responding automatically to the stimulus of movement and sounds produced by the returning scouts, there is evidence that the workers make decisions about whether or not to follow up the information they are provided with. For instance, Gould (1986, 1992) led a captive scout to a nectar source he had placed in a boat in the middle of a lake, and then released the bee. Despite the scout's dancing on returning to the hive, very few workers left the hive to investigate. Not only do bees dislike flying over water, but the prospect of finding food in the middle of a lake must seem remote. This seems a reasonable deduction, because when Gould next took the captive scout fully across the lake to the opposite shore, the scout was able to recruit workers by the waggle dance when it had returned to the hive. The basis of the honey bee's dance is believed to be even more complex than was first thought since it contains an amalgam of interacting signals (Kirchner and Towne 1994).

Understanding complex commands

Herman (1986) trained dolphins to carry out chains of instructions to earn a food reward. The instructions involved sequences of whistle sounds played into their tank. For instance, Herman was able to convey the message that he wanted the dolphin to touch a pipe floating on the surface with its tail by connecting the individual sounds which stood for *tail, touch* and *floating pipe*. The animals were able to carry out these commands successfully, which shows that they were able to interpret the complex chains of information they heard. The fact that different behaviours could be elicited simply by rearranging the individual command units ruled out the possibility that the dolphins were merely being conditioned to respond as though by use of some form of operant schedule of reinforcement (see Chapter 24 for details of operant conditioning).

In their natural environment, humpback whales have been observed to communicate in 'songs', which are sound phrases used to convey information over vast distances across the oceans. These songs change over time, with some being repeated on a seasonal basis. Although researchers have not as yet managed to translate these sounds, or find in them a basis of complex language, it is clear that we have a lot to learn about such communication (Payne and Payne 1985). Humans have always been eager to claim the faculties of intelligence and language as unique skills to our species. There is increasing evidence that such a view is not only anthropocentric; it is also plainly wrong.

Section summary

Communication occurs when one animal (the signaller) signals to another (the receiver) in such a way that it changes the behaviour of the receiver in some way. The environment and lifestyle of an animal determine the type of sensory channel that it most often uses. Signals have frequently become ritualized over time so that their current function has little in common with their original function. Deceptive communications have the advantage of manipulating the behaviour of another animal to the signaller's advantage.

Chapter summary

- Animals sometimes behave in ways that increase the reproductive fitness of the individual that is helped at some cost to the helper. This altruistic behaviour may, however, only be apparent, as animals may actually be acting in a way that benefits their own kin, and therefore their own genes. In reciprocal altruism animals may help another with the other animal returning the favour at some time in the future. Strategies such as 'tit for tat' ensure that defection from this need to return favours does not work to the advantage of the defecting animal.
- Animals frequently collaborate in social groups. The extra vigilance that is possible in social groups acts as protection against predators. Cooperation in foraging enables individual animals to profit from the information provided by successful foragers in the group.
- Imprinting and bonding are processes that enable young animals to stay close to their parents. Imprinting involves an inherited mechanism which predisposes a young animal to follow a moving object (usually the parent). This is vital in the short term, for protection, and in the long term, for species recognition, and is considered irreversible. Bonding is a more gradual process that may develop over months or years.

❖ Communication occurs when one animal (the signaller) signals to another (the receiver) in such a way that it changes the behaviour of the receiver in some way. The environment and lifestyle of an animal determine the type of sensory channel that it most often uses. Signals have frequently become ritualized over time so that their current function has little in common with their original function. Deceptive communications have the advantage of manipulating the behaviour of another animal to the signaller's advantage.

Examination questions

1 Describe and assess *two* genetic explanations for apparent altruism. *(24 marks)*

2 Describe and assess the reasons why animals live in groups. *(24 marks)*

3 (a) Explain the use of *two* different communication systems in non-human animals. *(12 marks)*

(b) Assess the advantages and disadvantages of *one* of these systems. *(12 marks)*

Further reading

Grier, J.W. and Burk, T. (1992) *Biology of Animal Behaviour* (2nd edn), St. Louis: Mosby.

A very comprehensive account of the topics in this chapter, and a text that deals critically with the issues discussed.

Ridley, M. (1995) *Animal Behaviour* (2nd edn), Oxford: Blackwell.

A very accessible and clear account of these topics and a very good introductory text on the subject of animal behaviour.

Chapter 24

Behaviour analysis

Roger Davies

Preview

In this chapter we shall be looking at:

- classical conditioning
- operant conditioning
- homing behaviour
- foraging
- animal language
- evolutionary explanations of human behaviour.

Introduction

The previous three chapters have all been concerned with evolutionary principles and influences on animal behaviour. The task outlined there was that of providing ultimate explanations for behaviour. This chapter includes a discussion of how the environment influences behaviour. There are two ways in which the term 'environmental influence' is meant in psychology. The first of these is where an immediate stimulus in the physical environment leads to some response in the individual. A second meaning treats the environment as an abstract construct which, during the course of our lives, moulds us into the people we become. Hence, large differences in personality, aptitudes, temperament or intelligence between people can be treated as attributable to environmental effects, or to differences in upbringing.

The importance of both these meanings of the term environment is that they are often commonly assumed to imply that:

- the main contribution psychology has to make is in investigating how such environmental variables affect people, and
- 'environment' offers an explanation which is a polar opposite to that based upon biological processes (e.g. physiology, genetics or evolution).

However, neither of these assumptions is true today, if they ever were. The point was made and reiterated throughout the previous three chapters that scientific explanations are by their nature multi-faceted: cause-and-effect relations in animal and human behaviour are necessarily complex and stratified (Timberlake 1993).

Behaviour analysis

According to the philosopher René Descartes (1596–1650), an individual is defined by self-awareness.

> *'But what, then, am I? A thing that thinks. What is a thing that thinks? That is to say, a thing that doubts, perceives, affirms, denies, wills, does not will, that imagines also, and which feels. Indeed, this is not a little, if all these properties belong to my nature'* (Descartes 1641/1968, p. 106)

Descartes, like most early psychologists, took for granted that consciousness, self-awareness, intelligence, emotion and personality are the main areas of study as far as understanding people is concerned. After all, it seems that these are the qualities that set humans apart from animals and also distinguish one person from another.

But the main problem with the approach of Descartes is that although such introspections seem to apply equally well to everyone's experience of their own mind, we can never really know, in a scientific sense, if what one person thinks or feels is similar to or comparable with what other people think or feel. For instance, though two English-speaking people may agree in their use of the word 'blue' to describe the colour of a particular object, this does not *prove* they are both perceiving the same thing. If one of these two individuals happens to be colour blind, his or her mental concept of the term 'blue' may be something resembling medium grey. In other words, abstract words do not make useful scientific terms even though in everyday use they may convey to others some rough semblance of how we think or feel, or what our aspirations in life happen to be. Probably the majority of concepts which we happily describe in the words of our everyday language are unamenable to scientific research for reasons of their ambiguity, abstraction and imprecision.

So, without such 'mentalisms', what are we left with? The only thing it seems we might readily agree upon are descriptions of what people do. For instance, if Jill's friend Mike trips her up as she is passing, then an observer might, in everyday terms, describe the event as being a 'practical joke'. But this would be a subjective interpretation based upon what the observer happens to know about Jill and Mike, as well as their countenances at the time. However, the observer might be a complete stranger to both, in which case the main clue towards making an accurate interpretation of events would be Jill's reaction to being tripped.

An objective explanation of what happened might be: 'When Mike extended his foot it coincided with Jill's passing by, and led her to stumble.' What is different about this objective description is that it records the events without referring to the intent or internal states of the people involved. If Jill and Mike were robots, the same statement would still hold true, but few people would explain a collision between two robots (or even animals) as the playing of a practical joke by one upon the other.

The early psychologists who were first faced with this issue of how to describe behaviour dealt with it in one of two ways. Either they cautiously ignored the problem and proceeded to use terms which they had carefully defined from the outset, or else they outlawed all concepts which could not be verified by observation alone. It is the mainly the work of this second group of theorists that is described in this chapter: the so-called 'behaviourists'.

The position of behaviourism could be characterized as 'I behave and therefore I am'. For instance:

> *'We are what we do. During the course of our lifetimes, we constantly engage in some type of behaviour. It is our behaviour that defines what kind of people we are, whether we are productive or wasteful, kind or cruel, and wise or foolish.'* (Grant and Evans 1994, p. 1)

Classical or Pavlovian conditioning

Classical conditioning was first described in detail by the Russian physiologist Ivan Pavlov (1927). Pavlov was investigating the salivatory reflex in dogs, a response which occurs automatically when food is placed on the animal's tongue. He observed that his animals salivated not just in response to this stimulus (which is the basic reflex action itself), but also in response to anything else which was regularly coinciding with the feeding routine, such as the presence of the food dish, or the person who regularly fed them. All animals are born with a host of reflexes, which may be either simple, such as a constriction of the pupil of the eye when strong light is seen, or complex, such as the righting reflex of the cat when it falls to the ground. The whole point about natural reflexes such as these is that:

- they are innate, i.e. they are present in the animal at, or soon after, birth
- they are triggered consistently and automatically by the occurrence of one kind of stimulus
- once such a response is triggered, it is not normally altered for its duration by subsequent events
- experience does little to alter the time course or pattern of the response.

In a typical classical conditioning experiment the researcher selects one of these naturally occurring reflexes of an animal and then deliberately and consistently presents an 'artificial' stimulus (that is, one which does not normally trigger the response or reflex itself) prior to the 'natural' stimulus (the one which does normally trigger off that reflex). Imagine for the purpose of this description this artificial stimulus to be the sound of a buzzer.

In his description of the procedure involved, Pavlov used a particular terminology to define these different components. The natural stimulus for any reflex (e.g. the object touching the tongue, in the case of salivation) is referred to as an 'unconditioned stimulus' (US), where the term 'conditioning' may be read as 'training'. In other words, an unconditioned stimulus is one which produces a response that is innate, or 'untrained'. When our eyes blink as an object approaches them at speed, this is not a trained response but one which we are born with. When the reflex is described as an 'unconditioned response' (UR), it means it occurs after an unconditioned stimulus. When training is taking place using an *artificial* stimulus, this is referred to as a 'conditioned stimulus' (CS).

At the start the CS does *not* bring about a reflex response by itself. However, after many pairings of CS followed by US, the situation changes. The animal's reflex of salivating arises at the onset of the buzzer and now works even though the dog's tongue is not stimulated. Pavlov realized that the salivation which occurs in response to the buzzer still has the properties of a reflex, but now happens as a learned response. Furthermore, the range of stimuli which can act as a CS seemed potentially infinite – being anything audible, visible, tactile or of any sensory modality which the subject (in this case, the dog) can detect.

In the case of innate reflexes it has already been stated that they are almost permanent features of the animal's behaviour repertory, however young or old the animal may be, and that they show little or no change over the lifespan. Pavlov examined the nature of the conditioned reflex to compare it with these aspects of the UR. Unlike the UR, he found that the CR is labile, i.e. does not become permanently established as a response. On the contrary, the CR does not long outlast the removal of the CS. So, for instance, although the dog may have been trained to salivate to the buzzer sound, if the buzzer is continually sounded without being followed by the food stimulus on the tongue, then salivation to the buzzer rapidly diminishes. This dying out of the CR when the US is no longer paired with the US is referred to as a process of 'extinction'. Experimentally, extinction is brought about by *unpaired* presentations of

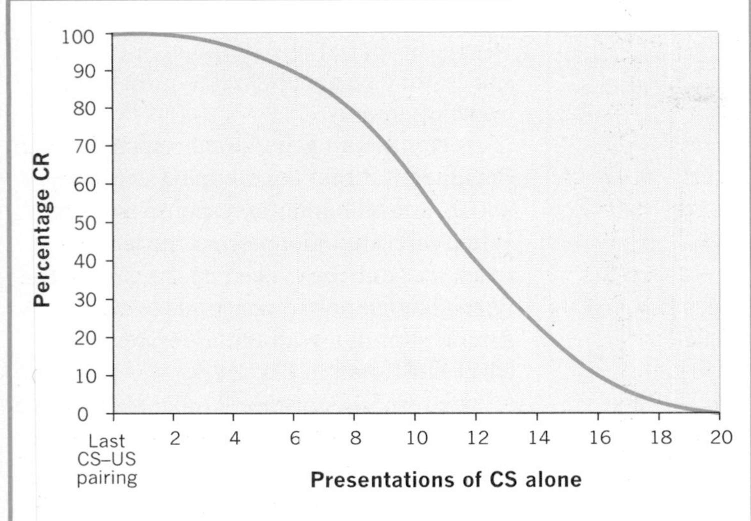

Figure 24.1
Extinction of CR when US no longer paired with CS

the CS. The extinction process can be seen by measuring the CR over experimental trials, with the response gradually diminishing until it eventually seems to disappear altogether (see Fig. 24.1). Figure 24.1 shows what happens when the trials proceed as with training, except that the US no longer follows the presentation of the CS. By the second presentation, the CR remains nearly the same as the last CS–US pairing, but by the tenth trial, the CR is now only one-half what it originally was. Likewise, by the twentieth trial the CR has further diminished, this time to the point where it is virtually 'extinct'.

However, Pavlov found that extinction is not like a process of forgetting. The unique thing about a CR that has become extinct is that is always liable to reappear suddenly, under the right conditions. This sudden reappearance is referred to as 'spontaneous recovery', and there are two main situations which bring it about:

- a postponement of training (i.e. a time lapse between one extinction trial and another), which is sufficient to reinstate the CR
- the subject being startled (e.g. any sudden event, such as loud noise, which occurs during the process of extinction training may bring back the CR, however transiently).

There is one more reason to doubt that extinction is analogous to forgetting. This is that when the subject is retrained by using the original CS–US pairings, the CR is quickly reinstated. This reinstatement occurs much faster that the original conditioning, which implies that the CR was not really 'lost'. To explain the process of response extinction, Pavlov described the CR as being inhibited, much like the energy that may be maintained in a coil spring by keeping your hand pressed down upon it. When the inhibition is removed, the response returns (in the metaphor of the coil spring, it rebounds into shape when your hand pressure is removed).

It is as though the nervous system has the property of being able to hold back a learned response until some 'releasing' event takes place. From what was known about the generally inhibitory action of the cerebral cortex (see Chapter 6 for a description of cerebral cortex) this suggested to Pavlov, and other neurophysiologists of his time, that much of the brain in complex animals was designed for suppressing learned responses until the occasion was right for their 'release'.

Pavlov also introduced a term called 'response generalization', which occurs when a stimulus is presented which is similar to the CS, but not identical to it. For instance, if conditioned to salivate at the sound of one buzzer, will the response occur when a *different* buzzer sound is played? The more similar the new buzzer is to the CS then the greater will be the similarity between the responses to this new sound and to the original one. For instance, if the salivatory response is measured in millilitres (ml) per minute, then the original CS will evoke the most saliva in that time. However, a similar-sounding buzzer will also evoke a similar amount, more so than a less-similar sounding buzzer, and so on. When plotted graphically, the effect is a bell-shaped curve, illustrated in Fig. 24.2. As this figure shows, stimuli at positions −1 and +1 are similar to the CS in their ability to evoke a CR – in fact each produces over 80 per cent of the response which the CS produces. In practice, the stimulus at

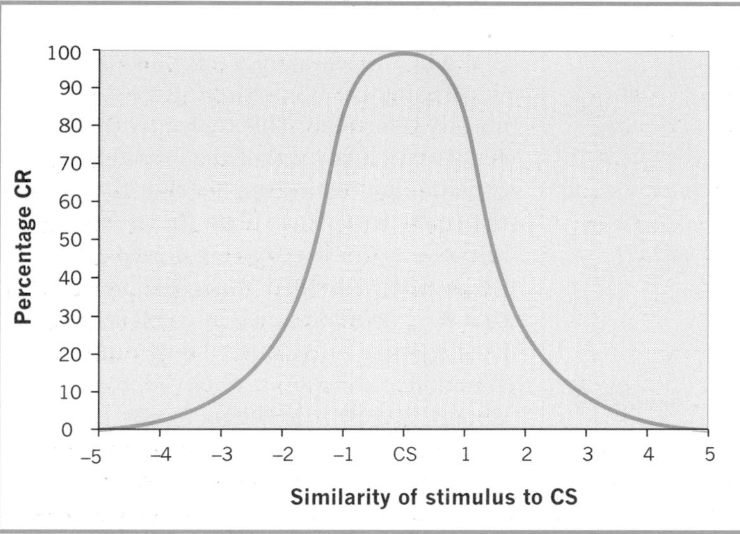

Figure 24.2
Generalization of CR to stimuli similar to CS

position –1 might be a buzzer with a sound of slightly lower pitch that the CS itself, and the one at +1 might have a slightly higher pitch. On the other hand, a stimulus at position –4 might be markedly lower in pitch to the CS, and as the graph shows, this stimulus produces only a small fraction (about 3 per cent) of the response which the CS evokes.

So, despite the fact that conditioning has involved only the use of one stimulus (CS), the response itself may be generalized to others. This is an important point to bear in mind in the application of this theory to psychological medicine, in particular with regard to the phenomena associated with people's experience of strong fear (phobia) where the fear of one stimulus, such as a spider, may be generalized to most of the crawling insects.

In contrast to generalized responses, Pavlov found that conditioning can bring about discrimination of response to the CS. When discrimination occurs the learned reflex can only be evoked by the CS, i.e. the typically generalized responses to other, similar stimuli are absent. Consider the effect illustrated in Fig. 24.3.

Figure 24.3
Discrimination of CR to CS

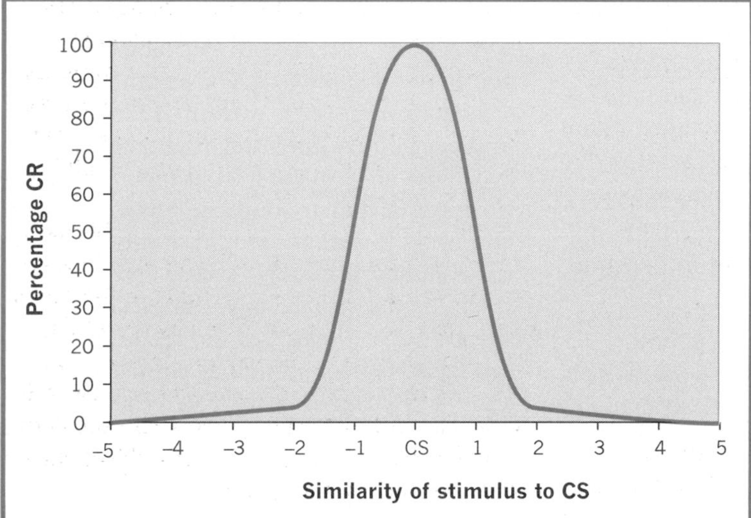

The response to stimuli other than the CS is now curtailed. For example, whereas the CR to stimuli at positions –2 and +2 were previously (see Fig. 24.2) over 20 per cent of the response to the CS, now these stimuli evoke less than 5 per cent of the CR.

The way in which discrimination training has been carried out is as follows. During the original conditioning, where the CS–US pairings were made, there needs to be a number of occasions when other stimuli, similar to the CS, are introduced. These other stimuli, however, are never paired with the US. The end result of this form of training is that the response which is conditioned to the CS is very specific to it. Now, the responses to almost all other stimuli are removed, with the CR being evoked by the CS and little else.

You may notice from Fig. 24.3 that the stimuli at positions –1 and +1 do still evoke a considerable proportion of the CR (about 60 per cent of it). This is because in practice the difference between the pitch of buzzer (in the example given here) of the stimulus at –1 and the CS, or +1 and the CS, is extremely slight. These differences in pitch may even be extremely difficult for the human ear to discern. The discrimination training can proceed until highly similar stimuli to the CS do not evoke much CR. In fact Pavlov reported in his experiments that if such training persists so that the distinction between stimuli is so fine that the subject's senses are hardly able to detect them, a condition of 'experimental neurosis' may arise in the subject being conditioned. In this case the subject's performance may break down altogether, with unpleasant consequences for their behaviour and general health. For instance, self-immolation may occur, where the animal may bite its own paws during the procedure. Discrimination training taken to this degree therefore, has the potential for inflicting psychological distress on the subject. Again, this has implications for the application of the theory to psychological medicine, as we shall discuss later in the chapter.

❖ Activity 1 ❖

From your own experience, can you recall any instances where your behaviour was influenced by classical conditioning. Try to identify the unconditioned and conditioned stimuli that were associated with this behaviour.

Section summary

In classical conditioning, a naturally occurring reflex (the US–UR reflex) is associated with another stimulus (the CR) that is not typically capable of producing the response in question. Following consistent association with the US, the new stimulus is able to trigger the original behaviour. If the US is no longer paired with the UR, however, the CR is extinguished. The CR might reappear under certain conditions in a procedure known as spontaneous recovery.

When a stimulus is presented which is similar to the CS, the response might generalize to it dependent on the degree of similarity. If other stimuli are never paired with the US, however, the organism will discriminate between them and only respond to the original CS.

Operant conditioning

Although the title of 'founding father of behaviour analysis' is attributed to B.F. Skinner (dating from the publication in 1935 of his book *The Behaviour of Organisms*), the roots of this approach go back at least to the nineteenth century. Skinner himself acknowledged the influence of Thorndike on his early work, especially Thorndike's description of a law of effect (Thorndike 1911). The law of positive effect states that any behaviour that leads to a positive outcome, such as a successful solution to a problem, or a state of 'satisfaction' in the organism, will tend to be retained and repeated in future. The increasing frequency of this behaviour by an organism will be reinforced by each further successful outcome that behaviour brings about.

Reinforcement

In terms of Thorndike's 'law of (positive) effect', the outcome of a behaviour will act so as to strengthen, or reinforce, that behaviour. For instance, consider an infant who is struggling to open a door that is obstructed by a toy. No amount of pulling on the door will open it, and so the child may resort to the favourite solution of all young children – yell long and loud. However, if neither the crying aloud nor any alternative works, then the problem of how to get through the door remains. The child may become distracted by playing with the toy for a while before resuming his efforts with the door. Then, by playing with the toy, the child moves its position so it is no longer an obstruction and 'magically', the door opens.

The removal of the toy has brought about the successful outcome of being able to leave the room and the action of moving the toy is therefore likely to be retained by the child. Not only has the child been reinforced by moving the toy, but the child's response will *generalize* in future situations where the door may be obstructed by a different object, such as a stool or a sleeping dog.

In Thorndike's view, behaviour is *reinforced* and maintained by its consequences, and so any behaviour which fails to bring about a successful outcome, such as the child's yelling or struggling against the obstacle in the above example, will go unreinforced, and should not reappear as frequently in that child's future behaviour patterns when he is placed in similar circumstances. In Thorndike's work the experimental demonstration of the law of effect was in giving animals problems to solve. For instance, a cat placed in a box from which it could only escape by operating a latch, would learn to do so eventually. Before learning the successful strategy the cat would have tried numerous other, unsuccessful behaviours, such as scratching and biting, and these would not have brought about its escape. Escape is itself a reinforcing outcome for the action of operating the latch and so, on being returned to the box again, the latch would become the focus of the cat's behaviour and actions directed at it would be those most in evidence.

Skinner devised an easier measurement technique for investigating how reinforcement acts upon behaviour. The Skinner Box was designed by him to reward the subject, not by allowing escape, but by providing food pellets. In this circumstance the animal (usually a rat or a pigeon) would also initially show only escape-seeking behaviour in the box. However, one of these actions, such as pressing downwards on a lever, would bring about a food reinforcer (see Fig. 24.4).

Figure 24.4
Skinner Box

This action would bring about reinforcement in the form of a food pellet delivered automatically from the hopper. This is much the same mechanism which delivers a chocolate bar from a machine when a coin is inserted. In the Skinner Box the subject's actions are easily (and automatically) recorded by measuring the number of food items obtained in a given interval of time. For instance, if twenty-five pellets of food were dispensed from the hopper in the first hour, and one hundred and fifty in the second hour, then the threefold increase in the subject's response rate is easy to monitor and record.

Using the Skinner box arrangement many interesting insights were gained regarding how reinforcement comes to control a subject's responses. For instance, the delivery of one food item for every lever press might seem to be the optimal way of ensuring the response is learned and maintained. But that is not what Skinner discovered. His greatest insight was in showing that reinforcement exerts subtle (though nonetheless predictable) effects on behaviour depending upon how the reinforcer is made contingent (i.e. dependent) upon the response.

Schedules of reinforcement

If a food reinforcer is not dispensed for every single response (e.g. lever press), but is arranged according to a predetermined 'schedule', such as one food pellet for every fifth lever press, then different response patterns arise depending upon the exact relationship between response and reinforcement.

There are four ways in which reinforcement may be scheduled:

- as a ratio of the number of responses, such as the 1:5 example above, or
- as a result of a time-base or time-interval criterion. For instance, this might mean the delivery of a food pellet at the end of, say, one minute *provided that the subject*

has responded in that interval (and not otherwise).

In addition to the above two forms of schedule, in which reinforcement may occur by either a time- or response-based criterion, reinforcement may also be applied in either a fixed or a variable schedule.

- A *fixed* schedule dispenses reinforcement on a reliable basis, e.g. in a 1:5 fixed-ratio (FR5) schedule the reinforcer is delivered after every fifth lever press. Similarly, a fixed-interval schedule of one minute (FI1) will deliver reinforcement at the end of every minute, provided that the subject has made the required response (e.g. lever pressing) in that time.
- *Variable* schedules dispense food on an erratic basis, e.g. a ratio schedule of 1:5 (VR5) will deliver food on average once every five responses, but during any one trial that number may vary from 5. Only over a large number of trials will the schedule be seen to have averaged one reinforcer per five responses. On a variable interval schedule of one minute (VI1) the interval is varied around the period of one minute, though this interval alters from trial to trial so that only over the long run does the one minute average become apparent.

Each of these forms of schedule has its own characteristic effects on the subject's responding. Some schedules, such as a low-fixed ratio, tend to bring about rapid initial learning of the required response, but the response rate itself does not accelerate as rapidly as it does with, say, a variable-interval schedule. The 'extinction' rates also differ markedly between schedules, i.e. extinction being the rate at which the conditioned response (such as lever-pressing in the Skinner Box) diminishes in frequency when the reinforcement is stopped altogether. Typically, a subject working on a VI schedule which has a relatively long interval will maintain their response rate far longer than will a subject working on one of the fixed-schedule types (i.e. FR or FI).

Because the above schedules all reinforce the subject for some, but not all, of their responses, they are referred to generally as 'partial reinforcement', to distinguish them from 'continuous reinforcement' (CRF), in which reinforcement is dispensed after every correct response. Typically, CRF schedules will induce rapid initial learning, a slower overall response rate, and rapid extinction. By comparison, partial reinforcement schedules generally induce slower initial learning, overall faster rates of responding, and slower extinction rates, though each of the four forms of partial schedule will vary in their effects on these aspects of learning, as has been pointed out above.

❖ Activity 2 ❖

What type of reinforcement schedule do you think 'one-armed bandits' operate on? How does that affect the behaviour of those who play them?

Punishment and negative reinforcement

In Thorndike's original formulation there was also a law of negative effect. By this he meant that if a subject's actions led to unwanted or unpleasant outcomes ('annoyers', as he called them), then those actions would diminish over time, i.e. the subject would become less likely on future occasions to reproduce those actions. This contingency between a behaviour and negative consequences is, however, less clear than that, as Thorndike himself found. One reason for this is that unpleasant outcomes may arise in a variety of ways, such as from:

- a failure to obtain a reward which was an expected consequence of some action the subject carried out
- a failure to avoid an unpleasant stimulus by taking appropriate avoiding action
- a direct consequence of the action itself.

For instance, a child may be playing behind a door when she hears the rattle of keys outside. If she remains behind the door when it opens against her she would be hurt. Her inaction brings about a negative consequence – had she moved in response to the rattle of keys the pain would not have been felt. On subsequent occasions the sound of keys may be sufficient to activate her into moving from the area. This key sound leads to avoidance behaviour, which is an example of negative reinforcement in that failure to make the correct response will lead to an unpleasant outcome.

Consider another situation where a child is reaching up to a table by leaning against a stool, and the stool topples under the child's weight. The pain is felt this time as a result of the child's actions, i.e. the outcome is a consequence of the child's action, rather than inaction, and has the effect of punishing the behaviour which preceded it.

Negative reinforcement has been generally regarded as being more effective than punishment in bringing about learning because it aims to activate a desired response rather to deactivate an unwanted one. Part of the problem with attempting to eradicate an undesirable behaviour is that it does not necessarily follow that a desired one will arise in its place. For instance, having learned not to reach to the table by leaning against the stool the child may then embark upon an even more risky behaviour, such as climbing upon an unstable chair. There is also the view that punishment fails to do more than just suppress a behaviour while the punishing agent is present, a view that has tended to prevail in institutions such as prisons, where sustained vigilance is required.

In negative reinforcement procedures the subject has actively to avoid the unpleasant event. The event itself, say, a mild electric shock delivered to the feet in a Skinner Box, has its onset signalled by the occurrence of a warning event such as a light or a buzzer. The shock is an aversive event and therefore the subject will soon learn to avoid it if possible, in much the same way as learning to obtain food or water by pressing a lever. The activity required of pressing the lever when, say, the buzzer plays, enables the subject to avoid the shock altogether. Failure to respond appropriately to the buzzer will bring about the aversive event. In 'Sidman avoidance' the subject is placed in a box which has two compartments. Shortly after the warning the subject has to move from one section of the box to another in order to avoid the aversive event (hence the name 'shuttle' box is sometimes used to describe this apparatus).

The theoretical question which negative reinforcement poses is: what is the reinforcer? For instance, when the subject responds to the lever so as to obtain a pellet the reinforcement is the food item itself. But in negative-reinforcement procedures the outcome is the avoidance of, not the contact with the reinforcer. To explain this conundrum some behaviourists reasoned that reinforcement of both positive and negative types acts upon 'drive reduction' mechanisms. A 'drive' is like a biological instinct – for instance, the experience of hunger is accompanied by a drive or motivation to find food in order to satisfy that hunger. To experience fear when expecting a shock to happen motivates or 'drives' the response of seeking safety so as to reduce that fear.

However, when shock is made unavoidable in a shuttle box, the subject will soon not only fail to attempt to avoid at all, but will also be less likely to learn an avoidance routine in future situations where the shock (or other aversive event) *is* avoidable. This failure to learn active avoidance after having experience of an unavoidable aversive stimulus has been suggested as an explanation for the onset of some forms of human depression (e.g. Beck 1991). The reasoning here is that having learned in one phase of life that personal difficulties are found to be irresolvable (e.g. following the death of a spouse or loss of employment) then this attitude will generalize to future occasions so that the person experiences feelings of helplessness when faced with what are, in reality, avoidable negative events. This situation has become known as 'learned helplessness'.

Section summary

Operant conditioning refers to learning that is dependent on the outcome of a behaviour. If behaviour is reinforced in some way, that behaviour will reappear more frequently in the future. This reinforcement may be positive, in that a behaviour is followed by a pleasant event, or negative, in that by responding in some way, an organism can avoid or escape from an unpleasant event. Reinforcement can also be presented in various schedules. These might be continuous or partial. Continuous reinforcement schedules produce more rapid initial learning and slower extinction rates. If a behaviour produces unpleasant consequences (punishment) it is less likely to be produced in the future.

Homing behaviour

A fundamental distinction between plant and animal life is the ability to move at will around the environment. Most plant life acts like a chemical factory, making up and breaking down chemicals into nutrient and waste products, and using one of a number of reproductive mechanisms to germinate and reproduce. Animals tend to move around in search of food (foraging), whether obtained from plants or other animal life (though some plants are also highly effective hunters and trappers of animals, too).

In animal species that build or otherwise manufacture a home (e.g. a nest, burrow or shelter) that is used more than once by them, they need to have some way of remembering not only where the home is, but also to have some form of navigational or direction-finding protocol for locating it from a distance. The means by which animals locate their home range from afar can be very impressive indeed, with some species able to do so as part of migratory pattern which may take them many thousands of miles each year (MacFarland 1993).

Migration is a generic term which usually describes the mass movement of members of a species from one location to another. The trigger for this behaviour may be seasonal changes in weather, air temperature or day length, or in response to fluctuations in the environment such as food supply. For instance, wildebeest on the African savannah move towards rain when they sense it during the dry season. They seem to be able to read the signs, such as darkened clouds or cool winds emanating from the direction of the rains. The distance over which animals migrate may range from one to two metres (e.g. the vertical movements of zooplankton in a lake, moving to different depths according to time of day) to several thousand miles, such as the albatross or the monarch butterfly. Usually these are return migrations, but not always. For instance, adult Atlantic salmon migrate from the Sargasso Sea (South Atlantic) to the lakes and rivers of Europe where they themselves were spawned.

In Focus

The monarch butterfly

The monarch butterfly lives mainly in North America. When the temperatures begin to fall, these large, strikingly coloured insects begin their amazing migration south to winter in the southern United States and Mexico. Although not all monarchs migrate south in this way, those who do, do so at astonishing speeds – with some tagged monarchs covering more than 80 miles in a single day. Although they may continue their free-living existence following this migration, when the weather turns colder, the butterflies aggregate into dense groups to keep warm. As they are cold blooded, it appears that this seasonal migration is driven by the need to be in a warm enough place to still maintain an active life.

After spawning near the site of their own birthplace, they perish, leaving the next generation to fight their way along the freshwater pathways back to the sea.

Though such migration may seem rather a pointless activity, the benefits are usually that the individuals exploit the best breeding or feeding conditions in both places. The seasonal changes which affect latitudes at some distance from the equator means that the climate, food or other resources fluctuate greatly with the seasons. The impetus to migrate may not be a *decision* left to individual animals – the so-called 'migration *instinct'* can markedly affect an animal's behaviour at the close of a season. On the other hand, many individuals of bird species seem to *decide* not to migrate in a given year (though of course, no 'reasoning' is implied here – the response may simply be one where the environmental cues have not been sufficiently strong to trigger off the behaviour seen in others of the species).

Birds which migrate over large distances are able to use a range of environmental cues to guide them, such as the smell of the sea while following a continental coastline, the sight of mountains or other landmarks, or by using the earth's magnetic field. The use of such landmarks is not confined to migratory journeys, however, since many animals utilize knowledge of their environment (a so-called 'cognitive map') to navigate during their daily forays from home.

For instance, Tinbergen and Kruyt (1938) demonstrated how the digger wasp uses the main features around its burrow to locate its home when returning from a foraging or hunting flight. The wasp makes its home by burrowing a short distance into soft dirt and, just prior to leaving each time, makes a hovering flight overhead, seemingly 'taking in' any changes in the environment in the vicinity of the burrow entrance. Tinbergen and Kruyt carried out an ingenious experiment by altering the position of landmarks (pine cones they had set out themselves) after the wasp had flown out of sight. When the resident wasp returned, it was deceived by the new placement of cones into searching for its burrow entrance in the wrong place entirely.

Insects such as the digger wasp show an ability to make use of memorized landmarks in finding their way back to a burrow. But how important is such compass orientation to navigation? In other words, migrating animals might always move in a certain direction relative to a point on a compass. To test whether birds were capable of true 'navigation' (i.e. showing the ability to reach their goal regardless of their starting point) or simply showing a compass orientation (always heading in one specific compass direction regardless of the 'correct' direction), a group of scientists carried out an ingenious experiment. They captured young starlings on their annual migration from their breeding grounds around the Baltic Sea to their wintering sites in southern England, Belgium and northern France. After tagging, the birds were taken, by aeroplane, to Switzerland, where they were released. After release, the birds continued on the same heading as before (south-west) despite the fact they had been displaced by nearly 500 miles from their original route! Instead of ending up in southern England, many of the birds arrived in northern Spain (see Fig. 24.5). Interestingly, adult birds that were captured and released in the same way compensated for the displacement and headed north-west, the proper direction for their wintering grounds. The juveniles, it appears, were relying on compass orientation, the adults on true navigation.

It has been long suspected that pigeons have a superb 'sense' of direction. When released into a completely unfamiliar environment they have the ability to orientate themselves (after a brief encircling flight) back to their home roosts, to which they often return before their human handlers have arrived! At least a part of this skill seems to be due to a magnetically sensitive substance found in the pigeon's brain. The use of a light bar magnet attached to the animal's head will disorientate it on cloudy days. The fact that on a sunny day the pigeon is able to 'override' the false magnetic information and to use the sun instead, shows that the navigational skill it has is neither simple, nor governed by a

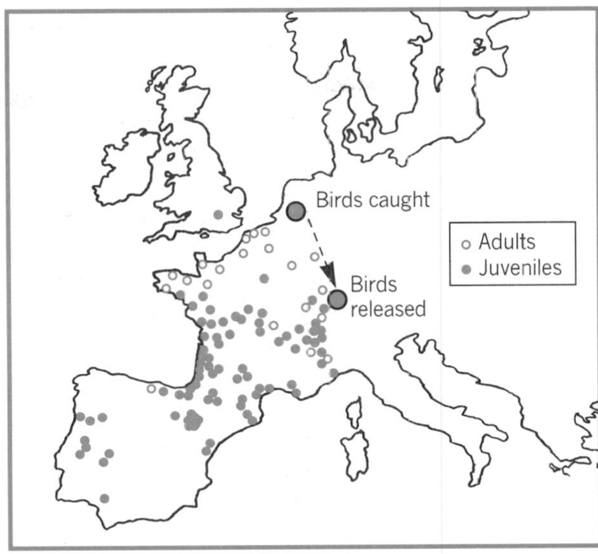

Figure 24.5 Results of experiment to detect whether birds use compass orientation or true navigation

single sense. The pigeon seems to collate information from a number of sources (sight, magnetism, smell, memory for visual landmarks, etc.) in order to determine the correct course of its homing flight.

None of this is certain, of course. Baker (1984) challenged the view that pigeons were really showing navigational skills. He suggested that when pigeons were released they were able to find their way home using familiar landmarks and other cues such as smells, visual landmarks and even magnetic fields. It appears, according to Baker, that pigeons are able to learn the direction on the outward journey so that when they are released for the inward journey, it is no longer unfamiliar. This cannot be the only explanation, however, as pigeons still seem able to find their way home when taken to the release point in enclosed vans, or even when under anaesthetic.

❖ Activity 3 ❖

Think of some of the different ways in which human beings navigate around their surroundings *without* the use technological assistance. Is there evidence for natural navigational skills in human beings?

Section summary

Animals migrate from one location to another for a variety of reasons, such as seasonal changes or fluctuations in the food supply. The benefits of migration are that individuals exploit the best breeding or feeding conditions in both locations. Migrating birds use a range of environmental cues to guide them, including landmarks or the earth's magnetic field. Some birds make use of compass orientation alone in their migration, others show true navigational skills.

Foraging

Animals are faced with the endless task of finding food to satisfy their own, and their nestmates' (i.e. siblings, mates, offspring) hunger. For instance, birds such as the great tit are constantly busy in provisioning their young with insects and grubs, barely finding enough time to replenish their own sapping energy. It has been estimated that the starling makes around 400 trips a day to furnish its nestlings. Kacelnik (1984) found that the starling manages this workload by trading off the amount of food it can carry in one flight against the number of journeys it must make. Clearly, it makes no sense for an individual to exhaust their bodily reserves in carrying one or two heavy loads when there is a full day's work ahead.

A similar problem faces other foraging animals such as the worker honeybee, which spends most of its life foraging and transporting nectar to the hive (Seeley 1993). Schmid-Hempel (1986) attached tiny weights to the thorax of individual foragers to test whether they would compensate by carrying lighter loads. If their foraging behaviour were fixed by an instinctive pattern which made them fill their nectar pouches regardless of practical circumstances, then their foraging habits should be unaltered. However, it was found that the bees not only adjusted their 'tare', but they did so in relation to the distance over which the nectar had to be transported. Furthermore, when the extra weight was removed from some workers at the point of their departure to the hive this made no difference to their overall foraging time, i.e. the bees acted as though their state of 'tiredness' (caused by foraging with additional weights on previous journeys) was affecting their individual estimation of the weight they were able to manage each trip.

Foraging, like many other behaviours which animals engage in which are critical to their survival, has been considered as having *optimality*. Optimal foraging means that the strategy an individual animal deploys will tend to be the most efficient of all the alternatives, given the circumstances in which they are operating (i.e. the physical limitations imposed by their own body structure and physiology, adverse environmental conditions, the need to avoid predation, and so on). Optimality models of behaviour have the advantage that, given the correct selection of parameters, they can make predictions ('hypotheses') about the way that individuals of a given species *should* behave if they are maximizing their gains and minimizing their losses in any particular situation.

These predictions made by a model can then be tested against reality when the fieldwork is undertaken to collect the relevant data. In the 1970s and 1980s optimal foraging models were very popular and generated a great deal of research interest (Harvey 1994). However, when a model was seen to fail when tested against what animals actually do, then it was often difficult to know whether the model was making incorrect assumptions or the animals concerned were not as efficient as they could be. Worse still, some closely related species were found to adopt quite different foraging strategies despite their diets being similar.

Krebs and Davies (1987) summarize the limitations of optimality modelling as follows:

- Models are sometimes untestable in the sense that when there is a mismatch between prediction and reality it is difficult to know whether it is the animal or the model which is behaving more optimally.
- When a model fails in its predictions it is often difficult to pinpoint where the weakness lies, e.g. which of the assumptions or parameters it employs is failing.
- Animals may not, after all, be optimizing! It is plausible that a successful strategy employed by an animal is nonetheless suboptimal if evolution has not brought about its fine-tuning. For instance, animals which are able to exploit a new ecological niche may have little competition and hence their current strategy may not be optimal despite its success for the individuals concerned. Conversely, animal species must sometimes become extinct for the very reason that their strategies are suboptimal ones in comparison with those of surviving species.

❖ Activity 4 ❖

Next time you watch wild birds feeding, try to establish any consistencies in their behaviour. How might you explain these consistencies? Are there pronounced differences between species?

Section summary

Animals must find sufficient food to satisfy their own and their nestmates' hunger. An individual deploys the strategy that tends to be the most efficient in the circumstances in which they are operating. These optimality models have a number of weaknesses in that they may not accurately predict how an animal will behave in a given circumstance. Animals may not always succeed in adopting the optimum strategy for a given circumstance in that sometimes their strategies are suboptimal. This puts them at a disadvantage compared with optimal foragers.

Animal language

One of the most provocative debates over recent years has been over whether language is an ability that is unique to humans. Research evidence from studies of chimpanzees and gorillas has begun to challenge this assumption of language being 'species-specific', although the debate has been looked upon with some amusement by some scientists and intense emotion by others.

Before we take a critical look at some of these projects, it would make sense to have a look at what is actually *meant* by language. This then gives us some criteria against which to assess whether, in fact, these researchers have succeeded in teaching language *per se*, or some other non-linguistic behaviour. One of the first major attempts to construct criteria for language were the 'design features' of language published by Hockett (1959). Hockett's sixteen features that define 'language' can be seen in Table 24.1 on p. 530.

Language is clearly the ability to speak of things that are not present or that have not yet happened. This immediately appears to rule out just about all animal language. Or does it? Foraging bees that have found a food source will communicate the whereabouts of the food source to the other bees in the hive through an elaborate 'dance'. If the forager does a *round* dance, it tells the other bees that food is nearby, although it does not tell them the direction of the food. If, on the other hand, the forager does a *waggle* dance (a figure of eight) this gives the other bees information about both the distance of the food source and also the direction. This appears to challenge one of the most basic assumptions of language, that non-humans are unable to show *displacement* in their communication (i.e. the ability to 'talk' of things that are removed in time or space). We will come back to these design features of language later as we assess whether these projects have succeeded in demonstrating the acquisition of 'language'.

There have been many different research projects that have attempted to demonstrate language ability in non-human species and these have taken one of two major approaches. Some researchers, such as Gardner and Gardner (1969) in their work with the chimpanzee Washoe, have attempted to teach their subjects a form of sign language known as American Sign Language (ASL). This same approach was taken by Patterson (1978) with her gorilla Koko, and by Terrace *et al.* (1979) with their chimpanzee Nim (an abbreviated form of its full name, Neam Chimpsky – not totally unlike the name of a famous psycholinguist, Noam Chomsky).

Gardner and Gardner (1969) taught their female chimp Washoe how to use ASL, a sign language used in the USA by deaf people. The Gardners used a variety of techniques, such as moulding Washoe's hands into the correct shape for a particular sign, modelling the sign themselves, and reinforcing her whenever she used an appropriate sign. Washoe showed herself to be a very able pupil. The Gardners devised a number of procedures to test whether she was using signs accurately or in a more random manner. In one situation, Washoe

Table 24.1 Hockett's design features of language

1	*Vocal/auditory*	Sounds are transmitted from one person to another.
2	*Broadcast/directional*	Sounds are 'broad' cast, although the listener can determine the direction of their origin.
3	*Rapid fading*	The signal fades away rapidly.
4	*Total feedback*	A speaker can hear what they themselves are saying.
5	*Interchangeability*	A sender can also receive signals as well as transmit.
6	*Specialization*	Language has a special communication function – it is not a by-product of some other behaviour.
7	*Semanticity*	Language has meaning.
8	*Arbitrariness*	The use of arbitrary units (e.g. words) means that they do not need to physically resemble the event they represent.
9	*Traditional transmission*	Language can be passed from one generation to the next.
10	*Learnability*	New forms of language can be learnt.
11	*Discreteness*	Language can be organized into discrete units (e.g. words) and the meaning of a communication determined by the organization of these units (e.g. sentences).
12	*Duality of patterning*	Language has more than one level of organization. Speech sounds can be organized into words and words can be organized into sentences.
13	*Displacement*	The speaker is able to refer to things that are not present in space (e.g. out of sight) or time (e.g. yesterday).
14	*Productivity*	A language user can produce an infinite variety of novel utterances.
15	*Prevarication*	Language can be used to deceive, to talk about things that are not true.
16	*Reflexiveness*	Language enables the user to talk about themselves, to describe their own experiences.

was shown a series of pictures and was required to respond with the appropriate signs. She signed correctly in 72 per cent of the trials. Washoe showed other evidence of Hockett's design criteria for language. When a small doll was placed in her drinking cup, Washoe made the signs for 'Baby in my cup'. In this way she was demonstrating Hockett's criterion of *productivity*, in that she was combining signs to produce a novel sentence. There was even evidence of *displacement* in her signing, at times she would refer to things that were not physically present (Gardner and Gardner 1969). Evidence of displacement was also found by Patterson (1979) with Koko the gorilla. In the following sequence, Penny Patterson and Koko are 'discussing' an incident that had happened some days earlier, in which Koko had bitten Patterson.

Patterson:	What did you do to Penny?
Koko:	Bite.
Patterson:	You admit it?
Koko:	Sorry, bite, scratch. Wrong bite.
Patterson:	Why bite?
Koko:	Because mad.
Patterson:	Why mad?
Koko:	Don't know.

The greatest setback to this type of research came with the publication, in 1979, of the results of Terrace's investigation with the chimpanzee, Nim. Not only did Terrace find that Nim's linguistic abilities were far short of a child of equivalent age (for example, he seemed not to be able to move beyond two word utterances), but also Nim seemed less interested in initiating conversation than in copying the signs made by his trainers. From films of other signing chimps, Terrace was able to show that they too were simply responding to the signs made by their trainers rather than using language spontaneously. Even Washoe's famous 'baby in my cup' sentence, claimed Terrace, was produced as a response to signs made an instant before by Washoe's trainers. Terrace suggested that what appeared to be sentence construction by chimpanzees such as Washoe may well be a result of the apes responding to subtle and unconscious cueing by the trainers (Terrace *et al.* 1979). Terrace believed that the Washoe phenomenon was a modern version of the 'Clever Hans effect'. Clever Hans was the name given to a supposed wonder horse that lived at the turn of the century. Hans was able to respond to mathematical problems by tapping out the answers with his hoof. It was subsequently discovered by the psychologist Oskar Pfungst that Hans could only perform these miraculous feats when his trainer also knew the question. Without his trainer knowing the question (the so-called 'double blind procedure') Hans was unable to perform in the same way. Without realizing it, his trainer had been unconsciously cueing Hans when to stop tapping. Terrace believed that this same explanation was appropriate for the signing apes as well.

In response to Terrace's criticisms, researchers such as Roger Fouts have claimed that Terrace's own failures with Nim could be attributed to the use of untrained and incompetent volunteers in Nim's training. Nim's environment was undoubtedly quite different to those of the other signing chimps and possibly not as conducive to learning. Fouts believed that Terrace had drilled Nim by the application of operant conditioning and, as a result, Nim had become passive and inactive, producing only those behaviours that had previously been reinforced rather than spontaneously generating new utterances. Claims that Washoe was merely responding to unconscious social cueing are also contradicted by the many successful double-blind experiments carried out by Gardner and Gardner.

An alternative approach to the study of ape language has been to use external objects such as keyboards and plastic signs that are associated with words. In these studies, the animal is first taught a set of names for familiar objects, persons and actions, by pairing the symbol with these objects and actions. After the association is learned, the researcher can note the ape's ability to use the symbol in an appropriate and spontaneous manner. The most recent, and indeed impressive example of this approach has been in Sue Savage-Rumbaugh's work with a pygmy chimpanzee (bonobo) called Kanzi (see *In Focus* on p. 532).

Is it really language?

Many of the criticisms of these ape studies have revolved around the fact that they do not demonstrate the features that are found in *human* language. Perhaps this is the wrong way to go about this type of evaluation. Reynolds (1981) argues that we should evaluate a species' *linguistic* competence in the light of its other cognitive and behavioural capacities. Terrace's claim that apes are not really inclined to spontaneously

In Focus

Kanzi

One of the most exciting research projects in the area of ape language has been that carried out with Kanzi, a pygmy chimpanzee (or bonobo) by Savage-Rumbaugh and her colleagues (Savage-Rumbaugh 1988). Kanzi was born in captivity in Atlanta in 1980. Right from the start the project was designed with all the criticisms from previous ape studies in mind so that the same criticisms could not be made about Kanzi's language abilities. For example, all the work was video-taped, and there were other careful control procedures to rule out any unconscious cueing from Kanzi's trainers.

Kanzi can communicate with his trainers by touching a symbol on a keyboard, which in turn is connected to a speech synthesizer so that the appropriate word is produced. To communicate with Kanzi, his trainers can use spoken English. In her 1988 publication concerning Kanzi's progress, Savage-Rumbaugh claimed that he had responded correctly 100 per cent of the time to 109 out of 194 spoken test words, and 75 per cent to another 40 test words. He also responded appropriately to 105 out of 107 action-object sentences ('Kanzi, go get me a coke'). Kanzi also appears to have some syntactic ability since he responds differently to a word depending on the way it is used in a sentence.

Unlike many of the earlier studies in this area which concentrated solely on the *production* of language, research with Kanzi has also focused on the *comprehension* of language. Is this ape acquiring *language*? Savage-Rumbaugh believes that he is.

comment on conversation topics introduced by others, says Reynolds, is consistent with other aspects of ape behaviour. In their use of tools and in other social behaviours, chimpanzees and other apes rarely show evidence of the coordination of individual actions to produce a common product. The fact that their sign language also lacks these features does not, therefore, seem surprising. These discrepancies do not prove that chimpanzees and gorillas lack language, but that they lack language as it is used by human beings in their everyday social interactions. Whether, then, the differences between humans and non-humans in the use of language is a quantitative or qualitative divide is not clear. What is clear, however, is that human language is much more than the type of language displayed by apes and other animals. Human language has shaped our species and is an integral part of our own consciousness. We might ask whether it is profitable to attempt to teach animals to use a language system for which they are not adapted. A more profitable endeavour, it would seem, might be to learn more about the communication systems that they themselves use.

Section summary

Debates over whether animals possess language have focused primarily on studies of apes. Early studies of Washoe and Nim using sign language have been criticized because of the possibility of methodological weaknesses in the testing procedures. Later research, particularly with Kanzi, has produced more convincing evidence that apes do, in fact, have the ability to both produce and understand some form of language. The discovery that ape language is deficient compared to human language is seen as a characteristic of the general behaviour of the species rather than a deficiency in the ability to learn and use some form of language.

The evolution of human behaviour

Psychology's main aim is to explain the complexities of human behaviour, but evolutionary roots will be difficult to trace if we confine our study only to humans. Although there are human societies alive today which possess little more than a Stone-Age culture and living a hunter-gatherer existence, they are unmistakably modern humans in every other sense. Furthermore, we have little enough insight into how people thought and felt just a few hundred years ago (even with ample documentary records to guide us), let alone be able to imagine what the thoughts and feelings were of our distant ancestors in pre-historical times. The question of how human behaviour evolved, when posed in this way, seems an insoluble one. Indeed, the whole enterprise of tracing the evolutionary roots of human behaviour would be fruitless unless we adopted a comparative approach. This is because, without the ability to test our hypotheses about where a given behaviour originates by empirical research, all we would have is what Gould and Lewontin (1979) refer to as 'evolutionary stories'. By referring to such accounts as 'stories', Gould and Lewontin mean that we are merely explaining away casual observations rather than relying upon a scientific quest for forming hypotheses, collecting evidence and devising formal theories.

The particular problem identified by these authors, in what they disparage as the 'adaptationist program' in recent accounts of evolution, is the tendency for theorists to try to explain every behaviour and body system as though it is explicitly designed for its current purpose. Their view is that in reality each living organism is made up of a hotch-potch of solutions which had some non-ideal starting point. To take an analogy, contrast the activities of a car manufacturer, who fashions every part from scratch, designing and making each component to serve its purpose in an optimal manner, with that of the car enthusiast, who simply collects whatever parts are available at the local scrapyard in order to piece together a 'special', i.e. a car made from the pre-existing components of scrapped vehicles. The point made by Gould and Lewontin is that an evolutionary process is never able to design organisms from scratch. Whenever a new structure or behaviour takes shape during natural selection it has been fashioned from structures and behaviours which existed before.

In addition to this problem, there are many structures, systems and behaviours which organisms possess that are merely 'left-overs' from previous forms, which have no immediate purpose despite being reproduced in the physiology or behaviour repertories of successive generations. One example of such a structure is the human appendix, a remnant of the time when our distant ancestors ingested large amounts of cellulose from a mainly vegetarian diet that needed the work of enzymes formed within this structure. In English, the very word appendix means something added on, i.e. that which contains material which is redundant to the main aim of an article. Many of the evolutionary accounts of behaviour written more than thirty years ago seem to be devising plausible stories to connect what were actually just anecdotes observed in animal watching. Books such as those written by Robert Ardrey in the 1960s and 1970s, which describe human evolution as one of epic struggles of hunter-gathering warrior tribes on the plains of Africa, those on the animal roots of human behaviour by Desmond Morris or the similar approach taken by Konrad Lorenz's *On Aggression* (1966), have all been accused of being speculations (or 'stories', in Gould's terms) on how human nature, and particularly its unfavourable side, has been determined by evolution. There has been some recent additions to this literature, such as the views of Elaine Morgan (1990) suggesting that the unique features of human sapiens were brought about by our African ancestors wading around in a lake and swamp environment in the flooded Rift valley. This is the so-called 'aquatic ape theory', which has received criticism for being as speculative as the earlier accounts mentioned above.

Since the 1970s, however, the scientific study of behavioural evolution, and particularly how it concerns humans, has changed radically. The essence of this change was the discovery that the most important process in evolution is the means by which genetic material is able to express itself in the control of behaviour, even of behaviour in its most complex forms. Previously it was thought that individuals and their genetic makeup had complementary aims, that of mutual survival, but it has become clear that this oversimplifies things. Whereas individuals are unique and have finite lives, genes are able to replicate themselves – although *finitely* in a given population, in potentially *infinite* way in evolutionary terms. When we talk here of genes, it is not the physical entity of the gene itself which is meant, but its effects (physiological, structural or behavioural) on the phenotype – that is, the fully developed organism.

The genetic effects we refer to as being 'selfish' are the *codings* which genes create, and not their physical entity – these codings being like a baton passed between runners in a relay race (Williams 1992). To illustrate the new ways in which Darwinian ideas have been applied to areas of human psychology, two areas will be discussed. These will show the way in which this approach has begun to generate new hypotheses and a new level of analysis. These two areas are:

- *parent–offspring conflict*
- *host–parasite relationships in disease states* (or 'Darwinian medicine', as it has come to be known).

Parent–offspring conflict

It may not seem, at first glance, that parents and offspring could have more than trivial reasons to fall out with one another. After all, a child is the biggest investment any person can make, taking up years of financial, emotional and intellectual commitment. For Atlantic salmon, breeding is a final act bringing about their death. Though less drastic than this, human parents usually make a lifetime's commitment to the children they bring into the world, and may even make careful plans to pass on whatever accumulated wealth they have long before the end of their lives.

However, human parent–offspring relationships are not always sweetness and light! They tend to follow remarkably similar patterns to those of some animals, both during the period in which the offspring depends on the parents for sustenance and care, and beyond. For example, antagonism between parent and offspring seems to grow at adolescence, which is also observed in other species at the point just prior to the independence of the young. In humans we characterize this period as the 'teenage' years. This phenomenon also occurs in chimpanzees, where juveniles sometimes act in a babyish way, such as by throwing temper tantrums, if they are not given their way by their mother (Goodall 1990). The conflict of interest here is that the mother may be ready to mate again (if she does not already have another youngster) and a near-grown offspring is a distraction from this activity. The juvenile, on the other hand, would gain in terms of its own reproductive success to have as protracted a period of provisioning from the parent as possible.

The fact is, then, that while there are many common and overlapping interests between parent and offspring there are also some important points of divergence, which themselves have interesting ramifications for the course of the relationship between the individuals concerned.

Let us start with a definition of 'parental investment'. This is any contribution to the reproductive success of an offspring at a cost to the remaining reproductive success of the parent. Examples of such investment might be in feeding, teaching, guarding, carrying around, and (maternally) foregoing reproduction. The prediction made by an evolutionary approach to this subject is that the offspring will make every attempt to maximize their reproductive success and to seek more parental investment than the parents are selected to give.

Does parent–offspring conflict begin prenatally?

In a paper showing remarkable insight into the issue, Trivers (1974) suggested that as far as he could see parent–offspring conflict would commence immediately after meiosis (see Chapter 22, pp. 479–80). Although both mother and fetus's interests coincide in most ways, there is not an exact match between them. The mother has to share her bodily resources with the fetus and in theory her best interests are served by providing sufficient, though not over-abundant resources. This is because she not only has her own state of health to consider – that of provisioning for her own bodily strength and wellbeing – but also that her own future reproductive potential may be threatened by too great a demand on her current physiological condition. For instance, she would not wish to have a massive baby to bring to labour (Trevathan 1987).

The fetus's interests are also in not damaging the mother's present state of health during the pregnancy (or for a relatively long period afterwards), but short of inducing ill-health in her the fetus has interests which make more demands on her resources than she might be adapted to supply.

Even before birth there have been a number of outcomes which have been explained in terms of mother-fetus conflict. Profet (1992) suggests that in order to protect itself from toxins in the mother's diet, the fetus is able to induce nausea in her which leads her to avoid food items which could bring about an accumulation of such poisons in her blood system (which is shared with the fetus). The craving of foods shown by many pregnant mothers may also have this as the cause – the demands for certain minerals and sugars made by the fetus. Haig (1993) has also studied the common ailments experienced by pregnant women. He has identified a number of symptoms which seem to arise as a result of the conflict of interests being expressed by mother and fetus at the time. For instance, pre-eclampsia, a condition in which the mother's blood pressure may remain alarmingly high for a time, seems to be caused by the fetus sending cells into the mother's arteries which dilate them. The effect of this is to garner more blood-borne resources for the placental supply. Normally, this condition is counteracted by the mother herself, but in extreme cases eclampsia may arise in which the mother convulses, sometimes progressing to abortion, and even threatening her own life.

Another symptom studied by Haig is that of gestational diabetes. Here the fetus secretes lactogen into the mother's bloodstream which has the effect of desensitizing her body cells to insulin. The action of insulin is to cause glucogen – the essential blood sugar of the body – to be taken up by body cells. If the cells are prevented from taking up glucose the life-threatening condition of diabetes can occur. One symptom of diabetes is the 'spillage' of glucose into urine – a waste system which a normal healthy body would never use for excreting glucose. In fact, glucose is so valued by the body that it would rather lay it down as fat reserves (glycogen) and make the person extremely obese than to waste it in this way. However, the condition of diabetes is a temporary one not unusual in pregnancy, and Haig believes that the fetus is producing this condition so as to ensure it has ready access to high levels of glucose in the mother's circulation. The cost to the mother is considerable, while the gain to the baby is in the layer of fat they are able to lay down as food reserves, ready for their very first birth-day! The amount of fat which the human neonate has at birth seems to give it optimum chance for survival. This fat may be needed should there be any delay in its being fed after birth has occurred. For instance, one baby in a Mexican earthquake was found alive after being buried for nearly two weeks.

It has been suggested by Badcock (1991) that the common occurrence of 'baby blues', or post-natal depression, in women, may have evolved as a natural 'test' of the baby's disposition, i.e. if the baby survives this initial ordeal then they may be nurtured with greater care. The layer of fat is one of the means by which the baby is able to pass this test. Conversely, the aquatic ape theory, discussed by Elaine Morgan and others, suggests that human babies are extraordinarily fat because they are adapted to a life in a watery environment – which goes to show how fertile different scientist's imaginations can be when applied to the same problem.

But as far as the problems which are commonly experienced by mothers during pregnancy are concerned these will also be discussed further later in this chapter, under the heading of 'pregnancy sickness'.

Parent–offspring conflict during early childhood

The child may employ a range of ploys to monopolize their parents' attention, with or without other sibling rivals. But their main disadvantage in any parent–offspring conflict is being smaller and weaker than either parent, and they therefore cannot win outright battles with them over the amount of investment they wish to receive. It is likely that, as a consequence of this disadvantage, the infant's strategy will work more at a psychological level. There are several such strategems:

1. *Crying.* Infants manage to exasperate and annoy parents who do not meet their demands. Crying begins as a biological, attention-gaining mechanism for indicating hunger, cold or other forms of distress (Barr 1990). However, as Darwin himself first observed, infants do not start to shed tears until the second month of life. *Weeping* produces a compelling stimulus of sight and sound which mobilizes adults to take action, but it is employed by infants so commonly that many adults realize its use as a *childish* ploy, and may not even respond to it when children are seen crying in the street.
2. *Regression.* Freud used the term 'regression' to indicate that when a person fails to progress satisfactorily in childhood, they may *fixate*. Fixation, which occurs at a given stage in development, has the outcome that the person may return (by regressing) to the psychological condition of that earlier stage, when they experience current stresses. Badcock also modifies this concept in applying an evolutionary argument in explaining the child's strategy. For instance, an older child may be able to obtain the resources normally reserved for a young child by appearing to be younger than it actually is. Unwitting parents may therefore respond to such *childish* behaviour (as many adult observers describe it) by giving more resources to it (time, attention, gifts, and so on).
3. *Smiling.* Like crying, the infant's early behaviour repertory includes the ability to smile. A 'social smile' is usually present by the end of the second month, long before the infant has consciousness of what it is signalling. Parents, on the other hand, respond very positively to an infant's smile, so much so that it would be a powerful strategy for attracting their interest (and other resources) to it.
4. *Temper tantrums.* Occasionally an infant behaves as though out of control. For instance, following a quarrel with a parent, a child may wander off, throw itself about as if to deliberately cause itself injury, hit out at objects, refuse help or otherwise behave dangerously in order to alarm its parents. An evolutionary analysis of all this wild activity is that it draws from the parents concern that it is at risk, and therefore they become more likely to respond by provisioning resources of some kind.

In mammals, where parental investment tends to be both intense and protracted, there are three phases over which parent–offspring conflict may extend. The exact limits of each phase depend upon, among other things, the parents' age. For instance, an older mother baboon will tolerate demands made on her by her offspring in wanting to be carried. Since her future reproduction would not be compromised by doing this, she may be willing to pay the additional cost for the extra protection afforded to her current, and probably last, offspring. In the first phase the parent will initiate all the investment supplied to the offspring. When very young the infant will be in no position to provide for itself, and would therefore be unable to survive if no protection and care were offered. As the infant matures, however, the mother will gradually begin withdrawing some forms of support. For instance, when the infant is able to feed itself the mother may show increasing resistance to its suckling. Later still, the infant will find the parent not only resistant to its attempts to garner their resources, but may even meet hostility in response to repeated demands it may make (see Fig. 24.6).

However, since each child has some investment in brothers and sisters (as we will go on to see), such behaviour would not continue forever. This is because the parent's reproductive fitness is only part of the 'inclusive fitness' of the child (which includes the transmission of genes through more indirect routes).

Figure 24.6
Initiation of parental investment (PI) by parent and offspring

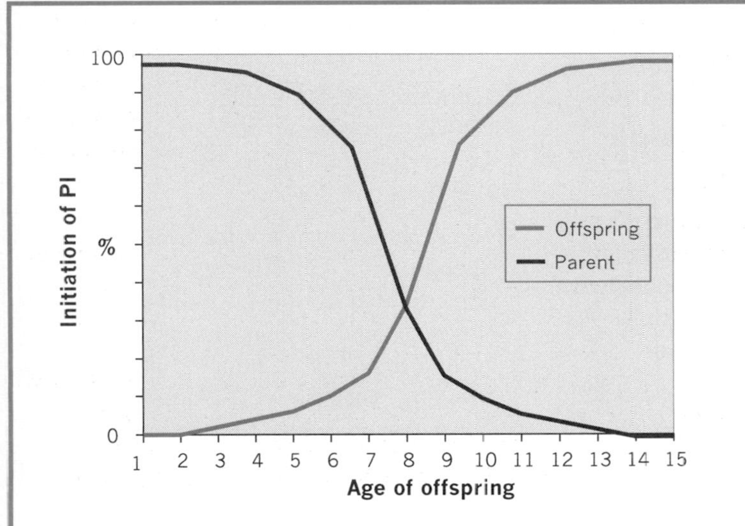

The medical treatment of disease states

Levels of explanation

A disease state is often a state of imbalance between a host and the numbers, or the behaviour, of the pathogens which normally reside inside them. Medical treatment of 'illness' has traditionally regarded health to be one of 'good' or 'bad', categories which assume infection is either present or not. In some cases this view is correct, in most it is not. An evolutionary viewpoint on disease takes an alternative position, and tries to examine the strategies used by a host and parasite as that between two species whose evolutionary interests have come into conflict. Traditional medicine considers principally the proximate causes of illness and disease, such as the cause of heart failure being deposits of fat in the person's arteries which have been impeding the flow of blood through them. Finding an ultimate cause of this condition would involve asking why such a fatal level of fat deposition occurs in such a body region. Evolutionary psychology aims to explain the ultimate causation for behaviour, and in this aim it complements, rather than contradicts, medical and biological theories of health (Nesse and Williams 1995, Rennie 1992).

An evolutionary perspective indicates that, far from being part of the illness, some symptoms such as fussiness over food may form a vital part of the body's adaptive response towards parasitic invasion. Similar responses affect body temperature increases (fever) and iron deficiency (anaemia).
For example, when lizards are affected by disease, they may seek a warm place to bask in the sun. Such basking is normal in cold-blooded animals as part of their thermo-regulation. However, they seem to tolerate much hotter conditions when ill than when in normal health, and the effect of this is to greatly increase their internal temperature. Kluger (1990) has shown that if lizards which are ill are prevented from this warming behaviour, then they are likely to die as a result of the illness.

In Focus

Pregnancy 'sickness'

A number of ailments are associated with pregnancy, one of the most common being feelings of nausea called 'morning sickness'. As mentioned earlier, Profet (1992) has suggested that feelings of nausea and sickness have the consequence of making pregnant women avoid certain foods that may themselves be toxic to the fetus. Symptoms of sickness may therefore be a natural response which has evolved to protect the fetus from the effects of certain foodstuffs the mother ingests. Since food aversions can be learned after a single trial mothers would tend to avoid foods which have led to this unpleasant reaction. The reason why food can be toxic to the fetus but not to the mother is that some natural foods, particularly plants, contain poisons to which humans gradually acquire immunity through their lifetime. The fetus does not have such immunity and may be adversely affected if the poisons accumulate in the blood. Evolution has therefore provided the fetus with a mechanism by which mother's appetite can be altered during the period of pregnancy, making her avoid certain foods of this type (containing the so-called 'teratogens', or natural toxins).

The symptom of nausea may therefore be seen as an important evolved response for protecting the fetus without causing too much discomfort for mother. However, as a medical complaint 'morning sickness' is counteracted by administering some form of anti-emetic. Such treatment, apart from possibly harming the fetus by suppressing the mother's aversive reaction to some foods, is typical of an approach which is orientated towards eradicating symptoms of illness. In fact, during many illnesses we tend to find some foods particularly disgusting to our palate – especially ones with a high fat content such as fried eggs and bacon. These food are high in iron content, a mineral which bacteria require for survival. Foods low in iron, such as normally bland foods like toast, are therefore generally favoured when we are ill.

In other words, increasing body temperature seems to be an effective treatment against pathogens. Similarly, a fever is a common symptom in a range of human illnesses and may well indicate that it is a part of the body's defensive response to pathogens, rather than being an indication of harm being done to the body from invasion (Ewald 1993a, 1993b).

Host's defences against parasitic invasion

In order to ward off attack from micro-organisms which threaten illness or death, humans have evolved a range of behavioural and biological strategies to reduce their susceptibility. Such strategies include:

- *Avoiding exposure.* We may regard sick people as undesirable and unattractive. Pale skin or haggard features may cause us to avoid close contact with those who look ill. Humans universally tend to regard the act of defecation as a private affair – often seeking places in private to perform this function. The outcome of this is that we do not have regular contact with one another's faeces. Also, the sight and smell of others' faeces is highly disgusting to us, which further leads to avoidance behaviour of a pathway which may contain contaminants. A similar response is found to nasal mucous, and contents regurgitated during nausea, possibly for the same purpose.
- *Erect barriers which deter invasion.* The human skin is constantly being regenerated from below, and we form a layer of dead cells on the surface which are sloughed off in huge numbers during the day. Bacteria which land upon this surface would need to keep burrowing into these layers in order to prevent being cast off with the dead layer. In other primates mutual grooming is frequently

done, and is essential to health. Without this regular concern over hygiene, the animals would soon become sick from a heavy parasite load.

❖ Activity 5 ❖

Read the section on human mate choice in Chapter 22. How do evolutionary theorists explain human reproductive behaviour?

Section summary

As you can see, the application of evolutionary principles has powerful implications for a range of human activity, including the very life forms which live on or inside us. Some of these micro-organisms have evolved a strategy to cope with the most ingenious defences which have been devised to repel them, and in some cases may even have evolved a capacity to take over the functional control of the host's brain, altering that host's behaviour pattern so as to optimize its own survival and reproduction (Moore 1984). Our relationship with most micro-organisms is that of a balance between our ability to tolerate them when we are healthy and their effects on us when our bodily defences are distracted by some other form of invasion. Furthermore, we are even dependent on the existence of some micro-organisms for our very survival. For instance, without those which live on our skin (which effectively keep our pores clear of debris), or those in our gut assisting in the catabolism of foods, we would not be able to function.

On the one hand an evolutionary approach to the study of the coexistences of organisms can help us to understand, and even exploit, these relationships for our own benefit. On the other hand, as the advent of Darwinian medicine shows, we may need to gain an understanding of some of these interrelationships which directly involve our species. For example, the application of these ideas may help us to reduce the virulence of some of our most threatening diseases (Krause 1992).

And so to return to the question of why it is necessary to take a comparative/evolutionary look at human psychology. We now know that we share the same basic processes and problems of replication and heredity as all biological systems. With some we have a fundamentally similar physiology. With some we have more than 98 per cent of our genetic makeup in common. Therefore, it is logical to expect that there are important clues in the variations and similarities which are seen in the ways in which animals (and, potentially, plants) from different species tackle the fundamental problems affecting the survival of their genetic make-up. In this regard, humans are, as much as any other extant species, the product of a slow process of change and adaptation made over the course of a long evolutionary history. We are inextricably linked with all other living species on this planet, and we, and they, are inextricably linked with our own evolutionary history.

Chapter summary

- Classical conditioning involves the association between a novel stimulus (CS) and another (US) that already produces a response (UR). After repeated pairings of these two stimuli, the new stimulus will be able to produce the response (CR) in the absence of the original stimulus. Repeated presentations of the CS without the US will eventually lead to extinction of the CR. Following conditioning, the CR may also be made to stimuli similar to the CS, or solely to the CS, depending on whether other stimuli are also associated with the US.

- Operant conditioning is a type of learning that is dependent on the outcomes of a behaviour. Behaviour that is followed by a pleasant event, or escape from an unpleasant one will appear more frequently in the future. Continuous reinforcement schedules produce rapid initial learning but also rapid extinction when the behaviour is no longer reinforced. Partial reinforcement schedules produce slower initial learning but also slower extinction rates. If a behaviour produces an unpleasant event, it is said to be punished and will appear less often in the future.
- Animals migrate for a number of reasons including seasonal changes and fluctuations in the food supply. Migration enables animals to exploit the breeding and feeding advantages of a particular location. Migrating birds use a range of environmental cues to guide them, including landmarks and the earth's magnetic field.
- Animals must find food to satisfy their own needs and the needs of their nestmates. Individual animals develop the strategy that tends to be the most efficient for the circumstances in which they are operating. The fact that animals sometimes behave suboptimally may indicate a weakness in optimality models or may indicate that animals are foraging inefficiently.
- Early studies of ape language demonstrated impressive language skills in apes but were criticized for their methodological weaknesses. Later studies have shown that some animals can both produce and understand some form of language. Whether this is the same as human language is still a point of considerable debate, although it is clear that such language skills do not have the same centrality of importance in non-human experience as they do in our own.
- Evolutionary explanations of human behaviour emphasize how genetic material is able to express itself in the control of behaviour. Two areas in which behaviour can be explained in this way are parent–offspring conflict and the medical treatment of disease states.

Essay questions

1. Describe and evaluate explanations of homing behaviour. *(24 marks)*
2. Discuss the view that animals other than humankind might possess the ability to use language. *(24 marks)*
3. Critically consider evolutionary explanations of any two aspects of human behaviour. *(24 marks)*

Further reading

Ridley, M. (1995) *Animal Behaviour* (2nd edn), Oxford: Blackwell.

An easy-to-read and accessible account of conditioning, homing and foraging behaviour.

Hayes, N. (1994) *Principles of Comparative Psychology*, Hove: Erlbaum.

This is a good introductory text on many of the topics in this chapter, with a particularly good section on animal language.

Archer, J. (1996) 'Evolutionary social psychology', in M. Hewstone, W. Stroebe and G.M. Stephenson (eds) *Introduction to Social Psychology*, Oxford: Blackwell.

A readable account of how evolutionary theory might help to explain a diverse set of human social behaviours.

Part 7

Perspectives in Psychology

Chapter 25

Approaches to psychology

Mike Cardwell

Preview

In this chapter we shall be looking at:

- assumptions and contributions
  - behaviourism
  - the psychodynamic approach
  - humanistic psychology
- free will versus determinism
- reductionism.

Introduction

When students first come across psychology they are often confused and frustrated by the very different and often seemingly contradictory approaches taken to the study and explanation of human behaviour. These different approaches, often referred to as 'perspectives', differ in the questions they ask about human behaviour, the assumptions they make about the processes behind this behaviour, and the explanations they offer of why human beings behave in the way they do. Although the three perspectives examined in this chapter represent only some of those found in psychology, they do provide a flavour of some of the very different assumptions and explanations that have characterized the development of psychology. *Behaviourism* offers a view of human behaviour as being infinitely malleable, fashioned and crafted by the rewards offered by the environment around us. *Psychodynamic theories* emphasize the hidden internal processes that underlie our behaviour, whilst humanistic psychology rejects the view of mindless human beings at the mercy of their immediate situation or their unconscious mind. Within the *humanistic perspective*, human beings have the potential to make more of themselves than might be presumed within the theories proposed by the other two perspectives.

Behaviourism

The behavioural approach emphasizes the importance of environmental stimuli in the way we act. As a result, behaviourists have concentrated on the processes of learning – that is, any lasting change in behaviour that occurs as a result of experience. The development of the behaviourist approach in psychology can be traced back to a paper written by John Watson, 'Psychology as the behaviourist views it' (Watson 1913). Watson put forward a point of view which emphasized the importance of the environment in our behaviour. The central ideas of this new science of behaviourism were:

- an emphasis on observable responses and environmental stimuli
- the rejection of any concepts that were not evident from direct observation
- a focus on learning and experience as fundamental to an understanding of behaviour.

Such was Watson's confidence in this approach that he claimed:

> *'Give me a dozen healthy infants, well-formed, and in my own specified world to bring them up, and I will guarantee to take any one at random and train him to become any type of specialist I might select – doctor, lawyer, artist, merchant-chief and yes, even beggar-man and thief, regardless of his talents, penchants, tendencies, abilities, vocations and race of his ancestors.'* (Watson 1930)

Although admitting that he was going beyond his facts, Watson never shifted from this extreme position, later known as 'radical behaviourism' to distinguish it from the behaviourist theories espoused by later advocates of this approach such as Burrhus Skinner (see Chapter 24). Nevertheless, Watson's ideas had a tremendous effect on thinking in psychology, and up to the 1950s, behaviourism was the dominant force in psychology.

Assumptions of behaviourism

First and foremost in behaviourist thinking people are seen as biological organisms, innately capable of responding to the environment in which they live. Whilst it is true that humans, in common with many other organisms, are capable of performing a wide range of complex responses, these are seen as combinations of simpler responses. Behaviourism assumes a continuity between human beings and all other animals, i.e. they all possess the capacity for making similar responses, although those of humans are more complex than those of other organisms.

Behaviourists have adopted a simple biological process as the fundamental model for explaining human behaviour – the reflex. All biological organisms that possess nervous systems are capable of reflexive action. These reflexes happen without our

In Focus

John Watson (1878–1958)

Generally regarded as the founder of behaviourism, Watson studied psychology at the University of Chicago and later became Professor of Psychology at Johns Hopkins University. His publications began in 1913 when he first outlined his behaviourist approach. Watson's confrontational approach gained him a good deal of notoriety, and when he turned his attention to the study of human sexual behaviour, he and Johns Hopkins University parted company. He took a job with an advertising firm, and applied much of what he had learned as a psychologist to the field of advertising. As with his career as a psychologist, his advertising career was equally eminent and successful.

having to think about them or decide what to do in that specific situation. To take this idea of reflexive behaviour further we need to look at what is involved in a reflex.

There are three essential elements to any reflex:

- the stimulus
- the response
- the connection between the stimulus and response.

Because of some quality that the stimulus possesses it tends to produce a response in the organism. For example, the smell of food may make us salivate, or a loud noise startle us. In this way, the stimulus and response are connected such that whenever the stimulus appears the response tends to follow. The connections between the stimulus and response ensure that this relationship is a reliable one, in that the stimulus nearly always produces that response in that organism. These connections are often referred to as S–R bonds because of this function.

The essence of this early view of behaviourist theory is in the explanation of how stimulus and response become bonded together such that when the stimulus (S) occurs, the response (R) follows. Although the stimuli and responses in the examples outlined earlier are not learned (i.e. they are reflexive), other stimuli and responses that are not normally associated can become so through the process of 'conditioning'. There are three factors that influence the conditioning process, namely:

1. *Contiguity* – i.e. two events occur together in time or space. A stimulus and response are contiguous events because they occur at nearly the same time and in the same place.
2. *Frequency* – i.e. if a stimulus occurs and is followed by the response on many occasions they are likely to become bonded together.
3. *Reinforcement* – in behaviourist theory, a connection between stimulus and response can be made stronger if the response results in some pleasant event. If this happens the response is likely to be repeated. Note that because of the power of contiguity, the response does not have to produce the pleasant event. It is enough for the pleasant event to appear closely after the response in order to reinforce it. We often find ourselves repeating actions because when we have performed them in the past something nice has happened.

One of the first theorists to explore this relationship between stimulus and response and the powers of reflexive learning was Pavlov (1849–1936). Pavlov observed that dogs in his laboratory would start to salivate at the sight of their food dish or even the sight of the assistant who fed them. Pavlov believed that when a neutral stimulus (such as the sight of Pavlov's assistant) regularly preceded a more significant event (such as the actual feeding) then an association would be formed between the two stimuli, and the previously neutral stimulus (now referred to as a *conditioned stimulus*) would be able to elicit the same response as the *unconditioned stimulus* (the food itself). Pavlov referred to this type of learning as *classical conditioning* (see Chapter 24 for a more complete account of this type of learning). Pavlov believed that an association was formed between the unconditioned and conditioned stimuli simply because they occurred closely together in time (contiguity) and that this was an arrangement that was repeated many times (frequency). More recent theorists (e.g. Rescorla 1988) have suggested that the importance of this association lies in the conditioned stimulus as a predictor of the coming unconditioned stimulus. When this association was no longer reliable (for example, if the assistant no longer fed the dogs), the association would be extinguished.

Watson proposed that the explanation of learning proposed by Pavlov could explain many of the mysteries of human behaviour. He believed that love for a parent was not that different to the learning shown by Pavlov's dogs. Watson explained that when babies are stroked and cuddled by their parents, for example, they will smile and gurgle. The presence of the parent would

In Focus

Classical conditioning – the case of Albert

'Albert' was a placid 11-month-old boy who rarely cried. Watson and Rayner gave him a live white rat to play with. He reacted with no fear, but was delighted with his new playmate. The two researchers next established that Albert did not like loud noises.

By striking a metal bar behind his head with a hammer, Albert was made to cry. When they next presented the child with the rat they struck the bar at the same time. Albert fell onto the mat and started to cry. After repeated presentations of the rat and the loud noise together, the rat was presented without the accompanying loud noise. Albert cried and tried to crawl away. He had become conditioned to fear the rat, which had become a conditioned stimulus for his fear.

Unfortunately, for reasons that are unclear, Watson and Rayner were unable to reverse this conditioning although other studies have shown that reversal is quite straightforward.

Source: Watson and Rayner (1920)

gradually become associated with this stroking and cuddling, and eventually the child would show the same 'loving' responses to the parent. Watson also showed how a phobia could be conditioned using the techniques of classical conditioning (see *In Focus* above).

Not all behaviourists accepted the view of learning championed by Watson. Skinner believed that most actions that people perform are not elicited directly by stimuli. He believed that whatever the reason for the behaviour appearing in the first place, if it was reinforced it would appear more frequently in similar situations. In this line of thinking, all people have been reinforced for doing certain things throughout their lives. In other words, they have a 'reinforcement history'.

Skinner's view of conditioning (known as *operant conditioning*) stressed the importance of the consequences of a behaviour. In this view of learning, the organism operates, or produces an effect on its environment. The effect produced would then determine the future probability of that response reappearing. This deceptively simple formula for learning contrasted with the model of learning proposed in Pavlov's theory. In classical conditioning the response is reflexive, an automatic response to something that happens in the environment. In operant conditioning the responses are not reflexive, and are more complex, frequently involving the whole organism. Imagine a child who is rewarded for throwing a temper tantrum in a supermarket. He is given sweets to try and calm him down and to save his parents' embarrassment. If his parents regularly respond to his outbursts in this way, the child's temper tantrums will become more frequent, and we can say that he has been operantly conditioned to produce this dreadful behaviour (see Chapter 24 for a more complete account of this explanation of learning).

Framed within this perspective of stimuli, responses and reinforcement, behaviourism offers a comprehensive view of all learning and therefore, it is claimed, an explanation for all behaviours. At the root of all these disparate behaviours is a common set of very simple processes.

The links between stimuli and responses can also be suppressed if the response is followed by something unpleasant. When this happens we say that the organism has been 'punished'.

Behaviourists also believe that these processes operate in much the same way in all species, thus providing a justification for studying the behaviours of other species (see Chapter 24). If the same processes occur in all other species, then it makes a lot of sense to study them in their simplest form. Behaviourists also favour the use of scientific methods (see Chapter 26) because of their emphasis on the observable aspects of the environment (that is, stimuli, responses and reinforcement).

Contributions of behaviourism

- *Classroom management*

  The use of conditioning techniques in modifying classroom behaviour has been demonstrated in a study by Wheldall and Merrett (1983). Children who were disruptive in class were rewarded for any evidence of attentiveness and general good behaviour. Prior to this study, these children spent a good deal of their time out of their seats and had this behaviour reinforced by the teacher who was forced to pay them attention because of it. As a result of this change of reinforcement patterns, the amount of disruptive behaviour dropped and the children spent a much greater amount of their time engaged in quiet and productive class work (Wheldall and Merrett 1983).

- *Programmed learning*

  Skinner pioneered the idea of self-paced, individual instruction with every child being taught by a 'teaching' machine that presented small amounts of information, asked questions and gave out reinforcement for correct answers. Later versions of this basic idea included programmes that could deliver remedial instructional loops so that learners could go back over steps that they had not successfully accomplished. By presenting information only one bit at a time, the learner was more likely to experience constant success rather than constant failure.

- *Token economy*

  Some behaviour-modification programmes involve rewarding people with tokens (items that have no real value themselves but can be later exchanged for other rewards) whenever they produce some desired behaviour. By using these tokens, it is possible to modify the behaviour of both children and adults. Once the desired behaviour is established, the tokens can be phased out, and replaced with more naturally occurring reinforcers such as praise from others. Such techniques have proved successful with, for example, disruptive children, brain-damaged patients and autistic children who may never before have spoken.

Evaluation of behaviourism

- Behaviourism clearly satisfies one of the criteria for a good scientific theory, in that its explanations are simple or parsimonious. There is no need to invent complex hidden processes (compare this approach with that of Freud) to explain why a behaviour happens.
- A fundamental belief in behaviourist theory is the belief that human behaviour does not just happen, but rather it is caused by environmental events (stimuli, reinforcers) that we cannot control. Because of this, behaviourism is strongly deterministic (see the later section on free will versus determinism, p. 557). The consequence of taking this deterministic position regarding human behaviour is to say that we do not control our own actions and therefore cannot be held responsible for them. Furthermore, it becomes possible for others to control our behaviour by the manipulation of environmental events. For many, however, this is a perfectly legitimate goal in psychology and, indeed, provides the justification for psychology (Skinner 1971).
- An important assumption of behaviourist theory is that human behaviour should be studied using the same methods as in the physical sciences. Furthermore, psychology should restrict itself to studying only those things that can be studied directly. An implication of this position is that anything that cannot be observed cannot be studied, and therefore cannot be used to explain human behaviour (Slife and Williams 1995). Slife and Williams point out that although stimuli, responses and reinforcements are essential in behaviourist explanations of behaviour, they are never observed directly. Although we can readily observe events in the environment, we have no way of knowing if they act as the stimulus for a

given response nor indeed whether they are acting as a reinforcer. Similarly, we have no way of knowing whether a particular response has been caused by a given stimulus. In fact, as can be seen in Chapter 26, we might question whether the scientific method can ever produce the certainty and confidence that we assume it does.

- The notion of reinforcement also poses considerable conceptual problems when we apply it to an explanation of human behaviour. If reinforcement serves to strengthen the bond between a stimulus and response, then it supposes that whatever we do, we do because it brings some pleasant consequence. When applied to human behaviours such as altruism and other aspects of self-sacrifice, behaviourist theory might suggest that somehow these behaviours are, in fact, producing some pleasant consequence for the person doing them. This may well be the case, and in fact some explanations of social behaviour and relationships are based on such a belief. This does cause us to review our previous acceptance that some people perform acts for no personal gain. To a behaviourist, all relationships must provide people with the opportunity of obtaining pleasant outcomes for themselves.
- You may remember from an earlier discussion that human beings are seen as learning in much the same way as any other species. By studying the behaviour of less complex species, we can infer how human beings learn. There are important implications of adopting this assumption about cross-species similarity. Slife and Williams (1995) point out that by reducing experiences such as 'loving' to its behavioural equivalent 'loving behaviours', behaviourists might argue that all animals that demonstrate, for example, parental care, do so for the same biological and environmental reasons. Accepting this point, they argue, means that human 'loving behaviours' such as our parental behaviour toward our children do not have the meaning that we thought they did, but are a product of our biology and our conditioning. To invest any other meaning on such behaviours, it would follow, would be merely illusory.

Section summary

Behaviourism was founded by John Watson. Watson believed that psychology should restrict its focus of study to only those things that were directly observable and emphasized understanding learning as being fundamental to understanding behaviour. Drawing on Pavlov's theory of classical conditioning, in which stimuli become associated because they constantly occur together, Watson advocated explanations of human behaviour based on the acquisition of learned stimulus–response relationships. Radical behaviourism, as this became known, was challenged by Skinner, who, in his operant conditioning theory, proposed that organisms learn as a result of the consequences of their actions when operating in their environment. If these consequences are desirable, a behaviour becomes more frequent; if they are undesirable, it becomes less frequent.

The psychodynamic approach

When people are asked to name the most famous figure in the history of psychology, they invariably come up with the name of Sigmund Freud. Freud's approach to understanding human behaviour, known as 'psychoanalysis', has had a profound effect within psychology, yet his approach is one of many that share some basic assumptions, whilst differing fundamentally in others. Contemporaries of Freud, such as Carl Jung and Alfred Adler, despite being inspired by Freudian theory, emphasized different issues

In Focus

Sigmund Freud (1856–1939)

Educated in Vienna, Freud spent most of his life there before fleeing Austria for London after the German invasion in 1938. Freud trained as a doctor, specializing in neurological disorders. In 1885, he won a six-month fellowship to study with Jean Charcot, a French doctor whose interests in hysteria (*physical* symptoms that appear to have no *physical cause*) had a profound effect on Freud's own theories. He began writing about psychoanalysis, as he called his theory, shortly after. In 1919 he was given the title of professor at the University of Vienna and became a prolific writer on psychology despite a long series of battles with cancer that he was eventually to lose at the age of 83.

Sigmund Freud

© Hulton Deutsch

in human development and experience. This wider theoretical framework is known as the 'psychodynamic approach'.

Figure 25.1 The iceberg representation of the human mind

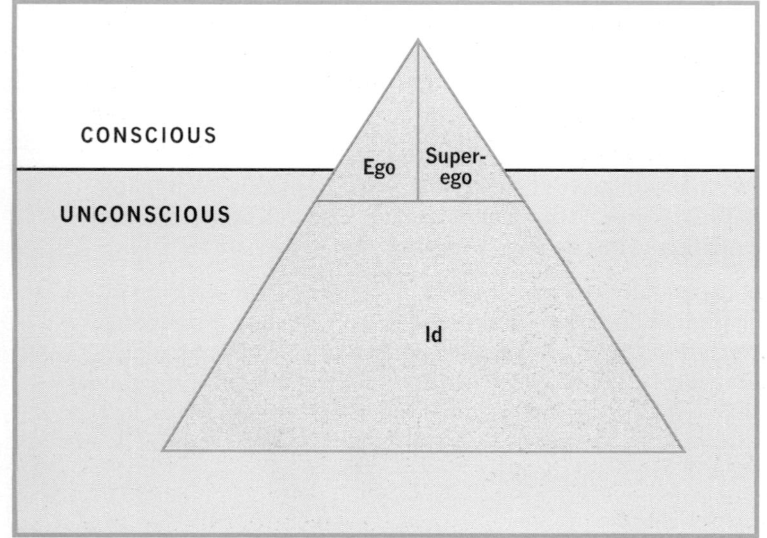

Freud's theory of psychoanalysis

Freud believed that the human mind had both conscious and unconscious areas. The unconscious part of the mind was seen as being dominated by the 'id', a primitive part of the personality that pursues only pleasure and gratification. The id is not concerned with social rules but only with self-gratification. This disregard for the consequences of a behaviour is referred to as 'primary process thinking'. The second area is the 'ego', which dominates the conscious mind. This is the part of our mind that is in contact with the outside world, the part that considers the consequences of an action, and as such carries out 'secondary process thinking'.

The third part of the mind is the 'superego'. This develops as we become more aware of the rules and conventions of society and specifically of our parents. It contains our social conscience, and through the experience of guilt and anxiety when we do something wrong, it guides us towards socially acceptable behaviour. According to Freud, the ego and the superego dwell largely in the conscious mind, while the id is in the unconscious area of our mind. This has led some writers to see the human mind as being rather like an iceberg, with the area above water being the conscious mind, and the part under the water the unconscious mind. This visual representation of this part of Freudian theory can be seen in Fig. 25.1. In this image, the id lurks totally below the surface of conscious awareness and cannot be seen (i.e. we are not aware of its influence). As with an iceberg, the majority of the mass of the iceberg (and hence its greatest potential influence) is under the surface. This analogy should not be overworked, but it does illustrate the relationship between consciousness and Freud's three aspects of the mind.

One of the more controversial aspects of Freud's theory, and the one that probably caused the greatest problem for his contemporaries, was his ideas of the sexual instinct and its importance in the development of the individual. According to Freud, human beings experience a cycle of arousal in their sexual instinct. When this cycle is at a high point, the id demands gratification and determines to carry out behaviours that will result in sexual gratification. In most civilized societies, however, sexual gratification is not something that can be achieved without a consideration of social morality. The superego may, therefore, *oppose* gratification with the result that the ego is caught between two conflicting demands: the id demands immediate gratification, while the superego demands conformity to the moralistic conventions of the society. The ego struggles to maintain a balance between these conflicting demands. How successful it is in achieving this goal ultimately determines both our everyday behaviour and also our mental health.

Another of the key aspects of Freud's theory is the claim that people move through a series of developmental stages (see Table 25.1 below).

Table 25.1 Freud's psychosexual stages of development

Stage	Description
Oral stage (birth to about 15 months)	The newborn child is governed only by its drives. Only the id is present at this stage and so the infant seeks immediate gratification, achieved through mouth its (i.e. through feeding, crying and oral exploration of its world).
Anal stage (15 months to about 3 years)	The focus of gratification shifts from the mouth to the anus. The child experiences pleasure from the elimination of faeces. This brings them into conflict with their parents. Random elimination (as demanded by the id) incurs parental displeasure, yet withholding elimination (as requested by the parents) is denying the demands of the id, which until this point has been the source of all motivation. The resolution of this conflict requires the development of the ego, and as such has important implications for personality in later life.
Phallic stage (3 years to about 5 years)	The focus of gratification is now on the genitals, although this gratification is not the same as experienced by adults. Children take an increasing interest in their own genitals, and show a curiosity about other people's bodies. The major conflict that children face during this stage is the Oedipal conflict, the resolution of which should result in the attachment to the parents, most notably the same sex parent and the development of a superego. The idea of the Oedipal conflict is central to Freudian theory and is outlined in the *In Focus* opposite.
Latency stage (around 5 years until puberty)	The drives that have been responsible for gratification in the previous stages appear relatively inactive (hence the reference to them being latent). This is partly due to the repression of sexual drives that is accomplished during the Oedipal stage. These repressed drives may be redirected into other activities, such as the formation of friendships, or hobbies.
Genital stage (puberty onwards)	With puberty, there is a re-emergence of the earlier drives. Drive energy is focused on the genitals once more, but this time with an adult expression of sexuality. Although the term 'genital' suggests that gratification during this stage must inevitably be sexual, Freud emphasized the importance of secondary process thinking as a form of symbolic gratification in this stage. Thus, forming loving relationships or assuming the responsibilities of adult life may all be seen as symbolic ways of satisfying the drive energy of this stage.

In Focus

The Oedipal conflict

The major conflict in the Freudian view of development is the Oedipal conflict. This is named after the Greek tragedy in which Oedipus unwittingly kills his own father and marries his own mother. The term was first used by Freud to describe the incestuous feelings that a young boy develops toward his mother, coupled with a jealousy and rivalry with his father for the affections of the mother. As the son comes to realize that the father is more powerful than he is, he begins to fear punishment, specifically that his father might castrate him for his incestuous feelings towards the mother. When the castration anxiety becomes intense, he represses his feelings for the mother and identifies with his father in a process called 'identification with the aggressor'. This lessens the chances of being castrated as the father will no longer see him as a rival. In this way, the boy will attempt to emulate his father, and in so doing he will internalize the father's moral standards, and so develop a superego.

In the female version of the Oedipus conflict, girls between the ages of 4 and 6 envy their father for possessing the penis that they have been denied. When the girl discovers that she lacks a penis, she is thought to blame the mother, and thus transfers her affections from the mother to the father. Because (according to Freud) both boys and girls value the penis, daughters choose their fathers as their primary love object. As they realize the unequal struggle to possess the father they must renounce these feelings and identify with their mother. This is the fundamental problem. Boys renounce their feelings for the mother because of the fear of castration, yet Freud suggested this would not be the case with girls, who had already been 'castrated' by their mother. Freud suggested that this conflict would simply fade away as girls realized they would never possess their father. Because the threat of punishment through castration is not present for girls, they would not be under the same pressure to renounce these feelings and identify with the moral standards of the mother.

Freud claimed that this conflict is forced (repressed) into the unconscious mind, and as a result, we are no longer aware of the feelings that we had previously experienced. This is commonly referred to as 'childhood amnesia' and explains why, other than a few fragmentary memories, we remember very little of our life before the age of 5.

Source: Adapted from Cardwell (1996)

Each of the stages described in Table 25.1 is characterized by different demands for sexual gratification and different ways of achieving that gratification. If we do not receive the right amount of gratification, receiving either too much or too little, we become fixated in a particular stage, that is we continue to have the same demand for gratification that we had at that stage throughout the rest of our life. This condition is thought to produce a variety of neurotic behaviours depending on the type of fixation. Freud believed that to deal with fixation at any particular stage (the fixation point), we must go back, or 'regress', to that stage and resolve the issues that led to the fixation.

To Freud, how well we deal with the demands of each of these developmental stages, and whether or not we receive the optimal amount of gratification, will determine how psychologically healthy we are as an adult.

Contributions of the psychodynamic approach

- Probably the most significant contribution of the psychodynamic approach has been in the development of psychotherapy. In Freud's psychoanalytic theory neurotic problems in adulthood were seen as the result of unresolved conflicts from childhood. These had been repressed because the immature ego was unable to deal with them at the time. The aims of psychoanalytic therapy are to create the right kind of conditions so that the patient is able to bring these conflicts into the conscious mind where they can be addressed and dealt with.

- Skal (1993) suggests that the attraction of horror films can be explained using psychodynamic concepts. The appeal of these films, argues Skal, is that they reflect unconscious anxieties about specific conditions in our own lives. By watching horror movies we can displace our own anxieties onto the movies themselves and overcome them. Skal supports his argument by pointing out that specific kinds of horror movies are popular at specific times in our history. After the First World War, films such as *The Phantom of the Opera* reflected the mutilation of many who lived through the war. After the Second World War, films about the horrors of the atomic bomb and about alien invasions (e.g. *Invasion of the Body Snatchers*) became widespread.
- Tavris and Wade (1995) suggest that the most important contribution of the psychodynamic approach may well be in showing us that because of unconscious patterns and needs, individuals tend to be the last to know the reasons for their own behaviour. There is an old joke about two psychoanalysts who meet in the corridor. 'You're all right', says the first psychoanalyst, 'How am I?'

Explanations based on the psychodynamic approach account for the unpredictability in our behaviour, the unwanted negative moods that arise for apparently no reason, and the emotional overreaction to innocent remarks (Tavris and Wade 1995).

Evaluation of Freud's psychoanalytic theory

- One of the most important implications of adopting this view of human behaviour is its reliance on the concept of an unconscious mind which influences our thinking and behaviour in ways about which we are unaware. If we are unaware of the forces that guide us, then it follows that we are not capable of intervening to change or go against them (Slife and Williams 1995).
- Of key importance in Freudian theory is the belief that all our behaviour is influenced in a causal way by an underlying sexual instinct. Freud felt that such was the power of the sexual instinct that it acted as the motivating force behind all our behaviours. The implication of this point of view is that our social behaviour, including our relationships with others, is ultimately connected with the fulfilment of sexual gratification, and a desire for pleasure. Other psychodynamic theorists such as Jung and Adler disagreed with Freud about the idea of such a pervasive sexual instinct, and proposed their own ideas of what motivated human behaviour.
- Related to the previous point is the belief that sexual motivation arises from the body, yet affects the mind, which must find ways of seeking gratification. While this might seem a fairly simple concept, it is far from being so. It is assumed that the body can, in some mysterious way, affect the mind in a causal way. This mind–body relationship is one that philosophers have struggled with for thousands of years, yet it has never been fully resolved. If there is such a link between body and mind, then it also follows that we should be able to cause our body to respond in a certain way by exerting control from our mind. We have all experienced situations where this simply does not work.
- According to Freud, we are in large part a legacy of our past. Our adult life is shaped by the way in which we have charted our stages of development and dealt with the conflicts presented in each. As Slife and Williams (1995) point out, this view of development makes us very much 'victims of our past'.

In psychoanalytic theory, not only are early experiences important, but they also influence and shape our present experience and behaviour. As all this is happening unconsciously, we are not only victims of our past, but are also totally aware of these influences.

- Because we are essentially trapped in the past, this poses real problems for an individual trying to escape from early repressive influences. If we are controlled by the past, then how do we manage to exert any sort of control over our lives? Psychoanalytic theorists take it for granted that a person can be freed from such influences through psychoanalytic therapy. Whether or not such therapy is effective in resolving psychological problems is a matter of intense debate. The relationship between how a person's problems might be defined and explained within the theory itself, and how they might be helped by psychoanalytic therapy is not always that clear. The problems associated with psychoanalytic therapy are dealt with more fully in Chapter 12.
- In order to be accepted as a scientific theory, we should be able to conceive of circumstances where the theory might be proved wrong. In other words, if we have no way of showing that a theory might be wrong, then we have no grounds for accepting that it might be right. Such a theory would lack 'falsifiability'. Freud's theory is often criticized for lacking this criterion of falsifiability. Ther[illegible] number of reasons for this. First, much of Freudian theory makes use of concepts or processes (such as the superego or the Oedipal conflict) that cannot be observed directly, but can only be inferred. This makes them more difficult to validate. Second, although offering a persuasive description of human behaviour, the theory fails to make predictions about behaviour that can be tested through use of scientific methods (see Chapter 26).

Section summary

The psychodynamic approach explains behaviour in terms of the unconscious processes operating in the mind, with an emphasis on the notion of motivation and of past experience. In Freud's psychoanalytic theory, behaviour is seen as a product of the constant interplay between the three parts of the personality: the id, ego and superego. Freud believed that people developed through five stages of development: the oral, anal, phallic, latent and genital. Each stage is marked by its own developmental conflict, but the most important of these, in terms of its impact on later development, is the Oedipal conflict. Failure to receive the correct amount of gratification in any of these stages may result in a fixation, with the individual later needing to regress to that stage in order to resolve the issues that were unresolved at the time.

Humanistic psychology

Humanistic psychology, often referred to as the 'third force' in psychology, developed in direct opposition to the theoretical approaches of behaviourism and psychoanalysis. Theorists such as Carl Rogers and Abraham Maslow totally rejected what they saw as the negative view of human behaviour put forward by behaviourism and psychoanalysis. Both of these two approaches see behaviour as being driven by forces outside the control of the individual they affect. Such ideas of human behaviour paint a rather pessimistic picture of human beings and make no allowances for progress and growth.

In Focus

◆

Abraham Maslow (1908–70)

Maslow was born in New York, the son of Jewish immigrants. He studied psychology at the University of Wisconsin, receiving his PhD in 1934. Although originally interested in primate behaviour (he studied with Harry Harlow, see Chapter 27) he gradually became more interested in human behaviour. After the Second World War, he became acutely aware how little psychology was contributing to solving social problems, and he began to specialize in social psychology and the study of personality. Maslow believed that psychology should focus on healthy people, a sharp contrast to the pessimism of Freud. In 1968, he wrote, 'To oversimplify the matter somewhat, Freud supplied to us the sick half of psychology, and we must now fill it out with the healthy half'. Maslow showed a particular interest in the application of psychology to business, and is still often quoted in that area. In 1951 he became chairperson of the Psychology Department of Brandeis University near Boston, and was President of the American Psychological Association in 1967–68. He died in 1970, aged 62.

Assumptions of humanistic psychology

An essential belief in humanistic theory is the idea that everybody is unique. Each of us has an innate potential that we can reach if we develop fully. Accompanying this innate potential is an inborn sense of identity that enables us to know what is best for us, and what we must achieve to become, as Rogers calls it, a 'fully functioning person'. In Maslow's theory, this process of fulfilling our potential is referred to as 'self-actualization'.

In contrast to the rather pessimistic view of human beings posited by psychodynamic theorists, humanistic theory sees human nature as being more or less good. By taking this optimistic view of human beings, humanistic psychologists encourage us to pursue growth and fulfilment, since without it we experience a lack of fulfilment and become psychologically unhealthy. The question becomes, of course, what do we have to do in order to to fulfil this potential. Slife and Williams (1995) identify three things that are important with regard to achieving our potential.

- We need freedom to develop in order to be able to pursue our potential. With psychodynamic and behaviourist theories, our behaviour is determined by influences outside our control. It is an essential part of humanistic psychology that individuals are free to make their own choices concerning their actions. Humanistic psychologists reject the hard determinism associated with psychodynamic and behaviourist theories and argue that freedom of choice is essential to becoming self-actualized.
- A second important aspect of the process of becoming self-actualized is being able to satisfy our needs. Maslow (1954) put forward the idea of a hierarchy of needs (see p. 167) with *biological* needs such as the need for food and shelter at the bottom of the hierarchy, above them the *belongingness* needs such as the need for love and acceptance by others. At the top of the hierarchy are the needs for *esteem* and *self-actualization*. Because these needs are hierarchical, we cannot address the higher needs until we have satisfied the lower ones. As self-actualization is so important (because without it we cannot fulfil our innate potential), we must fulfil all our lower needs so that we can pursue the goal of self-actualization.
- Slife and Williams' third point concerns how we might understand our own needs, to know what it is we need for growth and fulfilment. To stay psychologically healthy and to become self-actualized, a person must be aware of what is best for him or her, and then act

upon it. This may not be experienced as a process of conscious reasoning, but rather as a feeling of intuition. Because of the situations we are often forced into in our lives, and the influence of others upon us, we may be prevented from following a course of action that we feel is right for our own positive growth. In this sense, the environment may block our goal of self-actualization. In such situations, we may experience a conflict between what we feel that we need and the demands and expectations of others. If there is such a conflict, we may pay too much attention to the need to live by others' demands and expectations (and thus experience a sense of 'incongruence' between our feelings and the demands of others). Alternatively, we may resist the temptation to pursue our lives through the demands of others, and instead we may recognize what is right for us, give expression to our own feelings and act upon them. An important belief in humanistic theory is that we 'own' our own feelings and our lives, and we should be encouraged to be true to them, to pursue personal needs even if they appear wrong to others around us.

Contributions of humanistic psychology

Although the contributions that follow are detailed elsewhere in this book, it is also useful to outline them here. This outline gives a flavour of the influence of humanistic psychology, not only as an application of psychological knowledge, but also as an approach to the gathering of that knowledge.

- *Humanistic psychotherapy* (see Chapter 12)

  Humanistic psychologists maintain that we live in a world where restrictive personal, occupational and cultural pressures are frequently contrary to the achievement of our own personal fulfilment. As we have seen, conforming to the wishes and needs of others can produce a feeling of incongruence if, by these actions, we frustrate our own needs and fail to pursue our own potential. By seeking therapy, we might argue, we have taken the first step towards dealing with this incongruence. Although there are many different forms of humanistic therapy, all therapies share the same basic aim, that is to provide the right sort of therapeutic environment for the individual to once again move towards their own innate potential. By working through humanistic therapy, the individual becomes able to resist the pressures that have previously thwarted their own development.

- *Qualitative research methods* (see Chapter 30)

  Dissatisfaction with the use of scientific methods in psychological research (i.e. *quantitative* methods), together with a belief that human behaviour and experience were not *determined* in the mechanistic way implied by scientific psychology, has led to the development of *qualitative* methods (see Chapter 30). These enable psychologists to explore human experience with a good deal more sensitivity than is possible with traditional quantitative methods.

An evaluation of the humanistic approach

- You may recall how humanistic psychology developed, at least in part, as a reaction against the determinism of psychodynamic and behaviourist theories. However, as Slife and Williams (1995) point out, humanistic psychology cannot avoid the issue of determinism completely. A person's inborn potential is seen as exerting considerable influence over the way he or she acts. If this potential is based in our biology, Slife and Williams argue, there is not much we can do about it. Therefore, in the sense that this potential lies outside of our control, yet exerts an influence on our behaviour, the humanistic approach must be seen, to a certain extent, as being deterministic.

- One of the major assumptions of humanistic theory is that people have the ability to know their own nature, and to know what is best for them in order to reach their full potential. This knowledge does not appear to be available to our conscious mind, being more a matter of what Rogers refers to as 'intuition' or 'gut feeling'. Such knowledge is entirely subjective and, given the claims of humanistic theory, is not available to anyone other than the person who possesses it. A consequence of this position is that an individual's potential for conscious choice in their actions seems limited by both their inborn potential and also by their own needs which may lie outside of conscious recognition.
- Despite the 'breath of fresh air' appeal of humanistic psychology, there is a worrying consequence about at least one of the assumptions of such a position. In Maslow's theory, people are seen as pursuing self-actualization as their primary aim. Such single-mindedness in satisfying our own needs is not only justified, it is also encouraged. If we were to follow this idea to its extreme, Maslow appears to be advocating selfishness. Although, as Slife and Williams point out, humanistic psychologists strenuously deny that we should pursue our own fulfilment at the expense of others, there appears no argument within humanistic psychology that would explicitly exclude this kind of selfishness. If we attempt to block this personal goal of self-fulfilment, it appears, we introduce incongruence and thus increase the risk of psychological problems caused by the imbalance between the needs for personal fulfilment and meeting the needs of others. A further consequence of this need for self-fulfilment is that other people only serve as a means of obtaining our own personal fulfilment and satisfaction. True intimacy and the selfless concern for the needs of others would seem impossible under such circumstances.
- One final point made by Slife and Williams in their critique of humanistic theory concerns the morality of a person's behaviour. If, they argue, we are the only ones who know what is right for us, then we are the only ones able to judge the rightness or wrongness of our behaviour. If we must pursue our own needs, then we can only be held accountable for whether or not we are acting according to those needs. This introduces a moral position known as 'moral relativism' in that what is right or wrong can only be judged in terms of what is right or wrong for that particular person. According to this perspective, there can be no universal standards of right or wrong behaviour, with morality being regarded as unique to each individual and determined by their own unique needs. As each person is different, and we are denied knowledge of the unique potential and needs of any other, this is a further problem when applying humanistic principles to the explanation of intimate relations.

Section summary

The humanistic approach stresses the importance of an individual's unique potential to change in positive directions towards the goal of self-actualization. In contrast to the pessimistic view of human beings posited by the psychodynamic approach, humanistic theories see human nature as being more or less good. Within this approach we are encouraged to pursue growth and development, since without it, we experience a lack of fulfilment and become psychologically unhealthy. To stay psychologically healthy and to become self-actualized, people must be aware of what is best for their own development and must act on it. Sometimes the environment blocks our goal of self-actualization, and we may experience a conflict between what we feel we need and the demands and expectations of others. An important belief in humanistic theory is that we own our own feelings and lives, and we should pursue our own personal needs, even if they appear wrong to those around us.

Free will versus determinism

Free will

The idea that we are able to have some choice in how we act is fundamental in most commonsense theories of psychology. The notion of 'free will' allows us to separate out what is clearly the *intention* of an individual from what has been *caused* by some internal or external event. In the sense that we are freed from the causal influences of past events (e.g. of instinct or of our past reinforcement history), the concept of free will is of fundamental importance when explaining human behaviour. The idea of free will is inconsistent with the opposite idea of determinism, because under the latter view of human behaviour, individuals acts as a result of some prior cause.

Part of the scientific perspective in psychology is a belief in this causal determinism. Free will, therefore, would appear to be incompatible with the goals of scientific psychology. This is not, however, necessarily the case. If we examine the meaning of the term 'free will' we may find that the concept of human intention and planning is not that far removed from the ideas of scientific determinism. The term 'free' is taken to mean that a person or their behaviour is independent from the causal determinism of past events. The term 'will' refers to the idea that people make decisions about the goals they are seeking to achieve. This view that human beings behave 'for the sake of their intentions' can be seen as a form of 'final causal determinism'. In other words, the final goals (getting an A level, finding a birthday present for a friend) determine a person's present actions. This apparent contradiction need not be so. When most people talk about determinism, they are, in fact, talking about 'efficient causality', a definition of causality originally put forward by the philosopher David Hume (1951). To say that one event has been determined by another, wrote Hume, meant that the two events must be highly correlated (i.e. when one occurs, so does the other), they must appear in a certain chronological order (i.e. one after the other), and be located near to one another (Slife and Williams 1995). Although, as Hume admitted, the presence of these three criteria does not necessarily imply a cause–effect relationship, this belief in the importance of efficient causality has been enough to convince many scientists that the only appropriate way of determining the cause of events is to examine events in the past.

> **❖ Activity 1 ❖**
>
> Try to recall events that were related in the three ways described above. Did this necessarily mean that one of these events had caused the other?

If we accept this view of behaviour, that it is something that has been caused by events in the past, it becomes clear that we cannot accept the notion of free will. Free will, as Slife and Williams (1995) point out, enables people to choose a path that is inconsistent with their past. If we do not accept that we are bound to the past, but accept that we have the capacity to formulate plans and goals and act accordingly (a philosophical position known as 'human teleology') we are proposing the existence and influence of free will. As we have seen, the notion of free will is not inconsistent with the notion of determinism. A goal that is the product of our own free will can be responsible for our current thoughts and actions. For example, if I decide that I want to learn to play the piano, I might seek out a piano teacher, buy myself a piano and start practising. All these actions are clearly the product of my own conscious planning (i.e. my free will) but are determined by my final goal, that of being able to play the piano. Indeed, anyone who knew of my intention to learn to play the piano could very probably predict those very same actions mentioned above.

In Focus

'The DNA made me do it, M'lud...'

'Crime, and the fear of crime and violence, dominate much of politics in the US and Britain, stimulating a search for simple explanations and simple ways of dealing with the problem. One of the most heated debates is over claims that genetics and biology can help to explain the causes of crime and violence.

'What is the evidence linking biology to crime? A widely cited piece of research (van Dusen *et al.* 1983) is a Danish study of 14,427 people adopted as children by unrelated families. The theory is that if the biological parents have a heritable predisposition to crime, they might transmit these characteristics to their offspring. The research showed that as the 'criminality' of the biological parent increases from having no convictions on court records to three or more convictions, the proportion of adopted sons who are subsequently convicted themselves steadily increases from about 13 per cent to 25 per cent. This genetic predisposition is apparently for property crimes rather than violent crimes, and it is difficult to see how there could be a 'gene for theft'. Moreover, the findings are not clearly duplicated by a similar Swedish adoption study.

'The first problem with studies linking biology and crime is that most simply fail to demonstrate an association between the two, let alone a meaningful cause. The second flaw is that where a link *is* made, it is quite illegitimate to extrapolate these results to the population at large, even if the claims are hedged with qualifications about biology only 'predisposing' individuals to crime. The consequences of arguing that crime has a genetic component can only be authoritarian. The legal and moral implications are likely to be greater calls for authorities to contain and control those deemed to be genetically unfit or dangerous.'

Toby Andrew, *The Independent*, 23 January 1996.

The concept of free will is therefore not only compatible with a wider view of determinism, but is also very important if we are to view individuals as being morally responsible for their own actions. If our actions are merely the product of some past event or of our biological 'programming', then we cannot be held responsible for our behaviours. This is a view that has concerned many psychologists and politicians, and is illustrated by the *In Focus* above.

Determinism

One of the major debates within psychological thinking is the degree to which our behaviour is determined by factors over which we have no control. Some approaches tend to see the source of this determinism as being *outside* the individual, a position known as 'environmental determinism', whilst others propose the source of this determinism as coming from *inside* the organism, e.g. in the form of unconscious motivation or genetic determinism – a position known as 'biological determinism'. The position taken on this issue will have an important effect on the way that we explain human nature.

- *The psychodynamic approach*: In his psychoanalytic theory, Freud believed that we are controlled by unconscious forces over which we have no control and are largely unaware. An essential part of this theory is a belief in 'psychic determinism' (see Chapter 10), the view that events do not occur by chance, they are purposeful, being related to unconscious processes. This view of humankind as being unable to choose their course of action was in stark contrast to the previously held belief that we were rational, thinking beings, fully in control of our own actions. Because of this control by internal forces, and the belief that any perceived freedom of choice is in fact illusory, this theory is an example of biological determinism.

- *The behavioural approach*: As we have seen in the previous section, behaviourists believe that our behaviour is a product of the reinforcement provided by the environment. Within our own reinforcement history, we have been conditioned into behaving in specific ways. Although most of us accept that such conditioning clearly takes place, we still cling to the belief that we are free to plan our own actions. Skinner (1971) suggested that most human beings somehow believe that we are both free to choose and are controlled at the same time. For behaviourists, however, the position is much clearer: we have *no* freedom to choose our actions. They are determined by factors in our environment which, directly or indirectly, mould our behaviour. This approach is an example of environmental determinism.
- *The humanistic approach*: The antithesis of the two previous approaches, this approach believes that human beings are free to plan their own actions, and ultimately their own destiny. People are seen as struggling to grow and to make difficult decisions that will profoundly affect their lives (Rogers 1974). As a result of these decisions, each of us becomes unique and responsible for our own behaviour. Humanistic therapies such as client-centred therapy are based on the assumption of free will. The therapist helps clients to exercise free will in such a way as to maximize the rewards in their lives.

Determinism and science

The notion of current events being determined by something in the past is fundamental to scientific psychology. Indeed, we might argue that discovering the determinants of behaviour is the ultimate goal of psychology. When we speak of the determinants of an action, we are implying that the action has been caused by some specific past event. This, of course, has the inevitable consequence that, as scientists, we focus almost exclusively on past events. This is bound to be the case, we might argue, because causality can only work in this direction. Such a linear view of determinism is so deeply ingrained in scientific thinking that any other view of causality would seem inconceivable. Even theorists who differ fundamentally in their perspectives on human behaviour seem to share a common belief that we need to study past events in order to understand the present. Indeed, the essence of the experimental method in psychology is that we measure a behaviour before and after in order to explore the relationship between cause and effect. We have seen, however, the need for a broader view of causality that takes into account intention and decision-making. This is not incompatible with the idea of behaviour being caused, only with the traditional scientific view of behaviour being caused by past events.

Behavioural scientists who accept this view of humans being guided by their own conscious planning have embraced a less radical view of determinism. This 'soft' determinism proposes that people act consistently with their character. It is less difficult to reconcile this view of determinism with the idea of free will than it is with the 'hard' determinism views of behaviour being caused by environmental or biological factors.

It is perhaps obvious that there is a great deal of uncertainty about what is actually meant by the terms free will and determinism. We have seen that they are used in different ways within the behavioural sciences, and in implying that free will has a determining effect on behaviour, we are opening up questions that science has yet to answer.

❖ Activity 2 ❖

Turn to Chapter 12 on Therapeutic approaches. How do each of these therapies represent the cause of the psychological disorders they are treating?

Section summary

The notion of free will allows us to separate out what is the intention of an individual from what has been caused by some internal or external event. If we accept that behaviour is something that has been caused by events in the past, it becomes clear that we cannot accept the notion of free will. If we do not accept that we are bound to our past, but rather have the capacity to formulate plans and act accordingly, we are proposing the existence and influence of free will. The view that human beings might also behave for the sake of their intentions can be seen as a form of final causal determinism. The concept of free will is not only compatible with a wider view of determinism, but is also important if we are to view individuals as being morally responsible for their own actions. If our actions are merely the product of some past event or our biological 'programming', then we cannot be held responsible for our behaviours.

Reductionism

One of the notable developments in scientific thinking in the behavioural sciences has been the notion that the simplest explanations of events are generally the best. Sometimes known as 'Occam's razor' (after William of Occam, 1290–1349), this view has been with us for centuries as an important criterion for deciding which explanations are best. The essence of Occam's razor is that unnecessary constructs and levels of explanation can be cut away in order to find the simple explanation that lurks underneath. A more recent, but similar idea was suggested by Morgan (1852–1936). Morgan's law of parsimony states that we have no need to explain behaviour in terms of complex psychological processes when they can adequately be explained in terms of much simpler processes.

This tendency to simplify human behaviour to more biological or mechanical processes has persisted since then, with psychologists frequently reducing their level of explanation to its simplest level. This has become known as 'reductionism'. Following a reductionist line of thinking, we can suggest that we should always look for something more basic underneath whatever it is we are trying to explain – that is, the real cause of the event we are experiencing.

Biological reductionism

One of the most important influences on Western thought has been Darwin's theory of evolution. Darwin's theory offered a reductionist explanation of all the complex living phenomena in our world. All this had come about, he argued, through the principles of natural selection (see Chapter 21). Together with the principles (unknown to Darwin at the time he was writing) of Mendelian genetics, this provided a way of explaining how species change and how such variety is possible within the natural world.

In this theory, behaviours that can be shown to arise from genetic factors must have some 'survival value'. It is possible that many human behaviours have also evolved because of their survival value, or more generally, their ability to increase an individual's opportunities for passing on their genes (see Chapter 24). This view, that evolution has bred into us a tendency to act in such a way as to maximize our chances of passing on our genes has been championed by sociobiologists, a group of scientists who are interested in the evolution of social behaviours. The principles of kin selection suggest that in helping biological relatives, with whom we share genes, we are also ensuring the survival of our own genetic code. This, according to Wilson (1975), is the primary motivation behind much of human social behaviour from altruism (concern for others) to xenophobia (fear of strangers) (quoted in Tavris and Wade 1995). According to sociobiologists, nature 'selects' certain psychological traits and social customs (such as kinship bonds and taboos against female adultery) because they help to ensure the transmission of an individual's genes.

Evolutionary theory has also shown that species have a point of 'common origin', that is differences between species are not seen as 'qualitative' (i.e. implying differences in kind) but rather as 'quantitative' in that different species have evolved further than others along the evolutionary path. If, it is supposed, the forces of evolution work in the same way for all species, then it makes sense that we must share a number of natural processes with other species as well. Based on this idea of evolutionary continuity, behaviourists have chosen to study simpler species in order to understand more about these processes in a more basic form. An essential belief within behaviourism is the fact that all organisms learn and behave in essentially the same way, and therefore the processes of learning and conditioning must be the same in all species. This fact, suggest Slife and Williams (1995), provides the justification for studying subhuman species and then generalizing to human beings.

Problems with biological reductionism

Tavris and Wade (1995) suggest three errors that people typically make when accepting biological explanations for complex behaviour.

1. *Drawing premature conclusions*: Because dramatic breakthroughs in research make better headlines, the media may leap to conclusions on the basis of only limited studies. For example, research on the biological origins of schizophrenia has led to almost universal acceptance that this is a disease with physical origins. Research has implicated abnormalities in the biochemical transmitter dopamine, whilst there have even been claims that exposure to the influenza virus during prenatal development might be the main culprit. Twin studies have suggested an important genetic influence in the disorder. Enticing though these explanations might be, no one explanation can account for all cases and all types of schizophrenia. The truth, it appears, is only partial.
2. *Drawing unwarranted conclusions about cause and effect*: Although we commonly think of our biology as affecting the way we experience the world, the opposite may also be true. There are many studies that have shown how a stimulating environment can change the structure of an animal's brain (e.g. Rosenzweig 1984). Tavris and Wade also quote evidence from PET (positive emission tomography) scan studies (see Chapter 9) showing that during certain intellectual tasks, the brains of high performers appear less active and metabolize glucose more slowly than the brains of lower performers. The suggestion that an efficient brain is the *result* of superior performance rather than the cause of it is supported in research by Haier *et al.* (1992). In this study, participants who were allowed to play a computer game for a period of several weeks showed a slower glucose metabolism rate than a control group who did not play the computer game.
3. *Exaggerating the power of genes*: When we read about the role of genetics in a particular behaviour, we might assume that genes are the cause and the *only* cause. Even the words that we use to describe genetic influence, such as 'control' and 'determine' imply an inevitability that may not actually exist (Tavris and Wade 1995).

Recent research on the origins of homosexuality (see Chapter 27) has discovered a genetic link in homosexuality (Hamer *et al.* 1993). By studying forty pairs of gay brothers, Hamer showed that thirty-three of the forty pairs shared a common

> stretch of DNA on their X chromosomes. This research has created a great deal of interest given that other psychological perspectives have failed to find the origins of homosexuality.
>
> Previous attempts to discover the biological origins of homosexuality (such as hormonal deficiencies or levels of testosterone) also appear to have been unsuccessful. However, Hamer is quick to point out that 'sexual orientation is too complex to be determined by a single gene. The main value of this work is that it opens a window into understanding how genes, the brain and the environment interact to mould human behaviour' (Hamer 1993; quoted in Tavris and Wade 1995).

As regards applications of evolutionary reductionism, critics have been quick to point out the inadequacies of sociobiological thinking when applied to human behaviour. Given the importance attached to mating strategies by sociobiologists, we will review the arguments here.

Sociobiologists claim that the forces of evolution have made the males and females of most species profoundly different in terms of aggressiveness, social dominance and mating strategies (Buss 1994). According to this view, it pays a male to compete with others in order to obtain the maximum number of matings and therefore the maximum number of his genes passed on to the next generation. Females, on the other hand, must be choosy because they can only bear a limited number of offspring. According to sociobiologists, therefore, females are attracted to dominant males who possess resources and status. The result of these differences in strategy means that males require sex more than females do, are fickle and promiscuous, and relatively undiscriminating in their choice of partner. Females, on the other hand, are cautious and choosy in their choice of partner and are devoted and faithful once they have chosen (Tavris and Wade 1995). The observation that this arrangement also appears to apply to most human societies, argue sociobiologists, is no accident as people are governed by the same reproductive strategies as other species.

Critics of this position argue that although two species may behave in the same manner, this does not mean that the origins of these behaviours are the same. The existence of wide cultural differences in sexual behaviour, in male investment in childrearing and in attitudes to sexual infidelity casts doubt on the belief that such practices can be attributed solely to genetic influences.

Wilson (1978) argued that genes hold culture on a leash, but the problem, according to Gould (1987) is in determining the length of the leash. If it is only a foot long then society has very little room to manoeuvre and change, but if the leash is ten feet long, biology would only establish a broad range of possibilities. To sociobiologists, the leash is short and human nature inevitable; to many psychologists, however, given the enormous variation between cultures and individuals, the leash is long and flexible (Tavris and Wade 1995).

Environmental reductionism

From the earlier section on behaviourism, you may have reached the conclusion that people are constantly being controlled by forces outside of their control, and that, in the words of John Watson, given the right environment, anybody can be made into anything. The application of behaviourist principles in behaviour modification programmes can have spectacular success in training severely disturbed adults and those with severe learning difficulties to earn a living in the community. But is it all as simple as it sounds? Can we reduce everything to environmental influences in the way that behaviourists suggest?

In recent years psychologists have become more aware of the biological constraints on learning and have incorporated these considerations into their theories of the way in which organisms learn. These genetic dispositions and biological characteristics place limits on what individuals and species can learn. Of particular importance is the finding that all organisms appear to be biologically prepared to learn some responses more easily than others. Conditioning procedures that capitalize on these inborn tendencies are more likely to be successful than those which do not. When two psychologists turned animal trainers attempted to train animals to carry out actions for which they were not biologically prepared (i.e. the behaviour had no specific relevance in their evolutionary past and therefore they had no inborn tendency to learn it), they soon encountered problems (Breland and Breland 1961). In one example, a pig was trained to drop large wooden coins into a 'piggy bank'. The animal was then reinforced for its performance by being given food. The Brelands found that, after a while, the pig started to drop the 'coins' on the ground and push them along with its snout. As this delayed the onset of the reinforcer (which was given when the animal deposited the coin in the piggy bank), it posed a problem for a simple conditioning explanation. Breland and Breland explained this behaviour as 'instinctive drift', a reversion to an instinctive behaviour more usually associated with gaining food. In this case, the pig was reverting to its rooting instinct where it uses its snout to uncover edible roots.

The importance of biological preparedness is also evident in human behaviour. Research has demonstrated that many organisms (including human beings) are biologically prepared to associate sickness with a particular taste and develop a consequent food aversion (Garcia and Koelling 1966). We have all been in the situation where we think we have become sick shortly after eating something, regardless of the real cause of the sickness. As a result we carefully avoid the associated food or drink for quite a while afterwards. This phenomenon can also explain why children undergoing chemotherapy treatment (who may experience feelings of nausea as a result of their treatment) often develop food aversions at the same time (Bernstein 1985).

This is actually part of a larger problem within behaviourism. Restricting ourselves to the study of only one influence at a time may make perfect sense within the context of a laboratory science, but we may miss the complexity of influences on any one behaviour. A person is subject to many different influences with regard to any one specific behaviour. These interact in complicated ways and it can be frustratingly difficult trying to ascertain which, if any, of these influences really is causing the behaviour in question.

This oversimplification problem also applies when we adopt behaviourist principles in the real world. In a world dominated by either reinforcement or punishment, it might appear that the only way to motivate people is with the 'carrot and the stick'. Kohn (1993) argues that this sort of 'pop behaviourism' distracts us from asking whether the behaviour being reinforced is worthwhile in the first place. Skinner never believed that life should be reduced to the mindless use of extrinsic reinforcers that were merely 'bribes in disguise'.

> *'Too rarely are people reinforced for creativity, risk, participation, taking gambles. Too rarely are they given an opportunity to take pride in the products of their work, or to exercise initiative in their choice of pleasures.'* (Skinner 1987)

❖ Activity 3 ❖

Try to find examples of reductionist thinking in the explanations of behaviour offered in the chapters of this book. What do you feel are the implications of accepting these explanations?

Section summary

One of the most significant developments in scientific thinking is the notion that the simplest explanations are usually the best. The tendency to reduce human behaviour to simple biological or mechanical processes has become known as reductionism. According to this line of thinking, we should attempt to find the simple principles that inevitably underlie more complex behaviours. Biological reductionism includes the influence of genes on human behaviour. Sociobiologists believe that human beings behave according to the pressures of natural selection and act in such a way as to maximize the transmission of their genes. Behaviourist explanations of behaviour in terms of stimulus, response and reinforcement must be tempered by the knowledge that organisms are biologically prepared to learn some things more readily than others, particularly those things that have some survival value.

Chapter summary

- Behaviourists believe that psychology should restrict its study to only those things that are directly observable, and emphasize learning as being fundamental to an understanding of behaviour. The main explanations of learning under this perspective are classical conditioning, where two stimuli become associated because one predicts the coming of the other, and operant conditioning, where organisms learn as a result of the consequences of their actions.
- The psychodynamic approach explains behaviour in terms of the unconscious processes operating in the mind, with an emphasis on the notion of motivation and of past experience. Freud's psychoanalytic theory emphasizes the dynamic interplay between the id, ego and superego, and describes how people develop through five stages, each with its own conflict and its own consequences that arise if the conflict is not resolved.
- The humanistic approach stresses the importance of the individual's potential to grow and to change. Human beings are seen as basically good and we are encouraged to pursue positive growth and development because without this, we experience a lack of fulfilment and may become psychologically unhealthy. Sometimes the environment blocks our goal of self-actualization and we may experience a conflict between our own needs and the needs and expectations of others.
- Free will allows us to separate out what is the intention of an individual from what has been caused by some external or internal event. Determinism may be seen as congruent with the goals of scientific psychology, as it allows us to discover which past event has caused the behaviour in question. Free will and determinism are not mutually exclusive, however, in the sense that we act according to our intentions. If our actions are merely the product of some past event or of biological programming, we cannot justifiably be held responsible for our own behaviour.
- Reductionism is the tendency to reduce human behaviour to simple biological or mechanical processes. Biological reductionism includes the influence of genes on human behaviour. Sociobiologists believe that human beings behave according to the pressures of natural selection and act in such a way as to maximize the transmission of their genes. Behaviourist explanations of behaviour are tempered by the knowledge that organisms are biologically prepared to learn some things more readily than others, particularly if these things have survival value.

Essay titles

1 (a) Outline the main assumptions of the humanistic approach to an understanding of human behaviour. *(6 marks)*

(b) Describe and evaluate the contributions that have developed from this approach. *(18 marks)*

2 Discuss the freedom versus determinism debate as it applies to psychology. *(24 marks)*

3 (a) What is meant by reductionism as it applies to an understanding of human behaviour? *(3 marks)*

(b) Describe three examples of reductionist explanations of behaviour that are drawn from different areas of the syllabus. *(9 marks)*

(c) Critically assess the value of adopting a reductionist approach in psychology. *(12 marks)*

Recommended reading

Glassman, W.E. (1995) *Approaches to Psychology* (2nd edn), Buckingham: Open University Press.

A very thorough account of the different 'schools' of psychology.

Slife, B.D. and Williams, R.N. (1995) *What's Behind the Research? Discovering Hidden Assumptions in the Behavioural Sciences*, Sage: Thousand Oaks.

A clearly written and authoritative text that covers all the issues in this chapter.

Wadeley, A.E., Birch, A. and Malim, A. (1997) *Perspectives in Psychology* (2nd edn), Macmillan: Basingstoke.

A readable and accessible text that is targeted specifically at the AEB syllabus, so is especially relevant.

Chapter 26

Controversial issues in psychology

Mike Cardwell

Preview

In this chapter we shall be looking at:

- the psychology of advertising
- propaganda and psychological warfare
- psychometric testing
- psychology as science
- gender biases in psychological theory and research
- cultural biases in psychological theory and research.

Introduction

The aim of this chapter is to introduce you to some of the controversies within psychology. Some of these are concerned with the way in which psychological knowledge has been used by people outside psychology in what might be referred to as the 'technology of behaviour'. There is no set rule about what makes an application of psychological knowledge 'controversial' other than the fact that some applications have the potential for a greater impact on those who experience them than do others.

The applications discussed in this chapter are significant only in so far as they are defined by the AEB syllabus. However, they do give a flavour of the way in which psychology can be both applied and misapplied by the unscrupulous.

The psychology of advertising

'It was over in 30 seconds but 40 years later we are still living with the consequences. At precisely 8.12 p.m. on 22 September 1955, viewers of the new Independent Television Service looked in wonder as a tube of toothpaste burst out of a block of ice. They were watching the UK's first television commercial, for Gibbs SR. Over on the BBC Home Service, Grace Archer was being sacrificed to a blazing barn in a rather churlish early example of the spoiling tactic.' (Garrett 1995)

The television advert has become one of the icons of the consumer age, and, inevitably, psychologists have become increasingly fascinated by the art of persuading people to buy all manner of products and services.

The impact of advertisements

When we ask 'What was that advert all about?', we are implying that the advertisement had a definite and fixed meaning, and that its creators *intended* a very specific message to be transmitted to the recipients of the advertisement. When we talk in this way about advertisements, we often own up to 'missing the point', yet quite often there simply isn't one. The meaning of advertisements is actually a collaboration between the author of the advert and the receiver (i.e. you and me). What persuades people to buy, or whatever, is how the advert makes them feel, i.e. the meaning we attach to the advert. We may well interpret the advert in the way the author intended, we may adjust it in some way, or we may simply generate a meaning unique to us. Whichever of these is the case, the impact of any advertisement is in what it means to us. The author invites us to participate in constructing a meaning for the advert. O'Barr (1994) suggests that advertisers create an advertisement for us to use as a skeleton to add flesh to and breathe life into.

Activity 1

Take a long look at some of the advertisements around you. They might be on television, in magazines or on hoardings. Are the messages always clear? How do *you* receive the messages? What sort of messages do you think the author intended?

Another problem is that it is difficult to disentangle the impact of advertising from other influences that might be current at that time. Hedges (1982) points out that to the consumers, advertising is just part of their background – advertisements form just one part of the sensory bombardment that we experience every day. We cannot stop to evaluate every piece of sensory input, so for the most part, advertisements are relegated to fairly low levels of consciousness. Hedges suggests that advertisements can operate at a number of levels:

- by creating a sense of familiarity: people are more likely to buy a brand with which they are familiar, although that recognition might not be consciously associated with the advertisements for the product
- by surrounding the brand with particular associations, moods, feelings, etc.
- by conveying information about, for example, price or function
- by engaging the customer with rational arguments: it is mainly at this level that the customer's conscious attention is engaged.

Lannon and Cooper (1983) claim that consumers do not merely make a decision about whether or not to buy a product, they also endow the brands they buy with meanings, over and above their functional value. The task of advertisers, they suggest, is to communicate these possible meanings in ways which motivate and reinforce people. Lannon and Cooper suggest that advertising is increasingly dealing in symbolic communication. Examples of symbolism frequently used in advertising are class (e.g. in the After Eight mints adverts), sex, fun and sophistication. The *In Focus* that follows shows how the symbolic content of an advertisement is changed to accommodate the preferred associations of the target consumers.

In Focus

Bounty – a taste of paradise?

'We felt that the sun, sea and sand ads had become dreadfully clichéd. Generally, it's just an excuse to have half-naked females submissive before hunky men.'

'We sought to modernize the image but still wanted to capture the eating experience as a moment of escape. The press coverage so far has proved our point that the old ads were rather unsympathetic to women, as it's mainly been older men saying: 'Bring back our Bounty girls.' We have now tried to portray the Bounty consumer as a more sophisticated individual – not a passive woman – and have concentrated on the experience of eating, rather than on cleavage and half-naked bodies. The fact that it's set in an art gallery might lead you to over-intellectualize it, which we don't want. We selected that environment because of its natural air of peace and tranquillity, which is interrupted by something – the taste of Bounty. Research in France, where you'd think they'd prefer the old style of ad, has shown that this advert scores outstandingly highly with the public. We think the brand needed reinvigoration. We're happy that the viewer is no longer treated as a voyeur. I like to think we've moved the brand on in a responsible way.'

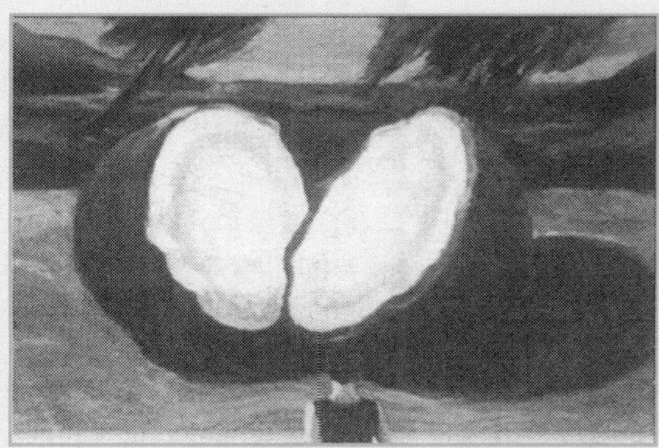

Source: Julian Ingram, Creative Director of Abbott Mead Vickers (*The Independent*, 30 April 1996)

❖ Activity 2 ❖

Many adverts, such as Bacardi rum, Saab cars and Coca-Cola, appeal to consumers because they associate their products with a certain 'symbolic' image. What other adverts seek to create the sort of symbolic image referred to earlier? What do you feel the authors of the adverts are trying to do?

The relationship between psychology and advertising

Banyard (1996) illustrates four ways in which psychology and advertising are intertwined.

Developing a need

Advertising must persuade people that they want or need a particular product. Sometimes this can be accomplished by creating the idea that specific events somehow go hand in hand with each other; for example 'Have a break, have a Kit-Kat' suggested that the only way to have a proper break from work was to consume a Kit-Kat bar. Other techniques, such as *subliminal advertising* (where messages appear on a TV or cinema screen at an intensity or duration that is too weak to reach conscious awareness) are more dubious, both in the ethics of their use and their effectiveness in changing behaviour. In 1957, James Vicary, an advertising expert, claimed to have flashed the words 'Eat popcorn' and 'Drink Coca-Cola' onto a cinema screen every five seconds during the showing of a feature film. As the exposure was very brief (1/3000th of a second) cinema goers were unaware of what was going on. Vicary reported that sales of popcorn rose by 60 per cent and Coca-Cola by 18 per cent during the trials, but as Banyard (1996) points out, the film showing at the time *(Picnic)* did contain lots of images about eating and drinking, so was obviously a contributory factor!

In an attempt to find out whether subliminal advertising really did work, Pratkanis and Aronson (1992) reviewed over 200 academic papers on the subject. In none of those papers was there clear support for the proposition that subliminal messages really do influence behaviour. Those studies that *did* find some effect were either severely methodologically flawed or the findings could not be reproduced. This is not to say that subliminal perception itself does not take place. Attention research (see Chapter 13) has demonstrated through the 'cocktail party effect' that we do process material that is outside conscious awareness.

Noticing the product

Advertisers have many different techniques for getting us to notice a product, including associating the product with a particular emotion or image. Neurological research (see Chapter 5) has shown us that the left hemisphere of the brain is more concerned with 'practical' functions such as language, and the right hemisphere with spatial and imaginative processing, and with feelings. Lannon and Cooper (1983) suggest that much advertising is 'right hemisphere communication'. Their representation of right and left hemisphere concerns is shown in Table 26.1

Banyard also suggests that many advertisers attempt to bypass the analytic side of our minds, and appeal directly to our emotions. This can be achieved by associating products with pleasant emotions such as the association of a cuddly puppy with toilet paper!

Purchasing the product

In order to get people actually to buy the product, advertisers have many different psychological tricks. Banyard quotes the study by Milliman (1982) who compared the effect of different types of music on sales in an American supermarket. Shoppers moved at a different pace depending on the tempo of the music, with sales rising by 40 per cent when the tempo was slow.

One of the new techniques that typifies the psychology of persuasion is known as *fastmarketing*. This is based on what psychologists have more usually called the 'boomerang effect'. When someone makes a decision to buy a product and you attempt to sell them an alternative, that person becomes defensive about his or her decision and effectively develops brand loyalty. This creates a problem for the advertiser, how *do* you persuade someone to change his or her mind? Advertisers believe that attitudes follow behaviour, and fastmarketing therefore presents a blitz of sampling opportunities so that nearly every consumer has the chance to try the product.

Table 26.1 Concerns of the right and left hemispheres of the brain (Lannon and Cooper 1983)

Styles of response

Left hemisphere	*Right hemisphere*
Conscious	Unconscious, intuitive
Communicable	Personal, idiosyncratic
Verbal	Feelings, images
Analytic	Diffuse
Convergent	Divergent

Having actually consumed, washed with, or simply read about the product, consumers are more likely to follow this by a change in their attitude. So, next time a free sample of coffee, hair shampoo or whatever pops through your letterbox, you will recognise the technique being used!

People are also more easily persuaded to change their minds about a product when they hear arguments from someone they admire or think is attractive (Pratkanis and Aronson 1992). As a result, advertisements frequently make use of beautiful models to advertise hair shampoo, sports heroes to advertise everything from tennis rackets to isotonic drinks, and 'experts' to validate the claims made about washing powders, dandruff removers, and so on.

Research by Janis *et al.* (1965) also showed that people are more likely to be convinced by persuasive arguments if they were given something to eat and soft drinks at the same time as they were exposed to the big sell. Perhaps this is why so many business deals and seductions take place over dinner!

Behaviour after the purchase

It is not enough for advertisers to persuade consumers to make a single purchase of their product, they must also persuade them not to change. In a sense, even consumer *inaction* is creating a sale. Consumers are more likely to repeat their behaviour later on than change to a different product. A famous study by Erlich *et al.* (1957) showed that people who buy a certain type of car are more likely to read advertisements for their car in the future than they are for any other type of car. Psychologists refer to the uncertainty we may feel after a purchase as *post-decisional dissonance* (timeshare salespeople call this *buyer's remorse*). By reading advertisements for their own type of car, and avoiding advertisements for different types of car, Erlich argued, these people were looking for further information to show that they had made the right decision in the first place.

How effective is advertising?

In order to test the effectiveness of advertising, researchers are increasingly turning to qualitative research (see Chapter 30). This involves interviewing a sample of consumers in some depth about the product in question and what it means to them. The role of the interviewer is to stimulate discussion rather than to ask a number of formal questions. There are several advantages in adopting this type of approach in the assessment of advertising effectiveness. This method:

- is relatively inexpensive and can be set up very quickly
- can uncover information that more structured quantitative methods, such as questionnaires, might not do. Particularly in group sessions, people are able to express things that by themselves they may be unable to communicate.

There are, however, disadvantages to the approach as well.

- The samples are usually small, therefore cannot be as representative as the much larger-scale quantitative research.
- Interpretation of the results can be very difficult, as it is often in the form of small pieces of conversation rather than precise, easily tabulated numerical data.

Although the effectiveness of advertisements can frequently be measured in this way, sometimes their impact is less tangible. Barthes (1979) writes about the effectiveness of symbolism in advertising. He gives the example of the advertising of soap and detergent products, in which foam acquires a set of 'desirable, mystical and spiritual characteristics'. What advertising is trying to do, claims Barthes, is to 'disguise the abrasive function of the detergent under the delicious image of a substance at once deep and airy...'. Advertisements pull us away from the product itself into some image or fantasy that is suggested by association. Cigarettes and alcohol are undoubtedly harmful and even anti-social, and fast cars are dangerous, yet we are presented with images that associate these products with exotic and desirable states such as drinking on tropical beaches or driving through sun-dappled vineyards.

Advertisements also present us with a set of shorthand signals about the products we are to buy and the circumstances in which we would use them. Because of this, they are a ready source of stereotypes, both sexual, regional and cultural. Families are always happy, adults are all fully employed, we are presented with a laundered world, where some types of character are repeatedly present, others not at all. Green (1991) highlights the apparent contradiction in cultural values when he quotes the advertising executive who claimed that in America, advertisers have no problem with images of a black woman barrister in an advertisement for toothpaste, but that the same advert in Britain would be unthinkable.

Propaganda

Propaganda refers to the 'dissemination of ideas and information for the purpose of inducing or intensifying specific attitudes and actions' (Childs 1994).

Propaganda is often accompanied by distortion of facts, appealing to passion and prejudice rather than rational, objective thought. Because of this, such information is often seen as being false – yet this is not always the case. Some forms of propaganda involve the delivery of information in a very objective and factual way. Education itself is a form of propaganda, but the main difference between persuasive propaganda and educational propaganda lies in the propagandist's intention to persuade an audience to adopt the particular attitude or style of behaviour being espoused.

In order to be considered as propaganda, a message must satisfy three criteria.

- There must be a conscious attempt to manipulate the behaviour of others.
- Only one side of an argument is presented to give the impression that it is an unquestionable truth.
- The fact that the message has this intention is disguised so that those receiving it do not recognize it as propaganda.

The essence of propaganda, then, is that it attempts to persuade recipients in such a way that they voluntarily accept the position being put forward as if it were their own (Pratkanis and Aronson 1992)

The routes to persuasion

Social psychologists have spent many years studying the use and abuse of persuasion and have discovered many of the techniques that make persuasive messages so persuasive.

When faced with a persuasive argument, do we merely accept it without thinking, or do we analyse it in great detail? How easily we are persuaded depends in part on our own characteristics as recipients. Petty and Cacioppo (1981), in their *elaboration likelihood model* suggest two routes to persuasion – which differ in the extent to which a recipient is likely to elaborate on the meaning of the message.

- The *central* route emphasizes the arguments related to the issue. If the recipient is motivated to think about the issue then this is the most effective route to persuasion. In this route, attempts to persuade are based on apparently solid arguments which are presented to an audience that is motivated to listen to them.
- The *peripheral* route plays upon the more tangential features of the message, such as the appeal of the sender or the medium of the message. This is more effective when the recipient of the message is not that interested in the message itself or lacks the expertise to analyse the content. Politicians gain a certain 'street cred' by being seen with pop-stars or sports personalities.

Although this may be totally irrelevant in terms of the content of their political agenda, it does give a tangential message that might be more readily assimilated by the viewers. In World War II, there was a continuous anti-Jewish theme in Nazi propaganda. As a result of World War I, the German economy was in deep decline and so Hitler and Goebbels proposed a series of propaganda messages that would blame this economic and social collapse on the Jews. In a 'documentary' film called *The Eternal Jew*, Nazi propagandists portrayed Jews as 'money grabbing villains' who were a drain on society and lacked proper German values. This message could only have been delivered via this peripheral route as it would not have stood up to careful scrutiny if the recipients of the message had been motivated to apply it.

In later research (Cacioppo and Petty 1986) showed that attitude change through the central route is more stable and long-lasting than attitude change through the peripheral route. The latter, according to Cacioppo and Petty is more volatile and subject to change in the opposite direction.

These two routes to persuasion raise a couple of important points.

- Because of our limited information-processing capabilities, we are forever trying to conserve our cognitive energy, – we are *cognitive misers* (see Chapter 1). We thus take the opportunity to simplify complex problems whenever possible. The strategies of the peripheral route take advantage of this fact. We often accept a message for no other reason than that it is accompanied by a simple persuasion device.
- Propaganda takes advantage of this tendency. Short messages embedded in symbolic content make it harder to think deeply about the issues being presented, and we are therefore less able to analyse the issues and are more open to the persuasive techniques of the propagandist.

Sometimes, however, attempts to persuade people to change their mind go beyond merely exposing them to a new idea and hoping they will embrace it. Attempts at *coercive persuasion* may use a whole different set of techniques.

Coercive persuasion

In popular terminology, the term 'brainwashing' has been used to describe the way in which some captives develop attitudes that are in sympathy with those of their captors, and the fanatical attachments that members of certain religious or political sects form with their leaders (Tavris and Wade 1995).

First, we need to make a distinction between coercive persuasion and other, more everyday types of persuasion, such as those we experience in advertising. Persuasion becomes coercive when it suppresses an individual's ability to reason and make choices in his or her best interests (Tavris and Wade 1995). A number of studies (e.g. Pratkanis and Aronson 1992) have identified the processes that cults might use to coerce their members. Although they are often shrouded in mystery, the persuasion tactics used by cult leaders are nothing more than the same propaganda tactics used in everyday life – except that they are applied in a more complete and systematic manner than we are accustomed to. Some of these techniques are presented in Table 26.2

It is difficult to appreciate the power of manipulation that such sessions can create. Compliant students are seen as 'good' and 'energized', whilst dissenters are 'negative' and 'blocked'. Nor do you have to be especially vulnerable to be manipulated in this way. Almost everyone, when under pressure from other group members and deprived of all external ways of testing the reality of what is being said, will conform to some degree (see Chapter 3). Freud provided some of the reasons why people are so likely to be affected in this way. We all play psychological 'tricks' on ourselves to resolve conflicts. For example, if the truth is

Table 26.2 Techniques of coercive persuasion used by cults (from Tavris and Wade 1995)

1	*The person is put under physical or emotional duress.*	They may be denied food or sleep before joining the group. People may be induced into a trance-like state through repetitive chanting or hypnosis. People who are already under stress, perhaps because they are lonely or troubled, are more vulnerable at this stage.
2	*The person's problems are defined in simple terms and simple answers offered.*	For example, if your parents are giving you a hard time, the answer might be to reject them completely.
3	*The leader offers unconditional love, acceptance and answers to personal problems.*	In return, the leader demands everyone's attachment, adoration and acceptance of his (or her) ideals. New recruits may constantly be presented with praise and encouragement so that they bathe in a sense of positive well-being.
4	*A new identity based on the group is created.*	The new recruits are told that they are part of the 'chosen' or the 'redeemed'. This may involve recruits going through an initiation rite, changing their name and wearing special clothes. They may be encouraged to hate 'evil' enemies, including non-believers.
5	*The person is subjected to entrapment.*	The recruit first agrees to small things, like spending a very enjoyable weekend with the group. During this first phase there is no pressure to join and gradually the person is drawn into greater and greater commitment to the group and its activities.
6	*The person's access to information is strictly controlled.*	Once a person becomes a committed follower, the group limits any choices, and denigrates any doubts or disbelief. The outside world is defined as evil, and any private distress is dismissed as lack of belief in the group. Total conformity in the group and its ideas has been imposed.

uncomfortable we employ *denial*, and when the going gets tough we use *regression*, a reversion to an earlier stage of child-like dependency.

Propaganda in warfare

The effectiveness of war propaganda can never be assessed directly, although there are certainly claims made about its power. Hitler frequently made reference to the effectiveness of Allied propaganda in the First World War and regarded it as one of the major reasons why Germany had lost the war. The relative ineffectiveness of German propaganda in both wars, and of Japanese propaganda in the Second World War was largely due to an inability to 'get inside the minds' of the enemy in the same way as the Allied forces had done.

For many years propaganda teams have carried out 'psychological profiles' of various countries. These have yielded information about local customs, religions and taboos, analysis of crime rates, popular culture, and so on. These profiles can be used by the propagandist in an attempt to take advantage of the people in the country in which he is operating. Many of the techniques derived from these profiles have been designed to undermine morale in the enemy, and to increase the probability of their surrender or defection.

During the Vietnam War, American propaganda teams played on the special significance of dates such as New Year's Day, death and funeral ceremonies and anniversaries of death. For example, on the eve of the Vietnamese New Year (Tet) it is important that all debts have been settled, as it is considered a bad omen to start the new year in debt. Propaganda messages attempted to make people feel extra guilty by reminding them of all their unsettled debts. It was also very important for Vietnamese to die in their homes. Leaflets would remind families of their relatives who had died far away in battle. If leaflet distribution coincided with significant dates (such as anniversaries of the death of relatives), its impact would be increased. An analysis of the use of leaflets in the Vietnam war makes interesting reading. Leaflets that emphasized emotions (such as fear) accounted for about 30 per cent of those dropped, but 69 per cent stressed ethnic differences or other social and political divisions. The *In Focus* that follows demonstrates another use of this kind of propaganda.

In Focus

Nazi propaganda in Holland

Prior to the D-Day landings posters were plastered over Dutch billboards representing the 'Allied liberators' as the bearers of a dangerous cultural heritage. The American GI was portrayed symbolically as an 'uncivilized Frankenstein' that had jitterbugging apes for its torso, a face hidden behind the mask of the Ku Klux Klan and black arms sporting a boxing glove on one hand and a jazz record on the other.

Racial fears were also aimed at occupied Europe through the suggestion that American soldiers would play a prominent part in the invasion. Goebbels' Nazi propaganda ministry produced a pamphlet entitled 'Greetings from England – The Coming Invasion'. Written in Dutch in the form of an Allied communiqué, it stated that the Germans had been duped into wrongly expecting a sea invasion and that half a million 'Negro paratroopers' would spearhead the attack.

'It will be an enormous humiliation for Hitler, the prophet of racial theories, when his warriors will be driven from western Europe by the black race. Dutchmen, your cooperation will be counted... make your old jazz records ready, because at the celebration of liberation your daughters and wives will be dancing in the arms of real Negroes.'

(Adapted from 'Sturm und Swing' by Les Back, *The Guardian*, 8 February 1995)

Psychological warfare

'All warfare is based on deception.' (Sun Tzu, *The Art of War*)

From the 1950s onwards, psychological warfare has come of age – although this particularly devious form of warfare has been around for a long time. The use of uniforms and drums to frighten the enemy has been a military strategy since time immemorial. In the 1960s, the then Liverpool Football Club manager, the late Bill Shankly, introduced the now famous all-red strip for European matches because it made his team look more physically imposing and more menacing to the opposition.

The modern age uses psychological warfare in many forms, many of which are not reported in mainstream psychology journals. We will now look at some of the ways in which psychological techniques have been used in the arena of war, and speculate on the future of the art of 'non-lethal warfare'.

The dehumanization of war

A good deal of psychological attention has been concerned with the way that people think and feel in times of war. The manipulation of those thoughts and feelings has become a prime concern in what has been referred to as the 'dehumanization of war'. Watson (1978) identifies three ways in which psychologists can help to dehumanize the enemy:

- exploring the habits, customs and personal characteristics of the enemy, and taking advantage of them. Because warfare is a battle for the human mind, targeting the values and beliefs of a opponent can be a devastatingly effective strategy
- using psychological techniques in interrogation to make brutality less visible and to inflict long-lasting damage that makes prisoners less able to fight and more vulnerable to future interrogation
- taking the fear out of killing. The use of special training techniques, such as the repeated showing of horrific films can be used to desensitize men in special combat units.

This last technique, known as 'battle-proofing' makes soldiers less emotional about what they are doing, and less afraid in combat situations. The consequence of the technique is that the natural deterrent of fear is removed from the field of conflict.

If the physiology of fear (or 'stress' as it tends to be referred to in this context) and its relationship to psychological effects can be understood, then military psychologists will be able to regulate stress and eliminate the psychological end-product (i.e. fear). The moral implications of this particular technique are profound.

Interrogation techniques

One of the most controversial applications of psychological warfare has been in the interrogation of prisoners of war. Many of the techniques used were of simple brutality, but others were more subtle and considered.

Sensory deprivation

One of the most effective types of interrogation techniques is to interfere with a prisoner's sense of time, place and self. This is often achieved by means of sensory deprivation techniques, that is the minimization of the normal range and frequency of sensory stimulation for a prolonged period of time. Whilst the British army (like most other armies) do not admit to using any form of torture, the Parker Report (Parker 1972) confirmed that techniques such as hooding, white noise, diet restriction and sleep deprivation had been used on IRA suspects when internment was first introduced in Northern Ireland.

Experimental studies of the effects of sensory deprivation typically involve techniques such as semi-immersion of subjects in tepid water and the playing of meaningless noise. Such techniques may produce hallucinations and subjects frequently find the experience too disturbing to finish the experiment. However, most studies have found the effects of sensory deprivation to be rather less terrifying than the public's perception of it. An interesting series of experiments by Myers (1971) illustrates some of the major effects of sensory deprivation (see *In Focus*).

Myers' work dispels some of the myths about the effects of sensory deprivation. It is clear from this research that although the effects of sensory deprivation can be unpleasant, there is little evidence of extreme distress. It also demonstrates the relevance of psychological study of the effects of social isolation in situations other than interrogation, e.g. in nuclear submarines and in space flight.

In Focus

Myer's experiments into sensory deprivation

At the Presidio of Monterey, an army base in California, subjects were confined to soundproofed cubicles which were kept at 22°C, lit with diffuse light at all times, and contained a rubber bed, a chemical toilet and a fridge with as much food as the men wanted. Subjects wore loose-fitting pyjamas to reduce sensation, and their watches and cigarettes were taken away.

The subjects were soldiers, ranging in age from seventeen to twenty-seven. There was no compulsion on the men to stay in the experiment, just the incentive of extra pay. The experiment was terminated after just four days.

- Subjects reported that they spent a great deal of time thinking and dreaming about the past. These thoughts and dreams were frequently unpleasant and frightening.
- 37 per cent of subjects withdrew before the four days were up. Most complained of tedium and boredom and said that they could no longer sleep.
- Many subjects showed evidence of time disorientation, and felt disturbed at not knowing how much longer they would spend in isolation.
- In some subjects, isolation also produced 'positive contemplation', i.e. constructive thinking and clearness of memories.
- On vigilance tasks (such as radar-screen monitoring), isolated subjects actually performed better than controls.

Other interrogation techniques

After the Korean War, Albert Biderman (1960) interviewed 220 United States Air Force internees who had been repatriated by the Chinese Communists. He found that over half the interrogations given by the Chinese had lasted more than 24 hours, and 10 per cent more than a month. Interestingly, the most effective methods of interrogation were not the coercive (involving physical pain) type, but the non-coercive type. Successful (for the interrogator) techniques included:

- asking short, simple questions in quick succession (for example, 'You are with the 357th Airborne, yes?'). As the interrogator already knew the answer to these questions, the prisoner was reduced to the role of a silent but compliant listener
- using the assumption that silence is incriminating, prisoners would frequently speak out to defend themselves
- the interrogator spending hours asking (or more usually shouting) impossible questions (e.g. asking for highly technical information). Finally, he would ask a question that the prisoner could answer, and the need to comply meant that prisoners would feel a strong sense of relief at being able to answer a question
- interrogators never returning a prisoner's hostility. This would mean that hostility was displaced onto the fellow prisoners, destroying the unity and support of the group
- interrogators making threats that were vague about time and degree of physical harm; these were more productive than death threats because they disorientated prisoners more and consequently made them more compliant.

Some of the techniques used in the Korean war would be very familiar to students of psychology. One such technique was the use of operant conditioning (see Chapter 24). A prisoner's behaviour could be modified by the reinforcements provided by the interrogator. The interrogator could, for example, only allow the prisoner to receive food when he gave the sort of information that the interrogator wanted. The use of verbal encouragement and approval could be used to 'shape' the prisoner's behaviour in the required direction.

Brainwashing

As a technique of persuasion, brainwashing attempts to direct and channel thoughts so that the target of the message thinks in a manner that is agreeable to the communicator's position. The tactic removes negative thoughts about this position and promotes positive thoughts instead. The use of this technique is shown in the *In Focus* below.

The techniques and images of 'brainwashing' have been portrayed in a thousand films, and it has achieved a perhaps undeserved notoriety concerning its use in the Korean War. The claims for the use and effectiveness of brainwashing reached their peak during this war, yet were rarely used effectively after it.

Brainwashing differs from interrogation in two important ways.

- The aim is not to extract information from a captive but rather to change his thoughts and beliefs. In this way a captive could be convinced that his enemies were actually fighting for a just cause and that his own side were the oppressors.
- Brainwashing may result in the captive actually collaborating with his captors through television broadcasts and false confessions – which might be used as propaganda against his own side.

In his book *Battle for the Mind* (Sargant 1957), Sargant discusses the work of the physiologist Pavlov who wrote extensively about the way in which behaviour could be changed through the processes of classical conditioning (see Chapter 24). Sargant identified four stages derived from the work of Pavlov that could explain the progressive dysfunctioning that is characteristic of brainwashing.

- In the *equivalent* stage, all stimuli, regardless of their strength or importance, are associated with the same response. Thus captives feel the same whether something trivial or very important happens to them.
- In the *paradoxical* phase, captives are made to feel more satisfaction from small events than from large ones. They might become very upset over minor events yet remain impassive over more important events.

In Focus

◆

Brainwashing during the Korean War

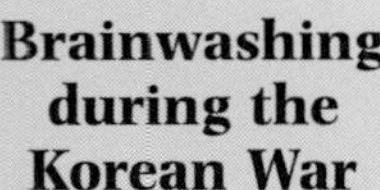

Major William Mayer, a US Army psychiatrist, researched almost 1,000 cases of prisoners of war who had been forcibly indoctrinated during the Korean War. During the indoctrination process, prisoners who might have expected torture or worse were relieved to find that they were not held responsible for their 'wrongdoings' by their Communist captors. The blame was very squarely aimed at their leaders and at American politicians. Prisoners could not help but be grateful for this reprieve. At this point the indoctrinators would attempt to 'unsell' America. They would present articles from *Time* magazine, the *Wall Street Journal*, and so on. These were carefully selected to show the unfairness of American life, pointing out the vast profits that were being made by businessmen back home while they fought in Korea. Post would be censored so that they only received bills and other bad news. Self-criticism was encouraged and soldiers invariably confessed the error of their ways to their fellow captives. It was, says Mayer, the first step to collaboration.

Source: Mayer (1956), reported in Watson (1978)

- In the *ultra-paradoxical* phase, the captive starts to dislike things that he previously liked and to like that which he had previously disliked. It is in this stage that the real impact of brainwashing begins to be felt.
- The brainwashed individual might also enter a fourth stage that Pavlov referred to as the *hypnoidal* phase. The combination of prolonged excitation of the nervous system and extreme fatigue means that individuals stop being critical of arguments and suggestions and receive commands and suggestions without question.

One of the major problems with brainwashing techniques, according to Bauer (1957), was that they frequently did not work. Many American servicemen who were subjected to brainwashing simply ended up being confused.

Psychological warfare and the future

One of the most important developments in psychological warfare in recent years has been the use of information technology. It is anticipated that by achieving information dominance over an opponent, it will be possible to end a war long before it escalates into prolonged and bloody conflict. Imagine playing a game of chess against a friend. They can see your pieces but you can't see theirs. No matter how strategically better placed you are, or how superior are your forces, you will lose, and quickly. That is the basic principle of 'information warfare', or to give the United States Air Force definition: 'Any action to deny, exploit, corrupt or destroy the enemy's information and its functions; protecting ourselves against those actions and exploiting our own military information functions.'

This type of warfare has a surprisingly long history. The Mongol armies in the twelfth and thirteenth centuries were able to subdue armies many times the size of their own by eliminating communication between elements of the opposing army. The enemy commanders would regard no news as good news and were often caught completely by surprise by the attacking Mongol armies. The Mongols themselves used a network of fast horsemen known as 'arrow riders' to keep their own commanders constantly aware of what was happening elsewhere. In the American Civil War, the telegraph was one of the main tactical weapons used by the Union troops. By the end of this war, half of the Union troops were deployed to protect these lines of communication. The use of information warfare in modern times was shown to its best advantage in the Gulf War between Iraq and the coalition forces. As with the Mongols centuries before, the coalition first targeted the enemy's communication networks, effectively making the Iraqis blind and deaf. By the start of the ground offensive the Iraqi leader, Saddam Hussein, no longer knew the location of his own armies, much less the location of coalition forces.

Once one side has an information advantage over another, there are many different techniques available in the psychological armoury, for example:

- computer viruses and other forms of 'malicious software'
- spoofing, i.e. sending a falsified message to someone through automated message systems
- 'video morphing', which can be used to make an enemy leader appear to say things he or she didn't say, thus undermining their credibility.

These are some of the new generation of psychological warfare techniques and are all established techniques. Others might appear more fanciful. According to Lewer (1995), there are plans for 'mind control' through subliminal audio and visual stimuli, 'psychotronic weapons' such as the projection of consciousness to other locations, and the use of holographic projection to disseminate propaganda and other information. Although many of these techniques remain only (perhaps) theoretical, they provide a chilling glimpse of what could be to come for this, the dawn of the cyber warrior.

❖ Activity 3 ❖

Consider the ethical issues that are raised by this application of psychological knowledge. What are the specific issues associated with research into psychological warfare and how might psychologists respond to them? You will find Chapter 27 helpful for this activity.

Psychometric testing

The nature of psychometric testing

'Metric' refers to measurement and so the term 'psychometric' test refers to testing of items which have been shown to measure competence in some other area of functioning. The performance scores that individuals obtain on these tests can then be compared to the scores of others on the same tests to illustrate the level of an individual's functioning.

A central belief of the psychometric model in psychology is that most things that people do are predictable to some degree. We can therefore make predictions relating to a person's abilities, personality, motivation, and so on. Many activities in working life (jobs, educational courses, etc.) require people with a certain set of characteristics. That is where psychometric tests have an important role to play.

Types of psychometric test

Ability tests

Ability tests attempt to measure human abilities, which can, in turn, be defined as the capacity to solve problems of various kinds in different areas of human endeavour (Kline 1992). This definition does not, however, mean that every human being has an almost infinite number of abilities, each specific to a different area of functioning. Could you claim, for example, that your high performance in maths, statistics and physics could be attributed to separate and highly specific abilities in each of those subjects? It is far more likely that there is an underlying mathematical ability that accounts for your performance in each of these related subjects. A statistical procedure known as 'factor analysis' enables test users to calculate the effect of a smaller number of factors (such as mathematical ability) on performance in a much wider range of human behaviour.

Most intelligence tests measure the general reasoning ability that is involved in many different types of problem-solving behaviour. Older types of intelligence test referred to this intelligence factor as *g* (general ability). More recent tests have tended to divide this general ability into two related factors, *fluid* intelligence and *crystallized* intelligence. Fluid intelligence is generally recognized as being a form of innate ability that is not particularly influenced by environmental experiences. Crystallized intelligence is the representation of the underlying fluid intelligence that is a product of environmental experience. In western industrialized cultures, technological and academic abilities are very important and so tests of crystallized intelligence would measure ability in these areas. In non-industrial cultures crystallized intelligence would take other forms, and the measurement of intelligence would therefore be different.

Bias in intelligence testing

With the advent of equal opportunities legislation in the UK and in other countries, it became illegal to select individuals on the basis of their racial group. Following this legislation, it was clear that many of the older tests of intelligence were unable to meet the exacting criteria for fairness when used with different racial groups. The Weschler Intelligence Scale for Children (WISC), for example, was outlawed in many states in the USA for just this reason (Rust and Golombok 1992). Since then, intelligence test development has paid special attention to the problem of eliminating test bias. Potential sources of bias include:

- *item bias*, where the bias exists in the items that make up the test. For example, items that are clearly asking for knowledge of one culture would not be appropriate within another. Items may also cause offence to those taking the test. For example, in the Stanford-Binet test, a child is shown two pictures of another child and asked which of them is ugly. Likewise, the use of gender or cultural stereotypes in tests may be seen as conveying expectations about what is normal (Rust and Golombok 1992)
- *intrinsic test bias*, which exists where the differences between two groups are due to the characteristics of the test rather than any real differences between the groups in the characteristic being measured. Thus, a test that has been designed to measure appropriate abilities and match them to occupational requirements may be valid for one group but not for another (see *In Focus* at the end of this section)
- *extrinsic test bias*, which is found when a test *does* find differences between members of different groups, yet the test itself is not biased. The consequence of this is that members of one group then receive preferential treatment compared with members of the other group, despite the fact that one group's performance may be due to deprivation or lack of opportunity. Once extrinsic test bias has been identified it is not sufficient to ignore it, or even (as is the case in some quarters) to see this difference as 'natural' or desirable. The use of compensatory educational programmes (see Chapter 17) has been a product of the information gleaned in this way.

Personality tests

Personality, as measured by personality questionnaires, is concerned with temperament (i.e. *how* people do what they do rather than *why* they do it – the latter being measured more by tests of motivation or interest). Temperament might be thought of as a collection of traits that characterize a person's behaviour. How people wash up, for example, illustrates temperamental traits quite vividly. Some people wash very methodically, large plates followed by small plates, followed by cutlery, all arranged in size and carefully rinsed in a separate bowl. Others wash with great speed, throwing everything in at the same time, and frequently breaking things. Meanwhile, others simply fill the bowl, put everything in to soak, and hope that it will mysteriously become clean. These behaviours illustrate differences in a number of underlying traits such as orderliness, speed, carefulness and even hopefulness (Kline 1992).

The major type of personality test used for assessment purposes is the personality questionnaire (sometimes called a 'personality inventory'). These are usually tests where respondents (the name given to those who undertake the test) must answer 'yes' or 'no', or perhaps 'true' or 'false' to a series of questions or statements. As with the ability tests discussed earlier, there is a problem concerning the sheer number of different traits that might be involved. Again, factor analysis has helped in this respect, isolating five major factors that account for much of the variation in personality:

Table 26.3 Advantages and disadvantages of personality questionnaires (Kline 1992)

Advantages

- They are easy to administer and can be given to large groups of subjects.
- They are easily and reliably scored (often by computer).
- Many of the best questionnaires have a great deal of evidence to support their predictive validity (that is, their ability to predict a person's performance in some related area of functioning).

Disadvantages

- Results are easily faked. If you wanted to go for a job as a deep-sea diver, you would not admit to being scared of water or being claustrophobic.
- They may produce response sets, i.e. stereotyped ways of responding to the items on the test. This may take the form of *acquiescence* (simply answering yes, regardless of the question) and *social desirability* (giving answers that you believe will present you in the best light). There are a number of techniques used to minimize these type of effects.
- Some questionnaires are derived from forced choice items (i.e. you select one statement from a number of different ones). Meaningful and valid comparisons of personality cannot really be made from such forced-choice questions.

- tough-mindedness
- extroversion
- neuroticism
- open-mindedness
- conservatism.

Some of the advantages and disadvantages of personality questionnaires are summarized in Table 26.3.

The use of psychometric tests in selection and appraisal

Intelligence tests

Of all the psychometric tests, intelligence tests of one sort or another have been most used to predict job success. Ghisella (1966) showed that the average correlation for intelligence test scores and job success was 0.3. Although this does not sound particularly high, it was based on 10,000 investigations and covered the whole spectrum of jobs. This is not to say that intelligence will always be an accurate predictor of job success – there are some occupations where high intelligence is a disadvantage to the worker. Kline (1992) mentions two in particular.

- Football pool checkers – before the advent of automation, it was found that quick and accurate checking of football pools coupons was hindered by high intelligence. Intelligent checkers quickly became bored, slowed up or made errors.
- Production line car workers – such work is generally extremely taxing, yet not particularly interesting. Modern car plants have adopted a completely different approach to car assembly that offers more possibilities for intelligent workers to use their intelligence to the organization's advantage.

It is also clear from work by Jensen (1980) that more intelligent people are better able to master new activities and instructions. This is clearly advantageous across all areas of functioning. Two examples of intelligence tests used in selection are:

- *Watson-Glaser Critical Thinking Appraisal (Watson and Glaser 1964)*

  This test is used for graduate recruitment and management selection. It involves drawing inferences from facts, recognizing assumptions implicit in statements and evaluating arguments. It is a test of crystallized intelligence, but differs from other intelligence tests in that it avoids short test-items and includes longer passages which test the skills outlined earlier.

- *The Alice Heim Intelligence Tests (Heim et al. 1970)*

  These tests measure both fluid and crystallized intelligence and have various versions for subjects of different ages and ability levels. The AH2 and AH3 are used for adults of average ability, whereas the AH5 and AH6 are used for adults of higher intellectual ability.

  Crystallized intelligence is measured by verbal reasoning items (such as analogies and working out complex family relationships), and fluid intelligence is measured by the use of non-verbal categorizations and analogies.

Personality questionnaires

There is considerable scientific evidence (Herriot 1989; Kline 1992) that personality differences play a very important role in job satisfaction, which, in turn, is related to job success.

There are three basic approaches to the use of personality tests in occupational psychology (Kline 1992). The assumption that underlies each of these approaches is that there is some ideal specification (in terms of personality characteristics) for each type of occupation.

1 *Matching*

Applicants for jobs can be matched to the scores of those currently doing that job. In this way it is possible to create a profile of successful workers in a particular job and match new applicants in terms of those characteristics. This method is not without its problems, however, not least of which is the assumption that those workers whose scores are being used to create the norms are *representative* of all workers in that position. This is particularly problematic when tests that are created in one country (for example, the United States) are used to select workers in another country (for example, the United Kingdom). The matching method should only be used when there are clear and representative norms.

2 *The regression method*

This method provides a means by which scores on personality questionnaires can be correlated with success in a particular job. If it is possible to show that successful workers tend to score more highly on particular aspects of a personality questionnaire (for example, the 16PF scales as shown in Table 26.4) then it is appropriate to use that type of measure to select workers for that position. Appealing and simple as this method appears, it is potentially problematic. First, the sample of workers used to create the norms must be representative of that occupation. Second, the regression data should not be out of date. The nature of certain occupations clearly changes over the years and what might be considered essential characteristics for successful performance in 1956 might not be as relevant in 1996. Third, it is clear that many jobs defy accurate assessment of 'job success'. Think how difficult it would be to accurately measure 'job success' among teachers, priests or even undertakers!

3 *Personality questionnaires and job analysis*

By a process of observation, interview and careful job analysis it is possible to judge the psychological demands of any particular job. For example, it would be clear from an analysis of stand-up comedians that their job requires a good deal of extroversion, and that the most successful comedians tend to display a fair amount of neurotic behaviour in their work. Personality questionnaires might then be used to select applicants with high scores in those areas. Although the correlation between occupational success and personality scores is quite small, even small correlations provide us with some relevant information that might be used in conjunction with information derived from other sources. When used in this selection context, however, these tests suffer from the problem of faking. It is probable that applicants will attempt to portray themselves as possessing the kind of personality characteristics that they see as important in that position. If you went for a job as brain surgeon, for example, you would be unlikely to admit to being careless and impulsive in your approach to your work! For this reason many tests (such as the Eysenck Personality Questionnaire) employ a lie scale that can filter out those applicants that are faking their responses.

Advantages and disadvantages of psychometric testing

Advantages

- On the whole, psychometric tests measure what they claim to measure (that is, they have acceptable *validity*). This makes them less prone to error than other types of assessment. Good tests must also demonstrate *reliability*. Test items should all be measuring the same thing with the same degree of accuracy (*internal reliability*) and maintain this accuracy on subsequent testing occasions (*test-retest reliability*).
- The interpretation of psychometric data requires the use of 'norms', against which the scores of a particular individual can be compared. Psychometric assessments tend to be the only measures for which norms are available.
- Psychometric tests are fairly short and are therefore time efficient. Many are group tests, and can be given to a number of people at the same time.
- Many modern tests can now be administered and scored by computer. This means that results are available very quickly and can form the basis for discussion.
- The use of psychometric tests is very cost efficient as it can prevent money being wasted in training personnel for jobs for which they are unsuitable. The most striking example of this is in the selection and training of pilots in the Air Force. Not all those who enter for fast jet training make it to the end of training

Table 26.4 Two personality tests commonly used in selection

1 *The Eysenck Personality Questionnaire, EPQ (Eysenck and Eysenck 1975)*

This contains 90 items to which respondents answer yes or no, and which scores them on four scales:

- Extroversion – Introversion
- Neuroticism – Stability
- Tough-mindedness – Tender-mindedness
- Telling lies (to detect those faking social desirability).

2 *The 16PF test (Cattell et al. 1970)*

This measures respondents on the 16 factors claimed by Cattell to underlie the variance in personality. The test consists of self-report statements concerning personality traits such as those detailed below.

- reserved *vs* outgoing
- trusting *vs* suspicious
- humble *vs* assertive
- affected by feelings *vs* emotionally stable
- shy *vs* venturesome
- relaxed *vs* tense.

because they lack the necessary characteristics for this arduous occupation. It can cost close to a million pounds to train a pilot to this level so mistakes at the selection stage are very expensive.

Disadvantages

- Test scores can be misused. The results of tests should not be used to withhold educational or occupational opportunities from those who may perform less well on tests of ability due to factors that have little to do with intelligence (see *In Focus*).
- There can be an undue reliance on the results of psychometric tests. Simply discovering that a person has an aptitude for a particular occupation does not *guarantee* that they will be successful at that job.
- Because of the cheapness and predictive success of many psychometric tests, there may be a failure to use other important information. Psychometric test results should really only be used alongside other reliable information about a person.
- The mystique of psychometric test results means that they are frequently not discussed with those who complete them. In this sense there is a failure to use psychological testing humanely.

In Focus

A fair test? Selecting drivers at British Rail.

A study of selection procedures at British Rail was undertaken following complaints of discrimination by eight Asian guards at Paddington who had been refused jobs as drivers. The study, carried out by psychologist Steve Blinkhorn, found that the psychometric tests used were biased against members of ethnic minorities, especially Asians. Blinkhorn found that many of the criteria used to choose drivers were irrelevant to the job. Employees found that if their first language was not English they were disadvantaged by the test. The report also found that Indian employees were slower and more careful in their answers to questions than non-Asian employees, yet the selection procedures failed to pick up this cultural idiosyncrasy. The result, claimed Blinkhorn, was that the selection procedures used were inadequate for the job.

Section summary

Controversial issues in psychology are those that tend to produce the greatest concern both within psychology and within society as a whole. Psychologists have contributed knowledge in ways that can be socially beneficial or socially divisive.

In areas such as advertising and propaganda, techniques of persuasion are used to manipulate people's behaviour in the direction desired by the perpetrator of the persuasive message. The use of psychological techniques in warfare is often shrouded in mystery and intrigue, but is well known in areas such as interrogation and battleproofing. Recent developments in psychological warfare have tended to focus more on the role of information warfare, and the contributions of the science of psychology have become merged with those of computer science. Psychometric tests have a long history of use in areas such as education and occupational selection. They are a quick and relatively successful method of assessment in these contexts, but can be abused if too much reliance is placed on their results or their results are misinterpreted.

Psychology as science

What is science? At first examination this may seem a fairly trivial question. We all know what science is, but what does it really mean to describe something as 'scientific', and can psychology really be considered scientific in the same way that the natural sciences are considered scientific.

The word 'science' comes from a Latin word which literally means 'knowledge'. Science can, therefore, be seen as concerned with what we *know* to be true, rather than what we *believe* to be true. Because of this we attach considerable importance to science as a way of distinguishing what is true and real from what is not (Slife and Williams 1995). In the contemporary use of the term, science is often seen as both a body of knowledge that we accept as being trustworthy, and also the method for attaining that knowledge (i.e. the *scientific method*).

The characteristics of science

Probably the most fundamental characteristic of science is its reliance on empirical methods of observation and investigation, i.e. observation through sensory experience rather than a reliance on thoughts and ideas. All scientific ideas must, at some point, be subjected to empirical test. Science has emerged as a trusted approach to the acquisition of knowledge because of this reliance on sensory experience. This does not mean, however, that science is purely empirical in nature. For science to 'make sense', it is necessary to explain the results of empirical observation. That means the construction of theories, which in turn can be tested and refined through further empirical observation. This cycle of scientific enquiry is shown in Figure 26.2.

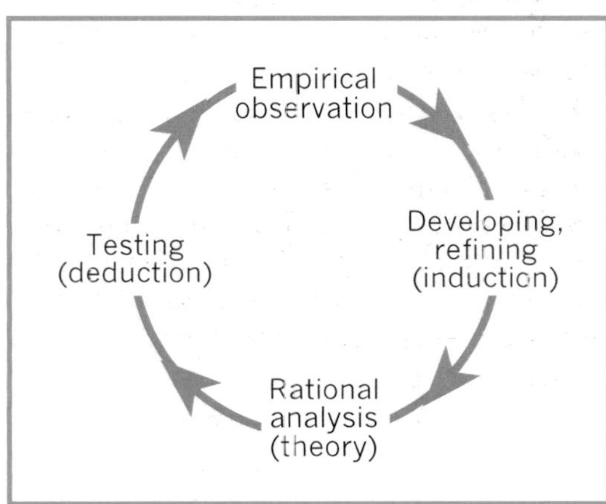

Figure 26.1 The cycle of scientific enquiry

Slife and Williams (1995) identify a number of further attributes that characterize science.

- Scientific observation is made under *objective* conditions. In other words, observation is not influenced by external factors such as bias or expectation, or the particular cultural values of the scientist.
- Scientific observation takes place under *controlled* conditions. This is often accomplished in the context of the experiment, where scientists can control the conditions under which they make their observations.
- Science involves making *predictions* about what is expected to happen under specified conditions. In this way the scientist is able to *validate* or *falsify* whatever theory or hypothesis led to the observations being made. This ability to control and predict behaviour in experimental settings gives us the expectation that we will also be able to control and predict behaviour in real-life settings. It is this expectation that drives psychology towards science as a chosen route to knowledge, and towards the establishment of a *technology* of behaviour.
- Scientific investigations are open to public scrutiny, i.e. the methods and results of scientific investigations are there for all to see and to check. Confidence in results can be increased when investigations can be *replicated*, and the results repeated.

Is psychology scientific?

There are two underpinnng views of science that might help us to decide whether psychology constitutes a science.

Science as knowledge

Science is a body of knowledge that explains the nature of the world (Slife and Williams 1995). Viewed from this perspective, scientific knowledge has two main characteristics:

- Scientific explanations reject, and are preferred to, other explanations of naturally occurring phenomena (such as magic or other supernatural explanations).
- Scientific explanations are often stated as laws or general principles about the relationship between different events. Because of the regularity of the way in which these events occur together, it then becomes possible to control and predict them.

Although most psychologists have certainly rejected the role of supernatural phenomena in determining human behaviour, it is perhaps a little hopeful to claim that psychology has led to the development of universal laws of human behaviour. Although psychologists accept the idea that behaviour tends to be determined, the inability to control all the myriad human variables that underlie behaviour means that accurate control and prediction is almost impossible.

Science as method

The second way of characterizing science is to see it as a method of studying phenomena. Scientific investigation involves empirical observation and the development of theories that in turn are constantly tested and refined in the light of further observation. When viewed from this perspective, it is clear that psychology probably *does* qualify as a science, because scientific methods are the preferred method of investigation. Indeed, the laboratory experiment has probably become the dominant mode of investigation in psychology, and therefore offers the psychologist opportunities for control and prediction that are absent in less 'scientific' methods. This raises various issues:

- Is the use of scientific methods sufficient cause for labelling psychology a 'science'? Slife and Williams quote the example of parapsychology (the study of paranormal phenomena) as an area that has been subjected to rigorous scientific study, yet few psychologists would accept parapsychology as 'scientific'.
- Would we accept that the traditional scientific methods as used in the natural sciences are necessarily the best means of studying human behaviour? We will return to this question later.

Problems of scientific psychology

Maintaining objectivity

We saw earlier that objectivity was an important characteristic of scientific enquiry. By that we mean that there is an assumption that any subjective influences (such as the values and expectations of the investigator) are excluded from the investigation. In this way, we can be sure that the results are not distorted in some way because of the subjectivity of the investigator. Thomas Kuhn (1970) believed that total objectivity is never possible. The view that any particular scientist holds about the world (in Kuhn's terms, their 'paradigm') makes them think about the world in a specific way. This influences what they investigate, the methods they use to investigate it, and the sorts of explanations that they see as acceptable for the results obtained. This is important if psychology is to be considered scientific according to the first perspective of science outlined earlier. As all scientific knowledge emerges from within a specific set of influences (the paradigm), and these lead scientists to think about a problem in their own special way, it is questionable whether it is possible to establish *universal* laws of human behaviour.

Operationalization

To carry out a scientific test, we must be able to observe whatever it is we are investigating. This may seem a straightforward requirement, but it is not always so. For example, there are many events (such as motivation or fear) that we cannot observe directly. Instead, we observe something else that we feel represents the thing we are really interested in. For example, we may choose to define fear in terms of some physiological change (such as pupil dilation) or motivation in terms of questionnaire responses. The trouble with these operational definitions is that they are not necessarily measurements of the thing we were interested in in the first place. The consequence of this is that psychologists often explore the relationship between two things (e.g. love and happiness) without ever being able to measure either of these directly. Instead, as is the case with many investigations in psychology, our observations are always one step removed from what we are really interested in studying.

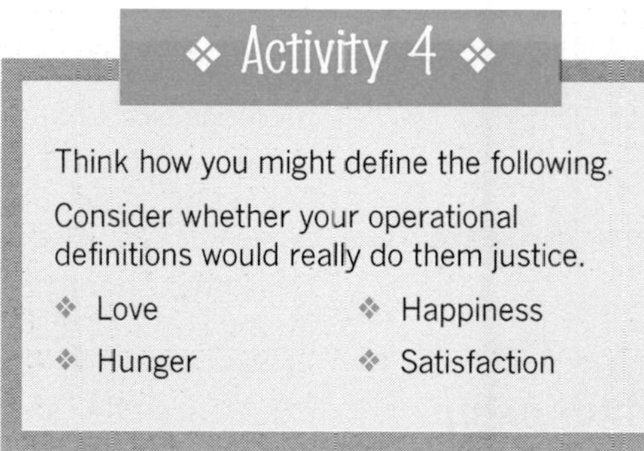

❖ Activity 4 ❖
Think how you might define the following.
Consider whether your operational definitions would really do them justice.
❖ Love
❖ Happiness
❖ Hunger
❖ Satisfaction

Establishing causality

It is generally accepted in scientific psychology that the only way of establishing causality is by carrying out an experiment. Experiments are often contrasted with correlational designs (see Chapter 28) because in the latter, the researcher merely observes that the two variables (e.g. amount of revision and examination success) are related, yet in the former, the researcher is able to manipulate one variable systematically (the *independent variable*) in order to see its effect on another (the *dependent variable*). In order to be confident that any change in the dependent variable had been caused by the manipulation of the independent variable, the researcher would need to control everything else that could possibly have a causal effect on the dependent variable. Clearly this is impossible when we are dealing with human beings. We have no way of knowing all the possible ways in which any one individual might be influenced to behave at any given time. Although this appears to make statements of causality redundant, it is, however, possible to observe that when X is manipulated in some way, Y tends to occur. In this way, we might *approach* the cause of a behaviour rather than being confident we *know* how it was caused.

Verification and falsification.

One of the classic problems in verifying hypotheses (i.e. showing that they are true) is the logical fallacy of *affirming the consequent*. Think about the following statements:

If this hypothesis is true then X will be observed.

X is observed (affirming the consequent), therefore the hypothesis is true.

In this example, the hypothesis (e.g. that watching violent videos makes children violent) is described as the antecedent, and the outcome (in this case a measurement of violence) is the consequent. If X is observed, then the consequent is said to be affirmed and we could conclude that watching violent videos does indeed make children violent.

Slife and Williams (1995) argue that empirical studies can only ever affirm the consequent, i.e. they can only show that the hypothesis given *might* explain the results of the investigation, but then so might many other possible explanations. Thus data cannot *prove* that a hypothesis is correct, nor can they indicate which of a range of possible alternative explanations is the most likely. Affirming the consequent thus always leads to a logically invalid conclusion (see 'Models of thought' in Chapter 16).

As scientists have considerable problems validating their hypotheses (i.e. proving that they are true), they may instead attempt to *falsify* them. According to Popper (1959), if we can prove things to be false, then we can rule them out as explanations and thus arrive at the truth by a process of elimination. The way in which scientists can falsify hypotheses is by *negating the consequent:*

If this hypothesis is true, then X will be observed.

X is not observed, therefore the hypothesis is not true.

In this way, the consequent (the observation of X) was not evident, therefore it follows that the antecedent (the hypothesis) is false.

❖ Activity 5 ❖

Sociobiologists tell us that animals grazing in larger herds look up less than those in smaller herds. This, they tell us, is all to do with the need for vigilance against predators. Do humans also act like this when eating? What might be an alternative explanation for this?

Alternative views on the science–psychology relationship

In the preceding section we explored the issue of whether science could establish 'truth' about human behaviour with any degree of certainty. This raises the question not about whether psychology might be considered scientific, but whether it should be scientific. It should be clear that some aspects of human behaviour might be more accessible than others to this type of empirical proof. For example, it may be a fairly straightforward endeavour to explore mundane issues such as the short-term memory span using scientific methods. However, psychology is concerned with human behaviour in all its richness and complexity, and scientific methods may not be the best route to investigating this area.

Slife and Williams (1995) present three positions on whether a science of human behaviour is possible or even desirable.

- Scientific methods might be seen as essential because of the need for empirical validation. All theories should be subject to rigorous tests to show that they are internally consistent (i.e. they make sense) and that they can explain a wide range of events consistent with the predictions of the theory. It is also important that the claims of a particular theory can be demonstrated through actual, observable behaviour.
- The study of human experience requires the development of methods that are quite different from those used in the study of the natural world. Human scientists would place a great deal of importance on the experience of their participants as a way of understanding their behaviour. The use of qualitative methods (see Chapter 30) avoids the measurement and quantification of behaviour, allowing participants to describe their own experiences within their own linguistic style. The role of the qualitative researcher would be to question, describe and interpret this experience (Slife and Williams 1995).
- The study of human behaviour and experience requires *methodological pluralism*. Researchers attempt to make sense of the world around them, and must make their choice of method based on the nature of the problem they are investigating. All methods open the door to knowledge in one way, but close it in another. On the basis of this, no one method might be considered superior to another.

Section summary

Science is concerned with the acquisition of knowledge that is considered trustworthy. The scientific method is the process by which explanatory theories are established through empirical observation and are constantly refined and updated in the same way. Although psychologists embrace the aims and methods of science there are some doubts over whether its subject matter and methods enable us to consider psychology as truly scientific. Recent developments in psychology have placed greater emphasis on the subjective experience of research participants than on restricting the collection of information to the gathering of numerical data.

Gender bias in psychological theory and research

❖ Activity 6 ❖

Self-assessment: Beliefs about women (*Adapted from:* Belk and Snell 1985)

For each of the statements listed below, write a number on the line to the right of the statement that describes your response to this statement. Your responses can range from strongly disagree (1) to strongly agree (5). Use the scale below to determine how to score your response.

Disagree		*Neutral*		*Agree*
Strongly	*Somewhat*		*Somewhat*	*Strongly*
1	2	3	4	5

Women are less decisive than men. ____
Women are less dominating than men. ____
Women are more passive than men. ____
Women have more emotional insight than men. ____
Women are more interpersonal than men. ____
Women are less career-interested than men. ____
Women are more vulnerable than men. ____
Women are less intelligent than men. ____
Women are less decisive than men. ____
Women are less sexual than men. ____
Women are more appearance-conscious than men. ____
Women are sexual teases. ____
Women are more moral than men. ____
Women act sillier than men do. ____
Menstruation debilitates women. ____

We will return to this assessment later, but for now it may be profitable to take a look at where some of these ideas may have come from in the first place.

Traditional views of men and women

Gender bias is not a new thing. For centuries we have accepted assumptions about the differences between the sexes. Even though the conditions under which these ideas were originally formed have changed, these outdated notions have tended to remain. For the psychologist who is trying to understand these ideas, a fundamental problem is trying to understand their origin. However, that isn't too hard to do, and we don't have to look very far to find representations of men and women that appear as old as time itself.

Both Aristotle and Plato wrote extensively about the role of women. Of the two, Aristotle (384–322 B.C.) was the more negative. He saw women's inferiority as being biologically based. 'We should look upon the female,' he said, 'as being a deformity, though one which occurs in the ordinary course of nature.' In Aristotle's philosophical writings, women are portrayed as not possessing fully developed rationality. Men, therefore, must both rule them and be responsible for them. Aristotle, it might be claimed, was also the perpetrator of that modern legacy, the gender stereotype. Women are frequently 'pathologized' because of their physical differences from men, for example their 'irrationality' or their emotionality is often attributed to pre-menstrual syndrome or to menopausal symptoms. In other words, their pathology is seen as inescapably connected to their femaleness.

Psychological theories and gender bias

'Throughout history people have knocked their heads against the riddle of femininity.' (Freud 1931)

Within psychology there have been two main approaches to gender-related characteristics. There are the theories that ignore the differences between men and women, and those which exaggerate them. Hare-Mustin and Marecek (1988) refer to these as *beta bias* and *alpha bias* respectively.

The alpha bias theories assume real and enduring differences between men and women. Sometimes alpha bias theories heighten the value of women, as in Chodorow's conception of women as more relational and caring (Chodorow 1978) and sometimes they are used to devalue women. Within sociobiology, for example, differences in male and female behaviour may be attributed to genetic determinism. Thus male social dominance or sexual promiscuity might be seen as a product of their evolutionary history.

Beta bias theories and research have traditionally ignored or minimized sex differences. They have done this either by ignoring questions about the lives of women or by assuming that findings from studies of males apply equally well to females. Such approaches, at best misguided, at worst arrogant, have resulted in what is essentially an androcentric view of human behaviour (based on and concerning males), rather than offering insights into what is essentially one half of the human race. These are not the only types of bias that lurk within the study of psychology. Worell and Remer (1992) identified other biases that also have their origins in outdated assumptions about men and women. They summarized six main types of gender bias that might be present in psychological theories.

Androcentric

Androcentric theories tend to offer an interpretation of women based on an understanding of the lives of men. Ideas of 'normal' behaviour may be drawn exclusively from studies of the development of males. A well-known example of an androcentric theory is Freud's account of male identity development, in which the young boy's identification with his father leads to the formation of a superego and of high moral standards. Girls, on the other hand, who do not experience the same Oedipal conflict as boys, cannot, it appears, develop their superego (and thus their moral standards) to the same degree as boys.

Gendercentric

Gendercentric theories see male and female development as following separate paths. Freud's theory can thus be seen as being both androcentric and gendercentric. Other theories that might be regarded as gendercentric do not devalue women in the way that androcentric theories might. Theories that might be described as gendercentric display an alpha bias in that they emphasize how males and females differ, rather than how their characteristics might intersect.

Ethnocentric

Ethnocentric theories assume that development and interaction are the same across cultures and races. Such theories are often characterized by an Anglo-European orientation, and as such may offer quite fixed sets of assumptions about 'normal' patterns of family functioning, and appropriate roles for males and females within the family structure.

Heterosexist

Most traditional theories of psychological development view heterosexual orientation as normal and therefore view orientation toward partners of the same sex as abnormal. In Freud's psychoanalytic theory, for example, a homosexual orientation was interpreted as a failure to achieve a normal gender identity, and was therefore treated as if it were a personality disorder. Homosexuality was diagnosed as a category of mental illness by the American Psychiatric Association up until 1973, when it was finally removed from the diagnostic classification system DSM II.

Intrapsychic

Intrapsychic theories tend to attribute all behaviour of an individual to factors within themselves. These theories tend to minimize the role of external influences, thus leading to the inevitable consequence of 'blaming' the victim for whatever happens to them. An example of an intrapsychic theory would be Nancy Chodorow's object relations theory where a later behaviour may be attributed to an earlier developmental failure. For example, a woman who stays in an abusive and unsatisfying marriage may be seen as the product of an earlier failure to separate herself from her own mother.

Deterministic

These theories assume that patterns of behaviour have developed as a result of past events and are thus more or less fixed. The consequence of this would be that ideas of gender role become an inflexible aspect of one's personality and are thus relatively unchangeable at a later stage of development.

❖ Activity 7 ❖

Turn to Chapter 19 and read about Lawrence Kohlberg's theory of moral development (p. 411). Which of these gender biases are characteristic of this theory?

Bias-free theories

There are a number of ways that psychological theories can avoid the biases described above. Worell and Remer (1992) offer four criteria by which theories might be evaluated in order to overcome the often detrimental models of women that develop from more traditional non-feminist models.

Gender-free

Gender-free theories see men and women as similar in their psychological makeup. Such theories avoid stereotypes or any labels that imply that one sex may be more valued than the other. Cast your mind back to Activity 6 at the beginning of this section. If you gave answers that were anything other than a 3 (neutral), you have stereotypes about women, and as such your conceptions of male and female behaviour are not gender-free. A gender-free theory attempts to avoid sexist and stereotyped concepts of the broader culture.

Flexible

A flexible theory uses ideas that can apply equally to individuals or groups of any age, race, gender or sexual orientation. Such theories emphasize within-sex differences in behaviour, as well as between-sex differences. These theories thereby offer a range of satisfying and fulfilling life styles for both men and women rather than devaluing one or the other as less mature, incomplete or unhealthy due to some preconceived notions of what might be considered normal or healthy (and therefore linked to one sex, age, etc. rather than another).

Interactionist

For a theory to be considered interactionist it should recognize the interaction between a range of individual-centred factors (including affective, cognitive and behavioural factors) and those which are more environmental (other people, institutions, etc.). Interactionist theories would recognize multiple influences on a person's behaviour, and accept that an individual could not be properly understood without consideration of all relevant factors.

Lifespan

The essential ingredient of a lifespan approach to development is the belief that behaviour changes can occur at any time during an individual's lifetime, rather than being restricted to specific periods that exert powerful influences on later behaviour. When applied to gender-related behaviour, such theories suggest that these behaviours are not fixed in people but may always be open to change. Individuals develop within a particular social-historical environment, and as such experience a range of influences that are specific to that time, but nevertheless remain capable of choice and thus self-determined change.

Gender bias in psychological research

'An experiment typically consists of a brief encounter among strangers in an unfamiliar setting, often under the eye of a psychologist. The question is whether this context is a valid one from which to make generalizations about behaviour.' (Riger 1992)

The main source of discontent with psychological research and its bias against women has centred around the use of traditional scientific method, most notably the use of the laboratory experiment. This technique has dominated psychological research and has become the normative research method in much of 'mainstream' psychology. In the eyes of the outsider, the laboratory experiment is the essence of scientific 'proof' about human behaviour. For some reason there is more credibility and prestige associated with the results of laboratory experiments than there is with other methods in psychology.

So, why is this a problem, and why is the experiment seen as being so gender biased? Nicholson (1995) identifies two main problems with this adherence to an experimental science of psychology.

- The experiment takes the *behaviour* of an individual research participant as the unit of study rather than the participant herself. This ignores the social, personal and cultural context in which the behaviour is enacted. In this way psychologists discover 'truths' about gender differences that are attributed to the characteristics of the participant rather than the characteristics of the research context.
- Experimental psychology characteristically disadvantages women. Stripped of their social power and knowledge, they are placed in a 'strange' environment, where they are expected to respond to the requirements of a (usually) male experimenter. Female participants are thus forced into a position of subordination in their interaction with a man who is in charge of the experiment.

As a result of 'scientific' research, women have been labelled as irrational, inappropriately volatile and easily depressed for no reason. They are accused of having more lapses of attention than men, and of generally performing more badly on both simple and complex cognitive tasks. Women are thus portrayed as being intellectually and emotionally deficient in relation to men because of their bodies. They have been pathologized through the use of the labels *pre-menstrual syndrome, post-natal depression* and *menopausal symptoms.* These have been identified by the medical profession and by psychologists as conditions, and therefore as incontestable facts.

The *In Focus* that follows illustrates the problems of applying this kind of reasoning in psychological research.

As well as criticizing the general experimental approach to psychology, feminists have shown that bias can appear at every stage of the experimental design, from formulating the research question to the interpretation of the data. Some examples of this research bias are given below.

In Focus

Women and the menstrual cycle

Feminist psychologists have identified that women's 'deficiencies' in behavioural, cognitive and emotional functioning are due to the conceptualization of the research question and the flaws in the methodologies used. Nowhere is this more noticeable than in the study of pre-menstrual syndrome (PMS). One extreme outcome of research in this area has been the attempts to use PMS as a legal defence to plead 'diminished responsibility'. PMS was seen as giving a woman an excuse for anything, including murder, while making her 'not responsible for herself'. What is the evidence for such a belief? Claims by scientists concerning the menstrual cycle are inevitably more to do with the male-dominated culture in which scientific enquiry is embedded than with the experiences and concerns of women themselves. Women are caught in the contradictions of the dominant culture which sees them as both biologically and psychologically inferior. A woman who does not display the characteristic qualities to suit her to the 'feminine role' is seen to be in need of treatment. Thus women are led to seek attributions for their 'unsatisfactory condition'. A medicalized concept such as PMS represents an appealing explanation to women themselves and to others. It serves to justify women's oppression and lack of achievement compared to men.

Source: adapted from Nicholson 1995

- *Formulating the research question*: Gross (1995) points out that topics that are studied in psychological research frequently reflect the prevalent gender stereotypes of the culture. For example, leadership is often defined by researchers in terms of dominance, aggression and other characteristics that are stereotyped as typically male characteristics.
- *Selection of research participants*: Social psychologists, for example, have typically developed theories from white, male undergraduates. This is then represented as 'human behaviour' (Fine and Gordon 1989). You might like to consider how some of the classic social psychology experiments mentioned in Chapters 1 to 4 have addressed this problem.

Alternative research strategies

If science is gender-biased and androcentric, what criteria should be considered when carrying out a study?

Worell (1992) suggests a number of research criteria that are particularly important to ensure non-gender-biased research investigations:

- *using alternative methods of inquiry*: expanding the boundaries of accepted scientific methodology to explore the personal lives of women
- *looking at meaningful contexts*: considering women in the natural settings in which they function
- *collaborating with research participants*: entering into a partnership with participants to explore personally relevant variables
- *soliciting diverse samples*: looking at women who vary by age, socio-economic class, partner preference, minority or ethnic group, etc.

Section summary

Gender bias is embedded both in psychology and in history. Philosophers such as Aristotle saw sex differences in behaviour as being biologically based. In more contemporary theories of psychology, there have been two main approaches to gender-related characteristics. Theories that ignore the differences between men and women have a beta bias and those that exaggerate the differences an alpha bias. There are a number of ways in which psychology can avoid these theoretical biases, including the need to avoid gender stereotypes and to consider the constant interaction between individual and environmental influences in a person's development.

Psychological research appears to disadvantage women through its reliance on experimental research. The construction of knowledge concerning female deficiency has typically been created within such a context. Alternative research strategies would move away from rigid experimental manipulations towards a consideration of the experiences of women in their own lives.

Cultural biases in psychological theory and research

What do we mean by culture? 'Culture refers to the collective programming of the mind which distinguishes members of one group from another.' (Hofstede 1980)

In attempting to distinguish one culture from another, we are attempting to draw definitive lines in terms of what is generally a characteristic in one culture but not, perhaps, a characteristic of another. Smith and Bond (1993) identify two major problems with this.

- Behaviour differences between any two countries may also be found between different subcultures within the same country.
- We assume that cultures are free from conflict and dissent in the behaviour of their members. It is clear that within any culture, there will be a great deal of divergence in the experiences of individuals that make up that culture.

A useful distinction between national cultures has been made by Hofstede (1980). He proposed that cultures could be classified in a number of ways, including their position on the dimension of *individualism–collectivism*. This measures whether an individual's identity is more defined by personal achievement and independence, or by collective achievement and interdependence.

Hofstede studied fifty national cultures and three regions, and ranked them in terms of their scores on the individualism–collectivism dimension. Examples of his findings can be seen in Table 26.5. Note that a high rank denotes a high *individualism* score and a low rank denotes a high *collectivism* score. Under this system, the United States would be the most individualist national culture and Guatemala the most collectivist.

In making this distinction between cultures, Hofstede was careful to avoid what is known as the *ecological fallacy*. This would be the (mistaken) belief that if two cultures differ in terms of their individualist or

Table 26.5 Examples of individualism–collectivism rankings for national cultures (Hofstede 1980)

Country	*Ranking*	*Country*	*Ranking*
United States	1	Jamaica	25
Australia	2	Hong Kong	37
Great Britain	3	Pakistan	47
France	10	Guatemala	53
India	21		

collectivist bias, then any two individuals taken at random from those cultures would also differ in that way.

Hofstede's work is not without its problems. It would be tempting, for example, to use these ideas as causal explanations of an individual's behaviour. If an individual is socialized within a collectivist culture, does that mean that they would always behave in a characteristic way? Clearly this would not be the case. Second, the techniques used to gather these data (a series of questionnaires) and the dimensions proposed to explain the results demonstrate a cultural bias specific to western scientific values (see previous section on the problems of using a scientific approach).

Cultural bias in psychology

The emic–etic distinction

This distinction, usually attributed to Berry (1969), focuses on the differences in our analysis of human behaviour.

- *Etic* analyses focus on the universals of human behaviour, for example the theory of moral development proposed by Kohlberg and discussed earlier, sees moral development as a universal process. That is, all individuals, regardless of culture, would experience the same developmental processes.
- An *emic* analysis of behaviour, on the other hand, would focus on the varied ways in which activities and development could be observed in any specific cultural setting.

Berry makes the point that psychology frequently involves an 'imposed etic', in that attempts to explain human behaviour in different parts of the world often involve using theories and research studies that have been developed within (predominantly) the USA. This imposed etic makes the assumption that whatever measures have been used in one cultural context (in this case the USA), will have the same meaning when applied in a different cultural context. Smith and Bond (1993) give the example of the F scale, a measure of intolerance toward minority groups that was developed by Adorno *et al.* (1950) in the USA. People who scored highly on this scale invariably showed greater prejudice against minority group members. Using the same scale with white South African participants, Pettigrew (1958) found that scores on the F scale did not correlate with anti-black prejudice. The *In Focus* that follows shows the difficulty of drawing direct comparisons across cultures with respect to one of the most controversial areas of social psychological research, obedience to authority.

Although these studies *appear* to show quite pronounced national differences in the degree of obedience, there are a number of reasons why we should not read too much into the results of this research.

- The experiments themselves varied in the way that they were carried out, and also in the type of 'victims' used in the research. For example, in Milgram's study the victims were all men, whereas in the Australian study (Kilham and Mann 1974) the female students were

In Focus

Obedience to authority and the problem of cross-cultural replication

In Milgram's study of obedience to authority (Milgram 1963), he found that 65 per cent of his American participants obeyed orders from an authority figure to give 'fatal' shocks to another person as part of an experiment on learning (see Chapter 3 for an extended discussion of Milgram's research). Although no shocks were actually given, the procedures used were convincing and participants were clearly under the impression that they had been giving real shocks.

Despite the outcry in the USA about the ethics of this research, at least eight studies were carried out in other countries after Milgram's results had been published. Extracts from these results are summarized below:

Study	*Country*	*Participants*	*Percentage obedience*
Milgram (1963)	USA	Males general population	65
Mantell (1971)	Germany	Males general population	85
Kilham and Mann (1974)	Australia	Male students	40
		Female students	16
Burley and McGuiness (1977)	UK	Male students	50
Shanab and Yahya (1978)	Jordan	Students	62
Meeus and Raaijmakers (1986)	Holland	General population	92

Source: adapted from Smith and Bond 1993

required to give shocks to a female victim. In the Dutch study (Meeus and Raaijmakers 1986) no shocks were given but the 'teacher' was instructed to harass and criticize the victim instead.

- With the exception of the Jordanese study (Shanab and Yahya 1978) all of these studies have been carried out in advanced industrial countries, so we are unable to conclude unequivocally that this is a universal aspect of human social behaviour.

The discussion above demonstrates some of the difficulties in replicating studies exactly across different cultures. In fact, we might argue that exact replication is rarely possible, particularly in areas such as social and developmental psychology. Many of the studies quoted throughout this book have been carried out as a result of a study in another country (usually the US) becoming well known, and researchers attempting to see if they could get similar results in their own country. Attempting to replicate a study brings with it many problems, including translation of questionnaires, samples of participants, and so on. Failure to ensure that participants and procedures are equivalent in different studies means that alternative explanations of the research findings (known as *plausible rival hypotheses*) must be addressed. Some of the problems of establishing equivalence in cross-cultural research are as follows (adapted from Smith and Bond 1993).

- *Translation*: Participants are instructed by spoken or written word and their verbal or written responses often constitute the main findings of the research. These instructions and responses must be faithfully translated for the purposes of comparison.
- *Manipulation of variables*: The operationalization of variables (see earlier in this chapter) and the impact of any manipulation must be the same in each cultural group being studied. For example, the expression of happiness might be different in different groups, and the impact of a specific independent

variable (such as an insult) dramatically different depending on the way it is interpreted by those involved in the study.

- *Participants*: Although these may be taken from similar social groups (university students, schoolchildren, etc.) they may have quite different social backgrounds and experiences in different cultural groups. To gain access to a university in some cultures, for example, does not involve the same criteria as it does in the West.
- *The research tradition*: In many cultures people grow up being used to the idea of scientific research and respond positively to participation in this tradition. Inherent in this positive attitude is the belief that their responses will remain confidential. This trust in the whole research process cannot be taken for granted in all other cultures where psychological research may be rare, if practised at all.

Racial bias in psychological theory and research

Perhaps more sinister and indefensible than cultural biases are the subtle (and sometimes not so subtle) influences that characterize the *racism of psychology*. The inclination to dismiss racial differences as being a product of 'bad genes' has a long history. In the 1800s the tendency for slaves to run away from their 'masters' was identified as being a mental illness, drapetomania. The idea that slavery itself might be the reason for this behaviour was dismissed and slaves seen as insane if they bucked the racist system (Howitt and Owusu-Bempah 1994). In his *Introduction to Social Psychology* (1908), William McDougall speaks of the 'deleterious consequences of unrestrained and excessive indulgence of the sexual appetite' and adds that 'it has often been maintained, and not improbably with justice, that the backward condition of so many branches of the Negro race is due to this state of affairs'. McDougall later found scientific 'evidence' for the 'defective character' of natives of India, and an 'instinct for submission' among American Negroes.

In the twentieth century there was a concerted attack on the assumptions of these bad-genes theories and of the interpretations of racial differences in intelligence test scores. This reached its controversial head with the publication of Arthur Jensen's notorious article on race and IQ. This questioned whether educational intervention could have any real effect on achievement among America's blacks. Jensen's arguments were based around the belief, supported by evidence from intelligence tests, that the intelligence levels of blacks were inferior to those of whites because of their inferior genes. This research stirred up a hornets' nest of criticism, only some of which was scientific. This was clearly not an issue that began and ended with scientific data. Jensen had based much of his argument on the data provided by the English psychologist, Cyril Burt. Burt, it transpired, had allegedly faked his data, and with that discovery went much of the evidence for the genetic basis of intelligence. Intelligence tests were no longer seen as objective measures of ability, but as 'weapons of subordination when used with society's disadvantaged' (Howitt and Owusu-Bempah 1994).

The publication of Jensen's research did have some beneficial effects within psychology. It made psychologists and non-psychologists sensitive to the issues involved and to the need for positive strategies to develop a psychology that was not embedded in racism. Owusu-Bempah and Howitt (1990) suggest a number of strategies that might help bring this about, including the following:

- ensuring that journal articles are monitored for unacceptable racist comments and interpretation of research findings.
- taking steps to encourage the recruitment of black people to psychology and making use of the different experiences and perspectives that they would bring to the profession.

In addition, Fernando (1989) argues that ethical committees frequently stand in the way of research oriented to the major concerns of black people. Researchers in this area are frequently misrepresented as being politically rather than psychologically motivated.

It is clear that we have an obligation to move toward a psychology that is both racism-free and that takes account of ethnic diversity. Ballard (1979) (quoted in Howitt and Owusu-Bempah (1993)) summarizes this obligation thus:

> 'For the practitioner the question of whether ethnic minorities ought, or ought not, to remain distinct should be irrelevant. The fact is that they are. Insofar as his specialism, whatever it is, demands that he should take into account the social and cultural worlds in which his clients live, he needs to make a response to ethnic diversity. If he does not, his practice is inadequate in purely professional terms.'

Section summary

Cultural biases in psychology may be evident through the 'imposed etic' whereby theories and research from one culture are used to explain the behaviour and experiences of members of another culture. Attempts to reproduce psychological studies in different cultures are rarely straight-forward. Failure to ensure equivalence in these studies means that alternative explanations of the research findings often have to be considered. Psychological theories have also been used to impose or to bolster particular social or political beliefs and practices. Psychology must address the need for a racism-free science and one that reflects a recognition of cultural diversity.

Chapter summary

- Controversial issues are generally regarded as those that produce the greatest concern from those within psychology as well as from the rest of society.
- Advertising and propaganda are related areas of persuasion. The former is often subtle and symbolic, focusing more on the way an advertisement makes us feel, whilst the latter can be more coercive and directed. Propaganda is one of the commonest types of psychological warfare, although its effectiveness is not always that easy to quantify.
- Psychological warfare may involve the use of battleproofing tactics to make soldiers into more fearless fighters as well as the use of interrogation devices such as sensory deprivation. Modern psychological warfare has moved more into areas of computer and communications warfare with the dawning of cyber-warfare.
- Science is concerned with the acquisition of knowledge that is trustworthy. Psychology seeks this type of knowledge and has therefore found the scientific methods the best route to psychological truth. Problems with the application of scientific methods in psychology have led some researchers to turn to the use of qualitative methods, which rely more on the subjective experience of research participants than on numerical data.
- Psychological theories may suffer from an alpha bias (exaggerating gender differences) or a beta bias (ignoring gender differences). Psychologists can avoid these and other gender biases by focusing more on explanations that are gender-free, flexible, interactionist and life-span oriented. Psychological research appears to disadvantage women by its over-reliance on experimental investigations. Alternative approaches would focus more on the subjective experiences of women.

- Cultural biases are evident in psychology through the imposition of ideas derived from the study of one culture onto the members of another. Replication of studies across cultures is often difficult because of problems of establishing equivalence. Psychological knowledge and practices might be used in a racist way, therefore there is a need for a psychology that is racism-free and acknowledges the importance of cultural diversity.

Essay titles

1 Critically consider the use of psychological techniques in advertising. *(24 marks)*

2 'The question is not about whether psychology *can* be a science, but rather whether it *should* be a science.' Discuss. *(24 marks)*

3 (a) Describe some of the ways in which psychological theories might be considered to be gender-biased. *(12 marks)*

(b) Assess any *two* theories in terms of their gender bias. *(12 marks)*

4 (a) What is meant by 'cultural bias in psychological research'? *(6 marks)*

(b) Critically consider the degree to which it might be possible to develop a truly universal understanding of human behaviour. *(18 marks)*

Further reading

Wadeley, A., Birch, A. and Malim, A. (1997) *Perspectives in Psychology* (2nd edn), London: Macmillan.

An updated, accessible and very relevant coverage of all the issues in this chapter.

Pratkanis, A.R. and Aronson, E. (1992) *Age of Propaganda: The Everyday Use and Abuse of Persuasion*, New York: W.H. Freeman.

A fascinating insight into the world of propaganda and other forms of persuasion.

Kline, P. (1992) *Psychometric Testing in Personnel Selection and Appraisal*, Kingston-upon-Thames: Croner.

An authoritative text dealing with the use of psychometric tests in selection and appraisal.

Slife, B.D. and Williams, R.N. (1995) *What's Behind the Research? Discovering Hidden Assumptions in the Behavioural Sciences*, Thousand Oaks: Sage.

An excellent source book on many issues relating to psychological research but particularly informative on the science of psychology.

Smith, P. and Bond, M.H. (1993) *Social Psychology Across Cultures: Analysis and Perspectives*, New York: Harvester Wheatsheaf.

An excellent account of the problems of carrying out cross-cultural research and of the cultural biases inherent in much of modern psychology.

Chapter 27

Ethical issues in psychology

Mike Cardwell

Preview

In this chapter we shall be looking at three areas of research which raise ethical issues:

- research with human participants
- research with non-human animals
- socially sensitive research.

Introduction

Because of the nature of psychological research there is a clear need to exercise the utmost care and consideration when dealing with both human and non-human subjects. Although originally a matter of individual morality and attention (it was expected that psychologists would consider ethical concerns alongside more purely methodological concerns), the need for a clear and unambiguous set of guidelines for research psychologists led to the development of the ethical principles that underlie all psychological research today. To describe something as 'unethical' therefore not only describes a practice that is morally wrong, but also one that is professionally unacceptable in terms of these guiding principles. The guidelines drawn up by the British Psychological Society (1990) stress that psychologists must carry out their work in a way that respects the rights and dignity of all research participants.

This concern for the rights and dignity of the participants of psychological research does not end with a consideration of the needs of human beings, but stretches to a consideration of the needs of non-human animals as well. This latter area of enquiry raises a commendable amount of concern and debate among students, and a good deal of entrenched opinion that often defies counter argument.

Socially sensitive research poses special ethical problems for the research psychologist. Research into issues of race and sexuality, for example, inevitably invites criticism from other psychologists and from the general public. It becomes obvious that psychological research has the potential not only for human betterment, but also for manipulation and exploitation.

Being a research psychologist then, requires an appreciation not only of how to deal with the immediate concerns and rights of our research participants, but also the more fundamental question of why the research is being carried out in the first place.

Research with human participants

In Focus

Krafft-Ebing's work with paretic patients

Around the middle of the nineteenth century, it had been established that many sufferers of general paresis (a degenerative mental disorder) had earlier contracted syphilis, a venereal disease. This led to the suggestion that general paresis was caused by syphilis. Despite the support for this link, many other explanations of general paresis were offered, including the alleged influence of coffee, tobacco and even sea-water!

In 1897, Richard von Krafft-Ebing set out to establish a causal link between syphilis and general paresis. Although most of his paretic patients denied ever having had syphilis, he was convinced that the answer lay in this direction. He believed that many of these paretic patients would be unaware of their own syphilis (the disease is a progressive one, beginning with open genital sores and then gradually leading to the destruction of specific areas of the brain) or might deny that they had ever had the disease. He injected them with material from the syphilitic sores of newly diagnosed syphilitics. If he was right, his paretic patients would not contract syphilis (because they already had it), but if he was wrong, his paretic patients would not only have the burden of their mental disorder, but the added distress of syphilis as well. Fortunately, none of the paretic patients injected with syphilis contracted the disease, and the link between the two diseases was established. Shortly after this, an effective way of diagnosing and treating syphilis in the early stages of the disease was discovered, and general paresis gradually disappeared as a known disorder.

The example given above is a true account of a study carried out towards the end of the last century. Although not strictly a psychological study in the true sense of the word, it does illustrate very nicely what a completely unethical study feels like. I use the word 'feel' here because even if you knew nothing about the professional guidelines used by research psychologists, you would get the 'feeling' that this study is completely unethical. You would be right, of course, but exactly what is it that makes a study unethical? In the UK this is laid out quite clearly in the guidelines published by the British Psychological Society (BPS) for research involving human participants. You may be wondering about the use of the rather clumsy title 'participants' when traditionally those that take part in a piece of research are referred to as 'subjects'. Although the term 'subject' was never meant to reflect a derogatory and impersonal stance towards those who take part in a study, to those outside this research tradition the term may appear to do just that. The term 'participants' is nowadays preferred in deference to that misconception.

The BPS constantly revises its *Ethical Principles for Research with Human Participants* and, in particular, it highlights a number of key issues that should be foremost in the minds of research psychologists. A summary of the full set of BPS guidelines is given in Table 27.1.

The guiding principles outlined in Table 27.1 are the 'rules' by which research psychologists operate, but what are the issues behind these principles? Let us focus on some of these to see why they are such an important part of the research process.

Consent

If someone volunteers for an experiment, we might believe that they are doing so because they know exactly what is going to happen to them. In other words, they are able to give their informed consent to take part in the study. Unfortunately this is not always

Table 27.1 A summary of the ethical guidelines for research with human participants (BPS 1990)

1 Introduction

Participants in psychological research should have confidence in the investigators. Good psychological research is possible only if there is mutual respect and confidence between investigators and participants. Although investigators are potentially interested in all aspects of human behaviour, for ethical reasons some areas of human experience and behaviour may be beyond the reach of psychological investigation. Ethical guidelines are necessary to clarify the conditions under which psychological research is acceptable.

2 General

In all circumstances investigators must consider the ethical implications and psychological consequences for the participants in their research. The essential principle is that the investigation should be considered from the standpoint of all participants; foreseeable threats to their psychological well-being, health, values or dignity should be eliminated. Where investigations involve individuals of different ages, gender and social background, the investigators may not have sufficient knowledge of the implications of any investigation for the participants. The best judges of whether an investigation will cause offence may be members of the population from which the participants in the research are to be drawn.

3 Consent

Whenever possible, the investigators should inform all participants of the objectives of the investigation. The investigators should inform the participants of all aspects of the research or intervention that might reasonably be expected to influence their willingness to participate. Research with children or with other vulnerable participants requires special safe-guarding procedures. Investigators are often in a position of authority or influence over participants who may be their students, employees or clients. This relationship must not be allowed to pressurize the participants to take part in, or remain in, an investigation. The payment of participants must not be used to induce them to risk harm beyond that which they risk without payment in their normal lifestyle.

4 Deception

Withholding information or misleading participants is unacceptable if the participants are typically likely to show unease once debriefed. Where this is in any doubt, appropriate consultation must precede the investigation. Intentional deception of the participants over the purpose and general nature of the investigation should be avoided whenever possible, although it may be impossible to study some psychological processes without withholding information about the true object of the study or without deliberately misleading the participants.

5 Debriefing

In studies where the participants are aware that they have taken part in an investigation, when the data have been collected, the investigator should provide the participants with any necessary information to complete their understanding of the nature of the research. The investigator should discuss with the participants their experience of the research in order to monitor any unforeseen negative effects or misconceptions.

6 Withdrawal from the investigation

At the outset, investigators should make plain to participants their right to withdraw from the research at any time, irrespective of whether or not payment or other inducement has been offered. In the light of experience of the investigation or as a result of debriefing, the participant has the right to withdraw retrospectively any consent given, and to require that their own data, including recordings, be destroyed.

7 Confidentiality

Except in circumstances specified by the law, information obtained about a participant during an investigation is confidential unless otherwise agreed in advance. Participants in psychological research have a right to expect that information they provide will be treated confidentially and, if published, will not be identifiable as theirs.

8 Protection of participants

Investigators have a primary responsibility to protect participants from physical and mental harm during the investigation. Normally the risk of harm must be no greater than in ordinary life. Where research may involve behaviour or experiences that participants may regard as personal and private, the participants must be protected from stress by all appropriate measures, including the assurance that answers to personal questions need not be given.

9 Observational research

Studies based upon observation must respect the privacy and psychological well-being of the individuals studied. Unless those being observed give their consent to being observed, observational research is only acceptable in situations where those observed would expect to be observed by strangers. Additionally, particular account should be taken of local cultural values and of the possibility of intruding upon the privacy of individuals who, even while in a normally public space, may believe they are unobserved.

10 Giving advice

During research, an investigator may obtain evidence of psychological or physical problems of which a participant is apparently unaware. In such a case the investigator has a responsibility to inform the participant if the investigator believes that by not doing so the participant's future well-being may be endangered. If the issue is serious and the investigator is not qualified to offer assistance, the appropriate source of professional advice should be recommended.

11 Colleagues

Investigators share responsibility for the ethical treatment of research participants with their collaborators, assistants, students and employees. A psychologist who believes that another psychologist or investigator may be conducting research that is not in accordance with the principles above should encourage that investigator to re-evaluate the research.

the case. Epstein and Lasagna (1969) discovered that only one third of participants volunteering for an experiment really understood what was involved. Gaining a participant's informed consent is a very important aspect of any research investigation. Without full disclosure prior to obtaining this consent it becomes impossible for participants to make an informed decision about their willingness to take part. Of course we might argue that full disclosure (of procedures to be used, reasons for the research and so on) is not a feasible requirement in a piece of psychological research, but to put it another way, would you accept a job when you did not fully know what you were required to do? Some participants may initially give their consent to take part in a study, but if they later realize that they would like to withdraw that consent (for whatever reason), they are free to do so, even if they have previously accepted payment for their participation. The issues of consent and withdrawal may appear compromised by the payment of participants. After all, we live in a society where people who accept payment are seen as entering into a contract to provide services. If a shopkeeper changed his mind about handing over your groceries after he had taken your money, you would be justifiably aggrieved. This 'I pay you – you do as you are told' relationship between investigator and participant can never be justified.

Deception

To those within the psychological profession, and to many outside it, the idea of deceiving research participants would be quite unacceptable. Quite apart from the immorality (or even illegality) of deception by a professional psychologist, the experience of deception can make research participants cynical about the activities and attitudes of psychologists. By deceiving research participants we may also remove their ability to give their fully informed consent to take part in the investigation we have in mind. This is not an open and shut case, however, as total honesty throughout an investigation may lead participants to modify their behaviour in some way because of the knowledge they have about the real aims of the investigation. You may like to consider the implications of total research honesty in an investigation such as that carried out by Stanley Milgram (1963) on obedience to authority (see *In Focus*, p. 605). There are clearly some situations where deception is inappropriate and some where it may be acceptable. There is a difference, for example, in withholding some of the research details, such as the hypothesis under test, and deliberately misleading the participants into believing the purpose of the research was more innocent than it actually was.

There are a number of issues here:

- It is evident that the consequences of some deceptions are more damaging than others. The amount of discomfort or anger expressed by participants when deception is revealed is normally a good guide to this.
- Deception in investigations of a trivial nature is less acceptable than investigations that make significant contributions to psychological knowledge. Although this may seem a case of the ends justifying the means, it should be clear that the importance of some research means that the ethical concerns spread far beyond the immediate context of the investigation. You might like to consider how Milgram might have justified deceiving his participants (see *In Focus*).
- There are alternatives to deception; deception should only be used if such alternatives are considered inappropriate. We may, for example, take a random sample of the population to be studied and introduce them to the research design, including knowledge of the deception to be used. If they agree that they would still have given their voluntary informed consent had they known the true aim of the investigation, then we may assume that they represent the views of the rest of their population group.

Debriefing

An important aspect of any research design, especially where deception has taken place, is the process of debriefing. Sometimes it is seen as sufficient merely to inform participants of the true nature of the investigation, but at other times such perfunctory debriefing would be inadequate. Consider again Stanley Milgram's research into obedience. His research participants either obeyed and gave the maximum electric shock, or disobeyed and declined to give further shocks. Either way the participants had done something that they may have perceived as being wrong. It was important that the obedient participants were reassured that their behaviour was the norm in that investigation (i.e. there was not anything wrong with them). Disobedient participants were reassured that their behaviour was actually socially desirable because they had stood up against a malevolent authority figure trying to coerce them into doing something they felt was wrong.

As a general rule, debriefing aims to restore the participant to the same state as when they entered the investigation. It also offers the researcher the opportunity to provide additional information about the research so that the whole thing becomes an educational experience for the participant. Debriefing does not, of course, provide a justification for any unethical aspects of the investigation. A good researcher regards participants as colleagues, not as objects to be used solely for the ends of the experimenter.

Protection of participants

Another general concern of the BPS is the protection of participants from undue risk during psychological research. The definition of undue risk is based on the risks that individuals might be expected to encounter in their normal lifestyle. Thus, the risks that an individual may be exposed to during a psychological investigation should not be greater than the risks they might already be expected to face in their everyday life. Such circumspection in the planning of research makes it possible to carry out significant research in those areas where some degree of risk is possible. It is clear that Godden and Baddeley's research into context dependent memory in scuba divers (i.e. divers were better able to remember instructions at depth if they had learned them at depth in the first place) was potentially risky for the participants, but only in so far as diving is a potentially dangerous activity anyway (Godden and Baddeley 1975).

Ethics and social responsibility

Some of the more notorious social psychology experiments such as Milgram's experiments on obedience to authority (see opposite) and Piliavin's research on bystander intervention in emergencies (see p. 74) illustrate the ethically thin ice that many psychologists have chosen to skate upon. But is this the one-sided affair that it might at first appear? Social psychologists such as the late Stanley Milgram and Irving Piliavin have an ethical responsibility to society as a whole, and we might argue that they would not be fulfilling that responsibility if they did not carry out such important research to the best of their ability. Elliot Aronson (1995) suggests that psychologists face a particularly difficult dilemma when their wider responsibility to society conflicts with their more specific responsibilities to each individual research participant. This conflict is greatest when the issues under investigation are issues of great social importance.

Is it just a coincidence that social psychological studies of obedience and bystander behaviour have attracted such adverse reactions from the public? It appears that the more important the issue and the more potential benefit a study might have for society, the more likely it is that the individual participant may experience some degree of discomfort or anxiety. Perhaps we are too short-sighted in sometimes condemning research for the more immediate impact that it has on the people that take part. Certainly the aftermath of Stanley Milgram's experiments produced reactions that were at both extremes of admiration and vilification. Consider the two quotes that follow, the first from psychiatrist Bruno Bettleheim, and the second from social psychologist Alan Elms.

> *'These experiments are so vile, the intention with which they were engaged in is so vile, that nothing these experiments show has any value.'*
>
> (Bruno Bettleheim, quoted in Miller 1986)

> *'Milgram, in exploring the external conditions that produce such destructive obedience, the psychological processes that lead to such attempted abdications of responsibility, and the means by which defiance of illegitimate authority can be promoted, seems to me to have done some of the most morally significant research in modern psychology.'*
>
> (Alan Elms, quoted in Miller 1986)

❖ Activity 1 ❖

Using the following *In Focus* and the two quotes above as a guide, consider what it was about Milgram's research that made Bettleheim describe it as 'vile' whilst, at the same time, others describe it as a study of great moral significance?

In Focus

Obedience to authority (Milgram 1963)

Milgram gathered together forty male subjects who had responded to newspaper advertisements to take part in a research project at Yale University in the USA. As each participant arrived at the laboratory he was introduced to the experimenter and to another participant who was actually an accomplice of the experimenter. The participants were told that the research was to investigate the effects of punishment on learning. They drew lots to see who was to be the teacher and who was to be the learner (this process was rigged so the real participant was always the teacher). The learner was strapped to a chair and electrodes were attached to his wrist. The teacher was instructed in the nature of his task which was to test the learner on word pairs.

Each time the learner gave a wrong answer the teacher was instructed to give him an electric shock by operating a shock generator. This had thirty switches, which went from 15 volts (marked as 'slight shock') through 'moderate' and 'danger, severe shock' until it finally reached an ominous 'XXX' at 450 volts. This was actually a dummy generator, so no shocks were really being given. With each wrong answer, the teacher was instructed to give a progressively higher shock. When the shock level reached 300 volts the learner pounded on the wall, and thereafter made no further responses. At this point the experimenter reminded the teacher that a non-response should be treated as a wrong answer and that the shocks should continue. The actual results obtained in this experiment showed that 65 per cent of participants gave the full 'fatal' shock of 450 volts.

Section summary

This section has introduced you to the major ethical considerations that underlie psychological research. All psychological research carried out in the UK is subject to the guidelines published by and regularly updated by the British Psychological Society. It is important to remember that psychological research does not take place within a social vacuum. The ethical responsibilities of researchers often conflict with their wider responsibilities as experts within society.

The use of non-human animals in research

Opposition to the use of animals in research has grown over recent years as the public have become increasingly aware of what is considered to be a cruel abuse of the power that one species has over another (a moral position that pro-animal welfare campaigners refer to as 'speciesism'). This is reflected in a general concern for the welfare of animals in all areas in which they are used. Demonstrations over the export of live calves to France in the mid-1990s showed how passionate were the emotions that could be raised over the human–animal power imbalance. This has often spilled over into violence against those who are involved in animal research. Laboratories have been broken into, animals have been removed and bombs have been placed under the cars of scientists who use animals in their work. These actions have grown out of the belief that animal research is both morally wrong and accomplishes very little that is justifiable, given the methods being used.

The reaction of the scientific world to these concerns has been divided. Some scientists such as Gray (1989) and Miller (1985) point out that opposition to animal research is contradictory in a society where the abuse of pets and the reliance on intensive farming methods pose moral questions far beyond those inherent in psychological research. Gray goes on to suggest that rather than having to justify the use of animals in research, scientists have a responsibility to use animals whenever their use could make a significant contribution to the alleviation of human suffering. Others have welcomed the increased concern for the welfare of animals in research and have offered suggestions about how animal research may be carried out in a way that minimizes stress and suffering (see Bateson's decision cube later in this section).

There has long been a tradition of using animals in psychology. Knowledge derived from this research has been instrumental in the development of many psychological theories and practices. Despite this long tradition, the popularity of animal research, particularly within the UK has diminished dramatically over the last fifteen years. The decrease in the use of animals has in part been due to the tightening of legislation concerning the use of animals. This is a direct result of the Animals (Scientific Procedures) Act of 1986, and also a result of the decrease in numbers of students choosing to follow psychology degree options that make significant use of non-human animals. This latter reason has inevitable consequences for the postgraduate interests of psychology students, and ultimately the research interests of psychology departments. The legislative changes surrounding the use of animals in research have also made university research review bodies more wary of the financial and moral constraints that underlie this avenue of research interest.

Table 27.2 contains the results of a survey carried out by Thomas and Blackman (1991) which compared the types and overall numbers of animals used in research in UK psychology departments for the academic years 1976–7 and 1988–9. It is clear from these results that there has been a significant decline in:

- the overall numbers of animals used
- the number of different species used
- the number of different procedures used.

It is significant that the only increase in any category is in the non-experimental research projects such as those involving the observation of animals.

The case for animal research

As psychology is, you might imagine, the study of *human* behaviour, why then do we bother studying *non-human* animals? There are several reasons why psychologists may choose to expend their research efforts on non-human animals.

- Animals may be studied simply because they are fascinating to study in their own right. The development of ethology (the biological study of behaviour) has been based on such goals, although some of the methods used are also open to ethical concerns (see later section).
- Animals offer the opportunity for greater control and objectivity in research procedures. Given the interest in and value of scientific methods in psychology, greater opportunities for experimental control exist with animals than with humans. Much of behaviourist theory was established using animal studies for just this reason. The scientifically desirable consequence of objectivity is more easily attained with non-human than human animals simply because it is difficult to remain completely objective when studying our own species. We may have expectations, biases and stereotypes of members of our own species that are not as evident when we work with another species.
- We may use animals when we can't use humans. Animals have been exposed to various procedures and events that

Table 27.2 Number of animals in 1988/9 academic year subjected to various types of research procedures (*Adapted from:* Thomas and Blackman 1991)

	Non-experimental	*Food/water deprivation*	*Other deprivation*	*Drugs*	*Surgery*	*Electric shock*	*Other exp.*	*Total 1989*	*Total 1977*	*1989 total as % of 1977*
Monkey	146				11		2	159	364	44
Cat									32	0
Rabbit									600	0
Rat	608	3495	355	3990	1431	490	403	10772	35560	30
Guinea pig									100	0
Gerbil									140	0
Mouse	600		30	610			262	1502	2614	57
Other mammals	50							50	221	23
Pigeon	40	621		48	61			770	1062	73
Chick									1600	0
Other birds	32							32	710	5
Reptiles	1							1	4	25
Fish									189	0
Total 1989	1477	4116	385	4648	1503	490	667	13286		
Total 1977	1174	8980	5916	6851	4761	3929	11585		43196	
1989 total as % of 1977 Standard	126	46	7	68	32	12	6			31

would simply not be possible with human beings. Harlow's deprivation work with rhesus monkeys (Harlow 1962; see *In Focus* below) could not have been carried out on humans. Often the need to establish cause and effect relationships in psychological research involves participants in procedures that they would not consent to take part in. This does, of course, raise the moral question of why we might expose animals to research procedures that we could not justify with human participants. We will return to this thorny question later.

- Human beings and non-human animals have sufficient of their physiology and evolutionary past in common to justify conclusions drawn from the one being applied to the other. Behaviourists such as Skinner saw sufficient similarity between rats and humans to warrant a special interest in rats as research opportunities. Similarities in the way rats and humans learn led Skinner to establish laws of learning based almost entirely on the study of rats (and other non-human animals) in controlled environments.

The case against animal research

We can usefully divide the arguments against animal research into two separate types. There are those that object to the use of animals in research on *practical* grounds, and those that object to such research on *ethical* grounds.

In Focus

Contact, comfort and attachment (Harlow 1962)

An important factor in the development of the attachment bond between infant and caregiver is the physical contact that exists between them. The research that first established this fact was carried out by Harry Harlow in the early 1960s. Harlow's original intention was not to explore the role of physical contact in attachment but rather to look at the effects of brain damage on learning. This was not the sort of experiment it would have been possible to carry out with human subjects. In order to maintain a sample of young rhesus monkeys free from disease, Harlow raised them alone away from their mothers. He noticed that these motherless monkeys formed strong attachments to small pieces of cloth in their cages and would protest loudly when they were removed. This led Harlow to wonder whether his infant monkeys needed physical contact with something soft for their normal development.

In an experiment to find out, he constructed artificial or 'surrogate' mothers. One of these was a bare wire frame, whilst the other one was covered in a soft terry towelling material. The motherless infants could only obtain milk from the 'wire' mother. The infants spent most of their time, however, clinging to the soft towelling mother and only went to the wire mother when they needed to drink. In subsequent research (Harlow and Harlow 1966) infant rhesus monkeys were exposed to various forms of rejection from their surrogate mothers. These included expelling strong jets of air and metal spikes that appeared from inside the towelling and pushed the monkey away. None of these seemed to have any lasting effects on the attachment of the infant to the surrogate mother, as they merely waited for the rejection episode to stop then moved back onto the mother.

From findings such as these Harlow concluded that at least in part, a monkey's attachment to its mother depends on the contact comfort that she provides. Evidence for such effects in human infants is mixed but does seem to suggest that they, too, have a need for contact, and the cuddling that is an integral part of the parent–infant relationship plays an important role in the formation of a lasting attachment bond.

The essence of a practical argument against the use of animals is that animal experiments would tell us nothing of any value about human behaviour because of the dissimilarities between humans and non-humans. Whilst it is true that some research is carried out on animals to discover facts about animals (these have their own problems, as we shall see later), the majority of animal studies in psychology are comparative, that is animals are being used because they may give us important insights into human behaviour.

The second type of argument is an ethical one. We may choose to take an extreme ethical stance over the issue of animal research. In other words, we may contend that pain or distress is never justifiable in animal research, regardless of the benefits to humankind. This position owes much to the work of people such as Peter Singer and Tom Regan (Regan and Singer 1976). Singer saw discrimination against animals as logically parallel to any other form of discrimination. In the same way that we would argue against racism and sexism as being morally indefensible, Singer suggests that 'speciesism' (discrimination against one species for the benefits of another) is also unacceptable. Regan, a champion of the animal rights movement, makes the point that current legislation which controls the use of non-human animals in laboratories does not go far enough in protecting the subjects of such research. What is needed, he claims, is not larger, cleaner cages, but empty cages.

The rest of this section develops an alternative ethical position, one that we might refer to as the relative view of the ethics of animal research. In such a position, animal research remains part of a much larger moral concern. We must weigh up several considerations before accepting that animal research is the answer.

Practical objections

If animals are used to tell us something about human behaviour, then it follows that there should be sufficient similarity between the brains and behaviour of non-human animals and those of humans. If this were not so, then the case for studying animals to gain insights into human behaviour would be very weak indeed. Critics of animal research will often suggest that these assumed similarities just do not exist. Green (1994) argues otherwise. The basic physiology of the brain and nervous systems of all mammals is essentially the same. Although the human brain might be more highly developed, its similarity to the brains of non-human mammals is far greater than critics of this approach would have us believe. Similarly the basic classifications of behaviour (affective, cognitive and motivational) are evident in all mammalian species.

This argument of 'similarity among mammals' appears at its weakest in the area of language. Human language is bound up with the whole idea of cultural transmission. Failure to accept that other animals might possess language weakens the useful comparisons that might be drawn between ourselves and our non-human counterparts. This is not a cut and dried case, however. Recent success in teaching what might conceivably be called language to pygmy chimpanzees has been instrumental in setting up the Great Ape Project (Singer and Cavalieri 1993). This initiative aims to extend the moral obligations that at present we restrict to human beings to all the great apes. The Declaration of Great Apes thus declares that it is indefensible to kill, torture or otherwise infringe the personal liberty of any of the great apes (including humankind). Such a momentous decision will inevitably have repercussions for how research psychologists come to view the rest of the non-human kingdom.

Ethical objections

As with the use of human beings in research, there are also guidelines for the use of animals. In the UK, the use of non-human animals is covered by the Animals (Scientific Procedures) Act 1986. Different bodies that are interested in the use of animals in research (such as the British Psychological

Table 27.3 Guidelines for the Use of Animals in Research: Extracts from the Animals (Scientific Procedures) Act 1986

1 The law

Within the United Kingdom there are specific laws protecting the rights of animals. Failure to comply with these laws leads to prosecution.

2 Ethical considerations

If animals are to be constrained, harmed or stressed in any way, investigators must consider whether the knowledge to be gained justifies the procedure. Alternatives to animal experiments should be considered wherever possible.

3 Species

If the research procedures used are likely to cause pain or discomfort, the investigator should bear in mind that some species may be less likely to suffer than others. Investigators should, therefore, have knowledge of a species' natural history as well as its special needs.

4 Number of animals

Laboratory studies should use the smallest number of animals necessary. Careful thought in the design of an experiment as well as the statistical analysis used can reduce the number of animals necessary in any given study.

5 Endangered species

Members of endangered species should not be collected or manipulated in the wild except as a serious attempt at conservation.

6 Caging and social environment

Caging conditions should take into account the social behaviour of the species. An acceptable density of one species may constitute overcrowding for a different species. In social animals caging in isolation may have undesirable effects.

7 Motivation

When arranging schedules of deprivation, the experimenter should consider the animal's normal eating and drinking habits and its metabolic requirements. However, differences between species must also be borne in mind. A short period of deprivation for one species may be unacceptably long for another.

8 Aversive stimuli and stressful procedures

Procedures that cause pain or distress to animals are illegal in the UK unless the experimenter holds a Home Office Licence and the relevant certificates. The investigator should be satisfied that there are no alternative ways of conducting the experiment without the use of aversive stimulation. If alternatives are not available, the investigator has the responsibility of ensuring that any suffering is kept to a minimum and that it is justified by the expected scientific contribution of the experiment. Any stressful procedures to be used have to be assessed and licensed by the Home Office.

Society, and the Association for the Study of Animal Behaviour) have generated their own guiding principles that are covered by the recommendations of this Act.

Criteria for assessing research on animals

Medical research has as its goals outcomes which are of direct benefit to human beings. The use of animals in such research is usually justified to the public because it contributes directly to the relief of human suffering. Developing a cure for a disease such as cancer or Alzheimer's disease can offset much of the terrible physical, social and economic suffering that inevitably accompanies such conditions. But how could *psychologists* justify the use of animals? Animals may be considered useful because they help us to understand natural principles (such as those involved in learning) and because they are a convenient way of developing and testing such principles.

As mentioned earlier, some people may hold the opinion that it is morally wrong to inflict any kind of pain or suffering upon non-human animals. If we are to find an acceptable way of using animals in research, what kinds of questions, over and above those covered by the Animals Act, should we be asking? In 1986, Professor Patrick Bateson, Secretary of the Ethical Committee of the Association for the Study of Animal Behaviour, proposed a system that would allow such questions to be asked. Bateson's decision cube (see Figure 27.1) assesses proposed research on three criteria.

The three criteria used to assess proposed research with animals are:

- the quality of the research
- the degree of animal suffering
- the certainty of benefit.

Figure 27.1
Bateson's decision cube

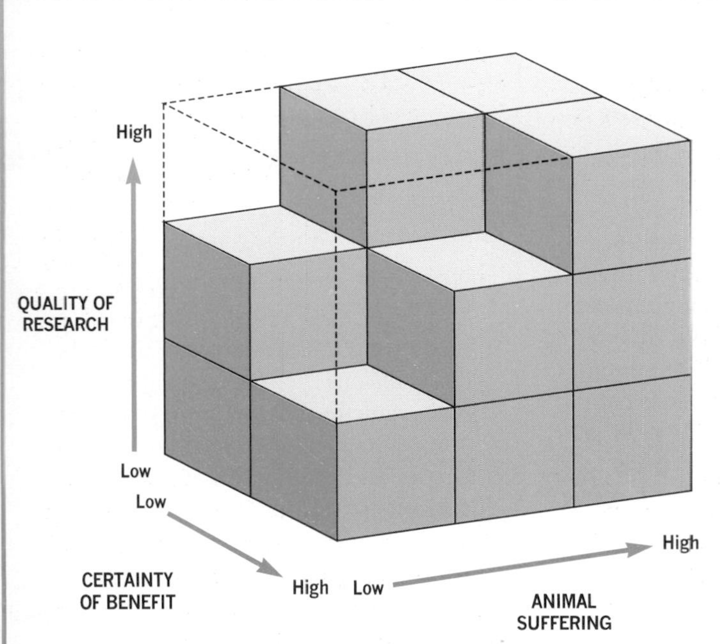

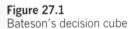

A cube for deciding whether a research project should proceed (clear space) or it should not (solid space) (from Bateson 1986). The most obvious case for proceeding is when the amount of suffering is negligible, the quality of the research is high and the benefit is certain. At the other extreme, the clearest case where research should not be done is when the suffering is likely to be great, the quality of the work and the benefit uncertain.

Quality of the research

Although the determination of quality in a piece of research may appear to be a very subjective assessment, there is actually a great deal of agreement among psychologists about what constitutes high quality research. The difficulties of obtaining research funding, together with the sheer expense of animal research means that institutional committees are likely to award research grants only to animal research of the highest quality.

Animal suffering

It is, of course, difficult to put oneself inside the mind of an animal and assess the degree to which a particular animal is or is not suffering as a result of the procedures to which we expose it. Some animals when threatened by danger remain rigid and silent because that is the safest thing to do. We may not recognize such behaviour as being a state of stress. As we increase our knowledge of how animals behave, we become more aware of what is and what is not likely to be stressful for a particular species.

Certainty of benefit

In the minds of many, if not most, people great human suffering is felt to be worse than the possibility of mild discomfort inflicted on an animal in the course of research. The funding of high quality psychological research may not always be seen in that light by its critics. It is difficult to predict exactly what the benefits of such research might be to the lives of humans and other animals. The case study that follows presents such an avenue of research. You might like to ask yourself, as you read this, whether in such cases the ends really can justify the means.

Comments on the Bateson model

This model provides a clear indication of when animal research may be tolerated and when it can not. When the quality of the

In Focus

Alzheimer's disease

One of the major social problems of the 1990s and onwards will be the increasing numbers, relative to the whole population, of old people. A proportion of these will suffer from senile dementia, the commonest form of which is Alzheimer's disease. In its severest form Alzheimer's produces severe memory loss, confusion, loss of the sense of self-identity, and double incontinence. Caring for sufferers is usually a family affair, 24 hours a day every day of the year, and involves watching your husband or wife, father or mother, degenerating in front of you.

There is as yet no cure for Alzheimer's disease. It is not linked to immoral behaviour or physical self-abuse of any sort, so lifestyle changes do not prevent it. We know from the brain changes seen at post-mortem that there is a particular pattern of damage to brain circuits, and we know from animal studies that these circuits are also involved in memory in rats and monkeys. Damage to these circuits in animals produces memory loss, and this model of Alzheimer's disease is being used to develop possible treatments. These include new drugs to restore brain function, and the use of grafts of brain cells to replace cells that have died. These latter techniques have already been used in the treatment of Parkinson's disease, a progressive movement disorder which is also caused by damage to a specific brain circuit. Animal research is also helping to reveal the biochemical abnormalities responsible for producing the brain damage.

There are encouraging signs that a treatment for Alzheimer's disease may emerge, which will have depended absolutely on the use of animal testing for its development. If successful it would have a dramatic impact, improving the quality of life for both those with Alzheimer's and those who would otherwise sacrifice their lives in caring for them. Is this potential benefit sufficient to justify the use of animals in psychological research?

Source: Green 1994, *Principles of Biopsychology*

research and the certainty of benefit are both high, the likelihood of animal research being considered acceptable is a great deal higher than when these are both low. It is also obvious that certain levels of animal suffering cannot be tolerated regardless of the quality of the research or the probability of benefit. The model would also permit research which has no direct benefit, yet was of high scientific quality and involved little animal suffering.

The effectiveness of a model such as that proposed by Bateson depends on any evaluation of quality, benefit and suffering being accurate. This is not as straightforward as it might appear.

- Evaluating the quality of the research – This should pose little or no problem to the scientist who should be aware of what constitutes high or not so high quality research. It is a routine part of any research application that it is assessed along these lines.
- Evaluating the benefits that might be derived from the research – This is a more difficult judgement to make. The aims of a particular piece of research should go beyond what is essentially curiosity about gaining real understanding.
- Measurement of animal suffering – Different species react differently to stress, and these reactions may be very different to those that might cause human beings to react in an avoidant manner. Dawkins (1985) suggests that three factors can be used to measure animal suffering: an animal's state of physical health, signs of stress and the animal's behaviour.

❖ Activity 2 ❖

Imagine you are part of a committee reviewing proposals for research involving animals. You receive an application for the Harlow study described earlier. How would you review it? What suggestions would you make to the researcher in the light of the Bateson model just outlined, and how would you justify your decision to turn the proposal down or to allow it to go ahead?

Field experiments in animal research

Ethical concern about the use of animals is normally focused on laboratory research with animals. This is due to the image of animal research in the field involving discreet observation and non-interference with the animals being studied. Occasional views of David Attenborough in natural history programmes tend to reinforce such a view.

However, field experiments (i.e. manipulating some part of the animal's natural habitat) have been an important part of ethological research since the beginning of this discipline. Consideration of the ethical concerns of this area of research is crucial for three major reasons:

- Ethologists are in a unique position to comment on how animals react to stress and suffering; their insights are, therefore, vital if animals are to be used in psychological research.
- Ethological research tends not to be of any direct benefit to human beings. If the justification of research is determined purely on that basis then ethological research would be considered to be very low priority.
- By their very nature, field experiments alter the natural environment of the animal in some way. This tampering with nature in order to understand it places great responsibilities on the researcher to ensure that the disruptive effects of any manipulation are kept to a minimum.

Cuthill (1991), in an analysis of over 930 research papers published in the journal *Animal Behaviour* between the years 1986 and 1990, calculated 46 per cent

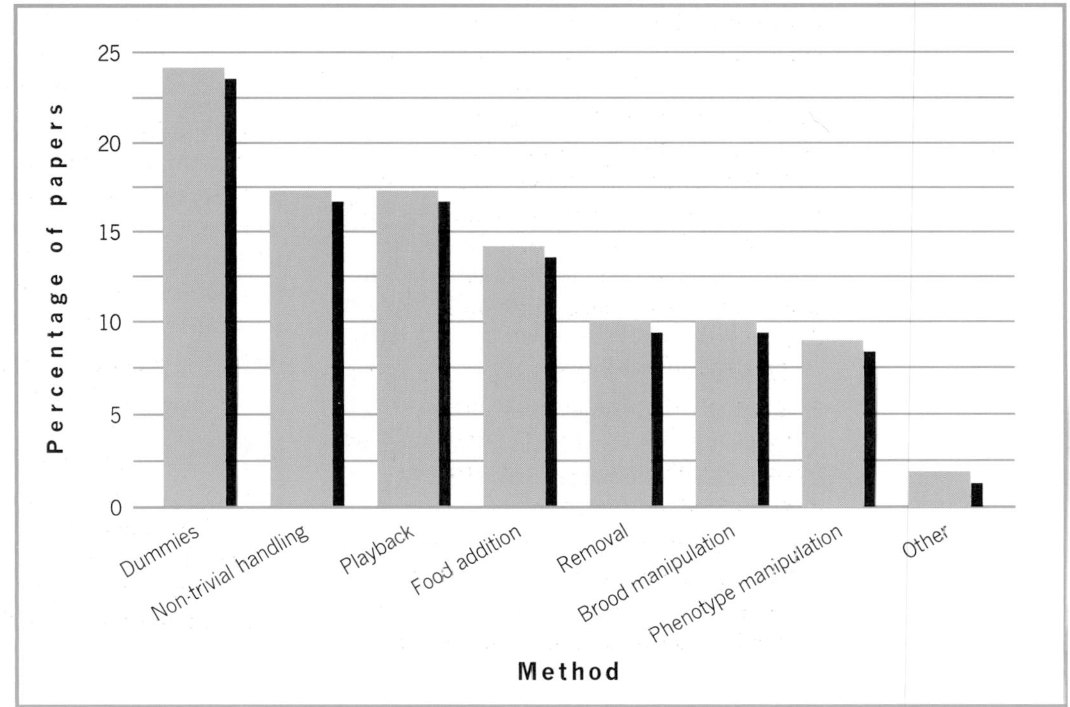

Figure 27.2 Methods employed in papers involving field experiments, published in *Animal Behaviour* from 1986 to 1990
Source: Cuthill 1991

(426) to be field studies. Of these 426 papers, one-third involved experimental manipulations. The main methods are broken down by percentage of papers in Figure 27.2.

Major types of experimental manipulation

1. *Dummies* – This involves the presence of a stuffed dummy predator. Although the appearance of a predator is within the normal experience of an animal, its presence can cause distress and in some cases, abandonment of its young.
2. *Non-trivial handling* – Repeated trappings in order for procedures such as radio tagging to take place can lead to distress from capture as well as the increased energy expenditure which is necessary for smaller animals (such as birds) to carry the transmitting device.
3. *Playback* – As used in studies of alarm calls (such as Seyfarth and Cheney's study of vervet monkeys 1990) playback of recorded signals can cause some distress. In extreme cases, the habituation that may develop to signals in the absence of a predator, may put the animals in danger should they fail to respond to alarm calls involving real predators.
4. *Food addition* – If food is provided to provoke territorial disputes or dominance encounters, there is a risk of injury from the aggression that this might cause. The artificial provision of extra food also upsets the natural ecology of the area, and leaves animals without the food on which they have come to depend once the experiment is over.
5. *Removal* – This may involve the temporary removal of an animal (e.g. the removal of one parent in studies of biparental care) or the release of an animal elsewhere from its normal territory. This may impair the survival chances of the animal on release, or may lead to an increased chance of starvation in the young that are left behind.
6. *Brood manipulation* – This is largely restricted to studies involving birds. It enables investigators to study the optimum clutch size in different species of birds by looking at the effects of brood manipulation upon the increased mortality through starvation. By interfering with the ecological conditions under which birds must survive, the investigator takes responsibility for the effects of any alteration.
7. *Phenotype manipulation* – By altering characteristics of certain animals (e.g. through altering plumage in some way, such as artificially extending tail length) it is possible to investigate the effects on reproductive success. It is difficult to assess the possible stressful effects that such alterations might have on the animals concerned. Males that are given extra plumage might find themselves the victims of aggression from other males who respond to the new adornment as if it were a 'badge of rank'.

Field experiments involving animals raise the concern that they also disrupt the animals' natural environment. This may create problems that persist long after the experiment is concluded. In order to minimize the disruptive effects of these studies, a number of procedures are necessary to assess the potential impact of the study. First, the use of pilot studies might go some way towards assessing the potential impact of the study. Second, animals that are not directly a part of the study should be monitored to check whether they are being affected by the manipulation. Finally, it is important to carry out follow-up studies to assess (and minimize) the disruptive effects of the experiment.

❖ Activity 3 ❖

Consider some of the field experiments reported in the comparative psychology chapters in this book. What are the ethical issues that these studies raise?

Section summary

The subject of animal research is unquestionably one of the most controversial issues within psychology. Public outcry against the abuse of animals has often blinded us to the potential advantages of high quality research that both minimizes animal suffering yet provides clear scientific benefits. Legislation concerning animal research appears to be focused more directly on laboratory studies, but is less clearly defined in field experiments that may also involve adverse effects on the subjects involved.

Ethical issues in socially sensitive research

Socially sensitive research refers to those studies where there are direct social consequences for those people who take part in the research or the class of people who are represented. Studies that examine the relationship between race and IQ, or the genetic basis of homosexuality can be considered socially sensitive. Research studies such as these create ethical dilemmas for the social scientist. In the same way that scientific knowledge can be used to enhance the quality of human life, it can also be used for exploitation and even social manipulation (see *In Focus*).

The dilemma posed by this sort of research is not covered by the BPS guidelines outlined earlier in this chapter. Psychologists are cautioned that some aspects of human behaviour are beyond the scope of psychological research

In Focus

The 'gay gene' (*The Independent*, 1 November 1995)

The 'gay gene' is back on the scene

The 'gay gene' has cruised back onto the scene. Homosexuality tends to run in families, according to Dean Hamer, the American scientist who has made a study of the genetic basis of human sexual preferences. His latest research, apparently confirming a genetic component to homosexuality, has once again rekindled controversy about the genetics of the more sensitive aspects of human behaviour.

Two years ago Dr Hamer had shown in a study of the family histories of 114 homosexual men that being gay tends to be inherited. The primary conclusion of his latest work, published in the journal *Nature Genetics*, is that there is a region on the X chromosome that influences variations in sexual orientation in men, but not in women.

The deep controversy stirred up by Dr Hamer's work is a rare phenomenon in the arcane world of genetics research, which usually concerns itself with identifying and eradicating or at least alleviating inherited diseases. Homosexuality, however, is not a disease nor an abnormality. Some disagree. When Dr Hamer's findings first appeared, a number of commentators, including at least one religious leader, appeared to countenance the prospect of a prenatal test for a gay gene, with the possibility of abortion.

'People are worried' said Hamer, 'that eventually someone – scientists, the military or insurance companies – might try to develop blood tests for sexual orientation, or a prenatal test so that expectant mothers could abort a foetus at risk of being gay. I think this would be wrong, unethical and a terrible abuse of research. It's wrong to discriminate on the basis of genes.'

This left some people asking what then was the point of doing such research? Dr Hamer's reply was that it furthered our understanding of an important aspect of human nature – sexual orientation. 'The AIDS epidemic has taught us, too bitterly, that we have more to fear from ignorance than from new knowledge about human sexuality.'

although it is largely left to individual psychologists as to how this caution is interpreted. This has resulted in some researchers avoiding sensitive areas altogether, and those who do pursue such areas often risk criticism from colleagues and others outside the discipline.

Ethical concerns in research

Sieber and Stanley (1988) suggest four main aspects of scientific activity that raise ethical points concerning socially sensitive research:

- formulation of the research question
- conduct of research and treatment of participants
- the institutional context
- interpretation and application of research findings.

Formulation of the research question

Posing a particular theory or research question can in itself have enormous implications for those who are directly or indirectly involved in the research process. For example, suggesting racial differences in IQ can be viewed as a socially damaging indictment of one racial group. Such claims, according to Sieber and Stanley, merely serve the purpose of 'adding scientific dignity to prevailing prejudice' (Sieber and Stanley 1988). Similarly research suggestions that attempt to link crime to genetics create both legal and moral implications, and inevitably a call for authorities to control those who are seen as being genetically dangerous.

Conduct of research and treatment of participants

One of the major problems in carrying out socially sensitive research is maintaining the confidentiality of information that might be revealed as part of the research process. In some areas of research, questions may reveal information of a sensitive nature (such as sexual habits or drug use). In such situations the issue of confidentiality is paramount. If confidentiality were broken, then participants would be less willing to divulge this information in the future and further research in this area would have been compromised.

It is clear, however, that the expectations that a participant may have concerning privacy and confidentiality of information must be balanced against the interests of society to be protected against deviant or criminal behaviour. In such cases there is a more convincing case for breaching confidentiality.

❖ Activity 4 ❖

Imagine you are carrying out research into patterns of transmission of AIDS. Some of your respondents reveal that they have AIDS and are still having unsafeguarded sexual relations with several partners. Furthermore, they intend to withhold from these partners the fact that they have AIDS. What is the role of the researcher in this dilemma? Should you:

- try to contact the respondents' partners directly to inform them of the risk, or
- respect the confidentiality of the information you have been given?

What are the implications of each decision?

Carrying out socially sensitive research also carries significant implications for the researchers themselves. Milgram's research (see *In Focus*, p. 605) created outrage both inside and outside the discipline of psychology. Why? Perhaps part of this was that he demonstrated something to people that they would rather not have known: ordinary people, it would appear, are capable of committing atrocities simply because they are instructed to do so by an authority figure. For his part in this revelation, Milgram was continuously harassed and criticized by the American press.

The institutional context

The context of the research can have substantial effects on the research participants. Quite apart from arguments about whether their behaviour would be 'true to life', there is an equally important concern over the way that the institution exerts a coercive effect on individuals to behave in a way that might be totally alien to them. Consider again the research setting of Stanley Milgram's 'obedience to authority' study. This was Yale University, one of the highly prestigious 'Ivy league' universities. When Milgram moved away from this setting the amount of obedience he could elicit from his participants dropped sharply.

Although the activities of research psychologists may be clearly defined and closely monitored within academic institutions, the activities of psychologists (or those engaged in quasi-psychological research) in other settings may expose participants to a completely different set of coercive influences. Occupational psychologists, for example, may obtain information from employees which is then used by the organization to make decisions regarding promotion or even redundancy.

Interpretation and application of research findings

A major concern in the interpretation and application of research findings in psychology is that they may be used for reasons other than those for which they were originally intended. Kelman (1965) suggests that it is the responsibility of all researchers to consider in advance the ways in which their research might be used. This is in sharp contrast to the view taken by many scientists, that knowledge is 'ethically neutral'.

An example of the way in which psychological research findings might be misused has already been suggested in Hamer's work on the inheritance of a gene connected with homosexuality (Hamer 1995). Hamer defends this work by claiming 'intellectual property rights' on the development of any test that might identify such a gene. Such 'ownership', it is suggested, would prevent the abuse of the scientific knowledge associated with such a test.

Not all such socially sensitive research issues are quite so controversial. Research into the accuracy of children as witnesses in allegations of sexual abuse has shown quite clearly that children are able to remember events with the same kind of accuracy that we might expect from adults. Contrast this finding with the accepted wisdom up until the 1980s when children's accounts of sexual abuse were generally regarded as unreliable and therefore inadmissible as evidence.

Socially sensitive research issues are more likely to have social applications in the real world – some desirable, some perhaps not so desirable. In the words of Sieber and Stanley (1988), socially sensitive research is not wrong in itself, but caution is needed at all stages of the research process.

Section summary

Socially sensitive research is research that has direct social consequences for either the people who take part in the research or the class of people whom they represent. Care needs to be taken at all stages of the research process: the formulation of the research question, the context of the investigation, the conduct of the research, the context of the research study and the way in which the results are used or interpreted. Failure to address these issues may lead the researcher to cause offence to a particular group or class of person, or worse, to use the research findings in a socially divisive way.

It is also clear that decisions regarding socially sensitive research need to involve more than just the scientists who carry out the research. Scientists may well doubt that those outside their profession have the technical expertise to make decisions about what should be studied and how it should be studied. Those outside the scientific community might likewise doubt the ability of scientists to make objective decisions about the wisdom of their own research.

Chapter summary

- Some areas of human behaviour and experience are more appropriate for psychological study than others. The ethical guidelines published by the British Psychological Society clarify the conditions under which psychological research is acceptable.
- Researchers must consider the ethical implications and psychological consequences for the participants of their research. Guidance is given regarding deception, confidentiality, consent, etc.
- The use of non-human animals in psychological research is seen as a potentially valuable source of insight into human behaviour. There has been a decline in the use of animals following the 1986 legislation which sets out strict guidelines for animal research.
- Psychologists generally operate a 'costs-benefits' analysis in their work with non-human animals. Research with animals is only considered appropriate where the quality of the research and certainty of benefit to be derived from the research are higher than the costs to the animals concerned.
- Some research issues are considered more socially sensitive than others: generally those that have direct social implications for the participants of the research or the class of people that they represent.
- In order to safeguard those who might be offended or abused as a result of this type of research, it is necessary to consider carefully all aspects of the research process, from questions about why it is being carried out, to how the findings might be interpreted or applied.

Essay questions

1 Describe and assess the ethical considerations that underlie the experimental study of human behaviour. *(24 marks)*

2 (a) Outline the reasons why psychologists might choose to use non-human animals in their research. *(6 marks)*
(b) Outline how animals have been used in two different areas of research. *(6 marks)*
(c) Assess the problems of using animals in psychological research. *(12 marks)*

3 'In the same way that scientific knowledge can be used to enhance the quality of human life, it can also be used for exploitation and even social manipulation.'
With reference to the issues in the above quotation, critically consider the problems faced by psychologists who carry out socially sensitive research. *(24 marks)*

Further reading

Association for the Teaching of Psychology (1992) *Ethics in Psychological Research: Guidelines for Students at Pre-degree levels*, Leicester: Association for the Teaching of Psychology.

Dawkins, M.S. and Gosling, L.M. (eds) (1992) *Ethics in Research on Animal Behaviour*, Association for the Study of Animal Behaviour Ethical Committee.

These provide invaluable information on the ethical issues raised in this chapter and should be consulted prior to any research projects in these areas.

Part 8

Research Methods

The nature of psychological enquiry
Graham Davies

Research design
Graham Davies

Data analysis
Graham Davies

Chapter 28

The nature of psychological enquiry

Graham Davies

Preview

In this chapter we shall be looking at some of the research methods used by psychologists, and in particular at:

- experimental investigations, including:
  - laboratory experiments
  - field experiments
  - natural experiments
- non-experimental investigations, including:
  - investigations using correlational analysis
  - naturalistic observational studies
  - case studies
  - interviews.

Introduction

The function of the wide range of research methods used in psychological investigations is to provide techniques which can help psychologists to gather and make sense of their data.

For many years the experiment, and in particular the laboratory experiment, has been a leading method used in psychology. However, dissatisfaction concerning the realism and applicability of the results achieved from experimental research has stimulated a search for alternative methods and has led to a recent increase in the use of non-experimental methods. Nevertheless, although the latter have increased in importance, it is true to say that the experiment still remains a vital research tool for psychologists. Both experimental and non-experimental approaches have their place and can be considered as being complementary to each other, since different types of research investigations require different methods. The different viewpoints of those advocating the use of experimental or non-experimental methods also reflect fundamental differences in perception about what psychologists should be doing and how they should go about it.

This chapter discusses only a selection of methods that the A level student is likely to encounter and makes no attempt to cover the complete range of methods used by the psychologist. The reader is asked to bear in mind that although research methods can be divided into specific categories, these methods often merge into each other. For example, the boundary between experimental and non-experimental research is far from clear-cut. What really matters, however, is that the appropriate method is used for a given research situation rather than the descriptive label placed on that method.

Experimental investigations in psychology

The experiment is regarded by many as the preferred method of scientific enquiry, and by using it a researcher can intervene directly in the situation which is being investigated. It is the most powerful of the research methods at the disposal of psychologists, with its greater potential to seek and find the causes of events than other methods. The true experiment has three key features:

- An independent variable is manipulated by the researcher to produce a change in a dependent variable.
- All other variables which might influence the results are held constant or eliminated.
- Participants are allocated to the experimental conditions randomly.

Each of these features will be discussed in turn.

A variable is, quite simply, anything which can change, and in the simplest form of an experiment, one crucial variable, called the *independent variable*, is deliberately manipulated by the researcher in an attempt to change the performance of participants on another variable, referred to as the *dependent variable*. For example, consider an experiment set up to investigate which of two methods is more successful at teaching children to read. In this case, the independent variable would be the teaching method that the participants (in this case the children who took part in the study) were exposed to, and the dependent variable would be some measure of their reading ability (such as scores derived from a standard test of reading ability).

However, if the experimenter is to be sure that it is the independent variable that has produced a change in the dependent variable, then it is necessary to ensure that all other variables which might provide alternative explanations for the results are either held constant or, if they cannot be held constant, eliminated. These unwanted variables are known as *confounding variables*, and might include the following:

- Differences in the instructions given by an experimenter or in the stimulus materials being used (which could be overcome by standardizing instructions and materials for all those taking part).
- Differences between participants, e.g. in their age (which could be eliminated as a variable by using a single age group, or alternatively it could be made constant by ensuring that the age structure of each of the groups taking part in the experiment is very similar).

A particularly important variable concerning the nature of the participants themselves is dealt with in the next chapter in the section on experimental design. The logic of the experiment is that if all other variables other than the independent variable have been successfully controlled or eliminated, then any change that is produced in the dependent variable must be the result of manipulating the independent variable.

As a principle of good design it is necessary either to allocate participants randomly to conditions (i.e. give all those taking part an equal chance of being selected for each), or permit all participants to experience each condition.

Sometimes, however, it is not possible to meet all the requirements for a true experiment. The prefix 'quasi' means 'resembling but not really the same as'. The term quasi-experiment is sometimes used for research which is broadly similar in approach to experimental research but in which the investigator lacks complete control over the independent variable and/or allocation of participants to groups that is a requirement in a true experiment.

The laboratory experiment

The laboratory experiment gives the researcher 'complete control over the experiment: the who, what, when, where and how' (McBurney 1983). It can be used to test theories, determine the conditions under which certain events occur, or extend current research by proposing new research problems.

Laboratory experiments provide the psychologist with the highest possible level of control. However, it must be remembered that not all experiments are carried out in laboratories and that not all investigations carried out in laboratories are experiments. For example, field experiments (see later in this chapter) are carried out in natural settings, and non-experimental techniques such as naturalistic observation may be carried out in a laboratory setting (e.g. an observational study of the strategies used by people to deal with boredom might be carried out in a laboratory).

Uses of the laboratory experiment

The laboratory experiment is used very widely as a research tool in psychology. Examples are the experiments by Broadbent (1954) on attention (see p. 288) and by Bousfield (1953) on memory (see p. 332).

See *In Focus* below for a detailed example of a laboratory experiment.

❖ Activity 1 ❖

Identify the independent and dependent variables in the above two studies? What variables did the researchers need to control in each case?

In Focus

Relation of cue to consequence in avoidance learning (Garcia and Koelling, 1966)

In this laboratory experiment the relationship between the sensory mode of a reinforcing cue and its consequences in an avoidance learning situation was investigated using groups of ten rats. Rats were placed in a box containing a drinking spout and in which light and sound were shielded. On licking the water spout, a rat received either a stimulus based on sound (a clicking noise), vision (a lamp was switched on), and/or taste (flavoured water was delivered).

The rats were then given an electric shock to their paws or poisoned by X-rays or lithium carbonate. The results showed that rats were able to associate the visual and auditory stimuli with electric shock but not with sickness, and would associate the taste stimulus with sickness but not with electric shock. The researchers concluded that the cues which an animal extracts from its environment in a learning situation are related to the consequences of the reinforcer. They suggest that the discriminations made may result from the process of natural selection which may have favoured mechanisms whereby taste is associated with internal discomfort.

Advantages of the laboratory experiment

- *Replicability of procedures*: A major advantage of the properly carried out and reported laboratory experiment is that its procedures can be repeated (replicated) by other researchers to see if they obtain similar results. Without this ability to replicate procedures, research might wait indefinitely for the precise set of circumstances which are obtained in the experiment to be repeated by chance.
- *Forcing the pace of research*: Experimentation allows the pace of research to be forced, making it unnecessary to wait for natural events to reproduce the appropriate scenario. As a result, it is possible to study behaviour which is uncommon, rarely observed by psychologists or which cannot be studied easily in another way, for example, bystander attitudes to an emergency. Also, it permits the researcher to select when and possibly where to undertake an experiment.

- *Control over variables*: The control of variables is less difficult in the laboratory than in other settings or with other research methods, so high levels of precision can be achieved. If all variables other than the independent variable are controlled successfully, then cause and effect can be established.
- *Generalizing results*: It is possible to generalize results to the rest of a population if a representative sample of participants has been selected.
- *Quantitative data*: An experiment yields quantitative data (numerical amounts of something) which can be analysed using inferential statistical tests (see Chapter 30). These tests permit statements to be made about how likely the results are to have occurred through chance.
- *Use of technical equipment*: The laboratory may be the only place where sophisticated technical equipment can be used and accurate measurements made. For some research at least, the artificiality of the laboratory situation does not really matter – examples here include research on newborn children, or on auditory perception.

Limitations of the laboratory experiment

- *Drawbacks of experimental designs*: Limitations of the laboratory experiment include the potential for order effects resulting from the order of presentation of the experimental conditions or, alternatively, the effects of individual differences between participants. These drawbacks are discussed in Chapter 29.
- *Loss of validity*: A serious problem with experiments is that by establishing high levels of control and narrowly defining independent and dependent variables, an experimental situation may become artificial and recognizably different from real-life situations. Ecological validity is concerned with the extent to which results may be generalized to settings other than the one in which the research took place, such as those outside the laboratory. For example, memory experiments have often been conducted using word lists, which are rarely learned in everyday life. A fuller discussion of ecological validity can be found in Chapter 29.
- *Demand characteristics*: Demand characteristics occur when participants try to make sense of the situation they find themselves in and act accordingly (Orne 1962). These may threaten the validity of an experiment seriously. The demands placed on participants in a laboratory situation are not helped by the experimenter sticking rigidly to a standardized procedure and acting in an unemotional way (necessary if confounding variables are to be avoided). Participants may respond to specific cues made by an investigator, such as differences in the tone of voice used, and this may present a problem. Another possible demand characteristic is that participants may try to behave in some way that they perceive as being helpful to the researcher (alternatively, if feeling awkward, they may set out deliberately to confound the results). With most participants, however, this is probably relatively unimportant. Other potential problems with those taking part may result from evaluation apprehension, where participants demonstrate concern over what an experimenter might find out about them, or social desirability effects, where participants change their everyday behaviour so that they may be perceived more favourably by others. A further possible problem concerns the level of public knowledge (or the lack of it) about psychology – how psychology is perceived by an individual may affect their responses in the research setting.
- *Sampling bias*: The participants in many experimental investigations reflect an over-representation of male participants and of specific cultures and have often been volunteers drawn from university campuses. This raises the question of the extent to which it is reasonable to generalize the results of such experimental studies to other groups of people.

- *Ethical issues*: Finally, ethical issues may present problems – for example, concern may arise over the issues of informed consent and deception of participants. It may be impossible to carry out an experiment without the researcher using some degree of deception or failing to provide full information on the procedures involved. These issues are discussed more fully in Chapter 27.

Good design can overcome many of the potential problems associated with laboratory experiments, and we will return to this issue in Chapter 29.

The field experiment

Field experiments are experimental investigations in which there is an attempt to improve realism by carrying them out in the natural environment of those being studied, e.g. in homes, schools or on the street. As with the laboratory experiment, the independent variable is still deliberately manipulated by the researcher. Therefore, much of what has been written in the previous section about the laboratory experiment also applies to the field experiment, so this part of the chapter will focus on a discussion of the key differences.

Uses of the field experiment

The field experiment is used in situations where it is considered particularly important for research to take account of the natural environment. For example, a field experiment by Andersson (1982) on the behaviour of the long-tailed widow bird is discussed in Chapter 22. A further example is provided by the study by Hofling *et al.* (1966) (see *In Focus* below).

Activity 2

Read the accounts of field experiments undertaken by Andersson (1982) (see Chapter 22) and Hofling *et al.* (1966) (see below). Suggest reasons why you think a field experiment was used in preference to a laboratory experiment in each case.

In Focus

Obedience in a natural setting

Hofling *et al.* (1966) carried out a field experiment on compliance within a hospital setting. The researchers placed boxes, claiming to contain 5 mg doses of a drug 'Astrofen', in the drug cabinets of twenty-two wards in American hospitals. In fact, the 'drug' was a harmless placebo.

A confederate of the researchers introduced himself over the telephone to the duty nurse as 'Dr Smith', and instructed the nurse to administer 20 mg of Astrofen to a patient 'Mr Jones'. The doctor claimed that he would visit the patient shortly and would sign the necessary authorization for the drug when he arrived. Administering the drug would result in serious breaches of hospital rules – written authority is required before drugs are administered; nursing staff need to be sure of the genuineness of such requests. The Astrofen was labelled that the maximum daily dose was 10 mg.

Twenty-one of the twenty-two nurses involved in the study actually complied with the request made by the bogus doctor and prepared the medicine and would have administered it if someone had not intervened. The nurses were stopped by a confederate, a real doctor, and the purpose of the study was explained to them.

The results – now widely discussed in nurse education programmes – provide an important insight into the power relationships within real-world settings and the level of compliance which can result. None of the nurses insisted on a written order or put up any resistance to the telephone request to administer the drug, in spite of the fact that the dose was twice that recommended.

Advantages of the field experiment

- *Improved ecological validity*: By avoiding the artificiality of the laboratory environment, the field experiment helps to eliminate the common criticism made of the laboratory experiment that it is difficult to generalize the findings to real-life situations. Therefore, validity is better.
- *Reduction of demand characteristics*: Participants may be unaware of taking part, and if this is the case, demand characteristics may be minimized.

Limitations of the field experiment

- *Establishing controls*: It is more difficult to establish high levels of control in a field experiment than it is in a laboratory setting. This applies to the precise control over the independent variable, measuring the dependent variable and controlling any potential confounding variables (for example, conversation from any non-participants or even their mere presence).
- *Generalization to other situations*: Although realism is higher in a field experiment, results cannot be generalized to other real-life situations which differ from the one in which the field experiment took place.
- *Ethical issues*: A particular ethical issue arises if participants are unaware of taking part in a psychological investigation (see Chapter 27).
- *Time and cost*: Field experiments may cost more than those undertaken in laboratory settings and may take longer to complete.
- *Use of technical equipment*: It may be more difficult to use sophisticated equipment than it is with experiments undertaken in a laboratory setting.
- *Replicability*: Due to the increased difficulty of establishing control, it may be harder to replicate a field experiment than a laboratory experiment.

❖ Activity 3 ❖

How would you feel if you had been one of the nurses studied by Hofling *et al.*? Do you think the results obtained from the investigation justified deceiving the twenty-two nurses who participated in the study?

The natural experiment

In a natural experiment the researcher exploits naturally occurring differences in the independent variable – therefore it is not directly controlled by the researcher. The approach can therefore best be described as quasi-experimental – indeed some purists might regard the method as non-experimental. For example, within a hospital setting one ward might be managed according to one management style with a second ward adopting a different style. A natural experiment might then be carried out which compares the two styles of management. This approach would not be a true experiment as the participants would not be allocated randomly to the two conditions.

Uses of the natural experiment

The natural experiment is a method used in situations in which the psychologist can exploit a naturally occurring event. Examples can be found in the adoption studies discussed in Chapter 11 and an example based on witnessing violent crime is included in Fig. 28.1. Occasionally an unforeseen event in the environment permits a natural experiment to be undertaken. Berkowitz (1970) hypothesized that witnessing violence makes people more violent. He recorded data on violent crime before and after the assassination in 1963 of President Kennedy in the USA, which appeared on TV in America and throughout the world, was examined. Berkowitz was able to demonstrate a sudden rise in violent crime after the assassination, thereby supporting his hypothesis.

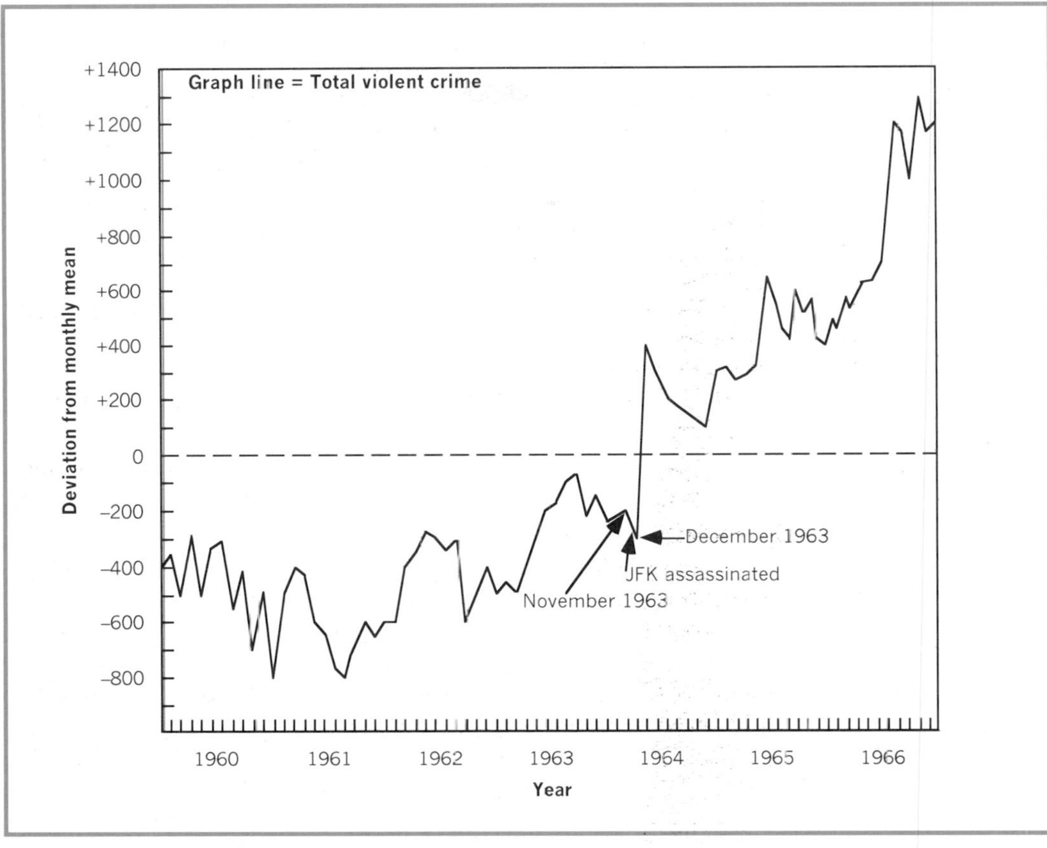

Figure 28.1 The assassination of President Kennedy and recorded levels of violence in the USA *Source:* Berkowitz 1970

Advantages of the natural experiment

- *Reduction of demand characteristics*: This approach has the advantage that participants may be unaware that they are taking part in an experiment, so demand characteristics may be avoided.
- *Lack of direct intervention*: The experimenter does not intervene directly in the research situation (although it is possible that the researcher's mere presence may still produce an effect).

Limitations of the natural experiment

- *Loss of control*: As the independent variable is not controlled by the investigator, the degree of control exercised by the researcher is less than in both the laboratory experiment and the field experiment.

Section summary

The experimental method is an important and powerful research tool available to the psychologist. A true experiment involves the deliberate manipulation of an independent variable by a researcher to produce a change in a dependent variable; complete control over potential confounding variables; and the random allocation of participants to conditions.

The greatest levels of control are possible in laboratory settings, but experimental research may take place outside laboratories as field experiments, or may investigate the effect of a naturally occurring event in a natural experiment. In cases such as these, the experimenter's control over events is reduced.

Non-experimental methods in psychology

This section examines research in which an independent variable is not deliberately manipulated by a researcher. The methods outlined here allow psychologists to study behaviour in more natural settings. This potential benefit is not without its costs: as a result of reduced levels of control, it is much harder for the researcher to reach any conclusions concerning cause and effect. The non-experimental methods discussed here are investigations using correlational analysis, naturalistic observations, case studies and interviews.

Investigations using correlational analysis

The term correlation refers to descriptive statistical techniques which measure the relationships between variables. Literally, these techniques measure 'co-relationships' between variables – i.e. the extent to which high values on one variable are associated with high values on another (known as a positive correlation) or the extent to which high values on one variable are associated with low values on another (a negative correlation). Many correlational techniques calculate a correlation coefficient, a statistic which has a value on a scale between +1 (which is known as a perfect positive correlation) and –1 (which is known as a perfect negative correlation). Correlation coefficients are discussed more fully in Chapter 30. The strength of the correlation increases as the obtained coefficient becomes closer to +1 or –1 (see Fig. 28.2).

As it is correctly a statistical technique, correlation is not strictly a research method in the truest sense of the word. Indeed, correlational techniques may be – and often are – used within experimental investigations. However, the term is also used to refer to the overall design of a non-experimental investigation which specifically attempts to identify relationships.

Uses of investigations using correlational analysis

Correlational analysis is often used to measure the extent of relationship between variables that are thought likely to co-vary. For example, research by Bryant and Bradley (1985) established a correlation between nursery school children's rhyming abilities and their later reading skills (see Chapter 9, p. 201). A further example is the research by Murstein on attractiveness (see *In Focus* on p. 630). Another major use of correlation is in the early stages of research into a particular area, especially where it is desirable to isolate relationships from a web of complex variables. An example involves the use of the Social Readjustment Rating Scale, a technique developed by Holmes and Rahe (1967) to measure the impact of life events. Studies using this measuring instrument have found correlations between life change units (scores derived from using the Social Readjustment Rating Scale) and, for example, the incidences of sickness and depression (see Chapter 20, pp. 446–7).

The correlational technique plays a major role in establishing the reliability and validity of psychological measuring instruments. For example, these techniques have played an important part in establishing the reliability and validity of psychometric tests of intelligence and personality (see Chapter 26).

Advantages of investigations using correlational analysis

- *Measuring the strength of relationships*: Correlational techniques provide valuable information on the strength of the relationship between specific variables.
- *Value to exploratory research*: Correlational techniques allow for the measurement of many variables and their relationships at the same time. They are useful, therefore, when trying to unravel complex relationships and a powerful tool for exploratory

Figure 28.2 Scattergraphs illustrating different correlation coefficients (calculated using Spearman's Rho)

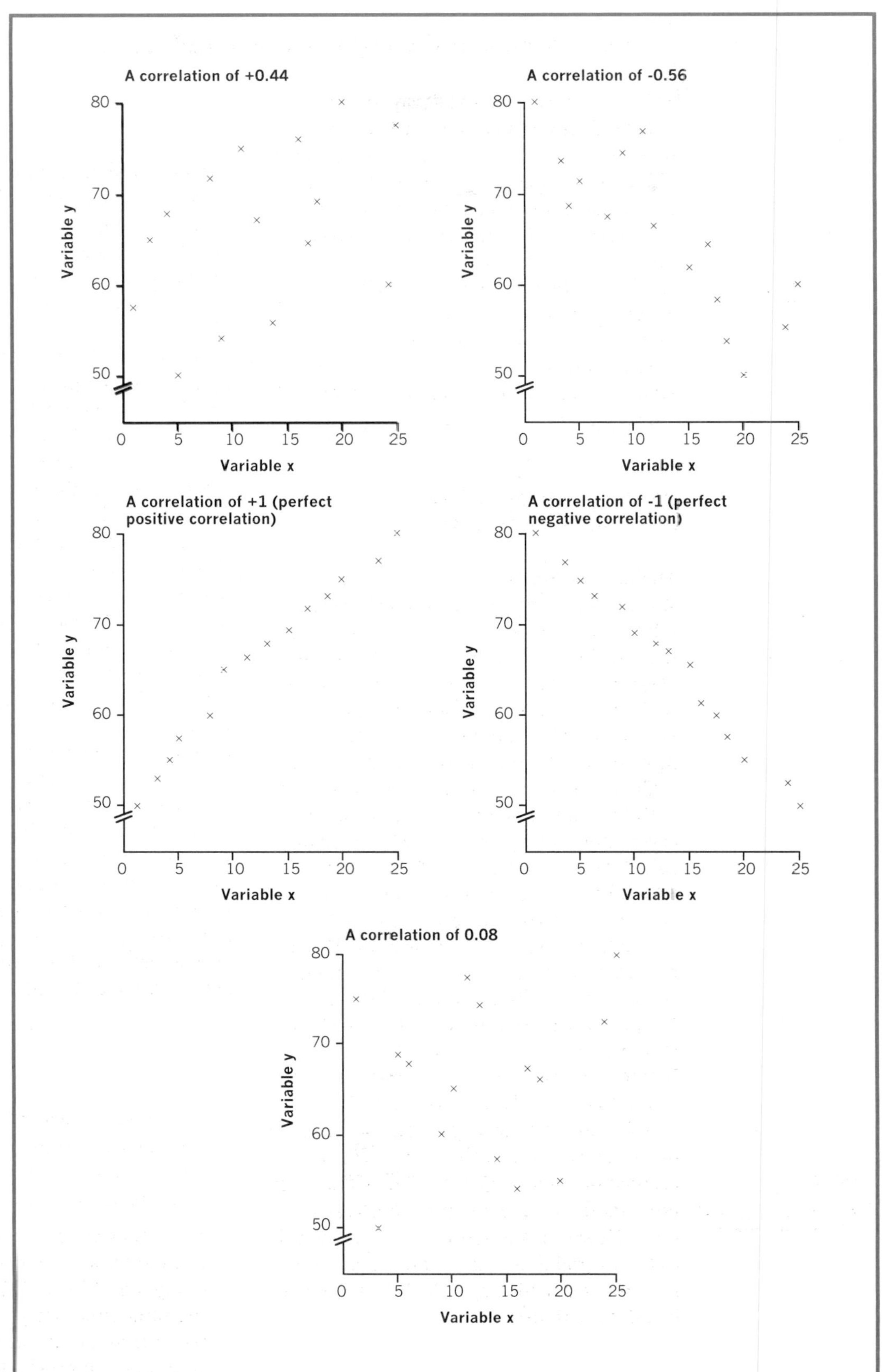

In Focus

Physical attractiveness and marital choice (Murstein 1972)

Murstein proposed the stimulus-value-role hypothesis of marital choice which proposed that individuals tend to select marital partners of comparable physical attractiveness to themselves. In two studies published in 1972, he set out to demonstrate that partners forming premarital couples show greater similarity with regard to physical attractiveness than one would expect by chance.

In the second of these studies, 98 couples described as 'engaged' or 'going steady' participated as paid volunteers. All participants were asked to rate the physical attractiveness of their partner and to estimate their own physical attractiveness, using a five-point scale. Photographs of each partner were also taken using a polaroid camera.

The following correlation coefficients were obtained:

Relationship between:	*Correlation coefficient achieved*
Male participants' perception of their own and their partners' attractiveness	+0.50
Female participants' perception of their own and their partners' attractiveness	+0.45
Independent judges' ratings of the physical attractiveness of partners	+0.38

All the correlations obtained were highly significant ($p < 0.01$), indicating support for Murstein's hypothesis (please note: statistical significance is discussed in Chapter 30).

research. Conducting tests of correlation in such circumstances may suggest appropriate directions for future research.

Limitations of investigations using correlational analysis

- *The issue of causality*: It is impossible to establish cause and effect through research investigations using correlational analysis, which can only measure the degree of interrelationship between different variables. That the technique only measures relationships is demonstrated by the presence of correlations which it would be very hard to explain causally. For example, Snedecor (1956) reported a correlation of –0.98 between production of pig iron in the USA and the birth rate in Britain for the years 1875 to 1920! This ability to detect spurious relationships is a real drawback of the technique, so it is important that there is some link to underlying theory when a researcher decides to analyse the correlation between specific variables.

  As an illustration of problems with the issue of causality, let us look briefly at the correlation which exists between the presence of symptoms of schizophrenia and the high availability of the neurotransmitter dopamine. This is a well-established correlation, but there is at the present time insufficient evidence to state that excess dopamine causes schizophrenia. It remains perfectly possible that it is schizophrenia which causes the increase in available dopamine, or indeed that there are other links in the causal chain which have yet to be discovered. Nevertheless, the existence of this correlation has provided an avenue for further research.
- *Measurement of non-linear relationships*: Non-linear relationships cannot be measured by commonly used techniques such as Spearman's Rank Order Correlation Coefficient. For example, Fig.28.3 shows the relationship between time of day and attention level in a group of students. Initially, there is a positive correlation between the two variables, but as lunchtime approaches this changes into a negative relationship. The result is that when such data are analysed, the positive and negative

relationships tend to cancel each other out, with the result that no meaningful relationship is indicated by the calculated correlation coefficient.

Naturalistic observation

Observation is a relatively loose term in itself, implying the scrutiny of ongoing behaviour. In this sense, it would be true to say that all psychological research involves observation. This section, however, will look at research where the deliberate manipulation of variables does not take place, and the research involves recording of behaviour in its natural setting. You will remember from the discussion of experimental research earlier in this chapter that rigidly controlled research methods can be criticized on the grounds of their artificiality. Research methods such as naturalistic observation provide a counter to this by placing the emphasis on how people or non-human animals behave in natural situations, with no attempt being made to influence the behaviour that is being investigated. Nevertheless, this does not imply that naturalistic observation cannot be laboratory based. For example, some species adapt well to laboratory conditions, and the behaviour displayed in laboratory settings may be considered to be natural. Also, although naturalistic observation is a relatively simple concept, it must be remembered that this kind of research presents its own particular difficulties.

A distinction is usually made between participant observation, in which the observer actually joins the group of people being studied and non-participant observation in which the observer remains external to those being observed. Observers may remain undisclosed (where those observed remain unaware of the research being undertaken) or may be disclosed to those taking part (where participants are aware of the research taking place).

Uses of naturalistic observation

The very wide range of uses of naturalistic observation includes driver behaviour, the behaviour of children in nursery settings and studies of the workplace. It is also useful where behaviour might be difficult to recreate in a laboratory setting or as a preliminary to laboratory investigation. Examples of naturalistic observational research include that by Rosenhan (1973) described in the *In Focus*. Also, naturalistic observation has always been popular in ethological research with non-human animals, for example, the classic research by Lorenz on imprinting (see Chapter 23), and the example contained in the *In Focus* on the acquisition of new behaviours in Japanese macaques by Kawamura (1963).

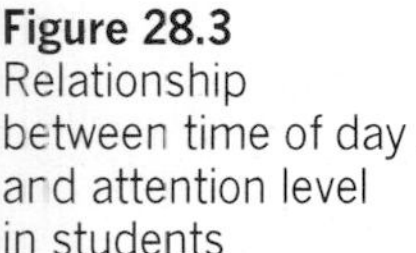
Figure 28.3 Relationship between time of day and attention level in students

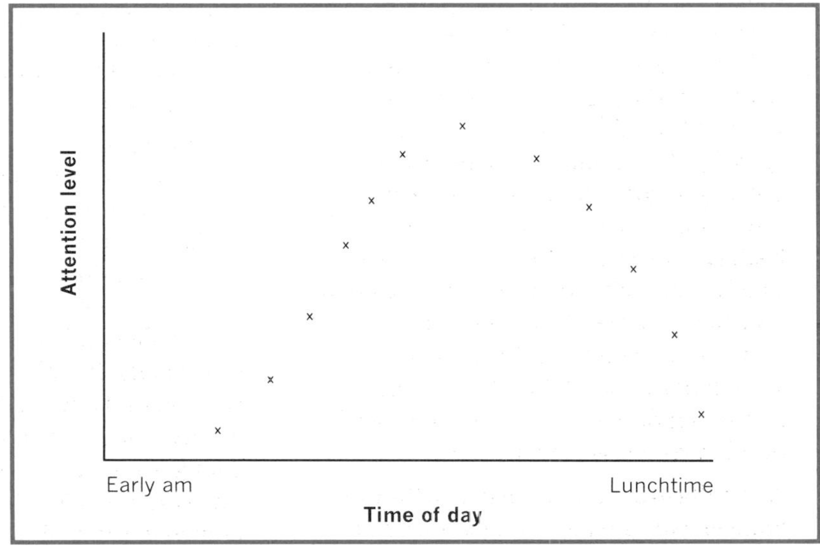

In Focus

Two examples of naturalistic observational research

On being sane in insane places (Rosenhan 1973)

Eight individuals, all free of any psychiatric symptoms, presented themselves at different psychiatric hospitals in the USA. All reported the same symptom – they said they heard a voice say 'dull', 'empty' and 'thud'. Apart from this single symptom they were instructed to behave normally, and give honest answers to any other questions asked. All were believed to be genuine patients and were admitted to the psychiatric hospitals concerned, seven with a diagnosis of schizophrenia. On admission, they immediately ceased reporting that they had been hearing voices. They were subsequently discharged 7 to 52 days later with diagnoses of 'schizophrenia in remission'. Rosenhan attributed these diagnoses to the context in which their behaviour was observed. None actually displayed symptoms of schizophrenia, but the context in which the symptoms were reported led to an expectation that these 'pseudopatients' were indeed mentally ill.

Study of Japanese macaques (Kawamura 1963)

This study recorded the spread of new behaviours through a population of Japanese macaques on Koshima Island. Researchers observing this group of monkeys spread sweet potatoes on a beach in an attempt to lure monkeys into a situation in which their behaviour could be observed more easily. One female macaque called Imo began to use a stream to wash sand from these sweet potatoes before eating them. This habit was imitated by other members of the group, and within ten years the behaviour had been acquired by the majority of the population. Subsequently, Imo started another procedure for washing food – cleaning handfuls of grain mixed with sand in the sea. This procedure was also learned by other members of the group in a similar way.

Advantages of naturalistic observation

- *Value as a preliminary research tool*: Careful observation can lead to the suggestion of appropriate hypotheses for further investigation or, on the other hand, may help to prevent time being wasted through the carrying out of unrealistic experiments. It is a useful technique for studying unknown or little known behaviour, for example, Clutton Brock and his research associates have provided much of our knowledge about the behaviour of red deer through their pioneering studies carried out on the island of Rum in the Hebrides (e.g. Clutton Brock and Albon 1979).
- *Validity*: Naturalistic observation can provide a useful check on whether experimental findings apply outside the laboratory. Realism and ecological validity can be good provided that the observer remains undetected. If this is so, then it is assumed that it is natural behaviour which is being displayed. The overall quality of the research may be improved through increased familiarity with the research setting, i.e. the researcher can become a 'predictable and familiar part of the environment' with both human and non-human participants (Coolican 1994), resulting, hopefully, in natural behaviours being observed.
- *Avoidance of demand characteristics*: Behaviour is affected neither by any anxiety nor by inhibition of behaviour resulting from being in a laboratory situation. Also, with undisclosed naturalistic observation, there will be no feeling of a need to impress the researcher (providing, of course, the observer remains undetected).

- *Use where experimentation is inappropriate*: The method can be used where experimental intervention is inappropriate (e.g. when studying weddings or funerals) or unethical (e.g. intervention with children). Also, it may be used where it is desirable to acknowledge the wider social context of observed behaviour.
- *Study of species which do not adapt to laboratory conditions*: With non-human animals, naturalistic observation is also of value when studying species which fail to thrive in laboratory conditions (e.g. red deer or marine mammals).

Limitations of naturalistic observation

- *Control*: Controls over extraneous variables are poor (although some degree of control is often possible), and cause and effect cannot be established with any certainty.
- *Observer effects*: It is possible that the presence of an observer may change behaviour, especially when it is a small group that is being studied. This can also be an issue when observing non-human animals – for example, breeding patterns may be disturbed by the mere presence of an observer (e.g. when recording the breeding patterns of seabirds on uninhabited islands).
- *Ethical issues*: Ethical issues such as deception and the invasion of privacy can be a problem, especially if the observation remains undisclosed to those taking part – the need to respect private behaviour in public places presents particular difficulties. As a general rule, an observer should not carry out research if it is considered that participants would refuse to take part if they were given the opportunity to do so (see Chapter 27 for a discussion of the ethical principles governing such research).
- *Observer bias*: The potential also exists for bias on the part of observers, deriving from their expectations or interpretations of events.

❖ Activity 4 ❖

Imagine you observe someone screaming in the street. Write down the different ways in which you might interpret this behaviour.

- *Costs*: There may also be problems with costs; for example, the costs of travel or of transporting recording equipment.
- *Difficulty of replication*: Replication may be difficult due to the problems which arise in controlling variables such as differences in naturalistic settings.
- *Structuring of data*: There may also be limitations concerning how any data gathered are structured, which places restrictions on the interpretations of behaviour which can be made (i.e. behaviour which doesn't fit into the categories which have been used).
- *Missing behaviour*: While the researcher is recording behaviour there is a potential problem that further behaviour may be missed. This problem may be minimised with the use of sound or video recordings.
- *Generalizability of the findings*: It may be difficult or impossible to generalize results to other occasions or other settings.
- *Studying unusual phenomena*: This may prove to be difficult – for example, the responses of individuals to events such as natural disasters. Indeed, even relatively common behaviours might not be produced within the timespan of an observational study.
- *Reliability*: Low inter-observer reliability may be a problem – even after observer training has taken place – since we all see the world from our own unique viewpoint. For example, identical behaviour in children might be classified as 'aggressive' by one researcher or as 'rough and tumble play' by another.
- *Study of non-human animals*: Certain practical difficulties exist when studying non-human animals – for example, when

individual members of a species appear very similar to each other (e.g. small brown birds), or when species live up trees, underground, under water, fly, move quickly or are nocturnal.

We will return to some of the ways in which some of these difficulties may be overcome in Chapter 29.

The case study

The case study method often involves simply observing what happens to, or reconstructing the 'case history' of, a single participant or a group of individuals (such as a hospital ward or a school class). This might be undertaken in various ways, for example, by using a person's own memories, the memories of friends and relatives, or records of various types. The range of potential approaches is vast and studies cannot be classified easily as they are often linked intimately to particular research areas. Most share the following characteristics:

- The method used is descriptive in nature.
- The research focus is narrow (often one aspect of a person's behaviour).
- A high level of detail is provided.

A case study is often carried out by the use of interviews or observation (or sometimes both). Both objective and subjective data may be gathered (e.g. reporting may not be confined to measurable 'facts', but may also include things such as beliefs and feelings).

Uses of the case study

The case study method permits the collection of detailed descriptive data which are usually qualitative in nature. It may provide information on the unique features of particular individuals. For example, the method is used widely in clinical psychology, where 'classic cases' are often described (see, for example, the case studies of post-traumatic stress disorder and anorexia nervosa in Chapter 11). The approach plays a major role in diagnosis and in the planning of therapy or treatment. Alternatively, case studies may be made of the typical representatives of groups. Examples which illustrate the uses of case studies include:

- the effects of isolation in young children, e.g. the cases of Isabelle, the Czech twins and Genie (see Chapter 17, p. 380)
- memory research, e.g. the study by Shallice and Warrington (1970) of KF, a young man who had a motorcycle accident leaving him with impaired short-term memory digit span (see Chapter 15, p. 326)
- case studies to illustrate different types of schizophrenia (see Chapter 11, p. 248).

The example of Dibs, a case study of play therapy reported by Axline (1971), is described in the *In Focus* on the next page.

Advantages of the case study method

- *Research in difficult areas*: The case study can increase the amount of information that is available on a topic area, especially when experimentation is an inappropriate or unethical technique (e.g. studies on topics such as physical abuse or mental illness). It also assists in the study of atypical individuals.
- *Ease of obtaining information*: It is relatively easy to obtain information and may involve grasping an opportunity provided by a 'one-off' situation which occurs at a particular time (for example, the studies of isolation in young children referred to above).
- *Valuable exploratory method*: The case study has an important role as an exploratory method, e.g. it may be useful in identifying variables which can be followed up using alternative research methods.
- *Confirming or challenging a theory*: Information from case studies can be useful in helping to confirm or challenge a theory (i.e. if a single case does not fit in, a theory can be challenged).

In Focus

The case study of Dibs (Axline 1971, first published in 1964)

Play therapy is a form of psychotherapy which assumes that children's play provides a window into their unconscious thought processes. It is assumed that in their play children may express wishes, fears and fantasies which are at the root of any current problem. In order to understand any current problems, previous events and unconscious thoughts need to be brought out into the open so that an insight may be gained into behaviour.

Dibs was a 5-year-old boy with behavioural difficulties who attended a private school. He was socially withdrawn and exhibited antisocial behaviours such as aggression and tantrums which the school pediatrician was unable to explain. During therapy, Dibs was permitted to direct his play activities and the therapist's function was to provide appropriate play materials and a safe and non-judgemental environment in which Dibs could express his feelings freely. After a series of weekly sessions, his self-esteem developed and he learned to respect and accept others. His problem behaviours gradually disappeared.

- *Depth of information*: The case study produces in-depth information, which is not contaminated in any way by the result of 'averaging' with other individuals – the information relates to a 'real' individual.
- *Permits study over time*: The case study allows for the study of behaviour over a period of time (e.g. the development of language in children).

Limitations of the case study method

- *Reliance on memory*: When reconstructing a case history, the heavy reliance on memory means that objectivity may be lacking.
- *Generalizability of the findings*: There are serious problems in generalizing the results as these are unique to a single individual and may not be representative of any particular population.
- *Potential for researcher bias*: The method involves reliance on the interpretation of the evidence by the person(s) undertaking the study.

The interview

Most research establishes some kind of distance between the researcher and the researched, but this kind of approach is challenged by the face-to-face nature of the interview which is inevitably both personal and public in its nature. The interview is an important tool for the research psychologist and needs an explicit purpose and aims to encourage the flow of information from the interviewee to the interviewer. In some instances the focus of an interview may be negotiated between interviewer and interviewee – notice the key difference here from the experimental approach, in which the research focus is always predetermined by the researcher. Consequently, interviews are both diverse in their nature and specific to a particular research situation. Their diversity also means that interviewing is a skill that requires careful development.

Interviews need careful planning and piloting, and vary in the extent to which they are structured or unstructured. At one end of this continuum, structured interviews usually aim to produce quantitative data and include questions which are decided in advance with the aim of structuring the interviewee's responses. The structured interview has several advantages. The interviewer and interviewee are less likely to deviate from the topic that is the subject of the interview. Also, data analysis may be simpler, results are easier to generalize, less training is needed for interviewers and there is less risk of the results being affected by interviewer bias since the interviewer is more likely to be objective. However, there are costs as well as benefits. The researcher cannot follow up any new lines of enquiry which become apparent during the interview, and validity may be threatened by participants reacting to the formality of the research situation.

At the other end of the continuum are unstructured interviews. These are far less rigid and very little, if anything, concerning their nature will be decided in advance. These can be more difficult to analyse, but have greater validity as interviewees will be more likely to report whatever they wish to say and the interviewers can be flexible in their approach.

The semi-structured interview is often the most successful approach, with the use of some prepared questions by the interviewer, supplemented by opportunities for the interviewee to expand the answers that have been given.

Uses of the interview

An interview may provide information which is additional to that obtained from other research methods. For example, Milgram (1963) enriched his work on obedience by interviewing his participants after they had completed the experimental procedure. Two areas where the approach has been of particular value are in social

❖ Activity 5 ❖

Try conducting two interviews on a topic of your choice. Obtain two volunteers; use a structured interview technique with the first and an unstructured interview technique with the other person. What differences do you note in your findings?

psychology and psychopathology (see, for example, the use of interviews in the research on conformity by Asch, discussed in Chapter 3, and in exploring the family histories of sufferers from anxiety disorders in Chapter 11). An example of the use of the method can be found in the *In Focus* (see below).

Two of the major reasons for using interviews have been outlined by Banister *et al.* (1994). First, interviews enable the researcher to gain subjective meanings (those that participants attribute to the topic of the interview) rather than obtaining responses within a standard format. Second, the interview can permit issues to be explored which are too complex to investigate through quantitative techniques, which may have resulted in an oversimplification of the issues in hand (i.e. making the participants' views hard to represent). The method may aim to explore precisely those

In Focus

Cognitive maps

Lynch (1960) was interested in environmental perception, and in particular in the cognitive maps people have of their home areas. He interviewed residents in three American cities (Boston, Jersey City and Los Angeles) about their feelings for local landmarks and also about major routeways and the areas that they passed through when driving around. From his interviews, he was able to produce a general image of each city that identified the basic units of the urban landscape. Often, participants were able to point out distinctive features of the urban landscape, which were not always the tallest or skyline features but rather things at a more human scale, such as a well-known building or open space. However, interviewees also tended to have areas of the cities which they were unable to describe. Knowledge gained in this way of the information that people have about their own cities has been used to practical effect in urban planning. For example, the work of Goodey (1971) on residents' cognitive maps of Birmingham was used to help planners develop their future vision of the city.

areas where other research methods present difficulties. The interviewer can tailor questions to the responses of the interviewee. This means that issues can be explored which have not been envisaged by the researchers. It allows response to and follow up of the issues raised.

The advantages of the interview

- *Flexibility*: A key advantage of the interview is that it can be a flexible research method. It can obtain perspectives which are unobtainable by other research methods or which have not been envisaged by the researcher prior to the investigation. This may benefit groups which have been disadvantaged by other research methodologies.
- *Identifying personal aspects of behaviour*: If carried out sensitively, the interview will permit knowledge to be gained about aspects of behaviour which are private or personal to the individuals concerned.

Limitations of the interview

'Conducting interviews is a complex, labour intensive and uncertain business, fraught with tricky issues that social scientific researchers, and particularly psychologists, are often ill-equipped to address' (Banister *et al.* 1994).

- *Interpreting data*: Misinterpretation or partial interpretation of data may take place. The interviewer needs to be detached from the interviewee, which can be difficult to achieve in face-to-face situations with their potential for bias.
- *Limitations in interviewees' responses*: A particular problem with interviews is that interviewees may be unable to put their thoughts precisely into words.
- *Ethical issues*: Ethical issues arise, e.g. participants may be deceived if the true purpose of the interview is disguised. There is a need to understand the position of power that the interviewer is in and to show respect for participants' views, particularly in relation to potentially sensitive topics such as asking parents about how they brought up their children, including the use of discipline within the home.
- *Interviewer effects*: The appearance of the interviewer may produce effects (e.g. as a result of their ethnic group, age, gender, physical attractiveness or their mode of dress).
- *Demand characteristics*: There may also be effects on the interviewees such as social desirability bias where a participant gives answers which are considered to be 'socially acceptable' and which may not actually represent their personal views on the topic under investigation.
- *Difficulties of analysing data*: Qualitative data obtained from unstructured interviews may not be easy to analyse.

Section summary

A wide range of non-experimental methods is used by psychologists to study behaviour. The aim of investigations using correlational analysis is to establish relationships between variables. Both naturalistic observation and the use of interview techniques have the advantage of increased ecological validity when compared with experimental methods. Case studies can be used to provide an in-depth analysis of the behaviours of an individual or group of individuals.

Chapter summary

- Psychologists have adopted a range of research methods when investigating their subject matter. No single method is appropriate or successful in all circumstances and in all contexts.
- Experimental methods provide the highest levels of control, but at the cost of a reduction in ecological validity.
- Investigations using correlational analysis allow researchers to obtain measures of the relationship between variables, but do not allow the research to establish cause and effect relationships.
- Naturalistic observational studies provide the researcher with an ecologically valid technique. However, establishing controls may be difficult, making it difficult to generalize the results.
- The production of case studies may involve the use of observation and/or interviews. The in-depth studies produced may assist the researcher in the study of ethically sensitive areas.
- Interviews allow the flexible exploration of detailed issues, some of which may not have been envisaged by interviewer or interviewee.

Exam questions

1 Explain one advantage and one disadvantage of each of the following research methods:

(a) The laboratory experiment *(4 marks)*
(b) Naturalistic observation *(4 marks)*
(c) Interviews. *(4 marks)*

2 Distinguish between a natural experiment and a field experiment. *(3 marks)*

Further reading

Banister, P., Burman, E., Parker, I., Taylor, M. and Tindall, C. (1994) *Qualitative Methods in Psychology: A Research Guide*, Buckingham: Open University Press.

An advanced text which covers observations and interviews.

Foster, J.J. and Parker, I. (1995) *Carrying out Investigations in Psychology: Methods and Statistics*, Leicester: BPS Books.

A detailed and advanced text which is useful for reference purposes.

Coolican, H. (1995) *Introduction to Research Methods and Statistics in Psychology*, London: Hodder and Stoughton.

A condensed version of the Coolican (1994) text.

Coolican, H. (1994) *Research Methods and Statistics in Psychology*, London: Hodder and Stoughton.

A clearly written text which covers the research methods included in the AEB syllabus.

Dyer, C. (1995) *Beginning Research in Psychology: A Practical Guide to Research Methods and Statistics*, Oxford: Blackwell.

A detailed text with useful sections on non-experimental methods.

Chapter 29

Research design

Graham Davies

Preview

In this chapter we shall be looking at the following aspects of psychological investigations:

- defining variables and formulating hypotheses
- methods of selecting participants
- the implementation of non-experimental research
- experimental design
- how the effects of situational variables may be minimized
- establishing reliability and validity.

Introduction

Chapter 28 discussed some of the research methods most widely used by psychologists. This chapter covers a wide range of issues associated with the design and implementation of experimental and non-experimental investigations.

It considers issues which are important once appropriate aims for a psychological investigation have been generated. It begins by considering operational definitions of relevant variables and the formulation of appropriate hypotheses. The chapter continues by discussing the major sampling methods used by psychologists in order to obtain their participants. The different ways of implementing non-experimental and experimental research investigations are then considered. The different decisions which need to be taken when undertaking non-experimental research are reviewed. Experimental designs are discussed, as well as the different ways in which the effects of situational variables may be minimized. Finally, the chapter examines the issues of reliability and validity in psychological research.

Defining variables

A variable is, quite simply, anything that may change or alter in any way. You may recall from Chapter 28 that the control, manipulation and observation of variables are central to psychological research. Psychologists need to be able to define variables successfully if their research is to be treated as scientifically worthwhile. This is not as easy as it may sound.

❖ Activity 1 ❖

Try writing down a definition for the term 'aggressive behaviour'.

❖ Activity 2 ❖

Imagine that you are about to undertake an observational study of aggressive behaviour in young children. Refine the definition of aggressive behaviour that you generated for Activity 1 into a fully operationalized definition that could be used in a research situation.

You probably included different forms of violent behaviour – but did you include things such as spitting, swearing, glaring or invading personal space? Even a smile can sometimes have aggressive intent!

It is even more difficult to define variables when they are less tangible, for example, 'stress' or 'concentration levels'. We may be able to measure the visible signs of their effect on a person, and we may endeavour to measure their effects on an aspect of behaviour, but can we be confident that we are actually measuring the variable?

Operational definitions

Operational definitions of variables or factors being investigated are precise descriptions of what researchers understand by particular terms.

In experimental research, the key variables are the independent variable and the dependent variable (see p. 622). Operationalizing these variables usually results in a narrowing-down of the research focus. For example, the general statement that 'mnemonics improve memory' might be refined into an independent variable that specifies the presence or absence of imagery, and a dependent variable that specifies the number of words correctly recalled. This process has wide implications for the extent to which research findings can be generalized, as it follows that the narrower the research focus, the narrower the area to which results can be generalized. Unwanted variables (i.e. those which can cause potential confounding) can result from either random error or constant error, and these need to be eliminated or controlled as far as possible (see *In Focus* opposite for a discussion of these).

The formulation of hypotheses

A hypothesis can be defined simply as a testable statement. It is essential for research purposes that the hypothesis is phrased carefully in such a way as to be clearly expressed and testable. This is the process of hypothesis formulation, i.e. stating it in precise terms. For example, consider the statement that 'leading questions affect eye witness testimony'. In the form presented here it begs too many questions to be tested precisely. For instance, what kind of leading question are we talking about, or in what ways is the testimony of witnesses affected? If this statement is to be converted into a format useful to the research psychologist, then its wording must be completely free from ambiguity.

In Focus

Random error and constant error

Unwanted variables (or extraneous variables) are those which obscure the effect of an independent variable on a dependent variable or which provide a false impression that the independent variable has produced changes when in fact it has not. If a variable other than the independent variable produces a change in a dependent variable, then results are said to be confounded.

The effects of **random error** cannot be predicted. Possible sources of random error might include:

- a participant's state of mind
- a participant's level of motivation
- incidental noise
- room temperature
- previous experiences on the day of the experiment.

It is hoped that errors which might result from variables such as these will not systematically affect one condition of an experiment more than another. By allocating participants randomly to experimental conditions, psychologists will assume that such errors balance out across the experimental conditions. Such error might, however, result in some loss of sensitivity.

Constant error affects the dependent variable in a consistent way and is, therefore, a much more serious problem for the researcher than random error since it may not affect all conditions of an experiment equally. Such errors might include:

- a failure to counterbalance or randomize the presentation order of experimental conditions
- participant differences
- errors of measurement which affect one condition more than another.

Wherever possible, such sources of error are eliminated by good experimental design (see the sections of this chapter on sampling techniques, experimental design and on minimizing the effects of situational variables).

Activity 3

Try to rephrase the above hypothesis about eye witness testimony in a precisely testable form.

You probably came up with a more specific statement – something along the lines of 'More witnesses report seeing a knife in a given scene when a leading question suggests the existence of a knife as a murder weapon'. This formulation process serves to highlight a fundamental issue concerning experimental research. On the one hand, the original statement is so general in its nature that it is difficult to test. On the other hand, the version based on operationalized variables, despite having the important advantages of being more clearly defined and testable, may lack more general application.

Null and alternative hypotheses

Researchers refer to two different hypotheses – the null hypothesis and the alternative hypothesis. The null hypothesis predicts that the results obtained from an investigation are due to chance alone. For example, in an experiment investigating the effect of an mnemonic on memory recall, the null hypothesis would predict that any differences in observed outcome are due to chance, rather than the effect of the independent variable (the mnemonic). The task of the researcher is to decide whether the null hypothesis should be retained or rejected. If the likelihood of the results occurring by chance is remote then the null hypothesis can be rejected and we may prefer to accept the alternative hypothesis (in an experiment this may be termed the experimental hypothesis). This predicts that something other than chance alone has played a part in producing the results obtained. Only if the design of the investigation is completely watertight will we be left with just one explanation for the results (i.e. that the independent variable is responsible for the outcome). In practice, reaching such a definite conclusion can be difficult.

Alternative hypotheses can be described as being directional or non-directional. A directional hypothesis predicts the direction in which results are expected to occur, for example, 'rehearsal using a mnemonic technique improves the recall of words'. A non-directional hypothesis, however, does not predict the expected direction of outcome. For example, 'there is a difference in the number of words recalled from word lists presented with or without background music'. Directional and non-directional hypotheses are referred to in many texts as one- and two-tailed hypotheses respectively (as they are tested by using one-tailed or two-tailed statistical tests, as we shall see in Chapter 30. However, the terms directional and non-directional hypothesis are preferred.

The null hypothesis can thus be regarded as the hypothesis which states that the alternative hypothesis is untrue. It is the most important of the hypotheses as it is the null hypothesis which is actually tested when inferential statistical tests are applied to data (see Chapter 30). A discussion of how a decision is made over whether or not a null hypothesis can be rejected can be found in Chapter 30.

❖ Activity 4 ❖

Select four areas of psychological research which you have studied. Devise null and alternative hypotheses which might be appropriate in these areas. Provide an example of a directional and a non-directional hypothesis in each case.

Selecting participants

When selecting participants to take part in research investigations, two key concepts are the population and the sample. A target population is a group of people that share a given set of characteristics, about which a researcher wishes to draw conclusions (e.g. *all* students registered for A-level psychology examinations in a given year). However, a target population is usually too large for each individual to be investigated, so a subset of the population – a sample – is investigated instead. A representative sample forms part of a target population, sharing the characteristics of the population despite its smaller size. Only if a sample is truly representative can it be used by psychologists as a basis for generalizing their conclusions to the remainder of the target population. If a sample is not truly representative, then time and effort may have been wasted.

As a general principle, the larger a sample is, the more likely it is to give an accurate estimate about the nature of the population from which it has been drawn. Deciding on the size of a sample therefore reflects a delicate balancing act between the need for accurate representation of the target population on the one hand, and practical considerations such as time and money on the other. In practice, if a sample is used instead of an entire population, some degree of sampling error is likely to result. The researcher's task is to minimize the sampling error. Generally, the larger the sample the better; the smaller the sample, the greater the potential bias. It is possible to determine sample size precisely – statistical tables exist which advise on the sample size needed to achieve acceptable levels of sampling error in target populations of different sizes.

There are several different ways in which samples can be taken and some of these will now be discussed.

Random sample

In a random sample, every person or item in a given target population stands an equal chance of being selected for inclusion. This means that it is necessary to have a list of every person or item in the population in order to generate a random sample. Selection must take place in a completely unbiased way. However, it is important to recognize that selecting a random sample does not guarantee the researcher a sample which is totally representative of the population concerned, nor does it guarantee that any two random samples which are drawn from the same target population will share identical characteristics. By its very nature, a random sample can only come with a guarantee that it has been selected in an unbiased manner (selection of random samples is discussed later in this chapter). However, as long as the target population and sample size have been chosen carefully, the laws of probability predict that the chance of selecting a biased sample through random sampling techniques is minimal.

Stratified sample

The term 'stratified' means 'arranged in layers'. A stratified sample is more complex than a random sample and its selection is undertaken through a multi-stage process. Firstly, factors (the 'strata') which are considered important to the research are identified by the investigator. Then the precise proportions of these factors in the total population are ascertained. A sample size is decided on and subsets of the sample are preselected which represent the distribution of these factors in the target population. For example, if social class was considered to be an important factor in a particular investigation, then the subsets selected for study would contain the exact proportions of people within each social class in the total target population. Within each of these subsets of the target population, the actual sample taken would then be selected on a random basis. The extra effort involved in taking this kind of sample will cost the researcher time and money, but the outcome is likely to be improved accuracy and more representative results.

Quota sample

A quota sample is similar to a stratified sample but a preset number of individuals (the quota) is drawn from each stratum. Random sampling is not involved and the sampling method can be used when a complete list of individuals in the target population is unavailable. For example, a quota sample could be selected representing A level and GCSE students. The sample would be proportional in size to the total number of students in each of these two groups. The quotas would then be selected proportional in size to the number of students who actually study each subject. The researcher, however, would have no way of knowing how representative the selected students were of their particular subject groups.

Systematic sample

A common way of selecting a systematic sample is to select as participants those present at fixed intervals, for example, every twentieth person from a list which represents the target population, such as a class register, or every tenth person alighting from a train. Strictly, this kind of sample should not be regarded as a random sample as each person does not stand an equal chance of selection. However, selection is substantially unbiased and the term quasi-random is sometimes applied to this kind of sample.

Self-selected sample

A self-selected sample (or volunteer sample) involves participants selecting themselves, often through replying to an advertisement. Much university research uses this kind of sample. A well-known example of this technique was Milgram's selection of participants for his research on obedience in the 1960s (see Fig. 29.1).

Figure 29.1 Milgram's advertisement

Public Announcement

WE WILL PAY YOU $4.00 FOR ONE HOUR OF YOUR TIME

Persons Needed for a Study of Memory

* We will pay five hundred New Haven men to help us complete a scientific study of memory and learning. The study is being done at Yale University.

* Each person who participates will be paid $4.00 (plus 50¢ carfare) for approximately 1 hour's time. We need you for only one hour: there are no further obligations. You may choose the time you would like to come (evenings, weekdays or weekends).

* No special training, education or experience is needed. We want:

Factory workers	**Businessmen**	**Construction workers**
City employees	**Clerks**	**Salespeople**
Laborers	**Professional people**	**White-collar workers**
Barbers	**Telephone workers**	**Others**

All persons must be between the ages of 20 and 50. High school and college students cannot be used.

* If you meet these qualifications, fill out the coupon below and mail it now to Professor Stanley Milgram, Department of Psychology, Yale University, New Haven. You will be notified later of the specific time and place of the study. We reserve the right to decline any application.

* You will be paid $4.00 (plus 50¢ carfare) as soon as you arrive at the laboratory.

- -

To: Prof. Stanley Milgram, Department of Psychology, Yale University,
New Haven, Conn.

I want to take part in this study of memory and learning. I am between the ages of 20 and 50. I will be paid $4.00 (plus 50¢ carfare) if I participate.

Name (Please print) ....

Address ....

Telephone No: .... Best time to call you ....

Age .... Occupation .... Sex ....

Can you come:

Weekdays .... Evenings .... Weekends ....

❖ Activity 5 ❖

Look at the advertisement in Fig. 29.1. What disadvantages can you think of for employing this kind of sample?

The potential disadvantages of using a self-selected sample are:

- selectivity of response (the majority of a given target population are unlikely to respond)
- biased response (those who do respond may be atypical of the target population in some way).

Opportunity sample

An opportunity sample (or opportunist sample) involves the researcher selecting anyone who is available to take part from any given population (such as available staff or students within a college). This type of sample is very widely used, despite the fact that such samples are very easily biased. However, the risk of bias is often acceptable, for example in research on the capacity of short-term memory it might reasonably be concluded that an opportunity sample of the general public would produce results that did not differ in important ways from those obtained from any other kind of sample.

Implementing non-experimental research

Non-experimental research includes investigations based on correlational analysis, naturalistic observation, the use of interviews and the production of case studies (these are discussed in Chapter 28). When undertaking non-experimental research, a number of decisions need to be taken. These may include the following (although some of these points apply also to research of an experimental nature).

- *Deciding on an appropriate research method to use*

  A decision needs to be made on the appropriate method(s) to be used and when it is appropriate to use them.

- *Deciding how many participants to use*

  Sometimes the non-experimental researcher will have no control over this and will need to use whoever is available. In some examples of qualitative research (e.g. research based on case studies or interviews), there will be only a single participant. However, there will be occasions when the researcher does have a choice. As a general rule, the larger the sample, the less biased it is likely to be. Twenty-five or thirty is often regarded as a reasonable number when quantitative data are to be collected and analysed.

- *Using an appropriate sampling method*

  Where a sample of participants is selected to represent some larger population, the researcher will need to decide on a sampling method that is appropriate for the task in hand. Also, the researcher will need to decide how representative the participants are of a particular target population.

❖ Activity 6 ❖

Consider the population in your local town centre on a weekday at 08.45, 11.00, 16.00 and 23.00. How might the population differ at these differing times of the day?

- *Deciding whether participants should be aware or unaware of taking part in research*

  This raises the ethical issue of informed consent (see Chapter 27). Sometimes researchers will disclose their intent to participants and spend a period of time getting to know them before the research is carried out. It is hoped that this will encourage more natural behaviour.

Figure 29.2 Sample coding sheet from an investigation on gender differences in the aggressive behaviour of schoolchildren *Source:* McIlveen *et al.* 1992, p. 120

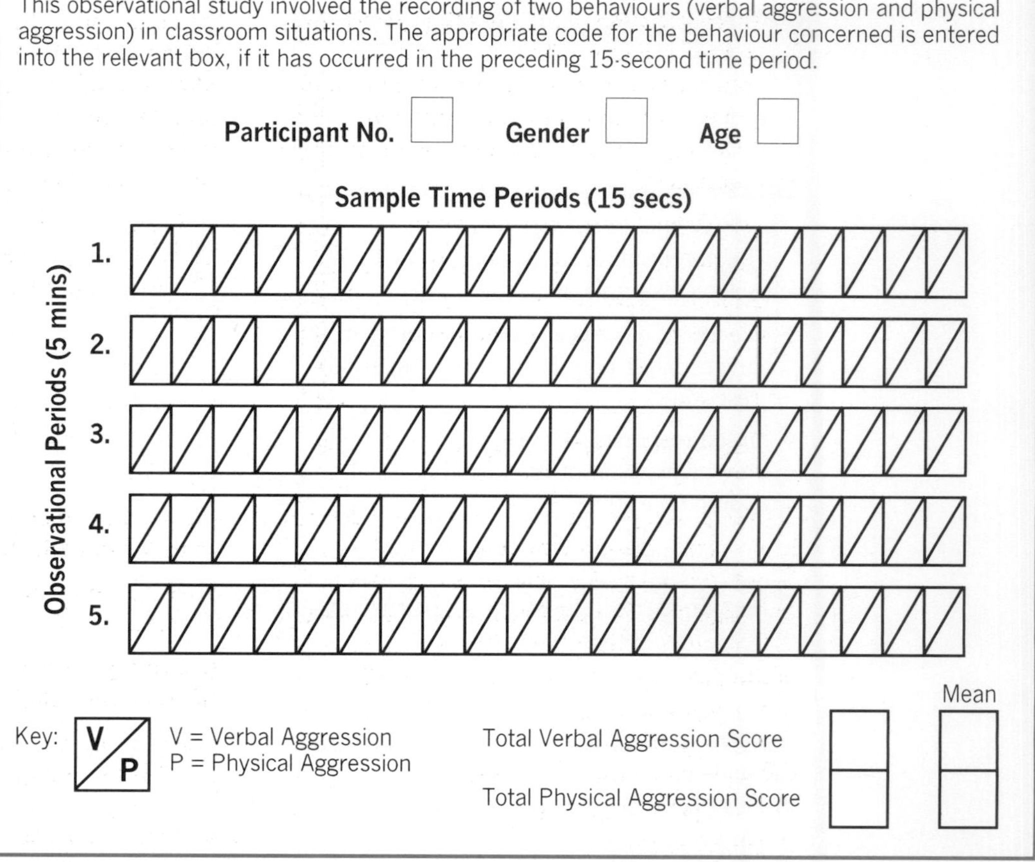

This observational study involved the recording of two behaviours (verbal aggression and physical aggression) in classroom situations. The appropriate code for the behaviour concerned is entered into the relevant box, if it has occurred in the preceding 15-second time period.

Participant No. ☐ **Gender** ☐ **Age** ☐

Sample Time Periods (15 secs)

Observational Periods (5 mins)

1.

2.

3.

4.

5.

Key: V/P V = Verbal Aggression P = Physical Aggression

Total Verbal Aggression Score

Total Physical Aggression Score

Mean

❖ *Deciding the medium for recording data*

The researcher will need to have a clearly defined medium for recording data. There are several possibilities here. A written record may be made, or behaviour may be recorded on videotape or speech on audiotape for subsequent analysis. A combination of these methods is commonly used. The researcher will need to decide which behaviour to record and which to ignore, and if a written record is made, the researcher may need to devise an appropriate coding system for recording behaviour (an example is provided in Fig. 29.2).

❖ *Deciding the techniques for recording behaviour*

The method used may be highly structured, as in some observational studies, or may be unstructured, as in some interviews. Likely methods are written notes, the production of a checklist or tally chart (see Fig. 29.3), or the use of a rating scale. The aim is to obtain data which are sufficiently explicit to enable appropriate analysis of the results.

❖ *Deciding how to sample the behaviour to be studied*

The possibilities include time interval sampling (observing and recording what

Figure 29.3 Specimen checklist of behaviours and tally chart (behaviour categories taken from Bee 1995, p. 90)

State of baby during 30-second time period	*No. of observations*
Deep sleep:	𝍸 𝍸 I
Active sleep:	𝍸 𝍸 𝍸 𝍸 I
Quiet awake:	𝍸 𝍸 𝍸 𝍸 𝍸 II
Active awake:	𝍸 III
Crying, fussing:	𝍸 𝍸 III

happens in a series of fixed time intervals), time point sampling (observing and recording the behaviour which occurs at a series of given points in time), and event sampling (observing and recording a complete event each time that it occurs).

- *Establishing inter-rater reliability*

  Ideally, in observational studies, more than one observer should be used. This procedure allows a researcher to measure the extent to which observers agree on the behaviours they have observed. Independent checks for reliability can often be made easier by the use of audiotaping or videotaping. Correlational analysis is often used to establish inter-rater reliability (see Chapter 30).

A checklist for interview planning and an example of an interview schedule are shown in Figs 29.4 and 29.5 respectively.

Experimental design

Selecting an appropriate experimental design is a crucial decision which is essential for the success or otherwise of an experimental investigation. The selection process involves balancing the advantages and disadvantages of the different designs which are available to the psychologist. When planning an experiment, it should be borne in mind that the aims of a successful design are to:

- provide an overall plan for the experiment
- try and ensure precision of measurement
- enable experimental results to be analysed to their full potential
- avoid any potential sources of ambiguity or confusion
- ensure high levels of control over the different variables.

When deciding on an appropriate design to use, it is necessary to consider carefully the precise nature of the experimental task to be undertaken, how relevant variables are to be controlled and the availability of participants.

Figure 29.4 Checklist for interview planning *Source:* Dyer 1995, p. 65

1 The preliminaries to the interview:

Have you:

- clearly described the research problem?
- stated the aim of the interview?
- linked the problem to an appropriate theory?
- identified the general categories of data which you will need to collect?

2 The questions:

Have you:

- generated an appropriate set of questions?
- planned the order in which the questions will be presented?
- planned the interview to obtain the required balance between structured and unstructured interviewing?

3 The interview procedure:

Have you:

- considered the issues of self-presentation?
- identified and approached potential respondents?
- planned the pre-interview meeting?
- planned the post-interview debriefing?
- decided how the information is to be recorded in the interview?
- considered the ethical issues raised by the proposed research and sought advice if necessary?

Figure 29.5
An example of an interview schedule
Source: Dyer 1995, p. 72

The following is an example of how a schedule of questions on the subject of the contribution of early school experience to the development of gender identity might look. The extreme right-hand column is used to place a tick against each question as it is asked, to prevent the embarrassing possibility of asking the same question twice. Note the heading to the schedule which ensures that you have a record of the basic details of the research stored with the questions, and the range of question types covered.

Title of project: A case study of the development of gender identity
Topic: Contribution of early school experiences
Date of interview:

1 Can you begin by giving me a general description of the school you attended at the age of five, so I can begin to understand what kind of a place it was?	
2 Looking back, how did your school deal with the issue of gender in general? For example, were boys and girls treated in very different ways? Could you give me some examples of that?	
3 How did this compare with what you experienced at home?	
4 How was children's behaviour dealt with? For example, was a clear distinction made between what was considered appropriate behaviour for boys compared to girls?	
5 Did the school generally reinforce or challenge stereotyped gender definitions? Examples?	
6 How do you now think this affected you during your early school life? Can you give some examples?	
7 Can you give me some examples of the kind of thing that would have happened if a boy behaved in a way the teachers thought was more appropriate to a girl?	
8 Can you give me any examples of the ways in which the rules about appropriate behaviour were enforced? How do you feel about them now?	
9 What would have happened if you had been found breaking a rule like that?	

This section will consider the three experimental designs that the AS or A level student is likely to come into contact with: the independent groups design; the repeated measures design; and the matched participants design. These are only three of the many designs available to the experimenter, and the reader seeking further information is directed to specialist texts such as those by Coolican (1994, 1995) or Dyer (1995).

Independent groups design

An independent groups design involves using different participants in each of the experimental conditions. (You may see this referred to as an independent measures/ participants/subjects/samples design or a between-groups/participants/subjects/ samples design.)

Experiments with this design may consist of:

- a control condition and one or more experimental conditions, or
- two (or more) experimental conditions.

In the former case, the group of participants that is given the experimental treatment is referred to as the experimental condition, and the group that exists for comparison and which receives no treatment is the control condition (see Fig. 29.6 for an example of how this design might appear in practice).

In true experiments, participants are allocated randomly to each of the conditions (i.e. allocated to conditions in such a way that each participant stands an equal chance of being selected for each condition). The aim of this random allocation of participants is to try to ensure that participant variables do not differ systematically between each group as a result of any individual differences which are relevant to the experiment concerned, and which otherwise might lead to results being confounded.

For example, if an experiment was carried out on learning ability, it would be undesirable to have all the fastest learners allocated to the same condition. However, you should not interpret this as suggesting that random allocation will produce groups of participants which have identical characteristics. You may still, through chance, fail to eliminate differences as a factor and allocate all the fastest learners to one group. However, the chance of this happening is minimal. For example, imagine the likelihood of the numbers one to six inclusive coming up in that order on the National Lottery, or the probability of dealing out all four suits of a pack of cards in both suit and number order. The chances of this happening are extremely remote – but of course a single combination, such as in the examples presented here, is as likely to happen as any other single combination. However, by randomly allocating participants, the researcher avoids any conscious or subconscious bias in participant allocation, and providing the independent groups design is suitable for the proposed experiment, the probability is high that individual differences will not be significant as a confounding factor.

The random allocation of participants to conditions can be achieved in several ways. The simplest method is to draw names from a hat. A more sophisticated way is to employ a random number table. (Appendix 1 contains a random number table together with an explanation of how to use it.)

In natural experiments (see Chapter 28), the allocation of participants to conditions is decided by the naturally occurring event which is treated as the independent variable. For example, if the independent

Figure 29.6 Allocation of participants in three different experimental designs

1 The independent groups design:

Participants (Ps) may be allocated to the conditions randomly. For example:

Condition A	*Condition B*
P1	P3
P2	P5
P4	P6 ..... and so on.

2 Repeated measures design:

Each participant undertakes all conditions of the experiment. For example:

Condition A	*Condition B*
P1	P1
P2	P2
P3	P3 ..... and so on.

3 Matched participants design:

Pairs of participants are matched on appropriate variables relevant to the experiment; the members of each pair are then allocated to each condition (sometimes randomly). For example:

Condition A	*Condition B*
P1a	P1b
P2a	P2b
P3b	P3a ..... and so on.

variable is the management style of two different hospital wards, then the experimenter will not have complete control over the allocation of participants to conditions. This kind of technique is properly regarded as quasi-experimental.

An independent groups design has a great advantage resulting from the different participants used in each condition – there is no problem with order effects. These occur when participants' performance is positively affected by their taking part in two or more experimental conditions. For example, their performance in a second or subsequent condition may be helped through the practice of a task which they undertook in a previous condition. Alternatively, order effects may have a negative effect occurring through fatigue or boredom. This freedom from order effects means that the independent groups design has a wide range of potential uses and can be used freely where problems with order effects would make a repeated measures design impractical.

However, the design also has disadvantages. The most serious is the potential for error resulting from individual differences between the groups of participants taking part in the different conditions. Also, if participants are in short supply, then an independent groups design may represent an uneconomic use of those available to participate, since twice as many participants are needed to obtain the same amount of data as would be required in a two-condition, repeated measures design.

Repeated measures design

A repeated measures design involves exposing every participant to each of the experimental conditions, so in effect participants are used as their own controls. (You may also see this referred to as related measures samples or within participants/ subjects design). Figure 29.6 provides an example of how participants might be arranged in an experiment using this design. One of the conditions in experiments using this design may be a control condition, which serves the same purpose as the control condition in an independent groups design, i.e. to provide a baseline against which responses from any experimental condition can be compared.

❖ Activity 7 ❖

Look back at the advantages and disadvantages of an independent groups design. Bearing in mind these strengths and weaknesses, what do you think are the advantages and disadvantages of the repeated measures design?

The key advantage of a repeated measures design is that individual differences between participants are removed as a potential confounding variable (you may recall that this was a major drawback of the independent groups design). Also, the repeated measures design requires fewer participants, since data for all conditions derive from the same group of participants.

This design also has its disadvantages. The range of potential uses is smaller than for the independent groups design. For example, it simply is not possible to use two different reading schemes to teach young children to read within the same group of children. Only an independent groups design could be employed. There is a potential disadvantage resulting from order effects which may result when participants take part in more than one experimental condition. You may remember that order effects can confound experimental results in two ways, either negatively through the effects of fatigue or boredom, or positively through the effects of learning or practice.

There are, however, ways in which the potential risks of order effects on results can be minimized. These are known as counter-balancing and randomization and are discussed later in this chapter.

Finally, before leaving the repeated measures design, it is worth pointing out that it is possible to combine an independent groups and a repeated measures design. Such mixed designs are in frequent usage.

For example, children from two different age groups might be given two different cognitive tasks. The independent element of the design would involve a comparison of the two age groups, and the repeated measures element would be a comparison of performance on the two cognitive tasks.

Matched participants design

A matched participants design (or matched subjects/pairs design) aims to gain the key advantages of both an independent groups design (no problems with order effects), and a repeated measures design (a greatly reduced risk of problems resulting from individual differences). It involves matching each participant in one of the experimental conditions as closely as possible with another participant in the second condition on variables which are considered to be relevant to the experiment in question. For example, pairs of participants might be matched for age, gender and their scores from intelligence or personality tests. Once pairs of participants have been identified, members of each pair should be randomly allocated to the conditions (see Fig. 29.6). The assumption made is that members of each pairing are so similar on the relevant variables that they can, for research purposes at least, be treated as if they are the same person. At the same time, however, participants perform in one condition of the experiment only.

Although this design combines the key benefits of both an independent groups and a repeated measures design, achieving matched pairs of participants is a difficult and time-consuming task which may be too costly to undertake. Successful use of a matched participants design is heavily dependent on the use of reliable and valid procedures for pre-testing participants to obtain the matched pairs. Complete matching of participants on all variables which might affect experimental performance can rarely be achieved. Even if an acceptable level of matching can be achieved, difficulties can arise – in particular the extensive pre-testing needed to identify suitable participants for potential matches. As a result of this difficulty, a matched participants design is relatively uncommon, with its use being restricted to specific situations where a matching process is highly desirable for experimental success to be achieved.

Minimizing the effects of situational variables

Situational variables are those aspects of the research setting which might influence the performance of participants. They include aspects of the task being undertaken, the physical environment in which the research takes place, and personal factors affecting the participants, such as their levels of tiredness. These situational variables are important factors for the investigator to take into account and minimize wherever possible, if the conclusions obtained from research are to be meaningful and not result from unwanted factors. Three major ways of reducing the effects of situational variables will now be discussed: standardization, counterbalancing and randomization.

Standardization

The function of standardization is to help ensure accuracy of measurement. The term has more than one meaning in psychology. One sense of the term refers to the standardization of the administrative procedures for a specific investigation. For example, the instructions given to participants in any investigation need to be identical in order to eliminate discrepancies in them as a potential variable that might influence the results. Likewise, the procedures used for all participants should be identical, as should the scoring techniques. It is also important to ensure that any equipment used is properly calibrated.

A second sense of the term refers to the establishment of a set of standards (norms) for a particular test. For example, scores obtained from psychometric tests such as IQ tests are compared against the norms obtained from particular target populations used to establish or construct the scale (see Chapters 18 and 26).

Counterbalancing

Counterbalancing provides a possible solution to the problem posed by order effects which may occur when a participant in an investigation performs in more than one condition (such as in an experiment using a repeated measures design). The concept is simple, and involves equal numbers of participants undertaking the tasks required of them in different orders. Figure 29.7 shows two examples of how this might take place, with participants performing the conditions alternately until all participants have been tested.

Notice from Fig. 29.7 that there needs to be an even number of participants if counterbalancing is to be implemented fully. In the first example, a multiple of two participants would be required and in the second a multiple of six, reflecting in each case the number of possible task orders.

Occasionally, however, it is not possible to apply counterbalancing as a strategy for minimizing order effects. Problems can occur when order effects impinge on one condition more than another. This can take place, for example, when performing one condition helps the performance of another more than the other way round.

Consider the following memory experiment:

- *Condition A:* Learning a set of words presented randomly.
- *Condition B:* Learning a matched set of words using a mnemonic technique to assist memory.

There may be no problem when participants undertake condition A first, followed by condition B. However, when condition A is presented after condition B, it is likely that participants still have the mnemonic technique fresh in their minds. As a result, condition B might help performance on condition A more than A helps B, which is likely to lead to confounding of the results. In such circumstances, counterbalancing would be inappropriate and a researcher would be advised to use an independent groups design.

Figure 29.7 Examples of how counterbalancing might take place in two and three condition experiments

Counterbalancing in a two condition experiment

Participant no.	*First condition undertaken*	*Second condition undertaken*
1	A	B
2	B	A
3	A	B
4	B	A ... and so on.

Counterbalancing in a three condition experiment

Participant no.	*First condition undertaken*	*Second condition undertaken*	*Third condition undertaken*
1	A	B	C
2	B	C	A
3	C	A	B
4	A	C	B
5	B	A	C
6	C	B	A ... and so on.

Randomization

Randomization provides an alternative strategy to counterbalancing for dealing with the potential problems resulting from order effects. Randomization decides the order of presentation of experimental conditions by adopting a random strategy such as drawing lots or tossing a coin. This procedure does not, however, guarantee that presentation order of conditions will not influence results, because it is still possible, through chance, that differences remain in the numbers of participants experiencing the conditions in particular orders.

Randomization can also be used as a technique for deciding the order of presentation of, for example, individual stimuli within experimental conditions. It works best when there are a large number of items within each condition. For example, suppose an investigation involves each participant rating 20 photographs for their attractiveness. If the same presentation order is followed by all participants then some biases in rating may occur (for example, the picture presented first is likely to be given an average rating by many participants, simply because they are rating this picture conservatively as they feel they may wish to use more extreme ratings for subsequent pictures).

Establishing reliability

The term reliability means dependability or consistency, which are vital attributes if the psychologist is to obtain meaningful data. The term can be applied in a general way to the findings from psychological research. If the findings are replicated consistently then the outcome can be said to be reliable. The term is used also in specific contexts. Establishing reliability often involves the use of correlational analysis (discussed in Chapter 30) in an attempt to assess the consistency of observer ratings or psychological measuring instruments such as psychometric tests. There are several ways in which reliability can be established, and we will now move on to consider some of these.

Establishing observer reliability

Observer reliability is concerned with the extent to which researchers, scoring the same participants, achieve consistency of measurement between each other. Scorers record their own data individually and then the sets of data obtained from each scorer are correlated. Scorer reliability is achieved if highly significant positive correlations are obtained between the scorers. Inter-rater reliability is a form of observer reliability which has already been discussed in the paragraph on 'establishing inter-rater reliability' earlier in this chapter.

Establishing test reliability

The *split half method* can be used to measure the extent to which individual items in a particular test or questionnaire are consistent with other items in the same test. The method involves splitting the test concerned into two parts after data have been obtained from the participants. This splitting might be done, for example:

- by comparing the results obtained from odd and even numbered questions
- by comparing the results from the first half of the test with those from the second half
- by splitting the test into two at random.

The two sets of responses (however they are obtained) are then correlated, and a highly significant positive correlation would indicate reliability.

The *test-retest method* is used to establish another important aspect of consistency: the stability of a test or questionnaire over time.

This method involves presenting the same participants with the same test or questionnaire on different occasions, with no feedback given after the first presentation. The time interval between presentations needs to be selected carefully. If it is too short, participants may remember their previous answers, but on the other hand if it is too long, then it is possible that the participants may have changed in some way relevant to the test or questionnaire over the intervening time period. Again, correlational techniques will indicate test stability if a highly significant positive correlation is obtained between the scores obtained from the test and retest phases.

Establishing validity

Validity is concerned with the extent to which something measures what it sets out to measure. This is not as simple as it first appears. For example, there is considerable debate over issues such as whether personality tests are valid measures of personality, or whether diagnostic classification schemes used in the mental health field such as ICD or DSM really are valid (see Chapter 10). There are several different techniques which are available to help the psychologist establish validity.

Face validity is the simplest and most subjective of these, and is concerned with assessing whether a measuring instrument looks correct in the eyes of independent experts. Due to its subjectivity, assessment of face validity usually only takes place in the earliest phases of constructing a measuring instrument.

Content validity is a procedure which is superficially similar to face validity. Again, independent experts are asked to estimate the validity of the measuring instrument concerned. This time, however, the procedures are more rigorous, and there is a detailed and systematic examination of all the component parts of the measuring instrument concerned.

Concurrent validity involves obtaining two sets of scores at the same time, one from the new procedure with unknown validity, and the other from an alternative procedure or experiment for which validity has already been established. The scores obtained from both of these measures will then be correlated with each other. If a highly significant positive correlation is obtained, this would suggest that the procedure of interest is valid. For example, a new diagnostic procedure for the diagnosis of a psychopathological condition might be compared with an existing method of diagnosis for which the success rate is already known.

Predictive validity involves a similar strategy to that used to establish concurrent validity. However, this time the two sets of data are obtained at different points in time.

This method might also be used in abnormal psychology where initial diagnoses may be correlated with information gained in the light of experience with the patients concerned over a period of time.

Construct validity involves a more complex procedure, concerned with the validation of hypothetical constructs which cannot be directly observed, for example, extroversion. It is important that this validation occurs, because if this does not take place, the construct concerned will remain purely hypothetical. When establishing construct validity, it is assumed that the constructs concerned are derived from a sound theoretical base, but this can be difficult to establish. One method which researchers have used to help them establish construct validity is factor analysis. This is the name given to a series of statistical procedures which are used to determine the smallest number of factors (dimensions) that can explain any correlations between participants and responses obtained on a large number of different tests. Readers wishing to know more about construct validity are referred to the discussion in Coolican (1994).

Chapter summary

- Psychologists must define precisely all the variables which they are investigating to ensure that they are clearly operationalized.
- Hypotheses are testable statements. A null hypothesis predicts that the results obtained from an investigation are due to chance alone. An alternative hypothesis attributes results to some factor other than chance, such as the independent variable.
- Different sampling techniques can be used to select participants for research investigations. These include random, stratified, quota, systematic, self-selected and opportunity samples.
- Implementing non-experimental research can involve the use of a range of different methods. A number of decisions need to be taken concerning participant sampling, data recording and the establishment of reliability.
- There are several experimental designs available to the researcher, including independent groups, repeated measures and matched participants designs.
- The effects of situational variables may be reduced through the processes of standardization, counterbalancing and randomization.
- Reliability refers to the consistency of a test or procedure. It is important to establish reliability when undertaking research. One aspect of reliability involves assessing the consistency of measurement between different observers. Another involves achieving consistent measuring instruments when developing tests.
- The validity of measuring instruments can be established by investigating the extent to which they measure what they set out to measure. There are several different techniques available to establish validity.

Exam questions

1 Two researchers carried out an experimental study to investigate whether there is a difference in reaction times to an auditory or a visual signal. An opportunity sample of forty participants was used in a repeated measures design. In condition A, participants were asked to press a computer key when a symbol appeared on a computer screen. In condition B, they were asked to press the key when a command word was relayed through headphones. The response times were recorded. Participants undertook ten trials in each condition, and order of trial presentation was randomized.

(a) What is the alternative hypothesis that the two researchers are investigating and is it directional or non-directional? *(2 marks)*

(b) Suggest an appropriate null hypothesis for this investigation. *(2 marks)*

(c) What is meant by the term 'opportunity sample' and how might an opportunity sample be generated? *(3 marks)*

(d) Name one alternative sampling method to an opportunity sample that would be suitable for this investigation and describe how this sample might be selected. *(3 marks)*

(e) Explain one advantage and one disadvantage of using a repeated measures design in this experiment. *(4 marks)*

(f) What is meant by the phrase 'order of trial presentation was randomized'. *(2 marks)*

2 (a) Distinguish between the split half method of establishing reliability and the test-retest method.

(4 marks)

(b) Distinguish between concurrent validity and predictive validity.

(4 marks)

Further reading

Banister, P., Burman, E., Parker, I., Taylor, M. and Tindall, C. (1994) *Qualitative Methods in Psychology: A Research Guide*, Buckingham: Open University Press.

An advanced text which covers observations and interviews.

Foster, J.J. and Parker, I. (1995) *Carrying out Investigations in Psychology: Methods and Statistics*, Leicester: BPS Books.

A detailed and advanced text which is of use for reference purposes.

Coolican, H. (1994) *Research Methods and Statistics in Psychology*, London: Hodder & Stoughton.

A clearly written text which covers the research methods included in the AEB syllabus.

Coolican, H. (1995) *Introduction to Research Methods and Statistics in Psychology*, London: Hodder & Stoughton.

A condensed version of the Coolican (1994) text.

Dyer, C. (1995) *Beginning Research in Psychology: A Practical Guide to Research Methods and Statistics*: Oxford, Blackwell.

A detailed text with useful sections on non-experimental methods.

Appendix 1: Random number table

Instructions for using a random number table to allocate participants to experimental conditions:

Allocate numbers, with the same number of digits, to all potential participants. For example, you might allocate participants with the numbers 01 to 50. Start at any point in the table below and move in any direction. As you reach numbers between 01 and 50 allocate them in turn to each condition. For example, if undertaking a two-condition experiment and starting at the top right hand corner of the random number table and moving down, the first number reached is 17, so participant 17 would be allocated to condition A. Next would come participant 46, who would be allocated to condition B and so on until all participants have been allocated.

36	45	88	31	28	73	59	43	46	32	00	32	67	15	32	49	54	55	75	17
90	51	40	66	18	46	95	54	65	89	16	80	95	33	15	88	18	60	56	46
93	41	90	22	48	37	80	31	91	39	33	80	40	82	38	26	20	39	71	82
55	25	71	27	14	68	64	04	99	24	82	30	73	43	92	68	18	99	47	54
02	99	10	75	77	21	88	55	79	97	70	32	59	87	75	35	18	34	62	53
79	85	55	66	63	84	08	63	04	00	18	34	53	94	58	01	55	05	90	99
33	53	95	28	06	81	34	95	13	93	37	16	95	06	15	91	89	99	37	16
74	75	13	13	22	16	37	76	15	57	42	38	96	23	90	24	58	26	71	46
05	66	30	43	00	66	32	60	36	60	46	05	17	31	66	80	91	01	62	35
92	83	31	60	87	30	76	83	17	85	31	48	13	23	17	32	68	14	84	96
61	21	31	49	98	29	77	70	72	11	35	23	69	47	14	27	14	74	52	35
27	82	01	01	74	41	38	77	53	68	53	26	55	16	35	66	31	87	82	09
61	05	50	10	94	85	86	32	10	72	95	67	88	21	72	09	48	73	03	97
11	57	85	67	94	91	49	48	35	49	39	41	80	17	54	45	23	66	82	60
15	16	08	90	92	86	13	32	26	01	20	02	72	45	94	74	97	19	99	46
22	09	29	66	15	44	76	74	94	92	48	13	75	85	81	28	95	41	36	30
69	13	53	55	35	87	43	23	83	32	79	40	92	20	83	76	82	61	24	20
08	29	79	37	00	33	35	34	86	55	10	91	18	86	43	50	67	79	33	58
37	29	99	85	55	63	32	66	71	98	85	20	31	93	63	91	77	21	99	62
65	11	14	04	88	86	28	92	04	03	42	99	87	08	20	55	30	53	82	24
66	22	81	58	30	80	21	10	15	53	26	90	33	77	51	19	17	49	27	14
37	21	77	13	69	31	20	22	67	13	46	29	75	32	69	79	37	23	32	43
51	43	09	72	68	38	05	77	14	62	89	07	37	89	25	30	92	09	06	92
31	59	37	83	92	55	15	31	21	24	03	93	55	97	84	61	96	85	45	51
79	05	43	69	52	93	00	77	44	82	91	65	11	71	25	37	89	13	63	87

Chapter 30

Data analysis

Graham Davies

Preview

In this chapter we shall be looking at:

- interpretation of the results of research investigations, including:
  - content analysis
  - data from case studies
  - data from interviews
  - observational studies
- descriptive statistical techniques, including:
  - measures of central tendency
  - measures of dispersion
- the use and interpretation of graphs and charts
- inferential statistical tests, including tests of difference, correlation and association.

Introduction

This chapter will look at some of the ways in which psychologists analyse their data and some of the issues which arise from this analysis. You may recall from Chapter 28 that the data derived from psychological investigations can be of different types. *Quantitative data* are measured on a numerical basis – for example, something is categorized, placed in rank order or measured in units of measurement. On the other hand, *qualitative data* do not have numbers attached to them, but consist of descriptions of what took place, e.g. transcripts of any conversations. It is possible that such data may subsequently be quantified, although it is their very qualitative nature that may help to provide insights that would not be apparent with a quantitative approach. To a certain extent, whether quantitative or qualitative data are obtained depends on the standpoint of the person conducting the research – an issue which has already been discussed in Chapter 28. It also depends on the aims of the research and the topic under investigation.

In considering the different ways in which psychologists analyse their data, this chapter will examine the quantitative methods widely used within psychology. It will also look briefly at the interpretation of qualitative data. Further key issues in data analysis – those associated with the reliability and validity of research – have already been discussed in Chapter 29.

Interpreting results

This section looks at ways of interpreting results from the following:

- content analysis
- case studies
- interviews
- observational studies.

Content analysis

Content analysis is a general term which covers a wide range of techniques used in the analysis of documents, messages or verbal discourse. Many would regard it as a research method in its own right. Content analyses often employ counting how frequently the particular item of interest occurs – for example, the frequency of particular words, phrases or gender-specific behaviours. This may involve the coding of behaviours or items in an attempt to provide an objective, systematic and descriptive record of events, to ensure a methodology which is replicable.

Content analysis can often be regarded as an observational technique which examines behaviour indirectly, e.g. through the analysis of published statistics, documentation or the media. Some of the very wide range of sources which have been investigated using content analyses include:

- literature, including books and magazines
- speeches, including looking at differences in their structure
- propaganda in wartime
- health records (e.g. the use of medical records to find the incidence of schizophrenia in particular families)
- TV programmes, e.g. the research on gender-role portrayal (Manstead and McCulloch 1981) and the analysis over a two-week period in 1990 of more than 500 prime-time advertisements (Cumberbatch 1990)
- toy catalogues.

Content analysis has its advantages as a technique. The technique can be regarded as valid because it is based on materials derived from real-world settings. Another important advantage is that an analysis of what is actually present may serve to point out what is absent. For example, content analysis might reveal the lack of representation of a particular group of people, items, themes or characteristics.

Despite its advantages content analysis also has important limitations. First, it may be difficult to avoid subjectivity in the scoring of behaviours. For example, there may be a problem in defining precisely what constitutes an aggressive act in research on aggression, or in research which requires the interpretation of graffiti. Second, because people are not observed directly and content analysis is based on the communications they have produced, their record may include evidence of bias and/or demand characteristics, e.g. research which involves asking children about bad behaviour at school, or asking adolescents about their attitudes to drugs.

❖ Activity 1 ❖

Spend a few moments considering how you might carry out content analysis of the number of aggressive acts in children's television programmes. How would you define an 'aggressive act'?

A problem such as this can be lessened by *operationally defining* behaviours, that is, by clearly defining them so that all involved in the investigation fully understand. Also, using more than one judge may improve reliability (an issue which is discussed in Chapter 29).

Another potential problem is that the motive for a particular behaviour may not be known or may be ignored. Also, in some research at least, content analysis fails to take account of the inter-relationships between events, resulting in an incomplete analysis of behaviour. The techniques employed do, however, often produce quantitative data that can be analysed using inferential statistics. (These are discussed later in this chapter.)

Interpreting data from case studies

Case studies have already been discussed in Chapter 28, and one of their features discussed in that chapter was their diversity. This, together with their frequent reliance on a single individual as their source of information, means that their interpretation can be a highly complex task. Case studies may contain many elements which need to be taken into account when interpretation takes place. These include description of features of interest, such as:

- the actual behaviour observed by the researcher
- the context(s) in which the behaviour occurs
- self-reports of behaviour by the participants in the case study
- self-reports of cognitions which cannot be observed directly, for example, the feelings, thoughts and attitudes of the participants in the study
- interpretations made by the researchers
- implications of the study for any theory.

From this list it can be seen that distinctions need to be made between these aspects of a report that:

- describe what actually happened
- are based on the interpretations and inferences made by the researcher
- are based on the interpretations and inferences of the participant(s).

If reporting is to be objective, the distinctions between these need to be made clear to the reader when a report of a case study is published. Inevitably, the potential for bias in reporting is considerable. For example, researchers might report only those aspects of behaviour which support their own theoretical standpoint, or are particularly relevant to their research.

The selection of participants for case-study research may be highly subjective. Also, decisions about what information to include and what to leave out may be subjective and highly dependent on who makes the decision. Carefully reported case studies will always make clear to the reader the criteria used to select participants and how decisions were made about what information to present.

The close, and often prolonged, relationship between the researcher and the participant(s) in case-study research may heighten the importance of interpersonal interaction. This interaction may be very productive or it may reduce objectivity.

Since no two case studies are the same, replication is not possible and reliability cannot, therefore, be established. Whilst the detail generated by case-study research may add to our existing understanding, it can also produce evidence that challenges theory or our existing understanding, thereby stimulating further research and, perhaps, a new theoretical perspective. For example, some of the work on amnesia has been done using case studies (see Chapter 15 for further details).

❖ Activity 2 ❖

Try to find a detailed report of a case study in your library. There are good examples in the texts by Gross (1994) and Banyard and Grayson (1996) – see the reading list at the end of this chapter. To what extent does the reporting of the case study make clear what is based on observation and what is based on inference? What implications does this have for how the case study should be interpreted?

Interpreting data from interviews

The use of interviews as a research method has already been discussed in Chapter 28. Interviews are often one of the techniques employed by the researcher who is gaining information for a case-study report, so much of what has been written in the previous section on interpreting data from case studies applies to interpreting interviews. They may also be used in association with other research methods, forming just one of the methods used in a particular piece of research. As such they may help to provide a validity check on the results obtained. Interpreting the information gained from interviews is a complex procedure.

The data obtained from interviews may be qualitative or quantitative in nature. The nature of the data obtained often reflects the extent to which the interview was structured or unstructured (see Chapter 28). Quantitative data are numerical data and may be interpreted using descriptive and inferential statistical techniques such as those discussed later in this chapter. Where data are qualitative (non-numerical), the researcher is able to present results more flexibly, but the problem exists of how to organize and present a mass of descriptive data in a meaningful way. Some of the issues the researcher might consider are listed below.

- Examine carefully the background theory for a study involving interviews before the research is undertaken and decide how the data can be categorized appropriately.
- Solicit opinions from the interviewees on how they would wish the material to be presented. Has material been presented in the spirit in which it has been told?
- Decide how any selection or paraphrasing of material is going to be undertaken. Particular care needs to be taken with this if bias in reporting is to be avoided.
- Decide whether quotations will be used to enrich the presentation of data. If so, how will they be selected?

Categorization of qualitative data is an important task for the person reporting an interview. It involves the grouping of like items together, e.g. statements by the interviewee concerning particular subjects. A good computer database can be an advantage here.

❖ Activity 3 ❖

Consider a series of interviews carried out to investigate patients' experiences in hospital. What categories might be used to group data when presenting results?

The interpretation of interview data is, perhaps inevitably because of their nature, partial or incomplete. Something may be lost in terms of reliability and something gained through the sensitivity and depth of the approach. They may have the important benefit of providing a new basis for interpretation. See, for example, the *In Focus* (on the following page) which provides interesting insights on the Bristol riots of the early 1980s derived from interviews.

Interpreting observational studies

Observational studies differ widely both in terms of the approach used and the ways in which behaviour is recorded and classified, so it is unsurprising that they also differ widely in terms of how behaviour is analysed and presented. Interpretation may also aim to produce ideas for hypotheses which can be tested using other research methods. The use of naturalistic observational techniques has already been discussed in Chapter 28.

As with interviews, observational techniques can produce either qualitative or quantitative data (or indeed a mixture of both). When quantitative data are presented, it is important that any categorization of observations is soundly based and is carried out carefully. Data derived from techniques such as time sampling and event sampling may be suitable for analysis using the

In Focus

Riots and representations: the Bristol riots of the 1980s (from Foster and Parker 1995)

Qualitative interviewing approaches can add a great deal to our understanding of social processes, and can illuminate events that appear, at first sight, to be incomprehensible. A series of street disturbances in Britain in the early 1980s, for example, raised the spectre of 'mob rule', and the idea that people who get together in crowds are overtaken by a 'group mind'. There is a close similarity here between the ways in which the popular tabloid press portrayed the disturbances and theories of the crowd in social psychology going back to the end of the last century. In both cases the perspective adopted is that of an 'outsider' who focuses attention on the crowd as a kind of mass irrational force. This is also an example, then, of how bad psychology can chime in with mistaken 'common sense'.

Journalists tend to see people in crowds, particularly when they attack the police, as if they were animals who have been stripped of the veneer of civilization that usually holds them in check. Social psychologists who have been influenced by the theories of the French writer Gustave LeBon have been just as negative. LeBon (1947, but first published in 1895) argued that the behaviour of people in crowds fell several rungs down the evolutionary ladder, to the level of 'beings belonging to inferior forms of evolution, women, savages, and children, for instance' (LeBon, 1947, p. 36). These ideas take on a quite nasty political flavour when they are used to describe 'riots' by black people in inner-city areas, and the task of the psychologist should be to look at how popular images work, and how people in the crowd understand their actions. Qualitative interviewing can move to an 'insider' perspective on these events, and so assist in this task.

One of the first 'riots' in the 1980s, in the St Paul's area of Bristol, was studied by Reicher (1984), a social psychologist whose training had been in the experimental tradition. Reicher was carrying out research on social identity at Bristol University when the April 1980 'riot' broke out, and he was able to interview participants. Their accounts did not correspond with either standard social psychological or journalistic images of people who had lost their minds, and the 'inside' story was of a community trying to defend itself against the police. One of the striking aspects of the insider accounts was that both black and white people who were in the crowd refused to accept the outsider claims that this was a racial disturbance. Private homes and shops within the community were left untouched, whereas the banks and the unemployment office were seen as legitimate targets. The stories collected in these qualitative interviews also corresponded with the descriptions of the damage given by the authorities. An examination of the accounts of outsiders and insiders by Reicher and Potter (1985) illustrated the ways in which traditional 'scientific' explanations of crowd behaviour fail to account for the insider perspective which, in the case of St Paul's, stressed the meaningfulness of crowd action, and the feelings of solidarity and emotional warmth that came with defence of the community.

descriptive and inferential statistical techniques discussed later in this chapter. Graphical techniques, depicting the frequency of occurrence of various behaviours are very commonly used.

Qualitative data may be presented in different ways, including diary descriptions and specimen descriptions of behaviour. An example of a diary description from an observational study is contained in the *In Focus* on the next page which illustrates the social rituals from which naming can arise.

Although ecological validity may be a strength of observational studies, the categorization of behaviours that takes place in them (and indeed in interview-based research) may challenge their validity. It might be asked whether the operational definitions used are the best ways of defining behaviours. For instance, are the definitions comprehensive enough or are they too comprehensive? It is important, therefore, that the structure of a study is fully justifiable in terms of its theoretical basis, and also sufficiently complete (i.e. it should include all the behaviours of interest). Other potential threats to validity are inadequate sampling (e.g. too few samples, or sampling undertaken at inappropriate times), mishandling or inadequate handling of the system used (e.g. through a pressure or lack of familiarity in a research situation). These challenges to validity serve to highlight the need for careful analysis and presentation of observational data if the benefits to be gained from the richness of the data gathered are not to be compromised.

Section summary

The data derived from case studies, interviews and observational studies can be analysed in a variety of ways, both qualitative and quantitative, reflecting the variety of possible individual research strategies. Content analysis permits the detailed analysis of documents, messages or verbal discourse. Case studies provide considerable detail on individuals or, sometimes, small groups of individuals. The use of interviews and observational techniques provides a richness of detail that may be absent when other research strategies are used.

In Focus

Diary description

Mary, aged 11 months: Mother takes Mary out of her high-chair and puts her on the potty. Her toys are all in a box on the table in front of her chair.

Mother (spontaneously): 'Do you want Teddy?'

Mary: 'aah'

Mother: 'Where is he?

Mary looks around and makes to get off her potty and go to the table, but Mother restrains her. Mary looks at the table and points.

Mother (going to table opposite and bringing down the box of toys): 'That's right, he's there, isn't he? Here he is. What does he say? What does Teddy say?'

Mary: 'aah'

Mother: 'Yes, he does, doesn't he?'

Mary: 'aah'

Mother pats Teddy.

Mary: 'aah'

Mary's attention moves to the box containing her other toys, which Mother has placed on the floor near her.

Mother: 'Oh, what can you see in there? Doggie? *(takes doggie out)* Let's see who else is in here. Who's that? Is it duckie? and what does the duck say?'

Mother squeaks the duck.

Mary: 'aah'

Mother: 'He doesn't! What does the duck say? What does he say?'

Mary: 'argh' *(reaching towards it)*

Mother: 'Yes, I know you want it. What does he say?

Mary: 'woraghagh'

Mother: 'He doesn't, he says *(she squeaks it concurrently)* "quack, quack, quack", doesn't he? "quack, quack, quack".'

Mary: 'gh, gh'

Mother: 'Yes, he does.'

Mary (looking at Teddy): 'aah'

Mother: 'And that's aah is it, that's aah Teddy.

Mary: 'aah'

Mother: 'And who's this, what does he say? What does doggie say? What does doggie say?'

No response from Mary. Mother squeaks duck.

Mary: 'gah'

Mother: 'quack!'

Mary: 'gah'

Mother: 'Ooh, aren't you clever.'

Source: Lock 1980, p. 110

Descriptive statistical techniques

Descriptive statistical techniques provide ways in which the researcher can obtain a summary description of sets of quantitative data. Two types of descriptive statistical techniques are measures of central tendency, which give average values, and measures of dispersion, which look at the spread of scores around the mean. Each of these techniques provides a single value which can help us to summarize a set of data which might otherwise be difficult to interpret. This potential benefit, however, is not without its cost. When any single value is obtained, the process of summation inevitably produces a loss of individual information.

Measures of central tendency and dispersion are also valuable to the psychologist in that they form the basis for analyses using inferential statistics, which are discussed later in the chapter.

This section also looks at some of the graphs and charts which can be used by psychologists to summarize and clarify their data.

Measures of central tendency

You are probably already familiar with measures of central tendency and refer to them as averages. A measure of central tendency provides a single value which is representative of a set of numbers by indicating the most typical value. Three measures of central tendency are discussed here:

- The *mode*, which is the most frequently occurring value.
- The *median*, which is the middle value of scores arranged in ascending or descending order.
- The *mean*, which is the arithmetic average.

Each of these has its own particular uses, and therefore advantages and disadvantages, for particular sets of data.

The mode

As previously mentioned, the *mode* is the value in any set of scores which occurs most frequently. For example, with the series of numbers:

2 4 6 7 7 7 10 12

The most frequently occurring number is 7, therefore the mode = 7.

Although the mode provides information on the most frequently occurring value, it has its limitations and is not widely used in psychological research. One reason for this is that when there are only a few scores representing each value, then even very small changes in the data can radically alter the mode. For example:

3 6 8 9 10 10 Mode = 10.
3 3 6 8 9 10 Mode = 3.

A further possible problem is that there may not be a single modal value. For example, take the series of numbers:

3 5 8 8 8 10 12 16 16 16 20

In this situation there are two modal values (8 and 16), known as the *bimodal values*. With cases such as this, the bimodal values may still provide a useful summary statistic. It is, of course, possible to have several modal values, in which case the distribution is referred to as *multimodal* and the value of the statistic becomes even more limited. For example:

2 2 4 7 7 8 8 10 11 11 13 13

Here, each of five values occurs twice.

The mode has an advantage in that it is a figure which actually does occur in a given sequence, which may not be true of other measures of central tendency. However, its disadvantage is that it tells us nothing about the other values in the distribution concerned.

The median

The *median* is the middle value of a set of numbers that has been placed in numerical order (i.e. in order from lowest to highest

Figure 30.1
Calculating the median

To calculate the median when there is an odd number of scores:

Scores placed in numerical order:

2 4 5 6 8 10 11.

Median = 6.

To calculate the median when there is an even number of scores:

Scores placed in numerical order:

2 4 5 6 8 10 11 13.

$$\text{Median} = \frac{6+8}{2}$$

Median = 7.

score, or highest to lowest). Therefore half of the scores in a given set of data will lie above the median, and half below it. When there is an even number of scores, however, there will be two middle values. In these circumstances, the median is calculated by adding the two central values together and dividing by two. Figure 30.1 provides an example of both situations.

When calculating the median you may find it helpful to cross out the lowest and highest values alternately until you are left with the middle value(s).

The main advantage of the median is that it remains relatively unaffected by any outlying values. It is therefore a safe measure of central tendency to use when we are unsure about the reliability of extreme values. Also, it can be used with data from skewed distributions (i.e. where there is a cluster of values at one end of the range, see *In Focus* on p. 666). Unlike the mean it can be used when data are on an ordinal level of measurement (see *In Focus* on p. 667) and we cannot be sure that our data are measured in fixed units with an equal distance between each point on the scale concerned.

The median, however, does not work well with small data sets and is affected by any alteration of the central values in a set of values. For example:

If we have two sets of data:

10 12 13 14 18 19 22 22 and
10 12 13 14 15 19 22 22.

The median would be 16 in the first case and 14.5 in the second, despite only one value being different in the two sets of data.

The mean

The *mean* is the arithmetic average of a set of data, and is probably the average with which you are most familiar already. It is calculated by adding all the values together and dividing the total by the number of scores. An example is shown in Fig. 30.2.

To find the mean of:

2 4 5 5 6 6 6 7 8 10.

Add all the values together:

2 + 4 + 5 + 5 + 6 + 6 + 6 + 7 + 8 + 10
= 59

Divide this sum by the number of scores (there are 10 scores).

$$\text{Mean} = \frac{59}{10}$$

Mean = 5. 9

Figure 30.2
Calculation of the mean

The main advantage of the mean is that it makes use of all the data that are available. As such, it is the most powerful of the measures of central tendency available. However, it needs to be used with a certain amount of caution.

One limitation of the mean is that when it has been calculated, decimal points may be less meaningful if all the data consist of whole numbers (as in the example in Fig. 30.2 above).

Also, the distribution of values needs to be taken into account. The mean can be used appropriately as the measure of central tendency with sets of data (such as normally distributed data – see *In Focus* on p. 666) which do not have extreme outlying values. When such extreme values are present the median should be used instead. For example: calculate the mean of 8, 10, 10, 12, 60. What does the mean tell us about any of these scores?

In Focus

◆

Normal and skewed distributions

A normal distribution curve is a bell-shaped curve which is symmetrical about its mean, median and mode (see diagram below). It is called normal

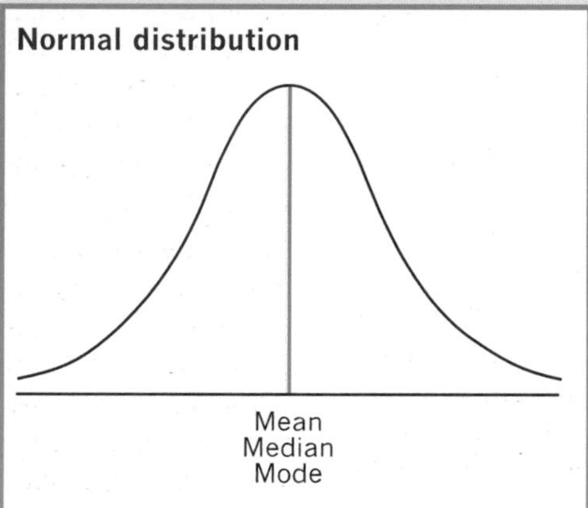

because it describes the theoretical distribution of a great many naturally occurring variables. Various characteristics of individuals are considered to be normally distributed (e.g. height and body weight) and sometimes a particular measure is deliberately constructed in a way that a normal distribution of scores results (e.g. some intelligence tests). In theory, a normal distribution curve should result when a large random sample of measurements is taken from an appropriate population. In practice, however, it would be very rare for a distribution to fit a normal distribution curve precisely – there are always likely to be at least some minor irregularities.

Notice the key features of this curve:

- The curve is symmetrical about its mean value which occurs at the central point of the distribution. (This value is also the median and mode.)
- The curve has a characteristic bell shape, curving downwards close to the mean and outwards further away.
- The outer extremities of the distribution (known as the tails) will never touch the *x*-axis.
- The properties of this distribution mean that certain statements about probability can be made – a very important feature when a researcher wishes to express clearly the relationship between sample data and data from the population which the sample represents.

However, all variables are not normally distributed – for example, some distributions can be best described as skewed (see below).

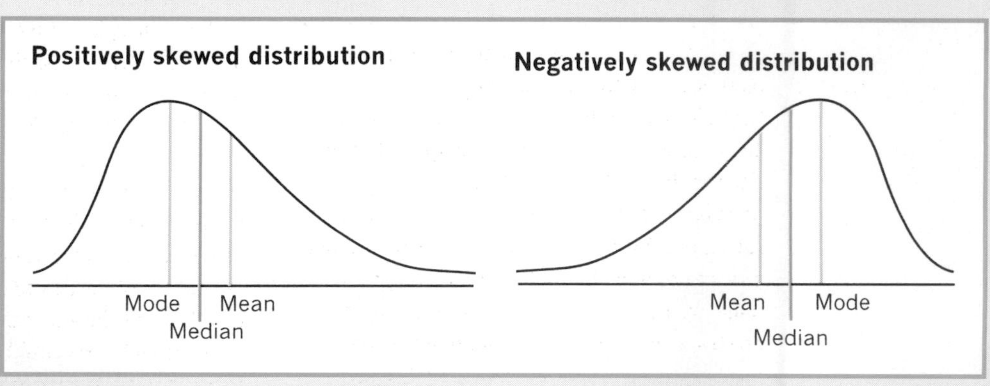

In Focus

Levels of measurement

The quantitative measurements that psychologists obtain from their research investigations can be made at different levels of measurement. These vary in terms of their precision and in how they can be used. The four most common levels of measurement will be discussed here.

The nominal level

Nominal level data provide the weakest level of measurement available to the psychologist, and are sometimes referred to as categorized or frequency count data. Data can be allocated into categories by counting frequency of occurrence within particular categories. An example might be the placing of research participants into categories based on their gender and the frequency with which they interpret a stimulus in different ways. For example:

	Interpretation A	*Interpretation B*
Female	25	15
Male	20	20

The ordinal level

Ordinal level data are capable of being placed into rank order (i.e. from highest value to lowest value or vice versa). This means the researcher can meaningfully compare scores with each other, although the extent of meaningful comparison is limited. It is possible to state that one value is higher than another, but it is not possible to assume more than this. For example, it is reasonable to assume that if children's helpfulness is rated on an eleven-point scale (with high numbers = high helpfulness) a child with a rating of 10 has been observed as being more helpful than a child with a rating of 5. However, it is unreasonable to conclude that the child with a rating of 10 is twice as helpful as the one with a rating of 5, as the points on such a rating scale are at intervals which are (or may be) arbitrary or unequal. It is impossible to tell precisely how much the points on the scale really differ, i.e. we cannot say that the difference between ratings of 1 and 2 and ratings of 9 and 10 are exactly equal. The most that we can achieve is the relative ranking of the children concerned.

Interval and ratio levels

The interval and ratio levels of measurement are more precise – they consist of data which are measured in fixed units with equal distances between all the points on the scale concerned. The key difference between interval and ratio scales lies in how zero values can be interpreted. Well-known examples of the interval level of measurement include temperature measured in degrees C or degrees F. In both of these cases 0 degrees is not meaningful because neither 0°C nor 0°F can be interpreted as a baseline for no temperature. Minus values are possible, and proportions are meaningless if calculated with zero as the baseline.

Ratio scales provide the strongest level of measurement of those discussed here, and on such scales zero really does provide a baseline which can be used for calculating proportions. Examples of data measured on ratio scales are distance in centimetres and time in seconds.

There is debate between statisticians about the interpretation of these levels of measurement. For example, some people treat numbers of words recalled in a memory task as interval data, whereas others treat such data as ordinal on the grounds that all words are not equally easy to recall. This raises the important point that data do not arrive with a label signifying the level of measurement attached to it – the researcher needs to decide the appropriate level at which data are to be treated.

For example, let us assume we have a series of times, such as the times taken for rats to run a particular maze (all times are in seconds):

20 28 29 30 30 31 34
40 42 44 46 47

These data consist of times – fixed units of measurement which we could treat, correctly, as being on a ratio scale. However, we could allocate rank orders to these scores, thereby treating our data as being on an ordinal scale. Alternatively, we could group the scores into categories such as 'number of rats running the maze in less than 40 seconds' and 'number of rats taking 40 seconds or more to run the maze'. In this case, we are now treating our data as nominal.

In this example, the mean is 20, which tells us very little about the four low scores and the single high score. In circumstances where such outliers occur it would be more appropriate to use the median (10), which at least would summarize the first four values reasonably successfully (coincidentally, 10 is also the mode in this example).

The mean can be used most successfully with data on interval or ratio levels of measurement. Caution needs to be used if the median is used with data on ordinal levels of measurement (levels of measurement are discussed in the *In Focus* on p. 667).

For example, consider the situation where a teacher rates pupils on a seven-point scale which measures how hard they have worked on their psychology coursework. Students are rated from 1 (very hard-working) to 7 (no effort). Given the arbitrary nature of the scale, we have no way of knowing for certain whether all those rated at 4 on this scale (average level of work) actually put in precisely the same amount of work, or whether all the points on the scale are at an equal distance apart.

❖ Activity 4 ❖

Examine sets of data in this textbook or from other sources and calculate their mode, median and mean. Try to work out which of these measures of central tendency would be most useful in each case.

Figure 30.3
The calculation of the variation ratio

To calculate the variation ratio of

2 3 6 6 6 7 7 8 8 10.

Mode = 6.

This value occurs three times in the ten scores.

Proportion of non-modal scores

$$= \frac{7}{10}$$

Therefore the variation ratio

= 70%

Therefore calculating the mean would be inappropriate. In a similar way it would be wholly inappropriate to work out a mean GCSE grade – these grades are measured on an ordinal level of measurement as some mark bands cover a wider range of marks than others.

Using a measure of central tendency is insufficient on its own to describe a set of data. Take, for example, the following scenario:

Data set A	*Data set B*
100	100
101	40
99	120
102	60
98	180
100	100

The mean for both sets of data is 100, yet the distribution of scores is very different in each case. In data set A the scores are all very close to 100 and in data set B they are dispersed much more widely.

Measures of dispersion

Measures of dispersion enable us to examine the variability within our data sets and help us to understand whether scores in a given set of data are similar to or very different from each other.

The variation ratio

The *variation ratio* is a measure of dispersion which complements the mode, and is simply the proportion of non-modal scores. An example is shown in Fig. 30.3 on the left.

The variation ratio is used infrequently in psychology for the same reasons that the mode is rarely used.

The range

The *range* is easy to calculate, being simply the difference between the highest and lowest scores in a given set of data, with one added if the scores are all whole numbers. A sample calculation is shown in Fig. 30.4 at the top of the next page.

Figure 30.4
Calculation of the range

> To calculate the range of:
>
> 3 7 8 10 11 16 18 21 22 26
>
> Find the difference between the highest score (26) and the lowest (3), and add one.
>
> Range = 26 – 3 + 1 = 24.

Similarly, if values are recorded to one decimal place then the range is the difference between the lowest and highest values with 0.1 added (to two decimal places, it is the difference plus 0.01, and so on), and if values are recorded to the nearest half unit, then the range has 0.5 added to the difference between the lowest and highest value.

The range has the advantage of being quick to calculate, but has some important limitations. It does not provide any idea of the distribution of values around the centre, nor does it take individual values into account (it is important to remember that the only values that are used when the range is calculated are the two most extreme values). Following on from this point, the range is seriously affected by any outlying values in a given set of data.

The interquartile range

In an attempt to overcome the potential effect of outlying values, calculating the *interquartile range* is often preferred. The interquartile range measures the spread of the middle 50 per cent of values when they are placed in numerical order. The top 25 per cent and the bottom 25 per cent of values are ignored, which has the effect of removing the influence of outlying values, and providing an indication of grouping around the central value. Figure 30.5 explains how this is achieved.

> Calculate the interquartile range for the following data:
>
> 2 3 7 8 10 11 16 18 21 22 26 26
>
> First of all, it is necessary to calculate the median:
>
> $$\text{The median} = \frac{11 + 16}{2}$$
>
> Median = 13.5.
>
> There are six scores above the median, and six below it. The interquartile range will therefore include the six scores which lie closest to the median, and exclude the remaining six. So, for the scores lying above the median, this means that 16, 18 and 21 will be included within the interquartile range, and 22, 26 and 26 excluded. The upper boundary of the interquartile range will therefore be the mean of the values immediately below it (21) and immediately above it (22), i.e. 21.5. Similarly, the lower boundary will be the mean of 7 and 8 (i.e. 7.5). The interquartile range is, therefore, the difference between 21.5 and 7.5 (i.e. 14).

Fig. 30.5
Calculation of the interquartile range

The standard deviation

The *standard deviation* is a measure of the variability (i.e. of the typical deviation) of a given sample of scores from its mean. Calculation, as with the mean, involves using all the scores in a given set of data, and this makes the standard deviation the most powerful of the measures of dispersion available to the researcher. Calculation involves working out the deviation of all the individual values in the sample concerned from the sample mean – in other words, we have to find the differences between each of these values and their mean.

The standard deviation can be calculated using the formulae in Fig. 30.6 (see next page). This is the first time in this book that we have encountered statistical formulae. If you don't like maths, please do not panic! The calculation is simple, and remember that you will not be asked to carry out any calculations of the standard deviation in the AEB examination. Most computer statistical packages will calculate standard deviation for you, as will most scientific calculators, so now is the time to learn how to use them!

The statistical symbols used in the formulae form part of a standard notation that will occur elsewhere, so it is worth the effort getting to know what these symbols mean.

Figure 30.6 Formulae used for calculating standard deviation

Formula 1: $S = \sqrt{\frac{\Sigma d^2}{N}}$

Formula 2: $s = \sqrt{\frac{\Sigma d^2}{N - 1}}$

where:

S or s = standard deviation (the statistic we are aiming to calculate)

√ = square root

Σ = sum of (ie add up)

d = the deviation of each value from the mean

N = the number of scores

Now for a few words on when to use the two different formulae. In order to explain this we need to refer to the concepts of population and sample – if you are not sure what these mean look back at Chapter 29.

- *Formula 1* is used for obtaining the standard deviation of values from a population where the whole population has been sampled. For example, when we are interested in, say, the data obtained from a psychology class and do not wish to say anything about any larger population.
- *Formula 2* is used for obtaining the standard deviation of values from a sample which constitutes part of a total population which you wish to say something about. This formula gives you an estimate of the standard deviation of the population – the difference between the two formulae allows for any sampling errors. It is most likely that you will need to use formula 2 since psychologists are most often interested in making inferences about a wider population,

A specimen calculation, using formula 2, is shown in Fig. 30.7 on the next page.

Notice that the formulae in Figure 30.6 involve squaring values – the function of this is to remove any minus signs (remember that when you multiply a minus by a minus the result is a plus). Later in the calculation a square root is calculated, which serves to restore the original units of measurement.

Interpreting standard deviation

The standard deviation allows us to make statements of probability about how likely (or how unlikely) a given value is to occur. This ability to make inferences is based on the relationship between standard deviation and a normal distribution curve. Therefore, the statistic is most informative as a measure of dispersion with data measured on interval or ratio levels of measurement which are approximately normally distributed. It becomes a less effective measure when there are outliers which skew the data distribution.

If you are unfamiliar with interval and ratio levels of measurement these are discussed in the *In Focus* on p. 667. Normal and skewed distributions are dealt with in the *In Focus* on p. 666.

The percentages of values which lie between the mean and a given number of standard deviations above and below the mean are fixed properties. These fixed properties are:

- 68.26% of all values lie within one standard deviation either side of the mean.
- 95.44% of all values lie within two standard deviations either side of the mean.
- 99.74% of all values lie within three standard deviations either side of the mean.

Figure 30.8 on p. 672 illustrates how this works with the data obtained from the example in Fig. 30.7. If you look again at Fig. 30.7, you can see that the calculated standard deviation was 10. As the mean value was 100, this means that 68.26% of values in the population can be inferred as lying between 90 (minus one standard deviation) and 110 (plus one standard deviation).

Figure 30.7 Calculation of the standard deviation (using formula 2)

Calculate the standard deviation of the following data:

85 86 94 95 96 107 108 108 109 112

These data could represent, for example, the psychology test scores of a sample of 10 students.

1 Calculate the mean of the data.

$$\text{Mean} = \frac{85 + 86 + 94 + 95 + 96 + 107 + 108 + 108 + 109 + 112}{10}$$

$$\text{Mean} = \frac{1000}{10}$$

$$\text{Mean} = 100$$

2 Place your data into the first column of a table organized as follows:

Psychology test scores	*d*	d^2
85	–15	225
86	–14	196
94	–6	36
95	–5	25
96	–4	16
107	7	49
108	8	64
108	8	64
109	9	81
112	12	144
		$\Sigma d^2 = 900$

3 Find the difference (d) between each of the values in the table and the mean (see d column in table above).

4 Square all the values of d (see d^2 column in table above).

5 Find the sum of all the values of d^2 (see Σd^2 above).

$\Sigma d^2 = 900$.

6 Substitute in the formula: $s = \sqrt{\frac{\Sigma d^2}{N - 1}}$

$$s = \sqrt{\frac{900}{10 - 1}} \qquad s = \sqrt{\frac{900}{9}}$$

$$s = \sqrt{100} \qquad s = 10$$

Knowing the standard deviation of a given sample of data also allows us to calculate a *standard score* (also known as a *z* score) which is the number of standard deviations a given value is away from its mean. Once a standard score is known, then it is possible to calculate the proportion of individuals between that standard score and the mean (see Appendix 1 at the end of this chapter for an explanation and example).

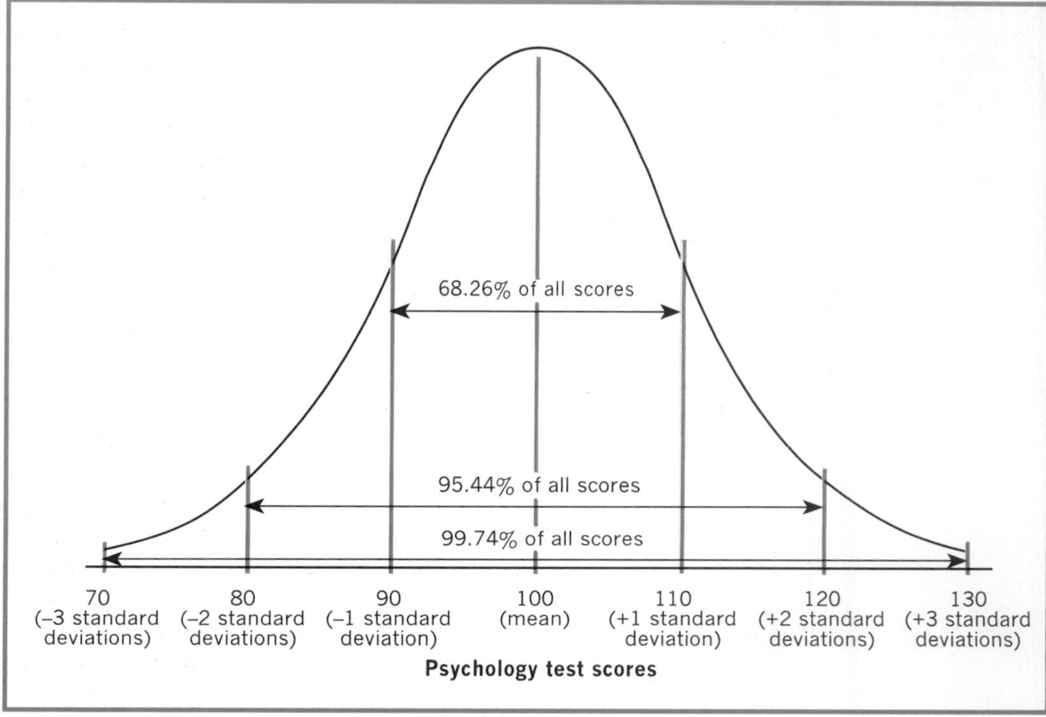

Figure 30.8
The percentage of scores which lie between a given number of standard deviations either side of the mean (using data derived from Fig. 30.7)

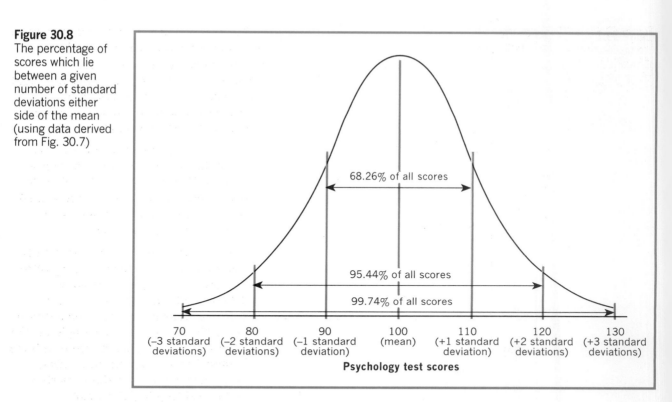

Using and interpreting graphs and charts

Graphs and charts act as visual aids which help us to make sense of the data obtained from psychological investigations. They aim to provide an overall picture which helps to summarize the results – when well constructed they can show us at a glance any patterns which occur in the data.

Be warned though that the careful manipulation of the way that the axes in graphs or charts are drawn can easily bias the interpretation. Before reading on, try the exercise in Activity 5 which illustrates the kind of visual deception that can occur.

❖ Activity 5 ❖

A psychology software publisher asks one of its sales representatives to present her sales figures for the last three years to the company's management. Her sales are:

1993	1,000 items,
1994	1,001 items and
1995	1,002 items (evidently a sales boom!).

The company is dissatisfied with the sales performance – the sales person is desperate to keep her job. Both parties decide to present the sales figures by means of a line graph, with the years 1993 to 1995 on the *x*-axis (horizontal) and number of items sold on the *y* (vertical) axis. The sales person draws a graph with 3 cm representing one year, the management opt for 8 cm = one year. The *y*-axis of the sales person's graph is 16 cm long and extends from 1,000 items sold to 1,002. However, the management draw their *y*-axis 10 cm long, and label it from 0 items sold to 10,000. Draw or sketch the two graphs and see the bias created.

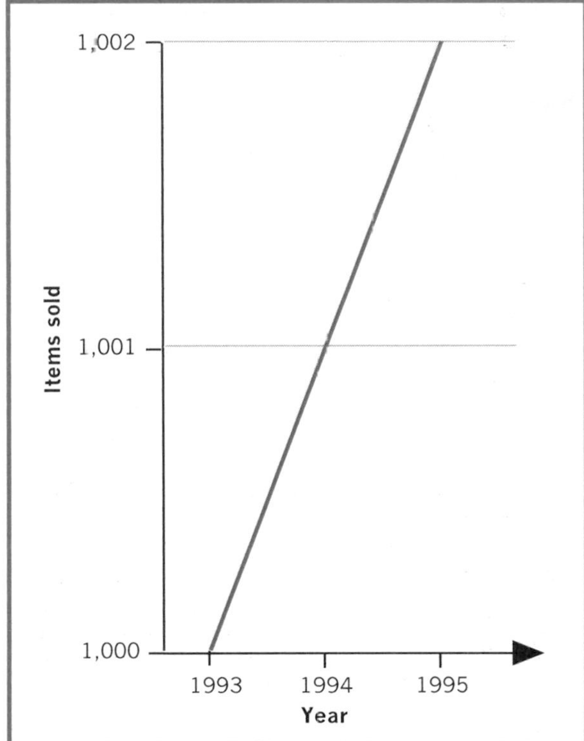

Figure 30.9 Graph produced by salesperson

The graphs will produce very different impressions, even though they are based on identical data (see Figures 30.9 and 30.10 respectively, which show the graphs at half size). Shortening or extending the axes in this way, or manipulating their labelling, can be used to convey a desired impression and may be highly misleading to the observer.

The moral of this exercise is that there is no single correct way to select the scales that are used on the axes of graphs. However, there are certain conventions that serve both to assist the drawer to present their information in an unbiased way and to reduce the risk of misunderstandings.

- Plot frequency of scores on the y-axis (as in the examples that you have just drawn). This is the conventional mode of presentation but is not a hard and fast rule – sometimes horizontal bars can provide a pleasing alternative.
- Adopt the three-quarter high rule. This states that when frequencies are plotted, the length of the y-axis should be determined in the following way. It should be organized so that the distance of the highest point on the graph (i.e. the point which represents the score with the highest frequency) from the x-axis is approximately equal to three-quarters of the total length of the x-axis.
- It is possible to break the x- or y-axis of a graph if labelling of the axis from zero would give a poor visual impression due to the large amount of empty space that would result.
- Remember that all graphs and charts need to have each axis clearly labelled and have an informative title.

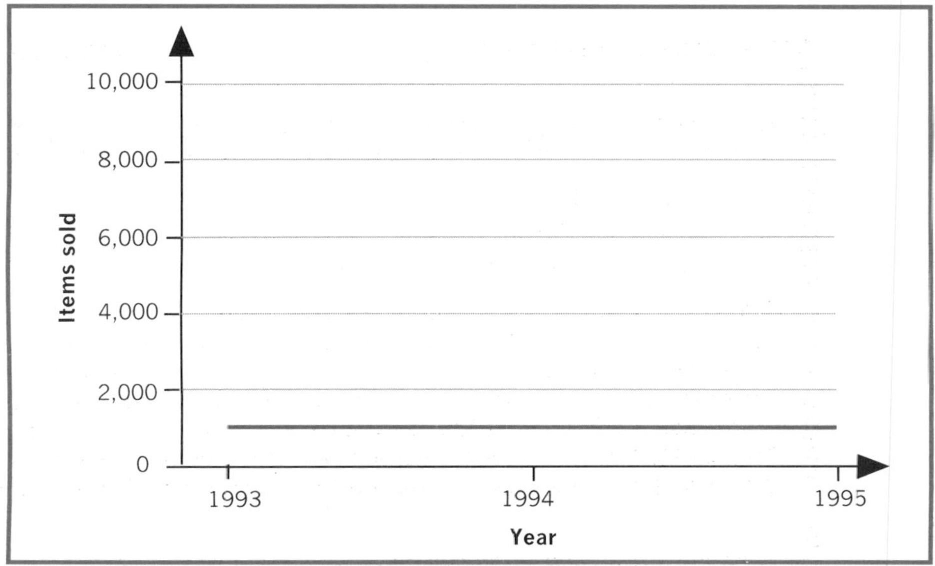

Figure 30.10 Graph produced by management

The ideal situation to aim for is that someone looking at a graph or chart should be able to understand what it is about without any additional explanation.

Histogram

Histograms and bar charts (which will be dealt with in the next section) are two of the most widely used graphical techniques. Simpler forms of these are discussed here, but it is worth remembering that alternative forms exist such as compound ones which show data from more than one condition simultaneously.

Histograms are a useful form of graphical representation which can be used when presenting data measured on interval or ratio levels (see *In Focus* on p. 667 if you need to remind yourself of these). A histogram consists of a series of vertical bars of equal width, which represent frequencies of the variable placed on the *x*-axis. The height of each bar represents the frequency of occurrence for each point on the scale or each category. A histogram is drawn with the bars representing the frequencies actually touching each other. An ideal number of bars to use is between six and eight. Sometimes, single values can be used for each bar, but if the scale used on the *x*-axis has a large number of points, then the data can be placed into class intervals. (This has been done in the example of a histogram shown in Fig. 30.11.)

Bar charts

A bar chart is superficially similar to a histogram, and consists of a series of vertical bars of equal width which can be used to illustrate the frequencies of a non-continuous variable on the *x*-axis. They are often used to depict data measured on nominal or ordinal levels of measurement or, for example, to illustrate the means from different samples. Unlike the histogram, it is usual to draw each bar separated from each of the others so that a continuous variable is not implied on the *x*-axis (see Fig. 30.12). When data are at a nominal level, bias should be avoided in the order in which the

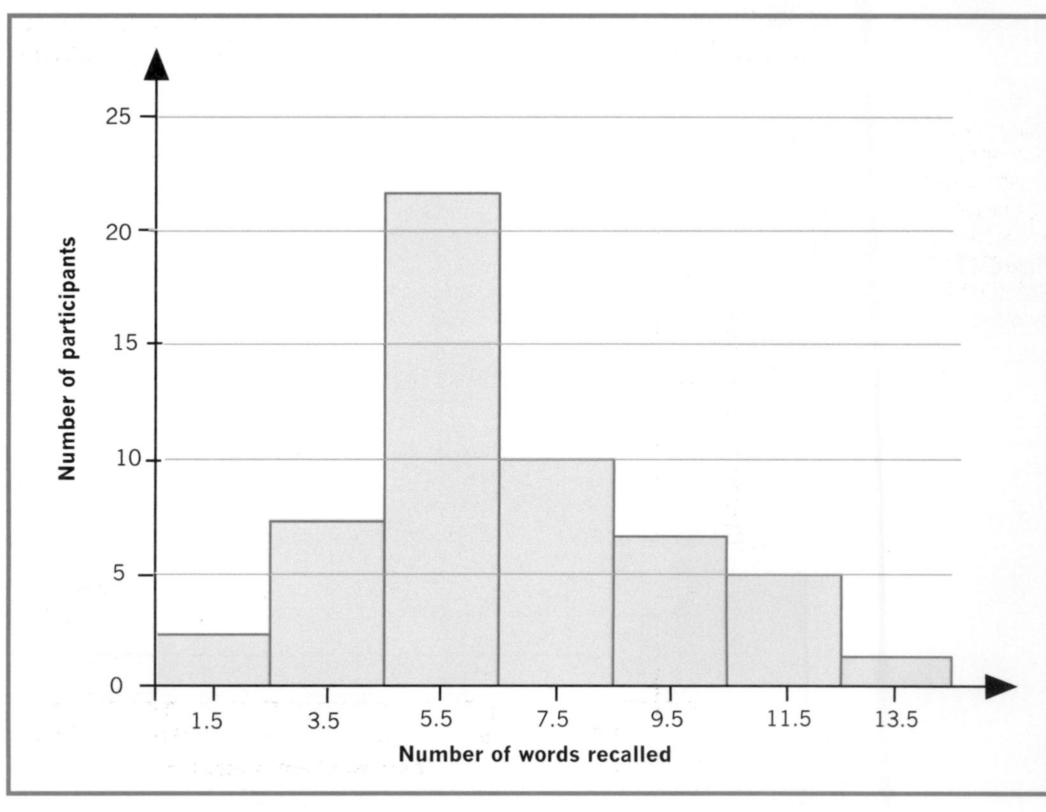

Figure 30.11 Histogram showing the number of words recalled in a memory experiment

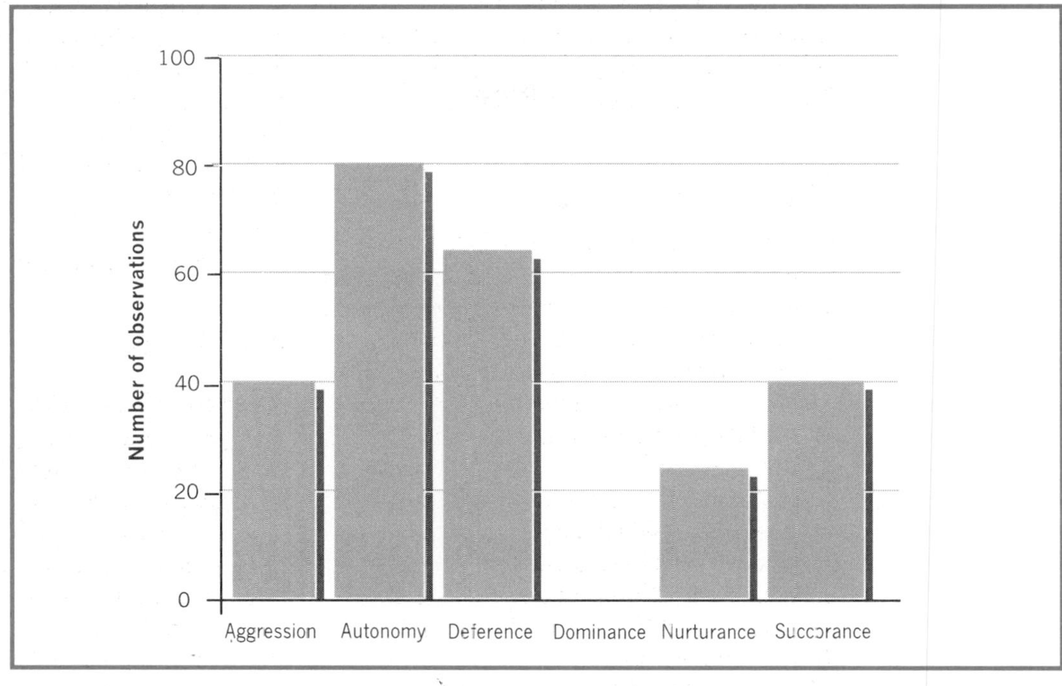

Figure 30.12 Bar chart showing the number of observations of different behaviours in a group of children

bars are presented, as these can logically be presented in any order. They are often presented in alphabetical order to avoid such bias. However, when data are treated at an ordinal level, the x-axis can be drawn using the order of the points on the scale concerned.

Frequency polygons

The frequency polygon is a particularly useful technique when it is desirable to compare two or more frequency distributions. It is used as an alternative to the histogram. Indeed a frequency polygon

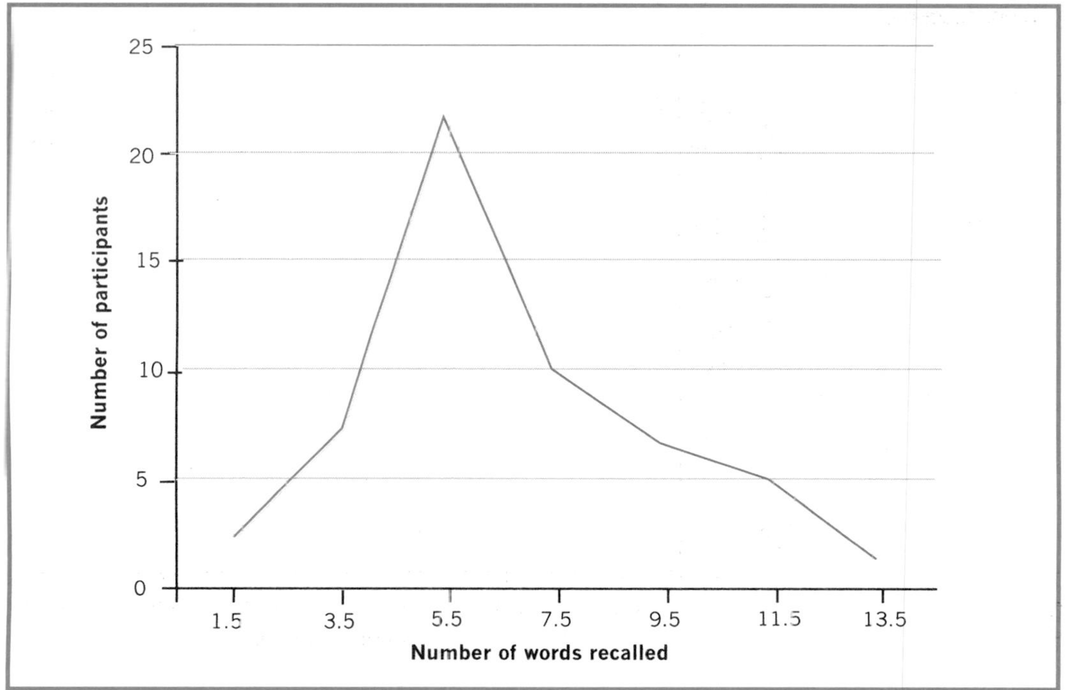

Figure 30.13 Frequency polygon showing the number of words recalled in a memory experiment

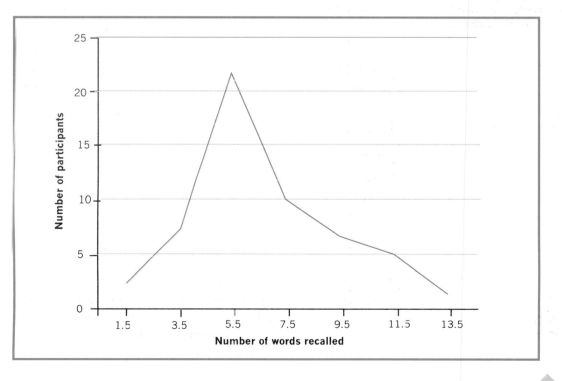

can be drawn by linking the midpoints from the top of each bar contained in a histogram, and this has been done in the example in Fig. 30.13. It may be the preferred technique when it is necessary to depict results from two or more conditions of an investigation at the same time.

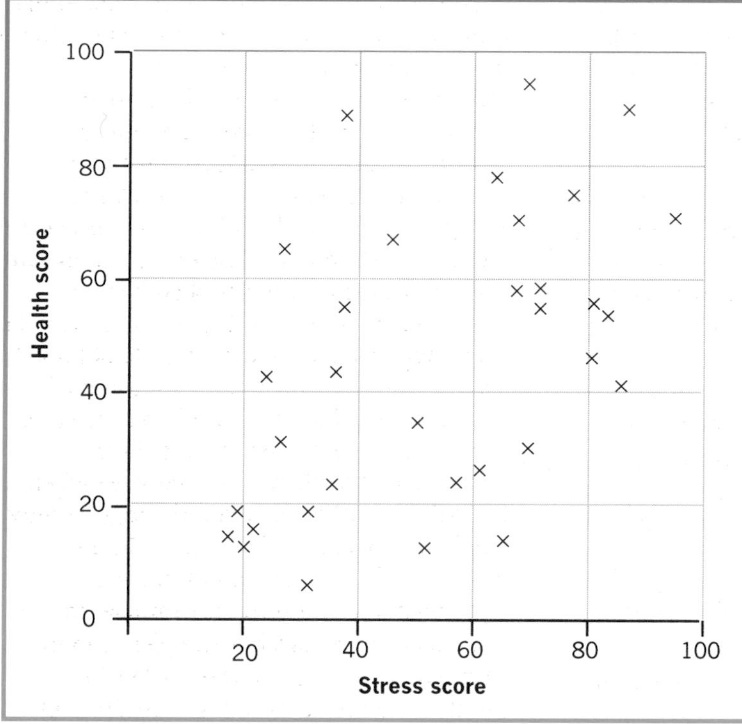

Figure 30.14 Scattergraph showing the relationship between scores derived from questionnaires measuring health and stress levels

Scattergraphs

A scattergraph (or scattergram) is a graphical technique which is used to illustrate sets of data that are being correlated with each other. Data from one of the variables being correlated are presented on the *x*-axis and data from the second variable on the *y*-axis (see Fig. 30.14).

Section summary

The use of descriptive statistical techniques helps psychologists to summarize quantitative data clearly. There are three principal measures of central tendency: the mean, the median and the mode, each of which provides an average figure to help summarize data and each with its own particular advantages and limitations.

Measures of dispersion permit the psychologist to describe the spread of a set of data by providing a single summary statistic. The most important of these measures are the range, and more particularly, the standard deviation. The calculation of the latter enables inferences to be made about probability.

Graphical techniques such as histograms, bar charts, frequency polygons and scattergraphs help the researcher to presents sets of data clearly.

Inferential statistics

Describing data in the ways outlined in the previous section are not the only statistical techniques available to the investigator. The use of inferential statistics enables a researcher to draw conclusions about the wider population from which a particular sample has been drawn. By using such inferential techniques, the researcher can, on the basis of data obtained from a particular sample, make statements of probability about the likelihood of obtaining a particular set of results by chance. Through such statements, reasoned conclusions can be reached by the researcher as to whether a null hypothesis can be retained or rejected, and following on from this, whether an alternative hypothesis may be accepted.

❖ Activity 6 ❖

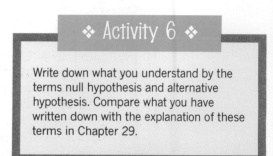

Write down what you understand by the terms null hypothesis and alternative hypothesis. Compare what you have written down with the explanation of these terms in Chapter 29.

Statistical significance

The concept of statistical significance is central to inferential statistics. A statistically significant result is one which is unlikely to have occurred through chance. In practice, we can never be 100 per cent certain that chance has not played a part. When, however, the likelihood of obtained results having occurred through chance is only slim, then researchers will prefer to reject their null hypothesis and accept their alternative hypothesis.

How do we know when to reject a null hypothesis and when to retain it? The answer to this question lies in the concept of level of significance, which can be defined as an arbitrary value used as a criterion for ascertaining whether a particular set of data differs from that which would be expected if only chance factors operate.

Significance levels may be written as percentages or in decimals. For example:

- The 5% level of significance is also written as $p = 0.05$ (where p = the probability of the results being due to chance).
- The 1% level of significance is also written as $p = 0.01$.

Be careful that you do not mix up the different ways of expressing levels of significance – a quite common error is for students to add a percentage symbol onto the end of a decimal version (e.g. $p = 0.05\%$ is a very different value to $p = 0.05$).
In practice, the normal way of expressing significance levels is to use the symbol ≤, which means less than or equal to. Thus, for example, the expression $p \leq 0.05$ refers to achieving a significance level of at least 5% – i.e. the probability of results such as these occurring through chance is no greater than 0.05 (or 5%).

As mentioned earlier, the choice of significance level is largely arbitrary. However, the 5% level of significance is regarded as being the minimum level which is acceptable for deciding results are significant. If the 5% level of significance is achieved (i.e. $p \leq 0.05$), this means that the likelihood of the results obtained having occurred through chance is one in 20 or less (i.e. such results are likely to occur 5% or less of the time). When this level of significance is used in experimental research, we are stating that any difference between sets of scores is so large that it is unlikely to have arisen due to chance. The researcher will conclude that the results are unlikely to have occurred because the null hypothesis is true and, provided some other unwanted variable has not intervened, that they are due to the effects of the independent variable. The alternative hypothesis can, therefore, be accepted.

The 5% level of significance is by no means the only one which is used. Less stringent levels (such as 10%) are occasionally employed, but it is sometimes important that more stringent levels of statistical significance are used – that is, we need to be even more certain that the results obtained are not due to chance. Can you think of situations in which this would be the case?

More stringent levels of statistical significance are likely to be required when a 5% risk of results occurring through chance would be unacceptable. Such a situation might be where harm might occur to participants as a result, for example, in some medical research. Examples of more stringent levels include the 1% level of significance (or $p \leq 0.01$), where the null hypothesis would only be rejected if the likelihood of the results obtained occurring through chance is 1% or less. Even more stringent levels are the 0.5% ($p \leq 0.005$) or 0.1% ($p \leq 0.001$).

Why has the 5% level of significance become the one which is conventionally used by psychologists? This significance level represents a reasonable balancing point between the chances of making a type one error and a type two error. A type one error is said to occur when a null hypothesis is rejected when in fact it is true, and the likelihood of making such an error is equal to the level of significance employed. For example, at $p \leq 0.05$ the risk of making a type one error is one in twenty or less. This type of error can occur when an insufficiently stringent significance level is adopted.

A type two error occurs when a null hypothesis is retained when in fact it is false, i.e. there is a failure to detect a difference or relationship that is really there. This can occur when significance levels are made too stringent.

It is often considered preferable to run a higher risk of making a type two error rather than make a type one error because it is better scientific practice to err on the side of caution. Before reading on, try Activity 6.

❖ Activity 7 ❖

What type of error would you be more likely to make if you were to use the following levels of significance instead of the 5% level ($p \leq 0.05$)?

- A 10% level of significance ($p \leq 0.1$).
- A 1% level of significance ($p \leq 0.01$).

If you used a 10% level of significance, you would be more likely to make a type one error. You would be rejecting your null hypothesis if the likelihood of results such as these occurring through chance was 10% or less. If you used a 1% level of significance a type two error would be more likely as the null hypothesis would be rejected only if you were at least 99% certain that results obtained were not due to chance.

Using and interpreting inferential statistical tests

In order to obtain the probability level of a particular set of results occurring through chance, we need to select and apply an appropriate inferential statistical test. To select the correct test we need to know the answers to certain questions concerning the nature of the data obtained (see *In Focus* below). These questions concern whether data are being tested for differences, relationships or associations, the level of measurement of the data and the design of the study.

In Focus

Selecting a statistical test

The following table shows the factors involved in choosing the correct test.

Level of measurement	**Two sample tests of difference**		**Two sample tests of correlation**
	Independent data	*Related data*	
Nominal	Chi-squared Test for Independent Samples (χ^2) (see p. 680)	Sign Test (see p. 684)	—
Ordinal, interval or ratio	Mann-Whitney *U* Test (see p. 679)	Wilcoxon Matched Pairs Signed Ranks Test (see p. 682)	Spearman's Rank Order Correlation Coefficient (r_s) (p. 685)

More powerful tests may be used when data are measured on an interval or ratio scale and certain other requirements are met. These tests include *t* tests and Pearson's Product Moment Correlation Coefficient. These are beyond the requirements of the AEB AS and A level syllabuses, but if you would like to find out more about the alternatives, you are directed to more detailed texts, such as those by Coolican (1994) and Dyer (1995) (see 'Further reading' at the end of the chapter).

The Mann-Whitney *U* Test

The Mann-Whitney *U* Test is a test of difference that is suitable for use with independent data. It can be used when at least an ordinal level of measurement has been achieved. It can therefore be used with data on an interval or ratio level of measurement which is converted to an ordinal level for the purposes of the test. Two versions of this test will be discussed here. The first is used when the larger of the two samples under investigation contains no more than twenty observations or when the size of each sample is equal, with up to a maximum of twenty observations in each. (See Chapter 29 for a discussion of independent data and *In Focus* p. 667 for a discussion of levels of measurement.)

Specimen calculation

Below is a specimen calculation of the Mann Whitney *U* test (where there are no more than twenty observations in each condition), using data obtained from a memory experiment

1 Place the data to be analysed into the appropriate columns of a table drawn up in a similar way to the one shown below.

	Condition 1			Condition 2	
Participant no.	*No. of words recalled (control condition)*	*Rank order*	*Participant no.*	*No. of words recalled (experimental condition)*	*Rank order*
1	7	2	10	20	19
2	6	1	11	14	11
3	8	3.5	12	14	11
4	12	8	13	18	17
5	9	5	14	15	13
6	14	11	15	17	16
7	8	3.5	16	13	9
8	11	7	17	16	14.5
9	10	6	18	19	18
			19	16	14.5
		47 Σ ranks for Condition 1			

2 Rank the data, from the lowest value (allocated rank one) to the highest value (rank *N*). Notice that both data sets are ranked in a single sequence and that the ranks are shared for any scores which are the same.

See Appendix 2 for how to rank your data.

3 Calculate the sum of the ranks for the smaller of the two samples and call this value *T*. If both samples contain the same number of observations, calculate the sum of the ranks for either sample.

In the example provided, $T = 47$.

4 Substitute in the following formula:

$$U = N_1 N_2 + \frac{N_1 (N_1 + 1)}{2} - T$$

Here, U = the observed (i.e. the calculated) value of the Mann-Whitney statistic.

N_1 = the number of values in the smaller sample (or in the sample for which the sum of the ranks has been calculated if both are the same size).

N_2 = the number of scores in the larger sample (or in the sample for which the sum of the ranks has not been calculated if both are the same size).

Here, $U = (9 \times 10) + \frac{9(9+1)}{2} - 47$

$U = 90 + \frac{90}{2} - 47$

$U = 90 + 45 - 47 = 88$

$U = 88$. This is the observed value of U.

5 Substitute in the following formula:

$U' = N_1 N_2 - U$

Here, $U' = (9 \times 10) - 88$

$U' = 90 - 88$

$U' = 2$. This is the observed value of U'.

6 Select the smaller of U and U'. In this example, U' has the smaller value of 2. Whichever is the smallest value becomes the value of U.

7 Consult the table in Appendix 3 to obtain the critical values of U (a critical value of U is the maximum value of U that is significant at a given level of significance). (Statistical significance is discussed earlier in this chapter.) In order to obtain this you need to know:

(a) The values of N_1 and N_2 (in this case 9 and 10 respectively)

(b) Whether a one-tailed or two-tailed test is required (in this case, let us assume a one-tailed test.).

(The concept of directional and non-directional hypotheses is discussed in Chapter 29.)

Take the smaller of the observed values of U and U'. In this case the smaller is U', which = 2. If this value is equal to or less than the critical value for a given level of significance, the null hypothesis can be rejected.

(Levels of significance are discussed on p. 677. Null and alternative hypotheses are discussed in Chapter 29.)

A minimum significance level of $p \leq 0.05$ will be assumed in this case. From Appendix 3, table 4, the critical value of U for $N_1 = 9$ and $N_2 = 10$ for a one-tailed test at $p = 0.05$ is 24. As the observed value of U (2) is less than the critical value (24) the probability of these results occurring through chance is less than 5%.

In this case, the null hypothesis could be rejected in favour of the alternative hypothesis.

Note: If the observed value had been greater than the critical value, then the probability of these results occurring through chance would have been greater than 5%. In this case the null hypothesis would not have been rejected.

Formula

The formula for the calculation of the Mann Whitney U test where one or more of the samples has more than twenty observations is shown below.

$$z = \frac{U - \frac{N_1 N_2}{2}}{\sqrt{\left(\left[\frac{N_1 N_2}{N(N-1)}\right] \times \left[\frac{N^3 - N}{12} - \Sigma T\right]\right)}}$$

This formula provides the researcher with a z score. (See Appendix 1 for how to interpret z scores.)

The Chi-squared Test for Independent Samples (χ^2)

The Chi-squared Test for Independent Samples (χ^2) is a test of association for use with independent data which are measured at a nominal level (in the form of frequencies). It tests for differences by examining the association which exists between data categorized into rows and columns. It compares observed frequencies (those actually obtained) with expected frequencies (the average frequencies which would be observed if the null hypothesis were true). (See *In Focus*, p. 667 for a discussion of levels of measurement and Chapter 29 for a discussion of the null hypothesis.)

You need to be aware of some cautions on the use of the Chi-squared test:

- The Chi-squared test should only be employed in situations where each observation is included in one category only. No overlap between categories is permissible.
- The observations used in the test must be actual frequencies of occurrence. Data such as averages, percentages or proportions should not be used.
- No individual participant should contribute more than one unit to a category. An exception to this is where all data relate to the same participant.
- The probability of making a type one error is increased when there are expected frequencies of less than 5, especially when the total sample size is small (i.e. less than 20). It is, however, possible to employ the Chi-squared test in such situations, although the potential for error increases with very small samples or an increase in the number of expected frequencies less than 5. This potential problem can be minimized by the use of a larger sample size. (Type one errors are discussed earlier in this chapter.)

Specimen calculation

Below is a specimen calculation of the Chi-squared Test for Independent Samples using data from an investigation into children's thinking.

1 Place the observed values to be analysed into the appropriate boxes of a table drawn up in a similar way to the table below. This kind of table is called a contingency table – in this case it is a 2 × 2 contingency table as there are two rows of data and two columns. Other numbers of rows and columns are possible using this same test.

	No. of children able to solve problem	*No. of children unable to solve problem*	*Row total*
4-year-old children	Cell 1 8	Cell 2 12	RT1 20
5-year-old children	Cell 3 17	Cell 4 3	RT2 20
Column total	CT1 25	CT2 15	GT 40

where RT1 and RT2 are row totals,
CT1 and CT2 are column totals and
GT is the grand total.

2 Calculate the expected frequency for each cell, using the formula:

$$\text{Expected frequency } (E) = \frac{\text{RT} \times \text{CT}}{\text{GT}}$$

For cell 1: $E = \dfrac{20 \times 25}{40} = \dfrac{500}{40} = 12.5$

For cell 2: $E = \dfrac{20 \times 15}{40} = \dfrac{300}{40} = 7.5$

For cell 3: $E = \dfrac{20 \times 25}{40} = \dfrac{500}{40} = 12.5$

For cell 4: $E = \dfrac{20 \times 15}{40} = \dfrac{300}{40} = 7.5$

3 Subtract the expected frequency (E) from the observed frequency (O) for each cell:

Cell 1: $O - E = 8 - 12.5 = -4.5$

Cell 2: $O - E = 12 - 7.5 = 4.5$

Cell 3: $O - E = 17 - 12.5 = 4.5$

Cell 4: $O - E = 3 - 7.5 = -4.5$

4 Calculate $(O - E)^2$ for each cell:

Cell 1: $-4.5^2 = 20.25$

Cell 2: $4.5^2 = 20.25$

Cell 3: $4.5^2 = 20.25$

Cell 4: $-4.5^2 = 20.25$

5 Calculate $\frac{(O - E)^2}{E}$ for each cell:

Cell 1: $20.25 \div 12.5 = 1.62$

Cell 2: $20.25 \div 7.5 = 2.7$

Cell 3: $20.25 \div 12.5 = 1.62$

Cell 4: $20.25 \div 7.5 = 2.7$

6 Add the answers to stage 5 to obtain the observed value of χ^2:

$1.62 + 2.7 + 1.62 + 2.7 = 8.64.$

This is the observed value of χ^2.

Note: Stages 2 to 6 can be represented by the following formula:

$$\chi^2 = \sum\left(\frac{(O - E)^2}{E}\right)$$

7 Calculate the number of degrees of freedom using the formula:

Degrees of freedom (df) = (No. of rows – 1)(No. of columns – 1).

(Degrees of freedom are the number of cell values which are free to vary, given that row totals and column totals are known.)

In the example above

$df = (2 - 1)(2 - 1)$

$df = 1.$

8 Consult the table in Appendix 4 to obtain the critical values of χ^2 (a critical value of χ^2 is the minimum value of χ^2 that is significant at a given level of significance). (Statistical significance is discussed earlier in this chapter.) In order to obtain this you need to know:

(a) The number of degrees of freedom (in this case $df = 1$).

(b) Whether a one-tailed test or two-tailed test is required

You should note that a one-tailed test should only be employed with a 2×1 contingency table and a directional hypothesis. Directional hypotheses and non-directional hypotheses are discussed in Chapter 29.

If the observed value of χ^2 is equal to or greater than the critical value for a given level of significance, the null hypothesis can be rejected. (Levels of significance are discussed on p. 677; null and alternative hypotheses are discussed in Chapter 29.)

A minimum significance level of $p \leq 0.05$ will be assumed in this case. From Appendix 4, the critical value of χ^2 for $df = 1$ and a two-tailed test at $p = 0.05$ is 3.84. As the observed value of χ^2 (8.64) is greater than the critical value (3.84) the likelihood of these results occurring through chance is less than 5%.

In this case, the null hypothesis could be rejected in favour of the alternative hypothesis.

Note: If the observed value had been less than the critical value then the probability of results such as these occurring through chance would have been greater than 5%. In this case, the null hypothesis would not have been rejected.

The Wilcoxon Matched Pairs Signed Ranks Test

The Wilcoxon Matched Pairs Signed Ranks Test is a test of difference that is suitable for use with related data. It can be used when at least an ordinal level of measurement has been achieved. It can therefore be used with data on an interval or ratio level of measurement which is converted to an ordinal level for the purposes of the test. Two versions of this test will be discussed here. The first is used when there is a maximum of 25 pairs of observations. (See Chapter 29 for a discussion of independent data, and the *In Focus* on p. 667 for a discussion of levels of measurement.)

Specimen calculation

Below is a specimen calculation of the Wilcoxon Matched Pairs Signed Ranks Test where there is a maximum of 25 pairs of observations, using data obtained from a memory experiment.

1 Place the data to be analysed into the appropriate columns of a table drawn up in a similar way to that in the table below, which represents the data obtained from a memory experiment.

2 Calculate the difference between each pair of scores (see the 'Difference' column in the table). Note that it is essential that the direction of any differences is recorded.

Participant no.	*No. of words recalled (control condition)*	*No. of words recalled (experimental condition)*	*Difference*	*Rank order*
1	17	20	–3	4
2	12	14	–2	2.5
3	16	14	+2	2.5
4	12	19	–7	9
5	16	15	+1	1
6	14	19	–5	6
7	13	13	0	(omitted)
8	11	16	–5	6
9	13	19	–6	8
10	11	16	–5	6

3 Rank the data in the difference column, from the lowest value (allocated rank one) to the highest value (rank N).

Notice that:

(a) any zero differences are disregarded
(b) positive and negative signs are disregarded
(c) the ranks are shared for any scores which are tied.

(See Appendix 2, p. 692, for how to rank your data.)

4 Calculate the sum of the ranks which correspond to:

(a) the differences with the + sign, and

(b) the differences with the – sign.

Call the smaller of these values T. In the example provided:

Sum of the ranks which correspond to the differences with the + sign = 2.5 + 1 = 3.5.

Sum of the ranks which correspond to the differences with the – sign = 4 + 2.5 + 9 + 6 + 6 + 8 + 6 = 41.5

The smallest sum of ranks is T.

Therefore, the observed value of $T = 3.5$.

5 Consult the table in Appendix 5 to obtain the critical values of T (a critical value is the maximum value of T that is significant at a given level of probability).

(Statistical significance is discussed earlier in this chapter.)

In order to obtain this you need to know:

(a) The value of N (the number of pairs of scores). NB. Note that pairs of scores with a difference of zero are not included. In this example, the number of pairs of scores = 9.

(b) Whether a one-tailed or two-tailed test is required. In this example, let us assume two-tailed.

(The concept of directional and non-directional hypotheses is discussed in Chapter 29.)

If the observed value of T is equal to or less than the critical value for a given level of significance, the null hypothesis can be rejected. (Null and alternative hypotheses are discussed in Chapter 29.)

A minimum significance level of $p \leq 0.05$ will be assumed in this case. From Appendix 5, the critical value of T for $N = 9$ for a two-tailed test at $p = 0.05$

is 5. As the observed value of T (3.5) is less than the critical value (5) the likelihood of the results occurring through chance is less than 5%.

In this case, the null hypothesis could be rejected in favour of the alternative hypothesis.

Note: If the observed value had been greater than the critical value, then the likelihood of results such as these occurring through chance would have been greater than 5%. In this case the null hypothesis would not have been rejected.

Formula

The formula for the calculation of the Wilcoxon Matched Pairs Signed Ranks Test when there are more than 25 pairs of scores is given below:

$$z = \frac{N(N+1) - 4T}{\sqrt{\left(\frac{2N(N+1)(2N+1)}{3}\right)}}$$

This formula provides the researcher with a z score (see Appendix 1).

The Sign Test

The Sign Test is a test of difference that is suitable for use with related data, which is measured at a nominal level of measurement. The test examines the direction of any difference between pairs of scores.

1 The example that follows uses data obtained from an investigation which set out to discover whether the perceptions of psychology held by students changed after following a GCSE psychology course. Place the data to be analysed into the appropriate columns of a table drawn up in a similar way to that in the table that follows.

Participant no.	*Attitude*	*Direction of difference*
1	More favourable	+
2	More favourable	+
3	No change	omitted
4	Less favourable	–
5	More favourable	+
6	More favourable	+
7	More favourable	+
8	No change	omitted
9	More favourable	+
10	More favourable	+

Note: It is perfectly possible to derive the direction of difference from numerical values (e.g. if actual ratings had been used in the example above, before and after taking a GCSE psychology course).

2 Enter a plus sign or a minus sign to indicate the direction of difference for each participant (see direction of difference column in the table above).

3 Add the number of times the less frequent sign occurs, and call this s. In the example above the less frequent sign is the minus sign, which occurs once. Therefore the observed value of $s = 1$

4 Consult the table in Appendix 6 to obtain the critical values of s. A critical value is the maximum value of s that is significant at a given level of probability. In order to obtain this you need to know:

(a) The value of N (the number of pairs of scores).

Note that pairs of scores with no + or – sign are not included. In this case, the number of pairs of scores = 8.

(b) Whether a one-tailed or two-tailed test is required (in this case, let us assume two-tailed). (The concept of directional and non-directional hypotheses is discussed in Chapter 29.)

If the observed value of s is equal to or less than the critical value for a given level of significance, the null hypothesis can be rejected. (Null and alternative hypotheses are discussed in Chapter 29.)

A minimum significance level of $p \leq 0.05$ will be assumed in this case. From Appendix 6, the critical value of s for $N = 8$ for a two-tailed hypothesis at $p = 0.05$ is 0. As the observed value of s (1) is greater than the critical value (0), the probability of results such as these occurring through chance is greater than 5%.

In this case, the null hypothesis cannot be rejected.

Note: If the observed value had been less than or equal to the critical value, then the likelihood of results such as these occurring through chance would have been less than 5%. In this case the null hypothesis would have been rejected.

Spearman's Rank Order Correlation Coefficient (r_S)

Spearman's Rank Order Correlation Coefficient (r_S) is a test of correlation that is suitable for use with pairs of scores. It can be used when at least an ordinal level of measurement has been achieved. It can therefore be used with data on an interval or ratio level of measurement which is converted to an ordinal level for the purposes of the test.

The example below uses data obtained from an investigation which set out to investigate the possible correlation between psychology test scores and biology test scores from a group of participants studying both subjects.

1 Draw a scattergraph of the data sets that you wish to correlate. This is important as this technique measures only straight-line relationships, and drawing a scattergram can help you to decide if this is the case (see p. 676).

2 Place the data to be analysed into the appropriate columns of a table drawn up in a similar way to that in the table below.

3 Rank each set of scores separately, giving the lowest score rank 1 and the highest score rank N.

Note: accuracy is diminished if this test is used when ranks are shared for any scores which are tied. In such cases, the appropriate procedure is to carry out the calculation for Pearson's Product-moment Correlation Coefficient on the two sets of ranks. This test is covered in more advanced texts such as Coolican 1994 and Dyer 1995) However, unless there are large numbers of ties, the effects on the outcome are likely to be very small.

Participant no.	*Psychology test score*	*Rank order*	*Biology test score*	*Rank order*	d	d^2
1	95	10	92	9	1	1
2	27	2	36	2	0	0
3	47	4	40	3	1	1
4	68	7	57	5	2	4
5	50	5	61	6	−1	1
6	94	9	91	8	1	1
7	33	3	41	4	−1	1
8	26	1	35	1	0	0
9	93	8	93	10	−2	4
10	59	6	70	7	−1	1
						d^2 14

(If the test is carried out where ranks are tied, then see Appendix 2, for how to rank your data.)

4 Find the difference (*d*) between each pair of rank order scores (see d column in above table).

5 Square each of the *d* values (see d^2 column in above table).

6 Calculate the sum of the d^2 values. This is the value described as d^2 in the above table. (The symbol Σ means 'sum of'.)

7 Substitute in the following formula:

$$r_s = 1 - \left(\frac{6\Sigma d^2}{N(N^2 - 1)} \right)$$

Here, r_s = the observed (i.e. calculated) value of Spearman's correlation coefficient

Σd^2 = the sum of the squared differences

N = the number of pairs of scores being correlated.

Here:

$$r_s = 1 - \left(\frac{84}{10(100 - 1)} \right)$$

$$= 1 - \left(\frac{84}{10 \times 99} \right)$$

$$= 1 - \frac{84}{990}$$

$$= 1 - 0.0848$$

$$= 0.9152$$

This is the observed value of r_s.

8 Consult the table in Appendix 7 to obtain the critical values of r_s (a critical value is the minimum value of r_s that is significant at a given level of probability). In order to obtain this you need to know:

(a) the value of *N* (the number of pairs of scores)

(b) whether a one-tailed or two-tailed test is required (in this case, let us assume one-tailed).

(The concept of directional and non-directional hypotheses is discussed in Chapter 29.)

If the observed value of r_s is equal to or greater than the critical value for a given level of significance, the null hypothesis can be rejected.

(Null and alternative hypotheses are discussed in Chapter 29.)

A minimum significance level of $p \leq 0.05$ will be assumed in this case. From Appendix 7, when N=10, the critical value of rs for a one-tailed hypothesis at $p = 0.05$ is 0.564. As the observed value of r_s (0.9152) is greater than the critical value (0.564), the likelihood of results such as these occurring through chance is less than 5%.

In this case, the null hypothesis can be rejected.

Note: If the observed value had been less than the critical value, then the likelihood of results such as these occurring through chance would have been greater than 5%. In this case the null hypothesis would not have been rejected.

Section summary

Inferential statistical techniques enable researchers to draw conclusions about the populations from which their samples have been drawn. By using these techniques, the researcher may reach reasoned conclusions concerning whether to retain or reject their null hypotheses. Reaching these conclusions is based on the probability of such results occurring through chance. The decision concerning which inferential statistical test to use is based on factors which include the level of measurement of the data, whether data are related or independent, and whether the researcher seeks to establish a difference, correlation or association.

Chapter summary

- Content analysis involves a wide range of research techniques used in the analysis of documents, messages or verbal discourse.
- Case studies are wide ranging and the variety of techniques used in them reflects this.
- Interviews and observational studies may produce qualitative or quantitative data. They can provide a richness of detail which may not be achievable with other methods.
- Descriptive statistical techniques for use with quantitative data include measures of central tendency (mode, median and mean) and measures of dispersion (variation ratio, range and standard deviation).
- Graphical techniques available to the researcher include histograms, bar charts, frequency polygons and scattergraphs.
- Significance levels are used as criteria for ascertaining whether a particular set of data differs from what would be expected if chance factors operated.
- Inferential statistical tests can be used to calculate the probability level of the obtained results occurring by chance. Tests may measure differences, associations or correlations between sets of data.

Exam question

A researcher carried out an investigation into the number of children from two different groups who were able to complete successfully two problem-solving tasks. An independent measures design had been employed with each child undertaking one of the two tasks. It was expected that there would be a difference in performance between the two tasks, although the researcher was unsure which task the children would be more successful at. The results obtained are shown in the table below.

Number of children able to complete two different problem-solving tasks at ages 4 and 8.

	Task A	*Task B*	*Total*
4-year-old children	10	15	25
8-year-old children	15	10	25
Total	25	25	50

1 (a) Name an appropriate graphical technique for displaying the data in the table above. *(1 mark)*

(b) Draw a sketch illustrating how this data would appear in graphical form. *(3 marks)*

(c) Suggest how the researcher might have interpreted the data presented in this way. *(2 marks)*

The researcher then carried out a statistical analysis of the results. Analysis using the chi-squared test for independent samples produced an observed (calculated) value of $\chi^2 = 2.0$. The critical (table) value of χ^2 at $p = 0.05$ for a two-tailed test is 3.84. The researcher was unable to reject the null hypothesis.

2 Suggest two reasons why the researcher selected the chi-squared test for independent samples in order to analyse the data. *(2 marks)*

3 What is meant by the term 'two-tailed test'? *(2 marks)*

4 Explain the term '$p = 0.05$'. *(2 marks)*

5 Explain why the researcher was unable to reject the null hypothesis. *(2 marks)*

6 Suggest an appropriate null hypothesis for this investigation. *(2 marks)*

Further reading

Banister, P., Burman, E., Parker, I., Taylor, M. and Tindall C. (1994) *Qualitative Methods in Psychology: A Research Guide*, Buckingham: Open University Press.

An advanced text which covers observations and interviews.

Banyard, P. and Grayson, A. (1996) *Introducing Psychological Research*, Basingstoke: Macmillan.

A text which contains shortened versions of key research studies.

Coolican, H. (1994) *Research Methods and Statistics in Psychology*, London: Hodder and Stoughton.

A clearly written text that covers the research methods included in the AEB syllabus.

Coolican, H. (1995) *Introduction to Research Methods and Statistics in Psychology*, London: Hodder and Stoughton.

A condensed version of the Coolican (1994) text.

Dyer, C. (1995) *Beginning Research in Psychology: A Practical Guide to Research Methods and Statistics*, Oxford: Blackwell.

A detailed text with useful sections on non-experimental methods.

Foster, J.J. and Parker, I. (1995) *Carrying out Investigations in Psychology: Methods and Statistics*, Leicester: BPS Books.

A detailed and advanced text which is of use for reference purposes.

Gross, R.D. (1994) *Key Studies in Psychology* (2nd edn), London: Hodder & Stoughton.

A further text which provides detailed examples from different methodologies.

Appendix 1: Standard scores

The table provided below gives the area beneath the normal distribution curve between the mean and any given standard score (i.e. *z* score). These values are therefore also the probabilities of finding a value within the area concerned.

To find the proportion of individuals between a given standard score and the mean:

1. Calculate the mean and the standard deviation for the sample concerned.
2. Calculate the standard score (or *z* score, i.e. the number of standard deviations a given score is away from its mean). For example, if a sample of test scores has a mean of 100 and a standard deviation of 10, then a test score of 80 would have a standard score of 2 (two standard deviations below the mean). Similarly, a test score of 107 would have a standard score of 0.7 (and so on).
3. Look up this standard score in the left hand column of the table provided and read off the value in the right hand column. This is the probability of a score occurring between the mean and the standard score.
4. If a percentage is required, the value obtained should be multiplied by 100. If a probability is required for a score occurring between the same number of standard scores either side of the mean, then the value obtained should be doubled.

Areas under the normal distribution

z	*p*	*z*	*p*	*z*	*p*
0.00	.5000	0.25	.4013	0.50	.3085
0.01	.4960	0.26	.3974	0.51	.3050
0.02	.4920	0.27	.3936	0.52	.3015
0.03	.4880	0.28	.3897	0.53	.2981
0.04	.4840	0.29	.3859	0.54	.2946
0.05	.4801	0.30	.3821	0.55	.2912
0.06	.4761	0.31	.3783	0.56	.2877
0.07	.4721	0.32	.3745	0.57	.2843
0.08	.4681	0.33	.3707	0.58	.2810
0.09	.4641	0.34	.3669	0.59	.2776
0.10	.4602	0.35	.3632	0.60	.2743
0.11	.4562	0.36	.3594	0.61	.2709
0.12	.4522	0.37	.3557	0.62	.2676
0.13	.4483	0.38	.3520	0.63	.2643
0.14	.4443	0.39	.3483	0.64	.2611
0.15	.4404	0.40	.3446	0.65	.2578
0.16	.4364	0.41	.3409	0.66	.2546
0.17	.4325	0.42	.3372	0.67	.2514
0.18	.4286	0.43	.3336	0.68	.2483
0.19	.4247	0.44	.3300	0.69	.2451
0.20	.4207	0.45	.3264	0.70	.2420
0.21	.4168	0.46	.3228	0.71	.2389
0.22	.4129	0.47	.3192	0.72	.2358
0.23	.4090	0.48	.3156	0.73	.2327
0.24	.4052	0.49	.3121	0.74	.2296

z	p	z	p	z	p
0.75	.2266	1.20	.1151	1.65	.0495
0.76	.2236	1.21	.1131	1.66	.0485
0.77	.2206	1.22	.1112	1.67	.0475
0.78	.2177	1.23	.1093	1.68	.0465
0.79	.2148	1.24	.1075	1.69	.0455
0.80	.2119	1.25	.1056	1.70	.0446
0.81	.2090	1.26	.1038	1.71	.0436
0.82	.2061	1.27	.1020	1.72	.0427
0.83	.2033	1.28	.1003	1.73	.0418
0.84	.2005	1.29	.0985	1.74	.0409
0.85	.1977	1.30	.0968	1.75	.0401
0.86	.1949	1.31	.0951	1.76	.0392
0.87	.1922	1.32	.0934	1.77	.0384
0.88	.1894	1.33	.0918	1.78	.0375
0.89	.1867	1.34	.0901	1.79	.0367
0.90	.1841	1.35	.0885	1.80	.0359
0.91	.1814	1.36	.0869	1.81	.0351
0.92	.1788	1.37	.0853	1.82	.0344
0.93	.1762	1.38	.0838	1.83	.0336
0.94	.1736	1.39	.0823	1.84	.0329
0.95	.1711	1.40	.0808	1.85	.0322
0.96	.1685	1.41	.0793	1.86	.0314
0.97	.1660	1.42	.0778	1.87	.0307
0.98	.1635	1.43	.0764	1.88	.0301
0.99	.1611	1.44	.0749	1.89	.0294
1.00	.1587	1.45	.0735	1.90	.0287
1.01	.1562	1.46	.0721	1.91	.0281
1.02	.1539	1.47	.0708	1.92	.0274
1.03	.1515	1.48	.0694	1.93	.0268
1.04	.1492	1.49	.0681	1.94	.0262
1.05	.1469	1.50	.0668	1.95	.0256
1.06	.1446	1.51	.0655	1.96	.0250
1.07	.1423	1.52	.0643	1.97	.0244
1.08	.1401	1.53	.0630	1.98	.0239
1.09	.1379	1.54	.0618	1.99	.0233
1.10	.1357	1.55	.0606	2.00	.0228
1.11	.1335	1.56	.0594	2.01	.0222
1.12	.1314	1.57	.0582	2.02	.0217
1.13	.1292	1.58	.0571	2.03	.0212
1.14	.1271	1.59	.0559	2.04	.0207
1.15	.1251	1.60	.0548	2.05	.0202
1.16	.1230	1.61	.0537	2.06	.0197
1.17	.1210	1.62	.0526	2.07	.0192
1.18	.1190	1.63	.0516	2.08	.0188
1.19	.1170	1.64	.0505	2.09	.0183

z	p	z	p	z	p
2.10	.0179	2.50	.0062	2.90	.0019
2.11	.0174	2.51	.0060	2.91	.0018
2.12	.0170	2.52	.0059	2.92	.0018
2.13	.0166	2.53	.0057	2.93	.0017
2.14	.0162	2.54	.0055	2.94	.0016
2.15	.0158	2.55	.0054	2.95	.0016
2.16	.0154	2.56	.0052	2.96	.0015
2.17	.0150	2.57	.0051	2.97	.0015
2.18	.0146	2.58	.0049	2.98	.0014
2.19	.0143	2.59	.0048	2.99	.0014
2.20	.0139	2.60	.0047	3.00	.0013
2.21	.0136	2.61	.0045	3.01	.0013
2.22	.0132	2.62	.0044	3.02	.0013
2.23	.0129	2.63	.0043	3.03	.0012
2.24	.0125	2.64	.0041	3.04	.0012
2.25	.0122	2.65	.0040	3.05	.0011
2.26	.0119	2.66	.0039	3.06	.0011
2.27	.0116	2.67	.0038	3.07	.0011
2.28	.0113	2.68	.0037	3.08	.0010
2.29	.0110	2.69	.0036	3.09	.0010
2.30	.0107	2.70	.0035	3.10	.0010
2.31	.0104	2.71	.0034	3.11	.0009
2.32	.0102	2.72	.0033	3.12	.0009
2.33	.0099	2.73	.0032	3.13	.0009
2.34	.0096	2.74	.0031	3.14	.0008
2.35	.0094	2.75	.0030	3.15	.0008
2.36	.0091	2.76	.0029	3.16	.0008
2.37	.0089	2.77	.0028	3.17	.0008
2.38	.0087	2.78	.0027	3.18	.0007
2.39	.0084	2.79	.0026	3.19	.0007
2.40	.0082	2.80	.0026	3.20	.0007
2.41	.0080	2.81	.0025	3.21	.0007
2.42	.0078	2.82	.0024	3.22	.0006
2.43	.0075	2.83	.0023	3.23	.0006
2.44	.0073	2.84	.0023	3.24	.0006
2.45	.0071	2.85	.0022	3.30	.0005
2.46	.0069	2.86	.0021	3.40	.0003
2.47	.0068	2.87	.0021	3.50	.0002
2.48	.0066	2.88	.0020	3.60	.0002
2.49	.0064	2.89	.0019	3.70	.0001

Appendix 2: Method used for ranking data in statistical tests

1 Organize data into ascending order of values (see specimen data below).

2 Allocate rank 1 to the lowest value.

3 Allocate ranks to the remaining values, averaging the ranks for any tied scores (see below).

Scores	*Rank*	*Notes*
10	1	
12	2.5	*Both scores of 12 are given the average rank of positions 2 and 3.*
12	2.5	*Note that the next score is rank 4, not 3.*
15	4	
17	5	
18	7	*Three scores of 18 are given the average rank of positions 6, 7 and 8.*
18	7	*Note that the next score is rank 9, not 8*
18	7	
20	9	
25	10	

Appendix 3

Table 1: Critical values of *U* for a one-tailed test at $p = 0.005$; two-tailed test at $p = 0.01$* (Mann-Whitney)

N_2 \ N_1	1	2	3	4	5	6	7	8	9	10	11	12	13	14	15	16	17	18	19	20
1	–	–	–	–	–	–	–	–	–	–	–	–	–	–	–	–	–	–	–	–
2	–	–	–	–	–	–	–	–	–	–	–	–	–	–	–	–	–	–	0	0
3	–	–	–	–	–	–	–	–	0	0	0	1	1	1	2	2	2	2	3	3
4	–	–	–	–	–	0	0	1	1	2	2	3	3	4	5	5	6	6	7	8
5	–	–	–	–	0	1	1	2	3	4	5	6	7	7	8	9	10	11	12	13
6	–	–	–	0	1	2	3	4	5	6	7	9	10	11	12	13	15	16	17	18
7	–	–	–	0	1	3	4	6	7	9	10	12	13	15	16	18	19	21	22	24
8	–	–	–	1	2	4	6	7	9	11	13	15	17	18	20	22	24	26	28	30
9	–	–	0	1	3	5	7	9	11	13	16	18	20	22	24	27	29	31	33	36
10	–	–	0	2	4	6	9	11	13	16	18	21	24	26	29	31	34	37	39	42
11	–	–	0	2	5	7	10	13	16	18	21	24	27	30	33	36	39	42	45	48
12	–	–	1	3	6	9	12	15	18	21	24	27	31	34	37	41	44	47	51	54
13	–	–	1	3	7	10	13	17	20	24	27	31	34	38	42	45	49	53	56	60
14	–	–	1	4	7	11	15	18	22	26	30	34	38	42	46	50	54	58	63	67
15	–	–	2	5	8	12	16	20	24	29	33	37	42	46	51	55	60	64	69	73
16	–	–	2	5	9	13	18	22	27	31	36	41	45	50	55	60	65	70	74	79
17	–	–	2	6	10	15	19	24	29	34	39	44	49	54	60	65	70	75	81	86
18	–	–	2	6	11	16	21	26	31	37	42	47	53	58	64	70	75	81	87	92
19	–	0	3	7	12	17	22	28	33	39	45	51	56	63	69	74	81	87	93	99
20	–	0	3	8	13	18	24	30	36	42	48	54	60	67	73	79	86	92	99	105

Table 2: Critical values of U for a one-tailed test at $p = 0.01$; two-tailed test at $p = 0.02$* (Mann-Whitney)

	N_1																			
	1	2	3	4	5	6	7	8	9	10	11	12	13	14	15	16	17	18	19	20
N_2 1	–	–	–	–	–	–	–	–	–	–	–	–	–	–	–	–	–	–	–	–
2	–	–	–	–	–	–	–	–	–	–	–	–	0	0	0	0	0	0	1	1
3	–	–	–	–	–	–	0	0	1	1	1	2	2	2	3	3	4	4	4	5
4	–	–	–	–	0	1	1	2	3	3	4	5	5	6	7	7	8	9	9	10
5	–	–	–	0	1	2	3	4	5	6	7	8	9	10	11	12	13	14	15	16
6	–	–	–	1	2	3	4	6	7	8	9	11	12	13	15	16	18	19	20	22
7	–	–	0	1	3	4	6	7	9	11	12	14	16	17	19	21	23	24	26	28
8	–	–	0	2	4	6	7	9	11	13	15	17	20	22	24	26	28	30	32	34
9	–	–	1	3	5	7	9	11	14	16	18	21	23	26	28	31	33	36	38	40
10	–	–	1	3	6	8	11	13	16	19	22	24	27	30	33	36	38	41	44	47
11	–	–	1	4	7	9	12	15	18	22	25	28	31	34	37	41	44	47	50	53
12	–	–	2	5	8	11	14	17	21	24	28	31	35	38	42	46	49	53	56	60
13	–	0	2	5	9	12	16	20	23	27	31	35	39	43	47	51	55	59	63	67
14	–	0	2	6	10	13	17	22	26	30	34	38	43	47	51	56	60	65	69	73
15	–	0	3	7	11	15	19	24	28	33	37	42	47	51	56	61	66	70	75	80
16	–	0	3	7	12	16	21	26	31	36	41	46	51	56	61	66	71	76	82	87
17	–	0	4	8	13	18	23	28	33	38	44	49	55	60	66	71	77	82	88	93
18	–	0	4	9	14	19	24	30	36	41	47	53	59	65	70	76	82	88	94	100
19	–	1	4	9	15	20	26	32	38	44	50	56	63	69	75	82	88	94	101	107
20	–	1	5	10	16	22	28	34	40	47	53	60	67	73	80	87	93	100	107	114

Table 3: Critical values of U for a one-tailed test at $p = 0.025$; two-tailed test at $p = 0.05$* (Mann-Whitney)

	N_1																			
	1	2	3	4	5	6	7	8	9	10	11	12	13	14	15	16	17	18	19	20
N_2 1	–	–	–	–	–	–	–	–	–	–	–	–	–	–	–	–	–	–	–	–
2	–	–	–	–	–	–	–	0	0	0	0	1	1	1	1	1	2	2	2	2
3	–	–	–	–	0	1	1	2	2	3	3	4	4	5	5	6	6	7	7	8
4	–	–	–	0	1	2	3	4	4	5	6	7	8	9	10	11	11	12	13	13
5	–	–	0	[illegible]	2	3	5	6	7	8	9	11	12	13	14	15	17	18	19	20
6	–	–	1	2	3	5	6	8	10	11	13	14	16	17	19	21	22	24	25	27
7	–	–	1	3	5	6	8	10	12	14	16	18	20	22	24	26	28	30	32	34
8	–	0	2	4	6	8	10	13	15	17	19	22	24	26	29	31	34	36	38	41
9	–	0	2	4	7	10	12	15	17	20	23	26	28	31	34	37	39	42	45	48
10	–	0	3	5	8	11	14	17	20	23	26	29	33	36	39	42	45	48	52	55
11	–	0	3	6	9	13	16	19	23	26	30	33	37	40	44	47	51	55	58	62
12	–	1	4	7	11	14	18	22	26	29	33	37	41	45	49	55	57	61	65	69
13	–	1	4	8	12	16	20	24	28	33	37	41	45	50	54	59	63	67	74	76
14	–	1	5	9	13	17	22	26	31	36	40	45	50	55	59	64	67	74	78	83
15	–	1	5	10	14	19	24	29	34	39	44	49	54	59	64	70	76	80	85	90
16	–	1	6	11	15	21	26	31	37	42	47	53	59	64	70	75	81	86	92	98
17	–	2	6	11	17	22	28	34	39	45	51	57	63	67	75	81	87	93	99	105
18	–	2	7	12	18	24	30	36	42	48	55	61	67	74	80	86	93	99	106	112
19	–	2	7	13	19	25	32	38	45	52	58	65	72	78	85	92	99	106	113	119
20	–	2	8	13	20	27	34	41	48	55	62	69	76	83	90	98	105	112	119	127

Table 4: Critical values of *U* for a one-tailed test at $p = 0.05$; two-tailed test at $p = 0.10$* (Mann-Whitney)

N_2 \ N_1	1	2	3	4	5	6	7	8	9	10	11	12	13	14	15	16	17	18	19	20
1	–	–	–	–	–	–	–	–	–	–	–	–	–	–	–	–	–	–	0	0
2	–	–	–	–	0	0	0	1	1	1	1	2	2	2	3	3	3	4	4	4
3	–	–	0	0	1	2	2	3	3	4	5	5	6	7	7	8	9	9	10	11
4	–	–	0	1	2	3	4	5	6	7	8	9	10	11	12	14	15	16	17	18
5	–	0	1	2	4	5	6	8	9	11	12	13	15	16	18	19	20	22	23	25
6	–	0	2	3	5	7	8	10	12	14	16	17	19	21	23	25	26	28	30	32
7	–	0	2	4	6	8	11	13	15	17	19	21	24	26	28	30	33	35	37	39
8	–	1	3	5	8	10	13	15	18	20	23	26	28	31	33	36	39	41	44	47
9	–	1	3	6	9	12	15	18	21	24	27	30	33	36	39	42	45	48	51	54
10	–	1	4	7	11	14	17	20	24	27	31	34	37	41	44	48	51	55	58	62
11	–	1	5	8	12	16	19	23	27	31	34	38	42	46	50	54	57	61	65	69
12	–	2	5	9	13	17	21	26	30	34	38	42	47	51	55	60	64	68	72	77
13	–	2	6	10	15	19	24	28	33	37	42	47	51	56	61	65	70	75	80	84
14	–	2	7	11	16	21	26	31	36	41	46	51	56	61	66	71	77	82	87	92
15	–	3	7	12	18	23	28	33	39	44	50	55	61	66	72	77	83	88	94	100
16	–	3	8	14	19	25	30	36	42	48	54	60	65	71	77	83	89	95	101	107
17	–	3	9	15	20	26	33	39	45	51	57	64	70	77	83	89	96	102	109	115
18	–	4	9	16	22	28	35	41	48	55	61	68	75	82	88	95	102	109	116	123
19	–	4	10	17	23	30	37	44	51	58	65	72	80	87	94	101	109	116	123	130
20	–	4	11	18	25	32	39	47	54	62	69	77	84	92	100	107	115	123	130	138

* Dashes in the body of the table indicate that no decision is possible at the stated level of significance. For any N_1 and N_2, the observed value of U is significant at a given level of significance if it is equal to or less than the critical values shown.

Source: Runyon, R. and Haber, A. (1976)

Appendix 4: Critical values of χ^2

Level of significance for a one-tailed test

df	*0.10*	*0.05*	*0.025*	*0.01*	*0.005*	*0.0005*
1	1.64	2.71	3.84	5.41	6.64	10.83

Level of significance for a two-tailed test

df	*0.20*	*0.10*	*0.05*	*0.02*	*0.01*	*0.001*
1	1.64	2.71	3.84	5.41	6.64	10.83
2	3.22	4.60	5.99	7.82	9.21	13.82
3	4.64	6.25	7.82	9.84	11.34	16.27
4	5.99	7.78	9.49	11.67	13.28	18.46
5	7.29	9.24	11.07	13.39	15.09	20.52
6	8.56	10.64	12.59	15.03	16.81	22.46
7	9.80	12.02	14.07	16.62	18.48	24.32
8	11.03	13.36	15.51	18.17	20.09	26.12
9	12.24	14.68	16.92	19.68	21.67	27.88
10	13.44	15.99	18.31	21.16	23.21	29.59
11	14.63	17.28	19.68	22.62	24.72	31.26
12	15.81	18.55	21.03	24.05	26.22	32.91
13	16.98	19.81	22.36	25.47	27.69	34.53
14	18.15	21.06	23.68	26.87	29.14	36.12
15	19.31	22.31	25.00	28.26	30.58	37.70
16	20.46	23.54	26.30	29.63	32.00	39.29
17	21.62	24.77	27.59	31.00	33.41	40.75
18	22.76	25.99	28.87	32.35	34.80	42.31
19	23.90	27.20	30.14	33.69	36.19	43.82
20	25.04	28.41	31.41	35.02	37.57	45.32
21	26.17	29.62	32.67	36.34	38.93	46.80
22	27.30	30.81	33.92	37.66	40.29	48.27
23	28.43	32.01	35.17	38.97	41.64	49.73
24	29.55	33.20	36.42	40.27	42.98	51.18
25	30.68	34.38	37.65	41.57	44.31	52.62
26	31.80	35.56	38.88	42.86	45.64	54.05
27	32.91	36.74	40.11	44.14	46.96	55.48
28	34.03	37.92	41.34	45.42	48.28	56.89
29	35.14	39.09	42.69	46.69	49.59	58.30
30	36.25	40.26	43.77	47.96	50.89	59.70
32	38.47	42.59	46.19	50.49	53.49	62.49
34	40.68	44.90	48.60	53.00	56.06	65.25
36	42.88	47.21	51.00	55.49	58.62	67.99
38	45.08	49.51	53.38	57.97	61.16	70.70
40	47.27	51.81	55.76	60.44	63.69	73.40
44	51.64	56.37	60.48	65.48	68.71	78.75
48	55.99	60.91	65.17	70.20	73.68	84.04
52	60.33	65.42	69.83	75.02	78.62	89.27
56	64.66	69.92	74.47	79.82	83.51	94.46
60	68.97	74.40	79.08	84.58	88.38	99.61

Calculated value of χ^2 must **equal** or **exceed** the table (critical) values for significance at the level shown.

Source: Abridged from Fisher, R.A. and Yates, F. (1974)

Appendix 5: Critical values of *T* for the Wilcoxon Matched Pairs Signed-Ranks Test

	Level of significance for a two-tailed test			
	0.10	*0.05*	*0.02*	*0.01*
	Level of significance for one-tailed test			
N	*0.05*	*0.025*	*0.01*	*0.005*
5	0			
6	2	0		
7	3	2	0	
8	5	3	1	0
9	8	5	3	1
10	10	8	5	3
11	13	10	7	5
12	17	13	9	7
13	21	17	12	9
14	25	21	15	12
15	30	25	19	15
16	35	29	23	19
17	41	34	27	23
18	47	40	32	27
19	53	46	37	32
20	60	52	43	37
21	67	58	49	42
22	75	65	55	48
23	83	73	62	54
24	91	81	69	61
25	100	89	76	68

Values of *T* that are equal to or less than the tabled value are significant at, or beyond, the level indicated.

Source: taken from Table 1 of McCormack, R.L. (1965). With permission of the publishers.

Appendix 6: Critical values of *s* in the Sign Test

	Level of significance for one-tailed test				
N	*0.05*	*0.025*	*0.01*	*0.005*	*0.0005*
	Level of significance for two-tailed test				
	0.10	*0.05*	*0.02*	*0.01*	*0.001*
5	0	–	–	–	–
6	0	0	–	–	–
7	0	0	0	–	–
8	1	0	0	0	–
9	1	1	0	0	–
10	1	1	0	0	–
11	2	1	1	0	0
12	2	2	1	1	0
13	3	2	1	1	0
14	3	2	2	1	0
15	3	3	2	2	1
16	4	3	2	2	1
17	4	4	3	2	1
18	5	4	3	3	1
19	5	4	4	3	2
20	5	5	4	3	2
25	7	7	6	5	4
30	10	9	8	7	5

Appendix 7: Critical values of Spearman's Rank Order Correlation Coefficient (r_s)

Level of significance for a two-tailed test

	0.10	*0.05*	*0.02*	*0.01*

Level of significance for one-tailed test

N	*0.05*	*0.025*	*0.01*	*0.005*
4	1.000			
5	.900	1.000	1.000	
6	.829	.886	.943	1.000
7	.714	.786	.893	.929
8	.643	.738	.833	.881
9	.600	.700	.783	.833
10	.564	.648	.745	.794
11	.536	.618	.709	.755
12	.503	.587	.671	.727
13	.484	.560	.648	.703
14	.464	.538	.622	.675
15	.443	.521	.604	.654
16	.429	.503	.582	.635
17	.414	.485	.566	.615
18	.401	.472	.550	.600
19	.391	.460	.535	.584
20	.380	.447	.520	.570
21	.370	.435	.508	.556
22	.361	.425	.496	.544
23	.353	.415	.486	.532
24	.344	.406	.476	.521
25	.337	.398	.466	.511
26	.331	.390	.457	.501
27	.324	.382	.448	.491
28	.317	.375	.440	.483
29	.312	.368	.433	.475
30	.306	.362	.425	.467

Values of r_s that equal or exceed the tabled value are significant at, or below the level indicated.

Source: Zar, J.H. (1972). *With permission of the author and publisher.*

Part 9

Putting it into Practice

Coursework
Graham Davies

Examination techniques
Mike Cardwell

Applied psychology
Phil Banyard

Chapter 31

Coursework

Graham Davies

Preview

In this chapter we will be looking at the different aspects of producing coursework for AS- and A- level psychology, including:

- the support documents available from the exam board
- how coursework should be organized and presented
- the ethical constraints which you will need to consider
- how to write up a coursework report.

Introduction

The aim of this chapter is to help you gain maximum benefit from your AS- or A-level psychology coursework. For A-level psychology, the requirement is to submit two pieces of coursework, one of which must be experimental in nature and one non-experimental. For AS level, you need to produce one piece which can be either experimental or non-experimental. For both AS- and A-level the coursework you conduct must be supervised by a teacher. It will account for 20 per cent of your final mark, so it is worth doing well. The piece(s) of coursework must be linked to the syllabus (for A-level candidates each piece must be linked to a different syllabus section).

Exam board documents

The AEB produces a series of documents to help you with your coursework reporting. You should have copies of, or access to, the following:

- *AS and A Level Psychology – Coursework Components: Notes for Guidance to Candidates*

  This document provides guidance on the examination requirements and on how coursework should be presented. It also contains the ethical guidelines for carrying out coursework produced by the Association for the Teaching of Psychology (ATP 1992) with which you will need to familiarize yourself.

- *Practical Report Mark Sheet*

  You will need to attach one of these, with the appropriate sections completed, to the front of each report submitted for marking.

- *Marking Scheme for Coursework*

  This is an important source of guidance. If you study the highest mark bands carefully, you can gain considerable insight into what is required for higher marks.

- *Malpractice in 'A'/'AS' Coursework*

  This document outlines the action that is taken for claiming that someone else's work is your own or for copying from textbooks or other candidates. It is not a nice thing to mention, but all AS- or A-level students are advised to read this document carefully, noting the contents.

Although it is aimed at teachers, you might also like to look at *Psychology A level and AS: Syllabus Support Materials for Teachers*. This book contains a number of marked examples of AS- and A-level psychology coursework (of varying standards), together with notes provided by the Principal Coursework Moderator on its strengths and weaknesses. Ask your teacher or lecturer if you can see a copy.

Organization and presentation

The maximum length for each coursework report is 2,000 words (exclusive of tables, graphs, charts or appendices) – you should remember that conciseness is an important report writing skill. Reports should be submitted on A4 paper, preferably secured by treasury tags or in a plastic document file. Please do not use bulky ring files, paper clips or plastic wallets from which the work has to be removed before it can be read – moderators dislike these!

The write-up of your investigation needs to be organized and produced in a manner appropriate for a scientific report. There is no single correct way of doing this, but the approach outlined in this chapter is one that is widely used and one that you may find helpful. The following tips may be useful:

- Avoid using the first person singular or plural ('I' or 'we'). Opinions differ on this point, but many students comment that they find it easier to write reports using the third person (i.e. 'the investigation was carried out' rather than 'I carried out an investigation').
- Keep to the past tense. Remember that your coursework is reporting what has taken place, rather than what you are about to do. Therefore you will find it much easier if you use the past tense, otherwise you might find yourself stringing together phrases such as 'The participants were about to have been able to have been...'
- Label all pieces of paper connected with a particular investigation with the report title – it can be hard to work out later on what odd fragments of data are if you do not do this.
- Write your report up as soon as you have completed the investigation. It is much harder if you leave it and return to it later on!
- Leave yourself enough time to write your report. It will probably take longer than you think, and rushed work often leads to careless errors. Don't forget that credit is given to the quality of your written expression.

Ethical considerations

Ethical issues have been discussed elsewhere in this book (see Chapter 27), but they warrant further discussion here as they arise whenever research is carried out in the name of psychology. It is vitally important that you are familiar with ethical guidelines before you carry out the investigations for your coursework, and you should familiarize yourself with both the ethical guidelines produced for practising psychologists by the British Psychological Society (BPS 1993) and those produced for students at pre-degree levels by the Association for the Teaching of Psychology (ATP 1992). These guidelines have been developed at least in part due to difficulties with ethical issues which have arisen in the past. If you are an AEB AS- or A-level psychology candidate you should have your own copy of the ATP ethical guidelines as they form part of the *Notes for Guidance to Candidates* published by the AEB.

Any work that you carry out for your psychology coursework must be approved by your examination centre. If you go ahead without this approval, the examination centre may refuse to accept it for marking. Ask your teacher or lecturer for advice.

The key ethical issues are laid out in Table 31.1.

Table 31.1 Ethical considerations when carrying out psychological research

General issues

- Should the study be carried out at all?
- Is it being carried out in the most ethical way?
- Do the ends justify the means?
- What are the 'costs' and 'benefits' of the work?

Consent

- Informed consent should be given by participants wherever possible.
- Deception of participants should be avoided.
- Debriefing of participants should take place.
- Participants have the right to withdraw from an investigation at any time.
- Participants completing an investigation have the right to refuse the use of their data.
- Participants may see a researcher as being in a position of power, so pressure should not be placed on people to continue to take part when they do not wish to do so.
- Right to privacy should be respected.
- Some participants may not be in a position to give informed consent themselves (these include children, elderly people and those with special needs).

Conduct

- Safety of self, those in the investigator's care and others the investigator comes into contact with must be maintained at all times.
- Physiological and psychological discomfort to others should be avoided.
- Act within the law.
- Do not copy data, copyright materials or other people's wording.
- Participants should leave the research situation in at least as good a psychological state as they entered it.

Competence

- Researchers should be sufficiently qualified to carry out the work undertaken.

Confidentiality

- Maintain confidentiality of data at all times.
- Do not name participants (numbers of pseudonyms may be used).

Source: Davies 1994a

❖ Activity 1 ❖

Before you undertake any of your coursework, read through the list of ethical issues in Table 31.1 and check that you understand why each is important. If you come across an issue that you do not understand then consult your teacher or lecturer for advice.

> 'Psychological research can be fun, but it should not be carried out just for fun.' (ATP ethical guidelines 1992)

Some psychological research is fun to do, but may involve costs to participants (e.g. in terms of potential discomfort or embarrassment) that are unjustifiable. The fact that research has been carried out in the past by qualified psychologists does not mean that it is an appropriate topic for study by AS- or A-level psychology candidates. For example, research on bystander behaviour, conformity or personal space may involve levels of deception or discomfort which are inappropriate. In such cases, do something else. Psychology has many fascinating possibilities for studies to be carried out which do not involve either deception or any physical or psychological discomfort.

You should not exploit others simply for your own interests. It is particularly important that you consider the rights of those who may not be in a position to give their full informed consent, for example those with special needs and people who are mentally ill. Children represent another vulnerable group – if you are studying them you *must* obtain informed consent from their parents, and it is also courteous to ask the children themselves. Remember that you will probably have to produce a simple and jargon-free way of doing this.

Sometimes, the fact that debriefing of participants takes place is seen as removing any risks that result from deception. You need to think carefully about this – sometimes deception can enter into the debriefing process, e.g. when participants ask 'how they did', as illustrated in the cartoon. If you feel that answering such questions honestly might upset your participants, then you should not embark on the study in the first place.

All the following scenarios could come from genuine psychological investigations, but how would you feel if...

- ❖ ... you are a parent with your children in the park. You see someone watching your children and making notes on their behaviour.
- ❖ ... you carry out a survey involving questions on activities such as under-age drinking or the taking of illegal drugs. Legitimate authorities (e.g. a head teacher, college principal or the police) then question you about your sources of information. In such circumstances you have no legal right to keep your participants' identities confidential.

Before carrying out any investigation as part of your psychology coursework, you should ask yourself the questions shown in Table 31.2 (derived from the ATP ethical guidelines).

Debriefing of participants can itself raise ethical issues

Table 31.2 Questions to ask before carrying out investigations

- Should I be conducting this kind of study at all?
- What is the most ethical way of carrying it out?
- Am I sufficiently competent to carry it out?
- Have I informed the participants of all that they need and would expect to know before taking part?
- Have they willingly agreed to take part?
- How do I ensure that all research records are confidential and anonymous, and will remain so?
- How do I ensure that my research is carried out professionally and in a way that protects the rights of those involved?

Source: Association for the Teaching of Psychology 1992

Writing up a coursework report

The following pages provide detailed guidance on what you might consider including in the different sections of a coursework report.

❖ Activity 2 ❖

Obtain two or three examples of research reports from journals or textbooks. As you read the suggestions for layout outlined here, review these in terms of good or poor practice.

Selecting an informative title isn't always as easy as it seems. You need to avoid a general title which gives the reader little information on the nature of the investigation, e.g. 'Short-term memory'. A useful way of thinking about titles is to consider the key variables involved in the investigation, for example, 'The relationship between health and stress levels', or 'The effect of imagery on encoding'.

The abstract

The aim of writing an abstract is to summarize the complete investigation briefly and clearly so that someone new to the topic being investigated can gain an idea of what actually happened. This should not be more than a paragraph or two long and merits careful writing – composing an abstract is a skill which needs to be practised if you are to perfect it. Within this short section you should provide information on:

- the background idea of the investigation (e.g. the previous research that it was based on)
- the aim(s) and/or hypothesis(-es)
- the research method/design
- the sample of participants
- the results of the investigation (including the statistical conclusion, where appropriate)
- how the findings were interpreted.

Given the short length of this section you have no more than a sentence or two on each of the above points. Although this section will appear at the beginning of your report, you will probably find it easier to write it last as it summarizes the whole investigation.

❖ Activity 3 ❖

Read one of the major studies for your AS- or A-level psychology course (or a detailed report of it). Try to write an abstract for this study.

The introduction

The introduction section aims to provide a rationale for the investigation that has been undertaken. It should contain relevant previous research or background material, developing logically into a discussion of the reasoning behind the current study, and end with a clear statement of the investigation's aim(s) and/or hypotheses. While you are reporting the introduction to a coursework investigation remember that the writing should progress smoothly and avoid sudden changes in direction. Coolican (1994) provides a helpful way of thinking about this process, suggesting that the introduction to an experimental report should be like a funnel (see Fig. 31.1a).

A good way to start an introduction is to outline briefly in broad terms the area that you are investigating. Once you have completed this, you should continue by discussing any previous research that has taken place on the topic in question. The key point here is to make sure that the research you are quoting is focused on the topic that is being investigated. You should not treat the introduction as an opportunity to write a general essay on the area concerned. Try not to fall into the trap of writing absolutely everything that you can find on the topic concerned – if you produce an introduction of excessive length then you are unlikely to obtain full marks for this section. Remember that the introduction can be regarded as a funnelling down

Figure 31.1a Coolican's concept of the introduction as a funnel compared to some less successful approaches (Fig. 31.1b and c)

Start with the general psychological subject area. Discuss theory and research work which is relevant to the research topic. Move from the general area to the particular hypotheses to be tested via a coherent and logical argument as to why specific predictions have been made. State the specific HYPOTHESIS

Figure 31.1b

Sometimes, however, the general topic area remains broad and the discussion is not focused specifically on the research topic in question. There is no real attempt to formulate the hypotheses and a sudden break in continuity occurs before the specific hypothesis is stated

Figure 31.1c

Another approach which fails to achieve the funnelling down achieved in Fig.31.1a is one in which general information on the research area in question occurs in various places throughout the introduction. Research studies on the area of interest are included, but not presented in a logical order, which makes the development of ideas hard to follow. Again, a break in continuity occurs before the specific hypothesis is stated process – as you write it, you move closer and closer to the specific aspect of the topic that you are investigating. So, end your introduction with the research that is closest to the area that you are researching.

Once you have reviewed relevant previous research, it is time to move on to develop the rationale behind your own investigation. How did your ideas develop from the previous research that has been outlined? Why was this considered to be an interesting area for investigation? What were the aims of your study? How did you formulate your hypothesis(-es)? If you have a specific reason for selecting either a one-tailed or two-tailed hypothesis, then this is the place to say what the reasons were behind your decision. It is very important to state clearly any null/alternative hypotheses investigated. These should be written in an operationalized form (i.e. one that is precisely testable) – a common problem with the phrasing of hypotheses in completed coursework reports is that they often read more like general aims.

If you re-read your introduction you should be able to see the logical flow of ideas.

The method section

In the method section you will need to state precisely how your investigation was carried out. An aim to keep in mind here is that you should be able to give your report to someone who is unfamiliar with the investigation concerned, who should then be able to replicate it from your description. You will probably find writing this section easier if you divide it into subsections. There is no single correct way of doing this – what follows is a common 'tried and tested' format. Each of these subsections may well be only one or two paragraphs in length.

Design

In the design subsection you will need to state the research method used (e.g. naturalistic observation or experiment). The best students will elaborate this and justify why this method was used. You should then go on to outline and justify the actual design used. For example, if your report is based on an experiment using a repeated measures design, you might briefly outline what the experimental conditions were and state why this design was used in preference to independent measures. Don't forget to mention such things as the number of participants per group or how many trials participants undertook. This is also the place to tell the reader what your key variables were. For example, in an experiment it is useful to report the independent and dependent variables here, remembering to avoid vague phrasing. How did you control or eliminate unwanted variables? Some students also like to use this section to report (and justify) the minimum level of statistical significance that they are prepared to accept when using inferential statistics to analyse their results.

A growing number of students include a report of any ethical issues associated with the design in this section. This is a welcome trend.

Participants

In the participants subsection you should state the number of participants that you have used. You might also report their age range and gender (but only if these are relevant to the investigation). You should also state the sampling method used to select your participants together with the population from which they were drawn. A common misconception here concerns random samples (see Chapter 29). Remember that taking every tenth person or using anyone that is available are not random techniques (although they may result in a representative sample) as every participant does not stand an equal chance of selection. Don't forget to say how your participants were allocated to different groups or conditions.

Apparatus and/or materials

This is a subsection where many students fail to do themselves full justice. Here you should report the details of any apparatus or materials used. If materials are in written form, then you may well find it useful to include a copy in an appendix at the end of your report. Also, you might find it helpful to refer to scoresheets or standardized instructions to participants here – it is vital to include the latter as this helps to ensure that the investigation that you are describing is fully replicable. However, don't include trivial details such as makes of pens or pencils, and remember that it is unnecessary to include every single response sheet or questionnaire – a specimen included in an appendix is usually sufficient.

Procedure

The procedure is the place to report exactly how the investigation was carried out. The key issue here is replicability. So if, for example, you are carrying out a case study, you will need to report it in such a way that someone else could carry out a similar study after reading your description. If it is an experiment, then you will need to say what the participants had to do. If you test each participant individually, you will probably find it easier to report the procedure for one participant and then state that this procedure was repeated x times. Some students prefer to present their standardized instructions to participants here. Alternatively, you may like to include them as an appendix, but if you do, remember to refer to them here.

The results section

Coursework assessors are often surprised by the indifferent quality of results sections when compared to the other sections of reports. Results sections often appear to have had less time and effort spent upon them. Once again, there is no single correct way of writing up this section. Alternative approaches are possible, all capable of earning full marks, so adopt the way that suits you best. For example, some candidates divide their material into two sections, headed 'results' and 'treatment of results' respectively, whereas others prefer to use a single section headed 'results'.

Organization

Whichever approach you decide to adopt, it is important to organize it in such a way that there is a logical flow of information presented to the reader (as with the rest of your report, it is important to express everything clearly, assuming that the reader is unfamiliar with the piece of work that you have undertaken).

First of all, decide which information you are going to present in your results section, and which you are going to place in an appendix.

Items which are best placed in an appendix are those which interrupt the flow of the text. For example, tables of raw data, specimen scoresheets, completed questionnaires or statistical computations. This does not mean that they cannot be mentioned in this section – it is good practice for every appendix to be referred to at some point in the text.

The best AS- and A-level students produce a results section which includes a text that guides the reader through the various elements of the results, and this greatly improves the accessibility of this section for the reader (remember that your examiner may be unfamiliar with the investigation undertaken). The results section might include the following:

- statement of how data have been obtained (for example, how questionnaires or observational studies have been scored – students frequently omit this, which means that it is difficult to achieve full marks for replicability
- reference to a table containing the raw data which should be included as an appendix to the report (e.g. 'A table showing the numbers of words recalled correctly by participants in the imagery and random list conditions can be found in Appendix 2.')
- an appropriate summary table of results – this table should also be referred to in the text of the results section

- reference to any graphs and/or charts which have been used to summarize the data
- the full reasons for using any inferential statistical test and what the results of its application are.

A *summary table* might include appropriate descriptive statistics. For example, relevant measures of central tendency (such as mean or median) or of dispersion (e.g. range or standard deviation) can often be used to good effect. Select the measures which are most appropriate for the particular investigation, and remember to state what these statistics actually tell us about the results of the investigation.

A good *graph* or *chart* can add greatly to the clarity of reporting your findings. It is useful to remember here that selectivity of the techniques employed is important. An appropriate technique for a particular investigation might be a scattergraph (in a study involving correlational analysis), a bar chart, histogram, frequency polygon or pie chart. This is not meant to be an exhaustive list, and many students use other specialized techniques which are appropriate in the context of the investigation concerned. The key factor is to assess your requirements *before* you begin to produce your illustrations; it is, unfortunately, quite common for candidates to include beautifully drawn graphs or charts which show little that is relevant in terms of the original aims and hypotheses of the investigation. Two things which you should try to avoid are:

- graphs or charts with 'Participant number' on their *x*-axes – these rarely show useful information, and indeed interpretations can sometimes be bizarre (e.g. 'participant 7.8 recalled 9.1 words')
- unnecessary repetition – you are very unlikely to gain extra marks for presenting the same information in several different ways (e.g. on a pie chart, frequency polygon and histogram).

Keep in mind that the specific aim of your illustrations is to add to the clarity (and quality) of your results. Your graphs or charts should, therefore, show something that can be related to the aims and hypotheses of your investigation. For example, they might compare the distributions of scores in the different conditions of an experiment, or show the relationship between sets of data which are being correlated.

The best coursework reports provide reasoned explanations for the choice of any *statistical test*, with students basing their reasons for selection on the nature of the data that they have obtained and what they are trying to demonstrate from its application. It may be useful, for example, to state whether the analysis is aiming to find a difference, correlation or association, as well as to provide comments on the nature of the data obtained (e.g. whether it is measured on a nominal, ordinal, interval or ratio scale). The results section is not the place to include your statistical calculations. They can be referred to here, but actual calculations should be consigned to an appendix.

You should always report the results of a statistical test if you have used one. It is important here that you have adopted an appropriate minimum level of statistical significance and reported the level of statistical significance actually achieved. Was your null hypothesis rejected or retained at your chosen level of significance?

Presentation of results

Care taken in the presentation of the results section can be rewarding. When drawing graphs or charts, it is helpful to use a sharp pencil or an appropriate pen (not an elderly felt tip or blobby ball-point). Alternatively, if you know that this is one of your weak areas, use computer-generated graphics. Try to think of appropriate titles for each of your graphs, charts or tables – you should aim to produce something which makes it immediately clear what the illustration is showing, without having to refer to the text. For example, 'results' or 'data' would be insufficient. 'Table showing the mean number of words recalled in the imagery and random list conditions' would be much more informative. Some students head their tables with terms such as 'Condition A' or 'Condition B' – but this does not make it easy for the reader (such as your coursework moderator) who has not been involved directly with the study to understand what is happening. It is also important to ensure that labelling of graphs, charts and tables is carried out to a high standard. You should ensure that, for example, headings of columns of data and labels on axes of graphs are meaningful, with the relevant units of measurement given wherever appropriate.

Discussion section

The discussion section often seems to be the place where, perhaps more than on any other section of the coursework report, the good candidate will score well and the weaker candidate poorly. With careful planning and by logically sequencing your ideas, it is possible to maximize your marks. It is useful to try and answer the following six questions in your reports.

1 What do your results actually mean?

Ideally, this first part of the discussion section will follow on logically from the end of your results section. In fact, a good way to start your discussion is to state the results that you obtained. How do these results fit in with the aims and/or hypotheses that you proposed at the start of your study? This is also the place to discuss, if necessary, any individual results, e.g. any atypical data that may have affected the outcome of your study. Be careful with your interpretation, keep in mind the nature of your sample of participants and that you should not generalize results inappropriately.

2 How do your results fit in with previous research?

In your introduction section you will have discussed the background research relevant to the investigation that you have undertaken. In your discussion, you should now move on to consider the ways in which your research supports or fails to support this previous research. Weaker candidates here will merely state that 'the results support the findings of research by...'. Better candidates, on the other hand, will be able to go on to compare the data obtained from previous investigations with those from their own study, discussing any similarities or differences. Selectivity of material is very important in the introduction sections of your coursework reports and if you have written an introduction which is suitably selective, this should benefit you here as you will be linking your results to those from appropriate theory or research.

If, however, your results do not fit in with those obtained from any previous research, then this is the place to suggest possible reasons why this might be so. You may need to examine any differences in methodology carefully if you are to do this well.

Remember that you should not need to introduce background studies into the discussion section that have not been mentioned previously in the introduction. If you find that you are doing this, then your selection of studies made in the introduction may need revising. Also, avoid making statements which are demonstrably untrue. Such statements might claim, for example, that your results 'prove the work of Bower to be wrong'.

3 What are the methodological limitations of your study?

This is your opportunity to criticize constructively the method that you have used in your study. It is important here that you confine yourself to factors which really are likely to have affected the outcome and not descend into trivia. The possible effects of any serious design weaknesses should be addressed here, for example, a failure to counterbalance in a repeated measures design or problems with observer reliability in a naturalistic observational study. Try to avoid potentially trivial points such as using a random sample instead of an opportunist one (when this is unlikely to have affected the results anyway), using more participants (when plenty were used), or minor issues such as time of day, light levels or room temperature. These should only be mentioned if you really do feel that they may have affected your results.

4 If you did the investigation again, how could you improve it?

You now have the opportunity to suggest how the problems that you have identified could be overcome if you were to undertake the investigation again. The suggestions that you make here should be both practical and ethical.

5 What are the wider implications of your results?

This is your opportunity to step back and assess the wider practical or theoretical implications of your findings. You might also review any ethical issues which arose in your investigation. It is difficult to give precise guidance here as the implications are often specific to a particular study, but you might consider whether, for example, there are implications for society, education, specific psychological theories or equal opportunities policies.

6 Can you suggest any follow-up studies?

You could now move on to suggest the possible direction for any further research. Given your findings, where could you go from here? What other research proposals could you make? How would you carry these out? Avoid simply stating the general area that might be investigated, but go a bit further and suggest the method or design that might be used to achieve your proposal. This will also serve to reinforce your knowledge of research methods which will be examined in the written papers.

Conclusion

The conclusion section should summarize briefly your main findings. These need to be described without the use of statistical notation.

References

You will need to include references for:

- all studies that you have quoted in your coursework report
- any books or journals that you obtained information from
- any computer packages that you have used.

References should be given in alphabetical order of author. For a book reference you will need to give the author (including the initials), date of publication, title of the book and the publisher. For example:

McFarland, D. (1985) Animal Behaviour, Pitman.

References for journal articles should provide the author and title of the article, the name of the journal concerned, the volume number and the relevant page numbers, thus:

Meddis, R. (1965) 'On the function of sleep', Animal Behaviour, 23, 676–691.

Occasionally you may need to give the reference for an article in a book that has been edited by someone else. This can be done as follows:

Moore, B.R. (1973) 'The role of directed Pavlovian reactions in simple instrumental learning in the pigeon', in R. A. Hinde and J. Stevenson-Hinde (eds) Constraints on Learning, Academic Press.

It is permissible to quote the references for studies by giving the full details of the text that you used – for example:

Marler, P. (1959) 'Developments in the study of animal communication', in P.R. Bell (ed.) Darwin's Biological Work: Some Aspects Reconsidered, Cambridge: Cambridge University Press.

There are conventions about how to present references:

- ❖ Titles of books and journals are normally underlined (as on the previous page) or, if you are using a word processor, italicized (as in the *References* section at the end of this book).
- ❖ Titles of articles or chapters in books are in roman (ordinary) letters, but are put inside quotation marks. These can be either single or double marks – it's up to you to choose, but once you have made your choice, use the same kind of quotation marks throughout.
- ❖ You can choose whether or not to include full stops after authors' initials. Again, be consistent – either put them all in or none at all.

❖ Activity 4 ❖

Practise giving references in the ways outlined above when you carry out your essay work. Developing the habit of providing good accurate references will stand you in good stead if you continue your studies into higher education.

Decide what conventions you will use to present references. You may find it useful to spend a few minutes looking at the list of references at the back of this book and working out what conventions have been used for this book.

Appendices

An appendix is the proper location for material that interrupts the readability of your report. For example, appendices might contain stimulus materials, diagrams of research layouts, tally charts from observational studies, specimen questionnaire surveys, raw data tables or statistical calculations. Do not, however, treat them as a repository for rough notes – everything that you place in your report will be marked. If you are including specimen response sheets or questionnaires, remember that you will not need to include every single copy – a specimen is normally quite sufficient.

Final checks

When you have finished writing your report:

- ❖ Carefully check that you have included everything necessary. You may like to use the checklist in the chapter summary to help you do this.
- ❖ Check your English (including the spelling). Don't forget that marks are awarded for quality of language.
- ❖ Complete a report mark sheet as far as possible and attach it securely to the front of your report.
- ❖ Remember to photocopy your report if you are likely to want to look at it again before you have completed your course.

Chapter summary

Checklist: AS- and A-level practicals

The checklist on the next two pages is designed to help you maximize your marks for practical work based on experimentation or correlational analysis. With a little ingenuity you can also adapt it for observational studies. Using the checklist as a starting point, create your own master copy which you can photocopy and use for each of your practicals. Remember, though, that not every question will apply to every study.

Name:

Title of practical work:

Abstract (summary)

Have you stated:

- ☐ the topic area studied?
- ☐ the aim/hypothesis?
- ☐ brief details of the method used?
- ☐ the principal findings?
- ☐ the main implications of your findings?

Introduction

Have you:

- ☐ stated the general area of your study?
- ☐ referred to relevant and carefully selected background studies?
- ☐ reported your reasons for studying this topic?
- ☐ precisely stated: (a) the alternative hypothesis(-es)
  (b) the null hypothesis(-es)?
- ☐ stated whether the alternative hypotheses are 1-tailed or 2-tailed?
- ☐ reported how you arrived at these aims/hypotheses?
- ☐ justified the direction of your hypotheses?
- ☐ organized your introduction in a logical way?

Method

Have you:

- ☐ divided this section into suitable subsections?

Have you stated:

- ☐ the design used?
- ☐ why this design was chosen?
- ☐ the nature of any experimental groups/conditions?
- ☐ the nature of any control groups/conditions?
- ☐ the IV and DV or the variables correlated?
- ☐ the variables that you controlled and how you controlled them?
- ☐ stated the minimum level of statistical significance you will accept?
- ☐ your number of participants?
- ☐ the population from which participants were drawn?
- ☐ how participants were selected/sampled?
- ☐ how participants were allocated to experimental groups/conditions?
- ☐ relevant characteristics of participants, e.g. age range, sex?
- ☐ details of all apparatus and materials used?
- ☐ any standardized instructions given to participants?
- ☐ the procedure followed in such a way that someone else could replicate it precisely using your description?
- ☐ any ethical issues which you took into account when designing and conducting your investigation?

Results

Have you:

- ☐ provided a summary table of results?
- ☐ provided titles for all graphs, charts and data tables?
- ☐ labelled appropriately all axes and columns of your graphs, charts and data tables?
- ☐ used appropriate descriptive/inferential statistical techniques?
- ☐ stated full reasons why a particular statistical test was selected to analyse your data?
- ☐ reported appropriately your observed and critical values?
- ☐ reported your level of significance?
- ☐ reported the outcome of your study in terms of the hypotheses tested?

Discussion

Have you discussed:

- ☐ your findings with reference to the studies quoted in your introduction?
- ☐ what your results mean in terms of your aims/hypotheses?
- ☐ the limitations of your study?
- ☐ how improvements could be made to the study if it was to be undertaken again?
- ☐ suggestions for follow-up studies?
- ☐ any wider implications of your findings?

Conclusion

Have you:

- ☐ provided full references for all sources used and all quoted by name in your report?
- ☐ written references in a conventional style?

Appendices

Have you:

- ☐ provided copies of such things as stimulus materials and experimental layouts which are referred to in the text but not included elsewhere?
- ☐ provided a table of raw data?
- ☐ included specimen statistical calculations?
- ☐ provided appropriate titles and labelling for all appendices?

Presentation

Have you:

- ☐ written your report in a concise scientific style?
- ☐ structured your report logically into sections?
- ☐ avoided unnecessary repetition or irrelevancy?
- ☐ provided a contents page and numbered your pages?
- ☐ presented your report in such a way that someone else could precisely replicate the study from your description?
- ☐ linked all graphs, charts and data tables into your text?

Further reading

Your key sources are likely to be the support materials produced by the Exam Board. However, you will find the following useful:

Association for the Teaching of Psychology (1992) *Ethics in Psychological Research: Guidelines for Students at Pre-degree Level*, Leicester: Association for the Teaching of Psychology.

British Psychological Society (1993) *Code of Conduct, Ethical Principles and Guidelines*, Leicester: British Psychological Society.

These sets of ethical guidelines are essential reading for any student undertaking coursework.

Coolican, H. (1994) *Research Methods and Statistics in Psychology* (2nd edn), London: Hodder and Stoughton.

Coolican, H. (1995) *Introduction to Research Methods and Statistics in Psychology*, London: Hodder and Stoughton.

These two textbooks provide valuable reference texts which give detailed information on the research methods that you are likely to be using in your coursework. The first text provides the greater detail, the second is briefer and more condensed.

Chapter 32

Examination techniques

Mike Cardwell

Preview

In this chapter we shall be looking at the following aspects of the examination process:

- examination preparation
- examination performance
- examination marking.

Introduction

Examinations are generally among the most feared times in our lives. The stress of the lead-up period, the pressure to do well, the impenetrable questions and those awful two months when we fear that examiners are doing their level best to undo our best efforts. As they say in the songs, it doesn't have to be that way. Like an athlete training for the Olympics, a student training for an A-level examination simply needs to know how to harness all that good intent in the most cost-effective way possible. The pressure? Well most of that is self-imposed anyway, and perhaps we all need to be reminded that in the great scheme of things, examination success is relatively unimportant compared to some of the more significant aspects of our life. Unlike some of those, you can always take your examination again.

One of the apparently most closely guarded secrets of the examination process is that it isn't a closely guarded secret! Apart from the actual questions, everything else is as predictable as a wet day at Wimbledon. And finally, what does happen to your examination paper after you emerge from the examination hall, your job done and the long wait for the results about to begin? Well, this chapter gives away all those mysteries of the examination process, and should ensure that all the good psychology from the rest of this book doesn't get wasted because of poor preparation or inadequate examination technique. Read on ...

Examination preparation

Revision strategies

'How do I revise?' This is probably one of the questions most often asked by students coming up to an examination. Some of the most common (and largely ineffective techniques) are as follows:

- Make yourself as miserable as possible. This involves sitting in your bedroom for long periods of time, staring at your notes, preferably being sullen and bad tempered towards the rest of the family at the same time. This is technically known as 'studying'.
- Read everything several times until it finally goes in. Textbooks are so wonderful nowadays, all students have to do is learn them off by heart and reproduce them verbatim in examinations. This is known as 'revision'.
- Make charts, timetables and revision plans. Spend a fortune at your local stationers on coloured pens and gummed paper shapes. Plan everything down to the last minute, but don't actually put any of it into practice. This is known as 'organization'.

Although all of these actions are well intentioned, can we really say that they contribute to examination success? Probably not. To do well in examinations takes more guile and planning. Let us look at some of the more useful things that you can do.

1 Revise carefully

The number of hours spent staring at a book is not directly proportional to examination success. There are a number of useful things you can do with your time however. Take a look at the syllabus. The syllabus is split into a number of options (Social, Developmental, Bio-psychology, etc.). You will also see that each of these options is split into a number of subsections (represented by the chapters in this book). Now for the good news. The AEB guarantee one question from each of these subsections. When planning what to revise, you should take this into account. It certainly has the effect of making your revision less stressful.

A word of warning though. If you do decide to concentrate your revision on certain subsections of the syllabus, make sure you cover everything in that subsection rather than just concentrating on the bits you like. This book has been constructed with this type of approach in mind. Each chapter should stand alone for revision purposes. In other words, if you read and absorb Chapter 1, you should be able to answer any question set on the social cognition subsection of the Social psychology part of the syllabus.

The other important aspect of careful revision is to check what you are revising against the requirements of the syllabus. Can you do what the syllabus asks you to do? If you can, then there should be no problem. If you went for your driving test, you would only expect to be tested on three-point turns, emergency braking and so on. The examiner is hardly likely to turn around suddenly and say 'I've got this Challenger tank out in the back, let's see how you get on with that then.'

2 Revise actively

Merely reading material in textbooks is not necessarily the most productive way of using your time. In an examination you will not be asked to 'write everything you can remember about perception'. Instead, you will be given a specific set of instructions which tell you what you should write about and which specific skills you should demonstrate in your answer. Students often do far worse than they deserve to do in examinations because they do not address the second of these points. They can often describe in great detail theories of perception or research on bystander behaviour, but cannot provide any evaluative commentary on that material. It is an inescapable fact in

A-level psychology that you will always be asked to provide narrative content (description, explanation, etc.) and commentary (evaluation, analysis, etc.). You should make a point in your notes of highlighting those points that are part of the narrative and those that are part of your commentary. In the sections that follow, you should become more familiar with how to play this 'skills' game more successfully.

3 Organizing your revision

None of us has enough time for all the things we plan to do and, as the exams get closer, that precious time seems to become scarcer than ever. It is never too early to plan your revision.

Decide (realistically) just how much of the syllabus you are going to revise and make a plan of what you are going to revise and when. Read the Introduction again (at the start of the book) and you will get more of an idea of the way that the syllabus is put together, and what you are expected to do in your revision. It is certainly permissible (perhaps even advisable) to concentrate on certain areas of the syllabus at this stage. If you find you are spending hours and hours dealing with the complexities of one particular subsection of the syllabus, then it might be worth taking a deep breath and dumping it in favour of a subsection where you feel more confident of doing well. Remember when you plan your revision that the heading 'Perception – 6 hours' on a piece of paper doesn't really help you when it comes down to spending those six hours profitably. Instead you might divide your revision time as follows:

- Theories of perception – 2 hours (1 hour description, 1 hour evaluation)
- Perceptual development – 2 hours (1 hour description, 1 hour evaluation)
- Perceptual organization – 2 hours (1 hour description, 1 hour evaluation).

Above all remember you are studying psychology, and try to use all those relevant bits of psychology to help you make this a profitable time. For example, don't cram too much into one session (maximum span of attention), nor expect to remember everything perfectly immediately after the revision session (the reminiscence effect). Reward yourself when you have had a productive session, and don't spend time worrying about what you *should* be doing, just do it and congratulate yourself on a job well done.

Skill A and Skill B

The AEB examination tests your ability in two main skill areas. These are known as Skill A and Skill B. Every examination question tests both of these skills and they are equally weighted in the marking schemes. So what do we mean by Skill A and Skill B?

The best way of thinking about them is to see Skill A as a narrative (i.e. giving information and showing understanding) and Skill B as a commentary (i.e. being able to offer some comments about the narrative, such as evaluating the points made or showing how they fit into a wider body of knowledge). Each question might ask you to offer a slightly different form of Skill A and Skill B, depending on the requirements of the question. Although most of the questions you will come across will use clearly recognizable terms (as in the *Glossary of Terms*), some will not. In some areas of the syllabus, notably comparative and bio-psychology, the requirements for Skill B might be slightly different. For example, imagine the following comparative psychology question from Section 2.1, Reproductive strategies.

Q: (a) Consider evolutionary explanations for parent-offspring conflict. *(12 marks)*

(b) What is the significance of this conflict for the animals concerned? *(12 marks)*

In this case there is no formal Skill B 'instruction' in part (b) although what is required (i.e. how does it affect the animals, and why is it important to each?) should be quite clear.

The 'instructions' on how to answer questions are contained in the terms used in the question wording itself, which are published by the AEB in the document *Glossary of Terms*. A simplified version of this *Glossary of Terms* is presented in Table 32.1.

It is well worth your while learning the differences between the different terms, particularly which are Skill A terms, which are Skill B, and which require a mixture of Skill A + B.

Table 32.1 Skill A and Skill B terms

Skill A terms	
Consider	show knowledge and understanding of the topic area.
Define	explain what is meant by a particular term.
Describe	show knowledge of the topic area.
Examine	present a detailed descriptive consideration of the topic area.
Explain	show understanding of a topic in a coherent and intelligible way.
Outline/State	offer a brief description (in summary form) of the topic area.
Skill B terms	
*Analyse/Critically analyse**	demonstrate understanding through a consideration of the different components of the topic area.
*Assess/Critically assess**	present a considered appraisal of the topic area through a judgement of the strengths and limitations of the information presented.
Criticize	evaluate in terms of the strengths and weaknesses of the topic area.
*Evaluate/Critically evaluate**	make an informed judgement of the value of a topic area.
Skill A + B terms	
Compare and contrast	consider both the similarities and differences between the topic areas.
Critically consider	show knowledge and understanding of a topic area, plus the strengths and limitations of the material used.
Distinguish between	consider the differences between two topic areas.
Discuss	describe and evaluate a topic area.

*These terms are used interchangeably and have the same meaning as each other.

(adapted from the Glossary of Terms, AEB)

Let's take a look at this in the context of a specific examination question:

Q: Discuss any two theories of moral development. *(24 marks)*

The 'instruction' in this question is *discuss*, which we can translate as requiring a description (the Skill A requirement) and an evaluation (the Skill B requirement) of two theories of moral development. This would mean that you must describe *and* evaluate *both* theories to gain maximum marks. This does raise another question. What is meant by a 'theory' and how does it differ from a 'model' or indeed from 'research'? The AEB *Glossary of Terms* also offers a translation of these terms (see Table 32.2) so that you can be quite sure what an examination question is asking you to do.

Question setting

When the Chief or Principal Examiners sit down to write an examination paper, they have to follow a number of basic rules and guidelines. The main guidelines are as follows:

- All questions must be drawn from the syllabus, with similar wording wherever possible.
- One question is set on each subsection of the syllabus (i.e. four from Social Psychology, four from Bio-Psychology and so on)
- All questions have an equal weighting of Skill A (12 marks) and Skill B (12 marks). No matter how many parts there are to a question, 12 marks will always be given for Skill A and 12 for Skill B.

Table 32.2 Other terms used in AEB examination questions

Term	Meaning
Applications	actual or possible ways of using psychological knowledge in an applied or practical setting.
Concept(s)	an idea or group of ideas that are often the basic units of a psychological theory.
Evidence	material drawn either from investigations or from theories in order to support or contradict an argument or theory.
Findings	the outcome of a research investigation.
Insights	perceptions from either investigations or theories that help us to understand or appraise a topic area.
Methods	the different ways in which research investigations can be carried out.
Model	used synonymously with 'theory' although it may be less elaborate or complex.
Research	the process of gaining knowledge and understanding either through theory construction and examination or through empirical data collection.
Studies	Empirical investigations.
Theory	a set of interrelated ideas or principles that can be used to explain observed phenomena.

(adapted from Glossary of Terms, AEB)

- Syllabus content which is preceded by the words 'should include' or 'including' can be specified in an examination question. Content which is preceded by the words 'for example' cannot be specified in a question.
- There are no rules regarding repetition of questions. The fact that a topic area is examined one year does not mean it will not be examined the next. Nor does the fact that a particular topic hasn't been examined for a year or two mean that it will automatically be examined soon.

When examination questions are set, the AEB employ a *Revisor* whose job is to check that the questions are appropriate in terms of standard and complexity, and could be answered within the time given. The Revisor must also check that the 'rules' outlined above are adhered to. For example, a question such as the following would be rejected by the Revisor:

Q: Describe and evaluate Piaget's theory of intellectual development. *(24 marks)*

This would not be an appropriate question because, although Piaget's name does appear under the appropriate subsection of the developmental psychology syllabus (cognitive development), it is included as an example of the theories that might be considered. It is not a prescription that Piaget must be studied, therefore questions cannot be asked specifically on this theorist. If you look through the syllabus you will see that sometimes theories or ideas are introduced as 'for example' and sometimes as 'including' or 'should include'. In the former case they cannot be specified in the examination question, in the latter they can.

Activity 1

Each of the following questions would be rejected by a Revisor. Can you work out why? (Answers at the end of the chapter.)

1 Describe any two theories of moral development. *(24 marks)*

2 Critically consider the use of electro-convulsive therapy in the treatment of depression. *(24 marks)*

3 (a) Describe any one theory of human aggression. *(12 marks)*

(b) Reflect upon the insights that might be gathered from this theory in order to reduce aggression. *(12 marks)*

Examination performance

Reading questions

One of the most elusive (it seems) skills for students in examinations is for them to interpret what is actually required from a particular question. This should not be as difficult as it might appear, given what you now know about the way that questions are actually set. The best way to illustrate this is by looking at some typical questions.

Q: Critically consider the contributions of the psychodynamic approach to human behaviour. *(24 marks)*

The 'instruction' for this question is *critically consider* which is a Skill A + B term. Referring back to Table 32.1, you will see that you are required to show 'knowledge and understanding' (Skill A) as well as the 'strengths and limitations' (Skill B) of the material presented. But what is the material required? Let's look more closely at the question. You are required to critically consider the *contributions* of the psychodynamic approach, rather than offer a critical consideration of the psychodynamic approach itself. There is a subtle yet important difference between the two. The contributions might include psychodynamic therapies (see Chapter 17), uses in advertising (see Chapter 26) or indeed in an explanation of other aspects of human behaviour (such as gender role or moral development). Note that the question also requests that any discussion is within the context of *human* behaviour rather than non-human behaviour. This shouldn't be a problem in this context but does often trap students in other areas (for example when talking about the ethical issues in human experimentation).

Q: Describe and evaluate research findings relating to divided attention. *(24 marks)*

The 'instruction' in this question is *describe* (Skill A) and *evaluate* (Skill B). This requires you to show your knowledge of research findings relating to divided attention, and also show the value of those research findings to an understanding of divided attention. Note that the instruction applies to research *findings* not to theories that explain divided attention. AEB questions do now tend to qualify plurals in questions (such as asking you to describe and evaluate *two* theories) but in this case you should assume that *findings* does refer to at least two.

Q: (a) Outline and evaluate research into the influence of the media on antisocial behaviour. *(12 marks)*

(b) Discuss the view that the media may also have a prosocial influence. *(12 marks)*

If you look closely at this question, you will see that it has 'instructions' in each part of the question. In part (a), you are asked to *outline* (Skill A) and *evaluate* (Skill B). This requires a summary description of research into the media/antisocial behaviour connection, as well as a judgement of the value of that research. The term research appears on its own here (i.e. without the qualifier 'evidence' or 'findings') so might include the results from empirical investigations and/or theoretical explanations. The term 'antisocial behaviour' is a broad one (taken from the syllabus) and is not restricted to the more usual aggression. Also relevant might be a consideration of the influence of the media on racism, crimes against women and many other behaviours that might be regarded as 'antisocial'.

In the second part of the question, the 'instruction' is to *discuss* which requires students to show their knowledge of possible links between the media and prosocial behaviour, and then to evaluate (i.e. show the value of) that material. There is no specific request for evidence or theories, nor is there any mention of specific types of media or specific types of prosocial behaviour (there cannot be, as these are not specified on the syllabus). This really gives you the chance to open up your discussion and write about anything that is relevant within the media/prosocial behaviour context. It is important to emphasize, though, that material should be broadly 'psychological' (as opposed to your own ideas and speculations) and that whatever you include, it is both described and evaluated.

❖ Activity 2 ❖

What specific skills are required in each of the following questions?

1 (a) Explain what is meant by the terms prejudice and discrimination. *(6 marks)*

(b) Outline any two strategies for the reduction of prejudice or discrimination. *(6 marks)*

(c) Critically assess the effectiveness of such techniques. *(12 marks)*

2 Critically consider the use of any two different signalling systems used by non-human animals. *(24 marks)*

3 (a) Consider any one approach to the classification of psychological disorders. *(12 marks)*

(b) What are the practical problems and ethical implications of such a classification system? *(12 marks)*

Time management

Having mastered the art of unravelling the requirements of the questions, the next hurdle is for students to manage their time effectively in an examination. This involves both time management *between* questions and *within* questions. The first of these really should present no problems to the well-prepared student. Each question is worth 45 minutes, so if you extend the time you give to one question, you are effectively stealing it from another. You should also remember that this 45 minutes includes thinking time, pencil sharpening and all those other time-consuming activities that we must do in an examination. This does mean that in reality, you tend only to have around 40 minutes of writing time for each question. There is no real reason, therefore, why you should spend more than 45 minutes on any one question. Imagine the following two scenarios.

A		B	
Time *(mins)* per essay	Mark	Time *(mins)* per essay	Mark
60	20	45	16
60	20	45	16
30	10	45	16
30	10	45	16
Total:	**60**	*Total:*	**64**

This is based on the reasoning that it is very much easier to push a mark up from 10 to 16 than it is to push it from 16 to 20. It is rarely cost-effective to push any one individual essay beyond the 45 minutes allocated to it within the confines of a three-hour (or one-and-a-half-hour) examination.

The second problem is to manage your time *within* a question so that all the different aspects and requirements of the question are covered.

Let us take a typical question as an example:

Q: (a) Outline and evaluate research into the influence of the media on antisocial behaviour. *(12 marks)*

(b) Discuss the view that the media may also have a prosocial influence. *(12 marks)*

With 45 minutes to answer this question, you may be tempted to start writing straight away and run the risk of only getting half or two-thirds through the whole question when the 45 minutes is up. To perform effectively and maximize your marks for any particular question, you need a strategy. There are many such strategies, although a particularly effective one is as follows:

- Decide what is required in each question, or part of a question.
- Calculate how much time should be allocated to each aspect of the question.
- Divide the answer into about eight paragraphs, about 5 minutes per paragraph.
- Plan what will go into each paragraph.
- Finally, stick to that plan, and don't go over the allocated time span.

For example, in the question given above, each part is worth the same number of marks, therefore is allocated four paragraphs (20 minutes) each. Each part of the question will be allocated 6 marks for Skill A and 6 for Skill B (therefore two paragraphs each). From then on, it is a simple matter of deciding on the content you want to fill those paragraphs.

❖ Activity 3 ❖

Take the example question given earlier, or any other question in this chapter, and plan an essay according to the eight paragraphs system just proposed.

Examination marking

Although this part of the examination process may not appear to be something that students can actively take part in, a knowledge of the vagaries of examination marking can certainly help you in your quest for the highest marks possible. The AEB uses a separate marking grid for Skill A and Skill B, but they work in the same way. A simplified version of these marking grids can be seen in Table 32.3.

Table 32.3 Marking grid used in AS- and A-level examinations

Mark band	*Marks*	*Skill A and Skill B marking criteria* (*NB: Each skill is marked out of 12 marks. When a part of a question is out of 6 marks, these marks are divided by 2.*)
Band 1	0 to 2	Very little or no psychological content that is relevant to the question. Material may be very weak, muddled and incomplete.
	3 to 4	Basic content which is of a restricted nature. Material may be flawed and lacks depth.
Band 2	5 to 6	Limited content which is generally accurate but lacks detail. Reasonable, although limited, commentary.
	7 to 8	Content is appropriate, accurate and reasonably detailed. Commentary is reasonable if slightly limited.
Band 3	9 to 10	Content is appropriate, accurate and only slightly limited. Commentary is informed and effective.
	11 to 12	Content is appropriate, accurate and well detailed. Material has been used and elaborated in a highly effective manner.

Source: Adapted from AEB marking guidelines

❖ Activity 4 ❖

The next time you write an essay, mark it yourself according to the marking guidelines given in Table 32.3. Try to place your answer in an appropriate mark band descriptor for each of the two skills (A and B). When you have done that, try to assess whether your answer is best described by the 'top' or 'bottom' criteria for that band. From there it should be fairly straight-forward to give yourself an appropriate mark. Next, you should justify the mark you have given. If you are not in the top band, why not? What would you have needed to gain a mark in the top band? If you get used to doing this, and following the guidance from your teachers, you will effectively become an examiner for your own work. It is hard to go backwards after that!

Contrary to popular opinion, examiners are not in the business of trying to find ways to award the lowest marks possible, but neither can they award 'sympathy' marks for essays that are good psychology yet not particularly relevant to the question set. There is a lot involved in examining at this level, but some of the basic rules are as follows:

- All answers are marked at the level of a notional 18-year-old who is writing for 45 minutes under examination conditions. What this means in practice is that examiners do not look for the 'perfect' answer, and are realistic in what they can expect a student to write in 45 minutes.
- Examiners engage in a process known as *positive marking*. This means that they do not look for opportunities to take marks

off (because of errors) but rather for opportunities to add marks *on* (for correct and appropriate material). If you write something that is wrong, the examiner effectively ignores it, and looks for content that can be credited under the terms of the question.

- There are no right or prescriptive answers. One of the features of this subject is that there are many ways to approach questions, and many different perspectives to take in answering them. Students often worry that they might be answering a question in the 'wrong' way. Provided that their answer is *relevant* to the question, it will be credited by the examiner. Examiners often learn things from students, so it is gratifying to know that your work is being marked by an appreciative audience.
- Examiners do not mark with ideas of pass and fail in their mind, nor of the grades they think an answer might be worth. Examiners will award marks according to the marking guidelines illustrated in Table 32.3 together with any special requirements of the question (for example, have the candidates included *two* theories if asked to do so?).
- Names and dates are not perhaps as important as you might imagine. Students spend a great deal of their time revising as many names and dates as they can, perhaps under the impression that it is the weight of such detail that gets the high marks. This impression is bolstered when you read learned academic journals, which appear top heavy with research names and dates. In this guise they do serve an important function, but they are far less important in A-level examinations. Including a researcher's name or the date of the research certainly helps to place the research in context, but so long as a piece of research is recognisable and is described in a way that is both accurate and relevant to the question, it will gain as many marks as if it were anchored to a name and date.
- Quality of language: each examination script is assessed as a whole and up to four marks (or two marks for module papers) awarded for the quality of language used. This involves the accurate expression of ideas, the precise use of specialist terms and good grammar, punctuation and spelling.

❖ Activity 5 ❖

Test your knowledge of the Glossary of Terms.

Knowing your Skill A instructions from your Skill B instructions is a vital part of examination success. Many students come unstuck in an examination simply because they respond inappropriately to the words in a question. The list below comprises a number of these terms. Some are Skill A terms, some Skill B and some Skills A + B. These are mixed in with some bogus terms that are not in the *Glossary of Terms*. Can you identify which are A, B, A + B, and which are bogus? (Clue: There are four of each.)

Admire	Analyse	Appraise	Assess
Compare and contrast	Consider	Critically consider	Critically evaluate
Criticise	Describe	Discuss	Distinguish between
Examine	Inspect	Outline	Slag off

Chapter summary

- Effective revision is more than good intentions and lots of time. It is more a question of being aware of the skills and topics of the syllabus, and structuring your revision in a way that is most likely to bring maximum rewards. This means knowing *what* to revise, *how* to revise and *when* to revise. Given that examinations are both predictable and fair, poor performance is often due to poor preparation.
- It is important to *read* the questions properly, looking in particular for the 'instructions' contained in the *Glossary* terms such as *Describe*, *Assess* and *Critically consider*. It is also important to respond to instructions about the *type* of material required (e.g. theories, research findings) and the *number* of theories, research findings, etc.
- Examiners are guided by a set of guidelines that underlie all AS- and A-level examination marking. There are no prescriptive answers, nor do examiners mark in terms of pass or fail. Examiners engage in positive marking, looking for opportunities to *give* marks for appropriate material rather than knocking them off for material that is wrong or inappropriate.

Answers to Activity 1

1 This question is only assessing Skill A (through the instruction *describe*). The revisor might suggest that an appropriate Skill B term such as *evaluate* is added.

2 The term 'electro-convulsive therapy' does not appear on the syllabus, therefore cannot be specified in a question. That doesn't mean that you cannot write about it (it is part of the *somatic approach* to the treatment of psychological disorders) but an examiner cannot request it.

3 The second part of this question uses a term that is not in the *Glossary of Terms*, nor is it clear exactly what is required. As the first part of the question is all Skill A, the second part should be all Skill B. It is not clear how a student would present Skill B material on the reduction of aggression without first describing those insights (a Skill A requirement).

Chapter 33

Applied psychology

Phil Banyard

Preview

In this chapter we shall be looking at:

- the relationship between psychological theory and its applications
- models of applied research
- some examples of successful and unsuccessful applications of psychology
- applying psychology to our understanding of crime.

Introduction

There are two ways of looking at how psychology has been applied. First, there are the established professional areas of applied psychology which have been developing since the early years of the twentieth century and which have grown considerably in influence in recent years. These are briefly described over the next few pages. The professional areas have developed their own terminologies and their own research traditions. As a result, each area has its own particular outlook and its own way of describing behaviour and experience.

The other way of looking at applied psychology is to consider how we can use psychological concepts in a range of professional situations. It is this second approach that is taken in this chapter. Both of the approaches raise issues about the relationship between theory and practice, and also challenge our models of social research.

The chapter goes on to look at one area where psychology can be applied – crime. There is a brief review of some of the many concepts that help us to understand crime better, and help us to deal with it or prevent it. With such a complex social issue it is not possible to provide the answer to all our concerns, but it is possible to give some insights into human behaviour and experience.

Professional areas of applied psychology

Since the beginning of the twentieth century, the professional areas of applied psychology have increased quite dramatically, and the concepts of psychology are being given wider and wider applications. Below is a brief outline of the main professional areas of psychology.

Industrial/organizational psychology

Industrial/organizational psychology is the scientific study of people in work organizations. These organizations include manufacturing industries such as the car industry, and also service industries such as health. Psychologists in this field are concerned with training, selection of staff, leadership, motivation of staff and co-ordinating diverse work groups.

Recently psychologists have been involved in a wide range of activities including developing a range of selection procedures, improving work practices and introducing techniques for reducing stress at work.

Clinical psychology

Clinical psychology is concerned with people in distress and how their stress can be alleviated. Clinical psychologists attempt to understand behaviour and experience using a variety of tests, observations and other sources of information. They use a range of interventions, such as psychotherapy and behaviour therapy, that have been developed from theory and refined through practice. Some of their interventions are direct (such as therapy) and some are indirect (such as developing community health programmes).

Clinical psychologists are quite distinct from psychiatrists although they often deal with similar issues. Psychiatrists are medically trained before they specialize in psychiatry, whereas clinical psychologists have a foundation in psychology before their specialization as clinicians.

Consumer psychology

One of the earliest applications of psychology was in the area of marketing and selling. When John B. Watson lost his job as a psychologist, he made his living with the J. Walter Thompson advertising company. From 1920 onwards he was very successful in creating advertising campaigns for, among other products, Johnson's Baby Powder and Pond's Cold Cream.

In affluent societies one of the most important influences on behaviour and experience is the 'consumer culture' (Featherstone 1991). The products we buy and display tell other people what sort of person we are, what values we hold, what our social position is and what groups we affiliate to. Identity is displayed, and sometimes acquired, through the clothes we wear and the way we wear them. Psychologists try to identify the factors involved in consumer choice so they can better understand what is happening and also so that business can develop more effective ways of encouraging us to buy expensive and sometimes useless products!

Educational psychology

Psychology can be applied to many aspects of education. It has a lot to say about how people learn and how best to organize educational activities. It also has a long history of developing tests to measure performance. Currently, however, psychologists are most commonly used to assess children who are having problems at school or with whom the school is having problems. The psychologist is asked to assess the child to see whether he or she needs specialist educational help and to identify the intervention which is likely to be most effective.

Children might be referred to a psychologist because of learning difficulties. The psychologist then tries to discover the nature of the difficulty which may be a language problem such as dyslexia (see Chapter 13).

Health psychology

Psychologists have been interested in health issues for many years but it is only since the 1980s that health psychology has developed as a separate field in the subject. The reason for the growth of health psychology is a growing realization that psychological factors play a large part in health and illness. An important policy-document on health from the British

Government, *The Health of the Nation* (The Secretary of State for Health 1992), identifies five key areas for action. The programmes for all these areas require behavioural change rather than medical intervention. For example, the number of deaths from coronary heart disease will reduce if people change their diets and stop smoking.

Health psychology is interested in questions such as why people are so reluctant to follow medical advice. The laboratory work on conformity and compliance by Asch, Crutchfield and Milgram (see Chapter 3) suggests that people are inclined to comply with requests from other people. The same is not true, however, in the real-life issues surrounding health. A survey of people with diabetes by Wing *et al.* (1986) reported that:

- 80% of patients administered insulin in an unhygienic manner
- 58% regularly administered the wrong dose of insulin
- 77% tested their urine incorrectly or made incorrect interpretations of the result
- 75% did not eat the prescribed foods
- 75% did not eat with sufficient regularity.

The problem for health psychologists is to discover why people make these health choices and what interventions can be used to encourage them to make healthy decisions.

Engineering psychology

Engineering psychology is concerned with investigating the relationship between people and machines, so that machines can be designed better and people can be trained in how to design them better. This is by no means as simple as it sounds and development often occurs through disastrous errors that only appear obvious with the benefit of hindsight.

An example of this comes from the experience of the American Air Force during the Second World War (1939–45). At the start of the war, the air force concentrated on training men to fly aircraft rather than designing aircraft that could be flown by men. However, they discovered that even very experienced pilots were prone to make errors with the poorly designed control systems. For example, on some B-25 bombers the landing gear and the steering flaps were operated by similar looking controls which were placed next to each other. The unfortunate consequence of this was that several B-25s were brought in to land without the landing gear in place and so landed on their bellies. The pilots believed that they had activated the landing gear, but in fact they had just steered the plane. Observation like this led to the psychologists helping to develop aircraft controls that more nearly match the capabilities of pilots.

Environmental psychology

Environmental psychology is concerned with issues like the impact of noise and air pollution on people, the effects of crowding, particularly in urban environments, and the changes that planners can introduce to make our environment more pleasant. The research looks at the interaction between the environment and our behaviour.

An example of the concerns raised in this area is sick building syndrome. It is now accepted as a problem by the British Government (see Oliphant 1995), though it is still quite controversial. Sick building syndrome refers to a work environment where a large proportion of the work force develop a range of symptoms such as lethargy and tiredness, dry throat, runny nose or blocked nose, difficulty in breathing, tight feelings in the chest, dry, itchy or watery eyes, headaches, coughs, nausea and mental fatigue. The controversy surrounds whether the syndrome is due to the environment of the building or whether it is due to some psychological factors. For example, Czander (1994) suggested that sick building syndrome is caused by the social dynamics of the work place (for example, bad management–worker relations) that increase the susceptibility of the workers to illness. On the other hand, Bauer *et al.* (1992) carried out a range of psychological measures on workers in sick buildings and found very few differences between workers with symptoms of the disorder and workers without the symptoms. This suggests that the illness comes from the building rather than from psychologically vulnerable people.

Other professional areas

There are a growing number of other professional areas in psychology including:

- sports psychology – which attempts to apply psychological knowledge to sporting performance
- forensic psychology – a special category of legal psychology which concentrates on the evaluation and treatment of criminal offenders
- the broader field of legal psychology – this also looks at a range of applications to the legal system of psychological research findings including those relating to eyewitness testimony and decision-making in juries. These issues are considered later in this chapter.

Theory and application

In make-believe land where trains run on time, love lasts for ever and Cornflakes don't go soggy, there is a clear relationship between *theory* and *application*. In this make-believe land, psychological theory is developed from observation, hypotheses are devised and tested, and applications spring from the loins of this intellectual activity. Application is seen to have a direct link to theory, and this link gives the application the authenticity of being scientific. Sadly, back in everyday life, the reality of this relationship is far less clear.

What then is the relationship between theory and practice? The diagram in Fig. 33.1 shows the *ideal model* of the research process. It is a model that is used to represent the development of knowledge in most sciences. For example, the research studies of physics and material science have helped people develop theories about forces and strains, and these theories have been applied in the construction of bridges. The performance of these bridges is studied and this leads to changes in the theories, and improved design of future bridges.

The question is whether this process occurs in the development of psychology. One of the issues concerns the role of theory in applied psychology. It is commonly thought that a theory should:

- be predictive
- generate hypotheses
- be a vehicle for improving our understanding
- provide models that help the further development of theory
- be testable.

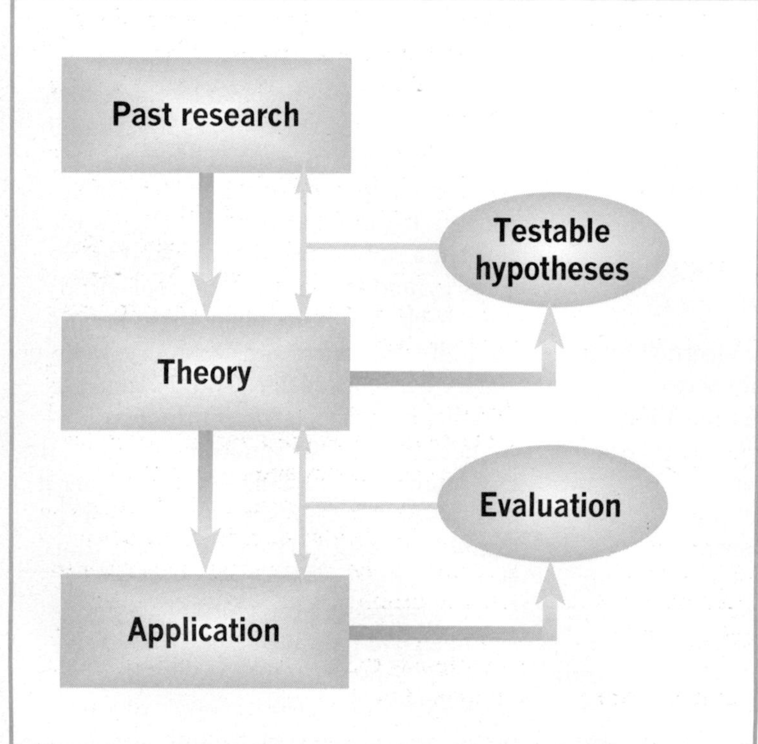

Figure 33. 1 Ideal model of psychological research

Do psychological theories have these qualities? The irritating answer to this question is 'yes, no and maybe'. The following sections look at one example from psychology that does follow the ideal pattern up to a point (locus of control), one that does not follow it at all (intelligence), and one that may have some connection to it (aversion therapy).

Locus of control

An example of the ideal research process is the work on locus of control. This concept comes from the general area of learning theory and was described by Rotter (1966). In brief, the theory suggests that the way we describe our control over events has an important effect on our behaviour and experience – in particular, whether we believe that we have personal control over events (*internal* locus of control) or that events are outside our control (*external* locus of control). An example of research on this theory is by Langer and Rodin (1976), who looked at the effect of locus of control on the health of elderly people in a residential home (see below).

The application of locus of control to the area of health led to the realization that the control beliefs we have about our health are different to the control beliefs we have about other aspects of our life. As a result, the original way of measuring locus of control (using a short questionnaire) was expanded

In Focus

Applying locus of control theory

Is it possible to enhance people's health by helping them experience a greater sense of control? This was the question investigated by Langer and Rodin (1976) in their study of a residential home for the elderly in the USA. The study compared the residents who were living on two different floors of the residential home. The researchers attempted to increase the sense of control in one group of residents through a talk given by the administrator of the home.

In the talk to the experimental group of residents the administrator made the following points:

- you have the responsibility of caring for yourselves
- you can decide how you want your rooms arranged
- you can decide how you want to spend your time
- it's your life
- it's your responsibility to make complaints known.

They were also offered a plant as a present, told that there was a movie showing in the home on Thursday and Friday, and asked which night, if any, they would like to go.

In the talk to the other group of residents, the administrator gave the same details about the home but did not emphasize their sense of control. These residents were given a plant rather than offered it, and were told which night they were to go to the movie.

Langer and Rodin measured the behaviour and experience of the residents through self-report questionnaires and also through the observations of the staff in the home who were not aware of the experimental manipulation. These measurements were made one week before the talk and again three weeks after it. The results showed some large differences between the two groups of residents. For example, the scores for individual residents showed that 93 per cent of the experimental group, but only 21 per cent of the control group, were judged to have improved their quality of life.

To check whether this manipulation had only a short-term effect on the residents, the researchers carried out a further study 18 months later (Rodin and Langer 1977). They found that the experimental group still showed considerable improvement when compared to the other group and were also in better health. This work suggests that a simple application of a psychological theory can improve the quality of life of residents in a nursing home.

by health psychologists such as Wallston *et al.* (1978). This new measurement goes beyond the simple internal–external dimension and looks at three dimensions of health locus of control:

- *internality:* the extent to which locus of control for health is internal
  Example statement: 'If I become sick, I have the power to make myself well again.'
- *chance:* the belief that chance or external factors are affecting the outcome of health problems
  Example statement: 'If I am going to get sick, I will get sick, no matter what I do.'
- *powerful others:* the belief in the control of powerful others (such as doctors) over our health
  Example statement: 'Following doctor's orders to the letter is the best way for me to stay healthy.'

The development of locus of control as a theory in psychology conforms to our ideas about ideal research. It originates from psychological theory and generates testable hypotheses (as in the study by Langer and Rodin). The findings from research lead to revisions of the theory which have further applications and lead to further revisions of the theory. However, some applications in psychology develop in very different ways.

Intelligence testing

Intelligence testing is perhaps the most famous, and controversial, application of psychology. It is discussed in more detail in Chapter 26, but our interest here is how the theory of intelligence relates to the practice of intelligence testing. If our ideal model of research was followed, then we would find the original theories of intelligence that produced testable hypotheses and look at how the research changed these hypotheses, producing better applications of the theory and also modifications of the theory.

The key concept here is *g* – the general factor of intelligence. The importance of this factor is that if we want to quantify a person's intelligence as one number (an IQ score), then there must be a *single factor* of intelligence, otherwise our IQ score is meaningless. So, the validity of IQ tests as a measure of intelligence depends on the existence of *g*.

The British statistician, Charles Spearman, developed the mathematical procedure known as factor analysis which seemed to show a unifying factor in a number of mental test results suggesting the existence of *g*. However, the American psychologist, Thurstone, was able to carry out similar mathematical calculations on the *same data* and make *g* disappear completely (for a review see Gould 1981).

The conclusion from these contradictory findings must be that we are unable to show that *g* exists. This means that the results of IQ tests tell us nothing more than how good we are at IQ tests. Nevertheless, they are used as measures of intellectual performance. As they cannot be mapped on to any psychological theory, we have a robust application of psychology without a theory to back it up. The various modern theories of intelligence that describe a number of separate factors, e.g. those of Guilford (1967) or Sternberg (1985), do not point towards a single number (IQ score) that can describe a person's intellectual ability.

❖ Activity 1 ❖

Think about the applications of psychology you have come across in other parts of the book. What theory are they connected to? How closely are they connected to that theory?

Aversion therapy

A commonly cited application of psychology is aversion therapy which, we are told, was derived from classical conditioning. The story often starts with a description of the work by Watson and Rayner (1920) with an unfortunate child named 'Albert B', more commonly known as Little Albert (see Chapters 8 and 16). Little Albert learnt to fear a white rat which he had previously liked. The little chap also generalized his fear response to hair, soft toys and a Santa Claus mask. Little Albert is described as learning by the process of classical conditioning to associate a neutral stimulus (the rat) with a reflex (fear response to unexpected loud noise). This is often described as an explanation of how phobias develop and how fear can be used to change behaviour.

Aversion therapy is thought to make connections between unpleasant reflexes and unacceptable behaviour (see Fig. 33.2). It was commonly used with sex offenders and alcoholics. Its use invariably involves giving noxious stimuli to people who carry out behaviour that the rest of society regards as deviant. So is this really a therapy based on psychological theory or is it a way of providing a scientific cover for attempts to punish social deviants?

There are a number of puzzles surrounding the use of aversive techniques:

- The theory of classical conditioning derives from the development of a dog's salivation response to a new stimulus (Pavlov 1927). This is remarkably removed from the complex sexual responses and drinking behaviour of adult humans.
- Aversive techniques are used on some behaviours, such as alcoholism and sexual deviation, but not on fraud or persistent parking violations.
- If aversion therapy were successful, then individuals would learn to be averse to alcohol after a number of episodes where they are ill following alcohol use. This is obviously not the case.

Figure 33.2
The relationship between classical conditioning and aversion therapy

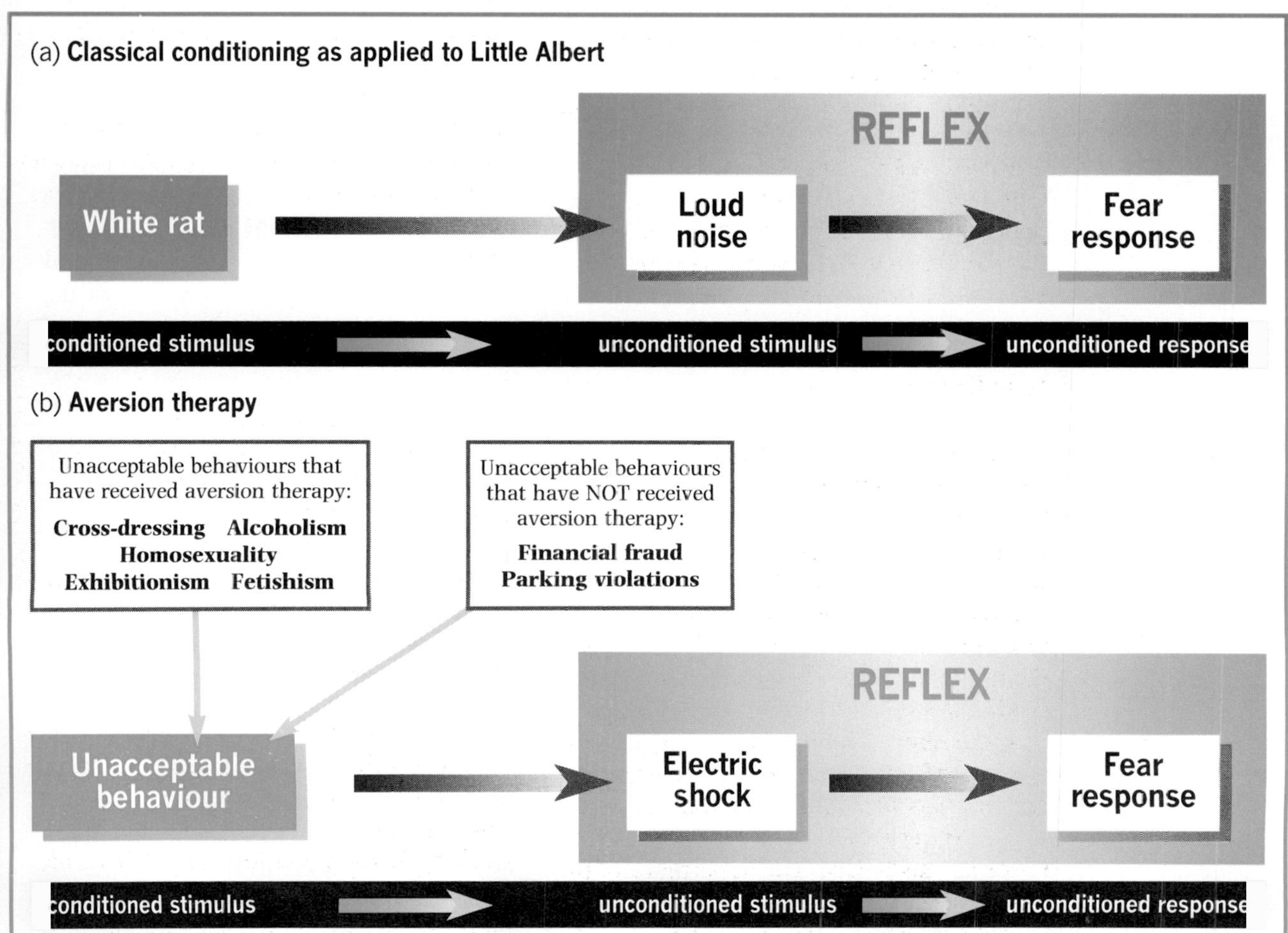

All this leads to an inconclusive answer about the relationship between classical conditioning and aversion therapy: there may or may not be a relationship – it's a matter of opinion. On the one hand, aversion therapy does offer a simple treatment that can have some dramatic short-term effects on behaviour. On the other hand, the treatment is only applied to a small number of behaviours and often does not have lasting effects (Marlatt and Gordon 1980). Programmes using aversion therapy techniques with alcoholics have claimed success rates as high as 60 per cent after one year, though as many as half of these people subsequently returned to drink (Wiens and Menustik 1983).

The above examples of locus of control, intelligence and aversion therapy, answer our question about whether there is a relationship between psychological theory and application with a 'yes', a 'no' and a 'maybe'. An alternative to the model of ideal research is to consider how research and application develop in the social context of our society.

Figure 33.3 Social model of psychological research

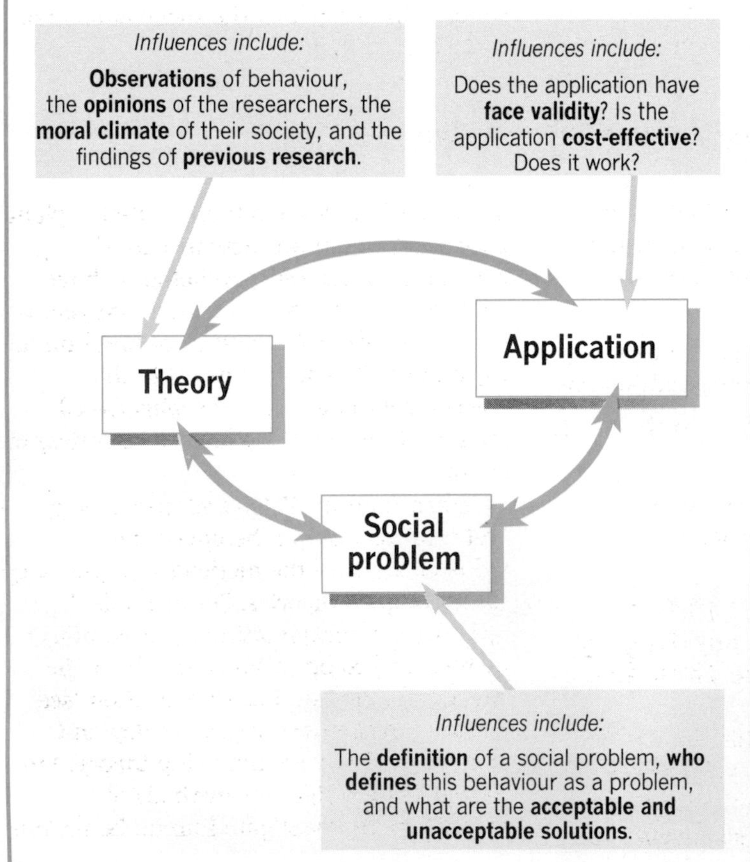

A social model of psychological research

The diagram in Fig. 33.3 shows a relationship between theory, application and social problems. The process of development can start at any part of this circle. It can be initiated by social concerns as easily as it can by psychological theory. The model identifies how theories, applications and social issues all have an effect on each other. Sometimes we study a psychological theory and develop an appropriate application, and sometimes we identify a social problem and look for a psychological theory to explain it. For example, there is currently a lot of concern about violent behaviour by people towards each other. In our society, we define this as a social problem and look for explanations and solutions. The explanations come from theory, and the possible solutions come from the range of psychological treatments currently in existence which may or may not be related to a specific theory. Alternatively, we might discover a useful technique in psychology and look around for something to apply it to. When we do this we must bear in mind that some solutions are unacceptable even if they are useful.

Rewards for drug users – an unacceptable application?

One of the applications of psychology that has the widest use is reinforcement. Reinforcement is one of the most effective ways of encouraging behavioural change, particularly in the short term. Perhaps we could encourage people to give up abusive drug habits by using reinforcement? A study that attempted just this was reported by Mestel and Concar (1994) who describe how cocaine abusers in the USA were encouraged to change their behaviour through the use of financial reinforcement.

The people who took part in the programme all had a history of serious cocaine abuse. During the programme they had several urine tests each week that looked for traces of cocaine. If their urine was clear of the drug they were given a voucher with a monetary value. If they had a second test that was also clear, they were given another voucher, but for a larger amount of money. The amount of money went up with every successive clear test, but if they were found to have any trace of cocaine they had to start building up the amount again from the lowest figure. The way to get the most money was, therefore, to stay clear as long as possible.

The voucher system was backed up by counselling to encourage constructive use of the money. This combined approach had unusually successful results for a drug rehabilitation programme. The norm for drug treatment programmes (according to Mestel and Concar) is a drop out rate of 70 per cent within 6 weeks. On this programme, however, around 85 per cent stayed in the programme for 12 weeks and around two-thirds stayed in for 6 months.

So, we have a successful application of psychological theory, but could we encourage a wider use of it? The answer is probably no because it is not difficult to imagine the hostile reaction of politicians and the general public to this sort of programme. This highlights the role of social factors in the development of psychological applications.

Section summary

The relationship between theory and application in psychology is not clear cut. Some psychological concepts, such as locus of control, offer clear testable hypotheses and show a close relationship to applications. Other concepts, such as aversion therapy and intelligence, have a weaker relationship to their applications. Some psychological techniques, however, derive directly from social concerns and may or may not be related to specific theories. The application of all these concepts is affected by the social climate of society.

Applying psychology: issues to consider

There are a number of issues to consider when we are examining the relationship between theory and application in psychology:

- whether the methods of psychology are more useful than the theoretical content
- who controls whom, when psychology is applied
- what the broader issues are that psychology has been applied to.

Are the methods of psychology more useful than the theories?

We have already seen in this chapter that the relationship between psychological theory and application is quite controversial. Human beings are so complex that it is difficult to develop theories that explain very much about our activities and experience. However, psychologists have studied people for over one hundred years, measuring behaviour and recording human experience. This study has led to the development of a range of sophisticated methods that have been used in a variety of contexts.

When John B. Watson left psychology and went to work in the advertising industry, he used the methods of psychology rather than its theories. For example, he used the methods of attitude measurement he had worked on in his research for the American Army on health education (see *In Focus* on the next page). Lashley and Watson (1921) were not using theory, but were using the rigorous methods of psychology to investigate human behaviour.

Psychology uses methods that aid the *valid measurement* of human behaviour and experience, and attempts to collect *reliable and verifiable data*. Perhaps it is these rigorous methods that are psychology's contribution to our understanding of human behaviour and experience.

Who controls whom?

If psychology can be applied effectively to people so that their behaviour can be changed, then who decides which people are changed and what parts of their behaviour should be changed? The application of psychological methods and knowledge raises a number of moral issues about control, and it is important to consider what uses psychological knowledge is put to. Some of these uses can be quite disturbing, for example the use of sensory deprivation on prisoners. Some psychologists, such as H.J. Eysenck, argue that psychology should be used to maintain the status quo of our society. He writes:

In Focus

The early use of psychological methods in health education

One of the first reported studies into the effectiveness of health education was carried out by Karl Lashley and John B. Watson (1921). At the request of the American military, they investigated the effectiveness of health education messages about venereal disease which were shown to the troops during the First World War (1914–18). They studied the impact of two films about venereal disease which were produced in the form of stories and had graphic images of the devastating medical and social effects of having sex with prostitutes and developing venereal disease. They surveyed and interviewed over one thousand people who saw the films and found that 70 per cent had a good knowledge of the points made in the film. Sadly, though, they found no evidence that the films had any effect on behaviour either in avoiding sex with prostitutes or in taking health precautions.

This research allowed Lashley and Watson to make a number of observations that are relevant today:

- If you try to get a message across in the form of a story, then viewers often concentrate on the story and miss the message.
- Young people tend to respond to information about sex in a flippant and jokey way, and so the best way to get the message across is to present it seriously and frankly.
- Many health education messages try to create fear in the viewers in order to encourage them to change their behaviour. However, fear does not seem to be very effective or, alternatively, does not have the desired effect. For example, Watson and Lashley found that 89 per cent of their research participants believed, after watching the film, that venereal diseases are easily transmitted and they should therefore not touch anything that had ever been touched by a prostitute!

It was the methods of psychology that allowed Lashley and Watson to collect and analyse so much data, and to make observations that have stood the test of time. The surprising, and rather disturbing, footnote to this is that these lessons were not heeded in subsequent health education campaigns. Baggaley (1991) points out that the various media campaigns on HIV/AIDS during the 1980s often used storylines, created a sense of fear and used amusing and dramatic styles to get the message across. The consistent ineffectiveness of these campaigns would have come as no surprise to Lashley and Watson.

'The problem to be discussed is: how can we engineer a social consent which will make people behave in a socially adapted, law-abiding fashion, which will not lead to a breakdown of the intricately woven fabric of society.'

Source: Heather 1976

Eysenck is suggesting that psychology should be used to maintain the status quo, whatever that happens to be. This is all very well if the 'intricately woven web of society' is one that most people would want to support. However, what if that society disregards the needs and aspirations of many of its members? In this case, shouldn't psychology be used to *change* the society? Take the issue of stress, for example. Stress is one of the most common health complaints in the UK as shown, for example, by the estimated number of days lost from work due to stress or stress-related illnesses. Arnold, Robertson and Cooper (1991) estimate they result in the loss of ten per cent of Britain's gross national product. One way of dealing with this is to maintain the 'intricately woven web of society' and encourage people to manage their stress and continue with their working life. An alternative approach might challenge the 'intricately woven web of society' and encourage employers to change their work practices, and encourage the government to change the economic structure of the country. Psychology, therefore, has to deal with the moral dilemma of the needs of the individual and the needs of the society. If psychology was used in the way Eysenck suggests, then our society would become fixed in its current ways and fixed in its current structures of power.

George Miller (1969), in his presidential address to the American Psychological Association, put forward a different view. He suggested that psychology should not be used by the powerful to control the weak, but by ordinary people so that they can better control their own lives and their own destiny. He writes:

'I believe that the real impact of psychology will be felt, not through the technological products it places in the hands of powerful men, but through its effects on the public at large, through a new and different public conception of what is humanly possible and humanly desirable.'

Miller uses the work of Freud as an example. The theories developed by Freud have been one of the major influences of the twentieth century, affecting psychological and general intellectual thought, as well as the views of ordinary people. On the other hand, the technology derived from the theory (the methods of psychoanalytic therapy) has had only limited success. Miller goes on to propose that psychologists should not try to become more powerful but should try to empower ordinary people. He writes:

'Our responsibility is less to assume the role of experts and try to apply psychology ourselves than to give it away to the people who really need it.'

Breadth of applications

Perhaps the most striking aspect of applied psychology is the sheer range of issues that it has made a contribution to. In the area of health, psychologists have developed a number of techniques for controlling pain without the use of drugs. They have also devised techniques to enhance the performance of sportsmen and -women. They have researched working practices in large companies and have been able to improve staff relations and also improve productivity. They have designed money: for example, the coins currently used in Britain were designed by psychologists at Nottingham University. In the area of the environment, psychologists have made a major contribution to road safety by, for example, devising visual displays that give drivers accurate feedback about their speed. They have also worked with planners and architects to design our living environment. The list of applications is almost endless, and the remarkable thing about it is the diversity of the applications, from personal therapy to the design of a housing estate. Any aspect of life that involves people can be enhanced by some positive contribution from psychology.

An example of psychological research that has a wide range of applications is the area of communication. Social skills training, for example, has been used to develop people's communication skills so that they can deliver a message more effectively. Research by Sutton (1979) looked at how non-verbal signals are used by social workers during interviews and identified a number of questions that should be considered in order to make the interview more effective (see Table 33.1).

On the whole we are not very good at remembering what we are told by our doctors. For this reason, medical consultations have also received a lot of attention from psychologists. In a study by Ley *et al.* (1973), patients attending a general practice surgery were given a list of medical statements and were then asked to recall them. The statements were either given in an unstructured way, or were preceded by information about how they would be organized. For example, a structured presentation might involve the researcher saying something like, 'I'm going to tell you three things: first, what is wrong with you; second, what tests we will be doing; and third, what is likely to happen to you.'

When the patients were tested to see how much they remembered, Ley *et al.* found that structuring the information had made a very clear difference. The patients who had received the information in a clearly categorized form remembered about 25 per cent more than those who had received the same information in an unstructured way. In subsequent work, Ley (1989) developed a booklet that gave advice to doctors on how to communicate with their patients. The patients of those doctors who had read the booklet showed a large improvement in their memory for what they had been told during the consultation.

Table 33.1 Non-verbal communication checklist for social workers

1 Am I punctual?
2 Do I smile at clients as we meet each other?
3 Do I make sure my client is not kept waiting, or, if this happens, do I apologize?
4 Are our chairs positioned to indicate equality?
5 If time is limited, do I make it clear how long we have?
6 Do I give my client my full attention or do I allow my gaze to wander?
7 Do I make sure I am not interrupted?
8 Do I sit in a relaxed, but not over-casual position?
9 Does my facial expression usually convey friendliness, tension, anxiety, aloofness, warmth? What does it convey?
10 Is my manner confident, over-confident, tentative, condescending, cold, aggressive, distant, anxious? What manner have I?
11 Do I avoid making notes as my client speaks, apart from purely factual information?

Source: Sutton 1979

Section summary

Applications of psychology are best understood in their social context. This context defines what behaviours need changing and how they can be changed. Psychological methods have wide application outside the field of psychology and arguably are more important than the theories of psychology. Applying psychology raises a number of moral issues including the responsibilities of psychologists when they develop techniques for controlling and changing people.

Applying psychology to crime

A growing concern in Western societies is the level of personal and property crimes that are being carried out. As a result, people look to psychology for explanations and solutions. Although there are no easy solutions to any social problem, psychology can increase our understanding in a number of ways. The psychological concepts covered below are just a sample of the wide range that can be applied to crime.

❖ Activity 2 ❖

Think about concepts from elsewhere in the book which can also be applied to crime. The choice in this chapter is very selective and can only give a flavour of the applications of psychology to crime.

Attention

Attention (see Chapter 18) has recently attracted a lot of research, and in particular our ability to concentrate on one task for a given amount of time. Psychologists have identified a syndrome of behaviours in children made up of poor attention, impulsivity and hyperactivity. The syndrome is known as Attention Deficit Disorder or ADD (see Chapter 13). Children with this syndrome of behaviours do badly at school and display a range of behavioural problems. It is thought that the problem has long-term effects for the individual and creates an above average risk of unemployment, marital instability and criminal behaviour. For example, Farringdon (1990) found that ADD in 8- to 10-year-old boys was a predictor of adult criminal behaviour. It is clearly not sensible to reduce discussions about criminal behaviour to simple qualities like attention span, especially since ADD is thought to interact with a number of factors including socio-economic deprivation and the quality of the home situation. However, ADD remains as a risk factor for criminal activity, so attention span and concentration remain an area for further investigation.

Bystanders

The research on bystander behaviour was initiated by reports of a brutal murder of a young woman in a New York street in 1964 (see Chapter 4). The feature of the murder which attracted the interest of some psychologists (for example, Rosenthal 1964) was the inactivity of the bystanders who did not intervene or even alert the police. The psychologists devised a range of laboratory studies to investigate the responses of bystanders to emergency situations. The emergency situations included hearing someone fall off a ladder, or being in a waiting room and finding that smoke was coming under the door. The studies suffered from a lack of ecological validity (were not true to life), and the participants often realized that the emergency was bogus. However, the researchers were able to introduce two new concepts into our understanding of social behaviour: pluralistic ignorance and diffusion of responsibility (see Chapter 4).

You may think that the behaviour of the bystanders is not the most important issue for psychologists to be studying after someone has been attacked. Why don't they direct their efforts towards trying to establish why women are violently attached or sexually assaulted by men? Might not these psychologists be accused of going to the theatre to study the audience, while ignoring the play?

Social scripts

The stories we tell about events affect the way we perceive them. For example, men who are convicted of rape do not necessarily believe that they have done anything wrong. Scully and Marolla (1984) interviewed over one hundred men who had been convicted of rape. The men described their behaviour as either being the fault of the woman, or being the result of diminished responsibility. About 40 per cent of the men denied they had raped and justified their behaviour by a combination of discrediting and blaming the victim, and so putting their own behaviour in a favourable light. These men described the women as willing, and would say things like 'women mean "yes" when they say "no"', 'most women eventually relax and enjoy it' and 'nice girls don't get raped'.

The other 60 per cent who actually admitted to rape described their behaviour in a way that reduced their personal responsibility. For example, they described their drug and alcohol problems, or their relationship problems. Scully and Marolla suggest that the rapists developed a set of actions and attitudes towards women including a social script that can be used to reduce their own responsibility and to maintain their view of themselves as non-deviant.

Attribution and sexual assault

The social scripts described above and the stories we tell about our behaviour affect our attributional judgements (the explanations we give for why events occur and why people behave in the way they do; see Chapter 1). One common social myth is that rape victims contribute to their victimization by the way they dress or behave. An attributional study by Krahé (1988) investigated this by presenting subjects with two simple stories of sexual assaults and asking questions that would discover how the subjects attributed blame for the assault. In one account the introductory sentence read, 'After having finished work in her office, the victim was on her way to the car park where her car was parked', whereas in the other account the introductory sentence read, 'After having had a drink on her own in a pub, the victim was on her way to the car park where her car was parked.' The research found that people who tended to accept the rape myth, responded to the information about the earlier behaviour of the woman, and attributed responsibility to her if she had been in the pub rather than the office.

If we are the victims of an assault rather than the assailant, then our attributions are also important. For example, the attributions made by victims of sexual assault have been shown to be important for their subsequent re-adjustment to everyday life. Frazier (1990) interviewed victims of rape and found that attribution of self-blame generally led to a range of negative feelings such as depression. The evidence also suggests that blaming other people does not improve the prospects of successful adjustment either and, in fact, is likely to have a negative effect. The factors that are associated with successful adjustment, on the other hand, are having a feeling of control over one's future life and a view of the event as bad luck. These cognitions mean that the woman will not doubt her own judgement, and her decision-making will not be overly affected.

Social perceptions: story-telling in court

Telling stories is an important component of the process of justice. We listen to a person's account of an event and we judge how accurate we believe it to be. Members of a jury are asked to decide whether an account is true or false. Juries listen to a number of stories from different witnesses and have to make an overall decision about the guilt or innocence of the defendant.

One question for psychologists to investigate is how good we are at spotting truth or fiction. Bennett and Feldman (1981) asked their student participants to tell true or false stories to a group of their peers. The listeners were asked to vote privately on whether they regarded the stories to be true or false. The results showed that their judgements were not related to the truth of the story. Interestingly, the judgements were also unaffected by presentation, so if the story teller appeared uncertain and paused a lot, it did not make the listeners any more likely to say the story was false. The crucial factor was how coherent the story was. If the story had a central piece of action to which the leading characters were connected, then the story was more likely to be believed. Stories that had ambiguous links were less likely to be judged true.

One of the important issues that comes from this observation is that not everyone tells stories in the same way, and some people or groups of people are less likely to be believed just because of the way they describe events. For example, people from groups that are under-represented in the criminal justice system, such as working-class people or black people, are likely to construct stories in ways that contain a coherence that is not familiar to the legal professionals and maybe the jury. This means that some people are more likely to be regarded as untruthful or even guilty, not because of their evidence, but because of the way they give it.

Memory for faces and events: eyewitness testimony

As early as 1932, Sir Frederick Bartlett showed that human memory isn't just a factual recording of what occurred. Instead, Bartlett argued that we make an 'effort after meaning' – we try to ensure that information fits in with what we already know; because of this, the information often becomes changed or adapted (see Chapter 19). Researchers (e.g. Loftus and Loftus 1975) have shown that expectations, even subtle ones generated by choice of language, can be enough to distort memories such that entirely new information is included and remembered as if it were fact. This tendency to distort memories is even more important when evidence has been gathered using hypnosis. Gibson (1982) discussed how the use of hypnosis in police investigations of eyewitness accounts in both America and Britain is disturbing in this respect, since the effect of hypnosis was to make subjects particularly co-operative. Since there is no way of distinguishing between a 'real' memory and one which has been constructed unconsciously by a co-operative subject during hypnosis, Gibson suggested that the use of hypnosis by police should be regarded as equivalent to tampering with the evidence.

Stephenson (1992) notes that psychologists have failed to publish anything from the perspective of the witnesses themselves. For example, there are a number of issues that might affect the quality of the witness report, not least coercion by relatives, pressure from lawyers, prejudice on the part of court personnel, threats from other players in the court drama. Memory researchers seem to assume that participants in their experiments will answer questions to the best of their ability. This may be true of laboratory studies of word list recall, but it can hardly be assumed of witnesses in the police station or the court.

One of the factors that influence eyewitness testimony is age. In a study by O'Rourke *et al.* (1989), the researchers showed people of varying ages a film of a robbery and asked them to identify the robber. The chart in Fig. 33.4 shows that younger people were able to make more accurate identifications than older people. It may well be that older people have too much experience and so rely on their stereotypes which distort their memories.

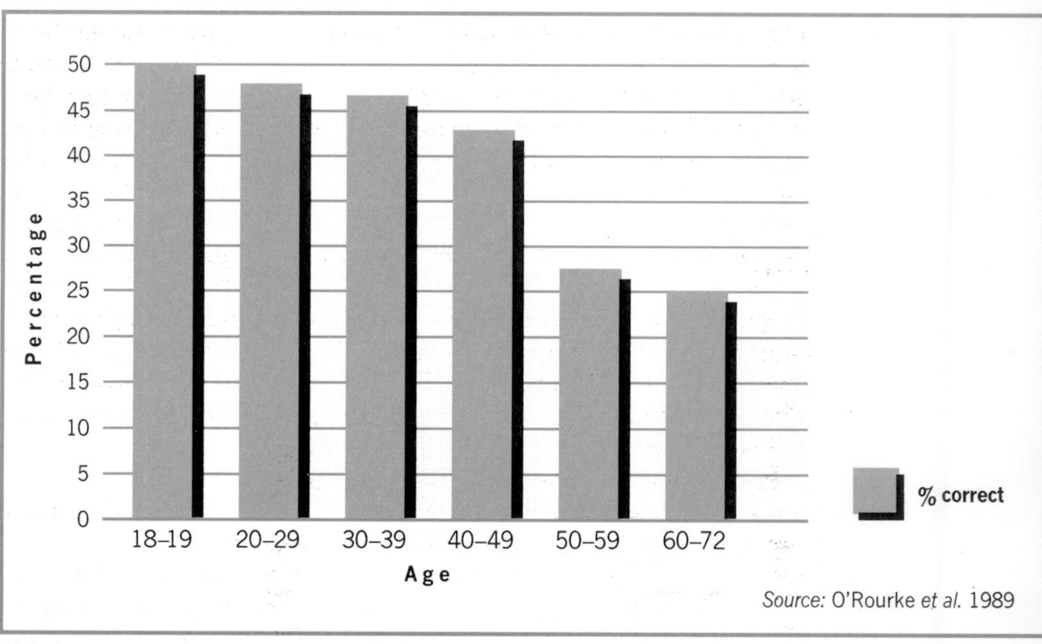

Figure 33.4 Percentage of correct identifications by people of different age

The identification parade

One of the important elements of many court cases is the identification parade where a witness is asked to pick out the suspect from a number of similar-looking people. These parades are not as accurate as we would like to believe and Stephenson (1992) describes a study which illustrates unconscious influences on the witness. The research participants were asked to take part in an identification task which was similar to an identity parade. The first 41 research participants were tested by the experimenter when he knew what the correct answers to the task were. When the remaining 30 research participants were tested, the experimenter was unaware of the correct answer. To the surprise of the experimenters, the second set of tests produced a substantially different result to the first set. The experimenters had unconsciously communicated their knowledge to the witnesses. Since the police officers who conduct witnesses to identity parades are usually aware of the identity of the suspect, this study implies that they may, unconsciously, bias the outcome of the parade in the direction of their own expectations.

Group decision-making and juries

Psychological studies of group decision-making usually involve laboratory groups of students making decisions about meaningless tasks. But what happens in real-life groups? Juries provide one example of everyday groups making real-life decisions. We usually imagine that the main task of the jury is to arrive at the truth, but in fact their major task is to reach an agreement, because they have to keep talking until they reach that agreement. In a study on actual jury decisions, Reskin and Visher (1986) looked at the results of 38 trials involving sexual assault and evaluated the strength and type of the evidence both during the trials and according to the press at the end of the trials. The results showed that where there was 'hard' evidence of assault (for example, injuries to the woman, or possession of a weapon by the assailant) then a guilty verdict was most likely. When 'hard' evidence was not available then the outcome was affected by various subjective responses by the jurors to the character of the woman victim (for example, whether she worked or not, how 'attractive' she was, whether she was 'careless' on the occasion of the assault, etc.). These factors are irrelevant to the task of applying the legal judgement of proof, but it appears that when a jury lacks conclusive 'hard' evidence it will turn to such factors to facilitate not the 'truth', but agreement.

Attitudes towards crime

Is there an increase in crime or is there just an increase in our concerns about crime? The simple answer is that both are rising, though our fear of crime sometimes distorts our perceptions about what is really happening. One source of information about our world is television and it is likely that it has some effect on our attitudes towards a range of social events. It could be that television intensifies our fear of crime and this is what Gerbner, Gross, Morgan and Signorielli (1980) looked at in their study of television viewers. They looked at the difference in attitude between people who were heavy watchers of television and those who were light watchers. The proportion of people who said that 'fear of crime is a very serious personal problem' was consistently greater for the heavy watchers in all categories.

One particular finding was that women who were heavy watchers of television were especially susceptible to fear of crime. This might well be because women are often the victims of television crime dramas. The reason for the general high level of fear in heavy viewers is debatable, though it might be because our modern life style tends to limit contact with ordinary people, especially strangers, so we have comparatively little positive social interaction to counteract the negative images from television.

Territorial behaviour

Ethologists, who study animal behavior, were the first to record territorial behaviour in their observations of animals. There have been some attempts, however, to describe human territory also. For example, Altman (1975) suggested that human beings have three types of territory, which differ in their importance to the individual or the group. Primary territories are the most important, followed by secondary territories and public territories (a summary of the three types is given in Table 33.2).

Table 33.2 Forms of territory and territorial behaviours

	Sense of ownership	*Personalization/Defence*
Primary Territory (for example, home or office)	**High:** perceived by all to be owned in a relatively permanent manner by the occupants	Extensively personalized/unwelcome entry to the space is a serious issue
Secondary Territory (for example, classroom)	**Moderate**: the occupant is perceived as one of a number of qualified users of the space	Could be personalized during occupancy/ some chance of defence when the person has the right to be there
Public Territory (for example, part of the beach)	**Low**: control is difficult to assert and the occupant is perceived as just one of many possible users	May be personalized in a temporary way/very little likelihood of defending the space

The concept of territory was applied to the design of housing estates by Newman (1972). He introduced the idea of 'defensible space' to identify the different social value of different parts of the estate. Newman observed that estates which suffered the greatest level of vandalism often had wide areas of public space, which did not belong to anyone in particular and which were also difficult to monitor. According to Newman, this invited vandalism, partly by making it easy for people to damage the property anonymously and partly by depersonalizing the property itself so that it didn't seem to matter. Newman believed that if defensible space – areas which were clearly defined and seemed to belong to the residents of the area – was created in housing estates, then vandalism would be less likely, and residents would feel more responsible for the area and more inclined to take care of it. It would also be likely to create greater social cohesion between neighbours.

Newman's ideas were supported in a study of vandalism in London housing estates (Wilson 1978). Data were collected from council repair records on a number of estates with a range of different building designs. Wilson found that the majority of damage was to public facilities rather than private, and the damage that did occur to private dwellings was mainly the breakage of windows on ground floor properties (see Fig. 33.5). She also found that the higher the block, then the greater the level of vandalism in the communal entrance areas. She suggested that this was due to the extensive semi-public space that could not be looked after by the tenants.

Other contributions to crime

Psychology has numerous applications to the topic of crime and we have only looked at a small selection. We could also examine the attempts by forensic psychologists to provide personality profiles of offenders, or the effect of deindividuation on the likelihood of offending. We could also broaden our view of crime to consider corporate crime as well as personal crime. For example, the Kings Cross fire in 1987 killed 31 people and seriously injured many others. There were a number of contributory factors to the disaster though it

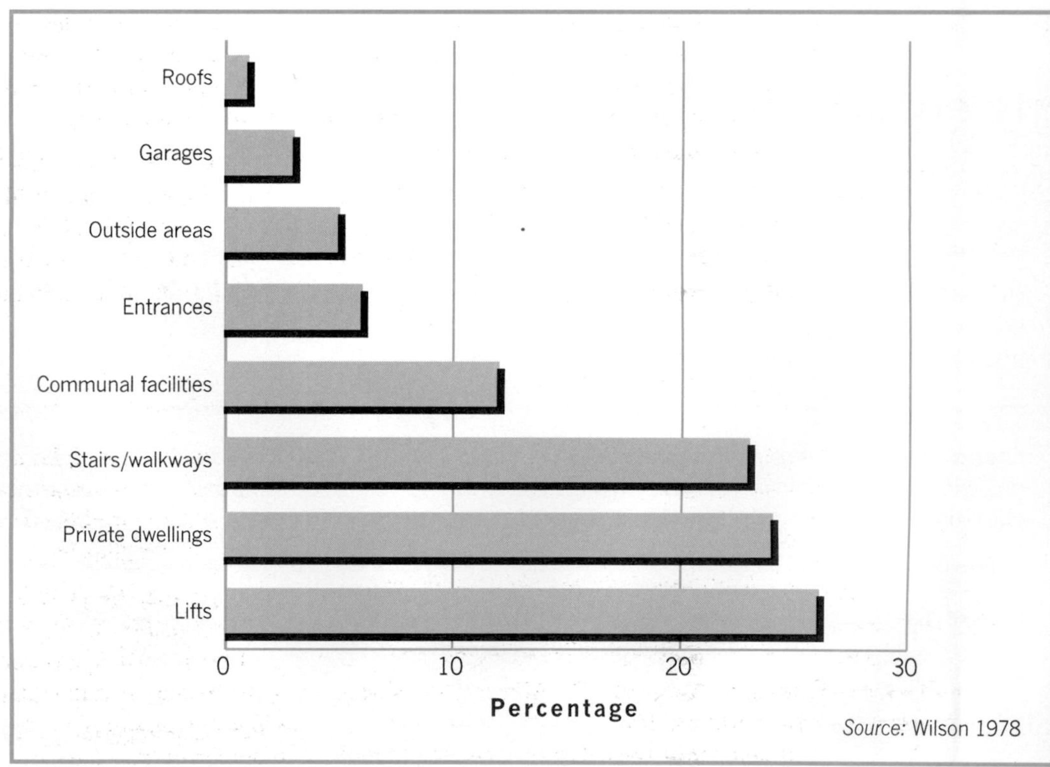

Figure 33.5 Location of damage in 6,200 reports of vandalism on London housing estates

is clear according to Reason (1990) that they were mainly due to the management failure of the London Underground. Overall, psychology can provide a range of explanations for the complex issues surrounding crime and offending.

Section summary

Psychology makes a contribution to our understanding of crime. Concepts such as attention, bystander behaviour, social scripts, attributions, social perceptions, memory, decision-making and perceptions of territory have all illuminated our understanding of this complex series of behaviours.

❖ Activity 3 ❖

Devise a piece of practical work that looks at some applied aspect of psychology. You could:

1 Devise a scale that measures fear of crime and investigate what factors affect responses to this scale, for example, gender, age, rural or urban life, ethnic background.

2 Use the methods of psychology to investigate product choice by consumers. Can people really tell the difference between different brand-named products? Investigate which factors affect their choice, for example, brand name, colour of packet, cost of the product.

3 Investigate how accurate people are at recognizing faces, either in identification parades or by using photographs. You could make a brief video of a simulated accident and ask people to identify the main actors after they have seen it.

Chapter summary

- ❖ The relationship between psychological theory and application is quite controversial. The theories and applications are affected by a range of social issues as well as scientific ones. Some applications develop as a response to social need rather than previous research.
- ❖ Psychology can be applied to a wide range of issues including health, environmental design, the world of work and various therapies. It is important to evaluate how useful and effective these applications are.
- ❖ Psychology has numerous applications to the topic of crime which help our understanding of this issue and help us to develop techniques for making our society more comfortable to live in.

Further reading

Banyard, P. and Hayes, N. (1994) *Psychology: Theory and Application*, London: Chapman and Hall.

This text provides brief summaries of psychological concepts and shows how they have been applied in the areas of sport, consumerism, health, education and work.

Gould, S. J. (1981) *The Mismeasure of Man*, New York: Norton.

If you are interested in the concept of intelligence and its mis-application in psychology, then this book is a must. It contains a very readable account of the development of testing as well as a critique of factor analysis.

Stephenson, G. (1992) *The Psychology of Criminal Justice*, Oxford: Blackwell.

A very readable account of the applications of psychology to crime that covers a wider range of topics in more detail than there was room for in this chapter.

Glossary

Action slips: a form of absent-mindedness where a person performs an action that was not intended. Action slips are caused by not paying attention to what is going on.

Activity theory: a theory of ageing that proposes that activity and involvement in later adulthood is likely to produce life satisfaction and psychological good health.

Adolescence: a period of development between puberty and adulthood. The concept of a distinct developmental period of adolescence has often been seen as a westernized phenomenon, with progression from childhood to adulthood in other cultures being more abrupt and marked by rituals and 'rites of passage'.

Adulthood: literally a period of maturity, but generally regarded as the period of post-adolescence. This has often been split by life-span theorists into early, middle and late adulthood, each with its own developmental tasks and conflicts.

Advertising: a form of persuasion where an attempt is made to change (or maintain) consumer behaviour with regard to a specific product or behaviour, through means of media images and messages.

Aggression: an action or a series of actions where the aim is to cause harm to another person or object.

Aims: when used in the context of psychological investigations, this refers to the general investigative purpose of the study.

Alternative sexualities: a term that alludes to the fact that one's sexual preference may not be for a partner of the opposite sex but for a partner of the same sex, or for both.

Altricial species: animal species that are relatively helpless at birth and therefore need considerable parental care if they are to survive to maturity.

Altruism (animal): an animal is considered to be engaging in altruistic behaviour when by so doing it increases the survival chances of another animal whilst decreasing its own.

Altruism (human): as with animal altruism, this involves some cost to the altruist and some benefit to the recipient. Unlike animal altruism, we often find evidence of 'kindly intent' on the part of the altruist.

Analyse/Critically analyse: show understanding by examining the different components of a topic area.

Animal language: this is a reference to the abilities that several species have demonstrated with respect to a 'language-like' form of communication, i.e. communicating about things removed in time and space, showing ability to combine signals to change meaning, and so on.

Antisocial behaviour: this is a general term used to refer to any behaviour that harms or offends another person. Common examples are aggression and discrimination.

Anxiety disorders: the most common of adult mental disorders, they are characterized by severe anxiety. Phobias are probably the most familiar of these disorders.

Anxiolytic drugs: a term used to describe any drug which serves to reduce anxiety.

Applications: actual or possible ways of using psychological knowledge in an applied or practical setting.

Assess/Critically assess: a considered appraisal of an area through a review of the strengths and weaknesses of the information presented.

Attachment: this refers to the result of a bonding process between two individuals (usually the mother and her offspring), characterized by mutual involvement and the desire to remain close to each other.

Attention-deficit hyperactivity disorder (ADHD): a disorder found in approximately 3 to 5 per cent of children, characterized by poor sustained attention, impulsivity and inappropriate overactivity.

Attribution: the way in which we infer the causes of our own or another person's behaviour according to a set of cognitive rules and biases. As a result of these strategies we are able to judge whether a person's behaviour is a result of his or her own stable characteristics, or whether it is a result of situational influences.

Attributional biases: the tendency to depart from the normal rules of attribution and make biased attributions about the behaviour of ourselves or others.

Autistic disorder (autism): a childhood disorder where sufferers are generally unresponsive to others, have poor communication skills and react to the environment in bizarre ways.

Automatic processing: a type of mental operation that is normally rapid, does not require conscious awareness and is a result of prolonged practice.

Autonomic nervous system: a division of the nervous system whose functions tend to be self regulating rather than being under conscious control.

Awareness: a state where we are conscious of both our inner self and the physical world around us.

Bar chart: a way of graphically representing scores on a discrete variable such as the number of cats belonging to different breeds in the UK.

Behaviour therapies: therapeutic techniques of changing behaviour that are based on the principles of classical conditioning. The term 'behaviour modification' is more usually used for techniques derived from operant conditioning.

Behavioural model of abnormality: the view that abnormal behaviours are maladaptive learned responses to the environment which can be unlearned and replaced by more adaptive behaviours.

Behaviourism: one of the major orientations in psychology that concentrates on overt (observable) events rather than covert (unobservable) mental processing. Behaviours are seen as being acquired through the processes of learning.

Biofeedback: a way of controlling physiological responses such as heart rate and blood pressure through monitoring and relaxation techniques.

Bodily (biological) rhythms: cycles of activity that occur with some regularity in an organism. *Infradian* rhythms less than once a day, *circadian* rhythms repeat themselves every 24 hours, and *ultradian* rhythms more than once a day.

Bonding: the process whereby the young of altricial species form a bond with their parent(s). In the bonding process, parents also bond with their offspring and thus safeguard them from abuse or abandonment.

Bystander behaviour: the behaviour shown by those who witness an emergency. This is often referred to as 'bystander *apathy*' because of the tendency of bystanders to ignore the emergency when in the company of others.

Case study: an investigative technique for studying the behaviour and experiences of an individual or small group of individuals.

Central nervous system: the part of the nervous system that comprises the brain and spinal cord.

Central tendency: a single value which is representative of a set of numbers by indicating the most typical value. Three measures of central tendency are the *mean*, *median* and *mode*.

Choice of goals: the aims/desired outcomes of therapy. Ideally the client and therapist will set the goals together. Sometimes they are set by the therapist alone.

Classical conditioning: an explanation of learning whereby one stimulus becomes associated with another and through that association is used to predict the coming of the second stimulus.

Cognitive development: refers to the development of cognitions such as language, intellect or thought.

Cognitive developmental theories: theories that stress the role of cognitive development in a range of other areas of functioning such as moral development or gender-role development.

Cognitive model of abnormality: this stresses the role of cognitive problems (such as illogical thought processes) in abnormal functioning.

Cognitive-behavioural therapies: these involve helping clients to identify their negative, irrational thoughts and to replace these with more positive, rational ways of thinking.

Collective behaviour: the tendency of people to behave in characteristic way (e.g. by suspending normal standards of individual thought and responsibility) when in groups or crowds.

Compare and contrast: consider both the similarities and the differences between two topic areas.

Competition for resources: an assumption that Darwin made in his theory of natural selection, that animals must compete for mates, foods, territories, etc. As resources are limited, those who are successful are better able to reproduce than those who are unsuccessful.

Comprehension of language: the mechanisms involved in the processing and understanding of spoken language (speech) and written language.

Concept(s): an idea or group of ideas that might be used as the basis for a psychological theory.

Confidentiality: the ethical concern that information gathered during psychological research or therapy should not be divulged to others.

Conformity: a type of social influence expressed through exposure to the views of a majority and our submission to those views. A persuasive minority may also exert a pressure to conform through the consistent and unwavering expression of a contrary point of view.

Consider: show knowledge and understanding of the topic area, as well as its strengths and weaknesses.

Content analysis: an investigative technique where people are not studied directly but through the artefacts that they produce, e.g. the analysis of documents, messages and verbal discourse.

Controversial issues: those applications of psychological theories and research that create considerable concern among psychologists and non-psychologists alike. For example, the use of psychometric tests to determine educational or occupational privilege might, according to this point of view, be socially divisive.

Correlation: the degree of relatedness between two sets of scores. If two sets of scores are correlated, it enables the researcher to predict (with varying degrees of certainty) the approximate value of one score if s/he knows the value of the other.

Cortical activity: neural activity in the cortex of the brain.

Counterbalancing: an experimental technique where the sequence in which different conditions are presented is varied to overcome any effect caused by the order of presentation.

Critically consider: show knowledge and understanding of the topic area as well as the strengths and limitations of the material presented.

Criticize: evaluate a topic area in terms of its strengths and weaknesses.

Cultural bias: a tendency in psychological theory and research to ignore the differences between cultures and impose understanding based on the study of one culture alone.

Cultural identity: the influence of one's culture on the development of identity. Individualist cultures stress the importance of personal achievement and independence while collectivist cultures stress the importance of collective achievement and dependence.

Decision-making: an area of cognitive research concerned with how individuals determine what is the correct course of action, or what is a correct or incorrect answer, or a valid or invalid conclusion.

Define: explain what is meant by a particular term.

Demand characteristics: the tendency for experimental participants to adjust their behaviour according to their own interpretation of the aims of the experiment.

Depression: a type of mood disorder where the person experiences feelings of great sadness, worthlessness and guilt, and finds the challenges of life overwhelming.

Deprivation: the loss of something. The term is most often used in the field of maternal deprivation, where the child is deprived of the love of the primary attachment figure.

Describe: show knowledge of a topic area.

Developmental dyslexia: a specific learning difficulty characterized by difficulties with written and spoken language. This form of dyslexia is thought to be caused by anomalies of development in childhood.

Diagnostic and Statistical Manual (DSM): a classification, definition and description of over 200 mental health disorders which groups disorders in terms of their common features.

Discrimination: a way of behaving towards members of a categorized group such that all members of that group are treated in the same (usually unfair) way.

Discuss: describe and evaluate a topic area.

Disengagement theory: a gradual decrease in social involvement and corresponding increase in self-absorption that is thought to be a characteristic of later adulthood.

Distinguish between: consider the differences between two topic areas.

Divided attention: the ability to divide attentional processing between more than one task.

Dream states: a stage of sleep characterized by rapid eye movements and the experience of visual imagery.

Dual task limitations: the impairment of functioning of one task caused by simultaneous performance of a second task.

Eating disorders: a serious disruption of healthy eating habits or appetite.

Ecological validity: the degree to which the findings from a study can be generalized beyond the context of the investigation.

Emotion: a complex interaction between subjective feelings and objective experiences that gives rise to an emotional response.

Empirical: almost any form of investigation where the aim is to collect some form of data based on observation or experience.

Endocrine systems: a set of internal glands that produce hormones and release them into the bloodstream.

Enrichment: attempts either to accelerate early learning ('hothousing') or to overcome early deprivation through the provision of compensatory education programmes.

Erikson, Erik: a post-Freudian psychoanalyst best known for his life-span theory of psychosocial development.

Ethical guidelines: prescriptive guidance on the conduct of psychologists in research and practice. These represent the key issues that face psychologists in their work with humans and animals and are regularly updated by the organizations that issue them.

Ethics: a branch of philosophy that is concerned with what is right or acceptable in the pursuit of a given goal.

Evaluate/Critically evaluate: make an informed judgement as to the value of an argument, theory or piece of research.

Evidence: material that might be drawn from theories or investigations and is used to support or contradict an argument or theory.

Evolution: the change over successive generations in the genetic make-up of a particular group or species. The dominant force in this change is natural selection.

Evolutionary psychology: the application of evolutionary ideas to the behaviour of human beings.

Examine: give a detailed descriptive account of a topic area.

Exchange theory: a theoretical model in social psychology which proposes that relationships are evaluated in terms of the rewards and costs that they bring.

Experiment: an investigative technique which involves the manipulation of an independent variable in order to see its effect on a dependent variable.

Experimental design: a procedure used within an experiment to control the influence of participant variables that might otherwise influence the outcome of the experiment.

Experimental validity: a measure of whether the experimental procedures actually worked, i.e. were the conclusions justified?

Experimental/alternative hypothesis: a testable statement made at the start of an investigation which serves as a prediction or explanation of events should statistical analysis dismiss the role of chance factors.

Experimenter effects: some aspect of the experimenter's behaviour or characteristics that has an effect on the participant and causes them to change their behaviour as a result of this effect.

Explain: show understanding of a topic through coherent and intelligible explanation.

Exploitation: an example of competition for resources whereby animals are distributed between different habitats according to the quality of the resources in each.

Eyewitness testimony: the study of the accuracy of memory following an accident or crime, and the types of errors that are commonly made in such situations.

Field experiments: an experimental manipulation of an independent variable that takes place in a natural setting rather than in the more artificial setting of the laboratory.

Findings: the outcome of a research investigation.

Focused attention: where the organism focuses on only one input from the environment, which is selected for further processing.

Followership: the influence exerted by followers on their leaders and which helps determine leadership effectiveness.

Foraging: the different ways in which animals satisfy their nutritional requirements.

Forgetting: the loss of the ability to recall or recognize something which has previously been learned.

Free will vs determinism: the debate between those who believe that behaviour is determined by external or internal factors acting on the individual (determinism), and those who believe that people respond actively to events around them (free will).

Frequency polygon: a frequency distribution that shows the peaks of each of the class intervals.

Fundamental attribution error: a tendency to see the behaviour of others as being due to their stable personality characteristics rather than the influence of situational factors.

Gender bias: the treatment of men and women in psychological research and/or theory in a way which offers a view of behaviour and experience that might not fully represent the characteristics of either one of these genders.

Gender role: those behaviours, attitudes and interests that are considered typical or appropriate for one gender yet atypical or inappropriate for the other.

Generalizability: the ability of researchers to offer a justifiable extension of their findings beyond the actual sample of participants used to a wider population of people.

Hemisphere asymmetries: refers to the fact that some functions of the cortex are located in one hemisphere only rather than being symmetrically organized across both hemispheres.

Histogram: a type of frequency distribution chart or diagram where the data are divided into proportional intervals.

Homeostasis: the process by which the body maintains a constant internal physiological environment, directing and controlling drinking, feeding and temperature regulation.

Homing behaviour: refers to the ability of animals to navigate toward a target that is normally their home range.

Humanistic model of abnormality: abnormality seen in terms of blocks and frustrations to an individual's self-growth and development.

Humanistic psychology: a view of human beings that sees every person as unique and possessing an innate potential for positive growth that we can achieve if we develop fully.

Humanistic therapies: the general name given to any therapy that attempts to help clients look at themselves more accurately and more acceptingly, and thus fulfil their full potential as human beings.

Hypnosis: the induction of a sleep-like state which represents an altered state of consciousness.

Hypothesis: a testable statement that enables a researcher to both predict and explain the results of a study.

Illusions: a perceptual experience that is not a true representation of the physical event that is experienced through the senses.

Imprinting: a type of early learning where a young animal forms an attachment to another animal that is difficult to change with subsequent experience (*filial imprinting*) or where they learn the characteristics of their own species (or a foster species) for later courtship and mating (*sexual imprinting*).

Independent behaviour: behaviour where a person resists the social influence imposed by those around them (e.g. by displaying *non*-conformity, or *dis*obedience to authority).

Independent groups: a type of experimental design where participants are randomly allocated to the different conditions of the experiment.

Information processing approach: a reference to the belief that the processing of sensory information takes place in a series of stages.

Informed consent: an ethical requirement that participants or clients should have sufficient information about an experiment or therapeutic intervention to enable them to make an informed judgement about whether or not to take part.

Insights: perceptions from theories or investigations that enable us to understand or appraise a topic area.

Intelligence: an underlying ability which enables an individual to adapt to and function effectively within a given environment.

Intelligence test: a type of assessment that purports to measure intelligence.

International Classification of Disorders (ICD): a classification of physical and psychological disorders published and regularly updated by the World Health Organization.

Interpersonal relationships: the study of factors and processes involved in the formation, maintenance and dissolution of relationships.

Interview: any face-to-face situation where one person (the interviewer) asks questions of another (the respondent).

Laboratory experiment: an investigative technique where the experimental manipulation of the independent variable takes place within such conditions that careful control of extraneous variables is possible.

Language acquisition: the study of the ways in which children acquire or develop human language.

Leadership: the process through which one member of a group influences other group members toward the attainment of specific group goals.

Learning difficulties: specific difficulties found in children of normal or above average intelligence. The most familiar of these specific difficulties is dyslexia.

Levinson, Daniel: an American psychologist best known for his book *Seasons of a Man's Life* in which he put forward the idea that human adult development was characterized by four different eras, each connected by transitional periods.

Life events: any events (such as widowhood or redundancy) that necessitate a significant transition or adjustment in various aspects of a person's life.

Localization of function: the principle that psychological functions are located in specialized areas of the brain.

Marcia, James: tested Erikson's ideas on adolescent identity formation. He claims that for a fully achieved identity, the young person must both have examined his or her values or goals and have reached a firm commitment.

Matched participants: an experimental design where each participant is matched on a specific variable with another participant in the other condition.

Mating strategies: the different arrangements between male and female animals that are concerned with mating. The most common of these are monogamy (one male and one female) polygyny (one male and more than one female) and polyandry (one female and more than one male). The particular strategy adopted within a particular species will be determined by many features including environmental pressures and the investment made by each sex in the rearing of the young.

Mean: the arithmetic average that is calculated by dividing the sum of all scores by the number of items or participants.

Media influences: the way in which the media (e.g. television, internet) might cause changes in behaviour in those who are exposed to it. Much of the debate concerning media influences has focused on its effects on aggressive behaviour.

Median: the middle value in a set of scores when they are arranged in rank order.

Medical model of abnormality: a view of abnormality that sees mental disorders as being caused by abnormal physiological processes such as genetic and biochemical factors. Abnormality, according to this model, is seen as an illness or disease.

Memory for medical information: our capacity to remember such things as advice from doctors and treatment instructions. Research has looked at new ways of maximizing the memorability of such information.

Measures of dispersion: a measurement of the spread or variability in a set of scores.

Methods: the different ways that research investigations can be carried out.

Mode: the most frequently occurring score in a set of data.

Model: a term that is used synonymously with 'theory', although it may refer to something that is less elaborate or complex.

Models of thought: cognitive psychologists usually use this term to refer to particular types of goal directed thinking, such as problem solving and reasoning.

Models of memory: different explanations concerning the nature of memory and the processes involved in remembering and retrieving information.

Moral development: the process by which children come to internalize standards of right and wrong, and ultimately make their own decisions concerning moral issues.

Motivation: literally, the study of why organisms act in the way that they do. This refers to an internal state of an organism that drives it to behave in a certain way.

Movement perception: refers to our ability to perceive accurately the movement of people and objects.

Natural experiment: an example of a 'quasi-experiment' where the allocation of participants to the different experimental conditions is outside the control of the investigator, but rather is manipulated fortuitously by some outside agency.

Natural observation: an observational technique where behaviour is observed in its natural context without intrusion by the person doing the observing.

Need satisfaction: the process by which a physical or psychological deficiency is corrected by motivated action.

Neural transmission: the process by which a nerve impulse passes along a neuron. This is achieved by a series of electrochemical changes in the nerve cell.

Null hypothesis: a statement that attributes the results obtained within a research investigation to chance or to some other event that is not covered by the research hypothesis under test.

Obedience: a type of social influence where an individual acts according to the orders of some authority figure. It is normally assumed that without such an order the person would not have carried out that behaviour.

One-tailed hypothesis: a predictive statement that specifies the direction of the relationship that will be found in a set of results, for example that participants in one condition will perform *better* than those in another, or that a correlation will be *positive* rather than negative.

Operant conditioning: an explanation of learning that sees the consequences of a behaviour as being of vital importance to the future appearance of that behaviour. If a behaviour is followed by a desirable consequence it becomes more frequent, if it is followed by an undesirable consequence it becomes less frequent.

Outline/State: offer a summary description of the topic area.

Parent–offspring conflict: a conflict between a feeding parent and its offspring whereby the offspring, in trying to maximize its own resources, will try to manipulate the parent into providing resources beyond the point where it is in its interests to do so.

Parental investment: an investment in an individual offspring that increases the chances of survival for the offspring whilst decreasing the parent's ability to invest in other offspring.

Participant reactivity: the tendency for participants in a research investigation to alter their behaviour because of the presence of the observer.

Participants: those people who are studied and contribute data in a research investigation.

Pattern recognition: a process of visual perception which enables us to recognize two-dimensional and three-dimensional objects in our environment.

Perception: the process by which we transform sensory information from the environment into the experience of objects, sounds, movement, etc.

Perceptual constancies: the tendency for objects to give the same perceptual experience despite changes in the viewing conditions.

Perceptual development: the systematic change of perceptual abilities and processes that develop as a result of maturation and experience.

Perceptual organization: the ability of an organism to organize the information that arrives via the senses into some meaningful perceptual experience.

Performance deficits: refers to the study of the processing and response limitations of the human organism. These include deficits associated with attention limitations, workload and the co-ordination of activities.

Phobia: a type of anxiety disorder where there is a persistent and unreasonable fear of an object or situation.

Physical handicap: the disadvantage that comes about as a result of some physical impairment.

Piaget, Jean: a Swiss psychologist whose major contribution to psychology was the belief that intelligence was the product of a natural and inevitable sequence of developmental stages and processes.

Post-traumatic stress disorder: a type of anxiety disorder that arises as a result of some traumatic event. The symptoms begin shortly after the event and may last for years.

Practical applications of memory research: the applications of memory research to practical situations such as eyewitness testimony and memory for medical information.

Precocial species: animals that can move about, feed and generally look after themselves shortly after birth.

Predator–prey relationships: pressures from one species that cause a change in behaviour in another such that predators become successful at catching their prey and prey become more successful at avoiding being killed and eaten.

Prejudice: prejudgement of somebody on the basis of their membership of a particular category or group. Prejudices tend to be resistant to reversal when faced with contradictory information about the object of the prejudice.

Prosocial behaviour: an act that benefits others but may appear to have no direct benefit for the person performing it.

Production of language: a goal-directed activity which is characterized by speaking or writing.

Propaganda: an attempt to persuade people to voluntarily accept a position being put forward as if it were their own.

Psychodynamic models of abnormality: models which see abnormal behaviour as being caused by underlying psychological forces of which the individual is probably unaware.

Psychodynamic theories: theories that emphasize change and development in the individual and where 'drive' is a central concept in the process of development.

Psychodynamic therapies: these therapies help clients to uncover past traumatic events and the conflicts that have resulted from them. These conflicts can then be resolved so that the client is able to restore an adaptive level of functioning.

Psychological disorder: a term used synonymously with 'mental disorder', it refers to a level of functioning that is harmful or distressing to the individual or to those around them. Psychological disorders are usually defined and described according to some current classification system such as DSM IV.

Psychological warfare: the use of psychological knowledge, skills and techniques in conflict situations. Techniques include the use of propaganda, interrogation techniques and battleproofing.

Psychology as science: the use of scientific methods to establish a body of psychological knowledge that is considered trustworthy and verifiable.

Psychometric testing: the testing of individuals in items that have been shown to measure competence in some other area of functioning.

Psychopathology: the study of the origins and course of psychological disorders such as schizophrenia and depression.

Qualitative analysis: a form of research analysis that stresses that the best interpretation of experience is through the analysis of what people say during a research investigation rather than attempting to convert their experiences into numbers or *quantitative* data.

Quality of language (QoL): an assessed skill in A and AS examinations. Maximum marks for QoL are give for clear and accurate expression of ideas, evidence of good grammar, punctuation and spelling, and appropriate use of specialist terminology.

Quantitative analysis: techniques that convert the outcome of a research investigation into numerical data.

Quasi-experiments: a type of experiment where the investigator does not directly allocate participants to the different research conditions but makes use of divisions that already exist in terms of the conditions of interest.

Race-related research: any research investigation which attempts to study differences in behaviour or functioning between members of different racial groups.

Randomization: a way of overcoming order effects by randomizing the order in which participants tackle the different conditions in an experiment.

Range: a measure of dispersion within a set of scores, this refers to the distance between the lowest and the highest score.

Reasoning: the cognitive processes involved in thinking, most notably in problem solving.

Reductionism: the tendency to reduce human behaviour to simpler levels of analysis such as the effects of genes or environmental reinforcement.

Reinforcement: the process by which a response is strengthened. This can be positive, in that a response produces a pleasant event, or negative in that the response leads to something unpleasant.

Reliability: the degree to which a description or score is consistent over time or across different observers.

Repeated measures: a type of experimental design where the same participants are used in all conditions of the experiment.

Research: the process of gaining knowledge, by either an examination of appropriate theories or through empirical data collection.

Resource defence: a strategy by which animals gain the best available territories and defend them against other conspecifics.

Scattergraph: a graphical representation of the correlation between two sets of measurements.

Schizophrenia: a serious mental disorder (psychosis) that is characterized by severe disruptions in psychological functioning.

Self-development: generally a development towards psychological maturity.

Self-serving bias: a type of attributional bias where people attribute failure to factors outside their control and success to their own ability or effort.

Sensory and motor processes: those physiological or psychological processes which relate to the senses (sensory) or to the actions (motor) of an organism.

Sensory handicap: the disadvantage that comes from having an impairment in one of the primary senses such as vision or hearing.

Sexual selection: the selection within nature of those characteristics that are solely concerned with increasing an animal's likelihood of mating. It covers two main processes, the development of characteristics that enable members of the *same* sex to compete with each other for access to mates, and characteristics that enable animals to attract members of the *opposite* sex.

Sign test: a statistical test of difference between two sets of related data.

Signalling systems: the different ways in which animals can stimulate the sense organs of other animals. These include the use of visual, auditory and olfactory signals.

Skill A: refers to 'knowledge and understanding' of psychological theories, investigations, arguments, issues, etc.

Skill B: refers to 'interpretation and commentary' concerning psychological theories, investigations, arguments, issues, etc.

Sleep: a loss of consciousness which is characterized by specific behavioural and physiological effects. Sleep can be non-REM or REM which is associated with dreaming.

Sociability: a child's willingness to interact with others and to seek their attention or approval.

Social control: the ways in which behaviour can be manipulated within a social setting. This may be achieved through the use of persuasion, reinforcement or even through the classification of mental disorders.

Social identity theory: a proposal that human beings categorize themselves and others into in-groups and out-groups. Because of the need to maintain a positive social identity unfavourable comparisons are made between the two and competition and discrimination develop.

Social learning theory: an explanation of the way in which people learn through observation and imitation of the behaviour of others.

Social organization in non-human animals: the different ways in which animals might organize themselves into groups, hierarchies or societies.

Social power: the influence that one person has over another whilst remaining relatively immune to the same effect in return.

Social representations: the ways in which ordinary people represent the world around them. These enable people to turn the unfamiliar into the familiar and the complex into the more easily understood.

Sociality in non-human animals: the tendency for animals to live in groups, primarily for the increased advantages relating to protection, foraging and an established order.

Socially sensitive research: any research that may have direct social consequences for those taking part in the study or the class of people who are represented.

Somatic therapies: an approach to the treatment of mental disorders that relies on the use of physical or chemical methods.

Space perception: the perception of the space in which we function, including our perception of depth, movement, etc.

Spearman's rho: a statistical test of correlation between two sets of measurements.

Split brain: the cutting of the corpus callosum resulting in the effective separation of the two hemispheres of the brain.

Standard deviation: a statistical measure of the variation from the mean in a set of scores.

Standardization: the technique whereby procedures using in carrying out and scoring the results from an experiment or a psychometric test are the same for all who take part.

Statistical significance: a conclusion drawn from the data collected in a research study that the results are unlikely to have been caused by chance, and can therefore be attributed to the particular relationship under study.

Stereotypes: a fixed and often simplistic generalization about a group or class of people. Stereotypes are frequently unflattering and may *underlie* prejudice and discrimination.

Stress: a lack of fit between the person and his or her environment. People experience stress when the perceived demands of the environment are greater than their perceived ability to cope.

Stress reduction: techniques used by an individual to cope with stress and reduce its adverse effects.

Studies: usually these refer to empirical investigations, although in a general sense they refer to any attempt to study a person or persons (or any other organism) in order to find out something about them.

Symbiotic relationship: a relationship between two animals where each derives some benefit from the arrangement.

Synaptic activity: the chemical process by which neurotransmitter substances are released at a synapse so they can stimulate the receiving neuron to initiate a new nerve impulse.

Theory: a set of interrelated ideas or principles that can be used to explain observed phenomena.

Treatment therapies: interventions by health practitioners that help people to overcome their psychological difficulties.

Two-tailed hypothesis: a statement made at the outset of a research study where a relationship is predicted but the direction of the relationship is not.

Validity: the degree to which a test, measurement or experimental manipulation is doing the job it has been designed to do.

Variation ratio: a way of comparing two variances (measures of dispersion) by dividing one by the other in order to obtain a ratio of the larger variance to the smaller.

Visual perception: the process by which we transform sensory information from the eyes to produce an experience of depth, distance, colour, etc.

Vygotsky, Lev: a Russian psychologist who believed that cognitive development was founded on social interaction, with a child's understanding of the world being derived from collaboration with others.

Wilcoxon matched pairs signed ranks test: a statistical test that tests for differences between two sets of related data.

References

Abrams, D. and Hogg, M.A. (1990) 'Social identification, self-categorization and social influence', *European Review of Social Psychology*, 1(8), pp. 195–228.

Abrams, R., Swartz, C.M. and Vedak, C. (1991) 'Antidepressant effects of high dose right unilateral electroconvulsive therapy', *Archives of General Psychiatry*, 48, pp. 746–8.

Abramson, L.Y., Seligman, M.E.P. and Teasdale, J.D. (1978) 'Learned helplessness in humans: critique and reformulation', *Journal of Abnormal Psychology*, 87, pp. 49–74.

Adorno, T.W., Frenkey-Brunswick, E., Levinson, D.J. and Sanford, R.N. (1950) *The Authoritarian Personality*, New York: Harper & Row.

Ainsworth, M.D.S. (1984) 'Attachment', in N.S. Endler and J.McV. Hunt (eds) *Personality and the Behavioural Disorders: Vol. 1*, New York: Wiley.

Ainsworth, M.D.S. and Bell, S.M. (1970) 'Attachment, exploration, and separation: illustrated by the behavior of one-year-olds in a Strange Situation', *Child Development*, 41, pp. 49–65.

Akiyama, M.M. (1984) 'Are language acquisition strategies universal?', *Developmental Psychology*, 20, pp. 219–28.

Allen, V.L. and Levine, J.M. (1968) 'Social support, dissent and conformity', *Sociometry*, 31, pp. 138–49.

Allport, D.A. (1980) 'Attention and performance', in G. Claxton (ed.) *Cognitive Psychology: New Directions*, London: Routledge Kegan Paul.

Allport, D.A., Antonis, B. and Reynolds, P. (1972) 'On the division of attention: a disproof of the single channel hypothesis', *Quarterly Journal of Experimental Psychology*, 24, pp. 225–35.

Allport, G. (1954) *The Nature of Prejudice*, New York: Double-Day Anchor.

Altman, I. (1975) *The Environment and Social Behaviour*, Monterey, California: Brooks Cole.

Ambrose, J.A. (1961) 'The development of the smiling response in early infancy', in B.M. Foss (ed.) *Determinants of Infant Behaviour* (Vol. 1), London: Methuen.

American Psychiatric Association (1994) *Diagnostic and Statistical Manual of Mental Disorders* (4th edn), Washington, DC: American Psychiatric Association.

Ames, A., *see* W.H. Ittleson (1952) *The Ames Demonstrations in Perception*, Princeton: Princeton University Press.

Anand, B.K. and Brobeck, J.R. (1951) 'Hypothalamic control of food intake in rats and cats', *Yale Journal of Biological Medicine*, 24, pp. 123–40.

Andersen, E.S., Dunlea, A. and Kekelis, L. (1993) 'The impact of input: language acquisition in the visually impaired', *First Language*, 13, pp. 23–49.

Anderson, J.L., Dodman, S., Kopelman, M. and Fleming, A. (1979) 'Patient information recall in rheumatology clinic', *Rheumatology and Rehabilitation*, 18, pp. 18–22.

Anderson, J.R. and Reder, L. (1979) 'An elaborative processing explanation of depth of processing', in L.S. Cermak and F.I.M. Craik (eds) *Levels of Processing in Human Memory*, Hillsdale, New Jersey: Erlbaum.

Andersson, M. (1982) 'Female choice for extreme tail length in widow bird', *Nature*, 299, pp. 818–19.

Andrew, T. (1996) 'The DNA made me do it, M'lud', *The Independent*, 23 January 1996.

Andrews, B., Morton, J., Bekerian, D.A., Brewin, C.R., Davies, G.M. and Mollon, P. (1995) 'The recovery of memories in clinical practice', *The Psychologist*, 8(5), pp. 209–14.

Antin, J., Gibbs, J. and Smith, G.P. (1978) 'Intestinal satiety requires pregastric food stimulation', *Physiology and Behavior*, 20, pp. 67–70.

Archer, D. and Gartner, R. (1976) 'Violent acts and violent times: a comparative approach to post-war homicide rates', *American Sociological Review*, 41, pp. 937–63.

Archibald, H.C.D., Long, D.M., Miller, C. and Tuddenham, R.D. (1963) 'Gross stress reactions in combat', *American Journal of Psychiatry*, 119, p. 317.

Arendt, H. (1963), *Eichmann in Jerusalem: A Report on the Banality of Evil*, New York: Viking Press.

Argyle, M. (1988) 'Social relationships', in M. Hewstone, W. Stroebe, J.P. Codol and G.M. Stephenson (eds) *Introduction to Social Psychology*, Oxford: Blackwell.

Argyle, M. (1992) *The Social Psychology of Everyday Life*, London: Routledge.

Argyle, M. (1994) *The Psychology of Interpersonal Behaviour*, Harmondsworth: Penguin.

Argyle, M. and Furnham, A. (1983) 'The ecology of relationships: choice of situation as a function of relationship', *British Journal of Social Psychology*, 45, pp. 481–93.

Argyle, M. and Henderson, M. (1985) *The Anatomy of Relationships*, Harmondsworth: Penguin.

Argyle, M., Furnham, A. and Graham, J.A. (1981) *Social Situations*, Cambridge: Cambridge University Press.

Argyle, M., Henderson, M. and Furnham, A. (1985) 'The rules of social relationships', *British Journal of Social Psychology*, 24, pp. 125–39.

Arms, R.L., Russell, G.W. and Sandilands, M.L. (1980) 'Effects of viewing aggressive sports on the hostility of spectators', in R.M. Suinn (ed.) *Psychology in Sports: Methods and Applications*, Minneapolis: Burgess Publishing Co.

Arnold, J., Robertson, I.T. and Cooper, C.L. (1991) *Work Psychology: Understanding Human Behaviour in the Workplace*, London: Pitman Publishing.

Arnold, M. (1960) *Emotion and Personality*, Vol. I, *Psychological Aspects*, New York: Columbia University Press.

Aronson, E. (1984 [4th edn], 1988 [5th edn], 1995 [7th edn]) *The Social Animal*, New York: W.H. Freeman.

Aronson, E., Stephan, C., Sikes, J., Blaney, N. and Snapp, M. (1978) *The Jigsaw Classroom*, Beverly Hills: Sage.

Asch, S.E. (1952) 'Effects of group pressure upon the modification and distortion of judgements', in H. Guetzkow (ed.) *Groups, Leadership and Men*, Pittsburg: Carnegie Press.

Ashurst, P.M. and Ward, D.F. (1983) 'An evaluation of counselling in general practice', Final Report of the Leverhulme Counselling Project.

Asso, D. and Beech, H.R. (1975) 'Susceptibility to the acquisition of a conditioned response in relation to the menstrual cycle', *Journal of Psychosomatic Research*, 19, pp. 337–44.

Association for the Teaching of Psychology (1992) *Ethics in Psychological Research: Guidelines for Students at Pre-degree Level*, Leicester: Association for the Teaching of Psychology.

Atkinson, R.C. and Shiffrin, R.M. (1968) 'Human memory: a proposed system and its control processes', in K.W. Spence and J.T. Spence (eds) *The Psychology of Learning and Motivation*, Vol. 2, London: Academic Press.

Attenborough, D. (1979) *The Trials of Life*, London: BBC Books.

Axelrod, R. and Hamilton, W.D. (1981) 'The evolution of cooperation', *Science*, 211, pp. 1390–6.

Axline, V. (1971) *Dibs: In Search of Self*, Harmondsworth: Penguin.

Ayres, J. (1983) 'Strategies to maintain relationships: their identification and usage', *Communication Quarterly*, 31, pp. 207–25.

Badcock, C. (1991) *Evolution and Individual Behaviour*, Oxford: Blackwell.

Baddeley, A.D. (1981) 'The concept of working memory: a view of its current state and probable future development', *Cognition*, 10, pp. 17–23.

Baddeley, A.D. (1992) 'What is autobiographical memory?', in M.A. Conway, D.C. Rubin, H. Spinnler and W.A. Wagenaar *Theoretical Perspectives on Autobiographical Memory*, Dordrecht, Netherlands: Kluwer Academic Publishers.

Baddeley, A.D. and Hitch, G. (1974) 'Working memory', in G.H. Bower (ed.) *The Psychology of Learning and Motivation*, Vol. 8, London: Academic Press.

Baddeley, A.D. and Lewis, V.J. (1981) 'Inner active processes in reading: the inner voice, the inner ear and the inner eye', in A.M. Lesgold and C.A. Perfetti (eds) *Interactive Processes in Reading*, Hillsdale, New Jersey: Erlbaum.

Baddeley, A.D. and Lieberman, K. (1980) 'Spatial working memory', in R. Nickerson (ed.) *Attention and Performance*, Vol. VIII, Hillsdale, New Jersey: Erlbaum.

Baddeley, A.D. and Warrington, E.K. (1970) 'Amnesia and the distinction between long- and short-term memory', *Journal of Verbal Learning and Verbal Behaviour*, 9, pp. 176–89.

Baddeley, A.D., Thomson, N. and Buchanan, M. (1975) 'Word length and the structure of short-term memory', *Journal of Verbal Learning and Verbal Behaviour*, 14, pp. 575–89.

Baggaley, J. (1991) 'Media health campaigns: not just what you say, but the way you say it', in World Health Organisation, *AIDS Prevention through Health Promotion: Facing Sensitive Issues*, Geneva: World Health Organisation.

Bain, D.J.G. (1977) 'Patient knowledge and the content of the consultation in general practice', *Medical Education*, 11, pp. 347–50.

Baker, R.R. (1984) *Bird Navigation: The Solution of a Mystery?*, London: Hodder & Stoughton.

Bales, R.F. and Slater, P.E. (1955) 'Role differentiation in small groups', in T. Parsons and R.F. Bales (eds) *Family, Socialization and Interaction Process*, Glencoe, Illinois: Free Press.

Balkwell, C. (1981) 'Transition to widowhood: A review of the literature', *Family Relations*, 30, pp. 117–28.

Ballard, R. (1979) 'Ethnic minorities and the social services: what type of service?', in V. Khan (ed.) *Minority Families in Britain: Support and Stress*, London: Macmillan.

Baltes, P.B. (1973) 'Prototypical paradigms and questions in life-span research on development and aging', *The Gerontologist*, 13, pp. 458–67.

Banaji, M.R. and Crowder, R.G. (1989) 'The bankruptcy of everyday memory', *American Psychologist*, 44, pp. 1185–93.

Bandura, A. (1965) 'Influence of a model's reinforcement contingencies on the acquisition of imitative responses', *Journal of Personality and Social Psychology*, 1, pp. 589–95.

Bandura, A. (1969) *Principles of Behaviour Modification*, New York: Holt, Rinehart & Winston.

Bandura, A. (1973) *Aggression: A Social Learning Analysis*, London: Prentice Hall.

Bandura, A. (1977) *Social Learning Theory*, Englewood Cliffs, New Jersey: Prentice-Hall.

Bandura, A. (1986) *Social Foundations of Thought and Action: A Social Cognitive Theory*, Englewood Cliffs, New Jersey: Prentice Hall.

Bandura, A. and MacDonald, F.J. (1963) 'Influence of social reinforcement and the behaviour of models in shaping children's moral judgements', *Journal of Abnormal and Social Psychology*, 67, pp. 274–81.

Bandura, A. and Menlove, F.L. (1968) 'Factors determining vicarious extinction of avoidance behaviour through symbolic modelling', *Journal of Personality and Social Psychology*, 8, pp. 99–108.

Bandura, A. and Walters, R.H. (1963) *Social Learning and Personality Development*, New York: Holt, Rinehart & Winston.

Bandura, A., Blanchard, E.B. and Ritter, B. (1969) 'Relative efficacy of desensitization and modelling approaches for inducing behavioural, affective and attitudinal changes', *Journal of Personality and Social Psychology*, 13, pp. 173–99.

Bandura, A., Ross, D. and Ross, S.A. (1961) 'Transmission of aggression through imitation of aggressive models', *Journal of Abnormal and Social Psychology*, 63, pp. 575–82.

Banister, P., Burman, E., Parker, I., Taylor M. and Tindall, C. (1994) *Qualitative methods in Psychology: A Research Guide*, Buckingham: Open University Press.

Bannister, D. and Agnew, J. (1977) 'The child's construing of self', in J. Cole (ed.) *Nebraska Symposium on Motivation*, Lincoln: University of Nebraska Press.

Banyard, P. (1989) 'Hillsborough', *Psychology News*, 2(7), pp. 4–9.

Banyard, P. (1996) 'Psychology and advertising', *Psychology Review*, 3, p. 1.

Banyard, P. and Hayes, N. (1994) *Psychology: Theory and Application*, London: Chapman and Hall.

Baran, S.J. (1979) 'Television drama as a facilitator of prosocial behaviour', *Journal of Broadcasting*, 23, pp. 277–85.

Barber, T.X. (1979) 'Suggested ("hypnotic") trance behaviour: the trance paradigm versus an alternative paradigm', in E. Fromm and R.E. Shor (eds) *Hypnosis: Developments in Research and New Perspectives*, New York: Aldine Press.

Barnes, P. (1995) *Personal, Social and Emotional Development of Children*, Oxford: Blackwell/Open University.

Baron, R.A. (1980) 'Olfaction and human social behaviour: effects of pleasant scents on physical aggression', *Basic and Applied Social Psychology*, 1, pp. 163–72.

Baron, R.A. and Bell, P.A. (1977) 'Sexual arousal and aggression by males: type of erotic stimuli and prior provocation', *Journal of Personality and Social Psychology*, 35, pp. 79–87.

Baron, R.A. and Byrne, D. (1994) *Social Psychology: Understanding Human Interaction* (7th edn), Boston: Allyn and Bacon.

Baron, R.A. and Ransberger, V.M. (1978) 'Ambient temperature and the occurrence of collective violence: the "long hot summer" revisited', *Journal of Personality and Social Psychology*, 36, pp. 351–60.

Baron, R.A. and Richardson, D.R. (1994) *Human Aggression* (2nd edn), New York: Plenum.

Baron-Cohen, S., Leslie, A.M. and Frith, U. (1985) 'Does the autistic child have a "theory of mind"?', *Cognition*, 21, pp. 37–46.

Barr, R.G. (1990) 'The early crying paradox: a modest proposal, *Human Nature*, 1, pp. 355–9.

Barrett, C.J. (1978) 'Effectiveness of widows' groups in facilitating change', *Journal of Consulting and Clinical Psychology*, 46, pp. 20–31.

Barthes, R. (1979) *Fragments d'un Discours Amoureux (A Lover's Discourse: Fragments)*, translated by Richard Howard, London: Cape.

Bartlett, F.C. (1932) *Remembering*, Cambridge: Cambridge University Press.

Bateson, G., Jackson, D.D., Haley, J. and Weakland, J. (1956) 'Toward a theory of schizophrenia', *Behavioural Science*, 1, pp. 251–64.

Bateson, P. (1986) 'When to experiment on animals', *New Scientist*, 109, pp. 30–2.

Batson, C.D., Duncan, B.D., Ackerman, P., Buckley, T. and Birch, K. (1981) 'Is empathic emotion a source of altruistic motivation?', *Journal of Personality and Social Psychology*, 40, pp. 290–302.

Batson, C.D., O'Quin, K., Fultz, J.L., Vanderplas, M. and Isen, A.M. (1983) 'Influence of self-reported distress and empathy on egoistic versus altruistic motivation to help', *Journal of Personality and Social Psychology*, 45, pp. 706–18.

Batson, C.D., Oleson, K.C., Weeks, J.L., Healey, S.P., Reeves, P.J., Jennings, P. and Brown, T. (1989) 'Religious prosocial motivation: is it altruistic or egoistic?', *Journal of Personality and Social Psychology*, 57, pp. 873–84.

Bauer, R.A. (1957) 'Brainwashing: psychology or demonology?', *Journal of Social Issues*, 13, pp. 41–7.

Bauer, R.M., Greve, K.W., Besch, E.L., Schramke, C.J., Crouch, J., Hicks, A., Ware, M.R. and Lyles, W.B. (1992) 'The role of psychological factors in the report of building-related symptoms in sick building syndrome', *Journal of Consulting and Clinical Psychology*, 60, pp. 213–19.

Baumrind, D. (1964) 'Some thoughts on ethics of research after reading Milgram's "Behavioural study of obedience"', *American Psychologist*, 19, pp. 421–3.

Bebbington P. and Kuipers, L. (1992) 'Life events and social factors', in D.J. Kavanagh (ed.) *Schizophrenia: An Overview and Practical Handbook*, London: Chapman & Hall.

Beck, A.T. (1963) 'Thinking and depression', *Archives of General Psychiatry*, 9, pp. 324–33.

Beck, A.T. (1976) *Cognitive Therapy and the Emotional Disorders*, New York: Penguin Books.

Beck, A.T. (1991) 'Cognitive therapy: a 30-year retrospective', *American Psychologist*, 46(4), pp. 368–75.

Beck, A.T. and Cowley, G. (1990) 'Beyond Lobotomies', *Newsweek*, 26 March 1990, p. 44.

Beck, A.T., Emery, G. and Greenberg, R.L. (1985) *Anxiety Disorders and Phobias: A Cognitive Perspective*, New York: Basic Books.

Beck, A.T., Freeman, A. and Associates (1990) *Cognitive Therapy of Personality Disorders*, New York: Guildford Press.

Bee, H. (1989) *The Developing Child* (5th edn), New York: Harper & Row.

Bee, H. (1995) *The Developing Child* (7th edn), London: HarperCollins.

Bee, H.L. and Mitchell, S.K. (1984) *The Developing Person: A Life-Span Approach* (2nd edn), New York: Harper & Row.

Bekerian, D.A. and Bowers, J.M. (1983) 'Eye-witness testimony: were we misled?', *Journal of Experimental Psychology: Learning, Memory and Cognition*, 9, pp. 139–45.

Belk, S.S. and Snell, W.E. (1986) 'Beliefs about women: components and correlates', *Personality and Social Psychology Bulletin*, 12, pp. 403–13.

Bell, P.A. and Baron, R.A. (1974) 'Effects of heat, noise and provocation on retaliatory evaluative behaviour', *Bulletin of the Psychonomic Society*, 4, pp. 479–81.

Bellugi, U. (1970) 'Learning the language', *Psychology Today*, 4, pp. 32–5.

Bellugi, U., O'Grady, L., Lillo-Martin, D., O'Grady-Hynes, M., Van Hoek, K. and Corina, D. (1990) 'Enhancement of spatial cognition in deaf children', in V. Volterra and C. Erting (eds) *From Gesture to Language in Hearing and Deaf Children*, London: Springer-Verlag.

Belsky, J. and Isabella, R. (1988) 'Maternal, infant, and social-contextual determinants of attachment security', in J. Belsky and T. Nezworski (eds) *Clinical Implications of Attachment*, Hillsdale, New Jersey: Erlbaum.

Belson, W.A. (1978) *Television Violence and the Adolescent Boy*, Farnborough: Saxon House, cited in G. Cumberbatch (1991) 'Is television violence harmful?', in R. Cochrane and D. Carroll (eds) *Psychology and Social Issues*, London: The Falmer Press.

Bem, S.L. (1981) 'Gender schema theory: a cognitive account of sex typing', *Psychological Review*, 88, pp. 354–64.

Bem, S.L. (1985) 'Androgyny and gender schema theory', in T. B. Sonderegger (ed.), *Nebraska Symposium on Motivation: Psychology and Gender* (Vol. 32), Lincoln: University of Nebraska Press.

Bem, S.L. (1989) 'Genital knowledge and gender constancy in preschool children', *Child Development*, 60, pp. 649–62.

Bem, S.L. (1991) 'The lenses of gender: an essay on the social reproduction of male power', Unpublished manuscript, Cornell University, Ithaca, New York.

Benewick, R. and Holton, R. (1987) 'The peaceful crowd: crowd solidarity and the Pope's visit to Britain', in G. Gaskell and R. Benewick (eds), *The Crowd in Contemporary Britain*, London: Sage.

Bennett, M. (1995) 'Why don't men come to counselling? Some speculative theories', *Counselling*, 6(4), pp. 310–13.

Bennett, W.L. and Feldman, M.S. (1981) *Reconstructing Reality in the Courtroom*, London: Tavistock.

Berger, H. (1929) 'Uber das Elektrenkephalogramm des Menschen', *Archiv für Psychiatrie und Nervenkrankheiten*, 87, pp. 527–70.

Bergin, A.E. (1971) 'The evaluation of therapeutic outcomes', in A.E. Bergin and S.L. Garfield (eds) *Handbook of Psychotherapy and Behaviour Change: An Empirical Analysis*, New York: Wiley.

Berglas, S. and Jones, E.E. (1978) 'Drug choice as a self-handicapping strategy in response to noncontingent success', *Journal of Personality and Social Psychology*, 36, pp. 405–17.

Berkowitz, L. (1962) *Aggression: A Social Psychological Analysis*, New York: McGraw-Hill.

Berkowitz, L. (1969) 'The frustration aggression hypothesis revisited', in L. Berkowitz (ed.) *Roots of Aggression: A Re-examination of the Frustration Aggression Hypothesis*, New York: Atherton Press.

Berkowitz, L. (1970) 'The contagion of violence: an S-R meditational analysis of observed aggression' in W.J. Arnold and M.M. Page (eds) *Nebraska Symposium on Motivation* (Vol. 18), Lincoln: University of Nebraska Press.

Berkowitz, L. (1983) 'Aversively stimulated aggression', *American Psychologist*, 38, pp. 1135–44.

Berkowitz, L. (1989) 'Frustration–aggression hypothesis: examination and reformulation', *Psychological Bulletin*, 106, pp. 59–73.

Berkowitz, L. and Daniels, L.R. (1963) 'Responsibility and dependency', *Journal of Abnormal and Social Psychology*, 66, pp. 429–37.

Berkowitz, L. and LePage, A. (1967) 'Weapons as aggression-eliciting stimuli', *Journal of Personality and Social Psychology*, 11, pp. 202–7.

Berman, J.J., Murphy-Berman, V. and Singh, P. (1985) 'Cross-cultural similarities and differences in perceptions of fairness', *Journal of Cross-cultural Psychology*, 16, pp. 55–67.

Bernard, C. (1856) 'Leçons de physiologie expérimentale appliquée à la médecine', *Cours du Semestre d'Eté*, 1855, 2, pp. 49–52.

Bernstein, B. (1962) 'Social class, linguistic codes and grammatical elements', *Language and Speech*, 5, pp. 31–46.

Bernstein, B.B. (1973) *Class, Codes and Control*, London: Paladin.

Bernstein, I.L. (1985) 'Learning food aversions in the progression of cancer and treatment', *Annals of the New York Academy of Sciences*, 443, pp. 365–80.

Berrettini, W.H., Golding, L.R. and Gelernter, J. (1990) 'X-chromosome markers and manic-depressive illness: Rejection of linkage to Xq28 in nine bipolar pedigrees', *Archives of General Psychiatry*, 47, pp. 366–73.

Berry, J. (1969) 'On cross-cultural comparability', *International Journal of Psychology*, 4, pp. 119–28.

Bhavnani, K.K. and Phoenix, A. (1994) *Shifting Identities, Shifting Racism: A Feminism and Psychology Reader*, London: Sage.

Bickman, L. (1972) 'Social influence and diffusion of responsibility in an emergency', *Journal of Experimental Social Psychology*, 8, pp. 438–45.

Biderman, A.D. (1960) 'Sociopsychological needs and "involuntary" behaviour as illustrated by compliance in interrogation', *Sociometry*, 23, pp. 120–217.

Bierbrauer, G. (1979) 'Why did he do it? Attribution of obedience and the phenomenon of dispositional bias', *European Journal of Social Psychology*, 9, pp. 67–84.

Bierhoff, H.W., Klein, R. and Kramp, P. (1991) 'Evidence for the altruistic personality from data on accident research', *Journal of Personality*, 59, pp. 263–80.

Billig, M. (1985) 'Prejudice, categorization and particularization: from a perceptual to a rhetorical approach', *European Journal of Social Psychology*, 15, pp. 79–104.

Binkley, S. (1979) 'A timekeeping enzyme in the pineal gland', *Scientific American*, 240, pp. 66–71.

Blakemore, C. and Mitchell, D.E. (1973) 'Environmental modification of the visual cortex and the neural basis of learning and memory', *Nature*, 241, pp. 467–8.

Blau, P.M. (1964) *Exchange and Power in Social Life*, New York: Wiley.

Blaye, A., Light, P., Joiner, R. and Sheldon, S. (1991) 'Collaboration as a facilitor of planning and problem solving on a computer based task', *British Journal of Educational Psychology*, 61, pp. 471–83.

Bloom, A. (1981) *The Linguistic Shaping of Thought*, Hillsdale, New Jersey: Erlbaum.

Blos, P. (1967) 'The second individuation process of adolescence', *Psychoanalytic Study of the Child*, 22, pp. 162–86.

Blumenthal, M., Kahn, R.L., Andrews, F.M. and Head, K.B. (1972) *Justifying Violence: The Attitudes of American Men*, Ann Arbor, Michigan: Institute for Social Research.

Bohannon, P. (1970) *Divorce and After*, New York: Doubleday.

Boker, W. (1992) 'A call for partnership between schizophrenic patients, relatives and professionals', *British Journal of Psychiatry*, 161 (Suppl. 18), pp. 10–12.

Bolger, T. (1989) 'Research and evaluation in counselling', in W. Dryden, D. Charles-Edwards and R. Woolfe (eds) *Handbook of Counselling in Britain*, London: Routledge.

Bongaarts, J. (1994) 'Can the growing human population feed itself?', *Scientific American*, 270, pp. 18–24.

Booth-Kewley, S. and Friedman, H.S. (1987) 'Psychological predictors of heart-disease: a quantitative review', *Psychological Bulletin*, 101, pp. 343–62.

Borbely, A. (1986) *Secrets of Sleep*, Harmondsworth: Penguin Books.

Borgia, G. (1985) 'Bower quality, number of decorations and mating success of male satin bowerbirds (Ptilinorynchus violaceus): an experimental analysis', *Animal Behaviour*, 33, pp. 266-71.

Borke, H. (1975) 'Piaget's Mountains revisited. Changes in the egocentric landscape', *Developmental Psychology*, 11, pp. 240–3.

Bousfield, W.A. (1953) 'The occurrence of clustering in recall of randomly arranged associates', *Journal of General Psychology*, 49, pp. 229–40.

Bower, G.H. and Hilgard, E.R. (1981) *Theories of Learning* (5th edn), Englewood Cliffs, New Jersey: Prentice-Hall.

Bower, T. (1966) 'The visual world of infants', *Scientific American*, 215 (6), pp. 80–92.

Bowlby, J. (1944) 'Forty-four juvenile thieves: their characters and home lives', *International Journal of Psychoanalysis*, 25, pp. 107–27.

Bowlby, J. (1951) *Maternal Care and Mental Health. Report to World Health Organisation*, New York: Shoken Books.

Bowlby, J. (1953; 2nd edn 1965) *Child Care and the Growth of Love*, Harmondsworth: Penguin.

Bowlby, J. (1969) *Attachment and Loss*, Vol. 1, *Attachment*, London: Hogarth Press.

Bowlby, J. (1973) *Attachment and Loss*, Vol. 2, *Separation, Anxiety and Anger*, New York, Basic Books.

Bowlby, J. (1981) *Attachment and Loss*, Vol. 3, *Loss, Sadness and Depression*, London: Hogarth.

Bowlby, J., Ainsworth, M, Boston, M. and Rosenbluth, D. (1956) 'The effects of mother–child separation: a follow-up study', *British Journal of Medical Psychology*, 29, pp. 211–47.

Braddick, O. J. (1980) 'Low-level and high-level processes in apparent motion', *Philosophical Transactions of the Royal Society of London, Series B*, 209, pp. 137–51.

Bradley, R.H. and Caldwell, B.M. (1984) '174 Children: A study of the relationships between the home environment and cognitive development during the first five years', in A.W. Gottfried (ed.) *Home Environment and Early Cognitive Development: Longitudinal Research*, New York: Academic Press.

Brady, J.V., Porter, R.W., Conrad, D.G. and Mason, J.W. (1958) 'Avoidance behavior and the development of gastroduodenal ulcers', *Journal of the Experimental Analysis of Behavior*, 1, pp. 69–72.

Brehm, S.S. (1985) *Intimate Relationships*, New York: Random House.

Breland, K. and Breland, M. (1961) 'The misbehaviour of organisms', *American Psychologist*, 16, pp. 681–4.

Bremer, F. (1977) 'Cerebral hypnogenic centres', *Annals of Neurology*, 2, pp. 1–6.

Bremner, J.D., Southwick, S.M., Johnson, D.R., Yehoda, R. and Charney, D.S. (1993) 'Childhood physical abuse and combat-related post-traumatic stress disorder in Vietnam Veterans', *American Journal of Psychiatry*, 150(2), pp. 235–39.

Bretherton, I. and Waters, E. (eds) (1985) *Growing Points in Attachment Theory and Research*, Monographs of the Society for Research in Child Development, 50(1–2), Serial No. 209.

Bretherton, I., Ridgeway, D. and Cassidy, J. (1990) 'Assessing internal working models in the attachment relationship: an attachment story completion task for 3-year-olds', in M.T. Greenburg, D. Cichetti and E. M. Cummings (eds) *Attachment During the Preschool Years*, Chicago: University of Chicago Press.

Breuer, J. and Freud, S. (1895) 'Studies in hysteria', in J. Stachey (ed.) (1955) *The Standard Edition of the Complete Psychological Works of Sigmund Freud*, Vol. 2, London: Hogarth Press.

Brewer, W.F. and Treyens, J.C. (1981) 'Role of schemata in memory for places', *Cognitive Psychology*, 13, pp. 207–30.

British Psychological Society (1993) *Code of Conduct, Ethical Principles and Guidelines*, Leicester: BPS.

Broadbent, D.E. (1954) 'The role of auditory localization in attention and memory span', *Journal of Experimental Psychology*, 47, pp. 191–6.

Broadbent, D.E. (1958) *Perception and Communication*, Oxford: Pergamon.

Broca, P. (1861) 'Remarques sur le siège de la faculté du langage articulé suivées d'une observation d'aphémie', *Bulletin de la Société Anatomique* (Paris), 6, pp. 330–57.

Bronfenbrenner, U. (1974) 'The origins of alienation', *Scientific American*, 231, pp. 53–61.

Bronfenbrenner, U. (1979) *The Ecology of Human Development*, Cambridge, Massachusetts: Harvard University Press.

Brooke, M. de L. and Davies, N.B. (1988) 'Egg mimicry by cuckoos *Cuculus canorus* in relation to discrimination by hosts', *Nature*, 335, pp. 630–2.

Broverman, I.K., Broverman D.M., Clarkson, F.E., Rosencrantz, P.S. and Vogel, S.R. (1981) 'Sex role stereotypes and clinical judgements of mental health', in E. Howell and M. Bayes (eds) *Women and Mental Health*, New York: Basic Books.

Brown, G.W. (1972) 'Influence of family life on the course of schizophrenic disorders: a replication', *British Journal of Psychiatry*, 121, pp. 241–8.

Brown, G.W. and Harris, T.O. (1978) *The Social Origins of Depression*, London: Tavistock.

Brown, J.A. (1958) 'Some tests of the decay theory of immediate memory', *Quarterly Journal of Experimental Psychology*, 10, pp. 12–21.

Brown, J.S. and Burton, R.D. (1978) 'Diagnostic model for procedural bugs in basic mathematical skills', *Cognitive Science*, 2, pp. 155–92.

Brown, R. (1965), *Social Psychology*, London: Collier McMillan.

Brown, R. and Hanlon, C. (1970) 'Derivational complexity and the order of acquisition in child speech', in J.R. Hayes (ed.) *Cognition and the Development of Language*, New York: Wiley.

Brown, R. and Kulik, J. (1977) 'Flashbulb memories', *Cognition*, 5, pp. 73–99.

Brown, R., Colter, N. and Corsellis, J.A.N. (1986) 'Post-mortem evidence of structural brain changes in schizophrenia: differences in brain weight, temporal brain area, and parahippocampal gyrus compared with affective disorder', *Archives of General Psychiatry*, 43, pp. 36–42.

Bruch, H. (1974) 'Anorexia Nervosa', in *American Handbook of Psychiatry* (2nd edn), New York: Basic Books.

Bruch, H. (1979) *The Golden Cage*, New York: Vintage Books.

Bruner, J.S. (1973) *Beyond the Information Given: Studies in the Psychology of Knowing*, New York: Norton.

Bruner, J.S. (1983) *Child's Talk: Learning to Use Language*, New York: Norton.

Bruno, N. and Cutting, J.E. (1988) 'Mini-modularity and the perception of layout', *Journal of Experimental Psychology: General*, 117, pp. 161–70.

Bryant, J.L. and Zillman, D. (1979) 'The effect of the intensification of annoyance through residual excitation from unrelated prior stimulation on substantially delayed hostile behaviour', *Journal of Experimental Social Psychology*, 15, pp. 470–80.

Bryant, P.E. and Bradley, L. (1985) *Children's Reading Problems*, Oxford: Blackwell.

Buchard, T.J. and McGue, M. (1981) 'Familial studies of intelligence: a review', *Science*, 212, pp. 1055–9.

Buchsbaum, M.S. (1990) 'The frontal lobes, basal ganglia, and temporal lobes as sites for schizophrenia', *Schizophrenia Bulletin*, 16, pp. 379–89.

Burger, J.M. (1992) *Desire for control: Personality, Social and Clinical Perspectives*, New York: Plenum.

Burman, E. and Parker, I. (eds) (1993) *Discourse Analytic Research*, London: Routledge.

Bushnell, I.W.R., Sai, F. and Mullin, J.Y. (1989) 'Neonatal recognition of the mother's face', *British Journal of Developmental Psychology*, 7, pp. 3–15.

Buss, A.H. (1961) *The Psychology of Aggression*, New York: Wiley.

Buss, D. (1989) 'Sex differences in human mate preferences', *Behavioural and Brain Sciences*, 12, pp. 1–49.

Buss, D. (1994) *The Evolution of Desire: Strategies of Human Mating*, New York: Basic Books.

Buss, T. and Redburn, F.S. (1983) Unpublished and untitled manuscript, Center for Urban Studies, Youngstown, Ohio: Youngstown State University.

Bussey, K. and Bandura, A. (1992) 'Self-regulatory mechanisms governing gender-development', *Child Development*, 63, pp. 1236–50.

Butler, R.A. (1953) 'Discrimination learning by Rhesus monkeys to visual-exploration motivation', *Journal of Comparative and Physiological Psychology*, 46, pp. 95–8.

Byrne, R.W. and Whiten, A. (1988) *Machiavellian Intelligence: Social Expertise and the Evolution of Intellect in Monkeys, Apes and Humans*, Oxford: Oxford University Press.

Cacioppo, J.T. and Petty, R.E. (1986) 'Central and peripheral routes to persuasion: an individual difference perspective', *Journal of Personality and Social Psychology*, 51, pp. 1032–43.

Cadoret, R.J. (1978) 'Evidence of genetic inheritance of primary affective disorder in adoptees', *American Journal of Psychiatry*, 135, pp. 463–6.

Caldwell, B.M. and Bradley, R.M. (1978) *Home Observation for Measurement of the Environment*, Little Rock: University of Arkansas.

Camino, I. and Trocolli, B. (1980) 'Categorization of violence, the belief in a just world and political activism', unpublished manuscript, University of Paraiba.

Camras, L. A., Malatesta, C. and Izard, C. (1991) 'The development of facial expression in infancy', in R. Feldman and B. Rime (eds) *Fundamentals of Non-verbal Behavior*, Cambridge: Cambridge University Press.

Cannon, W.B. (1929) *Bodily Changes in Pain, Hunger, Fear and Rage*, New York: Appleton-Century-Crofts.

Cannon, W.B. (1932) *The Wisdom of the Body*, New York: Norton.

Cannon, W.B. and Washburn, A.L. (1912) 'An explanation of hunger', *American Journal of Physiology*, 29, pp. 441–54.

Caraco, T. and Wolf, L.L. (1975) 'Ecological determinants of group size of foraging lions', *American Naturalist*, 109, pp. 343–52.

Cardwell, M.C. (1996) *The Complete A–Z of Psychology Handbook*, London, Hodder & Stoughton.

Cargan, L. and Melko, M. (1982) *Singles: Myths and Realities*, Beverly Hills, California: Sage.

Carlson, M., Marcus-Newhall, A. and Miller, N. (1989) 'Evidence for a general conduct of aggression', *Personality and Social Psychology Bulletin*, 15, pp. 377–89.

Carmichael, L., Hogan, H.P. and Walter, A.A. (1932) 'An experimental study of the effect of language on the reproduction of visually presented forms', *Journal of Experimental Psychology*, 15, pp. 73–86.

Carroll, B.J. (1982) 'The dexamethasone suppression test for melancholia', *British Journal of Psychiatry*, 140, pp. 292–304.

Carter, H. and Glick, P.C. (1970) *Marriage and Divorce: A Social and Economic Study*, Cambridge, Massachusetts: Harvard University Press.

Carver, C. and Scheier, M. (1992) *Perspectives on Personality* (2nd edn), Carver: Allyn & Bacon.

Case, R. (1992) 'Neo-Piagetian theories of intellectual development', in H. Beilin and P.B. Pufall (eds) *Piaget's Theory: Prospects and Possibilities*, Hillsdale, New Jersey: Erlbaum.

Cattell, R.B., Eber, H.W. and Tatsuoka, M.M. (1970) *The 16-Factor Personality Questionnaire*, Champaign: IPAT.

Cerletti, U. and Bini, L. (1938) 'L'elettroshock', *Archives of General Neural Psychiatry and Psychoanalysis*, 19, pp. 266–8.

Chandler, M.J., Greenspan, S. and Barenboim, C. (1973) 'Judgements of intentionality in response to videotaped and verbally presented moral dilemmas: the medium is the message', *Child Development*, 44, pp. 315–320.

Cherry, E.C. (1953) 'Some experiments on the recognition of speech, with one and two ears', *Journal of the Acoustical Society of America*, 25, pp. 975–9.

Cheyney, D.L. and Seyfarth, R.M. (1990) *How Monkeys See the World*, Chicago: University of Chicago Press.

Chi, M.T. (1978) 'Knowledge structures and memory development' in R.S. Siegler (ed.) *Child Thinking: What Develops?*, Hillsdale, New Jersey: Erlbaum.

Childs, H.L (1994) 'Progaganda', *Enkarta*, Microsoft.

Chiriboga, D.A. (1982) 'Adaptations to marital separation in later and earlier life', *Journal of Gerontology*, 37, pp. 109–14.

Chodorow, N. (1978) *The Reproduction of Mothering*, Berkeley: University of California Press.

Chomsky, N. (1957) *Syntactic Structures*, The Hague: Mouton.

Chomsky, N. (1965) *Aspects of the Theory of Syntax*, Cambridge, Massachusetts: MIT Press.

Christianson, S. (1992) 'Emotional memories in laboratory studies versus real-life studies. Do they compare?', in M.A. Conway, D.C. Rubin, H. Spinnler and W.A. Wagenaar *Theoretical Perspectives on Autobiographical Memory*, Dordrecht, Netherlands: Kluwer Academic Publishers.

Cialdini, R.B., Baumann, D.J. and Kenrick, D.T. (1981) 'Insights from sadness: a three-step model of the development of altruism as hedonism', *Development Review*, 1, pp. 207–23.

Cialdini, R.B., Kenrick, D.T. and Bauman, D.J. (1982) 'Effects of mood on pro-social behaviour in children and adults', in N. Eisenberg Berg (ed.) *Development of Prosocial Behaviour*, New York: Academic Press.

Cialdini, R.B., Schaller, M., Honlainhan, D., Arps, H., Fultz, J. and Beaman, A.L. (1987) 'Empathy-based helping: is it selflessly or selfishly motivated?', *Journal of Personality and Social Psychology*, 52, pp. 749–58.

Cicchetti, D. and Mans-Wagener, L. (1987) 'Stages, sequences, and structures in the organization of cognitive development in Down's Syndrome infants', in I. Uzgiris and J.McV. Hunt (eds) *Research with Scales of Psychological Development in Infancy*, Urbana: University of Illinois Press.

Clare, A.W. (1985) 'Hormones, behaviour and the menstrual cycle', *Journal of Psychosomatic Research*, 29, pp. 225–33.

Clark, M.S. and Mills, J. (1979) 'Interpersonal attraction and communal relationships', *Journal of Personality and Social Psychology*, 37, pp. 12–24.

Clark, R.D. and Word, L.E. (1974) 'Where is the apathetic bystander? Situational characteristics of the emergency', *Journal of Personality and Social Psychology*, 29, pp. 279–87.

Clarke, A. and Clarke, A. (1996) 'Varied destinies: a study of unfulfilled predictions' in B. Bernstein and J. Branner (eds) *Children and Social Policy*, London: Taylor and Francis.

Clutton-Brock, T.H. and Albon, S.D. (1979) 'The roaring of red deer and the evolution of honest advertisement', *Behaviour*, 69, pp. 145–70.

Clutton-Brock, T.H. and Vincent, A.C.J. (1991) 'Sexual selection and the potential reproductive rates of males and females', *Nature*, 351, pp. 58–60.

Cochrane, R. (1977) 'Mental illness in immigrants to England and Wales: an analysis of mental hospital admissions, 1971', *Social Psychiatry*, 12, pp. 25–35.

Cochrane, R. (1983) *The Social Creation of Mental Illness*, London: Longman.

Cochrane, R. (1988) 'Marriage, separation and divorce', in S. Fisher and J. Reason (eds) *Handbook of Life Stress, Cognition and Health*, Chichester: Wiley.

Cochrane, R. (1995) 'Mental illness and the built environment', *Psychology Review*, 1(4), pp. 12–15.

Cochrane, R. (1995) 'Women and depression', *Psychology Review*, 2(1), pp. 20–4.

Cochrane, R. and Sashidharan, S.P. (1995) 'Mental health and ethnic minorities: a review of the literature and implications for services', Paper presented to the Birmingham and Northern Birmingham Health Trust.

Cochrane, R. and Stopes-Roe, M. (1980) 'Factors affecting the distribution of psychological symptoms in urban areas of England', *Acta Psychiatrica Scandinavica*, 61, pp. 445–60.

Cohen, D. (1988) *Forgotten Millions: The Treatment of the Mentally Ill – A Global Perspective*, London: Paladin.

Cohen, G. (1986) 'Everyday memory', in G. Cohen, M.W. Eysenck and M.E. Le Voi *Memory: A Cognitive Approach*, Milton Keynes: Open University Press.

Cohen, J.E. (1995) 'The uniqueness of present human population growth', in J. Brockman and K. Matson (eds) *How Things Are: A Science Tool-Kit for the Mind*, London: Weidenfeld and Nicolson.

Cohen, K. (1992) 'Some legal issues in counselling and psychotherapy', *British Journal of Guidance and Counselling*, 20, Issue 1, pp. 10–25.

Cohen, N.J. and Squire, L.R. (1980) 'Preserved learning and retention of pattern-analysing skills in amnesia using perceptual learning', *Cortex*, 17, pp. 273–8.

Cohen, S. and Spacapan, S. (1978) 'The after-effects of stress: an attentional interpretation', *Environmental Psychology and Non-verbal Behaviour*, 3(1), pp. 43–57.

Coke, J.S., Batson, C.D. and McDavis, K. (1978) 'Empathic mediation of helping: a two-stage model', *Journal of Personality and Social Psychology*, 36, pp. 752–66.

Colby, A. and Kohlberg, L. (1987) *The Measurement of Moral Judgement*, Cambridge: Cambridge University Press.

Colby, A., Kohlberg, L., Gibbs, J. and Liebermann, M. (1983) 'A longitudinal study of moral development', *Monographs of the Society for Research in Child Development*, 48(1–2), No. 200.

Cole, M., Gay, J., Glick, J. and Sharp, D.W. (1971) *The Cultural Content of Learning and Thinking*, New York: Basic Books.

Coleman, J.C. (1974) *Relationships in Adolescence*, London: Routledge & Kegan Paul.

Coleman, J.C. and Hendry, L. (1990) *The Nature of Adolescence*, London: Routledge.

Collins, A. M. and Loftus, E.F. (1975) 'A spreading activation theory of semantic processing', *Psychological Review*, 82, pp. 407–28.

Collins, A.M. and Quillian, M.R. (1969) 'Retrieval time from semantic memory', *Journal of Verbal Learning and Verbal Behaviour*, 8, p. 244.

Comer, R.J. (1995) *Abnormal Psychology* (2nd edn), New York: W.H. Freeman.

Conners, K., Goyette, C. and Newman, E. (1980) 'Dose time effect of artificial colors in hyperactive children', *Journal of Learning Disabilities*, 13, pp. 512–16.

Conrad, R. (1979) *The Deaf Schoolchild*, London: Harper & Row.

Conway, M.A. (1991) 'In defense of everyday memory', *American Psychologist*, 46, pp. 19–26.

Conway, M.A. (1992) 'A structural model of autobiographical memory', in M.A. Conway, D.C. Rubin, H. Spinnler and W.A. Wagenaar *Theoretical Perspectives on Autobiographical Memory*, Dordrecht, Netherlands: Kluwer Academic Publishers.

Conway, M.A., Anderson, S.J., Larsen, S.F., Donnelly, C.M., McDaniel, M.A., McClelland, A.G.R. and Rawles, R.E. (1994) 'The formation of flashbulb memories', *Memory and Cognition*, 22, pp. 326–43.

Cook, M. (1978) *Perceiving Others*, London: Routledge.

Cooley, C.H. (1902) *Human Nature and the Social Order*, New York: Scribner.

Coolican, H. (1994) *Research Methods and Statistics in Psychology* (2nd edn), London: Hodder & Stoughton.

Coolican, H. (1995) *Introduction to Research Methods and Statistics in Psychology*, London: Hodder & Stoughton.

Cooper P.J. (1988) 'Non-psychotic psychiatric disorder after childbirth: a prospective study of prevalence, incidence, course and nature', *British Journal of Psychiatry*, 152, pp. 799–806.

Coopersmith, S. (1967) *The Antecedents of Self-esteem*, San Francisco: Freeman.

Corrigan, R. (1978) 'Language development as related to stage 6 object permanence development', *Journal of Child Language*, 5, pp. 173–89.

Corsini, R.J. and Wedding, D. (1995) *Current Psychotherapies* (5th edn), Illinois: F.E. Peacock Publishers.

Cosmides, L. (1989) 'The logic of social exchange: has natural selection shaped how humans reason?', *Cognition*, 31, pp. 187–276.

Council, J.R. and Kenny, D.A. (1992) 'Expert judgements of hypnosis from subjective state reports', *Journal of Abnormal Psychology*, 101, pp. 657–62.

Cox, T. (1975) 'The nature and management of stress', *New Behaviour*, 25 September, pp. 493–5.

Craik, F.I.M. and Lockhart, R.S. (1972) 'Levels of processing: a framework for memory research', *Journal of Verbal Learning and Verbal Behaviour*, 11, pp. 671–84.

Cramer, R.E., McMaster, M.R., Bartell, P.A. and Dragna, M. (1988) 'Subject competence and minimisation of the bystander effect', *Journal of Applied Social Psychology*, 18, pp. 1133–48.

Craske, M.G. and Barlow, D.H. (1993) 'Panic disorder and agoraphobia', in D.H. Barlow (ed.) *Clinical Handbook of Psychological Disorders: A Step-by-Step Treatment Manual* (2nd edn), New York: Guildford.

Crawford, H.J. and Gruzelier, J.H. (1992) 'A midstream view of the neuropsychology of hypnosis: recent research and future directions', in E. Fromm and M.R. Nash (eds) *Contemporary Hypnosis Research*, London: Guildford Press.

Cray, E. (1995) 'Teaching about racism', in *Psychology Teaching*, No. 4, Association of Teachers of Psychology, Leicester: BPS.

Crick, F. and Mitchison, G. (1983) 'The function of dream sleep', *Nature*, 304, pp. 111–14.

Crisp, A.H. (1967) 'Anorexia Nervosa', *Hospital Medicine*, 1, pp. 713–18.

Crooke, C. (1992) 'Cultural artefacts in social development: the case of computers', in H. McGurk (ed.) *Childhood Social Development: Contemporary Perspectives*, Hove: Erlbaum.

Crutchfield, R.S. (1955) 'Conformity and character', *American Psychologist*, 10, pp. 191-8.

Cumberbatch, G. (1987) *The Portrayal of Violence on British Television*, London: BBC Publications.

Cumberbatch, G. (1990) *Television Advertising and Sex Role Stereotyping: A Content Analysis*, Working Paper IV for the Broadcasting Standards Council, Communications Research Group, Birmingham: Aston University.

Cumberbatch, G. (1991) 'Is television violence harmful?', in R. Cochrane and D. Carroll (eds) *Psychology and Social Issues*, London: The Falmer Press, p. 179.

Cumming, E. and Henry, W. (1961) *Growing Old*, New York: Basic Books.

Cunningham, J.D. and Antrill, J.K. (1995) 'Current trends in non-marital cohabitation: in search of the POSSLQ', in J.T. Wood and S. Duck (eds) *Understudied Relationships: Off the Beaten Track*, Thousand Oaks, USA: Sage.

Curtiss, S. (1977) *Genie: A Psycholinguistic Study of a Modern-day 'Wild Child'*, London: Academic Press.

Cuthill, I. (1991) 'Field experiments in animal behaviour', *Animal Behaviour*, 42, pp. 1007–14

Czander, W.M. (1994) 'The sick building syndrome: A psychoanalytic perspective', *International Forum of Psychoanalysis*, 3, pp. 139–49.

Czeisler, C.A., Moore-Ede, M.C. and Coleman, R.M. (1982) 'Rotating shift work schedules that disrupt sleep are improved by applying circadian principles', *Science*, 217, pp. 460–3.

Dallenbach, K.M. (1951) 'A picture puzzle with a new principle of concealment', *American Journal of Psychology*, 64, pp. 431–3.

Dalton, K. (1964) *The Premenstrual Syndrome*, London: Heinemann.

Damon, W. and Hart, D. (1982) 'The development of self-understanding from infancy through adolescence' *Child Development*, 53, pp. 831–57.

Dana, C.L. (1921) 'The anatomic seat of the emotions: a discussion of the James-Lange Theory', *Archives of Neurology and Psychiatry (Chicago)*, 6, pp. 634–9.

Darley, J.M. and Latané, B. (1968) 'Bystander intervention in emergencies: diffusion of responsibility', *Journal of Personality and Social Psychology*, 8, pp. 377–83

Darwin, C. (1871) *Descent of Man and Selection in relation to Sex*, London: John Murray.

Darwin, C. For a general source book of Darwin's original writings, see Porter, D.M. and Graham, P.W. (eds) (1993), *The Portable Darwin*, Harmondsworth: Penguin Books.

Davie, R., Butler, N. and Goldstein, H. (1972) *From Birth to Seven*, London: Longman.

Davies, A. (1991) 'Piaget, teachers and education into the 1990s' in P. Light, S. Sheldon and M. Woodhead (eds) *Learning to Think*, London: Routledge/Open University.

Davies, G. (1994a) 'Ethical considerations', *Psychology Review*, 1(1), pp. 13–15.

Davies, G. (1994b) *AS and A level Practicals Checklist*, ATP Resource Item 203, Leicester: Association for the Teaching of Psychology.

Davies, N.B. (1992) *Dunnock Behaviour and Social Evolution*, Oxford: Oxford University Press.

Davies, N.B. and Brooke, M. (1991) 'Coevolution of the cuckoo and its hosts', *Scientific American* (January), pp. 66–73.

Davies, N.B. and Houston (1981) 'Territory economics', in J.R. Krebs and N.B. Davies (eds) *Behavioural Ecology: An AI Evolutionary Approach* (2nd edn), Oxford: Blackwell.

Davis, C.M. (1928) 'Self selection of diet by newly weaned infants', *American Journal of Diseases of Childhood*, 36, pp. 651–79.

Davis, J.D., Kane, J.M., Marder, S.R., Brauzer, B., Gierl, B., Schooler, N., Casey, D.E. and Hassan, M. (1993) 'Dose response of prophylatic antipsychotics', *Journal of Clinical Psychiatry*, 54(3), pp. 24–30.

Davis, K. (1947) 'Final note on a case of extreme isolation', *American Journal of Sociology*, 52, pp. 432–7.

Davison, G.C. and Neale, J.M. (1994) *Abnormal Psychology* (6th edn), New York: Wiley.

Dawkins, M.S. (1985) 'The scientific basis for assessing suffering in animals', in P. Singer *Defence of Animals*, Oxford: Blackwell.

Dawkins, R. (1976) *The Selfish Gene*, Oxford: Oxford University Press.

Dawkins, R. (1982) *The Extended Phenotype*, London: W.H. Freeman.

De Waal, F.B. (1986) 'The brutal elimination of a rival among captive male chimpanzees', *Ethology and Sociobiology*, 7, pp. 89–103

Deaux, K. and Lewis, L. (1983) 'Components of gender stereotypes', *Psychological Documents*, 13, 25 (Ms. No. 2583) (4, 13).

Deaux, K., Dane, F.C. and Wrightsman, L.S. (1993) *Social Psychology in the 90s*, Pacific Grove, California: Brooks/Cole.

DeCasper, A. J. and Fifer, W. P. (1980) 'Of human bonding: newborns prefer their mothers' voices', *Science*, 208, pp. 1174–6.

Dell, G.S. (1986) 'A spreading-activation theory of retrieval in sentence production', *Psychological Review*, 93, pp. 283–321.

Deluga, R.J. and Perry, J.T. (1991) 'The relationship of subordinate upward influencing behaviour, satisfaction and perceived superior effectiveness with leader-member exchanges', *Journal of Occupational Psychology*, 64, pp. 239–52.

Dement, W. and Kleitman, N. (1957) 'Cyclic variations in EEG during sleep and their relation to eye movements, body motility and dreaming', *Electroencephalography and Clinical Neurophysiology*, 9, pp. 673–90.

DeMyer, M.K., Barton, S. and Alpern, G.D. (1974) 'The measured intelligence of autistic children', *Journal Autism and Childhood Schizophrenia*, 4, pp. 42–60.

Dennis, W. (1973) *Children of the Creche*, New York: Appleton-Century-Crofts.

Descartes, R. (1641/1968) *Discourse on Method and The Meditations*, Harmondsworth: Penguin Classics.

Desimone, R., Albright, T., Gross, C. G., and Bruce, D. (1984) 'Stimulus-selective properties of inferior temporal neurons in the macaque', *Journal of Neuroscience*, 8, pp. 2051–62.

Deutsch, J.A. and Deutsch, D. (1963) 'Attention: Some theoretical considerations', *Psychological Review*, 70, pp. 80–90.

Deutsch, J.A., Young, G.W. and Kalogeris, T.J. (1978) 'The stomach signals satiety', *Science*, 201, pp. 165–7.

Deutsch, M. (1973) *The Resolution of Conflict: Constructive and Destructive Processes*, New Haven: Yale.

Deutsch, M. and Collins, M.E. (1951) *Interracial Housing: A Psychological Evaluation of a Social Experiment*, Minneapolis: University of Minnesota Press.

Devine, P.A. and Fernald, P.S. (1973) 'Outcome effects of receiving a preferred, randomly assigned or non-preferred therapy', *Journal of Consulting and Clinical Psychology*, 41(1), pp. 104–7.

Dindia, K. and Baxter, L.A. (1987) 'Maintenance and repair strategies in marital relationships', *Journal of Social and Personal Relationships*, 4, pp. 143–58.

Dirks, J. (1982) 'The effect of a commercial game on children's Block Design scores on the WISC-R test', *Intelligence*, 6, pp. 109–23.

Dodge, K.A. and Coie, J.D. (1987) 'Social information processing factors in reactive and proactive aggression in children's peer groups', *Journal of Personality and Social Psychology*, 53, pp. 1146–58.

Doise, W. (1986) *Levels of Explanation in Social Psychology*, Cambridge: Cambridge University Press.

Dollard, J., Doob, L., Miller, N.E., Mowrer, O.H. and Sears, R. (1939) *Frustration and Aggression*, Newhaven: Yale University Press.

Donaldson, M. (1978) *Children's Minds*, London: Fontana.

Donnerstein, E. and Wilson, D.W. (1976) 'Effects of noise and perceived control on ongoing and subsequent aggressive behaviour', *Journal of Personality and Social Psychology*, 34, pp. 774–81.

Drabman, R.S. and Thomas, M.H. (1974) 'Does media violence increase children's toleration of real-life aggression?', *Developmental Psychology*, 10, pp. 418–21.

Dryden, W. (1990) *Individual Therapy: A Handbook*, Milton Keynes: Open University Press.

Dryden, W., Charles-Edwards, D. and Woolfe, R. (1989) *Handbook of Counselling in Britain*, London: Routledge.

Duck, S. (1973) *Personal Relationships and Personal Constructs: A Study of Friendship Formation*, London: Wiley.

Duck, S. (1981) 'Toward a research map for the study of relationship breakdown', in S. Duck and R. Gilmour (eds) *Personal Relationships*, Vol. 3, *Personal Relationships in Disorder*, London: Academic Press.

Duck, S. (1988) *Relating to Others*, Milton Keynes: Open University Press.

Duck, S. and Sants, H.K.A. (1983) 'On the origin of the specious: are personal relationships really interpersonal states?', *Journal of Social and Clinical Psychology*, 1, pp. 27–41.

Dunbar, R. (1995) 'Are you lonesome tonight', *New Scientist*, 11 February 1995, pp. 26-31.

Duncker, K. (1945) 'On problem solving', *Psychological Monographs*, 58 (Whole No. 270).

Dunlea, A. (1989) *Vision and the Emergence of Meaning: Blind and Sighted Children's Early Language*, Cambridge: Cambridge University Press.

Dunn, J. and Kendrick, C. (1982) *Siblings: Love, Envy and Understanding*, Cambridge, Massachusetts: Harvard University Press.

Durkin, K. (1985) *Television, Sex Roles and Children*, Milton Keynes: Open University Press.

Durkin, K. (1995) *Developmental Social Psychology*, Oxford: Blackwell.

Dutton, D.C. and Aron, A.P. (1974) 'Some evidence for heightened sexual attraction under conditions of high anxiety', *Journal of Personality and Social Psychology*, 30, pp. 510–17.

Dworkin, B.R. (1987) 'Genetics and the phenomenology of schizophrenia' in P.D. Harvey and E.F. Walker (eds) *Positive and negative symptoms of psychosis*, Hillsdale, New York: Erlbaum.

Dyer, C. (1995) *Beginning Research in Psychology: A Practical Guide to Research Methods and Statistics*, Oxford: Blackwell.

Egeland, J.A., Gerhard, D.S., Pauls, D.L., Sussex, J.N., Kidd, K.K., Allen, C.R., Hosterer, A.M. and Houseman, D.E. (1987) 'Bipolar affective disorders linked to DNA markers on chromosome 11', *Nature*, 325, pp. 783–7.

Eggleston, J. (1985) *The Educational and Vocational Experiences of 15- to 18-year-old Young People of Minority Ethnic Groups*, Loughborough: University of Keele.

Eiser, J.R. (1986) *Social Psychology*, Cambridge: Cambridge University Press.

Elardo, R. and Bradley, R.H. (1981) 'The Home Observation for Measurement of the Environment (HOME) scale: a review of research', *Developmental Review*, 1, pp. 113–45.

Elgar, M.A. (1986) 'Food intake rate and resource availability: flocking decisions in house sparrows', *Animal Behaviour*, 35, pp. 1168–76.

Elicker, J., Englund, M. and Sroufe, L.A. (1992) 'Predicting peer competence and peer relationships in childhood from early parent–child relationships', in R. Parke and G. Ladd (eds) *Family–Peer Relationships: Models of Linkage*, Hillsdale, New Jersey: Erlbaum.

Elliott, J. (1977) 'The power and pathology of prejudice', in P.G. Zimbardo and F.L. Ruch, *Psychology and Life* (9th edn), Diamond Printing, Glenview, Illinois: Scott, Foresman.

Elliott, J. (1990) in *Discovering Psychology*, Program 20 [PBS video series], Washington, DC: Annenberg/CPB Program.

Ellis, A. (1962) *Reason and Emotion in Psychotherapy*, New York: Citadel.

Ellis, A. (1980) 'Discomfort anxiety: a new cognitive-behavioural construct. Part 2', *Rational Living*, 15(1), pp. 25–30.

Ellis, A. (1991) 'The revised ABCs of rational-emotive therapy', *Journal of Rational-Emotive and Cognitive-Behaviour Therapy*, 9, pp. 139–92.

Ellis, A.W. and Young, A.W. (1988) *Human Cognitive Neuropsychology*, Hove: Erlbaum.

Ellis, N.C. and Miles, T.R. (1977) 'Dyslexia as a limitation in the ability to process information', *Bulletin of the Orton Society*, 27, pp. 72–8.

Emlen, S.T. (1995) 'An evolutionary theory of the family', *Proceedings of the National Academy of Sciences of the USA*, 92, pp. 8092–99.

Emler, N. (1983) 'Morality and politics', in H. Weinreich-Haste and D. Locke (eds) *Morality in the Making: Thought, Action and the Social Context*, New York: Wiley.

Emmelkamp, P.M. (1994) 'Behaviour therapy with adults', in A.E. Bergin and S.L. Garfield (eds) *Handbook of Psychotherapy and Behaviour Change* (4th edn), New York: Wiley.

Emmerlich, W., Goldmann, K., Kirsh, K. and Sharabany, R. (1977) 'Evidence for a transitional phase in the development of gender constancy', *Child Development*, 48, pp. 930–6.

Endler, J. A. (1991) 'Interactions between predators and prey', in J.R. Krebs and N.B. Davies (eds) *Behavioural Ecology: An Evolutionary Approach* (3rd edn), Oxford: Blackwell.

Engel, M., Nechlin, H. and Arkin, A.M. (1975) 'Aspects of mothering: correlates of the cognitive development of black male infants in the second year of life', in A. Davids (ed.) *Child Personality and Psychopathology: Current Topics*, Vol. 2, New York: Wiley.

Engels, G.I., Garnefski, N. and Diekstra, R.F.W. (1993) 'Efficacy of rational–emotive therapy: a quantitative analysis', *Journal of Consulting and Clinical Psychology*, 61(6), pp. 1083–90.

Enquist, M. and Leimar, O. (1990) 'The evolution of fatal fighting', *Animal Behaviour*, 39, pp. 1–9.

Epstein, L.C. and Lasagna, L. (1969) 'Obtaining informed consent', *Archives of Internal Medicine*, 123, pp. 682–8.

Erikson, E.H. (1959) 'Identity and the life cycle', *Selected Papers: Psychological Issues 1 (Monograph 1)*, New York: International Universities Press.

Erikson, E.H. (1968) *Identity: Youth and Crisis*, London: Faber.

Erikson, E.H. (1980) *Identity and the Life Cycle*, New York: Norton.

Erlich, D. *et al.* (1957) 'Postdecision exposure to relevant information', *Journal of Abnormal and Social Psychology*, 54, pp. 98–102.

Eron, L.D. (1982) 'Parent–child interaction, television violence and aggression in children', *American Psychologist*, 37, pp. 197–211.

Eron, L.D., Huesmann, L.R., Brice, P., Fischer, P. and Mermelstein, R. (1983) 'Age trends in the development of aggression, sex-typing, and related television habits', *Developmental Psychology*, 19, pp. 71–7.

Ervin-Tripp, S. (1964) 'An analysis of the interaction of language, topic and listener', *American Anthropologist*, 66, pp. 94–100.

Evans, C. (1984) *Landscapes of the Night: How and Why We Dream*, New York: Viking.

Evans, G.W., Palsane, M.N. and Carrere, S. (1987) 'Type A behaviour and occupational stress: a cross-cultural study of blue-collar workers', *Journal of Personality and Social Psychology*, 52, pp. 1002–7.

Evans, J.St.B.T. (1989) *Bias in Human Reasoning: Causes and Consequences*, Hove: Erlbaum.

Evans, J.St.B.T. and Lynch, L.S. (1973) 'Matching bias in the selection task', *British Journal of Psychology*, 64, pp. 391–7.

Evans, M.D., Hollon, S.D., DeRubeis, R.J. and Associates (1992) 'Differential relapse following cognitive therapy and pharmacotherapy for depression', *Archives of General Psychiatry*, 49, pp. 802–8.

Evans, M.R. and Thomas, A.L.R. (1992) 'Aerodynamic and mechanical effects of elongated tails in the scarlet-tufted malachite sunbird', *Animal Behaviour*, 43, pp. 337–47.

Evans, P.D. (1990) 'Type A behaviour and coronary heart disease: when will the jury return?', *British Journal of Psychology*, 81, pp. 147–57.

Ewald, P.W. (1993a) 'The evolution of virulence', *Scientific American* (April), 56–62.

Ewald, P.W. (1993b) *The Evolution of Infectious Diseases*, Oxford: Oxford University Press.

Eysenck, H.J. (1952) 'The effects of psychotherapy: an evaluation', *Journal of Consulting Psychology*, 16, pp. 319–24.

Eysenck, H.J. (1979) 'The conditioning model of neurosis', *Behavioural and Brain Sciences*, 2, pp. 155–99.

Eysenck, H.J. and Eysenck, S.G.B. (1975) *The Eysenck Personality Questionnaire*, Sevenoaks: Hodder & Stoughton.

Eysenck, M.W. (1979) 'Depth, elaboration and distinctiveness', in L.S. Cermak and F.I.M. Craik (eds) *Levels of Processing in Human Memory*, Hillsdale, New Jersey: Erlbaum.

Eysenck, M.W. (1986) 'Working memory', in G. Cohen, M.W. Eysenck and M.E. Le Voi *Memory: A Cognitive Approach*, Milton Keynes: Open University Press.

Eysenck, M.W. and Keane M.T. (1995) *Cognitive Psychology: A Student's Handbook* (3nd edn), Hove: Erlbaum.

Falkai, P., Bogerts, B., and Rozumek, M. (1988) 'Limbic pathology in schizophrenia', *Proceedings of the National Academy of Science, USA*, 2, pp. 560–563.

Fantz, R.L. (1961) 'The origin of form perception', *Scientific American*, 204 (5), pp. 66–72.

Fantz, R.L., Fagan, J.F. and Miranda, S.B. (1975) 'Early visual selectivity', in L.B. Cohen and R. Salapatek (eds) *Infant Perception: From Sensation to Cognition: 1*, New York: Academic Press.

Farringdon, D.P. (1990) 'Implications of criminal career research for the prevention of offending', *Journal of Adolescence*, 13, pp. 93–113.

Fawcett, A. and Nicolson, R. (1994) *Dyslexia in children*, Hemel Hempstead: Harvester Wheatsheaf.

Featherstone, M. (1991) *Consumer Culture and Postmodernism*, London: Sage.

Feldman, N.S., Klosson, E.C., Parsons, J.E., Knoles, W.S. and Ruble, D.N. (1976) 'Order of information presentation and children's moral judgements', *Child Development*, 47, pp. 556–9.

Ferguson, T. J. and Rule, B. G. (1982) 'Influences of inferential set, outcome intent and outcome severity on children's moral judgements', *Developmental Psychology* 18, pp. 843–51.

Ferguson, T.J. and Rule, B.G. (1983) 'An attributional perspective on anger and aggresion', in R. Geen and E. Donnerstein (eds) *Aggression: Theoretical and Empirical Reviews*, Vol. 1, New York: Academic Press.

Fernando, S. (1988) *Race and Culture in Psychiatry*, London: Croom Helm.

Fernando, S. (1989) *Race, Culture and Psychiatry*, London: Routledge.

Festinger, L. (1954) 'A theory of social comparison processes', *Human Relations*, 1, pp. 117–40.

Festinger, L., Schachter, S. and Back, K.W. (1950) *Social Pressures in Informal Groups*, New York: Harper.

Fiedler, F.E. (1967), *A Theory of Leadership Effectiveness*, New York: McGraw-Hill.

Fiedler, F.E. and Chemers, M.M. (1984) *Improving Leadership Effectiveness: The Leader Match Concept*, New York: Wiley.

Fiedler, K. (1996) 'Processing social information for judgements and decisions', in M. Hewstone, W. Stroebe and G.M. Stephenson (eds) *Introduction to Social Psychology* (2nd edn), Oxford: Blackwell.

Field, R.H.G. and House, R.J. (1990) 'A test of the Vroom-Yetton model using manager and subordinate reports', *Journal of Applied Psychology*, 75, pp. 362–6.

Fine, M. and Gordon, S.M. (1989) 'Feminist transformations of/despite psychology' in M. Crawford and M. Gentry (eds) *Gender and Thought: Psychological Perspectives*, New York: Springer-Verlag.

Fischer, K. (1980) 'A theory of cognitive development: the control and construction of hierarchies of skill', *Psychological Review*, 87, pp. 477–531.

Fischer, M. (1971) 'Psychosis in the offspring of schizophrenic monozygotic twins and their normal co-twins', *British Journal of Psychiatry*, 118, pp. 43–52.

Fishbein, M. and Ajzen, I. (1975) *Belief, Attitude, Intention and Behaviour: An Introduction to Theory and Research*, Reading: Addison-Wesley.

Fisher, J. and Hinde, R.A. (1949) 'The opening of milk bottles by birds', *British Birds*, 42, pp. 347–57.

Fisher, R.A. (1930) *The Genetical Theory of Natural Selection*, Clarendon Press, Oxford.

Fisher, R.A. and Yates, F. (1974) *Statistical Tables for Biological, Agricultural and Medical Research* (6th edn), Harlow: Longman Group Ltd.

Fiske, S.T. (1989) 'Interdependence and stereotyping: from the laboratory to the Supreme Court (and back)', Invited address, American Psychological Association, New Orleans.

Fiske, S.T. and Neuberg, S.L. (1990) 'A continuum model of impression formation, from category based to individuating processes: influence of information and motivation on attention and interpretation', in M.P. Zanna (ed.) *Advances in Experimental Social Psychology*, Vol. 23, New York: Academic Press.

Fiske, S.T. and Taylor, S. (1992) *Social Cognition*, Reading: Addison-Wesley.

Fitzgibbon, C.D. and Fanshawe, J.H. (1988) 'Stotting in Thompson's gazelles: an honest signal of condition', *Behavioural Ecology and Sociobiology*, 23, pp. 69–74.

Flavell, J.H. (1985) *Cognitive Development* (2nd edn), Englewood Cliffs, New Jersey: Prentice Hall.

Foa, U.G. and Foa, E.B. (1975) *Resource Theory of Social Exchange*, Morristown, USA: General Learning Press.

Fok, Y.Y. and Bellugi, U. (1986) 'The acquisition of visiospatial script', in H. Kao (ed.) *Graphonomics: Contemporary Research in Handwriting*, Amsterdam: North Holland.

Fonagy, P., Steele, H. and Steele, M. (1991) 'Maternal representations of attachment during pregnancy predict the organisation of infant–mother attachment at one year of age', *Child Development*, 62, pp. 891–905.

Ford, C. and Neale, J.M. (1985) 'Effects of a helplessness induction on judgements of control', *Journal of Personality and Social Psychology*, 49, pp. 1330–6.

Forge, K.L. and Phemister, S. (1987) 'The effect of prosocial cartoons on preschool children', *Child Study Journal*, 17, pp. 83–8.

Foster, J.J. and Parker, R. (1995) *Carrying out Investigations in Psychology: Methods and Statistics*, Leicester: BPS Books.

Fourcin, A. J. (1975) 'Speech production in the absence of speech productive ability', in N. O'Connor (ed.) *Language, Cognitive Deficits, and Retardation*, London: Butterworth.

Fowler, A. (1988) 'Determinants of rate of language growth in children with Down's syndrome', in L. Nadel (ed.) *The Psychobiology of Down's Syndrome*, Cambridge, Massachusetts: MIT Press.

Fowler, W. (1990) 'Early stimulation and the development of verbal talents', in M.J.A. Howe (ed.) *Encouraging the Development of Exceptional Abilities and Talents*, Leicester: BPS.

Fraiberg, S. (1977) *Insights From the Blind: Comparative Studies of Blind and Sighted Infants*, New York: Basic Books.

Fraiberg, S. (1979) 'Blind infants and their mothers: an examination of the sign system', in M. Bullowa (ed.) *Before Speech*, Cambridge: Cambridge University Press.

Frazier, P.A. (1990) 'Victim attributions and post-rape trauma', *Journal of Personality and Social Psychology*, 59, pp. 298–304.

Freeman, D. (1983) *Margaret Mead and Samoa: The Making and Unmaking of an Anthropological Myth*, Cambridge, Massachusetts: Harvard University Press.

Freeman, N. H. (1974) *Human Infancy: An Evolutionary Perspective*, Hillsdale, New Jersey: Erlbaum.

French, C.C. and Richards, A. (1993) 'Clock this! An everyday example of a schema-driven error in memory', *British Journal of Psychology*, 84 pp. 249–53.

French, J.R.P. and Raven, B. (1959) 'The bases of social power', in D. Cartwright (ed.) *Studies in Social Power*, Ann Arbor, Michigan: Institute for Social Research.

Freud, A. (1936) *The Ego and the Mechanisms of Defence*, London: Chatto and Windus.

Freud, S. (1915–1918) *Introductory Lectures on Psychoanalysis*, London: Hogarth Press.

Freud, S. (1924) *A General Introduction to Psychoanalysis*, New York: Washington Square Press.

Freud, S. (1931, translated by J. Strachey 1977) *Three Essays on the Theory of Sexuality*, London: Hogarth Press.

Freud, S. (1937) 'Analysis terminable and interminable', in J. Strachey (ed.) *The Complete Psychological Works of Sigmund Freud*, London: Hogarth Press.

Freud, S. (1955) *Beyond the Pleasure Principle*, in J. Strachey (ed.) *The Standard Edition of the Complete Psychological Works of Sigmund Freud*, Vol. 18, London: Hogarth Press.

Freud, S. (1955) *The Interpretation of Dreams*, New York: Basic Books.

Freud, S. (1990, original work published in 1909) 'Case study of Little Hans' in *Sigmund Freud 8, Case Histories I*, London: Penguin Books.

Freund, L.S. (1990) 'Maternal regulation of the child's problem solving behavior and its impact on children's performance', *Child Development*, 61, pp. 113–26.

Friedman, M. and Rosenman, R.H. (1974) *Type A Behavior and Your Heart*, New York: Knopf.

Friedrich-Cofer, L. and Huston, A.C. (1986) 'Television violence and aggression: the debate continues', *Psychological Bulletin*, 100, pp. 364–71.

Frisch, K. von (1967) *The Dance Language and Orientation of Bees*, Cambridge, Massachusetts: Harvard University Press.

Frith, C.D. (1992) *The Neuropsychology of Schizophrenia*, Hove: Erlbaum.

Frith, U. (1989) *Autism: Explaining the Enigma*, Oxford: Blackwell.

Fromm-Reichmann, F. (1948) 'Notes on the development of treatment of schizophrenics by psychoanalytic psychotherapy', *Psychiatry* 11, pp. 263–73.

Fryer, D. (1985) 'Stages in the psychological response to unemployment: A (dis)integrative view', *Current Psychological Research and Reviews*, Fall, pp. 257–73.

Fryer, D. (1992) 'Editorial: Introduction to Marienthal and beyond', *Journal of Occupational and Organizational Psychology*, 65, pp. 164–75.

Fulton, R. (1970) 'Death, grief and social recuperation', *Omega: Journal of Death and Dying*, 1, pp. 23–8.

Funk, J.L. (1986) 'Gender differences in the moral reasoning of conventional and postconventional adults', Unpublished doctoral dissertation, University of Texas.

Furth, H.G. (1966) *Thinking without Language: Psychological Implications of Deafness*, London: Collier-Macmillan.

Fyer, A.J., Mannuzza, S., Gallops, M.S., Martin, L.Y., Aaronson, C., Gorman, J.M., Liebowitz, M.R and Klein, D.F. (1990) 'Familial transmission of simple fears and phobias', *Archives of General Psychiatry*, 40, pp. 1061–4.

Galotti, K.M. (1989) 'Gender differences in self-reported moral reasoning: a review and new evidence', *Journal of Youth and Adolescence*, 18, pp. 475–88.

Galotti, K.M., Baron, J. and Sabini, J.P. (1986) 'Individual differences in syllogistic reasoning. Deduction rules or mental model?', *Journal of Experimental Psychology: General*, 115, pp. 16–25.

Gamson, W.B., Fireman, B. and Rytina, S. (1982) *Encounters with Unjust Authority*, Homewood, Illinois: Dorsey Press.

Garcia, J. and Koelling, R.A. (1966) 'Relation of cue to consequence in avoidance learning', *Psychonomic Science*, 4, pp. 123-4.

Gardner, B.T. and Gardner, R.A. (1969) 'Teaching sign language to a chimpanzee', *Science*, 165, pp. 664–72.

Garland, H.A., Hardy, A. and Stephenson, L. (1975) 'Information search as affected by attribution type and response category', *Personality and Social Psychology Bulletin*, 1, pp. 612–15.

Garrett, A. (1995) 'Mid-life crisis for the TV ad', *The Observer*, 17 September 1995.

Garrett, M.F. (1988) 'Processes in language production', in F.J. Newmayer (ed.) *Linguistics: The Cambridge Survey*, Vol. 3: *Language: Psychological and Biological Aspects*, Cambridge: Cambridge University Press.

Garrett, T. (1994) 'Epidemiology in the USA', in D. Jehu (ed.) *Patients as Victims*, Chichester: Wiley.

Garrett, T. and Davis, J. (1994) 'Epidemiology in the UK', in D. Jehu (ed.) *Patients as Victims*, Chichester. Wiley.

Gavey, N. (1992) 'Technologies and effects of heterosexual coercion', *Feminism and Psychology*, 2(3), pp. 325–51, reprinted in S. Wilkinson and C. Kitzinger (eds) (1994) *Heterosexuality*, London: Sage.

Geen, R.G. (1968) 'Effects of frustration, attack and prior training in aggressiveness upon aggressive behaviour', *Journal of Personality and Social Psychology*, 9, pp. 316–21.

Geen, R.G. (1978) 'Some effects of observing violence upon the behaviour of the observer', in B.A. Maher (ed.) *Progress in Experimental Personality Research*, Vol. 8, New York: Academic Press.

Geiselman, R.E., Fisher, R.P., MacKinnon, D.P. and Holland, H.L. (1985) 'Eye-witness memory enhancement in police interview: cognitive retrieval mnemonics versus hypnosis', *Journal of Applied Psychology*, 70, pp. 401–12.

Gelfand, D.M. and Hartmann, P. (1980) 'The development of prosocial behaviour and moral judgement', in R.I. Ault (ed.) *Developmental Perspectives*, Santa Monica, California: Goodyear.

Gerbner, G., Gross, L., Morgan, M. and Signorielli, N. (1980) 'The "mainstreaming" of America', Violence Profile No. 11, *Journal of Communication*, 30, pp. 10–29.

Gergen, K.J., Morse, S.J. and Gergen, M.M. (1980) 'Behavior exchange in cross-cultural perspective', in H.C. Triandis and R.W. Brislin (eds) *Handbook of Cross-cultural Psychology: Social Psychology*, Boston, Massachusetts: Allyn & Bacon.

Ghiselli, E.E. (1966) *The Validity of Occupational Aptitude Tests*, New York: Wiley.

Gibson, E. (1969) *Principles of Perceptual Learning and Development*, New York: Appleton-Century-Crofts.

Gibson, E.J. and Walk, P.D. (1960) 'The visual cliff', *Scientific American*, 202, pp. 64–71.

Gibson, H.B. (1982) 'The use of hypnosis in police investigations', *Bulletin of the British Psychological Society*, 35, pp. 138–42.

Gibson, J.J. (1966) *The Senses Considered as Perceptual Systems*, Boston: Houghton Mifflin.

Gilberg, C. (1990) 'The neurobiology of infant autism', *Journal of Child Psychology and Psychiatry*, 29, pp. 257–66.

Gill, F.B. and Wolf, L.L. (1975) 'Economics of feeding territoriality in the golden-winged sunbird', *Ecology*, 56, pp. 333–45.

Gilligan, C. (1982) *In a Different Voice: Psychological Theory and Women's Development*, Cambridge, Massachusetts: Harvard University Press.

Gladue, B.A. (1991) 'Aggressive behavioural characteristics, hormones and sexual orientation in men and women', *Aggressive Behaviour*, 17, pp. 313–26.

Glenberg, A., Smith, S.M. and Green, C. (1977) 'Type I rehearsal: maintenance and more', *Journal of Verbal Learning and Verbal Behaviour*, 16, pp. 339–52.

Godden, D. and Baddeley, A. (1975) 'Context-dependent memory in two natural environments: on land and under water', *British Journal of Psychology*, 66, pp. 325–31.

Goffman E. (1968) *Stigma: Notes on the Management of Spoiled Identity*, Harmondsworth: Penguin.

Goldman-Eisler, F. (1968) *Psycholinguistics: Experiments in Spontaneous Speech*, London: Academic Press.

Goldstein, M.J. (1988) 'The family and psychotherapy', *Annual Review of Psychiatry*, 39, pp. 283–99.

Goodall, J. (1990) *Through a Window*, Harmondsworth: Penguin.

Goodey, B. (1971) *City Scene: An Exploration into the Image of Central Birmingham as Seen by Area Residents*, Research Memorandum No. 10, Birmingham: Centre for Urban and Regional Studies.

Gottesman, I.I. and Shields, J. (1982) *Schizophrenia: The Epigenetic Puzzle*, Cambridge: Cambridge University Press

Gould, J.L. (1986) 'The locale maps of honey bees: do insects have cognitive maps?', *Science*, 232, pp. 860–3.

Gould, J.L. (1992) 'Honey bee cognition', in C.R. Gallistel (ed) *Animal Cognition*, Cambridge, Massachusetts: MIT Press.

Gould, J.L. and Gould, C.G. (1989) *Sexual Selection*, New York: Scientific American Library.

Gould, R.L. (1978) *Transformations: Growth and Change in Adult Life*, New York: Simon & Schuster.

Gould, R.L. (1980) 'Transformation tasks in adulthood', in *The Course of Life*, Vol. 3, *Adulthood and Aging Processes*, Bethesda, Maryland: National Institute of Mental Health.

Gould, S.J. (1981) *The Mismeasure of Man*, New York: Norton.

Gould, S.J. (1989) *Wonderful Life: the Burgess Shale and the Nature of History*, Harmondsworth: Penguin.

Gould, S.J. (1994) 'The evolution of life on earth', *Scientific American*, 271, pp. 63–9.

Gould, S.J. and Lewontin, R.C. (1979) 'The spandrels of San Marco and the Panglossian paradigm: a critique of the adaptationist program', *Proceedings of the Royal Society of London*, Series B, 205, pp. 581–98.

Gouldner, A.W. (1960) 'The notion of reciprocity: a preliminary statement', *American Sociological Review*, 25, pp. 161–78.

Gove, W.R. and Howell, P. (1974) 'Individual resources and mental hospitalization: a comparison and evaluation of the societal reaction and psychiatric perspectives', *American Sociological Review*, 39, pp. 86–100.

Grafen, A. (1982) 'How not to measure inclusive fitness', *Nature*, 298, pp. 425–6.

Grafen, A. (1990) 'Do animals really recognize kin?', *Animal Behaviour*, 2, pp. 42–54.

Grant, L. and Evans, A. (1994) *Principles of Behaviour Analysis*, New York: HarperCollins.

Grant, P. (1994) 'Psychotherapy and Race', in Clarkson, P. and Pokorny, M. (eds) *The Handbook of Psychotherapy*, London: Routledge.

Gray, J.A. (1989) 'The ethics and politics of animal experimentation', in H.Beloff and A.M. Colman (eds) *Psychological Survey No. 6*, Leicester: British Psychological Society.

Gray, J.A. and Wedderburn, A.A.I. (1960) 'Grouping strategies with simultaneous stimuli', *Quarterly Journal of Experimental Psychology*, 12, pp. 180–4.

Green, S. (1994) *Principles of Biopsychology*, Hove: Erlbaum.

Greenberg, J. and Baron, R.A. (1995) *Behaviour in Organisations*, London: Prentice Hall.

Greene, J. (1986) *Language Understanding: A Cognitive Approach*, Milton Keynes: Open University Press.

Greeno, J.G. (1974) 'Hobbits and Orcs: acquisition of a sequential concept', *Cognitive Psychology*, 6, pp. 270–93.

Gregg, V.H. and Wagstaff, G.F. (1990) 'Hypnosis', in M.W. Eysenck (ed.) *The Blackwell Dictionary of Cognitive Psychology*, Oxford: Blackwell.

Gregor, A.J. and McPherson, D. (1965) 'A study of susceptibility to geometric illusions among cultural outgroups of Australian aborigines', *Psychologica Africana*, 11, pp. 1–13.

Gregory, R.L. (1972) *Eye and Brain* (2nd edn), London: Wiedenfield and Nicholson.

Gregory, R.L. (1973) 'The confounded eye', in R. L. Gregory and E.H. Gombrich (eds) *Illusions in Nature and Art*, London: Duckworth.

Gregory, R.L. and Wallace, J. (1963) *Recovery from Early Blindness*, Cambridge: Heffer.

Gregory, S. (1995) 'Psychology and deafness', in D. Bancroft and R. Carr (eds) *Influencing Children's Development*, Oxford: Blackwell Publishers.

Gregory, S. and Barlow, S. (1989) 'Interaction between deaf babies and hearing mothers', in B. Woll (ed.) *Language Development and Sign Language*, Monograph 1, International Sign Linguistics Association, University of Bristol.

Griffin, D.R. (1984) *Animal Thinking*, Cambridge, Massachusetts: Harvard University Press.

Griffin, D.R. (1991) *Animal Minds*, Chicago: Chicago University Press.

Grisso, T. and Applebaum, P.S. 'Mentally ill and non-mentally ill patients' abilities to understand informed consent disclosures for medication: Preliminary data', Law and Human Behaviour, cited in G.C. Davison and J.M. Neale (1994) *Abnormal Psychology* (6th edn), New York: Wiley.

Gross, R.D. (1992) *Psychology: The Science of Mind and Behaviour* (2nd edn), London: Hodder & Stoughton.

Gross, R.D. (1995) *Themes, Issues and Debates in Psychology*, London: Hodder & Stoughton.

Grossman, K., Grossman, K. E., Spangler, G., Suess, G. and Unzer, L. (1985) 'Maternal sensitivity and newborn's orientation responses', in Bretherton, I. and E. Waters (eds) *Growing Points in Attachment Theory and Research*, Monographs of the Society for Research in Child Development, 50, Serial No. 209, pp. 3–35.

Gualtieri, C. (1991) *Neuropsychiatry and Behavioural Pharmacology*, New York: Springer-Verlag.

Guilford, J.P. (1967) *The Nature of Human Intelligence*, New York: McGraw-Hill.

Gunter, B. and McAleer, J.L. (1990) *Children and Television: The One-eyed Monster?*, London: Routledge.

Gustafson, R. (1992) 'The relationship between perceived parents' child-rearing practices, own later rationality, and own later depression', *Journal of Rational-Emotive and Cognitive Behaviour Therapy*, 10(4), pp. 253–8.

Guzman, A. (1969) 'Decomposition of a visual scene into three-dimensional bodies', in A. Grasseli (ed.) *Automatic Interpretation and Classification of Images*, London: Academic Press.Haaga, D.A. and Davison, G.C. (1989) 'Outcome studies of rational–emotive therapy', in M.E. Bernard and R.D. DiGiuseppe (eds) *Inside Rational–Emotive Therapy*, San Diego, California: Academic Press.

Haaga, D.A. and Davison, G.C. (1993) 'An appraisal of rational–emotive therapy', *Journal of Consulting and Clinical Psychology*, 61(2), pp. 215–20.

Haier, R.J., Siegel, B.V., MacLachlan, A. and Soderling, E. (1992) 'Regional glucose metabolic changes after learning a complex visuospatial/motor task: a positron emission tomography study', *Brain Research*, 570, pp. 134–43.

Haig, D. (1993) *Quarterly Review of Biology*, 68, pp. 495–532.

Halgin, R.P. and Whitbourne, S.K. (1993) *Abnormal Psychology* (International edition), Orlando, Florida: Harcourt Brace Jovanovich, Inc.

Halliday, T. (1980) *Sexual Strategy*, Oxford: Oxford University Press.

Halpern, D. (1995) *More than Bricks and Mortar? Mental Health and the Planned Environment*, London: Taylor and Francis.

Hamer, D. (1995) in S. Connor 'The gay gene is back on the scene', *The Independent*, 1 November, 1995.

Hamer, D., Hu, S. and Magnuson, V.L. (1993) 'A linkage between DNA markers on the X chromosome and male sexual orientation', *Science*, 261, pp. 321–7.

Hamilton, D.L. (1981) 'Illusory correlation and stereotyping', in D.L. Hamilton (ed.) *Cognitive Processes in Stereotyping and Intergroup Behaviour*, Hillsdale, New Jersey: Erlbaum.

Hamilton, S., Rothbart, M. and Dawes, R.M. (1986) 'Sex bias, diagnosis, and DSM-III', *Sex Roles*, 15, pp. 269–74.

Hamilton, W.D. (1963) 'The evolution of altruistic behaviour', *The American Naturalist*, 97, pp. 354–6.

Hamilton, W.D. (1964) 'The genetic evolution of social behaviour I and II', *Journal of Theoretical Biology*, 7, pp. 1–52.

Hamilton, W.D. and Zuk, M. (1982) 'Hereditable true fitness and bright birds: a role for parasites?', *Science*, 218, pp. 384–7.

Harding, S. (1985) 'Values and the nature of psychological well-being', in M. Abrams, D. Gerard and N. Timms (eds) *Values and Social Change in Britain*, Basingstoke: Macmillan.

Hare-Mustin, R.T. and Maracek, J. (1988) 'The meaning of difference: gender theory, post-modernism and psychology', *American Psychologist*, 43, pp. 455–64.

Harley, T.A. (1995) *The Psychology of Language: From Data to Theory*, Hove: Erlbaum (UK), Taylor & Francis.

Harlow, H.F. (1950) 'Learning and satiation of response in intrinsically motivated complex puzzle performance by monkeys', *Journal of Comparative and Physiological Psychology*, 43, pp. 289–94.

Harlow, H.F. (1962) 'Heterosexual affectional system in monkeys', *American Psychologist*, 17, pp. 1–9.

Harlow, H.F. and Harlow, M.K. (1962) 'Social deprivation in monkeys', *Scientific American*, 207 (5), p. 136.

Harlow, H.F. and Harlow, M.K. (1966) 'Learning to love', *American Psychologist*, 54, pp. 244–72.

Harlow, H.F. and Zimmerman, R. R. (1959) 'Affectional responses in the infant monkey', *Science*, 130, pp. 421–32.

Harris, M. (1991) 'From gesture to language in hearing and deaf children', *First Language*, 11, pp. 181–7.

Harter, S. (1983) 'Developmental perspectives on the self-system', in P. H. Mussen (ed.) *Handbook of Child Psychology*, Vol. 4, New York: Wiley.

Harter, S. (1986) 'Processes underlying the construction, maintenance and enhancement of the self-concept in children', in J. Suls and A.G. Greenwald (eds) *Psychological Perspectives on the Self*, Vol. 3, Hillsdale, New Jersey: Erlbaum.

Harter, S. and Zigler, E. (1974) 'The assessment of effectance motivation in normal and retarded children', *Developmental Psychology*, 10, pp. 169–80.

Hartshorne, H. and May, M.S. (1928–1930) *Moral Studies in the Nature of Character: Studies in the Nature of Character*, New York: Macmillan.

Harvey, I.F. (1994) 'Strategies of behaviour', in P.J.B. Slater and T.R. Halliday (eds) *Behaviour and Evolution*, Cambridge: Cambridge University Press.

Haskins, R. (1989) 'Beyond metaphor: The efficacy of early childhood education', *American Psychologist*, 44, pp. 274–82.

Hatfield, E., Utne, M.K. and Traupmann, J. (1979) 'Equity theory and intimate relationships', in R.L. Burgess and T.L. Huston (eds) *Exchange Theory in Developing Relationships*, New York: Academic Press.

Hauser, M.D. (1988) 'How infant vervet monkeys learn to recognise starling alarm calls: the role of experience', *Behaviour*, 105, pp. 187–201.

Havighurst, R.J., Neugarten, B.L. and Tobin, S.S. (1968) 'Disengagement and patterns of aging', in B.L. Neugarten (ed.) *Middle Age and Aging*, Chicago: University of Chicago Press.

Hayes, J.R. (1989) 'Writing research: the analysis of a very complex task', in D. Klahr and K. Kotovsky (eds) *Complex Information Processing: The Impact of Herbert A. Simon*, Hillsdale, New Jersey: Erlbaum.

Hayes, J.R., Flower, L.S., Schriver, K.A., Stratman, J. and Carey, L. (1987) 'Cognitive processes in revision', in S. Rosenberg (ed.) *Advances in Psycholinguistics*, Vol. 2, *Reading, writing and language processing*, Cambridge: Cambridge University Press.

Hayes, L.A. and Watson, J.S. (1981) 'Neonatal imitation: fact or artifacts?', *Developmental Psychology*, 17, pp. 655–60.

Hayes, N. (1993) *Principles of Social Psychology*, Hove: Erlbaum.

Hayes, N. (1994) *Foundations of Psychology*, London: Routledge.

Hayes, P., Conway, M.A. and Morris, P.E. (1992) 'Evaluating the "cognitive structure of emotions" using autobiographical memories of emotional events', in M.A. Conway, D.C. Rubin, H. Spinnler and W.A. Wagenaar *Theoretical Perspectives on Autobiographical Memory*, Dordrecht, Netherlands: Kluwer Academic Publishers.

Hays, R.B. (1985) 'A longitudinal study of friendship development', *Journal of Personality and Social Psychology*, 48, pp. 909–24.

Heath, S.B. (1989) 'Oral and literate traditions among black Americans living in poverty', *American Psychologist*, 44, pp. 367–73.

Heather, N. (1976), *Radical Perspectives in Psychology*, London: Methuen.

Hedges, A. (1982) *Testing to Destruction*, IPA.

Heider, F. (1958) *The Psychology of Interpersonal Relations*, New York: Wiley.

Heim, A.W., Watts, K.P. and Simmonds S.V. (1970) *AH4, AH5 and AH6 Tests*, Windsor: NFER.

Hendry, L.B. (1989) 'The influence of adults and peers on adolescents' lifestyles and leisure styles', in K. Hurrelmann and U. Engel (eds) *The Social World of Adolescents: International Perspectives*, Berlin and New York: de Gruyter.

Hennigan, K.M., Heath, L., Wharton, J.D., Del Rosario, M.L., Cook, T.D. and Calder, B.J. (1982) 'Impact of the introduction of television on crime in the United States: empirical findings and theoretical implications', *Journal of Personality and Social Psychology*, 42, pp. 461–77.

Hepper, P.G. (1991) 'An examination of fetal learning before and after birth', *Irish Journal of Psychology*, 12, pp. 95–107.

Herman, L.M. (1986) 'Cognition and language competences of bottlenose dolphins', in A. Schusterman, A.J. Thomas and F.G. Wood (eds) *Dolphin Cognition and Behaviour. A Comparative Approach*, Hillsdale New Jersey: Lawrence Erlbaum.

Herriot, P. (ed.) (1989) *Assessment and Selection in Organisation*, Chichester: Wiley.

Hetherington, A.W. and Ranson, S.W. (1942) 'The relation of various hypothalamic lesions to adiposity in the rat', *Journal of Comparative Neurology*, 76, pp. 475–99.

Hetherington, E.M. and Parke, R.D. (1993) *Child Psychology: A Contemporary Viewpoint* (4th edn), New York: McGraw-Hill.

Hetherington, E.M., Stanley-Hagan, M. and Anderson, E.R. (1989) 'Marital transitions: A child's perspective', *American Psychologist*, 44, pp. 303–12.

Hewison, T. and Tizard, J. (1980) 'Parental involvement in reading attainment', *British Journal of Educational Psychology*, 50, pp. 209–15.

Hewstone, M. (1988) *Introduction to Social Psychology*, Oxford: Blackwell.

Hewstone, M., Jaspars, J. and Lalljee, M. (1982) 'Social representations, social attribution and social identity: the intergroup images of "public" and "comprehensive" schoolboys', *European Journal of Social Psychology*, 12(3), pp. 241–69.

Hewstone, M., Wolfgang, S. and Stephenson, G.M. (1996) *Introduction to Social Psychology*, Oxford: Blackwell.

Hilgard, R.E. (1973) 'A neo-dissociation interpretation of pain reduction in hypnosis', *Psychological Review*, 80, pp. 396–411.

Hilgard, R.E. (1977) *Divided Consciousness: Multiple Controls in Human Thought and Action*, New York: Wiley.

Hill, R. (1970) *Family Development in Three Generations*, Cambridge, Massachusetts: Schenkman.

Hinde, R.A. (1977) 'Mother–infant separation and the nature of inter-individual relationships: experiments with rhesus monkeys', *Proceedings of the Royal Society of London* (B), 196, pp. 29–50.

Hinde, R.A. (1979) *Towards Understanding Relationships*, New York: Academic Press.

Hinde, R.A. and Fisher, J. (1951) 'Further observations on the opening of milk bottles by birds', *British Birds* 46, 393–6.

Hiroto, D.S. and Seligman, M.E.P. (1975) 'Generality of learnt helplessness in man', *Journal of Personality and Social Psychology*, 31, pp. 311–27.

Hobson, J.A. (1988) *The Dreaming Brain*, New York: Basic Books.

Hobson, R.P. (1993) 'Perceiving attitudes, conceiving minds', in C. Lewis and P. Mitchell (eds) *Origins of an Understanding of Mind*, Hillsdale, New Jersey: Erlbaum.

Hockett, C.F. (1959) 'Animal "languages" and human language', *Human Biology*, 31, pp. 32–9.

Hodkinson, S. (1987) 'Molecular genetic evidence for heterogeneity in manic depression', *Nature*, 325, pp. 805–6.

Hoffman, M. (1979) 'Development of moral thought, feeling and behaviour', *American Psychologist*, 34, pp. 958–66.

Hofling, C.K., Brotzman, E., Dalrymple, S., Graves, N. and Pierce, C.M. (1966) 'An experimental study in the nurse–physician relationship', *Journal of Nervous and Mental Disorders*, 143, pp. 171–80.

Hofstede, G. (1980) *Culture's Consequences: International Differences in Work-related Values*, Beverley Hills, California: Sage.

Hogen, R.A. and Kirchner, J.H. (1967) 'A preliminary report of the extinction of learned fears via a short term implosive therapy', *Journal of Abnormal Psychology*, 72, pp. 106–11.

Hohmann, G.W. (1966) 'Some effects of spinal cord lesions on experimental emotional feelings', *Psychophysiology*, 3, pp. 143–56.

Hole, R.W., Rush, A.J. and Beck, A.T. (1979) 'A cognitive investigation of schizophrenic delusions', *Psychiatry*, 42, pp. 312–19.

Holland, A.J., Hall, D.J., Murrey, R., Russell, G.F.M. and Crisp, A.H. (1984) 'Anorexia Nervosa: A study of 34 twin pairs and one set of triplets', *British Journal of Psychiatry*, 145, pp. 414–18.

Hollander, E.P. (1985) 'Leadership and Power', in G. Lindsay and E. Aronson (eds), *The Handbook of Social Psychology* (3rd edn), New York: Random House.

Hölldobler, B. (1971) 'Communication between ants and their guests', *Scientific American*, 224, pp. 86–93.

Hollon, S.D., DeRubeis, R.J., Evans, M.D. and Associates (1992) 'Cognitive therapy and pharmacotherapy for depression: singly and in combination', *Archives of General Psychiatry*, 49, pp. 774–81.

Hollos, M. (1975) 'Logical operations and role-taking abilities in two cultures: Norway and Hungary', *Child Development*, 46, pp. 638–41.

Holmes, D.S. (1994) *Abnormal Psychology* (2nd edn), New York: HarperCollins.

Holmes, T.H. and Rahe, R.H. (1967) 'The social readjustment rating scale', *Journal of Psychosomatic Research*, 11, pp. 213–18.

Homans, G.C. (1961, 1974 revised edition) *Social Behaviour: Its Elementary Forms*, New York: Harcourt Brace Jovanovich.

Hopkins, C.D. (1977) 'Electrical communication', in T.A. Sebeok (ed.) *How Animals Communicate*, pp. 263–89, Bloomington: Indiana University Press.

Horne, J. (1988) *Why We Sleep*, Oxford: Oxford University Press.

Horne, J.M. (1983) 'The Texas Adoption Project: adopted children and their intellectual resemblance to biological and adoptive parents', *Child Development*, 54, pp. 266–75.

Horowitz, M.J. (1975) 'Intrusive and repetitive thoughts after experimental stress', *Archives of General Psychiatry*, 32, pp. 223–8.

House, R.J. (1971) 'A path-goal theory of leadership', *Administrative Science Quarterly*, 1, pp. 321–38.

Hovland, C. and Sears, R. (1940) 'Minor studies in aggression: VI: correlation of lynchings with economic indices', *Journal of Personality*, 9, pp. 301–10.

Howe, C., Tolmie, A. and Anderson, A. (1991) 'Information technology and group work in physics', *Journal of Computer Assisted Learning*, 7, pp. 133–43.

Howell, E. (1981) 'The influence of gender on diagnosis and psychopathology', in E. Howell and M. Bayes (eds) *Women and Mental Health*, New York: Basic Books.

Howitt, D. and Owusu-Bempah, J. (1994) *The Racism of Psychology: Time for Change*, New York: Harvester Wheatsheaf.

Hubel, D.H. and Wiesel, T.N. (1962) 'Receptive fields, binocular interaction and functional architecture in the cat's visual cortex', *Journal of Physiology*, 160, pp. 106–54.

Hubel, D.H. and Wiesel, T.N. (1979) 'Brain mechanisms of vision', *Scientific American*, 241, pp. 130–44.

Huffman, D.A. (1971) 'Impossible objects and nonsense sentences', in B. Meltzer and D. Michie (eds) *Machine Intelligence 6*, Edinburgh: Edinburgh University Press.

Hull, C.L. (1943) *Principles of Behavior*, New York: Appleton-Century-Crofts.

Hull, J.G. and Bond, C.F. (1986) 'Social and behavioural consequences of alcohol consumption and expectancy: a meta-analysis', *Psychological Bulletin*, 99, pp. 347–60.

Hultsch, D.F. and Deutsch, F. (1981) *Adult Development and Aging: A Lifespan Perspective*, New York: McGraw Hill.

Hultsch, D.F. and Plemons, J.K. (1979) 'Life events and life span development', in P.B. Baltes and O.G. Brim, Jr (eds) *Life-span Development and Behaviour*, Vol. 2, New York: Academic Press.

Hume, D. (1951) cited in L.A. Selby-Bigge (ed.) *Inquiries concerning the Human Understanding and concerning the Principles of Morals*, London: Oxford University Press.

Hunt, E. (1980) 'Intelligence of an information-processing concept', *British Journal of Psychology*, 71, pp. 449–77.

Huston, T.L., Ruggiero, M., Conner, R. and Geis, G. (1981) 'Bystander intervention into crime: a study based on naturally-occurring episodes', *Social Psychology Quarterly*, 44(1), pp. 14–23.

Hyde, T.S. and Jenkins, J.J. (1973) 'Recall for words as a function of semantic, graphic and syntactic orienting tasks', *Journal of Verbal Learning and Verbal Behaviour*, 12, pp. 471–80.

Iacono, W.G., Bassett., A.S. and Jones, B.D. (1988) 'Eye tracking dysfunction is associated with partial trisomy of chromosome 5 and schizophrenia', *Archives of General Psychiatry*, 45, pp. 1140–1.

Ineichen, B., Harrison, G. and Morgan, H.G. (1984) 'Psychiatric hospital admissions in Bristol: 1. Geographical and ethnic factors', *British Journal of Psychiatry*, 145, pp. 600–4.

Ingram, J. (1996) *The Independent*, 30 April 1996.

Insko, C.A., Smith, R.H., Alicke, M.D., Wade, J. and Taylor, S. (1985) 'Conformity and group size: the concern with being right and the concern with being liked', *Personality and Social Psychology Bulletin*, 11(1), pp. 41–50.

Irwin, M., Lovitz, A., Marder, S.R., Mintz, J., Winslade, W.J., Van Putten, T. and Mills, M.J. (1985) 'Psychotic patients' understanding of informed consent', *American Journal of Psychiatry*, 142, pp. 1351–4.

Isabella, R.A., Belsky, J. and Von Eye, A. (1989) 'Origins of infant–mother attachment: an examination of interactional synchrony during the infant's first year', *Developmental Psychology*, 25, pp. 12–21.

Isen, A.M. (1984) 'Toward understanding the role of affect in cognition', in R.S. Wyer and T.K. Krull (eds) *Handbook of Social Cognition*, Hillsdale, New Jersey: Erlbaum.

Izard, C.E. and Malatesta, C.Z. (1987) 'Perspectives on emotional development 1: Differential emotions theory of early emotional development', in J. Osofsy (ed.) *Handbook of Infant Development*, pp. 494–554, New York: Wiley.

Jackson, S.L. and Griggs, R.A. (1990) 'The elusive pragmatic reasoning schemas effect', *The Quarterly Journal of Experimental Psychology*, 42A, pp. 353–73.

Jacoby, L.L. and Craik, F.I.M. (1979) 'Effects of elaboration of processing at encoding and retrieval: trace distinctiveness and recovery of initial context', in L.S. Cermak and F.I.M. Craik (eds) *Levels of Processing in Human Memory*, Hillsdale, New Jersey: Erlbaum.

Jahoda, G. (1966) 'Geometric illusions and environment: a study in Ghana', *British Journal of Psychology*, 57, pp. 193–9.

James, W. (1884) 'What is an emotion?', *Mind*, 19, pp. 188–205.

James, W. (1890) *The Principles of Psychology: Vol. 1*, New York: Henry Holt.

James, W. (1892/1961) *Psychology: The Briefer Course*, New York: Harper Torch Books.

Janis, I.L., Kaye, D. and Kirschner, P. (1965) 'Facilitating effects of "eating-while-reading" on responsiveness to persuasive communications', *Journal of Personality and Social Psychology*, 1(2), pp. 181–6.

Jensen, A.R. (1969) 'How much can we boost IQ and scholastic achievement?', *Harvard Educational Review*, 39, pp. 1–123.

Jensen, A.R. (1980) *Bias in Mental Testing*, New York: Macmillan.

Jobanputra, S. (1995) 'Psychology and racism: views from the inside', in *Psychology Teaching*, No. 4, Association of Teachers of Psychology, Leicester: BPS.

Johansson, G. (1975) 'Visual motion perception', *Scientific American*, 14, pp. 76–89.

Johnson, H., Olafsson, K., Anderson, J. and Pledge, P. (1989) 'Lithium every second day', *American Journal of Psychiatry*, 146, p. 557.

Johnson, M.K. (1985) 'The origins of memories', in P.C. Kendall (ed.) *Advances in Cognitive Behavioural Research and Therapy*, London: Academic Press.

Johnson, M.K. and Raye, C. L (1981) 'Reality monitoring', *Psychological Review*, 88, pp. 67–85.

Johnson, M.K., Raye, C.L., Wang, A. and Taylor, T. (1979) 'Fact and fantasy: the role of accuracy and variability in confusing imaginations with perceptual experiences', *Journal of Experimental Psychology: Human Learning and Memory*, 5, pp. 229–40.

Johnson, T.J., Feigenbaum, R. and Weiby, C.R. (1964) 'Some determinants and consequences of the teacher's perception of causality', *Journal of Educational Psychology*, 55, pp. 237–46.

Johnson-Laird, P.N. and Byrne, R.M.J. (1991) *Deduction*, Hove: Erlbaum.

Johnston, W.A. and Dark, V.J. (1986) 'Selective attention', *Annual Review of Psychology*, 37, pp. 43–75.

Johnston, W.A. and Heinz, S.P. (1978) 'Flexibility and capacity demands of attention', *Journal of Experimental Psychology: General*, 107, pp. 420–35.

Johnstone, L. (1989) *Users and Abusers of Psychiatry: A Critical Look at Traditional Psychiatric Practice*, London: Routledge.

Jones, A. (1985) 'Psychological functioning in black Americans: a conceptual guide for use in psychotherapy', *Psychotherapy*, 22(3), pp. 363–9.

Jones, E.E. (1977) 'How do people perceive the causes of behaviour?', in I. Janis *Current Trends in Psychology*, Readings from *American Scientist*.

Jones, E.E. and Davis, K.E. (1965) 'From acts to dispositions: the attribution process in person perception', in I. Berkowitz (ed.) *Advances in Experimental Social Psychology 2*, New York: Academic Press.

Jones, E.E. and Nisbett, R.E. (1971) *The Actor and the Observer: Divergent Perceptions of the Causes of Behaviour*, Morristown, New Jersey: General Learning Press.

Jones, G.V. (1978) 'Recognition failure and dual mechanisms in recall', *Psychological Review*, 85, pp. 464–9.

Jones, M. (1953) *The Therapeutic Community*, New York: Basic Books.

Jordan, R. (1993) 'The nature of the linguistic and communicative difficulties of children with autism', in

D. Messer and G. Turner (eds) *Critical Influences on Child Language Acquisition and Development*, London: Macmillan.

Jouvet, M. (1969) 'Biogenic amines and the states of sleep', *Science*, 163, pp. 32–40.

Jusczyk, P.W. (1986) Speech perception', in K.R. Boff, L. Kaufman, and J. P. Thomas (eds) *Handbook of Perception and Human Performance*, Hillsdale, New Jersey: Erlbaum.

Just, M.A. and Carpenter, P.A. (1992) 'A capacity theory of comprehension. Individual differences in working memory', *Psychological Review*, 99, pp. 122–49.

Kacelnik, A. (1984) cited in J.R. Krebs and N.B. Davies (1987) *An Introduction to Behavioural Ecology*, Oxford: Blackwell.

Kagan, J. (1982) *Psychology Research on the Human Infant: An Evaluative Summary*, New York: W.T. Grant Foundation.

Kagan, J. and Klein, R.E. (1973) 'Cross-cultural perspectives on early development', *American Psychologist*, 28, p. 947–61.

Kahn, R.L. and Antonucci T.C. (1980) 'Convoys over the life course: attachments, roles and social support', in P.B. Baltes and O.G. Brim, Jr (eds), *Life-span Development and Behaviour*, Vol. 2, New York: Academic Press.

Kahneman, D. (1973) *Attention and Effort*, Englewood Cliffs, New Jersey: Prentice-Hall.

Kahneman, D. and Henik, A. (1979) 'Perceptual organization and attention', in M. Kubovy and J.R. Pomerantz (eds) *Perceptual Organization*, Hillsdale, New Jersey: Erlbaum.

Kahneman, D. and Treisman, A. (1984) 'Changing views of attention and automaticity', in R. Parasurama, and D.R. Davies (eds) *Varieties of Attention*, London: Academic Press.

Kanner, A.D., Coyne, J.C., Schaefer, C. and Lazarus, R.S. (1981) 'Comparison of two modes of stress measurement: daily hassles and uplifts versus major life events', *Journal of Behavioural Measurement*, 4, pp. 1–39.

Kanner, L. (1943) 'Autistic disturbances of affective contact', *Nervous Child*, 2, pp. 217–50.

Karlins, M., Coffman, T.L. and Walters, G. (1969) 'On the fading of social stereotypes: studies in three generations of college students', *Journal of Personality and Social Psychology*, 13, pp. 1–16.

Katz, D. and Braly, K.W. (1933) 'Racial stereotypes of 100 college students', *Journal of Abnormal and Social Psychology*, 28, pp. 280–90.

Kaufer, D., Hayes, J.R. and Flower, L.S. (1986) 'Composing written sentences', *Research in the Teaching of English*, 20, pp. 121–40.

Kaufman, K., Gregory, W.L. and Stephan, W.G. (1990) 'Maladjustment in statistical minorities within ethnically unbalanced classrooms', *American Journal of Community Psychology*, 18, pp. 757–65.

Kavanagh, D.J. (1992) *Schizophrenia: An Overview and Practical Handbook*, London: Chapman & Hall.

Kawamura, S. (1963) 'The process of sub-culture propagation among Japanese macaques', in C.H. Southwick (ed.) *Primate Social Behaviour*, New York: Van Nostrand, pp. 82-90.

Keesey, R.E. and Corbett, S.W. (1983) 'Metabolic defence of the body weight set-point', in A.J. Stunkard and E. Stellar (eds) *Eating and Its Disorders*, New York: Raven Press.

Kelley, H.H. (1972) 'Causal schemata and the attribution process', in E.E. Jones (ed.) *Attribution: Perceiving the Causes of Behaviour*, Morristown: General Learning Press.

Kelley, H.H. (1973) 'The processes of causal attribution', *American Psychologist*, 28, pp. 107–28.

Kelley, H.H., Berscheid, E., Christensen, A., Harvey, J.H., Huston, T.L., Levinger, G., McClintock, E., Pellau, L.A. and Peterson, D.R. (1983) *Close Relationships*, New York: W.H. Freeman.

Kelly, G.A. (1955) *The Psychology of Personal Constructs*, New York: Norton.

Kelman, H.C. (1958) 'Compliance, identification and internalisation: three processes of attitude change', *Journal of Conflict Resolution*, 2, pp. 51–60.

Kelman, H.C. (1965) 'Manipulation of human behaviour: an ethical dilemma for the social scientist', *Journal of Social Issues*, 21, pp. 31–46.

Kendler, K.S. Masterson, C.C. and Davis, K.L. (1985) 'Psychiatric illness in first degree relatives of patients with paranoid psychosis, schizophrenia and medical controls', *British Journal of Psychiatry*, 147, pp. 524–31.

Kendler, K.S., McLean, C., Neale, M., Kessler, R., Heath, A. and Eaves, L. (1991) 'The genetic epidemiology of bulimia nervosa', *American Journal of Psychiatry*, 148, pp. 1627–37.

Kenward, R.E. (1978) 'Hawks and doves: factors affecting success and selection in goshawk attacks on wood pigeons', *Journal of Animal Ecology*, 47, pp. 449–60.

Kerckhoff, A.C. and Davis, K.E. (1962) 'Value consensus and need complementarity in mate selection', *American Sociological Review*, 27, pp. 250–95.

Kihlstrom, J.F. (1985) 'Hypnosis', *Annual Review of Psychology*, 36, pp. 385–418.

Kilham, W. and Mann, L. (1974) 'Level of destructive obedience as a function of transmitter and executant roles in the Milgram obedience paradigm', *Journal of Personality and Social Psychology*, 29, pp. 696–702.

Kiloh, L.G., Gye, R.S., Rushworth, R.G., Bell, D.S. and White, R.T. (1974) 'Stereotactic amygdaloidotomy for aggressive behavior', *Journal of Neurology, Neurosurgery, and Psychiatry*, 37, pp. 437–44.

Kilpatrick, D.G. et al (1985) 'Mental health correlates of criminal victimization: a random community survey', *Journal of Consulting and Clinical Psychology*, 53, pp. 866–73.

King, F.A. and Meyer, P.M. (1958) 'Effects of amygdaloid lesions upon septal hyperemotionality in the rat', *Science*, 128, pp. 555–6.

Kingdon, D.G. and Turkington, D. (1994) *Cognitive-Behavioural Therapy of Schizophrenia*, Hove: Erlbaum.

Kirchner, W.H. and Towne, W.F. (1994) 'The sensory basis of the honey bee's dance language', *Scientific American*, (June) 270, pp. 52–9.

Kirkpatrick, S.A. and Locke, E.A. (1991) 'Leadership: do traits matter?', *Academy of Management Executive*, 5, pp. 48–60.

Klaus, M.H. and Kennell, J.H. (1975) *Maternal–Infant Bonding* (2nd edn), St Louis: Mosby.

Klaus, M.H. and Kennell, J.H. (1976) *Parent–Infant Bonding*, St Louis: Mosby.

Kleiner, L. and Marshall, W.L. (1987) 'Interpersonal problems and agoraphobia', *Journal of Anxiety Disorders*, 1, pp. 313–23.

Kleinginna, P.R.Jr. and Kleinginna, A.M. (1981) 'A categorised list of emotional definitions, with suggestions for a consensual definition', *Motivation and Emotion*, 5, pp. 345–79.

Klerman, G.L. (1988) 'Depression and related disorders of mood (affective disorders)', in A.M. Nicholi Jr (ed.) *The New Harvard Guide to Psychiatry*, Cambridge, Massachussets: Harvard University Press.

Klima, E. and Bellugi, U. (1979) *The Signs of Language*, Cambridge, Massachusetts: Harvard University Press.

Kline, P. (1988) *Psychology Exposed, or, The Emperor's New Clothes*, London: Routledge.

Kline, P. (1992) *Psychometric Testing in Personnel Selection and Appraisal*, Kingston upon Thames: Croner.

Klinger, E. (1977) 'Meaning and void: inner experience and the incentives in people's lives', Minneapolis: The University of Minneapolis Press.

Klopfer, P.H., Adams, D.K. and Klopfer, M.S. (1964) 'Maternal "imprinting" in goats', *Proceedings of the National Academy of Sciences USA*, 52, pp. 91–1-14.

Kluger, M.J. (1990) cited in P.A. MacKowiac (ed.) *Fever: Basic Measurement and Management*, New York: Raven Press.

Kluver, H. and Bucy, P. (1939) 'Preliminary analysis of functions of the temporal lobes in monkeys', *Archives of Neurology and Psychiatry*, 42, pp. 979–1000.

Kobasa, S.C. (1979) 'Stressful life events, personality, and health: an enquiry into hardiness', *Journal of Personality and Social Psychology*, 37, pp. 1–11.

Kobasa, S.C. (1986) 'How much stress can you survive?', in M.G. Walraven and H.E. Fitzgerald (eds), *Annual Editions: Human Development*, 86/87, New York: Dushkin.

Kohlberg, L. (1963) 'The development of children's orientations towards a moral order: 1. Sequence in the development of moral thought', *Vita Humana*, 6, pp. 11–33.

Kohlberg, L. (1966) 'A cognitive-developmental analysis of children's sex-role concepts and attitudes', in E.E. Maccoby (ed.), *The Development of Sex Differences*, Stanford, California: Stanford University Press.

Kohlberg, L. (1969) *Stages in the Development of Moral Thought and Action*, New York: Holt.

Kohlberg, L. (1976) 'Moral stages and moralization', in T. Likona (ed.), *Moral Development and Behaviour*, New York: Holt, Rinehart & Winston.

Kohlberg, L. (1978) 'Revisions in the theory and practice of moral development', *Directions for Child Development*, 2, pp. 83–8.

Kohlberg, L. (1985) *The Psychology of Moral Development*, San Francisco: Harper & Row.

Kohlberg, L. and Elfenbein, D. (1975) 'The development of moral judgements concerning capital punishment', *American Journal of Orthopsychiatry*, 54, pp. 614–40.

Kohn, A. (1993) *Punished by Rewards*, Boston: Houghton Mifflin.

Kolata, G. (1987) 'Associations or rules in learning language?', *Science*, 237, pp. 113–14.

Koluchova, J. (1976) 'A report on the further development of twins after severe and prolonged deprivation', in A.M. Clarke and A.D.B. Clarke (eds) *Early Experience Myth and Evidence*, London: Open Books.

Koneckni, V.J., Libuser, L., Morton, H. and Ebbesen, E.B. (1975) 'Effects of a violation of personal space on escape and helping responses', *Journal of Experimental Social Psychology*, 11, pp. 288–99.

Konner, M. (1977) 'Evolution in human behaviour development', in P.H. Leidermmans, S. Tulkin and A. Rosenfeld (eds) *Culture and Infancy: Variations in Human Experience*, New York: Academic Press.

Kosten, T.R., Mason, J.W., Giller, E.L., Ostroff, R. and Harkness, L. (1987) 'Sustained urinary norepinephrine and epinephrine elevation in post-traumatic stress disorder', *Psycho-neuroendocrinology*, 12, pp. 13–20.

Kowalowski, L. T. and Cutting, J.E. (1978) 'Recognising the gender of walkers from point-lights mounted on ankles: some second thoughts', *Perception and Psychophysics*, 23, p. 459.

Krahé, B. (1988) 'Attribution to victims of rape', *Journal of Applied Social Psychology*, 18, pp. 50–8.

Krause, R.M. (1992) *Science*, 257, pp. 1073–8.

Krebs, J.R. and Davies, N.B. (1987) *An Introduction to Behavioural Ecology* (2nd edn), London: Blackwell.

Krebs, J.R. and Dawkins, R. (1984) 'Animal signals: mind reading and manipulation', in *Behavioural Ecology: An Evolutionary Approach* (2nd edn), Sunderland, Massachussets: Sinauer.

Kremer, J.F. and Stephens, L. (1983) 'Attributions and arousal as mediators of mitigation's effects on retaliation', *Journal of Personality and Social Psychology*, 45, pp. 335–43.

Kruglanski, A.W. (1980) 'Lay epistemologic process and contents: another look at attribution theory, *Psychological Review*, 87, pp. 70–87.

Kübler-Ross, E. (1969) *On Death and Dying*, New York: Macmillan.

Kuhn, T.S. (1970) *The Structure of Scientific Revolutions* (2nd edn), Chicago: University of Chicago Press.

Kulik, J. and Brown, R. (1979) 'Frustration, attribution of blame and aggression', *Journal of Experimental Social Psychology*, 15, pp. 183–94.

Kurtines, W. and Greif, E.B. (1974) 'The development of moral thought: review and evaluation of Kohlberg's approach', *Psychological Bulletin*, 81, pp. 453–70.

Kvale, S. (1992) (ed.) *Psychology and Postmodernism*, Newbury Park, USA: Sage.

LaBerge, D. (1983) Spatial extent of attention to letters and words', *Journal of Experimental Psychology: Human Perception and Performance*, 9, pp. 371–9.

Labov, W. (1970) 'The logic of non-standard English', in F. Williams (ed.) *Language and Poverty*, Chicago: Markham.

Lack (1968) reviewed in Krebs, J.R. and Davies, N.B. (eds) *Behavioural Ecology: An Introductory Approach*, Oxford: Blackwell.

Lader, M.H. and Mathews, A.M. (1968) 'A physiological model of phobic anxiety and desensitization', *Behaviour Research and Therapy*, 6, pp. 411–21.

Lago, C. and Thompson, J. (1989) 'Counselling and race', in Dryden, W., Charles-Edwards, D. and Woolfe, R. *Handbook of Counselling in Britain*, London: Routledge.

Laing, R.D. (1965) *The Divided Self*, Harmondsworth: Penguin.

Lamb, M.E. (1977) 'The development of mother–infant and father–infant attachments in the second year of life', *Developmental Psychology*, 13, pp. 637–48.

Langer, E.J. and Rodin, J. (1976) 'The effects of choice and enhanced personal responsibility for the aged: a field experiment in an institutional setting', *Journal of Personality and Social Psychology*, 34, pp. 191–8.

Langley, T.L., O'Neal, E.C., Craig, K.M. and Yoat, E.A. (1992) 'Aggression-consistent, -inconsistent and -irrelevant priming effects on selective exposure to media violence', *Aggressive Behaviour*, 18, pp. 349–56.

Langlois, J.H. and Downs, C.A. (1980) 'Mothers, fathers and peers as socialisation agents of sex-typed play behaviours in young children', *Child Development*, 51, pp. 1237–47.

Langner, T.S. and Michael, S.T. (1962) *Life Stresses and Mental Health: The Midtown Study*, Illinois: Free Press.

Lannon, J. and Cooper, P. (1983) 'Humanistic advertising', *International Journal of Advertising*, July–September.

Larsen, K.S. (1974) 'Conformity in the Asch experiment', *Journal of Social Psychology*, 94, pp. 303–4.

Lashley, K. and Watson, J.B. (1921) 'A psychological study of motion pictures in relation to venereal disease', *Social Hygiene*, 7, pp. 181–219.

Lashley, K.S. (1929) *Brain Mechanisms and Intelligence*, Chicago: University of Chicago Press.

Latané, B. and Darley, J.M. (1970) *The Unresponsive Bystander: Why Doesn't He Help?* New York: Appleton Century Crofts.

Latané, B. and Nida, S.A. (1981) 'Ten years of research on group size and helping', *Psychological Bulletin*, 89, pp. 308–24 (11).

Latané, B., Williams, K. and Hawkins, S. (1979) 'Many hands make light work: the causes and consequences of social loafing', *Journal of Personality and Social Psychology*, 37, pp. 822–32.

Lazar, I. and Darlington, R. (1982) *Lasting Effects of Early Education: A Report from the Consortium of Longitudinal Studies*, Monographs of the Society for Research in Child Development, 47(2–3), Serial No. 195.

Lazarus, R.S. (1984) 'On the primacy of cognition', *American Psychologist*, 39, pp. 124–9.

Lazarus, R.S. (1991) Emotion and adaptation. New York: Oxford University Press.

Lea, M. and Duck, S. (1982) 'A model for the role of similarity of values in friendship development', *British Journal of Social Psychology*, 21, pp. 301–10.

Leary, M.A., Greer, D. and Huston, A.C. (1982) 'The relation between TV viewing and gender roles', Paper presented at the Southwestern Society for Research in Human Development, Galveston, Texas.

LeBon, G. (1947, first published 1895) *The Crowd: A Study of the Popular Mind*, London: Ernest Benn.

Lee, V.E., Brookes-Gunn, J., Schnur, E. and Liaw, F. (1990) 'Are Head Start effects sustained? A longitudinal follow-up comparison of disadvantaged children attending Head Start, no preschool, and other preschool programs', *Child Development*, 61, pp. 495–507.

Leifer, M. (1977) 'Psychological changes accompanying pregnancy and motherhood', *Genetic Psychology Monographs*, 95, pp. 55–96.

LeMagnen, J. (1981) 'The metabolic basis of dual periodicity of feeding in rats', *The Behavioral and Brain Sciences*, 4, pp. 561–607.

Lerner, M.J. (1975) 'The justice motive in social behaviour', *Journal of Social Issues*, 31(3), pp. 1–19.

Lerner, R.M. (1976) 'Pretty pleases: The effects of physical attractiveness, race and sex on receiving help', *Journal of Experimental Social Psychology*, 12, 409–15.

Leslie, A.M. (1987) 'Pretense and representation: the origins of Theory of Mind', *Psychology Review*, 94(4), pp. 412–26.

Levine, J. (1976) 'Real kids versus the average family', *Psychology Today*, June, pp. 14–15.

Levinger, G. (1983) 'Development and change', in H.H. Kelley, E. Berscheid, A. Christensen, J.H. Harvey, T.L. Huston, G. Levinger, E. McClintock, L.A. Pellau and D.R. Peterson (1983) *Close Relationships*, New York: W.H. Freeman.

Levinson, D.J. (1978) *The Seasons of a Man's Life*, New York: Knopf.

Levy, B.A. (1978) 'Speech processing during reading', in A.M. Lesgold, J.W. Pellegrino, S.D. Fokkema and R. Glaser (eds) *Cognitive Psychology and Instruction*, New York: Plenum.

Lewer, N. (1995) 'The future art of war', *Medicine and War*, 11, 2.

Lewin, K., Lippit, R. and White, R.K. (1939) 'Patterns of aggressive behaviour in artificially created social climates', *Journal of Social Psychology*, 10, pp. 271–99.

Lewinsohn, P.M. (1974) 'A behavioural approach to depression', in R.J. Friedman and M.M. Katz (eds) *The Psychology of Depression: Contemporary Theory and Research*, Washington, DC: Winston Wiley.

Lewis, C., Freeman, N., Hagestasdt, C. and Douglas, H. (1994) 'Narrative access and production in preschoolers' false belief reasoning', *Cognitive Development*, 9, pp. 397–424.

Lewis, J.L. (1970) 'Semantic processing of unattended messages using dichotic listening', *Journal of Experimental Psychology*, 85, pp. 225–8.

Lewis, M. (1990) 'Social knowledge and social development', *Merrill Palmer Quarterly*, 36, pp. 93–116.

Lewis, M. and Brooks-Gunn, J. (1979) *Social Cognition and the Acquisition of Self*, New York: Plenum Press.

Lewis, R.A. (1972) 'A developmental framework for the analysis of premarital dyadic formation', *Family Process*, 11, pp. 17–48.

Lewis, S.W., Harvey, I., Ron, M., Murray, R. and Reveley, A. (1990) 'Can brain damage protect against schizophrenia? A case report of twins', *British Journal of Psychiatry*, 157, pp. 600–3.

Ley, P. (1988) *Communicating with Patients: Improving Communication, Satisfaction and Compliance*, London: Chapman Hall.

Ley, P. (1989) 'Improving patients' understanding, recall, satisfaction and compliance', in A.K. Broome (ed.) *Health Psychology: Processes and Applications*, London: Chapman & Hall.

Ley, P., Bradshaw, P.W., Eaves, D. and Walker, C.M. (1973) 'A method for increasing patients' recall of information presented by doctors', *Psychological Medicine*, 3, pp. 217–20.

Leyens, J.-P. and Fraczek, A. (1984) 'Aggression as an interpersonal phenomenon', in H. Tajfel (ed.) *The Social Dimension*, Vol. 1, Cambridge: Cambridge University Press.

Leyens, J.P. and Dardenne, B. (1996) 'Basic concepts and approaches in social cognition', in M. Hewstone, W. Stroebe and G.M. Stephenson (eds) *Introduction to Social Psychology* (2nd edn), Oxford: Blackwell.

Liberman, A.M. and Mattingly, I.G. (1989) 'A specialization for speech perception', *Science*, 243, pp. 489–94.

Light, P.M., Buckingham, N. and Robbins, H. (1979) 'The conservation task as an interactional setting', *British Journal of Educational Psychology*, 49(3), pp. 304–10.

Lindauer, M. (1955) cited in D.R. Griffin (1992) *Animal Minds*, Chicago: Chicago University Press.

Linton, M. (1982) 'Transformations of memory in everyday life', in U. Neisser (ed.) *Memory Observed*, San Francisco: W.H. Freeman.

Lippman, M.F. (1972) 'The influence of grammatical transform in a syllogistic reasoning task', *Journal of Verbal Learning and Verbal Behaviour*, 11, pp. 424–430.

Littlewood R. and Lipsedge, M. (1982) *Aliens and Alienists*, Harmondsworth. Penguin.

Liu, L.G. (1985) 'Reasoning counterfactually in Chinese: are there any obstacles?', *Cognition*, 21, pp. 239–70.

Livingston, R.B. (1967) 'Brain circuitry relating to complex behaviour', in G.C. Quarton, T. Melnechuck and F.O. Schmitt *The Neurosciences: A Study Program*, New York: Rockefeller University Press.

Llewelyn, S. (1994) 'Trauma, child sexual abuse and survival', *The Psychologist*, 7(4), pp. 171–2.

Lock, A.J. (1980) *The Guided Reinvention Of Language*, London: Academic Press.

Locke, K.D. and Horowitz, L.M. (1990) 'Satisfaction in interpersonal interactions as a function of similarity in level of dysphoria', *Journal of Personality and Social Psychology*, 58, pp. 823–31.

Loftus, E.F. (1975) 'Leading questions and eye-witness report', *Cognitive Psychology*, 7, pp. 560–72.

Loftus, E.F. (1979) 'Reactions to blatantly contradictory information', *Memory and Cognition*, 7, pp. 368–74.

Loftus, E.F. (1993) 'The reality of repressed memories', *American Psychologist*, 48, pp. 518–37.

Loftus, E.F., Miller, D.G. and Burns, H.J. (1978) 'Semantic integration of verbal information into a visual memory', *Journal of Experimental Psychology: Human Learning and Memory*, 4, pp. 19–31.

Loftus, G.R. and Loftus, E.F. (1975) *Human Memory: The Processing of Information*, New York: Halsted Press.

Lopata, H.Z. (1973) 'Self identity in marriage and parenthood', *Sociological Quarterly*, 14, pp. 407–18.

Lorenz, K. (1937) 'The companion in the bird's world', *Auk*, 54, pp. 245–73.

Lorenz, K. (1966) *On Aggression*, London: Methuen.

Lott, B.E. (1994) *Women's Lives: Themes and Variations in Gender Learning*, Pacific Grove, USA: Brooks Cole.

Luchins, A.S. (1942) 'Mechanization in problem solving', *Psychological Monographs*, 54 (Whole No. 248)

Lugo, J.O. and Hershey, G.L. (1979) *Lifespan Development* (2nd edn), London: Macmillan.

Lujansky, H. and Mikula, G. (1983) 'Can equity theory explain the quality and stability of romantic relationships?', *British Journal of Social Psychology*, 22, pp. 101–12.

Luks, A. (1988) 'Helpers' high', *Psychology Today*, October, pp. 39–40.

Lundberg, I., Frost, J. and Peterson, O. (1988) 'Effects of an extensive program for stimulating phonological awareness in preschool children', *Reading Research Quarterly*, 23, pp. 263–84.

Luria, A.R. (1971) 'Towards the problem of the historical nature of psychological processes', *International Journal of Psychology*, 6, pp. 259–72.

Lynch, K. (1960) *The Image of the City*, Cambridge, Massachusetts: MIT Press.

McBurney, D.H. (1983) *Experimental Psychology*, Belmont, California: Wadsworth.

McClelland, D.C. (1961) *The Achieving Society*, Princeton, New Jersey: Van Nostrand.

McCormack, R.L. (1965) 'Extended tables of the Wilcoxon matched pair signed rank statistic', *Journal of the American Statistical Association*, 60, pp. 864–71.

McDougall, W. (1908) *An Introduction to Social Psychology*, London, Methuen.

McFarland, D. (1993) *Animal Behaviour* (2nd edn), Harlow: Addison Wesley Longman.

MacFarlane, A. (1975) 'Olfaction in the development of social preferences in the human neonate', in Ciba Foundation Symposium *Parent–Infant Interaction*, New York: Elsevier.

McGarrigle, J. and Donaldson, M. (1974) 'Conservation accidents', *Cognition*, 3, pp. 341–50.

McGee, M. and Wilson, D.W. (1984) *Psychology: Science and Application*, New York: West Publishing Co.

McGovern, D. and Cope, R. (1987) 'The compulsory detention of males of different ethnic groups, with special reference to offender patients', *British Journal of Psychiatry*, 150, pp. 505–12.

McGovern, L.P. (1976) 'Dispositional social anxiety and helping behaviour under three conditions of threat', *Journal of Personality*, 44, pp. 84–97.

McGrath, T., Tsui, E., Humphries, S. and Yule, W. (1990) 'Successful treatment of a noise phobia in a nine-year-old girl with systematic desensitization *in vivo*', *Educational Psychology*, 10(1), pp. 79–83.

McGregor, D. (1960) *The Human Side of Enterprise*, New York: McGraw-Hill.

McGuire, W.J. (1968) 'Personality and susceptibility to social influence', in E. Borgatta and W. Lambert (eds) *Handbook of Personality Theory and Research*, Vol. 3, Chicago: Rand-McNally.

McHugh, P.R. and Moran, T.H. (1985) 'The stomach: a conception of its dynamic role in satiety', *Progress in Psychobiology and Physiological Psychology*, 11, pp. 197–232.

McIlveen, R. (1995) 'Hypnosis', *Psychology Review*, 2 (November), pp. 8–12.

McIlveen, R. (1996) 'Applications of hypnosis', *Psychology Review*, 2 (February), pp. 24–7.

McIlveen, R. *et al.* (1992) *BPS Manual of Psychology Practicals*, Leicester: BPS Books.

MacKay, D.G. (1973) 'Aspects of the theory of comprehension, memory, and attention', *Quarterly Journal of Experimental Psychology*, 25, pp. 22–40.

McKenzie, B. and Over, R. (1983) 'Do neonatal infants imitate? A reply to Meltzoff and Moore', *Infant Behavior and Development*, 6, pp. 109–11.

MacLean, P.D. (1949) 'Psychosomatic disease and the "visceral brain": Recent developments bearing on the Papez theory of emotion', *Psychosomatic Medicine*, 11, pp. 338–53.

McNally, R.J. and Steketee, G.S. (1985) 'The etiology and maintenance of severe animal phobias', *Behaviour Research and Therapy*, 23(4), pp. 431–5.

Maier, S.J. and Seligman, M.E.P. (1976) 'Learned helplessness: theory and evidence', *Journal of Experimental Psychology: General*, 105, pp. 2–46.

Main, M. and Cassidy, J. (1988) 'Categories of response to reunion with the parent at age six: predicted from infant attachment classifications and stable over a one-month period', *Developmental Psychology*, 24, pp. 415–26.

Main, M., Kaplan, N. and Cassidy, J. (1985) 'Security in infancy, childhood and adulthood: a move to a level of representation', in I. Bretherton and E. Waters (eds) *Growing Points of Attachment Theory and Research*, Monographs of the Society for Research in Child Development, 50(1–2), Serial No. 209.

Mallik, S.K. and McCandless, B.R. (1966) 'A study of the catharsis of aggression', *Journal of Personality and Social Psychology*, 4, pp. 591–6.

Malthus, T.R. (first published 1798) *An Essay on the Principle of Population*, Harmondsworth: Penguin Books.

Mangel, M and Clark, C.W. (1988) *Dynamic Modeling in Behavioural Ecology*, Princeton, New Jersey: Princeton University Press.

Mann, L. (1981) 'The baiting crowd in episodes of threatened suicide', *Journal of Personality and Social Psychology*, 41, pp. 703–9.

Manstead, A.S.R. and McCulloch, C. (1981) 'Sex-role stereotyping in British television advertisements', *European Journal of Social Psychology*, 20, pp. 171–80.

Maranon, G. (1924) 'Contribution à l'étude de l'action émotive de l'adrénaline', *Revue Française d'Endocrinologie*, 2, pp. 301–25.

Marcia, J. (1980) 'Identity in adolescence', in J. Adelson (ed.) *Handbook of Adolescent Psychology*, New York: Wiley.

Marcia, J. E. (1966) 'Development and validation of ego identity status', *Journal of Personality and Social Psychology*, 3, pp. 551–8.

Marcia, J. E. (1968) 'The case history of a construct: ego identity status', in E. Vinacke (ed.), *Readings in General Psychology*, New York: Van Nostrand-Reinhold.

Marcus, J., Hans, S.L., Nagier, S., Auerbach, J.G., Mirsky, A.F. and Aubrey, A. (1987) 'Review of the NIMH Israeli Kibbutz-City and the Jerusalem infant development study', *Schizophrenia Bulletin*, 13, pp. 425–38.

Markovits, H. and Nantel, G. (1989) 'The belief-bias effect in the production and evaluation of logical conclusions', *Memory and Cognition*, 17, pp. 11–17.

Marr, D. (1982) *Vision: A Computational Investigation into the Human Representation and Processing of Visual Information*, San Francisco: W.H. Freeman.

Marsh, P., Rosser, E and Harre, R. (1978), *The Rules of Disorder*, London: Routledge.

Marshall, G.D. and Zimbardo, P.G. (1979) 'Affective consequences of inadequately explained physiological arousal', *Journal of Personality and Social Psychology*, 37, pp. 970–88.

Martin, C. and Halverson, C. (1983) 'Gender constancy: a methodological and theoretical analysis', *Sex Roles*, 9, pp. 775–90.

Martin, C.L. and Little, J.K. (1990) 'The relation of gender understanding to children's sex-typed preferences and gender stereotypes', *Child Development*, 61, pp. 1427–39.

Martlatt, G.A. and Gordon, J.R. (1980) 'Determinants of relapse: implications for the maintenance of behaviour change', in P.O. Davidson and S.M. Davidson (eds) *Behavioural Medicine: Changing Health Lifestyles*, New York: Brunner/Mazel.

Maruyama, G., Fraser, S.C. and Miller, N. (1982) 'Personal responsibility and altruism in children', *Journal of Personality and Social Psychology*, 42(4), pp. 658–64.

Marzluff, J.M., Heinrich, B. and Marzluff, C.J. (1996) 'Raven roosts are mobile information centres', *Animal Behaviour*, 51, pp. 89–103.

Maslach, C. (1979) 'Negative emotional biasing of unexplained arousal', *Journal of Personality and Social Psychology*, 37, pp. 953–69.

Maslach, C., Santee, R.T. and Wade, C. (1987) 'Individuation, gender role and dissent: Personality mediators of situational forces', *Journal of Personality and Social Psychology*, 53, pp. 1088–94.

Maslow, A.H. (1954) *Motivation and Personality*, New York: Harper & Row.

Maslow, A.H. (1968) *Toward a Psychology of Being*, New York: Van Nostrand-Reinhold.

Mason, M.K. (1942) 'Learning to speak after six and one-half years of silence', *Journal of Speech and Hearing Disorders*, 7, pp. 295–304

Massaro, D.W. (1989) 'Multiple book review of Speech perception by ear and eye: a paradigm for psychological inquiry', *Behavioural and Brain Sciences*, 12, pp. 741–94.

Masson, J. (1989) *Against Therapy*, London: HarperCollins.

Masters, J.C., Ford, M.E., Arend, R., Grotevant, H.D. and Clarke, L.V. (1979) 'Modelling and labelling as integrated determinants of children's sex-typed imitative behaviour', *Child Development*, 50, pp. 364–71.

Matas, L., Arend, R.A. and Sroufe, L.A. (1978) 'Continuity of adaptation in the second year: the relationship between quality of attachment and later competence', *Child Development*, 49, pp. 547–56.

Mathews, A. (1989) 'Cognitive aspects of the aetiology and phenomenology of anxiety disorders', in P.M.G. Emmelkamp, W.T.A.M. Everaerd, F. Kraaimaat and M.J.M. van Son (eds) *Fresh Perspectives on Anxiety Disorders*, Annual Series of European Research in Behaviour Therapy, Vol. IV, Amsterdam: Swets & Zeitlinger.

Matlin, M.W. (1993) *The Psychology of Women* (2nd edn), Orlando, Florida: Harcourt Brace Jovanovich.

Matlin, M.W. (1994) *Cognition* (3rd edn), Orlando: Harcourt Brace Publishers.

Matsuhashi, A. (1982) 'Explorations in the real-time production of written discourse', in M. Nystrand (ed.) *What Writers Know: The Language, Process and Structure of Written Language*, New York: Academic Press.

Mayer, W.E. (1956) 'Why did many GI captives cave in?', *US News and World Report*, 24 February 1956.

Maynard-Smith, J. (1976) 'Evolution and the theory of games', *American Scientist*, Cambridge: Cambridge University Press.

Mead, G.H. (1934) *Mind, Self and Society*, Chicago: University of Chicago Press.

Mead, M. (1928) *Coming of Age in Samoa*, New York: Morrow.

Meddis, R. (1977) *The Sleep Instinct*, London: Routledge and Kegan.

Meddis, R. (1979) 'The evolution and function of sleep', in D.A. Oakley and H.C. Plotkin (eds) *Brain, Behaviour and Evolution*, London: Methuen.

Meeus, W.H.J. and Raaijmakers, Q.A.W. (1986) 'Administrative obedience: carrying out orders to use psychological-administrative violence', *European Journal of Social Psychology*, 16, pp. 311–24.

Meichenbaum, D. and Cameron, R. (1983) 'Stress inoculation training: toward a general paradigm for training coping skills', in D. Meichenbaum and M.E. Jarenko (eds) *Stress Reduction and Prevention*, New York: Plenum.

Meichenbaum, D.H. (1975) 'A self-instructional approach to stress management: a proposal for stress inoculation training', in I. Sarason and C.D. Spielberger (eds) *Stress and Anxiety*, Vol. 2, New York: Wiley.

Meichenbaum, D.H. and Cameron, R. (1973) 'Training schizophrenics to talk to themselves: a means of developing attentional controls', *Behaviour Therapy*, 4, pp. 515–34.

Melhuish, E.C. (1993) 'Behaviour measures: a measure of love? An overview of the assessment of attachment', *ACPP Review and Newsletter*, 15(6), pp. 269–75.

Meltzoff, A. and Gopnik, A. (1993) 'The role of imitation in understanding persons and developing a theory of mind', in S. Baron-Cohen, H. Tager-Flushberg and D. Cohen (eds) *Understanding Other Minds: Perspective from Autism*, Oxford: Oxford University Press.

Meltzoff, A.N. and Moore, K. M. (1983) 'Newborn infants imitate adult facial gestures', *Child Development*, 54, pp. 702–9.

Meltzoff, A.N. and Moore, K.M. (1977) 'Imitation of facial and manual gestures by human neonates', *Science*, 198, pp. 75–8.

Melville, J. (1978) *Phobias and Obsessions*, New York: Penguin.

Menzies, R.G. and Clarke, J.C. (1993) 'A comparison of *in vivo* and vicarious exposure in the treatment of childhood water phobia', *Behavioural Research Therapy*, 31(1), pp. 9–15.

Messenger-Davies, M. (1989) *Television Is Good for Your Kids*, London: Hilary Shipman Ltd.

Messer, D.J. (1994) *The Development of Communication*, Chichester: Wiley.

Mestel, R. and Concar, D. (1994) 'How to heal the body's craving', *New Scientist*, 1 October 1994.

Metalsky, G.I., Halberstadt, L.J. and Abramson, L.Y. (1987) 'Vulnerability and invulnerability to depressive mood reactions: towards a more powerful test of the diathesis-stress and causal mediation components of the reformulated theory of depression', *Journal of Personality and Social Psychology*, 52, pp. 386–93.

Middleton, R. (1976) 'Regional differences in prejudice', *American Sociological Review*, 41, pp. 94–117.

Midlarsky, E., Bryan, J.H. and Brickman, P. (1973) 'Aversive approval: interactive effects of modelling and reinforcement on altruistic behaviour', *Child Development*, 44, pp. 321–8.

Milavsky, J.R., Kessler, R., Stipp, H. and Rubens, W.S. (1982) 'Television and aggression: results of a panel study', in D. Pearl, L. Bouthilet and J. Lazar (eds) *Television and Behaviour: Ten Years of Scientific Progress and Implications for the Eighties*, National Institute of Mental Health.

Milgram, S. (1963) 'Behavioural study of obedience', *Journal of Abnormal and Social Psychology*, 67, pp. 371–8.

Milgram, S. (1964) 'Issues in the study of obedience: a reply to Baumrind', *American Psychologist*, 19, pp. 848–52.

Milgram, S. (1970) 'The experience of living in cities', *Science*, 167, pp. 1461–8.

Milgram, S. (1973), *Obedience to Authority*, London: Tavistock.

Milgram, S. (1974) *Obedience to Authority*, New York: Harper & Row.

Miller, A.G. (1986) *The Obedience Experiments: A Case Study of Controversy in Social Science*, New York: Praeger.

Miller, D.T. and Ross, M. (1975) 'Self-serving biases in the attribution of causality: fact or fiction?', *Psychological Bulletin*, 82, pp. 213–25.

Miller, G. (1969) 'Psychology as a means of promoting human welfare', *American Psychologist*, 24, pp. 1063–75.

Miller, G.A. (1956) 'The magical number seven plus or minus two', *Psychological Review*, 63, pp. 81–97.

Miller, J.F. (1988) 'The developmental asynchrony of language development in children with Down's syndrome', in L. Nadel (ed.) *The Psychobiology of Down's Syndrome*, Cambridge, Massachusetts: MIT Press.

Miller, N. and Bugelski, R. (1948) 'Minor studies of aggression II: The influence of frustrations imposed by the ingroup on attitudes expressed toward outgroups', *Journal of Psychology*, 25, pp. 437–52.

Miller, N.E. (1985) 'The value of behavioural research on animals', *American Psychologist*, 40, pp. 423–40.

Milliman, R. (1982) 'Using background music to affect the behaviour of supermarket shoppers', *Journal of Marketing*, 46, pp. 86–91.

Mills, A.E. (1987) 'The development of phonology in the blind child', in B. Dodd and R. Campbell (eds) *Hearing by Eye: The Psychology of Lip-reading*, Hove: Erlbaum.

Minuchin, S., Rosman, B.L. and Baker, L. (1978) *Psychosomatic Families: Anorexia Nervosa in Context*, Cambridge, Massachusetts: Harvard University Press.

Mischel, W. (1970) 'Sex-typing and socialisation', in P.H. Mussen (ed.) *Manual of Child Psychology* Vol. 2 (3rd edn), New York: Wiley.

Mischel, W. and Patterson, C.J. (1976) 'Substantive and structural elements of effective plans for self control', *Journal of Personality and Social Psychology*, 34, pp. 942–50.

Mitchell, D.B., Hunt, R.R. and Schmitt, F.A. (1986) 'The generation effect and reality monitoring: evidence from dementia and normal aging', *Journal of Gerontology*, 41, pp. 79–84.

Mitchell, K.M. (1977) 'A reappraisal of the therapeutic effectiveness of accurate empathy, nonpossessive warmth and genuineness', in A.S. Gurman and A.M. Razin (eds) *Effective Psychotherapy: A Handbook of Research*, New York: Pergamon.

Miyake, K., Chen, S.J. and Campos, J.J. (1985) 'Infant temperament, mother's mode of interaction, and attachment in Japan: an interim report', in I. Bretherton and E. Waters (eds) *Growing Points in Attachment Theory and Research*, Monographs of the Society for Research in Child Development, 50(1–2), Serial No. 209.

Moghaddam, F.M., Taylor, D.M. and Wright, S.C. (1993) *Social Psychology in Cross-Cultural Perspective*, New York: W.H. Freeman.

Moller, A.P. (1992) 'Female preference for symmetrical male sexual ornaments', *Nature*, 357, pp. 238–40.

Moore, J. (1984) 'Parasites that change the behaviour of their host', *Scientific American*, 250, pp. 82–8.

Morgan, C.T. (1965) *Physiological Psychology*, New York: McGraw-Hill.

Morgan, E. (1990) *The Scars of Evolution*, London: Souvenir Press.

Morgan, E. (1994) *The Descent of the Child*, London: Souvenir Press.

Moriarty, T. (1975) 'A nation of willing victims', *Psychology Today*, April 1975, pp. 43–50.

Morris, W.N. and Miller, R.S. (1975) 'The effects of consensus-breaking and consensus-preempting partners on reduction of conformity', *Journal of Experimental Social Psychology*, 11, pp. 215–23.

Moscovici, S. (1981) 'On social representations', in J.P. Forgas (ed.) *Social Cognition: Perspectives in Everyday Understanding*, London: Academic Press.

Moscovici, S. (1985) 'Social influence and conformity', in G. Lindzey and E. Aronson (eds) *Handbook of Social Psychology* (3rd edn), New York: Random House.

Moscovici, S. and Hewstone, M. (1983) 'Social representations and social explanations: from the "naive" to the "amateur" scientist', in. M. Hewstone (ed.) *Attribution Theory: Social and Functional Extensions*, Oxford: Blackwell.

Moscovici, S., Lage, E. and Naffrechoux, M. (1969) 'Influence of a consistent minority on the responses of a majority in a colour perception task', *Sociometry*, 32, pp. 365–80.

Moss, M.K. and Page, R.A. (1972) 'Reinforcement and helping behaviour', *Journal of Applied Social Psychology*, 2, pp. 360–71.

Mulford, R.C. (1987) 'First word of the blind child', in M.D. Smith and J.L. Locke (eds) *The Emergent Lexicon: The Child's Development of a Linguistic Vocabulary*, London: Academic Press.

Munro, G. and Adams, G.R. (1977) 'Ego-identity formation in college students and working youth', *Developmental Psychology*, 13, pp. 523–4.

Munroe, R.H., Shimmin, H.S. and Munroe, R.L (1984) 'Gender understanding and sex role preference in four cultures', *Developmental Psychology*, 20, pp. 673–82.

Murray, H.A. (ed.) (1938) *Explorations in Personality*, New York: Oxford University Press.

Murray-Parkes, C. (1972) *Bereavement: Studies of Grief in Adult Life*, New York: International Universities Press.

Murstein, B.I. (1972) 'Physical attractiveness and marital choice', *Journal of Personality and Social Psychology*, 22, pp. 8–12.

Murstein, B.I., MacDonald, M.G. and Cerreto, M. (1977) 'A theory and investigation of the effects of exchange-orientation on marriage and friendship', *Journal of Marriage and the Family*, 39, pp. 543–8.

Myers, T. (1971) 'Human reaction to monotony', Paper presented at a symposium on the effects of reduced sensory stimulation at the American Association for the Advancement of Science, Philadelphia.

Nardi, P.M. (ed.) (1992) *Men's Friendships*, Newbury Park, USA: Sage.

Navon, D. (1977) 'Forest before trees: the precedence of global features in visual perception', *Cognitive Psychology*, 9, pp. 353–83.

Neisser, U. (1963) 'Decision-time without reaction time: experiments in visual scanning', *American Journal of Psychology*, 76, pp. 374–85.

Neisser, U. (1967) *Cognitive Psychology*, New York: Appleton-Century-Crofts.

Neisser, U. (1976) *Cognition and Reality*, San Francisco: W. H. Freeman.

Neisser, U. (1978) 'Memory: what are the important questions?', in M.M. Gruneberg, P.E. Morris and R.N. Sykes (eds) *Practical Aspects of Memory*, London: Academic Press.

Neisser, U. (1982) *Memory Observed*, San Francisco: W.H. Freeman.

Nelson, K. (1973) 'Structure and strategy in learning to talk', *Monographs of the Society for Research in Child Development*, 38 (Serial No. 149)

Nelson-Jones, R. (1995) *The Theory and Practice of Counselling* (2nd edn), London: Cassell.

Nesse, R.M. and Williams, G.C. (1995) *Evolution and Healing*, London: Weidenfeld and Nicolson.

Neugarten, B.L. (1968) *Personality in Middle and Late Life* (2nd edn), New York: Atherton Press.

Neugarten, B.L. (1980) 'Act your age: must everything be a midlife crisis?', in *Annual Editions: Human Development, 1980/1981*, pp. 289–90.

Newcomb, M.D. (1987) 'Cohabitation and marriage: a quest for independence and relatedness', *Applied Social Psychology Annual*, 7, pp. 128–56.

Newcomb, T.M. (1961) *The Acquaintance Process*, New York: Holt, Rinehart & Winston.

Newell, A. and Simon, H.A. (1972) *Human Problem Solving*, Eaglewood Cliffs, New Jersey: Prentice-Hall.

Newell, A., Shaw, J.C. and Simon, H.A. (1958) 'Elements of a theory of general problem-solving', *Psychological Review*, 65, pp. 151–66.

Newman, O. (1972) *Defensible Space*, New York: MacMillan.

Newson, E. (1994) 'Video violence and the protection of children', *The Psychologist*, 7(6) pp. 272–4.

Nicholson, P. (1995) 'The menstrual cycle, science and femininity: assumptions underlying menstrual cycle research', *Soc. Sci. Med.*, 41, pp. 779–84.

Nisbett, R.E. (1972) 'Hunger, obesity and the ventro–medial hypothalamus', *Psychological Review*, 79, pp. 433–53.

Norman, D.A. (1968) 'Towards a theory of memory and attention', *Psychological Review*, 75, pp. 522–36.

Norman, D.A. (1981) 'Categorization of action slips', *Psychological Review*, 88, pp. 1–15.

Norman, D.A., and Bobrow, D.G. (1975) 'On data-limited and resource-limited processes', *Cognitive Psychology*, 7, pp. 44–64.

Norman, D.A., and Shallice, T. (1980) *Attention to Action: Willed and Automatic Control of Behaviour* (CHIP Report 99), San Diego, California: University of California, San Diego.

Norman-Jackson, J. (1982) 'Family interactions, language development and primary reading achievement of Black children in families of low income', *Child Development*, 53, pp. 349–58.

Novick, L.R. (1988) 'Analogical transfer, problem similarity and expertise', *Journal of Experimental Psychology*, 14, pp. 510–20.

Novick, L.R. and Holyoak, K.J. (1991) Mathematical problem solving by analogy', *Journal of Experimental Psychology: Learning, Memory and Cognition*, 17, pp. 398–415.

Noyes, R., Crowe, R.R., Harris, E.L., Hamra, B.J., McChesney, C.M. and Chaudhry, D.R. (1986) 'Relationship between panic disorder and agoraphobia: a family study', *Archives of General Psychiatry*, 43, pp. 227–32.

Oakley, D.A. (1985) 'The plurality of consciousness', in D.A. Oakley (ed.) *Brain and Mind*, London: Methuen.

O'Barr, W.M. (1994) *Culture and the Ad*, Boulder, Colorado: Westview.

O'Brien, G.E. (1990) Youth unemployment and employment', in P.C.L. Heavan and V.J. Callen (eds) *Adolescence: An Australian Perspective*, Sydney: Harcourt Brace Jovanovich.

Ochs, E. and Schieffelin, B.B. (1984) 'Language acquisition and socialization', in R.A. Shweder and R.A. Levine (eds) *Culture Theory*, Cambridge: Cambridge University Press.

Ogilvie, J.C., Tulving, E., Paskowitz, S. and Jones, G.V. (1980) 'Three dimensional learning traces: a model and its application to forgetting', *Journal of Verbal Learning and Verbal Behaviour*, 19, pp. 405–15.

Ohbuchi, K., Kamdea, M. and Agarie, N. (1989) 'Apology as aggression control: its role in mediating appraisal of and response to harm', *Journal of Personality and Social Psychology*, 56, pp. 219–27.

O'Leary, K.D. (1980) 'Pills or skills for hyperactive children', *Journal of Applied Behavior Analysis*, 13, pp. 191–204.

Oliphant, J. (1995) 'Sick building syndrome?', *Occupational Safety and Health*, 25, pp. 14–15.

Olsen, S.L., Bayles, K. and Bates, J.E. (1986) 'Mother–child interaction and children's speech progress: a longitudinal study of the first two years', *Merrill-Palmer Quarterly*, 32, pp. 1-20.

Olson, R.K., Wise, B., Conners, F., Rack, J. and Fulker, D. (1989) 'Specific deficits in component reading and language skills: genetic and environmental influences', *Journal of Learning Disabilities*, 22, pp. 339–48.

Olton, D.S. (1976) 'Spatial memory', *Scientific American*, 236, pp. 82–98.

Orne, M.T. (1962) 'On the social psychology of the psychology experiment with particular reference to demand characteristics and their implications', *American Psychologist*, 16, pp. 776–83.

Orne, M.T. and Holland, C.C. (1968) 'On the ecological validity of laboratory deceptions', *International Journal of Psychiatry*, 6(4), pp. 282–93.

O'Rourke, T.E., Penrod, S.D., Cutler, B.L. and Stuve, T.E. (1989) 'The external validity of eyewitness identification research: generalising across subject populations', *Law and Human Behaviour*, 13, pp. 385–95.

Osterwell, Z. and Nagano-Hakamura, K. (1992) 'Maternal views on aggression: Japan and Israel', *Aggressive Behaviour*, 18, pp. 263–70.

Oswald, I. (1980) *Sleep* (4th edn), Harmondsworth: Penguin Books.

Overmier, J.B.L. and Seligman, M.E.P. (1967) 'Effect of inescapable shock upon subsequent escape and avoidance learning', *Journal of Comparative and Physiological Psychology*, 63, pp. 28–33.

Owen, F., Cross, A.J., Crow, T.J. and Poulter, M. (1978) 'Increased dopamine receptor sensitivity in schizophrenia', *Lancet*, 2, pp. 223–6

Owusu-Bempah, J. and Howitt, D. (1990) Racism and the British Psychological Society, Unpublished manuscript.

Packer, C. (1977) 'Reciprocal altruism in *Papio anubis*', *Nature*, 265, pp. 441–3.

Packer, C. (1986) 'The ecology of felids', in D.I. Rubenstein and R.W. Wrangham (eds) *Ecological Aspects of Social Evolution*, Princeton, New Jersey: Princeton University Press.

Packer, C., Scheel, D. and Pusey, A.E. (1990) 'Why lions form groups: food is not enough', *American Naturalist*, 136, pp. 1–19.

Papez, J.W. (1937) 'A proposed mechanism of emotion', *Archives of Neurology and Psychiatry (Chicago)*, 38, pp. 725–43.

Parke, R.D. and Slaby, R.G. (1983) 'The development of aggression', in E.M. Hetherington (ed.) *Handbook of Child Psychology*, Vol. 4, *Socialisation, Personality and Social Development*, New York: Wiley.

Parke, R.D., Berkowitz, L., Leyens, J.P., West, S.G. and Sebastian, R.J. (1977) 'Some effects of violent and non-violent movies on the behaviour of juvenile delinquents', in L. Berkowitz (ed.) (1977) *Advances in Experimental Social Psychology*, Vol. 10, New York: Academic Press.

Parker, G. (1979) 'Reported parental characteristics of agoraphobics and social phobics', *British Journal of Psychiatry*, 135, pp. 555–60.

Parkinson, J. (1817) 'Essay on the shaking palsy', reprinted in M. Critchley (ed.) *James Parkinson*, London: Macmillan, 1955.

Parson, E.R. (1993) 'Children of community trauma: Inner city violence, images of the media and therapists' perceptions and response', in J.P. Wilson and J. Lindy (eds) *Countertransference in the Treatment of Post-traumatic Stress Disorder*, New York: Guildford Press.

Patterson, F. (1978) 'The gestures of a gorilla: sign language acquisition in another pongid species', *Brain and Language*, 5, pp. 72-97.

Patterson, F. (1979) 'Conversation with a gorilla', *National Geographic*, 154(4), pp. 438–65.

Pavlov, I.P. (1927) *Conditioned Reflexes*, Oxford: Oxford University Press.

Pavlov, I.P. (1941) *Conditioned Reflexes and Psychiatry*, New York: International Publishers.

Pavlov, I.P. (1955) *Selected Works*, New York: Foreign Languages.

Paykel, E.S. (1981) 'Have multivariate statistics contributed to classification?', *British Journal of Psychiatry*, 139, pp. 357–62.

Payne, K. and Payne, R. (1985) 'Large scale changes over 19 years in songs of humpback whales in Bermuda', *Zeitschrift für Tierpsychologie*, 68, pp. 89–114.

Pearlin, L.I. (1980) 'Life strains and psychological distress among adults', in N.J. Smelser and E.H. Erikson (eds) *Themes of Work and Love in Adulthood*, Cambridge, Massachusetts: Harvard University Press.

Penfield, W. (1958) 'Functional localization in temporal and deep Sylvian areas', *Research Publications of the Association for Research into Nervous and Mental Disease*, 36, pp. 210–26.

Penrod, S. (1983) *Social Psychology*, Englewood Cliffs, New Jersey: Prentice-Hall.

Perlman, C. and Duck, S. (eds) (1987) *Intimate Relationships: Development, Dynamics and Deterioration*, Newbury Park, USA: Sage.

Perrin, S. and Spencer, C. (1981) 'The Asch effect: a child of its time?', *Bulletin of the British Psychological Society*, 32, pp. 405–6.

Perry, D.G. and Bussey, K. (1984) *Social Development*, Englewood Cliffs, New Jersey: Prentice Hall.

Peters, L.H., Hartke, D.D. and Pohlmann, J.T. (1985) 'Fiedler's contingency theory of leadership: an application', *Psychological Bulletin*, 97, pp. 274–85.

Peterson, L.R. and Peterson, M.J. (1959) 'Short-term retention of individual items', *Journal of Experimental Psychology*, 58, pp. 193–8.

Petkova, B. (1995) 'New views on the self: evil women – witchcraft or PMS?', *Psychology Review*, 2(1), pp. 16–19.

Petrie, M. (1994) 'Improved growth and survival of offspring of peacocks with more elaborate tails', *Nature*, 371, pp. 598–9.

Pettigrew, T.F. (1958) 'Personality and sociocultural factors in intergroup attitudes: a cross-national comparison', *Journal of Conflict Resolution*, 2, pp. 29–42.

Pettigrew, T.F. (1979) 'The ultimate attribution error: extending Allport's cognitive analysis of prejudice', *Personality and Social Psychology Bulletin*, 5, pp. 461–76.

Petty, R.E. and Cacioppo, J.T. (1981) 'Attitudes and Persuasion: classic and contemporary approaches', Dubuque, Iowa: Wm C. Brown.

Petty, R.E. and Cacioppo, J.T. (1986) 'The elaboration likelihood model of persuasion', in L. Berkowitz (ed.) *Advances in Experimental Social Psychology*, Hillsdale, New Jersey: Erlbaum.

Pi-Sunyer, X., Kissileff, H.R., Thornton, J. and Smith, G.P. (1982) 'C–terminal octapeptide of cholecystokinin decreases food intake in obese men', *Physiology and Behavior*, 29, pp. 627–30.

Piaget, J. (1932) *The Moral Judgement of the Child*, Harmondsworth: Penguin.

Piaget, J. (1954) *The Construction of Reality in the Child*, New York: Basic Books.

Piliavin, I., Rodin, J. and Piliavin, J. (1969) 'Good Samaritanism: an underground phenomenon?', *Journal of Personality and Social Psychology*, 13, pp. 289–99.

Piliavin, J.A., Dovidio, J.F., Gaertner, S.L. and Clark, R.D. (1981) *Emergency Intervention*, New York: Academic Press.

Plowden Report (1967) *Children and their Primary Schools* (Central Advisory Council for Education), London: HMSO.

Pollin, W. and Stabenau, J. (1968) 'Biological, psychological and historical differences in a series of monozygotic twins discordant for schizophrenia', in D. Rosenthal and S. Kety (eds) *Transmission of Schizophrenia*, London: Pergamon Press.

Pollock, K. (1988) 'On the nature of social stress: production of a modern mythology', *Social Science and Medicine*, 26, pp. 381–92.

Pomerantz, J. (1981) 'Perceptual organization in information processing', in M. Kubovy and J. Pomerantz (eds) *Perceptual Organization*, Hillsdale, New Jersey: Erlbaum.

Pomerlau, A., Bolduc, D., Malcuit, G. and Cossette, L. (1990) 'Pink or blue: environmental gender stereotypes in the first two years of life', *Sex Roles*, 22, pp. 359–67.

Popper, K. (1959) The Logic of Scientific Discovery New York: Basic Books.

Porter, D.M. and Graham, P.W. (eds) (1993), *The Portable Darwin*, Harmondsworth: Penguin Books.

Posner, M.I., and Snyder, C.R.R. (1975) 'Facilitation and inhibition in the processing of signals', in P.M.A. Rabbitt and S. Dornic (eds) *Attention and Performance: V*, London: Academic Press.

Pratkanis A.R. and Aronson, E. (1992) *Age of Propaganda: The Everyday Use and Abuse of Persuasion*, New York: W.H. Freeman.

Prentice, P. (1995) 'Rational–emotive therapy', *Psychology Review*, 2(2), pp. 28–31.

Price, L.H. (1968) 'The genetics of depressive behaviour', in A. Coppen and S. Walk (eds) *Recent developments in affective disorders, British Journal of Psychiatry* Special Publication No. 2.

Profet, M. (1992) 'Pregnancy sickness as adaptation: a deterrent to maternal ingestion of teratogens' in J.H. Barkow, L. Cosmides and J. Tooby (1992) *The Adapted Mind: Evolutionary Psychology and the Generation of Culture*, Oxford: Oxford University Press.

Pulliam, H.R. and Caraco, T. (1984) 'Living in groups: is there an optimal group size?', in J.R. Krebs and N.B. Davies (1987) *An Introduction to Behavioural Ecology* (2nd edn), London: Blackwell.

Quigley, S. and Paul, P. (1987) 'Deafness and language development', in S. Rosenberg (ed.) *Advances in Applied Psychologuistics*, Vol. 1, *Disorders of First Language Development*, Cambridge: Cambridge University Press.

Rack, J.P., Hulme, C., Snow, M.J. and Wightman, J. (1994) 'The role of phonology in young children's learning of sight words: the direct mapping hypothesis', *Journal of Experimental Child Psychology*, 57, pp. 42–71.

Rack, J.P., Snowling, M.J. and Olson, R.K. (1992) 'The nonword reading deficit in developmental dyslexia: a review', *Reading Research Quarterly*, 27, pp. 28–53.

Rack, P. (1982) *Race, Culture and Mental Disorder*, London: Routledge.

Randrup, A. and Munkvad, I. (1966) 'On the role of dopamine in the amphetamine excitatory response', *Nature*, 211, p. 540.

Ranta, E., Peuhkuri, N., Laurila, A., Hannu, R. and Metcalfe, N.B. (1996) 'Producers, scroungers and foraging group structure', *Animal Behaviour*, 51, pp. 171–5.

Rapoport, J.L., Buchsbaum, M.S., Zahn, T.P., Weingartner, H., Ludlow, C. and Mikkelson, E.J. (1978) 'Dextroamphetamine: cognitive and behavioral effects in normal prepubertal boys', *Science*, 199, pp. 560–3.

Raven, B. and Haley, R.W. (1980) 'Social influence in a medical context', in L. Bickman (ed.) *Applied Social Psychology Annual*, Vol. 1, Beverley Hills, California: Sage.

Read, T., Potter, M. and Gurling, H.M.D. (1992) 'The genetics of schizophrenia', in D.J. Kavanagh (eds) *Schizophrenia*, London: Chapman & Hall.

Reason, J. (1990) *Human Error*, Cambridge: Cambridge University Press.

Reason, J.T. (1979) 'Actions not as planned: the price of automatization', in G. Underwood and R. Stevens (eds) *Aspects of Consciousness*, Vol. 1, London: Academic Press.

Reason, J.T. and Mycielska, K. (1982) *Absent Minded? The Psychology of Mental Lapses and Everyday Errors*, Englewood Cliffs, New Jersey: Prentice-Hall.

Regan, T. and Singer, P. (eds) (1976) *Animal Rights and Human Obligations*, Englewood Cliffs, New Jersey: Prentice-Hall.

Reich, J. and Yates, W. (1988) 'Family history of psychiatric disorders in social phobia', *Comprehensive Psychiatry*, 29, pp. 72–5.

Reicher, G.M. (1969) 'Perceptual recognition as a function of meaningfulness of stimulus material', *Journal of Experimental Psychology*, 81, pp. 274–80.

Reicher, S.D. (1984) 'The St Paul's riot: an explanation of the limits of crowd action in terms of a social identity model', *European Journal of Social Psychology*, 14, pp. 1–21.

Reicher, S.D. and Potter, J. (1985) 'Psychological theory as intergroup perspective: a comparative analysis of 'scientific' and 'lay' accounts of crowd events', *Human Relations*, 38, pp. 167–89.

Reitman, J.S. (1974) 'Without surreptitious rehearsal, information in short-term memory decays', *Journal of Verbal Learning and Verbal Behaviour*, 13, pp. 365–77.

Rennie, J. (1992) 'Living together', *Scientific American*, 266, pp. 104–13.

Rescorla, R.A. (1988) 'Pavlovian conditioning: it's not what you think it is', *American Psychologist*, 43, pp. 151–60.

Reskin, B.F. and Visher, C.A. (1986) 'The impacts of evidence and extra legal factors in jurors' decisions', *Law and Society Review*, 20, pp. 423–38.

Rest, J.R. (1983) 'Morality', in J. Flavell and E. Markman (eds) *Handbook of Child Psychology*, Vol. 3, *Cognitive Development*, New York: Wiley.

Reynolds, P.C. (1981) *On the Evolution of Human Behaviour*, Berkeley and Los Angeles: University of California Press.

Rheingold, H.L. and Cook, K.V. (1975) 'The content of boys' and girls' rooms as an index of parent behaviour', *Child Development*, 46, pp. 459–63.

Richardson, J.T.E. (1984) 'Developing the theory of working memory', *Memory and Cognition*, 12, pp. 71–83.

Riger, S. (1992) 'Epistemological debates, feminist voices: science, social values, and the study of women', *American Psychologist*, 47, p. 730.

Roberts, L.G. (1965) 'Machine perception of three-dimensional solids', in J.T. Tippett, D.A. Berkowitz, L.C. Clapp, C.J. Koester and A. Vanderburgh (eds) *Optical and Electro-optical Information-Processing*, Cambridge, Massachusetts: MIT Press.

Robertson, J. and Bowlby, J. (1952) 'Responses of young children to separation from their mothers', *Courier Centre International L'Enfance*, 2, pp. 131–42.

Robertson, J. and Robertson, J. (1971) 'Young child in brief separation', *Psychoanalytic Study of the Child*, 26, pp. 264–315.

Robinson, J.A. (1992) 'First experience memories: contexts and functions in personal histories', in M.A. Conway, D.C. Rubin, H. Spinnler and W.A. Wagenaar *Theoretical Perspectives on Autobiographical Memory*, Dordrecht, Netherlands: Kluwer Academic Publishers.

Rodin, J. and Janis, I.L. (1982) 'The social influence of physicians and other health care practitioners as agents of change', in H.S. Friedman and M.R. DiMatteo (eds), *Interpersonal Issues in Health Care*, New York: Academic Press.

Rodin, J. and Langer, E.J. (1977) 'Long-term effects of a control-relevant intervention with the institutionalised aged', *Journal of Personality and Social Psychology*, 35, pp. 897–902.

Rogers, C.R. (1951) *Client-centred Therapy*, Boston: Houghton Mifflin.

Rogers, C.R. (1959) 'A theory of therapy, personality and interpersonal relationships, as developed in the client-centered framework', in S. Koch (ed.), *Psychology: A Study of Science*, Vol. 3, New York: McGraw-Hill.

Rogers, C.R. (1974) 'In retrospect: forty-six years', *American Psychologist*, 29, pp. 115–23.

Rokeach, M. (1960) *The Open and Closed Mind*, New York: Basic Books.

Rondal, J.A. (1988) 'Down's syndrome', in D. Bishop and K. Mogford (eds) *Language Development in Exceptional Circumstances*, Edinburgh: Churchill Livingstone.

Rose, G. and Marshall, T.F. (1974) *Counselling and School Social Work: An Experimental Study*, London: Wiley.

Rosenberg, M. (1979) *Conceiving the Self*, New York: Basic Books.

Rosenhan and Seligman (1995) *Abnormal Psychology* (3rd edn), New York: Norton.

Rosenhan, D.L. (1969) 'Some origins of concern for others', in P. Mussen, J. Langer and M. Covington (eds) *Trends and Issues in Developmental Psychology*, New York: Holt, Rinehart and Winston.

Rosenhan, D.L. (1973) 'On being sane in insane places', *Science*, 179, pp. 250-8.

Rosenthal, A.M. (1964) *Thirty-eight Witnesses*, New York: McGraw-Hill.

Rosenthal, R. (1985) 'From unconscious experimenter bias to teacher expectancy effects', in J. Dusek (ed.) *Teacher Expectancies*, London: Erlbaum.

Rosenzweig, M.R. (1984) 'Experience, memory and the brain', *American Psychologist*, 39, pp. 365–76.

Ross, L.D. (1977) 'The intuitive psychologist and his shortcomings: distortions in the attribution process', in L. Berkowitz (ed.) *Advances in Experimental Social Psychology*, Vol. 10, New York: Academic Press.

Ross, L.D., Amabile, T.M. and Steinmetz, J.L. (1977) 'Social roles, social control, and biases in social-perception processes', *Journal of Personality and Social Psychology*, 35, pp. 485–94.

Ross, L.D., Lepper, M. and Hubbard, M. (1974) 'Perseverance in self perception and social perception: biased attributional processes in the debriefing paradigm', *Journal of Personality and Social Psychology*, 32, pp. 880–92.

Rotter, J.B. (1966) 'Generalised expectancies for internal versus external control of reinforcement', *Psychological Monographs*, 80, pp. 1–28.

Rowe, E.J. (1974) 'Depth of processing in a frequency judgment task', *Journal of Verbal Learning and Verbal Behaviour*, 13, pp. 638–43.

Rubin, K.H. and Schneider, F.W. (1973) 'The relationship between moral judgement, egocentrism and altruistic behaviour', *Child Development*, 44, pp. 661–5.

Rubin, Z. (1973) *Liking and Loving*, New York: Holt, Rinehart & Winston.

Rubin, Z. and McNeil, E.B. (1983) *The Psychology of Being Human* (3rd edn), London: Harper & Row.

Ruble, D. (1988) 'Sex role development', in M. Bornstein and M. Lamb (eds) *Developmental Psychology: An Advanced Textbook* (2nd edn), Hillsdale New Jersey: Erlbaum.

Rumelhart, D.E. and Norman, D.A. (1983) 'Representation in memory', in R.C. Atkinson, R.J. Herrnstein, G. Lindsey and R.D. Luce (eds.) *Handbook of Experimental Psychology*, Chichester: Wiley.

Runyon, R. and Haber, A. (1976) *Fundamentals of Behavioural Statistics* (3rd edn), Reading, Massachusetts: McGraw Hill.

Rushton, J.P. (1989) 'Genetic similarity, mate choice and fecundity in humans', *Ethology and Sociobiology*, 9, pp. 329–33.

Russell, C.S. (1974) 'Transition to parenthood: Problems and gratifications', *Journal of Marriage and the Family*, 36, pp. 294–302.

Rust, J. and Golombok, S. (1992) *Modern Psychometrics: The Science of Psychological Assessment*, London: Routledge.

Rutter, M. (1976) 'Parent–child separation: psychological effects on the child', in A. M. Clarke and A.D.B. Clarke (eds) *Early Experience: Myth and Evidence*, London: Open Books.

Rutter, M. (1981) *Maternal Deprivation Reassessed* (2nd edn), Harmondsworth: Penguin.

Rutter, M., Graham, P., Chadwock, O. and Yule, W. (1976) 'Adolescent turmoil: fact or fiction?', *Journal of Child Psychology and Psychiatry*, 7, pp. 35–56.

Sachs, J., Bard, B. and Johnson, M.L. (1981) 'Language with restricted input: case studies of two hearing children of deaf parents', *Applied Psycholinguistics*, 2, pp. 33–54.

Sackeim, H.A. (1988) 'The efficacy of electroconvulsive therapy', *Ann. NY Academic Science*, 462, pp. 70–5.

Sackeim, H.A., Nordlie, J.W. and Gur, R.C. (1993) 'Effects of stimulus intensity and electrode replacement on the efficacy of the effects of electroconvulsive therapy', *New England Journal of Medicine*, 328, pp. 839–46.

Saegert, S., Swap, W. and Zajonc, R.B. (1973) 'Exposure, contact and interpersonal attraction', *Journal of Personality and Social Psychology*, 25, pp. 234–42.

Saks, M.J. and Krupat, E. (1988) *Social Psychology and its Applications*, New York: Harper and Row.

Sales, E., Baum, M. and Shore, B. (1984) 'Victim readjustment following assault', *Journal of Social Issues*, 37, pp. 5–27 and 40(1), pp. 117–36.

Sameroff, A.S. and Seifer, R. (1983) 'Familial role and child competence', *Child Development*, 54, pp. 1254–68.

Samerotte, G.C. and Harris, M.B. (1976) 'Some factors influencing helping: the effects of handicap, responsibility and requesting help', *Journal of Social Psychology*, 98, pp. 39–45.

Sarbin, T.R and Slagle, R.W. (1972) 'Hypnosis and psychophysiological outcomes', in E. Fromm and R.E. Shor (eds) *Hypnosis: Research, Developments and Perspectives*, Chicago: Aldine-Atherton.

Sargant, W. (1957) *Battle for the Mind: A Physiology of Conversion and Brainwashing*, New York: Doubleday.

Savage-Rumbaugh, S. (1988) 'A new look at ape language: comprehension of vocal speech and syntax', *Nebraska Symposium on Motivation*, 35, pp. 201–55.

Savin, H.B. (1973) 'Professors and psychological researchers: conflicting values in conflicting roles', *Cognition*, 2 (1), pp. 147–9.

Sawto, K.L. (1975) 'Social approval and helping', *Journal of Experimental Social Psychology*, 62, pp. 356–63.

Scandura, T.A. and Graen, G.B. (1984) 'Moderating effects of initial leader–member exchange status on the effects of a leadership intervention', *Journal of Applied Psychology*, 69, pp. 428–36.

Scarr, S. and Weinberg, R.A. (1976) 'IQ test performance of black children adopted by white families', *American Psychologist*, 31, pp. 726–39.

Scarr, S. and Weinberg, R.A. (1983) 'The Minnesota adoption studies: generation differences and malleability', *Child Development*, 54, pp. 260–7.

Schachter, S. (1971) 'Some extraordinary facts about obese humans and rats', *American Psychologist*, 26, pp. 129–44.

Schachter, S. and Singer, J.E. (1962) 'Cognitive, social, and physiological determinants of emotional state', *Psychological Review*, 69, pp. 379–99.

Schaffer, H.R. (1990) *Making Decisions about Children*, Oxford: Blackwell.

Schaffer, H.R. and Callender, W.M. (1959) 'Psychologic effect of hospitalisation in infancy', *Pediatrics*, 24, pp. 528–39.

Schaffer, H.R. and Emerson, P.E. (1964) *The Development of Social Attachments in Infancy*, Monographs of the Society for Research in Child Development, 29(3), Serial No. 94.

Schaie, K.W. (1965) 'A general model for the study of developmental problems', *Psychological Bulletin*, 64, pp. 92–107.

Schank, R. and Abelson, R. (1977) *Scripts, Plans, Goals and Understanding: An Enquiry into Human Knowledge*, New Jersey: Erlbaum.

Schank, R.C. (1982) *Dynamic Memor* Cambridge: Cambridge University Press.

Scheff, T.J. (1966) *Being Mentally Sociological Theory*, Chicago: Al

Scheper-Hughes, N. (1992) *Dect Weeping: The Violence of Every Brazil*, Berkeley: University o California Press.

Schlesinger, H.S. and Meadow (1972) *Sound and Sign: Childhood Deafness and Mental Health*, Berkeley: University of California Press.

Schmid-Hempel, P. (1986) 'Do honey bees get tired? The effect of load weight on patch departure', *Animal Behaviour*, 34, pp. 1243–50.

Schneider, B.H. (1991) 'A comparison of skill-building and desensitization strategies for intervention with aggressive children', *Aggressive Behaviour*, 17, pp. 301–11.

Schriesham, C.A., Hinkin, T.R. and Podsakoss, P.M. (1991) 'Can ipsative and single item measures produce erroneous results in the field studies of French and Raven's five bases of power? An impirical investigation', *Journal of Applied Psychology*, 76, pp. 106–114.

Schwartz, S. (1977) 'Normative influences on altruism', in L. Berkowitz (ed.) *Advances in Experimental Social Psychology*, Vol. 10, New York: Academic Press.

Scott M.J. and Stradling, S.G. (1994) 'Post-traumatic stress disorder without the trauma', *British Journal of Clinical Psychology*, 33, pp. 71–4.

Scott, J.P. (1992) 'Aggression: functions and control in social systems', *Aggressive Behaviour*, 18, pp. 1–20.

Scott, J.P. and Fuller, J.L. (1965) *Genetics and the Social Behaviour of the Dog*, Chicago: Chicago University Press.

Scoville, W.B. and Milner, B. (1957) 'Loss of recent memory after bilateral hippocampal lesions', *Journal of Neurology, Neurosurgery and Psychiatry*, 20, pp. 11–21.

Scully, D. and Marolla, J. (1984) 'Convicted rapists' vocabulary of motive: excuses and justifications', *Social Problems*, 31, pp. 530–44

Sears, D.O., Peplau, L.A. and Taylor, S.E. (1991) *Social Psychology* (7th edn), Englewood Cliffs, New Jersey: Prentice-Hall.

Secretary of State for Health (1992) *The Health of the Nation*, London: HMSO.

Seeley, T.D. (1993) 'The ecology of temperate and tropical honeybee societies', in P.W Sherman and J. Alcock (eds) *Exploring Animal Behaviour*, Sunderland, Massachusetts: Sinauer Associates.

Segal, L. (1990) *Slow Motion: Changing Masculinities, Changing Men*, New Brunswick, USA: Rutgers University Press.

Segall, M.H., Campbell, D.T. and Herskovits, M.J (1963) 'Cultural differences in the perception of geometric illusions', *Science*, 139, pp. 769–71.

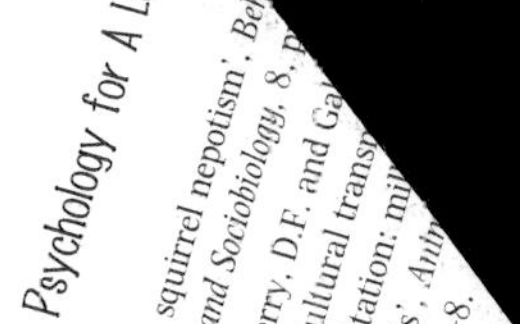

and ... *Depression: ...* Research, Washington, ... Wiley.

Seligman, M.E.P. (1975) *Helplessness: On Depression, Development and Death*, London: W.H. Freeman.

Selman, R. (1980) *The Growth of Interpersonal Understanding*, New York: Academic Press.

Selye, H. (1956) *The Stress of Life*, New York: McGraw–Hill.

Serbin, L.A., Powlishta, K.K. and Gulko, J. (1993) 'The development of sex typing in middle childhood', *Monographs of the Society for Research in Child Development*, 58(2), No. 232.

Seyfarth, D.M., Cheney, D.L. and Marler, P. (1980) 'Monkey responses to three different alarms: evidence for predator classification and semantic communication', *Science* 210, pp. 801–3.

Seyfarth, R.M. and Cheyney, D.L. (1992) 'Meaning and mind in monkeys', *Scientific American*, 267, pp. 122–8.

Shaffer, L.H. (1975) 'Multiple attention in continuous verbal tasks', in P.M.A. Rabbitt and S. Dornic (eds) *Attention and Performance: V*, London: Academic Press.

Shallice, T. and Warrington, E.K. (1970) 'Independent functioning of verbal memory stores: a neuropsychological study', *Quarterly Journal of Experimental Psychology*, 22, pp. 261–73.

Shanab, M.E. and Yahya, K.A. (1978) 'A cross-cultural study of obedience', *Bulletin of the Psychonomic Society*, 11, pp. 267–9.

Shepher, J. (1971) 'Mate selection among second generation kibbutz adolescents: incest avoidance and negative imprinting', *Archives of Sexual Behaviour*, 1, pp. 293–307.

Sherif, M. (1935) 'A study of some factors in perception', *Archives of Psychology*, 27.

Sherif, M., Harvey, O.J., White, B.J., Hood, W.R. and Sherif, C.W. (1961) *Intergroup conflict and cooperation: the robber's cave experiment*, Norman, Oklahoma: University of Oklahoma.

Sherman, M.A. (1976) 'Adjectival negation and the comprehension of multiply negated sentences', *Journal of Verbal Learning and Verbal Behaviour*, 15, pp. 143–57.

Sherman, P.W. (1981) 'Kinship, demography and Belding's ground

...avioral Ecology ...p. 251–59.

...ef, B.G. (1984) ...ission without ...k bottle opening by ...al Behaviour, 32, pp.

...R.M. and Schneider, W. (1977) ...trolled and automatic human ...formation processing II: Perceptual learning, automatic attending and a general theory', *Psychological Review*, 84, pp. 127–90.

Short, R.V. and Balban, E. (1991) *The Difference between the Sexes*, Cambridge: Cambridge University Press.

Shotland, R.L. and Huston, T.L. (1979) 'Emergencies: what are they and do they influence bystanders to intervene?', *Journal of Personality and Social Psychology*, 37(10), pp. 1822–34.

Shotland, R.L. and Straw, M.K. (1976) 'Bystander response to an assault: when a man attacks a woman', *Journal of Personality and Social Psychology*, 34, pp. 990–9.

Sieber, J.E. and Stanley, B. (1988) 'Ethical and professional dimensions of socially sensitive research', *American Psychologist*, 43 (1), pp. 49–55.

Simon, R.W., Eder, D. and Evans, C. (1992) 'The development of feeling norms underlying romantic love among adolescent females', *Social Psychology Quarterly*, 55(1), pp. 29–46.

Singer, P. and Cavalieri, P. (eds) (1993) *The Great Ape Project: Equality beyond Humanity*, London: Fourth Estate.

Sizemore, C.C. and Pittillo, E.S. (1977) *I'm Eve*, New York: Doubleday.

Skal, D.J. (1993) *The Monster Show: A Cultural History of Horror*, New York: Norton.

Skinner, B.F. (1938) *The Behavior of Organisms*, New York: Appleton-Century-Crofts.

Skinner, B.F. (1953) *Science and Human Behaviour*, New York: Macmillan.

Skinner, B.F. (1957) *Verbal Behaviour*, New York: Appleton-Century-Crofts.

Skinner, B.F. (1971) *Beyond Freedom and Dignity*, New York: Knopf.

Skinner, B.F. (1974) *About Behaviourism*, New York: Knopf.

Skinner, B.F. (1981) 'Selection by consequences', *Science*, 213, pp. 501–4.

Skinner, B.F. (1987) 'What is wrong with daily life in the Western world?', in B.F. Skinner *Upon Further Reflection*, Englewood Cliffs, New Jersey: Prentice-Hall.

Slater, A. and Morison, V. (1985) 'Shape constancy and slant perception at birth', *Perception*, 14, pp. 337–44.

Slater, E. and Sheilds, J. (1969) 'Genetic aspects of anxiety', *British Journal of Psychiatry*, 3, pp. 62–71.

Slater, P.J.B. and Halliday, T.R. (1994) *Behaviour and Evolution*, Cambridge: Cambridge University Press.

Slife, B.D. and Williams, R.N. (1995) *What's behind the Research? Discovering Hidden Assumptions in the Behavioural Sciences*, Thousand Oaks: Sage.

Slobin, D.I. (1985) 'Cross-linguistic evidence for the language-making capacity', in D. I. Slobin (ed.) *The Cross-linguistic Study of Language Acquisition*, Vol. 2, *Theoretical Issues*, Hillsdale, New Jersey: Erlbaum.

Smith, K.D., Keating, J.P. and Stotland, E. (1989) 'Altruism reconsidered: the effect of denying feedback on a victim's status to empathetic witnesses', *Journal of Personality and Social Psychology*, 57, pp. 641–50.

Smith, M.L. and Glass, G.V. (1977) 'Meta-analysis of psychotherapy outcome studies', *American Psychologist*, 32, pp. 752–60.

Smith, P. and Bond, M.H. (1993) *Social Psychology Across Cultures: Analysis and Perspectives*, Harvester Wheatsheaf: New York.

Smith, P. and Noble, R. (1987) 'Factors affecting the development of caregiver–infant relationships', in L.W. Tavecchio and M.H. van IJzendoorn (eds) *Attachment in Social Networks*, Amsterdam: North Holland.

Smith, P.B. and Peterson, M.F. (1988) *Leadership, Organisations and Culture*, London: Sage.

Smith, P.K and Cowie, M (1988, 1993 [2nd edn]) *Understanding Children's Development*, London: Blackwell.

Snarey, J.R., Reimer, J. and Kohlberg, L. (1985) 'Development of social–moral reasoning among kibbutz adolescents: a longitudinal cross-cultural study', *Developmental Psychology*, 21, pp. 3–17.

Snedecor, G.W. (1956) *Statistical Methods*, Iowa State University Press.

Snow, C.E. (1994) 'Beginning from baby talk: twenty years of research on input and interaction', in C. Gallaway and B. Richards (eds) *Input and Interaction in Language Acquisition*, Cambridge: Cambridge University Press.

Sodian, B. and Frith, U. (1990) 'The theory of mind deficit in autism: evidence from deception', in S. Baron-Cohen, H. Tager-Flusberg and D. Cohen (eds) *Understanding Others' Minds*, Oxford: Oxford University Press.

Solyom, L., Beck, P., Solyom, C. and Hugel, R. (1974) 'Some etiological factors in phobic neurosis', *Canadian Psychiatric Association Journal*, 21, pp. 109–13.

Spanos, N.P. (1982) 'A social psychological approach to hypnotic behaviour', in G. Weary and H.L. Mirels (eds) *Integrations of Clinical and Social Psychology*, New York: Oxford University Press.

Spender, D. (1980) *Man-made Language*, London: Routledge & Kegan Paul.

Sperling, G. (1960) 'The information available in brief visual presentations', *Psychological Monographs*, 74, pp. 1–29.

Sperry, R.W. (1982) 'Some effects of disconnecting the cerebral hemispheres', *Science*, 217, pp. 1223–6.

Spiegel, R. (1989) *Psychopharmacology* (2nd edn), New York: Wiley.

Spiegel, T.A. (1973) 'Caloric regulation of food intake in man', *Journal of Comparative and Physiological Psychology*, 84, pp. 24–37.

Spitzer, R.L. and Williams, J.B.W. (1985) 'Classification in psychiatry', in H.I. Kaplan and B.J. Sadock (eds) *Comprehensive Textbook of Psychiatry* (4th edn), Baltimore: Williams and Wilkins.

Sprafkin, J.N. and Rubinstein, E.A. (1979) 'A field correlational study of children's television viewing habits and prosocial behaviour', *Journal of Broadcasting*, 23, pp. 265–76.

Srole, L., Langner, T.S., Michael, S.T. and Opler, M.K. (1961) *Mental Health in the Metropolis*, New York: McGraw-Hill.

Sroufe, L.A. (1983) 'Individual papers of adaption from infancy to preschool', in M. Perlmutter (ed.) *Minnesota Symposium on Child Psychology*, Hillsdale, New Jersey: Erlbaum.

Staub, E. (1978) *Positive Social Behaviour and Morality*, Vol. 1, *Social and Personal Influences*. New York: Academic Press.

Steele, C.M. and Southwick, L. (1985) 'Alcohol and social behaviour. I. The psychology of drunken excess', *Journal of Personality and Social Psychology*, 48, pp. 18–34.

Stein, A.H. and Friedrich, L.K. (1972) 'Television content and young children's behaviour', in J.P. Murray, E.A. Rubinstein and G.A. Comstock (eds) *Television and Social Behaviour*, Vol. 2, *Television and Social Learning*, Washington DC: US Government Printing Office.

Steiner, W. (1991) 'Fluoxetine-induced mania in a patient with obsessive-compulsive disorder', *American Journal of Psychiatry*, 148, pp. 1403–4.

Stephenson, G.M. (1992) *The Psychology of Criminal Justice*, Oxford: Blackwell.

Stern, W.C. and Morgane, P.J. (1974) 'Theoretical view of REM sleep: maintenance of catecholamine systems in the central nervous system', *Behavioral Biology*, 11, pp. 1–32.

Sternberg, R.J. (1985) *Beyond IQ: A Triarchic Theory of Human Intelligence*, Cambridge: Cambridge University Press.

Stevenson, H.W. and Stigler, J.W. (1992) *The Learning Gap*, New York: Summit Books.

Stewart, D. A. (1992) 'Initiating reform in total communication programs', *Journal Special Education*, 26(1), pp. 68–84.

Stokoe, W.C. (1960) 'Sign language structure: an outline of the visual communicative system of the American deaf', *Studies in Linguistics*, Paper 8, University of Buffalo.

Stouffer, S.A., Suchman, E.A., Di Vinney, L.C., Starr, S.A. and Williams, R.M. (1949) *The American Soldier: Adjustment during Army Life*, Vol. 1, Princeton, New Jersey: Princeton University Press.

Stratton, P. and Hayes, N. (1993) *A Student's Dictionary of Psychology* (2nd edn), London: Edward Arnold.

Strongman, K.T. (1987) *The Psychology of Emotion* (3rd edn), Chichester: Wiley.

Stroop, J.R. (1935) 'Studies of interference in serial verbal reactions', *Journal of Experimental Psychology*, 18, pp. 643–62.

Strube, M., Turner, C.W., Cerro, D., Stevens, J. and Hinchey, F. (1984) 'Interpersonal aggression and the Type A coronary-prone behaviour pattern: a theoretical distinction and practical implications', *Journal of Personality and Social Psychology*, 47, pp. 839–47.

Strube, M.J. and Garcia, J.E. (1981) 'A meta-analytic investigation of Fiedler's contingency model of leadership effectiveness', *Psychologicial Bulletin*, 90, pp. 307–21.

Stuart, R.J. (1991) 'Kin recognition as a functional concept', *Animal Behaviour*, 41, pp. 1093–4.

Sue, D.W. and Sue, D. (1990) *Counselling the Culturally Different*, New York: Wiley.

Sugarman, L. (1986) *Life Span Development*, London: Methuen.

Suppes, T., Baldessarini, R.J. and Faedda, G.L. (1991) 'Risk of recurrence following discontinuation of lithium treatment in bipolar disorder', *Archives of General Psychiatry*, 48, pp. 1082–7.

Sutton, C. (1979) *Psychology for Social Workers and Counsellors: An Introduction*, London: Routledge & Kegan Paul.

Svejda M. J., Campos, J.J. and Emde, R.N. (1980) 'Mother–infant "bonding": failure to generalise', *Child Development*, 51, pp. 775–9.

Szasz, T. (1972) *The Manufacture of Madness*, London: Routledge and Kegan Paul.

Szatmari, P. and Jones, M. (1991) 'IQ and the genetics of autism', *Journal of Child Psychology and Psychiatry*, 32, pp. 897–908.

Tager-Flusberg, H. (1992) 'Autistic children's talk about psychological states: deficits in the early acquisition of a theory of mind', *Child Development*, 63, pp. 161–72.

Tajfel, H. (1970) 'Experiments in intergroup discrimination', *Scientific American*, 223, pp. 96–102.

Tajfel, H. (1982) *Social Identity and Intergroup Relations*, Cambridge: Cambridge University Press.

Taplin, J.E. (1971) 'Reasoning with conditional sentences', *Journal of Verbal Learning and Verbal Behaviour*, 10, pp. 219-25.

Tavris, C. and Wade, C. (1995) *Psychology in Perspective*, New York: HarperCollins.

Taylor, S.P. and Sears, J.D. (1988) 'The effects of alcohol and persuasive social pressure on human physical aggression', *Aggressive Behaviour*, 14, pp. 237–43.

Terrace, H.S., Petitto, L.A., Sanders, R.J. and Bever, T.G. (1979) Can an ape create a sentence?', *Science*, 206, pp. 891–902.

Thase, M.E., Frank, E. and Kupfer, D.J. (1991) 'Biological processes in major depression', in E.E. Beckham and W.R. Leber (eds) *Handbook of Depression*, Homewood, Illinois: Dorsey Press.

Thibaut, J.W. and Kelley, H.H. (1959) *The Social Psychology of Groups*, New York: Wiley.

Thigpen, C.H. and Cleckley, H. (1954) *The Three Faces of Eve*, Kingsport: Kingsport Press.

Thoma, S.J. (1986) 'Estimating gender differences in the comprehension and preference of moral issues', *Developmental Review*, 6, pp. 165–80.

Thomas and Blackman (1991) 'Are animal experiments on the way out?', *The Psychologist*, 4 (5), pp. 208–12.

Thomas, C., Stone, K., Osborne, M., Thomas, P., Fisher, M. (1993) 'Psychiatric morbidity and compulsory admission among UK-born Europeans, Afro-Caribbeans and Asians in Central Manchester', *British Journal of Psychiatry*, 163, pp. 91–9.

Thomas, J.C. (1974) 'An analysis of behaviour in the hobbits-and-orcs problem', *Cognitive Psychology*, 6, pp. 257-69.

Thompson, C.P. and Cowan, T. (1986) 'Flashbulb memories: a nicer interpretation of a Neisser recollection', *Cognition*, 22, pp. 199–200.

Thompson, R.F. (1986) 'The neurobiology of learning and memory', *Science*, 233, pp. 941–7.

Thorndike, E.L. (1911) *Animal Intelligence: Experimental Studies*, New York: MacMillan.

Thornhill, N.W. (1991) 'An evolutionary analysis of rules regulating human inbreeding and marriage', *Behavioral and Brain Sciences*, 14, pp. 247–93.

Tienari, P. et al (1987) 'Genetic and Psychosocial factors in schizophrenia: The Finnish adoptive family study', *Schizophrenia Bulletin*, 13, pp. 477–84.

Timberlake, W. (1993) 'Animal behaviour: a continuing synthesis', *Annual Review of Psychology*, 44, pp. 675–708.

Tinbergen, N. (1951) *The Study of Instinct*, Oxford: Oxford University Press.

Tinbergen, N. and Kruyt (1938) cited in Tinbergen N. (1951) *The Study of Instinct*, Oxford: Oxford University Press.

Tinbergen, N. and Perdeck, A.C. (1950) 'On the stimulus situation releasing the begging response in the newly hatched herring gull chick', *Behaviour*, 3, pp. 1–38.

Toch, H. (1985) *Violent Men* (revised edn), Cambridge, Massachusetts: Schenkman.

Tolman, E.C. (1948) 'Cognitive maps in rats and men', *Psychological Review*, 55, pp. 189–208.

Toon, F., Fraise, J., McFetridge, M. and Alwin, N. (1996) 'Memory or mirage? The FMS debate', *The Psychologist*, 9(2).

Tordoff, M.G., Novin, D. and Russek, M. (1982) 'Effects of hepatic denervation on the anorexic response to epinephrine, amphetamine, and lithium chloride: a behavioral identification of glucostatic afferents', *Journal of Comparative and Physiological Psychology*, 96, pp. 361–75.

Torgersen, S. (1983) 'Genetic factors in anxiety disorders', *Archives of General Psychiatry*, 40, pp. 1085–9.

Treisman, A. (1960) 'Contextual cues in selective listening', *Quarterly Journal of Experimental Psychology*, 12, pp. 242–8.

Treisman, A. (1964) 'Verbal cues, language and meaning in selective attention', *American Journal of Psychology*, 77, pp. 206–19.

Treisman, A. and Geffen, G. (1967) 'Selective attention: perception or response?', *Quarterly Journal of Experimental Psychology*, 19, pp. 1–18.

Trevarthen, C. (1979) 'Communication and co-operation in early infancy: a description of primary inter subjectivity', in M. Bullowa (ed.) *Before Speech*, Cambridge: Cambridge University Press.

Trevathan, W. (1987) *Human Birth: An Evolutionary Perspective*, New York: Aldine de Gruyter.

Trivers, R. (1985) *Social Evolution*, New York: Benjamin Cummings.

Trivers, R.L. (1971) 'The evolution of reciprocal altruism', *Quarterly Review of Biology*, 46, pp. 35–57.

Trivers, R.L. (1974) 'Parent–offspring conflict', *American Zoologist*, 14, pp. 249–64.

Tseng, Wen-Shing (1986) 'Chinese psychiatry: development and characteristics', in J.L. Cox (ed.) *Transcultural Psychiatry*, Beckenham, Kent: Croom Helm.

Tulving, E. (1972) 'Episodic and semantic memory', in E. Tulving and W. Donaldson (eds) *Organisation of Memory*, London: Academic Press.

Tulving, E. and Thomson, D.M. (1973) 'Encoding specificity and retrieval processes in episodic memory', *Psychological Review*, 80, pp. 352–73.

Turnbull, C.M. (1961) *The Forest People*, New York: Simon and Schuster.

Turner, J.S. and Helms, D.B. (1983) *Lifespan Development*, New York: Holt Rinehart & Winston.

Turner, R.H. and Killian, L.M. (1957), *Collective Behaviour*, Englewood Cliffs: Prentice-Hall.

Tversky, A and Kahneman, D. (1974) 'Judgement under uncertainty: heuristics and biases', *Science*, 815, pp. 1124–31.

Umbenhauer, S.L. and DeWitte, L.L. (1978) 'Patient race and social class: attitudes and decisions among three groups of mental health professionals', *Comprehensive Psychiatry*, 19(6), pp. 509–15.

Van der Kolk, B. (1988) 'The trauma spectrum: the interaction of biological and social events in the genesis of the trauma response', *Journal of Traumatic Stress*, 1, pp. 273–90.

Van Dusen, K.T., Mednick, S.A., Gabrielli, W.F. and Hutchings, B. (1983) 'Social class and crime in an adoption cohort', *Journal of Criminal Law and Criminology*, 74, pp. 249–69.

Van Orden, G.C., Pennington, B.F. and Stone, G. O. (1990) 'Word identification in reading and the promise of subsymbolic psycholinguistics', *Psychological Review*, 97, pp. 488–522.

Van Yperen, N.W. and Buunck, B.P (1990) 'A longitudinal study of equity and satisfaction in intimate relationships', *European Journal of Social Psychology*, 20, pp. 287–310.

van IJzendoorn, M.H. and Tavecchio, L.W. (1987) 'The development of attachment theory as a Lakatosian research programme', in L.W. Tavecchio and M.H. van IJzendoorn (eds) *Attachment in Social Networks*, Amsterdam: North Holland.

Vaughn, C.E. and Leff, J.P. (1976) 'The influence of family and social factors on the course of psychiatric illness. A comparison of schizophrenia and depressed neurotic patients', *British Journal of Psychiatry*, 129, pp. 125–37.

Vellutino, F.R. (1979) *Dyslexia: Theory and Research*, Cambridge, Massachusetts: MIT Press.

Veroff, J., Douvard, E. and Kulka, R. (1981) *The Inner American*, New York: Basic Books.

Voegelin, C.F. and Voegelin, F.M. (1977) *Classification and Index of the World's Languages*, New York: Elsevier.

von Krafft-Ebing, R. (1897) in R. von Krafft-Ebing (1902) *Psychopathia Sexualis*, Brooklyn, New York: Physicians and Surgeons Books.Back, L. (1995) 'Sturm und Swing', *The Guardian*, 8 February 1995.

Vroom, V.H. and Yetton, P.W. (1973) *Leadership and Decision-making*, Pittsburgh: University of Pittsburg Press.

Vygotsky, L.S. (original 1934, reprinted 1962) *Thought and Language* (translated by E. Hanfman and G. Vakar, 1962), Cambridge, Massachusetts: MIT Press.

Wadden, T. and Ancerton, C.H. (1982) 'The clinical use of hypnosis', *Psychological Bulletin*, 91, pp. 215–43.

Waddington, D., Jones, K. and Critcher, C. (1987) 'Flashpoints of public disorder', in G. Gaskell and R. Benewick (eds) *The Crowd in Contemporary Britain*, London: Sage.

Wagstaff, G.F. (1981) *Hypnosis, Compliance and Belief*, Brighton: Harvester Press.

Walker, L. (1984) 'Sex differences in the development of moral reasoning: a critical review', *Child Development*, 55, pp. 677–91.

Walker, L. (1989) 'A longitudinal study of moral reasoning', *Child Development*, 60, pp. 157–66.

Wallston, K.A., Wallston, B.S. and Devellis, R. (1978) 'Development of the multidimensional health locus of control (MHLC) scales', *Health Education Monographs*, 6, pp. 161–70.

Walster, E. and Piliavin, J.A. (1972) 'Equity and the innocent bystander', *Journal of Social Issues*, 28(3), pp. 165–89.

Walster, E.H., Walster, G.W. and Berscheid, E. (1978) *Equity Theory and Research*, Boston, Massachusetts: Allyn and Bacon.

Waltz, D. (1975) 'Understanding line drawings of scenes with shadows', in P. Winston (ed.) *The Psychology of Computer Vision*, New York: McGraw-Hill.

Ward, P. and Zahavi, A. (1973) 'The importance of certain assemblages of birds as "information centres" for food finding', *Ibis*, 115, pp. 513–34.

Warr, P.B. (1965) 'Proximity as a determinant of positive and negative sociometric choice', *British Journal of Social and Clinical Psychology*, 4, pp. 104–9.

Wartner, U.G., Grossman, K., Fremner-Bombik, I. and Guess, G.L. (1994) 'Attachment patterns in south Germany', *Child Development*, 65, pp. 1014–27.

Wason, P.C. (1960) 'On the failure to eliminate hypotheses in a conceptual task', *Quarterly Journal of Experimental Psychology*, 12, pp. 129–40.

Waterman, A.S. (1985) 'Identity in the context of adolescent psychology', *New Directions for Child Development*, 30, pp. 5–24.

Waterman, C.K. and Waterman, A.S. (1975) 'Fathers and sons: A study of ego-identity across two generations', *Journal of Youth and Adolescence*, 4, pp. 331–8.

Waters, E. (1978) 'The reliability and stability of individual differences in infant–mother attachment', *Child Development*, 49, pp. 483–94.

Watson, G. and Glaser, E.M. (1964) *Critical Thinking Appraisal*, New York: Harcourt Brace Jovanovich.

Watson, J.B. (1913) 'Psychology as the behaviourist views it', *Psychological Review*, 20, pp. 158–77.

Watson, J.B. (1930) *Behaviourism*, New York: Norton.

Watson, J.B. and Rayner, R. (1920) 'Conditioned emotional reactions', *Journal of Experimental Psychology*, 3, pp. 1–14.

Watson, P. (1978) *War on the Mind*, London: Hutchinson.

Weatherley, D. (1961) 'Anti-semitism and the expression of fantasy aggression', *Journal of Abnormal and Social Psychology*, 62, pp. 454–7.

Wehren, A. and DeLisi, R. (1983) 'The development of gender understanding:

judgements and explanations', *Child Development*, 54, pp. 1568–78.

Weinberger, D.R. (1988) 'Premorbid neuropathology in schizophrenia', *Lancet*, 2, 959–60.

Weiskrantz, L. (1986) *Blindsight: A Case Study and Implications*, Oxford: Oxford University Press.

Weisman, A.D. (1972) *On Dying and Denying: A Psychiatric Study of Terminality*, New York: Behavioural Publications.

Weisner, T.S. and Gallimore, R. (1977) 'My brother's keeper: child and sibling caretaking', *Current Anthropology*, 18, pp. 169–90.

Weiss, J.M. (1972) 'Influence of psychological variables on stress–induced pathology', in J. Knight and R. Porter (eds), *Physiology, Emotion and Psychosomatic Illness*, Amsterdam: Elsevier.

Weissman M.M. and Klerman, G.L. (1981) 'Sex differences and the epidemiology of depression', in E. Howell and M. Bayes (eds) *Women and Mental Health*, New York: Basic Books.

Wellman, B. (1985) 'From social support to social networks', in I.G. Sarason and B.R. Sarason (eds) *Social Support: Theory, Research and Applications*, Dordrecht: Nijhoff.

Wells, G. (1985) 'Preschool literacy-related activities and success in school', in D.R. Olson, N. Torrance and A. Hildyard (eds) *Literacy, Language and Learning*, Cambridge: Cambridge University Press, pp. 229–55.

Wender, P.H., Kety, S.S., Rosenthal, D., Schulsinger, F., Ortmann, J. and Lunde, I. (1986) 'Psychiatric disorder in the biological and adoptive families of adopted individuals with affective disorders', *Archives of General Psychiatry*, 43, pp. 923–9.

Wernicke, C. (1874) *Der Aphasische Symptomenkomplex*, Breslau: Cohn & Weigert.

West, S.G. and Brown, T.J. (1975) 'Physical attractiveness, the severity of the emergency and helping', *Journal of Experimental Social Psychology*, 11, pp. 531–8.

Whalen, C.K. (1989) 'Attention deficit and hyperactivity disorders' in T. Hollendick and M. Hersen (eds) *Handbook of Child Psychopathology*, New York: Plenum.

Wheeler, S. and McLeod, J. (1995) 'Person-centred and psychodynamic counselling: a dialogue', *Counselling*, 6(4), pp. 283–7.

Wheldall, K. and Merrett, F. (1983) 'Good behaviour', *The Times Educational Supplement*, 25 November 1983, in H. Coolican *et al.* (1996) *Applied Psychology*, London: Hodder & Stoughton.

White, M. (1990), cited in P. Barnes (1995) *Personal, Social and Emotional Development of Children*, Oxford: Blackwell/Open University, p. 206.

Whiting, B. and Edwards, C. (1988) *Children of Different Worlds: The Formation of Social Behaviour*, Cambridge, Massachusetts: Harvard University Press.

Whiting, J.W. (1966) *Six Cultures Series 1: Field Guide for a Study of Socialization*, New York: Wiley.

Whorf, B. (1941) 'The relation of habitual thought and behaviour to language', in L. Spier (ed.) *Language, Culture and Personality: Essays in Memory of Edward Sapir*, Utah: University of Utah Press.

Wickler, W. (1968) *Mimicry in Plants and Animals*, New York: McGraw-Hill.

Wiens, A.N. and Menustik, C.E. (1983) 'Treatment outcomes and patient characteristics in an aversion treatment program for alcoholism', *American Psychologist*, 38, pp. 1089–96.

Wilding, J.M. (1982) *Perception – From Sense to Object*, London: Hutchinson.

Wilkinson, G.S.(1984) 'Reciprocal food sharing in the vampire bat', *Nature*, 308, pp. 181–4.

Williams, G.C. (1992) *Natural Selection: Domains, Levels and Challenges*, Oxford: Oxford University Press.

Williams, R. L. (1972) *The BITCH Test (Black Intelligence Test of Cultural Homogeneity)*, St. Louis, Missouri: Washington University.

Williams, W.T. (1992) 'The relationship between male–male friendship and male–female marriage: American Indian and Asian comparisons', in P.M. Nardi (ed.) *Men's Friendships*, Newbury Park, USA: Sage.

Williamson, G.M. and Clark, M.S. (1992) 'Impact of desired relationship type on affective reactions to choosing and being required to help', *Personality and Social Psychology Bulletin*, 18, pp. 10–18.

Wilson, E.O. (1975) *Sociobiology, The New Synthesis*, Cambridge, Massachusetts: Harvard University Press.

Wilson, E.O. (1978) *On Human Nature*, Cambridge, Massachusetts: Harvard University Press.

Wilson, E.O. (1992) *The Diversity of Life*, Harmondsworth: Penguin.

Wilson, G. (1983) *QED: The Science of Sexual Attraction*, BBC Television.

Wilson, S. (1978) 'Vandalism and "defensible space" on London housing estates', in R. Clarke *Tackling Vandalism*, Home Office Research Study No. 47, London: HMSO.

Wing, R. R., Epstein, L.H., Nowalk, M.P. and Lamparski, D.M. (1986) 'Behavioural self-regulation in the treatment of patients with diabetes mellitus', *Psychological Bulletin*, 99, pp. 78–89.

Wispe, L.G. (1972) 'Positive forms of social behaviour: an overview', *Journal of Social Issues*, 28(3), pp. 1–19.

Wolpe, J. (1958) *Psychotherapy by Reciprocal Inhibition*, Stanford, California: Stanford University Press.

Wong, D.F., Wagner, H.N., Tune, L.E., Dannals, R.F., Pearlson, G.D. and Links, J.M. (1986) 'Positron emission tomography reveals elevated D2 dopamine receptors in drug-naive schizophrenics', *Science*, 234, pp. 1558–62.

Wood, J.T. and Duck, S. (1995) (eds) *Understudied Relationships: Off the Beaten Track*, Thousand Oaks, USA: Sage.

Wood, J.T., Dendy, L.L., Dordek, E., Germany, M. and Varallo, S. (1994) 'The dialectic of difference: a thematic analysis of intimates' meanings for differences', in K. Carter and M. Presnell (eds) *Interpretive Approaches to Interpersonal Communication*, New York: SUNY Press.

Wood, P.S., Wood, M.A. and Middleton, D.S. (1978) 'An experimental valuation of four face-to-face teaching strategies', *Internal Journal of Behavioural Development*, 1, pp. 131–47.

Wood, W., Wong, F.Y. and Chachere, J.G. (1991) 'Effects of media violence on viewers' aggression in unconstrained social interaction', *Psychological Bulletin*, 109, pp. 371–83.

Worell, J. (1992) 'Feminist journals: academic empowerment or professional liability?', in J.Williams (ed.) *Gender in Academe*, Tampa: University of South Florida Press.

Worell, J. and Remer, P. (1992) *Feminist Perspectives in Therapy*, Chichester: Wiley.

Wortman, C.B. and Brehm, J.W. (1975) 'Responses to uncontrollable outcomes: an integration of the reactance theory and the learned helplessness model', in L. Berkowitz (ed.) *Advances in Social Psychology*, New York: Academic Press.

Wulff, S.B. (1985) 'The symbolic and object play of a child with autism: a review', *Journal Autism and Development Disorders*, 15, pp. 139–48.

Yarrow, L. J. and Goodwin, M. S. (1973) 'The immediate impact of separation: reactions of infants to a change in mother figures', in L. J. Stone, H. T. Smith and L. B. Murphy (eds) *The Complete Infant*, New York: Basic Books.

Yeates, K.O., MacPhee, D., Campbell, F.A. and Ramey, G.T. (1979) 'Maternal IQ and home environment as determinants of early childhood intellectual competence: a developmental analysis', *Developmental Psychology*, 15, pp. 731–9.

Young, A.H, Blackwood, D.H.R., Roxborough, H., McQueen, J.K., Martin, M.J. and Kean, D. (1991) 'A magnetic resonance imaging study of schizophrenia: brain structure and clinical symptoms', *British Journal of Psychiatry*, 158, pp. 158–64.

Yukl, G.A. (1989) *Leadership in Organizations* (2nd edn), Englewood Cliffs, New Jersey: Prentice-Hall.

Zahavi, A. (1979) 'Ritualisation and the evolution of movement signals', *Behaviour*, 72, pp. 77–81.

Zajonc, R.B. (1968) 'Attitudinal effects of mere exposure', *Journal of Personality and Social Psychology*, 9, pp. 1–27.

Zajonc, R.B. (1984) 'On the primacy of affect', *American Psychologist*, 39, pp. 117–23.

Zar, J.H. (1972) 'Significance testing of the Spearman Rank Correlation Coefficient', *Journal of the American Statistical Association*, 67, pp. 578-80.

Zigler, E.F., Abelson, W.D. and Seitz, V. (1973) 'Motivational factors in the performance of economically disadvantaged children on the Peabody Picture Vocabulary Test', *Child Development*, 44, pp. 294–303.

Zihl, J., von Cramon, D. and Mai, N. (1983) 'Selective disturbance of movement vision after bilateral posterior brain damage, further evidence and follow-up observations', *Brain*, 114, pp. 2235–52.

Zillmann, D. (1983) 'Transfer of excitation in emotional behaviour', in J.T. Cacioppo and R.E. Petty (eds) *Social Psychophysiology: A Sourcebook*, New York: Guilford Press, pp. 215–40.

Zillmann, D. (1988) 'Cognition-excitation interdependencies in aggressive behaviour', *Aggressive Behaviour*, 14, pp. 51–64.

Zillmann, D. and Bryant, J. (1974) 'Effect of residual excitation on the emotional response to provocation and delayed aggressive behaviour', *Journal of Personality and Social Psychology*, 30, pp. 782–91.

Zimbardo, P. (1969/1970) 'The human choice: individuation, reason and order versus deindividuation, impulse and chaos', in W.J. Arnold and D. Levine (eds) *Nebraska Symposium on Motivation*, Vol. 17, Lincoln, Nebraska: University of Nebraska Press.

Zimbardo, P., Banks, P.G., Haney, C. and Jaffe, D. (1973) *A Pirandellian Prison*, New York Times Magazine, 814173.

Zimbardo, P., McDermott, M., Janz, J and Metaal, N. (1995) *Psychology: A European Text*, London: HarperCollins.

Index

E

F

N